Understanding
Politics

Ideas, Institutions, and Issues

TWELFTH EDITION

THOMAS M. MAGSTADT, Ph.D.
*The Johns Hopkins School
of Advanced International Studies (SAIS)*

CENGAGE
Learning·

Australia • Brazil • Mexico • Singapore • United Kingdom • United States

CENGAGE
Learning®

Understanding Politics: Ideas, Institutions, and Issues, 12th Edition
Thomas M. Magstadt

Product Director: Paul Banks

Product Manager: Carolyn Merrill

Content Developer: Amy Bither

Product Assistant: Michelle Forbes

Marketing Director: Michelle Williams

Marketing Manager: Valerie Hartman

IP Analyst: Alexandra Ricciardi

IP Project Manager: Farah Fard

Manufacturing Planner: Fola Orekoya

Art and Design Direction, Production
    Management, and Composition:
    Cenveo® Publisher Services

Cover Image©:
    Cover 1 (bottom image, Aung San Suu Kyi
    Addresses Her Supporters Following
    Release From House Arrest) Credit:
    ©CKN/stringer/Getty Images

    Cover 2 (top right image, BRITAIN-NATO-
    SUMMIT) Credit: **©SAUL LOEB/AFP/
    Getty Images**

    Cover 3 (top left image, Sao Paulo Prepares
    For Start Of World Cup) Credit:
    ©Mario Tama/Getty Images

Chapter opening image: Mario Tama/
    Getty Images

For product information and technology assistance, contact us at
Cengage Learning Customer & Sales Support, 1-800-354-9706

For permission to use material from this text or product,
submit all requests online at **www.cengage.com/permissions.**
Further permissions questions can be emailed to
permissionrequest@cengage.com.

Library of Congress Control Number: 2015947516

ISBN: 978-1-305-62990-5

Cengage Learning
20 Channel Center Street
Boston, MA 02210
USA

Cengage Learning is a leading provider of customized learning solutions with employees residing in nearly 40 different countries and sales in more than 125 countries around the world. Find your local representative at **www.cengage.com**

Cengage Learning products are represented in Canada by
Nelson Education, Ltd.

To learn more about Cengage Learning, visit **www.cengage.com**

Purchase any of our products at your local college store or at our preferred online store **www.cengagebrain.com**

Printed in the United States of America.

Print Number: 01   Print Year: 2015

CONTENTS

Contents

We live in a global age. Events anywhere in the world affect people everywhere. Terrorist acts, wars, natural disasters, economic downturns, banking crises, and volatile stock markets are everyday occurrences. Signs of entropy are all around us. Climate change and rapidly disappearing biodiversity threaten the planet and raise questions that cross over into a dark region where eschatology trumps science. Seismic events in the Indian Ocean, western Sumatra, or northern Japan are localized, but if they disrupt the global economy, the indirect effects can be far-reaching.

The same applies to political events. The 9/11 terrorist attacks happened in New York City—they were local—but led to costly wars in Afghanistan and Iraq. The "war on terror" is now a global phenomenon.

Things change with blinding speed in this age of globalization. We now have smart weapons that make it possible to use unmanned aerial vehicles (UAVs), called "drones," armed with guns and bombs to kill from a safe distance, one of the recent developments explored in Chapter 15. Remote-controlled warplanes take the risk out of flying combat missions—a big change in the art and science of war fighting.

The same technological revolution is also changing the way we make things—all kinds of things. For example, it's now possible to use a 3D laser printer to produce everything from medical implants to high-quality musical instruments, to racing-car parts, and, yes, guns.

Another big change is the rise of a global elite. There were more millionaires in the world than Australians in 2015—over 35 million according to Credit Suisse (a Swiss multinational bank and financial services holding company). An Oxfam study published in 2014 found that the world's wealthiest 1% control half of the world's wealth ($110 trillion). This global trend toward greater economic inequality and concentration of wealth is also happening in the United States, where the top 1% control 43% of the nation's wealth.[1]

The rise of a new global meritocracy is brain-power driven. In today's world, more than ever before, the wealth of nations and individuals is based on entrepreneurial science and engineering—that is, ideas converted into products for a global marketplace. For example, Chapter 14 looks at the role Facebook played in the Egyptian uprising in early 2011.

Technology is revolutionizing politics as well as business, but the basic nature of the decision makers—the people who run things—remains unchanged. Conflict in the world—the struggle for power—continues unabated, as does the search for peace, order, and justice.

Paradoxically, the limits of power, even in its most concentrated forms, are everywhere apparent—from ancient places, such as Palestine and Iraq in the Middle East and Afghanistan in Central Asia, to Europe, where the "euro crisis" threatens to undermine a supranational project six decades in the making, and the United States with its relatively short history and even shorter memory. The cost of failed policies and corrupt, incompetent leadership is also apparent in our world—and our nation's capital.

But when it comes to the quality of citizenship, the implications of recent advances in telecommunications, Internet access, and social networking are not so clear. It's easier than ever in our wired world to learn more about what's going on in the world, be more attuned to the news, and vote more intelligently than ever before. Despite this ease of learning, studies show a *decline* in civic knowledge and education in the United States.

This double deficiency—both at the top and bottom of political society—is a kind of stealth crisis, one that, not unlike a stealth bomber, gives ample evidence of its existence but continues to go largely unnoticed. Meanwhile, there is no absence of injustice, intolerance, misguided idealism, zealotry, and human suffering—proof enough that the ever-more polluted and crowded planet we inhabit has not changed for the better, even though the West's fortunate few are far more secure and comfortable than the vast majority who live in the so-called developing regions of the globe.

Since *Understanding Politics* made its debut in 1984, nothing has shaken my conviction that politics matters. I still believe now, as I did then, that as citizens in a country that claims to be a model democracy, students need to acquire a working knowledge of the political and economic forces that shape our world. Ironically, as news and information have become more and more accessible—thanks in no small part to the Internet—interest in public affairs and a willingness to get involved have declined. Indeed, many Americans are not engaged in the political process except perhaps to vote.

The study of politics is a gateway to a broader and better understanding of human nature, society, and the world. This idea is what originally inspired the writing of *Understanding Politics*. It is also what has sustained my own interest through multiple revisions—that, plus a sense that the book was, is, and always will be essentially a work in progress.

A successful introduction to politics must balance two key objectives: (1) dispel anxieties associated with the attempt to understand political science, especially for the uninitiated; and (2) provide the intellectual stimulation necessary to challenge today's college students. This book is testimony to the fact that the science and philosophy of politics fall squarely within the liberal arts tradition.

Mention of the science and philosophy of politics points to one of the deepest cleavages within the discipline: analysts who approach politics from the standpoint of science often stress the importance of power, whereas those who view it through the wide-angle lens of philosophy often emphasize the importance of justice. But the distinction between power and justice—like that between science and philosophy—is too often exaggerated.

Moral and political questions are ultimately inseparable in the real world. The exercise of power, in itself, is not what makes an action political; rather, what makes power *political* is the debate about its proper or improper uses and who benefits or suffers as a result. Thus, whenever questions of fairness are raised in the realm of public policy (for example, questions concerning abortion, capital punishment, or the use of force by police or the military), the essential ingredients of politics are present. Excessive attention to either the concept of power or that of morality is likely to confound our efforts in making sense of politics or, for that matter, in finding lasting solutions to the problems that afflict and divide us. It is necessary to balance the equation, tempering political realism with a penchant for justice.

Similarly, the dichotomy so often drawn between facts and values is misleading. Rational judgments—in the sense of reasoned opinions about what is good and just—are sometimes more definitive (or less elusive) than facts. For example, the proposition that "genocide is evil" is true. (Its opposite— "genocide is good"—is morally indefensible.) It is a well-known fact that Adolf Hitler and the Nazis committed genocide. We can therefore say that Hitler was evil *as a matter of fact* and not "simply" because mass murder is abhorrent to our *personal* values.

Other value-laden propositions can be stated with a high degree of probability but not absolute certainty. For example, "If you want to reduce violent crime, first reduce poverty." Still other questions of this kind may be too difficult or too close to call—in the abortion controversy, for example, does the right of a woman to biological self-determination outweigh the right to life? It makes no sense to ignore the most important questions in life simply because the answers are not easy. Even when the right answers are unclear, it is often possible to recognize wrong answers—a moderating force in itself.

This book gives due attention to contemporary political issues without ignoring the more enduring questions that often underlie them. For example, a voter's dilemma as to who would make the best mayor, governor, or president raises deeper questions: What qualifications are necessary for public office? What is wrong with a system that all too often fails to produce distinguished—or distinctive—choices? Similarly, conflicts between nation-states or social groups raise philosophical as well as empirical questions about why human beings continue to fight and kill one another on a mass scale.

Although I have tried to minimize the use of names and dates, political ideas cannot be fruitfully discussed in a historical vacuum. The choice of examples throughout the text is dictated by a particular understanding of the relationship between politics and history. The consequences of certain events in the first half of the last century—World Wars I and II, the October Revolution in Lenin's Russia, the Holocaust in Hitler's Germany—are still present today. We too seldom think or talk about "living history"—about all the ways antecedents (decisions and actions in the past) influence the present and constrain the future.

Inevitably, some themes and events are discussed in more than one chapter: The world of politics is more like a seamless web than a chest of drawers. In politics, as in nature, a given event or phenomenon often has many meanings and is connected to other events and phenomena in ways that are not immediately apparent. Emphasizing the common threads among major political ideas, institutions, and issues helps beginning students make sense of seemingly unrelated bits and pieces of the political puzzle. Seeing how the various parts fit together is a necessary step toward understanding politics.

Understanding Politics employs a foundation-building approach to the study of politics and government. It begins by identifying political phenomena, such as war and terrorism, that students find interesting and then seeks to describe and explain them. In an effort to build on students' natural curiosity, I try to avoid much of the jargon and many of the technical or arcane disputes that too often characterize the more advanced literature in the field of political science.

Rather than probe the deepest recesses of a single discipline, the book unapologetically borrows insights from various disciplines, including history, economics, psychology, and sociology, as well as philosophy. It is intended to be a true liberal arts approach to the study of government and politics. The goal is ambitious: to challenge students to begin a lifelong learning process that alone can lead to a generation of citizens who are well informed, actively engaged, self-confident, and thoughtful and who have a capacity for indignation in the face of public hypocrisy, dishonesty, stupidity, or gross ineptitude.

Chapter 1, "Introduction: The Study of Politics," defines the basic concepts of politics and centers on how and why it is studied. This chapter lays the groundwork for the remainder of the text and stands alone as its introduction. Chapter 2, "The Idea of the Public Good: Ideologies and Isms," deals with basic belief systems, including ideologies of the Right and Left, such as communism and fascism, and "isms" of the Right and Left, such as liberalism and conservatism.

Part 1, "Comparative Political Systems: Models and Theories," analyzes utopian, democratic, and authoritarian forms of government, as well as political systems caught in the difficult transition from authoritarian to democratic institutions. This part, which comprises Chapters 3 through 6, looks at different kinds of political regimes in a theoretical light.

Part 2, "Established and Emerging Democracies," consists of three chapters that examine parliamentary democracies (Chapter 7), transitional states (Chapter 8), and developing countries (Chapter 9). Virtually all governments in today's world either aspire to some form of democracy or claim to be "democratic." This amazing fact is itself irrefutable evidence of the power of an idea. Though often abused, the idea of democracy has fired the imaginations of people everywhere for more than two centuries. In an age when bad news is written in blood and body counts are more likely to refer to innocent civilians than armed combatants, we would do well to remember that democratic ideals have never before been so warmly embraced or so widely (if imperfectly) institutionalized.

In Part 3, "Politics by Civil Means: Citizens, Leaders, and Policies," four chapters (10 through 13) focus on the political process and public policy. The United States is featured in this section, which examines citizenship and political socialization, political participation (including opinion polling and voting behavior), political organization (parties and interest groups), political leadership, political ideologies (or divergent "approaches to the public good"), and contemporary public policy issues.

Part 4, "Politics by Violent Means: Revolution, War, and Terrorism," examines conflict as a special and universal problem in politics. It divides the problem into three categories: revolution, terrorism, and war (corresponding to Chapters 14, 15, and 16, respectively). Viewed from the aftermath of 9/11, when the president of the United States declared international terrorism to be the preeminent threat in the world and blurred the distinction between counterterrorist policy and all-out war, Part 4 is guaranteed to stimulate the curiosity of students and provoke spirited class discussions. Invading and occupying a country (Iraq) that had nothing to do with the 9/11 attacks, did not possess "weapons of mass destruction," and did not pose a threat to the United States was a curious response to the problem posed by the existence of a malevolent terrorist network (al Qaeda) harbored by a fundamentalist regime (the Taliban) in a land (Afghanistan) virtually impossible to subdue by conquest and notoriously impervious to outside influence. Indeed, this response affords ample opportunity for contemplation about the motives, causes, and consequences of war at the beginning of a new millennium.

Finally, Part 5, "Politics without Government," introduces students to key concepts in the study of international relations, describes key patterns, and discusses perennial problems. Chapter 17 examines the basic principles and concepts in international relations, the evolving structure and context of world politics, certain key global issues, international law, and role of the United Nations. The Afterword, "The Power of Knowledge," is a single paragraph. Students are encouraged to read it first and then read it at the end of the semester. My hope is that some will remember and apply it.

In this new edition—the twelfth!—I have retained the pedagogical features found in previous editions with one exception: a short list of learning objectives replaces chapter outlines in this edition. Each chapter ends with a summary, review questions, and websites and readings resources. For this edition, the glossary is posted on the book's website, which you can find at www.cengage.com/login. As in the past, endnotes for each chapter precede the index at the back of the book. In addition, the text contains a wide variety of photos, figures, maps, tables, and features, many of which have been revised or replaced with updated materials.

NEW IN THE TWELFTH EDITION

The twelfth edition has three kinds of features, one of which is totally new. I'm hoping that "Politics and Pop Culture" will stimulate class discussion and demonstrate how movies and music play an important role in reflecting or challenging our ideas and opinions, shaping our perceptions, and heightening our awareness of the issues. Key events and major achievements of enduring importance are highlighted in "Landmarks in History." The feature "Politics and Ideas" give students a bird's-eye view of perennial questions and key issues in political theory and philosophy.

As always, major developments in the United States and on the world stage have intervened since the last edition went to press. The previous edition covered the 2012 presidential campaign and the reelection of the country's first African American president; the battle of the budget and acrimonious partisan politics surrounding the so-called fiscal cliff; the use of the filibuster to block votes in the U.S. Senate; and the deep divisions in U.S. society over such issues as gun control, income inequality, immigration, abortion, health care, tax fairness, gay rights, and gender equality. The new edition covers the 2014 midterm election, the war in Ukraine, the rise of the Islamic State (ISIS) in the Middle East, and various recent events at home and abroad.

Coverage of the "euro crisis" is expanded and updated. The "agenda" samplers for the four liberal democracies featured in Chapter 7 (Great Britain, France, Germany, and Japan) reflect developments through 2012 and the first half of 2013. The material covering India and Israel, two of the world's most challenged representative democracies, is updated but, sadly, the existential circumstances—the predicaments and realities they face—have not changed for either country (and are not likely to change anytime in the expectable future).

There are other revisions, text enhancements, and new features too numerous to mention. I personally selected much of the art work appearing in recent editions—a lot of work, but worth the effort and fun to boot. Many of the photographers featured in these pages are amateurs with a good camera, a great eye, and a generous spirit.

Finally, I also encourage readers to visit my Facebook page, (https://www.facebook.com/thomas.magstadt), where I regularly post articles and comments.

Supplements for Students and Instructors

AUTHOR: Thomas M. Magstadt
ISBN: 9781305641174
TITLE: **Instructor Companion Website for Magstadt,** *Understanding Politics,* **12e**

This Instructor Companion Website is an all-in-one multimedia online resource for class preparation, presentation, and testing. Accessible through Cengage.com/login with your faculty account, you will find the following ancillaries available for download: book-specific Microsoft® PowerPoint® presentations; a Test Bank compatible with multiple learning management systems; an Instructor's Manual; Microsoft® PowerPoint® Image Slides; and a JPEG Image Library.

The Test Bank, offered in Blackboard, Moodle, Desire2Learn, Canvas, and Angel formats, contains specific Learning Objective multiple-choice and essay questions for each chapter. Import the test bank into your LMS to edit and manage questions, and to create tests.

The Instructor's Manual contains chapter-specific learning objectives, an outline, key terms with definitions, and a chapter summary. Additionally, the Instructor's Manual features a critical thinking question, lecture launching suggestion, and an in-class activity for each learning objective.

The Microsoft® PowerPoint® presentations are ready-to-use, visual outlines of each chapter. These presentations are easily customized for your lectures and offered along with chapter-specific Microsoft® PowerPoint® Image Slides and JPEG Image Libraries. Access the Instructor Companion Website at www.cengage.com/login.

AUTHOR: Thomas M. Magstadt
ISBN: 9781305641198
TITLE: **IAC Cognero for Magstadt,** *Understanding Politics,* **12e**

Cengage Learning Testing Powered by Cognero is a flexible, online system that allows you to author, edit, and manage test bank content from multiple Cengage Learning solutions, create multiple test versions in an instant, and deliver tests from your LMS, your classroom, or wherever you want. The test bank for *Understanding Politics,* 12e contains specific Learning Objective multiple-choice and essay questions for each chapter.

AUTHOR: Gale
TITLE: **CourseReader 0-30: Introduction to Political Science**
PAC ISBN: 9781133232162
IAC ISBN: 9781133232155

CourseReader: Introduction to Political Science allows you to create your reader, your way, in just minutes. This affordable, fully customizable online reader provides access to thousands of permissions-cleared readings, articles, primary sources, and audio and video selections from the regularly updated Gale research library database. This easy-to-use solution allows you to search for and select just the material you want for your courses. Each selection opens with a descriptive introduction to provide context, and concludes with critical-thinking and multiple-choice questions to reinforce key points. COURSEREADER is loaded with convenient tools like highlighting, printing, note-taking, and downloadable PDFs and MP3 audio files for each reading. COURSEREADER is the perfect complement to any Political Science course. It can be bundled with your current textbook, sold alone, or integrated into your learning management system. COURSEREADER 0-30 allows access to up to thirty selections in the reader. Please contact your Cengage sales representative for details.

ACKNOWLEDGMENTS

Through twelve editions and more than two decades, many individuals associated with several different publishing houses and universities have helped make this book a success. Among the scholars and teachers who reviewed the work for previous editions in manuscript, offering helpful criticisms and suggestions, were the following:

Donald G. Baker, Southampton College, Long Island University
Peter Longo, University of Nebraska at Kearney
Iraj Paydar, Bellevue Community College
Ruth Ann Strickland, Appalachian State University
Sean K. Anderson, Idaho State University
Daniel Aseltine, Chaffey College
Thomas A. Kolsky, Montgomery County Community College
Linda Valenty, California Polytechnic State University—San Luis Obispo
Andrei Korobkov, Middle Tennessee University
Ethan Fishman, University of South Alabama
Mack Murray, Seattle Community College
Lawrence Okere, University of Arkansas
Keith Milks, Nash Community College
Frank Bean, Garden City Community College
Jean-Gabriel Jolivet, South-Western College
Jose Lopez-Gonzalez, Towson University
Naomi Robertson, Macon State College

For the current edition, that vital role fell to reviewers: Julian Westerhout, Illinois State University; Abdalla Battah, Minnesota State University, Mankato; Kwame Dankwa, Albany State University; and Darlene Budd, University of Central Missouri.

I wish to express my appreciation to Amy Bither, my editor for this edition. Good editors are priceless, and Amy is one of the very best I've had the pleasure to work with over a span of more than three decades. Thanks are also due to Carolyn Merrill, Product Team Manager at Cengage, to Kay Mikel who handled the copyediting, and to Anupriya Tyagi for managing the process of moving the book from manuscript to market. Thanks to the entire Cengage team for getting this twelfth edition out in a timely fashion. Finally, as always, I owe a huge debt of gratitude to my family and friends, especially Mary Jo (who died in 1990), Becky, Michael, David, Amy, Alexa, Barbara, and, last but not least, the Coffee Boys of Westwood Hills: Dr. Stan Nelson (1928–2013), Glion Curtis, Grant Mallet, Hugh Brown, Dr. George Pagels, Howard Martin, Dr. Gary Ripple, Harris Rayl, and Professor Emeritus G. Ross Stephens.

ABOUT THE AUTHOR

Thomas M. Magstadt earned his doctorate at the Johns Hopkins School of Advanced International Studies (SAIS). He has taught at the Graduate School of International Management, Augustana College (Sioux Falls), the University of Nebraska at Kearney, the Air War College, and the University of Missouri–Kansas City, and, most recently, the University of Kansas. He has also chaired two political science departments, worked as a foreign intelligence analyst, served as Director of the Midwest Conference on World Affairs, and lectured as a Fulbright Scholar in the Czech Republic. In addition to publishing articles in newspapers, magazines, and professional journals, Dr. Magstadt is the author of *An Empire If You Can Keep It* (Washington, DC: Congressional Quarterly Press, 2004); *Nations and Governments: Comparative Politics in Regional Perspective*, fifth edition (Belmont, CA: Wadsworth/ Cengage Learning, 2005); *Contemporary European Politics* (Belmont, CA: Wadsworth/ Cengage Learning, 2007); and *The European Union on the World Stage: Sovereignty, Soft Power, and the Search for Consensus* (BookSurge, 2010).

CHAPTER 1

Introduction
The Study of Politics

Learning Objectives

1 Discuss the value of studying politics.

2 Identify the three basic elements of politics, as well as the dynamics of each.

3 Analyze the methods, models, and approaches for studying politics.

4 Evaluate whether politics brings out the best or the worst in human nature—or both.

Politics is not for the faint-hearted. There is virtually never a day without a crisis at home or abroad. Whenever we catch the news on our radio, TV, or computer, we are reminded that we live in a dangerous world.

In 2008, the spectacle of the world's only superpower paralyzed by extreme partisanship and teetering on the brink of a "fiscal cliff" loomed like a gathering storm. No sooner had that danger receded than a new threat arose in the Middle East in the form of the so-called Islamic State of Iraq and Syria (ISIS). There were even rumors of a coming end-of-the-world apocalypse—December 21, 2012, to be exact, the final day of the old Mayan calendar.

The politically charged atmosphere and the pervasive sense of an impending crisis was nothing new, but two events dominated the news in 2008. First, a financial meltdown and plummeting stock market wiped out fortunes and rocked the global economy to its very foundations. Second, Barack Obama became the first African American elected to the nation's highest office.

Political culture plays a big role in shaping public policy, and optimism is part of America's political DNA. Despite a deepening recession, there was a new sense of hope—perhaps it was the beginning of the end of two costly wars and the dawn of a new era in America. But by 2012 hope had given way to anger and disappointment.

What happened? In 2009, President Obama had moved to revive the U.S. economy, which had fallen into the deepest recession since the Great Depression of the 1930s. But the economic stimulus package he pushed through Congress, where the Democrats enjoyed a solid majority in both the House and Senate, was widely viewed as a Wall Street "bailout"—a massive multibillion dollar gift to the very financial institutions that had caused the problem. It was also criticized as a "jobless recovery"; unemployment rose to nearly 10% and youth unemployment (16- to 19-year-olds) rose about 25% in 2010. Nearly half of young people aged 16 to 24 did not have jobs, the highest number since World War II.

The conservative media (most notably FOX News) and the amorphous Tea Party movement eagerly exploited growing public discontent, handing the Democrats a crushing defeat in the 2010 midterm elections. Republicans regained control of the House and cut deeply into the Democrats' majority in the Senate (see especially Chapters 11 and 13).

Obama also spearheaded a controversial health care reform that satisfied few, confused everyone, and angered many voters on both sides of the acrimonious debate. His decision to order a "surge" in Afghanistan, committing 30,000 more U.S. troops to an unpopular and unwinnable war, did not placate Congress or greatly improve his standing in the opinion polls, nor did his decision to withdraw the last U.S. combat troops from Iraq in December 2011.

Despite a constant chorus of criticism and a vicious media campaign of attack ads from the right, Obama was elected to a second term in 2012. He defeated Republican Mitt Romney by a margin of 5 million votes (51% to 47% of the popular vote) while taking 61% of the electoral votes. The embattled president's troubles in dealing with a recalcitrant Republican majority in Congress, however, continued unabated. His decision in the fall of 2014 to launch a major bombing campaign against ISIS in Iraq and Syria—in effect, resuming a war that had officially ended three years earlier—did not appease the opposition or boost his popularity, which fell to new lows in 2014.

The president's popularity—or lack thereof—was a major factor in setting the stage for the Republican victory in the 2014 midterm elections when voters gave the GOP a majority in the Senate. Republicans also gained seats in the House (where they had won back control in 2010). But President Obama acted decisively in the days following the election, confounding his critics and commentators who had branded him a "lame duck."

We know politics is something that happens in Washington, D.C., or in Austin, Texas, and other state capitals, but some of us forget that politics is a pervasive fact of life— others never forget it. That very fact often gives those "others" a big advantage, which can be the difference between success and failure.

For any democracy to succeed in the long run, it is vital that citizens pay attention, learn to think for themselves, and vote intelligently. Political literacy is vital to a viable and sustainable representative government—what we commonly call "democracy."

The alternative is revolution, a drastic measure and a last resort—one American colonists chose in 1776 and the Confederate South chose in 1860. As we will see in Chapter 14, revolutions are convulsive and quixotic. They often result in less freedom for the people, not more.

A popular slogan (and bumper sticker) reminds us that "Freedom Isn't Free." It's true. At a minimum, being a good citizen requires us to have a basic understanding of the ideas, institutions, and issues that constitute the stuff of politics. This book is an attempt to foster just such an understanding.

WHY STUDY POLITICS?

The belief that anybody with a college education will have a basic understanding of political ideas, institutions, and issues is wishful thinking. There is a mountain of evidence showing it's simply not true; moreover, there is a mountain of empirical evidence to prove it. To begin to understand the power of politics—and the politics of power—we have to make a careful study and, above all, keep an open mind.

Self-Interest

Because personal happiness depends in no small degree on what government does or does not do, we all have a considerable stake in understanding how government works (or why it is not working). Federal work-study programs, state subsidies to public education, low-interest loans, federal grants, and court decisions that protect students' rights are but a few examples of politics and public policy that directly affect college students. For farmers, crop subsidies, price supports, and water rights are crucial policy issues. Environmental regulations are often the target of intense lobbying on the part of power companies, the oil and gas industry, and mining interests.

Taxes are a hot button for nearly everybody. Most people think they pay too much and others pay too little. Do you know *anybody* who wants to pay *more* in taxes? Can you think of one wealthy individual who argues that people in his income bracket ought to pay more? (*Hint:* His initials are W. B.)

Through the study of politics, we become more aware of our dependence on the political system and better equipped to determine when to favor and when to oppose change. At the same time, such study helps to reveal the limits of politics and the obstacles to bringing about any major change in a society. It is sobering to consider that each of us is only one person in a nation of millions (and a world of billions), most of whom have opinions and prejudices no less firmly held than our own.

The Public Interest

What could be more vital to the public interest in any society than the moral character and conduct of its citizens? Civil society is defined by and reflected in the kinds of everyday decisions and choices made by ordinary people leading ordinary lives. At the same time, people are greatly influenced by civil society and the prevailing culture and climate of politics. We are all products of our circumstances to a greater extent than most of us realize (or care to admit). Politics plays a vital role in shaping these circumstances, and it is fair to say the public interest hangs in the balance.

BASIC CONCEPTS OF POLITICS

politics
The process by which a community selects rulers and empowers them to make decisions, takes action to attain common goals, and reconciles conflicts within the community.

Politics has been defined as "the art of the possible," as the study of "who gets what, when, and how," as the "authoritative allocation of values," and in various other ways. Many people think politics is inherently corrupt and corrupting—hence the term "dirty politics." Is this true? Can you think of any exceptions?

We may not agree on how to define politics, but we know what it is when we see it—and we don't like what we see. We are quick to blame "politics" as the main cause of problems not only in society but also in families, schools, and the workplace. Likewise, college students are typically unaware of the anger and tumult that often animate campus politics.

Like other disciplines, political science has a lexicon and language all its own. We start our language lesson with three words that carry a great deal of political freight: *power, order*, and *justice*.

Power

power
The capacity to influence or control the behavior of persons and institutions, whether by persuasion or coercion.

Power is the currency of all politics. Without power, no government can make and enforce laws, provide security, regulate the economy, conduct foreign policy, or wage war. There are many kinds of power. In this book, we are interested in *political* power. Coercion plays an important role in politics, but political power cannot be equated with force. Indeed, the sources of power are many and varied. A large population, a booming economy, a cohesive society, and wise leadership—all are examples of quite different power sources.

We often define power in terms of national wealth or military spending. We once called the most formidable states Great Powers; now we call them "superpowers." Power defined in this way is tangible and measurable. Critics of this classical view make a useful distinction between "hard power" and "soft power." Hard power refers to the means and instruments of brute force or coercion, primarily military and economic clout. Soft power is "attractive" rather than coercive: the essence of soft power is "the important ability to get others to want what you want."[1]

Power is never equally distributed. Yet the need to concentrate power in the hands of a few inevitably raises three big questions: Who wields power? In whose interests? And to what ends?

The most basic question of all is "Who rules?" Sometimes we have only to look at a nation's constitution and observe the workings of its government to find the answer. But it may be difficult to determine who really rules when the government is cloaked in secrecy or when, as is often the case, informal patterns of power are very different from the textbook diagrams.

The terms *power* and *authority* are often confused and even used interchangeably. In reality, they denote two distinct dimensions of politics. According to Mao Zedong, the late Chinese Communist leader, "Political power flows from the barrel of a gun." Political power is clearly associated with the means of coercion (the regular police, secret police, and the army), but power can also flow from wealth, personal charisma, ideology, religion, and many other sources, including the moral standing of a particular individual or group in society.

Authority, by definition, flows not only (or even mainly) from the barrel of a gun but also from the *norms* society accepts and even cherishes. These norms are moral, spiritual, and legal codes of behavior, or good conduct. Thus, authority implies **legitimacy**—a condition in which power is exercised by common consensus through established institutions. Note this definition does not mean, nor is it meant to imply, that democracy is the only legitimate form of government possible. Any government that enjoys the consent of the governed is legitimate—including a monarchy, military dictatorship, or theocracy.

The acid test of **legitimate authority** is not whether people have the right to vote or to strike or dissent openly, but how much *value* people attach to these rights. If a majority of the people are content with the existing political order just as it is (with or without voting rights), the legitimacy of the ruler(s) is simply not in question. But, as history amply demonstrates, it is possible to seize power and to rule without a popular mandate or public approval, without moral, spiritual, or legal justification—in other words, without true (legitimate) authority.

A military power seizure—also known as a *coup d'etat*—typically involves a plot by senior army officers to overthrow a corrupt, incompetent, or unpopular civilian ruler. One well-known recent example happened in Egypt in July 2013, following many months of turmoil and the outcome of a presidential election that became unacceptable to the military.

Power seizures also occurred in Mauritania and Guinea in 2008 and in Thailand as recently as 2014; many contemporary rulers, especially in Africa, have come to power in this manner. Adolf Hitler's failed "Beer Hall Putsch" in 1923 is a famous example of an attempted power seizure. Such attempts often fail, but they are usually evidence of political instability—as the case of Weimar Germany illustrates.

Claiming authority is useless without the means to enforce it. The right to rule—a condition that minimizes the need for repression—hinges in large part on legitimacy or popularity.

authority
Command of the obedience of society's members by a government.

legitimacy
The exercise of political power in a community in a way that is voluntarily accepted by the members of that community.

legitimate authority
The legal and moral right of a government to rule over a specific population and control a specific territory; the term *legitimacy* usually implies a widely recognized claim of governmental authority and voluntary acceptance on the part of the population(s) directly affected.

Legitimacy and popularity go hand in hand. Illegitimate rulers are unpopular rulers. Such rulers are faced with a choice: relinquish power or repress opposition. Whether repression works depends, in turn, on the answer to three questions. First, how widespread and determined is the opposition? Second, does the government have adequate financial resources and coercive capabilities to defeat its opponents and deter future challenges? Third, does the government have the will to use all means necessary to defeat the rebellion?

If the opposition is broadly based and the government waivers for whatever reason, repression is likely to fail. Regimes changed in Russia in 1917 and 1992 following failed attempts to crush the opposition. Two other examples include Cuba in 1958, where Fidel Castro led a successful revolution, and Iran in 1978, where a mass uprising led to the overthrow of the Shah. A similar pattern was evident in many East European states in 1989, when repressive communist regimes collapsed like so many falling dominoes.

If people respect the ruler(s) and play by the rules without being forced to do so (or threatened with the consequences), the task of maintaining order and stability in society is going to be much easier. It stands to reason that people who feel exploited and oppressed make poorly motivated workers. The perverse work ethic of Soviet-style dictatorships, where it was frequently said, "We pretend to work and they pretend to pay us," helps explain the decline and fall of Communism in the Soviet Union and Eastern Europe, dramatized by the spontaneous tearing down of the Berlin Wall in 1989.

Order

Order exists on several levels. First, it denotes structures, rules, rituals, procedures, and practices that make up the political system embedded in every **society**. What exactly is society? In essence, society is an aggregation of individuals who share a common identity. Usually that identity is at least partially defined by geography, because people who live in close proximity often know each other, enjoy shared experiences, speak the same language, and have similar values and interests. The process of instilling a sense of common purpose or creating a single political allegiance among diverse groups of people is complex and works better from the bottom up than from the top down. The breakup of the Soviet Union and Yugoslavia in the early 1990s, after more than seven decades as multinational states, suggests new communities are often fragile and tend to fall apart quickly if there are not strong cultural and psychological bonds under the political structures.

The Russian-backed secessionist movement that threatened to break up Ukraine in 2014-15 also illustrates the obstacles to maintaining order in a newly independent country where a national minority group is geographically concentrated. Russian-speakers in parts of eastern Ukraine bordering on Russia constitute a solid majority and remain fiercely loyal to Moscow. The same is true in Crimea (previously part of Ukraine), where most people welcomed Russia's armed intervention. Russia annexed this strategically important region (the whole of the Crimean Peninsula) in March of 2014.

The idea that individuals become a cohesive community through an unwritten **social contract** has been fundamental to Western political thought since the seventeenth century. Basic to social contract theory is the notion that the right

---

order
In a political context, refers to an existing or desired arrangement of institutions based on certain principles, such as liberty, equality, prosperity, and security. Also often associated with the rule of law (as in the phrase "law and order") and with conservative values such as stability, obedience, and respect for legitimate authority.

society
An aggregation of individuals who share a common identity. Usually that identity is at least partially defined by geography because people who live in close proximity often know each other, enjoy shared experiences, speak the same language, and have similar values and interests.

social contract
A concept in political theory most often associated with Thomas Hobbes, Jean-Jacque Rousseau, and John Locke; the social contract is an implicit agreement among individuals to form a civil society and to accept certain moral and political obligations essential to its preservation.

to rule is based on the consent of the governed. Civil liberties in this type of community are a matter of natural law and natural rights—that is, they do not depend on written laws but rather are inherent in Nature. Nature with a capital *N* is a set of self-evident truths that, in the eyes of social contract theorists, can be known through a combination of reason and observation. A corollary of this theory is that whenever government turns oppressive, when it arbitrarily takes away such natural rights as life, liberty, and (perhaps) property, the people have a right to revolt (see Chapter 14).

Government is a human invention by which societies are ruled and binding rules are made. Given the rich variety of governments in the world, how might we categorize them all? Traditionally we've distinguished between **republics**, in which sovereignty (see below) ultimately resides in the people, and governments such as monarchies or tyrannies, in which sovereignty rests with the rulers. Today, almost all republics are democratic (or representative) republics, meaning political systems wherein elected representatives responsible to the people exercise sovereign power.[2]

Some political scientists draw a simple distinction between democracies, which hold free elections, and dictatorships, which do not. Others emphasize political economy, distinguishing between governments enmeshed in capitalist or market-based systems and governments based on socialist or state-regulated systems. Finally, governments in developing countries face different kinds of challenges than do governments in developed countries. Not surprisingly, more economically developed countries often have markedly more well-established political institutions—including political parties, regular elections, civil and criminal courts—than most less developed countries, and more stable political systems.

In the modern world, the **state** is the sole repository of **sovereignty**. A sovereign state is a community with well-defined territorial boundaries administered by a single government capable of making and enforcing laws. In addition, it typically claims a monopoly on the legitimate use of force; raises armies for the defense of its territory and population; levies and collects taxes; regulates trade and commerce; establishes courts, judges, and magistrates to settle disputes and punish lawbreakers; and sends envoys (ambassadors) to represent its interests abroad, negotiate treaties, and gather useful information. Entities that share *some* but not all of the characteristics of states include fiefdoms and chiefdoms, bands and tribes, universal international organizations (such as the United Nations), and regional supranational organizations (such as the European Union).

In the language of politics, state usually means **country**. France, for instance, may be called either a state or a country. (In certain federal systems of government, a state is an administrative subdivision, such as New York, Florida, Texas, or California in the United States; however, such states within a state are not sovereign.)

The term *nation* is also a synonym for *state* or *country*. Thus, the only way to know for certain whether *state* means part of a country (for example, the United States) or a whole country (say, France or China) is to consider the context. By the same token, context is the key to understanding what we mean by the word *nation*.

A **nation** is made up of a distinct group of people who share a common background, including geographic location, history, racial or ethnic characteristics, religion, language, culture, or belief in common political ideas. Geography heads this list because members of a nation typically exhibit a strong collective

government
The persons and institutions that make and enforce rules or laws for the larger community.

republic
A form of government in which sovereignty resides in the people of that country, rather than with the rulers. The vast majority of republics today are democratic or representative republics, meaning that the sovereign power is exercised by elected representatives who are responsible to the citizenry.

sense of belonging associated with a particular territory for which they are willing to fight and die if necessary.

Countries with relatively homogeneous populations (with great similarity among members) were most common in old Europe, but this once-defining characteristic of European nation-states is no longer true. The recent influx of newcomers from former colonial areas, in particular the Muslim majority countries of North Africa, the Arab world, and South Asia, and post–Cold War east-west population movements in Europe have brought the issue of immigration to the forefront of politics in France, Germany, the United Kingdom, Spain, Italy, the Netherlands, and even the Scandinavian countries. Belgium, on the other hand, provides a rare example of a European state divided culturally and linguistically (French-speaking Walloons and Dutch-speaking Flemish) from the start.

India, Russia, and Nigeria are three highly diverse states. India's constitution officially recognizes no fewer than eighteen native tongues! The actual number spoken is far larger. As a nation of immigrants, the United States is also very diverse, but the process of assimilation eventually brings the children of newcomers, if not the newcomers themselves, into the mainstream.[3]

The **nation-state** is a state encompassing a single nation in which the overwhelming majority of the people form a dominant in-group who share common cultural, ethnic, and linguistic characteristics; all others are part of a distinct out-group or minority. This concept is rooted in a specific time and place—that is, in modern Western Europe. (See "Landmarks in History" for the story of the first nation-state.) The concept of the nation-state fits less comfortably in other regions of the world, where the political boundaries of sovereign states—many of which were European colonies before World War II—often do not coincide with ethnic or cultural geography. In some instances, ethnic, religious, or tribal groups that were bitter traditional enemies were thrown together in new "states," resulting in societies prone to great instability or even civil war.

Decolonization after World War II gave rise to many polyglot states in which various ethnic or tribal groups were not assimilated into the new social order. Many decades later, the all-important task of **nation-building** in these new states is still far from finished. Thus, in 1967, Nigeria plunged into a vicious civil war when one large ethnic group, the Igbo, tried unsuccessfully to secede and form an independent state called Biafra. In 1994, Rwanda witnessed one of the bloodiest massacres in modern times when the numerically superior Hutus slaughtered hundreds of thousands of Tutsis, including women and children. In early 2008, tribal violence in Kenya's Rift Valley and beyond claimed the lives of hundreds of innocent people following the outcome of a presidential election that many believed was rigged.

In India, where Hindus and Muslims frequently clash and sporadic violence breaks out among militant Sikhs in Punjab and where hundreds of languages and dialects are spoken, characterizing the country as a nation-state misses the point altogether. In Sri Lanka (formerly Ceylon), Hindu Tamils have long waged a terrorist guerrilla war against the majority Singhalese, who are Buddhist.

Even in the Slavic-speaking parts of Europe, age-old ethnic rivalries have caused the breakup of preexisting states. The Soviet Union, Yugoslavia, and

---

state
In its sovereign form, an independent political-administrative unit that successfully claims the allegiance of a given population, exercises a monopoly on the legitimate use of coercive force, and controls the territory inhabited by its citizens or subjects; in its other common form, a state is the major political-administrative subdivision of a federal system and, as such, is not sovereign but rather depends on the central authority (sometimes called the "national government") for resource allocations (tax transfers and grants), defense (military protection and emergency relief), and regulation of economic relations with other federal subdivisions (nonsovereign states) and external entities (sovereign states).

sovereignty
A government's capacity to assert supreme power successfully in a political state.

country
As a political term, it refers loosely to a sovereign state and is roughly equivalent to "nation" or "nation-state"; *country* is often used as a term of endearment—for example, in the phrase "my *country* 'tis of thee, sweet land of liberty" in the patriotic song every U.S. child learns in elementary school; country has an emotional dimension not present in the word *state*.

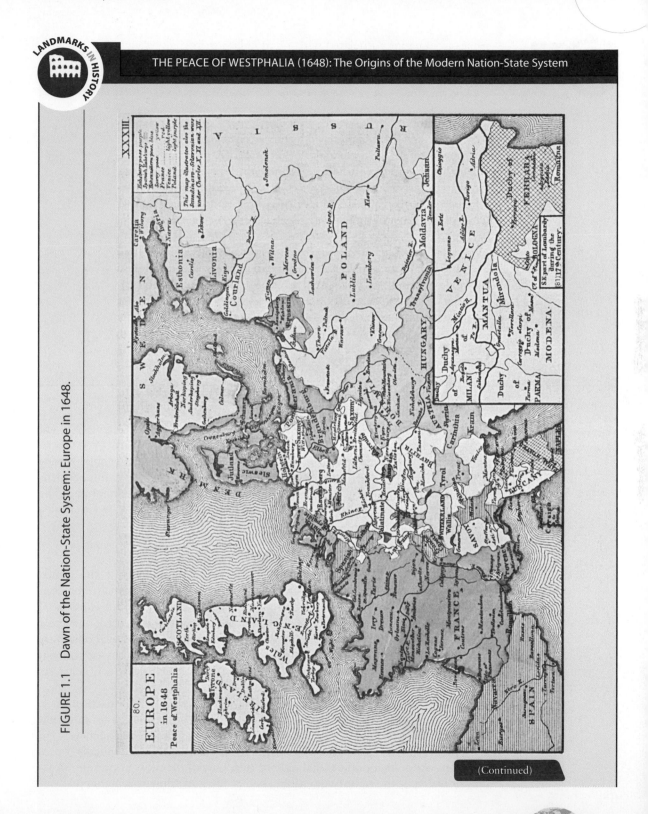

FIGURE 1.1   Dawn of the Nation-State System: Europe in 1648.

(Continued)

(CONTINUED)

Most historians believe the Peace of Westphalia marks the beginning of the modern European state system. The main actors in forging the peace, which ended the Thirty Years War in 1648, were Sweden and France as the challengers, Spain and the dying Holy Roman Empire as the defenders of the status quo, and the newly independent Netherlands.

At first glance, the map of Europe in the mid-seventeenth century does not look much like it does today. However, on closer inspection, we see the out-lines of modern Europe emerge (see Figure 1.1)—visual proof that the treaty laid the foundations of the nation-state as we see it in Europe today.

The emergence of the nation-state system trans-formed Europe from a continent of territorial empires to one based on relatively compact geographic units that share a single dominant language and culture. This pattern was unprecedented and it would shape both European and world history in the centuries to come.

France under Napoleon attempted to establish a new continental empire at the beginning of the nineteenth century but ultimately failed. Two other empires—Austria-Hungary and Russia—remained, but they were eclipsed by a rising new nation-state at the end of the nineteenth century and perished in World War I. After World War I, only the newly con-stituted Soviet empire existed in Europe. After World War II, what remained of Europe's overseas colonial empires also disintegrated. Today, the entire world, with few exceptions, is carved up into nation-states—the legacy of a treaty that, for better or worse, set the stage for a new world order.

Czechoslovakia are multinational states that self-destructed in the 1990s—in 2014-15 centrifugal tendencies threatened to split Ukraine in half.

Finally, **stateless nations** such as the Palestinians, Kurds, and Native Americans (known as First Nations in Canada) share a sense of common iden-tity but no longer control the homelands or territories they once inhabited. The tragic reality of nations without states has created highly volatile situations, most notably in the Middle East.

Justice

We willingly accept the rule of the few over the many only if the public interest—or common good—is significantly advanced in the process. The con-cept of **justice** is no less fundamental than power in politics, and it is essential to a stable order. Is power exercised fairly, in the interest of the ruled, or merely for the sake of the rulers? For more than two thousand years, political observers have maintained the distinction between the public-spirited exercise of political power on one hand and self-interested rule on the other. This distinction attests to the importance of justice in political life.

Not all states and regimes allow questions of justice to be raised; in fact, throughout history, most have not. Even today, some governments brutally and systematically repress political dissent because they fear the consequences.

Often, criticism of *how* a government rules implicitly or explicitly raises questions about its moral or legal *right* to rule. One of the most important meas-ures of liberty is the right to question whether the government is acting justly.

Questions about whether a particular ruler is legitimate or a given policy is desirable stem from human nature itself. The Greek philosopher Aristotle (384–322 BCE) observed that human beings alone use reason and language "to declare what is advantageous and what is just and unjust." Therefore, "it is the peculiarity of man, in comparison with the rest of the animal world, that he alone possess a perception of good and evil, of the just and unjust."[4]

The same human faculties that make moral judgment possible also make **political literacy**—the ability to think and speak intelligently about politics—necessary. In other words, moral judgment and political literacy are two sides of the same coin.

Anadolu Agency/Getty Images

Citizens unhappy about government policies at home or abroad can express themselves in any number of ways, including demonstrations and marches. Here in Washington, citizens are protesting the National Security Agency's mass surveillance, as revealed by Edward Snowden in 2013.

THE PROBLEM OF DIRTY HANDS

Based on everyday observation, it's easy to get the impression that politics and morality operate in separate realms of human experience, that power always corrupts, and that anyone who thinks differently is hopelessly naïve. Political theorists have long recognized and debated whether it is possible to exercise power and still remain true to one's principles. It's called the problem of "dirty hands."

In politics, anything is possible, including the unthinkable. When morality is set aside, justice is placed entirely at the mercy of raw power.

The rise and fall of Nazi Germany (1933–1945) under Adolf Hitler illustrates the tremendous impact a regime can have on the moral character of its citizens. At the core of Nazi ideology was a doctrine of racial supremacy. Hitler ranted about the superiority of the so-called Aryan race. The purity of the German nation was supposedly threatened with adulteration by inferior races, or *untermenschen*. Policies based on this maniacal worldview resulted in the systematic murder of millions of innocent men, women, and children. Approximately six million Jews and millions of others, including Poles, Gypsies, homosexuals, and people with disabilities, were killed in cold blood.

During the Nazi era, the German nation appears, at first glance, to have become little more than an extension of Hitler's will—in other words, the awesome moral responsibility for the Holocaust somehow rested on the shoulders of one man, Adolf Hitler. But some dispute this interpretation. For example, according to Irving Kristol,

> When one studies the case of The Nazi there comes a sickening emptiness of the stomach and a sense of bafflement. Can this be all? The disparity between the crime and the criminal is too monstrous.

nation
Often interchangeable with *state* or *country*; in common usage, this term actually denotes a specific people with a distinct language and culture or a major ethnic group—for example, the French, Dutch, Chinese, and Japanese people each constitute a nation as well as a state, hence the term nation-state; not all nations are fortunate enough to have a state of their own—modern examples include the Kurds (Turkey, Iraq, and Iran), Palestinians (West Bank and Gaza, Lebanon, Jordan), Pashtuns (Afghanistan), and Uighurs and Tibetans (China).

nation-state
A geographically defined community administered by a government.

We expect to find evil men, paragons of wickedness, slobbering, maniacal brutes; we are prepared to trace the lineaments of The Nazi on the face of every individual Nazi in order to define triumphantly the essential features of his character. But the Nazi leaders were not diabolists, they did not worship evil. For—greatest of ironies—the Nazis, like Adam and Eve before the fall, knew not of good and evil, and it is this cast of moral indifference that makes them appear so petty and colorless and superficial.[5]

One such person, according to the late German-born political theorist Hannah Arendt, was Otto Adolf Eichmann, the Nazi officer in charge of Jewish affairs in the Third Reich, who engineered and directed the genocide or extermination program known in history as the Holocaust. In Arendt's view, Eichmann was not a particularly unusual man.[6]

Following Eichmann's capture in 1960 and his subsequent trial for war crimes, Arendt wrote a famous series of articles for *The New Yorker* later published in a book entitled *Eichmann in Jerusalem: The Banality of Evil*. The subtitle of the book underscored Arendt's central argument: namely,

POLITICS AND POP CULTURE

SCHINDLER'S LIST

Not all Germans, or Europeans, were as indifferent or self-serving in the face of evil as Adolf Eichmann. One notable example was Oskar Schindler, who is now widely renowned thanks largely to the movie *Schindler's List*.

Schindler was a German businessman who belonged to the Nazi Party. Schindler was no saint, but he used his business and political connections to save the lives of the Jewish workers he had first exploited.*

No doubt most of us would identify more with Schindler and other Christians who rescued Jews than with Eichmann, but the disturbing fact remains that far more Germans (including tens of thousands of Hitler Youth), mesmerized by Hitler's message of hate, behaved more like Eichmann than like Schindler.

At his trial for war crimes, Eichmann claimed to have no obsessive hatred toward Jews. In fact, we know now that Eichmann's "little man" self-portrait was a clever act designed to save him from the gallows.

Although Eichmann was not the mere functionary or "cog" he claimed to be, many Germans who participated directly in the Holocaust do fit this description—they were following orders, full stop. The fact that so many Germans blindly obeyed Eichmann and Hitler's other top lieutenants illustrates the fine line between indifference and immorality—and how easily the former can lead to the latter.

Eichmann exemplifies the worst in human nature; Schindler exemplifies the best. Both men were caught up in the same set of circumstances. Except for a depraved but ingenious demagogue name Hitler, Eichmann would not have become a war criminal and Schindler would not have become a paragon. If Hitler does not deserve the credit for producing an exemplar like Schindler, does he deserve the blame for producing a monster like Eichmann? Think about it.

Hint: If we are all products of the circumstances we are born (or thrust) into, we are thereby absolved of individual moral responsibility. On the other hand, if there is such a thing as free will, then we cannot blame society for our misdeeds.

*To read more about Schindler and the courageous acts of other righteous Christians, see Eva Fogelman, *Conscience and Courage: Rescuers of Jews During the Holocaust* (New York: Doubleday, 1994). See also Samuel P. Oliner and Pearl M. Oliner, *The Altruistic Personality: Rescuers of Jews in Nazi Europe* (New York: Free Press, 1988).

that far from being one of the masterminds of the Holocaust, Eichmann was an ordinary man with no original ideas, great ambitions, or deep convictions. Rather, he had a strong desire to get ahead, to be a success in life. He took special pride in his ability to do a job efficiently.

Although not particularly thoughtful or reflective in Arendt's view, he was intelligent in practical ways, attentive to details, a competent administrator capable of managing a major operation like the systematic mass murder of millions of Jews and other "enemies" and "degenerates." Arendt also describes Eichmann as somewhat insecure, but not noticeably more so than many "normal" people (see "Politics and Pop Culture").

More recently, scholars have unearthed a treasure trove of research materials that challenge Arendt's thesis. In a well-documented 579-page tome entitled *Eichmann Before Jerusalem: The Unexamined Life of a Mass Murderer* (New York: Alfred A. Knopf, 2014), German philosopher Bettina Stangneth shows clearly that Eichmann was a thinking man, a fanatical believer in German racial superiority who believed himself to have been involved in "creative" work and who—as a fugitive hiding out in Argentina after the war—was determined to secure his rightful place as a hero in German history. The notion that in Kristol's words "he knew not of good and evil" is no longer credible. Eichmann did not lose any sleep over dirty hands; instead, he gloried in having bloody hands.

Nazi mass murderer Adolf Eichmann. An ordinary man? Pictured here is the Red Cross identity document Adolf Eichmann used to enter Argentina under the fake name Ricardo Klement in 1950. Have you ever known anyone who was loyal to a fault? Is blind obedience to authority uncommon? Why do people in the workplace often go along to get along?

HOW TO STUDY POLITICS

Aristotle is the father of political science.[7] He not only wrote about politics and ethics, but he also described different political systems and suggested a scheme for classifying and evaluating them. For Aristotle, political science simply meant political investigation; thus, a political scientist was one who sought, through systematic inquiry, to understand the truth about politics. In this sense, Aristotle's approach to studying politics more than two thousand years ago has much in common with what political scientists do today. Yet the discipline has changed a great deal since Aristotle's time.

There is no consensus on how best to study politics. Political scientists can and do choose among different approaches, ask different kinds of questions, and address different audiences. This fact is often a source of some dismay within the discipline, but it is hardly surprising and probably unavoidable given the vast universe of human activity the study of politics encompasses. Let us explore why and how contemporary political scientists study politics.

nation-building
The process of forming a common identity based on the notion of belonging to a political community separate and distinct from all others; often the concept of "nation" is based on common ethno-linguistic roots.

For What Purposes?

Some of the most important questions in politics are "should" and "ought" questions, the kind that scientists seeking objective truth tend to avoid. These are the great *normative* political questions that resonate throughout human history: When is war justified? Do people have a right to revolt? Is the right to life absolute? Is state repression always wrong? Does government have a right to keep secrets from the people? To invade the privacy of its citizens? What about censorship? Is government ever justified in placing limits on freedom of expression and freedom of the press? Should every citizen pay taxes at the same rate? If not, why not? Who should pay more and who less?

Such questions may seem too abstract or theoretical to have any practical value, but in fact they are behind the most controversial political issues of the day—abortion, gun control, gay rights, legalization of marijuana, capital punishment, and the list goes on. (See if you can think of more issues to add to this list and connect each issue to some fundamental question of justice or fairness.)

Some issues lend themselves to empirical analysis more than others. Studying elections, for example, can reveal flaws in the voting process—such as skewed voting districts or impediments to voter registration—and lead to appropriate changes or reforms, such as redistricting or switching from written ballots to voting machines. Opinion polls help leaders gauge the mood of the public and better understand the effect of government policies (see Chapter 11).

However, answers to many of the most basic questions in politics can only be discovered via a thorough knowledge of the facts and a rigorous process of analysis involving reason, logic, and dialogue. There are no shortcuts, and given that we are talking about the health and well-being of society, the stakes are too high to settle for anything less than our best efforts.

By What Methods?

Should political science strive to predict or forecast events? Is the study of politics a science akin to physics or chemistry? Answers to such questions lie in the realm of **methodology**. There are many ways to classify political scientists. We will focus on one basic distinction—the difference between *positivism* and *normativism*.

Positivism emphasizes empirical research (which relies on observation) and couches problems in terms of variables we can measure. **Behaviorism** is an offshoot of positivism that focuses mainly on the study of political behavior. Behaviorists use quantitative analysis to challenge the conventional wisdom—for example, what motivates voters or why a given election turned out the way it did. Following the facts—statistical data—wherever they may lead is the hallmark of the so-called hard sciences. The results of empirical research can cast long-standing "truths" into serious doubt or expose "facts" as fallacies.

Normativism is based on the idea closely associated with the German political philosopher Immanuel Kant. He stated that the "ought" and the "is" are inseparable from one another and that the "ought" cannot be derived from

stateless nation
People (or nations) who are scattered over the territory of several states or dispersed widely and who have no autonomous, independent, or sovereign governing body of their own; examples of stateless nations include the Kurds, Palestinians, and Tibetans (see also *nation*).

justice
Fairness; the distribution of rewards and burdens in society in accordance with what is deserved.

political literacy
The ability to think and speak intelligently about politics.

methodology
The way scientists and scholars set about exploring, explaining, proving, or disproving propositions in different academic disciplines. The precise methods vary according to the discipline and the object, event, process, or phenomenon under investigation.

positivism
A philosophy of science, originated by Auguste Comte, that stresses observable, scientific facts as the sole basis of proof and truth; a skeptical view of ideas or beliefs based on religion or metaphysics.

behaviorism
An approach to the study of politics that emphasizes fact-based evaluations of action.

the "is." Sticking strictly to the facts, a trademark of positivism, thus raises a serious problem for the adherents of normative theory, who are interested not only in describing actions and consequences but also in prescribing policies and remedies. Seen in this light, values are at the core of political analysis. In studying Congress, for example, value-based political science might ask: Did special interests unduly influence health care reform in 2009-2010? Or with respect to U.S. foreign policy: Was the invasion of Iraq in 2003 necessary?

Scholars and policy analysts seeking answers to such questions often resort to philosophy, history, constitutional law, court cases, treaties, declassified documents, and expert opinion. For example, in explaining why the Constitution adopted in 1787 did not abolish slavery, scholars often skip over the question of whether or why slavery is wrong. Instead, they examine the writings and speeches of the founding fathers, the economic interests they represented, the social class to which they all belonged, and the like. The reason they (we) don't dwell on the moral question is that today every sane and sensible person knows slavery is wrong. Slavery is an extreme case, but many political issues are at least as much about values as about facts.

In truth, it is not always easy to distinguish between a fact and a value. Moreover, in politics, values *are* facts. We all bring certain values to everything we do. At the same time, however, we can never get at the truth if we don't place a high value on facts.

For example, the belief that abortion is a sin, which is held by an influential segment of the population, is a *value* based on a religious belief or moral conviction. We can argue all day long whether abortion is an American's right or always wrong, but there is no escaping the *fact* that it is controversial and that politicians, government officials, and judges have no choice but to deal with it. No matter what legislation or jurisprudence is brought to bear on this question, it will have far-reaching consequences for society. This is but one simple example among many, illustrating the reality in which facts and values are entangled in the political life of every society, always have been, and always will be.

The Study of Human Behavior Political scientists tend to be wary of "subjective" value judgments that often fly in the face of objective facts. In the social sciences, so-called behaviorists use the type of quantitative methods common in the natural sciences such as biology, physics, and chemistry, asking questions that can only be answered empirically. Constructing a research design, collecting data, using the objective tools of statistical analysis to test hypotheses—these are the essential elements of the **scientific method**. In this manner, behavioral scientists develop mathematical models to try and explain voting behavior, coalition-building, decision making, even the causes of war.

In a study done nearly two decades ago but still relevant, researchers asked: Is it really true, as is widely believed, that high voter turnout favors Democrats?[8] The prevailing belief that Democrats benefit from high voter turnout assumes several things: (1) people with lower socioeconomic status (SES) vote less often than people with higher SES; (2) as voter turnout rises, more people on the lower end of the SES ladder vote; and (3) lower-end voters are likely to vote for the party they trust to advance working-class interests—namely,

normativism
Applying moral principles – norms – rooted in logic and reason to problems of politics and government; putting moral theory into political practice through good laws, wise legislation, and fair judges.

scientific method
Seeking empirical answers to questions through a rigorous process of constructing research designs, collecting data, and using the objective tools of statistical analysis to test hypotheses.

the Democratic Party. This belief is reinforced whenever low voter turnout coincides with Republican victories. It also explains why most Democrats favored (and Republicans opposed) the 1993 National Voter Registration Act—popularly known as the Motor Voter Bill—which eased voter registration procedures.

Researchers examined 1,842 state elections going all the way back to 1928: 983 for senator and 859 for governor. Applying a mathematical test, they concluded that from 1928 to 1964 high voter turnout did aid the Democrats, as generally believed, but after 1964 there was no such correlation either in senatorial or gubernatorial races.

Why? Although this question was beyond the scope of the study, its findings were consistent with another complex theory of voting behavior. The rise in the number of independents since 1964 (and the resulting decline in party identification and partisan voting) made it difficult to calculate which party would benefit from a large voter turnout in any given race. In 2011, a Gallup poll found that 40% of all voters identified themselves as independents, and **ticket splitting** and **swing voting** have become common (see Chapter 11). In the 2010 midterm elections, for example, Republicans were the beneficiaries of a huge swing vote, as they were once again in 2014.

Behaviorists, like other research scientists, are typically content to take small steps on the road to knowledge. Each step points the way to future studies.

Studying human behavior can be as frustrating as it is fascinating. There are almost always multiple explanations for human behavior, and it is often difficult to isolate a single cause or distinguish it from a mere statistical correlation. For instance, several studies indicate that criminals tend to be less intelligent than law-abiding citizens. But is low intelligence a cause of crime? What about social factors such as poverty, drug or alcohol addiction, or a history of being abused as a child? What about free will? Many reject the idea that society—rather than the criminal—is somehow responsible for the crime.

Political scientists often disagree not only about how to study politics but also about which questions to ask. Behaviorists typically prefer to examine specific and narrowly defined questions, answering them by applying quantitative techniques—sophisticated statistical methods such as regression analysis and analysis of variance.

Many broader questions of politics, especially those

ticket splitting
A voter who votes for candidates from more than one party; this is the opposite of straight-ticket voting.

swing vote
An independent voter who votes for the Republican Party in one election and votes for the Democratic Party in another.

Rob Crandall/Alamy

Political scientists analyze patterns and trends in voting behavior to learn more about who votes, how different segments of the population vote, and why people vote the way they do. Political strategists use this information to help clients (candidates for office) win elections. If you were running for the state legislature or Congress, what would you want to know about voters in your district?

raising issues of justice, lie beyond the scope of this sort of investigation. Questions such as "What is justice?" or "What is the role of the state in society?" require us to make moral choices and value judgments. Even if we cannot resolve such questions scientifically, they are worth asking. Confining the study of politics *only* to the kinds of questions we can subject to quantitative analysis risks turning political science into an academic game of Trivial Pursuit.

Given the complexity of human behavior, it is not surprising that experts argue over methodology, or how to do science. Although the lively debate sparked by the behavioral revolution has cooled, it divided the discipline for several decades and is likely to continue to do so for years to come.

The Political (Science) Puzzle

Political science, like politics, means different things to different people. The subject matter of politics is wide-ranging and thus difficult to study without breaking it down into more manageable parts and pieces. Subfields include *political theory, U.S. government and politics, public administration, public policy, political economy, comparative politics,* and *international relations.*

Political Theory The origins of what we now call political science are to be found in Greek philosophy and date back to Socrates and Plato (circa 400 BCE). The Socratic method of teaching and seeking Truth was to ask a series of pithy questions—What is the good life? Is there a natural right to liberty?—while questioning every answer in order to expose logical fallacies.

Political theory seeks answers to such questions through reason, logic, and experience. Famous names in the history of political thought include Aristotle, Thomas Hobbes, John Locke, Jean-Jacques Rousseau, and John Stuart Mill, among others. These thinkers ranged far and wide but met at the intersection of politics and ethics.

Because people on opposite sides of the political fence believe that they are right and the other people are wrong, understanding politics requires us, at minimum, to be open-minded and familiarize ourselves with pro and con arguments.[9] Knowledge of costs and the moral consequences in politics are essential to a clear sense of purpose and coherent policy.

Are we humans rational by nature or are we driven by passions such as love, hate, anger, and prejudice? Advocates of **rational choice** theory emphasize the role of reason over emotion in human behavior. Political behavior, arguably, follows logical and even predictable patterns. The key to understanding politics is self-interest. This approach, which forms the basis for a theory of international relations known as **political realism** (see Chapter 17), holds that individuals and states alike act according to the iron logic of self-interest.

Other political scientists argue that rational choice theory is an oversimplification because states and groups are composed of human beings with disparate interests, perceptions, and beliefs. The key is not self-interest pure and simple but culture and shared values. In this view, we cannot explain political behavior by reference to logic and rationality alone. Instead, the behavior of individuals and of groups is a product of specific influences that vary from place to place—in other words, political behavior is a product of **political culture**.

rational choice
The role of reason over emotion in human behavior. Political behavior, in this view, follows logical and even predictable patterns as long as we understand the key role of self-interest.

political realism
The philosophy that power is the key variable in all political relationships and should be used pragmatically and prudently to advance the national interest; policies are judged good or bad on the basis of their effect on national interests, not on their level of morality.

political culture
The moral values, beliefs, and myths people live by and are willing to die for.

Of course, it is not necessary to adhere dogmatically to one theory or the other. Both contain important insights and we can perhaps best see them as complementary rather than conflicting.

U.S. Government and Politics Understanding our own political institutions is vitally important. Because the United States is a federal system, our frame of reference changes depending on whether we mean national, state, or local politics. Similarly, when we study political behavior in the United States, it makes a big difference whether we are focusing on individual behavior or the behavior of groups such as interest groups, ethnic groups, age cohorts, and the like. Teaching and learning about one's own government is, in effect, an exercise in civic education.

Citizens in a democracy need to know how the government works, what rights they are guaranteed by the Constitution, and how to decide what to believe. We need to remember that the United States is home to the oldest written constitution, a behemoth economy, and the most potent military capability of all time. Prestige, power, and wealth have political and moral consequences: namely, an obligation to act responsibly as citizens of both a powerful country and an interdependent world.

Public Administration Public administration is all about how governments organize and operate, about how bureaucracies work and interact with citizens and each other. In federal systems, intergovernmental relations is a major focus of study. Students of public administration examine budgets, procedures, and processes in an attempt to improve efficiency and reduce waste and duplication. One perennial question deals with bureaucratic behavior: How and why do bureaucracies develop vested interests and special relationships (such as between the Pentagon and defense contractors, or the Department of Commerce and trade associations) quite apart from the laws and policies they are established to implement?

Political scientists who study public administration frequently concentrate on case studies, paying attention to whether governmental power is exercised in a manner consistent with the public interest. Public administration shares this focus with policy studies and political science as a whole.

Policy Studies and Analysis Public policy places a heavy emphasis on the outputs of government. However, the politics of public policy involves inputs as well. Before any policy can be formulated and finalized, much less implemented, all sorts of ideas and interests must be brought forward, congressional hearings held, consultants hired, and studies undertaken, published, digested, and debated. Not only special interests but also institutional interests and bureaucratic politics are further complicating factors. Once a policy is put into effect, policy analysts study the effects and look for signs—evidence—that it's working or not working. The whole process is highly political both because public policy carries a price tag denominated in taxpayer dollars and, not least, because it often carries a lot ideological freight.

Political Economy The study of political economy is a particularly well-developed discipline in the United Kingdom, but it has migrated across the

Atlantic and now occupies a prominent place in the curriculum at many colleges and universities in the United States. As the name implies, this subfield resides at the intersection of politics and economics. The genius of this marriage of two disciplines arises from the fact that so much of what governments do involves monetary and fiscal policy (taxes and spending), which have a major impact on the distribution of wealth in society, inflation and interest rates, employment levels, the business cycle, the investment climate, bank regulations, and the like.

Comparative Politics Comparative politics seeks to contrast and evaluate governments and political systems. Comparing forms of government, stages of economic development, domestic and foreign policies, and political traditions enables political scientists to formulate meaningful generalizations. Some comparativists specialize in a particular region of the world or a particular nation. Others focus on a particular issue or political phenomenon, such as terrorism, political instability, or voting behavior.

All political systems share certain characteristics. Figure 1.2 depicts one famous model, developed by political scientist David Easton in 1965. This model suggests that all political systems function within the context of political cultures, which consist of traditions, values, and common knowledge. It assumes citizens have expectations of and place demands on the political system, but they also support the system in various ways: They may participate in government, vote, or simply obey the laws of the state. The demands they make and supports they provide in turn influence the government's decisions, edicts, laws, and orders.

Countries and cultures differ in countless ways. Focusing on these differences makes it possible to classify or categorize political systems in ways that can aid our understanding of the advantages and disadvantages of each type. This book distinguishes among democratic, authoritarian, and totalitarian states.

Typologies change over time, reflecting new trends and seismic shifts in world politics or the global economy. For example, after the fall of Communism, the distinction between established liberal democracies and "transitional

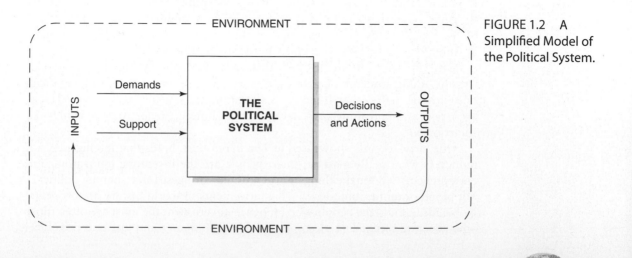

FIGURE 1.2   A Simplified Model of the Political System.

states" gained currency (see Chapter 8). It also became fashionable to distinguish between viable states and so-called failed states (see Chapter 9). The main types of totalitarian systems—the Nazi or Fascist model on the right and the Communist model on the left—are either defunct (most notably Hitler's Germany and Stalin's Russia) or depend on foreign investment and access to global markets (China and Vietnam). As a result, there is a tendency to gloss over or ignore the totalitarian model today even though some unreconstructed examples of this extremely repressive system still exist (North Korea and Cuba). And perhaps because many countries (including the United States and our NATO allies in Europe) are now locked in an interdependent relationship with China, there is also a tendency to sweep gross human rights violations under the rug.

International Relations Specialists in international relations analyze how nations interact. Why do nations sometimes live in peace and harmony but go to war at other times? The advent of the nuclear age, of course, brought new urgency to the study of international relations, but the threat of an all-out nuclear war now appears far less menacing than other threats, including international terrorism, global warming, energy security, and, most recently, the economic meltdown.

Although war and peace are ever-present problems in international relations, they are by no means the only ones. The role of morality in foreign policy continues to be a matter of lively debate. Political realists argue that considerations of national interest have always been paramount in international politics and always will be.[10] Others argue that enlightened self-interest can lead to world peace and an end to the cycle of war. Realists often dismiss such ideas as too idealistic in a dog-eat-dog world. Idealists counter that realists are too fatalistic and that war is not inevitable but rather a self-fulfilling prophecy. Still others say the distinction between the national interest and international morality is exaggerated; that democracies, for example, derive mutual benefit from protecting each other and that in so doing they also promote world peace.[11]

The Power of Ideas

In politics, money talks—or so people say. Listening to the news, it's easy to get the impression that Congress is up for sale. As a summer intern in the United States Senate many years ago, one of the first things I was told is, "Son, in Washington it isn't what you know but who you know."

Often we start out life being idealistic and then quickly run up against reality. For young students of politics, it is easy to fall into a trap, to lurch from one extreme to the other. If money is all that matters, justice is an illusion, ideas are irrelevant, and things can never change. But is it true? Are the cynics the smart ones?

One view, recently showcased in *The Economist*, holds that intelligence, not money, is what really matters: smart people are the inventors, innovators, and entrepreneurs who make things happen: "The strongest force shaping politics is not blood or money but ideas."[12] Big movements in world history are propelled by big ideas, and "the people who influence government the most are often those who generate compelling ideas." If true, ideas *do* matter and justice is possible.

According to this argument, intelligence is the great equalizer in a globalized and competitive world operating on market principles. The children of the poor can—and often do—have greater native intelligence than rich kids. Thus, a college dropout (Mark Zuckerberg) can have a bright idea, launch a social network called Facebook on the Internet, and become a billionaire in his mid-20s. Years earlier, another college dropout with an idea (Bill Gates III) started a computer software company called Microsoft and soon reached the top of the Fortune 400 list of the world's richest individuals. Gates remained at the top of that list in 2013.

But entrepreneurs who control billions of dollars in assets (Rupert Murdoch and the Koch brothers are a few other well-known examples) do not operate only in the business world and economy—they also invest heavily in politics and government. Do ideas still have a chance in today's political marketplace? Do smart people get elected to high office in the same way as they climb the corporate ladder to become CEOs and join the ranks of the super-rich? This book will challenge you to think about such questions.

And one word of caution: Don't expect to find easy answers. And don't expect the answers to be revealed suddenly in a burst of divine light. The role of education is to ask the right questions. The key to a life well lived is to search for the right answers—wherever that might take you.

SUMMARY

Understanding politics is a matter of self-interest. By exploring politics, we gain a better appreciation of what is—and what is not—in the public interest.

This chapter focuses on three fundamental concepts: power, order, and justice. It also explores the interrelationships between power and order, order and justice, and justice and power.

Political power can be defined as the capacity to maintain order in society. Whenever governments promulgate new laws or sign treaties or go to war, they are exercising political power. Whenever we pay our taxes, put money in a parking meter, or remove our shoes prior to boarding an airplane, we, in effect, bow to the power of government.

When governments exercise power, they often do it in the name of order. Power and authority are closely related: authority is the official exercise of power. If we accept the rules and the rulers who make and enforce them, then government also enjoys legitimacy.

Questions of justice are often embedded in political disputes. If the public interest is not advanced by a given policy or if society no longer accepts the authority of the government as legitimate, the resulting discontent can lead to political instability and even rebellion or revolution.

Political science seeks to discover the basic principles and processes at work in political life. Classical political theory points to moral and philosophical truths, political realism stresses the role of self-interest and rational action, and behaviorism attempts to find scientific answers through empirical research and data analysis. Most political scientists specialize in one or more subfields such as political theory, U.S. government and politics, comparative politics, international relations, political economy, public administration, or public policy.

Politics matters. This simple truth was tragically illustrated by the rise of Nazism in Germany. The bad news is that sometimes war is necessary to defeat a monstrous threat to world order and humanity. The good news is that there are often political or diplomatic solutions to conflict and injustice in human affairs. It is this fact that makes the study of politics forever obligatory and essential.

KEY TERMS

politics 4	state 7	positivism 14
power 4	sovereignty 7	behaviorism 14
authority 5	country 7	normativism 14
legitimacy 5	nation 7	scientific method 15
legitimate authority 5	nation-state 8	ticket splitting 16
order 6	nation-building 8	swing voting 16
society 6	stateless nation 10	rational choice 17
social contract 6	justice 10	political realism 17
government 7	political literacy 11	political culture 17
republic 7	methodology 14	

REVIEW QUESTIONS

1. "A basic understanding of politics is vital"—true or false?
2. On what three fundamental concepts is the study of politics based?
3. How does one identify a political problem? Why are some things more political than others? What does it mean to say something is "political"?
4. Given the pervasive presence of politics in society, how can the study of politics be made manageable?
5. In what ways can individuals benefit from the study of politics and government? Is there also a benefit to society as a whole?
6. Is politics a cautionary tale about human frailty? Or is that an oversimplification?

WEBSITES AND READINGS

A Google search produces millions of sites for the keyword *politics*. Fortunately, there are some cool gateways to politics on the Web, but you have to know where to look.

One good place to start is at http://www.politicalinformation.com/. This site contains thousands of political and policy websites in categories such as Campaigns and Elections, Parties and Organizations, Issues, and Research Tools, which are then broken down into subcategories, and so on.

Throughout the rest of the book, you will find more of these gateways, leading to a vast array of resources related to the material in a given chapter—everything from suggested search terms to the uniform resource locators (URLs) for specific websites. These gateways will prove useful in finding more information about various concepts, topics, and issues covered in the text or in doing research for term papers.

The URLs below relate to topics relevant to the whole book, but especially to Chapter 1. The Internet is constantly changing, so don't be surprised to discover that a site mentioned has a different name, is at a different address, or is no longer available. For example, the old URL for the Congressional Quarterly, http://cqpolitics.com/, will now take you too CQ's "Roll Call" blog at http://www.rollcall.com/politics/index.html?cqp=1.

Another useful CQ website is at http://www.governing.com/politics.htm, home to a monthly magazine for state and local government officials. The website at http://www.politics1.com/ claims to be "the most comprehensive guide to U.S. politics." Go to http://www.politicalwire.com/ for up-to-date coverage of news and commentary about politics. Finally, check out http://www.politico.com/ for comprehensive information on current affairs, especially the hot news from Capitol Hill and what Washington insiders are talking about.

Books and Articles

Arendt, Hannah. *Eichmann in Jerusalem: A Report on the Banality of Evil*. New York: Vintage Press, 1963. (Republished in paperback by Penguin in 2006).

Aristotle. *The Politics*. Edited and translated by Ernest Barker. New York: Oxford University Press, 1962. An account of the necessity and value of politics.

Crick, Bernard. *In Defense of Politics*. Magnolia, MA: Peter Smith, 1994. An argument that politics is an important and worthy human endeavor.

Drucker, Peter. "The Monster and the Lamb," *Atlantic* (December 1978): 82–87. A short but moving account of the effects of the Nazi government on several individuals.

Easton, David. *The Political System: An Inquiry into the State of Political Science*, 2nd ed. Chicago: University of Chicago Press, 1981. A pioneering book that laid the foundation for a systems theory approach to political analysis.

Lewis, C. S. *The Abolition of Man*. New York: Simon & Schuster, 1996. An elegant discussion of the necessity of moral judgments.

Tinder, Glenn. *Political Thinking: The Perennial Questions*, 6th ed. London: Longman, 2009. A topical consideration of enduring problems and controversies in politics.

CHAPTER 2

The Idea of the Public Good
Ideologies and Isms

Learning Objectives

1   Define the public good.
2   Identify the three kinds of political ideologies.
3   Identify the five core values.
4   Describe the difference between a liberal and a conservative, as well as how these terms have changed over time.
5   Determine whether or not one ideology or political persuasion better guarantees freedom, justice, and democracy.

I n Lewis Carroll's classic tale *Alice in Wonderland*, Alice loses her way in a dense forest and encounters the Cheshire Cat who is sitting on a tree branch. "Would you tell me, please, which way I ought to go from here?" asks Alice. "That depends a good deal on where you want to get to," replies the Cat. "I don't much care where," says Alice. "Then it doesn't matter which way you go," muses the Cat.

Like Alice lost in the forest, we too occasionally find ourselves adrift when trying to make sense of complex issues, controversies, and crises. Governments and societies are no different. Political leadership can be woefully deficient or hopelessly divided over the economy or the environment or health care or a new threat to national security. Intelligent decisions, as Alice's encounter with the Cheshire Cat illustrates, can take place only after we have set clear aims and goals. Before politics can effectively convert mass energy (society) into collective effort (government), which is the essence of public policy, we need a consensus on where we want to go or what we want to be as a society a year from now or perhaps ten years down the road. Otherwise, our leaders, like the rest of us, cannot possibly know how to get there. There are plenty of people eager to tell us *what* to think. Our purpose is to learn *how* to think about politics.

POLITICAL ENDS AND MEANS

In politics, ends and means are inextricably intertwined. Implicit in debates over public policy is a belief in the idea of the **public good**, that it is the government's role to identify and pursue aims of benefit to society as a whole rather than to favored individuals. But the focus of policy debates is often explicitly about means rather than ends. For example, politicians may disagree over whether a tax cut at a particular time will help promote the common good (prosperity) by encouraging saving and investment, balancing the national budget, reducing the rate of inflation, and so on. Although they disagree about the best monetary and fiscal strategies, both sides would agree that economic growth and stability are proper aims of government.

In political systems with no curbs on executive authority, where the leader has unlimited power, government may have little to do with the public interest.[1] In constitutional democracies, by contrast, the public good is associated with core values such as security, prosperity, equality, liberty, and justice (see Chapter 13). These goals are the navigational guides for keeping the ship of state on course. Arguments about whether to tack this way or that, given the prevailing political currents and crosswinds, are the essence of public policy debates.

IDEOLOGIES AND THE PUBLIC GOOD

The concept of Left and Right originated in the European parliamentary practice of seating parties that favor social and political change to the left of the presiding officer; those opposing change (or favoring a return to a previous form of government), to the right. "You are where you sit," in other words.

public good
The shared beliefs of a political community as to what goals government ought to attain (for example, to achieve the fullest possible measure of security, prosperity, equality, liberty, or justice for all citizens).

ideology
Any set of fixed, predictable ideas held by politicians and citizens on how to serve the public good.

Today, people may have only vague ideas about government or how it works or what it is actually doing at any given time.[2] Even so, many lean one way or another, toward conservative or liberal views. When people go beyond merely leaning and adopt a rigid, closed system of political ideas, however, they cross a line and enter the realm of **ideology**. Ideologies act as filters that true believers (or adherents) use to interpret events, explain human behavior, and justify political action.

The use of labels—or "isms" as they are often called—is a kind of shorthand that, ideally, facilitates political thought and debate rather than becoming a way to discredit one's political opponents. One note of caution: these labels do not have precisely the same meaning everywhere. Thus, what is considered "liberal" in the United Kingdom might be considered "conservative" in the United States (see Figure 2.1).

Conservatives in the United States traditionally favor a strong national defense, deregulation of business and industry, and tax cuts on capital gains (income from stocks, real estate, and other investments) and inheritances. They often staunchly oppose social spending ("welfare") on the grounds that giveaway programs reward sloth and indolence.

By contrast, liberals tend to favor public assistance programs, cuts in military spending, a progressive tax system (one that levies higher taxes on higher incomes), and governmental regulation in such areas as the food and drug industry, occupational safety and health, housing, transportation, and energy.

Prior to the Reagan Revolution of the 1980s, Republicans championed balanced budgets and limited government. In 2012–2014, Tea Party Republicans in Congress led the fight for deficit reduction, but insisted that it be done without raising taxes on the wealthy. Democrats countered by demanding that budget cuts be offset with targeted tax increases, in particular on individual earnings in excess of $400,000 and capital gains.

Compared to Europe's parliamentary democracies, the political spectrum in the United States is shifted to the right. Ideas and policies widely viewed as "socialist" in the United States—national health care, for example—are

FIGURE 2.1   Focus Conservative or Liberal?

	U.S. Conservatives*	British Liberals§
Constitutionalism	Yes	Yes
Religious tolerance	Yes	Yes
Market economy	Yes	Yes
Protectionism	No	No
Pacifism	No	No

* Values historically associated with the Republican Party in the United States, though not necessarily with the policies of any given administration or president

§ Values historically associated with the Whig Party in the United Kingdom, often called classical liberalism

mainstream in European countries. Any attempts to tamper with social programs in so-called welfare states are likely to provoke a public outcry, as the anti-austerity protests that have swept across Europe (notably, Greece, Spain, Ireland, Italy, and France) in recent years attest.

The word "liberal" is frequently associated with leftist views in the United States, where talking heads on FOX News routinely call President Obama's policy initiatives "socialist." But "liberal" has always meant something quite different in the United Kingdom, where it originated. There the term still denotes a desire to maximize individual liberty as the first principle of good government.

Leftists in Europe often belong to socialist parties, but there is no viable Socialist Party in the United States and never has been. In the May 2012 presidential election, for example, voters in France handed Socialist Party leader Francois Hollande a sweeping victory, giving the Socialists an absolute majority of 300 seats in the National Assembly. (What if that were to happen in the U.S.? You can't imagine it? That's because it can't happen here, which begs the question: Why?)

We'll learn more about European politics in general, and France in particular, in Chapter 7; for now, think of Socialists winning elections as a measure of the vast differences in the way Americans and Europeans define the public good.

In this chapter, we group ideologies under three headings: antigovernment ideologies, right-wing ideologies, and left-wing ideologies. Left and Right are very broad categories, however, and there are many shades of gray. Only when the political system becomes severely polarized, as it did, for example, in Germany between the two world wars, are people forced to choose between black and white.

In the two-party system of the United States, the choice is limited to red (Republican) and blue (Democrat). After September 11, 2001, the political climate became more polarized and partisan, as reflected in the charged rhetoric of media figures like Rush Limbaugh, Glenn Beck, and Sean Hannity on the right and of Keith Olbermann and Rachel Maddow on the left. Between 2010 and 2014, the most extreme partisanship since World War II gave rise to governmental paralysis and gridlock in Congress, which in turn exacerbated political polarization and gave birth to the Tea Party movement. History provides sobering examples of what can happen when a government is dysfunctional, wealth is extremely concentrated, and people become disillusioned.

Antigovernment Ideologies

Opposition to government *in principle* is **anarchism**. The Russian revolutionary Mikhail Bakunin (1814–1876), who reveled in the "joy of destruction" and called for violent uprisings by society's beggars and criminals, is often considered the father of modern anarchism. A close relative of anarchism is **nihilism**, which glorifies destruction as an end in itself rather than as a means to overthrow the existing system or rebuilding society. In Russia during the last half of the nineteenth century, anarchists helped to precipitate the discontent that led to the 1905 Revolution, sometimes called a dress rehearsal for the 1917 October Revolution.

anarchism
A system that opposes in principle the existence of any form of government, often through violence and lawlessness.

nihilism
A philosophy that holds that the total destruction of all existing social and political institutions is a desirable end in itself.

Ideologies of the Right

monarchism
A system based on the belief that political power should be concentrated in one person (for example, a king) who rules by decree.

fascism
A totalitarian political system that is headed by a popular charismatic leader and in which a single political party and carefully controlled violence form the bases of complete social and political control. Fascism differs from communism in that the economic structure, although controlled by the state, is privately owned.

Nazism
Officially called National Socialism, Nazism is a form of fascism based on extreme nationalism, militarism, and racism; the ideology associated with Adolf Hitler and the Holocaust.

Monarchism is at the opposite end of the political spectrum. Until the twentieth century, monarchy was the prevalent form of government throughout the world. Whether they were called kings or emperors, czars or sultans, or sheiks or shahs, monarchs once ruled the world. Aristotle regarded monarchy—rule by a wise king—as the best form of government (although he recognized that wise kings, as opposed to tyrants, were very rare).

However archaic it may look to modern eyes, monarchism is not dead. Jordan, Kuwait, Morocco, Saudi Arabia, and the oil-rich Persian Gulf ministates, as well as Bhutan, Brunei, and Swaziland, are still monarchies. Jordan and Morocco are limited monarchies; in both countries, the chief executive rules for life by virtue of royal birth rather than by merit, mandate, or popular election. Most other countries that still pay lip service to monarchism are, in fact, *constitutional* monarchies in which the king or queen is a figurehead. The United Kingdom is the example we know best in the United States, but Belgium, the Netherlands, Spain, Denmark, Norway, and Sweden all have monarchs as titular rulers.

After World War I, **fascism** supplanted monarchism as the principal ideology of the extreme Right. In Germany, National Socialism—more commonly known as **Nazism**—was a particularly virulent form of this ideology (see Chapter 6). Predicated on the "superiority" of one race or nation and demanding abject obedience to authority, fascism exerted a powerful influence in Europe and South America from the 1920s to the 1940s. The prime examples in history are the Axis powers (Germany, Italy, and Japan) in World War II, but other instances of authoritarian regimes bearing a close resemblance to fascism—including Spain (Francisco Franco), Portugal (Oliveira Salazar), and Hungary (Miklos Horthy)—existed in this period as well.

Argentina under Juan Perón (1946–1955) closely resembled the fascist model after World War II, as did military dictatorships in Brazil, Paraguay, and several other Latin American countries. However, Perón never engaged in the kind of violence and mass repression associated with General Augusto Pinochet in Chile (1974–1990) or General Rafael Jorge Videla in Argentina (1976–1981). More recent examples include Kim Jong-Il of North Korea (who died in December 2011), Hosni Mubarak of Egypt (overthrown in the 2011 Egyptian Revolution), Muammar Qaddafi of Libya (also overthrown in 2011 as part of the wider "Arab Spring"), Omar al-Bashir of Sudan, and Bashar al-Assad of Syria (see Chapter 5).

Fascism enjoyed mass support in many countries largely because of its appeal to nationalism, ethnicity, and (in the case of Nazi Germany) race. Other ideological roots of fascism can be found in romanticism, xenophobia, populism, and even a form of hierarchical socialism (discussed below).

One of the distinguishing features of many extreme right-wing ideologies is a blatant appeal to popular prejudices and hatred.[3] Such an appeal often strikes a responsive chord when large numbers of people, who are part of the racial or ethnic majority, have either not shared fully in the benefits of society or have individually and collectively suffered severe financial reversals. In turbulent times, people are prone to follow a demagogue, to believe in conspiracy theories, and to seek scapegoats, such as a racial, ethnic, or religious minority group; an opposing political party; a foreign country; and the like. Xenophobia and antipathy to foreigners, immigrants, and even tourists have been on the rise in many European countries (including France, Germany, the Netherlands, and the United Kingdom) and in the United States since the 1990s. Remnants of the American Nazi Party and the Ku Klux Klan (KKK) have lingered as well.

Belief in racial superiority supplies an underlying rationale for a whole range of radical policies dealing with immigration (foreigners must be kept out), civil rights (African Americans, Jews, and other minorities are genetically inferior and do not deserve the same constitutional protections as whites), and foreign policy (threats to white America must be met with deadly force). At the far-right extreme, these groups are organized along paramilitary lines, engage in various survivalist practices, and preach violence. Although the KKK has largely faded from view, it still has die-hard followers, including some

Hate groups like the Ku Klux Klan feed on ignorance, prejudice, and fear and often use racial or religious differences to create a scapegoat. As human beings, we want simple answers, quick fixes, and someone to blame when things go wrong.

in law enforcement. In February 2009, the Nebraska Supreme Court upheld the firing of State Highway Patrol trooper Robert Henderson for his ties to the KKK. The KKK's long history of violence toward African Americans—symbolized by the white sheets worn by its members and the crosses set ablaze at rallies—has made it synonymous with bigotry and racial intolerance.

The Religious Right The religious right in the United States emerged as an important nationwide political force in 1980. The election as president of a conservative Republican, Ronald Reagan, both coincided with and accelerated efforts to create a new right-wing political coalition in the United States. The coalition that emerged combined the modern political techniques of mass mailings, extensive political fundraising, and the repeated use of the mass media (especially television) with a call for the restoration of traditional values, including an end to abortion, the reinstatement of prayer in public schools, a campaign against pornography, the recognition of the family as the basis of U.S. life, and a drive to oppose communism relentlessly on every front.

This movement contained a core of fundamentalist or evangelical Christians, called the New Right, who saw politics as an outgrowth of their core religious values. Beginning in the 1980s, television evangelists such as the late Jerry Falwell (who spearheaded a movement called the Moral Majority) and Pat Robertson (who ran unsuccessfully for president in 1988) gained a mass

Petr Kratochvil/PublicDomainPictures.net

Evangelical Christians who embrace a strict interpretation of the Bible often vote on the basis of moral issues such as opposition to abortion and gay marriage rather than on economic issues like income inequality, tax reform, or job creation.

following. The far right suffered a setback in 1992 when Pat Buchanan's presidential bid also fizzled.

The election of George W. Bush, who openly courted the fundamentalist Christian vote, was widely viewed as victory for the religious right. Roman Catholics and Southern Baptists, along with other evangelical groups, joined forces in a new kind of coalition against what many regular churchgoers saw as an alarming upsurge in immorality and sinful behavior, including abortion, gay marriage, and the teaching of evolution in public schools. The last issue, along with stem cell research, pitted religion against science.

The Christian Coalition, another conservative group, has roots in the Pentecostal church. Boasting as many as one million members, the Christian Coalition produces and distributes a kind of morality scorecard, evaluating political candidates' positions on key issues from the perspective of religious dogma. Its members focus on getting elected to local school boards in order to advocate for patriotism (as opposed to multiculturalism), religion, and a return to the basics in education.

The Christian Coalition's success raised two serious questions. First, was the Christian Coalition best understood as a well-meaning effort by decent citizens to participate in the political arena or as a dangerously divisive blurring by religious bigots of the separation between church and state? Second, was it an interest group or a political party?

The 2008 and 2012 elections both pointed to the possibility that the political potency of the religious right in U.S. politics was declining. Some critics have suggested revoking the tax-exempt status of religious establishments that cross the line and transform themselves into political movements.[4] But the strength of religious fundamentalists, particularly in the South and Midwest, combined with an antiquated scheme of representation that gives small, sparsely populated states disproportionate voting power in Congress, makes it likely that religion will continue to play a huge role in American politics at all levels in the years to come.

Capitalism The dominant ideology in the United States, Europe, and Asia today is **capitalism**. Even in Communist China, where Maoism remains the official ideology, capitalism is the engine driving the amazing revitalization of the economy since the death of Mao Zedong in 1976. The collapse of communism and its explicit rejection of private property, the profit motive, and social inequality was a triumphant moment for proponents of free enterprise and the free-market economy. Indeed, the Cold War was in no small measure an ideological contest between the United States and the Soviet Union over this very issue.

In the contemporary world, capitalism is the ideology of mainline conservatives; at the same time, however, it is a basic feature of classical liberalism. In the United States, it is the Republican Party that most enthusiastically embraces capitalism, although few Democrats in Congress ever dare to denounce big business. However disappointing or frustrating this fact may be to some rank-and-file voters, it is not difficult to discern the reasons for it. Capitalism is the ideology of big business, as well as of powerful Washington lobbies, including the U.S. Chamber of Commerce and the National Association of Manufacturers. It also provides the moral and philosophical justification for the often ruthless practices of multinational corporations (MNCs) such as Walmart, Microsoft, McDonald's, and Wall Street financiers—practices that would otherwise appear to be based on nothing more high-minded than the idea that "greed is good." (The U.S. actor Michael Douglas won an Academy Award for his performance in *Wall Street*, a 1987 film in which his "Master of the Universe" character spoke those very words.)

What is capitalism? It means different things to different people. It can refer to an economic theory based on the principles found in Adam Smith's *Wealth of Nations* (discussed later in this chapter). Or it can mean an ideology that elevates the virtues of freedom and independence, individualism and initiative, invention and innovation, risk-taking and reward for success. We can also view it as an elaborate myth system used to justify the class privileges of a wealthy elite and the exploitation of the workers who produce society's wealth. The latter interpretation, of course, derives most notably from the writings of Karl Marx (see "Ideologies of the Left" section in this chapter).

As an economic theory, capitalism stresses the role of market forces—mainly supply and demand—in regulating economic activity; determining prices, values, and costs; and allocating scarce resources. In theory it opposes government interference, and in practice it opposes government regulation. It applauds the notion that, in the words of President Calvin Coolidge, "the business of America is business." Capitalism's proponents, however, often *assume* we have a free market operating solely on the principles of supply and demand; they seldom consider whether it really exists. In fact, the free market is a myth, useful for public relations or propaganda but not for understanding how modern economies actually work. No modern economy can function without all sorts of rules and regulations. The question is not whether rules are necessary but rather who makes the rules and in whose interests. The key to the success of a market economy is competition, not deregulation.

As an ideology, capitalism opposes high taxes (especially on business), social welfare, and government giveaways. Conservatives tend to believe wealth is a sign of success and a reward for virtue. Rich people deserve to be rich. Poverty is the fault of poor people themselves, who are lazy, indolent, and irresponsible. Relieving poverty is the job of charity and the church, not government. Capitalists also tend (or pretend) to believe in the trickle-down theory: if the most enterprising members of society are permitted to succeed and to reinvest wealth, rather than handing it all over to the tax collector, the economy will grow, prosperity will trickle down to the lower levels, and everybody will be better off.

capitalism
An economic system in which individuals own the means of production and can legally amass unlimited personal wealth. Capitalist theory holds that governments should not impose any unnecessary restrictions on economic activity and that the laws of supply and demand can best regulate the economy. In a capitalist system, the private sector (mainly business and consumers), rather than government, makes most of the key decisions about production, employment, savings, investment, and the like; the opposite of a centrally planned economy such as existed in the Soviet Union under Stalin and Stalin's successors.

Critics of capitalism argue that the free market is a fiction and that big business only pretends to support deregulation and the increased competition it fosters. Meanwhile, giant corporations routinely seek tax favors, subsidies, and regulatory concessions and fight antitrust legislation at every turn. Revelations of large-scale fraud and corruption in recent years, symbolized by such fallen corporate outlaws as Enron and WorldCom, had badly stained the image of U.S. business even before the financial meltdown in the fall of 2008. But then came the failure of major investment firms like Lehman Brothers, Wachovia, and Merrill Lynch in 2008, followed by bailouts of banks, automakers, and insurance giant AIG teetering on the brink of bankruptcy.

One measure of how far the corporate sector had fallen in the public esteem: the insurance giant AIG (American International Group) saw its stock plunge from a 52-week high of $52.25 to a low of $0.38 in February 2009. Sensational front page stories of fraud, misfeasance, and self-aggrandizement associated with such prominent financiers such as Bernie Madoff, Robert Allen Stanford, and Jamie Dimon—CEO of JPMorgan Chase & Company blamed for a $2 billion trading loss in 2012—further undermined public trust in business, banks, and Wall Street. Prominent pundits with national audiences—writers like Bill Moyers, Matt Taibbi, Paul Krugman, Joseph Stiglitz, and William Black—kept these stories from fading and furnished a steady stream of evidence about collusion between Washington and Wall Street, corruption in Congress, and crime in the suites.

Proponents of **libertarianism** generally agree with the axiom, "That government is best, which governs least." Like classical liberals, libertarians stress the value of individual liberty; but an obsession with fighting all forms of government regulation—even measures aimed at public safety or income security for the elderly—often leads them to embrace policies at odds with logic or common sense. Thus, for example, to quote libertarian Senator Rand Paul (son of 2012 presidential candidate Ron Paul) in a 2002 letter to the Bowling Green Daily News, "a free society will abide unofficial, private discrimination, even when that means allowing hate-filled groups to exclude people based on the color of their skin." Paul also opposed gun control, called for the United States to withdraw from the United Nations Human Rights Commission, and advocated abolishing the Federal Reserve System.

Ideologies of the Left

Left-wing ideologies propose a view of human beings living together harmoniously without great disparities in wealth or social classes. In contrast to capitalism, public goods take priority over private possessions. If equality is the end, state control is the means—control of everything from banking, transportation, and heavy industry to the mass media, education, and health care.

Socialism is fundamentally opposed to capitalism, which contends that private ownership and enterprise in the context of a competitive free-market economy is the best and only way to bring about prosperity. Socialism is "an ideology that rejects individualism, private ownership, and private profits in favor of a system based on economic collectivism, governmental, societal, or industrial-group ownership of the means of production and distribution of goods, and social responsibility."[5]

libertarianism
The belief that the state is a necessary evil best kept small and weak relative to society; libertarians typically value individual liberty above social services and security.

socialism
A public philosophy favoring social welfare and general prosperity over individual self-reliance and private wealth.

POLITICS AND POP CULTURE

THE RUSSIANS ARE COMING! "007" TO THE RESCUE

During the Cold War (1945–1991), Hollywood produced dozens of films aimed at addressing and sometimes exploiting movie-goers' fear of Communism. Among the most famous films of this genre are *Conspirator* (1949) starring Elizabeth Taylor; *Trial* (1955); *Rio Bravo* (1956), starring John Wayne; *The Manchurian Candidate* (1962); *Dr. Strangelove* (1964); *Seven Days in May* (1964); *The Spy Who Came in from the Cold* (1965), based on John le Carré's eponymous best-seller; *The Russians Are Coming, the Russians Are Coming* (1966); and *Three Days of the Condor* (1975).

Perhaps the most famous hero of the genre is "007." Ian Fleming created the fictional character of James Bond (aka 007) in 1953 as the Cold War was building and a hot war (in Korea) was raging. The character has since been adapted for all manner of popular culture uses, especially film. Starting with *Dr. No* in 1962, James Bond movies (23 so far!) are now the longest running and the second highest grossing film series in history. *Skyfall* (2012) and *Spectre* (2015) are the most recent installments.

The University of Washington Library has compiled a selective list of Cold War films ("The Red Scare: A Filmography"), which can be viewed online. Here is their brief introduction to this list:

> The films produced in Hollywood before, during and after the Cold War Red Scare make for an interesting study in the response of a popular medium caught in a political firestorm. . . . [Some] motion pictures played a role in fueling the Red Scare, in propagandizing the threat of Communism and in a few rare and rather veiled cases, in standing up to the charges of the House Committee on Un-American Activities (HUAC). . . .

HUAC interrogated many film industry people. In the end, countless careers were destroyed but only ten individuals actually went to jail. This group came to be known as "The Hollywood Ten.". . . An exhaustive analysis . . . indicated that none of the 159 films credited . . . to The Hollywood Ten contained Communist propaganda.

Similarly, since 9/11, countless films and TV series pander to the American public's fascination with terrorism—and seek to profit from it (see Chapter 16).

Spy-thrillers in book form and in films are extremely popular and often hugely profitable. They have the power to entertain us and also to shape our views of the world. Do films like the ones about Communism and the Cold War serve a useful purpose in society beyond entertainment? Is there a sharp distinction between art and propaganda? Think about it.

(Hint: It has been said that "propaganda is direct while art is reflective." In this view, art doesn't change us but rather makes us more aware of what we already know or think we know, and it can either intensify or challenge our preconceptions.)

Communism is sometimes used interchangeably with **Marxism,** named after its founder Karl Marx (1818–1883). Marx and his associate Friedrich Engels (1820–1895) envisioned a radical transformation of society attainable only by open class conflict aimed at the overthrow of "monopoly capitalism."

Marx and Engels opened the famous *Communist Manifesto* (1848) with the bold assertion, "All history is the history of class struggle." All societies, Marx contended, evolve through the same historical stages, each of which represents a dominant economic pattern (the thesis) that contains the seeds of a new and conflicting pattern (the antithesis). Out of the inexorable clash between thesis and antithesis—a process Marx called **dialectical materialism**—comes a

communism
An ideology based on radical equality; the antithesis of capitalism.

Marxism
An ideology based on the writings of Karl Marx (1818–1883) who theorized that the future belonged to a rising underclass of urban-industrial workers he called "the proletariat."

dialectical materialism
Karl Marx's theory of historical progression, according to which economic classes struggle with one another, producing an evolving series of economic systems that will lead, ultimately, to a classless society.

bourgeoisie
In Marxist ideology, the capitalist class.

proletariat
In Marxist theory, a member of the working class.

surplus value
Excessive profits created through workers' labor and pocketed by the capitalist or owning class.

law of capitalist accumulation
According to Karl Marx, the invariable rule that stronger capitalists, motivated solely by greed, will gradually eliminate weaker competitors and gain increasing control of the market.

monopoly capitalism
The last stage before the downfall of the whole capitalist system.

synthesis, or a new stage in socioeconomic development. Thus, the Industrial Revolution was the capitalist stage of history, which succeeded the feudal stage when the **bourgeoisie** (urban artisans and merchants) wrested political and economic power from the feudal landlords. The laws of history—or dialectic—which made the rise of capitalism inevitable, also make "class struggle" between capitalists (the owning class) and the proletariat (the working class) inevitable—and guarantee the outcome.

Marxist theory holds that the main feature of the modern industrial era is the emergence of two antagonistic classes—wealthy capitalists, who own the means of production, and impoverished workers, the **proletariat,** who are paid subsistence wages. The difference between those wages and the value of the products created through the workers' labor is **surplus value,** or excessive profits, which the capitalists pocket. In this way, owners systematically exploit the workers and unwittingly lay the groundwork for a proletarian revolution.

How? According to Marx's **law of capitalist accumulation,** the rule is get big or get out. Bigger is always better. Small companies lose out or are gobbled up by big ones. In today's world of mergers and hostile takeovers, Marx appears nothing less than prescient here. Eventually, the most successful competitors in this dog-eat-dog contest force all the others out, thus ushering in the era of **monopoly capitalism,** the last stage before the downfall of the whole capitalist system.

The widening gap between rich and poor is the capitalist system's undoing. As human labor is replaced by more cost-effective machine labor, unemployment grows, purchasing power dwindles, and domestic markets shrink. The result is a built-in tendency toward business recession and depression. It all sounded eerily familiar in the midst of the 2008–2009 global recession.

Countless human beings become surplus labor—jobless, penniless, and hopeless. According to the **law of pauperization,** this result is inescapable. For orthodox Marxists, the "crisis of capitalism" and the resulting proletarian revolution are equally inevitable. Because capitalists will not relinquish their power, privilege, or property without a struggle, the overthrow of capitalism can occur only through violent revolution.

The belief that violent mass action is necessary to bring about radical change was central to the theories of Marx's follower Vladimir Lenin (1870–1924), the founder of the Communist Party of the Soviet Union and the foremost leader of the Russian Revolution of 1917. Lenin argued that parliamentary democracy and "bourgeois legality" were mere superstructures designed to mask the underlying reality of capitalist exploitation. As a result, these revolutionaries disdained the kind of representative institutions prevalent in the United States and Western Europe.

With the fall of communism in the Soviet Union and Eastern Europe, **Marxism-Leninism** has lost a great deal of its luster. Even so, the doctrine retains some appeal among the poor and downtrodden, primarily because of its crusading spirit and its promise of deliverance from the injustices of "monopoly capitalism."[6] (See Ideas and Politics, Figure 2.2.) After World War II, communism spearheaded or sponsored "national wars of liberation" aimed at the overthrow of existing governments, especially in the Third World. Since the collapse

MARX IS DEAD; MARXISM—NOT SO MUCH

FIGURE 2.2   The leaders of three Latin American democracies (shaded here) have expressed Marxist ideas and adopted anticapitalist rhetoric and policies. Cuba (also shaded) has been a nondemocratic Marxist state since the late 1950s.

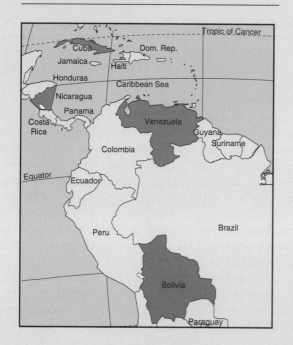

In contrast to what happened in many European democracies, Marxism has never gained a toehold in the United States. Yet, in many other parts of the world, Marxist parties have flourished at one time or another. In Castro's Cuba, most of Asia, and parts of sub-Saharan Africa, communist or socialist parties long dominated the political scene, and "national wars of liberation" were often spearheaded by self-avowed Marxists.

In many other countries, most notably in Western Europe, nonruling communist parties achieved democratic respectability. The communist parties of France and Italy, to cite two important examples, are legally recognized parties that regularly participate in national elections. Socialist parties are mainstream political parties throughout Europe. In the 1970s, communist party leaders in Italy and Spain led a movement called Eurocommunism. They renounced violent revolution and sought to change society from within by winning elections.

With the collapse of the Soviet Union in 1991, Marxist parties have declined but by no means disappeared. After the "Plural Left" coalition won the French parliamentary elections in May 1997, three communists were appointed to the cabinet of Socialist Prime Minister Lionel Jospin. In recent years, the elected leaders of Venezuela, Bolivia, and Nicaragua have all expressed sympathy with Marxist ideas and have embraced socialist policies. And China, now boasting the world's second largest economy, is still a communist one-party state. In addition, four other countries continue to be communist-ruled: Cuba, Laos, North Korea, and Vietnam.

Between 1928 and 1944 Norman Thomas was the Socialist Party's perennial candidate for president of the United States. In 1932, in the throes of the Great Depression, he garnered 884,885 votes. Thomas famously predicted: "The American people will never knowingly adopt socialism. But under the name of Liberalism, they will adopt every fragment of the socialist program until one day America will be a socialist nation without knowing how it happened." To what extent—if any—has this prediction come true? Why do conservatives and liberals often answer this question very differently? Think about it.

(Hint: Often the best way to win a televised debate or political argument, unfortunately, is to be highly selective—and inventive—in citing "facts" to underscore whatever strengthens the case you are making while ignoring or discrediting what doesn't.)

law of pauperization
In Karl Marx's view, the rule that capitalism has a built-in tendency toward recession and unemployment, and thus workers inevitably become surplus labor.

Marxism-Leninism
In the history of the Russian Revolution, Lenin's anticapitalist rationale for the overthrow of the czar (absolute monarch) and the establishment of a new political order based on communist principles set forth in the writings of Karl Marx.

Democratic Socialism
A form of government based on popular elections, public ownership and control of the main sectors of the economy, and broad welfare programs in health and education to benefit citizens.

gradualism
The belief that major changes in society should take place slowly through reform rather than suddenly through revolution.

welfare state
A state whose government is concerned with providing for the social welfare of its citizens and does so usually with specific public policies, such as health insurance, minimum wages, and housing subsidies.

of Communism in Europe, however, the revolutionary role played by the Soviet state and Marxist ideology on the world stage has given way to Islamism— not Islam, the religion, but Islamism, an anti-Western ideological offshoot that seeks to restore the moral purity of Islamic societies (see Chapter 15).

Democratic Socialism, the other main branch of socialist ideology, embraces collectivist ends but is committed to democratic means. Unlike orthodox Marxists, democratic socialists believe in **gradualism**, or reform, rather than revolution, but they hold to the view that social justice cannot be achieved without substantial economic equality. They also tend to favor a greatly expanded role for government and a tightly regulated economy. Socialist parties typically advocate nationalization of key parts of the economy—transportation, communications, public utilities, banking and finance, insurance, and such basic industries as automobile manufacturing, iron and steel processing, mining, and energy. The modern-day **welfare state**, wherein government assumes broad responsibility for the health, education, and welfare of its citizens, is the brainchild of European social democracy.

The goal of the welfare state is to alleviate poverty and inequality through large-scale income redistribution. Essentially a cradle-to-grave system, the welfare state model features free or subsidized university education and medical care, generous public assistance (family allowances), pension plans, and a variety of other social services. To finance these programs and services, socialists advocate high taxes on corporations and the wealthy, including steeply progressive income taxes and stiff inheritance taxes designed to close the gap between rich and poor.

Democratic Socialism has had a major impact in Western Europe. The United Kingdom and the Scandinavian countries provide the classic examples. The welfare state became the norm in Europe after World War II, but the aftermath of the 2008 global financial meltdown put its viability to a severe test. Many European Union (EU) governments, including Greece, Ireland, Portugal, and Spain, were running huge budget deficits in 2010. Greece, in particular, teetered on the brink of bankruptcy. Indeed, the EU was forced to bail out the governments of Greece, Ireland, and Portugal with massive infusions of euros to prevent them from defaulting and potentially causing the collapse of the euro zone itself.

The chronic deficits that led to the euro crisis were—and are—in no small measure a result of the generous welfare-state benefits, including health care and pensions, in place in these countries. Attempts to economize through austerity measures (spending cuts and tax increases) met with mass protests in Greece, Spain, Italy, and France, among others. Nor has the public mood in Europe greatly improved: in 2014, thousands of anti-austerity protesters took to the streets in Paris and Rome. In Italy, for example, youth unemployment had risen well above 40%—a figure that represents both a big drain on public spending and a big loss of labor productivity. Unlike France, Spain, and other European countries, the United States does not have a strong Socialist party nor has "socialism" ever lost the negative stigma most Americans attach to it. Even when Socialist Norman Thomas polled nearly 900,000 votes in the 1932 presidential election, that result amounted to only about 2% of the total votes cast.

Nonetheless, many entrenched social programs in the United States resemble measures associated with the welfare state. Examples include Social Security, Medicare, farm subsidies, family assistance, unemployment compensation, and federally subsidized housing. Compared with most Europeans, U.S. citizens pay less in taxes but also get far less in social benefits—except for high-level government employees, the professional military class, and, of course, members of Congress, who enjoy cradle-to-grave benefits that would make even the most ardent socialist blush.

IDEOLOGIES AND POLITICS IN THE UNITED STATES

U.S. politics is essentially a tug-of-war between **liberals** and **conservatives**. These two terms often generate more heat than light, but it is difficult to sort the central issues in U.S. politics without reference to the "liberals" and the "conservatives."

The Uses and Abuses of Labels

The political ideas virtually everyone in the United States embraces evolved from a 300-year-old liberal tradition in Western political thought that sees the safeguarding of individual rights as the central aim and purpose of government. Liberals and conservatives alike champion freedom and human rights, but they argue about which rights are fundamental. Liberals tend to favor narrowing the gap between rich and poor, whereas conservatives stress the virtues of free enterprise and tend toward a minimalist definition of equality (for example, equal rights = the right to vote; equal opportunity = the right to basic education and the like). In general, liberals typically define *equality* broadly in social, political, and economic terms; conservatives tend to confine *equality* to the political realm.

Several factors blur the distinction between liberalism and conservatism in the United States. First, although there are always plenty of impassioned liberals and conservatives eager to sound off on television talk shows, in practice voters tend to be more pragmatic than dogmatic. Voters want results, not rhetoric. Second, although politicians often make bold campaign promises, few are willing to go out on a limb by proposing any change that's likely to be controversial (for example, campaign finance reform, health care reform, or bank nationalization). Third, liberals and conservatives sometimes come down on the same side, but for different reasons. For example, conservatives are opposed to pornography on religious and moral grounds; many liberals, on the other hand, favor a ban on "dirty" books because pornography, they say, exploits and degrades women.

Common Themes

Liberalism and conservatism are both rooted in principles found in the political philosophy of John Locke[7] and enshrined in the Declaration of Independence—that all human beings are created equal; that they are endowed with certain

liberal
A political philosophy that emphasizes individualism, equality, and civil rights above other values (see also *conservative*).

conservative
A political philosophy that emphasizes prosperity, security, and tradition above other values (see also *liberal*).

unalienable rights, including the rights of life, liberty, and the pursuit of happiness (Jefferson's expansion of Locke's "right to property"); that government exists to protect these rights; and that governmental legitimacy derives from consent of the governed rather than from royal birth or divine right.

When government becomes alienated from the society it exists to serve, the people have the right to alter or abolish it. Indeed, the purposes of government are clearly spelled out in the preamble to the U.S. Constitution: to "establish Justice, insure domestic Tranquility, provide for the common defence, promote the general Welfare, and secure the Blessings of Liberty." As we are about to discover, however, these stirring words are also an invitation to debate.

Conservatives: Economic Rights and Free Enterprise

In stressing economic rights and private property, modern-day conservatives echo and expand on arguments first propounded by political philosophers in the seventeenth and eighteenth centuries. The dawning of the Age of Democracy brought doom to Europe's monarchies and unleashed the economic potential of a nascent middle class, thereby setting the stage for the Industrial Revolution.

commercial republic
This concept, found in the Federalist Papers, is most closely identified with Alexander Hamilton, who championed the idea of a democracy based on economic vitality, capitalistic principles, and private enterprise free of undue state regulation.

John Locke (1632–1704) Locke contributed greatly to the idea of the **commercial republic**, a concept that forms the core of modern conservatism. Locke is famous as an early champion of property rights. For Locke, protecting private property is one of the main purposes of government. Locke thus helped lay the foundations for free enterprise and the modern market economy, including such basic concepts as legal liability and contractual obligation.

Many earlier philosophers, from Aristotle to Thomas Aquinas (1224–1274), cautioned against excessive concern for worldly possessions. Locke, in contrast, imagined a society in which invention and innovation are rewarded, the instinct to acquire goods is encouraged, and money serves as the universal medium of exchange. Where wealth can be accumulated, reinvested, and expanded, Locke reasoned, society will prosper; and a prosperous society is a happy one.

Baron de Montesquieu (1689–1755) Although Locke developed the general theory of the commercial republic, the French political philosopher Baron de Montesquieu, in his famous *The Spirit of the Laws* (1748), identified a number of specific advantages of business and commerce. In Montesquieu's view, nations that trade extensively with other nations are likely to be predisposed toward peace because war disrupts international commerce. Montesquieu asserted that commerce would open new avenues for individual self-advancement; that focusing on wealth creation would combat religious fanaticism; and that a culture of commerce would elevate individual morality. A commercial democracy, Montesquieu believed, would foster certain modest bourgeois virtues, including "frugality, economy, moderation, labor, prudence, tranquility, order, and rule."[8]

Adam Smith (1723–1790) Following in the footsteps of Locke and Montesquieu, Adam Smith set forth the operating principles of the market economy. Known to many as the "worldly philosopher," Smith is the preeminent theorist of modern capitalism. In his famous treatise, *An Inquiry into the Nature and Causes of the Wealth of Nations* (1776), Smith explored the dynamics of a commercial society free of regulations or interference from the state. Like Locke, Smith observed that self-interest plays a pivotal role in human relations:

> It is not from the benevolence of the butcher, the brewer, or the baker that we expect our dinner, but from their regard to their own self-interest. We address ourselves, not to their humanity but to their self-love, and never talk to them of our own necessities but of their advantages.[9]

Smith famously theorized about the "invisible hand" of the marketplace, expressed in the *law of supply and demand*. This law, he argued, determines market value. Where supply is large and demand is small, the market value (or price) of the item in question will be driven down until only the most efficient producers remain. Conversely, where demand is great and supply is low, the market value of a given item will be driven up. Eventually, prices will decline as competition intensifies, again leaving only the most efficient producers in a position to retain or expand their share of the market. In this way, the market automatically seeks supply-and-demand equilibrium.

Smith believed self-interest and market forces would combine to sustain economic competition, which in turn would keep prices close to the actual cost of production. If prices did rise too much, producers would be undercut by eager competitors. In this view, self-interest and market conditions make prices self-adjusting: high prices provide an incentive for increased competition, and low prices lead to increased demand and hence increased production. Finally, Smith's free-enterprise theory holds that individuals voluntarily enter precisely those professions and occupations that society considers most valuable because the monetary rewards are irresistible, even if the work itself is not particularly glamorous.[10]

Taken as a whole, these concepts define what has come to be known as **laissez faire capitalism,** or the idea that the marketplace, unfettered by central state planning, is the best regulator of the economy.* Smith argued for the existence of a **natural harmony of interests**: what is good for the happiness of the individual is also good for society, and vice versa, because people will unintentionally serve society's needs as they pursue their own self-interests *without government intervention.*

Modern Conservatism Conservatives are generally opposed to big government and heavy taxes, especially on business and wealth. Conservative political parties and politicians typically appeal to commercial interests and corporate industry, as well as to voters for whom traditional family and religious values are paramount. Critics fault conservatives for opposing state regulation even at the cost of consumer safety, environmental protection, or minority rights.

Conservatives argue that the quest for individual affluence brings with it certain collective benefits, including a shared belief in the work ethic, a love of order and stability, and a healthy self-restraint on the part of government. These

laissez faire capitalism
An ideology that views the marketplace, unfettered by state interference, as the best regulator of the economic life of a society.

natural harmony of interests
According to Adam Smith, what is good for the happiness of the individual is also good for society, and vice versa, because people will unintentionally serve society's needs as they pursue their own self-interests without government intervention.

---

*Although the French term *laissez faire*—literally "let do" or "let be"—is often associated with Adam Smith's philosophy, Smith did not actually use the term. The first known use of this term in an English-language publication appeared in a book entitled the *Principles of Trade* (1774) written by George Whatley and Benjamin Franklin.

collective "goods" are most likely to result, they argue, from a political system that ensures the best possible conditions for the pursuit of personal gain.

Two of the most prominent conservative thinkers in the post–World War II period were Friedrich Hayek (1899–1992) and Milton Friedman (1912–2006). Hayek, a leading member of the Austrian School of Economics, won the Nobel Prize in Economics (with Gunnar Myrdal) in 1974. His book, *The Road to Serfdom* (1944), inspired a generation of Western free-market economists, and Hayek became an iconic figure for libertarians in the United States.

Friedman was the main architect behind the restoration of classical liberalism as the official economic orthodoxy in the United States (under Ronald Reagan), the United Kingdom (under Margaret Thatcher), Germany (under Helmut Kohl), and beyond. According to *The Economist*, Friedman "was the most influential economist of the second half of the twentieth century . . . possibly of all of it."[11] In his most famous work, *Capitalism and Freedom* (1962), Friedman argued forcefully that the secret to political and social freedom is to place strict limits on the role of government in the economy. In other words, capitalism is the key to democracy. In this view, it is desirable to minimize government by assigning to the public sector only those few functions that the private sector cannot do on its own—namely, to enforce contracts, spur competition, regulate interest rates and the money supply, and protect "the irresponsible, whether madman or child."

Liberals: Civil Rights and Social Justice

Liberals tend to hold civil rights most dear. They are often vigorous defenders of individuals or groups they see as victims of past discrimination, including racial minorities, women, and the poor. Rightly or wrongly, liberals are often associated with certain social groups and occupations such as blue-collar workers, minorities, gays and lesbians, feminists, intellectuals, and college professors. In general, liberals favor governmental action to promote greater equality in society. At the same time, however, they oppose curbs on freedom of expression, as well as on efforts to "legislate morality."

In the classical liberal view, respect for the dignity of the individual is a seminal value. In his treatise *On Liberty* (1859), John Stuart Mill eloquently stated the case for individualism:

He who lets the world, or his own portion of it, choose his plan of life for him, has no need of any other faculty than the ape-like one of imitation. He who chooses his plan for himself, employs all his faculties. He must use observation to see, reasoning and judgment to foresee, activity to gather materials for decision, discrimination to decide, and when he has decided, firmness and self-control to hold to his deliberate decision. . . . Human nature is not a machine to be built after a model, and set to do exactly the work prescribed for it, but a tree, which requires to grow and develop on all sides, according to the tendency of the inward forces which make it a living thing.[12]

John Stuart Mill (1806–1873). English philosopher and political economist.

Mill was at pains to protect individuality from the stifling conformity of mass opinion. Democracy by its very nature, Mill argued, is ill-equipped to protect individuality, as it is based on the principle of majority rule. Thus, following Mills, liberals point out that defenders of majority rule often confuse quantity (the number of people holding a particular view) with quality (the logic and evidence for or against it) and equate numerical superiority with political truth. In a political culture that idealizes the majority, dissenters are often frowned on or even persecuted.

Liberals value individualism as the wellspring of creativity, dynamism, and invention in society, the source of social progress. Protecting dissent and minority rights allows a broad range of ideas to be disseminated; keeps government honest; and sets up a symbiotic relationship between the individual and society, one that benefits both.

Differences Essential and Exaggerated

Liberals and conservatives often hold contrasting views on human nature. Liberals typically accent the goodness in human beings. Even though they do not deny human vices or the presence of crime in society, they tend to view antisocial behavior as society's fault. Thus, liberals believe that to reduce crime society must alleviate the conditions of poverty, racism, and despair. Human beings are innocent at birth and "go bad" in response to circumstances over which they have no control. If you are raised in a violent, drug-infested, inner-city neighborhood with inadequate police protection, you are far more likely to turn to a life of crime than if you are raised in a comfortable and safe middle-class neighborhood in the suburbs.

Conservatives take a dimmer view of human nature. They argue that human beings are not naturally virtuous; that coercion, deterrence, and punishment are necessary to keep people in line; that individuals differ in motivation, ability, moral character, and luck; and that it is not the role of government to minimize or moderate these differences. Consequently, conservatives are seldom troubled by great disparities in wealth or privilege. By the same token, they are generally less inclined to attribute antisocial behavior to poverty or social injustice. There will always be some "bad apples" in society, conservatives argue, and the only solution to crime is punishment. Liberals, on the other hand, maintain that alleviating poverty and injustice is the best way to reduce crime and that punishment without rehabilitation is a dead end.

Is change good or bad? Liberals generally take a progressive view of history, believing the average person is better off now than a generation ago or a century or two ago. They adopt a forward-looking optimism about the long-term possibilities for peace and harmony. As they see it, change is often a good thing.

Conservatives, by contrast, look to the past for guidance in meeting the challenges of the present. They are far less inclined than liberals to equate change with progress. They view society as a fragile organism held together by shared beliefs and common values. Custom and convention, established institutions (family, church, and state), and deeply ingrained moral reflexes are the keys to a steady state and stable social order. Like society itself, traditions should never be changed (or exchanged) too rapidly. As Edmund Burke put it, "change in order to conserve."

The differences between liberals and conservatives, though not insignificant, can be (and often are) exaggerated. Liberals and conservatives share a fundamental belief in the dignity of the individual; freedom of speech, the press, and religion; equality of opportunity; and other important values. In recent years, however, conservativism in U.S. politics has become associated with extreme right-wing groups and voting blocs such as the Tea Party movement, religious fundamentalists, and anti-immigration "nativists."

In the summer of 2011, political commentator Fareed Zakaria lamented:

> From Aristotle to Edmund Burke, the greatest conservative thinkers have said that to change societies, one must understand them, accept them as they are and help them evolve.
>
> Watching this election campaign, one wonders what has happened to that tradition. Conservatives now espouse ideas drawn from abstract principles with little regard to the realities of America's present or past.[13]

The "Values Divide" and the War on Terror

The tension between liberals and conservatives escalated into what came to be called a "culture war" or "values divide" in the 1980s.[14] In the 1990s, then Speaker of the House Newt Gingrich launched the "Contract with America"— a conservative agenda aimed at preventing tax increases and balancing the federal budget, as well as a series of congressional reforms. In 2001, a new divide was opened after the September 11 attacks. The ensuing **"war on terror"** was framed within a **neoconservative** worldview and carried out by a president intent upon making homeland security and a crusade against international terrorism the twin pillars of U.S. policy.

Deep divisions over emotionally charged social issues of a moral nature, such as abortion, gay marriage, and stem cell research, also contributed to the polarization of the U.S. body politic in the first decades of the new century. For many conservatives, morality is unambiguous and grounded in religion, whereas liberals tend to believe that morality is personal. Thus, many liberals oppose prayer in schools, favor broad legal and social rights for gays and lesbians, and are pro-choice on abortion. Most conservatives, on the other hand, argue that banning school prayer, allowing gay marriage, and legalizing abortion are morally wrong. Liberals counter that policies denying individual choice violate what is morally right.[15] For liberals, tolerance of diversity is a moral imperative; for conservatives, giving legal sanction to abortion and LGBT (Lesbian, Gay, Bisexual, and Transgender) marriage is itself immoral.

war on terror
After 9/11, President George W. Bush declared a worldwide "war on terrorism" aimed at defeating international terrorist organizations, destroying terrorist training camps, and bringing terrorists themselves to justice.

Courtesy of the Author, Thomas Magstadt

Anti-abortion sign among crosses set on imaginary burial plots of unborn babies on the grounds of a Roman Catholic church in the politically charged days leading up to the 2012 presidential election.

Lost in the din of angry voices was the inaudible voice of reason and the spirit of mutual tolerance. Lost, too, was a willingness to ask fundamental questions: What does the First Amendment separation of church and state mean? Does it work only in one direction—to protect religion from interference by the state? Or does it also protect the state and its political processes—above all, elections—from interference by tax-exempt (and thus, in effect, subsidized) religious organizations?

Conservatives have traditionally placed little trust in government, believing that less is more. Where tax-funded public programs are necessary, state and local governments are closer to the people and therefore better suited than the federal government to administer them. However, both major political parties have had a hand in the ever-expanding role of the federal government.

A somewhat harsh view of human nature predisposes conservatives to be tougher than liberals in dealing with perceived threats to personal safety, public order, and homeland security. Bush's military response to the 9/11 attacks, which at first greatly boosted his popularity ratings, was in keeping with this stance.

Liberals insist that the rights of the accused be protected even if it means some criminals will escape punishment. The war on terror gave rise to a new controversy over these rights when the Bush administration refused to classify captured alleged terrorists as criminals or prisoners of war, preferring instead to create a new category of detainee—illegal enemy combatants. As such, the government said, these people were entitled to none of the legal protections provided in the U.S. Constitution or under international law.

Conservatives typically do not share liberals' concern for protecting provocative speech, especially when they perceive the speakers as "radicals." Thus, in the war on terror, liberals expressed alarm at provisions of the Patriot Act that allow for increased surveillance powers, warrantless searches and seizures, and, in general, invasions of personal privacy long held to be barred by the Fourth Amendment. Section 215 of the act gives FBI agents pursuing an antiterrorism investigation broad power to demand personal information and private records from citizens. The law also contains a gag rule prohibiting public comment on Section 215 orders. Not surprisingly, libertarians have joined liberals in objecting to what they see as a blatant violation of the Bill of Rights (especially the First and Fourth Amendments).

Although Section 215 was set to expire in December 2009, President Obama backed its reauthorization. The Obama administration caused a furor in November 2010 when it authorized the Transportation Security Administration (TSA) to conduct full body scans of airline passengers—including pat downs.

President Obama vowed to pursue a very different (and more liberal) view in both foreign and domestic policy than his predecessor. But Obama's critics lament that he has failed to keep his promises—to close the Guantanamo prison (the notorious "Gitmo"), for example, or to renounce the practice of "extraordinary rendition," whereby suspected terrorists were grabbed anywhere in the world and taken to secret detention centers to be harshly interrogated and even waterboarded (a form of torture).

neoconservative
In the United States, a term associated with the ideology of top advisers and cabinet members during the presidency of George W. Bush; neoconservatives advocate a strong national defense, decisive military action in the face of threats or provocations, pro-Israeli policy in the Middle East, and a minimum of government interference in the economy. In general, neoconservatives are opposed to federal regulation of business and banking.

In foreign affairs, liberals tend to favor reduced defense spending, whereas conservatives are more apt to follow the adage, "Fear God and keep your powder dry." But, again, this generalization breaks down on close examination. Indeed, the so-called Blue Dog Democrats in Congress (Democrats who identify themselves as either moderate or conservative) are no less opposed to cuts in defense spending than most Republicans.

Choosing Sides versus Making Choices

Politics is often called a game, as in the "game of politics" or the "political game." In games, we typically choose sides; we cheer for our team and celebrate when we win. Most games have clear winners and losers. Ties are possible in European football (soccer) but not in most other sports.

Politics also has winners and losers—for example, in elections. But outcomes are not so simple or clear-cut. Winning an election means bearing the burdens of government as well as gaining power. When the winners abuse that power or use it for personal gain or make bad decisions with disastrous consequences, the whole country is the loser; and trust in government is damaged. Thus, choosing sides is a necessity, but it is not the same thing as making wise choices. One sides with conservatives and still votes for a Democrat, or vice versa. The character and qualifications of candidates are, arguably, more important than whether the candidate is a Republican or a Democrat.

Many voters in the United States prefer not to be identified as members of either major party. Independents tend to choose sides one election at a time. Whereas 30% of the U.S. electorate classified themselves as independent only a decade or so ago,[16] today that number has climbed to over 40%. For this reason, getting the "swing vote" has become crucial to winning elections in recent times. Independents tend to choose which candidate or party to support on the basis of issues, like the state of the economy, taxes, or health care reform, rather than on ideology. In politics, unfortunately, common sense is often uncommon—the exception rather than the rule.

We can easily fall into the trap of believing there are two (and only two) sides to every argument—one right and the other wrong. But the more adamant or partisan each side becomes, the more likely it is that the truth will elude both—that it will be found somewhere in the gulf between the two extremes. Why? Because politics, like life itself, is too complicated to be reduced to pat answers, populist slogans, or simple solutions.

SUMMARY

Governments seek to attain certain social and economic goals in accordance with some concept of the public good. How vigorously, diligently, or honestly they pursue these goals depends on a number of variables, including the ideology they claim to embrace. An ideology is a logically consistent set of propositions about the public good.

We can classify ideologies as antigovernment (anarchism, libertarianism), right-wing (monarchism, fascism), or left-wing (revolutionary communism, Democratic Socialism, radical egalitarianism). U.S. politics is dominated by two relatively moderate tendencies that are both offshoots of classical liberalism, which stresses individual rights and limited government. It is surprisingly difficult to differentiate clearly between these two viewpoints, principally because so-called liberals and conservatives in the United States often share fundamental values and assumptions. Conservatives stress economic rights; liberals emphasize civil rights. Conservatives are often associated with money and business, on the one hand, and religious fundamentalism, on the other; liberals are often associated with labor, minorities, gays and lesbians, feminists, intellectuals, and college professors. However, these stereotypes can be misleading: not everybody in the business world is conservative, and not all college professors are liberal.

Liberals look to the future, believing progress will ensure a better life for all; conservatives look to the past for guidance in dealing with problems. Liberals believe in the essential decency and potential goodness of human beings; conservatives take a less charitable view. These differences are reflected in the divergent public policy aims of the two ideological groups.

KEY TERMS

public good   25
ideology   26
anarchism   27
nihilism   27
monarchism   28
fascism   28
Nazism   28
capitalism   30
libertarianism   32
socialism   32
communism   33
Marxism   33
dialectical
   materialism   33

bourgeoisie   34
proletariat   34
surplus value   34
law of capitalist
   accumulation   34
monopoly
   capitalism   34
law of
   pauperization   34
Marxism-Leninism   34
Democratic
   Socialism   36
gradualism   36
welfare state   36

liberal   37
conservative   37
commercial
   republic   38
laissez faire
   capitalism   39
natural harmony
   of interests   39
war on terror   42
neoconservative   42

REVIEW QUESTIONS

1. What is the public good? How is it relevant to the proper aims of constitutional democracy?

2. How can the concept of core values be used to gauge the performance of a government?

3. What is ideology? Is it an aid to rigorous political analysis? Why or why not?

4. In twentieth-century Europe, Communism and Democratic Socialism vied for popular approval. What were (are) the main points of disagreement between these divergent strains of Marxism?

5. How can we distinguish between a liberal and a conservative in the United States? What economic and social factors help to explain why liberals and conservatives cannot agree on much of anything anymore?

WEBSITES AND READINGS

Websites

Anarchism: http://flag.blackened.net/revolt/anarchism/

Nihilism: http://www.counterorder.com/

Fascism: http://www.publiceye.org/eyes/whatfasc.html

Conservativism: http://www.heritage.org/initiatives/first-principles/conservatism

Libertarianism: http://www.libertarian.org/; http://www.libertarianism.com/; http://www.cato.org/

Socialism: http://www.lastsuperpower.net/

Communism: http://www.broadleft.org/; http://www.marxists.org/; http://www-formal.stanford.edu/jmc/progress/marxism.html

Religious right: http://www.cc.org/; http://www.theocracywatch.org/

Democratic Socialism: http://www.dsausa.org/; http://en.wikipedia.org/wiki/Social_democracy

Independents: http://www.whereistand.com/; http://www.independentvoter-project.org/; http://independentvoting.org/

Tea Party: http://www.teaparty.org/

Progressivism: http://www.progressive.org/

Blacklisted: http://www.crocker.com/~blklist/about_the_show.html

The Hollywood Ten: http://www.lib.msu.edu/spc/digital/radicalism/subj_struct.html#Hollywood

Readings

Bernstein, Edward. *Evolutionary Socialism: A Criticism and Affirmation.* Translated by E. C. Harvey. New York: Schocken Books, 1961. A classic work espousing nonrevolutionary socialism.

Friedman, Milton. *Capitalism and Freedom.* Chicago: University of Chicago Press, 1994. A classic argument in favor of minimal governmental participation in the private sector.

Galbraith, John Kenneth. *The New Industrial State,* 4th ed. Boston: Houghton Mifflin, 1985. A vigorous argument that concentrated economic power requires a powerful, active government.

Hayek, Friedrich. *The Road to Serfdom.* Chicago: University of Chicago Press, 1956. Perhaps the most definitive and influential critique of the welfare state ever written.

White, John Kenneth. *The Values Divide.* New York: Chatham House, 2003. Explores the role values play in American politics. Suggests that a deep cultural and political rift, one that cuts right down the middle of the electorate, was the root cause of the deadlocked 2000 presidential election between George W. Bush and Al Gore. Points to a paradigm shift in the political culture as a result of 9/11.

Packer, George. "The New Liberalism" *The New Yorker,* November 17, 2008. http://www.newyorker.com/magazine/2008/11/17/the-new-liberalism.

Roller, Emma. "Elizabeth Warren's 11 Commandments of Progressivism," *National Journal,* June 18, 2014. http://www.nationaljournal.com/politics/elizabeth-warren-s-11-commandments-of-progressivism-20140718.

PART 1

Comparative Political Systems
Models and Theories

CHAPTER 3

Utopias
Model States

Learning Objectives

1 Define utopia and discuss whether perfect justice is possible.

2 Describe utopian thought.

3 Evaluate the relationship between revolution and utopian thought.

4 Justify whether ideals are worth pursuing even if they are impossible to achieve.

5 Clarify whether all utopian thinkers are either idealists or revolutionaries, or explain if the authors of some utopias have a different purpose in mind.

What constitutes the public good and the good society?[1] To make meaningful comparisons between or among political systems, we first have to clarify what the public good *is* and is not. Ideas about utopia found in the writings of philosophers, theologians, and novelists give us a variety of possibilities for what a "perfect" society could look like. Imagining the best society leads inevitably to politics: What kind of a government would such a society have? Would a perfect society have any *need* for government? If politics is all about settling differences without violence, perhaps a society without conflict would be altogether *apolitical*.

The study of utopia raises questions about the limits of politics and about the possibility of rising above politics. Perhaps there is wisdom in the adage that "the best is the enemy of the good." History tells us that striving for too much can be as bad as—or, in extreme cases, far worse than—settling for too little.

The word *utopia* comes from the title of a book written by Sir Thomas More (1478–1535), the lord chancellor of England under King Henry VIII and an influential humanist. More coined the word from the Greek terms *ou topos*, meaning "no place," and *eutopos*, "a place where all is well." Hence, we might say that a **utopia** is a nonexistent place where people dwell in perfect health, harmony, and happiness.

The literature of Western political philosophy contains a number of elaborate utopian blueprints, each of which represents some thinker's best attempt at imagining the best political order. Thinking about a utopian society leads inexorably toward a critical examination of one's own society and gives us criteria for judging how well we measure up to the ideal. What it often fails to do is tell us how to get there or what dangers and sacrifices we might encounter along the way.

The American people are famous for taking a practical, no-nonsense, problem-solving approach to life. Starry-eyed idealism is for others. And yet, there have in fact been utopian experiments attempted in the United States. In 1826, for example, British industrialist Robert Owen attempted just such an experiment at New Harmony, Indiana. The experiment lasted only two years. Owen's son offered this colorful description of New Harmony society that hints at one reason it failed: "a heterogeneous collection of radicals . . . honest latitudinarians, and lazy theorists, with a sprinkling of unprincipled sharpers thrown in."

Our exploration of famous utopias begins with Plato's *Republic*, which we contrast with three later versions of utopia—Sir Francis Bacon's *New Atlantis*, Karl Marx's "classless society," and B. F. Skinner's *Walden Two*. Each author finds answers in a different place. For Plato, the answer lies in the realm of philosophy; for Bacon, in science; for Marx, in economics; and for Skinner, in psychology.

There are many other noteworthy examples of utopian literature, including More's *Utopia* (1516) and U.S. writer Edward Bellamy's *Looking Backward, 2000–1887* (1888). There is also a fascinating body of literature on dystopia— well-intended political experiments that went terribly wrong. The purpose of these works, which we review at the end of the chapter, is to demonstrate the danger of trying to build a perfect order in an imperfect world.

utopia
Any visionary system embodying perfect political and social order.

PLATO'S *REPUBLIC*: PHILOSOPHY IS THE ANSWER

Plato's *Republic* takes the form of a long dialogue between Socrates (c. 470–399 BCE) and several imaginary participants. Socrates, considered the first Western political philosopher, held that "the unexamined life is a life not worth living," an idea that has become a cornerstone of Western civilization (see "Ideas and Politics"—Figure 3.1). As portrayed by Plato (c. 428–348 BCE), Socrates's most brilliant student, Socratic philosophy—the notion that there is no higher purpose than the fearless pursuit of Truth—represents a fundamental alternative to the earlier works of Homer, who praised the virtues of courage and honor, and the later teachings of Jesus, who proclaimed belief in God and moral behavior in accordance with God's word to be the basis of the most exalted life.

Socrates lived for the sake of knowledge unadulterated by power, prejudice, politics, or religion; and in the end he died for it. The rulers of Athens mistrusted Socrates's relentless search for answers to penetrating philosophical questions. Eventually he was accused and convicted of undermining belief in the established gods and corrupting Athenian youth. His execution (by a self-administered drink of hemlock) stands as a poignant reminder of the tension between intellectual freedom and the political order.

In *The Republic*, Socrates begins with an inquiry into the meaning of justice and then proceeds to a discussion of the best political order, one in which there can be no tension between justice and power, philosophers and rulers.[2] There would be no reason for rulers to fear the teachings of philosophers, no need to choose between loyalty to the state and devotion to the truth.

The Perfect Polity

As Plato tells the story, a skeptical listener challenges Socrates to explain why it is better to be just than unjust. Is it not true, he asks, that the successful man who gains power and possessions from unjust actions is much happier than the just man who, like Socrates, has neither power nor possessions?[3]

Socrates first proposes that political life arises from the fact that no individual can be self-sufficient. He goes on to describe a very simple society with no government and no scarcity, whose farmers, shoemakers, and other artisans produce just enough for the perpetuation of a plain and placid way of life. In this society, which seeks to satisfy basic human needs (food, drink, and shelter), each person has a job, a special function essential to maintain the society and keep the economy going.

Prosperity feeds the ambitions and desires of the people for luxuries and more space. The *polis* (city-state) needs to expand to satisfy these demands and to defend itself from attack, and for these tasks, soldiers are necessary. The soldiers, who form the second class in the republic, are initially called guardians.

The education of the guardians encompasses the entire range of human activities, including the aesthetic, intellectual, moral, and physical aspects of life. Because the real aim of education is to teach the truth, censorship is necessary. Ideas that are deemed untrue or dangerous cannot be permitted. Strict discipline is maintained, and everything is held in common, including personal

ANCIENT GREECE—BIRTHPLACE OF WESTERN POLITICAL THOUGHT

FIGURE 3.1   The Beginnings of Historic Greece, 700–600 BCE

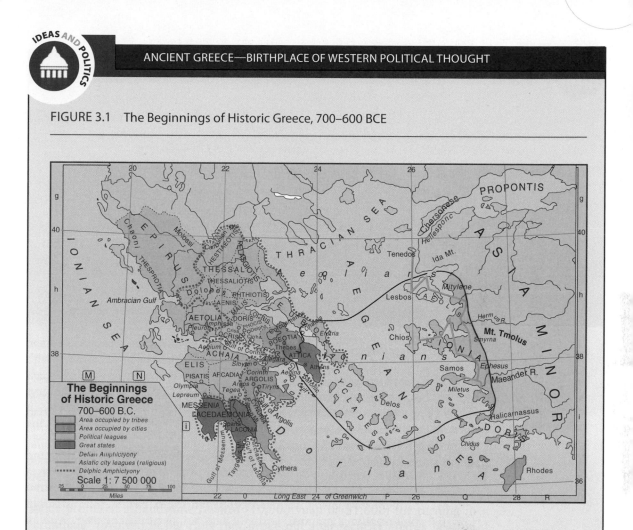

Ancient Greece was home to Socrates and Plato and is the birthplace of political philosophy, thanks in no small part to these two great thinkers. It was the Greeks who invented political philosophy and who placed justice at the very heart of political thought and practice.

Political philosophy is the study of fundamental questions about the state, government, politics, law, and, above all, justice. Indeed, justice is the common thread running through virtually all public policy issues today, but it is often implicit rather than openly acknowledged, despite the fact that we often closely associate justice and liberty. The U.S. Pledge of Allegiance, for example, speaks of "liberty and justice for all."

Of course, justice means different things to different people, depending on the culture and context in which it is used. In the Western tradition, its meaning often depends on whether we use it in a broad or narrow sense. Broadly speaking, justice is essentially a matter of distribution (who gets what, when, and how). In the narrower sense, it is about punishment for breaking the law and about rules of truth and evidence that determine judgments in the law. Today, justice is often couched in the language of political economy

(Continued)

(CONTINUED)

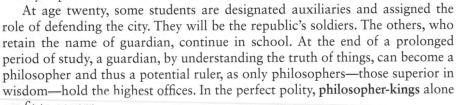

(property rights, taxation, contracts, fair trade practices, capital markets, and the like). Although "justice" has been adapted to fit the needs and values of modern society, the concept has been central to Western political thought since at least the time of the ancient Greeks, nearly two and a half millennia ago.

When people talk about "equal rights" or "human rights" today, it is often assumed that there can be no justice in this world without such rights—in other words, it is self-evident and, as such, requires no elaboration. Is this true? Think about it.

(Hint: In the Muslim world, to cite one example, women do not have the same rights as men. Many Muslim women claim to prefer it that way. Are they all ignorant, brainwashed, misguided, or simply too scared to express a dissenting opinion? Can "justice" have different meanings in different times and places?)

property and spouses. The public good takes precedence over private goods; society supersedes the individual.

At age twenty, some students are designated auxiliaries and assigned the role of defending the city. They will be the republic's soldiers. The others, who retain the name of guardian, continue in school. At the end of a prolonged period of study, a guardian, by understanding the truth of things, can become a philosopher and thus a potential ruler, as only philosophers—those superior in wisdom—hold the highest offices. In the perfect polity, **philosopher-kings** alone are fit to govern.

philosopher-king
Wise philosopher who governs Plato's ideal city in *The Republic*.

Plato's republic is a class society. The three classes—farmers and artisans, warrior-auxiliaries, and philosopher-guardians—each excel in one of three virtues essential to the ideal city-state: moderation (farmers and artisans), courage (warrior-auxiliaries), and wisdom (philosopher-guardians). Only the latter understand the true meaning of justice, the mother of all virtues.

Arguably, as long as each class does its job well (growing food and making things, defending the city, or ruling), the result is justice for all. According to one commentator, "all of Western man's aspirations to justice and the good life are given expression and fulfillment in Socrates' proposals."[4] This is a society based on merit, rather than on pedigree, where everyone's talents can find expression, and where the pursuit of the good life does not depend on personal wealth. It is a society where justice is watchword and wise men rule for the common good.[5]

To ensure that public servants place the public interest above private interests, family relationships are banned among the soldier and guardian classes. A eugenics program provides for state control of human sexual relations and ensures the continued existence of exceptional individuals. The guardian class propagates only through carefully orchestrated "marriage festivals" planned for the sole purpose of collective (and selective) breeding. Nothing is left to chance.

Stephen Bisgrove/Alamy

One of the greatest philosophers of ancient Greece, Plato believed that ideal state authority should rest in the hands of the philosopher-king: "Until philosophers are kings . . . cities will never have rest from their evils."

By now you are probably thinking that Socrates's idea of utopia is not a place where you would want to live. Socrates would probably not be surprised. After all, if Socrates was right, only a very few among us can ever understand the true meaning of justice. Which raises the question: How can the ruled be persuaded that the rulers know best? Socrates's surprising answer: Tell a big lie.

The Noble Lie

To convince the lower class of its proper status, the philosopher-kings are in charge of perpetuating the **noble lie**—an official myth or ideology—on which the just city depends. The myth is clearly designed to get citizens to see each other as members of a single family, (today what we call a nation), and to ensure the popular acceptance of the class system essential to the republic's existence. It goes as follows.

Everyone is taught at an early age that all memories of past experiences are only dreams, that they have actually been beneath the earth where they were fashioned and trained. When they were ready, mother earth sent them to the surface. But first, while still in her womb, where they gestated, they were given souls fashioned of gold (in the case of philosophers), silver (auxiliaries), or iron and bronze (farmers and artisans).

But in building his theoretical construct, Socrates uncovers serious difficulties. His model is highly impractical, if not impossible. It comes at too dear a price—the abolition of families, the establishment of censorship, and, of course, the big lie underpinning the legitimacy of the regime. Another difficulty arises from the fact that the ideal rulers, philosopher-kings, do not desire to rule—precisely what qualifies them to exercise supreme power! For Socrates, those who lust for power are not fit to rule; philosophers thirst after knowledge, not power, which is why they are best suited to be kings.

Although *The Republic* may not be an actionable blueprint for a political regime, it is valuable for its insights into the nature of justice, the roots of tyranny, and the key role of education in civil society. It is also interesting as a didactic tool and for the methodology Socrates employs. First he builds a utopia, then he tears it down by exposing the practical impediments to its implementation. In sum, *The Republic* is best understood as a philosophical exercise, not as a prescription. Socrates's excursion into utopia is an attempt to advance political thought, not to guide political action.

FRANCIS BACON'S *NEW ATLANTIS*: SCIENCE IS THE ANSWER

The idea that a utopia is possible first gained currency in the seventeenth century. In *The New Atlantis* published in 1627, Francis Bacon describes the imaginary voyage of travelers who discover an island called Bensalem. The travelers have suffered greatly during their long sojourn in the Pacific, and they need food and rest. At first the islanders warn them not to land, but after some negotiations, the travelers are allowed to disembark. Their negative first impressions fade as they come to see the island as it really is: a blissfully happy place.

The Noble Lie
To convince the lower class of its proper status, the philosopher-kings are in charge of perpetuating the noble lie—an official myth or ideology—on which the just city depends. The myth is clearly designed to get citizens to see each other as members of a single family (what today we call nation) and to ensure popular acceptance of the class system essential to the republic's existence.

Francis Bacon (1561–1626)—English philosopher, scientist, essayist, and statesman—promulgated the idea that science is the key to humanity's comfortable self-preservation: "Nature to be commanded must be obeyed."

Bacon merely sketched most of the practical details of day-to-day life in Bensalem. Although its envoys have made secret expeditions to Europe to learn about advances in science, the island is otherwise completely cut off from other societies, eliminating the need for self-defense. It is also economically self-sufficient, endowed with abundant natural resources.

Bensalem is a Christian society, but one that emphasizes religious freedom. Members of various religious faiths hold important positions, and toleration is the norm. The foundation of Bensalem society is the family, and marriage and moral behavior are celebrated. An ancient ruler named Solamona, renowned for his benevolence and wisdom, promulgated laws so perfect that some two thousand years later they still require no revision.

Bensalem is also a progressive society. Its best minds are assembled at a great college, appropriately called Solomon's House. There, through experimentation and observation, they apply the rules of science to the discovery of "knowledge of causes, and secret motions of things; and the enlarging of the bounds of human empire, to the effecting of all things possible." In contrast to Plato's Republic, Bensalem pursues knowledge not simply for its own sake, but also for the conquest of nature. Greater material comfort, better health, and a more secure and prosperous way of life make up the great legacy of the academy's laboratories, experimental lakes, medicine shops, and observatories. In Bensalem, science can and should be used for "the relief of man's estate."

In many respects, Bacon's seventeenth-century vision seems prophetic. Through science, for example, life expectancy on the island increases dramatically as whole strains of illness are eradicated. New types of fruits and flowers are produced, some with curative powers. Medical treatment undergoes a technological revolution. The Bensalemites' love of learning and science leads to remarkable discoveries that unlock some of nature's darkest secrets—for example, they can predict impending natural disasters.

Scholars debate Bacon's true intentions in *The New Atlantis*, but few dismiss him as a pie-in-the-sky dreamer. One noted authority sees him as the "first really modern utopian" because Bacon's ideal society was based on science rather than on religion or superstition.[6] Although his book was not meant to be a precise outline of the future, Bacon envisioned a time and place in which science and social progress, which in his mind go hand in hand, would proceed unimpeded. Bacon's vision of a technological utopia was not a protest against existing society so much as a key to the future and an invitation to imagine a world where science is set free to bring about the radical improvement of the human condition.

KARL MARX'S CLASSLESS SOCIETY: ECONOMICS IS THE ANSWER

Karl Marx (1818–1883) was also a utopian thinker, but in a different way from Plato or Bacon. Marx's predecessors began with elaborate descriptions of their paradises; and when they engaged in social criticism, it was usually implicit.

Marx, by contrast, began with an explicit criticism of existing society and sketched only the broadest outlines of his utopia.

As the originator of "scientific socialism," Marx based his historical analysis on rigorous empirical observation rather than on abstract reasoning. Nevertheless, the utopian element in Marxism is evident. Unlike earlier utopians, Marx believed his ideal society was not only possible but also inevitable. Class struggle is the means; the **classless society** is the inevitable end.

Why inevitable? Marx says it is because human history is a product of irresistible forces. Thus, one socioeconomic system—set of class relations—gives rise to an opposing class system, and out of the struggle between the two comes a new system, a synthesis of the two. This thesis-antithesis-synthesis process is the essence of Marx's theory of dialectical materialism.

The Centrality of Economics

The harsh working conditions and widespread suffering associated with capitalism in the mid-nineteenth century provoked Marx's attack on economic inequality. The wealthy commercial and industrial elites—the bourgeois capitalist class—opposed reforms aimed at improving the living conditions of the impoverished working class—the proletariat. Marx's *Das Kapital* is punctuated with vivid descriptions of employment practices that aroused his anger, such as the following:

> Mary Anne Walkley had worked without intermission for 26 1/2 hours, with 60 other girls, 30 in one room that only afforded 1/3 of the cubic feet of air required for them. . . . Mary Anne Walkley fell ill on the Friday [and] died on Sunday. . . . The doctor, Mr. Keys, called too late to the death-bed, duly bore witness before the coroner's jury that "Mary Anne Walkley had died from long hours of work in an overcrowded work-room."[7]

To Marx, the death of Mary Anne Walkley was no mere accident. The machinery of capitalism was remorseless: Mary Anne Walkley was just one of many children who would not live to adulthood.

Marx believed economics, or the production and distribution of material necessities, was the ultimate determinant of human life and that human societies rose and fell according to the inexorable interplay of economic forces. He believed Mary Anne Walkley's harsh life and premature death were dictated by the profit-driven economics of the mid-nineteenth century. But the internal progressive logic of capitalism made it equally inevitable, according to Marx, that the superstructures of power built on greed and exploitation would collapse in a great social upheaval led by the impoverished and alienated proletariat.

The Road to Paradise

Marx referred to the first stage in the revolution that would overthrow capitalism as the **dictatorship of the proletariat**. During this time, the guiding principle would be, "From each according to his abilities, to each according to his needs." Private ownership of property would be abolished. Measures would be put into

Karl Marx—German philosopher, economist, and revolutionary—believed a just world could be achieved only through the evolution of humanity from a capitalist to a socialist economy and society: "The history of all hitherto existing society is the history of class struggle."

SZ Photo/Scherl/DIZ Muenchen GmbH, Sueddeutsche Zeitung Photo/Alamy

classless society
In Marxist political theory, the ideal society in which wealth is equally distributed according to the principle "from each according to his ability, to each according to his needs."

dictatorship of the proletariat
Marx's first stage in the revolution that would overthrow capitalism; the guiding principle would be, "From each according to his abilities, to each according to his needs."

effect that set the stage for a classless society—including a very progressive income tax, abolition of the right of inheritance, state ownership of banks and communications and transportation systems, introduction of universal (and free) education, abolition of child labor, the "extension of factories and instruments of production owned by the State," and finally, "the bringing into cultivation of waste-lands, and the improvement of the soil generally in accordance with a common plan."[8]

Eventually, the state and government as we know it would vanish. In the absence of social classes, class antagonisms would disappear according to Marx's collaborator Friedrich Engels, the role of the state as the arbiter and regulator of social relations would become unnecessary, and "the government of persons [would be] replaced by the administration of things and by the direction of the processes of production." In the end, "The State is not 'abolished,' it withers away."[9] In Marxist theory, the political stage immediately following the workers' revolution, during which the Communist Party controls the state and defends it against a capitalist resurgence or counterrevolution; the dictatorship of the proletariat leads into pure communism and the classless society.

The Classless Society

The natural demise of government, Marx prophesied, would usher in a new and final stage—the classless society. Under capitalism, Marx wrote, "everyone has a definite, circumscribed sphere of activity which is put upon him and from which he cannot escape. He is hunter, fisherman or shepherd, or a 'critical critic,' and must remain so if he does not want to lose his means of subsistence."[10] Conversely, under communism,

> [when] each one does not have a circumscribed sphere of activity but can train himself in any branch he chooses, society by regulating the common production makes it possible for me to . . . hunt in the morning, to fish in the afternoon, to carry on cattle-breeding in the evening, also to criticize the food—just as I please—without becoming either hunter, fisherman, shepherd or critic.[11]

Marx believed that human beings come into the world with a clean slate, and what is subsequently written on that slate is determined by society rather than by genetic inheritance. Along with individual self-fulfillment, social bliss would blossom in the new order, which would be populated by "loyal, wise, and incorruptible friends, devoted to one another with an absolutely unselfish benevolence."[12] One student of Marxist utopianism observed that its description of communist society shares with most other utopian works a "single ethical core," characterized by "cooperative rather than competitive labor, purposeful achievement for societal ends rather than self-indulgence or private hedonism, and an ethic of social responsibility for each member rather than of struggle for survival of the fittest."[13]

The **withering away of the state** so central to Marxist ideology was thus based on a belief in the natural harmony of interests: Eliminate private property and the division of labor, and you eliminate social inequality. Eliminate social inequality, and you eliminate the cause of armed conflict. Obviously, no class

withering away of the state
A Marxist category of analysis describing what happens after capitalism is overthrown, private property and social classes are abolished, and the need for coercive state power supposedly disappears.

struggle is possible when classes no longer exist. Finally, eliminate armed conflict, and you eliminate the need for the state. After all, past societies were nothing more than human contrivances for the perpetuation of class dominance. With the disappearance of social classes, according to Marx, government as we have known it will simply atrophy as a result of its own obsolescence.

The picture of the future that Marx and Engels presented to the world was indeed captivating—and thoroughly utopian:

> Crime would disappear, the span of life would increase, brotherhood and cooperation would inculcate a new morality, [and] scientific progress would grow by leaps and bounds.

> Above all, with socialism spreading throughout the world, the greatest blight of humankind, war, and its twin brother, nationalism, would have no place. International brotherhood would follow. . . . With the socialist revolution humanity will complete its "prehistoric" stage and enter for the first time into what might be called its own history. . . . After the revolution a united classless society will be able for the first time to decide which way to go and what to do with its resources and capabilities. For the first time we shall make our own history! It is a "leap from slavery into freedom; from darkness into light."[14]

B. F. SKINNER'S *WALDEN TWO*: PSYCHOLOGY IS THE ANSWER

Psychologist B. F. Skinner (1904–1990) was perhaps the most influential contemporary writer on **behavioral psychology**. Skinner believed that all human behavior is environmentally determined, a mere response to external stimuli. His experiments, designed to control animal behavior (including the training of pigeons to play Ping-Pong), and his theories about the relationship of human freedom to behavior modification have been the object of both acclaim and alarm. In his fictional work *Walden Two* (1948), Skinner outlined his notion of a modern utopian society. He actually believed it possible to create the society described in Walden Two with the tools made available by the new science of human behavior.

The Good Life

As described in *Walden Two*, Skinner's imagined utopia is a world within a world. Its fictional founder, psychologist T. E. Frazier, has managed to obtain "for taxes" a tract of land that previously contained seven or eight rundown farms, conveniently self-enclosed, symbolizing its self-sufficiency.

Although concerned about the problem of creating a good society, Frazier disdains philosophy. Difficult questions such as "What constitutes the good life?" he dismisses as irrelevant. "We all know what's good, until we stop to think about it," he declares.[15] For Frazier, the basic ingredients of the good life are

behavioral psychology
A school of psychological thought that holds that the way people (and animals) act is determined by the stimuli they receive from the environment and from other persons and that human or animal behavior can be manipulated by carefully structuring the environment to provide positive stimuli for desired behavior and negative stimuli for unwanted behavior.

A pioneer in the field of behavioral psychology, U.S. psychologist B. F. Skinner described a utopian society fashioned by the modification of human behavior: "We simply arrange a world in which serious conflicts occur as seldom as possible."

obvious: good health, an absolute minimum of unpleasant labor, a chance to exercise your talents and abilities, and true leisure (that is, freedom from the economic and social pressures that, in Frazier's view, render the so-called leisure class the least relaxed of people). These goals are realized in *Walden Two's* pleasant atmosphere of noncompetitive social harmony.

The Science of Behavioral Engineering

Frazier summed up his view about how to produce individual happiness and group harmony in this way:

> I can't give you a rational justification for any of it. I can't reduce it to any principle of "the greatest good." This is the Good Life. We know it. It's a fact, not a theory. . . . We don't puzzle our little minds over the outcome of Love versus Duty. We simply arrange a world in which serious conflicts occur as seldom as possible or, with a little luck, not at all.[16]

The key word here is "arrange." The *kind* of world to be arranged is of only passing interest to Frazier; what commands his attention is the question of *how to do* the arranging. He is concerned not with ends, but with means, not with philosophy, but with scientific experimentation. He is the quintessential methodologist.

Because political action has not helped build a better world, "other measures" are required. What other measures? A revolution in the science of behavior modification:

> Considering how long society has been at it, you'd expect a better job. But the campaigns have been badly planned and the victory has never been secure. The behavior of the individual has been shaped according to revelations of "good conduct," never as the result of experimental study. But why not experiment? The questions are simple enough. What's the best behavior for the individual so far as the group is concerned? And how can the individual be induced to behave in that way? Why not explore these questions in a scientific spirit?[17]

The Walden Two experiment represents this kind of scientific exploration. Initially, Frazier develops an experimental code of good behavior. Everyone is expected to adhere to it under the supervision of certain behavioral scientists (such as Frazier) called managers. Positive reinforcement, rather than punishment, helps instill behavioral patterns; and a system of finely tuned frustrations and annoyances eliminates the destructive emotions of anger, fear, and lust. For example, to engender self-restraint, Frazier has the schoolteachers hang lollipops—which they are not to lick—around the children's necks. Such **behavioral engineering** will prove successful, Frazier asserts, not because it physically controls outward behavior, but because the conscious manipulation of stimuli effectively influences "*the inclination* to behave—the motives, the desires, the wishes."[18]

Children are placed in a scientifically controlled environment from infancy. They are raised in nurseries and never live with their parents. (Nor do their parents live with one another.) Private property is abolished, all eat together in common dining halls, and boys and girls marry and have children at fifteen or sixteen.

behavioral engineering
The carefully programmed use of rewards and punishments to instill desired patterns of behavior in an individual or an animal.

The Behavioral Scientist as God

Much that is familiar in the outside world is notably absent at Walden Two. Although its residents feel free, there is no freedom in this community. The idea of freedom is illusory, Frazier argues, because all behavior is conditioned. History is viewed "only as entertainment"; schoolchildren do not even study this "spurious science." Religion is not forbidden, but, like government in Marx's utopia, it has withered away through social obsolescence ("Psychologists are our priests," Frazier asserts). Moral codes of right and wrong have given way to

POLITICS AND POP CULTURE

WONDER WOMAN: UTOPIAN FICTION AND THE RISE OF THE FEMINIST MOVEMENT

Superheroes like Superman, Batman, and Wonder Woman are among the most popular and commercially successful comic book characters of all time. Superman was introduced to young readers in 1938, Batman in 1939, and Wonder Woman in 1941. Perhaps the real wonder here is how Wonder Woman managed to get a chance at comic book stardom seven years before the United Nations adopted the Universal Declaration of Human Rights, recognizing "the equal rights of men and women" and decades before the term "glass ceiling"—denoting the gender gap in work and pay—was invented. How did it happen? Here's how Jill Lepore, Harvard Professor of American History and author of *The Secret History of Wonder Woman* (New York: Knopf, 2014), explains it:

> Wonder Woman's origin story comes straight out of feminist utopian fiction. In the nineteenth century, suffragists, following the work of anthropologists, believed that something like the Amazons of Greek myth had once existed, a matriarchy that predated the rise of patriarchy. "The period of woman's supremacy lasted through many centuries," Elizabeth Cady Stanton wrote in 1891. In the nineteen-tens, this idea became a staple of feminist thought.*

And in case you're thinking that the early feminists were not really serious about challenging men for the right to run things, here's what Lepore has to say about that:

> The word "'feminism,'" hardly ever used in the United States before 1910, was everywhere

by 1913. The suffrage movement had been founded on a set of ideas about women's supposed moral superiority. Feminism rested on the principle of equality. Suffrage was a single, elusive political goal. Feminism's demand for equality was far broader. "All feminists are suffragists, but not all suffragists are feminists," as one feminist explained. They shared an obsession with Amazons.

Many popular Superman and Batman films have been made in the past four decades, but there has not been one starring Wonder Woman. But stay tuned: in December 2013, Warner Bros. announced a deal to produce three future Superman-Batman movies with a role for . . . (drum roll) . . . Wonder Woman! Feminism hasn't exactly conquered Hollywood—much less Wall Street or Washington—but putting a female superhero alongside Superman and Batman is surely overdue. Like putting a woman in the White House. . . .

***
*"The Last Amazon: Wonder Woman Returns," Jill Lepore, *The New Yorker*, September 22, 2014.

In your opinion, would the country or the world be better off if women were in charge? Think about it.

(Hint: Do men and women generally display differences in behavior that are relevant to politics? For example, are men by nature more aggressive or prone to violence than women? Are women by nature more emotional or less rational than men?)

"experimental ethics." Politics has no value: "You can't make progress toward the Good Life by political action! Not under any current form of government! You must operate upon another level entirely."[19]

Life at Walden Two has, in fact, been organized to create the most propitious circumstances for the managers' experiments in behavior modification. Although Frazier justifies this on the basis of increased human happiness, we are left with the gnawing sense that something significant is missing—some sort of check on the power of the behavioral engineers who run the community. Power will not corrupt the managers, we are told, for they "are part of a noncompetitive culture in which a thirst for power is a curiosity."[20] They do not use force (nobody does at Walden Two), and the offices they hold are not permanent. These reassurances have a hollow ring, however. Clearly, the love of power—an obsessive need to control others—is not absent from Frazier's own soul. As the founder of Walden Two, he appears to view himself as a kind of messiah who has discovered the secret to a whole new way of life: "I look upon my work and, behold, it is good."[21] Frazier is the ultimate "control freak"; a mere mortal who would be God.

UTOPIA REVISITED

Think about it: injustice, conflict, jealousies, rivalries, and individual frustrations—all are absent in these utopias. No deep-seated tensions divide individuals; no great antagonisms exist between society and the state. Each utopia, however, is inspired by a different vision and is ordered according to a different plan.

In *The Republic*, Plato explored the limits of human perfection; he sought not only to depict his idea of the best political order but also to make clear the problems in attempting to bring it about. Bacon wrote *The New Atlantis* to show not the limits of human achievement but the possibilities that a society wholly predicated on modern science might achieve. His is a hopeful work that promises tangible improvement in human welfare. For Marx, the path to utopia is class struggle and revolution. For Skinner, behavior modification is the solution.

To create a completely happy and harmonious world, a writer must postulate a breakthrough in the way society is constituted. As we have seen, Plato saw philosophy as the key. His republic could not exist until or unless the wisest philosophers ruled (an unlikely prospect at best). Bacon believed the scientific method, rather than logic and deduction, would blaze the trail to a better world. For Marx, philosophy and science were overshadowed by economics; public (collective) common ownership of the means of production, he believed, was the only way to achieve a peaceful and plentiful world. Finally, Skinner viewed the scientific manipulation of human behavior as the key to social and personal fulfillment.

With the advent of modern science and technology, some political thinkers began to take more seriously the practical possibility of achieving utopia. For thinkers like Bacon, Marx, and Skinner, the good life was a real possibility, not a pipe dream.

Utopias are futuristic blueprints for society. Underlying them are certain shared assumptions about human beings and what is best for them. Let's examine these assumptions.

Utopia and Human Nature

Even if an ideal state could be brought into existence, it would be ephemeral. Why? Simple logic, for one thing: if utopia is the best form of government possible, any change is to be resisted at all costs. But

If advances in behavioral science make it possible in theory to reprogram the human mind, who is to say that advances in genetic science will not make it possible one day soon to create the perfect mind in the perfect human body, one free of birth defects, weaknesses, and inherited traits deemed undesirable by society? If so, would the result be a true "master race"? Or would it be a nightmare? What do you think?

the world is constantly changing. So how can any society on earth remain static and still survive? The former Soviet Union, for example, failed to adapt to a rapidly changing world; the People's Republic of China did not. Both started out as revolutionary states with the goal of creating the kind of classless society Marx envisaged. Although neither succeeded in building a utopia (far from it), one has ceased to exist; the other is challenging the United States for world leadership.

Another big obstacle is human nature. Vices such as dishonesty, lust, greed, malice, and caprice are too common; virtues such as honor, fidelity, kindness, charity, and tolerance are too rare. Not surprisingly, utopian thinkers have often sought ways to reengineer the human makeup through **eugenics** or compulsory education or the abolition of private property. Utopian thinkers often blame institutions that protect, sanction, and perpetuate inequalities, and conclude that the only way to rid society of great disparities in wealth is to abolish established institutions. In many utopias, communal activities, common residences, and public meals replace private property ownership, and cooperation is valued above competition.

Josiah Warren, one participant in the New Harmony Society mentioned at the beginning of this chapter, reflected on the failure of Robert Owen's utopian project, "We had assured ourselves of our unanimous devotedness to the cause and expected unanimity of thought and action: but instead . . . we met diversity of opinions . . . entirely beyond anything we had just left behind us in common society." He added:

> We found more antagonisms than we had been accustomed to in common life. If we had demanded or even expected infinite diversity, disunion and disintegration we should have found ourselves in harmony with the facts and with each other on one point at least. We differed, we contended and ran

eugenics
The science of controlling the hereditary traits in a species, usually by selective mating, in an attempt to improve the species.

ourselves into confusion: our legislative proceedings were just like all others, excepting that we did not come to blows or pistols; because Mr. Owen had shown us that all our thoughts, feelings and actions were the inevitable effects of the causes that produce them; and that it would be just as rational to punish the fruit of a tree for being what it is, as to punish each other for being what we are.[22]

Utopia and the Rejection of Politics

If utopians are correct that environment can influence individuals so profoundly, then malleable humans are capable not only of moral perfection but also of moral corruption. Any flaw in the construction of a utopia—even a moral principle the great majority embrace—can therefore turn a dream into a nightmare. Thus, for example, Michael Young's 1958 book, *The Rise of the Meritocracy*, debunks the ideal of a social order based on pure merit.[23] Set in 2034, and written from the perspective of an academic social critic analyzing the development of post-aristocratic British society, this work (in which Young coined the term "meritocracy") was interpreted as a paean to the best and the brightest. In fact, says its author, it was "a satire meant to be a warning (which needless to say has not been heeded) against what might happen" if "those who are judged to have merit of a particular kind harden into a new social class without room in it for others."

In almost every utopia (for example, Marx's dictatorship of the proletariat), political power is centralized, giving the state powerful tools with which to reshape and control society. By themselves these tools are neutral; everything depends on how they are used—wisely or foolishly, efficiently or wastefully, for good or for ill. Utopian thinkers tend to assume power will always be used benignly. But in the absence of checks and balances, there is scant reason to believe it will be—and tons of evidence to the contrary.

Utopian thinkers typically display relatively little interest in politics, in the actual workings of government, or, for that matter, in reconciling opposing views. Truth and justice are treated as self-evident, and there is one—and only one—solution to all the problems that beset society. The solution is not to be found in politics but in the transcendence of politics.

DYSTOPIA: FROM DREAM TO NIGHTMARE

It is significant that the nightmare books of our age have not been about new Draculas and Frankensteins but about what may be termed dystopias—inverted utopias, in which an imagined megalithic government brings human life to an exquisite pitch of misery.

—Anthony Burgess

In a recent book of short stories tantalizingly entitled *The Persuasion Nation*, George Saunders creates a world "in which the oppressive force is not a totalitarian government but the all-seeing eye of targeted advertising." What makes both the "all-seeing eye" and targeted advertising so potent today is—Surprise!—the Internet and the new science of "virology"—that is, what makes a meme go viral on the web. For example, "My Flamboyant Grandson" is a story set in midtown Manhattan:

As the narrator and his grandson walk the street, devices implanted in the sidewalk mine digital information from strips in their shoes. Eye-level screens then show them "images reflective of Personal Preferences we'd stated," imploring them, for example to visit a nearby Burger King.[24]

The dangers of unchecked political power, and the more general theme of utopia-turned-nightmare, are vividly developed in such well-known works as George Orwell's *Nineteen Eighty-Four* (1949) and Aldous Huxley's *Brave New World* (1932). Such classic works, along with more recent literary utopias such as Margaret Atwood's *The Handmaid's Tale*, P. D. James's *Children of Men*, Cormac McCarthy's Pulitzer–Prize-winning *The Road*, and Lois Lowry's *The Giver*, provide graphic descriptions of a **dystopia**, or a society whose creators set out to build a perfect society only to discover that whoever promises the impossible is doomed to failure. And the people are like lambs being led to the slaughter.

A Right to Be Frightened

In 1962, British author Anthony Burgess published a novel with an odd-sounding title: *A Clockwork Orange*. The novel received little notice until 1971 when Stanley Kubrick's film adaptation of the book hit movie theaters around the world and it became an overnight sensation. The story is about a juvenile delinquent named Alex who is clever, predatory, and, oddly enough, a music lover (Beethoven, not the Beatles). His crimes of violence include robbery, vandalism, and rape.

Alex is arrested and imprisoned but the Home Office (the British equivalent of the Ministry of the Interior) decides to use "a form of aversion therapy guaranteed, in a mere two weeks, to eliminate criminal propensities forever."[25] Alex welcomes the opportunity to be "cured" of his violent tendencies, and he is confident the treatment won't tame his aggressive libido. He is given injections that induce extreme nausea and at the same time made to watch films about violence. Soon even thinking about a violent act makes him violently ill. The sight of a desirable woman nauseates him.

But the films also used symphonic music as "emotional heighteners" and now he cannot even stand to listen to Beethoven. Hearing a recording of the Ninth Symphony causes Alex to attempt suicide. We leave the story there. You will have to read the book or watch the movie to find out how it ends.

Burgess published a soul-searching commentary on this famous work in 1973.[26] In it he alluded to Huxley's *Brave New World* and Orwell's *Nineteen Eighty-Four*. He noted, "B. F. Skinner's book *Beyond Freedom and Dignity* came out at the very time that *A Clockwork Orange* first appeared on the screen, ready to demonstrate the advantages of what we may call beneficent brainwashing." Skinner was an advocate of positive reinforcement as a way to inculcate habits conducive to peace and harmony in society. "It is . . . conditioning of the wrong sort that turns the hero of *A Clockwork Orange* into a vomiting paragon of non-aggression," Burgess notes. He concedes that a good deal of conformity is necessary for a society to work, "But when patterns of conformity are imposed by the state, then one has a right to be frightened."[27]

dystopia
A society whose creators set out to build the perfect political order only to discover that they cannot remain in power except through coercion and by maintaining a ruthless monopoly over the means of communication.

Orwell's World

In *Nineteen Eighty-Four*, the totalitarian rulers (personified by a shadowy figure called Big Brother) retain power by manipulating not only the people's actions and forms of behavior, but also their sources and methods of thought. Thus, the Ministry of Truth is established for the sole purpose of systematically lying to the citizenry; a new language ("Newspeak") is invented to purge all words, ideas, and expressions considered dangerous by the government; and a contradictory kind of logic ("double-think") is introduced to make the minds of the citizenry receptive to the opportunistic zigzags of official propaganda.

According to the official ideology, the purpose behind state terror, strict censorship, and constant surveillance is to prevent enemies of the revolution from stopping the march toward full communism—a worker's paradise in which everyone will be happy, secure, prosperous, and equal. In theory, the masses are finally put in control of their own destiny; in practice, they become a new class of slaves whose fate is in the hands of the most ruthless tyrant(s) imaginable.

Utopia and Terrorism

In a later chapter, we explore the nature of terrorism and its impact on domestic and international politics in the contemporary world. Acts of terror are often associated with religious or ideological zeal, especially when they include the ultimate sacrifice, as in the case of suicide bombers. At least one scholar sees a close connection between the utopian quest for social justice and the Islamist glorification of martyrs.[28]

We might well wonder what could possibly motivate another human being to carry out a mission that is at once barbaric and self-destructive, like the September 11, 2001, attacks on the World Trade Center and the Pentagon, the horrific commuter train bombings in Madrid in March 2004, or the London subway bombings of July 2005. Indeed, terrorist attacks against civilians continue on a daily basis in Iraq and all too frequently in other parts of the world. Such acts are shocking and difficult to understand. What motivates a group of people to plan, prepare, and finally execute a mass murder based on a joint suicide pact?

There is no simple answer. It is quite likely that some terrorists are motivated by a perverted idea of the possible, a misguided sense of what could be if only the imagined source of all evil were annihilated.[29] The identity of the targeted "evil" is almost incidental. Extremists who imagine a time when, for example, Islamic societies were pure and unadulterated—a time before Western ideas, values, music, money, and military occupation corrupted the faithful—can too easily find a justification for killing innocent people in the name of a higher purpose. It is a disturbing fact that in modern history a longing for utopia, a place on earth where happiness knows no limits, is often associated with violence that knows no limits either.

SUMMARY

In the sixteenth century, Sir Thomas More coined the term *utopia* to signify an imaginary society of perfect harmony and happiness. More's *Utopia* was a subtle attack on the ills of English society under Henry VIII. The first important attempt to define the "perfect" political order, however, had been made by Plato in *The Republic*.

Four works stand out as representative of utopian thought in the history of Western political philosophy. In *The Republic*, Plato sought the just society through philosophical inquiry. In the seventeenth century, Francis Bacon's *New Atlantis* demonstrated how the human condition could be elevated through modern science. Karl Marx later propounded the view that only through the radical reorganization of economic relationships within society could true justice and an end to human misery be achieved. The ultimate aim of Marx's theory of social transformation is the creation of a classless society. Finally, in B. F. Skinner's *Walden Two*, a prime example of a contemporary utopian scheme, behavioral psychology holds the key to utopia. The form and content of the just society were of less concern to Skinner than the methods for bringing such a society into existence.

Thoughts of utopia have been inspired by idealism and impatience with social injustices. However, its presumed desirability conflicts with its practical possibility. The principal obstacle to utopian society is the unpredictability and selfishness of human nature, which utopian thinkers commonly have sought to control through eugenics programs, compulsory education, and the abolition of private property.

Utopian visionaries often blame politics for the failure to improve society. As a result, in many utopian blueprints, the role of politics in bringing about desired change is either greatly reduced or eliminated entirely. This leaves most utopian schemes open to criticism, for they could easily become blueprints for totalitarianism. Such blueprints often take shape in writings about dystopias—utopias that turn into nightmares.

KEY TERMS

utopia 51
philosopher-king 54
noble lie 55
classless society 57
dictatorship of the proletariat 57

withering away of the state 58
behavioral psychology 59
behavioral engineering 60

eugenics 63
dystopia 65

REVIEW QUESTIONS

1. What is the origin of the term *utopia*? What does the word mean?
2. How have utopian writers differed about the practicality of utopia?
3. Utopian writers often make certain basic assumptions about human nature and society. What are they? Which if any do you agree with and why?
4. What can the study of utopian thought teach us about politics?
5. In the twentieth century, novelists produced chilling stories that turn utopia upside down. What inspired these stores?
6. Choose one fictional dystopia you have read about. How did it come into being? Would you want to live there? If not, why not?

WEBSITES AND READINGS

Websites

Utopias: http://users.erols.com/jonwill/utopialist.htm

Utopian literature and artwork: utopia.nypl.org/Pt1exhibit.html

Bacon's *New Atlantis*: www.levity.com/alchemy/atlantis.html

Plato's *The Republic*: classics.mit.edu/Plato/republic.html

More's *Utopia*: www.luminarium.org/renlit/tmore.htm

Harrington's *The Commonwealth of Oceania*: www.constitution.org/jh/oceana.htm

Bellamy's *Looking Backward*: *From 200 to 1887*: xroads.virginia.edu/~HYPER/BELLAMY/toc.html

To do more research into utopias and dystopias, use the key words *utopia* or *dystopia* at two or three different search engines. Also, try combining these key words with other search terms, such as *utopia and ideology* or *utopia and terrorism*.

Readings

Atwood, Margaret. *The Handmaid's Tale*. New York: Houghton Mifflin, 1986. A dystopian novel that explores issues of power, gender, and religious politics.

Bacon, Francis. *The New Atlantis and the Great Instauration*, 2nd ed. Wheeling, WV: Harlan Davidson, 1989. Bacon's seventeenth-century account of a society blessed by scientific breakthroughs is surprisingly modern.

Berman, Paul. "Terror and Liberalism." *The American Prospect*, vol. 12, no. 18, October 22, 2001. An incisive piece on a topic that was timely when it first appeared and remains relevant as civil liberties in the United States have been sharply curtailed in the name of "homeland security."

Burgess, Anthony. *A Clockwork Orange* (1962). New York: W.W. Norton, 2012 (new hardcover edition). Called "A frightening fable of good and evil, and the meaning of freedom." A classic.

Gilison, Jerome. *The Soviet Image of Utopia*. Baltimore, MD: Johns Hopkins University Press, 1975. An insightful discussion of the idealist elements in Marxist-Leninist ideology.

Hertzler, Joyce. *The History of Utopian Thought*. New York: Cooper Square Publishers, 1965. A thorough discussion of utopian thinkers and their ideas throughout history.

Huxley, Alduous. *Brave New World* (1932). New York: Harper (reprint), 2006. A powerful story about a utopian world gone wrong.

James, P. D., *The Children of Men* (1992). New York: Vintage (reprint), 2006. Called "a story of a world with no children and no future."

Kateb, George. *Utopia and Its Enemies,* rev. ed. New York: Schocken Books, 1972. A sympathetic defense of the value and contributions of utopian thought.

Lowry, Lois. *The Giver* (1993). New York: Houghton-Mifflin (paperback), 2014. An award-winning novel about Jonas, a twelve-year-old boy, who lives in a seemingly ideal, if colorless, world of conformity and contentment—until he discovers the truth.

McCarthy, Cormac. *The Road.* New York: Vintage, 2007. A widely acclaimed story of a father and son on a journey through a burned, postapocalyptic America.

More, Thomas. *Utopia,* translated by Paul Turner. Baltimore, MD: Penguin, 1965. More's imaginary society inspired many later utopian writers; the work remains a charming account of one man's paradise.

Orwell, George. *Nineteen Eighty-Four.* New York: New American Library, 1961. A classic novel that brilliantly describes a dystopia modeled after Stalin's Soviet Union.

Plato. *The Republic,* translated by Allan Bloom. New York: Basic Books, 1991. Bloom's literal interpretation and interpretive essay helped make this edition of Plato's classic work especially valuable.

Popper, Karl. *The Open Society and Its Enemies.* Princeton, NJ: Princeton University Press, 1966. This work argues that Plato and Marx (among others) were advocates of totalitarian government and opponents of free, democratic societies.

Skinner, B. F. *Walden Two.* New York: Macmillan, 1976. A fictionalized account of a small community founded and organized according to the principles of behavioral psychology.

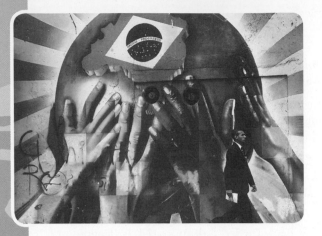

CHAPTER 4

Constitutional Democracy
Models of Representation

Learning Objectives

1 Define liberal democracy.

2 Evaluate whether "democracy" is the best form of government.

3 Identify and distinguish among four models of American democracy.

4 Determine whether the United States is really a democracy, what kind of democracy, and whether it is the best of its kind.

5 Describe the "tyranny of the majority" and how it can be avoided.

6 Identify why the rule of law and due process are fundamental to constitutional government.

Constitutional democracy is a form of government based on representation. In common usage, the term *democracy* is applied loosely—often too loosely to have any real meaning. Any government that does not operate openly and according to clearly established rules does not qualify as democratic. We tend to focus on the rules that govern the citizens (laws and regulations), but what is even more important is what rules govern the government—a constitution that functions as the supreme law, the law above ordinary statutory law.

Democracies rest on constitutional foundations and feature elections, representative assemblies (legislatures), an independent judiciary, a free press, and various other institutional constraints on executive power. Cultivating a political culture that places the constitution on a pedestal is a key factor stable democracies share in common.

LIBERAL DEMOCRACY: MODELS AND THEORIES

Democracy means different things to different people. One scholar has identified nine different models of democracy—four "classical" forms and five "contemporary" ones.[1]

One of the oldest models is **direct democracy**, which in ancient Greece encompassed a small city-state (Athens) wherein citizens (all those entitled to vote) participated directly in political deliberations and the decision-making process. Another classical model is the **republic**, a form of limited democracy more suitable to a large state and pioneered by the Romans in ancient times. Governance in the Roman Republic required elections and two representative bodies (a senate and an assembly), but it was not very democratic by today's standards.

Modern democracies typically invite wide citizen participation and promise a fair contest of ideas and interests. The modern form of republican government is **constitutional democracy**, which stresses political equality and individual liberties.

Political scientist Richard Katz has developed a useful "typology of liberal democratic theories."[2] Katz's typology asks two key questions. First, is a given society by nature stable or volatile? For a variety of historical, cultural, and demographic reasons, some societies are—or appear to be—more governable than others. Second, do the elites or the masses pose the greatest danger to democracy? Six different observers developed different theories of democracy corresponding to these two basic questions. Jeremy Bentham and Joseph Schumpeter viewed society as a single undifferentiated mass of individuals rather than as a collection of groups, classes, or factions. The others saw society as divided or segmented (differentiated), although they differed on exactly how, and what this differentiation means.

According to James Madison and Robert Dahl, society is pluralistic, containing many groups, but it's important to note that individuals belong to more than one group. This overlapping membership creates *crosscutting cleavages*.

direct democracy
A form of government in which political decisions are made directly by citizens rather than by their representatives.

republic
A form of government in which sovereignty resides in the people rather than with the rulers; the vast majority of democracies today are republics wherein supreme law-making power is exercised by elected representatives who are responsible to the citizenry.

constitutional democracy
A system of limited government, based on majority rule, in which political power is scattered among many factions and interest groups and governmental actions and institutions must conform to rules defined by a constitution.

In other words, individuals identify simultaneously with various groups and organizations, such as town, city, suburb, neighborhood, school, church, or synagogue. But John Calhoun saw society as segmented rather than fragmented, and Arendt Lijphart, a renowned political scientist, is famous for his theory of *consociationalism* involving ways democracies can resolve conflicts through power sharing. For theorists like Calhoun and Lijphart, overlapping affinities, interests, and loyalties will not break down the barriers that divide society on the basis of income, race, gender, regions, and the like without deliberate action and wise leadership.

The political implications of these different conceptions of society become clearer when we ask the second question: What is the greatest danger to democracy? For Bentham, who advocated "the greatest good for the greatest number," the economic and social elites threaten democracy; whereas for Schumpeter, the masses clamoring for socialism or a welfare state are the problem. In Schumpeter's view, democracy cannot endure without capitalism to spur economic growth. But because the masses see capitalism as the chief cause of inequality and democracy is based on majority rule, Schumpeter was pessimistic about the future of liberal-democratic government.

For the other four theorists, *pluralism* is more important than class distinctions, but they differ in terms of who and what poses the greatest threat to democracy. Madison and Calhoun saw the elites as the main danger; whereas for Dahl and Lijphart, the masses are the greatest threat.

Who is right? Clearly, it's a difficult question. And perhaps that's the key insight because it points to the conclusion that there are no simple answers, that there is some truth in each of these theories. The type of liberal democracy we choose depends on a larger political theory that takes account of human nature and makes a judgment about the main threat(s) to freedom—democracy's defining value. Next, we take a closer look at republics and constitutions.

REPUBLICS AND CONSTITUTIONS

Countries as diverse as France, Poland, India, South Africa, Brazil, and Mexico are all examples of constitutional democracy in action. Official names, such as the German Federal Republic or the Republic of South Korea, reflect the key importance of representation in the modern world. Nothing is more vital to a representative democracy than regular elections based on the right to vote and the secret ballot.

We take this right for granted, but it is a freedom that didn't exist anywhere else in the world when the United States came into being. Today, more people enjoy the right to vote in more places than at any other time in history. It's a right that some 1.3 billion people in the People's Republic of China, for example, do not enjoy.

Constitutions are necessary to impose limits on **majority rule** and protect minority rights, and to define the basic institutions, organization, and operations of the government. In the U.S. Constitution, for example, a detailed system of **checks and balances** assigns powers to each branch (executive, legislative, and judiciary) and sets limits to the exercise of those powers.

majority rule
The principle that any candidate or program that receives at least half of all votes plus one prevails.

checks and balances
Constitutional tools that enable branches of government to resist any illegitimate expansion of power by other branches.

Most contemporary democracies have written constitutions, but they differ greatly in age and length, as well as content. Some, like those of the United States and France, are models of brevity. Others are lengthy and detailed. India slices and dices governmental powers into federal (97), state (66), and concurrent (47) ones. Kenya allocates authority between the central and regional governments in elaborate detail (e.g., animal disease control, the regulation of barbers and hairdressers, and houses occupied by disorderly residents).

The United Kingdom, the "Mother of all Parliaments," does not have a formal written constitution. Instead, the British constitution is inscribed in the minds and hearts of the British people. It is a deeply ingrained consensual social contract consisting of custom and convention and certain bedrock principles found in historic documents, royal decrees, acts of Parliament, and judicial precedent.

Constitutional democracies must meet three competing, and sometimes conflicting, criteria. First, because such governments are democratic, they must be *responsive* to the people. Second, they must be *limited* in the goals they can pursue and the means by which they can pursue them. Third, they must be *effective*—for example, maintaining law and order, managing complex economies, protecting the people, and so on.

BOTTOMS UP: THE IDEA OF AMERICA

The United States is the birthplace of the first modern theory of representative democracy actually put into practice. (See Figure 4.1: "Landmarks in History: Philadelphia: Birthplace of Liberty"). Far from perfect at its inception (perpetuating slavery, for example), it nonetheless was a daring departure from the past and a bold attempt to reshape the future, which it did. The success of a political system based on a balance between "bottom-up" and "top-down" power is a defining moment in the history of the modern world.

The *idea* of America is a product of the eighteenth-century Enlightenment that, in turn, grew out of the Italian Renaissance of the late fifteenth century. The political views of the American Founders, including George Washington, Benjamin Franklin, John Adams, Thomas Jefferson, James Madison, and Alexander Hamilton, drew heavily on the contributions of famous thinkers who lived and wrote during that earlier time—Niccolò Machiavelli, Thomas Hobbes, Jean-Jacques Rousseau, John Locke, and Baron de Montesquieu, among others.

These modern political thinkers all agreed on at least one point: that the purpose of government is not, as Aristotle had claimed, to nurture virtue, but rather to combat vice. An unflattering view of human nature led these thinkers to stress the pursuit of realistic goals—liberty or security, for example, which is attainable, rather than virtue, which is not.

"America" has been synonymous with liberty in the minds of people all over the world. Arguably, it is the idea itself more than the reality that for many decades gave the United States vast reserves of "soft power" (the ability to get others to want what we want). But the unpopular and protracted Vietnam War eroded that soft power, as has the costly and controversial war in Iraq.

PHILADELPHIA: Birthplace of Liberty

FIGURE 4.1   Map of Colonial America. Philadelphia, Boston, and New York were the three major cities. Washington, D.C. did not come into being until after the U.S. Constitution was adopted in 1788.

Library of Congress

On July 4, 1776, the Continental Congress, which met in Philadelphia, Pennsylvania, adopted the Declaration of Independence—an audacious act of defiance against the king of England that was certain to provoke war with the world's preeminent naval power. The Declaration, which begins with the ringing words, "We hold these truths to be self-evident, that all men are created equal," followed a long struggle between the colonists and the colonizers over issues such as the power to tax, regulate trade and commerce, and quarter troops. At the root

(Continued)

(CONTINUED)

of all these disputes, however, was a thirst for liberty, a burning desire to escape unjust and arbitrary rule. Other grievances included "imposing Taxes on us without our Consent [and] depriving us in many cases, of the benefits of Trial by Jury."

Today, schoolchildren still recite the Declaration and, once learned, the key words are seldom forgotten. People, it asserts, have "unalienable Rights" (derived from the "Creator"). These rights are "Life, Liberty and the pursuit of Happiness." The "just powers" of governments derive "from the consent of the governed." This revolutionary manifesto—a stirring call to arms, by any measure— came at a time when absolute monarchies ruled all Europe. It preceded the French Revolution by thirteen years. Its creation was the act that led to the modern world's first, and oldest, constitutional democracy.

FOUR MODELS OF AMERICAN DEMOCRACY

The principle of majority rule is basic to constitutional democracy. Free elections decide who rules. Citizens play an important role in government—choosing who will hold high office and, therefore, who will make the laws, formulate the policies, and administer the programs on which well-ordered civil societies depend.

Alexander Hamilton: Federalism

Constitutional democracies cannot ignore the opinions and beliefs of the majority. However, a popular government is not necessarily a viable one. In the words of Alexander Hamilton (1757–1804), "a government ought to contain in itself every power requisite to the full accomplishment of the objects committed to its care, ... free from every other control, but a regard to the public good and to the sense of the people."[3]

What good is democracy if the government cannot protect its citizens, promote prosperity, and provide essential services such as education, law enforcement, water treatment, and firefighting? In Hamilton's view, checks and balances, however necessary in a democracy, should not be carried so far as to impede or impair the government's ability to act energetically. Madison noted that one of the "very important" difficulties encountered at the Constitutional Convention was "combining the requisite stability and energy in Government, with the inviolable attention due to liberty, and to the Republican form."[4]

Hamilton, the indomitable Federalist, argued the most passionately—and fought the most fiercely—for a

DMAC/Alamy

Alexander Hamilton (1757–1804). One of the principle authors of the Federalist Papers, published serially in two prominent newspapers in 1787–1788, he is still the most authoritative source for the interpretation of the U.S. Constitution. An unrelenting advocate of a strong federal government and an assertive executive branch, Hamilton was the first U.S. secretary of the Treasury and chief architect of the U.S. system of taxation, the plan for funding the national debt, and the first National Bank. Hamilton died at age 49 from a gunshot wound inflicted by his archenemy, Aaron Burr, in a duel. He is pictured on the U.S. ten dollar bill.

strong central government. With good reason, George Washington turned to Hamilton, the United States' first secretary of the Treasury, to put the fledging national government's finances in order and to create a tax system, a federal budget, a central bank, the Customs Service, and the Coast Guard. A brilliant administrator with a penchant for micromanaging everything he touched, Hamilton endeavored to construct a strong central government, one that would be financially solvent, stable, and competent to act without constantly having to secure agreement among the separate states or seek the lowest common denominator among them.

In a real sense, the U.S. Constitution stands as a monument to Hamilton's vision. The president as chief executive is given the power to conduct the nation's foreign affairs, veto legislation, and appoint judges (with the approval of the Senate). The Congress has the power "to make all Laws which shall be necessary and proper"—a formulation that underscores the Founders' determination to avoid the kind of political paralysis that had thrown the colonies into a crisis under the ill-fated Articles of Confederation. And under the so-called **Supremacy Clause** (Article VI, Paragraph 2), all treaties are entrenched as the "supreme Law of the Land; and the Judges in every State shall be bound thereby, any Thing in the Constitution or Laws of any State to the contrary notwithstanding."

Supremacy Clause
Article VI, Section 2, of the Constitution, which declares that acts of Congress are "the Supreme law of the Land . . . binding on the Judges in every State."

Stability and continuity are essential to the success of any government. Established procedures for changing leaders by regularized methods (elections and appointments) are vitally important and represent one of the principal advantages of democracy over modern dictatorships.

History and tradition, along with symbolism and ritual, reinforce the sense of continuity in governments. Citing the need for continuity, Madison opposed Thomas Jefferson's proposal for recurring constitutional conventions, on the grounds that because "every appeal to the people would carry an implication of some defect in the government, frequent appeals would, in a great measure, deprive the government of that veneration which time bestows on everything, and without which perhaps the wisest and freest governments would not possess the requisite stability" and that even "the most rational government will not find it a superfluous advantage to have the prejudices of the community on its side."[5]

Hamilton and other delegates at Philadelphia sought to create a powerful and unified executive branch capable of resisting both the encroachments of Congress and the centrifugal pull of the states. They understood that the absence of a hereditary monarch, regular elections, and the possibility of impeachment are all effective checks on executive power.[6]

For better or worse, Congress is well equipped to resist an over-reaching chief executive. Even a popular president can be impeded or even impeached. When the opposition party controls Congress, the danger of impeachment is often clear and present. Thus, for example, President Richard Nixon's attempt to use the IRS and the FBI to intimidate his opponents in 1972 backfired and led to his forced resignation.

Of course, less drastic methods of straight-jacketing a president are also readily available to Congress. When Republicans won control of the House of

Representatives in the 2010 midterm elections, they opposed and obstructed the Obama White House at virtually every turn, causing what many observers described as "gridlock." President Obama won reelection in 2012, but Republicans swept the 2014 midterm elections, regaining control of the Senate while keeping control of the House. The 2014 vote was widely interpreted as a repudiation of Obama's policies. What was worse, it held out the prospect of a federal government in limbo with a lame duck president for the next two years.

The American Founders deliberately set the stage for a contest. The document they adopted at Philadelphia left plenty of room for interpretation, maneuver, and debate. Its ambiguity is a source of both frustration and strength. Where the line between capabilities and constraints is drawn depends on a mix of history, political culture, and circumstances.

Thomas Jefferson: Anti-Federalism

The validity of democracy is far from self-evident. As Socrates pointed out some twenty-five centuries ago, faced with big decisions on important matters, people turn to experts. Why, then, if we want good government, would we trust ordinary citizens who, after all, tend to be apathetic and ill informed to make wise decisions? If you asked your physician whether or not to undergo an operation, "you would be appalled if he explained that his policy in such cases was to poll a random sampling of passersby and act in accordance with the will of the majority."[7] Yet that is what democracies do all the time, often with dire consequences.

Thomas Jefferson (1743–1826) had more faith in "We the People" than Socrates did or, for that matter, than did many of the other Founders, including Hamilton and John Adams. For Jefferson, the author of the Declaration of Independence, majority rule was the only way to run a democracy. Unlike James Madison and others at Philadelphia, Jefferson did not see the principle of majority rule as a danger to the stability of a future government. Indeed, it was Jefferson who, in 1787, wrote in defense of Shays' Rebellion: "The tree of liberty must be refreshed from time to time with the blood of patriots and tyrants."

Jefferson and Madison embraced quite different views of human nature. Jefferson believed in the basic goodness of the people, that presented with clear alternatives the majority would normally make a rational choice. Alexis de Tocqueville (1805–1859) offered a cogent defense of majority rule in his classic two-volume study *Democracy in America* (1835): "The moral authority of the majority is partly based upon the notion that there is more intelligence and more wisdom in a great number of men collected together than in a single individual." "The moral power of the majority," Tocqueville wrote, "is founded upon yet another principle, which is, that the interests of the many are to be preferred to those of the few."[8] Moreover, Tocqueville noted, the possibility that today's minority can become tomorrow's majority gives the principle of majority rule a universal appeal.[9]

The political principle of majority rule, therefore, finds support both in the ideal of equality and in self-interest. However, achieving it is not as easy, nor always as highly prized, as we might think. In the United States, where the two-party system is well entrenched, elections typically produce a clear majority in both state and national legislatures. They also produce the *appearance* of a clear majority in most presidential elections. But as we discovered in the 2000 presidential election, when Al Gore won the popular vote but lost the election to George W. Bush, the candidate who gets the most votes is not automatically assured of getting elected. The **winner-takes-all system** awards all the electoral votes in a given state to the candidate who gets the most votes, even if nobody gets a clear majority.

Unlike the United States, most democracies around the world are based on the British system. Parliamentary democracies typically have multiple political parties competing for votes in national elections. Multiparty systems often do not produce a clear majority in the parliament. The upshot is usually a coalition government consisting of two or more parties. The advantage of this system is that voters have more choices; the disadvantage is that no single party has a clear mandate and the very *possibility* of majority rule is called into question. No single party in a coalition government can hew to its own platform and ignore the wishes of its partners in the coalition. In these circumstances, the result is likely to be a government that reflects the lowest common denominator rather than the will of the people—and a disenchanted electorate.

Even in the United Kingdom, the world's foremost *two-party* parliamentary system, majority rule is problematic. British elections nearly always produce a clear majority in Parliament (see Chapter 7), but the winning party seldom garners more than 45% of the popular votes (and often significantly less). The reason is that the **plurality vote system**—which the British invented—is still in use there (as it is in the United States).

The distinction between majority and plurality voting raises a theoretical problem. If a candidate or government is chosen on the basis of a plurality, rather than a majority, it means more voters did *not* vote for that candidate or government than did vote—possibly many more. But critics of American or British democracy can easily take a wrong turn. More often than not, the reason the majority does not rule is not that the minority has usurped power but that *there is no clear majority*. Thus, to talk about the myth of the majority does not denigrate majority rule but recognizes the difficulty of putting it into practice.

The fact that the majority is often elusive raises a problem for democratic theory; the fact that it is often tyrannical raises a problem for democratic practice. Clearly, establishing government by majority rule is easier said than done. We turn next to this problem and how another great democratic theorist proposed to solve it.

James Madison: Balanced Government

Students are often surprised to learn many delegates to the Philadelphia Convention in 1787 did not fully share Jefferson's faith in the people. James Madison (1751–1836) stressed the natural tendency of society to fragment into factions based on self-interest, sectionalism, sectarian divisions, and the like. In Madison's view, Jefferson was naïve if he truly believed that nature predisposes human beings to live together in peace and harmony.

winner-takes-all system
Electoral system in which the candidate receiving the most votes wins.

plurality vote system
A system in which candidates who get the largest number of votes win, whether or not they garner a majority of the votes cast; in a majority vote system, if no candidate gets more than half the votes cast, a runoff election is held to determine the winner.

Both Madison and Hamilton expected individuals to act selfishly in politics, just as they do in personal matters, unless constrained by political arrangements designed for that purpose. The fairly clear distinctions that already existed between economic and social classes during the colonial period underscored Madison's fear of creating politically paralyzing or polarizing factionalism. How could a democratic government be structured to ensure the public interest would not be sacrificed to the selfish interests of factions?

The Madisonian solution was to ensure factions pursuing selfish ends would encounter as many hurdles as possible. It was this idea that won the day in Philadelphia. The **separation of powers** is one key; the other is **federalism**. For followers of Madison and Hamilton, good government requires a system of checks and balances, which in turn requires the right architecture.

The Architecture of Liberty

If people are not by nature virtuous and rulers are people, how can any system of rule *not* degenerate into tyranny? Here, in a nutshell, is the universal problem of politics. The Founders tried to solve this puzzle by developing what they called the "new science of politics," an ingenious arrangement of political institutions designed to permit a large measure of liberty while guarding against the arbitrary exercise of power by compartmentalizing the functions of government, thus preventing the concentration of power.

In *The Federalist*, Hamilton argued that the new U.S. Constitution would prevent "the extremes of tyranny and anarchy" that had plagued previous republics. He admonished his readers not to dwell on past examples: "The science of politics, like most other sciences, has received great improvement. The efficacy of various principles is now well understood, which were either not known at all, or imperfectly known to the ancients." Hamilton catalogued the structural improvements built into the Constitution by the pioneers of this new science:

James Madison (1751–1836). Fourth president of the United States (1809–1817). Author of many of the Federalist Papers, including several that many constitutional scholars consider seminal, Madison is often called the "Father of the Constitution" in recognition of his leading role in drafting that document. Madison is also credited with authorship of the Bill of Rights. An ally of Jefferson against the Federalists, Madison opposed various centralizing measures favored by Hamilton and John Adams. As president, Madison led the country into the War of 1812 against Britain. Perhaps more adept as a theoretician than as a practitioner of politics, Madison, as chief executive, changed his position on several key issues, favoring creation of a second National Bank (he had opposed the first), a strong military, and a high tariff to protect so-called infant industries.

GL Archive/Almay

> The regular distribution of power into distinct departments; the introduction of legislative balances and checks; the institution of courts composed of judges, holding their offices during good behaviour; the representation of the people in the legislature by deputies of their own election—these are either wholly new discoveries or have made their principal progress toward perfection in modern times. They are means, and powerful means, by which the excellences of republican government may be retained and its imperfections lessened or avoided.[10]

Because, as Madison noted, "enlightened statesmen will not always be at the helm," it was necessary to create and enshrine durable institutions capable of checking the ambitions of those in power.[11] Elections provide one such check, but "experience has taught mankind the necessity of auxiliary precautions."[12] The chief precaution was to set up a permanent rivalry within the

separation of powers
The organization of government into distinct areas of legislative, executive, and judicial functions, each responsible to different constituencies and possessing its own powers and responsibilities; the system of dividing the governmental powers among three branches and giving each branch a unique role to play while making all three interdependent.

federalism
A system of limited government based on the division of authority between the central government and smaller regional governments.

government: "The great security against a gradual concentration of the several powers in the same department, consists in giving to those who administer each department the necessary constitutional means and personal motives to resist encroachments of the others." In short, "Ambition must be made to counteract ambition."[13]

Checks and Balances In pursuit of this goal, the Founders attempted to make each branch of government largely independent of the other branches. Thus, the powers of each respective branch derive from specific provisions of the Constitution—Article I for the legislature, Article II for the executive, Article III for the judiciary. Each branch is given constitutional authority to perform certain prescribed tasks, and each is equipped with the tools to resist any illegitimate expansion of power by the other branches. These tools—called checks and balances—range from the mundane (the president's veto power) to the extraordinary (impeachment proceedings brought by Congress against a president). Together they make up the "necessary constitutional means" available to members of one branch of government for use against the encroachments of another.

As the authors of *The Federalist Papers* put it, "The interest of the [individual] must be connected with the constitutional rights of the place."[14] Protecting the powers and prerogatives vested in one branch would be motive enough to preserve the integrity of the whole tripartite system. Thus, Congress brought impeachment charges against President Nixon in 1974, alleging he had flouted the Constitution. (Nixon's abuse of power, including his role in the Watergate affair, was the main thrust of the case against him.)

Nearly a quarter of a century later, President Clinton was impeached after he resisted efforts by the Republican Congress to investigate his conduct in office. His opponents also charged he lied to a grand jury. But Congress spurned public calls for impeachment of President Bush in 2006–2008 over the Iraq War and other issues related to the "war on terror."

Most of the Founders were clearly motivated by a mix of idealism and realism. According to Hamilton, "Men are ambitious, vindictive, and rapacious."[15] Madison concurred, although less bluntly:

> It may be a reflection on human nature, that such devices [as checks and balances] should be necessary to control the abuses of government. But what is government itself, but the greatest of all reflections on human nature? If men were angels, no government would be necessary. If angels were to govern men, neither external nor internal controls on government would be necessary.[16]

Ideally, politicians would discover they could best serve their personal interests (getting reelected) by promoting the public interest. If not, however, Madison's system, like Adam Smith's theory of the "invisible hand" in the marketplace, came equipped with an automatic adjustment mechanism. Thus, it was not on the lofty plane of morality or religion that the new science of politics found its justification but, instead, on the firmer ground of institutionalized self-interest.

John C. Calhoun: Brokered Government

John C. Calhoun (1782–1850) was a younger contemporary of the Founders. In the first half of the nineteenth century, he was a leading political figure in the

South and served as vice president of the United States from 1825 until 1832, when he resigned over policy differences with President Andrew Jackson.

Contemporary political scientists often refer to Calhoun as the first prominent exponent of a pluralist model of democracy. In the 1820s, Calhoun championed a theory of **brokered democracy** based on the assumption of selfish motives in politics and what was, in his view, a universal tendency to interpret reality, and even *morality*, in self-serving ways—to put private interests *ahead* of the public interest.

Calhoun sought to tame this tendency through a mechanism he called the **concurrent majority**. In his model of U.S. democracy, there were (and are) many different economic, social, and sectional interests the government must mediate between and among. In a democracy, he reasoned, if one interest prevails over all the others because it has a majority of the votes on a given issue at a given time, neither justice nor the long-term survival of the system can be assured.

In his *Disquisition on Government*, Calhoun made an impassioned argument for protecting the interests of minorities against a steamrolling majority. The way to do so was to abandon the principle of majority rule in favor of government by concurrent majority. Thus, the decision-making model he advocated was one of *compromise* and *consensus* among all major competing interests on important policy questions of the day. If compromise failed and consensus could not be reached, the status quo would prevail indefinitely. In effect, Calhoun argued the case for protecting pluralism at all costs, granting a kind of veto power to minority groups.

Calhoun is a prime example of his own theory in action. As it turns out, he was not only a champion of concurrent majority decision-making but also the leading voice in the famous **nullification** controversy that divided the nation in the decades preceding the Civil War. Proponents of nullification, mainly southerners, held that a state could nullify acts of the Congress within its own borders—if Congress attempted to abolish slavery, for example, the southern states had the right to ignore it. This concept also came to be called "interposition," because it meant a state could interpose its own authority (or sovereignty) to void an act of Congress. Calhoun was, in effect, using the principle of minority rights *against* an oppressed racial minority, slaves.

For Calhoun and his southern cohort, "minority rights" and states' rights were inseparable. The tension between Federalists (favoring a strong national government) and Anti-Federalists (favoring states' rights) had been one of the major themes of the nation's founding and continued to be up to the Civil War.

In fact, the notion of **dual federalism** (near and dear to Calhoun's heart) prevailed between 1835 and 1860. Under dual federalism, the power of the national government was limited to its enumerated powers, Southern states claimed sovereign powers, and the all-important question of what would happen or who would prevail in a contest of wills between two "sovereign" governments (national versus state) remained unresolved. The upshot was, of course, the Civil War.

Federalism was at the heart of the fight between the North and South. The Union victory over the Confederacy was a triumph for the concept of a single sovereign seat of government, but it did not resolve the tension between

brokered democracy This theory holds that the interests of major groups cannot be steamrolled by the majority without jeopardizing democracy and that legislators and decision makers should act as brokers in writing laws and devising policies that are acceptable to all major groups in society.

concurrent majority John Calhoun's theory of democracy, which holds that the main function of government is to mediate between and among the different economic, social, and sectional interests in U.S. society.

nullification According to this controversial idea, a state can nullify acts of the U.S. Congress within its own borders; John Calhoun and other states' rights advocates put forward this doctrine prior to the Civil War.

dual federalism
Under this system, which prevailed in the United States between 1835 and 1860, the power of the national government was limited to enumerated powers; during this period, the southern states claimed sovereign powers.

federal authority and the states' rights. An attenuated form of dual federalism survived at least until the Depression Era of the 1930s, when President Franklin Delano Roosevelt launched what political scientists often call "cooperative federalism"—a series of federally funded programs that, in time, redefined the relationship between the national government and the states. From that time to the present, the federal government's power has expanded, and the states have taken a back seat. We turn next to a more detailed look at federalism.

Back to Basics: Federalism and the Separation of Powers

In theory, one way to limit constitutional government is through a division of powers, called federalism. In practice, however, it does not necessarily work that way. Modern examples of federal republics are the United States, Germany, Canada, India, Brazil, Mexico, and Nigeria. After World War II, federalism in Germany, for example, meant the states played a strong role in governing the country and truly did act as a check on central power (see "Ideas and Politics"). In the defunct Soviet Union, by contrast, federalism was a façade that allowed a tightly controlled and highly centralized dictatorship to pretend it was democratic.

Federalism By definition, federalism's distinctive feature is a division of power between the national government and regional subdivisions. These subdivisions are often called *states*, not to be confused with sovereign states or nation-states.

IDEAS AND POLITICS

FEDERALISM IN POSTWAR GERMANY

The link between federalism and liberty is particularly striking in the case of Germany. Democracy in Germany was reborn after World War II, when the nation was exhausted by war, defeated, and occupied by foreign armies. The Allied powers, led by the United States, were determined to prevent a new German state from again launching a campaign of military aggression in Europe. The best way to do that, they reasoned, was to inoculate Germany against the virus of dictatorship. The "vaccine" they decided to use was democratic federalism.

How could federalism possibly prevent the rise of a new Hitler? The key is the decentralized structure of Germany's government. The German states (called *Länder*) play an important role in governance on *both* the state and national levels. Delegates appointed by the sixteen state governments make up the upper house of the German parliament, the

Bundesrat. The upper house has veto power over legislation directly affecting the states, including new taxes. In addition, most of the governmental bureaucracy in Germany falls under the control of the *Länder*. Ironically, the German federal system, which was created under close U.S. supervision in the aftermath of Nazi Germany's defeat in World War II, is a good example of how federalism is supposed to work.

Do the fifty states in the USA still function as an effective counterweight to the national or central government? Is the federal government stronger or weaker than it was in the early years of the republic? Think about it.

(Hint: How did the Thirteenth, Fourteenth, and Sixteenth Amendments change the balance of power between the federal government and the states?)

The United States has a constitutional division of power between national and state governments. Article I, Section 8, of the Constitution, for instance, delineates many areas in which Congress is empowered to legislate. At the same time, the Tenth Amendment provides that all powers not granted to the national government are reserved for the states.

Originally, under the U.S. Constitution, states were empowered to maintain internal peace and order, provide for education, and safeguard the people's health, safety, and welfare—through the government's *police powers*. These powers were once exercised almost exclusively by the states. However, the role of the national (or federal) government has grown enormously since the 1930s when FDR launched a massive set of federal programs called the New Deal to create jobs and stimulate the economy in the midst of the Great Depression.

President Richard Nixon (1968–1973) tried to reverse this process with a policy called the *new federalism*, which was aimed at making government "more effective as well as more efficient." The two main elements of this policy were the use of so-called block grants to the states and general revenue sharing.

Both Ronald Reagan (1980–1988), a Republican, and Bill Clinton (1992–2000), a Democrat, paid lip service to *devolution* (transferring power back to the states), but did little to match words with deeds. President George W. Bush extended the federal government's law-enforcement and surveillance powers even as he reined in regulation of business and banking by various federal agencies created for that purpose.

Upon taking the oath of office, President Obama moved to reactivate departments and agencies charged with regulating energy and protecting the environment, but some critics on the left reproached him for making too many concessions to mining interests, big oil, builders of natural gas pipelines, and the like. Likewise, his failure to push for stricter regulation of the banking industry in the wake of the 2008 financial crisis also drew sharp criticism in the liberal media (to learn more, Google William Black or Matt Taibbi with key words such as "bailout" or "financial fraud").

President Obama also imitated his predecessor in other ways. For example, despite a campaign promise to bring greater transparency to government, he used executive privilege in the summer of 2012 in an effort to thwart a congressional investigation into a federal cross-border gun-tracking fiasco in Mexico called Operation Fast and Furious,. By the same token, Obama did not hesitate to exercise vast executive war powers during his first term, personally selecting targets for drone strikes and terrorist assassinations in Afghanistan and Pakistan from a "kill list," continuing the practice of "rendition" (capturing terrorist suspects abroad and handing them over to another government to be interrogated and tortured), detaining suspected terrorists without trial, and, of course, declining to close the notorious Guantanamo Bay military prison known as "Gitmo" (again despite a campaign promise to do so).

Why Federalism? The rationale for a division of power is to keep government as close to the people as possible. Thus, some delegates at the Philadelphia Convention argued that a federal system would create a first line of defense against a potentially tyrannical central government. Thus, the states were given equal representation in the newly created Senate, a key role in electing the president (the Electoral College), and an important role in amending the Constitution. Also, as noted earlier, the **reserved powers** provision in the Bill of Rights (the Tenth Amendment) was intended to protect and preserve states rights.

reserved powers
The reserved powers arise from the Tenth Amendment, which provides that powers not delegated to the federal government, "nor prohibited by it to the States, are reserved to the States respectively, or to the people."

The struggle to defend or extend states' rights is associated with major historic figures in the United States, including Thomas Jefferson, John Randolph, and John C. Calhoun. But Jefferson Davis, the institution of slavery, and the Civil War are also part of this story. A century later, southern segregationists like Strom Thurmond, George Wallace, and Lester Maddox unsuccessfully led the fight for states' rights against federal action to bring about desegregation in the South.

Federalism in the United States today is far weaker than it was originally. Great controversies once flared over the question of whether a state (for example, Virginia and Kentucky in 1798–1799 or South Carolina in the 1830s) or a region (the South in 1860) could resort to states' rights federalism to justify dissent from specific policies undertaken by the national government. When questions of interest or principle—the Alien and Sedition Acts of 1798, the tariff in the 1830s, slavery in the 1860s—divided the nation, political battles were often fought over the Supremacy Clause (Article VI) or the Tenth Amendment, over the constitutionality of national legislation or what level of government—national or state—had the right to decide.

Issues the Supremacy Clause could not settle, the Civil War did. Although there have been some notable clashes since then, especially in the South over school desegregation in the late-1950s and early-1960s, the federal government is now clearly in the driver's seat, with the states often competing for federal dollars in pursuit of policies hammered out at the federal level.[17]

In the 1990s, however, there was renewed competition between these two levels of government. For example, state governments experimented with educational reforms (charter schools, school vouchers, new ways to bring religion into the classroom) and a variety of anticrime measures (mandatory sentencing, three-strikes laws, victims' compensation). Some states also sought to roll back affirmative action.

After 2001, as the Bush administration rushed to deregulate business, California and some other states fought with the federal government over the right to enact tougher environmental standards than those mandated by Washington. In May 2009, the Obama administration announced that automakers and fourteen states led by California had agreed to a new national standard that by 2016 will match California's in reducing the CO_2 emissions from new vehicles by 30%. In taking this action and pledging to review and revamp federal environmental policies, Obama handed the states a rare intergovernmental victory.

These examples illustrate the sense in which federalism is *competitive,* as well as cooperative. Nonetheless, the federal government towers over the states by virtue of its vast powers to tax and borrow and spend, as well as its status under the Supremacy Clause.

The debate over federalism is ongoing. The Tea Party movement and libertarians who believe with Jefferson that "the government that governs least,

governs best"—a view most recently championed by 2012 presidential candidate Ron Paul—argue that the pendulum has swung way too far toward
centralization of power in Washington, D.C. Civil rights advocates counter by
pointing to the pivotal role of the federal government in promoting racial and
gender equality. (We examine the recent history of civil rights and the push for
racial equality in Chapter 13).

Federalism and Liberty Federalism helps protect civil and political liberties by
limiting the scope of national government.[18] Nonetheless, the post-9/11 expansion of federal law-enforcement powers under the provisions of the USA Patriot
Act raised questions about the proper balance between liberty and security in
the twenty-first century. As a main pillar underpinning the ponderous policy
architecture of the war on terror, the Patriot Act greatly enlarged the powers
of the executive branch to conduct domestic surveillance including warrantless
wiretaps against U.S. citizens.

In contrast to a **unitary system** of government (see "Ideas and Politics"), the
aim of a federal system is political-administrative decentralization. By "multi-
plying and simplifying the governments accessible" to ordinary citizens, "creating local organized structures capable of resisting centralized authority or
mitigating its excesses," and enabling "government to be adapted to local needs
and circumstances," decentralization allows "experimentation in the way problems are met." In short, federalism "is a vital safeguard to liberty and a way to
educate an energetic and competent citizenry."[19]

unitary system
A form of
government in
which most or all
power to make
and enforce laws
resides in the
central government;
opposite of a federal
system.

IDEAS AND POLITICS

THE UNITARY ALTERNATIVE

Most governments in the world today are not federal
systems. A far more common form of government is
the *unitary* system, such as that found in the United
Kingdom. It is called unitary because there is only one
primary unit of government, the central government,
which often turns over many affairs to local governments but is not required to do so. Notably absent
from these systems is an intermediate level of government between the center and local political-administrative units.

Some unitary systems, for example, those in
France and Italy, have guarded the powers and
prerogatives of the national government against
encroachment by local magistrates, mayors, and
politicians more jealously than have the British. In
France, *prefects*—officials appointed by the central government—mediate between the central

government in Paris and the local departments.
Until the socialist government of François Mitterrand instituted reforms in the early-1980s, the
prefects had vast powers of *tutelage* over local governments. The French system of public administration was so centralized and tightly controlled that
schoolchildren all over France studied the same
subject at the same time every day.

**Imagine the federal government mandating such a
system in the United States! Given the diversity of
schools, curricula, accreditation requirements, and
academic standards from state to state and school
district to school district, do you think people would
stand for it? If not, why not? Think about it.**

*(Hint: Start by taking a close look at the Tenth Amendment
of the U.S. Constitution.)*

Do we still have the necessary degree of decentralization, that "vital safe-guard to liberty"? For better or worse, the post-9/11 trend, growing out of the actions and decisions of two presidents and involving both major political parties, has been toward more centralization of power in Washington, not less. This point leads naturally back to one of the perennial questions facing democracy—namely, how to reconcile individual rights and majority rule. We revisit that question in the following section.

The Separation of Powers The U.S. Constitution assigns specific tasks to each branch of government. Congress, for example, is given the **power of the purse**. The president proposes a budget and attempts to influence congressional appropriations, but Congress always has the final word on governmental spending. This arrangement has not been widely copied by other liberal democracies, which typically give the executive branch the upper hand in setting the budget (expenditures), while giving the legislature the primary role on the revenue side (taxation).

In the U.S. model, power and authority are shared in a few areas. Overlapping responsibilities, for instance, characterize the government's **war powers**. Congress funds the armed forces (although the Constitution limits appropriations to two years) and declares war. However, the Constitution makes the president the commander in chief of the armed forces. Therefore, any significant military undertaking, declared or undeclared, requires the cooperation of both branches. Countries with similar institutions generally replicate this pattern, although the idea of civilian control over the military is nowhere more firmly established in principle or practice than in the United States. Even today, the possibility of a military takeover (a so-called coup d'état) in times of crisis remains a danger to civilian rule in some countries.

Members of the three branches in the U.S. government serve different terms of office and different constituencies. Under the Constitution, as amended, the president must stand for election every four years and is limited to two terms of office. The president and the vice president are the only two governmental officials in the United States who can receive a mandate from the entire national electorate (see "Ideas and Politics").

Members of the U.S. House of Representatives serve local constituencies in districts drawn by state legislatures (in most cases) and are elected for two-year terms. Senators represent states as a whole and serve six-year terms in office. The president, with the advice and consent of the Senate, appoints Supreme Court justices and all other federal judges. The Founders believed this method of selection was more likely to result in fair and impartial justice than requiring judges to stand for election.

The presidential term of office varies from country to country. Presidents in Russia and Brazil, for example, are elected to four-year terms and can run for a second consecutive term, as in the United States. The president of Mexico is elected to a six-year term but cannot run for reelection. Until recently, France's president was elected to a renewable seven-year term, reduced to five years in 2000.

power of the purse Under the U.S. Constitution, the provision that gives Congress the exclusive right to impose taxes and the final word on government spending.

war powers The U.S. Constitution gives Congress the power to raise and support armies, to provide and maintain a navy, to make rules regulating the armed forces, and to declare war; it makes the president the commander in chief of the armed forces.

PRESIDENTIAL DEMOCRACY

The U.S. government is often called a **presidential democracy** because the chief executive is elected in balloting separate from the vote for members of Congress. A presidential system is characterized by a separation of powers in which the legislative, executive, and judicial branches of the national government are each responsible to different constituencies for the exercise of their respective powers and responsibilities.

The government is formally organized along functional lines. Because all governments need to formulate, execute, and interpret laws, it is logical to create a legislature to perform the first of these functions (rule making), an executive to carry out the second (rule implementation), and a judiciary to oversee the third (rule interpretation).

The logic of this arrangement knows no political or geographic boundaries. Today it is reflected in the composition of many democracies in all regions of the world. Presidential democracies are especially common in Latin America, but in various forms they are also scattered in such far-flung places as Russia, France, Yugoslavia, Nigeria, South Africa, Indonesia, and the Philippines.

The major alternative to presidential democracy is parliamentary democracy, which is especially common in Europe and which we discuss at length in Chapter 7.

In recent years, the efficiency and viability of the U.S. system of government has been called into question. Why? By whom? Do critics deserve to be taken seriously? Think about it.

(Hint: Google "Washington gridlock dysfunction" and "Obama executive power.")

TOCQUEVILLE: THE TYRANNY OF THE MAJORITY

Imagine this Wild West scenario: A drifter falsely accused of the cold-blooded murder of a local citizen is jailed, pending trial by a judge and jury. An angry mob clamors for instant justice, but against this throng stand two solitary figures—a crotchety old deputy and the brave sheriff. The inevitable showdown takes place in the street in front of the sheriff's office. Led by the mayor and town council members (one of whom is the actual murderer), a lynch mob demands "the killer" be handed over immediately. Clearly, majority rule is at war with impartial justice. In the end, only heroic action by the sheriff saves the innocent man from being dragged off and hanged from the nearest tree.

When democratic government turns into mob rule, it becomes what Alexis de Tocqueville called the **tyranny of the majority**.[20] For this reason, political thinkers through the ages have often rejected democracy, fearing a majority based on one dominant class, religion, or political persuasion would trample the rights of minorities. The American Founders were conscious of this danger and sought to combat it by structural and procedural prescriptions written into the Constitution (see "Ideas and Politics").

presidential democracy
A form of representative government or republican rule in which the chief executive (or president) is elected in balloting separate from the vote for the legislative body (called a "congress" or "parliament" or "diet").

tyranny of the majority
The condition arising when a dominant group uses its control of the government to abuse the rights of minority groups.

MINORITY RIGHTS

The Founders of the U.S. political system were troubled by the possibility that the majority would trample the rights of the minority. A **bicameral** legislative branch was designed to prevent large and powerful states from steamrolling smaller and weaker ones. The presidential veto, the independence of the courts, and federalism were also intended as safeguards against the excesses inherent in majority rule.

Many of the world's federal systems are presidential. In most cases, presidents have veto power over legislation, but a determined and united legislature can override a veto. Courts are typically set up to be independent, but there is never any guarantee that judges will be impartial.

In most presidential systems, chief executives can veto legislation. But presidents with the power to reject discriminatory laws also have the power to ignore laws aimed at protecting victims of

discrimination. Institutional arrangements designed to curtail arbitrary rule and safeguard minority rights are necessary for democracy to work, but there is no substitute for a politically engaged citizenry and a vigilant electorate.

Representative democracy is built on the principal of majority rule, but in the U.S. even if a majority in both houses of Congress supports a proposed piece of legislation, it often faces serious obstacles to becoming a law. Is that a good thing or a bad thing? Think about it.

(Hint: In his famous treatise "On Liberty," John Stuart Mill argued that unpopular opinions need greater protection from the state than popular ones. Mill wrote, "The peculiar evil of silencing the expression of an opinion is, that it is robbing the human race. . . . " Mill fleshes out this idea near the end of the first paragraph in Chapter II.)

bicameralism
Division of the legislature into two houses.

The United States witnessed acts resembling mob rule in the fall of 2001 during the panic that followed the terrorist attacks in New York and Washington, D.C. When the perpetrators were identified as Muslim extremists, many citizens, horrified by the enormity of the crime, turned against Arab and Muslim minorities living in the United States.

Examples of popular tyranny in democratic countries are not uncommon. In Germany, for example, a sizable Turkish minority has never been granted equal rights. In the Czech Republic (and elsewhere in Eastern Europe), the Czech majority discriminate against the Roma. In Israel, the Arab minority (that is, Arab-Palestinians who are Israeli citizens rather than residents of the West Bank and Gaza) do not enjoy full political and social equality with the Jewish majority. In Turkey, the rights of the Kurdish minority have often fallen victim to the fears and prejudices of the Turkish majority (see Figure 4.2).

The French Revolution was the first revolt of the masses in modern history, but certainly not the last. In the period between the World War I and World War II, mass movements played an important role in bringing totalitarian regimes to power in Russia, Germany, and Italy—and crushing the seeds and seedlings of democracy.

FIGURE 4.2   Map of Turkey. The Kurds predominate on both sides of Turkey's borders with Syria, Iraq, and Iran.

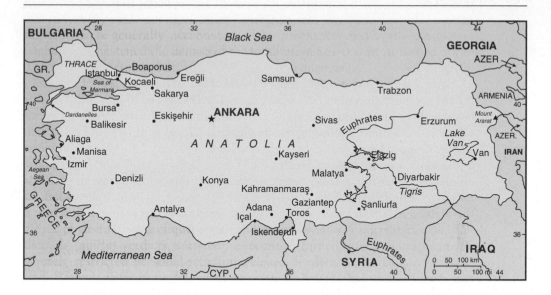

JOHN LOCKE: THE RULE OF LAW

The idea that nations ought to be governed by impartial, binding laws is not new. Aristotle embraced the **rule of law** because the law represents "reason free from all passion."[21] Therefore, a government of laws is superior to one of individuals, even though individuals (officials, judges, the police) interpret and enforce the laws.

More than two thousand years later, English philosopher John Locke (1632–1704) defended the rule of law on the basis of its close relationship to individual freedom. Locke believed freedom could not exist without written law and that good government must follow certain precepts (for instance, taxes should not be levied without the consent of the people).

To Locke, these rules constitute "laws" of the highest order because they embody what civil society is all about. They are laws above the law that place limitations on lawmakers. From Locke's concept of a higher law, the idea of **constitutionalism** evolved. As Locke noted (and as the inscription above the entrance to the Department of Justice building in Washington, D.C. reads), "Wherever Law ends, Tyranny begins."[22]

Locke was part of a proud English tradition that had long sought to establish limits on government. Rebellious barons forced King John to sign the famous **Magna Carta** in 1215. Originally, this document made concessions only to the feudal nobility, but it later became the foundation of British liberties. Containing some sixty-three clauses, it foreshadowed a system that replaced absolute monarchy with a power-sharing arrangement involving the Crown, aristocracy,

rule of law
The concept that the power and discretion of government and its officials ought to be restrained by a supreme set of neutral rules that prevent arbitrary and unfair action by government; also called *constitutionalism*.

constitutionalism
The concept that the power and discretion of government and its officials ought to be restrained by a supreme set of neutral rules that prevent arbitrary and unfair action by government; also called *rule of law*.

Magna Carta
A list of political concessions granted in 1215 by King John to his barons that became the basis for the rule of law in England.

and parliament. It obligated the king to seek the advice and consent of royal vassals on important policy matters, including taxation. Equally important was Clause 39, which guaranteed the accused an impartial trial and protection against arbitrary imprisonment and punishment. To that end it stated, "No free man shall be taken or imprisoned, or disposed, or outlawed, or banished, or in any way destroyed ... except by the legal judgment of his peers or by the law of the land."

Several landmarks in establishing the rule of law in Britain were achieved during the seventeenth century, in Locke's time. The Petition of Right (1628) further advanced the idea of due process of law while limiting the monarch's power of taxation. In addition, abolishing the dreaded Star Chamber in 1641 did away with a court that used torture to gain confessions and imposed punishment on subjects at the request of the Crown. Finally, the Habeas Corpus Act (1679) limited government's power to imprison people arbitrarily. It imposed substantial penalties on judges who failed to issue timely writs of *habeas corpus*, which demonstrated the accused had been legally detained and properly charged with a crime.

Also originating in the seventeenth century was a judicial precedent that came to have enormous influence in the United States. Renowned English jurist Sir Edward Coke's (1552–1634) opinion in Dr. Bonham's case (1610) asserted that English common law, including the Magna Carta, was the standard to which ordinary acts of Parliament, as well as the British Crown, should be made to conform.[23]

CONSTITUTIONALISM AND DUE PROCESS

Britain's democratic institutions evolved over many centuries. In the United States, it happened very differently—a constitution was hammered out over a period of four months in 1787 at a convention in Philadelphia. The U.S. Constitution and the Bill of Rights (the latter largely derived from English common law) became the standards against which popularly enacted laws would be judged.

Constitutionalism enshrines proper procedure. For instance, the Constitution as interpreted by the U.S. Supreme Court prohibits the president of the United States, even during wartime, from seizing or nationalizing industries, such as steel mills, without congressional approval.[24] Similarly, the concept of **due process**—prescribed procedural rules—dictates that a citizen accused of a crime shall be provided with an attorney, allowed to confront witnesses, informed of the charges brought against him or her, and so on. For the same reason, administrative agencies are compelled by law to provide public notice to those who might be adversely affected by a pending decision. In each instance, the rationale behind the idea of due process is the same: in any game, fairness requires that all the players play by the same rule and that the referee(s) not show favorites. If the winner of an election cheats and gets caught, the cheater is removed from office and can even face jail time. In fact, that was precisely the situation in 1974 when President Nixon was forced to resign (or face certain impeachment) following revelations about his role in the Watergate scandal.

Some critics argue that the principle of due process is taken to extremes in the United States. For example, if the suspect confesses to the crime without

due process
A guarantee of fair legal procedure; it is found in the Fifth and Fourteenth Amendments of the U.S. Constitution.

being informed that she has a right to remain silent, the confession will be inadmissible in court. In virtually every other liberal democracy in the world, including the United Kingdom, France, Canada, and Australia, to cite but a few examples, a confession is a confession as long as it is not extracted by torture or trickery. Conversely, critics at home and abroad condemn the United States for holding many suspected terrorists at "Gitmo" indefinitely without the right to habeas corpus and for using harsh, inhumane interrogation methods. What do you think?

It is not enough to proclaim the rule of law—words are important, but deeds are imperative if justice is to be done. After the Civil War, the Fourteenth Amendment explicitly guaranteed **equal protection** of the laws to all citizens, including former slaves living in the Deep South. But African Americans continued to be victims of discrimination for many years thereafter. By the same token, women did not gain the right to vote until 1920 and enjoyed few opportunities outside the confines of home and family until fairly recently.

In the United States, government is restricted as to how it can make laws or punish citizens accused of breaking laws. In practice, however, exactly how or where to draw the line between the state and society, between the public and the private, and between authority and liberty is often unclear. Citizens are free to express themselves, but this right is not absolute. Thus, freedom of speech does not give anyone the right to make obscene phone calls, to send death threats through the mail, or to incite a riot.

equal protection
The doctrine enshrined in the Fourteenth Amendment stating that the prohibitions placed on the federal government and the protections afforded American citizens under the Bill of Rights also apply to the states.

IDEAS AND POLITICS

VOTING: RIGHT, PRIVILEGE, OR OBLIGATION?

To vote or not to vote, that is the question—or is it? Until passage and ratification of the Nineteenth Amendment to the Constitution, granting women the right to vote, it was not an option for more than half the U.S. adult population. For a century after the Civil War, it was treated more like a privilege than a right in the Deep South, where "Jim Crow" laws effectively franchised African Americans. Today, although most historical barriers to voting have been taken down, millions of Americans don't bother to vote.

Observers often see low voter turnout as symptomatic of a serious sickness in democratic society. At least thirty-eight countries have gone so far as to prescribe a potent antidote: compulsory voting. Voting is obligatory in most of Latin America, including Argentina, Brazil, and Mexico (it was abolished in Venezuela in 1993). In Europe, Belgium and Greece

have mandatory voting, as does France (but only for the Senate); citizens have been required to vote in Australia since 1924. Sanctions for not voting often involve paying a fine or even disenfranchisement. In the United States, Article 12 of Georgia's 1777 constitution, which is still in effect, makes voting mandatory, subject to a fine, unless the person could provide a "reasonable excuse."

Chapter 11 examines voting behavior in greater depth. Here the question is one belonging to political philosophy: To what extent does a right—any right—also entail an obligation? Think about it.

(Hint: Think of practical rights that ordinary citizens like you exercise every day. For example, what, if any, obligations are entailed in the right to use the postal service, drive a car, or board an airplane?)

REMODELING DEMOCRACY: HAVE IT YOUR WAY

Political scientists frequently use models to illustrate or clarify a particular theory or to show a range of possibilities. The fact that so many countries became laboratories for democratic experimentation in the 1990s gave rise to renewed academic interest in democracy and provided a great variety of "specimens" to study. One upshot was the appearance of a new body of theories and models of democracy.

We give the most attention in this text to three existing models of democracy: the U.S. presidential model, the British parliamentary model, and the French half-and-half, or hybrid, model that combines features of the U.S. and British systems (see Chapter 7). All three are representative democracies and differ primarily in structural and procedural matters—in the way representatives are elected, the relationship between the executive and legislative branches, the role of political parties, and the way the national leader comes to power.

Another way of thinking about democracies is to focus on the role people and participation play under different models. After all, democracy is, by definition, a form of rule by the people. William Hudson, for example, identified four distinct theories of citizen participation and developed a model of democracy for each (see Figure 4.3).[25]

The main function of government in Hudson's **protective democracy** is to safeguard liberty rather than national security. Citizens may play a passive political role in this model, but they make up for it by playing an extremely active role in economics. The government is the guardian or protector of the free market, but not its master. According to Hudson, this theory holds that "democracy exists so that free competitive individuals may have and enjoy a maximum of freedom to pursue material wealth."[26] The limits on government are ensured through the elements so familiar to students of the U.S. Constitution, including the separation of powers, federalism, bicameralism, and the Bill of Rights.

protective democracy
A self-contradictory governing model put in place in the Unites States after the 9/11 terrorist attacks; a government that places national security above liberty and justifies curtailment of constitutional rights in times of crisis or war; an oxymoron.

FIGURE 4.3
Hudson's Typology of Democracy. Note that although all four models are democratic, the emphasis is different in each one. Does it matter?

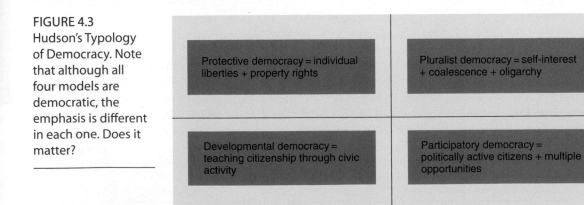

Protective democracy = individual liberties + property rights	Pluralist democracy = self-interest + coalescence + oligarchy
Developmental democracy = teaching citizenship through civic activity	Participatory democracy = politically active citizens + multiple opportunities

In Hudson's **developmental democracy**, the government's focus is on the development of virtuous citizens, not modern economies or political systems. This model views democracy as a kind of school for civic education and socialization. It sees indirect or representative democracy as a way to train citizens in those habits and virtues essential to progress, stability, and prosperity. Their broad participation through voting and expressing opinions is thus essential to making them *feel* closer to government and to help them gain a better understanding of the public good, even if they are not active decision makers in it. The paternalistic element is perhaps what most distinguishes it from Hudson's other models.

Pluralist democracy is the model most people recognize immediately. It features vigorous competition among various interests in a society where diversity is the norm. Hudson's model of pluralism, however, emphasizes its tendency to evolve into a hierarchical order dominated by economic elites. This tendency occurs naturally in a society where individuals are free to form associations or interest groups because the success of organizations depends on group cohesion, common purpose, and strong leadership. Thus, pluralistic democracy is inherently oligarchic. In a society that places a high priority on business, entrepreneurship, and amassing personal wealth, the natural result is social and economic inequality.

The final model—**participatory democracy**—is the most straightforward of the four and the closest to a practicable model of direct democracy. In theory, direct democracy means citizens themselves, not elected representatives, decide all major questions of public life. This model could perhaps work in a community or small city-state of a few hundred or even a few thousand citizens at most. It cannot easily work in a large modern state encompassing much territory, many towns and cities, and millions of inhabitants who may or may not even speak the same language.

Nonetheless, participatory democracy is based on the conviction that apathy is a conditioned response, not a trait inherent in human nature. Deprived of opportunities to participate in meaningful ways, people will naturally tune out or get turned off. The key to a vibrant citizenry—and therefore to a healthy democracy—is active participation on a large scale across a wide spectrum of issues. Participatory democracy goes further, arguing not only that citizens *would* participate actively in politics given the chance but also that they *should* participate—that is, that they have a right to do so.

Hudson's models of democracy, like all others, are just that—models. They do not represent actual democracies, nor are they necessarily the best way to characterize or categorize different types of democracy. But they do point to basic political questions that confront all contemporary democracies, which was precisely Hudson's intention in developing these models in the first place. The models become the basis for his book analyzing "eight challenges to America's future," namely, restoring the separation of powers, restraining the "imperial judiciary," combating "radical individualism," promoting citizen participation, reforming the "trivialized" election process, curbing the "privileged position" of business, addressing problems of inequality, and, finally, making the "national security state" more transparent and less threatening to its own citizens.

developmental democracy
A model of democracy that emphasizes the development of virtuous citizens; postulates that one essential role of representative government is to serve as a school for civic education to create a politically literate electorate.

pluralist democracy
A model of democracy that stresses vigorous competition among various interests in a free society; akin to the idea of market forces and the role of free enterprise in classic economic theory.

participatory democracy
A model of democracy that seeks to expand citizen participation in government to the maximum possible degree; emphasizes universal suffrage, transparency in government, and opportunities for direct action; includes elements of direct democracy.

Moving from theory to policy, as Hudson does, is, by its very nature, controversial. In matters of politics, scholars disagree on what the problems are, as well as on how to deal with them. Students may ask, if experts (including college professors) cannot agree on the questions facing democracy, much less on the answers, what is the point of theorizing about democracy? The short answer is that even if it does not provide clear-cut solutions, theory helps us think about political problems, identify different policy options, and anticipate their consequences. The study of politics is a *social* science, and there is seldom agreement on the vital issues facing society. The existence of different viewpoints is a trademark of constitutional democracy.

We turn, finally, to the future of democracy, and pose two questions. Are existing models of democracy still viable, or is a new one tailored to globalization and the new world order necessary and possible? Is democracy in America broken, as many close observers and a growing number of disillusioned citizens now believe?

THE FUTURE OF DEMOCRACY

Wherever people have access to computers, they are connected to the outside world. The physical distances that separate us are no longer the great barriers they once were to the spread of popular culture, capital, consumer goods, services, and ideas. Given (1) the transforming nature of the new information technologies, (2) an ever-expanding global economy undergoing a tectonic shift in the distribution of wealth from North America and Europe to Asia, and (3) the challenges posed by the new model of authoritarian capitalism propelling a rapidly rising People's Republic of China to prominence, is it possible that democracy as we know it is obsolescent?

Cosmopolitan Democracy

The word *cosmopolitan* in this context denotes a sense of belonging to the world rather than to a particular nation or state. A cosmopolitan individual is, by definition, a frequent traveler who is comfortable abroad, values cultural diversity, and respects the rights of others to live and worship as they choose. Cosmopolitans find the nation-state too confining; they blame nationalism and tribalism for the prejudice and patriotic fervor that divides the world into "us" and "them" and instead foresee a strengthening sense of community without borders.

cosmopolitan democracy
A model of democracy that sees the individual as part of a world order and not merely (or even primarily) as a citizen of a particular nation-state; often summarized in the slogan "Think globally, act locally."

Proponents of **cosmopolitan democracy** favor the extension of citizenship rights and responsibilities across supranational associations like the European Union (EU). In this way, "people would come . . . to enjoy multiple citizenships—political membership in the diverse political communities which significantly affect them." They would not only be citizens of a state but also fully empowered members of "the wider regional and global networks" that are shaping the world we all live in.[27]

But it is unclear what it would mean to be governed by the rules and institutions of cosmopolitan democracy or how such a political system would work in practice. Nor is it likely that national leaders or the citizenry anywhere will

SEIU Healthcare 775NW

An immigration reform rally in Seattle, Washington on April 10, 2010. The Washington Immigration Reform Coalition (WIRC) for America, an umbrella group of about sixty organizations, organized this national day of protest to urge Congress to pass a Comprehensive Immigration Reform Bill.

embrace the idea. In all probability, age-old loyalties, institutions, and ways of thinking will prove highly resistant to any fundamental change.

Democracy in America: Broke and Broken Beyond Repair?

Despite major changes in the international economy in the past half century, the world still pays close attention to what happens—and does not happen—in Washington. What it sees these days is a system that is not working very well, that many experts are saying is not only broke (a comment on the mounting multi-trillion-dollar public and private debt) but also broken. The evidence they cite ranges from gridlock in Congress to the role of money in elections to a panoply of policy fiascos—botched health care reform, tax cuts for the rich, a jobless recovery, chronic federal and state budget deficits, a sagging real estate market, and the "endless" war in Afghanistan, to cite but a few signs of what many see as an increasingly dysfunctional system.

Even the disclosure of classified U.S. documents on the Internet in the fall of 2010 by Wikileaks cofounder and editor-in-chief Julian Assange was widely viewed as Washington's fault for failing to manage and control the way classified documents are handled within the U.S. government. And then came Edward Snowden, the former CIA system administrator who began leaking classified information in June 2013. The leak was more like a hemorrhage that called into question the ability of the government—including the super-secret National Security Agency (NSA) responsible for decoding, translation, and analysis of massive amounts of foreign intelligence the United States collects around the globe by means of signals intelligence (SIGINT)—to protect its secrets. It also brought to light evidence that the U.S. government has engaged in domestic eavesdropping (warrantless wiretaps) and mass surveillance in violation of its solemn duty to protect citizens' privacy rights.*

Although it is possible, as some critics suggest, that we are witnessing the decline of the United States as a world power, it is not necessarily so. The problems are real and the machinery of government appears incapable of finding or following through on solutions. The question is not whether American democracy is working—it clearly is not working the way it did in the 1790s or the 1970s—but whether the system is broken beyond repair, whether it is still capable of adapting to a changed and changing world environment. Meanwhile, the rest of the world continues to look to Washington for leadership in meeting the challenges of pollution and global warming, population and urban overcrowding, energy security and conservation, nuclear proliferation and international terrorism, and the list goes on.

The rise of democracy in its many permutations has been a hallmark of the modern era. The number and variety of democracies multiplied during the course of the twentieth century, a process that greatly accelerated in the 1980s (in Latin America) and 1990s (Eastern Europe). Even so, it is too soon to declare victory for constitutional democracy, the open society, or free-market capitalism.

SUMMARY

In constitutional democracies, governments derive authority from the consent of the governed. Popular election, in theory, ensures that all viewpoints and interests will be represented. Such representation is the defining principle of a republic. Constitutions are designed to place limitations on what governments can and cannot do.

There is no one universally accepted model or theory of liberal democracy. The type of liberal democracy we choose implies a particular view of the basic nature of human society and the main threat(s) to peace and stability.

The idea of America is synonymous with representative democracy in the minds of people all over the world. For inspiration, the Founders drew upon the writings of political thinkers who lived and wrote from the time of the Renaissance to the Enlightenment and who were themselves inspired by classical political philosophy, particularly the writings of Plato and Aristotle from the time of ancient Greece. "The architecture of liberty" grew out of the new science of politics developed by the Founders. That new science was designed to prevent tyranny by compartmentalizing the functions of government (separation of powers) and ensuring that each of the compartments (branches) would have the means to defend itself against encroachment by the others (checks and balances).

---

*Glenn Greenwald, a lawyer turned blogger and author, has become Snowden's chief collaborator, apologist, and gatekeeper for what is possibly the largest cache of classified stolen documents in U.S. history. Assange and Snowden have sought and received political asylum—Assange in the Embassy of Ecuador in London; Snowden in Moscow. Greenwald lives in self-imposed exile in Brazil. A January 1, 2014, *New York Times* editorial opined that although Snowden had broken the law "he has done his country a great service."

We trace three distinct models of American democracy to the ideas of Thomas Jefferson (majority rule), James Madison (balanced government), and John C. Calhoun (brokered government). A fourth model of strong central government is associated with Alexander Hamilton. These early leaders disagreed about how much democracy was too much. Jefferson, for example, favored broad individual liberties and narrow limits on government, whereas Hamilton and others emphasized the need for an energetic national government. Madison falls somewhere between Jefferson and Hamilton. He recognized the danger of governmental paralysis, as well as the need for "energy," but he argued that the best way to achieve freedom and stability was by encouraging a vigorous pluralism, or competition among rival interests. Calhoun was a proponent of states' rights—his views contrasted most sharply with Hamilton's and were closer to Jefferson's.

The concept of popular control through majority rule is central to the creation of a responsive government and holds that the wisdom and interests of the majority are preferable to those of the minority. However, constitutional democracies also place limits on the powers of the government. Protection of individual rights, the rule of law (constitutionalism), and federalism are the principal strategies used to prevent the tyranny of the majority. Finally, we looked at four contemporary models of democracy and looked into the future of democracy in the light of globalization. A cosmopolitan model of democracy that has practical appeal is yet to be found, but there is no question that technology and globalizing forces have an impact on governments of all types, including democracies.

KEY TERMS

direct democracy   71
republic   71
constitutional
   democracy   71
majority rule   72
checks and
   balances   72
Supremacy Clause   76
winner-takes-all
   system   78
plurality vote
   system   78
separation of
   powers   80
federalism   80

brokered
   democracy   81
concurrent
   majority   81
nullification   81
dual federalism   82
reserved powers   84
unitary system   85
power of the purse   86
war powers   86
presidential
   democracy   87
tyranny of the
   majority   87
bicameralism   88

rule of law   89
constitutionalism   89
Magna Carta   90
due process   90
equal protection   91
protective
   democracy   92
developmental
   democracy   93
pluralist
   democracy   93
participatory
   democracy   93
cosmopolitan
   democracy   94

REVIEW QUESTIONS

1. Describe the model of democracy you prefer, and differentiate it from the others. Why did you choose the one you did?
2. What is a republic? Do you think republics are or are not *real* democracies? Explain.

3. Name at least three classical models of American democracy, and explain how they differ from one another.
4. What is federalism? What advantages does this form of government offer?
5. Why did Alexis de Tocqueville (among others) express certain reservations about majority rule?
6. Discuss John Locke's contribution to democratic theory. Can you locate Locke's influence in the U.S. Constitution? If so, where is it?
7. For the theorists involved in the debate over the U.S. Constitution, what was the philosophy behind the "new science of politics"?
8. Recapitulate William Hudson's typology of democracy, and relate it to the models of democracy discussed at the beginning of the chapter.
9. Define *cosmopolitan democracy*, and explain the political context of theoretical attempts to come up with a new, universal model of democracy.

WEBSITES AND READINGS

Websites

Constitutions for countries around the world: http://www.adminet.com/world/consti/; confinder.richmond.edu; http://www.constitution.org/cons/natlcons.htm

U.S. Congress: thomas.loc.gov

U.S. Executive branch: www.whitehouse.gov

Other democratic regimes: http://www.scaruffi.com/politics/democrat.html

One World, Many Democracies (for schools): www.abc.net.au/civics/oneworld

The Democracy Project (for kids): pbskids.org/democracy

All fifty state constitutions: http://codes.lp.findlaw.com/

Readings

Adair, Douglass. *Fame and the Founding Fathers.* New York: Norton, 1974. Argues that the key Founders were motivated by a strong sense of history and moral principles.

Brodie, Fawn. *Thomas Jefferson: An Intimate History.* New York: Norton, 1974. Interweaves two dimensions of Jefferson's life—the political and the personal.

Chernow, Ron. *Alexander Hamilton.* New York: Penguin Press, 2004. Examines Hamilton's key role as both a founder of the U.S. political system and an adroit political operator.

Corwin, Edward. *The "Higher Law": Background of American Constitutional Law.* Ithaca, NY: Cornell University Press, 1955. A brief account of the rise of constitutionalism in Great Britain and the United States.

Diamond, Larry. *The Spirit of Democracy: The Struggle to Build Free Societies Throughout the World.* New York: Holt, 2009. A hopeful book by a well-respected scholar who sees a bright future for democracy and makes an intelligent case.

Diamond, Martin. *The Founding of the Democratic Republic.* Itasca, IL: Peacock, 1981. An excellent and enlightening brief account of original ideas and first principles underlying the Constitution.

Dunn, John. *Democracy: A History.* New York: Atlantic Monthly Press, 2006. Traces the history of the word "democracy"; asks how and why the idea has persisted.

Friedrich, Carl. *Limited Government: A Comparison.* Englewood Cliffs, NJ: Prentice-Hall, 1974. A brief analysis of the nexus between constitutionalism and the idea of democracy.

Greene, Jack, ed. *The Reinterpretation of the American Revolution, 1763 to 1789.* Westport, CT: Greenwood, 1979. A collection of essays.

Hamilton, Alexander, John Jay, and James Madison. *The Federalist Papers.* New York: Modern Library, 1964. Original essays setting forth the ideas underlying the U.S. political system.

Held, David. *Models of Democracy.* 3rd ed. Stanford, CA: Polity and Stanford University Press, 2006.

_____. *Democracy and the Global Order: From the Modern State to Cosmopolitan Governance.* Stanford, CA: Polity and Stanford University Press, 1995. The emergence of fledgling democracies in the 1980s and 1990s inspired these two books by David Held.

Hudson, William E. *American Democracy in Peril: Eight Challenges to America's Future,* 4th ed. Chatham, NJ: Chatham House, 2003. On the prospects for American democracy on the eve of the worst gridlock in the federal government since World War II.

Irons, Peter. *A People's History of the Supreme Court.* New York: Penguin Books, 2006. A close-up look at the justices (warts and all) and the landmark cases they decided, as well as the lives and travails of the citizens who brought the cases before the Supreme Court.

Isaacson, Walter. *Benjamin Franklin: An American Life.* New York: Simon and Schuster, 2003. Biography at its best.

Mayo, H. B. *An Introduction to Democratic Theory.* New York: Oxford University Press, 1960. A thorough discussion of the advantages, limitations, and distinctive aspects of democracy.

McCullough, David. *1776.* New York: Simon and Schuster, 2005.

_____. *John Adams.* New York: Simon and Schuster, 2001. Both books are great reads by a gifted writer.

Zakaria, Fareed. *The Future of Freedom.* New York: W.W. Norton, 2007. Argues that democracy is not inherently good or bad; that it needs strong limitations to function properly.

CHAPTER 5

The Authoritarian Model
Myth and Reality

Learning Objectives

1 Identify the virtues of authoritarianism.

2 Identify the vices of authoritarian rulers.

3 Provide two present-day examples of authoritarian rule.

4 Recite the five myths about authoritarianism.

5 Analyze why the United States sometimes props up dictatorships and sometimes seeks to overthrow them.

History and logic point to a disturbing fact: dictatorship is more natural than democracy. But natural is not *always* better, especially in the realm of politics, where "nature"—especially *human* nature—is often the problem. The perennial challenge of politics is to temper the violent, antisocial side of human nature—greed, pride, deceit, lust, jealousy, and vengeance—with the kinder, gentler side associated with humility, empathy, honesty, civility, and a sense of fairness.

One way to compare political and economic systems objectively (that is, using common criteria, rules of evidence, and methods of data collection) is to ask whether some regimes are better than others at fostering the type of character traits most compatible with social harmony, happiness, and progress. Are people happier living under freely elected ("democratic") governments than authoritarian ones? Are they nicer to each other? If you think the answers to questions like these are obvious, think again. Surveys show that people in New Zealand (a constitutional monarchy) are happier than people in Greece or Spain (both democracies), but were people in Greece and Spain in 2012 happier than people in Oman or Bhutan (both monarchies)? Rather than rely on statistical indicators based on gross national product (GNP), Bhutan seeks to measure "Gross National Happiness" using these four categories: sustainable development, cultural values, natural environment, and good governance.

Until relatively recently, authoritarian states greatly outnumbered democracies in the world. Indeed, with a few notable exceptions (Australia, New Zealand, India, and Japan, for example), democracies were prevalent only in Western Europe and North America prior to the 1980s and 1990s when military dictatorships in Latin America and communist regimes in Eastern Europe gave way to multiparty civilian rule.

Authoritarian states come in various shapes and sizes. They can be traditional (monarchies and theocracies) or modern. Modern one-party authoritarian states often assume the form of military juntas (the "j" is pronounced like the "h" in hoop) or civilian dictatorships. At the other end of the spectrum are monarchies found mainly in the Arab Middle East. Examples include Morocco, Saudi Arabia, Jordan, Kuwait, Oman, Bahrain, Qatar, and the United Arab Emirates. In Iran after the fall of Shah Reza Pahlavi in 1979, a rigid and repressive anti-Western **theocracy** replaced a pro-U.S. modern dictatorship.

Whatever precise shape and form they assume, authoritarian states share certain telltale traits. Self-appointed rulers typically run the show, and all political power—in practice and often in principle—resides in one or several persons. In contrast to totalitarian rulers who typically use a utopian ideology to justify harsh or brutal acts of state repression, the most successful authoritarian rulers tend to be pragmatic, spurning ideological or religious dogmas, censoring the press, jailing dissidents, and, above all, encouraging trade, investment, and economic development.

Typically, authoritarian rulers do not try to control every aspect of society and the economy. Politically, they do what they think is necessary to keep themselves in power. Authoritarian regimes continue to be the main alternative to constitutional democracy. As such, they warrant closer examination.

authoritarian state
Wherever supreme political power is concentrated in one person (dictatorship) or a small group of persons (oligarchy), individual rights are subordinate to the wishes of the state, and all means necessary are used to repress dissent and crush opposition.

theocracy
A state like present-day Iran where religious leaders monopolize political power, legitimate authority derives from a common belief in one god, and there is no separation of church and state.

THE VIRTUES OF AUTHORITARIAN STATES

Virtues? Authoritarian regimes have had a great deal more success over a much longer period than democracies. Outside a few relatively brief historical periods—classical Greece and Rome, medieval and Renaissance Italy, and the contemporary age—monarchy as a political system has had few serious challengers (though many individual monarchs have been less fortunate). Even during the more "enlightened" eras, monarchy was the most prevalent form of government. In the golden age of the Greek city-state system, for example, the principal alternative to monarchy was another form of authoritarianism, oligarchy. Republics were rare.

Why? What are the advantages of authoritarian rule? First, unlike democratic systems based on constitutions and the rule of law, a dictatorship is relatively simple and efficient. There is less need to develop complex structures, procedures, and rules.

POLITICS AND POP CULTURE

A COMEDY THAT'S NO LAUGHING MATTER

The Dictator, a movie released in 2012 starring comic actor Sasha Baron Cohn, was described as "The heroic story of a dictator who risks his life to ensure that democracy would never come to the country he so lovingly oppressed."

The website TakePart has a photo gallery called "5 Real World Tyrants Most Like Sacha Baron Cohen's 'Dictator.'" The tagline says, "The 'Borat' star mocks the world's worst despots. In reality, the joke's been on us."

Three of the five "real world tyrants" are dead (Kim Jong-Il, North Korea; Muammar Gadaffi, Libya; and Saddam Hussein. Iraq), one is out of power (Mahmoud Ahmadinejad, Iran), and the only one still in power, Robert Mugabe of Zimbabwe, is 90 years old. Keep in mind that the list does not claim these five are the worst dictators the world has known in recent times, only that they most resemble the fictional General Aladeen, who rules Wadiya with an iron fist. A character laments, "Gaddafi, Saddam, Kim Jong-il, Dick Cheney … you're the last of the great dictators."

Two earlier films about tyrants are also worth noting. First is *The Great Dictator* (1940) starring Charlie

Chaplin as both main characters—the barber (a Jew) and Adenoid Hynkel (the dictator who strongly resembles Adolf HItler)—which has a five-minute final speech (available on YouTube) that is well worth watching. Also, check out *Bananas*, a 1971 Woody Allen film about a bumbling New Yorker, Fielding Mellish, who travels to a "banana republic" in Latin America and becomes involved in a rebellion against a military junta and winds up becoming the Castro-style dictator.

Why are films about serious political and social problems sometimes presented in the form comedy or satire? Think about it.

Hint: Watch The Daily Show and observe how "fake news" can provide valuable insights, perspective, and even information not available in the mainstream news.

SOURCE: http://www.takepart.com/photos/5-real-world-tyrants-most-sacha-baron-cohens-dictator/5-real-world-tyrants-most-like-sacha-baron-cohens-dictator

Second, dictatorships can act quickly. There is no need to bargain or compromise or cajole. Individuals loyal to the regime typically staff the bureaucracy. Recruitment is based on patronage and nepotism rather than on merit.

Third, neither special interest groups nor public opinion can block or blunt state action. Any serious opposition is suppressed; critics are silenced, jailed, exiled, or executed.

Fourth, a strong leader can collect taxes, build infrastructure (canals, roads, bridges, etc.), raise armies, and rally the nation for defensive purposes like self-preservation or offensive ones like expansion. Abraham Lincoln, one of our most admired and revered presidents, exercised dictatorial powers during the Civil War.

Fifth, unlike democracies, dictatorships often remain politically stable for a long time, even in the face of economic failure. In Cuba, for example, a dictatorship has survived for over half a century despite hardships and poverty due in no small part to strenuous U.S. efforts to isolate and overthrow Fidel Castro.

In contrast, democracies depend on economic prosperity and a robust middle class. Countries that can afford the luxury of schools and other social infrastructure essential to an informed citizenry are generally better candidates for democracy than are poor, less-developed countries, where people are caught up in a daily struggle for survival.

THE VICES OF AUTHORITARIAN RULERS

As Lord Acton (1834–1902) famously observed, "Power corrupts; absolute power corrupts absolutely." Power is intoxicating and addictive—a first drink often gives rise to an unquenchable thirst or—different metaphor, same idea—a ravenous hunger. Moreover, the appetite grows with the eating. Indeed, the tendency to use power as a means of gaining more power is well documented and all too human. There is thus a universal tendency in human relations toward concentration of power.

In authoritarian states, a single ruler or a ruling elite controls the government. The single-head form of government is called an **autocracy,** whereas the elite-group form is known as an **oligarchy,** sometimes referred to as a **junta** or ruling clique. Authoritarian rulers are the sole repositories of power and authority. In this type of regime, tenure in office depends less on elections, which are typically rigged to produce the desired outcome, and more on a combination of myth and might. Meanwhile, the people are often told that obedience to authority is a moral, sacred, or patriotic duty; at the same time, the rulers stand ready to use brute force whenever rebellion rears its head.

autocracy
Unchecked political power exercised by a single ruler.

oligarchy
A form of authoritarian government in which a small group of powerful individuals wields absolute power.

junta
A ruling oligarchy, especially one made up of military officers.

Hulton Archive/Getty Images

Lord Acton (1834–1902), the Baron John Emerich Edward Dahlberg-Acton, was a distinguished British aristocrat and historian. He greatly admired the American federal structure, which he believed to be the ideal guarantor of individual liberty; and as an ardent supporter of states' rights, he sympathized with the Confederacy in the American Civil War. Never one to engage in hero worship, Acton admonished that "Great men are almost always bad men."

FALLEN TYRANTS OF THE POSTWAR ERA: A Roll Call

Ruler	Country	Tenure	How Removed
Rafael Trujillo	Dominican Republic	1930–1961	Assassinated
François "Papa Doc" Duvalier	Haiti	1957–1971	Died in office
Idi Amin	Uganda	1971–1979	Ousted (fled)
Jean-Bedel Bokassa	Central African Republic	1965–1979	Ousted (fled)
Reza Pahlavi	Iran	1941–1979	Ousted (fled)
Augusto Pinochet	Chile	1973–1979	Lost election (fled)
Anastasio Somoza	Nicaragua	1967–1979	Ousted (fled)
Jean-Claude "Baby Doc" Duvalier	Haiti	1971–1986	Ousted (fled)
Ferdinand Marcos	Philippines	1972–1986	Ousted (fled)
Alfredo Stroessner	Paraguay	1954–1989	Ousted (exiled)
Mobutu Sese Seko	The Congo (Zaire)	1965–1997	Ousted (fled)
Slobodan Milosevic	Serbia (former Yugoslavia)	1989–1997	Resigned
Saddam Hussein	Iraq	1979–2003	Executed
Hosni Mubarak	Egypt	1981–2011	Ousted (jailed)
Ben Ali	Tunisia	1987–2011	Fled
Muammar Qaddafi	Libya	1969–2011	Ousted (killed)
Kim Jong-Il	North Korea	1884–2011	Died in office
Ali Abdullah Saleh	Yemen	1989–2012	Fled
Blaise Compaoré	Burkina Faso	1987–2014	Ousted (fled)

Authoritarianism and dictatorship go hand in hand. The dictators who came to power after World War II have nearly all died or been deposed (see "Landmarks in History"). Muammar el-Qaddafi of Libya was one exception until the start of 2011 when, facing heavy rebel opposition and having lost any claim to legitimate authority, his days in power were numbered; Fidel Castro of Cuba, now old and infirm, handed over the executive powers to his younger brother Raúl in 2008 but remained First Secretary of the Communist Party. Dictators in Syria and Nigeria died in the late 1990s.

In sub-Saharan Africa, the Congo remains in a prolonged state of turmoil after decades of rule by a thieving dictator named Mobutu. Nigeria's civilian government is plagued by corruption on all levels, threatened by internal ethnic and religious conflicts, and highly dependent on the military for security and stability. In the Middle East, Bashar al-Assad has repeatedly resorted to the use lethal force to put down popular antigovernment protests, killing thousands of civilians in the process. (Earlier reports that the Syrian Army and allied "Shabiha" militia were responsible for the May 2012 Houla massacre that claimed 108 victims—including 49 children and 34 women—have since been called into serious question, however.)

Until its turn toward democracy in the 1980s, Latin America had a long tradition of military rule. Indeed, after World War II, military dictatorships were common in most regions of the world, including Asia, the Middle East, and North Africa (the so-called Arab world), and sub-Saharan Africa. Thus, for example, prior to the Egyptian Revolution of 2011–2012, the way all three of Egypt's presidents came to power over a sixty-year period starting in 1952 was by rising to a high rank in the army (see "Ideas and Politics").

Where the military dominates the political system, it often rules as an *institution* rather than through a single individual. A ruling committee, or junta, consisting of generals headed by a "president" who is also a general, is the usual pattern. The military frequently claims legitimacy on the grounds that civilian leaders are corrupt and venal, or that only the military can maintain order and stability.

In many Latin American countries where popularly elected civilian presidents now govern, senior military officers continue to play an important governing role. In sub-Saharan Africa, hopeful signs two decades ago that civilian rule was the wave of the future soon faded, as violence, disease, and poverty—and official corruption on a scale rarely matched and seemingly impossible to eradicate—continue to plague many societies.

Authoritarian rulers generally do not respect individual rights when these rights interfere with the power or policy goals of the state. The interests of the state stand above the interests of society or the welfare of the rank-and-file citizenry.

Yet there are important differences among authoritarian rulers. They vary in the extent to which they impose conformity and suppress intellectual and artistic freedom. The amount of force, repression, and violence they employ also varies greatly. Some rulers use coercion sparingly, whereas others, appropriately labeled tyrants, display an enthusiasm for cracking down on dissenters.

Finally, although all tyrants are dictators, not all dictators are tyrants (see Figure 5.1). Some, like the Josip Broz Tito (1892–1980) in the former Yugoslavia and Anwar al-Sadat (1918–1981) in Egypt, pursue higher aims, even at great personal and political risk. Ambitious national programs undertaken to industrialize, reform, or modernize the economy—as demonstrated by Lee Kuan Yew, the no-nonsense political boss of Singapore for three decades (1959–1990), and Jigme Khesar Namgyel Wangchuk, a hereditary monarch who rules the tiny Himalayan kingdom of Bhutan (mentioned at the beginning of this chapter) under a constitution that places the people's "happiness" at its core—point to the possibility of a benevolent dictatorship.

But even benevolent dictators have limited tolerance for political opposition and often deal harshly with "trouble-makers." Dictators sometimes show surprising self-restraint so long as detractors and dissidents remain isolated, do not try to create an organized opposition or conspire to start a revolution, and pose no real threat to the regime. Some pathological tyrants are merciless toward opponents, whether real or imagined. Cambodia ("Kampuchea") under

THE RISE AND FALL OF HOSNI MUBARAK: The End of The World as We Know It?

Until the start of 2011, Egypt's leader, Hosni Mubarak, ruled as an elected president, but for all practical purposes he was a dictator. Mubarak, who followed in the footsteps of three previous military dictators ("president" was a euphemism in the context of Egyptian politics), came to power following the assassination of President Anwar al-Sadat in 1981.

Egypt is an Islamic society but has been a secular state since 1952 when Colonel Gamal Abdel Nasser and the Free Officers staged a coup against the monarch, King Farouk. Nasser ruled as a personal dictator from 1956 until his death in 1970. Soon after assuming the presidency, Nasser nationalized the Suez Canal, an act that led to war with the United Kingdom, France, and Israel (the Suez Crisis of 1956).

Anwar Sadat, another general, succeeded Nasser and ruled Egypt for nearly a decade before he met his untimely demise. Mubarak, his successor, was reelected by plebiscites (direct popular votes) in 1987, 1993, and 1999. As popular elections, these exercises were a farce—Mubarak ran unopposed until 2005. But that election, too, was rigged; the security apparatus, official state media, and ballot boxes remained firmly under Mubarak's control (his main rival, who dared to contest the outcome, was arrested and imprisoned).

Reporters Without Borders ranked the Egyptian media 133rd of 168 countries in the year immediately preceding Mubarak's overthrow. According to another measure, Egypt ranked 111th of 177 countries on the Human Development Index, which uses various economic and social standards and measures of comparison.

Egypt lacks the oil reserves that have made not a few other Arab states rich, and its economy relies heavily on agriculture and on a massive annual foreign aid package from the United States. Many Egyptians blamed Mubarak for the extreme social and economic inequality that allows a few wealthy Egyptians to live in luxury while the vast majority remain mired in poverty. Many also resented Mubarak's submissive stance toward the United States and his refusal to confront Israel—policies that contrast sharply with his strong-arm tactics in dealing with domestic opponents.

Mubarak's stunning overthrow in January 2011 left the generals in charge. After a turbulent sixteen-month transition, the country's military rulers finally allowed something bearing a resemblance to free elections to take place in May 2012, but not all would-be popular candidates were on the ballot. Votes were cast, and the outcome was announced a week later; meanwhile, the generals had dissolved the parliament and issued a new provisional constitution granting the military sweeping powers.

Notwithstanding these developments, Mohammed Morsi was eventually declared the winner. Morsi, a member of the Muslim Brotherhood, a militant Islamic group with a long history in opposition and a large popular following in Egypt, became the country's first civilian and Islamist president—a major break from Nasser's model of a modern military and resolutely secular regime. Morsi pledged to be "a president for all Egyptians" but remained in office for only one year before the military ousted him in July 2013.

The revolts in Egypt, Tunisia, Libya, and elsewhere in the Middle East were led by young people who constitute the majority of the population in all these countries. They are the best educated, most technologically sophisticated, and have the highest unemployment rate of all demographic groups—and they are less constrained by religion and tradition than previous generations have been.

Some observers believe that the tumultuous Arab Spring signaled the dawn of a new era in the Middle East; others see it as dangerously destabilizing in an already volatile region of the world. Who's right? Think about it.

Hint: What has happened in the Middle East since the Arab Spring? Has the region been more stable or less stable? More peaceful? Are some Arab states moving toward greater democracy?

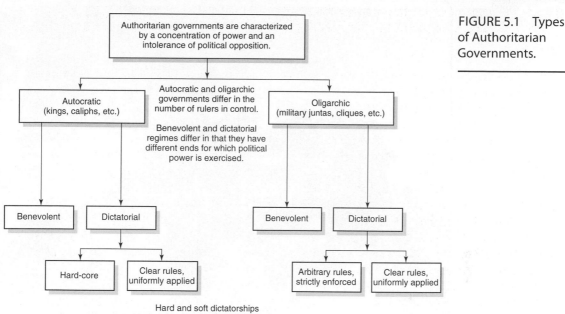

FIGURE 5.1 Types of Authoritarian Governments.

Pol Pot, Iraq under Saddam Hussein, and North Korea under Kim Jong-Il are three examples of what happens when dictators recognize no moral limits to the exercise of power.

Nonhereditary (or modern) autocratic rulers also use repression at times to maintain law and order (as do democracies), but they typically stage elections, pay lip service to constitutional norms, and show a degree of tolerance toward religious beliefs and cultural differences (think of Mubarak's Egypt). The inherent flaw in all dictatorships is that self-restraint never comes with any guarantees and rarely survives a serious challenge to the regime's existence. Arbitrary rules are strictly enforced—that is the immutable law and the very essence of authoritarianism.

CHARACTERISTICS OF AUTHORITARIAN STATES

Authoritarian rulers frequently come to power by force or violence, using the element of surprise to overthrow the government in a **coup d'etat**. Until quite recently, such power seizures were common in Asia, Latin America, the Middle East, and sub-Saharan Africa.

Maintaining a power monopoly is the main aim of authoritarian states. The army and the police are the principal instruments of coercion, hence the high incidence of military rule. Many civilian rulers of authoritarian states start out as military strongmen. In Egypt, for example, three of the past four leaders—Nasser, Sadat, and Mubarak—were military commanders before becoming president.

coup d'état
The attempted seizure of governmental power by an alternate power group (often the military) that seeks to gain control of vital government institutions without any fundamental alteration in the form of government or society.

Ramy Raoof

Jubilant demonstrators in Tahrir Square in Egypt during the Arab Spring in January 2011.

To frustrate actual or potential political opposition, authoritarian rulers often impose strict press censorship, outlaw opposition parties, and exert firm control over the legal system, which is manipulated to prosecute (and sometimes persecute) political opponents. Monopoly control of the mass media and the courts gives absolute rulers a potent propaganda tool and the means to suppress dissent in the face of official corruption and often egregious human rights violations. Repression is typically justified in the name of order and stability.

Until recently, authoritarian states with few exceptions were typically slow to modernize and were characterized by gross social inequality, rural poverty, and a host of related problems—official corruption on a grand scale, comparatively high illiteracy and high infant mortality rates, and low life expectancy. Authoritarianism "does not attempt to get rid of or to transform all other groups or classes in the state, it simply reduces them to subservience."[1] Indirect state control of the "commanding heights" (heavy industry, banking, energy, railroads, foreign trade) is far more common than outright state ownership of the means of production—a stark contrast with Stalinist *totalitarian* regimes during the Cold War (see Chapter 6).

Unlike totalitarian regimes, most dictatorships are indifferent to the way people live or what they do, as long as they stay away from politics. To be sure, dictators rarely make the lives of the people better—often, exactly the opposite. One contemporary case in point is Robert Mugabe, a 90-year-old dictator who has ruled the African nation of Zimbabwe since 1980—all the while presiding over one of the worst-managed economies in the world.

Though authoritarian rulers rarely do what is best for the people, they often do prevent the worst by maintaining law and order.[2] In Iraq, the bloody breakdown in civil society following the U.S.-led invasion in 2003 underscored this point, as did the violent breakup of Yugoslavia in the 1990s. Also significant is the fact that both Iraq and Afghanistan rank among the Top Ten most corrupt states in the world today.[3]

THE POLITICS OF AUTHORITARIANISM

Aristotle argued that all authoritarian forms of rule, despite important differences among them, are a perversion of good government. In his view, "Those constitutions which consider the common interest are *right* constitutions, judged by the standard of absolute justice," whereas "those constitutions which consider only the personal interests of the rulers are all wrong constitutions, or *perversions* of the right forms. Such perverted forms are despotic."[4]

This perversion of ends usually entails a like perversion of means. Despots (cruel dictators) often justify self-serving policies on the grounds that harsh measures are necessary to preserve order or protect the nation from its enemies. Or they may use brute force simply to mask or prevent criticism of their own failed policies. Throughout history, authoritarian rulers and regimes have been notorious for ruthlessly persecuting political opponents. Raising questions regarding who should rule or how is tantamount to treason. In short, where despotism thrives, politics does not.

AUTHORITARIANISM IN PRACTICE: A TALE OF TWO STATES

Despite a promising trend toward constitutional rule in the 1990s, much of Asia and sub-Saharan Africa continue to be ruled by authoritarian regimes. In this section we focus on two examples of authoritarian rule: China and Iran.

China since Mao has undergone a remarkable transformation from having a stalled Stalinist economy to becoming the most dynamic major economy in the world. Iran is a large country (population: 79 million) in Southwest Asia at the crossroads between continents and major countries—Russia, China, and India (to the north and east) and the Arab states, Israel, Africa, and Europe (to the south and west). Politically, Iran is a pariah state—a repressive theocracy with nuclear ambitions widely viewed in the West as a state sponsor of international terrorism.

China: Police-State Capitalism

In little more than three decades, the People's Republic of China (PRC) has transformed itself from an isolated totalitarian state with a dysfunctional command economy into the world's leading model of authoritarian capitalism. Today, China is a global power with a dynamic economy, achieving 10 to 12% annual growth rates every year since the early 1980s. China's economic miracle is the result of a cheap and abundant labor supply, pragmatic policies, skillful diplomacy aimed at opening Western consumer markets to Chinese exports, and special economic zones (SEZs) to attract foreign investment and create jobs for a rapidly expanding urban population. The SEZs combine liberal foreign-ownership policies with generous tax incentives.[5]

Measured in GDP per capita and despite having the second biggest national economy in the world, China remains a poor country compared to neighboring states such as Japan, South Korea, Taiwan, and Singapore (see Figure 5.2). At present, the United States and the European Union, China's two principal trading partners, have bigger economies and far exceed China in per capita GDP. An official U.S. intelligence assessment in December 2012 predicted that China will overtake the United States as the leading economic power before 2030, but the Conference Board, a respected business-research group, predicted in 2014 that China's annual growth rate will slow to 5.5% between 2015 and 2019, compared to 7.7% in 2013.

Although the PRC has shed its legacy of Maoist totalitarian rule (see below), China continues to be a monolithic police state. The path to power for Mao's Chinese Communist Party differed sharply from that of Lenin's Bolsheviks. Because Mao's victory followed a protracted guerrilla war against the Japanese and the Chinese Nationalist government of Chiang Kai-shek, the army played a much greater role in Mao's theory and practice of revolution than in Lenin's. When the Chinese Communists came to power in 1949, the army and the party were fused into a single organization.

Acting as a virtual government, the army was charged not only with fighting but also with administration, including maintenance of law and order,

FIGURE 5.2 The People's Republic of China. Note that many of China's greatest cities are in the east; note where Taiwan is located; note also the close proximity of Japan to the Korean Peninsula.

construction and public works, management of the economy, and education and indoctrination. In effect, the army became the nucleus of the new revolutionary government, the People's Republic of China (PRC).

The PRC was closely allied with the Soviet Union at first, but the era of friendship and cooperation between two communist behemoths lasted less than a decade. Mao's revolutionary quest and his bizarre penchant for self-destructive ideological purity found expression in the Great Leap Forward in 1957–1958. Less than a decade later, Mao's utopian obsession led to his decision to launch the Great Proletarian Cultural Revolution designed to smash the party-state bureaucracy. The Cultural Revolution destroyed what remained of the PRC's bureaucratic and managerial classes, as well as its infrastructure and industry. With the economy utterly ruined and the society in turmoil, the Chinese people were destitute and devoid of hope—until Mao's last act.

Changing of the Guard   Mao Zedong died in 1976. For China's long-suffering masses, it was, arguably, the best thing that ever happened—a watershed in modern Chinese history. According to one China scholar, "Mao's death marked the end of an era; what was not clear was who would lead China and in what direction in the era to come."[6]

After two years of halting reforms, the nation's post-Mao leadership under the direction of Deng Xiaoping (who had twice been purged by Mao for his alleged lack of revolutionary zeal) abandoned ideological fervor in favor of a sober, businesslike pragmatism symbolized by such slogans as "practice is the sole criterion of truth" and "seek truth from facts." Economic development replaced class struggle, and a welcome mat replaced the "no trespassing" sign that had impeded China's trade relations with the West for nearly three decades.

Banished were the mass campaigns, crash programs, hero worship, and ideological fanaticism that had been the hallmarks of Maoism. Expanding trade, especially with the industrial democracies, became a principal aim of Beijing's diplomacy. Deng's economic reforms—notably the SEZs mentioned above—were gradually implemented between 1978 and 1982, as he carefully and patiently consolidated his power within the ruling **Politburo Standing Committee**, the PRC's supreme decision-making body. By the fall of 1982, the reform-minded Deng was in full command.

Deng remained China's paramount ruler until his death, at the age of 92, in early 1997. His successors—first Jiang Zemin and, since 2003, Hu Jintao—continued Deng's pragmatic political and economic policies. Together with Prime Minister Wen Jiaobao, Hu guided China's rise to a position of unprecedented economic and political ascendancy in the new

politburo
A small clique that formed the supreme decision-making body in the former Soviet Union; some politburo members also belonged to the Secretariat and were ministers of key governmental departments.

In November 2012, President Xi Jinping was elevated to the role of Secretary General, the highest position in the Communist Party of China. In March 2013, Xi was named president of the People's Republic of China (PRC).

iStockphoto.com/EdStock

global economy. In a country currently second only to the United States as an economic and military power, and where only a very few top leaders make all key policy decisions, the changing of the guard is a matter of vital importance—not only for China but also for the United States and the world.

In November 2012, the Eighteenth National Party Congress elected a new Central Committee and chose the next generation of leaders. Xi Jinping succeeded Hu as China's supreme leader (head of state, party, and military). In economic policy, Xi shares the worldview and pragmatic approach of his predecessors; at the same time, he has maintained the Communist Party's iron grip on political power, including press censorship, crackdowns on dissent, and blockage of forbidden Internet sites.

Will China's late-stage transition from an insular state and walled-off economy to a global power open to the ever-expanding universe of information technology (IT), trade, and tourism eventually lead to greater personal freedoms and democratization? Or is China too big to be manageable except under strict rules and the harsh discipline of a one-party police state? Only time will tell.

The Two Faces of China China after Mao has shown two faces to the world: one turned outward and smiling, the other inward and frowning—upon dissent, that is. The external world sees the face of a reliable business partner; the face it shows its own people is stern and intimidating. Of late, however, China watchers in the West detect a disturbing policy shift in Beijing's dealings with the outside world. In the words of Richard Armitage, a key foreign policy official in the George W. Bush administration, "The smiling diplomacy is over." The fact that China's military spending rose at least fourfold in little more than a decade lends credence to this early warning.[7] (But keep in mind the United States spends four-and-a-half times as much on weapons and war every year—nearly as much as the rest of the world combined—and remains the world's largest arms producer, consumer, and exporter.)

China's Communist Party continues to maintain a monopoly on political power. Party members constitute a ruling elite that enjoys special privileges. The emergence of a class of *nouveau riche* entrepreneurs and a burgeoning middle class are changing the face of Chinese society, though with little impact on China's all-powerful party-state system thus far. High party ranking remains a prerequisite to membership in China's political class.

Before 1978, Maoism—a radical peasant-based brand of Communism that glorified revolution as a form of moral purification—was the official ideology of China. After 1978, Deng's pragmatic view prevailed—that economic growth, and not class struggle, ought to be the main measure of success for both the party and the state. In Deng's own words, "It matters not if a cat is black or white, as long as it catches mice." No longer would the party invoke Marxist ideology to justify its programs or policies or to legitimize the party's rule.[8]

A Communist Party that distances itself from communism is not only a novelty but also an anomaly—one that raises a key question: How long can China's leadership continue to restrict freedom of expression and the open exchange of ideas in the Information Age? China's engagement in the global economy has necessitated opening Chinese society to outsiders. Although the world now has

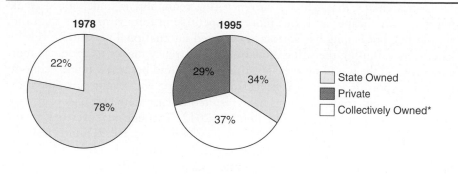

1978

22%

78%

1995

29%

34%

37%

☐ State Owned
■ Private
☐ Collectively Owned*

FIGURE 5.3 An Emerging Private Sector. Private ownership of business in China increased dramatically after Mao Zedong's death in 1976.

*Partly government owned

SOURCE: Originally published in *Newsweek*, March 3, 1997, vol. 89, no. 9, 27. The research is attributed to the Heritage Foundation and IMF, conducted by Anna Kuchment and Dante Chinni by The Heritage Foundation and the IMF.

far greater access to Mainland China than during the Maoist era, the political process remains off limits and shrouded in secrecy. Meanwhile, economic growth is slowing, the influx from poor rural areas to the cities continues unabated, and urban pollution and congestion worsen, aggravating otherwise difficult conditions and causing social stress to rise.

Market-Oriented Reforms In the post-Mao era, Beijing looked to the West for loans and direct foreign investment, thus violating a long-standing ideological taboo. The approach worked wonders; Western capital began pouring into the country in the 1980s and continued fueling China's modernization drive thereafter.

At the same time, agriculture was decollectivized. Under this system, the state makes contracts with individual households to purchase specified products; farmers can also sell produce in private markets. Not surprisingly, these reprivatizing, farm-friendly reforms have proven remarkably effective in boosting agricultural output.

In industry and commerce, too, China has moved toward a greater reliance on market forces. In 1978, there were no privately owned businesses in China; by 1995, approximately one-third of all businesses were privately owned (see Figure 5.3). Subsequently, the number of state-owned and state-controlled enterprises fell sharply between 1995 and 2001, while urban jobs in the state sector dropped from three-fifths to less than one-third of total urban employment.[9]

The results of China's agricultural and industrial revolution are impressive. China achieved "the most astonishing economic transformation in human history," to quote *The Economist*. "In a country that is home to one-fifth of humanity some 200 million people have been lifted out of poverty."[10] China's annual GDP now exceeds Japan's in size, making it the biggest in Asia, and the third biggest economy in the world, behind only the United States and the European Union. China is still relatively poor in terms of per-capita wealth, however. Japan's per capita income was four times that of China ($34,850 versus $8,390 at purchasing power parity) in 2010.

Exports continue to be a major source of China's economic dynamism. By 2003, China's trade surplus with the United States had surpassed Japan's. The overall U.S. trade deficit with China alone accounted for about one-fourth of the total. This imbalance jumped from $124 billion in 2003 to $318 billion a decade later, and China was garnering the largest trade surpluses in the history of the modern world.

Critics charge that China's currency (the renminbi) is undervalued (making its goods cheaper and thus more competitive in foreign markets than they should be), but Beijing has steadfastly resisted international pressure to revalue its currency. Raising the value of a country's currency makes its products more expensive on the world market. For this reason—and because China's economy is highly export-dependent—it seems unlikely Beijing will revalue any time soon.

China's huge trade surpluses have resulted in vast state holdings of foreign reserves totaling more than $3 trillion in 2012. Through its **sovereign wealth funds**, China invests heavily in U.S. Treasury bonds and T-Bills and is now the U.S. government's second-largest creditor (behind Japan). In effect, the United States and China have become economic codependents: the United States provides a major market for China's exports, and China provides the cash to cover Washington's annual budget deficits.

But, to coin a phrase from an old Johnny Mercer song, "something's gotta give." How long can the United States continue outsourcing and losing jobs to China? How long will U.S. consumers be willing and able to buy China's exports? Perhaps China can go on producing without consuming more, and the United States can go on consuming without producing more—but indefinitely? Perhaps not.

Beijing faces other economic challenges as well. Glaring income disparities exist for the first time since the Communist takeover in 1949. The coastal provinces of the east—Shanghai is a particularly striking example—are growing much faster than the rural provinces of central and western China and produce two to four times the income, according to official statistics. Costs of this rapid development include appalling air pollution in China's teeming cities, rivers that run thick with silt, mountains of industrial waste and sewage, and scenes of great natural beauty lost forever to dams and reservoirs for hydroelectric power generation (see "Ideas and Politics").

sovereign wealth funds
A state owned investment fund made up of financial assets such as stocks, bonds, precious metals, and property; such funds invest globally. China, for example, has invested huge sums in the United States via its sovereign wealth fund.

MARLBORO MAKERS SUE CHINA WEBSITES FOR COUNTERFEIT CIGARETTES

CHINA'S RISE: Economic Miracle or Environmental Nightmare?

The Chinese economy is on a collision course with the environment, argues writer David J. Lynch:

> Over the past two decades, China's economy has grown at an average annual rate of more than 9%. But the economic cost of environmental harm, measured in public health, worker absenteeism, and remediation efforts, is becoming prohibitively high. "This miracle will end soon because the environment can no longer keep pace," Pan Yue, deputy director of China's State Environmental Protection Administration, told the German magazine *Der Spiegel.*
>
> Environmental injury costs China 8% to 15% of its annual gross domestic product, Pan said. In the north, encroaching deserts are prompting human migrations that swell overburdened cities. In the south, factories have closed periodically for lack of water, according to [Elizabeth] Economy [of the Council on Foreign Relations], who wrote a book last year on China's environmental woes. The World Bank estimates such shutdowns cost $14 billion annually in lost output.

Since this article appeared, scientific evidence has mounted of global warming caused by excess carbon emissions released into the atmosphere. The international community has become increasingly alarmed about warnings that Earth is reaching a fateful tipping point—the moment when it will become impossible to reverse climate changes, and polar icecaps and glaciers will melt at an accelerating pace with disastrous consequences for the ecosystem. Meanwhile, in 2009 China and India—the two most populous countries in the world—were both continuing to build dozens of new carbon-emitting, coal-fired power plants each year to supply electricity for construction, transport, and industry.

In 2015, the United States ranked as the world's second largest carbon polluter. China, the largest polluter, produced well over one-quarter of the world's total CO$_2$ emissions, and China's annual carbon emissions were nearly 50% higher than the United States. Does this mean that China's leaders don't care as much about the environment as the United States does? Think about it.

Hint: Compare the size of the U.S. population with that of China and several other major economies, and weigh those numbers against annual CO2 emissions of each. Check out which country is the world's largest per capita carbon polluter.

SOURCE: From David J. Lynch, "Pollution Poisons China's Progress," *USA Today*, July 4, 2005 (electronic edition). For an in-depth analysis of this problem, see Elizabeth Economy, "The Great Leap Backward: The Costs of China's Environmental Crisis," *Foreign Affairs*, vol. 86, no. 5, September/ October 2007, pp. 38–59; see also, Carin Zissis and Jayshree Bajorie, "China's Environmental Crisis," *Foreign Affairs*, updated August 4, 2008, http://www.cfr.org/publication/12608/.

In sum, market-friendly reforms have produced a vibrant economy, rising incomes, and a new class of millionaires, but at the price of growing social inequality and severe damage to the environment. When China formally joined the WTO in 2001, the *Economist* asserted, "China's accession to the WTO . . . will be its biggest step since Communist rule began more than 50 years ago toward the integration of its economic system with that of the capitalist West."[11] More than decade later the West was still waiting for the other shoe to drop.

Political and Religious Repression Not long after the death of Mao Zedong in 1978, a phenomenon known as the **Democracy Wall** captured world attention. On a wall in the heart of Beijing, opinions and views at variance with the official line—including blunt criticisms of the existing system and leaders—were displayed with the government's tacit approval. But a government crackdown in 1979, complete with arrests and show trials, put an end to Beijing's brief dalliance with free speech. A decade later, the **Tiananmen Square massacre** came to epitomize the Chinese government's persistent hostility to human rights (see "Landmarks in History").

Tiananmen Square continues to symbolize China's persecution of critics and dissidents. Political prisoners in China can expect harsh treatment. Perhaps the most famous Chinese political dissident in recent times is Liu Xiaobo, winner of the 2010 Nobel Peace Prize. When the prize was announced, Beijing's reaction was swift and furious. The Chinese state media imposed a blackout of the ceremony in Oslo, and the country's draconian system of Internet censorship—the so-called Great Firewall of China—blocked news reports about the Nobel Prize. China warned that the award would harm relations with Norway, pressured other countries not to attend the event, and summoned Oslo's ambassador to Beijing to make a formal protest. Not only was Liu Xiaobo in prison when the honor was bestowed, but his entire family was also placed under house arrest.

Another famous Chinese dissident is Ai Weiwei, a painter and political activist who has openly criticized the Chinese government for failing to respect and protect human rights. Following his arrest at a Beijing airport in April 2011, he was jailed for more than two months without being charged, although officials hinted at allegations of tax evasion. He was later released, but he is not allowed to leave the country. In a widely publicized interview in April 2012, Ai said he considers himself "quite free" but warned against expecting big changes so long as artists are considered enemies. Even so, he noted, the Internet now provides artists and intellectuals access to the world.

Students in the United States would be shocked at the extent to which Chinese Web censors restrict access to the Internet. Forget Facebook, YouTube, and Twitter. More than two million "watchdogs" monitor Web activity on blogs and social media sites in China. Simply searching for information on religious or political topics, terminology, movements, and ideas the government opposes can get you into trouble. Imagine getting kicked off a server for trying to find a forbidden fact, name, or event.*

For the most part, the government controls religion by licensing and monitoring churches, monasteries, mosques, and other religious institutions. Beijing has been particularly ruthless in Tibet, according to Human Rights Watch and many other nongovernmental organizations (NGOs), where it has closed Buddhist monasteries and jailed and executed worshippers. Tibet's religious leader, the Dalai Lama, escaped into exile in northern India in 1959, and China brutally suppressed the national uprising in Lhasa, the capital.

---

*You can see for yourself how many websites are currently blocked in China by going to https://en.greatfire.org.

THE TRAGEDY OF TIANANMEN SQUARE

In May 1989, students and workers staged a mass march in Beijing to protest party privilege, official corruption, and the failure to democratize. The protest grew as throngs of demonstrators camped in Tiananmen Square, making speeches and shouting slogans. The rest of the world watched in rapt attention as the drama unfolded before Western television cameras. The fact that Mikhail Gorbachev, the father of "reform Communism," visited Beijing that same month for the first Sino-Soviet summit in three decades only added to the sense of high drama. When unrest spread throughout the country, Beijing declared martial law, but to no avail.

Army troops entered the Chinese capital with tanks and armor on June 3; it soon became apparent that the show of force was not a bluff. The crackdown that ensued brought the democracy movement to a bloody end as hundreds, possibly thousands, of protesters were killed or injured and many more arrested. Security forces later rounded up thousands of dissenters, and at least thirty-one were tried and executed. The atrocities against unarmed civilians in the Tiananmen Square massacre proved that China was still, at its core, a repressive state.

New Social Disorders China suffers some of the same problems affecting Western democracy. Corruption is widespread. With the blurring of the line between the public and private spheres, and with vast amounts of money circulating through China's burgeoning economy, business and politics have become tainted by routine acts of bribery, nepotism, and "unofficial favoritism." Since taking power in 2012, Xi Jinping has cracked down on official corruption, as well as on political dissidents and ethnic minority unrest.

In a village near Guangzhou in Guangdong Province, for example, one notice promised a handsome reward (10,000 yuan or $1,600) for turning in "criminals" involved in big riots that broke out after security guards beat up a street hawker. In a country where the press is tightly controlled by the state, such anecdotal evidence is often the only way to gauge what is actually happening outside of the capital and a few other major cities. Theft and robbery are also serious problems, as are drug-related crimes and prostitution—all represent the dark underside of China's economic expansion.[12]

In the fall of 2014, Beijing rejected popular demands for democratic elections to choose a new leader in Hong Kong. Two weeks of tumultuous pro-democracy street protests were portrayed in official propaganda as lawless rabble-rousing and proof of the need for constant vigilance against unnamed foreign enemies. Although the protests failed to force policy or leadership changes, they did focus world attention on the plight of Hong Kong, whose citizens lived happily under British rule for a century.

Back to the Future? Despite severe restrictions on political dissent, China is a less repressive society than it was during Mao's erratic totalitarian rule. People are relatively free to make personal choices about fashion and music. This freedom, however, stops short of civil rights and guarantees common in the West. Urban couples are limited by law to having only one child. Dissident artists and writers are often arrested and jailed.

Nor does it appear likely that China will more closely resemble the West in years to come. China's current supreme leader, Xi Jinping, has shown a strong inclination in the opposite direction: toward a greater reverence for what is authentically Chinese, including China's ancient sages, autocratic rulers, and time-honored ways. Traditions going back thousands of years, Xi declared in 2014, "can offer beneficial insights for governance and wise rule."

China: Rival or Partner? China is now a global power with a nuclear arsenal at its disposal. With the world's largest population, it has no difficulty finding conscripts for its armed forces, which total some three million troops. Since the late 1970s, China has sought to modernize its military capabilities. Today, it has the fastest-rising arms expenditures of any major world power. China also continues to test nuclear weapons and sell high-tech armaments on the international market. (But the United States is still by far the largest arms supplier to the world.)

Some analysts express alarm at what they see as China's massive arms buildup—its growing arsenal of cruise and ballistic missiles, its new and improved submarine fleet, its antiship ballistic missile program, and its electronic and cyberwarfare capabilities.[13] A view currently held by high level officials in Washington is that China's advances in cyberspace and antisatellite warfare "could threaten America's primary way to project power" and protect "our forward air bases and carrier groups" in the Pacific.[14]

Others caution against overreacting. They point out correctly that the United States is still far ahead in quantity and quality across the full range of state-of-the-art weapons, and annual U.S. defense spending is five or six times higher. Even as a percent of GDP, China devotes less than half as much to military spending as the United States.

In Asia, India's reluctance to forgo its nuclear weapons programs can be traced, in part, to its distrust not only of Pakistan but also of China. Japan is wary of China's military buildup, as is Russia. Bitter memories of the 1979 border war are still alive in Vietnam, and the Philippines, long a staunch U.S. ally in the western Pacific, have an unresolved dispute with the PRC over potentially oil-rich islands in the South China Sea.

Add to that the long-standing dispute over Taiwan. Beijing considers Taiwan a breakaway province of China, but the United States continues to back Taiwan's independence. Periodic Chinese naval exercises have reinforced this point, but so far Taiwan has continued to hold firm, buttressed by the U.S. Navy.

In 2012 a long-time dispute between Japan and China over uninhabited islands in the East China Sea caused a near-rupture in relations. Japanese exports to China were at risk, but there was a far worse fear that war would break out. In mid-January 2013, China flew a civilian surveillance plane near the islands. That action provoked Japan and soon escalated to the point where both Tokyo and Beijing ordered fighter jets into the area of the disputed islands.

According to one newspaper story at the time, "What began as a seemingly minor dispute is quickly turning into a gathering storm."[15]

In sum, China has replaced Russia as America's main rival, but that's where the similarity ends. China remains "inscrutable" to the rest of the world but no longer inaccessible. China continues its authoritarian ways in the realm of politics, but it has adapted with remarkable agility to the new global economy, opening its internal markets to foreign trade and investment and demonstrating flexibility and pragmatism in all things economic. Overall, the meaning of China's emergence as a global power is far from certain. Finally, China faces huge challenges at home and presents many new challenges to the rest of the world.

Iran: Petropariah in the Persian Gulf

As a political system, Iran is in an oxymoron—a modern theocracy. The words "modern" and "theocracy" are a contradiction in terms, but Iran proves that in politics everything is possible. As an authoritarian state, Iran is in a class by itself—unique and isolated both in the Islamic world and in the larger global system.

Historically, at the peak of Persian civilization during the period of the Sassanid Dynasty (224661 CE), Persia was a mighty empire encompassing all of today's Iran, Afghanistan, Iraq, Syria, the Caucasus (Armenia, Georgia, Azerbaijan, and Dagestan), southwestern Central Asia, part of Turkey, certain coastal parts of the Arabian Peninsula, the Persian Gulf area, southwestern Pakistan, and even stretched into India.

Iran is an Islamic state, but Persians are not Arabs. The language of Persia is Farsi, not Arabic. The dominant form of Islam in Iran is Shi'a, whereas most Arabs are Sunni. From the early 1950s until 1979, an absolute monarch called the Shah (from the Persian word *Shahansha* meaning "king of kings") ruled the country with troops and truncheons. Shah Mohammad Reza Pahlavi was a ruthless secular ruler committed to modernization and economic development. He was also a very close friend of the United States. Under the Shah, Iran provided the United States with a trusted ally in one of the most important strategic areas of the world, the Persian Gulf.

In 1979 the hated Shah was overthrown in a popular uprising now commonly known as the Iranian Revolution and inspired by the Ayatollah Khomeini, a charismatic religious leader. The revolution put paid to the monarchy and put Khomeini in the driver's seat.

Khomeini set about creating the modern world's first and only theocracy—a government run by religious leaders and based on a strict interpretation of the Koran. Thereafter, Islamic law became the law of the land. Ultimate authority fell to a "supreme legal guide," the ayatollah, responsible only to God. Religious leaders serve in the Majlis (parliament) and play an active role in the political life of the nation. The Council of Guardians acts as a high court, using the Koran, not the constitution, as the ultimate arbiter. Many of Iran's 80,000 clerics became local political agents of the Islamic Republican Party (IRP).

The first years of Ayatollah Khomeini's rule were chaotic. Following the seizure of the U.S. embassy in Tehran in November 1979, fifty-two U.S. citizens were held hostage until January 1981. To many Iranians, the long history of collusion between the United States and the shah justified a jihad against the United States (the "great Satan"). Nonetheless, the incident left Iran diplomatically isolated.

Internally, Khomeini launched a reign of terror; thousands of enemies of the Islamic state—intellectuals, former officials, military officers, and political figures—were arrested, tried, and executed. A series of bombings killed some Khomeini confederates, including the newly elected president (Khomeini had dismissed the first president). In retaliation, Khomeini crushed his political opponents.

In the midst of this instability, Iraq invaded Iran. The bloody war of attrition that followed led to appalling carnage and suffering, drained the economies of both countries, disrupted oil supply lines, and for seven years held the entire region under the threat of a wider war. When the fighting stopped in 1988, there was no winner or loser.

Within a year of the war's end, the ayatollah died, leaving a bitter legacy. He had inspired Iran to shed Western influences, but the price was a pariah state, a perpetrator of terrorism abroad and of human rights violations at home.

Iran's success in rebuilding its petroleum industries and armed forces after its prolonged war with Iraq, its refusal to condemn acts of aggression and international terrorism, and its success in developing sophisticated military capabilities to match Israel's, including nuclear weapons and medium-range missiles, all contributed to a renewed sense of alarm in the West (and, of course, Israel) from the early 1990s to the present.

Things have changed in the thirty-five years "since a senior American official last visited Iran," according to a 2014 report in *The Economist*:

> As people have moved from their villages to the cities, they have got richer and acquired a taste for consumer goods and Western technology. Over half of Iranians go to university, up from a third five years ago. The disastrous presidency of Mahmoud Ahmadinejad, the failed Green revolution—which sought to topple him in 2009—and the chaotic Arab Spring have for the moment discredited radical politics and boosted pragmatic centrists. The traditional religious society that the mullahs dreamt of has receded. With the passing of time, the mosques have started to empty. The muezzins' call to prayer is heard less often, because people complain about the noise. In Qom, the religious capital, seminaries are dwarfed by a vast shopping mall. As a caliphate takes root in Iraq and Syria, here is one Islamic state where religion is in retreat.[16]

Notwithstanding these changes, Iran has continued to develop "dual-use" nuclear technology (having both peaceful and military applications) despite intense Western pressures. In November 2011, the International Atomic Energy Agency (IAEA) issued a report saying it had "serious concerns regarding possible military dimensions to Iran's nuclear program . . . [point to the conclusion] that Iran has carried out activities relevant to the development of a nuclear explosive device."[17] In November 2014, reports of a possible breakthrough at the P5+1 talks in Vienna raised new hopes for an accord that will at last defuse a highly combustible issue in a region all too likely at any time to turn into a tinderbox. These hopes appeared closer to reality in April 2015 with the announcement of a new "historic" nuclear framework agreement in effect requiring Iran to shelve its nuclear weapons program for at least ten years in return for a lifting of crippling Western economic sanctions.

AUTHORITARIANISM IN THEORY: MYTH VERSUS REALITY

The stigma often attached to authoritarianism has given rise to various popular misconceptions. This section focuses on six common assumptions that, on closer examination, are half-truths at best—a blend of fact and myth.

Myth 1: Authoritarianism Is a Sign of the Times

Authoritarianism is neither abnormal nor unique to the modern era. Indeed, at least until the second half of the twentieth century, it was the norm. At the time of the American Revolution, *democracy* was abnormal and widely viewed as a kind of aberration.

In *The Politics*, Aristotle provided an impressive catalog of the political tactics designed to render individuals incapable of concerted political action. Persons thought to represent a political threat were eliminated. Autocratic rulers isolated individuals from one another by banning common meals, cultural societies, and other communal activities. Secret police spied on citizens, used informants to weed out dissent, and deliberately sowed seeds of mutual mistrust between friends and neighbors. Poverty, heavy taxes, and hard work monopolized the subjects' time and attention.* War was a yet another means of control, keeping "subjects constantly occupied and continually in need of a leader."[18]

Niccoló Machiavelli (1469–1527) expanded and updated Aristotle's impressive list of autocratic methods in a famous book, *The Prince* (1532). A virtual instructor's manual for dictators, *The Prince* is shockingly "Machiavellian"—in common usage, a pejorative term connoting cruelty, cunning, and everything commonly associated with "dirty politics." Those who would rule, Machiavelli contended, must practice "how not to be good." Rulers are advised to place expediency above morality, but to take pains to appear honest and upright.

Princes cannot operate according to the same moral code as subjects. Thus, deceit becomes a virtue and always keeping promises becomes a vice. It is good to be both feared and loved, but better to be feared; to cultivate the appearance of generosity but to give away mainly what belongs to others; to punish severely because anything less makes the ruler look weak and indecisive; and to dole out benefits little by little, so as to constantly remind those on the receiving end of the prince's benevolence.

It is hardly surprising that the word *Machiavellian* has come to be associated with ruthless, immoral acts. Yet Machiavelli did not invent the methods he prescribed. He simply translated a set of practices prevalent in the dog-eat-dog city-state system of sixteenth-century Italy into a general theory of politics.

---

*As an example, Aristotle cited the construction of the Egyptian pyramids. Recent archeological evidence, however, suggests the pyramid builders were paid laborers, not slaves. Perhaps, but talk about a hard life!

Niccolò Machiavelli (1469–1527). Renaissance Italy's most famous political philosopher, Machiavelli is also one of its most controversial characters. He approached the study of politics as a scientist, determined to record what he observed, not what others wanted to believe. The political arena was his laboratory. He was a remorseless realist. In *The Prince*, he offered shocking advice to rulers not to let moral inhibitions weaken them in the face of political necessity. But what is often forgotten or overlooked is that he also counseled prudence: "no prince has ever benefited from making himself hated."

Myth 2: Authoritarian Rulers Are Always Tyrannical

Aristotle distinguished between two different forms of authoritarianism. One form, by far the most common of the two, relies on cruelty and repression—crude methods of political control. The purpose of such policies is to intimidate the population, thus inoculating the ruler(s) against a mass revolt.

A second kind of authoritarian ruler displays concern for the common good and avoids ostentation, gives no sign of any impropriety, honors worthy citizens, erects public monuments, and so on. Such a "half-good" autocrat would clearly be preferable to a "no-good" one.

Some autocratic rulers imprison, torture, and even murder real or imagined political enemies; others govern with a minimum of force. Some run the economy into the ground; others give economic development the highest priority. In Iran, for example, the Shah Reza Pahlavi modernized Iran's military, economy, and society, but he also had his political opponents imprisoned, tortured, and sometimes executed.

Myth 3: Authoritarian Rulers Are Never Legitimate

In the United States, we agree with John Locke that legitimacy arises from the consent of the governed. But consent is not the only measure of legitimacy—in fact, for long periods in history, popular will was not even recognized as a criterion of legitimacy.

Instead, from the late Middle Ages through the eighteenth century, the prevalent form of government in Europe was monarchy, based on divine right conferred by religious belief or royal birth conferred by heredity. In Imperial China, the dynastic principle was one source of the emperor's legitimacy, but religion also played a major role; the Chinese emperor ruled under the "mandate of Heaven."

Many contemporary dictatorships have relied on a somewhat more informal and personal source of legitimacy—the popular appeal of a **charismatic leader**. Often charismatic rule is grounded in the personal magnetism, oratorical skills, or legendary feats of a national hero who has led the country to victory in war or revolution. Post–World War II examples include Egypt's Nasser (1956–1970), Indonesia's Sukarno (1945–1967), and Libya's Qaddafi (1969–2011). Many postcolonial Third World dictators came to power as "liberators" who led the struggle for independence and emerged as objects of hero worship.

Divine sanction, tradition, and charisma, then, are the historical pillars of autocratic rule. More often than not, these wellsprings of legitimacy have effectively sold the idea that the rulers have a *right* to rule without consulting the people. Having the right to rule does not mean the same thing as ruling rightly,

charismatic leader
A political leader who gains legitimacy largely through the adoration of the populace deriving from past heroic feats (real or imagined), personality traits, oratorical skills, and the like.

of course. And unfortunately, dictators and tyrants have too often used this "right" to commit serious wrongs.

But legitimacy, like beauty, is in the eyes of the beholder. If the people embrace an autocrat or dictator, no matter how brutal, evil, or corrupt he or she might be, that is what counts. What outsiders might think of a ruler like Cuba's Fidel Castro or Russia's Vladimir Putin is irrelevant.

Myth 4: Authoritarian Rulers Are Always Unpopular

Given a choice, people would choose to live in a democracy rather than a dictatorship, right? How then do we account for popular dictators?

First, difficult as it is for Westerners to understand, some dictators are loved as well as feared. In the aftermath of war or revolution, for example, autocratic rulers can and sometimes do guide a country through a difficult period of reconstruction. Stability and order set the stage for economic growth and prosperity. Former President Lee Kuan Yew of Singapore is one example in recent times; two historical examples are Catherine the Great of Russia and Frederick the Great of Prussia.

Personal charisma is another source of popularity. The prototype of the charismatic "man on horseback" was Napoléon Bonaparte (1769–1821). Napoléon seized power in a France convulsed by revolution and led it in a series of spectacularly successful military campaigns, nearly conquering the entire European continent. At the height of his military success, Napoléon enjoyed almost universal popularity in France.

Hitler, too, enjoyed broad support among the German rank and file. As one writer pointed out,

> It is sometimes assumed that one who rules with the support of the majority cannot be a tyrant; yet both Napoléon and Hitler, two of the greatest tyrants of all time, may well have had majority support through a great part of their reigns. Napoléon, in many of his aggressive campaigns, probably had majority support among the French, but his actions ... were nonetheless tyrannical for that. Hitler, for all we know, might have had at least tacit support of the majority of the German people in his campaign against the Jews; his action was nonetheless tyrannical for that. ... A tyrant ... may in many of his measures have popular support, but ... his power will not depend upon it.[19]

Good people will not necessarily stand in the way of bad rulers. As the great Russian writer Fyodor Dostoyevsky (1821–1881) observed, in an age of equality, the masses desire security above all else, and they will gladly accept despotism in order to escape the burdens that accompany the benefits of freedom.[20] The truth is that despotic government is often more popular than we care to believe.

Myth 5: Authoritarianism Has No Redeeming Qualities

Even the worst tyrants can bring order out of political chaos and material progress out of economic stagnation. Thus, in the 1930s, Hitler directed a massive military buildup that jump-started Germany's economy. Apologists for Benito Mussolini (1883–1945), Italy's fascist dictator in World War II, have noted that at least he made the trains run on time. Stalin industrialized Soviet Russia and thus set the stage for its rise to superpower status after World War II. Such public policy successes by no means justify the excesses of these tyrants, but they do help explain their domestic popularity.

Perhaps the most impressive example of an autocratic regime that succeeded in creating sustained social and economic progress comes not from Europe but from China. Baron de Montesquieu, Adam Smith, and Karl Marx were all moved to comment on the classical Chinese system of government.[21] The vast network of dikes, irrigation ditches, and waterways that crisscrossed the immense Chinese realm is particularly noteworthy. This hydraulic system represented a signal achievement, exceeding in scale and scope any public works ever undertaken in the West in premodern times. What kind of civilization could build public works on such a stupendous scale?

One modern scholar, Karl Wittfogel, theorized that the Chinese system, which he labeled "oriental despotism," owed its distinctive features to the challenges of sustaining a huge population in a harsh and demanding environment.[22] Rice has long been a staple in China, and rice cultivation requires large amounts of water under controlled conditions. Thus, to solve the perennial food problem, Chinese civilization first had to solve the perennial water problem. This meant building sophisticated flood control, irrigation, and drainage works. The result was a system of *permanent agriculture* that enabled Chinese peasants to cultivate the same land for centuries without stripping the soil of its nutrients.

Constructing such a system necessitated a strong central government. A project as ambitious as the transformation of the natural environment in the ancient world could not have been attempted without political continuity and stability, social cohesion, scientific planning, resource mobilization, labor conscription, and bureaucratic coordination on a truly extraordinary scale. Thus, the technology and logistics of China's system of permanent agriculture gave rise to a vast bureaucracy and justified a thoroughgoing, imperial dictatorship.

Private property ownership was rare and vast public works projects were designed and implemented by a centralized bureaucracy dedicated to efficient administration. Admission to the bureaucratic class was based on a series of examinations. At the apex of the power pyramid sat the emperor, who ruled under the mandate of Heaven and whose power was absolute.

What about the Chinese people under this highly centralized form of government? The rank-and-file traded labor for food and were treated as subjects, not citizens. The masses had duties in relation to the state but no rights. On the positive side, Imperial China lasted longer than any other system of government the world has ever known (from about 900 to 1800). As the saying goes, nothing succeeds like success.

Imperial China presents us with a paradox. On the one hand, it stands as an example of a ruling order more despotic than most traditional forms of Western authoritarianism.[23] On the other hand, its economic and technical achievements, along with its art, language, and literature, were extremely impressive by any standard. Significant material advances accompanied China's early economic development. Although Chinese rulers and scholar-officials were neither liberal nor enlightened by modern Western standards, China's system of hydraulic despotism resulted in a sufficient supply of food to support a large and growing population for centuries—though not without occasional famines.

Keep in mind that we often apply far tougher standards to "them" (dictatorships) than to "us" (democracies). No form of government is flawless or unfailingly fair, including constitutional democracy.

Myth 6: Authoritarianism Is the Worst Possible Government

Totalitarian states (the focus of the next chapter) go well beyond traditional autocracies in trampling on human rights—rounding up enemies, using slave labor, and carrying out acts of mass murder. One of the grim lessons of the last century is that the worst possible government is worse than most of us can imagine.

THE FUTURE OF AUTHORITARIANISM

Between 1974 and 1990, more than thirty countries in Latin America, Asia, and Eastern Europe shifted from a nondemocratic to a democratic form of government.[24] During the 1980s, Ecuador, Bolivia, Peru, Brazil, Uruguay, Argentina, Chile, and Paraguay replaced military rulers, opting for more democratic alternatives. Central American nations followed suit. In 1989, a wave of revolutions swept communist regimes from power across Eastern Europe.

Democracy also made inroads in parts of sub-Saharan Africa. In the early 1990s, many African countries held multiparty elections or adopted reforms designed to lead to such elections.[25] At the same time, South Africa's repressive **apartheid system,** based on a racist ideology of white supremacy, was abolished and replaced by majority rule.

How deep and enduring the trend away from authoritarian governments will be is still an open question. Can we look forward to a future when, for the first time in human history, democracy will be the global norm? Or will the inherit difficulties and defects of democratic rule give rise to growing disappointment until people become so disillusioned that they turn away?

Certainly, the contemporary world features many examples of successful democracies and failed dictatorships, and the prosperity common to many democratic states encourages imitators. But the reverse is also true: successful dictatorships and failed democracies. The People's Republic of China, for example, combines a rigidly authoritarian political system with a dynamic economy, whereas the government of Greece, a democratic country, faced bankruptcy in 2010.

The rise of Islamism, a fanatical, violent, anti-Western form of Islam, is a reminder that Western-style democracy continues to face major challenges in many parts of the world. Another is the return of the centralized authoritarian state in Russia, which is "run largely in the interests of a ruling clique."[26] Democracy has often suffered reversals even in the West, where popular rule has the deepest roots.[27]

In Latin America, democracy is widespread yet in places remains fragile and unstable. Several countries, including Colombia, Peru, and Mexico, face internal threats from guerrilla and terrorist groups. Back in 2004, a *New York Times* reporter painted this bleak picture:

> In the last few years, six elected heads of state have been ousted in the face of violent unrest, something nearly unheard of in the previous decade. A widely noted United Nations survey of 19,000 Latin Americans in 18 countries in

apartheid system
The South African system designed to perpetuate racial domination by whites prior to the advent of black majority rule there in the early 1990s.

April produced a startling result: a majority would choose a dictator over an elected leader if that provided economic benefits.[28]

He added, "Analysts say that the main source of the discontent is corruption and the widespread feeling that elected governments have done little or nothing to help the 220 million people in the region who still live in poverty, about 43 percent of the population."

Great disparities in wealth and living standards in today's world help explain popular discontent with democracy. There are many countries in Eastern Europe, Asia, Latin America, and sub-Saharan Africa where modern economies have yet to be created. Gross economic and educational inequalities persist and worsen with the passage of time. Stagnant economies and tribal or ethnic divisions destabilize many developing societies.

Even in countries where the military has relinquished power, generals often continue to exert a behind-the-scenes influence over civilian governments. Where the principle of civilian rule is open to question, the government is fragile and the fear of anarchy is real, the abrupt return of military dictatorship remains an ever-present possibility. Dictators come and go, but it is too soon to write the obituary for authoritarian rule.

AUTHORITARIANISM AND U.S. FOREIGN POLICY

Soon after the end of World War II, the United States found itself engaged in a cold war with the Soviet Union. The Cold War was not a natural rivalry between two great powers but rather a struggle to the death between two rival systems of morality, economics, and government. The ideologies of these two rivals were absolutely incompatible. The United States pursued a policy of "containment" based on the theory that Communism would eventually collapse of its own dead weight, while the Soviet Union drew upon Marx's prediction that capitalism was headed for the "dustbin of history."

The two principals in this contest divided the world into two halves—East and West, communist and capitalist, good and evil. One thing the implacable foes agreed on, however, was that neutrality was not an option: with few exceptions, the nations of the earth would have to choose between them.

In reality, the world was never so neatly divisible. Many developing countries preferred to remain nonaligned. Egypt, India, and Indonesia attempted to launch a nonaligned movement in the 1950s that, for a time, appeared to be getting off the ground. But the Cold War protagonists cajoled, pressured, and enticed the leaders of these fledgling states with foreign aid, weapons transfers, and cash. By the mid-1960s, most governments in Africa, Asia, and Latin America had chosen sides.

In the rush to recruit Third World leaders who would jump on the anticommunist bandwagon for a price, the United States frequently found itself using "dollar diplomacy" and other inducements to prop up right-wing dictatorships—and looking the other way when friendly regimes committed gross violations of human rights.[29]

Unfortunately, as events in the Balkans, West Africa, and elsewhere in the 1990s showed, when an autocrat dies or is ousted, the result is not always democracy, peace, and prosperity—that is one of the most important lessons of the post–Cold War era. Closer to home, as Robert Kaplan noted, "Look at Haiti, a small country only 90 minutes by air from Miami, where 22,000 American soldiers were dispatched in 1994 to restore 'democracy.' Five percent of eligible Haitian voters participated in [the last] election, chronic instability continues, and famine threatens." Kaplan continued,

> Those who think that America can establish democracy the world over should heed the words of the late American theologian and philosopher Reinhold Niebuhr: "The same strength which has extended our power beyond a continent has also . . . brought us into a vast web of history in which other wills, running in oblique or contrasting directions to our own, inevitably hinder or contradict what we most fervently desire. We cannot simply have our way, not even when we believe our way is to have the "happiness of mankind" as its promise.[30]

LANDMARKS IN HISTORY

THE DEMISE OF SADDAM HUSSEIN

In many respects the iron-fisted Saddam Hussein who ruled Iraq for twenty-four years was the "perfect" tyrant. Saddam's heroes were modern history's most ruthless dictators.

Saddam, called the Butcher of Baghdad, has been aptly compared with Joseph Stalin, the brutal Soviet dictator who summarily executed countless "enemies" and sent millions more to work and die in slave labor camps. Like Stalin, Saddam ruled through a tightly controlled monolithic political organization, the Ba'ath Party, which was virtually indistinguishable from the state. Like Stalin, he turned the country into a vast prison. And like Stalin, he perpetuated his rule through paralyzing fear, induced by highly publicized mock trials and police-state terror.

No one knows for certain how many Iraqis became victims of the Ba'athist regime during Saddam's twenty-four-year rule. That he routinely imprisoned all whom he suspected of disloyalty, that he used poison gas against whole villages to punish rebellious Kurds in the north, and that he tortured many of his victims without mercy are facts well known to Iraqis. Iraqi "traitors" and "enemies of the state" were not safe even abroad. At Saddam's behest,

secret agents murdered scores of dissidents in exile in the 1980s and 1990s. As Saddam put it, "The hand of the revolution can reach out to its enemies wherever they are found."*

Saddam emulated Stalin's use of ideology and propaganda to justify or legitimize his crimes against humanity by extolling the "historical mission" of the Ba'ath Party. If the regime brutalized and dehumanized anyone who got in its way, it was always for a "higher purpose."

In fact, Saddam's purposes were purely self-serving: to stay in power and live like a king while his people sank ever deeper into poverty. Between 1991 and 1995, he reportedly built fifty new palaces at a cost of $1.5 billion; the largest was bigger than Versailles. Saddam displayed no conscience and no remorse in doing whatever he deemed necessary to control Iraqi society while he plundered the economy.

In the wake of the U.S.-led invasion of Iraq in the spring of 2003, Saddam was captured, put on trial, and convicted of mass murder. He was hanged in Baghdad on December 30, 2006, defiant and unrepentant to the end.

*Quoted in Elaine Sciolino, *The Outlaw State: Saddam Hussein's Quest for Power and the Gulf Crisis* (New York: Wiley, 1991), p. 91.

These words proved prophetic. In early 2004, exactly a decade after Kaplan's warning about the dangers of anarchy in impoverished, out-of-the-way countries like Haiti was first published in the *Atlantic Monthly*, Haiti's elected president, Jean-Bertrand Aristide, was forced to flee as mob violence threatened to plunge the country into chaos. The crisis ended only after a U.S. Marine Corps contingent was deployed to restore calm.

Autocrats are often brutal and even sadistic. But where the fear and awe they inspire, and the ruthless methods they employ, prevent a descent into anarchy, it is quite possibly the lesser of two great evils. In Kaplan's words:

> The lesson to draw is not that dictatorship is good and democracy bad but that democracy emerges successfully only as a capstone to other social and economic achievements. . . . Tocqueville showed how democracy evolved in the West not through the kind of moral fiat we are trying to impose throughout the world but as an organic outgrowth of development.[31]

In recent times, the United States has invaded and occupied two countries, Iraq and Afghanistan, vowing to bring freedom and democracy to both despite the fact that the peoples of neither of these fractious societies had ever experienced anything of the sort. More than a decade later, it is clear that Iraq will not become a stable democracy and quite possible will not survive as a single state. Ditto for Afghanistan. In Iraq, as in Afghanistan and other troubled parts of the world, the choice is between the risk of anarchy and the reality of authoritarianism. It's a stark choice, but if history is any guide, it is one they and they alone can make.

SUMMARY

When one or more self-appointed rulers exercises unchecked political power, the result is a dictatorship. Benevolent autocrats (who are somewhat concerned with advancing the public good), ordinary dictators (who are concerned solely with advancing their own interests), and tyrants (who exhibit great enthusiasm for violence and bloodletting) all qualify as dictators, but even slight differences can make a significant alteration in the lives of the people who, by definition, have no voice in how they are governed.

Historically, authoritarian rulers have provided the most common form of government. Yet despite their prevalence, authoritarian regimes have been regarded as perversions of good government because they almost always place the ruler's interests ahead of the public good. Nigeria provides a good example of a contemporary authoritarian state.

Misconceptions about authoritarian regimes abound. It is not true that dictatorial rule is a modern phenomenon or that all authoritarian states are identical, illegitimate, or unpopular with their citizens. Further, we can differentiate such governments on moral grounds: Some seek to promote the public interest; others do not. Moreover, authoritarian regimes do not represent the worst possible form of government in all cases.

Finally, despite some evidence that authoritarian government is giving way to democracy, it is too early to draw any definitive conclusions. The record of U.S. relations with authoritarian states is replete with inconsistencies and contradictions. The latter have weakened the U.S. moral position in international politics, complicated its diplomatic efforts, and led to charges of hypocrisy.

KEY TERMS

authoritarian states 101	junta 103	Democracy Wall 116
theocracy 101	coup d'etat 107	Tiananmen Square massacre 116
autocracy 103	politburo 111	charismatic leader 122
oligarchy 103	sovereign wealth funds 114	apartheid system 125

REVIEW QUESTIONS

1. What are the two basic types of nondemocratic government? What are the chief characteristics of authoritarian governments?
2. Are authoritarian governments becoming less prevalent? Where are such governments found today?
3. Are all autocrats tyrannical? Explain.
4. What kind of "advice" did Machiavelli give to rulers bent on maintaining their power?
5. Summarize the six myths that surround authoritarian governments. What fallacies underlie these myths?

WEBSITES AND READINGS

Many countries discussed in this chapter have individual websites devoted to aspects of their political, historical, and social culture. To find a list of these sites, use the name of the specific country of interest as your search term. The Wikipedia entry for authoritarianism is a place to start. Click on the various terms such as *absolute monarchies, dictatorships, despotisms,* and *theocracies* for definitions and exegesis.

Websites

China: http://www.chinasite.com/

Saddam Hussein, Fallen Iraqi Dictator: http://www2.gwu.edu/~nsarchiv/special/iraq/

Nigerian Authoritarianism and Human Rights: http://www.amnesty.org/

"Despotism" Film: https://www.youtube.com/watch?v=dilk6FxkbHw

Nicolae Ceausescu, The Unrepentant Tyrant: https://www.youtube.com/watch?v=U_PP0dRbMFI

Readings

Boesche, Roger. *Theories of Tyranny, from Plato to Arendt.* University Park: Pennsylvania State Press, 1996. Many authoritarian rulers have been tyrants, and tyranny has been a subject of study for some of the greatest political thinkers. This book examines both.

Brownlee, Jason. *Authoritarianism in an Age of Democratization.* New York and London: Cambridge University Press, 2007. This book is based on fieldwork in Egypt, Iran, Malaysia, and the Philippines and seeks to explain the mixed record of democratic reforms in these countries by comparing how ruling parties originated.

Crick, Bernard. *Basic Forms of Government: A Sketch and a Model.* Magnolia, MA: Peter Smith, 1994. This short, yet comprehensive outline of types of governments contrasts authoritarian with totalitarian and democratic states.

Kaplan, Robert. *The Coming Anarchy: Shattering the Dreams of the Post Cold War.* New York: Vintage Books, 2000. A nicely arranged collection of insightful pieces on the challenges of the post–Cold War international system, featuring as its centerpiece the author's widely discussed article on the danger of anarchy—most notably in West Africa and the Balkans—originally published in the *Atlantic Monthly* in February 1994.

Latey, Maurice. *Patterns of Tyranny.* New York: Atheneum, 1969. A study that attempts to classify and analyze various tyrannies throughout history.

Machiavelli, Niccolò. *The Prince,* translated by Harvey C. Mansfield Jr. Chicago: University of Chicago Press, 1985. This classic study describes the methods tyrants must use to maintain power.

Moore, Barrington. *Social Origins of Dictatorship and Democracy.* Boston: Beacon Press, 1993. A general discussion of the relationship between social conditions and political systems.

Rubin, Barry. *Modern Dictators: Third World Coup Makers, Strongmen, and Political Tyrants.* New York: New American Library/Dutton, 1989. A good general discussion of various nondemocratic regimes that have held power in the post–World War II era.

Sassoon, Joseph. *Saddam Hussein's Ba'th Party: Inside an Authoritarian Regime.* New York: Cambridge University Press, 2011. From the publisher: "The true horrors of this regime have been exposed for the first time through a massive archive of government documents captured by the United States after the fall of Saddam Hussein."

Skierka, Volker. *Fidel Castro: A Biography.* Cambridge, UK: Polity Press, 2004. First published in German in 2000, this book is a well-researched narrative of Castro's life.

Szulc, Tad. *Fidel: A Critical Portrait.* New York: Avon Books, 1986. A highly acclaimed biography by a former *New York Times* foreign correspondent based on extensive interviews with Castro, as well as with friends and associates of the Cuban dictator.

CHAPTER 6

The Totalitarian Model
A False Utopia

Learning Objectives

1 Define totalitarianism.

2 Describe the role of ideology in totalitarian states.

3 Identify the three most infamous totalitarian rulers and how they earned that reputation.

4 Describe the three developmental stages in the life of a totalitarian state.

5 Determine the value of studying totalitarianism even though the world's worst examples of totalitarian rule have passed into the pages of history.

A new and more malignant form of tyranny called **totalitarianism** reared its ugly head in the twentieth century. The term itself denotes complete domination of a society and its members by tyrannical rulers and imposed beliefs. The totalitarian obsession with control extends beyond the public realm into the private lives of citizens.

Imagine living in a world in which politics is forbidden and *everything* is political—including work, education, religion, sports, social organizations, and even the family. Neighbors spy on neighbors and children are encouraged to report "disloyal" parents. "Enemies of the people" are exterminated.

Who are these "enemies"? Defined in terms of whole *categories* or groups within society, they typically encompass hundreds of thousands and even millions of people who are "objectively" counterrevolutionary—for example, Jews and Gypsies (Romany) in Nazi Germany, the *bourgeoisie* (middle class) and *kulaks* (rich farmers) in Soviet Russia, and so on. By contrast, authoritarian governments typically seek to maintain political power (rather than to transform society) and more narrowly define political enemies as individuals (not groups) actively engaged in opposing the existing state.

Why study totalitarianism now that the Soviet Union no longer exists? First, communism is not the only possible form of totalitarian state. The examples of Nazi Germany and Fascist Italy are reminders that totalitarianism is not a product of one ideology, regime, or ruler. Second, totalitarianism is an integral part of contemporary history. Many who suffered directly at the hands of totalitarian dictators or lost loved ones in Hitler's Holocaust, Stalin's Reign of Terror, Mao's horrific purges, or other more recent instances of totalitarian brutality are still living. The physical and emotional scars of the victims remain even after the tyrants are long gone. Third, totalitarian states demonstrate the risks of idealism gone awry. Based on a millenarian vision of social progress and perfection that cannot be pursued without resort to barbaric measures (and cannot be achieved even then), they all have failed miserably as experiments in utopian nation-building. Finally, as we will see, totalitarianism remains a possibility wherever there is great poverty, injustice, and therefore the potential for violence and turmoil—recent examples include Iran, North Korea, and Burma (Myanmar).

One of the lessons of 9/11 is that extremism remains a fact of political life in the contemporary world. It can take many malignant forms. Terrorism is one; totalitarianism is another. This chapter demonstrates clearly that totalitarianism and terror go hand in hand.

THE ESSENCE OF TOTALITARIANISM

Violence is at the core of every totalitarian state—at its worst, it assumes the form of indiscriminate mass terror and genocide aimed at whole groups, categories, or classes of people who are labeled enemies, counterrevolutionaries, spies, or saboteurs. Mass mobilization is carried out through a highly regimented and centralized one-party system in the name of an official ideology that functions as a kind of state religion. The state employs a propaganda and censorship apparatus far more sophisticated and effective than that typically found in authoritarian states. As the late sociologist William Kornhauser wrote in a highly acclaimed study, "Totalitarianism is limited only by the need to keep large numbers of people in a state of constant activity controlled by the elite."[1]

Totalitarian ideologies promise the advent of a new social order—whether a racially pure "Aryan" society envisioned by Adolf Hitler, or the classless society promised by Lenin and Josef Stalin, or the peasant society in a permanent state of revolution Mao Zedong imagined. All such totalitarian prophets "have exhibited a basic likeness . . . [in seeking] a higher and unprecedented kind of human existence."[2] We can trace the totalitarian leader's claim of political legitimacy directly to this self-proclaimed aim of creating a new utopian society.[3]

Totalitarian societies are "thoroughly egalitarian: no social differences will remain; even authority and expertise, from the scientific to the artistic, cannot be tolerated."[4] Thus, individualism is rejected and even criminalized. The rights of society are paramount, leaving no room at all for the rights of the individual.

At the heart of this harmonious community lies the concept of a reformulated human nature. The impulse to human perfection was reflected in Lenin's repeated references to the creation of a "new Soviet man" and in the Nazi assertion that party workers and leaders represented a new type of human being or a new breed of "racially pure" rulers. Mao Zedong displayed a near obsession with something he called **rectification**—the radical purging of all capitalist tendencies, such as materialism and individualism, at all levels of Chinese society.

The clearest examples of such utopian political orders have been Nazi Germany, the Soviet Union (especially during Stalin's Reign of Terror), and Maoist China. Other examples in recent history include Pol Pot's Cambodia (1976–1979) and Mengistu's Ethiopia (1977–1991), while North Korea is a contemporary case. In the following section we examine the stages in the evolution of totalitarian regimes.

rectification
In Maoist China, the elimination of all purported capitalist traits, such as materialism and individualism.

THE REVOLUTIONARY STAGE OF TOTALITARIANISM

How do totalitarian movements start? Typically, they emerge from the wreckage of a collapsed or collapsing state. In such turbulent times, a charismatic leader sometimes steps onto the scene. Leadership is crucial to the success of any revolution. In the case of *total* revolution, leadership is one of five key elements. Ideology, organization, propaganda, and violence are the other four.

Leadership

Perhaps the most conspicuous trait of total revolution has been reliance on what we may term the *cult of leadership*. Virtually every such revolution has been identified with—indeed, personified in—the image of a larger-than-life figure. The Russian Revolution had its Lenin, the Third Reich its Hitler, the Chinese Revolution its Mao, Cuba its Castro, and so forth. Each of these leaders became the object of hero worship. Without such a leader, observed Eric Hoffer, "there will be no [mass] movement":

It was Lenin who forced the flow of events into the channels of the Bolshevik revolution. Had he died in Switzerland or on his way to Russia in 1917, it is almost certain that the other prominent Bolsheviks would have joined a coalition government. The result might have been a more or less liberal republic run chiefly by the bourgeoisie. In the case of Mussolini or Hitler, the evidence is even more decisive: without them there would have been neither a Fascist nor a Nazi movement.[5]

Revolutionary leaders instinctively understand that the masses possess the raw power to change the world but lack the will and direction. Without a charismatic leader—one who can read their minds, capture their imagination, and win their hearts—there is nothing to act as a catalyst. A leader such as Lenin or Mao, then, is to a mass movement what a detonator is to a bomb.

Ideology

Whatever the quality of leadership, total revolutions depend in the final analysis on the willingness of converts to engage in extraordinary acts of self-sacrifice in the name of the cause. Such reckless devotion cannot be inspired by rational appeals. It must arise, rather, from the true believer's blind faith in the absolute truth provided by a comprehensive political doctrine.

Consider what an ideology must do for its followers if it is to be successful:

> It must claim scientific authority which gives the believer a conviction of having the exclusive key to all knowledge; it must promise a millennium to be brought about for the chosen race or class by the elect who holds this key; it must identify a host of ogres and demons to be overcome before this happy state is brought about; it must enlist the dynamic of hatred, envy, and fear (whether of class or race) and justify these low passions by the loftiness of its aims.[6]

The Need for a Scapegoat: Reinterpreting the Past As a critique of the past, ideology generally focuses on some form of absolute evil to which it can attribute all national (or worldwide) wrongs and social injustices. To the revolutionary ideologue, the true causes of economic recession, inflation, military defeat, official corruption, national humiliation, moral decadence, and other perceived problems are rooted in the mysteries and plots of a rejected past.

If an enemy does not exist, it is necessary to invent one. Usually it is an individual or a group that was already widely feared, hated, or envied. Lenin blamed the plight of workers on money-grubbing capitalists. Hitler blamed Jews and communists for the German loss in World War I and the economic crises that preceded his assumption of power. Mao found his enemy first in wealthy landlords and later in "capitalist roaders." Clearly, the purpose of these ploys was to focus mass attention on a readily identifiable scapegoat on whose shoulders all the nation's ills could be placed.

According to Hoffer, "Mass movements can rise and spread without a belief in God, but never without a belief in a devil."[7] Hate and prejudice, rather than love and high principle, seem the most effective forces in bringing people together in a common cause.

Revolutionary Struggle: Explaining the Present As a guide to the present, ideology provides the true believer with keys to a "correct" analysis of the underlying forces at work in contemporary society. Concepts such as class struggle for Marxist-Leninists, *Herrenvolk* (master race) for the Nazis, and "contradictions" for Mao's followers were used to explain and predict social reality. Yesterday the enemy was preeminent; today the enemy will be defeated.

Advocates of total revolution believe struggle is the very essence of politics. For Marxist-Leninists, class struggle was the engine of progress in history. For Maoists, struggle was a desirable end in itself; only through the direct experience of revolutionary struggle, they believed, could the masses (and especially the young) learn the true meaning of self-sacrifice. Hitler glorified the struggle for power by proclaiming war to be the supreme test of national greatness. (Revealingly, Hitler outlined his own path to political power in a book titled *Mein Kampf*, "my struggle.") Whether the aim is to overthrow monopoly capitalists or to purify a race, revolutionary struggle is always described in terms of good versus evil. It was common for leading Nazis to depict Jews not simply as enemies of the state but as *untermenschen* ("subhumans") and, frequently, as insects or lice.[8] The repeated use of such degrading characterizations dehumanizes the victims; it is a lot easier to justify the extermination of insects than human beings.

Utopia: Foretelling the Future As a promise of the future, ideology tends to paint a radiant picture of perfect justice and perpetual peace. Marxist-Leninists envisioned this utopia as a classless society, one from which all social and economic inequality would be abolished. Similarly, the Nazi utopia was a society from which all racial "impurities" would be removed through the extermination or enslavement of racial "inferiors."

Whatever its precise character, the vision of the future always included a radical redistribution of wealth and property. Marxism-Leninism promised to take from the rich (the bourgeoisie) and give to the poor (the proletariat). Hitler made a similar promise when he proclaimed his intention to provide *Lebensraum* ("living space") in the east; he would take land from the land-rich but slothful Slavs and give it to the land-poor but industrious Germans.

Marxism is based on a deterministic worldview in which the success of the proletarian revolution is dictated by inflexible "laws" of history. Hitler, too, was an unabashed determinist. In *Mein Kampf*, he wrote, "Man must realize that a fundamental law of necessity reigns throughout the whole realm of Nature."[9] Hitler also frequently ranted about "the iron law of our historical development," the "march of history," and the "inner logic of events." No less than Lenin, Stalin, or Mao, Hitler claimed that he (and the German people, or *Volk*) had a world-shattering mission to accomplish, and that success was inevitable. He expressed this notion in what is perhaps his most famous (or infamous) pronouncement: "I go the way that Providence dictates with the assurance of a sleepwalker."[10]

Ideology and Truth The past, present, and future as described by a given revolutionary ideology may seem far-fetched or even ludicrous to a disinterested observer. The racial theory put forth by the Nazis utterly lacked historical,

Image of Vladimir Ilyich Lenin, leader of the October Revolution, on a Soviet postage stamp. The letters "CCCP" stand for Union of the Soviet Socialist Republics (USSR) in the Russian-language Cyrillic alphabet.

iStockphoto.com/TZfoto

sociological, genetic, and moral foundations. By the same token, the economic facet of Hitler's ideology—the "socialism" in National Socialism—lacked any meaningful content. So watered down was Hitler's conception of socialism that in the words of one authority, "Anyone genuinely concerned about the people was in Hitler's eyes a socialist."[11]

Why would any sane person embrace such an ideology? First, it appealed to popular prejudices and made them respectable. Second, it was not the message that counted so much as the messenger— the leader's personal magnetism attracted a following, whether the words made sense or not. Third, certitude was far more important than rectitude. Fourth, ideologues can often get away with absurd allegations and gross falsehoods if they also address real problems faced by ordinary people.

Many Germans recognized the extremist nature of the Nazis' racial theories but probably believed Hitler would discard such absurdities once the work of unifying the country, reviving the economy, and restoring the nation's lost honor had been accomplished. By the same token, even if many of Lenin's followers did not truly believe the workers' paradise was just around the corner, the Russian peasants did believe in land reform, an end to Russia's disastrous involvement in World War I, and improvements in nutrition, medical care, and education as promised by Lenin.

Organization

Cohesive structure was one of the missing ingredients in pre-twentieth-century rebellions. Most such outbreaks were spontaneous affairs—they burst into flame, occasionally spread, but almost always burned themselves out. The October Revolution, however, was a different story.

Lenin founded the Bolshevik Party more than fourteen years before seizing power in 1917. Admitting only hard-core adherents into the party, Lenin reasoned the czar could be defeated through a long, clandestine struggle led by a small group of disciplined revolutionaries (a "vanguard") rather than by a large, amorphous mass of unruly malcontents.

To ensure secrecy, discipline, and centralized control, Lenin organized the Bolshevik Party into tiny **cells**. As the Bolsheviks grew in number and established cells in cities outside St. Petersburg (see "Landmarks in History"), however, intermediate layers of authority became necessary, although the principles of strict party discipline and total subordination of lower levels to higher ones were not relaxed. Factionalism was not tolerated; party members were still expected to place party interests above personal interests at all times. This spirit of self-sacrifice and total commitment to the party was called **partiinost**.

Unlike its Russian counterpart, the Chinese Revolution was primarily a rural uprising by a mass of discontented peasants. Mao's most pressing organizational problem was to mold the amorphous peasant mass into an effective military force capable of carrying out a protracted guerrilla war. His success

cells
Small, tightly knit organizational units at the grassroots level of V. I. Lenin's Bolshevik party.

partiinost
The spirit of sacrifice, enthusiasm, and unquestioning devotion required of Communist Party members.

THE OCTOBER REVOLUTION

In October 1917, the Russian capital of St. Petersburg (also called Petrograd) was in turmoil due to hardships and popular anger caused by the long years of World War I and the bitter capitulation to Germany. The October Revolution was led by Nikolai Lenin and the Bolsheviks, with the backing of the Mensheviks, the Left Socialist revolutionaries, and an assortment of anarchists.

There were actually two revolutions in Russia in 1917. The first, the so-called February Revolution, brought about three dramatic results: the ouster of Czar Nicholas II, the end of the Russian monarchy, and the creation of a power vacuum. Following a failed attempt by Aleksandr Kerensky to form a Western-style parliamentary democracy, Lenin and Trotsky masterminded a power seizure in the capital in October. This move had a dual character—half popular uprising and half *coup d'état*.

In fact, the revolution *did* spread, and it *was* fomented by Lenin's Bolsheviks. However, it was not entirely, or even mainly, a proletarian revolution of the kind Marx had imagined. Instead, it included disaffected soldiers and sailors, as well as land-hungry peasants. Russia did not have an extensive industrial labor force in 1917. It was still primarily a peasant society with an agrarian economy. Moreover, the "revolution" in St. Petersburg was actually led by Leon Trotsky, not Lenin.

Nonetheless, Lenin was the prime mover. His role in creating a conspiratorial organization, orchestrating events between February and October 1917, and inspiring the masses made him the undisputed leader of the revolutionary Soviet state—so much so that St. Petersburg was renamed Leningrad three days after Lenin's death in 1924. The name was changed back to St. Petersburg in September 1991, shortly before the Soviet Union was formally dissolved.

FIGURE 6.1 **Map of Russia.**

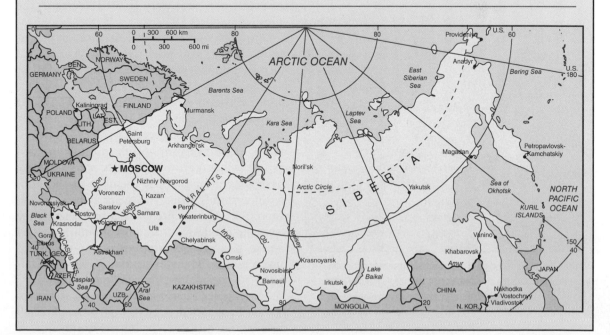

won over many leftists (especially in developing nations) who admired and even imitated Mao's theory and practice of peasant-based revolution in a poor and benighted rural society.

Mao's long march to power contrasts with Hitler's quixotic rise in Germany, which started with a violent, abortive coup in the early 1920s and culminated in a kind of constitutional *coup d'état* in the 1930s. A compliant organization in the form of the Nazi Party was crucial to Hitler's ultimate success. Hitler made extensive use of brute force to intimidate his opposition, but he also created numerous party-controlled clubs and associations. The Hitler Youth, a Nazi women's league, a Nazi workers' organization, a Nazi student league, and various other academic and social organizations gave the Nazis considerable political power even before Hitler took over the reins of government. Later, under an innocuous-sounding policy called **Gleichschaltung** ("coordination"), he destroyed virtually all preexisting social organizations and substituted Nazi associations in their place. Partly for this reason, Hitler's promises and threats carried great weight throughout German society. Like all modern revolutionaries, Hitler understood the value of a carefully constructed revolutionary organization.

Propaganda

As more people have become engaged in modern political life, **propaganda**—the dissemination of information based on falsehoods and half-truths designed to advance an ideological cause—has become a potent political weapon.[12] To be successful, as Hitler noted, propaganda must address the masses exclusively; hence, "its effect for the most part must be aimed at the emotions and only to a very limited degree at the so-called intellect."[13]

An avid student of the science of propaganda, Hitler proposed that "all propaganda must be popular and its intellectual level must be adjusted to the most limited intelligence among those to whom it is addressed." Hence, "the greater the mass it is intended to reach, the lower its purely intellectual level will have to be. . . . Effective propaganda must be limited to a very few points and must harp on these in slogans until the last member of the public understands what you want him to understand." Given these premises, it follows that the "very first axiom of all propagandist activity [is] the basically subjective and one-sided attitude it must take toward every question it deals with."[14] And the bigger the lie, the better.

Hitler theorized that the success of any propaganda campaign depends on the propagandist's understanding of the "primitive sentiments" of

AP Images

Through the implementation of an immense propaganda campaign in combination with the inculcation of the Nazi ideology, Adolf Hitler (1889–1945) was able to persuade the German people of the need to persecute Jews, the necessity of an eventual war, and the radical transformation of German society.

the popular masses. Propaganda cannot have multiple shadings: Concepts and "facts" must be presented to the public as true or false, right or wrong, black or white. In *Mein Kampf*, Hitler heaped high praise on British propaganda efforts in World War I and expressed contempt for German propaganda, which he faulted for not painting the world in stark black-and-white terms.

Unlike Hitler, who was a highly effective orator, Lenin was a master pamphleteer and polemicist who relied most heavily on the written word. In the infancy of his movement, Lenin's chief weapon was the underground newspaper. Endowed with such names as "The Spark" and "Forward," these propaganda tabloids were printed clandestinely or smuggled into the capital, St. Petersburg, in false-bottom briefcases.

Violence

The fifth and final characteristic of totalitarian revolution is the use of violence and terror as accepted instruments of political policy. According to the Nazi theorist Eugene Hadamovsky, "Propaganda and violence are never contradictions. Use of violence can be part of the propaganda."[15] Assassinations and kidnappings, indiscriminate bombings, and sabotage are all part of the totalitarian tool box. Sabotage is designed to disrupt production, transportation, and communications systems; terror is aimed at a greater, pervasive sense of insecurity (see Chapter 15).

State terror—violence perpetrated by the government—has played a prominent role in mass movements of both the Right and the Left. The notorious "combat groups" (*fasci di combattimento*) Italian Fascist Party leader Benito Mussolini formed shortly after World War I provide a striking example. After attempts to woo the working class away from the Socialist Party failed, Mussolini began to cultivate the middle classes and seek financing from wealthy industrialists and big landowners. One of the more novel forms of terror the fascists devised was the *punitive expedition*, in which armed bands conducted raids against defenseless communities. The local police would often cooperate by looking the other way.

Mussolini's aim was threefold: (1) to create an artificial atmosphere of crisis; (2) to demonstrate that the state was no longer capable of providing law-abiding, taxpaying citizens with protection from unprovoked attacks on their persons and property; and (3) to prod an increasingly fearful, desperate, and fragmented citizenry to turn for refuge and order to the very same political movement that was deliberately exacerbating the problem.

The Nazis in Germany used the same sort of tactics. The similarities between this kind of organized violence and plain gangsterism are obvious—the crucial difference has to do with ends rather than means: Gangsters seek to gain control over lucrative (and often illegal) businesses, not to overthrow the government.

THE CONSOLIDATION OF POWER

Once the old order has been overthrown or fatally discredited, the totalitarian leadership can operate from a solid power base within the government.

salami tactics
The methods used by Vladimir Lenin to divide his opponents into small groups that could be turned against one another and easily overwhelmed.

The next task it faces is to eliminate any competing political parties and factions. The final step in the consolidation process is the elimination of all those within the party who pose a real or potential danger to the totalitarian leader. At this stage, Machiavelli's advice is especially valuable: "One ought not to say to someone whom one wants to kill, 'Give me your gun, I want to kill you with it,' but merely, 'Give me your gun,' for once you have the gun in your hand, you can satisfy your desire."[16]

Eliminating Opposition Parties

Any opposition group, no matter how small or ineffectual, poses a potential danger to the ruler. By the same token, the mere existence of political opponents inhibits the kind of radical change mandated by the movement's ideology.

In dealing with rival political parties, Lenin famously employed **salami tactics**[17]—the practice of marginalizing or eliminating opposition by slicing it into pieces and playing one group off against the other. Thus, after the new Constituent Assembly (legislature) was elected, Lenin exploited an already existing division in the dominant Socialist Revolutionary Party by forming an alliance with its left wing. This alliance enabled Lenin to move against the party's more moderate wing, as well as against other rightist parties.

Lenin also repressed Russia's huge peasant population. The lack of peasant support for the Bolshevik regime became a particularly acute problem during the civil war (1918–1920), when foodstuffs and other basic necessities were extremely scarce. In response, Lenin "instituted in the villages a 'civil war within a civil war' by setting poor peasants against those who were less poor,"[18] thereby helping to undermine the political opposition.

Hitler employed a different strategy. Bolstered by his Nazi Party's steadily growing popularity in the polls (thanks to a formidable following of true believers), his superb oratorical skills, and a special group of shock troops known as storm troopers, he played a waiting game. Once in office, he gradually expanded his authority, first by gaining passage of new emergency powers and suspending civil liberties. Only then did he move to shut down all opposition parties. Hitler thus used the charade of legality to destroy his opponents politically before using the power of the state to destroy them physically.

Purging Real or Imagined Rivals within the Party

purges
The elimination of all rivals to power through mass arrests, imprisonment, exile, and murder, often directed at former associates and their followers who have (or are imagined to have) enough influence to be a threat to the ruling elite.

Political **purges** involve removing opponents from the party leadership or from positions of power, or rounding up whole (often fictitious) categories of people ("bourgeois capitalists" or "enemies of the people") but not necessarily killing them. Arresting people you don't trust and either imprisoning or exiling them can be just as effective as killing them—and ostensibly more civilized. In carrying out purges, totalitarian governments almost invariably accuse their victims of subversive activity or treason—a convenient rationale for eliminating individuals who are perceived as threats or political liabilities.[19] Thus, Hitler turned on Ernst Röhm and other party members who had been instrumental in the Nazis' rise to power; on the Führer's orders, the Röhm faction was murdered in June 1934. Blaming the whole incident on his political enemies, Hitler used the Röhm purge to solidify his popular support and give credence to his fear-mongering propaganda.

Purges played an even bigger role in the consolidation of power in the Soviet Union. In 1921, thousands of trade unionists and sailors, formerly the backbone of the Bolsheviks' popular support, were murdered by the secret police when they demanded free trade unions and elections. Next, Lenin purged the so-called Workers' Opposition faction of his own Bolshevik party, which demanded worker self-management of industry. Lenin pronounced the group guilty of "factionalism" and accused it of endangering both the party and the revolution. The members of the Workers' Opposition group were expelled from the party but not murdered.

Such relatively mild actions were not characteristic of Lenin's successor, Joseph Stalin, who, as the head of the Soviet Communist Party (1924–1953), did not hesitate to murder those whom he perceived to be his political enemies. How Stalin gathered total power in his hands is a textbook example of cutthroat power politics. He shrewdly adapted Lenin's salami tactics. However, whereas Lenin set rival parties against each other, Stalin set rivals within his own party—virtually all the great Bolshevik heroes of the October Revolution—against each other. Stalin purged and eventually murdered virtually the entire top party leadership after Lenin's death in 1924.

Creating a Monolithic Society

The totalitarian state stops at nothing short of total control over the economy, the arts, the military, the schools, the government—every aspect of society. As Nazi propaganda chief Joseph Goebbels (1897–1945) remarked, "The revolution we have made is a total revolution. . . . It is completely irrelevant what means it uses."[20] Ironically, the golden society at the end of the utopian rainbow is incompatible with intellectual freedom. Thus, one Nazi official asked this rhetorical question: "If the brains of all university professors were put at one end of the scale and the brains of the Führer at the other, which end, do you think, would tip?"[21]

Total control requires total loyalty. During the Nazi era, even in small towns, any magistrates and petty officials who had not publicly supported the Nazis were removed from power. Simultaneously, numerous "enemies of the people" were identified and punished by the brutal **Gestapo** or secret police.[22] The effectiveness of these terror tactics helps explain why there was so little overt resistance to the Nazi takeover, but it does not tell the whole story. Cowardice, apathy, and self-interest played important roles as well. A true story told by a German refugee who had been on the faculty of the prestigious University of Frankfurt speaks directly to this point.[23] Following the appointment of a Nazi commissar at the university, every professor and graduate assistant was summoned for an important faculty meeting:

> The new Nazi commissar . . . immediately announced that Jews would be forbidden to enter university premises and would be dismissed without salary on March 15. . . . Then he launched into a tirade of abuse, filth, and four-letter words such as had been heard rarely even in the barracks and never

Gestapo
In Nazi Germany, the secret state police, Hitler's instrument for spreading mass terror among Jews and political opponents.

before in academia. He pointed his finger at one department chairman after another and said, "You either do what I tell you or we'll put you into a concentration camp." There was silence when he finished; everybody waited for the distinguished biochemist-physiologist.

The great liberal got up, cleared his throat, and said, "Very interesting, Mr. Commissar, and in some respects very illuminating; but one point I didn't get too clearly. Will there be more money for research in Physiology?" The meeting broke up shortly thereafter with the commissar assuring the scholars that indeed there would be plenty of money for "racially pure science."[24]

The English philosopher Edmund Burke is reported to have said, "All that is necessary for evil to succeed is for good men to do nothing." Indeed.

THE TRANSFORMATION OF SOCIETY

The transformation stage generally coincides with the regime's assumption of control over the economy and requires active government planning and intervention.[25] In justifying the drive for a new social order, totalitarian regimes typically blame everything that is wrong with the country on counterrevolutionaries, spies, and saboteurs.

Carl Friedrich and Zbigniew Brzezinski, two respected students of this subject, have identified six characteristics shared by all totalitarian governments: (1) an official ideology; (2) a single, hierarchical party; (3) a secret police; (4) a tightly controlled armed forces; (5) a media monopoly; and (6) central control over the economy.[26] These characteristics derive from the main features and functions of the revolutionary movement we have discussed (leadership, ideology, organization, propaganda, and violence), now redirected to the state's day-to-day administration and transformation.

The attempted transformation of the state follows a predetermined ideological path, with some concessions to pragmatism where necessary. But practicality is rarely of prime importance for the total tyrant bent on transformation. Examples from the political careers of Stalin, Hitler, and Mao illustrate this point.

The Soviet Union under Stalin

In 1928, having defeated his political rivals, Stalin stood poised to launch his drive to collectivize and industrialize the Soviet economy. His first Five-Year Plan for the Soviet economy (1928–1932) marked the beginning of a cataclysm. Over the next ten years, millions of innocent people were killed or sent to labor camps, and a whole class of relatively well-to-do landholders, the **kulaks**, ceased to exist. In addition, the whole pattern of Soviet agricultural production was radically reshaped.

To understand why Stalin would inflict so much suffering on the Soviet farm population, we must first understand the role of ideology in totalitarian systems. Stalin's first Five-Year Plan, which instituted a highly centralized economic system designed to foster rapid development of the Soviet economy, was motivated by a lust for power. However, Stalin was also committed to creating an advanced industrial society based on collective, rather than capitalist, principles. The way to accomplish this remarkable feat in the shortest possible

kulaks
A class of well-to-do landowners in Russian society that was purged by Joseph Stalin because it resisted his drive to establish huge collective farms under state control.

time, Stalin reasoned, was to invest massively in heavy industry while squeezing every last drop of profit from agriculture, the traditional foundation of the Russian economy.

Private ownership of farmland, animals, and implements would have to be eliminated and farming "collectivized." Under Stalin's **collectivization** plan, most agricultural production took place in large cooperative units known as *kolkhozy* (collective farms), whose members shared whatever income was left after making compulsory deliveries to the state, or in *sovkhozy* (state farms), whose laborers received wages.

Soviet agriculture was collectivized to underwrite Soviet industrialization. Through a massive transfer of resources from farms to cities, Stalin believed industrial production could double or even triple during the period of the first Five-Year Plan. But doing so would necessitate crushing all pockets of rural resistance, herding the peasants into collective farms, and imposing a draconian system of "tax" collections, or compulsory deliveries of scarce food supplies to the state in order to feed the growing army of industrial workers and to pay for imported capital goods.

One reason the plan failed was the excessive and indiscriminate brutality Stalin employed. Stories spread through the countryside of how Stalin's agents had machine-gunned whole villages. Many Russian peasants deliberately burned their crops and killed their cattle rather than cooperate with Stalin's requisition squads. Despite an all-out national effort, industrial production grew only slightly, if at all. In the meantime, famine depopulated the countryside.

Stalin made no apologies and no policy adjustments. Instead, he fabricated statistics, which no one dared question, to "prove" that real progress was being made. In the words of one expert, "The Stalin regime was ruthlessly consistent: All facts that did not agree, or were likely to disagree, with the official fiction—data on crop yields, criminality, true incidences of 'counterrevolutionary' activities . . . were treated as nonfacts."[27]

In 1934, as the death toll mounted and the first Five-Year Plan came to an unspectacular end, the Soviet dictator declared he had uncovered a far-reaching conspiracy, orchestrated by foreign agents and counterrevolutionaries, to resurrect capitalism in Soviet Russia. This conspiracy theory gained credibility when Sergei Kirov, the dynamic young leader of the Leningrad party organization, was assassinated in December 1934. Harsh reprisals, numerous arrests, phony trials, summary executions, and large-scale deportations followed. Many of the victims were loosely identified as members of a fabricated conspiracy called the Leningrad Center. The alleged plot furnished Stalin with the pretext for a purge of Lenin's original circle of revolutionary leaders, the so-called Old Bolsheviks.

During the first phase of the Great Terror (January 1934 to April 1936)— also known as the Great Purge—Communist Party membership fell by nearly 800,000, or approximately 25%. The Soviet press denounced these ex-communicants as "wreckers, spies, diversionists, and murderers sheltering behind the party card and disguised as Bolsheviks."[28]

iStockphoto.com/Acprints

One of the most ruthless dictators of the twentieth century, Joseph Stalin (1879–1954) moved away from the Soviet model of an international communist revolution proposed by Marx and Lenin to focus on "socialism in one country." In pursuit of his aims, Stalin committed mass murders on a grand scale and enslaved millions in a vast system of gulags (forced-labor camps). It's amazing, even shocking given what we now know about Stalin, that he was named *Time* magazine's "Man of the Year" in 1942.

collectivism
The belief that the public good is best served by common (as opposed to individual) ownership of a political community's means of production and distribution; derived from "collective," denoting a form of community or commune in Marxist ideology.

THE GREAT PURGE

Between 1934 and 1938, Stalin ordered most of the Soviet political and military elite executed as enemies of the state, including:

- 1,100 delegates to the 17th Party Congress (more than half)
- 70% of the 139-member Party Central Committee

- 3 of 5 Soviet marshals (the highest-ranking generals)
- 14 of 26 army commanders
- All 8 admirals
- 60 of 67 corps commanders
- Half the 397 brigade commanders
- All but 5 of the 81 top-ranking political commissars

gulag archipelago
Metaphorical name for the network of slave labor camps established in the former Soviet Union by Joseph Stalin and maintained by his secret police to which nonconformists and politically undesirable persons were sent.

The second phase of the Stalin purges (1936–1938) was highlighted by the infamous *show trials*, in which the Old Bolsheviks, along with many other top-ranking party leaders, were placed on public trial and forced to make outrageous "confessions." The trials represented only the tip of the iceberg (see "Landmarks in History").

Nor were the rank-and-file workers spared. Throughout the mid- to late 1930s, Stalin collectivized the Soviet labor force by means of forced-draft or conscript labor. Work units were structured and regimented along military lines. This policy gave birth to the so-called **gulag archipelago**, a network of draconian slave-labor camps maintained and operated by the Soviet secret police where social and political undesirables were forced to live. Through the gulag system, railroads, canals, and dams were constructed in remote and inaccessible areas where workers would not voluntarily go. Aleksandr Solzhenitsyn, the celebrated dissident writer who chronicled life in the labor camps, estimated that they held as many as twelve million prisoners at any given time, perhaps half of them political prisoners. "As some departed beneath the sod," he noted, "the Machine kept bringing in replacements."[29]

At the close of 1938, Stalin stood alone at the top. Industrial development had been spurred, but the Soviet Union was anything but a worker's paradise. Terror had brought about great political changes, with many luminaries from the pages of Soviet Communist Party history uncovered as traitors and placed on public trial. The list of the accused read like an honor roll of the October Revolution. The military high command had been sacked, the party rank and file cleansed of all political impurities, and the "toiling masses" reduced to a new level of industrial serfdom. Although he ruled until his death in 1953, Stalin (and the legacy of Stalinism) would be identified, above all, with the bloody purges of the 1930s.

Germany under Hitler

The overriding theme of National Socialist (Nazi) Party ideology during the Third Reich (1933–1945) was the elimination of the Jews and other "social undesirables" and the ascendency of the "Aryan" race—a fiction that nonetheless obsessed Hitler and his followers. Through Nazi ideology and propaganda, the German people came to accept the persecution of the Jews, the necessity of eventual war, and the radical transformation of society. Every aspect of German life became politicized. Dissident artists, journalists, and academicians were silenced. New state organs, including the Reich chambers for literature, press, broadcasting, theater, music, and fine arts, were created for the primary purpose of censoring or quelling potentially "dangerous" forms of written or artistic expression.

In the realm of music, German folk tunes were exalted over "decadent" modern music and classical music written by composers of Jewish lineage, such as Felix Mendelssohn and Gustav Mahler. Modern art was likewise condemned, and the works of virtually every well-known contemporary artist were banned. Literature under the Nazi regime fared no better. According to one chronicler of the Third Reich, "Blacklists were compiled ceaselessly and literary histories were revised. . . . The 'cleansing' of libraries and bookstores presented some problems, but the destruction and self-destruction of German literature was achieved within a matter of months through the substitution of second- and third-rate scribblers for first-rate writers and by inhibiting contacts with the outside."[30]

The Nazi attack on the arts was indicative of the lengths to which Hitler would go to ensure that Nazi values were propagated. But perhaps no part of German life more vividly demonstrated Hitler's commitment to a new future than the Nazi school system. As Bracher pointed out, "While National Socialism could substitute little more than ideology and second-rate imitators for the literature and art it expelled or destroyed, its main efforts from the very outset were directed toward the most important instruments of totalitarian policy: propaganda and education."[31]

Nazi educational policy was implemented in three principal ways. To begin with, educators and school administrators who were suspected of opposing Hitler, Nazism, or Nazi educational "reform" were promptly removed from their positions. Then all academic subjects were infused with ideological content reflecting Hitler's anti-Semitic racial theories. History became "racial history," biology was transformed into "racial biology," and so on. Finally, the Nazis established special schools to train a future party elite, including military leaders, party officials, and government administrators. Students were assigned to these schools according to age group and career orientation. The Adolf Hitler Schools, to cite one example, taught 12- to 18-year-old students who wished to become high party functionaries. In general, all special schools taught certain basic core courses (such as racial history and biology) and emphasized military drill (for example, the training of the infamous Hitler Youth).

The Nazi educational program turned out to be all too successful. In the judgment of one authority, "Just as teachers and parents capitulated to the pressures of the regime, so on the whole did the indoctrination of the young succeed. The young, who were receptive to heroic legends and black-and-white oversimplifications, were handed over to the stupendous shows of the regime."[32] Education of the young was reinforced by carefully planned pomp and ceremony: "From

iStockphoto.com/Alatom

The overriding theme of Nazi Party ideology was the elimination of the Jews and other "social undesirables" and the subsequent creation of a "racially pure" Aryan nation. Between 1933 and 1945, at least six million European Jews plus countless others perished in Nazi death camps. The entrance to the infamous Auschwitz death camp is pictured here. The sign above the gate reads, "Work makes you free."

earliest childhood, they were exposed to flag raisings, parades, nationwide broadcasts in the schools, hikes, and camps."[33] Indoctrination and propaganda, not terror, became the instruments by which the children of the Third Reich were initiated into the new order.

Mass indoctrination combined with a preexisting anti-Semitism made it possible for Hitler to carry out the murderous racial policies that culminated in the Holocaust. After seizing power, Hitler implemented his anti-Jewish policy in stages, each more radical than the one before.[34] First came the attempt to define who precisely was and was not a Jew. Then the regime launched a systematic campaign to isolate Jews from the mainstream of German life and to expropriate their property. Next all Jews who had not fled the country between 1933 and 1938 were forcibly removed from German society and sent to the infamous concentration camps. This mass deportation presaged the fourth and final step—genocide.

Hitler's maniacal obsession was ultimately his undoing. Even on the brink of defeat, Hitler continued to divert resources needed to prosecute the war to the Final Solution (the liquidation of the Jews). In the end, some six million European Jews plus countless others, including the mentally ill, physically disabled, Soviet prisoners of war, gay men, Gypsies, Jehovah's Witness members, and Polish intellectuals, as well as many Polish Roman Catholics, were annihilated.

China under Mao

Mao Zedong's rise to power in China is an epic example of revolutionary struggle—a true mass movement in a poor, peasant-dominated society. For more than twenty years (1927–1949), Mao waged a bitter "war of national liberation" against the **Kuomintang**, headed by Chiang Kai-shek, as well as against the Japanese during World War II. In the mid-1930s, Mao was one of the leaders of the legendary Long March, a 6,000-mile trek, during which his ragtag band of guerrillas repeatedly evaded capture or annihilation by the numerically superior and better-equipped forces of Chiang's Nationalist army. By 1949, when Mao finally won the last decisive battle and assumed command of the Chinese nation, Mao had been waging class war in the name of the Chinese masses for more than two decades.

Kuomintang
The Chinese Nationalist Party, led by Chiang Kai-shek, defeated by Mao Zedong in 1949.

Mao prided himself not only on his revolutionary exploits but also on his political thought. In time, the "thoughts of Chairman Mao," compiled in his pocket-sized little Red Book, of which millions of copies were printed and mass distributed, attained the status of holy scripture in Chinese society. His vision of a new, classless state and of the exemplary communist cadres and comrades who would typify this morally reeducated society inspired the radical policies that have become known collectively as Maoism.

Although Mao's worldview was undoubtedly shaped by the basic tenets of Marxism, 1920s China was a preindustrial society without a true proletarian (industrial-worker) class or a "monopoly capitalist" class of the kind Marx had described in *Das Kapital*. The bane of China's peasant masses was not factory bosses but greedy landlords and bureaucratic officials preoccupied with the preservation of the status quo and of their own power and privilege. If the oppressed majority were to be liberated, those in power would have to be overthrown. To accomplish such a historic mission, Mao believed, violent revolution "from below" was an unavoidable necessity. "Political power," he wrote, "grows out of the barrel of a gun."[35]

As part of his adaptation of Marxism, Mao glorified the Chinese peasants—whom he described as "poor and blank"—as models of communist virtue because they had never been corrupted by "bourgeois materialism" and big-city decadence. Mao thus made the peasantry (not the proletariat) the cornerstone of his visionary utopian society.

Once in power, Mao turned China into a kind of social laboratory. The first step included campaigns to eradicate specific evils such as individualism and bourgeois materialism by "reeducating" the masses or exterminating undesirable social elements (landlords, counterrevolutionaries, and "bandits"). Accompanying mass reeducation was a sweeping land reform program culminating in the wholesale collectivization of Chinese agriculture. This bitter pill was administered with massive doses of propaganda, as well as brute force. In the early 1950s, a major push to industrialize China along Stalinist lines was also launched.

Alternating periods of freedom and repression marked Mao's rule. In 1956, for example, he announced the beginning of the **Hundred Flowers campaign**, which promised a relaxation of strict social discipline. As a high-ranking party official put it at the time, "The Chinese Communist party advocates [that] one hundred flowers bloom for literary works and one hundred schools contend in the scientific field... to promote the freedom of independent thinking, freedom of debate, freedom of creation and criticism, freedom of expressing one's own opinions."[36] What followed probably caught Mao by surprise. Public protests and anti-party demonstrations occurred at Beijing University and other campuses. Strikes and scattered riots, even isolated physical attacks on party officials, occurred in various parts of the country. Instead of a hundred flowers, thousands of "poisonous weeds" had grown in the Chinese garden. The incipient rebellion was rapidly suppressed in a brutal "anti-rightist" crackdown. The official party newspaper, *People's Daily,* announced the whole Hundred Flowers campaign had been a ploy to lure the enemies of the state into the open.

Hundred Flowers campaign
A brief period in China (1956) when Mao Zedong directed that freedom of expression and individualism be allowed; it was quashed when violent criticism of the regime erupted.

Peter Griffin/PublicDomainPictures.net

Following his successful war of national liberation against Chiang Kai-shek's Kuomintang, Mao's rule between 1949 and 1976 was characterized by periods of vast social experimentation, as well as by violent periods of political repression. Here a youthful looking Mao is depicted on Chinese currency officially known as the Renminbi (more commonly called the yuan).

In retrospect, the Hundred Flowers episode was a mere warm-up for Mao's **Great Leap Forward** (1957–1960)—a spectacular but ill-conceived attempt to catapult China onto the stage of "full communism" by means of mass mobilization. Mao set out to prove that anything is possible, and that subjective factors like human will can triumph over objective conditions such as poverty, illiteracy, and external dependency. Put differently, the idea "was to take advantage of China's rural backwardness and manpower surplus by realizing the Maoist faith that ideological incentives could get economic results, that a new spirit could unlock hitherto untapped sources of human energy without the use of material incentives."[37] Thus did Mao's brand of "Marxism" stand Marx on his head.

The most visible and dramatic symbol of the Great Leap was the establishment of communes—relatively large and self-sufficient residential, social, economic, and political-administrative units. Private plots were absorbed into the communal lands, and private belongings, including pots and pans and other domestic items, were pooled. In addition, as Fairbank noted,

> Many peasants for a time ate in large mess halls. All labor was to be controlled. Everyone was to work twenty-eight days of the month, while children went into day nurseries. This would bring large-scale efficiency to the village and get all its labor, including its womanpower, into full employment.[38]

Why were the unprecedented measures associated with Mao's grandiose concept instituted? According to China scholar John King Fairbank, "The result, it was hoped, would be agricultural cities with the peasants proletarianized and uprooted from their own land"—with an overall view toward giving the state increased control over labor resources and changing the peasants' attitudes.[39]

The Great Leap Forward was a colossal failure with disastrous consequences for the Chinese people, including severe crop failures and food shortages. But Mao was undeterred. After a brief period of retrenchment, he launched a second "revolution from above." From 1966 to 1969, the **Great Proletarian Cultural Revolution** shook Chinese society to its very foundations. In the first stage, designed to wash away all that was "decadent" in Chinese life, Mao closed all schools and urged his youthful followers, called the Red Guards, to storm the

Great Leap Forward
Mao Zedong's attempt, in the late 1950s and early 1960s, to transform and modernize China's economic structure through mass mobilization of the entire population into self-sufficient communes in which everything was done in groups.

Great Proletarian Cultural Revolution
A chaotic period beginning in 1966, when the youth of China (the Red Guards), at Mao Zedong's direction, attacked all bureaucratic and military officials on the pretext that a reemergence of capitalist and materialist tendencies was taking place. The offending officials were sent to forced labor camps to be "reeducated."

bastions of entrenched privilege and bureaucratic authority. Millions of Maoist youths obligingly went on a rampage throughout the country for many weeks. This phase of the revolution accomplished its intended purpose, as the Red Guards "smashed most of the Republic's bureaucratic institutions" and "invalidated [the government's] authority and expertise."[40] Officials were dragged out and put on public display to be ridiculed and humiliated, accompanied by purges and summary executions; temples and historical treasures lay in ruins, as did the party, government, and armed forces.

The second stage of the Cultural Revolution called for positive action to replace the previous order with a new and better one. Unfortunately, the economy and society, especially in urban areas, had been severely disrupted. Factories and schools, shut down by marauding Red Guards, did not reopen for months or even years.

The ultimate cost of the Cultural Revolution is incalculable. One fact, however, is clear: Mao's unrelenting efforts to prove that human nature is infinitely malleable—and society, therefore, infinitely perfectible—foundered on the rocky shores of political reality, not to mention the folly of eliminating a whole generation of educated citizens. His death in 1976 closed a unique chapter in the political history of the modern world.

THE HUMAN COST OF TOTALITARIANISM

Totalitarian regimes present a stark contrast between ends and means—diabolical deeds in pursuit of utopian dreams. The death camps of Nazi Germany and the labor camps of Stalinist Russia stand as the essence of twentieth-century totalitarianism.

All told, the three revolutions featured in this chapter—Nazi Germany, Stalinist Russia, and Maoist China—caused at least one hundred million civilian deaths by most estimates.[41] The number defies imagination; but these estimates, which include World War II casualties, are quite plausible and may actually be low.[42] War-related deaths in the European theater during World War II numbered "about six million for Germany and Austria, 20 million for the Soviet Union, and about 10 million for all other European countries, for a total of about 36 million."[43] Hitler's Final Solution was estimated to have resulted in the deaths of an estimated five to six million European Jews, not to mention an indeterminate number of non-Jews whom Hitler considered "social undesirables." All in all, perhaps forty-two million people died directly or indirectly as a result of Hitler's policies.

The Russian Revolution of 1917 and its aftermath were hardly less costly in terms of human life. Between 1918 and 1923, approximately three million Soviet citizens died of typhus, typhoid, dysentery, and cholera, and about nine million more disappeared, probably victims of the terrible famine that scourged the country in the early 1920s. Many perished in a severe drought in 1920–1921, but others died of direct or indirect political causes.

In the late 1920s, during Stalin's titanic industrialization drive, the kulaks were annihilated as a class. In addition, another killer famine—at least partially self-inflicted—occurred in the early 1930s. When deaths associated with the early stages of collectivization are combined with deaths brought on by famine, the mortality figures range in the millions for the period from 1929 to 1934.

But the worst was yet to come. After 1934, Stalin's purges directly claimed hundreds of thousands of lives and led to the premature deaths of some two million "class enemies" in Siberian forced-labor camps. Nor did the end of the great purges in 1938 stop the political hemorrhaging that, together with World War II, drained Soviet society of so much of its vitality. Millions of labor camp inmates died between 1938 and 1950 due to the inhumane treatment and harsh conditions they had to endure on a daily basis.

The human cost of the revolution in Maoist China exceeds that of Stalinist Russia. Between the time of the communist takeover in 1949 and the Great Leap Forward in 1957, several mass campaigns were launched to combat allegedly counterrevolutionary forces. After the Chinese Communist takeover, the land reform program cost the lives of several million "landlords" and rich peasants between 1949 and 1952. Other campaigns against counterrevolutionaries in the early 1950s cost another million and a half lives. Periodic anti-rightist campaigns and collectivization of agriculture after 1953 also took a toll.[44] According to scholar C. W. Cassinelli,

> Accurate information is not available—and often even informed guesses are lacking—on the cost of the *first decade* [emphasis supplied] of the People's Republic. An estimate of twelve million lives is modest but reasonable.[45]

These figures do not include deaths caused by hardship and privation, most notably those traceable to the dislocations that accompanied the Great Leap Forward in the late 1950s.

The Cultural Revolution (1966–1969) was another bloody episode in Chinese history, although firm estimates of the number of casualties are impossible to make. A much heavier toll was probably taken by the Chinese gulag system. As many as fifteen million may have perished as a direct result of inhumanly harsh labor camp conditions. When Cassinelli tallied the total number of politically related deaths, including "another million from miscellaneous causes," he arrived at the astonishing figure of "about 33.5 million."[46] Though unverifiable, this number is consistent with the available evidence. The mere fact that it is not implausible speaks volumes.

Totalitarian regimes typically refuse to concede that any goal, no matter how visionary or perverse, is beyond political reach. The compulsion to validate this gross misconception may help explain the pathological violence that marks totalitarian rule.

THE SANGUINARY IMITATORS

Stalin's Russia, Hitler's Germany, and Mao's China are the best-known examples of totalitarianism, but not the only ones. A surprising number of dictatorships have tried to copy or imitate totalitarianism's Big Three. Incredibly, one went to even greater extremes to purge society than either Stalin or Mao did, and in this case, to which we now turn, the tyrant committed genocide against his own nation.

Pol Pot governed Cambodia (renamed Kampuchea) from 1975 to 1979.[47] He and his followers sought to create a radically new society, based on the rustic and Spartan life of peasant cadres. All vestiges of the old order—everything from the calendar to the family—were eradicated. Pol Pot proclaimed 1978 "Year Zero," which turned out to be grotesquely appropriate, for at the end of his brief rule, some two million Cambodians (of a population of 7.5 million) would be dead—the victims of purges, starvation, or persecution.

Another example of totalitarian rulers is Ethiopia's Colonel Mengistu, who ruled from the mid-1970s until 1991.[48] Mengistu attempted to reorganize the nation by physically relocating its people into regimented population and refugee centers for the purposes of permitting intensive governmental surveillance as well as encouraging systematic propaganda and indoctrination. His efforts destroyed the nation's agriculture, and a killer famine resulted. Although the West made efforts to feed the starving children of Ethiopia, their government appeared curiously detached. While his people went hungry, Mengistu staged lavish military parades, sold wheat to neighboring nations, and used the money he received to buy weapons. In May 1991, with his regime under siege by a coalition of rebel forces, Mengistu fled the country.

North Korea is the last Soviet-style totalitarian state still in existence. Kim Il-sung ruled over the Hermit Kingdom (so named for the nation's self-imposed isolation from the outside world) until his death in July 1994. He was succeeded by his son, Kim Jong-il, who ruled from 1994 to 2011 as a brutal and lunatic tyrant bent on building nuclear weapons and indifferent to the suffering and starvation of his own people. The second Kim's claim to rule was hereditary—his father not only founded North Korea's totalitarian dictatorship after World War II but also established a ruling dynasty.

Kim Jong-il ruled North Korea the same way his father did—by perpetuating a personality cult similar to those once perpetrated in Russia by Joseph Stalin or in China by Mao Zedong. In a bizarre twist, when his father died, Kim Jong-il made him (the father) president for eternity. North Korean propagandists ascribe to Kim (the son) the authorship of a thousand books while he was a college student. When Kim Jong-il died in 2011, he was succeeded by (guess who) his son, Kim Jong-un.

North Korea maintains a huge army, entrenched along the 38th parallel that divides Korea, and poses a standing threat to South Korea, a close ally of the United States since the Korean War (1950–1953). That major war was started when northern Korea invaded the south, a fact that continues to shape Western perceptions of North Korea today. The war ended in a draw and without a peace treaty.

In stark contrast to the prosperous south, North Korea remains one of the poorest countries on earth. Malnutrition and even starvation threaten the population—children in North Korea are, on average, considerably shorter and weigh less than children of the same age in South Korea. North Koreans are not allowed to have contact with South Koreans, including family members.

After 9/11, President Bush declared North Korea to be part of an "axis of evil" along with Iraq and Iran. North Korea again found itself in the international spotlight when the late Kim Jong Il Jong-il defied the Bush administration's demand for a "complete, verifiable, and irreversible" halt to its nuclear weapons program. U.S. relations with North Korea did not greatly improve in the ensuing years. A preoccupation with the wars in Iraq and Afghanistan, as well as a deepening recession in the wake of the U.S. financial crisis in 2008–2009, led President Obama, like his predecessor, to seek an accommodation with Pyongyang (the capital).

North Korea conducted a nuclear test in 2006 and in April 2009 attempted to launch a long-range missile, but the test failed. Pyongyang is also thought to have stockpiles of chemical and biological weapons. North Korea's extreme self-isolation and secrecy make it impossible for the outside world to know where the country is headed, what the leadership is thinking, or even who's in charge. So if the Hermit Kingdom does have a nuclear "gun," nobody knows for sure whose finger is on the trigger.

Under the regime of Ayatollah Khomeini (1979–1989), Iran displayed most of the elements associated with totalitarian rule: an attempt to transform society; a dictatorship that demanded abject loyalty, obedience, and self-sacrifice; an all-encompassing creed that rationalized, explained, and justified arbitrary rule; press censorship; and secret police, show trials, summary executions, and holy wars.

Eventually, no aspect of life in Iran lay outside governmental control. Teachers, textbooks, education, entertainment, the legal system, even courtship and sexual mores were made to conform to fundamental Islamic beliefs. The regime declared war on civil servants, intellectuals, professional and entrepreneurial elements of the middle class, and all others who had endorsed modern Western ways and culture.

After Khomeini's death, his successors relaxed some of the strict moral and social controls but maintained a rigidly theocratic police state fiercely opposed to the West and, in particular, to the U.S. presence in neighboring Iraq and the Persian Gulf. In addition, Tehran launched a major nuclear research and development program, raising a general alarm in the international community and causing the United States to orchestrate a global campaign to stop Iran from building nuclear weapons.

When President Obama assumed office, he quickly attempted to break the diplomatic impasse with Iran. During the 2008 presidential campaign, Obama had roundly criticized President Bush for refusing to engage in direct talks with Tehran. In early 2009, the new administration expressed a willingness to meet with Iran "without preconditions." In April 2009, then President Mahmoud Ahmadinejad declared in a televised speech, "We have prepared a package that can be the basis to resolve Iran's nuclear problem. It will be offered to the West soon."[49] In 2015, the world was still waiting—and hoping—for that promise to bear fruit.

The Iranian case demonstrates three important points. First, totalitarian regimes, like democracies and traditional dictatorships, can share a single essence and assume many different guises. Second, although totalitarian regimes appear to be rigid and unchanging on the outside, they are, in fact, not impervious to change on the inside. Third, in the modern world of the twenty-first century, totalitarian regimes cannot succeed *economically* in isolation—that is, without access to global markets, the latest technological advances, and sources of investment capital.

Ironically, as totalitarianism disappeared in Russia and Eastern Europe, it reared its ugly head in Afghanistan—a country the Soviet Union had invaded in 1979. It is generally accepted that the protracted and costly conflict in Afghanistan hastened the demise of the totalitarian Soviet state. It turned out to be Moscow's Vietnam, but with more dire consequences.

In the 1990s, totalitarianism in a different guise arose from the ashes of the war that had ravaged Afghanistan during the previous decade. That regime—the Taliban—captured the world's attention after September 2001 because the mastermind behind the 9/11 operation, the actual perpetrators, and the organization that carried it out were all based in Afghanistan. The Taliban was providing sanctuary for Osama bin Laden, who had set up training camps for his stateless "army."

But the Taliban was not just *harboring* a terrorist organization; it was itself a terrorist organization—a full-blown totalitarian regime complete with a single all-powerful ruling clique, harsh and arbitrary laws, kangaroo courts, predictable (guilty) verdicts, summary executions turned into public spectacles, severely restricted personal freedoms, closed borders, and a captive population. Afghans were not allowed to emigrate or travel abroad. Girls were not allowed to go to school. Boys were not allowed to fly kites. Women had no rights, had to be completely covered in public, and could not work outside the home. Wife beating, no matter how severe, was not a crime—not even when the victim died.

After more than three decades of political upheaval, economic paralysis, and inconclusive civil war, Afghanistan remains one of the poorest of the least developed states in the world. None of the turmoil, however, has fundamentally changed the traditional structure and culture of Afghan society, which raises a serious question about outside intervention and whether revolutionary change is ever possible unless it comes from within.

TWILIGHT OF TOTALITARIANISM?

Hitler boasted that his would be a thousand-year empire, but it lasted less than a decade. In fact, in stark contrast to the great autocratic empires of ancient history, totalitarian regimes are short-lived. They tend to burst on the scene like a meteor and burn out. Why might that be?

Fatal wars with other nations, such as Hitler's defeat by the Allies in World War II, can bring a sudden end to totalitarian states. The death of a particularly charismatic or successful ruler—Mao or Stalin, for instance—can precipitate an extended downward spiral. Drab, indistinguishable successors who rule by coercion and terror rather than by consent may undermine the economic efficiency, moral vitality, and political idealism on

Comic fans know all about Captain America. Here, cartoonist Bryant Arnold depicts him as an old man. In real life he'd have to be in his 90s. (According to the legend, he enlisted in the U.S. Army in 1940 to fight the Nazis.) The 2011 movie *Captain America: The First Avenger* involves a Super-Soldier serum, a top secret research project, and a Nazi plot to take over the world. The Nazi era is over, but it's not forgotten.

state capitalism
An economy falling somewhere between a Soviet-style command economy and a Western-style market economy; the Communist China's economy after Mao is one contemporary example.

theocracy
A government based on religious dogma and dominated by clerics; Iran is the major example in the contemporary world.

which legitimate political power ultimately rests. Thus, the collapse of the Soviet Union was preceded by both a prolonged period of economic disintegration and a widespread loss of faith in the regime and its political ideals; a period of "totalitarianism in decline."[50]

The Peoples' Republic of China, to cite a key example, has morphed into a one-party authoritarian system with a transitional economy falling somewhere between a Soviet-style command economy and a Western-style market economy—a hybrid form sometimes called **state capitalism**. Iran after Khomeini remains a **theocracy** with limited personal freedoms, but it cannot in fairness be called totalitarian. North Korea alone still qualifies as unambiguously totalitarian. The totalitarian regimes in Kampuchea and Ethiopia are long gone—only the scars and bitter legacies remain.

In sum, the best thing about the worst regimes in today's world is that they tend to be short-lived. Unfortunately, totalitarian tyrants need only a little time to do a lot of damage.

SUMMARY

Totalitarian states attempt to realize a utopian vision and create a new political order. Like authoritarian states, totalitarian states are nondemocratic. Yet these two regime types differ in several important respects. In particular, totalitarian regimes seek total control over all aspects of their citizens' lives and demand active participation, rather than passive acquiescence, on the part of the citizenry.

The three major totalitarian states of the past century—Soviet Russia, Nazi Germany, and Maoist China—appear to have gone through several distinct stages of development. The first stage coincides with a period of violent revolution. The five major elements necessary for a successful revolution are charismatic leadership, ideology, organization, propaganda, and violence. During the second stage, power in the hands of the totalitarian ruler is consolidated, opposition parties are eliminated, the party faithful are put in charge, and real or imagined rivals within the party are killed.

The third stage attempts to bring about the total transformation of society. In the Soviet Union, Stalin launched this effort in 1928 with the first Five-Year Plan. In Nazi Germany, Hitler's goal of "racial purification" provided the rationale for a totalitarian drive that culminated in World War II and the Holocaust. In Maoist China, the first attempt to transform Chinese society, the Great Leap Forward, failed miserably in the late 1950s and was followed by the Cultural Revolution of the 1960s.

The human costs of totalitarianism have been staggering. Actual numbers cannot be verified, but even the roughest estimates suggest the totalitarian experiments of the twentieth century brought death or appalling hardship to many millions of people.

Totalitarian states appear in many guises, and there is no guarantee new ones will not emerge in the future. Indeed, the ousted Taliban regime in Afghanistan qualified as a new form of totalitarianism that used a perverted form of Islam as a political ideology.

KEY TERMS

totalitarianism   132
rectification   133
cells   136
partiinost   136
Gleichschaltung   138
propaganda   138
salami tactics   140
purges   140

Gestapo   141
kulaks   142
collectivization   143
gulag
   archipelago   144
Kuomintang   146
Hundred Flowers
   campaign   147

Great Leap
   Forward   148
Great Proletarian
   Cultural
   Revolution   148
state
   capitalism   154
theocracy   154

REVIEW QUESTIONS

1. What sets totalitarianism apart from other nondemocratic forms of rule?
2. What is required for a successful total revolution to take place?
3. How do totalitarian states consolidate power?
4. What are the basic characteristics of the totalitarian system of rule?
5. What were the primary aims of Stalin's drive to transform Soviet society in the 1930s? What methods did he use?
6. How and why did Hitler try to reshape German society?
7. What was the impetus behind the Great Leap Forward and the Cultural Revolution? What methods did the Maoists employ? What kind of a society did they envisage?
8. What have been the costs of totalitarianism, as measured in human terms?
9. "Totalitarianism passed away with the deaths of Hitler, Stalin, and Mao." Comment.
10. Name two or three recent examples of totalitarianism. Which one(s) are still in existence? Write a short essay on an existing totalitarian state, answering the following three questions. Who rules? How? To what ends?
11. Hitler's totalitarian state ceased to exist after a crushing military defeat. Does the evidence suggest that totalitarian regimes can ever change from within—that is, without being defeated in war—or not? Comment.
12. "As the world's oldest democracy, the United States government should never engage in direct talks with totalitarian states." Do you agree or disagree? Explain your position.

WEBSITES AND READINGS

Websites

Rise of Adolf Hitler and Timeline of Holocaust: www.historyplace.com/worldwar2/riseofhitler/index.htm

History of Totalitarianism in Europe 1919–1939: http://www.thecorner.org/home.htm

Biography of Mao Zedong: http://www.kirjasto.sci.fi/mao.htm

Marxist Internet Archive: http://www.marxists.org/subject

Cambodia Genocide Program: http://www.yale.edu/cgp/

Readings

Alpers, Benjamin J. *Dictators, Democracy, and American Political Culture: Envisioning the Totalitarian Enemy, 1920s–1950s*. Chapel Hill: University of North Carolina Press, 2003. A look at how totalitarianism was portrayed in U.S. books, movies, the news media, academia, and the political arena when it posed the greatest threat to Western-style democracy.

Arendt, Hannah. *Totalitarianism*. San Diego: Harcourt, 1968. A theoretical analysis of Nazi Germany and Stalinist Russia that spotlights totalitarian states' emphasis on terror, persecution, and mass murder.

Bracher, Karl Dietrich. *The German Dictatorship*. New York: Holt, 1972. A definitive study of Hitler's totalitarian state.

Browning, Christopher. *Ordinary Men: Reserve Police Battalion 101 and the Final Solution in Poland*. New York: HarperCollins, 1992. This study of a civilian Nazi police force engaged in mass murder argues that human beings commit the most evil acts imaginable when faced with tremendous social pressure to conform.

Bullock, Alan. *Hitler and Stalin, Parallel Lives*. New York: Knopf, 1992. A comprehensive and definitive account of the lives and character of these two tyrants.

Cassinelli, C. W. *Total Revolution: A Comparative Study of Germany Under Hitler, the Soviet Union Under Stalin, and China Under Mao*. Santa Barbara, CA: Clio Books, 1976. The writer argues that these regimes are fundamentally similar.

Chirot, Daniel. *Modern Tyrants: The Power and Prevalence of Evil in Our Age*. New York: Free Press, 1994. Hitler and Stalin are presented as the prototype of a new kind of ideological tyrant, who seeks to mold society according to specific "scientific" theories about how society should be constructed.

Conquest, Robert. *The Great Terror: A Reassessment*. New York: Oxford University Press, 1991. A detailed, carefully researched book that provides the definitive scholarly account of Stalin's bloodiest days.

_____. *The Harvest of Sorrow: Soviet Collectivization and the Terror-Famine*. New York: Oxford University Press, 1987. A chilling account of Stalin's war against the kulaks and the Ukrainians.

Friedrich, Carl, and Zbigniew Brzezinski. *Totalitarian Dictatorship and Autocracy*. New York: Praeger, 1965. A pioneering effort that attempts to classify and describe totalitarian states.

Fromm, Erich. *Escape from Freedom*. New York: Henry Holt, 1941. The author argues that human beings who cannot or will not accept the risks, dangers, and burdens of freedom will naturally turn to authoritarianism.

Gleason, Albert. *Totalitarianism: The Inner History of the Cold War*. Oxford and New York: Oxford University Press, 1997. Examines totalitarianism as a concept; this is a history of the idea behind a terrifying reality.

Goldhagen, Daniel Jonah. *Hitler's Willing Executioners: Ordinary Germans and the Holocaust*. New York: Knopf, 1996. A provocative and controversial argument that the Holocaust was predominantly carried out by ordinary citizens infected by a virulent anti-Semitism that was particularly rampant in Germany.

Hoffer, Eric. *The True Believer: Thoughts on the Nature of Mass Movements*. New York: Harper & Row, 1951. A perceptive examination of individuals who form the nucleus of mass movements.

Kiernan, Ben. *The Pol Pot Regime: Race, Power, and Genocide in Cambodia Under the Khmer Rouge, 1975–79*. New Haven, CT: Yale University Press, 1996. This detailed examination of one of the darkest periods of human history makes the controversial argument that race, and not ideology, motivated the Cambodian genocide.

Koestler, Arthur. *Darkness at Noon*. New York: Bantam Books, 1984 (First publication, 1940). A classic work of fiction about a totalitarian system in which a Bolshevik loyalist and true-believer is put on trial for treason, while his all-powerful tormentor, identified only as Number One, remains anonymous and without mercy.

Magstadt, Thomas. "Marx, Moral Responsibility, and the Cambodian Revolution," *The National Review*, July 24, 1981.

_____. "Bleeding Cambodia: The Great Leap Downward," *Reason*, July, 1982.

Menand, Louis. "The Devil's Disciples," *The New Yorker*, July 28, 2003. An excellent review of old and new books on totalitarianism that begins with this tantalizing observation: "Few puzzles in political philosophy are more daunting than the Problem of the Loyal Henchmen."

Menze, Ernest, ed. *Totalitarianism Reconsidered*. Port Washington, NY: Associated Faculty Press, 1981. A provocative collection of essays presenting different points of view on the usefulness of distinguishing between totalitarianism and other political orders.

Orwell, George. *Nineteen Eighty-Four*. New York: Knopf, 1992. The classic fictional caricature of Stalinist Russia that is full of insights regarding the nature of totalitarian societies.

Ponchaud, François. *Cambodia: Year Zero*. New York: Holt, 1978. A chilling historical account of Pol Pot's rule in Kampuchea.

Selznick, Philip. *The Organizational Weapon: A Study of Bolshevik Strategy and Tactics*. North Stratford, NH: Ayer, 1980. A penetrating study of Soviet institutions under Lenin and Stalin.

Shapiro, Leonard. *Totalitarianism*. New York: Praeger, 1972. An evenhanded and informative discussion of the scholarly controversy that surrounds the concept of totalitarianism.

Solzhenitsyn, Aleksandr. *One Day in the Life of Ivan Denisovich,* translated by H. T. Willetts. New York: Farrar, Straus and Giroux, 1992. A description of the Soviet labor camps that became a cause célèbre in the Soviet Union during Nikita Khrushchev's de-Stalinization program.

Wiesel, Elie. *Night*. New York: Bantam Books, 1982. A poignant autobiographical account of the suffering of the victims of totalitarian rule—in this case, the Jews under Hitler.

Established and Emerging Democracies

CHAPTER 7

Parliamentary Democracy
Pros and Cons of Perishable Governments

Learning Objectives

1 Describe Aristotle's concept of a mixed regime, and identify a modern political system that perhaps best embodies the Aristotelian model.

2 Compare the U.S. presidential model to British-style parliamentary systems.

3 Argue the case both for and against a powerful executive branch.

4 Compare and contrast the executives in the UK, Germany, and France.

5 Compare and contrast the British parliament and the U.S. Congress.

6 Explain the view that Japanese government and society is Western in form but Japanese in substance.

7 Identify the obstacles to parliamentary democracy in India and Israel compared to countries in Western Europe.

We have not only to study the ideally best constitution. We have also to study the type of constitution which is practicable [that is, the best for a state under actual conditions]. . . . The sort of constitutional system which ought to be proposed is one which men can be easily induced, and will be readily able, to graft onto the system they already have.

Aristotle, *The Politics*[1]

Long ago, the great Greek philosopher Aristotle made a compelling case for the systematic comparison of political systems. Today, the value of comparative political analysis is widely recognized in the discipline. We have seen that strikingly different forms of government are possible—democratic, authoritarian, and totalitarian—and that there are many permutations of each form. Authoritarian regimes, for example, can be monarchies, military juntas, theocracies, and so on. Democracies also vary widely, as we noted in Chapter 4. The form of democracy found in the United States is the one Americans know best, of course, but most Europeans are far more familiar with a very different model of democracy, one that originated in England—a country that is separated from the Continent by a narrow expanse of water and a wide expanse of history and culture.

In this chapter, we compare parliamentary democracies with a view to identifying how they differ between and among each other. We also ask what variations appear to result in dysfunctional systems and whether or not remedies are available. Finally, we ask how parliamentary systems compare to our own and revisit the question asked in Chapter 4: Which model of democracy works better?

GREAT BRITAIN: MOTHER OF ALL PARLIAMENTS

The British system has its origins in horticulture, not architecture. Unlike the U.S. Constitution, it is not based on a blueprint devised by rational minds. Instead, it grew out of England's unique history and geography and its evolving political culture. The organic nature of the British parliamentary system raises an obvious question about whether it can be transplanted, but first we take a closer look at this unique representative democracy.

The political system that formed after the American Revolution represented a sharp break with the European autocratic tradition, and it required a fresh political theory. Although there is no British counterpart to *The Federalist Papers*, we find a sort of homegrown theory of British-style democracy in the writings and speeches of Edmund Burke. Burke detailed Britain's long unbroken chain of political development, during which, significantly, economic equality and political liberty expanded together. As the monarchy declined in power, British government became increasingly democratic, evolving into a **parliamentary system**. It was gradually established that the British monarch would automatically accept Parliament's choice of prime minister (PM). In time,

parliamentary system
In contrast to the U.S. presidential model based on the separation of powers, parliamentary systems feature a fusion of powers in which parliament chooses the prime minister who then forms a government; parliament can in turn force the government to resign at any time by a simple majority "no-confidence" vote.

The United Kingdom's Queen Elizabeth II is a beloved monarch who reigns but does not rule. As the ceremonial chief of state, she has served a nation proud of its traditions with dignity and grace since 1952.

the PM eclipsed the monarch as the head of government. Today, the monarch Queen Elizabeth II is the head of state but with no executive power—a beloved figurehead.

A Mixed Regime

From the seventeenth century on, the British parliamentary system became a prime example of what Aristotle called a **mixed regime**, in which different institutions represent different classes. The House of Lords represented the interests of the traditional governing classes, whereas the House of Commons gradually came to represent the interests of the general electorate, expressed through free elections and increasing suffrage.

Great Britain's mixed regime historically promoted stability by providing representation for classes that otherwise might have become openly hostile toward one another. The famed British welfare state of today is designed to perpetuate a large middle class through an elaborate system of income redistribution. Although the traditional representation of separate social classes has become largely irrelevant, the two major parties—the Conservatives and Labour—continue to retain the distinctions, attitudes, and values of a class-conscious society.

The supreme legislative body is the popularly elected House of Commons (see below), while the aristocratic House of Lords has been reduced to little more than a debating society. The Parliament Acts of 1911 and 1949 made it impossible for the House of Lords to block legislation passed by the Commons. Today, the Lords can do no more than propose amendments or delay a bill from taking effect for one year.

About eight hundred individuals (including appointed life peers and hereditary peers, plus twenty-five Anglican bishops and archbishops) claim formal membership in the House of Lords, but only about three hundred play an active role.[2] The British upper house can easily be seen as an anachronism in the modern age, perhaps even a little ridiculous—and not only to outsiders.

A major reform bill to democratize the Lords by drastically reducing its size (to 450) and directly electing 80% of its members was introduced in the House of Commons in 2012. The Liberal Democrats and the Labour Party, along with some Tory backbenchers, demanded a popular referendum to decide the matter.[3] But the plan was abandoned after the Conservatives "broke the coalition contract," according to "Lib Dem" leader Nick Clegg (his Liberal Democrats joined David Cameron's Conservatives to form a coalition government when no party won a clear majority in the 2010 national elections).

Fusion of Powers

mixed regime
A nation in which the various branches of government represent social classes.

Under the British parliamentary system, the executive branch—the prime minister and the cabinet—is formed after each election and consists of the leaders of the victorious party within the House of Commons, endorsed by the Parliament and appointed by the queen. Although all members of Parliament, including those in the opposition party, are free to question and criticize, the victors control the government.

When a victorious party leader takes over in the United Kingdom, it is understood the new government will serve for no more than five years before seeking a new mandate from the voters. A British PM's job security entirely

POLITICS AND POP CULTURE

"YOU MIGHT THINK THAT . . .

. . . but I couldn't possibly comment." This is the famous line spoken by Ian Richardson's character, Francis Urquhart, in the *House of Cards* trilogy. The title is a clever wordplay on the British House of Commons. Urquhart is the cunning Chief Whip of the Conservative Party whose life ambition is to become prime minister. He will stop at nothing to get what he wants. An attractive young woman plays a key role in the story; she's a journalist who has ambitions of her own. They use each other. It's a fatal attraction fit for a plot in Shakespeare (think: *Macbeth* and *Richard III*).

House of Cards is a television drama that originally aired on the BBC in 1990. After much critical acclaim, two sequels were made: "To Play the King" and "The Final Cut." Andrew Davies adapted all three screenplays from books written by Michael Dobbs, a former Chief of Staff at Conservative Party headquarters when Margaret Thatcher was prime minister. The BBC series later aired on public television in the United States and again gained a wide audience and high praise. In 2013, a new adaptation of the story, starring Kevin Spacey as Francis "Frank" Underwood as the Majority Whip of the Democratic Party, was commissioned and released by Netflix.

In the United States, the public has long had a fascination with the American presidency—a fact that's reflected in a wide variety of films, plays, and novels, including: *The American President* starring Michael Douglas, *Election* (Reese Witherspoon), *Mr. Smith Goes to Washington* (Jimmy Stewart), *12 Angry Men* (Henry Fonda), *The Candidate* (Robert Redford), *Milk* (Sean Penn), *Lincoln* (Daniel Day-Lewis), and many more. Day-Lewis even won the Academy Award for best actor for his presidential role in 2012.

But Hollywood alone can't satisfy the public's appetite for stories about presidents. *The West Wing*, a political drama mainly set in the White House, is one of the most popular TV series in recent years. Martin Sheen, Stockard Channing, and Alan Alda play leading roles. The series ran from 1999 to 2006, encompassing 156 episodes. Consultants who helped ensure the accuracy of character portrayals as well as the action and atmospherics of life in the White House included former White House staffers Dee Myers, Marlin Fitzwater, Peggy Noon, and Gene Sperling. Netflix now offers viewers all seven seasons, and multiple Twitter handles for *West Wing* characters continue to keep the show alive.

So if your friends try to tell you that politics is boring, just say, "You might think that. . . ." Then invite them to the movies and wait for the curtain to go up.

Whether it's a play by William Shakespeare or a Steven Spielberg film about politics, the characters are always flawed, the plot involves intrigue and betrayal, and the endings are seldom happy. Dramatizations of politics in Shakespeare's day when monarchs ruled and today when democracy is well-established in many countries are not that different. What does that say about the success or failure of democratic institutions in creating a new kind of political culture, one conducive to "life, liberty, and the pursuit of happiness"? Think about it.

(Hint: "Democracy is the worst form of government, except for all the others." Is it true? Winston Churchill is often cited as the source of this comment. Assuming he said it, was he celebrating or denigrating democracy?)

depends on his or her ability to maintain "confidence"—an elusive but vital intangible in British politics. Think about what the ever-present possibility of falling from power means in practice.

In the United States, elections are held at regular intervals that never change; voters always know exactly when the next election will be held. Not so in the British system. Parliament is required to stand for election every five years, but the prime minister can call for elections earlier if it looks as though the mood of the electorate momentarily favors the ruling party. By the same token, Parliament can force the government to resign by a vote of "no confidence." In this event, either a new government is formed under new leadership or the queen dissolves Parliament and calls new elections.

The authority to decide when to call new elections can be a big advantage for the party in power. Prime Minister Margaret Thatcher made particularly shrewd use of this authority in 1983, for example. After serving only four years, the "Iron Lady" (as she was often called) capitalized on a surge of British patriotism, spurred by a war with Argentina over the Falkland Islands, to renew the Conservative Party's mandate to rule for another five years.

In 1987, Thatcher again called for an election four years into her term and won. Three years later, Thatcher's popularity fell as a result of her support for a poll tax that many Britons considered regressive and unfair. Under attack within her own Conservative Party, she resigned, turning over the reins of government to her successor, John Major. But by then she had already held the United Kingdom's highest office for more than a decade—a twentieth-century record.

More recently, Prime Minister Tony Blair was forced to resign due to his unstinting support for the U.S.-led war in Iraq—a war strongly opposed by the vast majority of British voters. In the summer of 2007, Blair gave way to his chief rival in the Labour Party, Gordon Brown. In 2010, Gordon Brown was ousted when the British voters deserted Labour in large numbers, giving the Conservatives and a third party, the Liberal Democrats, a sweeping victory in national elections (see Figure 7.1). The upshot, as noted earlier, was a coalition government under Conservative Party leader David Cameron in partnership with "Lib Dem" party leader Nick Clegg,

In the United Kingdom, the resignation of a chief executive who has lost public confidence is expected. Prime Minister Neville Chamberlain (1869–1940) resigned in 1940, despite the fact that his party still commanded a majority in the House of Commons. So widespread was his unpopularity after his "appeasement" of Adolf Hitler at Munich that he stepped aside and let another Tory leader take charge—a chap named Winston Churchill. The redoubtable, gravel-voiced, cigar-smoking Churchill, of course, proved to be one of history's great wartime leaders.

Other circumstances may cause a government to fall before its five-year term has expired. If the majority party's policy is unpopular or if the government becomes embroiled in a scandal, a motion of no confidence can be introduced. If the motion passes in a **no-confidence vote**, the government resigns. The prime minister then asks the monarch to dissolve parliament and call for new elections. In countries with multiparty parliamentary systems, governments come

no-confidence vote
In parliamentary governments, a legislative vote that the sitting government must win to remain in power.

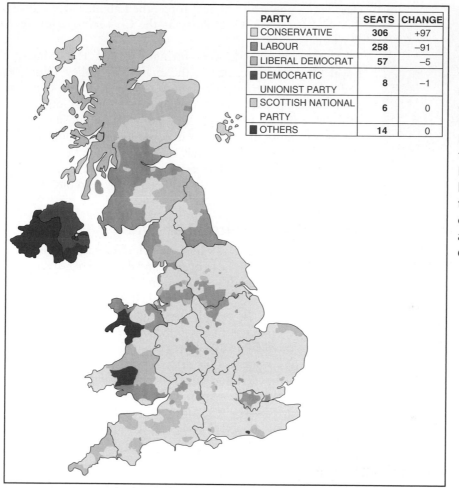

PARTY	SEATS	CHANGE
☐ CONSERVATIVE	306	+97
◼ LABOUR	258	−91
☐ LIBERAL DEMOCRAT	57	−5
◼ DEMOCRATIC UNIONIST PARTY	8	−1
☐ SCOTTISH NATIONAL PARTY	6	0
◼ OTHERS	14	0

FIGURE 7.1 Map of United Kingdom. Although the UK, like the United States, has two major parties, several other parties can and do win seats in Parliament. The Liberal Democrats are the major spoiler in British elections and became partners with the Conservatives in a coalition government after the 2010 elections.

and go frequently in this manner, but it is rare in the United Kingdom, where it has not happened since Prime Minister James Callaghan lost a no-confidence motion in 1979.

Disciplined Parties

Party discipline in the United Kingdom manifests itself in a ritual show of public unity, coherent party platforms, and bloc voting. British parties differ sharply in this respect from U.S. parties, which are more loosely organized and often less important to voters than are the personal traits of the candidates.

In Parliament, the government demands unwavering support from its majority-party members. Strong party discipline does not mean that MPs never cross the aisle to vote with the opposition, however. They can also abstain on an important vote or even engineer a party realignment. In the early 1900s, for example, when the trade union movement transformed the British working

party discipline
In a parliamentary system, the tendency of legislators to vote consistently as a bloc with fellow party members in support of the party's platform.

National Archives UK

Prime Minister David Cameron led the Conservative Party to victory in the May 2010 national elections. Failing to win a clear majority of seats in Parliament, he had to form a coalition government with the Liberal Democrats as the junior partner.

class into a powerful political force, the Labour Party eclipsed the old Liberal (or Whig) Party as the Conservative (or Tory) Party's chief rival.

The party-out-of-power—formally called Her Majesty's **Loyal Opposition**—criticizes the majority's policy initiatives and holds the government accountable for its actions. Criticism is usually tempered by civility, because the Opposition "thinks of itself as the next government, and a wise Opposition operates within those limits which it hopes its own opponents will respect when the tables are turned."[4] In fact, the Leader of the Opposition is considered an essential role player in the British system—and since 1937 given a special salary paid out of public funds.

Are Two Heads Better Than One?

Unlike the United States, where one chief executive (the president) serves as both the head of state and the head of government, Great Britain separates these functions. The British head of state is the reigning monarch. Queen Elizabeth II, "arguably the most famous person in the world," has occupied the British throne for over half a century. The monarch is a national symbol and a source of unity, personifying the state but not wielding its powers.

The actual head of the government is the prime minister, who, in close consultation with key cabinet members (often called the *inner cabinet*), sets domestic and foreign policy. National policy emerges from this leadership core, which then presents it to the cabinet as a whole. Cabinet members who are out of step with the government on an important policy matter are expected to resign quietly.

A Model with Legs

Most European democracies are patterned after the British system, although with mixed results. France under the Third and Fourth Republics (1876–1958) and Italy since World War II came to be dominated by political parties and a parliament. The political party system became fragmented, internal party discipline broke down, and the government fell victim to never-ending legislative skirmishes. Strong executive leadership was often missing in France before 1958 and remains a chronic problem in Italy to this day.

Such conditions have led to political stalemate in both countries at different times. In France, during the entire life span of the Third and Fourth Republics, no single party ever won a majority of seats in the National Assembly, and no fewer than 119 governments ruled the country, each with an average life of less than a year. A similar malaise has plagued Italy, which had more than forty prime ministers between 1945 and 1986 (one per year on average).

Yet today, parliamentary governments are found all over Europe, with few exceptions—a major triumph in a region divided by war, revolution, and totalitarian rule until recently. Parliamentary rule is Britain's gift to Europe and the world—a model with "legs."

Loyal Opposition
The belief, which originated in England, that the out-of-power party has a responsibility to formulate alternative policies and programs; such a party is sometimes called the Loyal Opposition.

THE BRITISH AGENDA: A Sampler

The Economy

Under Labour leadership, Britain developed a model welfare state in the 1950s and 1960s but was stricken by stagflation, or simultaneous recession and inflation, in the 1970s. In 1979, Margaret Thatcher led the Conservative Party to victory and set about reprivatizing state-run industries and systematically deregulating the British economy.

Voters turned the Conservatives out of office in 1997 for the first time in nearly two decades. Under Labour Prime Minister Tony Blair's market-friendly policies, the British economy outperformed Europe's other major economies (Germany, France, and Italy). Gordon Brown moved into 10 Downing Street when Blair moved out in 2007. As Chancellor of the Exchequer (or Finance Minister) in the Blair government, Brown was in charge of economic policy. Although few disputed his qualifications for the job, Prime Minister Brown's personal popularity hit a low ebb even before the 2008 global financial crisis took its toll.

Public confidence in Brown's economic crisis-management skills briefly boosted his standing in opinion polls, but his lackluster personality and a sluggish economy set the stage for a Conservative comeback in the May 2010 elections. The British economy has bounced back from the post-2008 global recession faster than the EU as a whole. The UK had one of the lowest unemployment rates in 2014-2015 and the highest rate of GNP growth among Europe's major economies. Britain's addiction to deficit spending and public debt continues despite unpopular austerity measures that the Conservatives under Prime Minister David Cameron have put into effect.

The Voting System

In a referendum held in May 2011, British voters roundly defeated a proposal to change the UK's tradition-bound first-past-the-post electoral system to a new Alternative Vote (AV) system. Under the AV system, voters rank candidates in order of preference; if no one gets 50%, the candidate with the least votes is eliminated and voters' second choices are allocated to the candidates; that process continues until a winner emerges. The Conservative "Lib Dem" coalition pushed for this change. Labour opposed it, fearing it was part of a larger Tory strategy aimed at changing constituency boundaries (called "redistricting" in the United States)

Paying for the Welfare State

In 2010, PM Cameron unveiled a plan calling for deep cuts in public spending as a cure for Britain's chronic budget deficits. This austerity plan came at a time when sluggish growth and rising unemployment prompted many economists to call for stimulus rather than austerity. Cameron's deficit reduction target for 2012 was missed, despite the Tory government's unpopular belt-tightening policies.

Even a steadily falling unemployment rate in 2013–2014 did not placate disgruntled voters. In 2014 by-elections, the populist UK Independence Party (UKIP) won 17% of the popular vote nationally—roughly the same share as Labour—taking half its votes from the Conservatives. That showing positioned UKIP to be the spoiler in the May 2015 national elections.

Northern Ireland

The four options for settling the decades-old civil war in Northern Ireland (Ulster) are (1) reunification of Ulster with Ireland, (2) independence from Britain, (3) devolution (home rule), or (4) integration with Britain. Before a 1994 cease-fire, the provisional Irish Republican Army (IRA) repeatedly carried out terrorist attacks in an effort to force the British from Northern Ireland and made bold attempts to assassinate both Thatcher and Major. By the time of the cease-fire, some three thousand people had been killed on both sides—Catholic and Protestant.

(Continued)

(CONTINUED)

In January 2013, news of loyalist youths "fighting street battles with police on an almost nightly basis over the last six weeks" shattered any illusions about an end to sectarian violence in Northern Ireland.

Scottish Independence

Scotland's independence vote was one of the biggest stories in 2014. Polls indicated that it would be a close vote. Money poured in; celebrities weighed in; the world looked in; the suspense mounted. When the results were announced on the morning after the September election, British loyalists had reason to rejoice: Scotland had voted to stay in.

"English Votes on English Laws"

On the morning after the Scottish independence vote, the *Economist* stated that David Cameron had "triggered a new constitutional crisis." Scotland, Northern Ireland, and Wales, he pointed out, have their own assemblies, but England continues to be run from Westminster (Parliament), where they all have representation and can vote on all bills, including ones that only affect England. This, he said, has to change.

One proposal is for a double majority system in Parliament whereby measures solely affecting England would have to be passed by a majority of the whole House of Commons *and* a majority of English MPs.

The European Union

The United Kingdom joined the European Union (EU) in 1973. However, its policy toward the EU has been characterized by continuing ambivalence. In the 1990s, when adoption of the euro went into effect, British popular opinion was strongly against a common currency, and London opted out. In the minds of most British voters, the euro crisis has vindicated the UK's decision not to join the euro zone.

Prime Minister Cameron is an outspoken Eurosceptic, saying there is "a lack of democratic accountability and consent that is . . . felt particularly acutely in Britain." In early 2013, he pledged to hold a national referendum—an in-or-out vote—on British EU membership. In October 2014, Parliament nixed a bill to establish a referendum vote in 2017. Meanwhile, even UK ally Denmark agreed that London should pay the EU the extra £1.7 billion the European Commission demanded.

Are All Parliamentary Systems Alike?

No. Most parliamentary systems function in ways similar to the British system, but in countries with multiple parties and proportional representation (see Chapter 11), the government often cannot count on a clear parliamentary majority. Where there are five or six parties in parliament—and none with a popular base to match either of Britain's two major parties—it often happens that no single party has enough seats to form a government. In this event, coalitions, or two or more parties joining forces, are necessary. Sometimes coalition governments work fairly well; in the worst cases such as Italy, however, parliamentary rule can be unstable and even chaotic.

FRANCE: PRESIDENT VERSUS PARLIAMENT

The U.S. presidential and British parliamentary systems represent two different approaches to democratic government. Under the Fifth Republic founded in 1958 and forged in the crucible of a constitutional crisis, France fashioned a unique form of representative democracy that combines elements of both models. Today, France is the world's fifth-ranked economy, sixth-ranked exporter; in the first half of 2012, it was the fourth-largest recipient of foreign direct investment and has more multinational corporations in the global *Fortune 500* than the United Kingdom.

In June 2012, French voters brought François Hollande's Socialists to power, replacing Nicolas Sarkozy's center-right government. It was a stunning victory for a party that in the United States is wrongly perceived as incompatible with a stable democratic order. Wrongly, because it's not the first time it's happened in France and, despite all sorts of dire Chicken Little predictions emanating from the land of the Anglo-Saxons, the sky over ancient Gaul has not fallen.

The Fifth Republic: A Hybrid System

The Fifth Republic was meant to overcome what its founder, Charles de Gaulle, understood to be the great nemesis of French politics: impotent executives dominated by fractious legislatures (see Figure 7.2). As de Gaulle was fond of pointing out, France's first three experiments in republican government all ended in dictatorship.

FIGURE 7.2 Map of France. Divided into 22 regions, 95 departments, and 36,851 communes, France is a political-administrative jigsaw puzzle. Mayors of major cities often become prominent national politicians and are often also members of the National Assembly (the French parliament) at the same time.

Under the Fourth Republic (1946–1958), governments had lasted an average of six months. A profusion of political parties, some of fleeting duration, turned France's parliamentary system into a travesty. Worse, parties at opposite ends of the political spectrum—Gaullists on the right and Communists on the left—both sought to undermine the Fourth Republic's constitution and force the resignation of weak coalition governments.

The Fifth Republic's constitution was short and simple. Its provisions were guided by de Gaulle, who, in a famous address twelve years earlier, declared:

> The unity, cohesion, and internal discipline of the Government of France must be sacred objects or else the country's leadership will rapidly become impotent and invalid. . . . The executive power should, therefore, be embodied in a Chief of State, placed above the parties . . . to serve as an arbiter, placed above the political circumstances of the day, and to carry out this function ordinarily in the Cabinet, or, in moments of great confusion, by asking the nation to deliver its sovereign decision through elections. It is his role, should the nation ever be in danger, to assume the duty of guaranteeing national independence and the treaties agreed to by France.[5]

In sum, the centerpiece of the constitutional system, de Gaulle insisted, would be a strong executive branch to counterbalance the perennially divided parliament. The centerpiece of the executive, however, would be the chief of state (president) rather than the prime minister.

France's Dual Executive

The basic elements of de Gaulle's diagnosis are etched into nearly every provision of the 1958 constitution that pertain to the organization of public powers. In accordance with the parliamentary model, the French executive is divided (a **dual executive**). On paper, the prime minister (or *premier*) is the head of government; the president is head of state. Unlike the British monarch, however, the French president is democratically elected and wields executive powers similar, though not identical, to those of the U.S. president. As France's leading political figure, the president is independent of the legislative branch, possesses a wide array of powers, and serves a fixed term in office (seven years from 1962 to 2000, but now five years).

France's constitution positioned the president as the arbitrator of conflicting interests and competing political parties. As the nation's chief diplomat and foreign-policy decision maker, the president appoints and dismisses the prime minister, dissolves the legislature, calls for new elections, declares a state of emergency, issues decrees having the force of law, and presides over cabinet meetings. In addition, the president can call for a national referendum, a device used a number of times since the 1960s. For example, in 1962, de Gaulle's popular referendum to replace the electoral college with direct election of the president passed by an overwhelming majority. In a democratic age, nothing gives a political leader more legitimacy or moral authority than a mandate from the voters.

Compared with the president, France's prime minister generally exercises less power and influence, although there is now a greater balance between these two offices than there was in de Gaulle's time. As head of the government, the

dual executive
In a parliamentary system, the division of the functions of head of state and chief executive officer between two persons; the prime minister serves as chief executive, and some other elected (or royal) figure serves as ceremonial head of state.

prime minister presides over the cabinet and is responsible to the legislature. Together, the prime minister and the cabinet oversee the running of government and the bureaucracy.

In general, however, the constitution of the Fifth Republic does not clearly delineate which powers or functions belong to the president and which belong to the prime minister. Due to his unrivalled stature in French politics, de Gaulle enjoyed considerable latitude in interpreting the constitution. Thus, during his tenure, the presidential powers were elastic—de Gaulle could, and did, stretch them to fit the needs of the moment.

No president after de Gaulle, however, has so dominated French politics. François Mitterrand, a Socialist, served as France's president for fourteen years (1981–1995), but he was no de Gaulle. Neither was his center-right successor, Jacques Chirac. Not until the election of Nicolas Sarkozy (2007–2012)—a one-term wonder—did France have a charismatic center-right president with a Napoleon-sized ego to match de Gaulle's (and a diminutive stature to match Napoleon's). By that time, France had endured (and the Fifth Republic had survived) three periods of cohabitation in which the president and prime minister were from opposing political parties.

Reduced Role of the National Assembly

If the presidency was clearly the big political winner under the Fifth Republic, the legislature was the loser. France's parliament is divided into two houses, the Senate and the National Assembly. The French Senate, which has only limited powers, is indirectly elected. The **National Assembly**, its parliament, is popularly elected from multimember districts in a double ballot (two-stage) election process. As the focal point of legislative power, the National Assembly must approve all proposed laws. However, the word *law* is rather narrowly defined by the 1958 constitution; in fact, many matters are left to the executive branch, which has the power to issue "decree laws."

The National Assembly is more interesting for the powers it does *not* have. For example, the French parliament has no power to introduce financial bills. If it fails to approve the government's budget by a certain deadline, the executive can enact the budget by fiat (presidential decree).

Rival Parties and Seesaw Elections

Unlike the United States, France has a wide spectrum of political parties. Rival parties exist on both the left and the right, as well as in the center, and both the Far Right and the Far Left often play a significant role in elections.

The two most important parties of the Left are the Communist Party and the Socialist Party. When left-leaning voters began turning away from the Communists in the late 1970s, the Socialist Party was the primary beneficiary on the left. In 1981, the Socialists won a resounding victory at the polls, and Socialist leader Mitterrand was elected president (a post he held for fourteen years after winning reelection in 1988).

In 1993, however, the center-right won a landslide victory, retaking control of the National Assembly; two years later, the neo-Gaullist candidate Jacques

National Assembly
Focal point of France's bicameral legislative branch that must approve all laws.

Chirac was elected president. Combined with the decisive center-right triumph in Senate elections that same year, Chirac's election put the conservatives back in the driver's seat—but not for long.

In the June 1997 elections, parties of the left, again led by the Socialists, won overwhelmingly. Chirac bowed to the will of the electorate and named Socialist Party leader Lionel Jospin the new prime minister. Jean-Marie Le Pen's far-right National Party received more votes than the Gaullist UDF (Union for French Democracy)—14.9% to 14.2%—and nearly as many as Chirac's RPR, which had 15.7%. Yet the two center-right parties garnered 242 seats in the National Assembly, while the National Party won but a single seat. Why?

France's electoral system stacks the deck against fringe parties by requiring a second round of balloting when no candidate receives an absolute majority of votes in the first round. In practice, this means parties with similar (and less uncompromising) ideological stances can form temporary alliances between the two balloting rounds. As a result, the influence of fringe or extremist parties is greatly diminished.

In 2002, Chirac's new center-right umbrella party called Union for a Popular Movement (UMP) won a clear majority in the National Assembly (357 seats, or 62% of the total) in the second round of balloting, but the result was misleading. The UMP, despite the preelection realignment that merged three center-right parties into one, received only 33% of the votes in the first round (just 7% more than the Socialists). The election outcome once again underscored the way France's two-step electoral process produces a parliamentary majority out of a fragmented party system.

When center-right candidate Nicolas Sarkozy was elected president in May 2007, French voters gave the center-right a solid majority in the National Assembly, but the Socialists were not shut out: in fact, they made a net gain of forty-six seats while the UMP actually lost forty-four seats. In the 2008 local and regional elections, the UMP lost numerous city mayoral races and eight departmental presidencies.

In the 2012 national elections, Sarkozy and the center-right parties suffered a stinging defeat. François Hollande was elected president in a runoff, and his Socialist Party won 314 parliamentary seats, 25 seats more than the 289 needed to command an absolute majority. Eighty percent of the people voted, a big turnout that significantly changed the composition of the new parliament: "younger, more feminine, and more ethnically diverse than the old one, which was dominated by grey hair and suits."[6] Many were first-timers, too—about 40%.

Constitution under Pressure: Testing the Balance

The Fifth Republic has brought stable democracy to France for more than six decades now. De Gaulle's influence has extended well beyond his presidency, and his broad interpretation of presidential powers prevails to this day. De Gaulle's preference for a strong national economy that mixes a large role for the state (a French tradition) with a healthy respect for free-market principles remains firmly fixed as a part of his legacy. Nonetheless, without de Gaulle's firm hand on the tiller, "long-range programs gave place to expediency, and party alignments obeyed the logic of electoral tactics rather than policy making."[7]

From the start of the Fifth Republic, France faced the danger of a **divided executive**: when the president and prime minister represented two different parties, embraced different ideologies, and advanced different policies. Although a deadlocked government remains a hazard in France's dual-executive system, France has survived three periods of cohabitation, most recently from 1997 to 2002.

divided executive
Situation in French government in which the president and the prime minister differ in political party or outlook.

Justice à la Française

The French judicial system is divided into two basic types of courts—ordinary courts and administrative courts—with different jurisdictions. Despite this rather routine distinction, France's legal system has some interesting twists. For example, the High Council of the Judiciary, chaired by the president, decides on judicial promotions and discipline, whereas the High Court of Justice has the power to try the president for treason and members of the government for crimes related to abuses in office.

IDEAS AND POLITICS

THE FRENCH AGENDA: A Sampler

The Economy

High taxes, mounting public debt, double-digit unemployment, an inflexible labor market, and a generally sluggish economy plagued France even before the global Great Recession brought a sharp downturn in the Europe's single-market economy. The 2008 Wall Street banking crisis exposed the dire financial straits of Greece and several other EU countries, which in turn put Europe's common currency—the euro—in jeopardy.

The euro crisis destabilized France not least because French banks held over 90 billion euros of Greek sovereign debt (government bonds) and Greece was teetering close to default (bankruptcy). If France's banks were crippled, the lumbering French economy would also be crippled.

Sarkozy faced a dilemma: adopt unpopular austerity measures or continue to pile bigger and bigger budget deficits on a rapidly rising national debt. With public spending approaching three-fifths of national output (57%) and chronic budget deficits rising above 90% of GDP, France was losing its competitive edge within the EU, making it too difficult for companies to lay off workers and running a risk that businesses would relocate to more business-friendly countries.

Of course, France's economic woes did not disappear when Sarkozy was turned out of office in 2012. It then fell to his successor, François Hollande and his Socialist party to pick up the pieces, including an 11–12% unemployment rate (double that for workers under age twenty-five).

The Welfare State

France's cradle-to-the-grave social spending model is facing huge challenges in the new era, which some are calling the decline of the West.

France's much-remarked thirty-five-hour workweek is immensely popular, but critics say it places France at a competitive disadvantage. France, they say, is paying the price for profligate spending and pandering to labor unions, farmers, pensioners, and other special interests. Without a major overhaul of pensions—a highly charged political issue—the French treasury faces a rising tide of red ink. Wealth, corporate profits, and high incomes are heavily taxed, a fact dramatized in early 2013 when famed French film star Gerard

(Continued)

Depardieu, protesting a new tax hike on the rich, left his native France for Russia where he will pay a flat 13% income tax rate rather than the 75% on income over 1 million euros ($1.3 million) in France.

Immigration and National Identity

There are an estimated fourteen million French citizens of foreign ancestry (about 23% of the total population) and more than three million Arabs, mostly from Algeria, Morocco, and Tunisia. High unemployment and urban decay have eroded traditional French hospitality toward political exiles, refugees, and asylum seekers, as well as immigrants in general. Immigrants are often willing to work for low wages, crowd into cities, and compete for scarce jobs.

The election of Nicolas Sarkozy, a hard-liner on immigration, put the issue of "national identity" high on the French government's policy agenda. In 2009, France's minister for Immigration and National Identity, Eric Besson, kicked off a three-month national debate on "what it means to be French." Muslim headscarves, citizenship classes, and a proposal to make schoolchildren sing France's national anthem ("La Marseillaise") were among the issues raised—symptoms of a deeper vein of race-tinged social tension in France that is not likely to disappear any time soon.

In 2010, 120,000 people became naturalized French citizens, but this number fell by more than 30% percent in 2011-2012. With an eye to the 2012 elections, the Sarkozy government deported 33,000 illegal immigrants in 2011 and moved to introduce a multiple-choice history and culture test for would-be citizens. But the new Socialist government scrapped this plan, easing the path to citizenship. A good proficiency in the French language is still required.

No one knows how many illegal immigrants reside in France now, but with the Socialists back in power, more will likely seek legal status.

Foreign Policy

De Gaulle's disdain for the "special relationship" between the United States and the UK and the mutual mistrust it fostered played a key role in shaping France's postwar foreign policy. France participated in the U.S.-led campaign against the Taliban regime in Afghanistan after the 9/11 attacks, but President Chirac opposed the invasion of Iraq in 2003, defiantly blocking U.S. efforts in the UN Security Council to get the United Nations to endorse the action.

A virtual partnership between France and Germany has been an essential pillar of the European Union from its origins. Differences over how to deal with the euro crisis has led to severe strains in Franco-German relations in recent years. How this bilateral relationship at the core of the European project is managed in a time of crisis will go a long way toward deciding the fate of France and Europe in the coming years.

President Sarkozy sought to repair France's strained relations with Washington and London. France rejoined NATO's integrated military structure in 2009 after a forty-year absence. In November 2010, Britain and France signed a landmark fifty-year treaty on defense and security, envisaging the joint use of aircraft carriers, a 10,000-strong joint expeditionary force, and unprecedented levels of collaboration on nuclear missiles. Whether this new look in French foreign policy will survive now that Sarkozy has left the scene only time will tell.

The Constitutional Council is composed of nine justices—three nominated by the president of the republic, three by the president of the National Assembly, and three by the president of the Senate—plus all the past presidents of the republic. This judicial watchdog plays several vital roles in the French system. It supervises presidential elections and can investigate and resolve contested legislative races.

Under certain conditions, it can also render opinions on laws and the constitution. The cases that come before the council deal with political issues brought by either the president of the republic, the prime minister, the two presidents of the legislature, or at least sixty members of the National Assembly or the Senate.

The Balance Sheet

From the social and political upheavals of the late eighteenth century to the launching of the Fifth Republic in 1958, France's quest for national unity and constitutional democracy was troubled and turbulent, but in the past half-century it has enjoyed the most stable government for the

Socialist Party leader Francois Hollande was elected president of France in May 2012; he succeeded center-right President Nicolas Sarkozy.

longest period since the French Revolution. This political system has proven to be more durable and adaptable than its predecessors, but the nation now faces big problems and avoiding unpopular solutions is not an option for Hollande's Socialist government.

Of course, France is not alone in facing many daunting challenges that call for creative policy responses. Europe is struggling, which only complicates

IDEAS AND POLITICS

HOLLANDE: Stimulate This . . .

Hollande promised to stimulate a sluggish economy and reduce France's chronic budget deficit by raising taxes on the rich, large companies, and financial transactions. The jobless rate remained above 10% in 2014-2015, and the GDP growth rate was flat—under 1.0%. In a desperate effort to stimulate the economy, Hollande reneged on his promise not to raise taxes on the middle class.

Meanwhile, Hollande was caught in another form of stimulating activity—namely, having an affair with a woman who was not the mother of his children. An opinion poll in the fall of 2014 found that 62% of French voters wanted Hollande to resign, but Hollande vowed to hang on, saying: "No poll, no political turmoil will make me go."

Scandals say a lot about cultural differences. Scandals in politics typically involve either money or sex. In parliamentary democracies like Britain, a sex scandal can bring down a government. In presidential systems based on the separation of powers, sex scandals can also be extremely disruptive. In Latin America, voters tend to be indifferent to the private lives of politicians. Does it matter how high-profile politicians and public figures behave in private? Think about it.

(Hint: Google any of the following names: Monica Lewinsky, Bill Clinton, Nelson Rockefeller, Megan Marshack, Christine Keeler, and John Profumo; also, Dominique Strauss Kahn, Francois Mitterand, Anne Pingeot, Felix Faure, and Marguerite Steinheil.)

matter for any country on the continent trying dig out of a deep hole. The big question now is whether the *dirigiste* (state-directed) French economic model is sustainable without dismantling the entrenched welfare state—a move almost certain to have profoundly destabilizing effects on a society accustomed to benefits its government can no longer afford.

GERMANY: FEDERALISM AGAINST MILITARISM

Modern Germany burst onto the scene in the second half of the nineteenth century with sweeping military victories over Austria in 1866 and France in 1871. Those two wars were a prelude to two world-shattering wars in the first half of the twentieth century.

The two world wars changed Europe in fundamental ways. Germany started both of these calamitous conflagrations—a fact Europeans will never forget and never let Germany forget. After World War II, Germany and its former capital were partitioned and divided between East and West for fifty years. In 1989 the infamous Berlin Wall was dismantled, and the country reunited following the collapse of the communist regime in East Germany.

Germany's postwar responsibility for Europe's condition is still costing Germans in all sorts of ways. In 2011-2012, for example, with the "euro crisis" threatening to spread like a contagion, Europe expected Germany to bear the burden of bailing out Greece and saving Europe's common currency. Meanwhile, in Greece and elsewhere, Germany was scorned and excoriated for demanding tough austerity measures as the price of bolstering the embattled euro. To understand Germany's turbulent history, it is necessary to go back to the bitter (for Germans) legacy of World War I.

The Weimar Republic

Hitler's Third Reich sprang from the ashes of the **Weimar Republic,** Germany's first experiment with constitutional democracy. The Weimar Republic was ill fated from the moment of its inception because it was associated with Germany's humiliating defeat and the harsh peace terms imposed by the Allied powers after World War I. Burdened by punitive reparations, Germany fell victim to high unemployment, widespread business failures, and rampant inflation.

In the face of such turbulence, German society became polarized between the extreme Right and the extreme Left. In the words of one authority, "Stable democratic government was in jeopardy throughout the life of the Weimar Republic. The country was governed . . . by unpopular minority cabinets, by internally weak Grand Coalitions, or finally, by extra-parliamentary authoritarian Presidential Cabinets."[8] Between the two world wars (1919–1939), the country's fragile political institutions were put to a test that proved fatal.

Weimar Republic
The constitutional democracy founded in Germany at the end of World War I by a constitutional convention convened in 1919 at the city of Weimar; associated with a period of political and economic turmoil, it ended when Hitler came to power in 1933.

Given this background, the founding of the Federal Republic of Germany in 1949 was risky. Whether democracy could ever be made to work in a country that had only recently bowed to a deranged dictator, served a totalitarian state, and looked the other way while millions of innocent people were systematically murdered was an open question.

Divided Germany: The Cold War in Microcosm

World War II destroyed Germany. The nation and its capital, Berlin, were subsequently bifurcated into the German Democratic Republic (GDR), or East Germany, and the Federal Republic of Germany (FRG), or West Germany. From 1949 to 1990, Germany and Berlin, the historical capital, became powerful symbols of the Cold War—the ideological rivalry between the United States and the Soviet Union—and the unbridgeable East–West divide.

The West German "economic miracle" in the 1950s was unmatched. In the 1960s, it was the main engine driving the newly established Common Market, a six-nation trading bloc that in time evolved into the world's largest single economy—the European Union. West Germany's success stood in stark contrast to the dismal Stalinist state of East Germany. The building of the Berlin Wall in 1961 aimed at keeping East Germans from escaping to the West highlighted the dramatic difference between the two Germanys. Berlin and "the Wall" became a metaphor for the Iron Curtain, proof that the peoples of the East living under communism were "captive nations" in the most literal sense, and a reminder to all in the West of the need for vigilance and unity in the ongoing struggle between freedom and tyranny.

The Great Merger: Democracy Triumphant

For three decades, East Germans, whose living standards were far below West Germans', had not been allowed to emigrate or even to visit relatives across the border.[9] It was the reform-minded Soviet leader Mikhail Gorbachev who opened the floodgates.

East Germany's end came at a time when rebellion was rife in Central and Eastern Europe: Poland and Hungary had already taken giant steps toward dismantling communist rule, and Czechoslovakia, Romania, and Bulgaria were not far behind. For East German Communism, the unraveling started with a mass exodus and ended with the bulldozing of the Berlin Wall following the collapse of the East German regime in late 1989.

Following free elections in the former GDR in the spring of 1990, the two Germanys entered into a formal union, with Berlin restored as the capital. Together, the nearly simultaneous collapse of Soviet power and German reunification set the stage for the eastward expansion of the European Union.

The remaking of Germany carried a big price tag. West Germans paid for the economic rehabilitation of East Germany with a 7.5% income tax surcharge and a higher sales tax. Nonetheless, unemployment in eastern Germany remained high in the 1990s, hovering around 18%, nearly twice the rate in western Germany.

German Federalism

Prior to 1989, the Federal Republic of Germany consisted of ten states, or *Länder* (singular, *Länd*), plus West Berlin. It was about equal in size to the state of Oregon. The merger of the two German states in 1989 added six new *Länder* to the federal structure (see Figure 7.3). Even so, no fewer than twenty-five countries the size of the united Germany would fit comfortably into the territory of the United States.

The main reason for German federalism is political rather than geographic— namely, to act as a barrier to overcentralization of power. The primary responsibility of the *Länd*, or state governments, is to enact legislation in specific areas, such as education and cultural affairs. They alone have the resources to implement laws enacted by the federal government, exercise police powers, administer the educational system, and place (limited) restrictions on the press. The federal government in Berlin has the exclusive right to legislate in foreign affairs, citizenship matters, currency and coinage, railways, postal service and telecommunications, and copyrights. In other areas, notably civil and criminal law, as well as laws regulating the economy, the central government and the *Länder* have shared powers, although the European Union plays a large and ever-greater role in regulating the economies of its twenty-eight member-states.

The *Länder* are more powerful and receive a larger proportion of tax revenues than U.S. states do. For example, individual and corporate income taxes are split between Berlin and the *Länder* in equal 40% shares; the remaining 20% goes to the cities. The *Länder* also receive one-third of the value-added tax, the large but hidden sales (or turnover) tax used throughout Europe.

The Executive

Germany has a parliamentary form of government with a divided executive. The most important government official is the chancellor, akin to a prime minister. The head of the majority party in the lower house of parliament becomes the chancellor; if no one party enjoys an absolute majority, as has often been the case, a coalition government chooses the chancellor. The chancellor, with parliamentary approval, appoints and dismisses cabinet members. In case of a national emergency, the chancellor becomes commander-in-chief of the armed forces (which are integrated into the NATO alliance structure) and is responsible for the formulation and implementation of public policy. In 2005, Angela Merkel became the first woman chancellor in German history.

The president, as the titular head of state, serves a largely symbolic function, except in the event of political stalemate in parliament. Chosen indirectly for a seven-year term, the president is, like the king or queen of Great Britain, above party politics.

The Legislature

The legislative branch of the German government is divided into a lower house, known as the **Bundestag**, and an upper house, called the **Bundesrat**. In this bicameral setup, as in France and Britain, the lower house is the more important

Bundestag
The lower house in the German federal system; most legislative activity occurs in this house.

Bundesrat
The upper house in the German federal system; its members, who are appointed directly by the *Länder* (states), exercise mostly informal influence in the legislative process.

FIGURE 7.3 Map of Germany. Note that Berlin, once again the capital, is located in the state of Brandenburg. During the Cold War and before Germany's reunification in 1990, it was deep inside East Germany. The provinces (now federal states) that comprised the former East Germany were Brandenburg, Mecklenburg-Vorpommern, Saxony-Anhalt, Saxony, and Thuringia.

of the two. In Germany, however, the upper house is a far bigger player than in France and Britain.

The Bundestag The presiding officer of the Bundestag is always chosen from the leadership of the majority party. Procedural matters are based on rules inherited from the Reichstag, the prewar legislature. Elections to the Bundestag are normally held every four years.

In Germany, the Basic Law (the constitution) requires a "constructive vote of no confidence," meaning a chancellor cannot be ousted by a no-confidence vote unless the Bundestag simultaneously chooses a successor. This provision was intended as insurance against a recurrence of the governmental instability associated with Hitler's rise to power.

Because the most important work is done in legislative committees, it is especially vital that political parties gain enough seats for a *Fraktion*, a block of at least fifteen legislative seats. It is only through this unit that deputies can be assigned to committees and political parties can receive formal recognition.

The Bundesrat   The upper house must pass to the lower house any measure that would alter the balance of powers between the national government and the *Länder*. Members of the Bundesrat are not directly elected; the *Länder* governments appoint them, and they must vote as a bloc. This arrangement gives the German states a powerful weapon to protect themselves against federal encroachment and makes the Bundesrat one of the most important upper houses anywhere in the world. Germany's state governments play a primary role in implementing federal policy as well as in helping to shape that policy in the concurrent areas designated under the Basic Law.

Political Parties

Germany's political party system was consciously designed to keep the number of parties from getting out of hand and to prevent tiny extremist groups from playing a significant role in the country's political life. To gain Bundestag representation, parties must receive a minimum of 5% of the national vote and must win seats in a minimum of three electoral districts.

Another factor strengthening the major parties is the mode of elections to the Bundestag. Each voter casts two votes, one for the individual and another for a *list* of names determined by the party. This method of election gives the major parties a significant role in determining the future of those who aspire to careers in politics and public service, because fully half the members of the Bundestag are elected from party lists in multimember districts by proportional representation.

Since 1949, the German Federal Republic has had two major parties—the center-left Social Democratic Party (SPD) and the conservative Christian Democratic Union/Christian Socialist Union (CDU/CSU). Because the two major parties have frequently evenly divided the popular vote (and the seats in the Bundestag), the small Free Democratic Party (FDP) has often held the key to forming a government. Both the SPD and the CDU/CSU have courted the FDP at different times but for the same reason. As a result, the FDP has had power disproportionate to its popularity at the polls and has been a junior partner in several coalition governments.

In recent years, the Green Party, which started as a social protest movement emphasizing environmental issues, has gained in popularity. In 1998, when the SPD defeated the CDU/CSU but failed to win a majority of the seats in the Bundestag, the Social Democrats, then led by Gerhard Schröder, entered into a coalition with the Green Party to form a center-left government. Schröder, who succeeded Christian Democrat Helmut Kohl (and preceded Angela Merkel) as chancellor, named Green Party leader Joschka Fisher as his foreign minister.

The Judiciary

Besides its ordinary judicial functions, the German court system is designed to act as a barrier against abuses of executive or legislative power and as a guardian of civil liberties. The regular judiciary, headed by the Supreme Court, operates alongside a set of four specialized federal tribunals: Labor Court, Social Court, Finance Court, and Administrative Court. From a political standpoint, the most important judicial structure is the Constitutional Court, which deals exclusively with constitutional questions and has the express power to declare the acts of both federal and *Länd* legislatures unconstitutional.

The Bundestag elects half the judges for the Constitutional Court, and the Bundesrat elects the other half. Most judges, however, are chosen on the basis of competitive civil service–type examinations and are appointed for life by the minister of justice, with the assistance of nominating committees selected by the federal and *Länd* legislatures. Indefinite terms help ensure judicial independence.

In some eyes, the Constitutional Court is Germany's most powerful institution. It is certainly the most popular: almost 80% of Germans trust it, whereas fewer than half express confidence in the federal government and the Bundestag. One big reason is that the court is widely seen as being above politics. Any German citizen can bring a case before the Constitutional Court, and over the years many have done so.

The Basic Law and Civil Liberties

In the realm of civil liberties, as one student of German politics declared, "The relevant historical experience was that of the Third Reich, with its oppressive flouting of all human liberties."[10] The first nineteen articles of the Basic Law—Germany's constitution—are devoted to a careful elaboration of the unalienable rights of every German citizen.

All forms of discrimination, including religious and racial discrimination, are expressly prohibited. Freedom of speech, movement, assembly, and association are guaranteed, except when used "to attack the free democratic order." This last proviso was clearly aimed at the two extremes—Communism on the

European Communities, 2009/Ec.Europa.eu

She has been called "the world's most powerful woman" and "the Chancellor of Europe." Angela Merkel, leader of the Christian Democratic Union, became the first female chancellor in German history in 2005. Chancellor Merkel's party won a major victory—and a third term—in national elections held in 2013. Her handling of the euro crisis—in particular, Germany's role in bailing out Greece and Ireland and support for a plan to create a euro zone rescue fund to recapitalize banks in Spain and Italy directly—dealt a serious blow to her prestige and popularity at home.

Reunification and Its Aftermath

Merging the two German states in the 1990s was costly, and West Germans had to pay the price. East Germany's infrastructure was inadequate, factories were obsolete, and unemployment was high due to numerous plant closings. More than two decades after the Berlin Wall came down, per capita GDP in eastern Germany pales in comparison with the western part; and while GDP has more than doubled in eastern Germany, the economic behemoth in western Germany still dwarfs the east.

Welfare State versus Competitive Economy

The German economy stalled in the mid-1990s and unemployment hit a postwar high of 12.8% in 1998, helping the Social Democrats win control of the government. By 2005, some 5.2 million Germans were jobless—a post–World War II record. German voters brought the center-right Christian Democrats, led by Angela Merkel, the first woman Chancellor in Germany's history, back to power.

Merkel engineered labor-market and pension reforms. The German economy bounced back strongly in 2010 despite the lingering effects of the 2008-2009 global recession. But chronic budget deficits and crushing public debt in Greece, Portugal, Ireland, and Spain dragged Europe's economy down and slowed the German recovery in 2011-2012. Not surprisingly, the euro crisis roiled German politics.

Even so, in the 2013 elections Merkel's CDU/CSU garnered 41.5% of the popular vote, nearly 8% more than in 2009. Germany's other major party, the SPD, gained 25.7%. The big surprise was the virtual disappearance of the FDP, the centrist junior partner in Merkel's governing coalition—having failed to get 5% of the popular vote required, the FDP went from ninety-one seats to zero! Merkel heads a "grand coalition" in which the two major parties form a ruling partnership; together these two parties control 80% of the Bundestag seats.

The Euro Crisis and the EU

Germany has been the bulwark for European unity and integration since the early 1950s, but bailing out EU governments teetering on the verge of bankruptcy was never part of the plan. Germany under Merkel and the Christian Democrats reluctantly agreed to go along with big (critics say not big enough) rescue plans for Greece and Ireland in the face of considerable domestic opposition.

To the chagrin of Keynesian economists, who favor strong state action and deficit spending to create jobs and boost consumer demand, Merkel has pushed for painful and unpopular austerity (spending cuts and tax increases). Critics abroad upbraided her for fiddling while Europe burned; the German public and her own party urged her not to bail out the prodigal Mediterranean member-states that caused the problem.

Merkel reluctantly backed two key measures to bolster the euro—a euro zone fiscal compact to impose a standard set of budget rules on member-states and a European Stability Mechanism (ESM) to provide emergency rescue funds. Some economists also argued for a third one—namely, creation of euro bonds and mutualization of euro debt (a transfer of debt obligations from debtor to creditor nations within the EU).

Germany is one of the world's largest exporters (behind only China and the United States in 2011) and benefits more than any other country from having free access to a single market of five hundred million consumers. Even in the 2012 slowdown, German exports were "buoyant." As reported in the Economist in 2012, "The German trade surplus is so huge—nearly €100 billion ($123 billion) in the first half of the year—that it has drawn flak from the OECD club of rich counties, and from the European Commission."

Climate Change and Energy Policy

Germany has been actively pursuing an ambitious policy of energy transformation (Energiewende) since the year 2000. This policy was accelerated after

(Continued)

the Fukushima disaster in March 2011 when Merkel order an immediate shutdown of seven reactors and reaffirmed Germany's clean-energy goals—to cut greenhouse gas emissions from 1990 levels by 40% by 2020 and by 80% by 2050 and to do so without nuclear power. That means Germany will have to make a major push to develop wind energy and solar power. Will it succeed? Nobody knows, but with German engineering prowess, it would not be surprising if Germany one-day soon emerges as a leading exporter of alternative energy technologies and systems.

Foreign Workers, Illegal Immigrants, Skinheads

Germany has been a magnet for temporary workers and illegal immigrants from Eastern Europe and elsewhere. Xenophobic extremists, including neo-Nazis and "skinheads," have tried in vain to capitalize on popular fears over immigration.

Germany between the United States and Russia

Edward Snowden's unauthorized release of classified information about an NSA surveillance program targeting foreign leaders caused a chill in U.S.-German relations in 2014 when the world learned, among other things, that the United States was wiretapping Angela Merkel's cell phone. Merkel said "spying between friends is simply unacceptable."

Germany's relations with Russia were also frayed in 2014 when Ukraine faced a serious secessionist threat in a region of eastern Ukraine that shares a common border with Russia. Russia encouraged the ethnic Russian rebels, provided weapons and material aid, and even sent ill-disguised military forces across the border.

The crisis in Ukraine served to underscore the continuing strategic necessity of the United States to Europe, in general, and to Germany, in particular. Objectively speaking, Germany and the United States are mutually dependent.

Old Country, New Century

The end of the Cold War signaled major changes in world politics. The 1990s war in Bosnia was the first time German soldiers had been sent abroad since World War II. In 1999, Germany contributed 8,500 combat troops to the NATO operation in Kosovo (Serbia), and after 9/11, it sent 2,000 troops to Afghanistan.

Germany's opposition to the U.S.-British invasion of Iraq in 2003, for example, was the first time Germany openly opposed the United States on a major foreign policy issue since World War II. Most Germans alive today were born after 1945, so any knowledge they have of that war of wars, Hitler, or the Holocaust is second-hand or from history books. That's another big change.

But some things haven't changed. Germany still needs NATO. Seven decades after the end of WWII, the United States still maintains military forces in Germany. NATO provides a reassuring framework for Germany's own modest military forces.

left, Nazism on the right. Fear of a right-wing resurgence has never been far beneath the surface. Indeed, in postwar Germany, neo-Nazi activity has generally been interpreted as constituting an "attack on the free democratic order."

Does Democracy in Germany Work?

One of the principal purposes behind the Basic Law was to arrange the institutional furniture in the "new Germany" to preclude a repeat performance of the "old Germany." By any standard, Germany's performance since World War II has been impressive.

THE EUROPEAN UNION

The **European Union (EU)** is an ambitious attempt to create an alternative to the war-prone nation-state system in Europe. A supranational body without parallel or precedent in world history, the EU encompasses twenty-eight countries. Nineteen member-states have given up national currencies and adopted the euro. In addition, it is now possible to travel freely and cross borders on the continent without passports and visas.

Origins and Evolution

The EU traces its origins to 1952, when Belgium, France, West Germany, Italy, Luxembourg, and the Netherlands founded the European Coal and Steel Community (ECSC). In 1957, these six countries met in Rome and agreed to launch the European Economic Community (EEC), and they formed the European Atomic Energy Community (Euratom) the following year. The ECSC, EEC, and Euratom were merged into a single entity—the European Community (EC), or Common Market, in 1967. Nine more states were admitted: Denmark, Ireland, and the United Kingdom in 1973; Greece in 1981; Portugal and Spain in 1986; and Austria, Finland, and Sweden in 1995. In 2004, the EU admitted eight former communist states in Eastern Europe (the Czech Republic, Estonia, Hungary, Latvia, Lithuania, Poland, Slovakia, and Slovenia, plus Cyprus and Malta). Romania and Bulgaria joined in 2007 and Croatia in 2013, bringing the total to 28.

Major Institutions

The EU's political institutions fulfill many functions of a supranational government. They include the European Council and Council of Ministers, the Commission, the European Parliament, and the Court of Justice. The European Council, Council of Ministers, and the Commission exercise executive powers; the European Council and Council of Ministers are intergovernmental, and the Commission is supranational. The Councils directly represent the interests of the national governments; the Commission represents the EU as a whole. On crucial issues, the two Councils vote on the basis of unanimity—everyone at the table has a veto. Increasingly, issues are decided by **qualified majority vote (QMV)**—reflecting a shift from intergovernmental to supranational decision making.

The European Parliament (EP) is a deliberative body that shares **co-decision** legislative powers with the Council of Ministers but remains the junior partner. Since 1979, its members have been elected by direct universal suffrage. The European Court of Justice (ECJ) interprets and applies EU treaties and adjudicates disputes between member-states and the EU bodies.

The 1993 Treaty on the European Union (TEU) created three pillars: the European Community (EC), the Common Foreign and Security Policy (CFSP), and the Justice and Home Affairs (JHA). Decisions on the economy (Pillar One) are made by supranational method (qualified majority voting). Decisions on foreign and security policy (Pillar Two) and justice and home affairs (Pillar Three) are made by the intergovernmental method (unanimity); however, some

---

European Union (EU)
The successor to the Common Market, or European Economic Community; the governing body that presides over a single economy that rivals the United States in size.

qualified majority vote (QMV)
In the European Union, a form of voting in the European Council and Council of Ministers in which no member -state has a veto, but passage of a measure requires a triple majority, including more than 70% of the votes cast.

co-decision
In the European Union, a method of legislation and rule-making that involves both the European Council (heads of government) and the European Parliament.

policy matters—for example, the internal open-border system, immigration, and asylum—formerly under Pillar Three (intergovernmental) have been shifted to Pillar One (supranational).

EU member-states agree to place the *acquis communautaire*—the total body of EU community law—over national law. The *acquis* comprises a billion words and have been translated into twenty-two official EU languages.

The **Common Agricultural Policy (CAP)** has been an EU fixture since the inception of the original common market in 1958. The CAP sets and collects tariffs on agricultural products coming into the EU and provides subsidies to EU farmers. In the past, agricultural expenditures (mainly subsidies) have accounted for nearly 50% of the EU budget. The CAP's share was projected to drop below one-third in 2013, but agriculture's share remained closer to 40% as France has resisted any reductions in subsidies to French farmers. Brussels also faces growing pressure from new member-states to reallocate EU resources to regional development programs and projects (called "structural" and "cohesion" funds) aimed at helping lagging areas—many in Central and Eastern Europe—catch up.

By far the gravest challenge to the EU in recent years, however, has been the sovereign debt crisis (aka, the "euro crisis") triggered by Greece's threat to default—to declare bankruptcy and leave creditors out in the cold (see "Landmarks in History: The Euro Crisis"). The danger of a panic in capital markets on the heels of the 2008 global financial crisis posed a policy dilemma for the EU Council: whether to evict Greece from the EU (the so-called Grexit option) or put together a financial rescue package (the bailout option). The problem with bailing out Greece was that Spain, Portugal, and Ireland were also sinking into insolvency. Eventually, the richer EU member-states agreed to bailouts for all four countries. But the bailouts came with strings attached—the givers (mainly Germany) made the recipients agree to tough and unpopular austerity programs. Nobody can say how this story will end; let's take a look at how it began.

The Single Market Economy

A landmark in the history of European integration, the Single European Act (SEA) of 1986 aimed to create a single market in the EU by 1992. It thus made several key institutional reforms, including a cooperative procedure giving the European Parliament a greater voice in legislation and extending qualified majority voting to new policy areas.

The SEA allowed wider and deeper integration of all the national economies, including the establishment of a European Monetary Union (EMU) and a new unit of currency—the euro. A treaty signed at the Maastricht summit in 1991 transformed the European Community (EC) into the European Union (EU) and paved the way for creating a European Central Bank (ECB) in 1998 and launching the euro in 1999. The euro went into circulation in twelve EU countries in 2002 and has now been adopted by a total of seventeen; the twelve countries that joined the EU from 2004 to 2007 are treaty-bound to join the euro area as soon as they meet the criteria for membership. Five of the seventeen

Common Agricultural Policy (CAP) An EU fixture since inception of the original Common Market in 1958. Sets and collects tariffs on agricultural products coming into the EU and provides subsidies to EU farmers.

THE EURO CRISIS

In December 2009, Greece's credit rating was downgraded by a leading rating agency, plunging the government into a financial crisis. In January 2010, Prime Minister George Papandreou ordered a second round of austerity measures, including public sector pay cuts, fuel increases, and a crackdown on tax evasion. EU leaders promised to help Greece meet its debt obligations but made no concrete pledges. General strikes and protests prompted by the unpopular austerity program continued into March, when Papandreou likened the budget crisis to a "wartime situation" and announced a third round of tax hikes and spending cuts. As the Greek government balanced precariously on the brink of default, the key euro zone countries stepped up with a €110 ($145) billion rescue package for the country; for its part, the Greek government agreed to still more stringent austerity measures. Trade unions called a general strike in protest.

In August 2010, Greece qualified for the second tranche of the EU/IMF bailout loan, and in October the Greek government unveiled an even tougher austerity budget for 2010 with new taxes and a higher value-added tax (VAT) rate. Finally, in November the EU and IMF approved the third tranche of rescue funding for Greece.

Greece's financial crisis deepened in 2011 and 2012 as mass protests destabilized the government. Worse, the crisis spread like a contagion to Ireland, Portugal, Spain, and Italy. In 2012, Spain's economy tanked, threatening to overwhelm euro zone efforts to save the euro. In January 2015, Greece elected a new government, and the EU faced the first anti-austerity ruling party, Syriza, led by Alexis Tsipras. Syriza claimed about 36% of the vote, enough to gain 149 seats in the 300-seat parliament and falling a gnat's eyelash short of an absolute majority. Prime Minister Tsipras moved quickly to bring the small right-wing Independent Greeks party with 13 seats into a governing coalition and made it clear that he did not intend to kowtow to the "troika" (the European Commission, the European Central Bank and the IMF) underwriting Greece's bail-out program. The fate of the euro (and global economy) hangs in the balance.

EU countries in the euro zone joined between 2007 and 2011: Slovenia, Cyprus, Malta, Slovakia, and Estonia.

The **Schengen area** grew out of a 1985 agreement among five countries (France, Germany, and the Benelux countries—Belgium, Luxembourg, the Netherlands) to create a passport-free zone. The Amsterdam Treaty incorporated the Schengen system into the EU *acquis* in 1997. Today twenty-five countries, including several not in the EU (Iceland, Norway, and Switzerland), belong to Schengen; and it is possible to travel from Finland to Greece by car, train, or bus without a passport, much like traveling within the United States.

The **Emissions Trading Scheme (ETS)** is Europe's major climate change project, a cap-and-trade system that sets limits on the volume of pollutants the five dirtiest industries in any given country can spew into the atmosphere each year. Companies that exceed allowances can buy pollution permits from other entities that have "credits" or unused permits. At first, the system did not work as intended because national governments bowed to domestic fears and gave away (rather than sold) permits and set the allowances too high. The EU has made adjustments aimed at tightening regulations and significantly reducing carbon emissions in the coming decades, but the cap-and-trade idea has yet to

Schengen area
The visa-free zone within the EU encompassing twenty-six countries, including several not in the EU (Iceland, Norway, and Switzerland), allowing more than five hundred million people to travel freely about Europe without being stopped at border crossings.

prove itself in practice. The global recession in 2008 and 2009 raised further questions about how vigorously national governments would push already stressed key industries to invest in cleaner technologies, as has the euro crisis since 2010.

The EU on the World Stage

The Atlantic Community forged after World War II was dominated by the United States, with Western Europe as a junior partner, but the distribution of power today is quite different. Asia and Europe—especially the European Union and China—play a larger role; the former superpowers play a smaller role (in the case of Russia, much smaller). The question is not *whether* the power picture will continue to change, but rather by how much.

Individually, the European countries cannot compete with the United States, China, Japan, and even India. Together, however, they most definitely can, as Europe's single market amply demonstrates. In 2010, only a decade after the euro was launched, the EU accounted for 28-29% of total global GDP, a larger share than either the United States or China.

There is a huge disparity between Europe's economic power and its political clout on the world stage. Achieving a Common Foreign and Security Policy (CFSP) has been a declared aim since the early 1990s, but so far the EU has rarely succeeded in presenting a united front to the world. One of the principal goals of the new Lisbon Treaty (also known as the Reform Treaty) that came into force in 2009 is to create a strengthened foreign policy post, as well as a more efficacious presidency. The EU has embraced the idea of a European Rapid Reaction Force (ERRF) to intervene where NATO is unable or unwilling to act. Since 2007, some sixty thousand soldiers have been committed to a rapid reaction force potentially deployable for one year.

The End of "Europe"?

Since World War II, peace and stability have been the norm in Europe. Not by chance, Western political theorists have posited a direct link between democratic institutions and war-avoidance and more than a few have placed the evolution of the European Union at the heart of Europe's "new normal." But as the EU struggled to recover from the Great Recession, questions began to be raised about the future of "Europe." Some observers even went so far as to predict the EU's demise. However, such dire predictions fly in the face of logic and history.

In politics, as in life, nothing succeeds like success. Economic integration has worked wonders

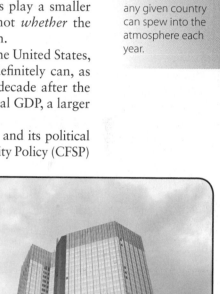

Emissions Trading Scheme (ETS) Europe's major climate change project; a cap-and-trade system that sets limits on the volume of pollutants the five dirtiest industries in any given country can spew into the atmosphere each year.

Daniel Roland/AFP/Getty Images

The euro crisis of 2010–2012 highlighted the importance of the European Central Bank (ECB) in restoring the fiscal solvency of dangerously indebted EU governments and monitoring the public finances of member-states.

in Europe. Europe's expansive—and until recently, expanding—markets create a space conducive to competition, investment, labor mobility, and commerce. The overall result has been an unprecedented era of peace and prosperity in a part of the world where for many centuries war was endemic. But the impetus for European integration is not solely economic; politics has also played a vital role.

Until the euro crisis cast a shadow over the single market economy, the EU was widely viewed as a great engine of economic prosperity and social progress. No less important is the political impact of the European project. Nearly every country in Europe has applied for membership in the European Union, but to gain admission, a country must demonstrate a commitment to constitutional rule, free elections, and human rights.

Putting dictators out of business is a remarkable achievement. No less remarkable is that within the twenty-eight nation EU, war is now unthinkable, a fact that has often been overlooked. The logic of integration is about perpetuating peace and promoting freedom in Europe, as well as achieving prosperity.

JAPAN: BETWEEN EAST AND WEST

When a powerful earthquake in the Western Pacific in 2011 caused one of the world's worst nuclear accidents and displaced more than 150,000 people living in the vicinity of the Fukushima nuclear power plant, it put Japan in the global spotlight—and not in a good way. Massive internal dislocations during the Fukushima reactor meltdown and questions surrounding the way high-level government officials handled the crisis focused international attention on Japan's hidebound political culture, its inaccessible power elite, and the opaque inner workings of its powerful and insulated bureaucracy.

Like other Asian societies, Japan had no democratic traditions prior to 1947. In fact, as an insular island nation (see Figure 7.4), Japan's history and culture often worked against Western democratic ideas. Yet today, Japan is one of Asia's oldest parliamentary democracies (the other, India, came into being at the same time but under very different circumstances). To see how this remarkable transformation came about, we start by sketching Japan's path from its feudal and imperial past to the present.[11]

Historical Background

Japan's feudal era lasted until the **Meiji Restoration** in 1868. At that time, under the guise of recapturing ancient glories, Japan crowned a new emperor, of the Meiji dynasty, and embarked on the path to modernization. Meiji Japan remained oligarchic, paying lip service to democracy. A group of elder statesmen, or *genro*, dominated the government, and the emperor, worshiped as a flesh-and-blood deity, personified national unity. He probably also played an important role in decision making on crucial issues.[12]

Domestically, Japan made great progress during the latter part of the nineteenth century. A modernizing elite promoted, protected, and subsidized a Western-style economic development program. Despite periodic opposition from rural landowners, the government force-fed the economy with infusions of capital designed to promote heavy industry. Only basic or strategic industries

Meiji Restoration
The end of Japan's feudal era, in 1868, when a small group of powerful individuals crowned a new, symbolic emperor, embarked on an economic modernization program, and established a modern governmental bureaucracy.

FIGURE 7.4   Map of Japan. Japan's population is 130 times larger than Montana (population: one million), but Japan would fit into a territory the size of Montana with room to spare. Note Japan's proximity to the Korean peninsula and, in the north, to Russia.

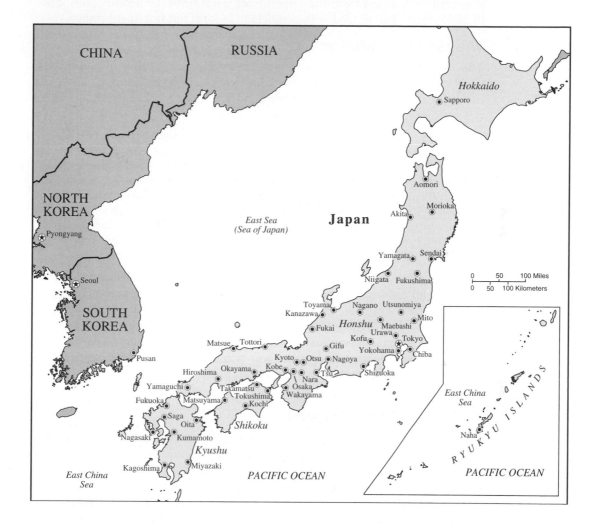

were state owned. Within a few decades, the leaders of the Meiji Restoration, according to one authority, "abolished feudal institutions, legalized private property in land, started a Western-style legal system, established compulsory education, organized modern departments of central and local government, and removed the legal barriers between social classes."[13]

After World War I, Japan entered a new phase of political development. Nationalism, taught in the schools, became a kind of religion. Governments blossomed and withered in a rapid and bewildering succession. All attempts at instituting democratic reforms were submerged in the tidal wave of militarism that swept over Japan in the 1930s. Alleging that ineffectual politicians infatuated with democracy had kept Japan down, ultranationalists looked to a strong military for leadership. Japan had never truly embraced Western concepts of constitutionalism and liberal democracy. Sovereignty, according to popular belief, issued from the emperor-deity, not from the people. Thus, prior to 1945, Japan had dallied with democracy in form but not in substance.

The 1947 Constitution

The 1947 Japanese constitution, imposed by the victors after World War II, sought to remake Japan's political system. Henceforth, sovereignty would reside in the Japanese people, not in the emperor. U.S. influence on the new Japanese constitution is readily apparent in its preamble:

> We, the Japanese people, acting through our duly elected representatives in the National Diet, determined that we shall secure for ourselves and our posterity the fruits of peaceful cooperation with all nations and the blessings of liberty throughout this land, and resolved that never again shall we be visited with the horrors of war through the action of government, do proclaim that sovereign power resides with the people and do firmly establish this Constitution. . . . Government is a sacred trust of the people, the authority for which is derived from the people, the powers of which are exercised by representatives of the people, and the benefits of which are enjoyed by the people.

Like weavers of a fine tapestry, the framers of the 1947 constitution sought to construct an elaborate system of representative democracy. Among the fundamental rights guaranteed by the constitution were the rights to receive an equal education and to organize and bargain collectively. In another extraordinary feature, the Japanese constitution explicitly renounced war and pledged, "land, sea, and air forces, as well as other war potential, will never be maintained." (This provision has not, however, prevented the government from building limited "self-defense forces.")

Parliament above Emperor

The constitution establishes a parliamentary form of government. The emperor remains the head of state, although as a merely ceremonial figure. The prime minister is the real head of government. The authors of the constitution, however, placed a preponderance of *formal* power in the new bicameral legislature. That body, called the Diet, is divided into a 480-member House of Representatives elected at least every four years (elections can be more frequent when the House is dissolved) and a relatively less powerful House of Councilors, whose 250 members serve six-year terms (half being elected every other three years).

Originally, members of each house were elected by universal suffrage from multimember districts (each having three to five seats, depending on population) in which voters made only one selection. This system endured until 1994, when calls for election reforms led to the redrawing of district boundaries and a major change in the electoral process for the lower house: there are now 300 single-seat constituencies, while the remaining 180 seats are decided by proportional representation.

The constitution explicitly states that popular sovereignty is to be expressed through the Diet, the only institution of the government empowered to make laws.

Whereas in the past the prime minister and cabinet were responsible to the emperor, they are now responsible to the Diet, the "highest organ of state power." Japan's Supreme Court is empowered to declare laws unconstitutional (which it rarely does), and justices are to be approved by the voters every ten years after their appointment, a process that has become virtually automatic.

As we will see, however, the Japanese have adapted Western institutions to fit Japan's own rich and resilient cultural traditions. The result is a unique system that combines democratic politics and market economics—the new—with political hierarchy, economic centralization, and social discipline—the old.

The Party System

With one brief exception in 1993-1994, the Liberal Democratic Party (LDP) dominated Japanese politics from 1955 to 2009. Among the smaller parties, the Socialists and Communists occasionally garnered significant numbers of votes, but their legislative role was to provide parliamentary opposition. For four decades, the actual governing of the country fell almost exclusively to the LDP.

When a single party retains a majority of seats in a freely elected legislative assembly over an extended time, it usually means the party has satisfied a broad range of social interests. In Japan, the LDP succeeded because it embraced pragmatism over ideological purity, enjoyed the backing of powerful special interests, and benefited from the sheer force of political inertia. According to two authorities,

> The changes they [the LDP] made toward a more strongly centralized system of government corrected some of the most obvious mistakes of the Occupation. The Liberal Democratic Party, being in power, also controlled a considerable amount of patronage and had the advantage when seeking the support of economic and professional interest groups. With the support of the majority of the rural vote and access to the resources of the business community, the party was in a strong position. It was on intimate terms with the bureaucracy, . . . [but these efforts] were not sufficient. . . . Beginning in 1955, the Liberal Democratic Party attempted to build up a national organization with mass membership.[14]

The LDP's consensus-building role became a defining feature of Japanese politics. Delegates to the LDP conference choose the party leader—called the president—before a national election. Until the 1990s, the LDP leader was assured of being elected prime minister. Getting elected president of the party, however, is not easy: A victor emerges only after intense bargaining by party factions, each of which has its own leader, its own constituencies to protect, and its own interests to promote.

The LDP nearly self-destructed in the early 1990s, after a series of political scandals severely tarnished the party's image. A rising tide of social discontent over the rigors of daily life, high prices, long workdays, and a sluggish economy also contributed to the party's unprecedented defeat in the historical national elections, shattering the one-party-dominant system. What followed was a chaotic period during which Japan would see five different governments come and go. The LDP was the clear loser, but there were no clear winners.

Promising reform "without any sacred cows," Junichiro Koizumi, an LDP maverick, won a hard-fought battle to become the LDP's new president in 2001.

He served as Japan's prime minister from 2001 to 2006. Reform-minded and opposed to cronyism, Koizumi was popular but unfortunately he did not enjoy the support of his own hidebound parliamentary party.

Under Koizumi, the country's economy revived. However, many members of his own party in the Diet opposed his proposal to privatize Japan's massive postal savings system. When the bill was defeated in the upper house in 2005, Koizumi dissolved the Diet and called new elections. The vote, which the LDP won by the largest majority since 1986, was a referendum on Koizumi's leadership and his move to privatize the postal savings system. Having won his biggest political battle (the privatization bill), Koizumi stepped down in 2006.

Although Japan has never fully recovered from the stock market crash in 1990-1991 (see "Ideas and Politics: The Japanese Agenda") and the subsequent implosion of its "bubble economy," it still boasts one the world's five largest national economies.

Patron–Client Politics

Japanese democracy is a unique blend of imported democratic ideals and native culture—in particular, Japan's traditional *patron–client system* that has long characterized Japanese politics. Factional leaders called patrons attract loyal followers or clients. The leader is expected to "feed" his faction, mainly by doling out campaign funds; in turn, faction members are obliged to vote as a solid bloc in the party conference and Diet.

Personal loyalty is the basis of financial support, intraparty power, and the prestige of individual leaders within the LDP. The vaunted political reform of 1994 that changed the electoral system temporarily disrupted the traditional behind-the-scenes collusion among government, bureaucracy, and the business elite, but it did not fundamentally change the patron–client system or practices. Nor is it likely to change the nation's preference for consensus seeking:

> This method rests on the premise that members of a group—say, a village council—should continue to talk, bargain, make concessions, and so on until finally a consensus emerges. . . . Despite the spread of democratic norms, this tradition of rule by consensus still has its appeal and sometimes leads to cries against the "tyranny of the majority"—for example, when the ruling party with its majority pushes through legislation over the strong protests of the opposition.[15]

When Japan's economic miracle gave way to a severe and prolonged slump in the 1990s, the LDP's popularity faded. After an eleven-month hiatus in 1993-1994, however, the LDP regained control of the government. The LDP's long run as Japan's ruling party appeared at an end in 2009 when voters handed the Democratic Party of Japan (DPJ) a stunning victory, giving the DPJ 308 seats and leaving the LDP with a mere 119 seats.

At long last, Tokyo's "iron triangle" of party bosses, bureaucrats, and business elites—a closed and corrupt system that was tolerated so long as Japan's economy was robust—was down but hardly out. (In a practice known as *amakudari*—literally, "descent from heaven"—retiring Japanese high-level bureaucrats often take lucrative jobs at firms they previously regulated. Sound familiar?)

A major earthquake (magnitude 9.0) in the ocean off Japan's east coast caused a massive tsunami in March 2011. The tsunami left more than 19,000 dead, destroyed or partly collapsed over a million buildings, and severely damaged three reactors at the Fukushima Daiichi nuclear power plant. When Prime Minister Naota Kan and his cabinet resigned in the fall of 2011—one more casualty of Japan's earthquake-induced perfect storm—the DPJ chose Yoshihiko Noda—Japan's sixth head of government in five years—to succeed Kan.

At the end of 2012, voters made yet another U-turn, giving the LDP a landslide victory in national parliamentary elections (294 seats in the 480-seat lower house). Naoto Kan lost his Diet seat to a relatively unknown LDP challenger. The LDP gave Shinzo Abe a second chance at running the government.

Abe, who had briefly served as prime minister in 2006-2007, called a snap election in late 2014 and the gamble paid off. The outcome, however, was not all positive for Abe. The LDP retained nearly all the seats it had won in 2012 and together with Komeito, its coalition partner, kept its two-thirds super majority in the 475-seat lower house: the good news. The bad news: voter turnout was very low—52.7% compared to 59.3% in 2012—and in the logic of parliamentary politics, a low turnout is tantamount to a weak mandate.

The Judiciary and Japanese Culture

The Japanese judicial system displays a curious combination of U.S. and European influences. The U.S. influence is evident in the name of Japan's highest judicial body, the Supreme Court. The Chief Justice is appointed by the Emperor but is nominated by the government; the cabinet appoints all other justices. The Supreme Court, like its U.S. counterpart, enjoys the power of judicial review, meaning it can declare acts of the legislature unconstitutional. Few other constitutional democracies permit judges to second-guess legislators.

Japan's legal system as a whole is modeled after the European civil law system, but again with some U.S. influences. Culturally, the Japanese are far less prone to sue each other than are U.S. citizens. They are also less likely to resort to the courts as a means of settling civil disputes or to seek redress for alleged injuries and injustices. In Japan, social, rather than judicial, remedies are still the norm. Often, successful intervention by a respected member of the community, the head of a family, or a supervisor at work makes legal action unnecessary.

Does Democracy in Japan Work?

Despite the turbulence of the 1990s, Japan has successfully blended Western political forms and Japanese political culture. As in Germany, economics played a key role in the success of the nation's shotgun democracy ("shotgun" because it was the result of defeat in war and military occupation).

Japan's economic revival after World War II was hardly less miraculous than Germany's, as bombed-out cities, symbolized by Hiroshima and Nagasaki, were turned into models of efficient and innovative industrial production. Deliberate planning by a modernizing entrepreneurial elite was important to Japan's resurgence; a rising volume of world trade and massive U.S. purchases during the Korean War (1950–1953) were also crucial. Within two decades, Japan's export-oriented mercantilist economic strategy produced huge advances in

THE JAPANESE AGENDA: A Sampler

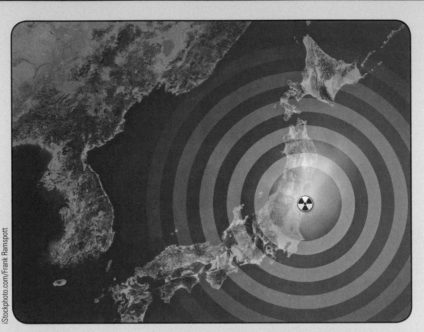

iStockphoto.com/Frank Ramspott

The map marks the spot where the tsunami that caused the Fukushima meltdown slammed into northeastern Japan and inundated the coastal city of Sendai in Kagoshima Prefecture.

Nuclear Power, Energy Security, and Public Safety

The earthquake and tsunami in March 2011—twin natural disasters compounded by a manmade disaster—raised questions about the wisdom of Japan's heavy reliance on nuclear reactors for electric power generation. What followed was intense public scrutiny and criticism of the government—in particular, its failure to monitor and enforce robust safety standards.

A blue ribbon panel of experts set up by the Japanese Diet issued a scathing report in July 2012, concluding, "The Fukushima nuclear power plant accident was the result of collusion between the government, the regulators and Tepco [Tokyo Electric Power Company, the owner of the six Fukushima plants] and the lack of governance. . . ." Further, the culpable parties, "effectively betrayed the nation's right to be safe from nuclear accident." And, finally, "the accident was clearly 'man-made.'"

The policy dilemma, however, is not easily solved. Japan's energy security is extremely tenuous: it has an export-oriented manufacturing economy, a modern, highly urbanized population, and at best modest indigenous fossil-fuel resources. Japan thus has to import almost all its coal, oil, and natural gas.

A Culture of "Reflexive Obedience"

The chairman of the above-mentioned expert panel, Kiyoshi Kurokawa, a medical doctor, declared Fukushima "a profoundly man-made disaster—that could and should have been foreseen and prevented." But he also placed blame on Japanese culture: "What must be admitted—very painfully," wrote Dr. Kurokawa, "is that this was a disaster 'Made in Japan.' Its fundamental causes are to be found in the ingrained conventions of Japanese culture; our reflexive obedience; our reluctance to question authority; our devotion

(Continued)

(CONTINUED)

to 'sticking with the program'; our groupism; and our insularity." The paradox of an open society with a closed culture impenetrable to outsiders is one key to understanding the challenges Japan faces in the new global economy of the twenty-first century.

"Abenomics"

Prime Minister Shinzo Abe advocates basic reforms in Japan's economy, especially in the rigid structure and culture of Japanese business—"Abenomics," it's called. His strategy for reviving Japan's creaky economy involves "three arrows"—fiscal policy (more spending, lower taxes), monetary policy (quantitative easing or "QE"), and structural reforms (opening Japan's protectionist economy to outside investment and competition). Abe's aim of "restoring Japan's earning power" is designed to reverse a negative trend—namely, that productivity in Japanese companies is lower on average (about 30% lower) than in the United States.

Sustaining a High Standard of Living

Despite its prolonged economic downturn, Japan remains an affluent society. Even so, it is a relatively small, mountainous country with a large urban-dwelling population and relatively little land suitable for agriculture or settlement. The problems of overdevelopment—stress-related health problems, rush-hour crowds, and traffic congestion—are readily apparent in present-day Japan. Japan's demographic crisis—steeply declining birthrates and high life expectancy—means that the ratio of workers to pensioners is getting steadily worse. Hence the question: Is Japan's ultramodern mass-consumption economy sustainable?

Asian Challengers

Japan has lost its position as the preeminent economic power in Asia. In the 1980s, its main challengers were the so-called newly industrialized countries (NICs): South Korea, Taiwan, Singapore, and Hong Kong. The GDP of the People's Republic of China, which registered double-digit growth rates for several decades, is now larger than Japan's. Indonesia, Malaysia, Vietnam, and, of course, India are among other countries in the region competing with Japan in global export markets.

A Troubled Partnership?

The United States is Japan's most important ally and trading partner. Until recently, the reverse was also true: Japan was America's most key trading partner in Asia. But the meteoric rise of China signifies a major strategic shift in the balance of power in Asia and the western Pacific. Today, China rivals Japan as a partner in U.S. foreign policy calculations, not only because of trade but also as America's largest creditor; in October 2012, China's official holdings of U.S. bonds rose to $1.1535 trillion. Japan was second at $1.1215 trillion. As Japan's largest export market, the United States is vital to Japan's economic health (and vice versa). The United States is also China's largest export market.

The U.S. air and naval bases in the western Pacific, as well as the massive U.S. Pacific Fleet, have enabled Japan to concentrate on development of high-technology consumer industries and overseas markets while spending less than 1% of its GDP on defense. Can the United States continue to subsidize Japan's security indefinitely?

The Tiger Next Door. . .

Fact: There is no love lost between China and Japan. Fact: In World War II, Japan committed terrible atrocities in China. Fact: China is a rising regional military power as well as a global economic superpower.

If China's resurgence poses major strategic challenges for the United States—which it does—imagine the view from Japan. In recent years, an escalating dispute with China over uninhabited islands in the East China Sea has threatened to erupt into a shooting war. The feud reached a dangerous new level in

(Continued)

(CONTINUED)

January 2013 when both sides scrambled jet fighters over the area in dispute.

Under the terms of the U.S.-Japan security treaty, Washington is obligated to defend the islands it handed back to Japan in 1972 along with the return of Okinawa. But China is a nuclear power. In a crisis, would Washington risk Honolulu—or San Diego, Los Angeles, San Francisco, Portland, and Seattle—to save Tokyo?

heavy industry—notably, automobile manufacturing, robotics, and consumer electronics. Despite "the loss of 52 percent of Japan's prewar territories, the return of five million persons to a country about the size of California, the loss of 80 percent of Japan's shipping, and the destruction of one-fifth of [its] industrial plants and many of [its] great cities,"[16] Japan is now a major global economic power. China, with a population more than ten times larger, is only now beginning to catch up with Japan in GDP; India, despite its impressive strides in recent times, remains far behind.

After the 1980s bubble burst, Japan's economic growth rate slowed dramatically under the impact of four recessions in a dozen years. When the 1997 "Asian flu" financial crisis hit, Japanese banks were trapped in circumstances they themselves had done much to create by lending vast sums for speculative investments in construction, real estate, and retail trade with little security or scrutiny—like a dress rehearsal for the global financial meltdown that started on Wall Street in September 2008.

Japan is and will remain a major economic power, but its technological prowess no longer sets it clearly apart from its Asian competitors. The worldwide recession derailed reforms aimed at lifting the economy out of its malaise after 2008.

INDIA AND ISRAEL: CHALLENGED DEMOCRACIES

Even if parliamentary rule works in Europe, where it started, and in Japan, where it was imposed by an occupying military power, can it work in other nations and regions where representative government has no roots in native traditions, or even in a country that finds itself in a perpetual state of war with its neighbors? The experiences of India and Israel suggest that it can.

Amazing India: A Parliamentary Miracle?

India is home to an ancient Hindu civilization and great empires, including that of the **Moghuls**, or Muslim conquerors. Colonized by Great Britain in the nineteenth century, India regained its independence after World War II. The questions then were: Would the former colony become one country or two? Or would it fragment into a dozen or more ethno-linguistic states?

Moghuls
Muslim invaders who created a dynastic empire on the Asian subcontinent; the greatest Moghul rulers were Babur (1526–1530), Akbar (1556–1605), Shah Jahan (1628–1658), and Aurangzeb (1658–1707); Shah Jahan was the architect of the Taj Mahal.

India is a paradox—an immense and extremely diverse established democracy in which poverty and illiteracy remain widespread despite great progress in recent times. With a population of 1.2 billion in 2014, it is the world's second most populous country. If current trends continue, India will overtake China by 2028—a distinction not to be desired.

Some 70% of India's people still live in villages, making India a rural society in a postindustrial world. Many children in rural India lack basic skills necessary to find productive work in a modern, urban economy; about two in five are physically stunted by malnutrition. Roughly half of all Indian women are still illiterate, compared with a ratio of about one in seven in China.

Two large and distinct populations—the larger one Hindu and the other Muslim—inhabited the subcontinent of India. The heaviest concentration of Muslims was (is) in the northwestern and eastern parts, whereas the vast lands in between constituting the bulk of the territory under the **British Raj** (the colonial ruler) were dominated by Hindus. To avoid conflict between these two religiously distinct communities, the retreating British created two states—India and Pakistan. The western part of Pakistan was separated from the eastern part with India in the middle (see Figure 7.5).

This geographic anomaly was only one of the problems the British left unresolved. Another was the Hindu-Muslim split within India: Although most Muslims inhabited the territory of Pakistan, a large Muslim minority remained within the territory of the newly independent state of India. Even more problematic was the fact that India is a mosaic of diverse ethnic and cultural minorities, each speaking a different language. There were also several religions, including Sikhism, Jainism, and Christianity, as well as Hinduism and Islam.

British Raj
British colonial rule on the Asian subcontinent from the eighteenth century to 1947, when India and Pakistan became independent.

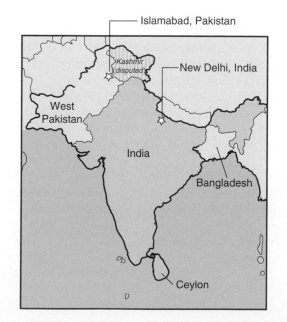

FIGURE 7.5 Pakistan at Independence in 1947. Note that West and East Pakistan (present-day Bangladesh) were on opposite sides of India. In 2012, the population of India was 1.2 billion and Pakistan had 180 million people.

Finally, no account of contemporary India is complete without mentioning poverty and population. Next to China, India is the most populous country in the world, with more than one billion souls. To this day, tens of millions are illiterate, and hundreds of millions are desperately poor, living in rural areas with little or no access to basic services, schools, health clinics, jobs, and the like.

Indeed, millions of India's poor have no identity—literally—because they lack birth certificates and school records. Imagine if you had no way to prove who you are. You could not open a bank account, get a job, enroll in college, get a post office box, travel abroad (sorry, no passport), or get a driver's license—to cite but a few examples. In 2010, India launched the Unique Identity (UID) project aimed at providing an exclusive number, based on biometrics (photo, all ten fingerprints and iris scans) to every resident in the country—more than a billion people.

India *is* changing. After decades of sluggish growth barely keeping pace with the "exploding" population, economic reforms put in place by Prime Minister Manmohan Singh in the 1990s galvanized the Indian economy. "The Indian tiger is on the prowl," wrote the *Economist* in 2007, and "at some point, India's growth rate could even outpace China's; and if you measure things by purchasing power parity, India should soon overtake Japan and become the third-biggest economy, behind only America and China."[17]

Perhaps, but India still has a lot of catching up to do. The Indian economy was racing along at nearly 9% a year for a time, but India's GDP slowed to under 5% in 2014. On the other hand, China's GDP (in current US$) was roughly five times larger than India's in 2013.

India faces huge challenges. Ethnic clashes and communal conflict among Hindus, Muslims, and Sikhs have plagued the country since independence. The bitter dispute between India and Pakistan over the territory of Kashmir (see the map) has never been resolved. One of the most dangerous moments came in the early 1970s, when East Pakistan broke away and became the present state of Bangladesh. India and Pakistan both possess nuclear weapons. India's border dispute with China, which erupted in a shooting war in 1962, is on the back burner, but irredentist (territorial) claims on both sides and various other unresolved issues remain potential triggers of future conflict.

Despite signs of progress, modernization and the rise of a prosperous middle class have failed so far to pull hundreds of millions at the bottom out of poverty. People in rural India still "waste hours queuing for drinking water," children still have no chance to go to school, and "around half of all Indian women are still illiterate."[18]

And yet, there it is—a parliamentary democracy (see "Ideas and Politics: India's Federal Government"), functioning for more than six decades in a society faced with staggering challenges and presented with such extremes of size and diversity that its very existence as a single state under a single form of government—*any* form of government—is nothing short of miraculous. Except for one brief interlude in the late 1970s, when Prime Minister Indira Gandhi declared a state of national emergency and assumed dictatorial powers, India's leaders, starting with the great Jawaharlal Nehru, have operated within the framework of a British-style parliamentary democracy.

Lok Sabha
The lower house of India's Federal Parliament; the directly elected House of the People; in India, as in the United Kingdom and other parliamentary systems, governments are formed by the majority party (or a coalition of parties) in the lower house following national elections (see also *Rajya Sabha*).

Rajya Sabha
The upper house of India's Federal Parliament; the indirectly elected Council of States (see also *Lok Sabha*).

IDEAS AND POLITICS

INDIA'S FEDERAL GOVERNMENT

On the face of it, the idea of India as an independent republic is absurd. And yet there it is: India is a federal system comprising twenty-eight states and seven union territories. Power resides in a freely elected parliament and a prime minister who is the leader of the majority party (as in other parliamentary systems). The prime minister chooses a cabinet that is presented for approval to the **Lok Sabha**, the lower house. The **Rajya Sabha**, or upper house, is indirectly elected; it plays second fiddle to the lower house, but it debates and can delay passage of legislation, thus giving its members a real voice in the policy-making and law-making processes.

If a political system as complicated as parliamentary democracy can be transplanted from the outside into a society as diverse as India, why has it not worked for the United States in Afghanistan and Iraq, for example? Think about it.

(Hint: What is different about the British colonial presence in India and the U.S. presence in Iraq and Afghanistan? Contrast the world in the nineteenth century with the world today. Compare cultures and ask whether some are more receptive or resistant to change and external influence than others.)

India's 2014 national elections held in May were a mandate for change. In a record turnout (66.38%), the National Democratic Alliance swept to a "historic victory" taking 336 seats. The Congress Party with Rahul Gandhi as its candidate won a mere 44 seats. What's more, the BJP (Bharatiya Janata Party) alone won 282 seats (51.9%), ten more than needed for an absolute majority.

What had happened to turn two-thirds of India's 550 million voters in this election against the ruling Congress Party? Chiefly, two things: the economy (especially high inflation) and, above all, official corruption.

India's new business-friendly leader, BJP boss Narendra Modi, has vowed to jump-start the economy and root out corruption. Modi is a charismatic figure. As such, he represents a strong contrast to the phlegmatic octogenarian Manmohan Singh who was his predecessor. But he came into office with some troubling baggage—namely a callous disregard for India's 172 million Muslims (14.2% of the population). As we have seen, India has a history of communal violence between Hindus and Muslims. But his election also holds out the hope of a new dawn in India politics. After all, who better to address the explosive issue of communal violence than a Hindu nationalist leader with a popular mandate for change?

Cuneyt Karadag/Anadolu Agency/Getty Images

Voters gave India's new leader, Narendra Modi, a huge mandate in 2014. Mr. Modi is a Hindu nationalist who, as Chief Minister in Gujarat, displayed little sympathy for Muslims who constitute a large minority in India.

Zionism
The movement whose
genesis was in the
reestablishment, and
now the support of, the
Jewish national state of
Israel.

Balfour Declaration
Named for the British
foreign secretary who, in
1917, declared that the
United Kingdom favored
"the establishment in
Palestine of a national
home for the Jewish
people" and pledged
to "facilitate the
achievement of this
object, it being clearly
understood that nothing
shall be done which
may prejudice the civil
and religious rights
of the existing non-
Jewish communities in
Palestine or the rights
and political status
enjoyed by Jews in any
other country."

Israel: Permanent State of War?

The term "state of war" can mean either (1) an existential condition of armed conflict whether or not war has been officially declared or (2) a legal condition arising from a declaration of war that in theory brings international law—specifically, the rules of warfare—into play. This distinction is vital to an understanding of Israel, the "Arab World," and the so-called Arab-Israeli conflict.

Like India, Israel came into being after World War II. The trouble is that most of today's Jewish Israelis are relatively recent immigrants to the territory once known as Palestine. Surprisingly, there are 1.6 million Arab Israelis—fully 20% of the population.

But unlike India, Israel is a small state; its total population is only 8.2 million and its total territory is roughly the size of New Jersey. From its inception in 1948, Israel (see Figure 7.6) was enmeshed in controversy and surrounded by hostile Arab neighbors. In fact, Israel's very birth was violent, resulting from a bitter and prolonged struggle with the indigenous population of Palestinian Arabs.

Israel is a secular state but a Jewish society. A great influx of Jews into Palestine followed on the heels of Hitler's rise to power in Germany in the 1930s; however, the movement for a Jewish state in the modern era dates back to the 1890s. **Zionism,** as this movement was called, gathered momentum in 1917 with the famous **Balfour Declaration,** named for the then British foreign minister who authored the first official endorsement of the idea of a Jewish state. (At the time, Palestine was a virtual colony of Great Britain.)

Israel and the Holocaust are inextricably intertwined. The original idea backed by the United States, the United Kingdom, and the United Nations after World War II was to carve two states out of the historic territory of Palestine—one for Jews and the other for Palestinian Arabs—and to make Jerusalem, sacred to three religions (Judaism, Christianity, and Islam), an international city under the auspices of the United Nations. That idea died when the Palestinian Arabs rejected the deal they were offered in 1947—though the Jewish side accepted it.

The Western Wall ("Wailing Wall")—a sacred relic of the ancient Jewish temple and courtyard in Jerusalem destroyed by the Romans in the first century (CE). Ultra-orthodox Hasidic Jews are recognizable by their long beards and braids and traditional black attire.

FIGURE 7.6   The Land (?) of Israel. Israeli Jews and Palestinian Arabs claim the same historic land of Palestine, which has been at the epicenter of the Middle East conflict since the state of Israel was founded in 1947. President Obama gave a major speech on the Middle East in May 2011 calling on Israel to return the lands it seized in the 1967 Six-Day War to the Palestinians, but Israeli Prime Minister Benyamin Netanyahu vowed that Israel would never give up control of a "united Jerusalem" and blamed Hamas and Palestinian extremists for the long-standing stalemate in peace negotiations. In 2012, the bloody protracted civil war in Syria threatened to spill over into neighboring states; in 2014 war broke out between Israeli and Palestinians in Gaza.

As a result of the ensuing war, most Palestinian Arabs were displaced by Jewish settlers and became refugees living in squalid camps in the Gaza Strip, the West Bank of Jordan, and Lebanon (see Figure 7.6).

This situation left a legacy of bitterness and despair that has inscribed itself indelibly in modern Middle Eastern history, pitting the Arab-Islamic world against a diminutive but invincible Jewish state. Facing hostile Arab neighbors on all sides, Israel fought and won three wars of self-defense with Egypt, Syria, Jordan, and Lebanon: the Suez Crisis in 1956, the Six Days' War in 1967, and the Yom Kippur War in 1973. In the 1967 war, Israel seized and kept control of the Gaza Strip and the Sinai Desert (Egypt), the West Bank (Jordan), and the Golan Heights (Syria). In the 1973 war, Israel was in a position to conquer all of Egypt but—under heavy diplomatic pressure from the United States—decided

Camp David Accords
A 1979 agreement by which Israel gave the Sinai back to Egypt in return for Egypt's recognition of Israel's right to exist; the two former enemies established full diplomatic relations and pledged to remain at peace with one another.

intifada
An Arabic word meaning "uprising"; the name given to the prolonged Palestinian uprising against Israeli occupation in the West Bank and Gaza in 1987–1993 and again in 2001–2002.

against doing so. In 1978, President Jimmy Carter brokered the **Camp David Accords**—a peace treaty between Egypt and Israel. This historic deal included large U.S. subsidies to both parties, but it worked: Egypt and Israel have not exchanged blows since 1973.

Israel and Palestine   Sadly, the Middle East and Palestine continue to be cauldrons of conflict and violence. In the 1980s and 1990s, a protracted Palestinian uprising called the **intifada** in the occupied territories (disputed Arab lands Israel seized in the 1967 Six Days' War) caused deaths and suffering on both sides. Although it is common to speak of two separate uprisings, it is ongoing to this day.

Relations between Israel and the Palestinians went from bad to worse in 2006 after voters in the West Bank and Gaza gave Hamas a mandate—an outsized majority in the new Palestinian parliament. The outcome set the stage for a struggle between militant Hamas and the more moderate Fatah. The struggle split the territories politically, with Fatah controlling the West Bank (under the leadership of Palestinian President Mahmoud Abbas) and Hamas controlling Gaza.

Thereafter, Israel bombed and invaded Gaza twice, once at the end of 2008 in retaliation for rocket attacks and again in 2014. Residences believed to be harboring Hamas fighters were targeted in 2014, but there was much "collateral damage." Many Palestinian civilians were killed or injured, many buildings including schools and hospitals were damaged or destroyed, and much of impoverished and isolated Gaza was left in ruins.

In 2009, parliamentary elections in Israel resulted in a virtual tie between Tzipi Livni, the centrist leader of the Kadimi Party, and Benyamin Netanyahu, the right-wing leader of Likud. The hawkish Netanyahu, who as prime minister in the 1990s had turned his back on a possible peace settlement with the Palestinians, was once again in the political cockpit.

True to form, Netanyahu encouraged expansion of Jewish settlements in the West Bank and was unyielding to such issues as the status of Jerusalem and Arab-Israeli civil rights. Israel has effectively annexed Jerusalem (the 1980 Basic Law refers to the Holy City as the country's undivided capital)—a *fait accompli* not recognized by any other country in the world. In 2014, the Israeli cabinet approved a nationality bill entitled "Israel, the Nation-State of the Jewish People." If the Knesset approves this bill without amendment, only Jews will have basic rights. (Most Arab-Israelis have refused formal citizenship in a state they consider illegitimate. As such, they do not enjoy "national rights," including the right to vote in parliamentary elections.)

The dramatic events in the Arab World—including the Arab Spring and Egyptian Revolution, the overthrow of Muammar Qaddafi in Libya, Iran's nuclear ambitions, and the civil war in Syria—again brought that troubled region to the brink of war in 2011 and 2012. In the Middle East, the more things change, the more they stay the same.

Israel: A Problematic "Democracy"   Clearly, Israel has a functioning parliamentary form of government, but is it a democracy? Like the United Kingdom, it does not have a written constitution. But that's where the similarity ends.

In Israel, Jewish ancestry and national security take precedence over all other values, including the rule of law. Thus, to protect the 6.2 million Jews who comprise the 75% majority, there are severe restrictions on the civil liberties of Israeli's roughly 1.6 million Arabs (more than 20% of the population) who, as noted earlier, are not citizens and do not enjoy the right to vote in national free elections.

In one sense, however, Israel is *too* democratic for its own good. Elections based on a wide-open system of proportional representation, in which even small upstart parties have a chance to win a few seats, mean Israel's **Knesset**, or parliament, is a free-for-all that is often confusing and chaotic. The upshot is that governments are cobbled together, sometimes from center-left coalitions and, more often, from a wide range of right-wing Zionist parties, including the far-right. The elections in January 2013 kept the right-wing Likud coalition, but "the tepid vote for Netanyahu" surprised even close observers.[19]

Ironically, permanent crisis has probably saved Israel from the consequences of a contentious political culture and a chaotic party system. The examples of India and Israel do not prove that popular self-government can work everywhere, but they do demonstrate it can work in some very unlikely places.

Knesset
The unicameral Israeli parliament.

THE ADAPTABILITY OF DEMOCRACY

The examples of France, Germany, Japan, India, and Israel suggest that democracy is surprisingly adaptable. There are always idealists and dreamers who choose to believe it can be made to work everywhere, but that is probably not the case. One of the lessons of Vietnam, Iraq, and Afghanistan is that democracy can seldom be imposed on a society against its will. The imposition of democratic rule in Germany and Japan after World War II occurred under extraordinary circumstances—these two defeated powers were at the mercy of the victors and, as such, were only too grateful to have a second chance at self-governance. At the same time, the fact that democracy has now taken root in these two countries points to its adaptability.

Virtually every government in the world today, no matter how tyrannical, tries to give the *appearance* of constitutionalism and claims to be democratic. Indeed, democracy is, by definition, popular. It is no surprise that the idea of government "of the people, by the people, and for the people" has broad appeal—broad, but by no means universal.

The Islamic societies of North Africa, the Middle East, and South Asia, for example, have religion-based cultures and legal systems incompatible with the individualism, secularism, religious tolerance, and permissiveness inherent in the idea of liberal democracy. If it's true that people cannot be forced to be free, it's equally true that starving people cannot eat freedom. For people who are starving, democracy is as a vague and meaningless abstraction. Any government that can alleviate the misery of daily existence is a good government.

But it would also be a mistake to sell democracy short. Many commentators attributed the failure of Germany's Weimar Republic to an allegedly ingrained antidemocratic passion for order and authority among the Germans. By the same token, Japan had virtually no experience with democracy before World War II, and its consensus-based patron–client culture appeared to be at odds with the basic principles of democracy. And who would have thought that democracy had any chance of succeeding in India?

Are these nations exceptions that prove the rule? The experiences of such diverse countries as France, Germany, Japan, India, and Israel suggest that constitutional democracy is a surprisingly adaptable form of government that can work in a variety of social, cultural, and economic contexts. But the fact that it has yet to take root in the Islamic world or Africa is a cautionary note—one we ignore at our own peril.

PARLIAMENT OR PRESIDENT? A BRIEF COMPARISON

The purpose of legislatures in both systems is to enact laws, levy taxes, control expenditures, and oversee the executive. But, despite these similarities, the British parliament is surprisingly different from the U.S. Congress.

In the British tradition, Parliament is sovereign. According to Sir William Blackstone (1723–1780), the famed British jurist, Parliament can do "everything that is not naturally impossible." In the words of another authoritative writer, "This concept of **parliamentary sovereignty** is of great importance and distinguishes Britain from most other democratic countries. Parliament may enact any law it likes, and no other body can set the law aside on the grounds that it is unconstitutional or undesirable."[20] In contrast, the U.S. system places the Constitution above even Congress. Ever since the 1803 case of *Marbury v. Madison*, in which Chief Justice John Marshall used an obscure provision in the Judiciary Act of 1789 to establish the principle of **judicial review**, the U.S. Supreme Court has successfully asserted its right and duty to overturn any law passed by Congress it deems unconstitutional.[21]

In both systems, of course, legislatures can pass or defeat proposed new laws, both confirm new cabinet ministers, and both have oversight powers. But there is nothing in the U.S. Congress to compare with the **Question Time** in the British Parliament, when the various government ministers are required to answer questions submitted by MPs. Question Time occurs Mondays through Thursdays. On Wednesdays, the prime minister answers questions from 12:00 to 12:30 p.m. The questions, which run the gamut from the trenchant to the trivial, are aimed at clarifying issues, focusing public attention, eliciting information, and holding the government accountable for its actions (or its failure to act). Question Time is when the Opposition can and does go on the attack. It is representative democracy at its best.

A key difference between the two political systems lies in the extent to which the legislature determines the makeup of the executive branch. As we noted earlier, the prime minister is the leader of the majority party in Parliament. Government ministers—the cabinet—are prominent members of the majority party. Because the parliamentary system blurs distinctions between legislative and executive powers, it is often difficult to determine where the authority of one branch begins and that of the other leaves off.

parliamentary sovereignty
In the United Kingdom, the unwritten constitutional principle that makes the British parliament the supreme law-making body; laws passed by Parliament are not subject to judicial review and cannot be rejected by the Crown.

judicial review
The power of a court to declare acts by the government unconstitutional and hence void.

Question Time
In the United Kingdom, the times set aside Monday through Thursday every week for Her Majesty's Loyal Opposition (the party out of power) to criticize and scrutinize the actions and decisions of the government (the party in power); twice each week, the prime minister must answer hostile questions fired at him or her by the opposition or backbenchers.

No such fusion of powers exists under the presidential system of government. Unlike senators and representatives, presidents enjoy a *national* popular mandate, and the presidency derives its powers from a separate section of the Constitution. But Congress can refuse to confirm cabinet appointments, hold public hearings, subpoena government officials, censure those who violate the law or the public trust, and, in extreme cases, impeach presidents for abuse of power (the Constitution cites "treason, high crimes, and misdemeanors").

Unlike Parliament, however, Congress does not have the power to bring down the executive by a vote of no confidence. Even if Congress votes down a key program proposed by the White House, the president will normally remain in office for a full four-year term. Unless a president dies in office or resigns, he or she can be removed only by impeachment, and no U.S. president has ever been impeached *and* convicted.

The executive branch of government comprises the head of government and the head of state, the cabinet, and the bureaucracy. In the U.S. system, the president is the head of government *and* the chief of state; in the British system, the executive is divided between the prime minister (head of government) and the monarch (head of state).

Presidents in the United States also enjoy the security of a fixed term. By contrast, the British prime minister's position depends on his or her ability to retain the confidence of a majority in the House of Commons. Prime ministers frequently are forced to step down either because public opinion turns against them or because they lose on a key vote in Parliament.

Despite significant differences in the structures of their court systems, both the United States and Great Britain share what is generally known as the common law tradition. **Common law** is based on decisions made by judges rather than laws promulgated by legislatures. The idea dates back at least as far as the twelfth century, when Henry II sought to implement a system by which judges were charged with enforcing the king's law while taking into account local customs. In the process of resolving disputes, each judge made, and sent to London, a record of the legal proceedings. Over the years, certain common themes and legal principles emerged from these records, and magistrates turned to certain celebrated judicial decisions for guidance. In time, these precedents and decisions were codified by judicial commentators—the most famous being William Blackstone—and were carried to all corners of the globe, including the American colonies.

Notwithstanding this shared common law background, the legal systems of the United States and Great Britain differ with respect to selection of judges, organization of the judiciary, powers of judicial review, and other key structural matters.

Perhaps the most important *political* difference between the two judicial systems has to do with the power of judges to uphold or strike down legislative or executive actions. In the United States, both state and federal courts review the acts of the other branches of government—state courts on the basis of state constitutions and federal courts on the basis of the U.S. Constitution.

In contrast, British judges play only a limited role in governing. Whereas the question of constitutionality hovers over every legislative and executive act in the United States, in Great Britain the judiciary does not possess the power

common law
In Great Britain, laws derived from consistent precedents found in judges' rulings and decisions, as opposed to those enacted by Parliament. In the United States, the part of the common law that was in force at the time of the Revolution and not nullified by the Constitution or any subsequent statute.

to overturn an act of Parliament. Nor do British judges act as constitutional guardians of civil liberties, as U.S. judges do whenever they assert the primacy of individual rights over legislative acts. Only rarely do British judges rule that the executive branch has overstepped its legal bounds.

In the view of one scholar, "The parliamentary system is a Cadillac among governments" and the presidential system is a "Model T."[22] Parliamentary systems are often highly sensitive to public opinion. Political parties campaign on distinct, well-defined platforms. If the election outcome results in a strong mandate for one party, the resulting government is likely to succeed in pushing its program through the parliament. If government policies prove unpopular or impracticable or if the government falls into disrepute for any reason whatsoever, the prime minister or the ruling party can be replaced with no major shock to the political system as a whole. Party discipline in the British parliamentary system makes it more efficient than the often deadlocked U.S. Congress.[23]

The U.S. presidential system, critics have asserted, is too often marked by deadlocks stemming from the checks and balances built into its tripartite structure. Too often, one party controls the presidency and another controls the Congress. Moreover, it is very difficult to remove an incompetent or unpopular president from office. In addition, an ossified two-party system leaves many groups and interests underrepresented in the Congress.

Finally, many critics contend that the Electoral College is a dinosaur that makes the popular election of the president a farce. In this view, the practice of choosing electors on a winner-takes-all basis puts the will of the people in jeopardy—witness the 2000 election in which Al Gore won the popular vote but George W. Bush won the White House.

SUMMARY

The British parliamentary model features a fusion of powers, indefinite terms of office, disciplined parties, and a dual executive. This model of constitutional democracy has been imitated more widely (except in Latin America) than the U.S. model. It is especially influential in Europe, where it has inspired most of the constitutional democracies in existence.

France is a hybrid form of constitutional democracy, combining features of both the U.S. and the British systems. Germany features a parliamentary system but differs from both France and Great Britain in that it is federal (comprising states called *Länder*), rather than unitary. The EU is a supranational organization of 28 sovereign states with a legal framework enshrined in the Lisbon Treaty (2007); all member-states are representative democracies by design – authoritarian states need not apply. Japan is a parliamentary democracy with a Japanese twist. Politically, it differs from Europe in its political culture rather than its political structure. Japan has incorporated a consensus-based society with informal, highly personal networks of political power based on patron–client relations into a set of political institutions that, on the surface, appear to be made in Europe. (Actually, they were made in America during the U.S. occupation after World War II.)

India and Israel are two unlikely candidates for republican rule, yet they have both survived as parliamentary democracies for more than half a century. Their examples suggest the parliamentary model is highly adaptable and has wide application, even in places that appear too troubled or turbulent for elections to occur or stable governments to endure.

The U.S. and British systems invite comparisons and offer provocative contrasts in the legislative, executive, and judicial areas. It is difficult to say which system is better in the abstract; the answer exists only within the specific context and circumstances of each nation.

KEY TERMS

parliamentary system 161
mixed regime 162
no-confidence vote 164
party discipline 165
Loyal Opposition 166
dual executive 170
National Assembly 171
divided executive 173
Weimar Republic 176
Bundestag 178
Bundesrat 178

European Union (EU) 184
qualified majority vote (QMA) 184
co-decision 184
Common Agricultural Policy (CAP) 185
Schengen area 186
Emissions Trading Scheme (ETS) 186
Meiji Restoration 188
Moghuls 196
British Raj 197
Lok Sabha 199

Rajya Sabha 199
Zionism 200
Balfour Declaration 200
Camp David Accords 202
intifada 202
Knesset 203
parliamentary sovereignty 204
judicial review 204
Question Time 204
common law 205

REVIEW QUESTIONS

1. Why is the British political system often considered a model of parliamentary democracy?
2. What are the basic operating principles of the parliamentary system?
3. How can the British manage without a written constitution?
4. When did the current French republic come into being and under what circumstances?
5. Compare and contrast democracy in France with democracy in the United States and the United Kingdom. (Trick question: Which country did France model its own political system after?)
6. Compare and contrast the European Union and the United States as political systems and governing bodies.
7. When did Japan adopt the parliamentary system and under what circumstances?
8. Compare and contrast democracy in Japan with democracy in France and Great Britain.
9. Comment on the significance of parliamentary democracy in India and Israel.
10. Compare the strengths and weaknesses of parliamentary versus presidential rule.

WEBSITES AND READINGS

Websites

British government and politics: http://www.ukpolitics.org.uk/; http://www.historylearningsite.co.uk/british_politics.htm

French government and politics: http://www.gksoft.com/govt/en/fr.html; http://wessweb.info/index.php/French_Politics_%26_Government

German government and politics: http://www.germany-info.org; http://www.princeton.edu/~achaney/tmve/wiki100k/docs/Politics_of_Germany.html

European Union: http://europa.eu/index_en.htm

Japan government and politics: http://www.mofa.go.jp

India government and politics: http://india.gov.in/; http://www.asianinfo.org/asianinfo/india/politics.htm

Israel government and politics: http://countrystudies.us/israel/; http://www.goisrael.com/tourism_eng

Palestinian policy network: http://al-shabaka.org/

Readings

Bailey, Sydney. *British Parliamentary Democracy,* 3rd ed. Westport, CT: Greenwood, 1978. A comprehensive introduction to the functioning of the British democracy.

Birch, Anthony. *Concepts and Theories of Modern Democracy,* 3rd. ed., New York: Routledge, 2007.

_____ *The British System of Government,* 10th ed. New York: Routledge, 1998. A good reference to British government.

Diamond, Larry. *The Spirit of Democracy: The Struggle to Build Free Societies Throughout the World.* New York: Holt, 2009. A hopeful and optimistic book about the prospects for democracy in the world by a highly respected, first-rate political scientist who makes an intelligent and well-researched argument that will make most readers want to stand up and cheer.

Diamond, Martin, Winston Fisk, and Herbert Garfinkel. *The Democratic Republic: An Introduction to American National Government.* Skokie, IL: Rand McNally, 1970. An introductory text that contains an extraordinarily insightful discussion of the relationship between the American Founders and political institutions.

Dicey, A. V. *Introduction to the Study of the Law of the Constitution.* Indianapolis: Liberty Fund, 1982. A classic account of the British political tradition.

Ornstein, Norm E., and Thomas G. Mann. *The Broken Branch: How Congress Is Failing America and How to Get It Back on Track.* New York: Oxford University Press, 2006. The authors argue cogently that Congress no longer performs its critical constitutional functions and offer a well-conceived pre-scription for change.

Packer, George. "The Quiet German." *The New Yorker*, December 1, 2014, pp. 46–63. An article about the "astonishing rise of Angela Merkel, the most powerful woman in the world" whom Germans call "Mutta" (Mommy) and a biographer dubs "the Chancellor of Europe."

Tilly, Charles. *Democracy*. New York: Cambridge University Press, 2007. A comparative study of the processes of democratization at the national level over the past several hundred years. The author explores the processes involved in both the rise and fall of democracies.

CHAPTER 8

States and Economies in Transition
Between Democracy and Yesterday

Learning Objectives

1   Discuss the idea that the system of rule in Russia under Putin has more in common with tsarist Russia than Western-style democracies.

2   Define the term "transitional state" and describe what changes in the world have caused or incentivized states to undertake major economic and political reforms.

3   Compare and contrast the progress of various East European countries in making the transition from a centrally planned to a market-based economy.

4   Identify key Asian transitional states and characterize the political system in each country before and after the transition.

5   Name several transitional states in Latin America and explain the pressures for change as well as the historical and cultural obstacles to liberalization in these countries.

On December 31, 1991, something incredible happened, something only a few years earlier nobody believed ever could or would happen. The Soviet Union, one of two superpowers that had dominated world politics for nearly half a century, ceased to exist.

The collapse of the mighty Soviet superpower stands as one of the most momentous political events of the twentieth century. It ushered in a new era in world politics. It pointed to fatal flaws in centrally planned economies—structural rigidity, systemic inefficiencies, and a lack of incentives common to competitive markets.

In Russia today, the tradition of autocratic rule continues to cast a long and dark shadow over a society that has never known the civil liberties taken for granted in the West. Our main focus in this chapter is on the politics of transition from central planning and totalitarian rule to capitalism and parliamentary democracy in Russia and Eastern Europe. We also look briefly at a few transitional states in Asia and Latin America.

For all practical purposes, the Communist World ceased to exist in 1989. In 1988, before the end of the Cold War, fifteen states could be classified as communist. A decade later, the number had shrunk to only five or six states—China, Cuba, Laos, North Korea, Vietnam, and perhaps Cambodia—each pursuing independent policies. Only North Korea remains an unreconstructed Stalinist state. It no longer makes any sense to talk about a "Communist threat." What happened?

Eastern Europe abruptly abandoned Communist rule in 1989, ahead of the collapse of the Soviet Union in 1991. Thereafter, democracy and privatization (the process of turning formerly state-run enterprises over to the private sector) advanced rapidly in Poland, Hungary, the Czech Republic, and Slovakia, as well as in the Baltic States (Latvia, Lithuania, and Estonia). Romania and Bulgaria have followed suit, but at a slower pace. The former East Germany is a special case, having merged with West Germany in 1990.

RUSSIA: OLD HABITS DIE HARD

As the 1990s began, the Soviet Union stood as one of the last of the world's great empires (see Figure 8.1). The Stalinist state that remained in place until 1991 displayed all the classic features of totalitarian rule, including centralized control over the armed forces, the media, and the economy; a dominant monopoly party; an official ideology; and a systematic program of terror against suspected political opponents and the mass murder of innocents deemed unworthy (or dangerous) by the regime. The story of how the former Soviet Union emerged from the long dark winter of totalitarianism provides the essential background for understanding the nature of Russian politics today.

The Decline and Fall of a Superpower

When Mikhail Gorbachev became General Secretary of the Communist Party in 1985, the Soviet Union faced daunting political and economic problems. The USSR was falling behind the West and, looking east, the People's Republic of China was stirring. Gorbachev recognized the need for radical reforms; and

FIGURE 8.1   Sixty percent of Russia (including Siberia) is located east of the Urals, in Asia. Russia is so vast that if you board a train in St. Petersburg and go all the way Vladivostok, you pass through no less than eleven time zones!

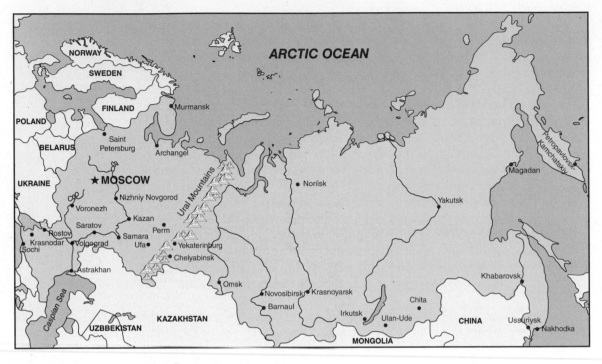

because the Communist Party monopolized power, he made a risky decision—a kind of wager with the devil—to transfigure the Soviet political system in order to save it.

From the time Lenin assumed power in 1917, the Soviet Union had featured a *command economy* in which all important economic decisions (such as what and how much was to be produced and so on) were made at the uppermost level of the Communist Party. Competition, the pursuit of profits, and most forms of private ownership were forbidden as inconsistent with the tenets of Communism.

This system of central planning succeeded in making the Soviet Union a first-rate military power, but at a crushing cost to the consumer economy, which was all but nonexistent. Grossly distorted budget priorities and mounting debt were disguised by artificial prices, press censorship, and secrecy. By the mid-1980s, the Soviet Union was at a huge competitive disadvantage with industrialized democratic nations such as the United States, Japan, and the members of the European Union, and it was falling further behind all the time.[1]

Most Soviet citizens led relatively austere lives with few of the conveniences Westerners took for granted. Soviet economists estimated about one-fourth of all grain harvested each year was lost before it got to the market. As a result, meat and dairy consumption for the average Soviet citizen declined nearly 30%.[2]

Store shelves were often empty and spare parts unavailable. According to one estimate, women spent an average of two hours a day, seven days a week, waiting in line to purchase the few basic goods available.[3] In the twilight of the Soviet era, an estimated 28% of the Soviet population lived below the official Soviet poverty line.[4]

While the Soviet economy decayed and the quality of life for the general populace deteriorated, growing social problems threatened the very fabric of Soviet society. Among the worst were alcoholism and corruption. Another major problem was a widening technology gap. Soviet managers had little encouragement to invest in new technologies (computers, cell phones, robotics), and the party feared (rightly, it turned out) that the coming Digital Age and Internet (already on the horizon in the 1980s) would jeopardize its information monopoly.

At the root of these problems was central planning, which discouraged initiative. Plant managers and directors of government-run farms remained tied to a central plan that imposed rigid quotas on factory and farm production. Plan fulfillment was the highest priority for all Soviet economic administrators. The Stalinist system sacrificed quality for quantity. Because of relentless pressures to meet overly ambitious production quotas, managers often took shortcuts and cooked the books to conceal failures or to paper over problems.

The cynicism of the managers was matched by the low morale of the Soviet workers, who were underemployed, unhappily employed, or simply not motivated to work. "The party pretends to pay us, and we pretend to work." This cynicism was fed by the hypocrisy of high party officials, who espoused egalitarian ideals but lived in secluded luxury while the proletariat they glorified had to stand in long lines to buy bread and other staples.[5] The result was appallingly low productivity, shoddy work, and poor quality.

An entrenched elite known as the **nomenklatura** occupied all the top positions in the Soviet system.[6] Included in this system of power and privilege were key members of the party and state bureaucracy. The hidden world of luxury apartments, specialty shops, vacation resorts, hospitals, health spas, and schools was an open secret—one that stood in sharp contrast to the bleak existence of ordinary Soviet citizens and made a mockery of the "classless society" Marx had envisioned.

In short, Gorbachev faced a stark choice: push reforms or preside over the death of the Soviet state. In the end, he did both.

The Politics of Reform

Gorbachev's reforms became known to the world as **perestroika** (restructuring) and **glasnost** (transparency), plus a promise of **democratization**. Clearly, what Gorbachev had in mind was nothing less than a state-controlled revolution from above. Unfortunately, the revolution spun out of control.

The goal of perestroika was to revitalize the ossified system of central planning. Gorbachev endeavored to reduce power of the entrenched party and state bureaucracy, improve worker productivity, change the culture of cheating, stealing, and cynicism, et cetera. But serious market reforms—breaking up the woefully inefficient state enterprises, introducing real competition, or privatization—were

nomenklatura
The former Soviet Communist Party's system of controlling all important administrative appointments, thereby ensuring the support and loyalty of those who managed day-to-day affairs.

perestroika
Term given to Mikhail Gorbachev's various attempts to restructure the Soviet economy while not completely sacrificing its socialist character.

glasnost
Literally "openness"; this term refers to Mikhail Gorbachev's curtailment of censorship and encouragement of political discussion and dissent within the former Soviet Union.

democratization
Mikhail Gorbachev's policy of encouraging democratic reforms within the former Soviet Union, including increased electoral competition within the Communist Party.

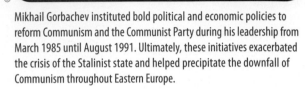

Mikhail Gorbachev instituted bold political and economic policies to reform Communism and the Communist Party during his leadership from March 1985 until August 1991. Ultimately, these initiatives exacerbated the crisis of the Stalinist state and helped precipitate the downfall of Communism throughout Eastern Europe.

not in the picture. Hence, perestroika became a catchy political slogan rather than a coherent economic policy. By 1989, the Soviet economy was rapidly disintegrating, and within two years it had plunged into a depression.

Glasnost brought a major relaxation of media censorship, and for a time won popular sympathy for Gorbachev, while distracting public attention from the disastrous war in Afghanistan, the poor economy, and the disarray in the party and state bureaucracies. It also held a wide appeal beyond Soviet borders, making Gorbachev the darling of the world press and a popular figure in many Western countries.

The real purpose behind glasnost was to expose the official corruption and incompetence Gorbachev blamed for the country's economic malaise. He wanted to shake the change-resistant Soviet bureaucracy out of its lethargy and change the public attitude toward work and the workplace.

But glasnost quickly became a force unto itself. Previously censored books and movies flourished; the state-controlled mass media dared to criticize the government; newspapers and magazines published scorching articles challenging the official version of history and current events. By allowing public dissent, glasnost severely undermined the legitimacy of the ruling Communist Party and dispelled the fears that kept the Soviet system afloat.

Finally, Gorbachev also called for democratization of the political system, including elections that allowed voters a limited choice at the polls. Taken together, these reforms, in effect, let the genie out of the bottle.

The Empire Strikes Back—And Breaks Up

Gorbachev's reforms failed miserably. Popular expectations rose while living standards fell dramatically, creating a politically volatile situation. Galloping inflation and labor strikes, both previously unheard of, dangerously destabilized the Soviet state.

As the end of the Soviet empire drew near, the so-called Nationality Question loomed ever larger. In 1991, the seventeen largest nationalities accounted for more than 90% of the Soviet population (about 294 million people). The majority Russians accounted for only slightly more than half the total. Some twenty ethnic groups numbered more than one million. Among the largest were the fifteen nationalities for whom the union republics are named, plus the Tatars, Poles, Germans, Jews, and others less familiar to the outside world (see Table 8.1). In total, the Soviet Union encompassed more than 100 different nationalities, speaking some 130 languages.

Historically, the Kremlin was not averse to the use of brute force to assimilate non-Russian groups. Another primary instrument of state policy was the education system. All schoolchildren throughout the Soviet Union were required

TABLE 8.1   Major Nationalities in the Soviet Union at the Time of Its Demise (1989).

Nationality	Percent of Total Population[a]	Nationality	Percent of Total Population[a]
1. Russian	50.78	11. Moldovan	1.17
2. Ukrainian	15.47	12. Lithuanian	1.07
3. Uzbek	5.84	13. Turkish	0.95
4. Belarusian	3.50	14. Kirgiz	0.85
5. Kazakh	2.84	15. German	0.71
6. Azerbaijani	2.38	16. Chuvash	0.64
7. Tatar	2.32	17. Latvian	0.51
8. Armenian	1.62	18. Jewish[b]	0.50
9. Tajik	1.48	19. Bashkir	0.50
10. Georgian	1.39	20. Polish	0.39

[a]These figures are adapted from the last official census of the Soviet Union.
[b]The former Soviet Union classified Jews as a nationality.
SOURCE: Based on Population Today, November 1991, Population Reference Bureau.

to learn Russian; at the same time, however, schools in the non-Russian "social-ist republics" were allowed to teach in the native (or national) language of the indigenous people.

Gorbachev's reforms emboldened non-Russian nationalities to demand self-determination. Glasnost, in particular, encouraged criticism of local officials. The independence movement broke out in the Baltic states first. The spirit of rebellion swept across the Soviet empire, as republic after republic declared its independence.

In August 1991, a group of eight hard-line Communist Party traditional-ists with ties to the army and the KGB (the Soviet secret police) staged a coup, which ultimately failed. Boris Yeltsin, the president of the Russian republic, saved the day, rallying demonstrators who had taken to the streets to fight for democracy. The Soviet Union ceased to exist on the last day of 1991.

Contemporary Challenges

A downsized Russian state and a loose, face-saving confederation consisting of all former Soviet republics except the Baltic states emerged from the ashes of the extinct Soviet Union. Boris Yeltsin turned out to be a colorful but quixotic character, ill-suited to the big tasks he faced as the new Russia's first elected president. By contrast, his successor is the exact opposite: a no-nonsense politi-cal boss with little imagination and a notable lack of charisma, but an iron will (see "Ideas and Politics: Putin: The Black-Belt Tsar").

PUTIN: The Black-Belt Tsar

Many Russians express admiration for strong leaders like Stalin, Nicolas II, or Ivan the Terrible. Vladimir Putin is the latest incarnation of such a leader. A former KGB agent with a black belt in karate, Putin has earned a reputation for ruthlessness.

Several examples illustrate his no-nonsense style of leadership. The day after the United States withdrew from the antiballistic missile (ABM) treaty in June 2002, Putin withdrew from the START II treaty (Strategic Arms Reduction Treaty signed in 1993). A few months later, when fifty Chechen rebels seized eight hundred hostages inside a Moscow theater, Putin ordered Russian commandos to move in and use poison gas to incapacitate the guerrillas. Nearly all the guerillas died in the ensuing firefight—as well as 129 hostages.

In October 2003, Putin ordered that Mikhail Khodorkovsky, the richest man in Russia at the time, be arrested and jailed on charges of tax evasion. Khodorkovsky was sentenced to nine years in prison in 2005. Having served seven years of his original term, Khodorkovsky was again put on trial in 2010 on new charges of embezzlement, convicted, and sentenced to an additional fourteen years in prison. Why? In 2003, Khodorkovsky had been a potential rival for president. What better way to deal with a would-be challenger than to lock him up and throw away the key?

From 2008 to 2012, Putin ruled Russia as prime minister rather than president (under the Russian constitution, a sitting president can serve no more than two consecutive terms) while his lackey, Dimitry Medvedev, served as titular president. As planned, in 2012 Medvedev and Putin again traded places.

Putin tightly controls the mass media, especially television. His government has been called a "kleptocracy," and he's been rumored to be the world's richest leader, but there's no way of knowing. The Kremlin is a walled fortress, and secrecy is the watchword.

When Putin's reelection in 2012 occasioned mass protests in Russia, the world press generally treated the

Vladimir Putin is Russia's second president since the fall of Soviet Communism.

election as a sham. And in early 2014, in the midst of a crisis in Ukraine, Putin seized Crimea. World opinion was outraged at this violation of Ukraine's territorial integrity.

Russians, however, saw it differently. Ethnic Russians constitute a majority of Crimea's population (58%). Voters in Crimea overwhelmingly approved a hastily arranged referendum on joining Russia. In Russia proper, a wave of Great Russian nationalism swept across the land, and Putin's popularity soared.

It's likely that Putin's success in taking back Crimea emboldened him to give military and economic aid to ethnic Russian separatists in eastern Ukraine in 2014—even sending thinly disguised Russian soldiers across the border. In response to Moscow's intervention in Ukraine, the West imposed economic sanctions on Russia; at the end of 2014, oil prices plummeted—a one-two punch that caused the ruble to collapse and plunged the Russian economy into a crisis.

(Continued)

IDEAS AND POLITICS

(CONTINUED)

In an attempt to save the ruble and head off a stampede to the exits (capital flight topped $100 billion by mid-December 2014), the Russian Central Bank raised interest rates to 17% (!), thus presaging a deep economic recession. Russian GDP was expected to fall by 4.5% in 2015.

It was anybody's guess how Vladimir Putin—the Black-Belt Tsar—would react to this crisis. Dangerous creatures are often most dangerous when they are cornered.

Russia is no longer a communist state and therefore no longer a threat to the West. True or false? Think about it.

(Hint: Mikhail Khodorkovsky, Putin's archrival, was released from prison in December 2013. His release proves how different Russia is today from the days when Stalinists ruled in the Kremlin, say the Putin sympathizers. Find out where Khodorkovsky is now and what he's doing. Then decide for yourself.)

Russia has roughly three-fourths the landmass, about half the population, and approximately three-fifths the GNP of the Soviet Union. Even so, it is still by far the world's largest country, encompassing an area roughly twice the size of Canada, the United States, or China, and possesses the massive nuclear arsenal it inherited from its superpower predecessor. Ukraine, Kazakhstan, and Belarus fell heir to the nuclear weapons deployed outside Russia proper. Ukraine and Kazakhstan promised to relinquish control of these weapons to Moscow, but they demanded economic and financial concessions in return. Belarus demurred. All three eventually came around to the view that possessing nuclear weapons was a liability. The 9/11 terrorist attacks on the United States raised new fears that weapons of mass destruction might fall into the hands of international terrorists. Fortunately, by that time all ABC weapons (atomic, biological, and chemical) stamped "Made in the USSR" had reportedly been removed to Russia.

Economic Dislocations In the 1990s, the Russian economy went from bad to worse. By the middle of the decade, output dropped by one-third and hyperinflation stalked Russian consumers like a great plague.[7] Year after year, the vital statistics—GDP growth, productivity, prices, wages—told a grim story.[8] Failure to crack down on organized crime was partially to blame for the deep malaise, as was official corruption that, among other things, turned the privatization program into a bonanza for crooks.

A grossly mismanaged privatization program allowed crooks—operating behind the scenes, greasing palms, and using Kremlin connections—to gain control of huge chunks of the Russian economy. In this way, the sell-off of state assets at fire sale prices created multimillionaires ("oligarchs") while most Russians sank deeper into poverty. Meanwhile, Russia lacked the legal and financial structures necessary for the development of a diversified economy capable of competing in a global marketplace.

Under Yeltsin, most Russians perceived they were worse off than under Communism. A decade later with Putin at the helm, the picture was much brighter.[9] The reason: a sudden steep rise in oil and natural gas prices on the world market in the post-9/11 period. A major producer and exporter of fossils fuels (oil and natural gas), Russia reaped windfall profits before the global recession drove world oil prices down in 2008.[10]

In short order, Russia paid off its external debt and amassed the world's largest foreign currency surpluses during this period of irrational exuberance, but ultimately failed to capitalize on it. By failing to diversify the Russian economy or to create a business environment attractive to foreign investors, Putin squandered Russia's energy-export windfall. The downside of Russia's extreme dependence on energy exports became evident when world oil and gas prices collapsed and export revenues plummeted in 2008-2009, a prelude to the current economic crisis rocking Russian civil society to its core.

Ethnic Conflict Civil war, religious persecution, and ethnic strife followed in the wake of the Soviet breakup in 1991. Centrifugal forces—antagonistic ethnic groups, demands for independence, and terrorist acts—have taxed the Kremlin's patience and resources and marred its image in the eyes of the world.

Under the 1993 constitution, ethnic groups form the basis for the twenty-one republics in the new Russian Federation (successor to the USSR). These federal units, similar to state governments in the United States, are represented as *republics* in the upper house of the Russian legislature.

Unfortunately, enmities rooted in history and culture, along with prejudice born of rivalry, injury, and envy are not easily erased. Russia's nationality problem was put on display in December 1994, when Russia attacked Chechnya, a Muslim republic the size of Connecticut. When Chechnya declared independence and talks failed to produce a settlement, Yeltsin sent troops to put down the revolt. In the ensuing war, Russian warplanes bombed the Chechen capital of Grozny, but Russian ground forces suffered heavy casualties.

Faced with a formidable enemy, a failing economy, a demoralized public, and a rising tide of negative world opinion, Yeltsin moved to end the dirty war in Chechnya. A truce signed in late 1996 put the question of Chechnya's independence on the back burner; in other words, it settled nothing. In 1999, it was Yeltsin's deputy, Vladimir Putin, who directed the brutal crackdown that subdued the Chechen rebels. Putin's success made him a hero to nationalists still fighting mad over Russia's lost empire.

Family Matters: Ukraine For Russian nationalists, losing Ukraine was the biggest blow, akin to losing a family member, because Russians and Ukrainians come from the same ethnic stock and (to a larger extent than Ukrainian nationalists care to admit) share a common history, religion, and culture.

Family feuds can become very nasty, very fast. Nations are no different. In 2005-2006 in the middle of a cold hard winter, when Moscow announced a fourfold increase in the price of natural gas, Kiev balked. Putin cut off natural gas supplies to Ukraine but eventually agreed to a compromise somewhat more acceptable Kiev.

Russia again cut off natural gas supplies to Ukraine in the winter of 2008-2009. Why? Putin used an economic tool (natural gas) as political leverage. Specifically, Ukraine's dependence on Russia for its energy supplies meant

OLEG NIKISHIN/AFP/Getty Images

The wars in Bosnia and Chechnya are often called "dirty wars" because uniformed soldiers (not insurgents or "terrorists") deliberately attacked and targeted civilians as a matter of strategy and policy. Such acts are outlawed under the rules and conventions of warfare going at least as far back as the Geneva Convention of 1864. No wars are civilized; the wars in Bosnia and Chechnya were particularly barbaric (hence the term "dirty").

(means) the Kremlin could (and still can) punish Kiev at will for being too pro-EU, pro-NATO, and pro-Western—a classic example of one state using economic means to coerce or blackmail another state.*

Tensions between Russia and Ukraine, which erupted into a virtual state of war in 2014, are rooted in the intertwined history of these two closely related nations. In fact, Russia and Ukraine are so closely related that it is possible to see them as one nation with two states. Indeed, many Russian nationalists see Ukraine in this way—as an integral part of Russia. They have a point: the earliest Russians on record were the "Kievan Rus."

Ukraine, and specifically the city of Kiev, is the ancient birthplace of Russia. It is one of the largest countries in Eastern Europe, with a population of approximately forty million, roughly the size of neighboring Poland's population.

Crimea, a strategic peninsula in the Black Sea, was part of Ukraine from 1954 to 2014, when Russia reclaimed it as part of a larger campaign to punish Kiev for leaning toward the West and, in particular, for seeking membership in the European Union. Crimea's current inhabitants are Great Russians, who replaced the indigenous population after Stalin sent the Crimean Tatars (famous as formidable warriors) into internal exile to Siberia in the 1930s.

---

*It's not nice, but in politics nothing succeeds like success. Economic coercion often works better than military coercion (think USSR in Afghanistan in the 1980s, the United States in Iraq from 2003 to 2011, or the United States in Afghanistan today).

FIGURE 8.2   Map of
Georgia.

A dispute in the mid-1990s over control of former Soviet naval facilities and forces at Sevastopol, a historic Crimean port city, arose from ambiguities and conflicting interests. Although it was resolved peacefully in 1997 (Russia got 80% of the fleet but conceded the port to Ukraine), it resurfaced in 2008 during Russia's war with Georgia (see Figure 8.2) and again in February-March 2014 when Moscow seized control of Crimea. Alarmed and facing a bloody secessionist movement in a pro-Russian region in eastern Ukraine, Kiev applied for NATO membership in August 2014.

Relations between Russia and other former republics—for example, Kazakhstan and Moldova—are often strained as well. Troubled ethnic relations on Russia's borders continue to be mirrored by tensions inside the Russian Republic. Chechnya is by no means the only potential internal trouble spot: In fifteen of the twenty-one ethnic republics in Russia today, the titular nationality is in the minority.[11]

No Trespassing: Georgia* Russia's military invasion of Georgia, a small country of less than five million on its southern flank, rekindled memories of the Cold War when the United States and the Soviet Union were bitter rivals. In happier times, the United States made a show of promising Georgia it would not stand alone as it embarked on the path of democracy.

But when Russia attacked in August 2008, the United States was embroiled in two dirty wars (Iraq and Afghanistan) of its own. George W. Bush—a lame duck president already badly overextended in the Middle East and Central Asia—was in no position to do anything but join the chorus of feckless diplomatic protests. On its own, tiny Georgia was no match for the Russian Goliath.

Georgia's desire to join NATO gave Moscow a motive to match its means, a powerful mixture of geopolitics and national pride. From the Kremlin's vantage

---

*Adapted from the author's op-ed article in the *Kansas City Star*, August 18, 2008, p. B6.

point, the West had profited at Russia's expense, using NATO and the EU to fill the vacuum created by the Soviet collapse. Any further encroachment on Russia's periphery was a provocation to be met with deadly force. Seen in this light, the attack on Georgia put the West on notice: No (more) trespassing!

Nor was the war just about politics. It was also about control of vital oil and natural gas pipelines to the West, about Russia's debut as a post-Soviet global power (which it clearly is by any geopolitical reckoning), and about drawing a line in the sand on Russia's western and southern frontiers. Georgia always has been important to Russia because of its strategic position on the Black Sea, the gateway to the Mediterranean, and its proximity to Iran, Turkey, and the Middle East.

Russia's use of force against a sovereign state friendly to the West was reminiscent of the Cold War. Some things never change.

State Building   Putin recentralized state power at great cost to Russia's fragile democratic institutions. We can summarize the effect of his reverse reforms as follows:

- *A Tattered Constitution*. Putin has greatly enhanced the powers of the executive at the expense of the legislative branch and used the judicial system to intimidate and punish his opponents.

- *Feeble Parties and Fewer Elections*. The Russian party system is weak and badly fragmented. Putin places formidable obstacles in the path of political parties and party leaders who dare to oppose his policies; he abolished elections for regional governors altogether (he handpicks them now).

- *Organized Crime*. According to one estimate, organized crime employed some three million people in the mid-1990s; it infiltrated the police and bureaucracy; it also clouded Russia's relations with the West on many levels.[12] Organized crime remains a major blight on civil society in Russia to this day.

- *Disrespect for the Law and the Police*. Crime, corruption, and collusion have contributed to a culture of illegality that's been called "Russia's biggest blight."[13]

Putin: President or Tsar?

In August 1999, Yeltsin named Putin, a political unknown, to be his new prime minister; eight months later Putin was the newly elected president of the Russian Federation. As the new boss in the Kremlin, Putin quickly moved to put his personal stamp on Russia's domestic and foreign policies. At home, he moved against Russia's notorious "oligarchs" (wealthy tycoons who gained control over gigantic pieces of the old Soviet economy in the botched privatization program carried out during the Yeltsin era). Abroad, he gave Russia's foreign policy a new look, strongly backing the U.S. campaign against terrorism in the fall of 2001.

Putin also paid tribute to economic reforms, including changes in the tax laws and creation of a financial intelligence service to fight money laundering.

Buoyed by high oil prices, the Russian economy revived. But the basic structures of Russia's protectionist, cartel-dominated, red tape-ridden economy, including such key sectors as utilities, banks, and state-owned enterprises, remain largely unchanged.

Putin's instincts are authoritarian; his methods are Machiavellian. He has eviscerated the independent news media. He relies heavily on the so-called *siloviki* (antidemocratic hard-liners from the old KGB, police, and the army) to run the country and maintain his grip on power.

The fatal poisoning of Alexander Litvinenko in a London restaurant in November 2006 was a chilling reminder that the ghost of Stalin lives on. Litvinenko, who had defected to the United Kingdom six years earlier, was a former colonel in the Russian secret service (the FSB, successor to the KGB) and a vitriolic critic of Putin. Other Putin critics and mischief makers have been murdered, including Stanislav Markelov, a lawyer who defended Chechens and dissident journalists, and Anastasia Baburova—one such dissident journalist. Baburova became one of at least fifteen journalists killed execution-style (shot in the head on a Moscow street in broad daylight) since Putin took power. A month before the Litvinenko incident, Anna Politkovskaya, a popular investigative journalist and Putin critic, was shot dead in what appeared to be a cold-blooded contract killing.

Politkovskaya wrote for *Novaya Gazeta*, one of the few independent Russian newspapers still in existence. She's one of five journalists at *Novaya Gazeta* who have been murdered. In June 2012, a high-ranking police official arranged to have deputy editor Sergei Sokolov taken to a forest outside Moscow where he threatened to kill the newspaperman. A few months later, that same official charged Alexander Navalny, another Putin critic, with embezzlement (stealing sixteen million rubles worth of lumber)—a crime that carries a maximum prison sentence of ten years. On the same day, the feminist punk rock band Pussy Riot went on trial for blasphemy against the Russian Orthodox faith (see "Politics and Pop Culture").

Such incidents illustrate the severe limits to press freedom in Putin's Russia. As we are about to see, the same can be said of political opposition.

The Two Faces of Post-Communist Russia

Clearly, Russia has emerged from the dark days of its totalitarian past. Stalin is dead, but the legacy of Stalinism is still present in the political culture and the courts of law are tools of state power. The fate of journalists such as Politkovskaya Baburova and Putin opponents such as Litvinenko and Khodorkovsky attests to the continuing use of police-state tactics and a corrupt judicial system reminiscent of the Stalinist show trials to suppress dissent.

One piece of legislation in the summer of 2012 imposes heavy fines on protestors who attend unsanctioned street demonstrations. Another forces NGOs receiving funding from abroad to declare themselves "foreign agents" and submit to extraordinary financial audits. A third recriminalizes libel, with fines as high as five million rubles (over $150,000). A fourth creates a "blacklist" of websites to be blocked—a thinly disguised form of state censorship. These recent laws are Putin's way of dealing with problems inherent in the rise of a new middle class in Russia.

WHAT'S NEW, PUSSY CAT?

"Pussy Riot" is the name that a group of young Russian feminists with an attitude chose when they decided to form a punk rock band in 2011. Within a year, they were famous far beyond the borders of Russia—perhaps no group since the Beatles has made a more sudden and spectacular entrance on the world stage. But unlike the Beatles, Pussy Riot's fame was not from making hit records or doing world tours; it was from a brief singing "prayer."

In August 2012, three Pussy Riot members—known to fans as Nadia, Masha, and Katya—were sentenced to two years in prison after staging a thirty-second anti-Putin performance they called a "punk prayer" in a near-empty church in Moscow. The title of the "prayer" in question was "Mother of the Lord, Chase Putin Out." Putin was not amused: the three women had been kept in pretrial detention since being arrested the previous March.

The women, all between twenty-two and thirty years of age, were put on trial and, to no one's surprise, were found guilty. Guilty of what? Of violating "conceivable and inconceivable rules" and "emphatically vulgar" and "deliberately provocative" gesturing. Of "crossing themselves in a parodied way." Of wearing clothing "inappropriate in a church." And of other impious acts that "offended the feelings of religious believers."

Among the protestors outside the courthouse was Garry Kasparov, a former world chess champion turned political activist. A political culture that reveres strong rulers, state control of television, and strong backing from the Russian Orthodox Church all worked in Putin's favor. In the eyes of the world, however, Putin again showed his true colors—the colors of a true tyrant.

During the old Stalinist days, any open expression of dissent was typically characterized as criminal hooliganism endangering the public order. In Putin's Russia, it seems, the more things change, the more they stay the same.

When Pussy Riot got into trouble in Moscow and landed in jail, it was the result of a "performance" many true believers considered blasphemous or sacrilegious. Plus, it happened in a church! Should artists be allowed to do or say anything in the name of art no matter how offensive to the morals and/or religious beliefs of others? Does not the state have a right and duty to draw the line somewhere? Think about it.

(Hint: Search your memory (if that fails, try the Internet) for examples of outrageous songs, poems, and books; rock, rap, and hip hop artists; paintings, movies, and YouTube videos that are (or once were) deemed deeply offensive to people of certain religious sects, political persuasions, and social classes.)

Even so, Putin is not Stalin, and today's Russia is not the Soviet Union. Queuing up for a loaf of bread or a kilo of meat in freezing cold is no longer part of daily life. The dreaded knock on the door in the middle of the night is a thing of the past, as is the infamous Soviet gulag archipelago—the vast chain of forced labor camps in the Siberian wilderness. Gone too is the Soviet ban on foreign travel.

The horrors of Soviet history are no longer locked away: "*Gulag Archipelago* and other literature, fiction and nonfiction, about Stalin's terror are easily available in bookstores and libraries; academic research is unconstrained."[14] In 2007, Putin visited Butovo, one the sites where mass executions occurred under the Stalin terror in 1937 and 1938, calling it "insanity"; and in November 2010 the Kremlin admitted that the Soviet Union—*not* Nazi Germany—carried out the atrocity known as the Katyn Forest massacre near the Russian city of Smolensk in 1943.[15]

But Putin continues to rely heavily on Russia's law enforcement agencies—specifically the Federal Security Service (the FSB) and the new Investigative Committee under a Putin crony—to maintain his grip on power. FSB officers and veterans still proudly call themselves *chekisty*—heirs of the Cheka (Lenin's secret police). Putin himself got his start as a KGB officer under the old Soviet system.

Putin's relations with Europe and the United States are strained. In the eyes of the West, Russia has consistently backed the wrong side, be it Iran's nuclear ambitions, the civil war in Syria, or the secessionist movement in eastern Ukraine.

The Economy: Neither Fish nor Foul

In the early 1990s, Russians dared to hope that Russia was finally shedding its stifling autocratic political institutions and uncompetitive, anti-consumer economy. But that hope soon faded. With Putin at the helm, it all but vanished. Putin restored order and recentralized power, but he failed to take advantage of windfall profits from Russia's oil and gas exports to modernize and diversify the Russian economy. At the same time, he allowed cronies and corrupt insiders—so-called oligarchs—to amass fortunes and divert billions of rubles into private bank accounts abroad.

By 2014, Russia's emerging middle class constituted 42% of the population. In Russia's major cities, notably Moscow and St. Petersburg, these numbers were even higher. Arguably, Putin and his old-style Russian politics are out of step with this fundamental change in the class structure of Russian society.

At first, high oil prices allowed Putin to restore a measure of popular trust in the paternalistic state, which fell into disrepute in the turbulent 1990s. But in 2014, Western sanctions designed to punish the Kremlin for its support of east Ukrainian separatists began to take a heavy toll on the Russian economy (see Table 8.2). As the price of crude oil went into free fall (trading at $71.00 a barrel in early December 2014), and with the ruble losing value (down 40%), the nation braced for a new round of budget cuts and belt-tightening.

Given the dire circumstances, the Russian economy was expected to contract at least 0.8% in 2015 (a worst-case scenario—oil falling to $60 a barrel—put that figure at 3.5–4.0%). Capital flight was draining the nation's bank reserves. Meanwhile, Russia's banks and state-run companies "that constitute the heart of the Russian economy," reportedly owed nearly $700 billion to Western banks.

TABLE 8.2   Russia's Roller Coaster Economy, 1992–2014 (% annual change).

	1992	1996	2000	2004	2006	2008	2010	2012	2014
GDP	−14.5	−6.0	9.0	6.4	7.5	6.0	3.5	3.7	0.8
Inflation	2323	21.8	20.2	12.7	9.2	14.1	7.0	5.1	9.0

SOURCE: World Bank and *The Economist* ("Emerging Market Indicators"), July 1, 2000; December 7, 2002; March 27, 2004; February 19, 2005; and December 2, 2006. Data for 2008 and 2010 from Economist Intelligence Unit estimates, *The Economist*, January 31, 2009, p. 101, and December 11, 2010, p. 117.

"But sanctions imposed by the United States and Europe over Russia's annexation of Crimea and adventurism in southeastern Ukraine have blocked access to Western financing."[16]

Revitalizing the economy was one of the big challenges facing Putin even before oil prices dropped and relations with the West soured. Corruption—fraud, bribery, blackmail—are pervasive problems. Bureaucratic red tape is yet another. Foreign investors were reluctant to take the risks associated with doing business in Russia even before the falling out (and fallout) over Putin's aggressive moves in Crimea and eastern Ukraine. In 2014, the United States froze the assets of a Russian bank and several Russian oligarchs, foreign direct investment (FDI) in Russia fell sharply, venture capital all but dried up, and the ruble sank to record lows for the decade.

But Russia is a big country with a well-educated population, vast natural resources, and much potential for economic growth and development. In 2007, a new "state corporation" called Russian Technologies (RT), or "Rostec," was created to spearhead a drive to reindustrialize.[17] Since that time, hundreds of industrial firms and some 900,000 employees have been transferred to Rostec, whose goals are to innovate, develop new technologies, and eventually float high-quality companies on the stock market. Rostec is required to find new jobs for any workers laid off.

Moscow is making a bid to create a Russian Silicon Valley at a place called Skolkovo outside Moscow. This ambitious project is a special economic zone (SEZ), modeled after China's SEZs (see Chapter 5), credited with catapulting the PRC to the front ranks of the world's major economies in the short span of three decades. Whether Skolkovo will materialize into something more than a pipedream remains an open question. Nonetheless, it is a sign of the times and of Putin's sense of urgency in the face of new forces and rising powers in the global economy that are rapidly leaving Russia in the dust.

In 2012, Russia joined the World Trade Organization (WTO), normally a big step toward opening a national economy to global competition and normalizing trade relations with the West. But more recent events have had a chilling effect and given rise to fears of a new Cold War in Europe—a development no one, least of all Vladimir Putin, would or should welcome.

Will Russia Ever Change?

Does Russia represent the remains of a great empire in decay or will it reemerge as a major world power? Is it unalterably authoritarian?

The answer to the first question is probably "neither"—Russia will neither self-destruct as the Soviet Union did nor will it recapture the status of world-class superpower the Soviet Union achieved. The answer to the second question is probably "yes"; there is little reason to believe Russia's governmental institutions, power structure, or political culture will change any time soon.

Though the era of totalitarian rule has ended, Russia remains a riddle. The show trial of the rock band Pussy Riot in 2012 for blasphemy (a *crime*!?) underscored the tenuous and tentative status of democracy in Putin's Russia, as well as the collusive ties reminiscent of pre-Soviet Russia between church and the state, patriarch and potentate. Given centuries of despotism and centralized rule, the political culture necessary for liberal democracy to take root and flourish is too weak and the inertia of the past too strong.

Russia's post-Soviet constitution created a federation based on republican principles (aka, representative democracy). Today, Russia is neither federal nor democratic in character—one Western journalist has called Russia under Putin a "mafia state."[18]

We turn next to a brief look at Eastern Europe, a region of nations in transition. No two countries have approached the problems of political and economic reform in exactly the same way.

EASTERN EUROPE: TWO-TRACK TRANSITION

The newly independent states of Eastern Europe were Communist-ruled during the Cold War era, which lasted for more than four decades. All were saddled with centrally planned economies patterned after that of the Soviet "Big Brother." Just as central planning did not work in the long run in the Soviet Union, neither did it work anywhere else. But it is easier to demolish than to construct; for rebuilding, Eastern Europe had to look to the West. The West stood ready to help, but first the former communist states would have to create democratic institutions and market-based economies.

Poland

The boldest reforms were adopted in Poland, the Czech Republic, and Hungary. (The Baltic states of Estonia, Latvia, and Lithuania also moved quickly to jettison all vestiges of the Stalinist police state and central planning following the breakup of the Soviet Union.) Poland showed the way, launching "shock therapy" policies designed to create a functioning market and to privatize the notoriously inefficient state enterprises that were a legacy of Communist rule. Unlike the Soviet Union, Poland had never banned small-scale private enterprise, and a decade after its democratic revolution, private enterprise was flourishing as never before (with some two million registered businesses).

Poland's tough approach to reform yielded impressive results in the 1990s, when its economy grew faster than that of its ex-communist neighbors, averaging over 5% a year between 1995 and 2000. Poland also managed to tame inflation, a major threat to social and economic stability throughout the region. As a direct result of these market-friendly reforms, Poland attracted infusions of foreign investment that were, in turn, a tonic to its reviving economy.

However, double-digit unemployment (nearly 25% among young workers in 2014) remains a nettlesome problem, especially in a country where jobs had been guaranteed to all adults during two generations of Communist rule. A growing wealth gap is also a problem, as the relatively poor rural populations continue to lag behind the urban middle class. Because Polish agriculture was never collectivized (as in the Soviet Union), many of Poland's impoverished villagers still live and work on its two million family farms.[19]

Although polls show crime and official corruption have undermined public confidence in government, the Polish economy continued to improve year after year, turning in steady growth rates (5–7%) with modest inflation (2–4%) prior to the global recession in 2008. Poland's economy was projected to grow at a modest 2.3% in 2014. Poland joined NATO in 1999 and the European Union in 2004—before the euro crisis cast a pall over Europe's single market.

Poland is a parliamentary democracy with a popularly elected president. Prime Minister Donald Tusk's center-right Civic Platform won the 2011 elections with nearly 40% of the popular vote and gaining sixty-three seats in the Sejm (parliament). The Civic Platform (PO) and the agrarian Polish People's Party (PSL) formed a coalition government, with the PSL as a very junior partner. President Lech Kaczynski, leader of the main opposition party, called Law and Justice, was killed in a plane crash in April 2010. Bronislaw Komorowski (a Civic Platform leader from 2001–2010) was elected president in August 2010.

The Czech Republic

Unlike Poland, caught between two totalitarian states (Nazi Germany and Soviet Russia) in World War II, Czechoslovakia was betrayed at the Munich meeting between British Prime Minister Neville Chamberlain and German Reich Chancellor Adolf Hitler. (It's fair to call the Munich Pact a betrayal because Britain and France chose not to honor a preexisting military alliance with Czechoslovakia.) Hitler's Wehrmacht invaded and occupied Czechoslovakia in 1939. In 1945, as the war was drawing to a close, it was the Red Army, ironically—not the U.S. Army—that "liberated" most of Czechoslovakia, thus helping to boost the image of the Czech Communist Party. In the 1947 elections, Czech Communists won a majority of seats in the national parliament, formed a government, and quickly moved to establish a Stalinist dictatorship.

This bit of history is especially important both because the Communists came to power in a free election rather than a revolution (the only such instance in European history) and because Czechoslovakia was the *last* country where anyone who knew anything about Eastern (or Slavic) Europe would have expected that to happen.

Czechoslovakia came into being after World War I as a full-fledged parliamentary democracy—the only instance of popular self-government in Eastern Europe prior to 1989. In the Czech Republic, Prime Minister (now President) Václav Klaus extolled the virtues of the marketplace and implemented an ambitious coupon-redemption scheme that theoretically gave all Czech citizens shares of newly privatized (formerly state) enterprises. But the distribution was done without adequate safeguards and thus failed to accomplish one of its primary aims—to give Czechs a stake in the new market economy. In fact, crooks and insiders (a distinction without a difference) grabbed up the high-quality stocks, most of which never became available to the public, and used connections to get operational control of the "hottest" properties.

Unsurprisingly, this bungled attempt at reform soured many ordinary Czechs toward democracy and capitalism rather than solidifying popular support as it was intended to do. Inflation, fear of job losses, corruption in high places, a growing gap between the *nouveaux riche* and the majority, and a heightened awareness of how far behind the West Eastern Europeans in general—and Czechs in particular—had fallen all contributed to a deepening disillusionment.

In the eyes of the people, the shady entrepreneurs and self-aggrandizing politicians became synonymous with "the system."

Despite popular dissatisfaction with politics, the Czech Republic is a free country with a popularly elected president and parliament and an independent judiciary. The Czech economy, having stumbled along for most of the 1990s, made a good recovery following the recession of 1997–1999. Structural reforms (for example, in the banking sector) helped achieve this result. Voters strongly endorsed the Czech Republic's entry into the EU in 2004, a move that opened Europe's huge Single Market to Czech-built automobiles, armaments, machinery, and other exports and could well make the Czech Republic a magnet for foreign investment.

In the five-year period from 2003 to 2008, the Czech economy grew at an annual rate of 5.2%, while inflation averaged just below 3%. The manufacturing-based economy was especially hard-hit by the global recession in 2008-2009—industrial output fell by over 17.4% in November 2008, the highest of any EU country. (Spain was close, but the overall drop in industrial activity for the EU as a whole was a less dramatic 7.7%.) Due to budget constraints at home and Europe's painfully slow recovery from the global recession—exacerbated by the euro crisis after 2010—the Czech economy contracted in 2012 and 2013 but was on track to grow a mere 2% in 2014.

After more than two decades of freedom and independence, Czechs embrace constitutional democracy as an ideal but remain cynical about the existing political system and the politicians who run it. And for good reason: the Czech party system is fragmented (no fewer than nine political parties contested the 2010 elections), the Czech parliament is fractious (five parties claimed seats in the new parliament), and coalition governments are often unstable.

In 2012, the Czech parliament passed a constitutional amendment providing for popular election of the president. Previously, the president was chosen by parliament. This first direct presidential election in January 2013 required a second round runoff, in which Milos Zeman was elected president. But he soon fell afoul of public opinion for cozying up to Russia and China, among other things. Zeman is combative and vulgar by nature—the very opposite of the soft-spoken, diplomatic, and conciliatory Vaclav Havel, the Czech Republic's first president, a playwright famous for choosing his words carefully. In November 2014, during celebrations in Prague commemorating the twenty-fifth anniversary of the Velvet Revolution that ended Communist rule in Czechoslovakia, an unruly crowd pelted Zeman with eggs, shouting, "Resign! Resign!" True to form, he vowed to stay in office, and his exact words don't bear repeating.

Hungary

In 1968, the same year as the ill-fated Prague Spring ("socialism with a human face") in Czechoslovakia, the Budapest government launched the New Economic Mechanism (NEM). The NEM, aimed at limited decentralization of the economy and other market-oriented reforms, was a promising experiment in

Miloš Zeman—the Czech Republic's popularly elected—but unpopular—president.

CTK/Alamy

the early going. Production of consumer goods (always a low priority in Soviet-type economies) rose, and the quality of life for Hungarians generally improved. But hard-line Communists at home and abroad (particularly in the Soviet Union) opposed these reforms, and in the 1980s the NEM was abandoned.

Even so, as the economy steadily declined, Hungary turned to the West for trade, aid, and investment. The liberalization that accompanied this policy included a new tolerance of private businesses and partnerships with foreign multinational companies. Thus, Hungary's reform efforts—though limited in scope and scale by a combination of politics, ideology, and Soviet interference—gave it a head start when Communism self-destructed at the end of the 1980s.

After 1989, Hungary's popularly elected government accelerated the pace of free-market reforms. In particular, as the leading emerging market in the region, Hungary attracted more than half of all direct foreign investment in Eastern Europe, even though its population (about ten million) was a mere 25% of Poland's and a tiny fraction of Russia's.

Post-communist Hungary moved swiftly to break up and privatize its huge state-owned enterprises; by 1993 the private sector's share of the GDP was about 50%. The pace of privatization slowed temporarily when the Socialists gained a majority in the parliament in 1994, but the following year the same parliament passed legislation to speed the sale of state-owned enterprises and prepare to sell off public utilities and strategic industries such as steel and electricity.

Despite these bold restructuring efforts, Hungary has suffered high levels of inflation and unemployment. In the five years preceding the 2008 global recession, Hungary's economy grew at an annual rate of only 2.8%, while inflation averaged more than 5%. In 2009, the economy was in dire straits as demand for the country's manufactured goods crumbled—exports account for about 80% of Hungary's GDP, and industrial output fell by almost 30% in February.

To make matter worse, Hungary's currency (the Forint) dropped sharply. Because it depends so heavily on exports to the EU (and especially Germany), Hungary was particularly vulnerable as Europe and the world sank into recession in 2009. Hungary's struggling economy showed signs of recovery in 2014, growing 2.4%, but the nation's extreme energy dependence on Russia, which supplies 80% of its natural gas, made it hostage to the Ukraine crisis.

Like Poland and the Czech Republic, Hungary is a multiparty parliamentary democracy. In the first three free elections after 1989, a different party won control of the government each time—a sign of party competition and political pluralism at work.

Both president and prime minister are leaders of the right-wing Fidesz Party, which won a two-thirds majority in Hungary's unicameral legislature in the 2010 national elections—the biggest electoral margin since the end of communist rule. The first acts of the new government under Prime Minister Viktor Orban, including a tough new law aimed at restricting the independent media, left many observers questioning its commitment to liberal democracy. Voters handed Fidesz a second victory in the 2014 parliamentary elections. But in November, an estimated ten thousand Hungarians gathered outside the parliament in Budapest to protest against the Orban government's alleged corruption and abuse of power.

In sum, Hungary's political future remains under a cloud while its economic problems are raising tensions within Hungarian society. Will Hungary's fledgling democratic institutions survive? Now that Hungary is part of the EU, will Brussels stay on the sidelines if Hungary slides toward a police-state dictatorship?

The Changing Face of Europe

Most former communist states in Eastern Europe have joined NATO and the European Union, including Slovakia, Slovenia, the Baltic states (Estonia, Latvia, and Lithuania), Bulgaria, Romania, and, most recently, Croatia. Tiny Slovenia (population two million) has outshined all the others, achieving a per capita GDP that puts it well ahead of the Czech Republic, Poland, and Hungary—and even one Western European country, Portugal. All have made—or are in the process of making—the transition from authoritarian one-party rule and Soviet-style command economies to pluralistic representative democracy and market economies. Failure to make this transition means the door to the European Union remains shut.

Among the countries standing in line to join the West are Albania, Montenegro, and Serbia. Ukraine and Georgia have also expressed a desire to join both NATO and the EU. But the euro crisis, which started with a small country (Greece) and now threatens to spread and possibly call into question the survival of common currency, has created new burdens for EU members (especially Germany) and a collective sense of self-doubt in Brussels. Whether the new realities translate into a greater reluctance to admit new members only time will tell.

Amid all of Europe's "negatives" in these difficult times, it's easy to lose sight of the positives. For all practical purposes, totalitarianism (Communism, Nazism, Fascism) has disappeared from the map of Europe. There are still countries where elections are a farce and freedom of the press is a fairytale (Russia and Belarus, for example), but they are now few and far between.*

ASIA: AGING TIGERS—STILL STRONG OR ENDANGERED?

Like the former communist states of Eastern Europe, Asia's "four tigers"—South Korea, Hong Kong, Taiwan, and Singapore—were also in transition in the 1990s. (Under the terms of an 1898 treaty, control of Hong Kong reverted to China in 1997.) Other Asian "tigers" were emerging as well, including Thailand, Malaysia, and Indonesia. All competed with Japan, Asia's "economic miracle" and model of an export-driven economy. But already in the 1990s, the rise of China—combined with Japan's sinking economic fortunes—signaled a big change in the global balance of power and put Asia's tigers on notice: *Beware of the Dragon!*

*Belarus is a perennial Putin nemesis. Historically part of the Kremlin's "inner empire" from the time of Catherine the Great (1762–1796) to the breakup of the Soviet Union in 1991, Belarus has blocked Putin's efforts to resurrect the Old Russian Empire, resisted Putin's move to create a customs union (with Kazakhstan), and refused to recognize the independence of South Ossetia, Abkhazia (two provinces of Georgia that seceded with Russia's military backing).

South Korea: Beleaguered but Resilient

The economic transformation of South Korea, from a poor country dependent on agriculture to a modern industrial state powered by a technologically advanced manufacturing sector, was complete by the turn of the twenty-first century. South Korea achieved an impressive economic growth rate of more than 7% a year between 1971 and 2014.

The Economy: Down but Not Out Although China now has the world's second largest national economy, South Korea's per capita national wealth (GDP) was roughly six times mainland China's and twenty times that of Pakistan in 2010. To put South Korea's achievement in even better perspective, South Korea's GDP per capita is far larger than that of Chile, the richest country in Latin America, and more than double that of Brazil.

It has come very far in the half-century since World War II and the Korean War left its economy in a shambles and its people traumatized and destitute. But it has a long way to go to catch up with Japan. Indeed, Japan's GDP per capita ($45,680 in 2013) still far exceeds that of South Korea ($24,590).

In the 1990s, huge industrial conglomerates and largely unregulated big banks dominated South Korea's economy. These special interests had become powerful and entrenched, stifling competition.

Although Asia's financial crisis of 1997-1998, known as the **Asian flu,** did not start in South Korea, it had a devastating impact there. Big banks had been lending money to big business without regard to the underlying financial condition of the borrowers. This situation, as well as the general need to revitalize the country's economy, compelled the government to intervene aggressively—not to put the state in control of the economy but to give greater play to free-market forces.

Seoul launched a program of bold reforms in the late 1990s. The reforms proved to be a tonic: South Korea's economy grew 4% a year on average between 1995 and 2008. The country's resilient export-driven, trillion-dollar economy was slowed by the 2008 global recession but bounced back quickly thanks in no small part to a $38 billion economic stimulus program. South Korea's economy has slowed in recent years, averaging 3–4% annually.

Who Rules? New Times, Old Habits Korea's political traditions are authoritarian. North Korea has been Communist-ruled since World War II, while South Korea, a close ally of the United States, is anti-communist and theoretically a "republic" (see Figure 8.3). The official name "Republic of South Korea" was, in effect, the mask of a pro-Western police state for half a century. Then, in 1997, the impossible happened: Kim Dae Jung was elected president—the first opposition candidate ever to win (or be allowed to win) the country's highest office. Kim was awarded the Nobel Peace Prize in 2000 for his efforts to improve relations between the two Koreas.

South Korea's institutional reforms are tenuous, as Kim Dae Jung's successor, Roh Moo Hyun, found out when opposition parties that dominated a raucous National Assembly impeached him in 2004. After a sixty-three-day hiatus, the Korean Constitutional Court threw out the impeachment and reinstated Roh, thus ending a perilous political crisis in one of East Asia's pivotal states.

Asian flu
A term used to describe the widespread financial turmoil in Asian stock markets, financial institutions, and economies in 1997.

FIGURE 8.3   Map of South Korea. Note the vulnerable geostrategic location of the capital, Seoul, perilously close to the Demarcation Line (border zone) with South Korea's archenemy, North Korea.

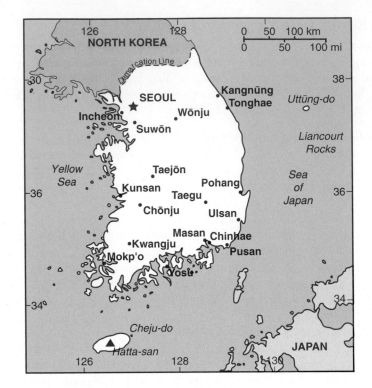

Business executive and former mayor Lee Myung-bak won the December 2007 presidential election, but five years later his approval rating had plummeted to an abysmal 30%. Rising food and gas prices, high education and housing costs, inadequate job opportunities for university graduates, and a weak social safety net were among the primary sources of public disenchantment with the government.

Despite the initial predictions of a landslide victory for the main opposition Democratic United Party (DUP) in the 2012 national elections, the ruling conservative Saenuri Party staged an upset, winning 152 seats, enough for a clear majority in the 300-member national assembly (the DUP won 127 seats).

Park Geun-hye, the daughter of General Park Chung-hee (South Korea's ruler from 1961 to 1979) was credited with engineering a major makeover of the conservative party in the run-up to the 2012 parliamentary elections. Her reward was to become her party's (successful) presidential candidate.

The nation's the first female president, she faced daunting challenges. South Korea's export-led economy, still suffering from the lingering effects of the global recession, faces stiff competition from China and Japan, as well as the other Asian tigers. Sluggish growth has been accompanied by declining living standards. The number of South Koreans living in relative poverty jumped 10% between 2006 and 2012, while one-fifth earned less than half the national average income.

Although Korea remains a divided peninsula, change is afoot. It is no longer fair to describe South Korea as an authoritarian state with a democratic veneer.

Thanks to a reformed political system that features competitive elections, civilian authority, and the rule of law, South Korea is making the transition from republic-in-name-only to just plain republic.

Taiwan: Asia's Orphan State

Taiwan is another of Asia's success stories, but it exists in a kind of diplomatic twilight zone. For more than three decades, despite determined efforts by the People's Republic of China to isolate it on the global stage, Taiwan has managed to prosper.

Taiwan: Beyond Recognition . . . Taiwan became an independent state after World War II when the Chinese Communists, led by Mao Zedong, defeated Chiang Kai-shek's Kuomintang. Until 1972, the United States recognized Taiwan as the legitimate government of China, although it was clear the communist regime in Peking was in control of the mainland. In 1972, the People's Republic of China replaced Taiwan at the United Nations and the United States decided to "derecognize" Taiwan in order to normalize diplomatic relations with Beijing for the first time since 1949.

The decision was a devastating blow to Taiwan. Although it has remained independent, it no longer enjoys diplomatic recognition by other sovereign states and is no longer a member of the United Nations. The reason for this unique state of affairs is that the People's Republic of China has successfully pressed its claim that Taiwan is part of China, there is only one China, and Beijing is its capital. Even so, Taiwan—officially the Republic of China– continues to enjoy the military protection and diplomatic goodwill of the United States, as well as close economic ties.

The Economy: A Little Tiger with Teeth Compared to mainland China, Taiwan is Lilliputian, but its per capita GDP, only slightly lower than South Korea's, dwarfs the PRC's. Exports—especially electronics, machinery, and petrochemicals—are the main drivers of Taiwan's economic growth.

A heavy dependence on exports makes Taiwan's economy, like Japan's and South Korea's, especially sensitive to fluctuations in global demand, turmoil in global stock markets, and downdrafts in the global economy. Little surprise, then, that in the year following the 2008 Wall Street meltdown, Taiwan's GDP fell to under 2%.

In 2010, exports bounced back and the economy raced ahead by over 10%. The GDP growth rate dropped to less than half that level in 2011, fell as low as 1.3% in the fourth quarter of 2013, but bounced back at around 4% in 2014.

Taiwan's economy grew at an average annual rate of 4–5% from 2003 through 2008—before the financial meltdown that plunged the world into the Great Recession. That's the kind of "normal" to which most countries would be only too happy to return.

Politics: Where Abnormal Is Normal Taiwan's economic success is nothing new, but its fretful movement toward liberal democracy *is* new. The country finds itself in a unique and unenviable position. For more than four decades, Taiwan has existed in a kind of international legal-political-diplomatic twilight zone.

Governments wishing to have normal relations with the PRC are forced to pretend that Taiwan doesn't exist. They can trade with Taiwanese companies but cannot exchange ambassadors or have official political or diplomatic relations with Taipei.

In 1988, Lee Teng-hui became the first native Taiwanese leader to assume the office of the presidency, and in the 1996 election he became the first popularly elected president in Taiwanese history. Lee instituted sweeping political reforms during his twelve-year tenure, continuing a process initiated in the mid-1980s by his predecessor, Chiang Ching-kuo (Chiang Kai-shek's son). In 2000, Taiwan's voters elected Chen Shui-bian president—the first time ever that the Taiwanese government was not headed by the leader of the Kuomintang.

Taiwan's political parties and electorate are polarized. The Pan-Blue Coalition favors eventual Chinese reunification, whereas the Pan-Green Coalition favors an official declaration of Taiwan independence. In September 2007, the Democratic Progressive Party (leader of the Pan-Green Coalition) approved a resolution asserting Taiwan's separate identity from China, expressing a desire to become a "normal country" under a new constitution and calling for general use of "Taiwan" as the island's name.

Chen assumed office pledging to clean up government, but his tenure was marred by allegations of corruption against a background of public discontent over a sluggish economy and legislative gridlock. Chen and his family allegedly embezzled millions of dollars while he was in office, charges that led to a high-profile trial, conviction, and a seventeen-year prison sentence in 2009.

The Kuomintang increased its majority in Taiwan's parliament in January 2008, and its nominee Ma Ying-jeou won the presidency that year, promising a more robust economy and the pursuit of closer relations with the People's Republic of China. Ma made good on the latter promise, but closer trade ties with the mainland raised fears that Ma's pro-China policies would jeopardize Taiwan's independence. Despite these fears, President Ma was elected to a second term in 2012.

Prime Minister Jiang Yi-huah and his cabinet resigned at the end of 2014 when the pro-China KMT party suffered big losses in local elections across the country—in all, twenty thousand candidates ran for eleven thousand positions. Ma, who is also KMT chairman, felt compelled to apologize to party supporters "for making everyone disappointed."

LATIN AMERICA: A NEW DAY DAWNING?

Whereas Asia's transitional states started with economic reforms, Latin America's led with political change. Democracy has finally taken root, but most countries in Latin America still have not found a recipe for economic revitalization.

The states of Latin America (formerly colonies of Spain or Portugal) gained independence in the 1820s—long before Europe's colonial empires were dismantled elsewhere. With few exceptions, military-bureaucratic rule was the norm in Latin America until quite recently. Only in a few countries, such as Colombia, Venezuela, and Costa Rica, had popularly elected civilian government ever succeeded. The wave of liberalizing reforms that swept across Latin America in the 1980s ushered in a whole new age in the region's history and opened a fresh page in its politics.

The ABCs of Reform: Argentina, Brazil, and Chile

In the 1980s, one Latin American military dictatorship after another stepped aside in favor of a democratically elected civilian government. Today, virtually every government in the region qualifies as a liberal democracy.

What drove these regime changes was the need for economic reforms, evidenced, above all, in the huge foreign debts many Latin American countries had amassed. The burden of these debts, combined with outmoded economic structures and uncompetitive (protected) industries, high inflation, mass unemployment, widespread poverty, and gross inequality between the rich and poor plunged the region into a crisis of self-confidence and underconsumption. Millions of people, especially *campesinos* (peasants) in rural areas, continue to struggle to survive at a bare subsistence level.

Chile Although in most of Latin America political change preceded economic reforms, Chile instituted market reforms *before* it democratized its political system. Under General Augusto Pinochet, who seized power in a bloody coup in 1973 by overthrowing the elected Marxist government of Salvador Allende, was one of the harshest military dictatorships in the region.

Pinochet's seventeen-year rule was a reign of terror in which more than 3,200 people were executed or disappeared. But the Chilean economy—spurred by market forces and a cozy relationship with the United States—marched ahead.

Chile is the most prosperous country in South America. Despite the persistence of official corruption and a uneven distribution of wealth reminiscent of feudal societies, the economy has continued to grow. Income inequality has started to shrink in recent times, but the top 10% still take $42 out of every $100 of disposable income in Chile (compared to $30 in the United States).

Exports are a major factor in this success story. The country's main exports are copper, fish, fruit, paper and pulp, and chemicals. Chile signed free-trade agreements with the EU in 2003, and similar agreements with the United States and South Korea went into effect in 2004.

Pinochet gradually eased his iron grip on the Chilean political system in the 1990s. Today Chile holds free elections and civilians run the government. In 2005, Michelle Bachelet, a Socialist, became Chile's fourth elected president since the end of the Pinochet era—and the country's first female chief executive. Her popularity fell sharply in the first year when massive demonstrations involving high school students broke out all over the country. The students were difficult to dismiss as a bunch of rebellious teenagers when what they demanded was a better education!

Camila Villejo, a twenty-three-year-old university student, is a prominent figure in the protest movement; she is also one of many young, university-educated Chileans who openly embrace communism two decades after its

She is called the "angel of liberty" by her admirers. Camila Villejo led mass university student protests against social injustice and inequality in Chile. There are many YouTube videos of Ms. Villejo on the Internet.

widely (but perhaps prematurely) celebrated death. According to opinion polls, 70% of Chileans supported the students' demands, even though some respondents had reservations about the students' methods.

But Bachelet won most Chileans back in the second half of her four-year term—according to one opinion poll, she had a record 84% approval rating when she left office in the spring of 2010. Under Chile's constitution, however, presidents cannot have consecutive terms, no matter how popular they are.

Billionaire businessman Sebastián Peñera, leader of the opposition center-right Alliance Party and the man Bachelet narrowly defeated in the 2005 election, was elected president in 2009. Peñera faced his first major test as president in the aftermath of the devastating 2010 earthquake. Peñera directed the dramatic rescue of thirty-three trapped miners—a story that was closely followed by the media around the world for many months. His approval rating soared to 63% in late 2010; over the next two years it plunged to under 30%.

What happened? In 2011, a Chilean winter of discontent followed the tumultuous Arab Spring. Often the causes of social unrest are rooted in a failed or failing economy, but Chile's economy was growing at a brisk pace. So what *was* the problem? In a word: fairness. In 2010, Chile joined the Organization of Economic Cooperation and Development (OECD), an exclusive club consisting of the world's most advanced economies. Among the OECD's thirty-four members, Chile "boasts" the biggest gap between rich and poor. The upshot is a pervasive sense of unfairness.

Evidence of this roiling discontent was not long in coming: in national elections at the end of 2013, Michelle Bachelet, now for running president again after a four-year hiatus, won in a landslide, the biggest margin of victory since Chile's return to democracy. Bachelet promised to tackle social and economic inequality through tax and education reforms, as well as constitutional changes.

Brazil In Brazil, the generals finally relinquished control of the government in 1985. Three years later, the country adopted a new constitution that provides for direct election of the president. Fernando Henrique Cardoso, an economist, was elected in 1995, promising to reform and restructure Brazil's economy. Despite his best efforts, Brazil continued to be plagued by heavy external debts, chronic budget shortfalls, extensive rural poverty, and glaring inequalities when Cardoso left office in 2002.

Cardoso's successor, Luis Inácio Lula da Silva, presented a stark contrast in both political philosophy and leadership style. A charismatic union leader and reformer, the new president was affectionately known as "Lula" to millions of

Brazilians. Under Lula's direction, the state ratcheted up pensions and the minimum wage by 50%. In 2006, Brazilians rewarded Lula's efforts by reelecting him to a second term.

Lula was ineligible to run again in 2010, but such was his popularity that any candidate he endorsed would have a good chance of winning. He chose a woman, Dilma Rousseff, who ran and won, becoming Brazil's first female president.

Lula was a tough act to follow. As president from 2003 to 2010, he managed to balance economic reforms and social justice. With Lula at the helm, the richest Brazilians (top tenth) got 11% richer, while the poorest (bottom tenth) gained 72%, thanks in part to the *Bolsa Familia* (Family Allowance), a plan that uses tax revenues to give cash subsidies to the poorest Brazilians provided they send their kids to school and get regular checkups at free public health clinics.

Despite a sluggish economy slowing to a nearly zero growth rate, Rousseff's personal approval rating hit record highs in the summer of 2012. "We are living in a period of crisis for the advanced economies," Rousseff wrote in an article on the Brazilian model. "Debt accumulation is no substitute for rising wages, and market self-regulation is no substitute for government regulation. The rich world is now searching for a more balanced economic model and there are some common policies we should all pursue in 2012." According to Rousseff, in the short span of eight years, more than forty million Brazilians were lifted "out of poverty and into the middle classes, with access to health, education, credit and formal employment."[20]

Notwithstanding bureaucratic obstruction, corruption, poverty, illiteracy, and inequality remain major obstacles to a Brazilian economic miracle. Yet Brazil *does* have a lot going for it. Measured by both population and landmass, it is the seventh-largest country in the world.

Thanks to Lula's popularity and political skills, Rousseff inherited a strong and stable government, a fiscally sound state, and a large, diversified service sector and modern industries including automotive, aeronautical, and electronics. That's the good news. The bad news is that Mother Nature is paying a heavy price.

Brazil has made a commitment to reduce the deforestation of its Amazon rain forest by 80% by 2020. The Amazon rain forest is one of the natural wonders of the world and a major mechanism for the exchange of carbon dioxide and oxygen in the earth's atmosphere. But clear-cutting for roads and agriculture is massively reducing the area it covers. In 2013, the government ordered an inventory of the trees in the Amazon—perhaps a step in the right direction.

Along with China and India, Brazil is one of three major economic powers to rise to prominence on the world stage in recent times (see Figure 8.4). But it turns out that even being on a glide path of economic growth and development is not a cure-all. Rising expectations, demographic realities, and energy demands all contribute to an ecological conundrum now often oversimplified in terms such as "climate change" and "global warming." These are problems not only for ecologically challenged BRICs (Brazil, Russia, India, and China) but also for the richest countries. The BRICs have the most to gain; the West has the most to lose.

FIGURE 8.4   Map of Brazil. With the exception of Ecuador and Chile, every country in South America borders on Brazil, the fifth-largest country in the world by total landmass.

Rousseff did not cover herself in glory during her first four years in office. Far from it. Yet despite a legacy that "includes recession, inflation above the Central Bank's target, opaque public accounts, rising public debt and a looming downgrade in Brazil's credit rating, as well as a current-account deficit that, at 3.7% of GDP, is the widest since 2002," she was reelected in 2014—but by slim 3%margin.[21] It was not an auspicious start to her second term. Even less so because—with charges of corruption in the air—her Workers' Party (PT) is reported to have financed the campaign in part with money stolen from Petrobas, the state-owned oil company.

Nevertheless, Brazil stepped onto center stage as a rising global power in 2014 when it hosted the World Cup, a wildly popular international sports event. As if that were a mere dress rehearsal, Brazil will also host the 2016 Olympic Games, which are expected to draw 600,000 visitors to Rio de Janeiro, the capital. Organizers expect to sell nine million tickets.

Argentina Argentina's military rulers bowed out in 1982 after the country's humiliating defeat by the British in the Falklands War. Argentina was then the richest country in South America in per capita GDP, but in the years that followed, corrupt politicians and economic mismanagement reduced its economy to ruins.

To hold down inflation and budget deficits, the government had little choice but to adopt unpopular policies, including high taxes and spending restraints. This policy of fiscal austerity, in turn, led to rising unemployment and social unrest. But the government feared that if it relaxed fiscal discipline, foreign investors would turn away. This dilemma led to a political crisis in 2001 as the slumping economy went from bad to worse. With the country on the verge of economic collapse, popular anger boiled over. Argentina became the scene of widespread riots and looting. Then it defaulted on its $155 billion foreign debt payments—the largest default of its kind in history. One president resigned, another could not calm the storm.

Néstor Kirchner, the governor of Santa Cruz, was elected president on a vow to reform the courts, police, and armed services and prosecute perpetrators of the dirty war (see "Landmarks in History"). Argentina's economy rebounded, growing at an impressive rate of 8% a year under Kirchner's guidance. In March 2005, Kirchner announced the successful restructuring of the country's debt. In January 2006, Argentina paid off its remaining multimillion dollar IMF debt ahead of schedule.

Kirchner chose not to run again in 2007, endorsing the candidacy of his wife, Cristina, instead. She won. This marital succession had a precedent in Argentina—Isabella Perón famously succeeded her husband, Juan Perón, in 1974. Néstor Kirchner died in 2010 amid calls for his wife's impeachment. She easily won reelection to a second term in 2011 with 54% of the popular vote, beating her nearest rival by 22%.

Cristina Kirchner's presidency has been marked by controversy over policy and marred by persistent questions over the family's personal finances, which reportedly have increased exponentially since they acceded to the presidency. Her attempt to dismiss the Central Bank president failed when he refused to step down and a judge annulled the decree. Kirchner used a 1983 truth-in-advertising law dating back to the days of military dictatorship to levy stiff fines on maverick economists for allegedly misleading consumers and deployed the national tax agency against some of her critics (tax evasion is common in Argentina).

Mass demonstrations in 2013-2014 attested to her unpopularity. For most Argentines, the presidential election scheduled for 2015 could not come too soon.

By all accounts, Cristina Kirchner mismanaged Argentina's economy, running up big deficits year after year and borrowing heavily. The inflation rate soared from 28% in 2013 to more than 40% in 2014, and real wages were declining. Car sales dropped 35$ and spending at supermarkets fell by more than 4%. When consumers start cutting back on groceries, it's a sure sign of hard times—an economy teetering on the brink of a deep recession. Another ominous sign: Argentina defaulted on its public debt in mid-2014. The Economist Intelligence Unit described Argentina as "a time bomb with multiple fuses."

The problems facing Brazil and Argentina are fairly typical for the region as a whole. In Latin America, political reforms have often proven easier to implement than economic reforms. The reasons are many and varied, but the most intractable problems are rooted in a history of injustice and extreme inequality. The potential for social and political instability inherent in such conditions goes far to explaining the appeal of radical populist and socialist ideas, as evidenced

THE ARREST OF LEOPOLDO GALTIERI

Following a military coup in 1976, Argentina's junta (ruling clique) declared martial law and began the "dirty war" to restore order and eradicate opponents. No one will ever know how many people perished in this brutal campaign of repression, but the Argentine Commission for Human Rights charged the junta with 2,300 political murders, more than 10,000 political arrests, and the disappearance of 30,000 people.

Blanket amnesty laws protected the perpetrators of Argentina's dirty war for many years. In July 2002, former junta leader Leopoldo Galtieri and forty-two other military officers were arrested and charged with the torture and execution of twenty-two leftist guerrillas during the country's seven-year military dictatorship (1976–1983). In June 2005, the Supreme Court ruled the amnesty laws unconstitutional. The following year, numerous military and police officials went on trial. But it was too late to save the victims or to find any trace of the "disappeared."

in the rise to power of Hugo Chávez in Venezuela and Evo Morales in Bolivia, as well as the persistence of violent Marxist and Maoist insurgent groups, most notably in Colombia and Peru.

Mexico

Institutional Revolutionary Party (PRI)
The dominant political party in Mexico from 1929 to the present. The PRI had never lost an election until 2000, when Vicente Fox of the National Action Party won the presidency.

National Action Party (PAN)
The main opposition party in Mexico; the PAN's candidate, Vicente Fox, was elected president in 2000.

North American Free Trade Agreement (NAFTA)
Agreement signed in 1994 by the United States, Mexico, and Canada that established a compact to allow free trade or trade with reduced tariffs among the three nations.

Mexico and the United States have been aptly called the "distant neighbors."[22] The two countries are geographically close but only for residents of one region, namely, the Southwest border states (California, Arizona, New Mexico, and Texas), all of which were once part of Mexico.

In other ways, Mexico is a foreign country to North Americans, many of whom have never been to Mexico and most of whom don't speak Spanish. No less important is the often troubled history of relations between the United States and Mexico, a history that includes war, annexation, and, of course, the legendary Alamo.

In more recent times, problems in bilateral relations have involved drug trafficking, gun-running, and illegal immigration. People north of the border often see Mexico as not only distant but also dangerous.

Historically, Mexico exemplifies a contradiction common throughout Latin America—a yearning for a "man on horseback" to lead a popular revolution coexisting with an authoritarian regime disguised as a republic. On paper, Mexico has been a liberal democracy since World War I. In reality, competitive elections in Mexico were a pipedream until the year 2000 when, after decades of one-party rule under the **Institutional Revolutionary Party (PRI)**, Mexican voters were given a real choice. The result was a first: opposition candidate Vicente Fox, representing the **National Action Party (PAN)**, won in a runoff election and the results were allowed to stand.

The **North American Free Trade Agreement (NAFTA)** boosted Mexico's economic prospects in the 1990s, but internal market reforms had been half-hearted, at best, due to Mexico's inefficient state-owned companies (for example,

PEMEX, the oil monopoly), entrenched interests, and a corrupt bureaucracy fearful of losing its privileges. Membership in NAFTA gave Mexico easy access to U.S. markets, but it also gave the United States leverage to pressure the Mexican government into accelerating economic reforms.

President Fox came into office vowing to do just that. It would not be any easier in Mexico than elsewhere in Latin America, but Mexico had to agree if it wanted to compete as an equal NAFTA partner with the United States and Canada. The 2003 national elections produced no clear majority in Mexico's federal legislature—for the third time in a row.[23] President Fox's efforts to reform Mexican government and economy were effectively blocked. In 2006, the PAN candidate, Felipe Calderón, was elected president in the closest Mexican election ever, with a 0.58% lead over a center-left opponent. His opponent, Andrés Manuel López Obrador, claimed fraud, calling for "pacific civil resistance," but an electoral tribunal upheld the outcome.

Calderón pledged to fight crime and corruption. His campaign slogan, "Clean hands, firm hands," struck the right chord, but changing a political culture is easier said than done. In office, Calderón placed a high priority on illegal immigration and security policy—especially the drug war and narcoterrorism (drug-related murders and kidnappings). His answer to rising world corn prices, the main food staple of Mexico's poor, was the Tortilla Price Stabilization Act. Unfortunately, it did not work—at least not well enough to satisfy voters. Similarly, Calderón's well-intended First Employment Program, aimed at creating new jobs for first-time new entrants into the labor force, was criticized for not going far enough.

Enrique Peña Nieto, leader of the Institutional Revolutionary Party (PRI) that ruled the country for seventy years until 2000, was elected president in July 2012. The PRI also won the most seats in Congress, but fell short of a clear majority. Peña pledged transparency in government; action to curb organized crime (drug-trafficking and drug-related violence against citizens); economic revitalization; and improved relations with the United States.

Too good to be true? If the past is any guide, Peña will be the latest in a long line of leaders who overpromised and underperformed. Mexico's economy has recently rebounded, growing 2.5% in 2014 and expected to jump 4% in 2015. Other vital signs pointed to improving health—inflation was moderate and falling, as was the unemployment rate. Politically, Mexico has undertaken significant reforms, and democracy is no longer just a dream.

But drug-related violence—executions, kidnapping, and random murders—are all too common. In November 2014, the federal government disclosed a shocking crime. Drug traffickers murdered forty-three students who had disappeared from a teacher-training college in southern Mexico (Guerrero state) in late September. The police had kidnapped the victims on orders from the town's mayor! Such an unspeakable crime points to a frightening fact: in Mexico, the rule of law has not taken firm root in the society, and police protection is at best sporadic, at worst nonexistent.

Official corruption, fiscal mismanagement, gross social inequality, and endemic poverty are problems by no means unique to Mexico. They are prevalent throughout Latin America—and not just Latin America. When people do not have good jobs or benefits or steady income, they lack the kind of security middle-class Americans north of the border tend to take for granted.

Without a circulation of wealth throughout the whole society, it is difficult, if not impossible, to complete the transition from a rural-based, slow-growth, inward-looking protectionist economy to a modern, urban, market-based, mass-consumption, export-oriented economy. The latter is where Latin America is headed, but for the region's poor, it is taking too long to get there.

In sum, Latin America has made a turn toward political pluralism, but the social and economic transition is incomplete. In the year 2000, around 225 million people were considered poor (43.9% of the total population), according to the Economic Commission for Latin American and the Caribbean (ECLAC); by 2012 that number had fallen to 167 million (28.9%)—the lowest in three decades. For millions of Latin Americans, the promise of a better life is no longer an empty one.

SUMMARY

With the demise of the Soviet Union in 1991, Communist rule ended nearly everywhere in the world. Nonetheless, a few exceptions remain, including China, Cuba, and North Korea. The collapse of Communism brought the problems of transition in the former Soviet-bloc states to the fore. Other countries launched major political and economic reforms in the 1990s, including South Korea and Taiwan in Asia and Argentina, Brazil, and Chile in Latin America.

The Soviet political system was an outgrowth of the Stalinist totalitarian model. In trying to reform and restructure this system, Mikhail Gorbachev followed in the footsteps of an earlier Soviet leader, Nikita Khrushchev. In the Soviet system, the Communist Party ruled, and a person's ranking in the party was the best indication of that individual's political power. When Gorbachev rose to the top post in the Communist Party in 1985, he faced both acute economic problems and associated social problems, each related to the failure of central planning.

Gorbachev's reforms proved inadequate to save the former Soviet Union. His successor, Boris Yeltsin, failed to guide Russia through a smooth transition. Then his successor, Vladimir Putin, inherited a mess—economic dislocations, ethnic fragmentation, and poorly established state institutions. Putin turned out to be a decisive leader who was twice elected by large majorities but has ruled as a traditional strong Russian boss.

China instituted major free-market reforms and downplayed much of its communist ideology after Mao's death, but remains a country headed by a single party that tolerates no political or religious dissent. As China modernizes its armed forces and attempts to become a world power, it faces increasing social problems as well as economic and border tensions among its provinces.

India, South Korea, and Taiwan are three other examples of Asian societies in transition. All three countries made the transition to market-based (though semi-protectionist) economies first, but have more recently instituted meaningful political reforms.

The transition process in Latin America is the reverse of the pattern found in Asia. Argentina, Brazil, Chile, and Mexico are four key countries in the region. In three of the four, political reforms came before economic reforms (Chile is the exception). In Venezuela and Bolivia, market reforms have taken a back seat to social reforms—a reversal of what has happened elsewhere in the region and the world. The extremely unequal distribution of wealth and official corruption remain obstacles to progress.

KEY TERMS

nomenklatura   213
perestroika   213
glasnost   213
democratization   213
Asian flu   231

Institutional
   Revolutionary Party
   (PRI)   240
National Action Party
   (PAN)   240

North American Free
   Trade Agreement
   (NAFTA)   240

REVIEW QUESTIONS

1. What problems did the Soviet Union face in 1985, when Mikhail Gorbachev came to power, and how did Gorbachev respond? With what consequences?
2. "One of the most important questions facing Russia today is whether it can become a stable democracy." What do you think? Explain.
3. What countries in Eastern Europe, Asia, and Latin America have made the most successful transitions so far? Explain your choices.
4. Comment on the economic transition in China since Mao's death. What reforms did Mao's successors institute and with what results?
5. Compare and contrast the transitions in Eastern Europe with the transitions in Latin America relative to: (a) economic reforms; (b) political stability; (c) the rule of law; and (d) human rights.
6. Compare and contrast the transitions in Asia with transitions in Latin America relative to: (a) economic reforms; (b) political stability; (c) the rule of law; and (d) human rights.
7. What region of the world has experienced the most success in making the transition from dictatorship to democracy in the past two decades? Justify your view.
8. Has Russia or China been more successful in making the transition from a centrally planned economy to a market-oriented economy? Compare and contrast the way the two countries have approached problems and assess the economic reform strategies of each. Which country has had a better outcome so far? What is the evidence?

WEBSITES AND READINGS

Websites

New York Times "Russia" page: http://topics.nytimes.com/top/news/international/countriesandterritories/russia/index.html

Reuters News Service's "Russia" Page: http://www.reuters.com/places/russia

"Russia on the Web": http://www.valley.net/~transnat/

English-Language Newspaper Published in Prague: http://www.praguepost.com/

The Economist's **Articles on Taiwan and the Two Koreas:** http://www.economist .com/topics/south-korea; http://www.economist.com/topics/north-korea; http://www.economist.com/topics/taiwan

Latin American Information Network: http://lanic.utexas.edu/

Political Science Database of the Americas: http://pdba.georgetown.edu/

Readings

Baker, Peter, and Susan Glasser. *The Kremlin Rising: Putin's Russia and the End of the Revolution.* New York: Scribner, 2005. A highly readable account of Russian politics in the Putin era written by two former *Washington Post* bureau chiefs.

Brass, Paul. *The Politics of India Since Independence.* New York: Cambridge University Press, 2008. A concise study of political, economic, and culture change in India over the past half century.

Camp, Roderic et al. *Politics in Mexico: The Democratic Transition,* 4th ed. New York: Oxford University Press, 2003. A rich introduction to Mexican politics that continues to withstand the test of time.

Gessen, Masha. *The Man Without a Face: The Unlikely Rise of Vladimir Putin.* New York: Penguin/Riverhead Books, 2012. Gessen is that rare Russian journalist who has dared to criticize Putin and (so far) lived to tell about it.

Goldman, Marshall. *Petrostate: Putin, Power, and the New Russia.* New York: Oxford University Press, 2008. Russia is major power, but addiction to energy exports and extreme dependence on a single export market are major obstacles to growth and diversification.

Guha, Ramanchandra. *India after Gandhi: A History of the World's Largest Democracy.* New York: Harper Perennial, 2008. An expert chronicle of India's history and politics following the untimely assassination of Mahatma Gandhi, the leader of country's non-violent mass movement for independence from British colonial rule, in January 1948.

Kynge, James. *China Shakes the World: A Titan's Rise and Troubled Future— and the Challenge for America.* New York: Houghton Mifflin, 2006. A treasure trove of information and insight into contemporary China by a former *Financial Times* bureau chief in Beijing.

Lucas, Edward. *The New Cold War: Putin's Russia and the Threat to the West.* New York: Palgrave Macmillan, 2009. The threat is plausible. Think: Georgia, Crimea, and Ukraine.

Luce, Edward. *In Spite of the Gods: The Strange Rise of Modern India.* New York: Doubleday, 2007. A good, balanced account of contemporary India's emerging economy, the problems India still faces in its modernization drive (including pervasive corruption and criminality in government and society alike), and the sheer complexity of this wondrously diverse society.

Politkovskaya, Anna. *Putin's Russia: Life in a Failing Democracy.* New York: Henry Holt, 2004. Reprinted in 2007 in paperback (Owl Books) after the author, one of Russia's best-known dissident journalists, was murdered in what appeared to be a contract killing.

Preston, Julia, and Samuel Dillon. *Opening Mexico: The Making of a Democracy.* New York: Farrar, Strauss, and Giroux, 2005. A good read by two former *New York Times* Mexico bureau chiefs.

Reid, Michael. *Brazil: The Troubled Rise of a Global Power.* New Haven: Yale University Press, 2014. Brazil is to South America as China is to Asia, but the country faces big problems.

Shirk, Susan. *China: Fragile Superpower.* New York: Oxford University Press, 2008. One of the best books on contemporary China.

Wilpert, Gregory. *Changing Venezuela by Taking Power: The History and Policies of the Chavez Government.* New York: Verso, 2006. The title captures the book's contents.

Wolpert, Stanley. *A New History of India,* 8th ed. New York: Oxford University Press, USA, 2008. The title says it all.

CHAPTER 9

Development
Myths and Realities

Learning Objectives

1 Explain the concept of development in the study of politics and economics.
2 Discuss the challenges involved in building a new nation-state.
3 Compare and evaluate India and Nigeria as models of economic development.
4 Identify and elaborate on five obstacles to development.
5 Choose one failed state, describe how it failed, and analyze the failure.
6 Explain why failed states pose problems for regional stability and world order.

This chapter focuses on the problems arising in the context of too little development too late, rather than too much too soon. We use the term **least developed countries** (LDCs), a term adopted by the United Nations, instead of "developing countries" (see Table 9.1). LDCs encompass the poorest of the poor.

During the second half of the last century, the West lumped Africa, Asia, and Latin America together into what was commonly called the Third World. In this

least developed countries (LDCs) Countries where the ratio of population to land and jobs is unfavorable to growth, where the economy is not diversified, and where literacy rates are low; three criteria used to classify LDCs also indicate the challenges they face: (1) low income; (2) human resource weakness (nutrition, health, education, adult literacy); and (3) economic vulnerability.

TABLE 9.1   The World's Least Developed Countries*

Africa (33)			
1	Angola	18	Madagascar
2	Benin	19	Malawi
3	Burkina Faso	20	Mali
4	Burundi	21	Mauritania
5	Central African Republic	22	Mozambique
6	Chad	23	Niger
7	Comoros	24	Rwanda
8	Democratic Republic of the Congo	25	São Tomé and Príncipe
9	Djibouti	26	Senegal
10	Equatorial Guinea	27	Sierra Leone
11	Eritrea	28	Somalia
12	Ethiopia	29	Sudan
13	Gambia	30	Togo
14	Guinea	31	Uganda
15	Guinea-Bissau	32	United Republic of Tanzania
16	Lesotho	33	Zambia
17	Liberia		

Asia and Pacific (15)			
1	Afghanistan	9	Samoa
2	Bangladesh	10	Solomon Islands
3	Bhutan	11	Timor-Leste
4	Cambodia	12	Tuvalu
5	Kiribati	13	Vanuatu
6	Lao People's Democratic Republic	14	Yemen
7	Myanmar	15	Maldives
8	Nepal		

Latin America and the Caribbean (1)	
1	Haiti

*This is the list drawn up by the United Nations' Office of the High Representative for the Least Developed Countries. It can be accessed on the Internet at http://www.unohrlls.org/en/home/. Click on "least developed countries" and "country profiles" on the drop-down menu.

SOURCE: United Nations Office of the High Representative for the Least Developed Countries. http://www.unohrlls.org/en/home/.

narrative, the First World was epitomized by the United States, Western Europe and Japan, plus Canada, Australia, and New Zealand—rich countries with stable societies and well-established democratic political institutions. The citizens of these fortunate states were free to criticize the government. The communist states—Soviet Russia and Eastern Europe—comprised the Second World. All the rest were known as the Third World, collectively referred to as "underdeveloped" or "less developed" countries.

Today it is considered politically incorrect to use such pejorative terms. Indeed, the term "developing countries" is rarely used to describe the former colonies. Many of these countries now have diversified economies, meaning they are no longer simply agrarian or nomadic but have industries and service sectors as well. Indeed, major companies in the United States and Europe outsource manufacturing and services to China, India, Malaysia, and Indonesia where labor costs (wages) are low.

In fact, *all* countries are developing, no matter how rich or how poor. Indeed, if some countries are not developed enough to sustain themselves, other countries are, arguably, not sustainable for the *opposite* reason: development driven by the latest advances in science and technology has given rise to major new problems and huge challenges (carbon pollution, climate change, pandemics, water wars, nuclear accidents, etc.).

By definition, LDCs display all or most of the following features: endemic poverty; ethnic, religious, or tribal conflict; widespread illiteracy; political turmoil; and glaring inequalities. Although the picture is changing in much of Asia and, to a lesser extent, in Latin America, many sub-Saharan African nations continue to face great obstacles on the path to full political, economic, and social development.

In the worst cases, the economy goes into a tailspin, the government collapses, societies erupt, and entire populations are plunged into anarchy. In the 1990s, this chilling possibility became a reality in places like the former Yugoslavia, Rwanda, Sierra Leone, and the Côte d'Ivoire (Ivory Coast); more recently, forces of anarchy have ravaged societies in the Middle East, Central Asia, and West Africa.

In the upheavals of 2011-2012 known as the "Arab Spring," rulers in Egypt and Tunisia were overthrown following bloody confrontations between demonstrators and security forces. In Libya, where civil war broke out, Dictator Muammar Gadaffi fled, but rebels captured and killed him. A full-scale civil war in Syria dragged on through 2012 and into 2015 with no end in sight.

In 2014, a jihadist group called the Islamic State of Iraq and Syria (ISIS) cut wide swathes of death and destruction across a vast territory, gaining control of towns and cities in northern Iraq and eastern Syria, engaging in violent clashes with Kurdish fighters, threatening Baghdad, and prompting President Obama to redeploy U.S. military forces there. In December 2014, thirteen people were killed when U.S. Special Forces attempted to rescue hostages in Yemen—among the dead were a woman, a ten-year-old boy, an American journalist, and a local al Qaeda leader.

West Africa has been in crisis for more than two decades. Insurgencies, atrocities, kidnappings, "child soldiers"—these horrors were the stuff of daily life in this all-but-forgotten corner of sub-Saharan Africa during the 1990s. Although troubles persisted into the 2000s, a modicum of stability and peace was restored. But in 2012, a new crisis boiled over when jihadist insurgent groups in northern Mali seized the country's largest city, Gao, and the fabled town of Timbuktu.

The background to the crisis in Mali involved a military coup d'etat in 2012 that overthrew an elected president and scrapped the country's constitution. France sent troops to help Mali's army put down the Islamist rebellion in 2013.

Given the endemic instability in the region, there was a danger that the conflict would spill over to neighboring states. Across the border in Algeria, jihadists attacked a BP gas facility and seized hostages. A shootout with Algerian security forces left some sixty-nine people dead, including thirty-nine foreigners and an Algerian, presumed to be hostages.

Pakistan, a big country (population: 170 million) located in one of the most volatile regions of the world, perennially teeters on the edge of open rebellion. Pakistan's per capita GDP is lower than India's and roughly one-tenth that of New Zealand or South Korea.

With few exceptions, endemic poverty is the root cause of the worst problems facing most of the least developed countries—some three billion people, almost half the world's population, live on less than $2.50 a day (see Figure 9.1). According to the World Bank, the poorest 40% of the world population account for 5% of global income; the richest 5% account for 75%. Over one-fourth of the children in LDCs are stunted or underweight due to chronic malnutrition; about two-thirds live in South Asia or sub-Saharan Africa—two of the most conflict-ridden regions on the planet.

Nearly one billion people entered the twenty-first century unable to read or write, but the correlation between poverty and illiteracy is just part of the story. In the least developed countries, unemployment is the norm and only the most fortunate few have access to a health clinic or doctor. Preventive health care is also beyond reach. The lack of mosquito nets is a major reason there are half a billion new cases of malaria and as many as two million deaths, mostly children, in the LDCs each year. Add an estimated 50–100 million cases of dengue fever and approximately 25,000 deaths annually, and the magnitude of the problem of poverty becomes all too apparent.[1] One of the biggest stories in 2014 involved the Ebola epidemic. First discovered in 1976, the Ebola virus is fatal in half the cases, and there are no licensed vaccines. The West African countries of Guinea, Liberia, and Sierra Leone were the most severely affected in the latest outbreak. All suffer from a lack of doctors and nurses, medical facilities and supplies, and public health infrastructure. Although the disease is not highly contagious and can only be transmitted through direct person-to-person contact, ill-informed and irresponsible headline news stories gave rise to a scare bordering on hysteria for a time in the United States.

Poverty, malnutrition, illiteracy, tribal and ethnic rivalries, official corruption, and violence against women are among the many problems we often associate with the regions formerly known as the Third World. What we often forget is that these problems are related to the bitter legacy of colonialism, and they continue to be exacerbated by the fact that many of the world's poor countries

FIGURE 9.1   Percent of People in the World at Different Poverty Levels, 2005.
How many people in the world are poor? The answer depends on who is counting
and how national governments and international organizations define poverty.
At $1.00 a day, "only" about 880 million people were poor in 2005; but if we draw
the poverty line at $2.00, that number climbs to 2.6 billion.

The 1990 poverty rate was cut in half in 2010—five years ahead of the
UN goal—but the number of people still living in extreme poverty remains
"unacceptably high." In 2011, 17% of people in the developing world lived at or
below $1.25 a day (down from 43% in 1990 and more than 50% in 1981); and just
over one billion people lived on less than $1.25 a day (compared with 1.91 billion
in 1990).

According to the World Bank, even at the current rate of progress, "some 1
billion people will still live in extreme poverty in 2015—and progress has been
slower at higher poverty lines. In all, 2.2 billion people lived on less than U.S. $2 a
day in 2011, the average poverty line in developing countries [indicative of deep
deprivation and] only a slight decline from 2.59 billion in 1981."

SOURCES: World Bank Development Indicators, 2008; and "Poverty Overview" (October 2014) at http://
www.worldbank.org/en/topic/poverty/overview#1.

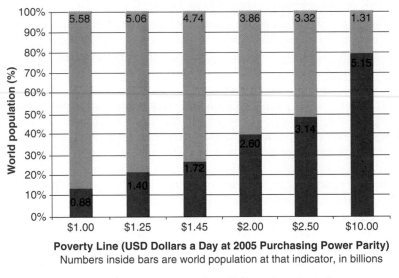

Poverty Line (USD Dollars a Day at 2005 Purchasing Power Parity)
Numbers inside bars are world population at that indicator, in billions

■ Below the poverty line   ■ Above the poverty line

contain resources that the world's rich countries desire—a mixed blessing, to be
sure, as the turmoil in the conflict-ridden Middle East attests.

World poverty amidst Western affluence raises serious moral issues. In this
chapter, we focus on two basic questions. First, what are the causes of poverty
and instability in least developed countries? Second, is a world divided between
rich ("us") and poor ("them") sustainable? A closer look at the obstacles to
progress and good government in these countries will shed light on the extreme
challenges they face.

DEVELOPMENT AS IDEOLOGY

During the Cold War, the Third World was also called the South, which highlighted the great disparities between the industrially developed states in temperate climates above the equator (North), and the former colonies in the tropical and semitropical zones below it (South). According to a view known as **neocolonialism,** the rich nations of the North continued to exploit the poor nations of the South even after the latter gained independence in the post-World War II period. This view both reflected and fed into notions about the existence of an ill-defined **North-South conflict.**

Several Third World countries promulgated the idea of a Manichean struggle between the rich (north) and the poor (south) in the 1950s and 1960s. Ghana's Kwame Nkrumah published a book in 1956 entitled *Neo-Colonialism, The Last Stage of Imperialism.* "Faced with the militant peoples of the ex-colonial territories in Asia, Africa, the Caribbean and Latin America," Nkrumah wrote, "imperialism simply switches tactics." Nkrumah called for solidarity among the former colonial peoples, railing against the "extended tentacles of Wall Street" and Washington (in particular, the Pentagon and the CIA) as the "very citadel of neo-colonialism."

However, all such attempts to bring about solidarity among the LDCs were doomed to fail. As memories of colonial rule fade, the anti-imperialist rhetoric that resonated throughout much of Africa, Asia, and Latin America has lost its relevance. More than half a century after independence, blaming the old overlords for new problems no longer rings true. Official corruption and mismanagement are widespread and well-known facts. Even more telling is the fact that some former colonies are racing ahead and others are sliding into the abyss.

The West countered neocolonialist ideology with its own capitalist ideology, extolling the virtues of freedom, democracy, and commerce. The fact that capitalism grew out of the Western experience and was tainted by its close association with colonialism made it a hard sell in the Third World. But strategic grants of foreign aid and trade concessions, and the implicit or explicit threat to intervene militarily, provided the West with a good deal of leverage nonetheless.

THE IDEA OF DEVELOPMENT

What exactly does development mean in a global economy undergoing such rapid change? For better or worse, the definition is based on the Western experience and the yardstick in common use is a Western measure of economic and political success. That doesn't make it good or bad, right or wrong, but it does raise questions about its applicability and acceptability outside the West.

In the least developed countries, the vast majority still do not enjoy access to education, jobs, health care, or the other good things in life that are the hallmarks of modernity in the West. Moreover, few LDCs have governments that are accountable, stable, and clean (as opposed to corrupt). Although some of these countries have made great strides while others continue to languish, even the most successful continue to have massive poverty and unemployment rates.

When we in the West say a country is "developing," we are usually thinking of a LDC, and what we mean is that it is not *yet* truly modern—that is,

neocolonialism
A theory holding that unequal and exploitative economic arrangements created by former colonial powers continued to be used to maintain control of former colonies and dependencies long after they gained formal independence in the 1950s and 1960s.

North-South conflict
A shorthand term for the tensions and disputes that arose between the rich industrialized countries and the former colonies during the Cold War era.

resembling the Westernized world. Westerners tend to assume that as, or if, these countries develop, they will look increasingly like us—urbanized, secularized, materialistic, and technology-dependent—and will want what we want.

LDCs come in all shapes and sizes. Some are huge—Brazil has a territory of three million square miles (larger than the continental United States) and a population of over 200 million; India's territory of one million square miles supports a population of 1.2 billion. Others are tiny—the Pacific island of Nauru, for example, has 8,000 people living on eight square miles of land.

Nauru is small but not poor, thanks to a brisk trade in phosphate exports. Most of the poorest countries depend primarily on agriculture. LDCs are often dependent on a single commodity or raw material for export, but a few, such as the oil-rich states of the Persian Gulf—Bahrain, Kuwait, Oman, Qatar, Saudi Arabia, and the United Arab Emirates—rely largely on a single natural resource, as does Russia, a country much poorer than Saudi Arabia and the others, who are anything but poor.

The world's poorest countries generally have the highest population growth rates; the richest often have the lowest. The world's population, surpassing 7.3 billion in 2015, has more than doubled since 1969. As Figure 9.2 and Figure 9.3 show, population growth rates have been steadily declining since the 1960s, but the world's total population continues to climb and is projected to reach nine billion by 2050.

Population pressure places onerous burdens on economic, social, and political structures in many poor countries, but comparisons can be misleading and often yield surprises. The Gaza Strip—one of the most wretched places on earth—has one of the fastest growing populations in the world. Arab and sub-Saharan countries generally have higher birthrates than Asian or Latin American nations. Asia is by far the most densely populated part of the globe. China and India alone account for roughly 37% of the world's total population. Asia as a whole is home to almost three-fifths of the people but has only about 18% of the landmass.

FIGURE 9.2   World Population Growth Rates, 1950–2050.

SOURCE: U.S. Census Bureau, International Data Base, June 2011 Update.

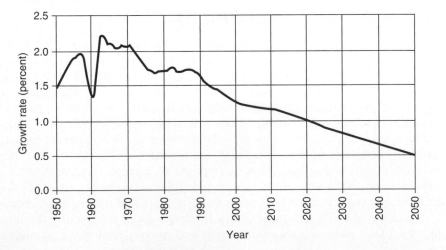

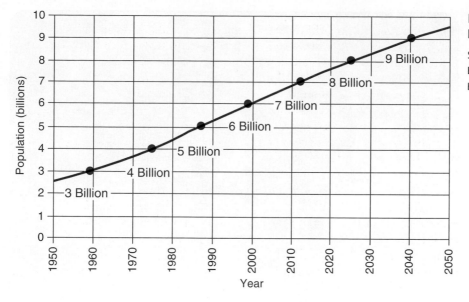

FIGURE 9.3 World Population, 1950–2050.

SOURCE: U.S. Census Bureau, International Data Base, June 2011 Update.

Apart from Asia, however, population density in least developed countries is relatively low. Africa's average population density is only 24 per square kilometer, as opposed to India's 296, the United Kingdom's 646, Japan's 880, and Singapore's 5,571. Africa has more arable land per capita than any other so-called developing region.

Why are so many of the least developed countries in the world located in sub-Saharan Africa? There is no simple answer, but no doubt the legacy of colonialism—enslavement, foreign intrusions, cultural genocide, and shameless exploitation—plays a major role.

THE LEGACY OF COLONIALISM

Only twenty-three countries among the current United Nations membership were independent in 1800. More than half of these states were in Europe, with Afghanistan, China, Ethiopia, Japan, Iran, Nepal, Oman, Russia, Thailand, Turkey, and the United States rounding out the list.[2] Since then, the number of independent states has risen to more than 190. World War II (1939–1945) was a watershed because it led to the rapid deconstruction of the European colonial empires (see "Landmarks in History"). Most of the countries existing today came into being during this recent period, and all but a few were least developed countries. Also, the breakup of the Soviet Union led to the creation of some twenty-five new independent states in Eastern Europe, Transcaucasia, and Central Asia by 1994.[3]

For centuries, the great powers of Europe competed for colonial holdings, ruling and administering over weaker and technologically less-advanced peoples and territories located in faraway places around the globe. These colonial empires were a source of great prestige and wealth. In the nineteenth century, European powers scrambled to colonize Africa. At the beginning of the

Ethnic strife is an all-too-common legacy of colonialism and remains a problem for many developing nations. Here a member of the Luo tribe is being attacked by a Kikuyu gang in January 2008 in the northeast Nairobi slum of Huruma.

Bloomberg/Getty Images

colonialism
The policy of seeking to dominate the economic or political affairs of underdeveloped areas or weaker countries (see also imperialism).

imperialism
A policy of territorial expansion (empire building), often by means of military conquest; derived from the word *empire*.

nonviolent resistance
A passive form of confrontation and protest; also called civil disobedience at times.

twentieth century, Britain, France, Belgium, Germany, Portugal, Holland, Italy, Spain, and Turkey all possessed overseas colonial empires (see Figure 9.4). This European intrusion—which came to be known as **colonialism** or **imperialism**—became synonymous with subjugation and exploitation in the minds of the indigenous peoples.

Colonialism *did* include Europeans dominating native peoples, and it *was* based on implicit or explicit notions of racial superiority or religious zeal (or both). However, there were great differences in the methods and means employed by the colonial powers. For instance, the British approach was far milder than Spanish colonial rule, which was notorious for its rapacity and cruelty. The Portuguese and French tried to assimilate colonized peoples. France even granted Algerians seats in the national legislature and positions in the national cabinets. The Dutch in Indonesia allowed native rulers to remain in power. Great Britain pursued both strategies, relying on local authorities to maintain law and order and allowing natives to pursue careers in public administration, attend British schools and universities, and enter the professions.[4]

Nonetheless, the idea of being governed by a distant country was repugnant to most colonial peoples. In many cases, independence and violence went hand in hand. In India, however, Mahatma Gandhi led a nationwide mass campaign of **nonviolent resistance** (*satyagraha*), a strategy later adopted by Martin Luther King Jr. in the United States. (Ironically, both Gandhi and King were assassinated.)

Colonialism's legacy remains controversial. Any advances in health (hospitals), education (schools), and transportation (roads) generally came at a high price for the native peoples—including disruption of traditional ways of life and

THE AGE OF IMPERIALISM

FIGURE 9.4 The World in 1914. Note how many European countries, including small countries such as Belgium, Denmark, and Holland (the Netherlands), had far-flung colonial empires at the beginning of the twentieth century. Note also that these empires encompassed nearly all of Africa and much of Asia but had all but disappeared from Central and South America.

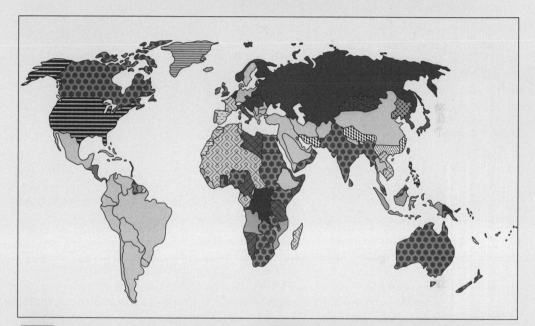

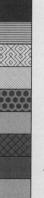

Belgium	
Denmark	
France	
Germany	
Great Britain	
Holland	
Italy	
Japan	
Portugal	
Russia	

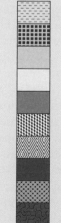

Spain	
United States	
Independent States	
Bodies of Water	
American sphere of influence	
British sphere of influence	
French sphere of influence	
German sphere of influence	
Japanese sphere of influence	
Russian sphere of influence	

(Continued)

(CONTINUED)

A new wave of European colonial expansion occurred in the second half of the nineteenth century, sometimes called the Age of Imperialism. Earlier in that century, popular revolutions in the Americas against England, Spain, and Portugal had led to disillusionment with empires and colonies. Industrialization diverted attention from external expansion in favor of internal development, and the new emphasis on free trade removed much of the rationale for global empire building. British Prime Minister Benjamin Disraeli expressed the tenor of the times in 1852. "These wretched colonies," he said, "will all be independent too in a few years and are a millstone around our necks."

But as industry grew, Europe's economic and political leaders began to seek new sources of raw materials and new markets for their products. After 1870, free trade gave way to protectionist policies, and soon a race for new colonies began. Various theories defending colonial expansion were expounded. Alfred T. Mahan's geopolitical concepts were used to "prove" great powers could not survive without overseas possessions. Charles Darwin's concept of the survival of the fittest was used to "prove" colonialism was in accordance with the inexorable laws of nature. Rudyard Kipling wrote about the "white man's burden" of spreading civilization to a benighted world. Even U.S. President William McKinley claimed God had spoken to him on the eve of the Spanish-American War (1898), commissioning the United States to take the Philippines and Christianize "our brown brothers."

By the end of the nineteenth century, all of Asia and Africa had been colonized. Even China had lost its sovereign status: It was subjugated through a series of treaties that gave various European powers special rights and prerogatives. Africa in 1914 was under the colonial sway of no fewer than seven European nations—Belgium, France, Germany, Great Britain, Italy, Portugal, and Spain. In fact, only two independent nations remained—Ethiopia and Liberia.

epidemics caused by the introduction of European germs into populations with no resistance.[5]

The extent to which Western countries continued to exploit former colonies *after* independence is debatable. Today, trade issues top the political agenda in relations between the rich and poor countries. Although agriculture constitutes only 8% of the world's total merchandise trade, exports of food and fiber so vital to the LDCs are among the hardest hit by protectionist policies of rich countries.

The consequences of colonialism are still with us. Colonial empires were created without regard to preexisting ethnic identities, territorial boundaries, and the like. When the European powers withdrew, they typically created artificial new states by stitching together a crazy quilt of incompatible peoples and cultures. (Iraq, Sudan, and Nigeria are three prime examples.) Chronic political instability, coups, revolutions, civil wars, and even genocide—these are the bitter fruits of colonialism. Simply listing *some* of the least developed countries that have been wracked by conflict in recent years proves the point: Afghanistan, Angola, Burma, Burundi, Cambodia, Chad, the Democratic Republic of the Congo (formerly Zaire), Côte d'Ivoire, Ethiopia, Iraq, Liberia, Nigeria, Pakistan, Rwanda, Sierra Leone, Somalia, Sudan, and Sri Lanka.

The fragility of these societies has led to dire warnings about the "coming anarchy" in Africa and elsewhere.[6] Raising the specter of anarchy is perhaps overly pessimistic, but Somalia has experienced a calamitous breakdown in civil order in recent times, as have Sudan, the Congo (DRC), and Syria.

NATION-STATE NEWBIES: FOUR CHALLENGES

Building a new nation-state is an exercise in **political development**. Rich countries often display certain common traits: a stable government, a merit-based civil service system, basic public services (police and fire protection, education, health, and sanitation), and legal structures (law codes and courts). All these traits are typically lacking in poor countries. Imagine growing up in a society where not only schools but also drinking water and basic sanitation do not exist. How can people who have no money, no police protection, and who cannot read or write lift themselves out of poverty or demand decent government?

The development process can be—and often is—destabilizing. It is therefore no great surprise that governments in least developed countries are often authoritarian, prone to coups, and beset by crises. Poor countries typically face four fundamental developmental challenges: (1) nation building, (2) state building, (3) participation, and (4) distribution.[7]

The first and most basic challenge is **nation building**—the process of forming a common identity based on the notion of belonging to a political community separate and distinct from all others. Often the concept of "nation" is based on common ethno-linguistic roots. The countless conflicts in Africa and Asia in the post–World War II era testify to the extreme difficulty (if not impossibility) of artificially building something as natural as a nation within a territory containing multiple ethnic and religious communities. The lessons of recent U.S. attempts at nation building in Iraq and Afghanistan also point to the conclusion that it cannot be done from the outside by outsiders.

Having a *charismatic* leader present at the creation is a key variable in the initial nation-building stage (try to imagine the founding of the United States without George Washington). Notable examples include Egypt's Gamal Abdel Nasser (who ruled from 1954 to 1970), Kenya's Jomo Kenyatta (1964–1978), India's Jawaharlal Nehru (1947–1964), Indonesia's Sukarno (1945–1967), and Libya's Muammar el-Qaddafi (1969–2011). Flags and celebrations also help instill a sense of national identity, and threats from a neighboring state—real, imagined, or manufactured—can galvanize unity, at least until the perceived danger subsides.

The second challenge, **state building**, is the creation of political institutions—in particular, a central government—capable of exercising authority and providing services throughout the length and breadth of society. A functioning state bureaucracy promotes economic development and social unity by such mundane means as creating the infrastructure (roads, bridges, telephone lines) necessary for an integrated national economy. To achieve this essential result, the government must be capable of levying and collecting taxes. But in countries with traditional economies based on subsistence agriculture, there is often little

political development
A government's ability to exert power effectively, to provide for public order and services, and to withstand eventual changes in leadership.

nation building
The process of forming a common identity based on the notion of belonging to a political community separate and distinct from all others.

state building
The creation of political institutions capable of exercising authority and allocating resources effectively within a nation.

or nothing to tax, which leads to a vicious cycle that can only be broken with infusions of foreign capital (trade, aid, and investment).

But foreign investment (an external variable) depends on political stability (an internal variable). It turns out that in the least developed countries, there are all sorts of vicious cycles.

A third challenge facing the LDCs is *participation*. For new societies to prosper and grow economically, the people must be actively engaged in the development process. This kind of mobilization gives rise to a political dilemma: As people become more actively involved and feel the effects of government (good and bad), they begin to demand a greater voice in determining who governs and how. But what if rising expectations strain the capacity of the state to respond? Hence, the challenge of participation is how to harness popular energies without setting in motion the forces of political disintegration or revolution.

The fourth and final challenge is *distribution* to reduce the extreme inequality that often characterizes **traditional societies**. Extremes of wealth and poverty can easily lead to a pervasive sense of injustice and, in turn, to mass revolt (see Chapter 14), as Marxism's popular appeal in the Third World during the Cold War demonstrated. In some cases, attempts have been made to address the challenge of distribution through land reform, but often only half-heartedly. Readjusting tax burdens and instituting income redistribution are two other obvious approaches to this problem, but the cost of Western-style social welfare programs is prohibitive for least developed countries.

Problems arising from the unequal distribution of wealth are now also arising in some of the world's most advanced economies. The United States, where the extreme concentration of wealth now resembles Argentina and other Latin American countries, is a prime example.

THE STRATEGY OF DEVELOPMENT

As we have seen, political development and popular participation often go hand in hand. But not all forms of popular participation are bottom-up (democratic); some are top-down (coercive). The latter are associated with authoritarian or totalitarian regimes. Democratic states are, by definition, limited in what they can do by constitutions, laws, and public opinion. For this reason, democracy and development often do not easily coexist, and dictatorships have been (and still are) all too common in the LDCs.

To say that democracy is a sign of development is true, but it begs the question: what explains development? In fact, democracy is a sign of wealth. Not all democracies are rich (although most are), nor are all rich nations democratic (although, again, most are). But there are precious few examples of democracy and poverty coexisting for very long.

Democracy and Development

Why does democracy work in many rich countries but not in most poor countries? One way to approach this question is to look for factors most democracies have in common—in other words **democratic correlates**. In theory, where these correlates exist in the greatest number and measure, the probability of

traditional societies
A common term for often resource-poor societies that continue to observe premodern ways of life, work, and worship; often associated with high infant mortality rates, low life expectancy, poverty, illiteracy, hunger, and lack of the most basic medical services.

democratic correlates
A condition or correlate thought to relate positively to the creation and maintenance of democracy within a nation.

democracy is greatest; conversely, where they are largely absent, democracy has the smallest chance of succeeding.[8] But in the real world, theory and practice often diverge.

Economic correlates include:

- *National Wealth*. Prosperity and democracy are often found in the same place, as are poverty and autocracy, but not always. India, for example, has been democratic since independence, despite being poor and extremely diverse, whereas oil-rich Saudi Arabia is autocratic.

- *A Market Economy*. Market economies generally favor private enterprise over state ownership of the means of production. Competition rewards efficiency and innovation. Supply and demand drive decisions about what to produce and how. Self-interest and the need for self-reliance encourage savings and investment.

- *A Middle Class*. A sharp class division with no buffer between rich and poor is not conducive to a sustainable democracy. Sooner or later, the many will strike back against the few—either rising up in open rebellion or simply slacking off on the job, placing either the state or the economy—or both—in grave jeopardy.

- *The Internet*. Access to the latest knowledge and information is vital to economic success; in the age of globalization, access to the Internet is essential.

There are also certain political, cultural, historical, and geographic correlates of democracy. Political correlates include civilian control over the military, a strong independent judiciary, and the existence of a differentiated civil society (civic clubs, trade unions, business organizations, and the like).[9] *Cultural* correlates, such as tolerance of diversity, respect for the rule of law, and belief in democracy are also important. Obviously, the greater the distribution of wealth and education in a given society, the more likely that the seeds of democracy will spread.[10] But that doesn't solve the problem for the LDCs that, by definition, lack the resources to build schools or the wealth to spread around.

Development and Democracy

What comes first: democracy or development? The stunning success of China in reducing poverty provides dramatic proof that development without democracy is possible. Indeed, civil rights are hardly a top priority for people who are starving, sick, or homeless.[11] A vibrant economy is more likely to have an immediate impact on the quality of life, social services, infrastructure, and educational opportunity than, say, free elections.

The reforms necessary to spur economic development inevitably have spillover effects on society and the political system. Thus, privatization and foreign investment give rise to a nascent middle class. To be competitive, it is necessary to cultivate a professional class with the same type of educational opportunities and financial rewards. To gain access to foreign markets, least developed countries face pressures to open up their own markets. Western products and services—from music to fashion—give rise to individualism, materialism, and a desire for freedom of expression, especially among the youth. In these and countless other ways, market-oriented economic reforms impart a bias toward democratization. Where such reforms bring new hope and prosperity, they help ensure that if and when democracy finally arrives, it does so without plunging society into a state of anarchy.[12]

Sub-Saharan Africa: Neither Democracy nor Development?

Between 1974 and 1990, more than thirty countries in southern Europe, Latin America, East Asia, and Eastern Europe replaced authoritarian with democratic governments. One noted observer wrote that it was "probably the most important political trend in the late twentieth century."[13] Everywhere, that is, except Africa.

Then in the early 1990s, a democracy wave rolled across sub-Saharan Africa, and at least nine countries—including Benin, Cape Verde, and Gabon in West Africa—held free elections, in most cases for the first time ever.[14] It was South Africa that witnessed the most stunning changes, however, as black majority rule supplanted apartheid (white-supremacist rule). Democratic reforms were changing the face of politics in Benin, Botswana, Guinea-Bissau, Madagascar, Mali, Namibia, and Sao Tome as well during this time.[15]

Elsewhere in Africa, however, things fell apart. In 1993, Nigeria's military rulers rescinded election results that displeased them. Côte d'Ivoire's government did the same. Elections in Kenya, the Cameroon, and Gabon were marred by irregularities and corruption. Rwanda was the scene of genocidal violence in 1994. In 1996, military governments in Chad, Gambia, and Niger rigged national elections to achieve the outcomes they desired. During the 1990s, Somalia sank deeper into chaos and anarchy. Bloody civil wars wrought havoc in Liberia and Sierra Leone, and the conflict in the Democratic Republic of the Congo (formerly Zaire) was accompanied by unspeakable atrocities. More than a decade later, the Congo is still a war zone. Thus, despite democratic gains, clan or tribal tensions destabilized much of sub-Saharan Africa in the 1990s.[16]

NIGERIA VS. INDIA: TWO CASE STUDIES, ONE RIDDLE

Nigeria is a giant with few equals on the African continent, but India dwarfs Nigeria in nearly every category. The world's tenth largest oil exporter, Nigeria is resource rich; India, the world's seventh largest oil importer, is not. Nigeria's natural wealth to population ratio is favorable to successful nation-state building; India, with well over a billion people, is not so fortunate.

And yet India has had a long run as a parliamentary democracy, interrupted only once (in 1975) by then Prime Minister Indira Gandhi who declared a state of emergency amid escalating riots. She allowed free elections in 1977 and was voted out of office. Nigeria, on the other hand, was under military rule during most of its post-independence history. When the military finally relaxed its chokehold on the government in 1999, it ushered in a decade of turmoil and misery.

Today, India is not only more democratic than Nigeria, but it is also achieving more rapid and diversified development. Why? Let's take a closer look at these two countries in search of clues to solving this riddle.

Nigeria: A Poor Oil-Rich Country

A large country in West Africa, Nigeria includes several distinct ethnic groups that predominate in different parts of the country, has many smaller tribes, and several hundred distinct languages are spoken.[17] Potentially one of sub-Saharan Africa's great powers, Nigeria endured inept military rule for much of its brief history as an independent state. Although the country accounts for only 3% of Africa's landmass, its population (estimated at 178 million in 2014) makes up some 20% of sub-Saharan Africa's total.

Nigeria is not a natural nation-state. Originally a British colony, it was drawn up for the administrative convenience of its colonial rulers who were only dimly aware of the ethnographic map of Africa at the time. Within its borders are peoples divided by region, religion, ethnicity, language, and culture. Nigeria's astonishing diversity also makes it a breeding ground for social conflict. The country is also divided along religious lines: Muslims dominate in the north and Christians in the south.

Tensions simmer between Christians and Muslims. Regional animosities, exacerbated by religious, ethnic, and linguistic differences, erupted in a bloody civil war in 1967, when eastern Nigeria seceded as the independent state of Biafra. The war, which lasted about three years and ended in defeat for the rebels, claimed at least 600,000 lives.

After 1967, corrupt and incompetent military regimes ruled Nigeria. Despite huge state-owned oil reserves that produced a steady flow of export revenues, the nation's economy sank into a deepening morass with the vast majority of the population living in abject poverty.

In the 1990s, Nigeria's economy stagnated, growing by less than a half percent per year while corruption reached new heights. A 1996 U.N. fact-finding mission did not mince words: Nigeria's "problems of human rights are terrible, and the political problems are terrifying." A succession of military dictators and ruling cliques enriched themselves shamelessly while neglecting the country's economic and social needs. According to Transparency International, a research institute based in Berlin, Nigeria had the most corrupt government in the world in the mid-1990s.[18]

By this time, bribery and extortion had become a way of life in Nigeria, where the system of "patronage" (with the military rulers bestowing government jobs and other favors on supporters of the regime) produced a bloated, inefficient, irresponsible, and unresponsive bureaucracy that absorbed more than 80% of the annual budget. Even today, it is not unusual to find petty civil servants sleeping at their desks or asking visitors for cash. Higher-level officials routinely inflate the contracts for everything the state procures and embezzle untold sums of money.

The average per capita income in oil-rich Nigeria (about $2,700 at purchasing power parity in 2013) is only about half that of India, which has a population more than six times larger. High world oil prices have boosted Nigeria's oil-dependent economy in recent years, but most Nigerians have experienced few benefits.

There is no good reason for Nigeria or Nigerians to be poor. In 2014, Nigeria's GDP (estimated at $509 billion) overtook South Africa's to become the largest national economy in sub-Saharan Africa. Nigeria is a major oil producer, but its petrodollar bounty has not been invested in infrastructure, public works projects, or job-creating private business enterprise. In addition to suffering atrocious macroeconomic mismanagement, the country has been plagued by tribal and ethnic rivalries.

The complexity and diversity of Nigerian society partially explains the failure of two previous experiments with democracy and elected civilian government (in 1960–1966 and 1979–1983). Nigeria's military rulers repeatedly promised free elections, but these promises were not kept. When elections were held in 1993, the results displeased the generals, who nullified the election, imprisoned the winner, and charged him with treason. Thereafter, many other critics of the military regime were also imprisoned and persecuted; some were even executed.

In 1999, a former military leader, Olusegun Obasanjo, became Nigeria's first democratically elected president since 1983. Obasanjo was a rarity in Nigeria—a public figure with a military background and a reputation for personal integrity. His promise to root out corruption, however, was wishful thinking. Here is how one *New York Times* reporter described the situation at the end of 2005:

> Corruption touches virtually every aspect of Nigerian life, from the millions of sham e-mail messages sent each year by people claiming to be Nigerian officials seeking help with transferring large sums of money out of the country, to the police officers who routinely set up roadblocks, sometimes every few hundred yards, to extract bribes of 20 naira, about 15 cents, from drivers.[19]

Corrupt military regimes ran the country almost continuously from 1967 to 1999. The generals would promise—and occasionally stage—a national election, but it would turn out to be a sham (as in 1993). Mounting international pressure no doubt played a large role in compelling Nigeria's military rulers to allow free elections in 1999 and to permit the results—the election of the first popular presidential candidate in nearly twenty years—to stand.

But corruption did not end with the return of civilian government, and a decade later the morally debasing effects of easy money from a grossly mismanaged oil industry with few links to the national economy were still apparent everywhere. For a time Nigeria—a major oil producer—was actually *importing* gasoline. Although the country has extensive fossil fuel resources, crooked officials who control the state-monopoly oil company have used it as a cash cow for personal enrichment rather than a resource for national economic development.

Hopes for a new beginning in Nigeria were dashed in 2007 by widespread reports of fraud in local and parliamentary elections and a sham election for president. What some called "gangster politics" eclipsed outgoing Obasanjo's attempted reforms.[20] When Umaru Yar'Adua succeeded Obasanjo as president in 2007, he inherited an improved economy but not a particularly healthy one. Nearly halfway through his first term, nothing was yet being done about the country's inadequate infrastructure, nationwide electricity cuts were still a common occurrence, and continuing attacks by militants in the oil-rich Delta region were severely disrupting oil production, which provides 95% of Nigeria's export revenues. Meanwhile, all but a few Nigerians continued to languish in poverty—and frequently darkness as well.

Yar'Adua died in office after an extended illness that left him incapacitated and the government in limbo. Vice-president Goodluck Jonathan (yes, that's his real name) formally succeeded Yar'Adua as president in May 2010, pledging to fight endemic corruption, clean up the electoral process, and fix the electricity grid. As a member of the Ijaw, an ethnic group native to the Niger delta where rebels have engaged in a prolonged and bloody battle for a bigger share of the oil income that makes up 80% of the central government's revenues, Jonathan is perhaps Nigeria's best hope of ending this bitter dispute.

Jonathan won the presidential election in 2011, a mixed blessing for any Nigerian civilian leader intent upon improving the life of the long-suffering Nigerian people. Four years later, in late March 2015, General Muhammadu Buhari defeated Goodluck Jonathan in a lopsided vote. It was the first time in Nigerian history that an incumbent president was defeated. General Buhari vowed to defeat the Boko Haram Islamist insurgents responsible for attacks on civilians and mass kidnappings. Nigeria continues to be plagued by a dysfunctional economy and a corrupt state bureaucracy.

Nigeria's oil-wealth has not led to diversification of its economy or any significant redistribution of income. The unemployment rate was almost 30% (!) in 2013 and most Nigerians—as much as 70% of the population—live below the poverty line.

As noted earlier, Nigeria is a diverse society with deep ethnic and religious divisions that frequently erupt in violence. The absence of a well-established rule-of-law culture and dependable law enforcement puts life and property at constant risk. In 2014, a militant Islamist group called Boko Haram seized control of towns and territory in northeast Nigeria and declared it a caliphate—an Islamic theocratic state—with the city of Gwoza, a city of close to half a million people, as its capital. "Few outsiders dare to visit. A trader who recently returned after making a delivery approved by the militants described it as an abattoir after hours: 'cold, calm and full of blood'."[21]

Boko Haram is the same group that abducted more than two hundred school-girls earlier in 2014 in the town of Chibok. Government officials announced a cease-fire with the group in October and claimed to have extracted a promise to release the girls, but the Boko Haram attacks continued and the girls' fate remains in the hands of the jihadists. By the spring of 2015, the terrorist group had taken an estimated 2,000 captives, including a high percentage of girls and women.

Boko Haram, which targets Muslims and Christians alike, killed at least 4,000 civilians in 2014 and at least 1,500 in the first three months of 2015, according to Amnesty International, which estimates that the real number could be much higher. The Jonathan government's failure to protect the people, unchecked official corruption, and gross economic mismanagement were all key factors explaining the verdict of the voters in the 2015 election.

India: Elephant or Cheetah?

With its 1.2 billion people—17% of the world's population—India accounts for only about 2% of global GDP and about 1% of trade.[22] India has the second-largest population in the world and one of the most diverse. In geographic size (3 million square miles) it ranks seventh, behind Australia (7.7 million square miles, population 22 million) and ahead of Argentina (2.7 million square miles, population 40 million) (see Figure 9.5).

The Indian constitution recognizes sixteen languages, though census data indicates more than 1,500 languages are spoken, including dialects. The "big three" official languages are English, Hindi, and Urdu. Hindi is spoken by about one-third of all Indians. English is the elite language, spoken by all university-educated Indians. Urdu is the language of Indian Muslims, the nation's largest minority group.

India is also home to various religions. Hinduism predominates, but there is also a large Muslim population (about 12% of the total), as well as Sikh, Jain, Parsi, Buddhist, and Christian minorities. Since Indian independence in 1947, communal violence—between Hindus and Muslims or Hindus and Sikhs—has erupted periodically. In some instances, members of one religious group have massacred members of another. In 1984, Prime Minister Indira Gandhi was assassinated by her Sikh bodyguards. In 1991, her son, former Prime Minister Rajiv Gandhi, was assassinated while campaigning to regain office.

The traditional caste system in India also created a barrier to development—everyone was born into a particular caste and remained there for life.

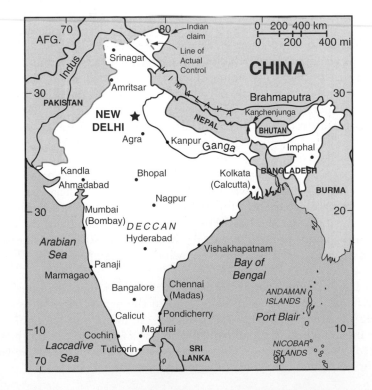

FIGURE 9.5 Map of India. Note India's lengthy border with Pakistan; note also the geographical triangle formed by New Delhi (north central) and Mumbai (formerly Bombay) on the Arabian Sea and Calcutta on the extreme eastern edge by the Bay of Bengal.

LANDMARKS IN HISTORY

INDIA: A Political Miracle

After World War II, Germany and Japan were often called economic miracles. Few noticed that during this same period a political miracle was happening on the Asian subcontinent.

India gained its independence in 1947, thus becoming one of the very first former colonies to break away. Mahatma Gandhi's leadership, exemplified by the strategy of nonviolent resistance, was a major factor in India's successful campaign against the British *raj*. India's extreme poverty and diversity at the time of independence made any attempt to create a democracy in the power vacuum that resulted from the British departure precarious. Even so, India's early leaders, including Gandhi (who was assassinated in 1948) and Jawaharlal Nehru, India's first elected president,

resolved to bring India into the world as a democracy. And so they did.

India's achievements since independence include:

- Maintaining a parliamentary democracy
- Reducing poverty by more than half
- Bringing about a "green revolution"; becoming a net exporter of grain
- Quadrupling literacy rates
- Vastly improving health care delivery; more than doubling life expectancy
- Achieving high annual GDP growth rates
- Emerging as a global player in pharmaceuticals, steel, information and space technologies, and telecommunications

SOURCE: The World Bank, "India Country Overview 2014."

Professions, occupations, and social status were all governed by the rules of the caste system. Members of a lower caste could not aspire to a profession or occupation reserved for a higher caste, nor could anyone marry outside his or her caste. Obviously, this rigid framework greatly impeded social mobility—the very mobility needed to transform a traditional society into a modern one. A vast underclass, called the untouchables, had no rights or opportunities in traditional India. The Indian government has since outlawed untouchability, but old attitudes die slowly, especially in tradition-bound rural societies. (Seven in ten Indians still live in small villages.)

Societal divisions tend to be reinforcing rather than crosscutting. Thus, Indian Muslims practice their own distinct religion and live in their own insular areas, have a distinct ethnic heritage, and speak their own language. Much the same can be said of Sikhs, Jains, and other groups. In extreme cases, these divisions can lead to calls for separatism or communal violence. Militant Sikhs have called for an independent state in northwestern India (where they are concentrated).

Hindu-Muslim hatred has led to periodic massacres. In the state of Gujarat in March 2002, Hindus slaughtered as many as 2,000 Muslims. In August 2003, two bombs blamed on Muslim militants killed 52 people in Mumbai (formerly Bombay). On November 26–29, 2008, ten coordinated shooting and bombing attacks occurred in Mumbai, killing at least 173 people and injuring more than 300. The split between Hindus and Muslims continues to destabilize India—and therefore South Asia as a region—more than six decades after independence.

India was long the indigent giant of Asia, a society with a rich history and a civilization symbolized by the splendor of the Taj Mahal but unable to cope with the challenges of the modern world. Just as Hong Kong, Taiwan, South Korea, and Singapore were often called "dragons" or "tigers" not long ago, India was likened to an elephant—huge and magnificent, but encumbered by the weight of its massive body. Anyone familiar with the contemporary Asian scene, however, is more likely to think of India as a cheetah than an elephant. Neither image quite fits; paradoxically, each is half true.

Despite gains and an impressive growth spurt in recent years, India remains a poor country even by comparison with China (the only country with more people). One reason: India's population is growing much faster than China's. Until recently, demography has overwhelmed development in India.

Although a recent five-year growth spurt saw India's economy grow by nearly 9% a year, China's GDP was still 3.5 times larger than India's in 2008-2009. China needs 8% annual growth to provide jobs for the roughly seven million new members of its workforce each year; India's workforce is growing by about fourteen million a year—that is, it is producing about 25% of the world's new workers. Like China, India is vulnerable to a drop in global demand for its exports. And when the Indian economy retreated in 2008-2009, Delhi's ability to provide the needed stimulus was hampered by a budget deficit approaching 8% of GDP.[23]

Today's India is a study in contrasts. In the 1990s, Manmohan Singh, then prime minister, opened India's economy by privatizing publicly owned enterprises, easing protectionist trade practices, cutting red tape, and making it possible for foreign firms in certain sectors to set up operations in India for the first time since independence.

India's economy is growing but its population is growing even faster, threatening to overwhelm all efforts to provide a better life for millions of Indians with little or no education and mired in poverty. The young woman pictured here ekes out a living by selling brooms on the street.

Piotr Wojtkowski/PublicDomainPictures.com

India's five-year plan set in 2007 called for a sustained growth rate of 9%. The downturn in 2008-2009 put a dent in the plan (the projected growth rate in 2012 was 6 to 7%, well below both the inflation and unemployment rates). Despite all, India's road to prosperity is strewn with potholes, including woefully underdeveloped infrastructure (roads, bridges, airports, electricity, and clean water), runaway inflation, overextended commercial bank credit, and a chronic double (trade and budget) deficit.

Great inequities continue as a blight on Indian society. Thus, in 2014 the World Bank observed: "Disadvantaged groups will need to be brought into the mainstream to reap the benefits of economic growth, and women—who "hold up half the sky"—empowered to take their rightful place in the socioeconomic fabric of the country."[24] Despite the "Green Revolution," some 217 million children in India still suffer from malnutrition. Less than 10% of the working-age population has completed secondary education. The World Bank describes India's infrastructure needs as "massive":

> One in three rural people lack access to an all-weather road, and only one in five national highways is four-lane. Ports and airports have inadequate capacity, and trains move very slowly. An estimated 300 million people are not connected to the national electrical grid, and those who are face frequent disruptions. And, the manufacturing sector—vital for job creation—remains small and underdeveloped.[25]

OBSTACLES TO DEVELOPMENT

The steeplechase is a challenging track-and-field event, of course, a race over fences and ditches and hurdles—in a word, an obstacle course. As such, it's an apt metaphor for the problems facing developing nations. They, too, are in a race—against the clock and the competition. And they, too, face all sorts of obstacles.

Self Identity: Who Am I? Where Do I Belong?

When modernization occurs, traditional ties are undermined, people are uprooted, and beliefs are challenged. Villagers tend not to trust strangers; social interaction is generally confined to family, clan, or village members. Fear of the unfamiliar, fatalism in the face of nature's accidents, and a low sense of individual efficacy combine to make traditional peasants and villagers averse to risk taking. Modernization often forces villagers to move to cities in search of work; to interact with strangers; and to redefine themselves. Traditional people are less time-conscious than modern urbanites. Punching a clock is alien. Personal success and the spirit of free enterprise associated with entrepreneurship and competition are also alien to people accustomed to thinking in group terms (family, clan, or tribe).

Status in traditional societies is **ascriptive**; that is, it is *ascribed* by society on the basis of religion, age, and the like. In contrast, modern societies are (or claim to be) merit based. The Indian caste system is an extreme example of ascriptive status.

Gender is another key status factor. Male dominance is prevalent in most traditional societies, where a low level of technology, ranging from the lack of modern machines to absence of birth control, combines with high infant

ascriptive societies
A society in which an individual's status and position are ascribed on the basis of religion, gender, age, or some other attribute.

War, revolution, ethnic rivalry, famine, drought, and epidemics cause widespread human misery and destabilize the governments on the African continent every year. Pictured here are Somali women and children in the Dadaab refugee camp in Kenya; thousands of Somalis fled from hunger and starvation in 2011.

mortality rates to reinforce traditional gender roles and attitudes. Thus, in developing nations, the communal nature of traditional life precedes, and often precludes, individualism, entrepreneurship, and self-expression.

Greed: West Africa's Deadly Diamonds

Wars interfere with a nation's development efforts by diverting the government's attention and sapping its limited resources. Nearly all the wars since World War II have been fought in the Middle East, Africa, and Asia. Rivalries in the Middle East and Asia have also culminated in wars at various times, including those between Iran and Iraq, Pakistan and India, Vietnam and China, and China and India. Many Latin American countries also have long-standing disputes and rivalries with neighbors. Chile, for example, has engaged in military clashes with all three adjacent states: Argentina, Bolivia, and Peru.

In the 1980s, a conflict between Ethiopia and Somalia over the Ogaden region, worsened by a famine that spread across the Horn of Africa, led to a humanitarian crisis for some 1.5 million Somali refugees. This conflict was the background for the ill-fated 1992–1994 intervention by U.S. military forces, which was ostensibly to safeguard food deliveries to the starving (see discussion later in this chapter). Anarchy stalked West Africa during these years. In Sierra Leone, the diamond trade drove the violence. For years, so-called conflict diamonds from rebel-held mines allowed the brutal Revolutionary United Front (RUF) to arm and equip armies.

Between 1994 and 2007, sub-Saharan Africa was the scene of four major wars (conflicts causing at least 800,000 deaths each)—in Rwanda, Sudan,

Congo, and Angola—and eighteen smaller wars. Armed conflicts in sub-Saharan Africa have not only taken a terrible toll in human life, they have also destroyed and disrupted fragile economies.

Ethnic Hatred: Taming the Tigers

Many least developed countries were carved out of former colonial holdings with little concern for the geography or history of the area or indigenous ethnic, religious, tribal, or linguistic patterns. Too often the result has been interethnic strife and even civil war.

Modernization (another name for development) poses daunting problems for indigenous peoples. Western concepts of "nation" and "nationalism" have little relevance, and yet success in forging a single national identity is crucial. Often, militant groups or movements hostile to social integration and modernization (Westernization) obstruct efforts at nation building. For example, Islam's emphasis on piety, devotion to Allah, prayer five times each day, and strict rules of moral conduct are at odds with secularization, the sexual revolution, materialism, and self-gratification—in other words, the kinds of social change associated with modernization in the West.

Specific examples best illustrate the practical problems associated with diverse populations. Nigeria and India are both least developed countries with very diverse populations. Although we have focused on India and Nigeria, many other least developed countries face similar problems. Take Sri Lanka, for example.

Sri Lanka is split between the majority Sinhalese (74%), who are mostly Buddhist, and the Tamils (18%), who are mostly Hindu and predominate in the northern and eastern parts of the country. Militant Tamil groups seeking to secede—notably the Tamil Tigers—have carried out terrorist acts and conducted guerrilla warfare against the central government since 1983, when an outbreak of communal riots left at least two thousand Tamils dead.[26] Sri Lanka's long and brutal civil war finally ended in 2009. During a decade in power, President Mahinda Rajapaska brought peace and progress to a country in great need of both. Having entrenched himself in power, he called for early elections in November 2014. In what one close observer has called a "miracle election," Sri Lankan voters quietly turned Rajapaska out of office. Like India, Sri Lanka displays a pattern of cultural diversity that impedes the search for a national consensus, but the recent election demonstrates the power of elections to revitalize government and spur social change.

Rwanda and Burundi became genocidal killing fields in 1993–1994 as a result of hatred and mistrust between Hutu and Tutsi tribes. A decade later, a tragedy of similar proportions unfolded in eastern Sudan, where a government-sponsored campaign to crush rebels turned into a policy of **ethnic cleansing**, the unconscionable practice of rape, pillage, and mass murder, in the remote Darfur region. Some two million refugees—mostly women and children who managed to escape—were displaced during the genocidal civil war.

Peace talks finally produced an accord in 2005 calling for a six-year period of autonomy for South Sudan followed by a referendum on independence. The outcome was no surprise: the people of South Sudan voted overwhelmingly to divorce Sudan. South Sudan became independent in July 2011.

ethnic cleansing
The practice of clearing all Muslims out of towns and villages in Bosnia by violent means; the term has also been used to characterize genocidal assaults on minority populations in other parts of the world, including the Darfur region of Sudan.

Development is necessary, but it is no guarantee of peace or prosperity. But as the case of South Sudan demonstrates, the reverse is also true: peace does not necessarily bring development and prosperity.

In sum, ethnically diverse societies are the rule in the LDCs. Over half of the nations created by decolonization in the postwar period are home to more than five major ethnic groups.[27] Ethnic diversity has made the problems of nation building in these countries complex and conflict an all-too-common occurrence.

Poverty: First Things First

Despite significant differences in economic development and national wealth, many former colonies are still poor more than half a century after independence. Why?

Premodern economies are based on agriculture and mining. Excessive dependence on agricultural commodities and raw materials makes these societies vulnerable to the ups and downs of global markets. Some poor countries raise only one major export crop. Bangladesh, for example, produces nothing but jute for export. When the price of jute declines, Bangladesh—one of the poorest developing nations—has nothing to fall back on. Ethiopia's monoculture economy is based on coffee exports; Cuba mainly produces sugar for export; Honduras exports bananas, and so on.

Some LDCs are economically addicted to illegal cash crops: peasants in Colombia, Ecuador, and Peru, for example, produce coca (cocaine) for export; Afghanistan is the world's primary source of heroine (made from poppy seeds). Though many LDCs have more than one crop or mineral resource, few are highly diversified in both agriculture and industry. And even some oil-rich countries are poor despite having an abundance of "black gold." As a result, great economic disparities still exist, not only from one country to another but also from region to region (see Table 9.2).

TABLE 9.2   Per Capita Gross National Income* by Region in 2013.

Region	Per Capita GNI (US$)
Arab World	9,577[†]
Sub-Saharan Africa	3,161
Latin America	14,186
South Asia	5,005
Euro Area	37,156
United States	53,960[‡]

*Purchasing power parity (PPP)
[†]2011 (figures for 2013 not available)
[‡]GNI for Canada (population 35 million) was $42,610 in 2013; for Mexico (population 120 million) it was $16,110.
SOURCE: World Bank 2014. http://data.worldbank.org/country?display=graph

Jose Manuel Lima de Silva

This young man in Angola is pushing a cart by hand. Angola is poor despite being one of sub-Saharan Africa's largest oil-producing countries.

To modernize, poor countries need to import industrial goods. To pay for manufactures, LDCs need to export food, fiber, and minerals. But the **terms of trade** tend to work against them—the price of industrial goods is high, while the price of agricultural products and raw materials is often low. Commodity prices on the world market fluctuate wildly at times, creating uncertainties and mounting foreign debt.

Some LDCs also face a serious population problem. The industrial democracies have population growth of less than 1%, and several western European countries reached zero or negative population growth by 1990. By contrast, many of the poorest countries still have birthrates in the range of 2 to 3% annually (compare Figure 9.6 and Figure 9.7). In some African countries (Niger and the Democratic Republic of the Congo), as well as in parts of the Middle East (notably the Palestinian territories and Yemen), annual birthrates are greater than 3%.

Rapid urbanization poses acute problems because LDCs do not have the resources to support public services, build roads and bridges, or create new schools, hospitals, housing complexes, and most important, jobs. Many people do not have easy access to a water pump, much less indoor plumbing. Open sewers and contaminated drinking water pose a standing threat to public health.

Tens of millions of people go to bed hungry every night. The United Nations Food and Agriculture Organization put the number suffering from malnutrition or chronic undernourishment in 2010–2012 at 817 million, most of whom live in the least developed countries. These numbers have been falling in Asia and Latin America but are still on the rise in Africa. Many malnourished children

terms of trade
In international economics, the valuation (or price) of the products (commodities, manufactures, services) that countries buy on the world market relative to the valuation of the products they sell; the structure of prices for different kinds of goods and services in international trade—for example, if manufactures are generally high-priced relative to minerals and agricultural products, then the terms of trade are unfavorable for countries that produce only farm commodities or raw materials.

FIGURE 9.6   World Population, 1995: 5,692,210,000.

SOURCE: Boyce Ransberger, "Damping the World's Population: Birthrates Are Falling Now but More Needs to Be Done in the Long Term," *Washington Post National Weekly Edition.* September 12–18, 1994, 10–40. ©1994 The Washington Post. Reprinted with permission.

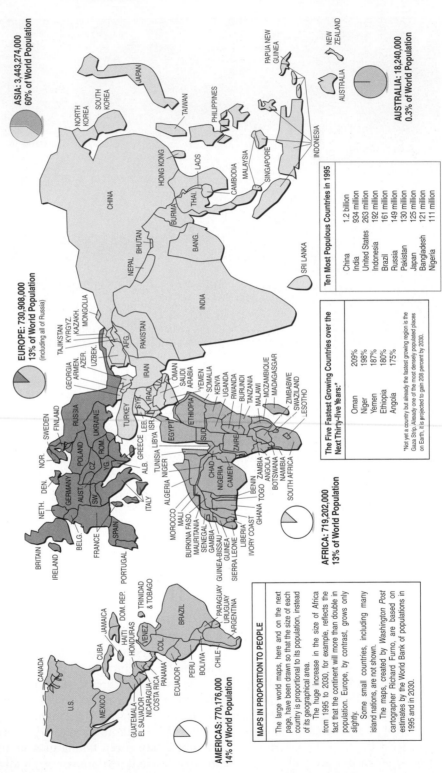

ASIA: 3,443,274,000
60% of World Population

EUROPE: 730,908,000
13% of World Population
(including all of Russia)

AUSTRALIA: 18,240,000
0.3% of World Population

AFRICA: 719,202,000
13% of World Population

AMERICAS: 770,176,000
14% of World Population

Ten Most Populous Countries in 1995

China	1.2 billion
India	934 million
United States	263 million
Indonesia	192 million
Brazil	161 million
Russia	149 million
Pakistan	130 million
Japan	125 million
Bangladesh	121 million
Nigeria	111 million

The Five Fastest Growing Countries over the Next Thirty-five Years: *

Oman	209%
Niger	198%
Yemen	187%
Ethiopia	180%
Angola	175%

*Not yet a country but already the fastest growing region is the Gaza Strip. Already one of the most densely populated places on Earth, it is projected to gain 208 percent by 2030.

MAPS IN PROPORTION TO PEOPLE

The large world maps, here and on the next page, have been drawn so that the size of each country is proportional to its population, instead of its geographical area.

The huge increase in the size of Africa from 1995 to 2030, for example, reflects the fact that the continent will more than double in population. Europe, by contrast, grows only slightly.

Some small countries, including many island nations, are not shown.

The maps, created by *Washington Post* cartographer Richard Furno, are based on estimates by the World Bank of populations in 1995 and in 2030.

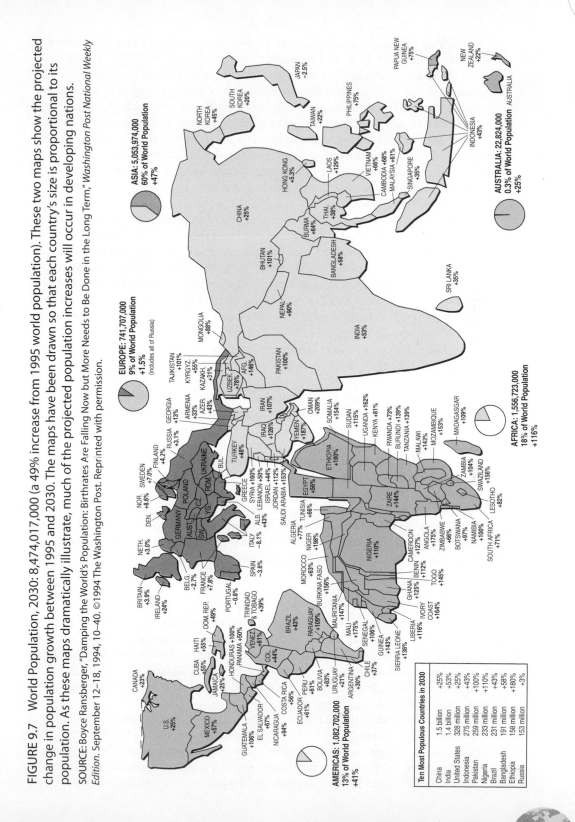

FIGURE 9.7 World Population, 2030: 8,474,017,000 (a 49% increase from 1995 world population). These two maps show the projected change in population growth between 1995 and 2030. The maps have been drawn so that each country's size is proportional to its population. As these maps dramatically illustrate, much of the projected population increases will occur in developing nations.

SOURCE: Boyce Ransberger, "Damping the World's Population: Birthrates Are Falling Now but More Needs to Be Done in the Long Term," *Washington Post National Weekly Edition*, September 12–18, 1994, 10–40. ©1994 The Washington Post. Reprinted with permission.

Green Revolution
A dramatic rise in agricultural output, resulting from modern irrigation systems and synthetic fertilizers, characteristic of modern India, Mexico, Taiwan, and the Philippines.

are sick up to 160 days in a year, and chronic hunger plays a role in at least half the 10.9 million child deaths annually.[28]

The main obstacles to ending world hunger today are political, not economic. The so-called **Green Revolution**—that is, the application of agricultural technology and modern irrigation and synthetic fertilizers to produce high-yield strains of wheat, rice, and corn—has helped ease the food-population crisis in India, Mexico, the Philippines and elsewhere, but at a high cost to the environment.[29] People who subsist on severely limited diets do not have the energy to be productive, leaving many developing nations caught in a vicious cycle: they are poor because they are not productive enough, and they are not productive enough because they are poor.

Land tenure also poses a significant problem in many least developed countries. In some areas, land ownership—and local power—is highly concentrated; in others, land is fragmented into parcels too small to be profitable. In Africa, communal ownership of rural land is (or was) common. But as commercial plantations encroach on village land, cash crops such as maize, rice, and coffee replace traditional food crops. Young men and women are forced leave in search of work. Many become migrant farm workers, earning paltry wages during the crop-growing season.

Finally, damage to the environment is an ever-growing problem in the least developed countries. Native plants and animals are disappearing in many places, water and air pollution is rising, soil degradation and deforestation are occurring at an alarming rate from Indonesia to Brazil and in many parts of sub-Saharan Africa, causing floods, soil erosion, and loss of wildlife habitat.

The idea of progress and the closely related concept of development are both outgrowths of the Western experience. But we now know that societies in the throes of modernization are also, paradoxically, among the most vulnerable to disintegration and decay—from better to worse. As the famed political scientist, Samuel Huntington, wisely observed, "Modernization in practice always involves change in and usually the disintegration of a traditional political system, but it does not necessarily involve significant movement toward a modern political system. . . . Yet the tendency is to think that because social modernization is taking place, political modernization must also be taking place."[30]

FAILED STATES

The promise of development all-too-often collides with the realities of poverty, corruption, and ethnic hatred in the former colonial areas. In recent decades, the world has witnessed a grim spectacle of states and societies self-destructing and in the process destabilizing neighboring states. Clearly, development has its discontents and comes with no guarantees, no owner's manual. In many parts of the world, it has not come at all.

The most dysfunctional ("failed") states are wretched places where extremes are the norm, where government is either repressive or too weak to maintain a modicum of law and order. Under such circumstances, the most violent elements in society take over. Both criminal and political violence stalk the city streets and threaten villages unprotected by police or a vigilant free press.

When the world is not watching, atrocities can go unnoticed for days, weeks, even months. This image may be disturbing, but it is all too real. Among the world's most dysfunctional states, Haiti is the one geographically closest to the United States. In this section, we look at Haiti and four other examples of failed states: Somalia, Sierra Leone, Afghanistan, and Zimbabwe. These examples by no means exhaust the list of candidates. Before the collapse of Communism (1989–1991), Soviet Russia and the Central and Eastern European countries probably belonged on that list as well. After the collapse, the former Soviet Union, Czechoslovakia, and Yugoslavia broke apart—in other words, failed.

Haiti

Haiti banished French colonial control and slavery in a series of wars in the early nineteenth century. In so doing, it became the first republic ruled by people of African descent in world history, as well as the first independent Caribbean state. But after decades of poverty, environmental degradation, and political instability—as well as a series of brutal dictatorships and natural disasters—Haiti is the poorest country in the Western Hemisphere and one of the poorest in the world—even before the devastating 2010 earthquake in which nearly 300,000 people were killed.

That catastrophic event left the capital of Port-au-Prince in ruins and prompted a major international aid effort. Later that same year, the country was hit by a major cholera outbreak. Meanwhile, despite massive outside aid, the rubble had still not been cleared away. For a time, 1.5 million out of a population of 10.2 million were living in tents.

UPI/Joshua Lee Kelsey/U.S. Navy/Landov

Following the 7.0 magnitude earthquake that hit Haiti's capital city of Port-au-Prince in January 2010, some 1.5 million people were housed in temporary shelters. Many families were still living in tents one year later.

Somalia

The Horn of Africa is home to several of the poorest countries on earth, including Sudan, Somalia, Eritrea, and Ethiopia. In the 1980s and 1990s, this region was afflicted by drought, famine, international conflict, civil wars, and all manner of violence. In the early 1990s, the most critical food shortages occurred in Somalia, where civil war and drought conspired to cause terrible human suffering. In August 1992, the United Nations Children's Fund (UNICEF) triggered a massive international relief effort when it warned that two million Somalis, of a total population of slightly more than eight million, faced starvation within six months.

Against this backdrop of violence and misery, rebels ousted Somalia's long-time dictator, Siad Barré, in January 1991. Fighting and famine followed, leaving 300,000 people dead and millions at risk of starvation. A near-total breakdown of law and order plunged the country into anarchy and placed women and children at the mercy of armed bandits, who disrupted relief efforts by international agencies, stole food intended for starving children, and murdered relief workers.

At the end of 1992, outgoing U.S. President George H. W. Bush ordered a military intervention to safeguard relief supplies and workers. The scene was so chaotic that restoring law and order proved impossible. Long after the U.S.-led UN forces departed in March 1995 (following the brutal killing of several U.S. soldiers), Somalia remained a country without a national government. Maps showing which areas were controlled by which factions looked more like a jigsaw puzzle than a political configuration.

Somalia was one of the poorest countries in Africa in the 1990s, with a per capita GNP of less than $500 and an illiteracy rate of more than 75%. Moreover, it is underdeveloped both politically and economically. The structure of Somali society is based on kinship ties, or clans—in fact, the civil war was a clan war. If Somalia cannot find a formula for political stability, it cannot rebuild its economy. The reverse is also true: stability depends on economic and social progress.

Somalia today remains a failed state. Anarchy is a boon to thieves, and Somalia is the world's number-one haven for pirates. In 2009, Somali pirates seized a merchant ship flying the U.S. flag and held the captain hostage, prompting President Obama to authorize the use of force. Three of the hostage takers were killed by sharpshooters and a fourth was captured and put on trial in the United States. The rescue operation succeeded: the captain's life was saved. But who will rescue Somalia?

Sierra Leone

We have seen that political stability and the rule of law are rare in sub-Saharan Africa. Even where it once appeared to be working, it has failed—nowhere more so than in Sierra Leone.

When legislative elections were held in Sierra Leone in 1986, the aptly named All People's Party approved 335 candidates to contest 105 elective seats. The party typically offered at least three contestants for each seat, a common practice among one-party states in sub-Saharan Africa. Voters in Sierra Leone actually had more choices—relative to personalities, at least—than voters in most U.S. legislative races.

Nonetheless, in the 1990s, Sierra Leone began a steady descent into anarchy. Between 1996 and 1998, the government changed hands four times. Then all hell broke loose, and rebel members of the so-called Revolutionary United Front began chopping off hands right and left. They chopped off heads too. They kidnapped small boys and girls and abused them in unspeakable ways. The RUF was notorious for turning boys into drug-addicted killers and sex slaves—so-called child soldiers. Kidnapped girls became sex slaves and sometimes fighters as well.[31]

The conflict officially ended in January 2002. It is estimated that 50,000 people were killed in the decade-long civil war, but there is no way of knowing for sure and no way of measuring the cost in shattered lives. The United Nations installed a peacekeeping force of 17,000 troops—the largest ever. The incumbent president, Ahmad Tejan Kabbah, was reelected with 70% of the vote in May 2002. Some 70,000 soldiers were disarmed and a war crimes tribunal convicted three former rebel leaders of rape and enlisting child soldiers—the first time a world court ever ruled on the recruitment of child soldiers under age 15.

War crimes trials in The Hague continued for the next five years, including the highly publicized trial of Charles Taylor, the former Liberian president, for "crimes against humanity"—specifically, aiding and abetting the violent rebel group (RUK) mainly responsible for the atrocities committed in the civil war. (A gruesome practice of the RUK was to terrorize the population by hacking off victims' hands or feet.) The last case ended in The Hague in April 2012, with judges finding Taylor guilty as charged.

Sierra Leone is an object lesson in what can happen when a failed state sinks into anarchy. Neither the civil institutions nor the political culture necessary to support and sustain democracy were present. For a time, the appearance of democracy masked the reality of a society capable of erupting into volcanic civil violence at any moment. Today, the UN classifies Sierra Leone as one of the world's "least livable" countries.

Zimbabwe

Robert Mugabe has been the face of Zimbabwe since its inception in 1980. Mugabe was born in 1924 in what was then the British colony of Southern Rhodesia. He rose to prominence in the 1960s as the leader of the Zimbabwe African National Union during a long and bitter guerrilla war against white minority rule. In 1980, he became the prime minister of the new Black African government of Zimbabwe and gradually gathered dictatorial powers in his own hands, assuming the presidency in 1987. As president, Mugabe has enriched himself and his cronies while plunging his country into a degrading and desperate state of poverty. Today Zimbabwe is a failed state.

At first hailed as a symbol of the new Africa, Mugabe, a lifelong Roman Catholic, has presided over one of the worst and most corrupt governments in the world, while utterly mismanaging Zimbabwe's postcolonial economy.

Under his despotic rule, the health and well-being of the people has dropped dramatically, in a natural result of widespread poverty, unemployment, malnutrition, and the absence of medical care—as well as a costly war with the Democratic Republic of the Congo (1998–2002).

The government's chaotic land reform program, which seized white-owned farms with the avowed aim of redistributing the land, effectively destroyed the only functioning sector of the economy and turned Zimbabwe into a net importer of food. Mugabe's response to the economic crisis he created was to print money to cover soaring government deficits while stubbornly refusing to institute economic reforms. The IMF eventually stopped lending to Zimbabwe because of arrears on past loans.

With humanitarian food aid from the United States and the EU, the World Health Organization states that life expectancy in Zimbabwe has improved in recent years but remains low (under 52 years)—only slightly higher than Afghanistan or Somalia. In 2008, cholera claimed the lives of 4,282 people in the country; the number of suspected cases soared above 95,000. The outbreak was due to a lack of basic infrastructure—safe drinking water and sewage systems.

Runaway hyperinflation rendered the country's currency worthless: in January 2009, a newly released $50 billion note was just enough to buy two loaves of bread! Zimbabwe's annual GDP per capita in 2010 was estimated at a paltry $169 (PPP).

Elections in Zimbabwe are empty exercises in "democracy" designed to put the stamp of legitimacy on dictatorship. In 2002, for example, Mugabe had his leading opponent arrested for treason. A popular opposition leader named Morgan Tsvangirai was beaten and hospitalized in 2007 after Mugabe ordered police to break up a protest rally in the capital of Harare. When, despite all, Tsvangirai managed to beat Mugabe in a popular vote, Mugabe unleashed a spasm of violence that saw 163 people killed and some 5,000 tortured or brutally beaten.

Under enormous international pressure and facing a reenergized domestic opposition, Mugabe agreed to a power sharing deal, allowing Tsvangirai to become prime minister in a new dual-executive arrangement—but true to form, he installed his cronies in every ministry. In 2013, the 90-year-old autocrat *PARADE* magazine once named the world's worst living dictator was reelected to a seventh term. When outgoing Prime Minister Tsvangirai declined to attend the inaugural ceremonies in 2013, a spokesman was quoted as saying, "Expecting Tsvangirai to attend the inauguration is like expecting a victim of robbery to attend a party hosted by the robber."

During his three decades in power, Mugabe has plunged Zimbabwe into utter ruin. When he finally goes, he will leave a bitter legacy of chronic unemployment, hyperinflation (the highest in the world), and an impoverished society where the oft-repeated promise of democracy was repeatedly broken.

Mugabe is an example of the kind of corrupt and incompetent leadership that has plagued sub-Saharan Africa since the end of the colonial era. Sadly, at the end of the first decade of the twenty-first century, what distinguishes Zimbabwe's government from that of most other countries in the region is a difference in degree, not in kind.

Afghanistan

The United States invaded Afghanistan when it became known that the 9/11 attacks were carried out by a militant Islamic group called al Qaeda and that the Taliban, Afghanistan's fundamentalist political regime, was allowing al Qaeda's leader, Osama bin Laden, to use Afghanistan territory as a base of operations. What was less well known at the time (and what decision makers in Washington appear to have forgotten or overlooked) is the historical background. For nearly three decades prior to the landing of U.S. Special Forces on Afghan soil, Afghanistan had been one of the world's most dysfunctional states. Even prior to the overthrow of the monarchy in the 1970s, the country was poor and backward, but thereafter it spiraled into two decades of bloody turmoil. By 2001, the entire country was in shambles and millions of people—especially women and children—were living on the very edge of a precipice.

Home to many ethnic groups, Afghanistan reflects the disparate populations around its periphery—Pakistan, Iran, Turkmenistan, Tajikistan, Uzbekistan, and China. The largest group, the Pashtuns, constitute about 40% of the total population (about 26 million people). Thus, there is no majority group, only minorities of different sizes. Roughly 99% of all Afghans are Muslims; about 15% are Shi'ite Muslims (as are most Iranians).

Afghanistan was a monarchy from 1747 to 1973, when the country came apart at the seams. Various factions fought for supremacy after 1973, until the Soviet Union made the fateful decision to intervene on behalf of its favorite thug (a Communist) in 1979. A brutal and protracted war ensued; the Soviet Union finally withdrew in defeat in 1989 after a decade of debilitating (and humiliating) warfare. The United States had secretly backed the Islamic resistance, called the mujahedeen, by supplying weapons and other aid to the rebel forces. Amazingly, the United States and Osama bin Laden were fighting side by side at this time.

Opponents overthrew the communist regime and seized power in 1992. The new strongman refused to relinquish power when his term officially expired, but Taliban forces assaulted the capital and ousted him in 1996. The Taliban regime instituted a totalitarian system of rule couched in the language and concepts of Islam but based on a perversion of the Qur'an (holy scripture) and Sharia law (based on the teachings of Muslim clerics or mullahs). Women and girls were forced to wear the burka (a one-piece, head-to-toe garment) in public and were forbidden to work outside the home, to go to school, or to express opinions at variance with the government. The government banned television, movies, music, dancing, and most other forms of "decadent" entertainment.

The Taliban was a brutal and repressive regime that clearly did not enjoy the support of the people. It seized control of a fragile and dysfunctional state and turned it into a tool of domestic and international terrorism. Instability in Afghanistan poses a grave danger to neighboring Pakistan as well. As a failed state, Afghanistan illustrates a stark and sobering lesson: dysfunctional states can become a threat to regional stability and world order. The solution—economic growth and development—is obvious but elusive.

Afghanistan was not Barack Obama's war. As a presidential candidate, he opposed the war and promised to end it if elected. As the nation's newly elected commander-in-chief in 2009, he ordered a troop surge. At that point there were 32,800 troops on the ground in Afghanistan. By the fall of 2010, that number had risen to 98,000. Nearly three-fourths of U.S. combat fatalities in Afghanistan occurred after the start of the Obama troop surge.

In June 2011, President Obama unveiled his plan for withdrawal of all U.S. combat forces from Afghanistan by the end of 2014. But it was not to be. In May 2014, Obama said it was "time to turn the page on a decade in which so much of our foreign policy was focused on the wars in Afghanistan and Iraq," and announced that the last U.S. troops would be withdrawn by the end of 2016. Under the new timetable, the 32,000 U.S. troops still in Afghanistan would be reduced to 9,800 in 2015. But after decades of war, the prospects for peace and stability were bleak—with or without a U.S. military presence.

In December 2014, the government released the Senate Intelligence Committee's "torture report," detailing the CIA's use of "enhanced interrogation" methods against suspected terrorists. Many of the torture victims were captured abroad through an extralegal process called "extraordinary rendition"—that is, without being charged or offered legal representation—and taken to "black sites" where they were held indefinitely and brutalized ("water-boarding" was only one of the ways it was done).

The CIA use of torture to extract information was previously known to the public but had never before been officially acknowledged and admitted in this way. There was fear in some quarters that release of this report would provoke extremists to launch yet another wave of international terrorism.

In retrospect, everything associated with the war on terror has led to extremes and involved extremism on all sides. The costs have been extremely high, the results have been extremely unsatisfactory, and the use of torture is not only embarrassing but also extremely antithetical to the principles enshrined in the U.S. Constitution.

DEVELOPMENT: TONIC OR ELIXIR?

In the West, we think of development as a good thing. But we are seeing lots of signs that point to a different and disturbing conclusion: that it's possible to get too much of a good thing, that *overdevelopment* can be as detrimental to the health and sustainability of a state and society as underdevelopment. Signs and symptoms of overdevelopment are all around us but are often too easily ignored unless we happen to be visiting Beijing during an "orange smog" alert; or living on the Jersey Shore when a super storm like Hurricane Sandy makes landfall; or caught in an afternoon rush-hour traffic jam on a Los Angeles freeway in mid-July. You can probably think of examples close to home. Go ahead. Try. (Start with what you know from firsthand experience. One example: massive multiacre high school parking lots filled with cars. You won't see anything like it anywhere else on the planet. By the way, there were about twenty million students in grades 9 through 12 in the United States in 2012. If, say, one-third of these students drive to school . . .).

All societies are in a constant state of flux, rising or falling. They develop in different ways, at different rates, and at different times. In the modern era, Western societies have led the way, developing economically and technologically along lines congruent with the political institutions that evolved at the same time. In this sense, development was a natural process originating *within* these societies.

For least developed countries, development is often just the opposite: an alien process that originates from the outside. Development is always disruptive, but even more so when it is forced on societies, whether by foreign powers or by external circumstances.

The story of development does not end with the arrival of the postindustrial state. Most rich states boast high-tech economies offering a vast array of commercial and financial services. They still engage in agriculture, mining, and industry, but these sectors of the economy are eclipsed in importance by high-tech goods that drive the global economy—computer software, pharmaceuticals, and financial services.

The new global economy brings a higher quality of life to consumers but comes with a price—outsourcing of jobs and chronic unemployment, urban congestion and crowding, air and water pollution, epidemics and stress-related illnesses, illegal drug use, overconsumption, energy shortages, waste disposal problems, global warming, extinction of countless plant and animal species, and others.

Thus late-stage development is no more free of challenges than early-stage development. The challenges are different, but no less daunting. Over-developed countries—where development has outrun society's capacity to deal with undesirable side effects of rapidly accelerating technological and social change—might do well to focus more attention on solving the problems they face and less on telling so-called underdeveloped countries what to do and how to do it.

In the West, politicians and scholars alike often uncritically accept the proposition that development is the answer to all the world's problems. Sometimes, in an effort to be politically correct, political scientists use the term *premodern* to describe societies in an early stage of development. Development theory often *assumes* development is good—always and everywhere—and that tradition and superstition, the "dead hand of the past," are impediments to progress. Critics argue that musings on development often amount to little more than praise for all things Western, and that Western experts on the subject are guilty of ethnocentrism.

In 1750, the French philosopher Jean-Jacques Rousseau observed, "Our souls have been corrupted in proportion to the movement of our sciences and arts towards perfection."[32] Rousseau's political philosophy sprang from the notion that science and technology were eroding, rather than enhancing, our humanity. Overstated? Perhaps, but there's no denying that development—what we often equate with the greatest advances in modern civilization—can be a double-edged sword.

SUMMARY

The least developed countries (LDCs) are so named because they are poor and lack basic feature of modern postindustrial states. Although generalizations and clichés are common (for example, rural poverty and urban crowding), these nations are highly diverse. The enduring legacy of European colonialism is a political map that makes little sense: borders that do not reflect indigenous ethnic, religious, and tribal patterns. The upshot in many cases is chronic instability: social unrest, rebellions, civil wars, and even genocide.

State building requires leaders that effectively unify the population (nation building), political institutions that respond to people's needs and encourage citizen participation, and an honest government that can transfer power smoothly.

Democracy correlates with the existence of certain identifiable economic, political, social, and attitudinal variables. In most LDCs, the failure of democracy and development have gone hand in hand.

Development is an arduous task and often fails. Socially, populations are often fragmented. Psychologically, individuals are heavily dependent on tradition and frequently oppose change. Economically, problems range from unfavorable terms of trade and high foreign debt to rapid population growth, a low level of technology, entrenched land tenure problems, and environmental difficulties.

States and societies frequently disintegrate rather than develop. The Soviet Union provides the most stunning example in recent decades. Other examples include Iraq, Congo, Ethiopia, Haiti, Lebanon, Liberia, Sudan, Somalia, Sierra Leone, Zimbabwe, and Afghanistan.

Overdevelopment (the opposite of "underdevelopment") is a problem afflicting many Western societies today. Contemporary ideas about development tend to assume its desirability despite such postindustrial problems as pollution, congestion, and drug addiction, as well as overpopulation, climate change, and pandemic diseases.

KEY TERMS

least developed
  countries   247
neocolonialism   251
North-South
  conflict   251
colonialism   254
imperialism   254

nonviolent
  resistance   254
political
  development   257
nation building   257
state building   257
traditional societies   258

democratic
  correlates   258
ascriptive   267
ethnic cleansing   269
terms of trade   271
Green Revolution   274

REVIEW QUESTIONS

1. What are the salient characteristics of the so-called Third World? How do these relate to the development process?
2. Are most WTO members rich or poor? Do the majority of the world's nations and peoples have fair access to global markets?

3. Elucidate the correlates of democracy. How compelling is this line of analysis? Comment.
4. What are the incentives for modernization? What sources of resistance can you identify?
5. Does development always lead to democracy? Is the reverse true? List some examples.
6. All things considered—India's political system, the current state of the Indian economy, and the broader question of social justice—would you say India's successes outweigh its failures or vice versa? Explain.
7. Nigeria is most likely to become sub-Saharan Africa's first major global power. Do you agree or disagree with this statement? Explain.
8. What are the barriers to development? If development is so difficult, why do nations undertake it?
9. How are development and decay related? Are states and societies ever static? Comment.
10. Name three dysfunctional states and use one as an example to illustrate the nature of this type of state.

WEBSITES AND READINGS

Websites

UN Development Program: http://www.undp.org/

World Hunger Page of Bread for the World: http://www.bread.org/hunger/

Global Service Corp: http://www.globalservicecorps.org/

World Bank: http://www.worldbank.org/

Group of 77: http://www.g77.org/

Providing Safe Drinking Water: http://water.org/

Failed States Index: http://global.fundforpeace.org/index.php

U.S. Census Bureau International Database: http://www.census.gov/population/international/

World Trade Organization: http://www.wto.org/english/thewto_e/whatis_e/tif_e/org6_e.htm

Readings

Acemoglu, Daron, and James Robinson, *Why Nations Fail: The Origins of Power, Prosperity, and Poverty.* New York: Crown, 2012. Attempts to answer a big question: Why are some nations rich and others poor?

Beah, Ishmael. *A Long Way Gone: Memoirs of a Boy Soldier.* New York: Sarah Crichton Books, 2007. A shocking firsthand account of the horrors of Sierra Leone's descent into anarchy in the 1990s and how children were both innocent victims and brutal perpetrators of violence. The factual accuracy of the author's account has been called into question, but not the authenticity of his ordeal.

Binder, Leonard. "The Crises of Political Development." In *Crisis and Sequences in Political Development*, edited by Leonard Binder et al. Princeton, NJ:

Princeton University Press, 1971. A groundbreaking study that identifies five "crises of development": identity, legitimacy, participation, distribution, and penetration.

Brass, Paul. *The Politics of India Since Independence*, 2nd ed. New York: Cambridge University Press, 2004. A concise but broad study of political, economic, and culture change in India since 1947.

Casper, Gretchen. *Fragile Democracies: The Legacies of Authoritarian Rule.* Pittsburgh, PA: University of Pittsburgh Press, 1995. Explores why democracy "remains problematic" in the Philippines and other states with a history of authoritarian rule.

Chomsky, Noam. *Failed States: The Abuse of Power and the Assault on Democracy.* New York: Henry Holt and Company, 2006. A critique of U.S. policy toward the Third World. Argues that the United States is a failed state that's armed to the teeth and trigger-happy.

Collier, Paul. *The Bottom Billion: Why the Poorest Countries are Failing and What Can Be Done About It.* New York: Oxford University Press, 2008. A book on world poverty variously described by reviewers as "thought-provoking," "path-breaking," and "insightful."

Diamond, Jared. *Guns, Germs, and Steel: The Fate of Human Societies.* New York: Norton, 1999. Argues that geography and environment are the critical variables that determine winners and losers in world history; that Western civilization flourished for reasons that had nothing to do with the racial superiority; and that Europeans are no smarter than the peoples they colonized—just luckier.

_____. *Collapse: How Societies Choose to Fail or Succeed.* New York: Viking Penguin, 2005. In this sequel to *Guns, Germs, and Steel,* Diamond turns the question around and asks, "What causes great civilizations and thriving societies to decline or disintegrate?"

Easterly, William. *The White Man's Burden: Why the West's Efforts to Aid the Rest Have Done So Much Ill and So Little Good.* New York: Penguin, 2007. An incisive analysis of failed Western aid policies in the Third World by a former senior economist at the World Bank.

Godwin, Peter. *When a Crocodile Eats the Sun: A Memoir of Africa.* New York: Little, Brown and Company, 2008. About the death of the author's father and the dictator Robert Mugabe, Zimbabwe's president-for-life, who Godwin holds responsible. A gripping personal account written by a professional journalist.

Guha, Ramanchandra. *India after Gandhi: A History of the World's Largest Democracy.* New York: Harper Perennial, 2008. Chronicles the nation's trial and tribulations but also celebrates its achievements.

Huntington, Samuel P. "How Countries Democratize." *Political Science Quarterly* 106 (1991-92): 578–616. Examines how various nondemocratic regimes (classified as one-party systems, military regimes, and personal dictatorships) democratized between 1974 and 1990, with an emphasis on Third World nations.

Kaplan, Robert D. *The Coming Anarchy.* New York: Vintage Books, 2001. A best- selling book on the tragedy and travail of West Africa and beyond.

_____. "Will More Countries Become Democratic?" *Political Science Quarterly* 99 (1984): 193–218. Articulates the economic, cultural, and social factors assumed to be associated with democracy.

Kaplan, Seth. *Fixing Fragile States: A New Paradigm for Development.* Westport, CT: Praeger Security International, 2008. Argues for placing policy emphasis on institution building instead of sending troops and foreign aid. Gives special attention to seven dysfunctional places, including West Africa.

Lipset, Seymour. *American Exceptionalism: A Double-Edged Sword.* New York: W. W. Norton, 1996. The thesis that the United States was "born modern," having shed all vestiges of feudalism at birth, and that it remains fundamentally different from European societies.

_____. *Political Man: The Social Bases of Democracy,* rev. ed. Garden City, NY: Doubleday, 1983. Argues that national wealth is the most reliable predictor of democracy.

Luce, Edward. *In Spite of the Gods: The Strange Rise of Modern India.* New York: Doubleday, 2007. All about India's emerging economy, the problems India still faces in its modernization drive (including pervasive corruption and criminality in government and society alike), and the sheer complexity of this wondrously diverse society.

Piketty, Thomas (translator: Arthur Goldhammer). *Capital in the 21st Century.* Cambridge, MA: Harvard University Press, 2014. One of the most talked-about nonfiction books of 2014. "Thomas Piketty analyzes a unique collection of data from twenty countries, ranging as far back as the eighteenth century, to uncover key economic and social patterns. His findings will transform debate and set the agenda for the next generation of thought about wealth and inequality."—Amazon

Rostow, Walt Whitman. *The Stages of Economic Growth: A Non-Communist Manifesto,* 3rd ed. Cambridge: Cambridge University Press, 1991. Posits that all developing economies pass through the same developmental stages. The theory suggests that eventually all societies will become industrialized, capitalist, and democratic—in other words, thoroughly Westernized.

Sachs, Jeffrey. *The End of Poverty: Economic Possibilities for Our Time.* New York: Penguin, 2005. An exploration of how societies emerge from poverty by an internationally renowned scholar. Sachs is the director of Columbia University's Earth Institute. *Time* magazine has called him "the world's best-known economist."

Wolpert, Stanley. *A New History of India,* 8th ed. New York: Oxford University Press, 2008. The title says it all.

PART 3

Politics by Civil Means
Citizens, Leaders, and Policies

Political Socialization
The Making of a Citizen

Learning Objectives

1 Describe the model citizen in democratic theory and explain the concept.

2 Define socialization and explain the relevance of this concept in the study of politics.

3 Explain how a disparate population of individuals and groups (families, clans, and tribes) can be forged into a cohesive society.

4 Demonstrate how socialization affects political behavior and analyze what happens when socialization fails.

5 Characterize the role of television and the Internet in influencing people's political beliefs and behavior, and evaluate their impact on the quality of citizenship in contemporary society.

The year is 1932. The Soviet Union is suffering a severe shortage of food, and millions go hungry. Joseph Stalin, leader of the Communist Party and head of the Soviet government, has undertaken a vast reordering of Soviet agriculture that eliminates a whole class of landholders (the *kulaks*) and collectivizes all farmland. Henceforth, every farm and all farm products belong to the state. To deter theft of what is now considered state property, the Soviet government enacts a law prohibiting individual farmers from appropriating any grain for their own private use. Acting under this law, a young boy reports his father to the authorities for concealing grain. The father is shot for stealing state property. Soon after, the boy is killed by a group of peasants, led by his uncle, who are outraged that he would betray his own father. The government, taking a radically different view of the affair, extols the boy as a patriotic martyr.

Stalin considered the little boy in this story a model citizen, a hero. How citizenship is defined says a lot about a government and the philosophy or ideology that underpins it.

THE GOOD CITIZEN

Stalin's celebration of a child's act of betrayal as heroic points to a distinction Aristotle originally made: The *good citizen* is defined by laws, regimes, and rulers, but the moral fiber (and universal characteristics) of a *good person* is fixed, and it transcends the expectations of any particular political regime.[1]

Good **citizenship** includes behaving in accordance with the rules, norms, and expectations of our own state and society. Thus, the actual requirements vary widely. A good citizen in Soviet Russia of the 1930s was a person whose first loyalty was to the Communist Party. The test of good citizenship in a totalitarian state is this: Are you willing to subordinate all personal convictions and even family loyalties to the dictates of political authority, and to follow the dictator's whims no matter where they may lead? In marked contrast are the standards of citizenship in constitutional democracies, which prize and protect freedom of conscience and speech.

Where the requirements of the abstract good citizen—always defined by the state—come into conflict with the moral compass of actual citizens, and where the state seeks to obscure or obliterate the difference between the two, a serious problem arises in both theory and practice. At what point do people cease to be real citizens and become mere cogs in a machine—unthinking and unfeeling subjects or even slaves? Do we obey the state, or the dictates of our own conscience?

This question gained renewed relevance in the United States when captured "illegal combatants" were subjected to "enhanced interrogation techniques"—an Orwellian euphemism for torture—during the Bush administration's war on terror following the 9/11 attacks. One prisoner was waterboarded 183 times (strapped to a board with towels wrapped around his head while water was poured slowly onto the towels until he smothered).[2] Other harsh interrogation methods were also used.

citizenship
The right and the obligation to participate constructively in the ongoing enterprise of self-government.

ZERO DARK THIRTY

The *New York Times* called the 2012 film *Zero Dark Thirty* "a national Rorschach test on the divisive subject of torture." Jessica Chastain plays the starring role as "Maya," a brilliant young CIA analyst who is obsessed with al Qaeda and hunting Osama bin Laden. Maya is assigned to an office in Pakistan where she's introduced to the netherworld of unconventional warfare and CIA black-site torture. At first, she's uncomfortable with what she learns, but she soon sets aside her reservations. Her intensity is pathological. She follows every lead, pursues every possibility, and never lets up or backs down. In her extreme commitment to defeating the enemy, she's the anti-terrorist equivalent of a terrorist. In the end, her tenacity pays off.

The film realistically portrays the CIA's brutal methods used to interrogate al Qaeda prisoners. It drew harsh criticism from certain quarters for suggesting that waterboarding and other forms of torture graphically depicted in the film helped track down Osama bin Laden, who was killed in Pakistan by special ops airborne commandos in May 2011. Critics of the war on terror argue that torture is not only illegal and immoral but also ineffectual—that is, it doesn't work.

One question left unasked is whether Maya acted honorably. Arguably public servants ought to set a good example for us as private citizens. Maya may be a model intelligence analyst, but she is hardly a model citizen.

We now know for certain that beginning in 2002 the U.S. Government sanctioned the use of torture in the war on terror. Can anyone in any position of authority who orders the use of torture be justified in so doing? Can anyone who carries out such an order—or collaborates with those who do—be a good citizen? Is it ever right to obey orders that are wrong—that is, illegal and (or) immoral? Think about it.

(Hint: There were massive student demonstrations against the war in Vietnam in the 1960s and early 1970s. Historians often point to these protests as a major factor in forcing the United States to end the war. Consider whether those students were troublemakers or good citizens. Here are a few relevant facts: Over 58,000 U.S. soldiers died in the Vietnam War and another 150,000 were wounded, many severely. More than 33,000 battlefield fatalities were young men of college age (21 or younger). Of these, over 14,000 were 20 years old (more than any other age group). Most were drafted into the army. We lost the war and Congress abolished the draft in 1973.)

The Third Geneva Convention (1949), to which the United States is a party, outlaws torture, as does the U.S. Code (Title 18, Chapter 113C). In addition, torture is a gross violation of the *moral* code we are taught to observe in our everyday lives from earliest childhood. As a presidential candidate, Barack Obama denounced torture and the use of "extraordinary" methods and procedures in the war on terror. As president, he ordered an end to waterboarding but, to the dismay of his critics on the left, failed to close the Guantanamo Bay ("Gitmo") detention camp.

President Obama's decision to sign the 2012 National Defense Authorization Act (NDAA) disappointed and angered many of his erstwhile supporters, not least because he had threatened to veto it. "The fact that I support this bill as a whole does not mean I agree with everything in it," he said. "In particular, I have . . . serious reservations with certain provisions that regulate the detention, interrogation, and prosecution of suspected terrorists." Few friends of the U.S. Constitution and Bill of Rights—in particular the Fourth, Fifth, and Sixth Amendments—were placated.

In January, 2010, members of a group called Witness Against Torture, wearing orange jumpsuits and black hoods, staged a protest in Washington, D.C., and called on the Obama Administration to close down the Guantanamo detention camp. At the end of 2014, the Senate Intelligence Committee released a damning report on the U.S. Government's post-9/11 anti-terror program, in particular, the CIA's extralegal detention of suspects and brutal interrogation methods. The report's release led to a new round of human rights protests at home and abroad and raised new doubts about the efficacy and morality of U.S. anti-terror policies.

Defining Citizenship

Throughout history, people of diverse moral character have claimed to be models of good citizenship. The relationship between the moral character of citizens and different forms of government underscores Aristotle's observation that the true measure of a political system is the kind of citizen it produces. According to this view, a good state is one whose model citizen is also a good person; a bad state is one whose model citizen obeys orders without regard for questions of good or evil. Simple though this formulation may sound, it offers striking insights into the relationship between governments and citizens, including, for example, the fact that we cannot divorce civic virtue or public morality from our personal integrity or private morality.

It is little wonder that different political systems embrace different definitions of citizenship. In many authoritarian states, people can be classified as citizens only in the narrowest sense of the word—that is, they reside within the territory of a certain state and are subject to its laws. The relationship between state and citizen is a one-way street. Ordinary citizens have no voice in deciding who rules or how, or even whether they have a vote. In general, the government leaves them alone as long as they acquiesce in the system.

By contrast, in totalitarian states, where the government seeks to transform society and create a new kind of citizen, people are compelled to participate in the political system, but popular participation is meaningless because it is not voluntary and stresses duties without corresponding rights. Loyalty and zealotry form the core of good citizenship in such states, and citizens may be forced to carry out orders they find morally repugnant.

In democratic societies, people define citizenship very differently. In elementary school, the good citizenship award typically goes to a pupil who sets a

Fringe right-wing opponents of Barack Obama have claimed that he was not born in the United States and therefore is not eligible under the Constitution to serve as president. The so-called Birthers refused to drop this spurious objection to his presidency even after Obama published this official long-form birth certificate proving that he was, in fact, born in the state of Hawaii.

good example, respects others, plays by the rules, and hands in assignments on time. Adults practice good citizenship by taking civic obligations seriously, obeying the laws, paying taxes, and voting regularly, among other things. In a democracy, the definition of good citizenship is found in the laws, but the legislators who write the laws are freely elected by the people—in other words, a true republic at its best erases (or at the very least eases) the tension between citizenship and moral conscience.

Many individuals, including civil libertarians, emphasize that the essence of citizenship lies in individual rights or personal liberties. Citizenship in the United States requires little in the form of duties and obligations, and affords its beneficiaries an enviable array of opportunities (hence, the steady flow of immigrants into the United States, compared with the trickle of U.S. citizens emigrating to other countries). According to the Fourteenth Amendment, "All persons born or naturalized in the United States, and subject to the jurisdiction thereof, are citizens of the United States and of the State wherein they reside." Note that citizens of the United States are distinguished from aliens not on the basis of how they act or what they have done but simply on the basis of birthplace—to be born in the United States is to be a U.S. citizen. Moreover, the presumption is once a citizen, always a citizen, barring some extraordinary misdeed (such as treason) or a voluntary renunciation of citizenship.

A Classical View

The minimalist view of citizenship described in the "Ideas and Politics" feature may provide a convenient way of distinguishing citizens from aliens (foreigners), but it does not do justice to a time-honored concept in Western civilization. To the ancient Greeks, the concept of citizenship was only partly related to accidents of birth and political geography; rather, responsible and selfless participation in the public affairs of the community formed the vital core of citizenship. Aristotle held that a citizen "shares in the administration of justice and in the holding of office."[3] The Athens of Aristotle's time was a small political society, or city-state, that at any given time accorded a proportionately large number of citizens significant decision-making power (women and slaves were excluded). Citizenship was the exalted vehicle through which public-spirited and properly educated free men could rule over, and in turn be ruled by, other free men and thereby advance civic virtue, public order, and the common good.

In eighteenth-century Europe, the Greek ideal reemerged in a modified form. *Citizen* became a term applicable to those who claimed the right to petition or sue the government. Citizens were distinguished from slaves, who had no claims or rights and were regarded as chattel (property). Citizens also differed from subjects, whose first and foremost legal obligation was to show loyalty to and obey the sovereign. According to the German philosopher Immanuel Kant (1724–1804), citizens, as opposed to slaves or subjects, possessed constitutional freedom – that is, the right to obey only laws to which they consented. Kant also contended that citizens possessed a civil equality, which relieved them of any obligation by law or custom to recognize a superior moral authority, and political independence, meaning a person's political status stemmed from

MILITARY CONSCRIPTION: Democracy, Duty, and the Draft

Apart from paying taxes and obeying laws, citizens in the United States have few obligations to anyone or anything but themselves. One big obligation for males of a certain age—namely, military service—ended in the wake of the Vietnam War as a result of the backlash against the **Selective Service System** (often called "the draft"), which many considered unfair. Although males over the age of 18 are still required to register for the draft, the practice of military conscription in the United States ended in 1973, with the establishment of an all-volunteer military.

Defenders of an all-volunteer military argue that it is more professional and proficient, that willing recruits are likely to make better soldiers than are conscripts, and that the military provides excellent opportunities for young men and women from minority and low-income groups to acquire the self-confidence, discipline, and technical skills that can lead to high-paying jobs in the civilian economy.

Many veterans of past U.S. wars, among others, decry the ending of the draft. Others advocate making at least one year of national service mandatory for young adults who do not enlist in the armed forces. Supporters of the draft stress that military service builds character, teaches teamwork, and inculcates important moral values such as honor, duty, self-discipline, respect for authority, and courage.

Some who argue for bringing back the draft do so on the surprising ground that it would make war less likely. Why? Because voters are often apathetic when an issue does not affect them directly and are too easily swayed when patriotism is invoked—as it always is in war. This issue resurfaced in 2003 when President George W. Bush, in effect, declared a "presidential war"—defined as the use of force outside the United States without a formal declaration of war by Congress as required under the Constitution—on Iraq.

Was President Bush justified in ordering U.S. troops to invade a country that did not directly threaten and could not attack the United States? Is it fair to ask the sons and daughters of minorities and the low-income families to fight our wars, while the rich are called upon to make no such sacrifices? Why not reinstitute the draft or at least a universal national service of some sort? Think about it.

(Hint: Google "The Argument: Should America Reinstate the Draft?" and read the opposing opinions of Congressman Charles Rangel and Professor James Lacey.)

Library of Congress Prints and Photographs Division [LC-USZC4-595]

After the unpopular Vietnam War, the United States abolished the draft in favor of an all-volunteer armed forces.

fundamental rights rather than from the will of another.⁴ No longer were citizens to be ruled arbitrarily by the state.

Republican government came the closest to this ideal of citizenship. In the final analysis, as Kant and other eighteenth-century thinkers recognized, the freedom and dignity of the individual inherent in the concept of citizenship could flourish only under a republican government, and such a government could function only if its rank-and-file members understood and discharged the responsibilities of citizenship.

One distinguishing feature of the modern era is the extension of citizenship. In the United States, for instance, it took many years for racial minorities, women, and individuals without property to gain the right to vote and the right to protection under the law in the exercise of their civil rights. Yet, as the number of citizens (and of people in general) has risen, effective political participation for individuals has often become more difficult. It is one thing for society to embrace ideas such as citizenship for all and equal rights in theory; it is quite another to provide the civic education and social development necessary to make the ideal of a society of political equals a practical reality.

POLITICAL CULTURE: DEFINING THE GOOD

The Greek view of what constituted the good citizen was a reflection of the way the Greeks defined the word *good*. Every language in the world has a word meaning "good," and it is arguably the most important word in any language. But every language is embedded in a culture, and no two cultures are identical. We are all products of the culture into which we are born. From our earliest infancy, and long before we know how to read or write, we learn to talk.

Along with the language, we also learn about our environment, which includes both tangible and intangible things. Among the most important intangibles are values—that is, what our parents or other guardians say is "good" or "bad." In the process of learning the difference between good and bad (picking up our toys is "good" and not eating our vegetables is "bad"), we also learn about right and wrong. Crossing the line from "good" and "bad" in word and deed to "right" and "wrong" in thought and sentiment is a giant step across a great chasm—it is the difference between outward behavior and inner motives, beliefs, and desires. Culture, in the sense that anthropology and political science use the word, is all about established norms, customs, and traditions—in other words, how *society* defines right and wrong and about what "the good life," or the word *good* itself, means in a given place and time. There is no universally accepted definition of "the good life" in this world for the simple reason that there is no universal culture.

Culture has many meanings. Here we are interested primarily in the aspects of culture that are related to politics—what scholars often call **political culture**. Political culture encompasses the prevailing moral values, beliefs, and myths people live by and are willing to die for. It also includes the collective memory of a society—the history we learn about in grade school; what we come to know about our leaders, about crises we have survived as a nation, and about wars we have fought. Virtually anything and everything that shapes our shared

political culture
The moral values, beliefs, and myths people live by and are willing to die for.

perceptions of reality is part of our political culture. This collective memory and these shared perceptions differ depending on the specifics of geography, climate, terrain, and other physical circumstances, as well as certain accidental factors—for example, the presence or absence of hostile and aggressive neighbors.

Small nations often have a history of being subjugated by powerful neighbors. Island peoples, such as the British and the Japanese, have a history that differs in fundamental ways from landlocked nations, owing to the absence of shared borders. The success of the thirteen American colonies in breaking away from the British Empire, as well as the United States' historic isolationism, would not have been possible without the benevolent presence of two great oceans. Clearly geography matters.

Religion plays a major role in shaping political cultures. We cannot understand Western civilization without reference to Roman Catholicism, the Reformation, and Christianity. By the same token, Islam forms the moral core of life in the Arab Middle East, as well as in much of South, Central, and Southeast Asia (see Figure 10.1). The same is true of Hinduism in India; Buddhism in Cambodia, Tibet, and Thailand; Taoism and Confucianism in China and other Asian countries; and Shinto, as well as Buddhism, in Japan. Even where secularization has eroded religious beliefs (as in the West), the stamp of religion on political culture is both undeniable and indelible (see "Ideas and Politics").

We are often bemused, perplexed, or outraged by the reactions and perceptions of others. We wonder what they must be thinking. How could anyone,

FIGURE 10.1   Map of Islamic Faith. Religion exerts a powerful influence on the political ideas, values, and aspirations of people all over the world. With an estimated 1.5 billion adherents, Islam is the second-largest body of believers in the world. (Christianity is the first, with roughly 2.1 billion.)

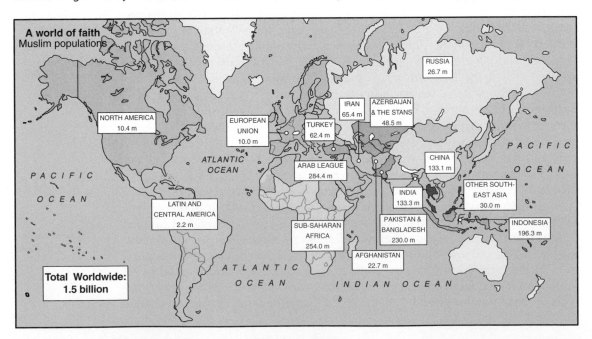

THE TAO AND THE CLASH OF CIVILIZATIONS

In his provocative little book *The Abolition of Man* (New York: Macmillan, 1947), C. S. Lewis argued that "the Tao" could be found in civilizations, cultures, and religions the world over. Taoism originated in China in ancient times. The Tao is "the way"—the source of all knowledge about nature and truth, the key to inner peace and social harmony. Lewis noted that this type of metaphysical reasoning and the moral values it fostered are found in religions and ethical systems all over the world. He cites many "Illustrations of the Tao" drawn "from such sources as come readily to the hand of one who is not a professional historian."

Lewis makes a powerful case for humanistic education—that is, for teaching people to love truth and justice. Learning to love truth and justice, Lewis suggested, is the key to civil society, because people are not simply rational beings and do not naturally behave according to reason. It is necessary, therefore, that society finds ways to link human emotions with positive attitudes and good acts, which brings us back to the Tao. What Lewis called the Tao teaches respect for authority, humility, honesty, charity, generosity, and so forth—in short, the way to live in harmony with oneself, others, and nature.

Political culture cannot be distilled from moral and religious teachings alone; indeed, politics is not what Lewis's book is about. But his views on the role of public education in developing a sense of right and wrong—a civic culture that supports democratic

processes and institutions—have significant implications for students of politics.

The late Harvard scholar Samuel Huntington wrote a best-selling book in the mid-1990s titled *The Clash of Civilizations and the Remaking of the World Order*. The book's thesis highlights the prevalence and intensity of faith-based politics in today's world. Indeed, the nexus between education and values, the province of religion and morality, remains an important question—one involving a global battle for the hearts and minds of people with little understanding of international politics.

Historians, political theorists, and social scientists of all types often make a distinction between the proximate and root causes of dramatic events such as wars and revolutions. We focus on war and revolution in later chapters, but the distinction between surface and deep-seated factors can be applied to everyday politics—and everyday life—as well. How we react to events is important, but how we see the world is even more important. Why? Think about it.

(Hint: Ask yourself where your own ideas about the greatest values in life come from. To a greater extent than most of us realize, what we are is inseparable from where we are—and where we were born. Try to imagine what you would think of Jews and/or Christians if you had been born in a Palestinian refugee camp or lived in Gaza. Now reverse the example: Imagine what you would think of Arabs and/or Muslims if you were Jewish.)

for example, condone the actions of terrorists whose victims are often innocent bystanders? We tend to assume that anyone with extreme views is ignorant, misguided, or even depraved. In fact, however, profound differences in perception, outlook, and behavior can often be traced to differences in national history, personal experience, and political culture.

A political culture is like a filter for our personal experiences—without it we lack any common interpretation of reality. Without a shared reality, we lack the basis for a community or society.

We can study political culture in several different ways. We can look at its sources in society (geography, climate, history, religion, and the like), at its manifestations (attitudes, perceptions, beliefs, and prejudices), or at its effects (actions and public policies). As is often the case, however, the closer we look, the more complicated the picture becomes.[5]

Another way to think about political culture is in terms of one national political culture and many regional and local political *subcultures*. College students have an opportunity to research this question themselves by simply engaging classmates from different states or regions of the country—and from different countries—in conversations about growing up. Comparing your own upbringing with those of others from different backgrounds can be both fun and enlightening.

In the next section, we look at the ingenious ways societies sow the seeds of political culture. Consider this: are our ideas about "first things" (good and bad, right and wrong) really *our* ideas at all—or were they implanted at a young age, long before we had any idea of them?

POLITICAL SOCIALIZATION: FORMING CITIZENS

Though we can dispute the proper definition of citizenship, most people agree that good citizens are made, not born. Children grow up to be responsible citizens through the interplay of various influences and institutions—including family, religion, school, peer groups, the mass media, and the law. The process of being conditioned to think and behave in a socially acceptable manner is called *socialization*.

Every self-sustaining society inculcates in its citizens certain basic values necessary to establish and perpetuate a political order. Even as staunch an individualist as the British philosopher John Stuart Mill (1806–1873) acknowledged that the sense of citizen loyalty or allegiance "may vary in its objects and is not confined to any particular form of government; but whether in a democracy or in a monarchy its essence is always . . . that there be in the constitution of the state something which is settled, something permanent, and not to be called into question; something which, by general agreement, has a right to be where it is, and to be secure against disturbance, whatever else may change."[6]

Political socialization is the process whereby citizens develop the values, attitudes, beliefs, and opinions that enable them to support the political system.[7] This process begins with the family.

The Family

The family exerts the first and most important influence on the formation of individual values. Different political regimes view the family in different ways. Some governments support and nurture the family; others choose to remain indifferent toward it; a few seek to undermine it and regard the love and loyalty that flow from family ties as subversive to the state. Despite these varying reactions, all governments recognize the importance of the family in the socialization process.

Even nations that publicly proclaim the value of the traditional family, however, may not be able to ensure its success in society. The number of children living in single-parent households in the United States, for example, has risen

political socialization The process by which members of a community are taught the basic values of their society and are thus prepared for the duties of citizenship.

dramatically since the 1960s due to rising divorce rates, changes in sexual mores, teenage pregnancies, and other social changes. Whereas in 1980 single-parent households constituted 19.5% of the total, that figure had risen to 29.5% by 2008. Another sign of the times: In 2009, 7.8 million children lived with at least one grandparent, a 64% increase since 1991, according to a U.S. Census Bureau report released in mid-2011.

Poverty and lack of education are major causes of divorce. Moreover, the problem is self-perpetuating. Studies confirm that children raised in single-parent families are at greater risk than those in two-parent families to drop out of school, to become involved with crime and illegal drugs, to be unemployed (or underemployed) and poor, and to have failed marriages and personal relationships as adults—a vicious cycle.[8] Of course, single-parent families are often successful, and many children raised by single parents become well-adjusted adults. Indeed, if one parent is physically or emotionally abusive, it is often better for a child to be nurtured (and protected) only by the parent who is not.

Children are first socialized at home, within the family structure, learning what is and what is not permissible, with rewards and punishment to reinforce daily behavior. In this manner, parents make the obligations of children to the family and to others clear. Slowly, children become citizens of the family, often with clearly defined responsibilities and occasionally with rights or privileges. Parents emphasize moral ground rules, even if they don't always specify the reasons for them ("Do it because I said so"). Trust, cooperation, self-esteem, respect for others, and empathy, each rooted in family relations, bear on the behavioral and moral development of individuals.[9]

U.S. Navy photo by Photographer's Mate 1st Class Arlo K. Abrahamson

Where discipline is lacking and parents are overly permissive, children are given rights and privileges with few if any responsibilities. In such cases, socialization is impeded to the extent it fails to produce behaviors conducive to social harmony, civility and civic duty, or leads to narcissism, self-promotion, and a tendency to exploit others.

The family also helps determine the direction the ultimate political socialization of children takes and how successful it will be. Party orientation and even affiliation often derive from the family, especially when both parents belong to the same party. In the United States, about 70% of children whose parents both have the same party affiliation favor that party too.[10] In addition, the family exerts a powerful influence on religious persuasion, which tends to correlate highly with party affiliation, as well as with certain political opinions (fundamentalist Protestants tend to oppose abortion; Jews tend to support Israel; and so on).[11] However, studies

A young boy awaits the arrival of the late president's funeral motorcade at the gate of the Ronald Reagan Presidential Library in Simi Valley, California, on June 7, 2004. This picture illustrates that children begin learning to be good citizens and to show respect for legitimate authority—important lessons in political socialization—at an early age.

indicate that when it comes to opinions about more abstract political issues, parental influence is quite limited.[12] As adults, we often find ourselves at odds with our parents' ideas about politics (among other things), a fact often attributed to "generational" differences.

Social Class and Minority Status Family interest in politics tends to increase with social standing. Middle- and upper-class children are most likely to become actively engaged in politics; children from lower-class families are typically uninformed about politics and participate less often.[13] There are many exceptions, however, including Abraham Lincoln, Harry S. Truman, Richard Nixon, William Jefferson Clinton, and Barack Obama, all arising from humble origins to become president of the United States.

Former Secretary of State Madeleine Albright, current president of Liberia Ellen Johnson Sirleaf, and Josephine Baker, the first African American female to star in a major motion picture, are examples of women not born to privilege who rose to great heights. Josephine Baker was born in St. Louis in 1902 and dropped out of school at the age of 12. She is best known as a recording artist and stage performer, but she was decorated for her undercover work in the French Resistance during World War II. When she died in Paris in 1975, she became the first American woman to receive French military honors at her funeral. Condoleezza Rice, born in Birmingham, Alabama, in 1954 at a time when blacks were not allowed to have a hamburger at Woolworth's, became the first black woman (and only the second woman) ever to serve as U.S. Secretary of State (2005–2009).

Minority status can play a significant role in political socialization. Some researchers have found that in the United States, African American children tend to place less trust in government, and to feel less confident of influencing it, than do white children.[14]

Not surprisingly, such attitudes correlate with political opinions; thus, holding social-class differences constant, black adults in the United States tend to be less conservative than whites on most economic and foreign policy issues, although not on the issue of crime. Politically, though not necessarily socially and culturally, Asian Americans tend to resemble white ethnic groups more closely than black groups, particularly on domestic social issues. Hispanic Americans tend to fall between blacks and whites. However, family socialization and the transmission of political beliefs have exerted an influence on Cuban Americans, who, as a group, tend to be more hard-line conservative, especially on foreign policy questions, than are other Hispanic-American groups, including Mexicans and Puerto Ricans. One reason is that after Cubans fled to the United States at the time of the Cuban Revolution, Cuban leader Fidel Castro confiscated their property and persecuted family members they had left behind.

Gender and Politics Like class and race, gender differences can be important independent correlates of political behavior and opinions. In the United States, the so-called **gender gap**—differences in the ways men and women think and vote in the aggregate—has gotten a lot of attention in recent decades. For instance, in the 1992 general elections, Bill Clinton won the women's vote by

gender gap
Differences in voting between men and women in the United States; this disparity is most obvious in political issues and elections that raise the issue of the appropriateness of governmental force.

In the race to succeed in business, politics, and most professions, women in economically advanced societies have made substantial gains in recent decades, but men still enjoy a big advantage at the highest levels of government and the corporate world.

Peter Griffin/PublicDomainPictures.net

8 points, but won the men's vote by only 3. Women thus helped a challenger defeat a sitting president. In 1996, the gender gap was even bigger. In 2008, women favored Barack Obama over John McCain by a wide margin despite the fact that McCain's running mate was a woman, Sarah Palin. But that number does not tell the whole story: in all, 8 million more women voted for Obama than for McCain, and women voters accounted for 53% of all the votes cast. Obama thus received a double boost from women voters—a larger percentage of a bigger vote. The pattern is different in congressional races, however, where the gender gap is seldom apparent.

Some researchers tie gender differences to early family experiences and expectations; others contend there are innate differences in the way men and women develop moral and political awareness. One theory postulates that due to some combination of socialization and biology, women—as mothers and primary caregivers for children—tend to develop a moral and political perspective that emphasizes compassion and the protection of human life.[15] An alternate theory holds that gender-based political differences are rooted in *some* women's later life experiences.[16] For example, working women who have been paid less than men doing the same job are likely to vote for a party or candidate that stresses fairness and equal rights.

One important political difference between the sexes revolves around the government's use of force. Women tend to be more reluctant to support war, more opposed to capital punishment, and more inclined to support gun control. Women also tend to give more support to social welfare programs intended to help families, the working poor, and the economically disadvantaged. These differences help explain why the gender gap has aided Democrats in recent years. We turn now to a factor that has greatly aided Republicans in recent times.

Religion

Either the church or the state may present itself as the true source of moral authority, which makes religion particularly important in the socialization process. And just as religion can influence a young person's developing political opinions, so can politics decisively shape the role of religion within the family and the place it ultimately occupies within the larger political order.

Sometimes religion can legitimize existing practices and lend stability to a society in transition. Hinduism in India, for instance, has proved compatible with changing political institutions. Described by one expert as having "a multi-layered complexity allowing for the existence of many gods, many incarnations, many layers of truth,"[17] Hinduism has tended, historically, to support the status quo. Even when the status quo allowed systematic discrimination against a lower, "untouchable" class, Hinduism counseled patience and perseverance in anticipation of future lives to come. In other parts of the world, however, religious doctrine has ignited aggressive policies. In Libya and Iran, for instance, Islamic fundamentalism has helped fuel belligerent foreign policies and contributed to a periodic fervor for war.

Religion and politics sometimes conflict. In Nazi Germany, the government steamrolled the Lutheran and Catholic churches. In the former Soviet Union, the regime allowed the historically entrenched Russian Orthodox Church to continue functioning but restricted and monitored its activities, frequently persecuting believers.[18]

In the United States, religion and politics reinforce one another at a number of levels. Although the Supreme Court has interpreted the Constitution to prohibit government from directly supporting religion, the First Amendment also clearly prohibits government from denying an individual's free exercise of religion. Religion continues to flourish in the United States. In the mid-1980s, "More than 90 percent of all Americans identify with some religious faith, and on any given Sunday morning more than 40 percent are to be found in church"; furthermore, by "most measurable indices the United States is a more religious country than any European nation except Ireland and Poland."[19] But this picture appears to be changing—about 15% of survey respondents in the United States say they have "no religion."[20]

The Judeo-Christian tradition continues to be dominant in the United States, yet there is significant diversity within that tradition. Census data show numerous Protestant denominations constitute about 51% of the population (with Baptists constituting the largest groups at about 16%); Roman Catholics, 24%; and Jews, 1.7%. After the terrorist attacks of September 11, both the public reaction and the mass media focused attention on the fact that there is also a Muslim minority in the United States, although it is relatively small (0.6%). There are more Buddhists in the United States than Muslims.

Important political differences correlate with these differences in religious orientation, some even arising from the religious doctrines themselves. Quakers and Mennonites tend to be pacifists, whereas, as previously mentioned, fundamentalist Protestants tend to oppose abortion and Jews generally favor Israel. By the same token, members of black Protestant churches tend to be more politically liberal than are Protestants affiliated with mainstream churches, and members of mainstream churches tend to be more politically liberal than their evangelical Protestant counterparts.

More generally, on a scale measuring political conservatism and liberalism, Protestants tend to be somewhat more conservative than Catholics and much more conservative than Jews. Jews, Catholics, and religiously unaffiliated voters have historically identified more with the Democratic Party, whereas Protestants have leaned toward the Republican Party, though the correlation between religion and party affiliation appeared to be weakening until George W. Bush received 56% of the Protestant vote and Al Gore (the Democratic candidate) only 42% in the 2000 presidential election. (Gore won among Roman Catholic voters, however, with 50% to Bush's 47%.) In 2010, Roman Catholics joined Protestants in voting Republican in the midterm elections, a shift reflecting the Vatican's staunch "pro-life" (anti-abortion) position. But in 2012, a majority of Roman Catholics voted for Obama despite a strong pro-choice stance on the part of the church hierarchy. (The literal meaning of the word "hierarchy" is "holy government").

Religion can be used to edify and elevate as well as divide. Sometimes political leaders draw on religious imagery to unite citizens in a common understanding of the present or point them toward a more noble vision of the future.[21] For example, the famous U.S. clergyman and civil rights leader Martin Luther King Jr. inspired the nation with his dream of a day "when all of God's children—black men and white men, Jews and Gentiles, Protestants and Catholics—will be able to join hands and sing in the words of the old Negro spiritual 'Free at last! Free at last! Thank God Almighty, we are free at last!'" The tragic assassination of King, like the assassination of Abraham Lincoln a century earlier, helped rally the U.S. people to the cause of racial equality.

The role of religion in U.S. national politics has risen sharply in recent years. As part of his "faith-based initiative," George W. Bush asked Congress to allow religious organizations to compete for government contracts and grants without a strict separation of religious activities and social service programs.

But it was the shock of September 11, 2001, that changed everything. Suddenly, religion was at the heart of a great menace, namely, international terrorism. The late Osama bin Laden and his al Qaeda terrorist network gave the

Courtesy of the author, Thomas Magstadt

The separation of church and state is a principle enshrined in the Bill of Rights. Thomas Jefferson famously described it as a "wall of separation." Nonetheless, religion has always played a big role in U.S. politics and still does. Indeed, some critics, alarmed at what they see as an improper and increasingly aggressive use of the pulpit to influence voters, argue that overtly political religious institutions deserve to lose their tax exempt status. The sign in this picture was planted amidst rows of crosses symbolizing the graves of aborted fetuses on the grounds of a Roman Catholic church in a midwestern city only days before the 2012 election. What do you think?

civic education
The process of inculcating in potential citizens the fundamental values and beliefs of the established order.

world a horrifying glimpse of religion's dark side when they attempted to unite the world's 1.5 billion Muslims against the "Crusaders" (Christians and Jews) in a jihad, or holy war. Al Qaeda obliterated the distinction between religion and ideology and used Islam as an instrument of war against the West.

Schools

Schools play a vital role in **civic education**. In effect, the state uses schools as instruments of political socialization. Some governments merely prescribe one or two courses in civics or history, require students to salute the flag, and hang a few pictures of national heroes on school walls. Other governments dictate the entire school curriculum, indoctrinate the children with slogans and catch phrases, heavily censor textbooks and library acquisitions, and subject teachers to loyalty tests.

Different regimes inculcate different values. Under some regimes (for example, the Soviet Union in the 1930s), blind obedience to authority is the norm. In others, patriotism is encouraged, but so is the habit of critical and independent thinking. One other key variable is the *priority* given to education (see "Ideas and Politics").

IDEAS AND POLITICS

CONFUCIAN VS. CONFUSION: A Reverence for Education

An international study, published in December 2010, compared students in sixty-five countries representing all different faiths in math, science, and reading. The winner? Confucianism!

China's Shanghai was at the top of all three lists by a wide margin. The *New York Times* columnist Nicolas Kristof observed, "Three of the next top four performers were also societies with a Confucian legacy of reverence for education: Hong Kong, Singapore and South Korea."*

Finland was the only non-Confucian country in the mix. The United States came in 15th in reading, 23rd in science and 31st in math.

No less worrying is a study published a month later, in January 2011, reporting that 45% of undergraduates in the United States show almost no gains in learning in the first two years.† The research indicated that colleges don't make academics a priority, that professors are primarily interested in research, and that students spend 50% less time studying compared with students several decades ago.

Other details in the research: over a third of U.S. students surveyed reported spending no more than five hours per week studying alone (research shows

that students who study in groups learn less); half report never taking a course where they wrote more than twenty pages; nearly one-third say they never took a course where they read more than forty pages per week.

Problems in society are often a product of a particular culture, perhaps one that is changing too fast or one that is too resistant to change. Such problems also are a product of public policy, which may reflect the values of an elite social class or a dominant religious sect. Why are students in the United States—a country with many of the best schools and universities in the world—falling behind students elsewhere in the world? Think about it.

(Hint: Many teachers in the United States blame parents and a certain approach to parenting for many of the problems they encounter in the classroom. To learn more, Google "America education falling behind." Try it again and add the word "parents.")

* Nicolas Kristof, "China's Education System", *New York Times*, January 15, 2011; http://kristof.blogs.nytimes.com/2011/01/15/chinas-education-system/.

† Richard Arum et al., *Academically Adrift: Limited Learning on College Campuses* (Chicago, IL: University of Chicago Press, 2011).

Socialization studies tell us a lot about how children learn civic values in school.[22] During the elementary school years, children develop positive *emotional* attachments to key political concepts, such as liberty and democracy and respect for others. Young children also learn to think of the government in terms of an authority figure—a police officer, the president, and so on.

As we mature, *cognition* comes into play; we begin to grasp abstract concepts such as democracy. During adolescence and early adulthood, our attitudes toward authority often change radically. We cease to obey authority without question. Increasingly, we want to decide things for ourselves—a sentiment readily transferable to the political realm.

High school civics classes are probably less important than the total educational experience.[23] Lessons and stories on the nation's history, formal rituals such as reciting the Pledge of Allegiance, patriotic music, and extracurricular activities like sports, band, debate, and writing for the school newspaper all can convey the importance of responsible participation and working toward a common goal. Electing class officers and participating in student government is typically our first exercise in democracy.

In general, higher education and political participation go hand in hand. Higher education also correlates positively with personal self-confidence and trust in others—personality traits that democratic political systems, based on citizen participation, require.[24]

In the United States, the college curriculum often represents a blend of vocational training and liberal arts—with the latter, which includes literature, philosophy, science, history, and linguistics, placing great emphasis on the development of critical thinking.[25] Advocates of the liberal arts stress the importance of education not only for citizenship, but also for leadership. What such an education does, at its best, is produce *politically literate* adults. Evidence suggests it tends to produce more liberal adults, as well.[26]

The ideal of **liberal education** fits easily with constitutional guarantees that protect the right to question authority. It also prepares citizens to do so.[27] With rare exception, democracies alone tolerate independent thinking and dissent. Recall that the Greek philosopher Socrates was considered subversive and sentenced to death—not for teaching his students *what* to think but for teaching them *how* to think.

Peer Groups

A **peer group** can refer either to a group of people who are friends, or to people of similar age and characteristics. The concept of peers itself arises from "the tendency for individuals to identify with groups of people like themselves."[28] Peer groups exert considerable influence over our political activities and beliefs, but there has been little research on the influence of peer groups in politics.[29]

The relationship between gang membership and the development of antisocial attitudes by adolescent male lawbreakers, for example, is a matter of more than academic interest. Studies indicate that gang membership and teenage crime are linked. According to one study, peers and gangs "can affect the value a person assigns to the rewards of crime (by adding the approval of colleagues

liberal education
A type of education often associated with private colleges in the United States; stresses the development of critical thinking skills through the study of literature, philosophy, history, and science.

peer group
A group of people similar in age and characteristics—for example, college students.

to the perceived value of the loot or the direct gratification of the act)."[30] But it's still not clear whether gangs *cause* teenagers to commit crimes or attract teenagers predisposed to criminal behavior in the first place. In all probability, the answer is both.

Psychologically, peer groups satisfy our need for approval. Peer groups are often formed voluntarily and informally, but organizations such as the Girl Scouts, the Young Democrats, or a high school journalism club are also peer groups. As such, they also satisfy the same need for approval and a sense of belonging, one totalitarian tyrants like Hitler, Stalin, and Mao deftly exploited (see Chapter 6).

The state can create peer-group structures for youth, as well as adults. These involuntary associations are typically designed to infuse ideological fervor and abject loyalty into young hearts and minds. Under the Nazi Party, for example, German life was organized through an elaborate network of state controlled associations of peers to ensure that every German would, in time, adopt correct political attitudes and be properly socialized into the new Nazi order. Similarly, the Communist Party of the Soviet Union created an all-encompassing set of centrally controlled peer organizations in the guise of clubs and civic associations.

In liberal democracies, the state plays a role in the socialization process but does not control it. Peer groups form naturally and civic associations are independent of the state.

The Mass Media and Internet

The media and Internet also play a significant role in political socialization. In nondemocratic states, the **mass media**—that is, television, radio, newspapers, and large-circulation magazines—are almost always owned or controlled by the state, and the Internet is monitored and websites the government finds objectionable are often blocked (as in China, North Korea, and Iran). Even some democratic governments monopolize radio and television broadcasting (as in Denmark) or own and operate television networks (as in Great Britain) but strive to ensure fairness and objectivity.

The Internet is especially crucial in shaping attitudes now because young people generally have a high level of computer skills and spend more hours each day on the Internet than watching TV. For American youth between the ages of 12 and 24, one recent study found that in "daily time spent," the Internet soared from 10% in 2000 to 30% in 2010. The same respondents reported watching TV almost as much, but spending almost no time reading newspapers and magazines.[31]

Television is still popular most everywhere in the world, of course, even in some strict Islamic societies, where the state now uses this otherwise "decadent" source of Western pop culture to inculcate Islamic moral values. Thus, in Saudi Arabia, a traditional monarchy, state-owned television holds an annual "Miss Beautiful Morals" pageant that is the exact opposite of our beauty pageants— the physical appearance of the contestants is irrelevant (in fact, they are covered from head to foot). Rather, the winner is the contestant who is judged to have the most devotion and respect for her parents.[32]

mass media
The vehicles of mass communication, such as television, radio, film, books, magazines, newspapers, and the Internet.

IDEAS AND POLITICS

FREE SPEECH: The FCC vs. FOX Television

The late comedian George Carlin created a sensation when he did a stand-up routine about the "seven dirty words" you cannot say on television. That routine secured Carlin's place as one of the most famous nightclub and television comedians in recent U.S. history. But it was more than a knee-slapping shtick; it was also political satire at its most biting, for Carlin was raising a serious question: Does the state's action in restricting indecent speech on television violate the citizen's right to free speech?

For several decades, the FCC's restrictions on indecent speech allowed a fleeting swear word or curse word—that is, so long as it was not repeated. In 2003, the FCC changed the rule to make even a fleeting indecent word impermissible, and to impose severe penalties in the form of steep fines for violations. FOX TV then sued the FCC, and in November 2008, the case came before the U.S. Supreme Court.

The issue was determining whether the FCC provided an adequate explanation, or instead acted arbitrarily and capriciously, in changing its policy regarding televised use of isolated expletives considered indecent under federal law. The Court narrowly backed the FCC in a 2009 ruling, but sent it back to the court of appeals for further consideration of the First Amendment question. It remains unclear whether and under what conditions the state can censor speech on radio and television, much less the Internet.

Does the state's action in restricting indecent speech on television violate the citizen's right to free speech? Think about it.

(Hint: Do not shout "fire" in a crowded theater.)

In the United States, where the mass media are privately owned, the Federal Communications Commission (FCC) regulates radio and television. FCC rules are designed to discourage ideas, attitudes, or behavior the agency considers undesirable or unhealthy. For example, certain words cannot be uttered on television in the United States (see "Ideas and Politics"), full nudity is banned from 6:00 a.m. to 10 p.m. daily, and broadcasters are not permitted to air commercials for cigarettes.

The FCC is also charged with promoting and preserving media competition, but in December 2007, it lifted the so-called cross-ownership ban in the twenty largest U.S. markets. Radio and television broadcasters are now allowed to own newspapers as well. Critics contend that consolidation of the media has greatly harmed competition and undermined the quality of news and the diversity of views available to the public.

The Internet and television have become critical sources of information as U.S. adults read fewer newspapers and attend fewer political party functions.[33] The high cost of television advertising—and, therefore, of running for office—adversely affects the quality of campaigns and candidates (see Table 10.1) The same is true of the content. Attack ads are often intentionally unfair, misleading, and manipulative (see "Ideas and Politics: Opposition Research"). They typically impugn the character and motives of the other candidate and deliberately misrepresent his or her voting record.

How news is presented, particularly on television, is important. Fairness and objectivity are vital. Some conservative critics contend that television news

TABLE 10.1   Campaign spending by candidates, parties, and outside groups hit a record high of $7 billion in 2012. The figures in the chart below do not include over two billion dollars independently donated by outside groups on behalf of candidates, issues, and partisan causes. Altogether, candidates spent $3.2 billion; parties spent $2 billion; and outside political committees accounted for another $2.1 billion. In 2014, the U.S. Supreme Court opened the door to raising the aggregate limits corporations and wealthy individuals are allowed to contribute to political campaigns.

An Incomplete Picture of Spending in 2012 E(US$)			
	House	Senate	President
Republicans	$532 million	$408 million	$1.019 billion
Democrats	$447 million	$331 million	1.123 billion
Total	$979 million	$739 million	2.142 billion

SOURCES: Open Secrets.Org at http://www.opensecrets.org/overview/index.php and POLITICO at http://www.politico.com/story/2013/01/7-billion-spent-on-2012-campaign-fec-says-87051.html.

shows a liberal bias. The media's emphasis on rumor and innuendo—as well as the ranting of popular media personalities on both the right and left—has blurred the line between sensationalism and straight news.

One view holds that media consolidation (especially for radio and news-papers) is leading to homogenized news, keyed to conservative audiences and corporate agendas. Critics fear the daily news will reflect right-wing biases while also becoming more and more like tabloid journalism or mind-numbing entertainment.

There is no denying that radio and television media are often superficial and sensationalistic. Television coverage of election campaigns, for example, stresses candidates' attempts to gain strategic advantage instead of focusing on issues and policy differences. One mainstream political scientist argues, "the United States cannot have a sensible campaign as long as it is built around the news media."[34]

Television executives know that conflict and confrontation are entertaining and that, as a rule, bad news makes good ratings. For this reason also, television almost always emphasizes the "horse race" aspect of presidential elections, dwelling on who is ahead, who gained, and who lost because of this gaffe or that revelation. The networks all want to be the first to call every contest. The race becomes an end in itself, and the "product" (where the candidates stand on the issues) takes a back seat to the process.

In one study of network news coverage between 1968 and 1988, the average length of presidential quotations shrank from 45 seconds to 9 seconds—truncated sound bites.[35] The old form of coverage—a short setup and a relatively long presidential comment—was reversed. By the late 1980s, reporters were regularly upstaging the president, commenting on his comments rather than letting him speak for himself. The ratio of paid political ads to political news

IDEAS AND POLITICS

OPPOSITION RESEARCH

Increasingly, the mass media broadcast negative political advertisements. These ads may or may not be entirely truthful, but they are often very effective. Sometimes viewed as a kind of political ambush, they are the product of extensive research into the backgrounds of political opponents and are aired at strategic times during the campaign. The Internet has made this kind of dirty work much easier for those who do it. Dirt diggers can request (and often obtain) telephone records, credit checks, and court records. Opposition research—or "oppo"—is a multimillion-dollar business employing investigators, consultants, lawyers, pollsters, and media experts.

Go to a website operated by Investigative Research Specialists, LLC touting "The Opposition Research Handbook" to get a better idea of what these for-profit dirt-dealing firms actually do (http://researchops.com/ or simply Google "research ops").

What's wrong with digging up dirt on politicians and wannabe politicians? What's right about it? What good can it do? What harm? Think about it.

(Hint: Ask yourself whether you have ever done anything you wouldn't want your parents or teachers or friends to know about or whether someone you know once got caught—or got away with—cheating on a test but regrets having done it and is basically a good person.)

SOURCE: Michele Norris, "Opposition Research: Know Thine Enemies," National Public Radio (NPR), *All Things Considered*, February 6, 2007.

has also shifted dramatically. In 2006, a study at the University of Wisconsin-Madison found that "local newscasts in seven Midwest markets aired 4 minutes, 24 seconds of paid political ads during the typical 30-minute broadcast while dedicating an average of 1 minute, 43 seconds to election news coverage."[36] In-depth analysis, critics say, has become a casualty of Madison Avenue marketing techniques, the Nielsen ratings, and outright manipulation by highly paid professionals—political gurus, media consultants, and spin doctors (public relations specialists).

In short, a drift toward tabloid journalism and the use of the airways as a vehicle for propaganda have severely compromised the integrity of television news reporting and talk radio. This type of coverage, pandering to prurience and prejudice, increasingly crowds out honest attempts to fulfill the vital "news and information" function of the mass media.[37] To make matters worse, newspapers—long the main source of information on current events for most citizens—are rapidly losing readership (see "Ideas and Politics").

Consumers are also to blame for the state of the news. The news is "dumbed down" and entertaining because that is what attracts the largest number of viewers. Knowing the average viewer has a short attention span, television news directors spotlight the razzle-dazzle of video technology, flashy computer graphics, fast-paced interviews, and rapidly changing stories, locations, and camera angles. After a hard day's work, most viewers are not in the mood for an in-depth story or analysis that confuses, upsets, or makes them think too much. The problem is that the most important political issues tend to do all three.

The media's tendency to focus on negative news serves as a reminder that freedom of speech and criticism of the government are protected rights in

MEDIA CONSOLIDATION

Who needs newspapers or media competition? Either Congress or the FCC are asleep at the switch—or they are looking the other way. The facts speak for themselves:

- In early 2009, the *Seattle-Post Intelligencer* shut its printing presses after 146 years in business; two weeks later, the *Rocky Mountain News* folded. The *Tucson Citizen* suffered the same fate.
- Daily print circulation dropped from a peak of 62 million circa 1990 to around 49 million two decades later. Online readership has risen faster, to almost 75 million people and 3.7 billion page views in January 2009, according to Nielsen Online.
- In 1950, the total daily paid circulation relative to the number of households in the United States was 120%; by 2010, this figure had dropped to under 40%; similarly, total daily circulation of *national* dailies in the United States fell from just under 60% in 1995 to well below 40% in 2010.
- In the middle of the twentieth century, 80% of all newspapers were independently owned. By 2004, more than 7,000 cities and towns had no locally owned newspaper.
- There are 2,500 book publishers in the United States, but five giant companies produce most of the revenue; two retail chains (Barnes & Noble and Amazon.com) accounted for well over half of all retail book sales in the United States in 2008.
- Four major companies account for half the movie business.
- Six companies account for at least 90% of all domestic music sales, and Apple (iTunes)

became the biggest single U.S. music retailer in 2008 (19%), beating out Walmart (15%) for the first time.

- The 1996 Telecommunications Act doubled the number of local radio stations a single company can operate and removed all limits on how many one company can own nationwide; a single company—Clear Channel Communications—owns more than 1,200 radio stations.
- By one count, the forty-five top-rated talk radio shows ran 310 hours of conservative talk to a mere five hours that were not patently right wing.

Visiting Stalinist Russia during the Cold War with a group of my very own students, our Intourist guide proudly announced that the Soviet Union had more newspapers than we have in the United States. "Yes," I replied, "and less news." Why do you suppose Soviet tour guides emphasized the *quantity* of newspapers available to Soviet citizens to visitors from the West? Do Western governments also sometimes use facts and statistics to deceive rather than to enlighten or inform the public? Think about it.

(Hint: Many Americans who remember what television network news was like in the days of Edward R. Murrow or Walter Cronkite now decry what they believe to be a decline in the quality of nightly news broadcasts, as well as newspapers. CNN was once the "go to" source for breaking world news. Compare CNN today with the BBC.)

SOURCE: NOW with Bill Moyers on PBS, February 13, 2004, http:// www.pbs.org, and author's updates from various Internet databases.

liberal democracies. Indeed, the content and quality of the daily news in any given country is one indicator of how much freedom exists there. Where criticism of the government is allowed, freedom is usually the norm. In the final analysis, the mass media in democratic states are both gauge and guarantor of individual freedom.

The Law

The law plays an important role in socialization. Some laws are designed to promote public order (by having cars drive on the right side of the street, for example). Other laws prohibit violent or antisocial behavior in society, such as murder, false advertising, theft, and racial discrimination. Equally important, the very idea of "law and order" is ingrained in us at an early age and the "rule of law" is an essential feature of liberal democracy. Thus, the law conditions our behavior in all sorts of subtle and not-so-subtle ways.

SOCIALIZATION AND POLITICAL BEHAVIOR

Fortunately, most citizens who participate in the political process choose, most of the time, to do so legally.

Political Behavior

Most of us participate in politics in largely symbolic, passive, or ritualistic ways—for example, by attending a political rally, responding to a political poll, watching a candidate on television, or putting a bumper sticker on our cars. Some volunteer on political campaigns (witness the huge volunteer "army" that helped Barack Obama get elected in 2008) or join liberal public interest groups such as the Sierra Club, the American Civil Liberties Union, or MoveOn.Org, or conservative ones such as the National Right to Life Committee, the National Taxpayers Union, or the Christian Coalition. Others participate in political protests of one kind of another.

Even during the turbulent Vietnam War era, however, only 2% of U.S. citizens surveyed believed violence was justified to achieve political aims.[38] Support for milder forms of protest is much higher, but this support falls off sharply as the action in question approaches the line between legal and illegal behavior. In general, protests, mass marches, and street demonstrations are far less common in the United States today than in Europe and elsewhere in the world.

Civil Disobedience

Some illegal acts—in particular, those classified as civil disobedience—are intended to stir a nation's conscience. Taking his cue from Mahatma Gandhi, Martin Luther King Jr. advocated civil disobedience in the struggle for racial equality in the 1960s. Civil disobedience stresses nonviolence and encourages demonstrators to accept the consequences of breaking the law, including arrest and detention.

Whether a particular form of illegal political behavior is morally wrong depends on the context—and the beholder. Where people are victimized by government or by a dominant class or ethnic group, the moral basis for law and authority often erodes. Even in the United States, illegal forms of political behavior have not always been considered "un-American." Agitating for independence from Great Britain in colonial times, for example, was treasonous. Had the American Revolution failed, Benjamin Franklin, Thomas Jefferson, and George Washington, among other leaders of the revolt, would probably have gone to the gallows.

Students marching for freedom of speech in Caracas, Venezuela, after then President Hugo Chávez shut down a popular television channel that dared to criticize him. Note that many of the student demonstrators' hands are painted white as a sign of peaceful intentions, but the government nonetheless accused them of being violent. Chávez died of a massive heart attack in the spring of 2013; mass protests against the rule of his handpicked successor, Nicolas Madura, in 2014 turned violent and threatened to plunge the country into chaos.

AP Images/Howard Yanes

Before the Civil War, the "underground railroad" that helped fugitive slaves escape bondage was a clear violation of federal law by many otherwise law-abiding citizens, especially in northern states like Massachusetts and New York. The underground railroad could not have existed without a network of activists who considered slavery a desecration of a "higher law," nor could these activists have themselves escaped prosecution without the cooperation of family, friends, and neighbors.

That the legal system does not always serve the cause of justice is, in fact, a kind of cliché even in the United States, where most people express a strong belief in the rule of law. It's the theme of popular books, movies, and television shows. Thus, for example, in the popular TV series *Person of Interest*, a billionaire computer genius and a former Green Beret and CIA field officer who have lost faith in the system go outside the law to protect intended victims from violent crimes that fall outside the government's narrow definition of a terrorist threat.

But, of course, illegal political behavior—sabotage, assassinations, and terrorist acts—aimed at elected officials and legitimate governments cannot be tolerated. Examples of such acts are all too common even in stable democracies. The attack on Arizona Congresswoman Gabrielle Giffords at a shopping mall in Tucson, Arizona, in early 2011 resulting in the death of six people, including a 9-year-old girl, is a recent case in point.

WHEN POLITICAL SOCIALIZATION FAILS

A nation's political culture reflects the fundamental values its people hold dear. These values need not be entirely consistent and may even conflict at times. Nor will day-to-day political beliefs and actions of individual citizens always conform to the ideals people hold dear in the abstract.[39] But a steady state requires an established political culture consisting of shared values. In democracies, these values set a very high standard—too high, in fact, to be fully attainable. And yet the standard is kept at the forefront, and it is the striving for a perfection never achieved that, in many ways, defines democracy and distinguishes it from its alternatives.

In the United States, private values correlate highly with key public (or civic) values.[40] Accordingly, U.S. adults generally profess a strong belief in basic liberal values: personal freedom, political equality, private ownership of property, and religious tolerance. Not only are these values expressed in the nation's fundamental documents and writings, including the Declaration of Independence, the Constitution, and *The Federalist Papers*, but they are also instilled in U.S. youth by a variety of socialization strategies.

In other democratic societies, the process of socialization works the same way and serves the same purposes. But the *expression* of such core values as liberty, equality, security, prosperity, and justice (see Chapter 13), as well as the precise content and balance among them, vary significantly from one country to another. In Europe, "equality" is more often about class-consciousness than civil rights. As a result, the state provides a much wider range of social services (including guaranteed universal health care) than in the United States. By the same token, love of liberty in Europe does not impede the police in criminal investigations the way it often does in the United States, nor does it entail the right of private citizens to own deadly weapons.

When a multiethnic nation fails to politically socialize large numbers of citizens as members of a single community—in effect, a new nation—the consequences are far-reaching. If there are multiple communities, there will be multiple processes going on and multiple political cultures being perpetuated. Members of the various subnational communities will not be successfully integrated into the political system, and they will not share the norms, rules, and laws of the society.

Some citizens may never become fully socialized politically. A state's failure to socialize its citizens may result from its unequal or unfair treatment of them. Citizens may then become angry, cynical, or embittered, or they may even turn to crime or revolution. In extreme cases of unjust, tyrannical government, citizens' "crimes" may be viewed as actions taken justifiably. Thus, while the failure of political socialization is always detrimental to the government in power, the moral and political implications of that failure are not always as easy to evaluate.

SUMMARY

Different governments treat the concept of citizenship in different ways. All states demand adherence to the rules (laws), of course, and most treat birth in, or naturalization into, the political order as a requirement of citizenship. In democratic states, the concept of citizenship is also tied to the ideas of equality and liberty, as well as to meaningful participation in politics, such as voting in periodic elections. This ideal of democratic citizenship dates back to the ancient Greek city-states, which were small enough to permit direct democracy (self-representation of enfranchised adults through public assemblies and plebiscites).

Political socialization is the process whereby citizens develop the values, attitudes, beliefs, and opinions that enable them to relate to and function within the political system. Specific influences on the developing citizen include the family, religion, public education, the mass media, the law, peer groups, and key political values. Political socialization is of paramount importance; if a nation fails to socialize its citizenry on a large-scale basis, its political stability can be endangered.

KEY TERMS

citizenship   289

political culture   295

political
   socialization   298

gender gap   300

civic education   304

liberal education   305

peer group   305

mass media   306

REVIEW QUESTIONS

1. Why was the concept of citizenship of central importance to Aristotle and other political thinkers?
2. In what contrasting ways can we define citizenship? Which definition best describes your understanding of citizenship? Explain your choice.
3. It is sometimes argued that true citizenship can be found only in a democracy. What does this statement mean? Do you agree with it? Why or why not?
4. What factors influence the political socialization of citizens? Which ones do you think have been most influential on you? On your peers? Your parents?

WEBSITES AND READINGS

Websites

University of Michigan: http://www.icpsr.umich.edu/icpsrweb/content/ datamanagement/quality.html; http://home.isr.umich.edu/centers/cps/; http:// home.isr.umich.edu/

National Elections Studies: electionstudies.org/index.htm http://

Money in Politics Databases: http://www.politicalmoneyline.com/; CQPolitics.com

Primary and Secondary Teacher Resources: http://www.educationworld .com/a_curr/curr008.shtml

Los Angeles Times **on Citizenship:** http://www.latimes.com/opinion/editorials/ la-ed-citizenship-part-1-20141005-story.html#page=1; http://www.latimes .com/opinion/editorials/la-ed-citizenship-sg-storygallery.html

Readings

Almond, Gabriel, and Sidney Verba. *The Civic Culture: Political Attitudes and Democracy in Five Nations.* Newbury Park, CA: Sage Publications, 1989. An influential comparative study of politics and political culture in the United States, Great Britain, former West Germany, Italy, and Mexico.

Alterman, Eric. *What Liberal Media? The Truth About Bias and the News.* New York: Basic Books, 2003. The author refutes the charge that the news has a liberal bias and makes a compelling (albeit controversial) argument that it reflects the corporate culture of the giant media conglomerates who control the industry.

Bennett, Lance W. *News: The Politics of Illusion,* 8th ed. (White Plains, NY: Longman, 2008. An intriguing analysis of television news. Raises the central question: How well does the news serve the needs of democracy?

Dalton, Russell J. *Citizen Politics: Public Opinion and Political Parties in Advanced Industrial Societies.* 5th ed. Washington, DC; CQ Press, 2008. A popular comparative study of political attitudes and behavior in the United States, Great Britain, France, and Germany.

Franken, Al. *Lies and the Lying Liars Who Tell Them: A Fair and Balanced Look at the Right.* New York: Dutton, 2003. A best-selling book that started out as a class project for Harvard graduate students.

Glendon, Mary Ann, and David Blankenhorn, eds. *Seedbeds of Virtue: Sources of Competence, Character, and Citizenship in American Society.* Lanham, MD: University Press of America, 1995. Thoughtful essays discuss the role of virtue and values in the contemporary formation of the American character.

Graber, Doris. *Media Power in Politics.* Washington, DC: CQ Press, 2007. This book looks at recent scholarship on traditional and new (electronic) media and analyzes role of "media power" in American politics.

Holloway, Harry, and John George. *Public Opinion,* 2nd ed. New York: St. Martin's Press, 1985. A thoughtful general introduction to American political culture.

Kern, Montague. *Thirty-Second Politics: Political Advertising in the Eighties.* Westport, CT: Greenwood, 1989. A detailed and disturbing analysis of contemporary political advertising on television. Even more relevant today than when it was published.

Lipset, Seymour Martin. *American Exceptionalism: A Double-Edged Sword.* New York: Norton, 1996. According to Lipset, American exceptionalism resides in its culture and its creed, including liberalism, individualism, egalitarianism, populism, voluntarism, and moralism.

Moore, Barrington. *The Social Origins of Dictatorship and Democracy: Lord and Peasant in the Making of the Modern World.* Boston, MA: Beacon Press, 1993. A classic study. The *New York Times Review of Books* calls it "A landmark in comparative history and a challenge to scholars of all lands who are trying to learn how we arrived at where we are now."

Patterson, Thomas E. *Out of Order.* New York: Vintage, 1994. The author makes a convincing case—in a book published two decades ago!—that the media has distorted and undermined the integrity of U.S. elections.

Putnam, Robert. *Bowling Alone: The Collapse and Revival of American Community*. New York: Touchstone, 2001. Argues that Americans are becoming ever-more disconnected from each other and social structures are disintegrating.

Reichley, A. James. *Religion in American Public Life*. Washington, DC: Brookings Institution, 1985. The best discussion available of religion's historical influence in the United States.

Roelofs, H. Mark. *The Tension of Citizenship: Private Man and Public Duty*. New York: Rinehart, 1957. Explores the development of various conceptions of citizenship.

Skocpol, Theda, *Diminished Democracy: From Membership to Management in American Civic Life*. Norman, OK: University of Oklahoma Press, 2004. Argues that participation by citizens and activists is being replaced by paid professionals.

Wald, Kenneth. *Religion and Politics in the United States*, 3rd ed. Washington, DC: CQ Press, 1996. A comprehensive account of the relationship between public life and religion in contemporary America.

Walzer, Michael. *Obligations: Essays on Disobedience, War, and Citizenship*. Cambridge, MA: Harvard University Press, 1982. A collection of philosophical essays dealing with the meaning of citizenship by one of the leading socialist thinkers in the United States.

Westin, Drew. *The Political Brain: The Role of Emotion in Deciding the Fate of the Nation*. New York: Perseus, 2007. A study on a topic of enormous relevance to the viability of democracy at a time when the spectacle of zealots taking center stage in politics is all too familiar—both at home and abroad.

Wilson, James Q. *The Moral Sense*. New York: Free Press, 1995. How is it that people come to act morally? Wilson fuses theory and social science research in the search for an answer.

CHAPTER 11

Political Participation
The Limits of Democracy

Learning Objectives

1 Discuss how ordinary people can participate meaningfully in politics.

2 Cite examples of successful citizen participation in politics and analyze why direct action worked in these instances.

3 Identify who participates and who doesn't and distinguish between their two opposing theories.

4 Explore whether political parties impede, orchestrate, or facilitate political participation.

5 Identify different kinds of interest groups and suggest criteria for distinguishing between good and bad ones.

We begin with a checklist of sorts. Many of us hold certain basic beliefs about participation and the political process:

- Participation is a right.
- Voting matters.
- Every vote is equal in value.
- A large voter turnout is good.
- Elections are fair.
- Majority rule determines outcomes.

These assumptions are worth examining, but first let's look at the various ways ordinary citizens can participate in the political process.

DEFINING PARTICIPATION

Citizens in democracies participate in politics by expressing opinions and casting votes. Polls focus attention on public opinion and give it clear definition (see "Ideas and Politics: Public Opinion")

IDEAS AND POLITICS

PUBLIC OPINION: Just How Stupid Are We?

In *Just How Stupid Are We?* (New York: Basic Books, 2008), historian Rick Shenkman asks, "Why do we value polls when most citizens do not know enough to make a reasoned judgment?" He is not alone in wondering.

"Americans are too ignorant to vote." That was the conclusion of a report from the Intercollegiate Studies Institute on the state of civic literacy in the United States, published in late 2008.* Nearly half the 2,500 voting-age adults in the study (including college students, elected officials, and other citizens) flunked a 33-question test on basic civics. Consider these results:

- Only 17% of college graduates knew the difference between free markets and central planning.
- Only 27% of elected officials could name a right or freedom guaranteed by the First Amendment.
- Asked what the Electoral College does, 43% of elected officials were stumped.
- Almost half of the elected officials (46%) in the study did not know that the Constitution gives Congress the power to declare war.

The authors of this study recommend reforms in the higher-education curriculum to correct the problem. Shenkman, founder of George Mason University's History News Network, suggests requiring students to read newspapers and giving college freshmen weekly quizzes on current events. He would subsidize newspaper subscriptions and college tuition for students who perform well on civics tests.*

In the meantime, don't expect government to do anything about the problem. After all, many—if not most—elected officials can't pass a basic civic literacy test themselves.

In theory, the idea of using civic literacy tests to decide who is qualified to vote and who is not makes sense. You can't get a driver's license without taking a test, for example. Voters who are ignorant of economics and don't know much about the issues or the candidates cannot vote intelligently. Isn't voting more important than driving? Think about it.

(Hint: Find out how literacy tests were used in the electoral process in the United States from the late 1800s to the 1960s.)

*Kathleen Parker, "Disheartening Finds about Civic Literacy," *Washington Post*, November 26, 2008, http://www.washingtonpost.com.

IDEAS AND POLITICS

STRATEGIC POLLING

Traditionally, polls measured public opinion *after* political leaders took positions or enacted legislation. Increasingly in election campaigns, however, polling has become future oriented, to determine what positions candidates *ought* to take or how positions are to be advanced or what advertisements will project positive candidate images. This use of public opinion is *strategic polling*.

To gauge whether a political advertisement or position will be popular, *focus groups*—small numbers of people led by a professional communications expert—are asked to react to and discuss particular agenda items. Electronic polling has made possible the *dial group*, in which individuals use a dial to register instant approval or disapproval.

Strategic polling, even among incumbents, has become a fact of political life. In the 2008 presidential election, the Obama campaign was particularly adept in using polls to determine how to frame not only the issues but also the message, including slogans like "Yes, we can" and "Change you can believe in."

What's wrong with candidates for public office using polls to get inside the minds of the voters? Think about it.

(Hint: Ask yourself whether you really need to know what a candidate is passionate about, where she or he stands on the issues, what she or he believes.)

Public Opinion

In theory, citizens in a democracy have a powerful voice in shaping government policies. In practice, it's not so simple. The public is often divided; attitudes change over time, vary from place to place, and are difficult to measure accurately. Different polls on the same issue or candidate often produce conflicting results.

Politicians do pay attention to opinion polls, but is public opinion a reliable guide? (See "Ideas and Politics: Strategic Polling.") Should elected officials follow or lead? As we will see in Chapter 12, this fundamental question is at the root of two opposing theories of representation.

What is **public opinion**? Is it a fine blend of collective wisdom and rational thought or a witch's brew of gut feelings, prejudices, and preconceptions based on scant information? The short answer is: both. Let's look a little deeper.

Polls

The first attempts to measure public opinion were **straw polls**—unscientific opinion samples nineteenth-century newspapers used to predict a winner in the run-up to elections. Local news sources still sometimes use straw polls today.

But there is never any guarantee that the sample in such a poll is representative of the population as a whole. The *Literary Digest* poll that predicted Alf Landon would defeat Franklin D. Roosevelt in 1936 is a famous case in point. Although the *Literary Digest* had correctly predicted the outcome of the three previous presidential elections, in 1936 its poll missed by a mile: Roosevelt

public opinion
In general, the ideas and views expressed by taxpayers and voters; when a majority of the people hold strong opinions one way or the other on a given issue or policy question, it tends to sway legislators and decision makers who know they will be held accountable at the next election.

straw poll
Unscientific survey; simple, inexpensive poll open to all sorts of manipulation and misuse.

random sampling
A polling method that involves canvassing people at random from the population; the opposite of stratified sampling.

stratified sampling
A manner of polling in which participants are chosen on the basis of age, income, socioeconomic background, and the like, so that the sample mirrors the larger population; the opposite of random sampling.

exit polling
Stratified polling technique that permits television networks to predict political winners as the polls close by surveying departing voters.

tracking poll
Repeated sampling of voters to assess shifts in attitudes or behavior over time.

won big. Where did this particular poll go wrong? The names in the sample were taken from the telephone directory and automobile registration lists—two very unrepresentative rosters at the time, because only rich people could afford telephones and cars during the Great Depression. Incidentally, that was the end of the *Literary Digest*'s polling and, for all practical purposes, of the *Literary Digest* itself. In 1938, it went out of business.

Over the past few decades, opinion polling has improved. To obtain the most objective results, a **random sampling** of citizens is drawn from the entire population, or universe, being polled. (Statisticians have deemed that a sample of 1,500 respondents is ideal for polls of large numbers of people.) In a cross-section of this kind, differences in age, race, religion, political orientation, education, and other factors approximate those within the larger population.

Because it is not always possible to conduct hundreds of separate interviews, pollsters sometimes use a method called **stratified sampling** in which they select small population sets with certain key characteristics (age, religion, income, party affiliation, and so on) in common. **Exit polling**, which permits television networks to predict political winners as the polls close by surveying departing voters, illustrates two levels of stratified polling. Pollsters first identify precincts that statistically approximate the larger political entity (a congressional district, a state, or the nation) and then try to select a sample that reflects the overall characteristics of the precinct.

Tracking polls repeatedly sample the same voters during the course of a campaign to identify shifts in voter sentiment and correlate them with media strategy, voter issues, candidates' gaffes, et cetera. To discover which campaign strategies are working and which are not, candidates often use tracking polls in conjunction with focus groups and other campaign instruments (see "Ideas and Politics: Strategic Polling").

Polls predict who will win an election before voters cast ballots. But they are not infallible. The same can be said of voters who often pay little attention or spend little time studying the issues and vote mindlessly. Only fourteen of the fifty states allow straight-ticket voting—for example, selecting all the Democrats or Republicans on the ballot by checking a single box.

Jewel Samad/Getty Images

Polls are useful predictive instruments, but they are not infallible. The exact wording of a given instrument is important for issues about which most people do not have well-formed opinions. Given a choice between two policy alternatives (for example, "Should the federal government see to it that all people have housing, or should individuals provide for their own housing?"), some respondents can be so influenced by the order in which the policies appear that a 30% variance between them may result, depending solely on which comes first in the question.[1] The *way* a question is phrased can also make a big difference. For example, "Do you support a woman's rights over her own body?" is likely to produce very different results from, "Do you support the right to terminate a pregnancy in the first trimester?"

Polls not only *measure* public opinion but also *influence* it. A question that frames smoking in terms of freedom to exercise a personal choice will yield a higher rate of approval for smoking than a question that mentions the health risks of secondhand smoke. Candidates, corporations, and organized interest groups of all kinds can often obtain the results they want through careful phrasing of their questions. Unfortunately, stacking the deck this way is a common practice in both the public and the private sectors.

Today, literally hundreds of polls are taken in a presidential election year. More polls do not necessarily mean better results,[2] although in the last three presidential elections they have been quite accurate. Indeed, the "poll of polls" (the average of all the major surveys) in the 2008 presidential election was right on the money. Polls taken on the eve of the election projected an Obama advantage of 7.52 percentage points on average; Obama's actual margin of victory was 7.2%.[3]

Political polling presents certain hazards. First, polls are only snapshots of public opinion, and public opinion is subject to rapid change. Second, as polling has become more widespread and intrusive, citizens are becoming less cooperative (despite pollsters' assurances of anonymity) and probably less truthful as well. Third, there are important methodological differences among the various polls. The biggest is the way polling organizations count the "undecided" voter and how they predict who the "likely" voter will be. Even the most scientific polls typically have a margin of error of 3% at the .05 level of confidence, which means 95 in 100 times the error is no more than 3% in either direction.

Elections

Polls and elections are closely related. In fact, elections *are* polls—the most accurate ones of all because the "sample" includes everybody who actually votes. Free elections are tied to the concept of representation—indeed, *representative democracy* and *republic* are synonymous.

Limitations of Elections Ideally, elections should enable a democratic society to translate the preferences of its citizens into laws and policies. In reality, elections often produce disappointing or indecisive results for a long list of reasons, including the following:

- If public opinion is ill defined or badly divided, elected officials get mixed signals.

- The great expenditure of time and money required to run for public office gives a huge advantage to incumbents and discourages many potential challengers.
- To attract as many voters or interest groups as possible, candidates often waffle on issues, giving voters a choice between Tweedledee and Tweedledum.
- Powerful lobbies and a convoluted budget process preoccupy, and occasionally paralyze, Congress.
- Politicians frequently say one thing and do another.

Despite these limitations, elections are indispensable to democracy. Contrary to popular opinion, campaign promises are often kept.[4] Elected officials sometimes turn out to be duds or disappointments, but seldom are they total surprises. In this sense, voters often get what they deserve.

Electoral Systems

Electoral systems vary greatly. We begin with the familiar and then look at some of the alternatives.

Winner-Takes-All Systems Most voters in the United States would have difficulty explaining how the U.S. electoral system works. Members of Congress are elected by plurality vote in single-member districts—that is, in the **winner-takes-all system,** which means that only one representative is elected from each electoral district, and the candidate who gets the most votes in the general election wins the seat. Because a state's two senators are elected in different years, entire states function as single-member districts. The fifty states are each single-member districts in presidential races as well, because *all* the electoral votes in any state are awarded to the electors of the presidential candidate who receives the most popular votes in that particular state.

The practical implications of such a system are wide-ranging. In any election within a single-member district, if only two candidates are seeking office, one of them necessarily will receive a **plurality,** defined as the largest bloc of votes. If three or more candidates are vying for a seat, however, the one who receives the greatest number of votes is elected. In a five-way race, for example, a candidate could win with 25% (or less) of the votes. As we shall see, this method of election strongly favors the emergence of a two-party system.

The effects of winner-takes-all, also known as **first past the post,** electoral systems are graphically illustrated by the hypothetical U.S. congressional race depicted in Table 11.1. This system has at least one important advantage: it produces clear winners. A plurality—as opposed to a majority (over half the total

TABLE 11.1 Hypothetical Political Race.

Party	Candidate	Votes Received	Percent of Vote
Democratic	John Liberal	25,800	43
Republican	Jane Conservative	24,600	41
Independent	Ima Nothing	9,600	16

votes cast)—decides who will represent the district. In the table, John Liberal is the clear winner. But there is a price to be paid for this convenient result—a majority (57% of the electorate) did not vote for him. For all it mattered, they might as well have stayed home. Neither the policies advocated by candidates Jane Conservative or Ima Nothing, nor the preferences of the majority in this congressional district, will be represented.

Under this system, one of the two major parties in every election invariably gains seats disproportionate to the actual percentage of the total votes it receives—a built-in bonus that comes at the expense of the other major party and any minor parties in the race. Hence, a party receiving, say, 42% of the popular vote may win a clear majority of legislative seats, as normally happens in British elections. In the United Kingdom a major party receiving fewer than half the votes can sometimes win in a landslide (an election resulting in a huge parliamentary majority). A referendum on electoral reform was overwhelming rejected in May 2011.

The winner-takes-all electoral system encourages the emergence of two major political parties and hampers the growth of smaller political parties and splinter groups. The advantage is greater political stability, compared with many multiparty systems. But critics argue that stability in this case is achieved at too high a price. Because the winner-takes-all system does not represent the total spectrum of voter opinions and interests, they point out, it severely limits voter choice and stifles attempts of minor parties to compete in elections.

PR Systems The main alternative to a winner-takes-all system is **proportional representation (PR)**. PR systems typically divide the electorate into *multimember* districts, with a formula awarding each district's seats in proportion to the fractions of the vote the various parties receive in that district. The result is that representation in the legislature accurately mirrors the outcome of the election. Hence, if a party wins 42% of the vote, it will get 42% of the seats—in other words, not enough to form a government without the support of at least one other party.

Among the many countries using this system are Israel, Italy, Belgium, Norway, and Ireland. Germany also uses proportional representation to elect half the members of the Bundestag (the lower house of parliament). Candidates in a district win office if they receive at least a specified number of votes, determined by dividing the number of votes cast by the number of seats allocated. For example, assume in Table 11.1 that a proportional representation system is in place, the district has been allocated three seats, and 60,000 votes have been cast. A representative will thus be elected for every 20,000 votes a party receives. According to this formula, John Liberal and Jane Conservative would both be elected, because each received more than 20,000 votes.

But no votes are wasted. The district's third representative would be determined by a regional distribution, which works like this: 5,800 Democratic votes, 4,600 Republican votes, and 9,600 Independent votes are forwarded to the region, to be combined with other districts' votes and reallocated. Where regional distributions fail to seat a candidate, a final *national* distribution may be necessary. In this manner, proportional representation guarantees that everyone's vote will count.

proportional representation (PR) Any political structure under which seats in the legislature are allocated to each party based on the percentage of the popular vote each receives.

list system
Method of proportional representation by which candidates are ranked on the ballot by their party and are chosen according to rank.

Hare plan
In parliamentary democracies, an electoral procedure whereby candidates compete for a set number of seats and those who receive a certain quota of votes are elected. Voters vote only once and indicate both a first and a second choice.

coalition government
In a multiparty parliamentary system, the political situation in which no single party has a majority and the largest party allies itself loosely with other, smaller parties to control a majority of the legislative seats.

plebiscite
A vote by an entire community on some specific issue of public policy.

legislative referendum
The state legislature puts a proposal to repeal an existing law or policy on the ballot.

popular referendum
A vote through which citizens may directly repeal a law.

Some countries have modified this system to prevent the proliferation of small fringe parties, requiring that minor parties receive a certain minimum of the national vote to qualify for district representation. In Germany and Russia, this figure is 5%; in other countries, it can be 15% or even higher.

The **list system** is by far the most common. Parties choose the candidates and rank them on the ballot in each electoral district. If a party receives enough votes to win one seat, the candidate ranked first on the list gets that seat; if it garners enough votes to elect two, the candidate ranked second also gets a seat; and so on. The list system strengthens political parties significantly because citizens vote primarily for the party (as opposed to the candidate), and the party controls the ordering of the candidates on the ballot.

The **Hare plan** is based on a single transferable vote and emphasizes individual candidates or personalities rather than parties. Voters indicate a first and second preference. A quota—the number of votes required to win a seat—is set, and when a candidate has met the quota, the remainder of votes cast for that candidate are transferred to the second preference on those ballots, and so on until all available seats have been awarded.

Electoral Systems Compared Proportional representation systems have certain advantages over the winner-takes-all method. Few votes are "wasted," more parties can gain seats in the legislature, and fairness—to voters, candidates, and parties—is emphasized because seats are apportioned according to the vote totals that each party actually receives.

The winner-takes-all system has the advantage of stability. It effectively bars the door to upstart and single-issue splinter parties. By frequently magnifying a plurality of votes into a majority of seats, it often obviates the need for **coalition governments**. Finally, it boils down choices for the voters, typically between two or three middle-of-the-road parties.

Direct Democracy

Voters can also be legislators. Perhaps the most easily recognized model of direct democracy is the New England town hall meeting. By providing for elected representatives, however, the U.S. Constitution rejects the idea of a direct democracy in favor of a representative one.

Today, direct democracy coexists with representational democracy in many places. In some democracies, such as Switzerland and Australia, as well as a number of U.S. states, citizens can bypass or supersede the legislature by voting directly on specific questions of public policy in a **plebiscite**. In the United States, a plebiscite can take three forms.

A **legislative referendum** occurs when the state legislature puts a proposal to repeal an existing law or policy on the ballot; in states that allow for a **popular referendum**, citizens can petition to repeal a law by a direct vote. Sometimes the vote is merely advisory, indicating the electorate's preferences; in other cases, voter approval is required before a ballot item can be enacted into law. In an **initiative**, the voters themselves put a measure on the ballot by filing petitions containing a stipulated number of valid signatures (see "Ideas and Politics: Initiative and Referendum").

INITIATIVE AND REFERENDUM

There are two types of initiative—direct and indirect—and two types of referendum—popular and legislative. Legislative referendum is divided into two categories: amendments and statutes. Twenty-three states give their legislatures *discretionary power* to place statutes on the ballot. Delaware is the only state that does not *require* placement of *constitutional amendments* on the ballot.

- Twenty-seven states have some form of initiative or popular referendum.
- Twenty-four states have a form of initiative.
- Twenty-four states have popular referendum.
- Eighteen states allow citizens to fire state officials by means of the recall.
- All fifty states have some form of legislative referendum.
- The first state to hold a legislative referendum to adopt its constitution was Massachusetts, in 1778.
- The first state to adopt the initiative and popular referendum was South Dakota, in 1898.
- The first state to place an initiative on the ballot was Oregon, in 1904.

- The first state to allow cities to use initiative and popular referendum was Nebraska, in 1897.
- The first state to provide for initiative and popular referendum in its original constitution was Oklahoma, in 1907.
- Four states have adopted initiative or popular referendum since 1958.

People often use the term "democracy" to describe any political system that isn't a dictatorship, but in reality there are no true democracies. All the world's so-called democracies elect representatives to make and execute the laws. In some states in the United States, voters sometimes get to decide some questions directly, but never on the federal level. Why? Think about it.

(Hint: In classical Greece, Athens was a true democracy. At that time, Athens was an independent city-state, not a nation-state. Compare the size of the population in ancient Athens with any major city in today's world. Find out what percentage of the population qualified to vote.)

SOURCE: Adapted from Initiative and Referendum Institute, "Quickfacts," http://www.iandrinstitute.org/factsheets/quickfacts.htm.

The **recall** is a political device intended to remove an elected official from office. It works much like an initiative and is also placed on the ballot by the signatures of a predetermined number of citizens. One famous example in recent history was the recall of California Governor Gray Davis in 2003 and his replacement by the move star, Arnold Schwartzenegger (aka "The Terminator").

Some major issues decided by direct vote in Europe include the following:

- French President Charles de Gaulle used a referendum to amend the French constitution to provide for the direct election of the president (de Gaulle himself) in 1962.
- The United Kingdom held its first referendum in 1973 to decide whether the nation should join the Common Market (a narrow majority voted in favor); in its second ever referendum in 2011, voters rejected a proposal to change the way MPs are elected.

initiative
A mechanism by which voters act as legislators, placing a measure on the ballot by petition and directly deciding whether or not to make it a law on election day.

recall
Direct voting to remove an elected official from office.

- Denmark, Ireland, and Sweden, among others, have put issues such as whether to join the **euro area**—the EU countries that have adopted the euro—on the ballot. (Danish voters rejected it, but Denmark plans to hold another referendum on it; Irish voters said yes, and Swedish voters said no.)
- Direct popular vote in several Central and East European countries determined whether they would join the European Union. (All countries invited said yes.)

We can trace the modern era of direct democracy in the United States to 1978 and California's passage of the famous Proposition 13, which not only halved property taxes there but also spurred many initiatives and referendums throughout the nation.

Many direct democracy measures are divisive and "too hot to handle" for elected representatives seeking to avoid alienating voters on either side of the issue. In 1996, for example, voters approved Proposition 209 (aka, the California Civil Rights Initiative) limiting affirmative action programs by amending the state's constitution to prohibit discrimination against, or preferential treatment of, "any individual or group on the basis of race, sex, color, ethnicity, or national origin in the operation of public employment, public education, or public contracting."

Opponents of the initiative challenged the new law in federal court on grounds it was unconstitutional, but lost. In 2012, Proposition 209 was again challenged in a federal appeals court (the outcome is uncertain at the time of this writing). Michigan voters passed a similar amendment in 2006, but a three-judge panel of the 6th Circuit Court of Appeals voted to overturn Michigan's affirmative action ban in 2011.

Even more controversial is Proposition 8, another California ballot initiative, passed in 2008, which amended the state constitution to restrict the definition of marriage to opposite-sex couples and eliminate same-sex couples' right to marry. The "yes" vote overrode portions of a California Supreme Court decision affirming marriage as a fundamental right earlier in 2008. In December 2012, the U.S. Supreme Court agreed to consider a constitutional challenge to Proposition 8.

Direct democracy is often championed as a means of revitalizing public faith in government, improving voter participation, and circumventing corrupt, cowardly, or incompetent officeholders.[5] Opponents argue that money and special interests can too easily engineer the outcome of an initiative or referendum. They also say ballot measures are often so complex and technical the average voter cannot understand the issues. At least one student of plebiscites disagrees: "On most issues, especially well-publicized ones, voters do grasp the meaning . . . and . . . they act competently."[6]

But opponents of direct democracy argue that too much democracy can perhaps be as bad as too little. When measures are too numerous and issues are complex, the opportunity for demagoguery grows, and the possibility of rational voter choice diminishes. For these reasons, direct democracy is, at best, a supplement to, rather than a substitute for, representative democracy—one that should be used sparingly and with caution.

Opponents of direct democracy argue too much democracy can be as bad as too little. The anger displayed in this photo is inimical to reason or calm deliberation.

WHO VOTES FOR WHAT, WHEN, AND WHY?

The right to vote is not a foolproof defense against tyranny and oppression, but it is the best one available. Yet later generations often take for granted rights that earlier generations won at a very dear price. The United States offers no exception.

Voting in the United States

Voter turnout in the United States is often low by comparison with many other democracies.[7] In Europe, voter participation in national elections typically averages over 80%. Imagine a U.S. presidential election with an 85% voter turnout (that was the actual turnout in France in April 2007).

In 1996, a presidential election year, fewer than half of voting-age adults in the United States voted (see Figure 11.1); by contrast in the 1960 Kennedy-Nixon election, nearly 63% of eligible adults voted. In recent elections, however, turnout has climbed back up but still remains well below 60%.

In 2000, a slightly larger turnout in Florida (where less than half the voting age population cast a ballot) might have changed the outcome—and the course of U.S. history (see "Landmarks in History: Bush v. Gore 2000"). In the hotly contested 2004 presidential election (George W. Bush vs. John Kerry), as the electorate became polarized over the war in Iraq, voter turnout climbed to 55% and in 2008 reached nearly 57%, the highest since 1968.

Midterm elections (when there is no presidential race) provide another measure of voting behavior in the United States. In general, turnout is low in these years (see Figure 11.2). Even in the highly charged 2006 midterm elections, only 37% of the eligible population turned out to vote; in 2010 the figure was a bit higher—about 41%.

Year	Voting age	Voter registration	Voter turnout	Voting-age turnout
2012	240,926,957	180,345,625	129,085,403	54.8%
2010	235,940,406	NA	90,732,693	37.8%
2008	231,229,580	150,000,000	132,618,580	56.8%
2006	220,600,000	135,889,600	80,588,000	37.1%
2004	221,256,931	174,800,000	122,294,978	55.3%
2002	215,473,000	150,990,598	79,830,119	37.0%
2000	205,815,000	156,421,311	105,586,274	51.3%
1998	200,929,000	141,850,558	73,117,022	36.4%
1996	196,511,000	146,211,960	96,456,345	49.1%

FIGURE 11.1 Voter Turnout in U.S. National Elections 1996–2012. Color indicates presidential election years. Voting-age turnout in 2014 was estimated at a mere 33.2%, the lowest in over seventy years (since 1942). SOURCE: Federal Election Commission. Data drawn from Congressional Research Service reports, Election Data Services, Inc., and state election offices.

FIGURE 11.2 Midterm Election Turnout, 1962–2014, based on House Votes Cast (percentage of voting-age population).
SOURCE: Adapted from Congressional Quarterly Weekly Report, February 23, 1991, p. 484; and the United States Elections Project, George Mason University, http://elections.gmu.edu/Voter_Turnout_2006.htm.

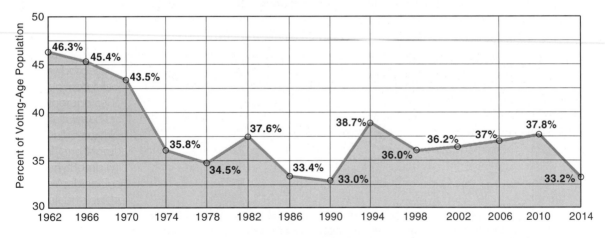

The voter turnout rate in midterm elections remains low. It fell abruptly after the voting age was lowered to 18 in 1971 and has trended downward, with a mild reversal in the recession year of 1982 and a significant upturn in 1994. In Tennessee, Mississippi, and Louisiana (where only one district was decided in November), the turnout rate did not reach 20 percent. In only four states did a majority of the voting-age population participate in voting for the House: Maine (55.6 percent), Minnesota (54.8 percent), Montana (54.6 percent), and Alaska (52.5 percent).

As noted earlier, low voter turnout remains the pattern in the United States despite changes that ought to have brought more voters to the polls. Laws and rules designed to block or burden access to the ballot, such as poll taxes, literacy tests, and lengthy residence requirements are gone. The voting age has dropped to 18. The potential for virtually all U.S. adults to vote now exists.[8] Moreover, since passage of the **motor voter law** in 1993, new voters can register while obtaining or renewing their driver's licenses. In sum, low voter participation flies in the face of "broad changes in the population [that] have boosted levels of education, income, and occupation, all associated with enhanced rates of turnout."[9]

Who votes is a key question in any democracy. Perhaps even more important, however, is the question many nonvoters ask: "Why bother?" Unless the defenders of democracy can continue to give them a meaningful answer, there is a danger that liberty itself will lose its hold on the popular imagination.

People who believe it is possible to make a difference, who are self-confident and assertive, are more likely to become engaged in public affairs, including political activity, than people who lack these attributes. Why then do some people lack a sense of **political efficacy** and why do so many U.S. adults not even vote?

motor voter law
A statute that allows residents of a given locality to register to vote at convenient places, such as welfare offices and drivers' license bureaus; the idea behind laws of this kind is to remove technical obstacles to voting and thus promote better turnouts in elections.

LANDMARKS IN HISTORY

BUSH V. GORE 2000: Winning the Vote, Losing the Election

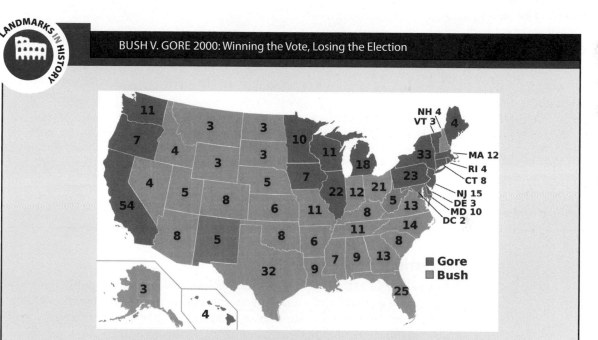

SOURCE: 2000 Electoral College Map, public data.

In the 2000 presidential election, Al Gore won over half a million more popular votes than George Bush (48.38% for Gore, 47.87% for Bush). But Gore lost the election. How and why? The answer lies in an anomaly called the Electoral College.

The 2000 presidential election came down to 537 votes separating the "winner" (Bush) from the "loser" (Gore) in one state, Florida, where the chief election official, Katherine Harris, was also co-chair of the Florida Bush campaign. In that race, thousands of Florida voters were "wrongly purged" according to the *New York Times**

Florida was the most notorious case of voting list irregularities in the 2000 election, but it was not the

(Continued)

LANDMARKS IN HISTORY

(CONTINUED)

only one, nor was it the most egregious. The *New York Times* cited another example:

> In Missouri, St. Louis election officials kept an "inactive voters list" of people they had been unable to contact by mail. Voters on the list, which ballooned to more than 54,000 names in a city where only 125,230 voted, had a legal right to cast their ballots, but election officials put up enormous barriers. When inactive voters showed up to vote, poll workers had to confirm their registration with the board of elections downtown. Phone lines there were busy all day, and hundreds of voters travelled downtown in person, spending hours trying to vindicate their right to vote. The board admitted later that "a significant number" were not processed before the polls closed.

What happened in Florida and Missouri in 2000 could happen elsewhere. According to the *New York Times*, "Voters would have no way of knowing [if there was a problem] because of the stunning lack of transparency in election operations." Election board officials often make decisions about removing voters from the rolls without any written rules or procedures.

The power to decide who gets to vote has both social and political implications. In both Florida and St. Louis, disenfranchised voters were disproportionately black. In Florida, African Americans are one of the strongest Democratic voting groups.

In the 2012 election, liberals accused Republican strategists of attempting to prevent high voter turnout especially in key "swing states" (Ohio, Virginia, North Carolina, Wisconsin, Colorado, and Florida, among others). How? By putting strict photo ID laws in place (thus, critics claim, targeting minorities, the poor, and elderly citizens) and restricting early voting, for example.

What is to be done? The *New York Times* recommends a three-step remedy: (1) clear standards—the policy for purging voting lists ought to be based on clear, written guidelines; (2) transparency—the public has a right to know when voting list purges are under way; and (3) nonpartisanship—election board officials should not be connected to candidates or parties.

Editorial, "How America Doesn't Vote," New York Times, February 15, 2004, http://www.nytimes.com/2004/02/15/opinion/how-america-doesn-t-vote.html?

Patterns of Participation

Most people in the United States value private property over public goods—from national parks and vital water resources to the air we breathe. Oddly, citizens who belong to service clubs and donate to charities are often reluctant to get involved in "politics" or community action or to run for local office. A pioneering 1950 study by Julian L. Woodward and Elmo Roper revealed that about 70% of U.S. adults were politically inactive.[10] A later study found approximately 26% of the U.S. population could be classified as activists; the rest either limited participation to voting or avoided politics altogether.[11]

The rate of political literacy—people with the knowledge, skills, and values essential to make informed decisions and participate effectively in the democratic process—is low in the United States and falling. According to one study by the UCLA Higher Education Research Institute, a mere 29.4% of college freshman considered political awareness a "very important" or "essential" life goal in 1996, down from 38.8% in 1992 and 57.8% in 1966. (If you were to take an informal poll in your dorm or dining hall, do you expect today's college students to be as apathetic as they were in 1996? Less? More?)

political efficacy
The ability to participate meaningfully in political activities; relevant factors include education, social background, and sense of self-esteem.

Who votes in the United States? According to U.S. census data, women are more likely to vote than men, and whites more likely than blacks or Hispanics. People over 65 are much more likely to vote than young adults 18 to 24. Midwesterners are more likely to vote than people in the South or West. People with a college education vote more than people who never finished high school, and white-collar workers vote more than blue-collar workers. Clearly, socioeconomic factors affect participation rates.

The 2008 general election, however, "the most diverse in U.S. history," saw a marked difference in certain voting patterns. Minorities and youth voted in record numbers. African Americans cast nearly 3 million more ballots in 2008 than in 2004 (up 21%); 1.5 million more Latinos voted in 2008 than in 2004 (up 16%); and the youth vote (aged 18–29) climbed by 1.8 million votes (a 9% rise). Black women had the highest voter turnout rate (68.8%)—a first.[12]

Whether 2008 was indicative of a trend toward greater diversity in elections is unclear. Voter turnout in 2012 was indeed higher than in 2010, but lower than in the two preceding presidential elections—57.5% compared to 62.3% in 2008 and 60.4% in 2004. (It was only 54.2% in 2000, however.) There were some 219 million eligible voters in the United States in 2012. Postelection estimates put the number of votes cast at 26 million, meaning 93 million "eligibles" failed to vote.

Generational factors are increasingly important in U.S. elections. In three recent general elections—2004, 2006, and 2008—voters 18–29 were "the Democratic party's most supportive age group. In 2008, 66% of those under age 30 voted for Barack Obama, making the disparity between young voters and other age groups larger than in any presidential election since exit polling began in 1972."[13] In 2012, exit polls had Obama carrying 60% of the youth vote, less lopsided than in 2008, but still far above Mitt Romney's 36%. Voters 18–29 represented 19% of the total turnout in 2012.

Until recently, observers tended to blamed low voter turnout rates on the lowering of the voting age to 18. But this explanation is too simplistic. Other relevant factors include a declining sense of civic duty, lengthy campaigns that dull the senses, voter cynicism over the rising role of Super PACs and stories in the press about billionaires who pour millions into candidates and causes they favor,[14] and negative television ads that turn people off.

Private Pursuits and the Public Good

In the 1830s, French writer Alexis de Tocqueville observed that wherever a widespread belief in equality exists, and established sources of moral instruction like religion, family, monarchy, and tradition fail to carry the weight they once did, individuals tend to be morally self-reliant.

For Tocqueville, the resulting **individualism** is detrimental to a sense of social and civic duty and thus diminishes the life of the community. "Individualism," he wrote, "is a mature and calm feeling, which disposes each member of the community to sever himself from the mass of his fellow creatures; and to draw apart with his family and friends; so that, after he has thus formed a little circle of his own, he willingly leaves the society at large to itself."[15] People live in a state of constant agitation arising from personal ambitions, he noted. "In

individualism
According to Alexis de Tocqueville, the direction of one's feelings toward oneself and one's immediate situation; a self-centered detachment from the broader concerns of society as a whole. According to John Stuart Mill, the qualities of human character that separate humans from animals and give them uniqueness and dignity.

America the passion for physical well-being . . . is felt by all" and "the desire of acquiring the good things of this world is the prevailing passion of the American people."[16]

Tocqueville thought that individualism in the United States was counteracted, to some extent, by the fact that people belonged to an enormous number and variety of civic associations. But participation in groups and group activities of all kinds has declined in the United States. Observing that the number of bowlers had increased 10% whereas league bowling decreased 40% between 1980 and 1993, Robert Putnam concluded in the mid-1990s that bowling symbolized life as we know it in the United States.[17] Putnam also pointed out that participation in organized religion, labor unions, the PTA, traditional women's groups such as the League of Women Voters, and service clubs such as the Shriners and Masons had declined during the past thirty years, as had volunteering.

In April 2009, President Obama signed the Edward M. Kennedy Serve America Act committing $5.7 billion over five years to promoting volunteerism. It is doubtful whether this program will make much of a difference, but in an age when a "wireless culture" is transforming the character of postmodern societies, there can be no denying the importance of civic-minded citizens in the life of a community—or a nation.

Affluence and Apathy

Political apathy and indifference, expressed as a lack of curiosity about what is going on in Washington or the world, persisted in the United States even after 9/11 and the invasions of Afghanistan and Iraq. The apathy turned to alarm, if only momentarily, in 2008 when the financial crisis suddenly jeopardized the fortunes and future of millions of U.S. workers with investments in mutual funds and retirement plans. The conclusion that wallets are more important than wars in the public mind is difficult to escape (see "Ideas and Politics: Australia's Mandatory Voting Law").

Perhaps thinking we can afford to be nonchalant about politics so long as we ourselves are not insecure or oppressed is just human nature. Or maybe Tocqueville was right: people in the United States are too predisposed to individualism to care if somebody they don't know is fighting a war in a place they can barely find on a map.

Political apathy is the luxury of an affluent society where the majority does not feel threatened and people's basic needs are met. Under such circumstances, apathy is understandable, predictable, and perhaps even rationale. But when people who are normally indifferent or inattentive to politics grow restive, however, it's a sure sign that all is not well. In the 1850s, for example, apathy gave way to antipathy between North and South over slavery and states' rights, leading to secession and the Civil War. In the 1930s, the Great Depression galvanized the nation.

In 2008-2009, the deepest recession since the 1930s briefly banished voter apathy in the United States. But voters quickly shrugged off the Great Recession: as noted previously, voter turnout in 2012 was well below 2008 and even 2004 despite a bitterly contested cliffhanger presidential race, an estimated $6 billion spent in campaigns, and 8 million more eligible voters.

political apathy
Lack of interest in politics resulting from complacency, ignorance, or the conviction that "my vote doesn't really count" or "nobody cares what I think anyway."

AUSTRALIA'S MANDATORY VOTING LAW

Noted scholar and political observer Norm Ornstein* wants to make voting mandatory in the United States. He believes lower turnout is the cause of "ever-greater polarization in the country and in Washington, which in turn has led to ever-more rancor and ever-less legislative progress." He makes a persuasive case.

With participation rates of about 10% or less of the eligible electorate in many primaries, to 35% or so in midterm general elections, to 50 or 60% in presidential contests, the name of the game for parties is turnout—the key to success is turning out one's ideological base. Whichever party does a better job getting its base to the polls reaps the rewards of majority status. And what's the best way to get your base to show up at the polls? Focus on divisive issues that underscore the differences between the parties.

Ornstein points out that several countries, including Austria, Belgium, and Cyprus, as well as Australia and Singapore, have adopted mandatory voting. In Australia (see Figure 11.3), "no-shows" at the polls pay a modest fine of about $15 the first time and more with each subsequent offense. The result: a turnout rate greater than 95%. "The fine, of course, is an incentive to vote. But the system has also instilled the idea that voting is a societal obligation." No less important, "It has elevated the political dialogue," and it places a premium on "persuading the persuadables."

Ornstein surmises, "If there were mandatory voting in America, there's a good chance that the ensuing reduction in extremist discourse would lead to genuine legislative progress." But, he argues, political reform is urgent: "These days, valuable congressional time is spent on frivolous or narrow issues (flag burning, same-sex marriage) that are intended only to spur on the party bases and ideological extremes. Consequently, important, complicated issues (pension and health care reform) get short shrift."

Why not require citizens to vote? How about fining people who don't vote or penalizing them in some

FIGURE 11.3   Map of Australia. Australia is a continent, as well as a country, that is roughly the size of the "lower 48" (the continental United States minus Alaska). It is a parliamentary democracy with a mandatory voting requirement.

other way (say, with a 1% income-tax penalty or by putting a "delinquent" bumper sticker on the cars of all nonvoters)? Think about it.

(Hint: Maybe there's a better way. Find out what countries that have a consistently higher voter turnout compared to the United States do.)

SOURCE: Norm Ornstein, "Vote—Or Else," *New York Times*, August 10, 2006 (online edition).

*Norm Ornstein is a scholar in residence at the American Enterprise Institute and the co-author (with Thomas Mann) of *The Broken Branch: How Congress Is Failing America and How to Get It Back on Track* (New York: Oxford University Press, 2006).

In sum, participation is not always a good thing. But neither is apathy. If the only time we take a keen interest in politics is when we are personally affected, if our *only* motive is self-interest as opposed to the public interest or the common good, that points to a serious defect in our national character—one that, over time, will manifest itself in undesirable ways. Try explaining what went wrong on Wall Street in August 2008, for example, without mentioning the role of greed. A steady and sober interest in public affairs stemming from a well-ingrained sense of civic duty is a healthy antidote to excessive individualism—and a far better solution to the problem of apathy than an aroused but ignorant majority.

PARTICIPATING AS A SPECTATOR: OUTSIDERS

In the competitive "game" of politics, most people are outsiders. As outsiders, we are at a disadvantage because (a) we don't understand the game very well; (b) we don't get to make the rules; and (c) unlike the insiders, we can't break the rules and get away with it.

One study in the 1990s found nearly half of respondents did not know the Supreme Court has final authority to determine whether a law is constitutional, and three of four were unaware senators serve six-year terms.[18] Can government by majority rule work if the majority—the outsiders—do not know *how* it works (or why it doesn't work the way we want it to or think it should)?

Many believe politicians rarely, if ever, say what they mean or mean what they say. Studies of voter awareness paint a portrait with few distinct lines. First, whereas only a minority of the voting-age population votes, those who do vote generally are better informed than are those who do not. Second, U.S. adults as a whole probably know as much about politics today as they did in the 1940s.[19] Third, many find it more worthwhile to engage in private pursuits and leave politics to others.[20] Fourth, candidates often take no clear political stance, so many citizens may wonder, What's the point? Finally, many voters make reasonable judgments about issues and candidates despite being poorly informed.[21]

According to a theory called **low-information rationality**, ill-informed voters use shortcuts (for example, does a candidate look the part?) and simplifying assumptions (such as party identification) to make political judgments.[22] This theory assumes picking a candidate for office is like buying a car. But when voters go to the polls, they have a far narrower range of choices than car buyers and far less information about the "product"—problems that can be fixed only by elected representatives, who unfortunately often have a vested interest in *not* fixing them.

Why do supposedly rational voters almost always reelect incumbents while mistrusting Congress as an institution? According to rational actor theory (which holds that human behavior is a product of logical reasoning rather than emotion or habit), they are "voting for the devil they know rather than the devil they don't" and for representatives with seniority who have proven they can produce "pork" (federal funding) for local projects.

Enlightened or not, this type of voting behavior is rational in the short term and on the local level. The dilemma for democracy arises from the fact that

low-information rationality
The idea that voters can make sensible choices in elections even though they lack knowledge and sophistication about public policy, candidates, and current events.

"comfort zone" voting is not necessarily rational in the aggregate or in the long run—that is, on the national level, where the big-picture decisions, laws, and policies are made.

PARTICIPATING AS A PLAYER: INSIDERS

Some say a power elite controls the political process from top to bottom. The most popular version of this theory holds that ordinary citizens never exercise much influence, elections and public opinion polls notwithstanding, and the political system is manipulated from above rather than below. The manipulators are the power elite, a small group of plutocrats who go back and forth through a "revolving door" between the commanding heights of the economy (megabanks and multinational corporations) and the rarefied echelons of government, exercising enormous power over the nation's destiny. The status, wealth, and power of this self-perpetuating political class ensure that access to the levers of government is monopolized by the few to pursue private interests, not the public interest.

The close links between personal business interests of the Bush family and the oil industry gave new credence to this theory (especially after the ill-fated invasion of Iraq), as did the fact that Halliburton, the huge multinational corporation formerly headed by Vice President Cheney, was awarded billions of dollars in no-bid contracts to operate in Iraq. The nomination of venture capitalist and multimillionaire Mitt Romney as the Republican candidate for the presidency in 2012 gave rise to numerous books and articles about the rise of a Super-Rich, plutocratic, and self-perpetuating "meritocracy" in American politics.

Elitist Theories: Iron Laws and Ironies

Elitist theories of democracy hold that neither the voters nor public opinion nor a variety of competing interests, but rather a small number of wealthy individuals, governs democracy. This theory was propounded most influentially in the 1950s by sociologist C. Wright Mills and has recently been expanded and updated by a growing number of distinguished journalists, economists, and policy analysts—Robert Reich, Christopher Hayes, Joseph Stiglitz, Paul Krugman, and Matt Taiibi, to name a few.[23] By putting the power elite in the spotlight, Mills challenged the idea of "government by the people" and called into serious question whether it exists (or ever existed) in the United States. Contemporary critics focus on the erosion of the middle-class and the great divide between the "plutocracy" (the so-called super-rich) and the rest of us.

Robert Michels, a German sociologist, also advanced a theory of elitism, but his study applied to all modern bureaucratic organizations. His findings were distilled from an analysis of the German Social Democratic Party, which before the outbreak of World War I had been the largest socialist party in the world. Michels reasoned that because the party favored equality in wealth and status, it should be sufficiently committed to democratic principles to put them into practice. He found instead that elite groups that derived their power and authority from well-honed organizational skills ran the party.

elitist theory of democracy
In political thought, the theory that a small clique of individuals (a "power elite") at the highest levels of government, industry, and other institutions actually exercise political power for their own interests; according to elitist theories, ordinary citizens have almost no real influence on governmental policy.

iron law of oligarchy
According to this theory, the administrative necessities involved in managing any large organization; access to and control of information and communication inevitably become concentrated in the hands of a few bureaucrats, who then wield true power in the organization.

This discovery led Michels to postulate his famous **iron law of oligarchy**, which holds that all large organizations, including governments, are run in the same fashion. He believed organizations naturally become increasingly oligarchic, bureaucratized, and centralized over time, as those at the top gain more information and knowledge, greater control of communications, and sharper organizational skills, while the great mass of members (or citizens) remain politically unsophisticated, preoccupied with private affairs, and bewildered by the complexity of larger issues. According to this view, the people, for whose benefit democratic institutions were originally conceived, are inevitably shut out of the political or organizational process as corporate officers or bureaucratic officials govern in the name of the rank-and-file shareholder or citizen.

In elitist theories, democracy is seen as a sham or a myth; it does not matter what the people think, say, or do because they have no real influence over public policy. If most people believe public opinion matters, it is only because they are naive and do not really understand how "the system" works.

Logically, "democracy for the few" is a contradiction in terms incompatible with the core principle of government by consent. But some close observers argue that the many are unfit to govern themselves. The "masses are authoritarian, intolerant, anti-intellectual, atavistic, alienated, hateful, and violent."[24] The irony of democracy is then clear: allowing the people real power to rule will only result in the expression of antidemocratic preferences and policies.

Pluralists versus Elitists

Pluralists and elitists agree that in any society there are gradations of power and certain groups or individuals exercise disproportionate influence. They disagree, however, about the basic nature of the political system itself.

According to pluralists, the U.S. political system is decentralized. They concede that organized interest groups with lots of money to dole out, by concentrating on a single issue, can exert disproportionate influence in that specific policy area. They also admit that from time to time certain disadvantaged or unpopular groups may not be adequately represented. Nonetheless, no single individual or group can exercise total power over the whole gamut of public policy. The political system is too wide open, freewheeling, and institutionally fragmented to allow for any such accumulation of power. In the opinion of one prominent pluralist,

> The most important obstacle to social change in the United States, then, is not the concentration of power but its diffusion. . . . If power was concentrated sufficiently, those of us who wish for change would merely have to negotiate with those who hold the power and, if necessary, put pressure on them. But power is so widely diffused that, in many instances, there is no one to negotiate with and no one on whom to put pressure.[25]

Pluralists don't deny that those who hold the highest positions in government and business tend to have similar backgrounds and characteristics. Admittedly, many are males from well-to-do WASP (white Anglo-Saxon Protestant) families who have had Ivy League educations. However, that wealth, status, and education correlate closely with political influence does not prove the system is closed, they argue, nor does it mean participatory democracy is a sham. In fact, there are opportunities for most everyone to exert political pressure at the local, state, and national levels. The public interest—defined as the aggregation of private interests—is generally better served under constitutional democracy than under any other system. So say the pluralists.

So who's right? There is more than a grain of truth in elitist theory, as the concentration of wealth in the United States, with its market economy and business-friendly tax system, attests. But politicians and public policy *are* affected by public opinion. There's no denying that widespread and steadily growing popular sentiment against the Vietnam War was instrumental in pressuring the government to withdraw from that conflict. In 2006, growing opposition to the war in Iraq cost the Republicans control of the Congress. Similarly, in 2010 voters turned against the convoluted "ObamaCare" plan in large numbers, helping Republicans to win a solid majority in the House of Representatives. Republican presidential candidate Mitt Romney tried to capitalize on this divisive issue in 2012, but the effort was awkward because as governor he had signed a similar plan into law in Massachusetts—one that served as a model for the Affordable Care Act of 2010 (aka, ObamaCare).

Public opinion in the United States is often fragmented, but that does not render it nonexistent or irrelevant. Whether elections are meaningful or the outcomes rational, however, are very different questions (ones we take up later in this chapter).

Jim West/Alamy

Interest groups take many different forms. Some, like labor unions, are formal and highly structured with dues-paying members and professional staffs; others, like these demonstrators on behalf of health care reform, are informal, spontaneous, narrowly focused, and often short-lived. Public opinion has the potential to influence elected officials and force action on pressing issues, but it plays little or no role when the citizenry is deeply divided.

PARTICIPATION AND POLITICAL PARTIES

One major purpose of a **political party** is to select, nominate, and support candidates for elective office. Another is to bring various interests under one tent—a process called **interest aggregation**. Political parties have become permanent fixtures in all liberal democracies, including the United States.

American Democracy: No Place for a Party?

The Constitution makes no mention of political parties; some Founders abhorred them. George Washington sought to avoid partisanship by forming a cabinet composed of the best available talent, including Thomas Jefferson as secretary of state and Alexander Hamilton as secretary of the treasury.

political party
An organization whose adherents share a political philosophy and common interests and whose primary reason for existing is to win control of government.

interest aggregation
A term political scientists use to describe how the interests, concerns, and demands of various individuals and groups in society are translated into policies and programs; in constitutional democracies, a major function of political parties.

Washington's noble attempt to avoid partisan politics ultimately failed. Personal animosities developed between Jefferson and Hamilton, in large part due to conflicting understandings of government and public policy, and the two became fierce rivals. In the late 1790s, Jefferson and his followers founded a loosely organized Republican Party to oppose the strong anti-French policies of Federalists such as Hamilton and John Adams. Yet in 1789, Jefferson himself had written, "If I could not go to heaven but with a party, I would not go there at all."[26]

Why did so many statesmen of Jefferson's generation distrust political parties? In Jefferson's case, dislike stemmed from a peculiarly American brand of individualism that has survived to this day. "I never submitted the whole system of my opinions to the creed of any party of men whatever, in religion, in philosophy, in politics, or in anything else, where I was capable of thinking for myself," he observed, concluding that "such an addiction is the last degradation of a free and moral agent."[27] Other thinkers of Jefferson's generation believed political parties fostered narrow self-interest at the expense of the general or public interest. They saw parties as the public extension of private selfishness.

Fast forward to the present. Partisanship in U.S. politics still has a bad name. Witness the calls for a "bipartisan" approach to legislation in Congress, often by the very politicians who are the least willing to compromise or work with a president of the opposing party.

Many commentators see Republican leaders such as Speaker of the House John Boehner, House Majority Leader Eric Cantor, 2012 vice presidential candidate Paul Ryan, and several state governors, including Scott Walker of Wisconsin and Bobby Jindal of Louisiana, in this light. For example, Andrew Sullivan, a conservative *Daily Beast* political columnist appeared on Comedy Central's *Colbert Report* (August 26, 2012) and denounced Republicans in Congress because, in his words, he expected them "to have the good grace and patriotism to cooperate with an incoming president" but instead "they set out to destroy this guy from the get-go."

Sullivan's criticism was remarkable mainly because his is the voice of a popular conservative with a big amplifier. But polls consistently show that the spectacle of a mudslinging Congress and a dysfunctional government is repulsive to citizens on both sides of the partisan divide.

General Aims

Political parties strive to gain or retain political power; in practical terms, this means capturing control of the government. Because voters decide who rules, political parties concentrate on winning elections, but they also engage citizens as volunteers, recruit candidates, raise money, and launch media campaigns. In the party platform, proposals and policies are formulated to appease key interest groups, which, in turn, support the party's candidates with money and votes.

In the United States, candidates frequently appeal for votes by promising to deliver on bread-and-butter issues rather than taking strong stands on ideological issues or advancing bold domestic and foreign policy proposals. The idea is to build a consensus around a vague set of principles rather than detailed policies. The presidential candidate perceived to be closest to the political center is usually elected. An opposing strategy is to offer voters clear alternatives, which is how elections are structured in most democratic countries—and, arguably, how the Obama campaign won in 2008 and how the Romney campaign lost in 2012.

In Europe's parliamentary systems, multiple parties vie for votes and each formulates more or less distinctive policy alternatives. Parties are generally more important than personalities because winning a majority of seats in parliament is the key to controlling the government. Where the stakes are so high, party discipline is at a premium and mavericks rarely prosper.

Political Party Systems

By definition, liberal democracies have competitive party systems. In theory, more competitive party systems are better than less competitive ones—democracy, after all, implies meaningful choices. Thus, multiparty systems have this advantage over two-party systems: they offer voters real choices. Two-party systems sometimes do offer "a choice, not an echo," but often the choice is between Tweedledee and Tweedledum (two middle-of-the-road parties). On the other hand, two-party systems often result in more stable governments than multiparty systems.

At one time or another, **one-party dominant** systems existed in Mexico (the Institutional Revolutionary Party), Japan (the Liberal Democratic Party), India (the Congress), Taiwan (the Nationalist Party), and the U.S. Deep South (the Democratic Party). One-party dominant systems resemble the one-party systems found in authoritarian states, but they hold regular elections, allow open criticism of the government, and do not outlaw other parties.

However, the line between authoritarian and democratic rule is not always clear. In Mexico, for example, the Institutional Revolutionary Party long maintained its dominant position through corruption, intimidation, and voting fraud. One-party dominant systems invite official interference in elections—including ballot box stuffing and other blatantly unfair practices.

The nearly century-long dominance of the Institutional Revolutionary Party (PRI) in Mexico is a notorious example of the correlation between concentration and corruption, and the corrosive effects of this nexus on a society (see Chapter 8). But Americans north of the border too often failed to recognize that official corruption is not confined to Latin America or the Southern Hemisphere.

Excessive concentrations of wealth are closely linked to a narrow distribution of political power manifested in cozy arrangements among business leaders, bankers, entrenched bureaucrats, and top government officials. This is the message of the Occupy Wall Street (liberal) and Tea Party (conservative) movements in the United States, where the copious mixing of money and power is perfectly legal under the U.S. Supreme Court's interpretation of the First Amendment right of free speech (the "corporations are people" argument).[28] To understand how and why things happen the way they do in Washington, the best advice is "follow the money." When and where the exchange of votes for money (say, in Congress) follows the exchange of money for votes (say, in campaigns), how is that different from bribery? How can the conflation of private motives and public service fail to foster corruption?

one-party dominant
One-party dominant systems are different from authoritarian one-party systems in that they hold regular elections, allow open criticism of the government, and do not outlaw other parties; until recently, Japan operated as a one-party dominant system, as did Mexico; South Africa is one current example.

Designing Democracy: Electoral Systems

Political parties allow citizen participation; they are thus an important part of the architecture of democracy. But this architecture is not entirely accidental—in fact, party systems are not an accident of nature. Rather, they are the result of human engineering.

The design element is found in the *rules* governing elections, sometimes spelled out in a constitution, that limit the number of political parties that can exist and thus shape the choices available to voters. The success of minor parties is discouraged in systems based on single-member districts, where any candidate with a one-vote advantage (a plurality) wins the only available seat. Smaller parties find it difficult to attract voters simply because their candidates have such a small chance of winning. By contrast, in PR systems, where several candidates are elected from each district, minor parties enjoy a far greater chance of being elected. Thus, to repeat a key point, proportional representation is far more likely than the first past the post system to produce a multiparty political system.

Another structural consideration is whether the political system is centralized or decentralized. Parties in federal systems organize themselves along the federal structure of the government. In the United States, vote totals in presidential elections are determined nationally but counted (and weighted) state by state in winner-take-all contests, as illustrated when George W. Bush won the 2000 election despite the fact that Al Gore received more total votes nationwide.

Presidential candidates in the United States and the political parties they lead face the challenge of winning not one election but fifty. And though the United States has only two major parties, fifty state parties exist alongside each *national* party. Thus, for example, the Democratic Party in Massachusetts has borne little resemblance to the Democratic Party in Mississippi historically. Strong state-level party organizations help elect senators, representatives, and state and local officials. Thus, in 2012, the Republicans won thirty-three more seats in the U.S. House of Representatives then Democrats despite the fact that Democratic candidates received over a millions more votes.

The U.S. federal structure also strongly favors small states over large and gives small-state voters far greater weight in Congress. In the Senate, Rhode Island and Texas have the same weight. The twenty-six smallest states have a mere 18% of the population but a majority of the votes; conversely the nine states with a majority of the population have only 18% of the votes. States reshape congressional districts every ten years (called reapportionment) so the party that controls the legislature can stack the deck by a method called "gerrymandering" (drawing up voting districts most likely to produce the desired outcome). And the electoral college can hand the White House over to a candidate who loses the popular vote (as happened in 2000).[29]

Structural factors are clearly important, but culture also influences a nation's form of government and the party system it designs by the electoral rules it prescribes. Multiparty systems are most likely to thrive in countries that value ideology and group solidarity over compromise and stability.

Is the Party Over?

Some now say neither major party reflects U.S. society's values or diversity.[30] Others see the rancor between the two parties as evidence of a dysfunctional political system.

Ironically, opportunities to participate are at an all-time high. State primary elections, once the exception, have become the rule. States now compete to hold the earliest primaries. (The elections themselves have become a bonanza for some states, attracting revenue and wide media attention.) Other states hold party caucuses, where rank-and-file party members choose delegates who later attend state conventions that, in turn, select delegates pledged to support particular candidates at the party's national convention.

On the other hand, presidential campaigns are costly and prolonged in the United States; the nomination and election process can last well over a year. (By contrast, British parliamentary elections often last less than a month and cost a tiny fraction of what U.S. elections cost.) Fundraising is a full-time endeavor, not only for presidential hopefuls but also for serious candidates in Senate and House races, prompting cynics to remark that U.S. elections have become non-stop events.

The 2012 campaigns saw record spending (both presidential candidates spent over $1 billion, for example—Obama: $1.123 billion; Romney: $1.019 billion). No other liberal democracy in the world spends so much time and treasure choosing its chief executive. Parties play a role in elections, but money plays a far bigger role. Where do candidates turn for financial backing? Next we look at the role of interest groups in contemporary U.S. politics.

PARTICIPATION AND INTEREST GROUPS

Interest groups—also known as special interest groups, pressure groups, and advocacy groups—try to influence legislation, policy, and programs. Interest groups that operate in Washington, D.C. or state capitals are known as lobbies. They often concentrate on specific areas or issues, including corporate taxes and subsidies for big business, banking regulations, farm subsidies, federal aid to education, or wildlife conservation, to name a few.

One way to categorize interest groups is to distinguish between those that represent special interests and those that represent the public interest. The Audubon Society, the Aspen Institute, Greenpeace, Friends of the Earth, the Sierra Club, the Fund for Peace, Worldwatch Institute, and the Earth Policy Institute are examples of familiar public interest advocacy groups in the United States. The Royal Society for the Protection of Birds, with more than a million members, is the largest advocacy group in Europe. Public interest groups promote causes they believe will benefit society as a whole. The Sierra Club, for example, backs environmental causes and sound conservation policies.

Special interest groups differ not only in the issues they emphasize but also in scope. Most ethnic groups (the National Italian American Foundation, for example), religious groups (the American Jewish Congress), occupational

interest group An association of individuals that attempts to influence policy and legislation in a confined area of special interest, often through lobbying, campaign contributions, and bloc voting.

lobbies Interest groups that operate in Washington, D.C. or state capitals.

special interest An organization or association that exists to further private interests in the political arena; examples in the United States are the U.S. Chamber of Commerce or the National Association of Manufacturers (business), the AFL-CIO (labor), and the National Farmers Organization (NFO).

public interest The pursuit of policies aimed at the general good or the betterment of society as a whole; in contrast to special interests that pursue laws or policies more narrowly favoring individuals or groups.

groups (the American Association of University Professors), age-defined groups (AARP), and a variety of groups that cannot be easily categorized (such as the Disabled American Veterans) are narrowly focused. Each fights for laws and policies that benefit the exclusive group it represents—for private rather than the public interest.

One common classification scheme distinguishes four basic types of interest groups.

- Associational interest groups have a distinctive name, national headquarters, professional staff, and political agenda tied to specific group characteristics, goals, beliefs, or values. Examples include the National Association of Manufacturers (NAM), the National Rifle Association (NRA), the National Association for the Advancement of Colored People (NAACP), the United Auto Workers (UAW), the Christian Coalition of America (CCA), the Sierra Club, and AARP (formerly the American Association of Retired Persons).
- Nonassociational interest groups lack formal structures but reflect largely unvoiced social, ethnic, cultural, or religious interests capable of coalescing into potent political forces under the right circumstances. Informal groups are most common in the developing countries of Asia, the Arab world, Latin America, and sub-Saharan Africa.
- Institutional interest groups exist mainly within the government, although some outside groups—major defense contractors, for example—are so intertwined in the operations of government that we can include them in this category. In the United States at the federal level, departments and agencies have vested interests in policies and programs for which they lobby from the inside, often out of public view. The Pentagon lobbies for new weapons systems, airplanes, warships, and the like, while Labor, Agriculture, and Education become captives of the special interests most directly affected by the programs they administer.
- Anomic interest groups sometimes develop spontaneously when many individuals strongly oppose specific policies. The nationwide student demonstrations against the Vietnam War in the late 1960s and early 1970s are one example. Political scientist Gabriel Almond suggested that street riots and even some assassinations also fit this category.[31]

Sources and Methods of Influence

Interest groups attempt to sway public policy by influencing elected officials and public opinion at the national or state level in three primary ways: (1) by seeking the election of representatives they trust, (2) by seeking access to elected officials, and (3) by mounting mass media campaigns.

Interest groups prize access to decision makers, especially on a one-on-one basis. Many employ **lobbyists,** who cultivate credibility and influence with legislators in various ways. They testify before legislative committees on the basis of their expert knowledge and arrange for intermediaries—close personal friends or constituents—to advance their viewpoints. Lobbyists also mount public relations, fax, telephone, telegraph, or Internet campaigns; cooperate with other like-minded lobbyists for common legislative objectives; and increase

lobbyist
A person who attempts to influence governmental policy in favor of some special interest.

communication opportunities between themselves and legislators (for example, by throwing a party or sponsoring a charitable event).[32]

Money and membership are vital to the success of interest groups. Organizations representing a large and distinct group of citizens with identical interests have a clear advantage. AARP is a prime example, with tens of millions of like-minded members (some 36 million) and clear aims (for example, protecting senior-citizen entitlement programs for like Social Security and Medicare).[33] Roughly half of all U.S. adults over the age of 50 (some 20% of all voters) belong to AARP, making it the second-largest nonprofit organization in the country, trailing only the Roman Catholic Church. Employing 18 registered lobbyists and a staff of 1,800 people, maintaining a budget of nearly $600 million, and portraying itself as the guardian angel of the U.S. elderly, AARP is a key player on legislation affecting pensions, health care, and the rights of the elderly.

The American-Israel Political Action Committee (AIPAC), the National Right to Life Committee (NLRC), and the National Rifle Association (NRA) are three powerful single-issue interest groups. Each focuses on a single objective: support for Israel (AIPAC), opposition to abortion (NLRC), and the right to bear arms (NRA).

A highly motivated mass membership is important, but money is crucial. Major corporations, interest groups, and wealthy private citizens can exert great influence on the political process by launching expensive media campaigns or contributing large amounts to political campaigns. In addition, the personal networks and political contacts of the super-rich are often advantageous in influencing elected officials.

Interest groups are sometimes closely tied to political parties. In Western Europe, the giant trade unions maintain close ties with working-class political parties. (The British Labour Party and Trades Union Congress have the support of some 85% of organized labor in Great Britain.) In the United States, by contrast, interest groups increasingly bypass political parties entirely, providing direct financial support to candidates they favor. Indeed, in a recent landmark decision the U.S. Supreme Court ruled that under the First Amendment the funding of independent political broadcasts in elections cannot be limited (see below).

Thomas M. Magstadt

In September 2012, the City Council of Overland Park, Kansas, passed a law permitting residents who are at least 18 years old to openly carry a gun without even completing a gun safety or weapons training class. Such laws are applauded by the National Rifle Association (NRA), but the Overland Park City Council had second thoughts when the new law created a public outcry. Only two months earlier in neighboring Colorado, a gunman entered a movie theater and opened fire, killing 12 people and injuring 58 others. Three months later, another gunman killed 20 children and 6 adults at an elementary school in Newtown, Connecticut. Meanwhile, the NRA, which claims to have nearly 4 million members, calls itself "the most powerful lobbying organization in the country."

Soliciting funds through computerized direct-mail appeals and the Internet is one key to interest-group success, but personal connections are also important. In Washington, it's often said, "It isn't *what* you know, but *whom* you know that counts." For this reason, interest groups often compete to hire former presidential advisers, ranking civilian and military Pentagon officials, and members of Congress as "consultants." A rose by any other name is still a rose, and lobbyists by any other name are still lobbyists, paid handsomely by defense contractors, arms manufacturers, oil companies, and the like to open doors on Capitol Hill, at the Pentagon, wherever power resides, policies are shaped, and decisions are made (see "Ideas and Politics: Clean Government vs. the Best Congress Money Can Buy").

Upon taking office, President Obama laid down a marker for members of his administration: "If you are a lobbyist entering my administration, you will not be able to work on matters you lobbied on, or in the agencies you lobbied during the previous two years." Ironically, it was soon disclosed that Obama's choice for Secretary of Health and Human Services, former Senator Tom Daschle, a liberal and longtime advocate of universal health care, had not paid all the federal income tax he owed and after leaving the Senate had lobbied for clients in the health care industry, among others—using his personal contacts and political ties in Congress to line his own pockets.

The Great Race: Getting Ahead of the PAC

Although estimates differ significantly, experts agree the number of interest groups in the United States, and the lobbyists they employ, has increased by at least 50% over the past three decades. Today, lobbying is the third-largest industry in Washington, D.C., behind only government and tourism. There were about 5,000 registered lobbyists in the nation's Capital in 1956. One source estimated that in 1991 there were still fewer than 6,000.[34] That number jumped to 20,000 by 1994 and kept rising; in 2005, there were 34,750, whereas the fees lobbyists charged clients rose by as much as 100%.[35]

Why this population explosion? It results from the dramatic increase in government benefits, the declining influence of political parties, the increasing diversity of U.S. society, and the rise of single-issue movements.[36] At the same time, mass mailings and computer technology make new start-ups relatively easy. Higher levels of education have increased individuals' interest in such associations, and relative prosperity has made them better able to pay dues.

In the early 1970s, a new kind of interest group, known as **political action committees (PACs)**, became prominent in the United States. In 1971, Congress attempted to curb election abuses by prohibiting corporations and labor unions from contributing directly to political campaigns. However, the law did not prohibit special interests from spending money *indirectly* through specially created committees. The number of PACs rose dramatically until the mid-1980s. Interest groups with large and influential PACs include the American Medical Association; the National Association of Realtors; the National Automobile Dealers Association; the National Association of Letter

political action committee (PAC) Group organized to raise campaign funds in support of or in opposition to specific candidates.

CLEAN GOVERNMENT VS. THE BEST CONGRESS MONEY CAN BUY*

In January 2007, the new U.S. Congress then controlled by the Democrats launched a major drive to curb unethical ties between Washington lobbyists and legislators. House Democrats pledged to crack down on the use of corporate jets by members of Congress and adopt stricter rules on gifts and travel.

Not to be outdone, President George W. Bush, taking aim at the widespread use of "earmarks" by Congress, denounced "the secretive process by which Washington insiders are able to get billions of dollars directed to projects, many of them pork barrel projects that have never been reviewed or voted on by the Congress." This issue became a major bone of contention at the end of 2010 when the senators on both sides of the aisle stuffed 6,000 earmarks totaling $8 billion into the proposed budget bill, while blaming each other and vowing to cut the deficit. In the midst of all the mudslinging and mayhem in Congress, budget stalemates threatened to shut down the federal government and drive the economy over a "fiscal cliff." All too often when lawmakers find out how much a given vote in Congress is worth, they sell it to the highest bidder.

Both Republicans and Democrats in Congress use lobbyists and earmarks to get what they want—including enough money and votes to get reelected. Who or what is to blame when money corrupts the political process, and how can it ever be fixed? Think about it.

(Hint: Check out the websites "Move to Amend" (https://movetoamend.org/) and "Free Speech for People" (http://www.freespeechforpeople.org/).)

*Based on Carl Hulse and David D. Kirkpatrick, "Ethics Overhaul Tops the Agenda in New Congress," New York Times, January 4, 2007 (electronic edition).

Carriers; the American Institute of Certified Public Accountants; the American Dental Association; and the American Federation of State, County, and Municipal Employees.

PACs have played a key role in financing candidates and causes at both the national and state level as the cost of elections, increasingly dependent on television advertising, has escalated. Dianne Feinstein, a Democratic senator from California, raised $22,000 a day during the seven months before the 1994 election; if "Feinstein Inc. were a business, its projected revenue would place it among the top 5% of U.S. corporations."[37] Incredibly, Feinstein was outspent by her wealthy Republican opponent, Michael Huffington, who squandered $29 million of his own money in a losing campaign.

Given the high cost of campaigns, it is hardly surprising to find more, not less, PAC involvement in elections. In the 2005-2006 election cycle, industry group PACs alone gave $311 million to federal candidates, an increase of $45 million since the 2003-2004 election cycle.[38]

Many observers decry the growing influence of money in U.S. politics. Although money has always been a factor in politics, in recent decades it has become *the* factor without which winning is virtually impossible. The average cost of winning a House seat jumped from $73,000 in 1976 to $680,000 in 1996, and to roughly $1 million in 2004; for a Senate seat, it rose from $595,000 to more than $7 million during the same period.[39]

MONEY, MONEY, MONEY: A Tale of Two Elections

Political campaigns in the United States are by far the longest and most expensive in the world. Every election sets new spending records as corporations and wealthy individuals have discovered that investing in political office-seekers yields big dividends. The U.S. Supreme Court has ruled against efforts to limit the amount of money special interests can pour into campaigns on the ground that campaign spending is a form of free speech protected under the First Amendment.

- The 2010 midterm election was the most expensive ever, costing more than $4 billion. The 2006 midterm cost $2.6 billion.
- According to the nonpartisan Center for Responsive Politics, $293 million came from so-called political action committees (or PACs) – groups operating independently of the candidates or political parties. Under the Supreme Court's controversial *Citizens United* ruling, these groups, including PACs and Super PACs, 527 organizations, and 501(c) organizations, are free to spend without limits and accept unlimited donations from corporations, trade associations, and unions.
- Slightly less than half of the independent money ($138 million) came from 501(c) and 527 organizations that are not required by law to disclose donor names when they file spending reports with the Federal Election Commission (FEC).
- Independent money, including donations made in secret, was instrumental in election outcomes. Figures compiled by Public Citizen show independent groups spent an average of $764,000 on behalf of the winners and just $273,000 on behalf of the losers.
- Republicans were the major beneficiaries of secret 501(c) money; these groups spent some $183 million on behalf of GOP candidates.
- Democrats were the biggest beneficiaries of donations by 527 organizations to political party committees; these groups can accept unlimited corporate and union funds; they spent $102.7 million on behalf of Democratic candidates. Most 527 contributions focused on a single issue or a particular ideology. Money spent by

union-aligned 527s—over $42 million in 2010—is subject to FEC disclosure requirements.
- Independent money, including some $252 million from 527 groups, also figured prominently in campaigns for governor and other state and local races. The 2012 general election set an all-time spending record, estimated at $7 billion, compared to $5.4 billion in 2008.
- The $7 billion total breaks down as follows: $3.2 billion in spending by candidate committees, $2 billion from party committees, and at least $2 billion from outside groups (the major source of "dark money," that is, money from undisclosed sources).
- Obama for America reported receipts of $746.9 million in the 2012 presidential campaign; ROMNEY FOR PRESIDENT, INC. reported receipts $485.8 million.
- Political action committees (PACs) reported giving $48.9 million to House and Senate candidates in 2012, including $29.9 million (61%) to Republicans and $18.8 million (39%) to Democrats.
- Democrats spent $919.3 million on advertising in 2012, including payroll, TV, and radio ads ($420 million), online ads ($118 million), telemarketing ($35.2 million), fundraising, and polling.
- Republicans spent $885.6 million on ads, including $270 million for TV and radio ads, $100.6 million for online ads, and $74.5 million for telemarketing.

Compared to the United States, no other country in the world spends nearly as much on campaigns and elections. Why? How do other countries manage to do the same thing only better—that is, to hold free elections with a better turnout and fewer obstacles to a fair contest—for much less money? Think about it.

(Hint: Find out how much it costs to buy TV ads in prime time; compare the length of campaigns in the United States with campaigns in France, Germany, and the United Kingdom.)

SOURCES: Common Cause, Public Citizen, the Center for Responsive Politics, Political MoneyLine, and the Sunlight Foundation, plus various major news outlets. http://www.commoncause.org/, see "Money in the 2010 Election."

As a rule, Republicans raise more money than Democrats, and incumbents have a huge financial advantage over challengers. In 2004, 98% of House incumbents and 96% of incumbent senators won reelection. In 2008, five U.S. senators lost their seats to challengers, but only 23 incumbents in the House of Representatives were defeated (6 Democrats and 17 Republicans), from a total of 435.

In the 2006 midterm election, the incumbent senators raised, on average, $11.3 million, compared with the average challenger's $1.8 million. In House races, incumbents raised an average of $1.27 million, compared with $283,000 for challengers. According to the Pew Charitable Trusts, "Money is the fuel that powers the current campaign system. In a circular fashion, interest groups, candidates, and parties raise money to pay consultants to launch expensive television ad campaigns."[40]

Interest groups are essential, but in the absence of any effective curbs on **soft money**—money given to political parties ostensibly for purposes other than campaigning and money spent independently *on behalf* of candidates or parties—they are increasingly drawn into a kind of systemic corruption for which there currently are no adequate legal or political remedies. To expect the very politicians who benefit most from the existing system to change it is unrealistic. So long as voters continue to elect incumbents who don't want to fix the system, the system will not get fixed.

Citizens United v. Federal Election Commission

The Bipartisan Campaign Reform Act of 2002 (BCRA)—commonly known as the McCain-Feingold Act—prohibited corporations and unions from making campaign contributions out of their general treasury fund, to include "any broadcast, cable, or satellite communication" that "refers to a clearly identified candidate for Federal office" and "is made within 30 days of a primary election." McCain Feingold allowed corporations and unions to establish a political action committee (PAC) to express advocacy through media ads.

In January 2008, Citizens United, a nonprofit corporation, released a documentary critical of then Senator Hillary Clinton, a candidate for her party's presidential nomination. Anticipating that it would make the *Hillary* documentary available on cable television through video-on-demand within thirty days of primary elections, Citizens United produced television ads to run on broadcast and cable television. To head off civil and criminal penalties for violating federal law, it sought injunctive relief, arguing that the McCain-Feingold Act is unconstitutional. The District Court denied Citizens United a preliminary injunction and ruled in favor of the Federal Election Commission (FEC) summary judgment.

In a landmark decision in 2010, the nine-member U.S. Supreme Court overturned the lower court ruling by a vote of 5 to 4, holding corporate campaign spending cannot be limited under the First Amendment. Critics argued that this ruling places elective office on the auction block and a "for sale" sign on Capitol Hill.

The upshot of the controversial *Citizens United* ruling is to reaffirm the status of corporations as "citizens" under the U.S. Constitution, declaring that

soft money Campaign contributions to U.S. national party committees that do not have to be reported to the Federal Election Commission as long as the funds are not used to benefit a particular candidate; the national committees funnel the funds to state parties, which generally operate under less stringent reporting requirements. Critics argue that soft money is a massive loophole in the existing system of campaign finance regulation and that it amounts to a form of legalized corruption.

money donated to political campaigns is a form of speech, and giving businesses with billions of dollars in assets such as Walmart, Exxon Mobil, and General Electric the same First Amendment rights as individuals. Given the huge sums corporations can and do spend electing candidates, influencing Congress, and swaying public opinion (think TV ads), critics point out that it's impossible for ordinary citizens, individually or collectively, to compete with corporations in today's political arena. Indeed, record spending in the 2010 and 2014 midterm elections approached $4 billion—a figure that exceeds the gross national product of Georgia and Armenia, as well as more than sixty other small countries.

IDEAS AND POLITICS

OPEN SECRETS

According to OpenSecrets.org:

A January 2010 Supreme Court decision (*Citizens United v. Federal Election Commission*) permits corporations and unions to make political expenditures from their treasuries directly and through other organizations, as long as the spending—often in the form of TV ads—is done independently of any candidate. In many cases, the activity takes place without complete or immediate disclosure about who is funding it, preventing voters from understanding who is truly behind many political messages. The spending figures cited are what the groups reported to the FEC; it does not account for all the money the groups spent, since certain kinds of ads are not required to be reported.

Here's a glance at "outside spending" in the 2012 election cycle, much of which can be done anonymously. In other words, not all the open secrets of campaign finance are open anymore.

What is the point of trying to hide who gives how much to whom, what, when, or why? Is "transparency" in politics necessary? Is it possible? Think about it.

(Hint: The Center for Responsive Politics publishes extensive campaign finance data online on its Open Secrets website. Find out how much Super PACs spent on opposing candidates in the last presidential election, compare candidate spending, find out who gives what and who funds your representatives in Congress, what lobbies spend the most, where the money goes, and so on.)

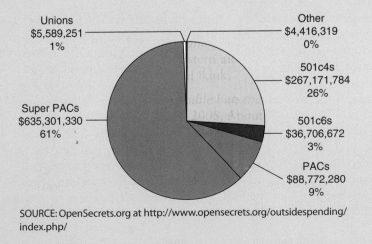

SOURCE: OpenSecrets.org at http://www.opensecrets.org/outsidespending/index.php/

Birth of the Super PAC: Death of the Republic?

In the aftermath of the Citizens United ruling and following the outcome of a federal court case known as *SpeechNow.org v. Federal Election Commission* in July 2010, a new kind of political action committee, known as the Super PAC, came into being. Super PACs are free to raise unlimited sums of money from corporations, unions, associations, and individuals. There are no limits to the sums Super PACs may spend electing or defeating targeted candidates. But they must report the names of donors to the Federal Election Commission on either a monthly or quarterly basis, and they cannot donate money directly to—or coordinate with the campaigns of—candidates.

By contrast, 501(c)(4) organizations do not have to disclose the names of donors. In theory, they operate exclusively to promote "social welfare"—that is, to further, in some way, the common good and general welfare of the people of the community. But here theory and practice part company—a major loophole in the law allows these organizations to engage in lobbying and to promote political causes and candidates without jeopardizing their tax-exempt status. The only "catch": the donations they receive are not tax-deductible donations.

The impact of Super PACs and 501(c)(4)s was tested for the first time in the 2012 elections. Big contributions from a small number of individuals loomed larger than ever, but in the end they failed to achieve what for a few ultra-conservative billionaires like Charles and David Koch and Sheldon Adelson was the desired outcome: namely, defeating Obama's bid for a second term and electing a slate of Tea Party Republicans who campaigned against abortion, gay marriage, ObamaCare, state regulation—and higher taxes for the super-rich.

Thomas M. Magstadt

Many wealthy individuals who back political candidates prefer not to disclose to whom or how much they shell out. Here's one example of the exact opposite. The person who paid for this billboard located on I-70 near Fort Riley in Kansas is obviously proud of it and wants the world to know what she thinks of President Barack Obama.

THE INTERNET: POWER TO THE PEOPLE?

Until the advent of the Computer Age, few advances in technology have had a more profound or sudden impact on politics than television. In the United States, television became available in most homes in the 1950s, computers only in the 1980s. When the first desktop computers started showing up in people's homes, however, they were usually not connected to the outside world, which meant that TV and telephones were still essential to remain "connected." How the world has changed!

Imagine living without your "tablet" and "handheld device" today. Staying connected without email, Facebook, and Twitter would be like going back to the horse and buggy days. Getting the information you want and need is so easy now compared to the "good old days" when college students had to trudge to the library and go to the card catalog, search through stacks for books that may or may not contain the information they needed, go through reels of microfiche to find archived newspaper stories, and the like.

Just as the Internet has transformed the way we study, play, and learn about the wider world, it has also transformed politics. In theory, this transformation is a great victory for democracy, transparency, and participation.

Information is power—a cliché to be sure, but one worth pondering. By placing massive amounts of information at the fingertips of anybody with a computer and a "wifi" hookup, the Internet gives potential power to the previously powerless. The Internet also makes it much harder for governments to hide inconvenient truths or to censor the news. It also greatly facilitates bottom-up, grassroots political action; it is now possible to spark a mass movement with little or no money using existing social networks. The Tea Party movement that played a crucial role in the 2010 midterm elections is one example. Another example, the huge demonstrations in Cairo, Egypt, in January 2011 aimed at overthrowing the autocratic rule of President Hosni Mubarak, which began on a popular Facebook page with some 90,000 pledges to participate. Fearing a spillover effect, China blocked "Egypt" from Internet searches, as a growing number of Chinese relied on microblogging sites for news and information.

But it works both ways: governments can use the Internet to monitor the activities of ordinary citizens. Or they can block certain Internet sites—witness Google's recent troubles operating in the China. Then, too, international terrorists can use it to plan and coordinate attacks and hackers to steal your credit card information.

Finally, the Internet is changing the way political campaigns are conducted. In 2008, Barack Obama's campaign demonstrated the power of the Internet to reach masses of people and coordinate grassroots political action across the length and breadth of the fifty states. Few observers dispute that the Obama campaign changed politics, that presidential campaigns in America will never be the same. Thus, "by using interactive Web 2.0 tools, Mr. Obama's campaign changed the way politicians organize supporters, advertise to voters, defend against attacks and communicate with constituents."[41] Obama's campaign videos were watched on YouTube for 145 million hours. To buy the same amount of exposure on broadcast TV would cost $47 million.[42]

The Internet has changed the way we live and learn. Will the tenor and tone of politics change for better or worse? So far, at least, the vulgar partisanship that has characterized the political scene in recent years does not bode well.

THE ECLIPSE OF THE PUBLIC INTEREST

Often, when citizens complain about influential "special interests," they mean lobbyists or pressure groups that advocate *other people's* interests. Farmers back the farm lobby in Washington, millions of senior citizens (defined as anybody over 50 years of age) join AARP every year, and so on.

What problems do interest groups *objectively* pose to the public interest? Some critics argue that the power of interest groups imposes a particular hardship on the most disadvantaged segments of society. The poor have too little influence and the rich have too much, in this view.

Critics also express alarm at the number of government officials who leave high positions to lobby on behalf of major corporations and defense contractors. In 1978, Congress banned high-ranking, ex-government officials from any contact with the agencies for which they previously worked for a year and prohibited them from attempting to influence the government on policies for which they had "official responsibilities" for two years. But the rules did not prevent government officials from going back and forth between the public and private sectors in a kind of revolving door. Thus, Dick Cheney, a former secretary of defense under George H. W. Bush, left his job as CEO of Halliburton, a major defense contractor, to become George W. Bush's running mate in 2000. This practice raises serious ethical issues involving conflicts of interest and the public trust. President Obama issued an executive order aimed at stopping this practice, but whether anything will change is open to question.

When a single-issue interest group champions an obscure regulation or law, there is little incentive for lawmakers or bureaucrats to resist pressures from special interests. In a large country with numerous levels of government, important matters, especially tax laws in the United States, are decided with little debate or media attention.[43] When well-financed lobbies operating under the radar or behind the scenes push for laws and regulations that bear little, if any, relationship to the public interest, the policy process is likely to be corrupted.

In politics, money talks. To the extent that participation and democracy go hand in hand, it follows that the super-rich can participate to a far greater degree than the rest of us. If so, and if the trend is toward an ever-greater concentration of wealth (as it has been at least since the early 1980s), then democracy becomes less and less meaningful for the vast majority of Americans—the middle class long recognized as the backbone of democracy. Can anything reverse the trend toward an ever-greater concentration of wealth and power? Or is the coin of democracy in America destined to be permanently debased?

The same technology that has revolutionized political campaigns is also revolutionizing the way government works. At this point, it's anybody's guess what that means for the future of democracy.

SUMMARY

Citizens can participate in politics in a variety of legal ways: conventionally, by voting and taking part in public opinion polls; organizationally, by joining political parties or interest groups; or professionally, by working full time for such organizations. Street demonstrations and economic boycotts are unconventional forms of participation. Illegal participation runs the gamut from nonviolent actions (civil disobedience) to extremely violent acts (terrorism).

Public opinion polls can influence the political process in various ways. Elections, despite inherent limitations, are the democratic way to translate mass preferences into public policy. The two major types of electoral systems are first past the post (found in the United States and Great Britain) and proportional representation (used in most representative democracies). In democratic republics, voters elect legislators, chief executives, and sometimes judges. Forms of direct democracy include referendums, initiatives, and recalls.

Voting rates in the United States are low, especially in midterm elections. Voters are generally ill informed. According to elitist theories, political power is always concentrated in the hands of the few. Madisonian pluralists, who argue that power in democratic societies is diffused, dispute this elitist theory.

Political parties perform several key functions in republics. They facilitate participation, aggregate interests, recruit qualified candidates for office, raise money for political campaigns, and help organize governments by building a national consensus and offering alternatives, especially during the election process. One-party systems are generally associated with authoritarianism. Multiparty systems typically offer voters clearer alternative than do two-party systems. The type of party system found in a given country is determined by its traditions, constitution, and culture.

In modern democracies, interest groups and lobbies play an important role in influencing public policy. Some say they distort the democratic process and serve special interests rather than the public interest. Defenders say they offset one another and ensure a competitive political system.

The Internet has transformed politics. It both facilitates popular participation and places a new control tool in the hands of governments.

KEY TERMS

public opinion   319
straw poll   319
random sampling   320
stratified
   sampling   320
exit polling   320
tracking poll   320
winner-takes-all
   system   322
plurality   322
first past the
   post   322

proportional
   representation
   (PR)   323
list system   324
Hare plan   324
coalition
   government   324
plebiscite   324
legislative
   referendum   324
popular
   referendum   324

initiative   324
recall   325
euro area   326
motor voter
   law   329
political efficacy   329
individualism   331
political apathy   332
low-information
   rationality   334
elitist theory of
   democracy   335

REVIEW QUESTIONS

1. How do citizens participate in politics?
2. What are the different forms of electoral systems? What are the advantages and disadvantages of each?
3. Some say apathy is a problem in democratic societies. Do you agree or disagree? Explain.
4. How do the elitist theories of democracy differ from the pluralist model? What political implications follow from the elitist theories?
5. What assumptions do we generally make about political participation in democracies? Are they correct? Explain.
6. What kinds of party systems are found in democracies? How do they differ? Why do the differences matter? Finally, in your opinion, which one is best?
7. To what extent does the functioning of interest groups depend on the political system in which they operate?
8. Why has the power of interest groups increased as the power of political parties has decreased? To what extent are these two phenomena related?
9. What does the statement "Not all interest groups are created equal" mean?

WEBSITES AND READINGS

Websites

National Elections Studies at the University of Michigan: http://www.electionstudies.org/

Nonpartisan American Public Opinion Trends: http://www.pollingreport.com/

CQ MoneyLine (formerly PoliticalMoneyLine): http://www.fecinfo.com/

Money in U.S. Politics: http://www.opensecrets.org/bigpicture/stats.php

Affirmative Action (California Civil Rights Initiative): http://plato.stanford.edu/entries/affirmative-action/; http://www.washingtonpost.com/wp-srv/politics/special/affirm/affirm.htm; http://ballotpedia.org/California_Affirmative_Action,_Proposition_209_%281996%29; http://www.streetlaw.org/en/landmark/home; http://www.pbs.org/wnet/supremecourt/rights/landmark_regents.html

Pew Charitable Trusts: http://www.pewtrusts.org/en

U.S. Federal Election Commission: http://www.fec.gov/index.shtml

Voice for Independent Journalism: http://www.truth-out.org/

Grassroots Movement to Overturn Citizens United: http://www.amendmentgazette.com/how-spending-money-became-a-form-of-speech/; https://movetoamend.org/; http://freespeechforpeople.org/

Readings

Asher, Herbert. *Polling and the Public: What Every Citizen Should Know,* 7th ed. Washington, DC: CQ Press, 2007. A solid introduction to polling and polling techniques.

Caplan, Bryan. *The Myth of the Rational Voter: Why Democracies Choose Bad Policies*. Princeton, N.J.: Princeton University Press, 2008. The author blows gaping holes in rational choice theory.

Cigler, Allan, and Burdett Loomis, ed. *Interest Group Politics*, 8th ed. Washington, DC: CQ Press, 2011. A comprehensive account of the roles and influences of interest groups in contemporary U.S. politics.

Cronin, Thomas. *Direct Democracy: The Politics of Initiative, Referendum, and Recall.* Cambridge, MA: Harvard University Press, 1999. A measured examination of the history, advantages, and disadvantages of direct democracy.

Dye, Thomas. *Who's Running America? The Bush Restoration,* 7th ed. Englewood Cliffs, NJ: Prentice-Hall, 2001. A detailed examination of the political and corporate elites who decisively influence U.S. politics.

Erikson, Robert, and Kent Tedin. *American Public Opinion: Its Origins, Contents, and Impact,* 9th ed. Englewood Cliffs, NJ: Prentice-Hall, 2015. An excellent summary and discussion of the literature.

Gais, Thomas. *Improper Influence: Campaign Finance Law, Political Interest Groups, and the Problem of Equality.* Ann Arbor: University of Michigan Press, 1998. An empirical study that concludes business PACs are too powerful and have too much influence due to weak campaign finance laws.

Goldwin, Robert, ed. *Parties U.S.A.* Skokie, IL: Rand McNally, 1964. A stimulating collection of essays that present important and contrasting interpretations regarding the theory and practice of U.S. political parties.

Hillygus, D. Sunshine, and Todd G. Shields. *The Persuadable Voter: Wedge Issues in Presidential Campaigns.* Princeton, NJ: Princeton University Press, 2009. The authors identify persuadable voters and microtargeting techniques and show how candidates and parties frame messages around wedge issues on which elections often hinge.

Hofstadter, Richard. *The Idea of a Party System: The Rise of Legitimate Opposition in the United States, 1780–1840.* Berkeley: University of California Press, 1969. A historical examination of the origins of the American party system.

Jacobson, Larry. *The Politics of Congressional Elections,* 8th ed. New York: Pearson, 2012. This edition brings things up to date through the 2010 elections.

Lippmann, Walter. *Public Opinion.* New York: Simon & Schuster, 1997. This book, written by one of the greatest American journalists of the twentieth century, explores the relationship between public opinion and democracy. A classic originally published in 1922, which has been republished many times over the years.

Maisel, Sandy. *American Parties and Elections: A Very Short Introduction.* New York: Oxford University Press, 2007. A little book on a big topic.

Michels, Robert. *Political Parties.* Translated by E. Paul and P. Paul. New York: Free Press, 1966. The original study that produced the Iron Law of Oligarchy.

Mills, C. Wright. *The Power Elite.* New York: Oxford University Press, 1959. The original formulation of the power elitist thesis.

Ornstein, Norman J., and Thomas E. Mann. *The Broken Branch: How Congress Is Failing America and How to Get It Back on Track*. New York: Oxford University Press, 2006. A rigorous critique of the U.S. Congress; the title nicely captures the content and intent of the book.

Tocqueville, Alexis de. *Democracy in America*. New York: Schocken Books, 1961. A classic study of American democracy in the nineteenth century.

Wagner, Michael, and William Flanigan. *Political Behavior of the American Electorate,* 13th ed. Washington, DC: CQ Press, 2014. A general but comprehensive account of voting in the United States.

Wattenberg, Martin P. *The Decline of American Political Parties: 1952–1994.* Cambridge, MA: Harvard University Press, 1996. A scholarly study neatly capsulated by the book's title.

CHAPTER 12

Political Leadership
The Many Faces of Power

Learning Objectives

1 Define and discuss the concept of statesmanship in politics.

2 Identify a few exemplary leaders in history and explain why you admire them.

3 Explain what Rómulo Betancourt and Anwar al-Sadat have in common with Abraham Lincoln and Winston Churchill.

4 Parse the role and relevance of leadership in politics.

5 Define the word "demagogue," and compare and contrast demagogues with ordinary politicians.

6 Accurately describe two opposing theories of representation, explain how they differ, and reflect on why it matters.

7 Explain the distinction between a great leader and a good leader, then reflect on U.S. presidents and world leaders who were one or the other, both, or neither.

The implied meaning of words we use in everyday language and life is often more important than their dictionary definitions. Contrast the implied meanings of the words "physician" and "politician." Both denote a practitioner of a profession, but that's where the similarity ends. One is accorded automatic respect; the other is often a term of derision and disdain.

Perhaps more than any other group, politicians are lumped together and stereotyped. We rarely see politicians in a positive light—as leaders with the knowledge, experience, and strength of character to guide the nation in times of crisis, to find solutions to big problems, and to act in the public interest even when it means taking political risks. Imagine parents saying, "Our daughter is in college now and wants to become a cardiologist, but we're hoping she goes into politics."

For a long time politics was off limits to women, but not anymore. Women now occupy key positions of leadership in many countries. Nancy Pelosi was the first woman in U.S. history to become the Speaker of the House (2007–2011); Madeleine Albright became the first woman to serve as U.S. Secretary of State (1997–2001), and two others, Condoleezza Rice (2005–2009) and Hillary Clinton (2009–2013), have followed in her footsteps.

In President Barack Obama's first term (2009–2013), women held four cabinet posts and several other key positions, including EPA administrator and White House Senior Advisor. Elizabeth Warren, a Harvard Law School professor, led the effort to establish a federal Consumer Financial Protection Bureau in the wake of the tumultuous 2008 financial crisis (and won a U.S. Senate seat in 2012). Gender roles and attitudes in the United States and the world (including the Middle East and North Africa) are changing in ways with profound implications for politics and society.

Whether we know it or not, politics plays a huge role in our lives, and what politicians do with the power we give them matters a great deal. When we make a campaign contribution or cast a ballot in an election, we are not only choosing one politician over another but also one political path over another. Few things are more important than the wisdom, knowledge, character, and judgment of the people we elect to high office.

The news headlines constantly remind us that the fate of the nation and the world depends on the capacity of leaders to choose wisely and act prudently. History offers many examples of misguided policies leading to tragic consequences. Thus, President Lyndon Johnson's decision to escalate the Vietnam War in the mid-1960s—eventually committing more than 500,000 U.S. troops, alienating friends and allies abroad, and damaging the nation's prestige in the eyes of the world—cost him his job but also cost the lives of 58,193 U.S. military personnel. And it was all for naught: the United States lost the war and a whole lot more.

The Vietnam War proved the undoing of Johnson's successor, Richard Nixon, as well. The Watergate affair involving dirty tricks in the 1972 presidential campaign led directly to impeachment proceedings—and Nixon's resignation. Now let's look at a very different set of foreign policy decisions with very different consequences.

After World War II, President Truman made a series of historic decisions: to rebuild Europe by means of the Marshall Plan, to create new military alliances

Sir Winston Churchill (1874–1965) was an indomitable wartime leader who opposed the policy of appeasement toward Hitler and, when his dire warnings turned out to be true, led his country through its darkest days to its finest hour. As bombs fell on London and other British cities, Churchill declared, "We shall not flag or fail. We shall go on to the end. . . . We shall never surrender."

such as the North Atlantic Treaty Organization (NATO), and to confront the Soviet Union's perceived expansionism with a strong policy of containment. Few historians doubt that firm and decisive leadership was a crucial factor in shaping the postwar world and in creating the structures at home and abroad whereby the West eventually prevailed in the Cold War.

The late political scientist and historian Robert C. Tucker said that "Politics in essence is leadership,"[1] which is at once a timeless truth and wishful thinking. Political leaders have the potential for doing good or evil on a vast scale. Once in office, however, politicians often fail miserably as leaders or positive role models. For good or ill, elected officials *are* role models for civil society; they set a moral tone that affects the behavior of the citizens they purport to serve. A chronic and conspicuous absence of civility in public life (such as mudslinging and smear tactics in political campaigns) inevitably infects the way people treat each other. Because power corrupts and most people are not naturally evil, leaders are often not worthy of the people they lead.

In this chapter, we examine four types of leader—the **statesman, demagogue, politician,** and **citizen-leader**. These leadership types are different in many ways, including methods used and purposes pursued. A few are notable for the good they accomplish. Some are placeholders who do no harm. Still others are remembered for audacious abuses of power. You will encounter some household names; others will be new to you. All are chosen because they illustrate certain problems, pathologies, and patterns of leadership behavior—and how power corrupts many who exercise it but raises a few to sublime heights and even a kind of immortality.

Often these distinctions are easier to make in theory than to apply in practice. Nonetheless, there are enormous differences between the best and the worst of leaders. Thus, most observers would agree that Adolf Hitler, a mass-murdering madman who led Germany to disaster in World War II, exemplifies the worst. On the other hand, few would dispute that Winston Churchill—who recognized the dangers of totalitarianism in Nazi Germany earlier than most, led his nation's heroic defense in the darkest days of the war, and played a major role in shaping the postwar world—exemplifies the best.

THE IDEAL LEADER

The concept of the ideal leader has been around for a long time. Plato and Aristotle both examined it. Indeed, Plato depicted Socrates engaging in a dialogue about *statesmanship*, the term often used to refer to the role of a gifted leader or national hero. Typically, it is only after a leader has departed the scene that he or she comes to be regarded as a statesman in the popular mind.

statesman
Political architects who create new states, peacemakers who resolve conflicts, and orators who inspire the popular masses in times of national crisis—they are yesterday's founders, today's pathfinders, and tomorrow's legends

demagogue
Someone who uses his or her leadership skills to gain public office through appeals to popular fears and prejudices and then abuses that power for personal gain.

politician
A public officeholder who is prepared to sacrifice previously held principles or shelve unpopular policies to get reelected.

citizen-leader
An individual who influences government decisively even though he or she holds no official government position.

Great men and women in history are often exemplars of **statecraft**—the art of leading in difficult times. Founders of new nations are often revered and remembered as heroes. George Washington is such a larger-than-life figure, but many nations have iconic leaders steeped in legend and lore. Examples include Simon Bolivar (1783–1830), a Venezuelan statesman, who led the revolt against Spanish rule in Latin America; Kwame Nkruma (1909–1972), who led Ghana to independence from the United Kingdom in 1957; Nelson Mandela

IT'S A MAN'S WORLD, RIGHT?

Until quite recently, politics and government were male dominated, but to coin a phrase from a Bob Dylan song, "the times they are a-changin." The lyrics from this famous song spoke to the so-called Baby Boomer generation of alienated youth who rebelled against a morality they saw as hypocritical and a military duty—to fight in Vietnam—they saw as immoral and unnecessary.

The Vietnam era witnessed a sea of change in attitudes affecting race relations, sexual mores, and women's rights. It was not the beginning of the "sexual revolution" or "women's liberation"—that actually dates back to the late nineteenth century, but it was a kind of rebirth. Even so, the "glass ceiling" is still a fact of life in the United States today.

Many countries in the world now have (or have had) women as chief executives—presidents or prime ministers—including Germany, the United Kingdom, Norway, Poland, Israel, India, Pakistan, Bangladesh, South Korea, the Philippines, Argentina, Brazil, Chile, Peru, and Liberia, among others, whose personal charisma, political skills, and leadership qualities propelled them to national or even international preeminence.

Hillary Clinton, Nancy Pelosi, and Elizabeth Warren are three prominent examples of women in politics in the United States today. In 1997, Madeleine Albright became the first woman ever to serve as a U.S. Secretary of State; two other women (Condoleezza Rice and Hillary Clinton) would follow her in that role in the next decade.

Women constitute more than 50% of all eligible voters in the United States, yet they held only 18.7% of the House and Senate seats in the U.S. Congress

following the 2014 midterm elections. The gender gap is also apparent in voting patterns. In 2014, women favored Democrats 51% to 47%; men favored Republicans by a huge 16-point margin (57% voted for the GOP, 41% for Democrats). Of the 80 women who serve in the House of Representatives, 61 are Democrats and only 19 are Republicans.

Nancy Pelosi became the first woman ever to be elected Speaker of the House in 2007. In 2010, women voters joined men in ousting her, but it's men who kept Democrats in the minority in 2012 and 2014. In 2012, women voters favored Obama by 12 percentage points and men favored Mitt Romney by 8 points—that 20-point gender gap was the largest in U.S. history. Women outnumber men by five million (161million to 156 million) and vote in larger numbers than men.

Bottom line: it's still a man's world—until women decide to change it.

In 2008, the turnout among African American women voters was 68.8%, the highest of all racial, ethnic, and gender groups. In 2011, the year before the next presidential election, more than thirty state legislatures introduced voter suppression legislation. These laws make it harder for an estimated five million eligible voters to cast ballots. Who gains and who loses? Think about it.

(Hint: Proponents of strict voter ID laws also tend to oppose same-day voter registration; they argue that voter fraud has to be stopped to ensure that elections are fair. Find out as much as you can about ballot box stuffing and other forms of voter fraud.)

(1918–2013), who led the struggle to end *apartheid* (white minority rule and strict racial segregation) in South Africa; and Ho Chi Minh (1890–1969), Vietnam's "George Washington" who masterminded a protracted guerrilla war for national independence from France and subsequently led the war against the United States to unite North and South Vietnam. (Think of other examples and ask yourself what special qualities these heroic figures have in common.)

Even the most revered and admired leaders are not above reproach, however. Washington and the founders did not abolish slavery (or free their own slaves), nor did they see fit to give women the right to vote. Nearly a century later, Abraham Lincoln was instrumental in freeing the slaves, but the Civil War did not advance the cause of women's suffrage (voting rights) in America. Between the Civil War and World War I, women's rights activists arose to fight for the franchise. The names of these courageous leaders—Isabella Baumfree (aka, Sojourner Truth), Susan B. Anthony, Louisa May Alcott, Mary Baker Eddy, and Jeannette Rankin, to name a few—until recently were often absent in standard American history textbooks. The rise of the Suffragettes in England paralleled this historic women's rights movement in the United States.

Statesmanship

Defining the ideal leader is not easy. Most of us would agree that we want our leaders to possess certain qualities or virtues we look for in our friends, qualities others look for in us. We want our friends to be fair-minded and faithful, generous and compassionate. Intelligence is important, but common sense is essential. Some of the most gifted and famous people—geniuses and virtuosos of all kinds—are deeply flawed. The bravado of a Donald Trump may be useful in high-stakes business dealings, but it does not translate into political appeal or leadership potential. The brilliance of Albert Einstein did not overbalance the eccentricities that made him unfit for high office (to which, fortunately, he never aspired).

In *A Preface to Morals*, the late Walter Lippmann, a famed American philosopher and columnist, attempted to isolate the key factors and character traits that distinguish leaders from run-of-the-mill politicians. Lippmann suggested that most politicians work only "for a partial interest." Examples include politicians who feather their own nests or slavishly follow the party line. The word *statesmanship*, in contrast, "connotes a [person] whose mind is elevated sufficiently above the conflict of contending parties to enable him to adopt a course of action which takes into account a great number of interests in the perspective of a longer period of time."[2]

Lippmann recognized that the line between an ordinary politician and a real leader is often blurred. In a democracy, even the most high-minded leaders have to be politicians to gain and hold office. A trenchant observation attributed to H. L. Mencken (1880–1956) speaks directly to this point: "The men the American people admire most extravagantly are the most daring liars; the men they detest most violently are those

The late Golda Meir (1898–1978), who served as Israel's prime minister from 1969 to 1974, is remembered today as an exceptional leader; in her public life, she exemplified the traits of personal charisma, practical wisdom, political skills, and moral integrity often associated with statesmanship.

AP Images

who try to tell them the truth." Nonetheless, a true leader is not content merely to satisfy the momentary wishes of his or her constituents. The wiser course is to persuade voters that the pursuit of the public interest is in everyone's interest and that private interests are not (and ought not to be) the primary concern of public policy.

Pursuit of the Public Good The best leaders are motivated not by crass self-interest but by the public good. By choosing what "the people will in the end find to be good against what the people happen ardently to desire," Lippmann contended; true leaders resist opinion polls and popular impulses. In refusing to promise the impossible, they choose honesty and moderation over self-flattery. Such a decision, he continues, requires the "courage which is possible only in a mind that is detached from the agitations of the moment," as well as the "insight which comes from an objective and discerning knowledge of the facts, and a high and imperturbable disinterestedness."

Virtue in public life is not identical to virtue in private life. Honesty is a virtue, but in political life it is not always possible. When the stakes are high, when complete honesty is an impediment to success, and when the best interests of the nation are served by stealth or dissimulation, a true leader will some-times resort to deception. For example, both before and during the Civil War, President Lincoln consistently downplayed the slavery issue, preferring to keep the political spotlight on the overriding importance of preserving the Union. Lincoln understood that a call for immediate abolition risked alienating many moderates in both the North and South, ultimately harming the cause of both black emancipation and the Union.[3]

Practical Wisdom Belief in the public good is useless without a way of achieving it. Effective leaders display common sense—a quality not always present among wielders of much power. They understand the relationship between ideals and implementation, between actions and consequences. Statecraft—the art of diplomacy—distinguishes between the possible and the unattainable. In this sense, political leaders are a lot like physicians, whose success is ultimately measured not in dollars and cents they earn but in the health of the community they serve.

Political Skills Law and policies (and in the case of elections, the leaders themselves) require the consent of the governed. Reconciling wisdom and consent in the often-turbulent public arena is one of the primary tasks of leadership in a democracy.

Successful leaders are also good judges of talent and know how to delegate. Managing a vast bureaucracy, directing a large personal staff, working with the legislature to ensure a majority for the passage of the administration's programs, and rallying public opinion behind the administration's policies—these complex and demanding tasks are too much for any one individual to handle.

Of course, political skills are not always put at the service of the public good. Demagogues often seek to remove obstacles to needed social reforms by ruining, jailing, or killing opponents; even when they bring about progress and a measure of prosperity, the ends do not justify the means.

Perilous Times Historians have frequently observed that great times make great leaders. To become an iconic figure like Washington or Lincoln, it is necessary to guide the nation in a time of war or revolution. At such times, moral inspiration and political expertise are essential if the nation is to endure; such a situation is tailor-made for the exercise of statecraft. During times of "politics as usual," even the most capable leader will lack the opportunity to become a hero in history.

Good Fortune The final prerequisite of exceptional leadership is good luck. No political leader can be successful without a certain amount of good fortune. A turn in the tide of a single battle, a message thought about but not sent (or sent too late), or any number of other seemingly unimportant incidents or actions may prove decisive. Great leadership can never be attributed entirely to good luck, but considering the complex environment in which such leaders operate, good luck often makes the difference between success and failure.

The Lure of Fame Officeholders often get into politics at significant cost to themselves, relinquishing more lucrative careers and facing constant public scrutiny. The question inevitably arises: Why would men and women of outstanding ability devote the best years of their productive lives to the pursuit of political excellence? What would inspire such individuals to work for the public good, often at the expense of more obvious and immediate self-interests?

According to historian Douglass Adair (1912–1968), the Founders were motivated primarily by the idea of fame. For George Washington, James Madison, Alexander Hamilton, and Benjamin Franklin, narrow self-interest, defined in terms of personal power or wealth, was not an overriding concern. Nor was individual honor, which Adair defined as a "pattern of behavior calculated to win praises from [one's] contemporaries who are [one's] social equals or superiors."[4] Rather, the Founders' great motivating force was a desire for fame—a concept that, according to Adair, has been deeply embedded in the Western philosophical and literary tradition since the classical era. Applying this interpretation to the U.S. Founders, Adair wrote:

> Of course they were patriots, of course they were proud to serve their country in her need, but Washington, Adams, Jefferson, and Madison were not entirely disinterested. The pursuit of fame, they had been taught, was a way of transforming egotism and self-aggrandizing impulses into public service; they had been taught that public service nobly (and selflessly) performed was the surest way to build "lasting monuments" and earn the perpetual remembrance of posterity.[5]

Alexander Hamilton observed that a love of fame is "the ruling passion of the noblest minds."[6] The desire for immortality was a powerful elixir in Hamilton's time, when only wealthy, property-owning white men dared aspire to high office.

But times have changed. Today you don't have to be rich to get into politics in America, but it helps (witness Wilbur Mitt Romney). On the other hand, an African American named Barack Hussein Obama, whose father was born in Kenya and who was raised in a small Kansas town (by his grandparents), can become president. But he couldn't have done it without raising millions and millions of dollars. As we noted in Chapter 11, Obama raised a lot of money in small donations using the Internet; but he also had the backing of billionaires like George Soros in 2008 and Jon Stryker, David Shaw, Anne Cox Chambers, Irwin Jacobs, Haim Saban, and Stephen Spielberg in 2012.

National politics is now a very lucrative profession. Former Senator Tom Daschle is one example among many. When Daschle went to Washington as a freshman congressman in 1979, he had no money. An unknown even in his home state of South Dakota, he had campaigned by going house to house, knocking on doors, and introducing himself to the voters: people called him "door-to-door Daschle." But in Congress he prospered. In 1987, he was elected to the Senate, where he rose to become Senate majority leader. Having lost his bid for reelection in 2005, he left the Senate but did not leave Washington. He became a "consultant" (a euphemism for lobbyist)—like his second wife, Linda, a former deputy Federal Aviation Agency (FAA) administrator, known as "one of Washington's most prominent aviation lobbyists" whose clients notably include American Airlines. Linda Daschle, a former Miss Kansas, was so successful that she started her own lobbying firm, LHD and Associates, in January 2009. It goes almost without saying that today the Daschles are multimillionaires.

GREAT LEADERS IN HISTORY

We all know something about great rulers in history. In some cases, it's ridiculously easy to identify them: Alexander the Great (356–323 BCE), Asoka the Great (c. 304–232 BC), Darius the Great (550–486 BC), Peter the Great (1672–1725), Frederick the Great (1712–1786), Catherine the Great (1729–1796), and the list goes on. Such heroic figures in history are often called "great" because they fought and won military battles and conquered new lands. But that's not how we use the term in this book.

At least since the dawn of the Nuclear Age at the end of World War II, militarism and expansionism are no longer associated with virtuous leadership. As we saw in Chapter 6, the most militaristic leaders of the twentieth century were totalitarian dictators bent on conquest—greatly cruel, greatly destructive, and greatly evil, but not great. The adverb works, but not the adjective.

If not conquest, what is it that distinguishes great leaders from all the others in today's world? Obviously, leaders are not all cut from the same cloth. Some are courageous and incorruptible. Others are cowardly and crooked. Most of them fall somewhere in the middle. Here we reserve the term "great" for the best ones.

It is easy to become cynical about the possibility of good government or honest leaders (two sides of the same coin). If we believe politicians are *all* alike or power *always* corrupts, we run the risk of creating a self-fulfilling prophecy. If we have low expectations and reward elected officials by reelecting them *automatically*, we devalue the very idea of leadership.

Good leaders do not come along every day; great ones are rare. Throughout history, exemplary leaders—the best of the best—have appeared at various times and places. As the following political biographies of four world-famous leaders demonstrate, the backgrounds, qualities, and motives of those who have risen to the first rank of leadership display both remarkable similarities and wide disparities. Setting a good example is the mark of a good leader—hence the term *exemplary* to characterize the best of them.

Rómulo Betancourt (1908–1981)

Venezuela's President Hugo Chávez was a left-leaning populist and strident critic of U.S. foreign policy. As such, he is reminiscent of a certain type of leader in Latin American history, namely the *caudillo* (in Spanish, a strong leader, especially a military dictator). Thus, despite his image as part demagogue and part Robin Hood, Chávez was not really so different from other leaders in Venezuelan history. Indeed, the famous "liberator" of Latin America was a charismatic, populist Venezuelan military leader named Simon Bolivar.

Against this backdrop of populist dictators, the story of Rómulo Betancourt (1908–1981), a towering figure in the checkered history of Latin American democracy who remains little known in the United States, appears all the more remarkable.

Venezuela became a nation in 1830. From then until 1959, when Betancourt assumed the elected presidency, no democratic ruler had survived in office for even two years. Yet not only did Betancourt survive, battling seemingly insurmountable obstacles, but his public career also prospered, giving life to his country's fledgling democracy.

Betancourt's political career began when he was still a university student. At that time, a military dictator named Juan Vicente Gómez ruled Venezuela. In 1928, at the age of 20, Betancourt became a student leader in a failed revolution, eventually ending up in jail. After his release, he went into exile in Costa Rica for eight years, returning to Venezuela shortly after the death of the dictator in 1935. Afterward, Betancourt became a prominent political figure, though from the mid-1930s until 1959, he was a political maverick—often on the run, active in the underground, and sometimes living in exile as he continued his opposition to the dictator of the day. During his early years in opposition, he sympathized with the Communists, but he moderated in time, favoring democratic socialism instead. Betancourt's most notable achievement during this time was laying the groundwork for what would become Venezuela's leading party—Acción Democratica.

Rómulo Betancourt (1908–1981), president of Venezuela, 1945–1948 and 1959–1964. Betancourt first became president of Venezuela in the old-fashioned Latin American way: by a military coup. Today he is most often remembered as the "Father of Venezuelan Democracy," one of Latin America's great post–World War II statesmen and a vigorous defender of constitutional government. Among his most notable achievements in office are the declaration of universal suffrage, many progressive social reforms, restructuring of Venezuela's oil contracts to keep over half the profits in the country and for the public benefit, and, finally, the famous "Betancourt Doctrine," which denied diplomatic recognition to any government that came to power by military force. Betancourt's last major contribution as president was to direct what is generally believed to have been the most honest election in Venezuela's history; and in March 1964, he handed over the reins of government to the winner, Raul Leoni. Betancourt thus became the first elected Venezuelan president ever to serve a full term in office and the first to transfer power constitutionally from one elected chief executive to another.

Throughout most of his years in opposition, both Betancourt and his party consistently championed broad democratic participation for all citizens, agrarian reform, guaranteed universal education, national health care, and economic diversification (Venezuela was heavily dependent on oil exports). Betancourt joined and, according to some versions, headed a group of military reformers in a coup d'état (power seizure) against Venezuela's military government in October 1945. He ended up as president.

In office Betancourt championed a foreign policy in which Venezuela refused to extend diplomatic recognition to dictatorships and urged other governments in the region to follow suit. Domestically, he decreed that the large oil companies in Venezuela turn over half their income, enabling the government to undertake a far-reaching program to establish schools, hospitals, public water and sanitation facilities, and low-cost housing developments. He sponsored a new constitution in 1947, promoted elections, and declared he would not be a candidate for office. The candidate who succeeded Betancourt lasted only nine months before being ousted by another military coup. It was not until Betancourt was elected president in 1959 that democracy returned to Venezuela.

During his five-year term, Betancourt pursued the progressive policies he had always advocated. Particularly notable were his efforts to encourage foreign investment and improve urban housing. Betancourt also initiated a program of land reform. His economic and political achievements were all the more remarkable because, when he took office, his nation was facing an economic crisis, the military did not support his rule, and coup attempts from both the Left and the Right punctuated his term. (Betancourt survived more than one assassination attempt.)

Although he was decisive and governed with a firm hand, Betancourt exemplified the differences between democratic leadership and dictatorial abuse of power. He encouraged the politics of moderation, compromise, and toleration. He heeded the powers and prerogatives of the other two branches of government, followed the constitution, respected the rights of citizens, and did not use his high office for material advantage (or permit anyone under him to do so).[7]

Betancourt prevailed in the end and was beloved by his people. What accounted for his success as a democratic leader in a country with an autocratic tradition? Betancourt appears to have possessed an uncanny ability to judge the motives and character of others; almost unerring judgment about when to stand firm and when to compromise; a capacity to listen to advice but to keep his own counsel; an ability to make difficult decisions; self-control; and great personal valor, both moral and physical. He combined all these qualities with a high degree of practical idealism—a clear vision of what he wanted to accomplish for his country and a commitment to values that, together with ambition, had motivated him in national politics for decades.[8]

Betancourt can justly be considered the founder of Venezuelan democracy. As one of his foremost biographers, Robert J. Alexander, observed, "No other Venezuelan political leader of his time could have succeeded under all these circumstances."[9] A historian who specialized in Latin America wrote, "If moral authority and high principles counted, Rómulo Betancourt loomed as a titan in the history of Venezuela."[10] In the end, he did what no Venezuelan had ever done before, something demagogues never do: he bowed out gracefully, handing power over to a democratically elected successor.[11]

Winston Churchill (1874–1965)

Winston Churchill became Britain's prime minister in May 1940, at a time of great peril to his country. A colorful personality, Churchill was brilliant, charming, and witty; he was also courageous, controversial, and cantankerous. In the 1930s, he recognized and warned Britain of the menace posed by the rise of Nazi Germany in the heart of Europe. When war broke out, Churchill had already had his share of ups and downs in government, but his career reflected a steadfast devotion to the cause of freedom.

Churchill was born into a prominent English family that traced its lineage directly back to John Churchill, the first duke of Marlborough. Winston's father had been a distinguished member of Parliament and cabinet minister; his mother was an American. He himself was elected to Parliament at the tender age of 25 and almost immediately acquired a reputation as an eloquent and outspoken maverick. In 1911, he was appointed First Lord of the Admiralty, a high office he held through the first year of World War I. He was forced to resign in 1915, after the dismal failure of an amphibious attack on Turkey, by way of the Dardanelles, that he had sponsored. Churchill's political prestige then fell to an all-time low, although he managed to recoup sufficiently to be appointed minister of munitions in 1917.

Churchill remained a Conservative Member of Parliament (MP) throughout most of the 1920s and even held the prestigious position of chancellor of the exchequer (comparable to the U.S. secretary of the treasury) for an extended period. Despite a solid record of public service, he entered the 1930s as something of a political outcast, having alienated the leadership of his party. Even though the Conservatives held power, he was excluded from the government, and he found himself increasingly isolated in Parliament. At the age of 56, he was facing a premature end to his political career.

But Churchill had a kind of clairvoyance rare in politics. From the time of Hitler's ascent to power, he tried to alert Britain, Europe, and the United States, warning of the danger posed by Nazi Germany's rapid rearmament and the comparative weakness of Britain's armed forces—especially its air power. Many mainstream politicians and commentators ridiculed him as an alarmist. In the words of his foremost biographer, Churchill was a voice in the wilderness.[12]

As the 1930s progressed and Churchill's alarms began to arouse the nation, there still was no place for him in his party's cabinet. Only after Britain entered World War II was he asked to return to the government, initially in his former post as First Lord of the Admiralty, and then as prime minister.

After France had fallen and before the United States relaxed its policy of strict neutrality, Britain was the only power standing between Hitler and his goal—the total conquest of Europe. Churchill's inspiring words and example proved decisive. As Churchill later wrote, "Alone, but up-borne by every generous heartbeat of mankind, we had defied the tyrant in his hour of triumph."[13]

Churchill had rare leadership qualities. He understood the darker side of human nature and thus grasped the danger Hitler posed to civilization. Churchill had the courage of his convictions, never yielding to the voices of appeasement in his own party or the pressures of public opinion. His rhetoric inspired the nation in the face of a mortal threat and relentless bombardment. Above all, events proved him tragically right—right about the imminent threat, right about the malignant evil Hitler represented, and right about the urgent need for military preparedness. His message—that another terrible war was coming—was one his compatriots did not want to hear, but he never confused what the nation wanted to hear with what it *needed* to hear. And so he became the savior of his country.

Abraham Lincoln (1809–1865)

Churchill saved Britain from Hitler's Germany; Abraham Lincoln saved the United States of America from itself. The pivotal political issue in Lincoln's time was slavery. The South's economic dependence on it, along with the persistence of racial prejudice in the North, meant that advocating the immediate abolition of slavery was incompatible with winning the presidency. But preventing the "westward" spread of slavery, as it turned out, was incompatible with maintaining the peace.

This was the context in which Lincoln decided to run for president, a decision that culminated in his election to the nation's highest office in 1860. Lincoln's politics were guided by a basic moral precept and a profoundly practical judgment. The moral precept, which he repeatedly voiced in his debates with Stephen Douglas during his 1858 campaign for the Senate, held that slavery was wrong in principle, everywhere and without exception. In declaring slavery unjust and immoral, Lincoln did not resort to abstract philosophy; rather, he based his judgment squarely on the Declaration of Independence, which states, ". . . all men are created equal." Thus, for Lincoln, slavery violated the most basic principle of the U.S. political order.

Lincoln exercised uncommon practical judgment in evaluating the conditions under which slavery might be eradicated in the United States. He believed above all that it was necessary to maintain the Union as a geographic entity, as well as to preserve its integrity as a constitutional democracy. Only through a single central government for North and South alike could slavery be ended, although this was by no means inevitable. Conversely, any breakup of the Union would mean the indefinite extension of slavery, at least in the South.

Lincoln's belief in political equality and his conviction that such equality could be achieved only by preserving the Union help explain the pre–Civil War stands he avoided taking, as well as the ones he adopted. Although he believed slavery was morally wrong, he did not propose its immediate abolition; he knew such a proposal would prompt the South to secede and ensure the survival of slavery in that region. Nor did he support northern abolitionists who sought to disassociate themselves from the Union so long as it continued to countenance slavery. Here again, Lincoln recognized that such a policy would only entrench the very institution it was designed to eliminate. Finally, he opposed Stephen Douglas's formula of popular sovereignty, under which each new state would be allowed to declare itself for or against slavery. The question of slavery, Lincoln believed, was too fundamental to be submitted to the vagaries of the political marketplace.

Rather than pursue any of these policies, Lincoln favored an end to the extension of slavery into the territories, so that from then on, only free states would be admitted to the Union. In Lincoln's mind, this was the only antislavery policy that had any chance of gaining popular acceptance. The keys to his strategy were patience and perseverance. Adoption of his plan would ultimately bring about an end to slavery in the whole United States, as the relative weight and legislative strength of the slaveholding states diminished with the passage of time and the admission of new non-slaveholding states.

When it became evident that Lincoln's policy would not win the day, he accepted the Civil War as inevitable. Yet during the course of this conflict, his approach to the slavery question varied according to the circumstances of the war. As noted earlier, when the tide of battle ran against the Union and victory seemed to depend on not alienating several of the slaveholding Border States, Lincoln went out of his way to soft-pedal the slavery issue. The North needed military victories, not pious pronouncements, if the Union were to endure. It could not endure, he believed, if it remained "half slave and half free." In the final analysis, the reason Lincoln was willing to countenance civil war was, paradoxically, to preserve the kind of Union the Founders had intended.

Both before and during the Civil War, Lincoln's policies were aimed at achieving the maximum amount of good possible within the confines of popular consent. As commander in chief, he pushed his constitutional authority up to, and arguably beyond, its legal limits. But just as his ultimate political purposes were not undermined by the compromises he accepted to save the Union in time of peace, so too his moral integrity was not corrupted by the dictatorial powers he wielded in time of war. For all these reasons, Lincoln stands out as an exemplary political leader whose resolute actions and decisions under fire were instrumental in saving the Union.

Anwar al-Sadat (1918–1981)

The Middle East is one the world's most unstable and violent regions. Miraculously, in late 1993, Israeli Prime Minister Yitzhak Rabin and Palestine Liberation Organization leader Yasir Arafat, bitter enemies, agreed to a deal that gave limited autonomy to the Palestinians in the Israeli-occupied West Bank and Gaza Strip. The agreement was a big step toward a possible peace, but it was not the *first* step. In fact, there was a precedent in the Middle East, one that suggested even the deadliest of enemies can live together in peace. Anwar al-Sadat was the political architect of that peacemaking precedent.

Sadat was president of Egypt from 1970 until his assassination in 1981. He succeeded Gamal Abdel Nasser, the acknowledged leader of the Arab world and a prime mover in the post–World War II anti-colonialist movement. Nasser was an autocratic ruler who governed Egypt with an iron fist and staunchly opposed the existence of the state of Israel. When Nasser died in 1970, Sadat succeeded him. (As vice president, Sadat was Nasser's handpicked successor.)

Like Nasser, Sadat was a fighter for Egyptian independence from Great Britain. His anti-British activities during World War II included contacts with Germans aimed at collaboration against the British imperialists. For these efforts, Sadat spent two years in a detention camp. Later he would spend three more years (1946–1949) in prison, charged with attempting to assassinate a British official. In pursuit of a nationalistic strategy that sought to capitalize on anti-British sentiment in Egypt, Sadat and Nasser cooperated closely. It was Sadat who publicly announced the overthrow of the Egyptian monarchy and the establishment of the new, independent republic of Egypt under Nasser's leadership in July 1952.

Given this history, it seemed inevitable that, as president, Sadat would continue Nasser's policies. Events seemed to bear out this expectation. In 1971, he was instrumental in forging the Federation of Arab Republics, an alliance of Egypt, Libya, and Syria motivated by Nasser's policy of uniting the Arab world. The federation ultimately failed, but not for want of trying on Sadat's part.

In 1973, Sadat led Egypt in a war against Israel. Although Egypt was defeated, Sadat stressed that the Egyptian army had won a major battle at the outset of the war; this victory, he maintained, restored Egypt's national honor. In the aftermath of the war, Sadat switched from belligerent Arab nationalist to committed advocate of peaceful coexistence. This transformation was capped by a precedent-shattering state visit to Israel, where Sadat delivered a memorable speech before the Israeli Knesset (parliament) on November 20, 1977. More important than the speech was the symbolic significance of his official presence in the Israeli seat of government: Egypt had become the first Arab country to recognize Israel as a sovereign state.

This dramatic act of conciliation by Sadat paved the way for the Camp David Accords between Egypt and Israel the following year. The Egyptian-Israeli agreement at Camp David, Maryland, which set the stage for Israel's withdrawal from the Sinai peninsula, caught foreign observers by surprise and stunned the Arab world. Sadat was bitterly attacked by many of his fellow Arab rulers as a traitor to the Palestinian cause. To the Arabs, and to many of the most astute observers, Sadat's bold step toward a lasting Arab-Israeli peace was as unexpected as it was unprecedented.

Why did Sadat take this extraordinary step? Given the serious economic and social problems (poverty, overpopulation, urban crowding, and a growing generation gap) facing Egypt, Sadat, some argue, had little choice but to seek peace with Israel. Others emphasize Israel's value as a source of intelligence about Libya, Egypt's neighbor and rival in North Africa. A more plausible explanation is that Sadat the pragmatist concluded the only way Egypt was ever going to regain the Sinai (which Israel had occupied since 1967) was by signing a peace treaty.

Pragmatism explains Sadat's political-strategic calculations, but not the intensity of his peace efforts or the magnitude of the personal and political risks he was willing to take. He knew his actions would alienate most of the Arab world, including many of his fellow citizens. It seems likely that just as the young Sadat was moved by the ideal of a free and independent Egypt, which he helped to bring about, so too an older Sadat was inspired by an even more noble vision. As he expressed it on the occasion of the signing of the Camp David Accords:

> Let there be no more wars or bloodshed between Arabs and Israelis. Let there be no more suffering or denial of rights. Let there be no more despair or loss of faith. Let no mother lament the loss of her child. Let no young man waste his life on a conflict from which no one benefits. Let us work together until the day comes when they beat their swords into plowshares and their spears into pruning hooks.[14]

The eradication of hatred, religious bigotry, and incessant warfare from a region where they had been a way of life for as long as anyone could remember would indeed be a great act of statecraft. The attempt to bring peace to the Middle East may well have been Sadat's own personal bid for immortality. He may or may not have been aware of Alexander Hamilton's views on the subject of leadership, but through his actions, Sadat bore out the truth of Hamilton's observation that love of fame is the "ruling passion" of history's most exceptional leaders.

Like Lincoln, Sadat was assassinated by one of his own countrymen. Oddly, such is often the fate of history's peacemakers. Thus, Mahatma Gandhi, the charismatic leader of India's independence movement and a champion of non-violent resistance, was himself assassinated.

Paradoxically, making peace often entails greater political and personal risks than making war. The tragic fate that befell Sadat also befell Israeli Prime Minister Rabin who was gunned down in Tel Aviv in 1995. The assassin was Yigal Amir, 25 years of age, a fanatical Zionist opposed to the Oslo Peace Accords (for which Rabin, along with Shimon Peres and Arafat, won the Nobel Peace Prize). A lasting peace in the Middle East has been elusive, but Egypt and Israel have been at peace for more than two decades thanks to the treaty that stands as a fitting memorial to the wisdom and courage of Anwar al-Sadat.

Benazir Bhutto (1953–2007)

In December 1988, Benazir Bhutto of Pakistan became the first female prime minister in a Muslim country in history. She was born into politics in a country where politics was off limits to women, but broke through the plate glass ceiling that still reserves most professions and most well-paying jobs for men. Her father, Zulfikar Ali Bhutto, founded the Pakistan People's Party, the largest political party in Pakistan, and served as Pakistan's president (1971–1973) and prime minister (1973–1977).

 The Army deposed Zulfikar Ali Bhutto in a coup in 1977 and affected his judicial execution (by hanging) two years later (allegedly for ordering the assassination of a political opponent). Educated in the United States (Berkeley) and the UK (Oxford), Bhutto favored Western-style progressive economic policies. Such policies are often controversial in tradition-bound Islamic societies. In addition, the generals did not like playing second fiddle to a modernizing civilian leader.

 Benazir Bhutto returned to Pakistan when her father was arrested and jailed. She removed to England in 1984, but became the joint PPP leader in exile. In 1986, she returned to Pakistan and led a successful nationwide campaign for open elections. In 1988, Benazir Bhutto, at the ripe young age of 35, led the PPP to victory. Like her father, Bhutto was educated in the United States (Radcliffe and Harvard) and the UK (Oxford). And like him, she embraced modernity, democracy, and liberalism.

As prime minister, one of her first acts on taking the oath of office was to lift the ban on student unions and labor unions. She also directed negotiations leading to three peace agreements with India, Pakistan's archenemy since independence in 1947. But in 1990, her government was accused of corruption and dismissed under a controversial provision of the Constitution (Amendment Eight) that allows the president (usually a military figure or a civilian under the Army's boot heel) to take such action at virtually any time he chooses.

Bhutto's PPP won the elections in 1993 and she again served as prime minister until 1996 when her government, in the face of fierce opposition from conservative politicians and the Army, was again dismissed. Threatened, she again went into self-imposed exile only to be accused in absentia of corruption and sentenced to three years in prison. Unable to return to Pakistan, she continued to work for liberal reforms and social justice from abroad.

Bhutto returned to Pakistan in October 2007 after President Musharraf (a former Army general) granted her amnesty on all corruption charges. A suicide attack at her homecoming rally killed 136 people, but she survived by ducking down behind her armored vehicle. When Musharraf imposed a state of emergency in early November, Bhutto pronounced it Pakistan's "blackest day" and threatened to call on her supporters to stage mass demonstrations. In the showdown that followed, Musharraf place Bhutto under house arrest; she, in turn, called for his resignation. Under heavy Western pressure, Musharraf lifted emergency rule in December.

Bhutto was assassinated and twenty-eight others died in a suicide attack after an election campaign rally in Rawalpindi on December 27, 2007. The attack left at least another hundred wounded. Some died in a hail of bullets; others were killed in the bomb blast.

The attack plunged Pakistan into turmoil. Bhutto's supporters went on a rampage in several cities. The fact that Pakistan and India both have nuclear weapons added drama and danger to the crisis.

The political murder of Benazir Bhutto was a tragedy on many levels—her family, her country, the war-torn region of Central Asia (Afghanistan is Pakistan's next-door neighbor), and the turbulent Muslim world. But it was also a tragedy for the West and for women the world over. Because her life and work were cut short, we will never know what might have been. But it is clear that Benazir Bhutto was an uncommonly courageous woman who dedicated her life to making Pakistan a better place for her people and the world a better place for us all. To that end, she fought and died.

Aung San Suu Kyi (b. 1945)

"It is not power that corrupts, but fear. Fear of losing power corrupts those who wield it and fear of the scourge of power corrupts those who are subject to it."

Like Benazir Bhutto, Aung San Suu Kyi was born into politics. Her father, Aung San, a major military and political leader in Burma's struggle for independence after World War II, was assassinated by rivals for power in 1947. Suu Kyi earned degrees from Oxford (BA, 1969) and the University of London (PhD, 1985).

From 1962 until 1988—that is, during Suu Kyi's entire adult life to that point—Burma (also known as Myanmar) was ruled as a military dictatorship under Genera Ne Win. During the Ne Win dictatorship, Suu Kyi lived abroad in the UK (London) and in the United States (New York City). In 1988, two events signaled a watershed in Burma's history: Ne Win stepped down, and Suu Kyi returned from her long self-imposed exile. In August, she addressed a huge throng (estimate at half a million people) in the capital, Rangoon, calling for democracy. In September, even as a military junta usurped power, Suu Kyi and others launched the National League for Democracy (NLD). Placed under house arrest, the junta invited her to leave the country in July 1989. She refused.

When the military called a general election in 1990, the Aung San Suu Kyi's NLD received 59% of the popular vote and, in theory, 80% of the assembly seats. The balloting turned out to be a feckless exercise because the military promptly nullified the elections and again placed Suu Kyi under house arrest, where she would remain for fifteen of the next twenty-one years. During these years, however, she continued a solitary fight for democracy in personal isolation, against all odds, in poor living conditions, and under constant threat from the military rulers.

Finally released from house arrest in November 2010, she plunged right back into the roiling waters of Burmese politics. In a 2012 by-election, she ran for a seat in parliament and won.

During the two decades she was barred from politics and kept a prisoner in her own home, Aung San Suu Kyi became the stuff of legend. Many honors and awards were bestowed on her (in absentia, of course), including the Nobel Peace Prize and the Congressional Gold Medal. Today, she is the face of a newly emerging Burma (much as Nelson Mandela became the face of the new South Africa), a living symbol universally admired for her courage and resistance to continuing tyranny in her native land.

WHERE HAVE ALL THE LEADERS GONE?

Living politicians have a lot in common with the late comedian Rodney Dangerfield: they get no respect. In politics, sometimes "losers" come to be admired as leaders, and winners suffer the opposite fate. When politicians are beholden to special interests and use focus groups to formulate messages that will sell in a ten-second television sound bite, courageous political leadership often seems like a distant ideal.*

Leadership as a concept has virtually disappeared from the language and literature of U.S. politics. Significantly, while the 1934 edition of the *Encyclopedia of the Social Sciences* included a brief but incisive essay on statesmanship by a celebrated British scholar, a more recent edition omits all mention of statesmanship as a category of political thought.

*Historians sometimes seek to refute the conventional wisdom about history's most famous figures. In the United States, recent books have cast doubt on the character and motives of even our most revered national icons, including George Washington and Thomas Jefferson.

In an age of equality, there is a danger that the idea of excellence will be debunked and dismissed as elitist.[15] To the debunkers, vague historical determinants or narrow self-interest, not free will, are the true motive forces in history, and it is naive to believe some leaders really care about the public good. This cynical view leads to a drastically reduced opinion of outstanding leaders in world history. It is as if "the old histories full of kings and generals whom our ancestors foolishly mistook for heroes are, we suppose, to be replaced by a kind of hall of fame of clever operators."[16]

One consequence of this tendency is that it makes political life less attractive to capable and conscientious individuals. By denying public officials the respect they are due, a democratic society can do itself considerable harm. As noted earlier, a pervasive belief that corrupt and mediocre politicians are the norm can become a self-fulfilling prophecy, causing only the corrupt or mediocre to seek public office.

DEMAGOGUES IN AMERICAN HISTORY

Originally, in ancient Greece, a demagogue was a leader who championed the cause of the common people. Today, the term *demagogue* is applied to a leader who exploits popular prejudices, distorts the truth, and makes empty promises to gain political power. In general, demagogues combine unbridled personal ambition, unscrupulous methods, and great popular appeal.

If true leaders represent the ideal, demagogues represent the perversion of both truth and leadership. Statesmen genuinely care about justice and the public good; demagogues only pretend to care in order to gain high office whence they inevitably betray the public interest they previously championed.

Demagogues are rarely long remembered. Occasionally, they leave an indelible mark.

Aaron Burr (1756–1836)

His name is one of the most notorious in the annals of early U.S. history. Schoolchildren learn at an early age that Aaron Burr was a "bad guy," that he shot and killed Alexander Hamilton in a duel. But the reason he was a danger to the young republic he claimed to serve is often glossed over.

Burr had a tragic childhood. Born into a wealthy and famous family, he lost both his parents at a very early age. He was beaten by his guardian and ran away from home more than once. At the age of 10, he tried to stow away on a ship. Desperate not to be taken back to live with his tormentor, he climbed the ship's mast and refused to come down. In the end, he was delivered once again into his guardian's "care."

Burr was a precocious child and a brilliant student. In time, he became a lawyer and then went into politics. He had an uncanny ability to beguile, to pretend he was someone other than who he really was. He was also an eloquent speaker and an agile debater, skills that served him well in a court of law. A great admirer of Thomas Jefferson, he was a candidate for president in 1800, the year Jefferson was elected. Because of the peculiar workings of the Electoral College, however, no candidate received the absolute majority required by the Constitution to claim the presidency, so the decision was thrown into the House of Representatives, dominated by the lame-duck Federalists, where the delegations from the various states each cast one vote. The contest in the House of Representatives was between Jefferson and Burr. The Federalists were determined to "elect" Burr, who refused to withdraw even though Jefferson was clearly the popular choice. Finally, after five long days, on the thirty-sixth ballot, a delegate from Virginia changed his vote, giving Jefferson the one additional state vote he needed to put him over the top. Thus, Burr became the vice president, having nearly stolen the presidency.

In Jefferson's time, vice presidents had very little to do. Burr kept himself busy, however, by undermining the president and the republic. The story of his seditious activities is too long and convoluted to be told here, but they included trying to organize a secession movement in New England and the territory north of the Ohio River, later plotting to assassinate Jefferson, and trying to lead an insurrection in New Orleans and what was then the Mississippi Territory. (His plans included creation of a western empire, under his control, in the lands acquired through Jefferson's leadership in the famed Louisiana Purchase.)

Burr was eventually captured and arrested on charges of treason. Brought to trial in Richmond, Virginia, in 1807, he was acquitted by the Chief Justice of the Supreme Court, John Marshall, who was also acting as federal court judge. Marshall was a die-hard Federalist and a rival of Jefferson's. Seldom, if ever, has there been a more blatant case in U.S. jurisprudence of politicizing a trial and showing contempt from the bench for the integrity of the Constitution. The evidence against Burr was abundant and damning, but neither Jefferson nor the Republican-controlled Congress had the stomach to see Burr hang once Marshall had rendered his verdict.

In sum, Burr failed to achieve his seditious intents, but his demagoguery had come dangerously close to catapulting him into the presidency in 1800. The fact that he became a U.S. senator and vice president shows that demagogues have long played a role at the highest levels of government. Burr's personal charisma and political skills in the end also probably helped him escape the gallows.

Theodore Bilbo (1877–1947)

As governor and senator, Theodore Bilbo dominated Mississippi politics from the 1920s through the 1940s. He campaigned equally hard against blacks and his political opponents, linking them whenever possible. His campaign rhetoric was colorful and outrageous. In the heat of one political campaign, he denounced his opponent as a "cross between a hyena and a mongrel . . . begotten in a [racial slur deleted] graveyard at midnight, suckled by a sow, and educated by a fool."[17] Although Bilbo's white supremacist politics and down-home language endeared him to a great many Mississippians, not everyone was impressed. Even political allies viewed him as a self-serving political operator.

According to one writer, Bilbo was "pronounced by the state Senate in 1911 'as unfit to sit with honest upright men in a respectable legislative body,' and described more pungently by his admirers as 'a slick little bastard.'"[18] And in the eyes of the editor of the *Jackson Daily News*, Bilbo stood "for nothing that is high or constructive, . . . nothing save passion, prejudice and hatred, . . . nothing that is worthy."[19] Bilbo was reelected to a third Senate term in 1946, but this time the Senate refused to seat him because of his alleged incitement of violence against blacks who tried to vote. Bilbo died of cancer a few months later at the age of 69.

Huey Long (1893–1935)

Theodore Bilbo has mercifully escaped the attention of most U.S. historians; Huey Long, a politician from the neighboring state of Louisiana, has not. Known to his Cajun constituents as the Kingfish, Long was far more ambitious than Bilbo. Of humble origins, he completed the three-year law program at Tulane University, passed a special examination from the Louisiana Supreme Court, and became a licensed attorney at the age of 21. In his own words, he "came out of the courtroom running for office."[20] Three years later, he was elected state railroad commissioner, and in 1928, he gained the Louisiana governorship.

Long governed Louisiana with an iron hand during his four-year reign (1928–1932) and during his subsequent term as U.S. senator, which was cut short by his assassination in 1935. As governor, Long controlled every aspect of the state's political life. Surrounded by bodyguards and aided by a formidable political machine, he used state police and militia to intimidate voters, handed out patronage and political favors, created a state printing board to put unfriendly newspapers out of business, ordered a kidnapping on the eve of a crucial election vote to avoid personal political embarrassment, and generally

AP Images

As Governor of Louisiana, Huey Long seized control and acted as a virtual dictator. Then as senator during the Great Depression, he cast himself as a radical populist social reformer and had great ambitions on the national scene. But an assassin's bullet abruptly ended his career and his life in 1935. It is said that his last words were, "God don't let me die. I have so much left to do."

acted more like a despotic ruler than a democratically elected governor. Under his autocratic rule:

> Men could be—and were—arrested by unidentified men, the members of his secret police, held incommunicado, tried, and found guilty on trumped-up charges. A majority of the State Supreme Court became unabashedly his. . . . A thug, making a premeditated skull-crushing attack upon a Long opponent, could draw from his pocket in court a pre-signed pardon.[21]

Despite these excesses and a penchant for luxury, Long always took care to portray himself as "just plain folks." The true villains in U.S. society, he said, were rich corporations such as Standard Oil, which consigned ordinary people to lives of poverty while enriching a few corporate officers.

To counteract this alleged thievery by big business and to create a popular platform for the upcoming presidential race in 1936, Long developed an unworkable (but popular) "Share the Wealth" program, tailor-made to appeal to people suffering through the Great Depression. Long's proposal included restrictions on maximum wealth, mandated minimum and maximum incomes, so-called homestead grants for all families, free education through college, bonuses for veterans, and pensions for the aged—as well as the promise of radios, automobiles, and subsidized food through government purchases. However implausible and impractical this program seems, it's worth remembering that the people to whom Long was appealing were not inclined to quibble or question. They needed someone to believe in.

Like many other demagogues, Long gained power by promising hope to the hopeless. Demagogues generally vow to defeat the forces of evil that, according to them, are solely responsible for the people's plight. Of course, those forces—blacks in the case of Bilbo, corporations for Long—invariably do not exercise anything like the controlling influence attributed to them. Nonetheless, once accepted as the champion of the little people against enemies they themselves have conjured up, demagogues often have been able to manipulate the unsuspecting populace for their own illicit ends.

Joseph McCarthy (1906–1957)

During the 1950s, an obscure politician from Wisconsin named Joseph McCarthy identified a demon that greatly alarmed the U.S. people and then claimed to find evidence of this malignant force in all areas of public life.

While serving as a Republican senator from Wisconsin, McCarthy attracted national attention by making the shocking "revelation" that the U.S. Department of State was infiltrated by Communists. For approximately four years, he leveled charges of treason against a wide array of public officials, college professors, and Hollywood stars. Using his position as chair of the Senate Committee on Investigations, McCarthy badgered, intimidated, and defamed countless people in and out of government. As his accusations helped create a national climate of fear, his power grew, and those who opposed him did so at their own risk.

In 1954, McCarthy accused the secretary of the Army of concealing foreign espionage operations. That accusation, along with innuendos aimed at General

ALL THE KING'S MEN . . .

The life and death of Huey Long has inspired popular books and films and, ironically, made a lot of money for writers, publishers, movie studios, filmmakers, and actors, among others. It all started back in 1946 with the publication of Robert Penn Warren's novel, *All the King's Men*, which won the Pulitzer Prize. It was adapted for film and won the Academy Award for Best Picture and Best Actor (Broderick Crawford) in 1949. Not bad for a story named after a nursery rhyme!

"All the King's Men" is a *roman à clef* (literally, novel with a key) inspired by the life and legend of Huey Long, who becomes Willie Stark in the screenplay. Stark is a backwoods southern lawyer who rises to power in Louisiana as a corruption-fighter. A young, idealistic journalist helps him create a captivating narrative and public image. As governor, Stark shows his true colors. A serial philanderer, he's more venal and dishonest than the crooks he's replaced. He's also ruthless, with a fascist bent for using the police to do his dirty work; "accidents" conveniently befall his detractors and rivals.

He's a consummate demagogue, a champion of the poor who funnels money into the school system and public works to keep the voters on his side. And he can be disarmingly charming; he possesses that magical quality in a leader—charisma. He craves a bigger stage. His ambition is boundless. Nothing can stop him—except a bullet.

All in all it's a great story, a work of fiction based on a real person and real events that captures a real truth about the corrupting effects of unchecked political power. Few stories—and fewer politicians outside the presidency—have etched a deeper impression on the public mind or had a greater impact on popular culture in America than this one. Indeed, Warren's novel would later be adapted into a stage play, a Ken Burns TV documentary, and even an opera.

"Power corrupts; absolute power corrupts absolutely." It's one of the best known quotes about politics in the English language, one that's easy to demonstrate with historic examples like Huey Long and virtually impossible to dispute without appearing naive. But is it true? Is a little power less corrupting than a lot of power? Are leaders with dictatorial ("absolute") power always absolutely corrupt? Do counterexamples exist? Think about it.

(Hint: Try to explain how a given country has survived a time of great peril—war, revolution, natural disaster—without reference to a strong leader, one who grabs or is given dictatorial powers at least for a limited time. Is such a power grab or grant always a sign of cynicism and corruption, or can it be necessary and rational? Do leaders always use these powers to enrich themselves, silence dissent, or destroy opponents?)

George C. Marshall—next to President Dwight D. Eisenhower perhaps the most respected public servant in the United States—marked a turning point. McCarthy had gone too far. Ironically, his unscrupulous methods were exposed in Senate investigations that resulted from his own irresponsible accusations. The hearings received national radio and television coverage and made front-page headlines in every major newspaper in the country. In the end, McCarthy was cast into obscurity as rapidly as he had been catapulted into national prominence.

Tom DeLay (b. 1947)

Texas Republican Tom DeLay was first elected to the U.S. House of Representatives in 1984 and served as House majority leader from 2003 to 2006, having been the House majority whip in the 1990s and subsequently serving as deputy majority leader. DeLay became known as "The Hammer" for his ruthless methods and questionable ethics. As House majority whip, he demanded strict party discipline and made anyone who crossed him pay. When he became House majority leader after the 2002-midterm elections, he rallied—or bullied—House Republicans to close ranks behind President George W. Bush's neoconservative agenda.

In the early 2000s, DeLay played a key role in a plan to gerrymander state legislative districts and later to redraw Texas's congressional districts in favor of the Republican Party. However, in October 2004, the House Ethics Committee voted unanimously to admonish DeLay on two counts relating to ethics violations, though it deferred action on another count related to fundraising while that matter was under criminal investigation in Texas.

In 2005, a Texas grand jury indicted DeLay on criminal charges of conspiring to violate campaign finance laws by engaging in money laundering during that period. Although he denied the charges, claiming they were politically motivated, he had no choice under existing rules but to step down temporarily as majority leader. Under heavy pressure from within his own party, he later announced he would not seek to return to his leadership position in the House. About this same time, two of DeLay's former aides were convicted in the Jack Abramoff influence-peddling scandal involving Native American gambling casino interests.*

DeLay ran for reelection in 2006 and won the Republican primary but subsequently resigned his seat in Congress. He tried to have his name removed from the ballot to avoid a humiliating defeat, but he lost a court battle and had to remain, even though he had withdrawn from the race. In the annals of U.S. politics, there are few more ignominious endings to a politician's career. (The demise of Richard Nixon is one.)

Abramoff is now serving a prison sentence for defrauding American Indian tribes and for corruption of public officials. DeLay was sentenced to three years in prison in January 2011. As the saying goes, the bigger they are, the harder they fall.

LEGISLATORS

Solon was the great lawgiver of ancient Athens, the wise legislator who framed the laws of the city-state that became the first democracy in the history of Western civilization. Words like *great* and *wise* are seldom used in the same sentence as *legislator* these days; sadly, many today delegate and consider the very idea of a "great legislator" to be an oxymoron.

Most politicians are fairly average. On a day-to-day basis, they do the best they can, given the pressures and constraints they face. Much of the time, they want to do the right thing, although they have difficulty keeping moral or ethical issues in clear focus and even more difficulty taking political risks. Generally

---

*The scandal involved lobbyists Jack Abramoff, Ralph E. Reed Jr., Grover Norquist, and Michael Scanlon. Abramoff and Scanlon were accused of extorting $85 million from Native Americans clients they pretended to work for. As part of the scheme, they orchestrated a lobbying effort against allowing casinos on reservations! The wrong-doing also involved campaign donations and gifts to legislators in return for votes. Representative Bob Ney (R-OH), as well as aides to House Majority Whip Tom DeLay (R-TX), were directly implicated in the conspiracy.

they are not corrupt, but they often *are* corruptible. They are no better, and no worse, than most people, but they are in a position to do more harm (or good) than most ordinary citizens.

As citizens, we often scorn "politicians."[22] They, in turn, lament the fact that voters fail to understand how the system really works—that without logrolling (trading votes) the legislative process would grind to a halt. The would-be leader in a democratic society faces the choice of whether to act as a delegate, carrying out the voters' (presumed) wishes, or to act as a trustee, exercising independent judgment on behalf of his or her constituents. The political system itself requires elected representatives to be responsive if they wish to be reelected. But those to whom the people have entrusted power are duty-bound to lead—and therein lies the politician's dilemma.

Legislators as Delegates

According to the **delegate theory of representation**, a legislature "is representative when it contains within itself the same elements, in the same proportion, as are found in the body politic at large. It is typical of us; we are all in it in microcosm."[23] In this model of representative democracy, elected representatives are obliged to act as instructed delegates.

The delegate theory thus tends to legitimize the use of focus groups and opinion polls to help legislators decide what stands to take on important issues. One notable advocate of this theory holds there is a "relative equality of capacity and wisdom between representatives and constituents," it would be "arbitrary and unjustifiable for representatives to ignore the opinions and wishes of the people," and that political issues often involve "irrational commitment or personal preference, choice rather than deliberation, [making it all] the more necessary . . . that the representative consult with the people's preferences."[24]

Legislators as Trustees

Detractors say the delegate theory of representation requires elected officials to be too passive—in effect, to act as followers rather than leaders. One famous critic of this theory was Edmund Burke (1729–1797), the famed eighteenth-century British writer and legislator.

Burke believed legislators ought to retain a certain independence of thought and action. Specifically, according to Burke, the elected representative needs to isolate specific complaints about real problems from the grumbling of an irascible (and possibly irrational) electorate. He contended that the politician as legislator must listen to the complaints of constituents but not give all complaints equal weight: competent legislators distinguish between legitimate grievances and those that arise from defects in human nature.[25] For Burke's ideal lawmaker, public opinion is a useful barometer rather than a guidepost.

Burke believed a natural aristocracy made up of the best and the brightest should govern and that elected officials should act as trustees, not puppets. As he declared in a famous speech to his own constituents, "Your representative owes you not his industry only, but his judgment; and he betrays, instead of serving you, if he sacrifices it to your opinion."[26] Burke's views were elitist:

delegate theory of representation According to this theory, elected officials should reflect the views of the voters back home rather than following their own conscience or substituting their own judgment for that of their constituents. In other words, elected representatives should be followers rather than leaders.

he posited a wide gulf in knowledge, wisdom, and virtue between those fit to be legislators and ordinary constituents. Seen in this light, true legislators are leaders rather than followers.

Burke's so-called **trustee theory of representation** fits into his larger philosophy of government. Good government, he argued, must include not only goodwill but also "virtue and wisdom." Burke's Parliament is a place where "*one* nation, with *one* interest, that of the whole—where not local purposes, not local prejudices, ought to guide, but the general good, resulting from the general reason of the whole" prevails.[27] Did it ever exist, or did Burke fall victim to wishful thinking? Looking at the U.S. Congress today, what do *you* think?

CITIZEN-LEADERS

Occasionally, an individual can decisively influence the course of political events without holding an official position in the government. An individual's unique dedication to a cause, personal magnetism, or even outright courage can garner an impressive political following. Such a person is called a *citizen-leader*. In the following section, we look at five examples of such grassroots leadership.

Václav Havel (1936–2011)

In the mid-1960s, at the age of 29, Václav Havel gained worldwide acclaim for his satirical absurdist plays, including *The Garden Party* (1964) and *The Memorandum* (1965). In the summer of 1968, Havel and thirty other Czech cultural figures signed a statement calling for the revival of the outlawed Social Democratic Party in communist-controlled Czechoslovakia. In August of that same summer, the increasing, but cautious, trend toward liberalization within Czechoslovakia that had begun in 1963 was swiftly and successfully thwarted when the Soviet Union invaded the country to reassert hard-line Soviet control.

During the conflict, Havel played a key role in putting Czech Radio Free Europe on the airways and using this underground radio broadcast to direct daily commentary to Western intellectuals as a plea for assistance. Over the next two decades, he became Czechoslovakia's most famous playwright. His plays often contained biting satire aimed at the Communists who ruled in Prague. But his writings were not the only reason for his increasing notoriety. He also became Czechoslovakia's foremost dissident and human rights champion. In 1977, Havel coauthored the Charter 77 Manifesto, which denounced Czechoslovakia's Communist rulers for failing to abide by Basket Three of the 1975 Helsinki Accords, in which all signatories promised to respect civil and political rights. For such acts of political defiance, Havel was jailed repeatedly, serving sentences that often included hard labor. Despite these punishments, he was not silenced.

In December 1989, after Czechoslovakia's Communist regime collapsed under the crushing weight of popular civilian discontent, Havel became president by popular consensus. His rise from prison to the presidency in 1989 was unprecedented. But then, no other public figure in Czechoslovakia could come

Václav Havel at Columbia University in November 2006; president of Czechoslovakia (1989–1993) and the Czech Republic (1993–2003). Havel led the revolution against Czechoslovakia's Communist regime in 1989 and was instantly elevated to the presidency by popular acclamation. A courageous playwright and lifelong human rights activist who had been persecuted and imprisoned for daring to dissent against tyranny, Havel in office was even more poplar abroad than at home. As president, he was content to exercise moral power through his words and ideas and, to the chagrin of critics and admirers alike, readily conceded political power to others. Renowned for his credo of "living in truth," Havel was, and remains, the conscience of his country and a highly respected world leader.

Dennis Van Tine /Landov

close to matching the moral authority Havel had accumulated during three decades of courageous citizen-leadership.

Havel remained in office for more than three years. Then, on the verge of Czechoslovakia's disintegration into two ethnic nation-states (the Czech Republic and Slovakia), he resigned. But he did not long absent himself from public life. On January 26, 1993—little more than six months after his resignation—the Czech parliament elected Havel to a five-year term as president of the Czech Republic.

Despite his prominent position, Havel did not always take an active role in governing his nation, yet he remained an important national figure. Although most Czechs distrusted and disavowed politicians, many respected Havel as the only living Czech leader who not only talked and wrote about "living in truth," but also practiced what he preached.

Martin Luther King Jr. (1929–1968)

An outstanding citizen-leader was the renowned civil rights champion Martin Luther King Jr. (1929–1968). From the moment he became president of the newly formed Southern Christian Leadership Conference in 1957, King's national prominence grew. He led sit-ins, marches, demonstrations, and rallies throughout the South, all aimed at ending racial segregation and overcoming racial discrimination in jobs and housing. Practicing nonviolent civil disobedience, protesters under King's leadership openly broke the law, which sanctioned segregated lunch counters, required parade permits, forced African Americans to sit at the back of buses, and so on, and then accepted punishment for their actions. King intended to stir the conscience of the nation by reaching legislators and judges and, in the end, the U.S. people. As he stated in his famous 1963 "Letter from Birmingham Jail":*

> I submit that an individual who breaks a law that conscience tells him is unjust, and willingly accepts the penalty by staying in jail to arouse the conscience of the community over its injustice, is in reality expressing the very highest respect for law.[28]

*King had gone to Birmingham, Alabama, to lead an economic boycott aimed at desegregating public facilities and was jailed for organizing an unlicensed parade.

King's hope was clear:

> We must see the need of having nonviolent gadflies to create the kind of tension in society that will help men to rise from the dark depths of prejudice and racism to the majestic heights of understanding and brotherhood.[29]

The influence of King and other African American civil rights leaders has been decisive. Although extremely controversial at the time, their courageous efforts proved crucial to the passage of the landmark 1964 Civil Rights Act, which banned discrimination in public accommodations and employment. Later, other civil rights legislation was passed, further ensuring equal treatment under the law for all citizens. In 1964, King was awarded the Nobel Peace Prize for his efforts. Four years later, at the age of 39, he was assassinated.

Rosa Parks (1913–2005)

Rosa Parks (1913–2005) stirred the conscience of a nation with a single act of courage. On December 1, 1955, she left work after spending a long day as a tailor's assistant at a department store in Montgomery, Alabama. Boarding a bus to go home, she found a seat. Soon, however, a white man who was standing demanded her seat. (Montgomery's customary practice required that all four blacks sitting in the same row with Rosa Parks would have to stand in order to allow one white man to sit because no black person was allowed to sit parallel with a white person.)[30] Parks stayed put:

> I was thinking that the only way to let them know I felt I was being mistreated was to do just what I did—resist the order. . . . I had not thought about it and I had taken no previous resolution until it happened, and then I simply decided that I would not get up. I was tired, but I was usually tired at the end of the day, and I was not feeling well, but then there had been many days when I had not felt well. I had felt for a long time, that if I was ever told to get up so a white person could sit, that I would refuse to do so.[31]

The bus driver had Parks arrested.

Many historians date the origin of the U.S. civil rights movement to the Montgomery Bus Boycott—a reaction to the arrest of Rosa Parks. Her simple but courageous act of defiance is remembered today as one of political valor that drew attention to racial injustice and led to a chain of events that eventually changed the nation forever.

Nelson Mandela (1918–2013)

Born in Transkei, South Africa, on July 18, 1918, Nelson Mandela (1918–2013) was the son of a tribal chief. He joined the African National Congress in 1944 and was engaged in resistance against the ruling National Party's apartheid policies after 1948. He went on trial for high treason in 1956 and was acquitted in 1961. Meanwhile, resistance to apartheid grew,

AP Images/Jim Mcknight

Rosa Parks in Montgomery, Alabama, in 1956, after the Supreme Court banned segregation in public transportation.

mainly against the new Pass Laws, which dictated where black people were allowed to live and work.

When the government banned the ANC in 1960, Mandela went underground. As one of the top leaders of the ANC, Mandela launched a campaign of economic sabotage and even advocated creation of a military wing within the ANC. He was arrested in 1962 and sentenced to five years' imprisonment with hard labor. Mandela and other ANC militants were brought to stand trial for plotting the violent overthrow of the government, and in June 1964, eight of the accused, including Mandela, were sentenced to life imprisonment. At his trial, he said: "I have cherished the ideal of a democratic and free society in which all persons live together in harmony and with equal opportunities. It is an ideal which I hope to live for and to achieve. But if needs be, it is an ideal for which I am prepared to die."

While in prison, Mandela became the symbol of the anti-apartheid movement. "In prison," he later confessed, "you come face to face with time. There is nothing more terrifying." And yet, for more than a quarter of a century, he refused to compromise with South Africa's white minority government. "Only free men can negotiate. Prisoners cannot enter into contracts."[32]

Mandela was finally released on February 11, 1990. In 1991, Mandela was elected president of the newly legalized ANC. He was awarded the Nobel Peace Prize in December 1993. Five months later, as a widely revered statesman who was jailed for twenty-seven years and yet managed to lead the anti-apartheid struggle, Mandela emerged to become the country's first black president when, for the first time in South Africa's history, all races voted in democratic elections. He retired from politics—and largely from public life—in 1999.

Every community and every country is profoundly affected by the quality of its political leadership. The 75-year-old Mandela, who was self-taught, widely trusted, and world renowned, led a peaceful political transition, ending the rule of the white supremacist government.

Wael Ghonim (b. 1980)

In the early days of the Egyptian uprising that ended the rule of dictator Hosni Mubarak at the beginning of 2011, Google executive and political activist Wael Ghonim was arrested and held in detention for eleven days. Ghonim quickly became a symbol of the anti-Mubarak movement and a national hero. Protest organizers gave speeches in Cairo's central Tahrir Square vowing they would not leave the square until Ghonim was freed, while the government-controlled media suggested that Ghonim's political activities made him a traitor to the nation.

Ghonim's role in organizing the January 25 protest movement is unclear, but there is no doubt that his use of an Internet-based social network—Facebook—to communicate with a vast social network of Egyptian activists in the months preceding the uprising played a key role. Part of a cadre of young activists in Egypt who set the stage for the massive demonstrations in Cairo, Ghonim wrote on his personal Facebook profile for friends, "I said one year ago that the Internet will change the political scene in Egypt and some Friends made fun of me:).” He posted this comment two days into the crisis that brought the Egyptian dictator down. The next day, January 28, Ghonim disappeared.

> Ghonim was one of four administrators running the first of the major Facebook pages that became a virtual headquarters for the protest movement, according to a collaborator in the political opposition, and also according to an Internet activist familiar with the situation. Ghonim also set up the official campaign website for opposition leader Mohamed ElBaradei and volunteered as a tech consultant for other opposition groups, according to Ziad Al-Alimi, a senior aide to Mr. ElBaradei.
>
> Online activists including Ghonim have played a central role in electronically sowing the seeds of the current protests. Ghonim joined ElBaradei's political campaign as a volunteer about a month before Mr. ElBaradei, winner of the 2005 Nobel Peace Prize and former head of the International Atomic Energy Agency, made a dramatic return to Egypt last February amid speculation he was seeking a wider political role. Ghonim's Facebook profile, which he updated often, lists Mr. ElBaradei as someone he admires along with Microsoft founder Bill Gates, billionaire investor Warren Buffett and Apple founder Steve Jobs.[33]

On March 2, 2011, Ghonim gave a ten-minute “TED” talk that was beamed to seventy locations around the world on closed-circuit television. He said that one reason the protestors succeeded in ousting Mubarak was because “we didn't understand politics.” Another: the Egyptian people were no longer paralyzed by fear. Why? Because, he said, they finally had a way to talk to each other (Google, Facebook, Twitter), and they discovered that they were not alone, that they were part of a community of people who desired freedom, and that they had the power to act on that desire.

One of the virtues of modern democracies is that citizenship is universal and leadership arises from the rank and file. Leadership can take many different forms—from the highest office to working at the local level. Exemplary leadership at the national level always has local consequences, but, as we have seen, it is also true that exemplary leadership on the local level can have national consequences. The quality of a nation reflects the quality of its leaders; in a democracy, where voters make choices, the quality of the nation's leaders reflects on its citizens too.

SUMMARY

We can classify political leaders who occupy government positions as statesmen, demagogues, or ordinary politicians. Citizen-leaders hold no official office but can exert significant political influence.

Exceptional leaders who display an overriding concern for the public good, superior leadership skills, and keen practical wisdom in times of crisis were long called statesmen; today this term is not considered politically correct in some quarters, so it has fallen into disuse. The lure of fame has been one of the motivating forces for many great leaders. Modern neglect of the concept of statecraft has led some observers to view it as a dying art.

Most prevalent in representative democracies are ordinary politicians. All elected officials must decide whether to exercise positive leadership or merely represent the views of their constituents. According to the delegate theory of democratic representation, politicians should act primarily as conduits for the expressed wishes of the electorate; the trustee theory, by contrast, stresses the importance of independent judgment in political office. Politicians who seek to combine these two concepts of representation are called *solons* in the text, in honor of the Roman statesman and lawgiver, Solon. The demagogue combines reckless personal ambition, unscrupulous methods, and charismatic appeal. Demagogues are most prevalent in democracies, and their fall is often as sudden and spectacular as their rise to power.

Citizen-leaders combine dedication to a cause, personal ability or magnetism, and opposition to governmental policy (or established practice). They inspire others and attract a sympathetic following, frequently on a worldwide scale. They exert a moral force generated by the power of the cause they personify.

KEY TERMS

statesman   358

demagogue   358

politician   358

citizen-leader   358

statecraft   360

delegate theory of
  representation   379

trustee theory of
  representation   380

REVIEW QUESTIONS

1. How do we classify political leaders? Explain the differences between the various categories.
2. Why is the study of political leadership an important aspect of the overall study of politics?
3. What accounts for the rarity of exemplary leadership?
4. Describe two competing theories of representation. Which one makes the most sense to you and why?
5. Is it fair to lump all politicians together? Do politicians generally have a good reputation? Can they be found all over the world or only in certain countries? Explain your answers.
6. What is a demagogue? Name some demagogues. What motivates them?
7. Does democracy have any natural defenses against demagoguery? If so, what are they?
8. What is the nature of exemplary leadership? Name four exemplary leaders and explain in detail what makes any one of them exemplary.

WEBSITES AND READINGS

Websites

For information on political leaders, past and present, enter the name of the leader as the keyword in any browser or search engine. A search using "Winston Churchill" as the keyword, for example, returned the following URL, which includes sspeeches, famous quotes, photographs, and a links page: http://www.winstonchurchill.org/

Notable/Notorious Twentieth-Century Leaders: www.time.com/time/time100/leaders/index.html

Harvard's Center for Public Leadership: http://www.centerforpublicleadership.org/

World Political Leaders: http://zarate.eu/countries.htm

Forbes **Qualities of a Great Leader:** http://www.forbes.com/sites/tanyaprive/2012/12/19/top-10-qualities-that-make-a-great-leader/

Readings

Adair, Douglass. "Fame and the Founding Fathers." In *Fame and the Founding Fathers: Essays by Douglass Adair*. New York: Norton, 1974. Adair's essay on the relationship between fame and statecraft in the founding of the United States is a classic.

Alexander, Robert J. *Rómulo Betancourt and the Transformation of Venezuela*. New Brunswick, NJ: Transaction Books, 1982. An admiring biography of Venezuela's leading democratic statesman.

Burns, James Macgregor. *Leadership*. New York: HarperCollins, 1982. An exhaustive study of all facets of the leadership phenomenon.

Frisch, Morton, and Richard Stevens, ed. *American Political Thought: The Philosophic Dimension of American Statesmanship*, 2nd ed. Itasca, IL: Peacock, 1983. A collection of essays on U.S. statesmen that features a brief, but outstanding, introduction.

Gardner, Howard E., and Emma Laskin (contributor). *Leading Minds: An Anatomy of Leadership*. New York: Basic Books, 2011. The author is a leading scholar (no pun intended) in the field of leadership.

Garrow, David J. *Bearing the Cross: Martin Luther King, Jr., and the Southern Christian Leadership Conference, 1955–1968*. New York: Random House, 1988. An in-depth examination of the life and accomplishments of America's greatest twentieth-century citizen-leader.

Gilbert, Martin. *Churchill: A Life*. New York: Henry Holt, 1991. A comprehensive one-volume biography written by his foremost biographer.

Havel, Vaclav. *The Art of the Impossible: Politics as Morality in Practice*. New York: Knopf, 1997. A collection of essays on politics, morality, and leadership by a brilliant Czech playwright and the former president who led the popular uprising that ended Communist rule in the Czechoslovakia.

Jaffa, Harry. *Crises of the House Divided: An Interpretation of the Issue*. Chicago: University of Chicago Press, 1982. Documents the political wisdom that characterized Abraham Lincoln's statecraft.

Kouzes, James M., and Barry Z. Posner. *A Leader's Legacy*. San Francisco, CA: Jossey-Bass, 2006. One of many recent books on the essence and importance of leadership. Many such books are motivational in nature, and most are highly perishable. This one is unusually insightful and, not surprisingly, gets rave reviews.

_____ *The Leadership Challenge,* 4th ed. San Francisco, CA: Jossey-Bass, 2008. A book about ordinary people achieving "individual leadership standards of excellence."

Long, Huey. *My First Days in the White House.* New York: Da Capo Press, 1972. A fanciful and amusing piece of propaganda written by one of America's foremost demagogues.

Meer, Fatima. *Higher Than Hope: The Authorized Biography of Nelson Mandela.* New York: HarperCollins, 1991. A detailed account of the life of a former political revolutionary who has become one of the world's most distinguished leaders.

Pitkin, Hannah, ed. *Representation.* New York: Atherton Press, 1969. A rich collection of essays with a straightforward and enlightening introduction by the editor.

Tucker, Robert C. *Politics as Leadership.* Columbia: University of Missouri Press, 1995. A thought-provoking essay on politics in the best sense of the word and a reminder that beneath the sordid realities of everyday politics lie the sublime possibilities that leadership alone can uncover.

White, Richard D., Jr. *Kingfish: The Reign of Huey P. Long.* New York: Random House, 2006. The most recent biography of a political figure with a genius for populist politics and a demagogic streak. He continues to fascinate students of American politics more than seven decades after his untimely exit.

Wicker, Tom. *Shooting Star: The Brief Arc of Joe McCarthy.* New York: Harcourt, 2006. Joe McCarthy is one of America's legendary demagogues, and Wicker is a first-rate storyteller. Good story. Good writer. Result: a real page-turner.

Wildavsky, Aaron. *The Nursing Father: Moses as a Political Leader.* Tuscaloosa: University of Alabama Press, 1984. A thoughtful analysis of political leadership in a biblical context.

Williams, T. Harry. *Huey Long.* New York: Alfred A. Knopf and Vintage Books, 1981. Still the most authoritative biography of Huey Long available.

CHAPTER 13

Issues in Public Policy
Politics, Principles, Priorities, and Practices

Learning Objectives

1 Elaborate on the four "P's" that frame the study of public policy in this chapter.

2 Discuss security as a policy priority and judge where it ranks relative to other priorities.

3 Discuss perennial questions and key issues affecting prosperity and the U.S. economy.

4 Elaborate on the importance of the First Amendment in the U.S. Constitution.

5 Identify and discuss current policy issues related to the pursuit of liberty in the United States.

6 Explain the need for the Fourteenth Amendment even though a Bill of Rights already existed.

7 Explain the role of "due process" and "equal protection" in reshaping U.S. race relations.

The law locks up the man or woman
Who steals the goose from off the common
But leaves the greater villain loose
Who steals the common from off the goose.

—Seventeenth-century poem (author unknown)

In Chapter 2, we identified five core values: security, prosperity, equality, liberty, and justice. Translating values into law and public policy is the essence of politics. In this chapter, four words all beginning with the letter "P" provide the analytical framework for evaluating just how—and how effectively—our own government processes collective values into corrective policies.

In democratic societies, dialogue and debates over public policy are an integral part of the process. The quality of the process is critical to the quality of product. When the tenor and tone of politics are debased by politicians and pundits with personal agendas, the public interest is undermined and democracy itself is placed in jeopardy.

Although this chapter focuses on contemporary issues in the United States, many of the same problems arise in other democracies as well. Some are part of a pattern—a kind of postmodern syndrome—such as high-consumption, affluent Western societies. Others, such as wildlife conservation, climate change, and pandemics, are universal. Still others are uniquely American—the Senate filibuster, race relations, gerrymandering, the length and cost of political campaigns, and issues surrounding health care and health insurance, for example. Problems facing many non-Western countries (such as overpopulation, hunger, and illiteracy) are discussed in Chapter 9.

THE PURSUIT OF SECURITY

Every independent state seeks to safeguard the security of its population and territory. The famous political philosopher Thomas Hobbes (1588–1679) argued that safety from harm constituted the chief justification for a government's existence. For Aristotle, too, the first goal of political life was the protection of life itself.[1]

Security from Foreign Enemies

In the aftermath of World War II, the high priority Washington gave to **national security** was (and still is) reflected in staggering levels of defense spending. Today, the United States accounts for roughly half of world arms expenditures; China, now America's chief rival for world leadership, follows at less than 10% (see Figure 13.1). Nearly two decades after the Cold War has ended, the United States still spends more on arms than the next fourteen countries combined.

From 1945 to 1991, foreign policy debate in the United States focused on the Soviet threat. Portraying the Soviet Union as an expansionist power bent on world domination, politicians of both major parties made support for ever-expanding arms expenditures into a virtual loyalty test. Today, the U.S. Department of Defense maintains hundreds of military bases overseas, plus thousands

national security
Protection of a country from external and internal enemies.

FIGURE 13.1   Global Distribution of Military Expenditures in 2012. The United States alone accounts for roughly 40% of the world's total military spending every year. By comparison, Europe spends less than half as much as the United States and a mere fifth of global military outlays. Russia, the world's other superpower only two decades ago, now spends one-tenth as much as the United States on defense and only one-fourth as much as the European Union.* Globally, military spending has leveled off in recent years after an annual average increase of 4.5% between 2001 and 2009. The United States, the UK, France, Germany, India, and Brazil cut military budgets in 2011, but arms expenditures rose markedly in China and Russia. SOURCE: Stockholm International Peace Research Institute (SIPRI) Military Expenditure Database, 2013, http://www.globalissues.org/article/75/world-military-spending.

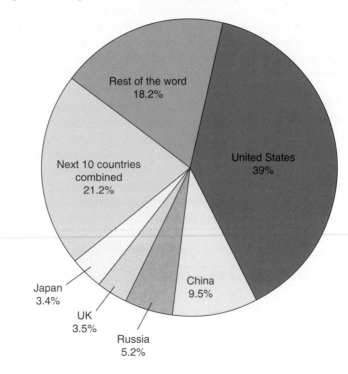

of military bases and facilities in the United States and its territories. In 2010, there were more than 1.4 million men and women in uniform. The Pentagon's natural constituents and biggest stakeholders are defense contractors who provide a vast array of arms and services to the military and profit from budget-busting military outlays.

In his 1961 farewell address to the nation, President Dwight D. Eisenhower, one of the most celebrated generals in U.S. history, warned of a growing "military-industrial complex":

> In the councils of government, we must guard against the acquisition of unwarranted influence, whether sought or unsought, by the military-industrial complex. The potential for the disastrous rise of misplaced power exists and will persist.

*For all practical purposes, Europe minus Russia.

We must never let the weight of this combination endanger our liberties or democratic processes. We should take nothing for granted. Only an alert and knowledgeable citizenry can compel the proper meshing of the huge industrial and military machinery of defense with our peaceful methods and goals, so that security and liberty may prosper together.[2]

President Eisenhower echoed James Madison who way back in 1795 observed:

Of all the enemies to public liberty war is, perhaps, the most to be dreaded because it comprises and develops the germ of every other. War is the parent of armies; from these proceed debts and taxes . . . known instruments for bringing the many under the domination of the few. . . . No nation could preserve its freedom in the midst of continual warfare.[3]

With the collapse of the Soviet Union, the justification for Cold War levels of defense spending suddenly evaporated. President George H. W. Bush promised a "peace dividend" in the early 1990s.*

Defense budgets in the mid-1990s were a reflection of the "peace dividend" (scaled-down military commitments) when the Cold War ended in 1989–1991 (see Figure 13.2). Thus, from the Cold War peak in 1986, Pentagon personnel—active, reserve, and civilian—declined by almost 20%. Active-duty military also underwent a 20% reduction, from 4.4 million to 3.5 million. But these figures are misleading. The Clinton administration contracted out to the private sector many services previously performed in-house (within the federal government); these outsourced services included military combat roles that in the past had been kept strictly under the executive branch's control.[4]

This practice was continued and extended under the Bush administration following the terrorist attacks of September 11, 2001. Congress and the country were back in the Cold War groove, ready to spend "whatever it takes" to make the world safe for democracy. Gone was the euphoria of the 1990s. Gone, too, was the illusion of invulnerability. *They* (international terrorists) had attacked *us* in our own front yard.

Security from Enemies Within

This new climate of fear gave rise to a homeland security state similar to the national security state that came into being after World War II. Just as the National Security Act of 1947 had restructured the federal government to meet the perceived threat of Communism, the USA Patriot Act of 2001 (officially the Uniting and Strengthening America by Providing Appropriate Tools Required to Intercept and Obstruct Terrorism Act) restructured the machinery of the state to fight international terrorism (see "Ideas and Politics").

September 11, 2001, placed a premium on the role of government in protecting the lives and property of U.S. citizens from the enemies amongst us. But just how far does the Constitution allow the government to go?[5] Is terrorism a crime or an act of war? Are terrorists covered under the Geneva Convention (see Chapter 17)

*However, a behind-the-scenes group of conservative hard-liners, the so-called neocons, remained adamantly opposed to big defense cuts in the 1990s. When George W. Bush ran for president in 2000, members of this group, calling themselves the "Vulcans," served as Bush's team of foreign policy advisors.

FIGURE 13.2   Annual U.S. Military Budgets: The 9/11 Effect. In 2004, total military spending in the United States was about $534 billion, including $87 billion for military operations in Iraq and Afghanistan passed by Congress and other arms-related expenditures. In that year "national security"—including the portion of the national debt attributable to past defense budgets, totaled more than $700 billion. In 2006, military spending rose to $626 billion; total spending for national security past, present, and future totaled about $800 billion. In 2008, defense spending alone climbed to $710 billion (an increase of 25% since 2004), and dropped to $612 billion in 2012. Even so, in 2013-2014, the United States spent over four times more than China, the world's second biggest military spender.

SOURCE: The author wishes to thank G. Ross Stephens, Professor emeritus at the University of Missouri–Kansas City for supplying much of the information shown in this graph. Most of the data are based on official U.S. budget reports; some are taken from the *Stockholm International Peace Research (SIPRI) Yearbook 2012.*

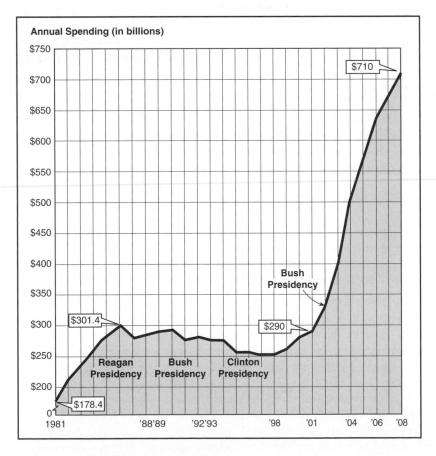

on the humane treatment of captured enemy combatants or "POWs" (prisoners of war)? Is the use of torture to extract information ever not a crime?

Crime and Punishment There is little agreement about what causes crime, what society ought to do about it, and whether some crimes ought to be

WAR ON TERROR OR WAR ON THE CONSTITUTION?

The USA Patriot Act, passed by Congress in response to the September 11, 2001, attacks, was signed into law by President George W. Bush on October 26, 2001. In May 2011 and to the dismay of his liberal base, President Obama extended several key provisions of this act due to expire. Critics contend it severely erodes privacy rights long upheld by the U.S. Supreme Court, for the following reasons:

- **It expands the power of the federal government to conduct surveillance of U.S. citizens**. The government can monitor individual Web-surfing records, use wiretaps to monitor phone calls of persons "proximate" to the primary person being tapped, access Internet service provider records, and investigate anyone who participates in a political protest.
- **It is not limited to terrorism**. The government can add samples to DNA databases for anyone convicted of "any crime of violence." Wiretaps are now allowed for suspected violators of the Computer Fraud and Abuse Act, offering possibilities for government spying on any computer user.
- **Intelligence agencies can more easily spy on citizens**. Domestic eavesdropping powers under the existing Foreign Intelligence Surveillance Act (FISA) are broadened. The Patriot Act partially repeals legislation enacted in the 1970s that prohibited pervasive surveillance of citizens by U.S. agencies created to gather foreign intelligence.
- **It reduces government accountability**. The balance between the need for secrecy in government and the need for transparency (the public's right to know what the government is doing) is shifted sharply in favor of secrecy.
- **It authorizes the use of sneak-and-peek search warrants**. Such warrants authorize

law-enforcement officers to enter private premises without the occupant's permission or knowledge and without informing the occupant that such a search was conducted. These warrants can be used against anyone suspected of a federal crime, including a misdemeanor.

Hence the question: Is the USA Patriot Act a declaration of war on terror or on the Constitution? Defenders say it's the former; critics—liberals and conservatives alike—fear it's the latter. The American Civil Liberties Union (ACLU), the American Conservative Union, Americans for Tax Reform, and other interest groups on both the right and the left have joined forces to push for a major overhaul of federal laws that allow the NSA and the FBI to engage in warrantless domestic spying operations. The White House and Congress have turned a deaf ear.

In January 2012, journalist Chris Hedges and six other plaintiffs sued President Obama over Section 1021(b)(2) of the National Defense Authorization Act (NDAA), which authorizes the military to detain U.S. citizens indefinitely without due process. In September 2012, a federal district judge ruled for the plaintiffs and issued a permanent injunction—in effect, declaring the law unconstitutional—but an appeals court overturned the lower court ruling on October 3, 2012.

Section 215 of the Patriot Act gives the FBI power to order any person or entity to turn over "any tangible things," so long as the order is pursuant to "an authorized investigation . . . to protect against international terrorism or clandestine intelligence activities." According to the ACLU, Section 215 "vastly expands the FBI's power to spy on ordinary people living in the United States." Ordinary people are law-abiding citizens, so who cares? Think about it.

(Hint: Peruse the Bill of Rights. See if you can find anything—any single amendment—that Section 215 contravenes.)

IDEAS AND POLITICS

DEFINING CRIME DOWN

Why has the United States accepted such a high level of crime? The late Daniel Patrick Moynihan (1927–2001), a former U.S. senator and noted scholar, suggested one intriguing answer in the controversial article "Defining Deviancy Down: How We've Become Accustomed to Alarming Levels of Crime and Destructive Behavior."* Faced with a high crime rate, Moynihan contended, U.S. citizens have denied its importance by redefining (defining down) what they consider to be normal. Years ago, a high crime rate was understood to be a severe social pathology; now it has become accepted as a normal condition of society about which little can be done.

Moynihan supplied a striking example. On February 14, 1929, four gangsters gunned down seven rivals in the infamous St. Valentine's Day Massacre. Moynihan observed that the nation was shocked, the event became a legend meriting two entries in the *World Book Encyclopedia*, and the "massacre" inspired an amendment to the Constitution that ended Prohibition (a policy thought to have caused much gang violence).

Moynihan noted that with illegal drug trafficking this form of violence has returned, but "at a level that induces denial." Inured, U.S. adults now accept violence they once rejected as deviant and unacceptable. Sadly, concluded Moynihan, "Los Angeles has the equivalent of a St. Valentine's Day Massacre every weekend."

Beginning in the 1960s, the rate of incarceration in the United States rose sharply for four decades. The United States currently has the largest prison population in the world. Young black males constitute the largest group by gender, age, and race or ethnicity. The likelihood of an African American male going to state or federal prison in his lifetime is over 30%, compared to about 5% for while males. How society defines crime is to some extent political. How many business and banking executives ever go to jail? Is it because rich old white men never break any laws? Think about it.

(Hint: Find out what types of crimes most African American males in prison have committed; ask yourself whether the laws are uniformly enforced or consistent across the length and breadth of the country. Consider whether some laws are counterproductive or if alternatives to incarcerating people for certain types of law violations are available.)

*American Scholar, Winter 1993.

The end of Prohibition.

The late Daniel Patrick Moynihan (1927–2001), U.S. senator and noted scholar.

decriminalized (the buying and selling or mere possession of marijuana, for example). What is not in dispute is that the long-term crime rate in the United States has risen steadily over the past fifty years (see "Ideas and Politics"). Why?

According to some experts, crime is a social phenomenon, a reflection of personal frustration or alienation caused by poverty and neglect, racial discrimination, and unequal economic opportunity. Others stress the decline of the traditional family and community. Still others blame popular culture and the mass media.[6]

Some social critics would reduce crime by redefining it—for example, by decriminalizing prostitution. Advocates of this approach say it's illogical and unjust to punish "victimless" crimes. In this view, nobody is harmed when adults freely choose to engage in prostitution, for example. In 2003, the U.S. Supreme Court ruled state sodomy laws unconstitutional and unenforceable (*Lawrence v. Texas*), a sign of the times and a deepening "values divide" along fault lines of religion, region, and sexual orientation.

Many violent crimes in the United States are drug-related.[7] The problem may be clear, but the solution is not. Drug addicts sometimes rob and steal to support a habit made artificially expensive by state action rather than market forces. Legalize drugs, some argue, and the price will drop dramatically, drug trafficking will become less profitable, and drug-related crime will decrease. That's what happened when the sale of alcohol was legalized. The Eighteenth Amendment and Volstead Act established nationwide Prohibition (making the manufacture, sale, transport, import, or export of alcoholic beverages a crime), which led to the rise of the mafia in the 1920s and 1930s. In December 1933, the Eighteenth Amendment was repealed, but by that time gangsters like Al "Scarface" Capone, Charles "Lucky" Luciano, and John Dillinger had written new pages in the history of organized crime in Chicago and other major cities.

Of course, times have change. Alcohol is legal everywhere now, but it is regulated in various ways in the fifty states. Marijuana, however, is a different story.

Why Not Pot?

Opponents fear that legalizing marijuana would increase the number of addicts and corrode the moral standards of the community. Perhaps, but the historical evidence and recent experience demonstrate clearly that criminalizing a popular social activity such as drinking or smoking pot creates a highly lucrative, unregulated black market where violence-prone thugs often thrive and places a heavy burden on law enforcement and the penal system without solving the problem.

Between 1980 and the mid-1990s, the U.S. prison population more than tripled, due in large part to a nationwide crackdown on illegal drugs, and rose from 1.1 million in 1995 to 1.6 million in 2010. Thereafter, it dropped for three years straight to about 1.57 million in 2012.

The United States had the world's highest rate of imprisonment, with 743 persons per 100,000 incarcerated in 2011-2012. With only 4.5% of world population, the United States accounts for 23% of all prison inmates. California, Texas, and Florida lead the states in the rate of imprisonment, but the federal government is by far the nation's largest jailer.

Drug laws and drug-related crimes account for a major share of all the criminal trials and convictions in the United States. About half of all inmates in federal prisons are there for drug-related crimes. The social and economic costs of this zero-tolerance policy have been very high, by any measure, but have failed to produce the promised results.

Decriminalization of drugs and prostitution is extremely controversial in the United States, but the Netherlands has already done it. In the capital city of Amsterdam, "soft drugs" (including marijuana) and prostitution are allowed, but only in restricted areas under no-nonsense police supervision and control. Prostitutes are required to have frequent medical checkups, and social problems linked to illegal drug trafficking have been alleviated.

But the times are changing. Colorado began licensing medical marijuana dispensaries in 2010; a year later there were more than four hundred marijuana businesses in Denver alone. In 2012, voters in Colorado, Washington, and Oregon were given the chance to legalize marijuana for recreational use by adults. Polls showed that Colorado's Amendment 64 legalizing recreational marijuana use for adults age 21 and older enjoyed the support of more than 60% of the voters. Why? One of the most compelling arguments for many voters is one most advocates overlook: tax revenue. If it's legal and transactions take place in the open, marijuana (like liquor and gasoline) can be taxed. Voters in Colorado and Washington approved the ballot initiative, but it failed by a large margin (went up in smoke?) in Oregon. Colorado collected $60 million in marijuana taxes and licensing fees in 2014, not to mention the estimated $145 million it did not spend fighting illegal use of marijuana.

Guns "R" Us

In January 2011, a tragic shooting in a shopping mall in Tucson, Arizona, refocused national attention on the problem of gun control. The attack by a 22-year-old killer brandishing a 9mm Glock pistol with a 33-round magazine resulted in the death of six people, including a 9-year-old girl, and left Congresswoman Gabrielle Giffords in critical condition with a gunshot wound to the head at point blank range. In July 2012, at a midnight showing of Batman 3 (*The Dark Knight Rises*) in Aurora, Colorado, a lone gunman set off tear gas grenades and sprayed the theater with gunfire, killing twelve movie-goers and wounding fifty-eight, in the bloodiest mass shooting in U.S. history. Four months later, in December 2012, another mass shooting occurred, this time at an elementary school in Newtown, Connecticut. The shooter killed twenty children and six adults and then committed suicide.

Since the Newtown massacre, some 1,500 state gun bills have been introduced across the country, 178 passed at least one chamber of a state legislature, and 109 have become law. Nearly two-thirds of the new laws (70) actually *ease* restrictions and expand the rights of gun owners. With few exceptions, these laws were passed in states where the Republican Party controls the legislature and governorship. Most of the 39 bills that tighten regulations were passed in states where Democrats are firmly in control.[7]

In the run-up to the November 2012 election, the presidential candidates of the two major parties, incumbent Obama and the challenger Romney, avoided

December 14, 2012	Sandy Hook Elementary School in Newtown, Connecticut: 20 children, 6 adults dead, plus gunman Adam Lanza.
July 20, 2012	Movie theatre in Aurora, Colorado: 12 movie-goers killed and 58 injured by gunman James Holmes.
January 8, 2011	Shopping mall in Tucson, Arizona: 6 killed and 14 wounded, including Congresswomen Gabrielle Giffords who was critically injured with a gunshot wound to the head by gunman Jared Lee Loughner.
April 3, 2009	Immigration services center in Binghamton, New York: 13 dead plus gunman Jiverly Wong.
November 5, 2009	Soldier Readiness Processing Center at Fort Hood, Texas: 13 killed by Nidal Malik Hasan.
April 16, 2008	Virginia Tech campus, Blacksburg, Virginia: 32 dead plus gunman Seung Hui Cho.
April 20, 1999	Columbine High School in Littleton, Colorado: 13 dead plus gunmen, students Eric Harris and Dylan Klebold.
October 16, 1991	Luby's Cafeteria in Killeen, Texas: 23 dead plus gunman George Hennard.
August 20, 1986	Post office in Edmond, Oklahoma: 14 dead plus gunman Patrick Sherrill.
July 18, 1984	McDonald's restaurant in San Ysidro, California: 21 dead plus gunman James Oliver Huberty.
August 1, 1966	University of Texas at Austin: 16 dead plus gunman Charles Whitman.
September 6, 1946	Camden, New Jersey: 13 killed by Howard Unruh.

FIGURE 13.3   The Terrorists Within: Mass shootings in the United States, 1946–2012.

the issue—one indication of the extent to which "gun control" has become a litmus test of freedom in the eyes of many Americans. After the election, however, President Obama came out strongly in favor of an assault weapons ban—in other words "gun control." Despite a rising commentariate demanding action and opinion polls showing a public solidly in favor of restricting the sale of assault weapons and high-capacity magazines (see Figure 13.3), Congress dithered, holding hearings and making speeches but putting off any definitive changes in the gun laws that would antagonize constituents or risk incurring the wrath of the NRA.

The United States is the only postindustrial society in which private ownership of handguns is considered normal and private arsenals are not unusual.

TABLE 13.1   Privately Owned Guns Per Capita in Selected Countries

Country	%	Rank
United States	90	1
Switzerland	46	4
Saudi Arabia	35	6
Sweden	32	9
France	31	11
Canada	31	12
Germany	30	14
New Zealand	23	22
Czech Republic	16	38
South Korea	1.1	149
Japan	0.6	164

Accurate data of this kind is difficult to obtain and even more difficult to verify; data on gun ownership in many non-Western developing countries is simply not available.

SOURCE: Small Arms Survey 2007, Graduate Institute of International and Development Studies, Geneva, Switzerland; http://www.smallarmssurvey.org/publications/by-type/yearbook/small-arms-survey-2007.html.

In the United States, the right to bear arms is guaranteed by the Second Amendment. Some 40% of households in the United States report having a gun (or guns), compared with only 4.7% in the United Kingdom, and a mere 2% in the Netherlands. Other countries vary considerably. Among the countries that make these figures publicly available, not one comes close to U.S. levels. (See Table 13.1.) Current estimates put the number of private firearms in the United States at three million or close to 90 guns per 100 residents.

Changing gun laws to restrict access is controversial. Gun control activists argue that guns contribute to violent crime and point out that the murder rate in the United States is the highest in the Western world. Moreover, they argue, the Second Amendment says nothing about the right of individuals to own semi-automatic weapons with large-capacity magazines (such weapons did not exist when the Constitution and Bill of Rights were drafted). Nor does say anything about the right of individual to bear arms of any kind. Rather, it says "a well-regulated militia being necessary to the security of a free state, the right of the people to keep and bear arms shall not be infringed." Until the Reagan Revolution of 1980s, it was generally understood that the Second Amendment protected the right of state militias, not individuals, to bear arms. Then Chief Justice Warren Burger scoffed at this interpretation, calling it "a fraud."

Opponents of gun control, led by the National Rifle Association, began to push hard for the "individual-rights" doctrine in the late 1970s. Gun enthusiasts and the NRA point out that most gun owners have never committed a crime; that most private firearms are used for hunting, recreational shooting, and home defense; and that the non-gun murder rate in the United States is higher than the total murder rate in many European countries.

But facts are stubborn and by the numbers, with the sole exception of Turkey, the United States is by far the most violent major OECD* country, with a homicide rate much higher than most societies at a comparable stage of political-economic development. The gun culture in the United States not only correlates positively with a high homicide rate but also correlates with an incarceration rate about seven times higher than the median rate for other OECD countries.

Social Security

When Americans think of social security, they think of the mandatory federal pension program established in 1935: the concept of social security is narrowly defined and limited. Contrastingly, Europeans take it for granted that the state has an obligation to provide a cradle-to-the-grave social safety net for all its citizens. Oddly enough, voters and taxpayers in the United States have long been staunchly opposed to a European-style "welfare state" or anything that smacks of "socialism."

What is the state's proper role in helping members of society in need? Food stamps, farm subsidies, pensions, health and unemployment benefits, and student aid are all forms of public assistance. In general, Americans disdain "welfare" (defined as any subsidies or benefits for which they themselves are not eligible) on the grounds that "giveaway" programs reward lazy people. Welfare reform was a big issue in the 1990s, when the federal government gave states more authority (and flexibility) to require welfare recipients to perform public service (called "workfare").

Social Security and Medicare are by far the biggest and most expensive public assistance programs in the United States. These are *compulsory* insurance programs, however, not "welfare." Thus, U.S. workers are required by law to pay into the Social Security pension fund until they retire (normally around age 65). Payouts from the fund are called **entitlements**, not to be confused with subsidies— government payments to a particular industry or sector (agriculture, for example) deemed vital to the economy. So-called entitlements are politically sensitive, not least because senior citizens typically turn out to vote in large numbers.

In the 2012 election, entitlements were at the center of a bitter political debate over how to cut deficit-spending and balance the federal budget. Republicans insisted it be done by cutting social spending (Social Security, Medicare, and Medicaid); Democrats wanted to extend the Bush tax cuts for households making less than $250,000. So vitriolic was the fight that in the weeks after the election Republican leaders in Congress vowed to let the country go over a "fiscal cliff" (triggering automatic tax hikes and across-the-board spending cuts of 10%) if President Obama did not back down.

The Social Security Administration made monthly remittances totaling $863 billion to over 59 million beneficiaries in 2014. Social Security, Medicare,

entitlements Federal- and state-provided benefits in the United States such as Social Security and Medicare funded by mandatory tax contributions; such benefits become a right, rather than a privilege, in the public mind because recipients typically pay into the system for many years before they are eligible to take anything out.

*OECD is the acronym for the Organization for Economic Cooperation and Development, which comprises thirty-four of the world's wealthiest countries.

and Medicaid programs have grown dramatically in recent decades and are projected to rise even faster in the future. Social Security and Medicare distributions (payments to beneficiaries) totaled more than $1.5 trillion, accounting for 46% of the federal budget, in 2013.[8] (Medicare costs rose sharply after Congress approved a prescription drug benefit in 2003.)

Social Security and Medicare expenditures are rising faster than projected revenues; at present depletion rates and without changes, the Social Security trust fund will be empty by 2033. One reason is that U.S. adults are living longer, making the programs more expensive. An even bigger reason is the large number of people born in the years immediately following World War II (the "baby boomers") who have now reached retirement age and are eligible to draw monthly benefits.

Medicare has been hit hard by the demographic tidal wave as well as by escalating health care costs. When it was established in 1965, there were 5.5 people paying money into Medicare for each recipient drawing money out. Since then, the ratio has dropped to about 3 to 1 and is still falling. Since 1980, Medicare has been the fastest-growing federal program. At President George W. Bush's urging, Congress passed a controversial law in 2003 adding a prescription drug plan to Medicare at a projected long-term cost of as much as $8 trillion.[9] According to current projections, Medicare will run short of funds in as early as 2030.

What happened to the Social Security trust fund? When the federal government spends more than it raises in taxes and other revenues, it borrows money to cover the shortfall. Since the 1980s, the Treasury has quietly "borrowed" from the Social Security trust fund. This transaction is not reflected in the official federal budget balance sheet (these borrowings totaled $2.7 trillion in 2011). Thus, using standard accounting rules, the real deficit in 2005, for example, was $760 billion—more than double the official figure of $318 billion.[10]

The use of Social Security funds to offset the deficit dates back to the start of the Reagan era in the early 1980s. In 1983, Congress "voted to raise Social Security taxes, changing it from a pay-as-you-go system to one in which people were required to pay 50 percent more than the retirement and disability program's immediate costs, to build a trust fund to pay benefits more than three decades into the future."[11]

So far, partisan politics in the nation's Capitol have thwarted all efforts to place Medicare and Medicaid on solid, long-term financial footing as well. Doing so will necessitate unpopular changes: later retirement, less generous cost-of-living adjustments, and payroll tax increases. Not doing so will make it impossible to deal with the chronic federal deficit and risk a Greek-style debt crisis that would have disastrous consequences for the United States and the global economy.[12]

Security and the Environment

Hazards caused by humans can also endanger the health and safety of the public. Mandatory clean air standards, environmental impact statements, increasingly stringent waste disposal requirements, and vigorous recycling efforts all seek to protect the environment. Most scientists now agree global warming is

iStockphoto.com/Barnaby Chambers

China and India are the two most populous countries and two of the fast-growing economies in the world. As such, they are the two leading examples of Asia's rapid rise in the global economy. But the price of progress in an overpopulated world comes very high. It creates massive problems of its own, which can easily overwhelm the resources and capabilities of governments. Here, in one of China's many burgeoning cities with millions of migrants from poor rural areas, pedestrians wear masks in thick smog that makes breathing a health hazard.

a major threat to the security of the planet (and therefore to the life-forms that inhabit it) in the coming century. Greenhouse gas (GHG) emissions, mainly from automobiles and coal-fired power plants, trap heat in the earth's atmosphere, causing climate change. The likely consequences, say the experts, are that glaciers will continue to melt at an accelerating rate, sea levels will rise, and ocean currents will be altered and degraded.

The European Union has adopted an **Emission Trading Scheme (ETS)** as part of a larger set of policy goals aimed at significantly reducing Europe's "carbon footprint" by 2020. In one of his first acts as president, George W. Bush announced that he was taking the United States out of the **Kyoto Protocol** (see "Landmarks in History"), which had been signed by his predecessor, Bill Clinton. The Bush White House favored corporate oil and energy interests over the environment and was generally at odds with the green movement, but the Obama administration has pledged cooperation with the global community to combat climate change.

Critics argue rightly that the United States alone cannot make a dent in the problem; unless China, India, and other Third World countries take action to cut GHG emissions, there is not much the United States can do to curb global warming. Advocates of **sustainable growth** point out that the United States ranks first in the world in total volume of GHG emissions. However, China and India both outrank the United States in emissions intensities (metric tons of carbon equivalent per million dollars of economic output), and energy-related carbon emissions increased not only in the United States but also in six of the nine biggest polluting countries in recent decades.[13] One sign of the growing alarm over the dangers posed by global warming: in 2005, researchers at Yale and Columbia universities, in collaboration with the World Economic Forum and the European Union, published an Environmental Sustainability Index that

Emission Trading Scheme (ETS)
In the European Union, part of an antipollution drive aimed at significantly reducing Europe's carbon footprint by 2020 by assigning carbon-emission allowances to industries and factories and creating a carbon exchange, or a market where "clean" companies (ones that do not use their full allowances) can sell the credits they accumulate by not polluting to "dirty" companies (ones that exceed their allowances).

LANDMARKS IN HISTORY

THE KYOTO PROTOCOL AND CLIMATE CHANGE

The Kyoto Protocol is an addendum to the UN Framework Convention on Climate Change (UNFCCC). Countries that ratify this protocol agree to cut emissions of carbon dioxide and five other greenhouse gases or to engage in emissions trading if they exceed a certain cap. The protocol, which went into effect in 2005, now covers some 160 countries and more than 55% of GHG emissions worldwide. The United States has signed, but not ratified, the agreement. After Australia embraced it toward the end of 2007, the United States was more isolated than ever. Upon taking office in 2009, President Obama pledged U.S. support for global efforts to curb climate change, but his critics say he has waffled on the issue and relegated it to the back burner.

Under Kyoto, developed countries are obligated to reduce GHG emissions to an average of 5% below 1990 levels by 2008–2012. For many countries, including EU member-states, meeting this goal means cutting to roughly 15% below 2008 GHG emissions levels. The Kyoto caps expire in 2013.

Parties to the UNFCCC agreed to a set of "common but differentiated responsibilities." The largest share of GHG emissions has originated in developed countries, and per capita emissions in developing countries were relatively low in the 1990s (and still are). China, India, and other developing countries were exempted from the Kyoto Protocol caps because, at least until recently, they have not been major contributors to GHG emissions nor, therefore, to past and present climate change. But critics of Kyoto argue that climate change is, above all, a future threat, and that developing countries—especially China and India—will be major contributors in the twenty-first century. In addition, unless developing countries are brought into the global warming tent, polluting industries in developed countries will simply move to the Third World, resulting in little or no net reduction in carbon pollution.

As a presidential candidate in 2008, Barack Obama pledged to renew U.S. leadership in the fight against global warming. But the issue of climate change in was derailed by the global banking crisis after 2008. In the 2012 presidential debates, climate change did not get so much as a nod from either candidate.

Ironically, the devastating impact of Hurricane Sandy put climate change back on the national agenda just days before the election. But in his election-night victory speech, President Obama said his second-term goals were "reducing our deficit, reforming our tax code, fixing our immigration system, freeing ourselves from foreign oil." Climate change was mentioned only in a passing reference to "the destructive power of a warming planet." Having still not ratified the Kyoto treaty, the United States is the only holdout among the world's major countries.

ranked countries using a range of scientific indicators—the United States ranked forty-fifth, behind Japan, Botswana, Bhutan, and most of Western Europe.[14]

Environmentalists, naturalists, and conservationists around the world also seek to protect endangered species of wildlife, to prevent clear-cutting of tropical rain forests (sometimes called slash-and-burn agriculture), and to curb the use of deep-sea fishing nets, among other commercial fishing activities such as whaling. Although the 2008 presidential election pointed to growing public support for environmental action, the green movement in the United States still pales in comparison to Europe's. Meanwhile, the global recession that started with the meltdown on Wall Street in August 2008 is proving to be the biggest immediate threat to coordinated action on climate change—deflecting attention, derailing efforts, and dampening public enthusiasm for environmentalism on both sides of the Atlantic.

Security and Self-Determination: Sweetening the "Pot"

Many states have adopted laws requiring motorists to wear seatbelts, motor-cyclists to wear safety helmets, and small children to be strapped into special infant seats in cars. Examples of local, state, and federal attempts to legislate morality include Prohibition, pornography, prostitution, and, of course, "pot."

Many people agree that society should not encourage bad behavior, but what does that mean? Do we want a "nanny state" that treats adults like children? What about the right to privacy and self-determination? Alaska, Colorado, Oregon, and Washington are states that now allow adults to buy and sell marijuana for recreational purposes. Libertarians, among others, argue that the state has no right to interfere in citizens' private lives.

Marijuana is still a banned substance under federal law. Nebraska and Oklahoma have challenged the Colorado law in court arguing that it has "created a dangerous gap" in federal drug-control efforts and places an undue burden on law enforcement in neighboring states. This issue promises to be contentious for many years to come because it involves a "mind-bending drug" and raises fundamental questions about limits and where to draw lines when public safety, morality, privacy, and self-determination are in conflict.

THE PURSUIT OF PROSPERITY

James Madison famously labeled the United States a commercial republic—salient characteristics include self-reliance, upward mobility, and the profit motive. There is a close link between the political philosophy of Madison, the nation's fourth president and a founding father, and Madison Avenue, a symbol of U.S. capitalism.[15]

The Founders launched a political experiment long championed by great thinkers like Locke and Montesquieu. The idea was compelling: a republic that encouraged entrepreneurship and innovation, protected private property, and rewarded hard work would generate great wealth, a burgeoning middle class, and a robust economy.

During the nineteenth century, the Industrial Revolution ushered in modern capitalism—the private ownership, manufacture, and distribution of goods and services free of heavy-handed state intervention or regulation. In the early twentieth century, the federal government enacted new laws to curb monopolies and encourage competition. The Great Depression of the 1930s witnessed a sudden expansion of the state's role in the economy. That legacy has coexisted with an aversion to state intervention and "welfare" ever since.

Beginning in the 1980s, a conservative backlash—often called the Reagan Revolution—swept the country. Reagan—and a decade later, Republican House Speaker Newt Gingrich—suggested government had gone too far down the road to becoming a "welfare state" (never mind that federal budget deficits soared to record heights during the Reagan presidency). In fact, however, the level of state intervention and social spending was still far below that found in most Western democracies.

The prosperity of the 1990s and early 2000s made many in the United States wealthy—at least on paper—as the stock market hit historic highs and

Kyoto Protocol
Countries that ratify this treaty, which went into effect in 2005, agree to cut emissions of carbon dioxide and five other greenhouse gases or to engage in emissions trading if they exceed a certain cap. The United States signed it under President Bill Clinton, but President George W. Bush renounced it shortly after taking office in 2001. President Barack Obama, who was sympathetic to the Kyoto pact as a candidate, has shown little inclination to push for a new global climate change treaty.

sustainable growth
A concept popular among environmentalists and liberal economists that emphasizes the need for economic strategies that take account of the high-cost and long-term impact on the environment (including global warming) of economic policies aimed at profit maximization, current consumption, and the like.

federal budget deficit
In the United States, the difference between federal revenues and federal expenditures in a given year; the national debt is the cumulative sum of budget deficits over many years.

the number of people investing in it through mutual and pension funds rose dramatically. Much of that paper wealth temporarily shrank in the bear market of 2001–2003 and then disappeared in the recession of 2008–2009, which saw the sharpest stock price declines since the 1930s.

Budget Deficits and the National Debt

Total federal spending as a share of gross domestic product (GDP) increased from about 17% in the mid-1960s to 24% in 1983, following the massive Reagan tax cut of 1981 and returned to Reagan-era levels under President George W. Bush (see "Ideas and Politics"). Not surprisingly, the **federal budget deficit** rose sharply in the 1980s and again after 9/11. In 2001, annual interest payments on the national debt amounted to $360 billion; in 2008, the last year of the Bush-Cheney administration, interest payments came to a record $451 billion.

IDEAS AND POLITICS

AN ILL-FATED BALANCING ACT

Between 1993 and 2000, President Bill Clinton, a Democrat, and the Republican-controlled Congress addressed the problems posed by the mushrooming national debt. As a consequence, budget deficits declined sharply in the 1990s. Later in the decade, amid a generally robust economy, Democrats and Republicans joined forces in Congress to pass the historic **Balanced Budget Act of 1997**, which mandated a balanced federal budget by 2001. But tax revenues increased faster than expected due to the strong economy, resulting in budget surpluses—using official accounting rules—earlier than expected or required by law. In fact, the only real surplus, when borrowing from the Social Security is factored in, was in 2001.

All that changed suddenly after September 11, 2001, when Congress under President Bush voted huge sums for cleanup and reconstruction efforts in New York City, bailing out hard-hit airlines (among others), and prosecuting the "war" against international terrorism at home and abroad. The budget surplus quickly vanished, as did all talk of a balanced budget. At the same time, the Bush administration pushed hard for across-the-board tax cuts, which Congress approved.

Then came the financial crisis of 2008 followed by a deep recession, prompting President Obama to launch a massive **economic stimulus** program resulting in the nation's first trillion-dollar budget deficit. In 2009, the federal deficit hit $1.4 trillion but has since returned to prerecession levels, falling to about $483 billion in 2014. Big deficits, however, continue to be a fact of life, and a massive federal debt has not deterred Congress and the White House from extending the Bush tax cuts for millionaires and billionaires.

Most conservatives are proponents of free markets, deregulation, and balanced budgets, whereas most liberals favor deficit spending, wealth redistribution, and regulations to protect consumers, wage-earners, the environment, and the like. Are liberals (aka, Democrats) mainly responsible for the mounting national debt, or are conservatives (aka, Republicans) big spenders too? Is the main source of conflict between Democrats and Republicans over the size of the budget or how to spend the taxpayers' money? Think about it.

(Hint: Find a current pie chart showing how federal spending is divided up, then ask which party, social class, or income bracket different categories of expenditure favor most. Also, check out how much of the budget involves discretionary spending versus ongoing programs both major parties consider untouchable.)

Losing Interest: The National Debt
The U.S. federal budget for 2010—the first Obama budget—was about $3.4 trillion. In the fall of 2014, the national debt —that is, the accumulated annual federal budget deficits—had climbed to over $18 trillion, rising at a rate of more than $2.4 billion a day. Each citizen's share came to over $56,000. The national debt hit a record in 2008 and climbed above 100% of GDP in 2012 (it stood at 31% in 1975).

The national debt represents a burden on future generations. The federal government borrows from the Social Security trust fund and replaces it by selling Treasury bonds. That's not the same as paying it back with liquid dollars. Meanwhile, the debt continues to mount, and the government is obligated to pay interest—a lot of interest (over $430 billion in 2014 alone)—on the *entire* debt. In the twenty years between 1994 and 2014, interest on the national debt cost U.S. taxpayers over $7.8 trillion.

Debt payments are currently the third-largest line-item expenditure in the federal budget (Social Security/Medicare and defense are first and second).* Social Security now owns about one-fifth of the national debt; foreign governments hold a little less than half; and China holds the most, about 8%, more than U.S. citizens own.

The Tax Burden: Who Pays What, When, and How?
Until recently, most U.S. citizens shared three mutually reinforcing aversions: socialism, state ownership, and high taxes. Of these, tax aversion is the oldest.

Taxes are a perennial issue. One easy way for a presidential candidate to win votes is to promise tax cuts, as did both Ronald Reagan and George W. Bush in their successful bids for the White House. In 1988, George H. W. Bush made a campaign promise not to raise taxes and was elected; four years later, he was turned out of office after going back on that promise. In the 2008 campaign, Barack Obama pledged to keep the Bush tax cuts except for those making more than $250,000 a year; as president, he succumbed to pressure by Republicans in Congress to accept an extension of the Bush cuts for all, including the richest of the rich.

Few political issues in the United States are inherently more complex—or surrounded by more deliberate obfuscation and statistical subterfuge—than taxes. Revelations of corporate fraud, greed, and stock swindles following the 2008 Wall Street meltdown caused a furor and fueled a short-lived debate over tax fairness.

Tax loopholes allowing the super-rich to avoid paying millions of dollars in income tax every year have been shifting the overall tax burden downward since the early 1980s. A slogan commonly attributed to Benjamin Franklin says the two things nobody can avoid are death and taxes, but some of the richest people in the United States *do* manage to avoid taxes. What's more, it's perfectly legal in most cases.

Balanced Budget Act of 1997
Passed by Congress in 1997, this historic measure mandated a balanced federal budget by 2001 but was ironically undone in that very year by the events of 9/11.

economic stimulus
A fiscal tool of government designed to bolster a weak economy and create jobs via public works projects and deficit spending.

*Who's to blame for the Washington's addiction to deficit spending? The two parties blame each other. In truth, they are both to blame. To find out more about the national debt and Obama's efforts to revive the economy, use an Internet search engine to look up "Obama by the Numbers," by Mark Warren and Richard Dorment, *Esquire* magazine, October 2012, which contains graphs and charts illustrating changes to the U.S. economy in recent years.

Taxes for the vast majority of middle-class taxpayers rose during the 1990s, while the tax burden on the super-rich fell.[16] In the words of David Cay Johnston, a Pulitzer Prize-winning journalist who covers taxes for the *New York Times*:

> [In 1997] Congress passed what its sponsors promoted as a tax cut for the middle class and especially for families with children. Buried in that law were many tax breaks for the rich, some subtle and some huge, notably a sharp reduction in the tax rate on long-term capital gains, the source of two-thirds of the incomes of the top 400.[17]

Both major political parties are to blame. The trend toward downloading the tax burden began in the 1980s, when Ronald Reagan (a Republican) was president but the Democrats controlled the Congress, and accelerated in the 1990s, when Democrat Bill Clinton was president but Republicans were in the majority. The result of this bipartisan failure at tax reform—which steadily made taxes more unfair to the middle class—is that "wealth in America today is more highly concentrated than at any time since 1929." Astonishingly, "the richest 1 percent of Americans [own] almost half of the stocks, bonds, cash, and other financial assets in the country. The richest 15 percent control nearly *all* of the financial assets."[18]

According to a Federal Reserve survey in 2012, the net worth of a median American family fell almost 40% from 2007 to 2010—from $126,400 to $77,300. Collapsing real estate values accounted for most of that loss. Median family income in 2010 was about the same as in the mid-1990s (but, of course, indebtedness and prices of everything from groceries to gasoline were much higher).

The beneficiaries of the tax bonanza for the rich include many members of Congress, a body that collectively posted a 16% gain on stocks alone during the steep market downturn in 2008-2009. Roughly half of all members of Congress are millionaires compared to 1% of the population at large—eight are multimillionaires with stock portfolios valued above $100 million.[19]

That most voters don't understand tax issues is hardly surprising. President Franklin Roosevelt once said the federal tax code "might as well have been written in a foreign language." The federal income tax rules are a taxpayer's nightmare but an accounting firm's dream come true.

Attempts at "tax simplification" have failed. In 1986, the U.S. Congress passed a law directing the IRS to fix the system. A few years later, a "hypothetical" tax return listing family income and expenses was sent to fifty tax experts. The result was fifty different "bottom lines" ranging from a tax bill of $12,500 to nearly $36,000.[20] Clearly, the Byzantine tax code is too complicated, but that's not the only—or worst—thing critics say is wrong with it (see Figure 13.4).

The U.S. tax system currently favors the rich over the middle class and poor. Due to various loopholes and tax shelters, the *actual* taxes its wealthiest citizens pay are low in comparison with other industrial democracies. Sales taxes hit the middle class much harder than the rich. If X and Y pay the exact same amount of sales tax in a year, but X earns 100 times more than Y, then X pays far less in sales tax than Y in proportion to income. For this basic reason, sales taxes are regressive.

FIGURE 13.4 Business Tax. The tax burden in the United States is lower than in most developed countries, but critics point out that U.S. taxpayers do not get key benefits, such as national health insurance, that taxpayers in most other developed countries do get. Critics also point out that corporations pay a relatively small portion of the total tax bill, smaller by far than they did in the first decade after World War II. Big business pays a lot less of the total tax bill than in 1950. Guess who pays a lot more? If you guessed the middle class and lower-income wage earners, you're right on the money.
SOURCE: OMB.

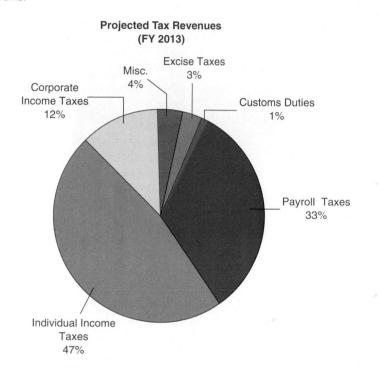

**Projected Tax Revenues
(FY 2013)**

- Excise Taxes 3%
- Misc. 4%
- Corporate Income Taxes 12%
- Customs Duties 1%
- Payroll Taxes 33%
- Individual Income Taxes 47%

Throughout the fifty states, sales taxes are common; in Europe, a *value added tax* (VAT) is the principal form of taxation. Unlike a sales tax, VAT is assessed at every stage in the manufacture and sale of a product—in this manner, the total tax "take" is built into the price of a finished product and passed along to the consumer. VAT rates among the twenty-seven countries of the EU range from 15 to 25%, but a high percentage of tax revenues are recycled into social welfare programs. By contrast, sales taxes in the United States are rarely more than 6%; in Minnesota, for example, groceries are exempt (eating in restaurants, however, is not), and in New Jersey there is no sales tax on clothing.

Just under 60% of all federal revenue in the United States comes from personal and corporate income taxes, but the tax burden on individuals is far heavier than on corporations. In fact, corporate income tax amounts to only 13% of federal revenues today, a dramatic decline from the 1950s and 1960s,

FIGURE 13.5   Federal Revenues by Source, Fiscal Year 2013. Individual income and payroll (Social Security) taxes together account for more than 80% of the U.S. government's annual revenues. Corporations pay only 13%. Today corporations with powerful Washington lobbies get big tax breaks, and middle-class taxpayers foot the bill for Big Business and Big Government.
SOURCE: The National Priorities Project. http://nationalpriorities.org/en/budget-basics/federal-budget-101/revenues/

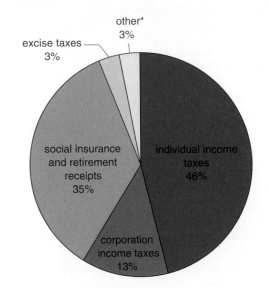

*Estate and gift taxes (1%), custom duties (1%), and miscellaneous receipts (1%).

when it stood at about 25% (see Figure 13.5). Pro-business interests decry the fact that the *maximum* corporate tax rate in the U.S. is 39.2%—the "highest in the world." But what most corporations actually pay is a mere 12%, thanks to exemptions and a long litany of loopholes in the tax code. In 2011, for example, the ten richest corporations in the United States paid an average rate of 9%. Meanwhile, Social Security payroll taxes, which every worker has to pay, were the fastest-growing source of federal revenue (about one-third of the total).

U.S. taxpayers tend to think taxes are too high, yet the United States has low tax rates relative to other developed countries, especially the Scandinavian countries, but also to France, the Netherlands, Germany, and the United Kingdom (see Table 13.2). But, as noted earlier, in Europe income is widely redistributed through cradle-to-grave benefits to all citizens. In the United States, the federal income tax instituted shortly before World War I has become less and less progressive (or redistributive) since the early 1970s.

Comparisons between taxes and benefits in the United States and Europe raise two fundamental questions. First, is the tax system fair? Second, what do citizens actually get in return for the taxes they pay? Answering these questions necessitates a closer look at public policy in such areas as health and education.

TABLE 13.2   Total Tax Revenue as a Percentage of GDP by Country in 2013

Country	Tax Revenues (% of GDP)
India	07.4
Pakistan	10.1
United States	24.8
Australia	20.9
Japan	28.8
Switzerland	29.8
Canada	31.0
Spain	31.7
Poland	31.8
United Kingdom	35.0
Germany	36.3
EU27	40.0
Italy	43.0
France	42.9
Sweden	45.8
Denmark	48.2

SOURCE: "2013 Index of Economic Freedom," the Heritage Foundation at http://www.heritage. org/index/explore?view=by-variables, and Eurostat at http://epp.eurostat.ec.europa.eu/statistics_explained/index.php/Tax_revenue_statistics.

Educational Malaise

We tend to measure the value of education primarily in monetary terms—how much more the average college graduate earns over a lifetime than someone with only a high school diploma. We want to know the practical value of a particular course, major, or degree and implicitly we reject the inherent value of an education—knowledge for its own sake. "What can you do with a History major?" "There are no jobs for Philosophy majors." These are the kinds of questions and comments college students hear frequently if they are not pursuing a course of study that leads to a definite profession or occupation, such as prelaw, premed, nursing, accounting, and the like.

Critics frequently talk about the "crisis in education." In some schools, guns, drugs, and gangs endanger students and teachers alike. Declining college entrance examination scores, studies showing our students score worse on mathematical tests than comparable European and Asian students, and high failure rates on elementary-level literacy tests administered to job applicants by many large corporations all testify to the seriousness of the problem. Studies have long shown that U.S. high school students consistently score lower than students in many other countries at a comparable level of development in

English, mathematics, science, history, geography, or civics—even though the public schools are well funded.[21]

Grade inflation is widely recognized as a pervasive and corrosive force in education at all levels. Critics charge that teachers pamper students more and more and expect less and less. U.S. business spends billions of dollars every year training students in skills they should have learned in school. Who is to blame, and what is to be done?

Until passage of the Elementary and Secondary Education Act of 1965 (ESEA), control of education had fallen primarily to the states. The 1965 law enhanced the role of the federal government. In 2001, Congress passed the No Child Left Behind Act (NCLB), which requires schools across the nation to administer standardized proficiency tests in reading and math and to improve on a yearly basis or face penalties. This law ties federal funding for public schools to compliance with federal educational policy, thus redefining—and greatly expanding—the federal role.

States and municipalities must now meet academic performance standards set by the federal government and measured by standardized tests administered yearly nationwide. Critics say NCLB was ill conceived from the start; that it forces teachers to change what and how they teach; that it is yet another example of the federal government burdening financially hard-pressed state governments and public schools with unfunded mandates; and that the requirements are unrealistic. They also point out that this movement toward frequent standardized testing (the magic word is "assessment"), which is now universally hated by teachers, was invented in Texas, where (they say) the educational system is an anomaly—state-controlled despite the fact that Texans are famously obsessed with private rights and fiercely opposed to big government.*

Although the Constitution prohibits Congress from making laws that would either establish religion or restrict its free exercise, many social conservatives favor a voucher system. Under such a system, parents with school-age children would first get money (vouchers) from the state, then freely choose a school—any accredited school (public, private, or parochial). Champions of free choice argue that competition would force all schools to excel or face extinction. Opponents argue that public support for private schools violates the First Amendment separation of church and state, discriminates against the poor and minorities, and perpetuates racial segregation.

In recent years, the idea of charter schools has gained ground in many states. As nonsectarian institutions independent of local school districts, charter schools are an attempt to revitalize public education while maintaining the "wall of separation" between church and state. Following Minnesota's lead, forty other states and the District of Columbia have passed laws allowing the creation of charter schools—Alabama, Kentucky, Maine, Montana, Nebraska, North Dakota, South Dakota, Vermont, Washington, and West Virginia are the only ten holdouts. In 2010, over 1.7 million students were enrolled in thousands of charter schools across the country.

*If you want to know more about the bogus theory behind your own experience in the public schools, you can't do better than to read Gail Collins's delightful, tongue-in-cheek, *As Texas Goes. . . . How the Lone Star State Highjacked the American Agenda.*

Are charter schools the answer? One study found that fourth-grade students in charter schools do no better than those in public schools on math and reading assessments. Good charter schools are often very good; bad ones are sometimes egregiously bad. Some simply fall by the wayside: between 1991 and 2004, more than four hundred charter schools went out of business.

Public school administrators and teachers have generally opposed fundamental reforms. They contend that standardized tests are poor indicators of educational performance or potential. The whole idea of educational privatization, they argue, is politically motivated and pecuniary; the aims are to break teachers unions (notably, the National Education Association [NEA]) and to shift billions of tax dollars from public schools to the private sector. Significantly, hundreds of charter schools are now run by for-profit education management organizations (EMOs).

Educators and researchers argue that problems in our public schools are reflections of the larger society—including crime, broken homes, bad role models, and drug use—which public schools are powerless to solve. They have a point.

Health Care: A Sick System?

A healthy society and a vibrant economy are two sides of the same coin. Individuals who suffer from malnutrition or are too ill to work are not productive. Societies ravaged by hunger and disease are not prosperous.

The question can be simply put: is health care a business like, say, hair care or auto repair? Or is it a fundamental right inseparable from "life, liberty, and the pursuit of happiness" as enshrined in the Declaration of Independence and the U.S. Constitution? After all, without good health, there can be little happiness, rights are moot, and life itself is in jeopardy.

Modern postindustrial states, with one notable exception, guarantee basic health care to every citizen. The sole exception is the United States, where the bitterly partisan controversy over the Affordable Care Act (often called "ObamaCare") demonstrates anew that health care is still widely viewed as a private good rather than a public right. In the field of health care, the United States is an "outlier" among rich countries. Health care facilities are among the very best in the world, the quality of medical care is generally high, the federal government spends far more money on biomedical research and development than any other country in the world, and, finally, its citizens spend more money on medical care than anybody else. And—outlays for Medicare and Medicaid are the largest single drain on the federal budget—larger than Social Security and larger than defense.

The United States is the only developed country in the world that does not treat basic health care as a fundamental human right. Total private spending on health care in the United States is much higher than in Europe, and public spending under Medicaid and Medicare is also rising at what many (especially opponents of public health insurance) say is an unsustainable rate.

In Europe, health care—like education—is something citizens expect in return for paying taxes. (In fact, university education is also free or highly subsidized in Europe.) Many countries provide medical services comparable to those available in the United States but at far lower overall costs. France, for example, provides universal health care for its 62 million citizens, is healthier than the United States, and spends only about half as much per capita on health care—less than 11% of GDP compared to 16.5% in the United States. France's system is a mix of public and private provision of health care that has produces a healthy population at one-half the per capita cost in the United States and has shorter waiting lists than in the UK. And the French live longer on average than both the British and the Americans.[22]

The Affordable Care Act, which requires most Americans to have health insurance, reduced the estimated number of citizens with no health insurance from 18% at the end of 2013 to 13.4% in 2014. Although the number was falling, some 41 million Americans still have no health insurance at all. Most middle-class U.S. workers have some sort of private health insurance now, but policies vary widely in cost and coverage. Studies show that almost a third of uninsured adults in the United States go without needed medical care due to cost.

At least twenty countries have lower infant mortality rates than the United States, and impoverished Cuba has a higher life expectancy. In the United States, health care costs have risen much faster than inflation rates or personal incomes, and patients often pay exorbitant prices for prescription drugs compared with the prices of the same drugs in other countries.

Who is to blame? The medical profession points to costly malpractice insurance, hospitals to costly new life-saving technologies, and pharmaceutical companies to research and development (R&D) costs. Critics tend to dismiss these arguments, pointing out that consumers of medical care are *patients*, not customers shopping for a new pair of shoes. Sick people do not choose to be sick. In this view, compassion and common sense argue that sick people with health insurance ought not to be driven into bankruptcy, and taxpayers should not have to foot the bill for "uncompensated" medical services hospitals and clinics provide to the uninsured.

Physicians point out that many people seek medical attention for trivial reasons, ask for prescription drugs they see advertized on TV, and are too ready to sue when something goes wrong. As more people live to ripe old age, hospitals and health care professionals are being asked to devote more and more time and resources to geriatric care involving fragile patients facing end-of-life medical crises. In 2010 the elderly constituted 13% of the population and accounted for 34% of national health expenditures.

Campaigning in 2008, Barack Obama promised to reform the system and tried to keep his promise after he was elected. But Republicans in the House and Senate opposed what right-wing ideologues stigmatize as "socialized medicine"—in particular, mandatory health insurance and cost controls. The result was a watered-down law that finally passed as the Affordable Care Act (ACA) of 2010.

The new law pleased few and did not fix the problem it purported to address—namely, to provide "affordable care" for all members of society. There is growing support for doing so among doctors and even within the traditionally conservative business community. In February 2007, the chief executives of retail giant Walmart and three other major U.S. companies joined hands with union leaders in calling for health care coverage for "every person in America and raising the value it [America] receives for every health care dollar." Walmart

CEO Lee Scott declared, "We believe Americans can have high-quality, affordable, and accessible health care by 2012."[23] A 2007 New York Times/CBS News survey found that 90% of respondents believe the system needs either fundamental changes (54%) or a major overhaul (36%).[24]

Health care reform remains a major issue in U.S. politics. Critics denounce ObamaCare as a budget-busting step toward European-style socialism. Twenty-five challenges were filed in various states in 2010; in four separate cases, two federal judges found the law unobjectionable, two overturned all or part of it on constitutional grounds. A crucial test came in June 2012 when the U.S. Supreme Court upheld the constitutionality of the Affordable Care Act by a narrow 5 to 4 vote. The key question was over the law's controversial provision requiring everyone to buy health insurance and providers to insure individuals without regard to "pre-existing conditions" (previous health problems).

Pursuant to the new law, health insurance exchanges have been established in all fifty states, but fewer than half are state-run; twenty-seven others have "federally facilitated" exchanges because the states chose not to cooperate. All health insurance providers on these exchanges are in the private sector, resulting in a wide range of plans and policies. Moreover, insurers can (and do) change the terms and premiums. Policy holders are left to sort it all out and shop around for the best deal at the end of each year. This reshuffling of the deck adds to the confusion.

Many public interest advocates want a nationwide single-payer system patterned after the British, French, or Scandinavian models. Opponents want the new law struck down.

Many Americans are still ambivalent about health care reform. A Rasmussen Reports national telephone survey in January 2011 found that 55% of likely voters favored repeal of the new health care law. The stage was set for the 2012 presidential contest to be a referendum on health care reform. Tea Party Republicans in general and Mitt Romney in particular believed they could parlay opposition to ObamaCare into a winning strategy. They were wrong.

THE PURSUIT OF EQUALITY

A century before the Declaration of Independence was written, English political philosopher John Locke argued that "life, liberty, and property" are natural rights to which all human beings are entitled. The principle of *equal rights*—as distinct from equal results—has deep roots in the Anglo-American political tradition. Yet principle and practice often diverge, as the history of slavery in the United States attests.

Income Distribution: Who Gets What, When, and How?

Thomas Jefferson's declaration that "all men are created equal" was not a formula for the radical redistribution of property or wealth. It was an existential idea about how we start out, not how we end up. Far from it. But how much inequality is too much?

Prosperity depends not only on the amount of wealth in a society but also on its distribution. Unless income is distributed widely in society, there will be

Talia Felix/PublicDomainPictures.net

How wealth is distributed in a society says a lot about the character of its political institutions as well as the viability and sustainability of its economy.

too few consumers, or consumers with too little money to afford the goods and services the economy can produce, creating a vicious cycle in which everybody loses. Thus, recession (falling demand) causes unemployment, resulting in less demand (fewer consumers with money to spend), causing business profits to fall, and so on.

But the health of the economy is not simply an economic question. A faltering economy can also undermine political stability and governmental authority. Riots and revolts often have economic roots, as the American and French revolutions showed (see Chapter 14).

Glaring economic inequalities are difficult to justify from a moral standpoint as well. Indeed, in the United States, no politician seeking reelection would dare challenge the idea of "an honest day's work for an honest day's pay."

Yet, since 1980, the disparity between the incomes of the richest members of society and all the rest has grown. From 1949 to 1974, the share of family income of the poorest one-fifth of the labor force rose 26.7%, while that of the richest 5% of income earners fell more than 12%. Between 1980 and 2008, this trend was dramatically reversed, as the bottom one-fifth's share of family income fell almost 25%, while that of the top one-twentieth climbed nearly 44%.[25]

A Congressional Budget Office (CBO) study in 2011 found that the share of national income taken by the top 1% of earners had more than doubled since 1979: "The equalizing effect of federal taxes was smaller [because] the composition of federal revenues shifted away from progressive income taxes to less-progressive payroll taxes." According to a Federal Reserve survey released in the summer of 2012, the median family's net worth fell nearly 40% between 2007 and 2010, due in large part to collapsing real-estate prices. Median family income also continued to decline in 2010, a year in which 93% of the increase in total income went to the top 1%.[26]

Such numbers are startling, but they are not an accident of nature or an economy operating on autopilot—there is no such thing as a free market.[27] On the contrary, government plays a major role through its power to tax—or not to tax. The taxes paid by the richest four hundred taxpayers in the "roaring nineties" fell from about 26 cents on every dollar of reported income to 22 cents, while the overall federal income tax burden actually increased. Narrowing the gap between what the super-rich pay and what everybody else pays constitutes a major upward redistribution of income.[28]

The Bush tax cuts enacted between 2000 and 2006 greatly benefited the wealthy.[29] Studies show that middle-class workers have been running in place since the early 1970s. Between 1970 and 2000, average wages in the United States adjusted for inflation were flat. Meanwhile, the family income of the top 1% was 23 times that of typical families in 1997 compared to 10 times in 1979; incomes of the top *one-tenth* of 1% climbed astronomically.[30]

CAPITALISM IN THE TWENTY-FIRST CENTURY: POTENTIALLY TERRIFYING?

Perhaps the most talked-about new nonfiction book in 2014 was, believe it or not, a book about economics—"the dismal science." The book by Thomas Piketty and innocuously titled *Capitalism in the 21st Century* is a wide-ranging study of economic trends—in particular, income distribution—in thirty countries, including the United States.

Piketty drew on the "World Top Incomes Database," which he and several colleagues created to study in depth what they believed to be a "potentially terrifying" global trend. Using the database, which covers some thirty countries, Piketty found that the rising income share of the richest families continued unabated during and after the Great Recession. By 2012, the top 1% of households enjoyed 22.5% of total income—the highest figure since 1928.

Nor is the trend toward ever-greater concentration of wealth unique to the United States. On the contrary, Piketty shows that it's happening in other countries too. Many economists have missed this global paradigm shift because they failed to pay sufficient attention to capital accumulation—the many ways wealth begets wealth—a phenomenon that greatly impressed Karl Marx, as well as David Ricardo and John Stuart Mill.

Unlike Marx, Piketty does not believe monopoly capitalism and revolutions are inevitable. Indeed, between 1945 and 1973, low-income and middle-class living standards increased steadily in the United States. What has happened since then?

In a word, politics. Piketty writes, "The forces of divergence can at any point regain the upper hand, as seems to be happening now, at the beginning of the twenty-first century." If things don't change, "the consequences for the long-term dynamics of the wealth distribution are potentially terrifying."

The publication of Karl Marx's "The Communist Manifesto" and *Das Kapital* represent a landmark in world history because they inspired mass revolutions, social change, and economic reforms in the twentieth century. It's too soon to say if the publication of *Capitalism in the 21st Century* will become a landmark or suffer the fate of most books—even best-sellers—too soon relegated to the dustbin of history. Marx is one exception. Will Piketty be another?

Some economists even argue the American middle class is disappearing. The top 20% of the populace, they point out, hold 93% of the country's total financial assets, while the top 1% control approximately 43%. The middle 20% of the population owns a mere 6% of the nation's wealth, but even this small slice of the pie dwarfs the bottom 40%, who get along on less than 1%. One sign of the times: less than 10% of U.S. workers are employed in manufacturing now compared to just under 30% in 1960.

Many conservatives take a different view of economic inequality. Rather than focusing on the extreme differences in income, they argue that the United States has always had a large middle class, still has, and it would be self-defeating to level society through legislative action aimed at redistributing incomes. Rather, policies that benefit those who work hard, take economic risks, invest wisely, and provide goods and services people want are proven to work best. Helping the poor is not the government's job, and "giveaway" programs only perpetuate poverty by rewarding laziness. In this view, charity belongs in the private sector—philanthropists, religious institutions, and charitable organizations.

Debates over income distribution in a given society are really about equality. Liberals and conservatives agree that equality is important in some sense, but they do not agree on what *kind* of equality is necessary or how much inequality is desirable—or tolerable.

Racial Discrimination

Until the 1860s, slavery made a mockery of the U.S. commitment to liberty. On the eve of the Civil War, in the infamous *Dred Scott v. Sandford* (1856) case, the Supreme Court ruled that African Americans, whether slave or free, were not citizens. Chief Justice Roger Taney argued that "Negroes" were "so inferior" that they had "no rights which the white man was bound to respect."

The outcome of the Civil War meant an end to slavery, but it did not ensure equality under the law. Nor did enactment of the Fourteenth Amendment, which, among other things, guaranteed that no person shall be denied "the equal protection of the laws." Ironically, it was the Supreme Court, the supposed guardian of the Constitution, that largely nullified the intent of this amendment.

Two Landmark Cases In the *Civil Rights Cases* (1883), the Court ruled that an act of Congress prohibiting racial discrimination in public accommodations (restaurants, amusement parks, and the like) was unconstitutional.[31] The Equal Protection Clause of the Fourteenth Amendment, the justices held, was intended to prohibit only *state* discrimination, not private discrimination. Discriminatory acts committed by individuals having no official connection with state government, in other words, were beyond the range of the federal government and, therefore, of the federal courts. If, for example, a restaurant owner turned away black citizens, the owner would merely be exercising the rights of a private individual, and no congressional remedy would be constitutional.

Thirteen years later, in *Plessy v. Ferguson* (1896), the Court went even further.[32] In upholding the constitutionality of a state law mandating racially segregated railway carriages, the Court in *Plessy* devised the notorious *separate-but-equal doctrine.*

Plessy (described by the Court as being of "seven-eighths Caucasian and one-eighth African blood") had taken a seat in the white section of a train, only to be told he was required to move to the "colored" section. A nearly unanimous Court rejected Plessy's claim that the segregation law violated his right to equal protection of the law, arguing that the law was neutral on its face; that is, it provided equal accommodations for persons of both races. The Court majority went so far as to suggest that if "the enforced separation of the two races stamps the colored race with a badge of inferiority," that "is not by reason of anything found in the act, but solely because the colored race chooses to put that construction upon it."

In both the *Civil Rights Cases* and *Plessy v. Ferguson*, only Justice John M. Harlan dissented. On each occasion, he argued the Court's decision had the effect of defeating the egalitarian purpose behind the Fourteenth Amendment, which, he declared, had "removed the race line from our government systems." Because he believed no government, at any level, possessed the constitutional power to pass laws based on racial distinctions, Harlan viewed the

Constitution as "color-blind." His dissenting opinion in *Plessy* would not become law, however, for another fifty-eight years. Through the decisions handed down in the *Civil Rights Cases* and *Plessy v. Ferguson*, the Court not only sanctioned strict racial segregation in the South but helped legitimize a social system in which blacks were discriminated against, brutalized, and even murdered.

Racial Equality: Free at Last? Systematic racial segregation under law was the norm throughout the South well into the twentieth century; *de facto* segregation (neighborhoods and schools) was also widespread in the North, especially in urban areas. Beginning in the late 1940s, however, the Supreme Court began to reinterpret the old legal formulas with a view toward promoting racial equality. In *Shelley v. Kraemer* (1948), the Court held that judicial enforcement of discriminatory private contracts was unconstitutional.[33] The Court ruled that legal enforcement of such agreements amounted to "state action" for the purpose of discrimination, which was prohibited by the Fourteenth Amendment. In addition, though it declined to outlaw them outright, the Court began to insist that segregated state facilities be *truly* equal.

Dr. Martin Luther King Jr., president of the Southern Christian Leadership Conference, at the Civil Rights March on Washington, D.C., August 28, 1963.

Thus, in *Sweatt v. Painter* (1950), it held the University of Texas law school had to admit blacks because the state could not provide a black law school of equal quality and reputation.[34]

In the famous case *Brown v. Board of Education of Topeka* (1954), the Court finally overturned the separate-but-equal doctrine,[35] declaring segregated schools unconstitutional because "separate educational facilities are inherently unequal." The *Brown* decision sparked a heated political debate over the meaning of "equality" in the United States.

Congress eventually passed the Civil Rights Act of 1964, the first of a series of federal laws aimed at realizing racial equality. It was a sign of the changing times that the 1964 act contained an equal accommodations section very similar to the one ruled unconstitutional in the *Civil Rights Cases*.[36] By the late 1960s, after a decade of intense civil rights activities and the most serious civil disorders since the Civil War, the government was fully committed to ensuring equal rights under the law for all citizens. The public policy battle between advocates of racial equality and of white supremacy thus gave way to an increasingly complex and heated debate over the appropriate means to the goal of equality.

The Busing Controversy The question of how far the government could and should go to promote equal rights was crystallized in the school busing controversy of the 1970s and 1980s, which grew out of an ambiguity in

Brown v. Board of Education. But most blacks lived in the inner city and most whites in the suburbs—*de facto* segregation.

In 1971, the Supreme Court in *Swann v. Charlotte-Mecklenburg Board of Education* unanimously ruled in favor of a controversial remedy: to integrate school districts by transporting schoolchildren across district lines.[37] Court-ordered school busing met with strong opposition from parents and school administrators on various grounds and coincided with a national "crisis of confidence" in the public schools.

Was busing a good idea? It *did* put pressure on local officials and school boards to improve facilities and conditions in inner-city schools. But busing often did nothing more than reshuffle minority schoolchildren from one part of the inner city to another. The Supreme Court invalidated most plans that involved reshuffling between black inner-city neighborhoods and white suburbs.[38]

Marriage Equality The gay rights movement in the United States is part of a social revolution dating back to the turbulent 1960s. But it's a latecomer to the party.

Few believe racial and gender equality are fully realized goals in America. Still, court-ordered and/or legislated social reforms have led to significant change.

Until recently, however, most homosexuals remained "in the closet." Gays were equal only in the sense that gay men and women of all ages, creeds, and colors faced the same sort of persecution, discrimination, and alienation not only within society but also, often, within their own families.

In recent years, these attitudes have started to change. In December 2011, the lame duck Congress repealed the "don't ask, don't tell" rule, the policy restricting the military from inquiring into sexual preferences of service members or applicants, while barring openly LGBT (gay, lesbian, bisexual, or transsexual) individuals from military service.

In 2013 in *United States v. Windsor* , the Supreme Court overturned the 1996 Defense of Marriage Act (DOMA) on grounds that it violated the Fifth Amendment due process clause.[39] Justice Kennedy wrote: "The federal statute is invalid, for no legitimate purpose overcomes the effect to . . . injure those whom the State, by its marriage laws, sought to protect in personhood and dignity."

In 2008, California became the second state, after Massachusetts, to issue same-sex marriage licenses after the California Supreme Court ruled the state's ban on same-sex marriages unconstitutional. Later in 2008, however, California voters passed Proposition 8, a constitutional amendment intended to supersede the Court's ruling.

By 2015, same-sex marriage was legalized in thirty-seven states, including California. It was banned in Arkansas, Georgia, Kentucky, Louisiana, Michigan, Mississippi, Missouri, North Dakota, Ohio, South Dakota, Tennessee, Texas, and Nebraska. Court challenges to restrictive marriage laws put those states at odds with changing social attitudes—and the U.S. Supreme Court.

Opinion polls in 2013 showed that more Americans favor same sex marriage now than oppose it. In another sign "the times they are a-changin',"

President Obama dared to note the struggle for civil rights of "our gay brothers and sisters" in his nationally televised Inaugural Speech on January 21, 2013.

Prejudice cannot be legislated out of existence, but societies can change. There is no better way to initiate that process than through fair laws and impartial judges.

Affirmative Action or Reverse Discrimination?

If the Constitution permits preferential treatment of minorities, does it also provide the majority with protection against **reverse discrimination**? The Supreme Court wrestled with this question in 1978 in a suit brought by a white student, Allan Bakke, who had unsuccessfully sought admission to the medical school of the University of California at Davis.[40]

Bakke contended that the medical school had unfairly undercut his chances of acceptance simply because of his race. In a close decision, the Court ruled rigid **affirmative action** quotas unconstitutional but said preference for minorities were allowable under certain circumstances.[41]

The Supreme Court has upheld broad-based preferential hiring programs, while drawing the line at preferential protection against layoffs.[42] It has upheld affirmative action for women in the workforce to improve gender balance in industry and many professions.[43] But the Court struck down governmental preferences for minority-owned businesses.[44]

In 2003, the Supreme Court in *Grutter v. Bollinger* ruled that race can be used in university admission decisions, voting 5-4 to uphold the University of Michigan Law School's affirmative action policy, which favors minorities—thus apparently reversing the decision in *Bakke*. But in a parallel case, *Gratz v. Bollinger*, the justices struck down the university's undergraduate affirmative action policy (which awarded twenty points to blacks, Hispanics, and Native Americans) on the grounds that the policy was not "narrowly tailored" to achieve the goal of diversity—thus apparently confirming the *Bakke* decision.

Exactly where affirmative action ends and reverse discrimination begins in the eyes of the Supreme Court is unclear. The Court adjudges the Constitution to give Congress more latitude than state and local governments to remedy discrimination past and present. Color-conscious affirmative action programs at the state and local levels are most likely to be upheld where there is clear evidence of specific (and not general social) discrimination against minorities.[45]

Who Deserves Preferential Treatment?

African Americans and Native Americans have historically been victims of injustice and discrimination. So, too, have Asian Americans.

During World War II, more than 120,000 Japanese Americans living on the West Coast were herded into concentration camps surrounded by barbed wire and armed guards until the end of the war. In the name of national security, whole families who had done nothing wrong were forced into internal exile, losing everything they had in the process. Not until 1988 did the U.S. Congress pass a law acknowledging "a grave injustice was done" and giving each victim $20,000 in compensation, along with an official letter of apology signed by the president.

reverse discrimination
In effect, going overboard in giving preferences to racial minorities and victims of gender discrimination in hiring, housing, and education; the U.S. Supreme Court has ruled that in some cases affirmative action quotas are unconstitutional.

affirmative action
Giving preferential treatment to a socially or economically disadvantaged group in compensation for opportunities denied by past discrimination.

Women, gays and lesbians, and Arab Americans are three other groups with a claim to preferential treatment based on past discrimination. After 9/11, Arab Americans were insulted, threatened, and in some cases physically attacked. The FBI placed many Arabs and Muslims under surveillance, questioned others, and arrested thousands, holding them without charges or access to an attorney for longer than the law allowed.[46]

Gender-based discrimination became a front-burner issue only in the 1970s. For a time, the debate centered on the ill-fated equal rights amendment, which would have guaranteed that "equality of rights under the law should not be denied or abridged by the United States or by any State on account of sex." Do women need special protection as a historically disadvantaged "minority"? Are they entitled to preferential treatment to remedy the effects of past gender discrimination?

Gays and lesbians have long been the object of discrimination too. In 1992, Colorado voters passed a measure prohibiting the state from enforcing specific legal protections or extending preference to gay citizens who believed they were disadvantaged or discriminated against. The referendum was overturned in 1996 when the Supreme Court held the measure discriminatory and therefore unconstitutional.[47]

THE PURSUIT OF LIBERTY

What rights and legal protections are due all citizens? Do implied rights—for example, the right to privacy—deserve the same protection as expressed or enumerated rights? What does the U.S. Constitution have to say about liberty, and how can it guarantee all citizens equal protection of the laws? What are the limits of individual freedom? Can a state prevent gay marriages? Can it allow the sale of marijuana for recreational purposes?

Liberty is often equated with freedom from governmental restraint. Free enterprise is necessary for a creative society and dynamic economy. Without freedom, the spirit of invention and innovation is stifled. Freedom of expression keeps citizens informed and governments honest. When the state encroaches on anyone's liberty, it threatens everyone's liberty.

Liberty and the First Amendment

In the United States, legal questions about individual freedom often turn on the First Amendment, which provides:

> Congress shall make no law respecting an establishment of religion, or prohibiting the free exercise thereof; or abridging the freedom of speech, or the press, or the right of the people peaceably to assemble, and to petition the Government for a redress of grievances.

The First Amendment protects four **civil liberties**: freedom of speech, freedom of the press, freedom of religion, and freedom of assembly. Because the language of the First Amendment is brief and intentionally vague, the first three rights in particular have required an unusual amount of judicial interpretation.

Freedom of Speech   Most constitutional experts agree the overriding purpose behind the First Amendment is the protection of *political* speech. In a republic,

civil liberties
Basic constitutional rights guaranteed to all citizens, including the right to life and freedom of speech, religion, and association, as well as freedom from arbitrary arrest and incarceration, torture, and slavery. But there is no universally accepted definition or list.

open debate between political opponents is vital to the effective functioning of the political system. Most of the time, the *exercise* of free speech is not controversial, even though the speech itself might be.

Freedom of speech can become a hotly contested issue even in the most open societies. Extremists often arouse strong passions, especially within minority groups they have victimized (Jews against Nazis, for example, or African Americans against the Ku Klux Klan). In what one contemporary writer calls "the greatest defense of freedom of speech ever written," John Stuart Mill argued that "the free contest of ideas, even bad ones, is necessary to discover the truth of things."[48]

In the United States, people often associate protesters and demonstrators with extremists and troublemakers. During the early days of the Vietnam War, youthful protesters were often depicted as unpatriotic and disloyal. Several years later, after the war had become unpopular, defenders of the U.S. role in Vietnam were booed and shouted down when they spoke on college campuses. But the First Amendment safeguards the right of all citizens to express political opinions, no matter how repugnant or unpopular. However, freedom of speech is not absolute. For example, it does not entail the right to shout "Fire!" in a crowded theater, foment a riot, plot a terrorist act, or use "fighting words" in a dispute.

During the Vietnam War, the federal government engaged in domestic spying under the secret Counter Intelligence Program (COINTELPRO), which was aimed at monitoring the activities of antiwar activists. Subsequently, the FBI was banned from monitoring public events involving religious or political groups unless it had a specific reason for doing so. After September 11, 2001, the FBI again began collecting information on antiwar demonstrators.[49]

iStockphoto.com/Stuart Sipkin

Antiwar protesters in masks demonstrate at the Colorado state Capitol during the 2008 Democratic National Convention in Denver, Colorado.

In early February 2004, a county deputy sheriff working closely with the FBI's Joint Terrorism Task Force served subpoenas on Drake University in Des Moines, Iowa, to turn over "records relating to the people in charge, or to any attendees" of an antiwar conference held on the Drake campus.[50] The public was alarmed. Senator Tom Harkin of Iowa likened this action to "Vietnam when war protestors were rounded up [and] grand juries were convened to investigate people who were protesting the war."[51] The matter was dropped.

The Supreme Court has placed a broad interpretation on the word "speech," defining it as synonymous with any form of expression. This broad interpretation has opened the door to big campaign contributions—the five conservative members of the Court have repeatedly ruled that giving money to politicians is a form of free speech.

In *Snyder v. Phelps*, the Supreme Court ruled that free speech extends to antiwar street demonstrations at military funerals.[52] At issue was whether the First Amendment protects such speech no matter how "outrageous" against tort liability. Albert Snyder, the father of Matthew Snyder, a Marine who died in the Iraq War, filed a lawsuit seeking redress for intentional infliction of emotion distress against Fred Phelps and the Phelps family, as well Phelps's Westboro Baptist Church (WBC). The Court ruled 8-1 in favor of Phelps, holding that speeches about public issues on public sidewalks are covered under the First Amendment.

Flag burning has been upheld as a protected form of **symbolic speech**.[53] The context of symbolic free speech is almost always constitutionally more important than its content. The Ku Klux Klan, for example, has the right to burn a cross in an isolated field.[54] Burning a cross on someone's lawn, however, is prohibited.[55]

Freedom of the Press The First Amendment protects publishers from almost all forms of official censorship. Newspapers and periodicals can publish what they wish, including criticisms and indictments of the government. The same holds true for the broadcast media. A free press is crucial to a democracy because every citizen is a decision maker at election time and because the glare of publicity helps keep elected officials honest.

In the aftermath of 9/11, freedom of the press became a bone of contention as the Bush administration advocated for greater governmental secrecy to prosecute the war on terror. But journalists and media executives expressed alarm at the way the Freedom of Information Act (FOIA) was being flouted.[56]

Historically, the Supreme Court has vigorously protected a free press, ruling that except in times of war or grave national emergency the government cannot use **prior restraint** to prevent publication of information—even classified documents.[57] Nor are public officials protected from criticism or calumny ("character assassination"). In the final analysis, however, only a free press and an alert public can prevent the abuse of executive power.

Freedom of Religion By prohibiting the establishment of a state-sponsored religion, the First Amendment requires the government to be neutral in religious matters—to neither help nor hinder any religion. This requirement complements

symbolic speech
Symbolic speech includes forms of expression other than words: for example, flag-burning, provocative gestures, black armbands, and the like.

prior restraint
The legal doctrine that the government does not have the power to censor the press, except in cases of dire national emergency.

the guarantee of the free exercise of religion. Taken together, these two clauses ensure that citizens may practice any religion in any manner they like, within reasonable limits.

When religious practices pose a threat to society, however, government has the power to outlaw them. The free exercise of religion, for instance, does not include ritual murder or even certain religious practices that do not present any obvious danger to society, such as polygamy.[58] The Supreme Court has ruled the free exercise clause does include the right of conscientious objectors not to bear arms, Amish children not to attend public schools, and Jehovah's Witness schoolchildren not to salute the flag.

On the controversial issue of school prayer, the Supreme Court has held that prayer, even if nondenominational, and Bible-reading in public schools violate the Establishment Clause of the First Amendment.[59] Prayers at high school graduation exercises have also been ruled out.[60] Even a moment of silence in the public schools is outlawed if a teacher suggests it be used for prayer.[61] Thus, the Court has consistently ruled that school prayer unconstitutionally involves the state in the establishment of religion.

The Establishment Clause also plays a role in the debate over state aid to private schools. In 2002, the U.S. Supreme Court ruled in *Zelman v. Simmons-Harris* that a school voucher program in Cleveland, Ohio, did not violate the Constitution because the vouchers were intended for the secular purpose of helping children of low-income families attending failing schools. But in 2004, the Colorado Supreme Court ruled a school voucher program violated a provision of the Colorado Constitution. Similarly, in January 2006, the Florida Supreme Court struck down a school voucher plan on grounds that it violated a section of the Florida Constitution providing "for a uniform, efficient, safe, secure and high-quality system of free public schools." In 2009, at the urging of the NEA, Democrats in Congress effectively killed the D.C. voucher program in a compromise plan one critic called "choosing attrition over summary execution."[62]

Although the National Education Association (NEA) is a staunch opponent of voucher plans, the idea of an alternative to dysfunctional public schools is not likely to fade away. Even so, polls continue to show most voters still don't support school voucher programs that compete with public schools for tax dollars.

Privacy and the Right to Life

In 1973, the Supreme Court ruled in *Roe v. Wade* that most laws against abortion violated the right to privacy under the Due Process Clause of the Fifth Amendment. Since then, a more conservative Court has ruled that a woman's right to an abortion does not require the use of public funds to reimburse poorer women for the cost of abortions, nor is the state required to pay public employees for performing or assisting in abortions.[63]

Objections to *Roe v. Wade* have come largely from right-to-life groups, whose members believe human life begins at conception and abortion therefore amounts to legalized murder. Anti-abortion protesters have picketed and sometimes blockaded abortion clinics, actions that are illegal under a federal law passed in 1994. The same year, the Supreme Court held that anti-abortion activists could be sued under the Racketeer Influenced and Corrupt Organization (RICO) law if blockading abortion clinics inflicted economic harm on those performing abortions.[64] But in 1997 the Court appeared to contradict itself when it ruled that anti-abortion demonstrators also enjoy constitutional protection under the First Amendment.[65]

Since the 1973 Supreme Court's ruling in *Roe v. Wade*, pro-choice and anti-abortion activists in the United States have demonstrated vocally and sometimes violently. On a Sunday morning in late May 2009, a gunman entered the foyer of a church in Wichita, Kansas, then shot and killed Dr. George Tiller, a licensed physician who performed abortions at his local clinic. It was not the first instance of its kind, and law-enforcement officials fear it will not be the last.

In 2004, the Bush administration served medical subpoenas on hospitals and clinics demanding lists of patients who had undergone certain types of abortions.[66] The federal government nonetheless sought the medical records of 2,700 patients from a public hospital and six Planned Parenthood clinics in San Francisco alone.[67] The dispute involved legal challenges to an anti-abortion law many legal experts argued was in conflict with a Supreme Court decision in a Nebraska case.[68] A federal judge in San Francisco denied the Justice Department access: "There is no question that the patient is entitled to privacy and protection." The information sought, the judge ruled, was potentially "of an extremely intimate and personal nature." [69]

In 2007, the conservative Roberts Court (*Gonzales v. Carhart*) upheld a 2003 law banning "partial birth" (late-term) abortions. In so doing, the Court rejected the rulings in four Federal District Courts and three Federal Circuit Courts, all of which found the law unconstitutional.

Several Supreme Court justices have defended the pro-choice position by developing a new concept of privacy based on a right "to define one's own concept of existence, of meaning, of the universe, and of the mystery of human life."[70] On this basis, some also claim people under some circumstances choose death over life, as in a medically assisted suicide. In 1997, the Supreme Court unanimously refused to recognize a constitutional right to die.[71]

THE PURSUIT OF JUSTICE

In a just society, laws are applied fairly and the punishment fits the crime. Viewed in this way, justice is not a pie-in-the-sky ideal but a realistic political end achievable by means of proper courts and legal systems.

Crime and Punishment

No society can afford to let seriously antisocial or criminal behavior go unpunished. The four main most commonly cited reasons for punishment are **incarceration, deterrence, rehabilitation**, and **retribution**. The first can protect society by taking dangerous criminals off the streets; the other three are less clear-cut. Does punishing one crime deter another? Are prisons conducive to rehabilitation? Is retribution a good thing?

incarceration
The isolation of criminals in an effort to protect society and to prevent lawbreakers from committing more crimes.

deterrence
In criminal justice theory, punishing a criminal for the purpose of discouraging others from committing a similar crime; in international relations, the theory that aggressive wars can be prevented if potential victims maintain a military force sufficient to inflict unacceptable punishment on any possible aggressor.

rehabilitation
Education, training, and social conditioning aimed at encouraging imprisoned criminals to become normal, productive members of society when they are released.

retribution
The punishment of criminals on the ground that they have done wrong and deserve to suffer as a consequence.

Justice as Fair Procedure

An old legal cliché holds that 90% of fairness in the law is fair procedure. Procedural safeguards are essential to prevent the innocent from being falsely accused and the accused from being falsely convicted. These safeguards—called **due process of law**—are outlined in the Fourth, Fifth, and Sixth Amendments of the Bill of Rights. Under the Constitution, citizens have the legal right:

- Not to be subjected to unreasonable searches and seizures by the state,

- Not to be tried twice for the same offense,

- Not to incriminate themselves,

- To receive a speedy and public trial by an impartial jury,

- To be informed of the nature of any charge made against them,

- To be confronted by any witnesses against them,

- To obtain witnesses in their favor, and

- To have legal counsel.

As a group, these guarantees represent the heart of the U.S. justice system. Meticulous (and, at times, exasperating) adherence to the rules of "due process" is essential to protect defendants from miscarriages of justice. [72]

The Limits of Legal Protection

Despite all safeguards, the criminal justice system is far from perfect. The poor cannot afford high-priced lawyers, nor has justice always been color-blind. Historically, injustice in the United States has been closely associated with race. The plight of both African Americans and Native Americans as a group illustrates this point.

For a long time after slavery was abolished, black men in the South convicted (often falsely) of raping white women were sentenced to death or life in prison, whereas whites accused of similar crimes against black women were often not even brought to trial. Even today, the prison population reflects the history of race relations: in 2008, 1 in 9 black men ages 20 to 34 was behind bars in the United States; for the population as a whole, it was 1 in 100.

Native Americans have also been victims of historical injustices. Driven off ancestral hunting grounds during the westward expansion, cheated by treaties ignored and promises broken, nearly all the indigenous Indian tribes that survived the arrival of Europeans in the New World were eventually confined to reservations on marginal lands.

But recognizing injustices and flaws in the legal system is easier than correcting them. Virtually every due process guarantee has been the object of bitter controversy. For example, the Constitution grants a defendant the right to an attorney. But what if the accused cannot afford an attorney? Is the state required to provide an attorney for an indigent person accused of a felony? (Yes.) What about a defendant who wishes to appeal a verdict? (Yes.) Only for the first appeal? (Yes.)[73]

due process of law
The established legal and court procedures aimed at ensuring that arrests, interrogations, jury selection, the rules of evidences, verdicts, and sentencing are fair, uniform, and bent toward a common result: justice.

An Oglala Sioux Indian farmstead on the Pine Ridge Reservation, South Dakota, one of the poorest areas in the United States.

Winston Barclay

The United States is the world's number one jailer. With 5% of the world's population, the United States has 25% of the world's prisoners. Also, there is a racial dimension to the administration of justice in the United States. Black men are 6 times as likely as white men to be incarcerated, according to a recent Pew Research Center study. Studies show that 1 in 3 African American males can expect to spend some time in jail. Blacks constitute 13% of the general population but more than 40% of the prison population (1.57 million in 2012).[74]

The shooting death of Michael Brown in the St. Louis suburb of Ferguson, Missouri, and the choking death of Eric Garner in New York City—both unarmed black men killed by white police officers—sparked nationwide protests and charges of racially motivated police brutality in 2014. In December, two white New York City police officers were ambushed and killed in an apparent act of revenge. These and other incidents raised tensions between whites and blacks to a level not seen in many cities since the civil rights protests of the 1960s and 1970s, quite possibly striking a severe blow to the cause of racial justice and social harmony in a country still weighed down by the heavy legacy of slavery.

Obviously, there are limits to the scope of legal safeguards. Apply them too broadly and it becomes next to impossible to convict anyone accused of anything, due process becomes self-defeating, and justice itself is undermined. In the end, the courts must balance the procedural rights of the accused against the obligation of government to punish lawbreakers.

In wartime, constitutional guarantees and due process are circumscribed in ways not acceptable under any other circumstances. During the Civil War,

Ten days after the Staten Island Grand Jury failed to indict the police officer who killed Eric Garner, thousands of people marched in protest of the recent police brutality in New York City, chanting the slogans "Black Lives Matter" and "Ferguson is Everywhere."

Stacy Walsh Rosenstock/Alamy

President Lincoln even suspended habeas corpus. At one point, the chief justice of the Supreme Court, Roger Taney, was frozen in an eyeball-to-eyeball confrontation with the U.S. military over this very issue and had to back down when it became clear that the chief executive was on the side of the generals.

Fast-forward to the fall of 2001. In the aftermath of 9/11, Congress passed sweeping new antiterror legislation that gave the Justice Department unprecedented powers of investigation and interrogation, search and seizure, arrest and detention, and surveillance (including telephone wiretaps and email monitoring), provided these activities were carried out for purposes of combating terrorism. The Patriot Act was rushed through the Republican House of Representatives and passed with minor modifications in the Democratic Senate, with only one opposing vote from Senator Russell Feingold of Wisconsin. Many of Europe's democracies require all citizens to carry ID cards, but this practice has long been resisted in both the United States and the United Kingdom.

The Exclusionary Rule This rule holds that when evidence has been illegally obtained, it cannot be entered in a court of law. In the absence of such a rule, the Supreme Court has declared, the Fourth Amendment prohibition against illegal searches and seizures would be unenforceable.[75] Thus, the **exclusionary rule** provides an indispensable barrier to deliberate abuse of police powers.

Critics of this rule (including several Supreme Court justices) see it as an impediment to law enforcement and focus on the problems it causes for police officers, crime scene investigators, and prosecutors.[76] Few searches and seizures, they point out, conform to textbook cases; often police officers have to make

exclusionary rule
In judicial proceedings, the rule that evidence obtained in violation of constitutional guidelines cannot be used in court against the accused.

spur-of-the-moment decisions. Police officers face harrowing situations without the luxury of time to deliberate in the safe circumstances enjoyed by judges and juries. Others, however, argue that law-enforcement officers are often overzealous. They view the exclusionary rule as vital protection against arbitrary arrest, false accusation, and wrongful conviction.

The Supreme Court has tried to find a middle ground by carving out a "harmless error" exception that admits illegally obtained evidence in certain situations.[77] But striking the proper balance between the rights of the accused and effective law enforcement is easier said than done.

Judicial Discretion Prevailing legal theory long favored wide discretion for prosecutors (to prosecute, plea-bargain, or not prosecute), judges (to pronounce indeterminate sentences), and parole boards (to determine how much actual time a convicted criminal should serve). Critics argue inconsistency from case to case creates doubts about the impartiality of the justice system and dilutes the deterrent effect of punishment; sentencing, for example, often depends on circumstances that ought to be irrelevant, such as which judge tries which case.

In 1986, Congress enacted mandatory minimum sentence laws in a number of states to reduce or eliminate indeterminate (discretionary) sentences. But experience shows there are no easy answers. Take the example of mandatory sentences aimed at drug traffickers. The law allows sentence reductions when defendants provide "substantial assistance" (rat on other drug dealers). The drug kingpins are in the best position to provide such assistance. As a result, the biggest offenders sometimes get off easy; the drug mules or street dealers, who have little information to give, often get the stiffest sentences.

Mandatory minimum sentences are criticized as a cause of prison overcrowding, for punishing too few high-level dealers, and for sending to prison record numbers of women and people of color. In 2005, the Supreme Court ruled that federal judges are not bound by mandatory sentencing guidelines.

Capital Punishment Thirty-two states still have capital punishment on the books. Between 1976, when the death penalty was reinstated, and 2014, 150 people who were convicted and sentenced to death were subsequently exonerated, and at least 20 people on death row were released on the basis of exonerating DNA evidence.[78]

Experts differ about whether capital punishment actually deters murders. The evidence has been so fragmentary, and the interpretations so diverse, that a definitive answer is unlikely. But the bitterest controversy surrounds the whole question of whether or not capital punishment is morally defensible.

Are whites as likely as blacks to be convicted in capital crimes? If potential jurors who do not believe in capital punishment are dismissed in *voir dire* (the jury selection process), does that stack the deck against the accused?

Both sides emphasize the sanctity of human life. Defenders of capital punishment say justice demands the death penalty precisely because society is morally obligated to condemn the murder of innocent persons in the harshest possible way. Opponents say not even the state has the right to take a human life. Here's one startling fact seldom mentioned in the United States: all twenty-eight members of the European Union have outlawed the death penalty.

GOALS IN CONFLICT

Certainly, the five core values examined in this chapter—security, prosperity, equality, liberty, and justice—are not always easy to translate into public policy. Many times, the goals themselves conflict. The war on terror was a grim reminder of the tension between liberty and security in times of crisis.[79]

Moderation and tolerance are keys to good government and a vibrant civil society. Together, they guard against the temptation to pursue one end of government at the expense of all the others.

SUMMARY

Public policy issues attempt to satisfy five basic goals: security, prosperity, equality, liberty, and justice. Security is the most fundamental goal of government, because a country cannot pursue or preserve other values without it. In pursuing security, government attempts to protect citizens from foreign enemies, from fellow citizens, from natural enemies, and, in some instances, from themselves.

In the United States, the goal of prosperity has historically been associated with a free-enterprise economy based on the idea of the commercial republic. In the twentieth century, however, the government has attempted to promote the economic well-being of individuals through social welfare and other programs. These programs have sparked heated debate over the proper role of government in economic matters, especially as the budget deficit has increased. Problems in the educational system endanger U.S. competitiveness in the international economy. Income distribution also made for a lively topic of national debate in recent years and became a front-burner issue after the Wall Street meltdown in the fall of 2008. The election of Barack Obama and the economic recession have made extravagant executive bonuses and income disparities front-page news.

The goal of equality in the United States has been closely identified with the effort to end racial discrimination. Two landmark Supreme Court cases in the post–Civil War period helped perpetuate state laws and public attitudes upholding established patterns of racial inequality. Later, *Brown v. Board of Education* (1954) spearheaded the civil rights movement, which culminated in legislative, judicial, and administrative measures aimed at bringing about genuine racial equality. These civil rights gains were followed by new controversies over mandatory school busing to achieve racial integration and affirmative action guidelines designed to rectify past inequalities. Other major public policy issues related to equality have addressed the rights of various ethnic groups, women, and the poor and disadvantaged.

The pursuit of liberty is a core value of U.S. society. Among the personal liberties protected explicitly by the First Amendment are freedom of speech, freedom of the press, and freedom of religion. The right to privacy, or freedom of choice, is another significant aspect of personal liberty in the United States.

We can narrowly define the pursuit of justice as the government's attempt to ensure fair and impartial treatment under the law. In the United States, the criminal justice system strives to uphold a commitment to due process, or fair procedure. The controversial exclusionary rule attempts to balance the defendant's right to due process against society's right to be protected against criminals. Debates about judicial discretion and capital punishment also attempt to balance defendants' and society's rights.

Conflicts among these five goals prevent any one of them from being fully realized. A moderate, well-informed, and fair-minded citizenry is thus essential to sound public policy and a sustainable democratic order.

KEY TERMS

national security   389
entitlements   399
Emission Trading
   Scheme (ETS)   401
Kyoto Protocol   401
sustainable
   growth   401
federal budget
   deficit   404

Balanced Budget Act of
   1997   404
economic
   stimulus   404
reverse
   discrimination   419
affirmative action   419
civil liberties   420
symbolic speech   422

prior restraint   422
incarceration   424
deterrence   424
rehabilitation   424
retribution   424
due process of
   law   425
exclusionary
   rule   427

REVIEW QUESTIONS

1. What are some political issues that arise from security concerns?
2. What internal and external economic problems face the United States today? What triggered the current recession? What measures has the Obama administration taken to deal with it?
3. Contrast the ideal and the practice of equality in U.S. history.
4. Explain the idea of affirmative action. What groups, if any, deserve protection, and why?
5. What is reverse discrimination? How has the Supreme Court ruled in cases alleging discrimination of this kind? Do you agree or disagree with these rulings? Explain.
6. Why is liberty valuable? How is it protected in the United States?
7. What challenges currently plague the U.S. criminal justice system? Is the law color-blind? Comment.
8. Is mandatory sentencing a good idea in your opinion? Explain your point of view.
9. What is the relationship between the public good and moderation?

WEBSITES AND READINGS

Websites

Leadership Conference on Civil Rights and the Leadership Conference on Civil Rights Education Fund: http://www.civilrights.org/

National Education Association Legislative Action Center: http://www.nea.org/

Budget and Fiscal Policy Simulator: http://www.nathannewman.org/nbs/

Cumulative Trade Deficit Moment by Moment: http://www.americaneconomi-calert.org/ticker_home.asp

U.S. Census Bureau Foreign Trade Statistics: https://www.census.gov/foreign-trade/statistics/highlights/index.html

National Debt Clock Showing Each Citizen's Share: http://brillig.com/debt_clock/

Current Year and National Debt History: http://www.treasurydirect.gov/govt/reports/pd/histdebt/histdebt_histo5.htm

Analysis Behind and Beyond Government Economic Reporting: http://www.shadowstats.com/

Affirmative Action and Diversity Project: http://vos.ucsb.edu/browse.asp?id=143

Public Policy Information: http://www.policyalmanac.org/

National Health Expenditures Fact Sheet: http://www.cms.gov/Research-Statistics-Data-and-Systems/Statistics-Trends-and-Reports/NationalHealthExpendData/NHE-Fact-Sheet.html

Readings

Because public policy questions are forever changing, exposure to current information and thoughtful opinion is vital. Appropriate reading would include highly respected newspapers (such as the *New York Times* and the *Washington Post*), weekly news magazines (such as *Time* and *Newsweek*), magazines of opinion (including the *Nation, New Republic, Atlantic, Harper's, Commentary,* and *National Review*), and certain scholarly journals that specialize in public policy questions (such as *The Public Interest*). One collection that covers themes discussed in the last several chapters is Henry Aaron et al., eds., *Values and Public Policy* (Washington, DC: Brookings Institution, 1994).

Alexander, Michelle. *The New Jim Crow: Mass Incarceration in the Age of Colorblindness.* New York, NY; The New Press, 2012. The author argues persuasively that government efforts to stem criminal activity in the U.S., including the illegal drug trade, are racially motivated and have had devastating effects in African–American urban neighborhoods.

Altman, Nancy J. *The Battle for Social Security: From FDR's Vision To Bush's Gamble.* Hoboken, NJ: Wiley, 2005. A well-researched study of Social Security from its inception to the Bush administration.

Dahl, Robert. *On Political Equality.* New Haven, CT: Yale University Press, 2007. A thoughtful essay; Dahl is among the most esteemed political scientists of his generation.

Eric Laursen. *The People's Pension: The Struggle to Defend Social Security Since Reagan.* Oakland, CA: AK Press, 2012. A provocative study of the most deeply rooted and broad based social program in U.S. history, the forces arrayed against it, and the battle to save it.

Keller, Bill. "Prison Revolt," The New Yorker, June 29, 2015, pp. 22–28. A penetrating article on conservative efforts to bring about enlightened prison reforms in the U.S., rare bipartisan cooperation on this issue, and the problems deep prison reform poses for policy-makers.

Moghalu, Kingsley. *Global Justice: The Politics of War Crimes Trials*. Stanford, CA: Stanford University Press, 2008. A topic given renewed prominence and relevance in 2014.

Paust, Jordan. *Beyond the Law: The Bush Administration's Unlawful Response in the "War" on Terror.* New York: Cambridge University Press, 2007. On the legal and moral implications of "enhanced interrogation" (torture) and "extraordinary rendition" (abduction without extradition) used against "unlawful combatants" (prisoners of war).

Piketty, Thomas. *Capital in the Twenty-First Century.* Harvard, MA: Harvard University Press, 2014. Argues that if global current trends toward ever-greater inequality continue the consequences are "potentially terrifying." Acclaimed as a "watershed" in economic thought.

Shenkman, Rick. *Just How Stupid Are We? Facing the Truth About the American Voter.* New York: Basic Books, 2009. Argues that most Americans are too ignorant and ill informed to vote intelligently and urges reforms in higher education aimed at civic literacy.

PART 4

Politics by Violent Means
Revolution, War, and Terrorism

CHAPTER 14

Revolution
In the Name of Justice

Learning Objectives

1. Explain how the American and French Revolutions differed.

2. Compare and contrast Edmund Burke's and Thomas Paine's view of revolution.

3. Demonstrate the connection between John Locke's political theory and the American Revolution more than seventy years after his death.

4. Identify and discuss the causes of revolution.

At the beginning of 2011, the eyes of the world were riveted on the turbulence in Egypt; then in 2012, all eyes were on Syria. Many in the mass media called the upheaval in Egypt a revolution and the one in Syria a civil war. What happened in Egypt was a mass uprising on a scale not witnessed in the Arab world at any time in recent memory. But was it a **revolution**? And what about Syria? When does a "civil war" morph into a "revolution"?

It's true that Egypt's dictator Hosni Mubarak was forced to flee the country, a victory for the antigovernment protesters in Tahrir Square. But the Egyptian military did not relinquish formal control of the government for a full year after the Arab Spring and even then the generals kept a tight rein on the election process, media outlets, and state security organs. Given the long history of military rule in Egypt, the acid test comes down to whether or not real political power is transferred from military to civilian hands. By the same token, until Syria's ruthless ruler Bashir Assad abdicates or is forced out of power, there will be no regime change and therefore no revolution no matter how much blood is spilled in Syria.

What exactly is a revolution? Few words are used more loosely than "revolution" and "revolutionary." Television commercials abound with descriptions of "revolutionary" new antiaging skin creams, Internet-enabled cell phones, or hybrid cars that represent a "revolution" in transportation. *Real* revolutions, however, are deadly serious business.

Revolutions are not to be confused with revolts. Any mass action that does not result in a fundamental change in the form of government is quite possibly a revolt, but it is not enough to qualify as a revolution. Revolts are often accompanied by violence and social upheaval, but they rarely result in a revolution. That's the reason it was premature to call the turbulence in Egypt a "revolution" before anyone knew the final outcome, or *dénouement*. Nor is violence a sure sign of revolution. Some recent revolutions—in the former Soviet Union and Eastern Europe—have brought little or no bloodshed. In other cases, a great deal of social upheaval—and, yes, violence—has not resulted in a change of regime (for example, Syria in 2012).

The eighteenth century witnessed two great revolutions—one in the New World (the American Revolution) and one in the Old World (the French Revolution). But it was not until the twentieth century that revolutions swept across the globe—from Russia (1917) to China (1949) to the Third World (1960s and 1970s) to Eastern Europe (1989) and, coming full circle, back to (Soviet) Russia (1991). Great technological advances filled the years following World War II: space travel, organ transplants, computers, and the Internet. Those same years—coinciding with the Cold War—witnessed an eruption of revolutions in the Middle East, Africa, Asia, and Latin America.

The period after World War II saw the fastest and most far-reaching changes in world history so far. During this age of revolution, the dizzying pace of change was changing the nature of revolution itself. The Russian and Chinese revolutions occurred in agrarian societies. Although revolutions in the Third World were typically associated with Marxist ideologies and opposition to Western colonial rule, ethnic and religious conflicts often played a major role as well.[1] Unlike many anti-colonial independence struggles, the largely peaceful

revolution
A fundamental change in the rules and institutions that govern a society, often involving violent conflict in the form of mass action, insurrection, secession, or civil war.

OH, THOSE REVOLTING MOVIES!

Dozens of movies on revolution have been made, some dating back to the early years of the modern film industry. Famed Russian film director Sergei Eisenstein made two such movies in the 1920s, *The Battleship Potemkin* (1925) and *October: Ten Days That Shook the World* (1928).

Here are ten additional movies on revolution for you to watch at your leisure:

> *Zapata* (1952)
> *Doctor Zhivago* (1965)
> *Bananas* (1971)
> *Reds* (1980)
> *Missing* (1982)
> *Divided We Fall* (2000)
> *Good Bye Lenin!* (2003)
> *The Motorcycle Diaries* (2004)
> *Carlos* (2010)
> *John Adams* (2008)

These movies portray a wide variety of nations and time periods. For example, *Good Bye Lenin!* is a German film set in 1989–1990. The movie spans the amazing year during which the Berlin Wall was dismantled and Germany was reunified. It's a story about a young man who creates an elaborate ruse, pretending that the Berlin Wall is still standing so that his diehard Communist mother, emerging from a nine-month coma, is spared the shock of learning that her beloved East Germany no longer exists. In other words, it's about a fragile old revolutionary who wakes up in the midst of a robust new revolution—and a son who fears that it will kill her.

If revolution is such a bad thing, as Americans were led to believe during the Cold War—and many Americans still do believe—why is it the subject of countless popular books and movies, many of which make out rebels to be the good guys—heroic figures and often tragic victims of an unjust system? Think about it.

(Hint: Ambivalence is common in politics and life. Revolutions are violent and unpredictable. The three world-shaking revolutions of the twentieth century were particularly violent and gave rise to totalitarian regimes. Even so, many Americans are disposed to sympathize with underdogs, the oppressed, and "popular liberation movements." Contemplate possible reasons for this paradox.)

revolutions in Eastern Europe following the collapse of Communist rule led to democratization and liberal reforms (see Chapter 8).

Studying the contexts, causes, and consequences of revolution is essential to understanding the political forces that shape today's world. We begin with a look at the incidence of revolution in the modern world.

THE FREQUENCY OF REVOLUTIONS

Revolutions have occurred throughout human history, particularly during times of strong population expansion and rapid economic change.[2] Significant changes in governmental structure took place in many Greek city-states in the seventh and sixth centuries BCE, in Rome in the first century BCE, in the Islamic world in the eighth century CE, and in Europe, particularly from 1500 to 1650 and from 1750 to 1850.

In the twentieth century, revolutions occurred more frequently. In a sense, revolutions were part of a surge in national violence that marked most of the century. In the 1930s, the renowned Harvard sociologist Pitirim Sorokin studied "internal disturbances" in eleven political communities. In Western Europe alone, he was able to identify no fewer than 1,622 such disturbances in the post–World War I era, of which fully 70% "involved violence and bloodshed on a considerable scale."[3] Moreover, in each country studied, for every five years of relative peace, Sorokin found one year of "significant social disturbance." He concluded that the twentieth century overall was the bloodiest and most turbulent period in history—and he made that judgment *before* World War II.

Subsequent events bore out his judgment. From 1945 to 1970, fully forty of the approximately one hundred developing countries witnessed at least one military takeover. Between 1943 and 1962, attempts to overthrow an existing government occurred in virtually every country in Latin America, in two-thirds of the countries of Asia, and in half the African countries that had gained independence.[4] Although the world has witnessed many revolutions, rebellions, and civil disturbances since the 1970s, the incidence of military coups has decreased in more recent decades. The *New York Times* reported that between 1946 and 1959, however, there were 1,200 separate instances of "internal war," including "civil wars, guerrilla wars, localized rioting, widely dispersed turmoil, organized and apparently unorganized terrorism, mutinies, and coups d'état."[5]

Not all revolutions are violent. In Eastern Europe, one country after another broke away from the Soviet Union in 1989, and most turned toward a market economy and parliamentary democracy. In all but a few instances—Romania, for example—these revolutions came about with a minimum of violence and bloodshed. In the former Czechoslovakia, it even came to be called the Velvet Revolution, because the changeover from communist dictatorship to constitutional government was so smooth. The newly independent Baltic republics of Estonia, Latvia, and Lithuania are also notable examples of peaceful mass revolution. In each, a process of political transformation was initiated without great upheaval, destruction of property, or loss of life.

MODERN REVOLUTIONS: TWO TRADITIONS

Although revolutions date to the slave revolts of antiquity, we can trace to the late eighteenth century the idea of modern revolution—the belief "that a nation's people, by concerted political struggle, could fundamentally transform the political order that governed their lives and, with it, the social and economic structure of society."[6] Modern revolutions possess a distinctive attribute: the use of the anger of the lower classes not merely to destroy the prevailing social order but also "to create a new and different one in which the traditional forms of oppression did not exist."[7] For this reason, they are usually "characterized by a set of emotion-laden utopian ideas—an expectation that the society is marching toward a profound transformation of values and structures, as well as personal behavior."[8]

Modern revolution, and its desire to establish a new, just, social order, usually is traced to the **French Revolution** of 1789. But the **American Revolution**, begun in 1776, provides another model. Both revolutions, among the most important political events of the modern age, influenced the destiny of generations to

French Revolution
(1789) Brought down the Bourbon monarchy in France in the name of *"liberté, egalité, et fraternité"* (liberty, equality, and fraternity); introduced the contagion of liberalism in a Europe still ruled by conservative, aristocratic, and royalist institutions; and ushered in the rule of Napoléon Bonaparte. Prelude to the First Republic in France and to the Napoleonic Wars.

American Revolution
(1775–1783) Also called the War of Independence and the Revolutionary War, this epoch-making event led to the end of British rule over the thirteen American colonies and to the formation of the United States of America in 1787–1789; usually dated from the Declaration of Independence in 1776.

come. Both championed profoundly important political changes animated by visions of a new kind of political order. Yet they differed dramatically in many other respects. As one astute observer contended:

> It is certainly indisputable that the world, when it contemplates the events of 1776 and after, is inclined to see the American Revolution as a French Revolution that never quite came off, whereas the Founding Fathers thought they had cause to regard the French Revolution as an American Revolution that had failed. Indeed, differing estimates of these two revolutions are definitive of one's political philosophy in the modern world: there are two conflicting conceptions of politics, in relation to the human condition, which are symbolized by these two revolutions. There is no question that the French Revolution is, in some crucial sense, the more "modern" of the two. There is a question, however, as to whether this is a good or bad thing.[9]

The American Revolution

There was no doubt in the minds of the Founders that the American War for Independence against the British Crown (King George III) was a revolution, or that signing the Declaration of Independence was an act of treason. Nor did they have any illusions about the grim fate that awaited them if the revolution failed. As Benjamin Franklin is reputed to have said, they needed to all hang together or they would hang separately.

In waging a war against England in the 1770s, the American colonists became the instigators of the modern world's first successful anti-colonial revolution. In time, the colonists' break with Great Britain became complete and irreparable. For that reason, it is tempting to say the American **Revolutionary War** created a model for later wars of national liberation. However, it differed decisively from subsequent revolutions prior to 1989.

Historical Significance To understand the historical significance of the American Revolution, we must first examine the political opinions of its leaders. They saw the Revolutionary War as a special and unique experience. "From the very beginning," according to one authority, "it was believed by those who participated in it—on the western side of the Atlantic—to be quite a remarkable event, not merely because it was their revolution, but because it seemed to them to introduce a new phase in the political evolution of mankind, and therefore to be touched with universal significance."[10] The Founders were well acquainted with world history and with the writings of the great political philosophers, including Montesquieu, Locke, Rousseau, David Hume, and Voltaire.[11] Given this familiarity, they were not inclined to overestimate the value of new or experimental approaches to politics.

The revolutionaries of 1776 believed the divorce they demanded had universal meaning and that the Declaration of Independence was the timeless expression of it. In other words, they perceived an intimate relationship between the words (the "truths") they promulgated and the deeds they performed.[12] Thus, to discover what was truly revolutionary about the American Revolution, we first focus on what the revolutionaries wrote about government and then observe what they did about it.

Revolutionary War
The American War of Independence (1775–1783).

The Battle of Lexington. The "first blow for liberty" in America's War for Independence was struck at the Battle of Lexington in April 1775; the American Revolution was the world's first successful anti-colonial uprising.

Hulton Archive/Getty Images

Justification The clearest exposition of the American revolutionary credo can be found in the Declaration of Independence. In addition to proclaiming separation from Great Britain, the Declaration enunciated the reasons for it.

The British government, it asserted, had grievously violated the principles of good government. Following Locke's lead, Thomas Jefferson (the chief author) argued that those principles were twofold: (1) government must conform to the will of the majority (according to the Declaration's precise language, such a government must be based on "the consent of the governed"), and (2) it must protect the inalienable rights of all individuals to "Life, Liberty, and the pursuit of Happiness." These principles, in Jefferson's view, established the criteria by which to measure the legitimacy of all governments in all times and places. A good (or legitimate) government, in other words, draws its authority from the consent of the governed and acts to ensure the inalienable rights of all its citizens.

By making human rights the philosophical basis of good government, the Declaration departed significantly from past precedent and contemporary practice. Formerly, governments had come into existence to guarantee order, to build empires, to punish impiety, or to enforce obedience. Now, for the first time in history, a political regime dedicated itself unequivocally to the principle of securing popular rights and liberties.

It followed from the Declaration's principles that governments that repeatedly jeopardized, rather than protected, those rights forfeited their claim to rule. Having stated this conclusion in the Declaration, the colonists continued to wage their war for independence.

Although initially they desired only to be treated as equal British subjects, with the drafting of the Declaration they insisted on complete self-government. Nor would just any government do; they wished ultimately to create a government consistent with the self-evident truths they had pronounced in the Declaration. And these truths, they believed, were applicable far beyond the boundaries of the thirteen colonies. Jefferson found *universal* meaning in the enduring words of the document he had drafted:

> May it be to the world, what I believe it will be (to some parts sooner, to others later, but finally to all), the signal of arousing men to burst the chains under which monkish ignorance and superstition had persuaded them to bind themselves and to assume the blessings and security of self-government.[13]

Social and Political Changes Jefferson's sentiments were expressed in language that ranks with the best revolutionary rhetoric of his or any other time; certainly, it stirred citizens to fight and die for the cause. Even so, it would be a mistake to view the American Revolution solely in the context of the fighting that ensued. While the historic battles raged, great social, economic, and religious changes took place. Restrictive inheritance laws, such as primogeniture and entail, were abolished; large British estates were confiscated and redistributed in smaller holdings; royal restrictions on land settlements were repealed; important steps to secure religious equality and separation of church and state were taken; and old families lost power, their places "taken by new leaders drawn from younger men, from the common people, and from the middle classes."[14]

Political changes also occurred, as every colony wrote a new constitution. Drafted in the heat of war, these constitutions perpetuated existing systems of local self-government, especially the executive branch, while protecting individual liberties. The concepts and principles incorporated in these documents were then reflected in the Articles of Confederation and, eventually, in the U.S. Constitution. It is impossible to overemphasize the importance of this preoccupation with the rule of law, or legality, and procedural correctness.

The *constitution-writing process* culminated in the creation of a government by majority rule, at a time when Europe was still largely subject to the autocratic rule of monarchs. Moreover, the colonists' steadfast concern for constitutionality helped defuse or prevent conspiracies and cabals that could have divided the new nation into many feuding political subdivisions.

"A Revolution of Sober Expectations" In retrospect, the American Revolution was marked by a "rare economy of violence when compared to other revolutions."[15] In comparison with later revolutionary conflicts (such as the French Revolution, the Russian Revolution, and the Spanish Civil War), civilian reprisals between insurrectionists and loyalists were mild. In addition, the leaders of the American Revolution were never purged or murdered, as so many instigators of later revolutions would be. To the contrary, the "military chief [Washington] became the first president of the Republic and retired at his own choice; the author of the Revolutionary Manifesto [Jefferson] was its first Secretary of State."[16]

What accounted for the unique orderliness of this revolution? Most important, the colonial leaders combined a Lockean attitude toward revolution with the pursuit of realistic, down-to-earth political goals. By "Lockean attitude," to which we will return later, we mean that, with few exceptions, the Founders regarded the revolution as a necessary evil. It was necessary because they knew of no other way of achieving independence from Great Britain, but it was evil insofar as it caused suffering, bloodshed, and devastation. The American Revolution remains unique precisely because it was not led by fanatics and zealots who embraced an inflexible ideology or who thought any means were appropriate to achieve their political ends. Rather, its leaders were contemplative individuals who continually questioned themselves (and one another) about the correctness of what they were doing.

Although there was no lack of enthusiasm on the part of the revolutionary leadership, "this enthusiasm was tempered by doubt, introspection, anxiety, and scepticism."[17] In short, the American Revolution never took its own goodness for granted. Its tempered revolutionary values were placed in the service of sober and clear-eyed goals. Essentially, what the colonial leaders wanted from the revolution was to separate from England and found a government on consent and respect for the rights and liberties of the people.

These objectives were ambitious but not unattainable, in contrast to the utopian aims of the French Revolution. The intertwined concepts of self-government and the protection of citizens' rights had been evolving in the colonies at both the state and township levels in advance of the revolutionary conflict. Unlike later revolutionaries, the colonial leaders did not attempt to immediately institute something radically new and different. Understanding the dangers inherent in quixotic or utopian idealism, they knew that "the political pursuit of impossible dreams leads to terror and tyranny in the vain effort to actualize what cannot be."[18]

Far from being an event marked by such terror and tyranny, the American Revolution was, in the words of one authority, "a revolution of sober expectations."[19] Sobriety, moderation, and prudence were the watchwords of this revolution and the chief characteristics of the "well-ordered union" the Constitution would later ordain.

The French Revolution

The French Revolution was quite a different affair. For years, France had experienced growing political instability and popular dissatisfaction. Seeking to preserve the sharp class distinctions that marked French society, the aristocracy had repeatedly frustrated attempts at economic and political reform. Furthermore, the government had demonstrated a clear inability to cope with changing circumstances.

Even a skilled and intelligent monarch, which Louis XVI (1754–1793) certainly was not, would have found it difficult to overcome the liability of governmental institutions that were decentralized and hard to coordinate. By the late 1780s, the government faced increasing difficulties in raising taxes to pay off massive debt from earlier wars. Then, just at the wrong time for those in power, economic reversals occurred.

Although the economy had been growing, the fruits of growth were terribly maldistributed. Many urban poor and peasants faced crushing material deprivation rather than the promise of economic development. By 1789, eddies of discontent had swelled into a sea of dissension. Middle- and upper-class reformers demanded both political and social changes, including restrictions on

The Storming of the Bastille. This bold mob action on July 14, 1789, was a direct attack against the monarchy. Louis XVI conceded too little too late, and a revolutionary tidal wave in the name of "liberty, equality, and fraternity" swept France.

class privileges and reform of the tax system. Some leaders wanted more radical changes, including the creation of a political order governed by the principles of popular sovereignty.

All these demands were put forward at the May 1789 meeting of the **Estates-General**, a giant parliament elected by broad male suffrage and divided into three estates, or houses, representing the clergy, nobility, and commoners. After considerable debate (and a good deal of turmoil), a majority of the delegates, led by the numerically preponderant Third (commoner) Estate, formed a popular National Assembly. In addition to asserting the right to approve or reject all taxation, the members of this body demanded an end to aristocratic privileges.

These actions constituted a direct attack on the monarchy. Louis XVI responded with predictable ineptitude, applying just enough force to incense his opponents. When he marshaled his troops in an effort to bar the National Assembly from meeting, the delegates promptly moved to a nearby indoor tennis court, where they resolved to draft a constitution. The king promised tax reforms later but refused to abolish the privileges of the aristocracy. At the same time, he deployed troops in strategic positions. Sporadic outbursts of violence, including the storming of the **Bastille**, followed swiftly, and Louis XVI, having lost control of the streets, was forced to accede to demands for a constitution.

An Ill-Fated Constitution Between 1789 and 1791, as the citizens of France awaited the unveiling of the new constitution, an egalitarian spirit swept the land. Aristocratic privileges were abolished, and church land was confiscated. A political document of fundamental importance, the **Declaration of the Rights of Man**, enshrined a slogan epitomizing the egalitarian spirit of the times: "liberty, equality, fraternity." The new constitution created a constitutional monarchy. No longer would Louis XVI rule autocratically according to divine right. Although the constitution placed the king at the head of the armed forces and charged him with responsibility for foreign affairs, it assigned most legislative powers to the National Constituent Assembly, which was given the power of the purse, as well as the power to declare war. A new elective administration was also created, and voting laws were liberalized. Thus, a stunning democratization of French political and social life was achieved in an amazingly brief period. The king's almost unlimited power had been undermined and radical social reforms implemented.

The constitutional monarchy set up by the 1791 constitution lasted less than one year, during which time the nation foundered without effective political leadership. Naturally, Louis XVI despised the new government imposed on him.

Estates-General
Prior the French Revolution, a quasi-legislative body in France in which each of the three estates (clergy, nobility, and commoners) was represented; it convened in 1789 for the first time since 1614.

(At one point, he even tried to flee the country to join opponents of the new government, but he was caught and returned to Paris.) The constitution barred former members of the National Constituent Assembly from serving in the new legislature, which meant inexperienced lawmakers held sway. Additional problems arose when the newly elected local administration failed to perform efficiently and interests that had lost power, especially the Catholic Church and the aristocracy, began to oppose the new regime. A war with Austria and Prussia exacerbated existing difficulties, and expected economic improvements were not forthcoming. Persistent rumors of the king's imminent return to absolute power swirled through Paris, inspiring a widespread fear of counterrevolution that undermined the political optimism brought on by the reforms.

Robespierre and the Reign of Terror   In the chaotic political and social environment of the early 1790s, events moved swiftly. Louis XVI was convicted of treason, deposed, and then beheaded in June 1793. A committee of political radicals intent on refashioning French society and unafraid to use violence took over the reins of government. The first priority of the new leader, Maximilien Robespierre (1758–1794), was to win the war against Austria and Prussia. In this atmosphere of external emergency, national unity at home was made paramount and all political opposition was considered treasonous. Then as now, political repression during times of war was common. But Robespierre was not satisfied simply to enforce national unity; he also wished to create a regime of virtue—to rebuild French society from the ground up, so to speak, by remaking the French citizenry in the image of moral perfection. According to one authority:

> Robespierre wanted a France where there should be neither rich nor poor, where men should not gamble, or get drunk, or commit adultery, cheat, or rob, or kill—where, in short, there would be neither petty nor grand vices—a France ruled by upright and intelligent men elected by the universal suffrage of the people, men wholly without greed or love of office, and delightedly stepping down at yearly intervals to give place to their successors, a France at peace with herself and the world.[20]

However grandiose, Robespierre's utopian idealism was not merely a statement of what *ought* to be; for him, it represented a call to action. Determined to create a "new citizen," Robespierre could not countenance the goal of individual freedom or the individual pursuit of happiness, as the American revolutionaries had. He was committed to a "despotism of liberty," rather than to a free society.

Institutionalizing virtue, however, was only one aspect of utopian idealism. Freedom from want, and even the promise of permanent abundance, became an important goal of Robespierre's revolution, waged in the name of the poor and oppressed against the greed and avarice of the oppressors.[21] Only through a policy motivated by compassion for the downtrodden, Robespierre believed, could a virtuous and contented citizenry emerge. Thus, the Biblical promise that "the meek shall inherit the earth" was an important part of his credo.

To advance virtue and end poverty in the shortest possible time, Robespierre proposed a sweeping reformulation of French life. Governmental institutions,

Bastille
At the time of the French Revolution (1789), the Bastille was the infamous royal prison in Paris; the mass storming of the Bastille on July 14, 1789, and the freeing of the prisoners constituted a direct attack against the monarchy and symbolized the end of an era in French history; the revolutionaries then used the guillotine against none other than the reigning Bourbon monarch, King Louis XVI, and his extravagant wife, Queen Marie Antoinette.

Declaration of the Rights of Man
Enacted by the French National Assembly in August 1789, this brief manifesto was intended as the preamble to a liberal-democratic constitution to be written later; it affirmed the sovereign authority of the nation but limited that authority by recognizing individual rights to life, property, and security.

legal arrangements, and social practices—everything was to be changed. Even a new calendar was proposed, as a symbol that a new era of history had dawned. The spirit of change was total, and heaven on earth was the ultimate goal. One observer has noted that the reigning spirit was that of "undiluted, enthusiastic, free floating messianism . . . satisfied with nothing less than a radical transformation of the human condition."[22]

But Robespierre and his compatriots soon discovered it was one thing to proclaim a new order and quite another to *keep* order. Policy disputes emerged as disillusionment reacted with unlimited expectations in a volatile mix. Active opposition to the new rulers began to spread.

Robespierre's response was to reinforce the regime of virtue with mass executions, which became known as the **Reign of Terror**. Executions by guillotine ordered by the Committee of Public Safety became commonplace, particularly in Paris. Originally aimed at active opponents, governmental violence soon gained a momentum of its own. It came to include people who shared Robespierre's vision but disagreed with his methods, and later, those merely suspected of dissenting became victims of the guillotine. Deep distrust enveloped those in power, as survivors feared for their safety. Eventually, collective fear led to the overthrow and execution of Robespierre himself. During his yearlong rule, some 40,000 people were summarily executed—an astonishing number in the eighteenth century.

Reign of Terror
During the French Revolution, Robespierre and his Committee of Public Safety arrested and mass executed thousands of French citizens for the "crime" of opposing the revolution or daring to dissent.

The King Is Dead, Long Live the Emperor   The results of the French Revolution are not easy to evaluate. Clearly, it did not achieve its desired ends. After Robespierre's fall, a corrupt and incompetent government known as the Directory assumed power. In 1799, that regime gave way to the dictatorship of Napoléon Bonaparte, who managed to restore order and stability and crowned himself emperor in 1804. Under him, France tried to conquer all Europe in a series of ambitious wars that ultimately led to defeat and Napoléon's downfall.

Thus, no popular government followed on the heels of the French Revolution. After Napoléon's deposition, in fact, the monarchy was reinstituted. Many worthwhile and long-lasting changes did come about, however. For instance, the monarchy installed in 1815 was significantly limited in its powers. Important social and political reforms stemming from the revolutionary era were retained, and the government was more centralized and more efficient. Despite these changes, however, the restored monarchy stood in sharp contrast to the egalitarian vision of a new society that had inspired Robespierre and his followers.

The Two Revolutions Compared

If the American Revolution was a revolution of sober goals, the French Revolution was one of infinite expectations. In the beginning, the French revolutionaries believed everything was possible for the pure of heart. The extremists' goals were utopian, and to realize them they were forced to use extreme means, including terror. Incredibly, America's best-known radical, Thomas Paine, found himself in a French prison during the revolution because his politics were not sufficiently extreme. In the thirteen colonies, most of the revolutionaries were political moderates. In France, moderates were executed or imprisoned.

The American Revolution, with its more modest aims, managed to produce the first great example of republican government in the modern age. France had no such luck. Yet the many revolutionary movements of the twentieth century were influenced far more by the French than the American example.[23] It is understandable why the French Revolution—with its desire to eradicate poverty and its compassion for the oppressed—has fired the imagination of revolutionaries everywhere. But if concrete and lasting results are to be achieved, political ends must be realistic; otherwise, impossible dreams can turn into inescapable nightmares.

REVOLUTION—A RIGHT OR ALL WRONG?

"The tree of liberty must be refreshed from time to time with the blood of patriots and tyrants." These words were penned by Thomas Jefferson, who believed revolution was necessary to "refresh" democracy, as well as to establish it in the first place. But was he right? Is revolution more likely to improve the lot of the people or make things worse? British conservative Edmund Burke and American revolutionary Thomas Paine, Jefferson's contemporaries, engaged in a memorable debate over this very question during the early phase of the French Revolution. The pivotal issue was whether that revolution was really in the interest of the French people, in whose name it was waged, and, more generally, whether revolutions were beneficial or detrimental to society.

Burke's "Reflections"

The French Revolution inspired Edmund Burke (1729–1797) to write perhaps the most famous critique of revolution in the English language, *Reflections on the Revolution in France* (1790). Burke did not believe the French Revolution resulted from deep-seated economic and social forces. To his mind, the real revolutionaries were the philosophers who had expounded the subversive doctrine of rationalism and worshiped the god of science. By teaching that government existed to fulfill certain simple goals (for example, to secure individual rights), revolutionaries, Burke argued, created misleading impressions—most important, that radical change almost always brought great improvements. This way of thinking undercut what Burke believed were among the most important foundations of political society: religion and tradition.

Burke argued that dangerous political abstractions were at the heart of the French Revolution. By grossly oversimplifying politics and engendering unwarranted expectations at odds with French history and tradition, simplistic concepts such as "liberty, equality, fraternity" endangered the public order, on which all other political values and virtues ultimately rested. Good order, Burke noted, was the foundation of all good things.

The science of good government—how to run, maintain, or reform it—could not be mastered through philosophical speculations, Burke contended. He saw government as an "experimental science" whose practitioners needed the wisdom and insight born of experience. And experience, by its very nature, he argued, could not be acquired overnight; rather, it was accumulated, nurtured, cherished, and above all transmitted from generation to generation. Burke's

Edmund Burke (1729–1797). Born in Dublin, Ireland, Burke is best known to the world as a British statesman and philosopher who abhorred revolution and advocated gradual change in order to conserve core values and institutions without which, he argued, societies risk descending into chaos and anarchy. "Our patience," Burke opined, "will achieve more than our force." Among his many quotable quotes, this one is perhaps the most famous: "All that is necessary for the triumph of evil is that good men do nothing."

view implied a veneration of the past, as well as a respect for age and achievement. Society, to his mind, was an intricate tapestry of laboriously handcrafted institutions possessing an inner logic and perpetuated by the force of habit, custom, and convention.

This sober view of government, and of human capacities and limitations, led Burke to stress the importance of pragmatism and prudence in politics. Prudence, he said, was the "first of all virtues." As for pragmatism, he maintained that given the complexity of humanity and society, no simple, all-embracing political formula could work the kind of profound changes promised by the French theorists.

Finally, Burke criticized the extreme impatience of those who glorified revolution. Arguing in favor of gradual and deliberate reform, he warned that unless political change occurred slowly and circumspectly, the main mass of the population would end up in worse straits than ever: "Time is required to produce that union of minds which alone can produce all the good we aim at. Our patience will achieve more than our force."[24]

By promising more than any political order can ever deliver and raising unrealistic expectations for some immediate utopian breakthrough, revolution may both dazzle the masses with visions of a bountiful (but unattainable) future and blind them to the wisdom of the past. In short, though politics can be understood as the "art of the possible," in the distorted mirror of revolution, it becomes the science of the impossible.

Paine's Rebuttal

Thomas Paine (1737–1809) attempted to refute Burke's view of revolution in his *Rights of Man*, written in two parts in February 1792 and addressed specifically to Burke. In defining the legitimacy of popular revolution, Paine stressed the many injustices perpetrated by the British monarchy on the American colonists. For him, tyranny and monarchy were as one. Monarchies, he declared, thrive on ignorance and are wrong in principle:[25]

> All hereditary government is in its nature tyranny. A heritable crown, or a heritable throne, or by what other fanciful name such things may be called, have no other significant explanation than that mankind are heritable property. To inherit a government, is to inherit the people, as if they were flocks and herds.[26]

In another passage, Paine wrote:

> When we survey the wretched condition of man under the monarchical and hereditary systems of government, dragged from his home by one power, or drived (sic) by another, and impoverished by taxes more than by enemies, it becomes evident that those systems are bad, and that a general revolution in the principle and construction of government is necessary.[27]

Thomas Paine (1737–1809) is best remembered for his ringing call to revolution in 1776 and his denunciation of monarchy in a pamphlet called *Common Sense*. Because this pamphlet inspired the American Revolution, Paine's place in history is secure, even though his role has often been overlooked in favor of iconic figures such as Thomas Jefferson, George Washington, John Adams, and Benjamin Franklin. This sign at a Tea Party rally features immortal words from another of Paine's revolutionary pamphlets called *The American Crisis*.

Paine cited numerous examples of royal injustice and corruption. The greatest, he believed, was denial of the people's right to choose their own government. It seemed obvious to him that people should in no way be bound by their ancestors' decisions. "Every age and generation must be free to act for itself, in all cases, as the ages and generations which preceded it. . . . The vanity and presumption of governing beyond the grave is the most ridiculous and insolent of all tyrannies."[28]

Paine saw revolution in France as emphatically just. In seeking to overthrow the monarchy, he contended, the French were merely exercising a fundamental right, which grew out of their equal, natural right to liberty. Paine possessed an almost religious faith in the essential goodness and wisdom of the people. This pushed him to conclude that when the French Revolution is compared with that of other countries, it becomes apparent "that *principles* and not *persons* were the meditated objects of destruction."[29]

Locke's Right to Revolt

While Burke abhorred popular revolution, Paine glorified it.[30] Roughly a century earlier, John Locke had taken a middle ground between their two extremes in his *Second Treatise of Government*. Locke began with the premise that to escape the inconveniences of anarchy in the state of nature, human beings consent to be governed. Consent formed the basis for both civil society and formal government, with government existing chiefly to protect the rights deemed essential to human life. Locke then raised this question: What happens if the government endangers the life, liberty, and property of its citizens? In such a case, he concluded, the government has exercised "force without right," and the people have the right to resist and defend themselves. In Locke's words:

> The end of Government is the good of Mankind, and which is *best for Mankind*, that the People should be always expos'd to the boundless will of Tyranny, or that the Rulers should be sometimes liable to be oppos'd, when they grow exorbitant in the use of their power, and imploy (sic) it for the destruction, and not the preservation of the Properties of their People?[31]

Locke did not glorify revolution; he cautioned that popular rebellion should not be launched on a mere impulse. People will accept individual errors and instances of misrule, he asserted, but not "a long train of Abuses, Prevarications, and Artifices."[32] Locke even suggested his doctrine of rebellion could serve as a deterrent to revolution, by causing governments to respect the people's rights. Whether or not governments choose to recognize the *right* of the people to revolt, he pointed out, the people *will* revolt against a wicked government:

> If the majority of the people are persuaded in their Consciences, that the Laws, and with them their Estates, Liberties, and Lives are in danger, and perhaps their Religion, too, how they will be hindered from resisting illegal force used against them, I cannot tell. This is an Inconvenience, I confess that attends all Governments.[33]

In proclaiming the **right to revolution**, Locke may seem to have done little more than endorse what he saw as a fact of political life. But that does not diminish the importance of his doctrine of rebellion, which was itself revolutionary in the late seventeenth century. Even in England, where a few decades earlier King Charles I had been beheaded, the question of whether dynastic rulers had a divine right to wield the scepter and command the sword was still being debated. In most other European nation-states, monarchs took the doctrine of divine right for granted. Not surprisingly, these kings did not trifle with anything so mundane as the will of the people, for they believed their authority stemmed from the will of God.

Locke's theory of revolution helped sound the death knell for the doctrine of divine right. Revolution, Locke claimed,

·JOHN LOCKE Eſ.

John Locke (1632–1704), English philosopher. Locke's magnum opus, *An Essay Concerning Human Understanding*, offers great insights into the limits of science and reason relative to what we can truly know about God, the natural order, and the self—and what we can never know. In Locke's view, the role of civil government is to preserve the life, health, liberty, and property of its subjects. When government fails, when it loses the consent of the majority, it naturally loses its legitimacy and risks overthrow. Locke's theory of revolution is not a prescription, but rather a description—based on reasoned analysis of the conditions likely to give rise to rebellion.

becomes necessary when government acts contrary to its reason for being. Does revolution ensure good government? Of course not. It may lead to anarchy followed by a worse form of tyranny. But, Locke argues, popular revolution does create the *possibility* of government based on respect for life, liberty, and property.

Thus, Locke made no utopian claims about the relationship between revolution and political revitalization. As he saw it, revolutions may stem from the desire for better government, but they cannot guarantee that happy result. Like Aristotle before him, Locke assumed the existence of a finite number of governmental forms. New governments, he argued, are invariably new only in the sense that they supersede previous governments.[34]

Revolution, thus defined, hardly seemed a romantic endeavor. In Locke's view, it meant the exchange of one imperfect form of government for another, perhaps less imperfect form; it invariably encompassed great changes in the larger society; and it almost always implied the use of political force and violence. The tendency of revolutions toward upheaval meant the process was to be feared, even if the goal was desirable. Locke's sober view of rebellion has not been eclipsed; as one leading contemporary scholar pointed out, "A period of terror and the emergence of coercive and aggressive regimes are the outcomes of revolutions."[35]

THE CAUSES OF REVOLUTION

Locke held that revolutions are necessary and proper when citizens simply cannot endure any more. But what specifically is it they cannot endure? What causes citizens to discard ingrained political habits and support revolution?

The Classical View

To many observers, history and common sense suggest that injustices perpetrated by government over a prolonged period foster the conditions in which the seeds of revolution can germinate. This explanation of the cause of revolution originated with Aristotle, who observed in the fourth century BCE that although sedition may spring from small occasions, it ordinarily does not turn on small issues. The spark that ignites a revolution, in other words, should not be confused with the underlying causes of revolt.

Under every political order, competition for honors and wealth may give rise to the popular belief that one or both have not been fairly distributed. In most cases, Aristotle postulated, revolutions are caused by the administration of unequal justice.

Aristotle's concern with the perennial tension between rich and poor in political life established a theme in Western political thought that has gained importance over time. James Madison, for example, declared in *The Federalist*, no. 10, that the "most common and durable source of faction is the various and unequal distribution of property" and then set out to develop a theory of government that might lessen this common source of political tension.

A half century later, Karl Marx declared inequality in wealth to be the ultimate cause of all revolutions. According to Marx, revolution is synonymous with class warfare and invariably stems from pervasive injustice. As the economic distance between wealthy capitalists and impoverished workers increases, so does the possibility of revolution.

What persuades the ordinary individual to disregard the strong social pressure for conformity and participate in a revolutionary movement? Marx held that desperation caused by poverty and social alienation is the chief psychological spur to revolutionary action, and his explanation has been widely accepted in modern times. A few years before Marx outlined this position in *The Communist Manifesto* (1848), however, Alexis de Tocqueville offered an alternative view. In studying the French Revolution, Tocqueville observed, "It was precisely in those parts of France where there had been the most improvement that popular discontent ran the highest. There, economic and social improvement had taken place, and political pressure had lessened, but still there existed the greatest amount of unrest."[36]

Tocqueville concluded that economic improvement leads to revolution because once the people see that some improvement is possible, they inevitably yearn for more. No longer are they willing to put up with inconveniences and annoyances—only *real* improvement, *immediate* improvement, will satisfy them. Thus is the incentive for revolution born, he argued.

Modern Theories

The positions of Marx and Tocqueville seem incompatible, but in 1962, James C. Davies wrote a celebrated article suggesting "both ideas have explanatory and possibly predictive value, if they are juxtaposed and put in the proper time sequence."[37] Davies came to this provocative conclusion after careful study of Dorr's Rebellion of 1842, the Russian Revolution of 1917, and the Egyptian Revolution of 1952. After seeing a remarkably similar pattern of revolutionary development, he concluded that revolutions are most likely to erupt when conditions have been getting better for a prolonged period of time and then suddenly take a sharp turn for the worse.

Elaborating on Davies's thesis, two authorities later argued that the rates of earlier economic growth (and the speed of any economic decline) are especially significant factors. The higher the growth rate in per capita GNP prior to a revolutionary upheaval and "the sharper the reversal immediately prior to the revolution," they declared, "the greater the duration and violence of the revolution."[38] In other words, revolutions stem not so much from terrible suffering as from crushing disappointment. Intense discontent, bred by the failure to acquire the goods and experience the conditions of life to which people believe they are rightfully entitled, induces them to revolt.[39]

A pervasive sense of injustice is typically at the core of revolutionary mass movements. But great social and economic injustice does not *always* lead to revolution. Modern theorists have tried to identify *specific* causes that can become the incubator of revolution. One way to go about this kind of academic detective work is through methodical case studies.[40]

According to political scientists Ted Gurr and Jack Goldstone, a revolution is best conceptualized as an interactive process that continues over time.[41] The machinery of government breaks down in stages as political crises ensue; both influential citizens and government leaders become alienated. Governmental leaders are increasingly perceived as inept: unable to exercise effective authority, incapable of stabilizing the economy, powerless to ensure domestic order, weak and irresolute in the face of external threats. Thus, nearly everyone (including the elites) comes to see the established government as illegitimate, and it loses its right to rule.[42] Precisely for these reasons, successful revolutionaries usually have the support of wealthy (possibly even aristocratic) patrons and are able to mobilize many discontented people as well.

Conceptualizing revolution as an interactive process is compatible with the traditional theory of revolution. It helps explain how injustice, or the perception of injustice, is at the root of revolution. Contemporary scholarship details how this process takes place. It examines the types of crises facing prerevolutionary states, the factors leading to a general loss of confidence in government, and the besieged governments' often hapless responses.

Invariably, societies on the verge of revolution face peril. Economic hardships can be particularly debilitating. Rapid population growth can slow or reverse economic growth and promote inequality. Ethnic, racial, or religious tensions may plunge a society into civil war, especially when one group grows or prospers at a faster rate than others. Rapid urbanization can create social problems, including inadequate housing, sanitation, and medical and educational services. Crime usually increases, particularly when there is a high percentage of alienated young males.[43]

Losing a war can be another prelude to revolution, because it is typically associated with severe economic hardships. In these circumstances, any government can lose its legitimacy in the eyes of the people.[44] Finally, upheavals in neighboring states can spill into and affect vulnerable governments in the vicinity.

Mounting economic, demographic, and political pressures in prerevolutionary nations can lead to criticism, lawlessness, riots, and acts of terrorism, forcing governments to act. If the bureaucracy includes officials from the landholding class, they may block or inhibit reforms designed to defuse a potentially revolutionary domestic crisis.[45] Or action may be inhibited by widespread internal corruption. But no government can tolerate long-term criticism, lawlessness, or acts of terrorism. If its response is unjust or inept, or if it fails to act at all, government risks losing the confidence of its supporters and becomes vulnerable to revolutionary demands.

Surprisingly, unpopular governments that equivocate or temporize in the face of a rebellion, rather than taking swift and decisive action to it in its infancy, are often at risk of being overthrown. In a study of the French Revolution, Tocqueville noted that French citizens took up arms against the government precisely when it began easing its crackdown. He concluded, "Generally speaking, the most perilous moment for a bad government is one when it seeks to mend its ways."[46]

Tocqueville believed that underlying this paradox (as well as his contention that reform, not repression, is the great accomplice of revolution) is a psychological truth:

> Patiently endured so long as it seemed beyond redress, a grievance comes to appear intolerable once the possibility of removing it crosses men's minds. . . .

For the mere fact that certain abuses have been remedied draws attention to the others and now appears more galling; people may suffer less, but their sensibility is exacerbated.[47]

In sum, tyrants cannot afford to institute reforms because to do so would be to admit past injustices and activate "the rancor and cupidity of the populace."[48]

Modern studies provide some support for Tocqueville's observations. In a major analysis of the role of the armed forces in revolutionary episodes, one writer argued that revolution never succeeds when the armed forces remain loyal to the government in power and can be effectively employed.[49] When internal security measures are applied too late, too haphazardly, or as the last resort of a desperate government, there is a good chance that official acts of repression may only make matters worse. Apparently, governments that shrink from the systematic use of physical force in revolutionary situations run the greatest risk of being overthrown.

Some Tentative Conclusions

Theories of revolution abound, but despite many attempts, there is still no definitive *general theory* of revolution. Nonetheless, we can draw some generalizations based on historical and sociological evidence.

For revolutions to occur, charismatic leaders must be willing to take the deadly risks associated with overthrowing an established (often repressive) regime.[50] They need the support of others in high positions and those with technical skills. The right moment to win over the elites is when the government offends, threatens, or undermines them in some way. Elite alienation poses the greatest danger to the prerevolutionary government when it occurs within the armed forces.[51] If the generals and other senior military officers withdraw support from or turn against the ruler(s), it is almost always fatal for the government in power.

Revolutionary change is frequently organized from above. However, all such change depends on the new government's success in gaining or holding a mass following, which, in turn, often depends on the degree of citizen discontent prior to the revolutionary events. The causes of popular discontent can include "widespread dissatisfaction over economic conditions, especially among urban peoples; frustration about the lack of opportunities for real political participation, especially among young students and the middle classes; widespread anger about foreign interventions and official corruption; and rural hostility toward the predatory and repressive policies of urban-based regimes."[52] In short, it is the popular perception of injustice, whether true or false, that fuels the fires of all-out revolution in the modern era.

Finally, revolutions are not likely unless most or all of the factors we discussed earlier exist simultaneously. Thus, even a nation with economic and social problems would probably not be prone to revolution unless it came also to display the other elements of prerevolution, such as the existence of revolutionary leaders, strong elite and citizen support for radical action, and a general loss of public confidence in the existing government's capacity to rule. It is the coincidence of these factors that makes revolutions happen.

The Spanish philosopher José Ortega y Gasset (1883–1955) published his famous book *The Revolt of the Masses* in 1930, after the fascists had taken over Italy, shortly before Hitler's accession to power in Germany, and just about the time Stalin was consolidating his power in Soviet Russia.[53] Ortega y Gasset wrote with horror about "the accession of the masses to complete social power" and argued that "the masses, by definition, neither should nor can direct their own personal existence, and still less rule society in general, [which means] that actually Europe is suffering from the greatest general crisis that can afflict peoples, nations, and civilizations."[54]

The twentieth century witnessed the bloodiest mass movements in history. All failed. The words of Ortega y Gasset are particularly poignant in the light of the calamitous results of modern revolutions:

> As they say in the United States: "to be different is to be indecent." The mass crushes beneath it everything that is different, everything that is excellent, individual, qualified, and select. Anybody who is not like everybody, who does not think like everybody, runs the risk of being eliminated.[55]

At the same time, the modern history of revolution provides significant counterexamples. Ironically, the United States would become the self-appointed global defender of the status quo after World War II, the archenemy of revolutionary movements in the Third World, where former colonies were fighting for independence as we ourselves had done nearly two centuries earlier. Those in the United States came to associate revolution with terror, totalitarianism, and tyrants. But when the Cold War finally drew to a close, the face of revolution suddenly changed as dozens of dictatorships were swept away.

Today, democracies flourish where Communist police states ruled for nearly half a century, thanks to a series of stunning revolutions that occurred simultaneously with very little violence (with the exception of the Balkans). It was as if a massive earthquake shook Russia and Eastern Europe to their foundations but left nearly everything intact; instead of causing great death and destruction, it actually set the stage for a political and economic resurgence.

IDEAS AND POLITICS

NONVIOLENT REVOLUTION

History teaches that violent regimes are often the offspring of violent revolutions. Between World War I (1914–1918) and the end of the Cold War (1989–1992), Russia (Lenin and Stalin), Germany (Hitler), Italy (Mussolini), Spain (Franco), China (Mao Zedong), Cuba (Castro), Cambodia (Pol Pot), Ethiopia (Mengistu), and Iran (Khomeini) endured bloody revolutions. Other notable revolutions after World War II occurred in Egypt (Nasser), Algeria (Ahmed Ben Bella), and Indonesia (Sukarno). All witnessed large-scale violence in varying degrees.

In sharp contrast, the overthrow of Dictator Slobodan Milosevic (also known as the "Bulldozer Revolution") was the culmination of a long, sustained campaign of civil resistance—in other words, a nonviolent revolution. The overthrow was led by a largely

(Continued)

student-based mass organization called *Otpor* ("Resistance" in Serbian). Nine years later, Mohamed Abdel, a 20-year-old Egyptian blogger, frustrated at the failure of one previous attempt to launch a similar nationwide uprising against the autocratic rule of Hosni Mubarak, traveled to Belgrade, Serbia.* Abdel was on a mission:

> The Serbian capital is home to the Center for Applied Non Violent Action and Strategies, or CANVAS, an organization run by young Serbs who had cut their teeth in the late 1990s student uprising against Slobodan Milosevic. After ousting him, they embarked on the ambitious project of figuring out how to translate their success to other countries. To the world's autocrats, they are sworn enemies—both Venezuela's Hugo Chávez and Belarus's Aleksandr Lukashenko have condemned them by name.

Abdel went to Serbia to take "a week-long course in the strategies of nonviolent revolution." He did not need to learn how to communicate with others using Facebook or Twitter. He already knew that. In his own words, "I got trained in how to conduct peaceful demonstrations, how to avoid violence, and how to face violence from the security forces . . . and also how to organize to get people on the streets." Above all, he learned how to teach others.

Back in Egypt, Abdel began training young people. Out of these training sessions emerged two youth groups that "led the charge in actually getting organized and onto the streets," according to one report from Stratfor, a geopolitical analysis group.

Viewed in this light, the overthrow of Hosni Mubarak is one link in a lengthening chain of popular revolts using the strategy and tactics of civil resistance to bring about regime change. Before 1989, the Baltic states of Latvia, Lithuania, and Estonia were essentially Communist dictatorships ruled from Moscow. East Germany, Poland, Hungary, Czechoslovakia, Romania,

and Bulgaria were also ruled by Soviet-style dictatorships. When Hungary revolted against Soviet rule in 1956, the Red Army quelled the uprising. In 1968, Moscow brutally suppressed a spontaneous mass revolt known as the Prague Spring in Czechoslovakia.

But two decades later, the Kremlin boss (Mikhail Gorbachev) looked the other way as Stalinist rulers in Eastern Europe tumbled like falling dominoes when the people streamed into the streets and refused to go home. The political map of Europe looks nothing like it did before 1989. Hungary is an independent country with a parliamentary democracy, as are Poland and the Baltic states. East Germany has merged with the Federal Republic of Germany (West Germany). Czechoslovakia has split into two separate states, both democratically ruled. All are members of NATO and the EU. Romania and Bulgaria joined the EU in 2007 (see Figure 14.1).

In Serbia, an organized and energized popular uprising ousted a brutal dictator. Remarkably, the protestors did it by adapting principles found in Lenin's revolutionary playbook (see Chapter 6). Three keys taught in the CANVAS seminars on nonviolent revolution are unity, discipline, and planning. Unlike Marxism-Leninism, however the emphasis on discipline in the Serbian and Egyptian uprisings was directed toward self-restraint in confrontations with security forces.

The triumph of democracy in Eastern Europe testifies to the possibility of nonviolent regime change. But the failure of the nonviolent revolution in Egypt and the brutal suppression of peaceful protests there is a cautionary tale. There's no guarantee of a happy ending.

Violence often begets violence, but it seldom works the other way around. Why, then, does nonviolence

*See Tina Rosenberg, "Revolution U," *Foreign Policy*, February 16, 2011; http://www.foreignpolicy.com/articles/2011/02/16/revolution_u.

(Continued)

(CONTINUED)

sometimes work? How can a nonviolent popular movement prevail over a government predisposed to use whatever degree of force is necessary to stay in power? Think about it.

(Hint: Consider how the world changed in the second half of the twentieth century and why the idea of globalization has captivated so many minds in the first decade and a half of the twenty-first century.)

FIGURE 14.1 Political Map of Europe. In 1989, the Communist regimes in Eastern Europe were overthrown in rapid succession and replaced by democratically elected governments. Except in Romania, this remarkable transformation was accomplished without bloodshed, and today, these emerging democracies belong to NATO and the European Union. EU members as of 2015 are highlighted in this figure.

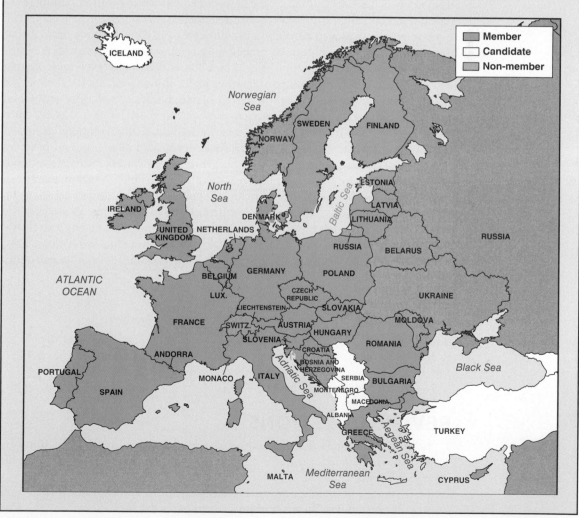

Eastern Europe is not the only place where revolutions have occurred on the quiet. Several Asian states, including South Korea and Taiwan, have achieved major regime change with relatively little violence. Clearly, the notion that revolutions are *always* violent or that they are *always* inimical to peace and stability is false. Perhaps that is the most revolutionary change (and lesson) of all.

SUMMARY

Revolution brings significant changes in the form of a nation's government. There are two basic revolutionary traditions, the American and the French. The American Revolution was more limited and sought more moderate goals. The French revolutionary leaders, unlike their more pragmatic American counterparts, sought complete and radical change in the social, political, and moral fabric of their country.

Whether revolution is desirable has been fiercely debated since the late eighteenth century, when Edmund Burke stressed its many dangers and Thomas Paine its many benefits. Earlier, John Locke had taken a moderate position, calling revolution necessary and justified when directed against an oppressive government.

The precise causes of revolution are difficult to isolate. Aristotle argued that injustice is at the root of popular rebellion. But what convinces the ordinary citizen to participate in a revolution? Karl Marx contended that worsening economic and social conditions lead to participation in revolutions. Alexis de Tocqueville asserted that improving conditions are to blame, because they cause individual hopes to outrun social reality. A modern view put forth by James C. Davies combined Marx's and Tocqueville's positions in arguing that revolutions are most likely to erupt when sharp economic or social reversals follow a period of rising expectations and moderate improvements. More recent studies characterize revolution as an ongoing process, reflecting a crisis of government's legitimacy.

Facing difficult economic, political, or social problems, governments often act ineptly or unjustly. When they lose the confidence of elites in society, the masses are mobilized as revolutionary leaders plan the government's overthrow and the creation of a new political order. Mass-movement revolutions have ultimately all failed, and in the process they have ironically victimized many innocent people.

KEY TERMS

revolution 435	Revolutionary	Declaration of the
French Revolution 437	War 438	Rights of Man 442
American	Estates-General 442	Reign of Terror 444
Revolution 437	Bastille 442	right to revolution 448

REVIEW QUESTIONS

1. In politics, what is the meaning of the word *revolution*? Did revolutions become more or less prevalent in the twentieth century when compared with previous eras?
2. In what important respects were the American Revolution and the French Revolution similar? In what important respects did they differ?

3. In the debate over the desirability of revolution between Edmund Burke and Thomas Paine, what position did each take? What were Burke's chief arguments? How did Paine respond?

4. What was John Locke's view of revolution? Why did he assert the right of citizens to overthrow their government? In what sense does Locke occupy a middle ground between Paine and Burke?

5. According to Aristotle, what is the principal cause of revolution? How have modern social scientists sought to go beyond Aristotle's philosophical insights into revolution?

6. Has contemporary research shed any new light on the causes of revolution? If so, have any common elements arisen from recent theoretical research, or are the findings contradictory? What theories have been advanced to explain how and why individuals become sufficiently disenchanted to join a revolutionary movement?

WEBSITES AND READINGS

Websites

PBS Series on the American Revolution (Liberty!): www.pbs.org/ktca/liberty

Companion Site to PBS: revolution.h-net.msu.edu

Chronology of French Revolution: userweb.port.ac.uk/~andressd/frlinks.htm

Documents on the French Revolution: chnm.gmu.edu/revolution

October Revolution Timeline of Events: http://www.marxists.org/history/ussr/events/revolution/

Russian Revolution: www.fordham.edu/halsall/mod/modsbook39.html

BBC News Special Report on the Chinese Revolution: news.bbc.co.uk/hi/english/static/special_report/1999/09/99/china_50/tiananmen.htm

Official U.S. Government History of the Chinese Revolution: http://www.state.gov/r/pa/ho/time/cwr/88312.htm

Cuban Refugees and Exiles Accounts of the Cuban Revolution: http://www.miamiherald.com/video/?genre_id=4920

Cuban Revolution, 1952 to 1958: http://www.latinamericanstudies.org/cuban-revolution.htm

Latin American Movements and Revolutions: www.uoregon.edu/~caguirre/revol.html

Readings

Ash, Timothy Garton. *The Magic Lantern: The Revolution of '89 Witnessed in Warsaw, Budapest, Berlin, and Prague.* New York: Vintage, 1993. The author is a scholar who thinks like an intelligence analyst and writes like a journalist.

Barone, Michael. *Our First Revolution: The Remarkable British Upheaval That Inspired America's Founding Fathers.* New York: Crown, 2007. Something happened in England that whetted the American colonists' appetite for liberty and independence a century later.

Brinton, Crane. *The Anatomy of Revolution*. Magnolia, MA: Peter Smith, 1990. A classic study of revolution.

Davies, James C. "Toward a Theory of Revolution," *American Sociological Review* (February 1962): 5–18. Contends that sudden economic reversals—a widening gap between what people expect and what they get—creates the conditions for revolution.

Goldstone, Jack A., ed. *Revolutions: Theoretical, Comparative, and Historical Studies,* 3rd ed. Boulder, CO: Westview Press, 2007. A collection of readings on revolutions.

Gurr, Ted. *Why Men Rebel*. Princeton, NJ: Princeton University Press, 1970. Argues that citizens' perceptions of relative deprivation cause revolution.

Kenney, Padraic. *A Carnival of Revolution: Central Europe 1989*. Princeton, NJ: Princeton University Press, 2003. From the publisher: "This is the first history of the revolutions that toppled communism in Europe to look behind the scenes at the grassroots movements that made those revolutions happen."

Ortega y Gasset, José. *The Revolt of the Masses*. New York: Norton, 1993. (First published in 1930.) A trenchant essay on the downside of the rise of "mass man" in the twentieth century.

Skocpol, Theda. *States and Social Revolutions: A Comparative Analysis of France, Russia, and China*. Cambridge: Cambridge University Press, 1979. A study that stresses the importance of community structure and international pressure.

Wolfe, Eric R. *Peasant Wars of the 20th Century*. New York: Harper and Row, 1969. Looks at the six major popular revolutions of the last century—in Russia, Mexico, China, Algeria, Cuba, and Vietnam—from the perspective of the peasant peoples who rose up.

CHAPTER 15

War
Politics by Other Means

Learning Objectives

1 Identify and discuss three theories on the causes of war (Hobbes, Rousseau, Locke).

2 Contrast World Wars I and II with previous wars in history.

3 Explain how and why war has fundamentally changed since World War II.

4 Identify the different types of war most relevant in world politics now, and explain one or two in detail.

5 Expand on the "just war" theory.

6 Explain the role of ethics and morality in the conduct of modern warfare.

7 Make a case for or against the relevance of international treaties on rules and limits in war.

war
Organized violence, often on a large scale, involving sovereign states or geographic parts of the same state or distinct ethnic or social groups within a given state (civil war).

interstate war
Armed conflict between sovereign states.

civil war
A war between geographical sections or rival groups within a nation.

guerrilla warfare
The tactics used by loosely organized military forces grouped into small, mobile squads that carry out acts of terrorism and sabotage, then melt back into the civilian population.

low-intensity conflict
Internal warfare that is sporadic and carried out on a small scale but is often prolonged and debilitating to the state and society in which it occurs.

War is the central problem of world politics. In the famous words of Prussian military theorist Carl von Clausewitz (1780–1831), "war is a continuation of politics by other means." If anarchy is the absence of government and the rule of law, then world politics is an arena where anarchy reigns. Small wonder that state actors are always conscious of war as an ever-present possibility and view peace as a precarious and perilous condition.

When people think of war, they usually have in mind **interstate wars**—that is, conflicts between two or more nation-states. **Civil wars** are conflicts within a single country; they have become more common than international wars today. **Guerrilla warfare** is a low-tech form of fighting usually waged in rural areas by small, lightly armed mobile squads (often fed and sheltered by sympathetic villagers). Guerrillas typically carry out selective acts of violence, primarily against the army, the police, and the government, in an attempt to weaken or topple the ruler(s). **Low-intensity conflicts**, a fourth category, occur when one state finances, sponsors, or promotes the sporadic or prolonged use of violence in a rival country (by hiring mercenaries or underwriting guerrillas, for example).

In terms of lives lost, property damaged or destroyed, and money drained away, war is undeniably the most destructive and wasteful of all human activities. One recent study of conflict in today's world found that 13.4% of global GDP ($14.3 trillion) went into fighting wars in 2014, while 180,000 people were killed in various conflicts (compared with 49,000 in 2010).* Estimates of the war dead in the last century alone fall in the range of 35 million, including 25 million civilians.[1] General William Tecumseh Sherman knew firsthand the horror of war. As a military leader, he had, in fact, been a fearsome practitioner of it. In a speech delivered fifteen years after the American Civil War, Sherman declared, "There is many a boy who looks on war as all glory, but boys, it is hell."

But not everyone sees war the way an older and wiser General Sherman did. Some of history's most illustrious (or infamous) personalities have reveled in the "glory" of war or acknowledged its perverse attractions. In the eighth century BCE, the Greek poet Homer noted that men grow tired of sleep, love, singing, and dancing sooner than they do of war. In his poetry, he celebrated the self-sacrifice and courage war demanded. The Greek philosopher Aristotle, writing some five hundred years later, listed courage as the first, though not the foremost, human virtue. To Aristotle, courage in battle ennobled human beings because it represented the morally correct response to fear in the face of mortal danger—danger that, in turn, imperiled the political community.

Perhaps no writer in modern times rationalized war better than the German philosopher G. W. F. Hegel, who argued, "If states disagree and their particular wills cannot be harmonized, the matter can only be settled by war." Hegel argued war is necessary because "corruption in nations would be the product of prolonged, let alone 'perpetual' peace." During times of peace, Hegel reasoned, society too easily grows soft and contentious: "As a result of war, nations are strengthened, but peoples involved in civil strife also acquire peace at home through making war abroad."[2]

*Global Peace Index 2015, Institute for Economics and Peace at http://economicsandpeace.org/wp-content/uploads/2015/06/Global-Peace-Index-Report-2015_0.pdf; also, see, "Global conflicts 'cost 13% of global GDP', BBC News at http://www.bbc.com/news/world-33161837.

Hegel contended that "world history is the world court." For Hegel, the measure of a nation is not some abstract moral standard, but power and prowess. It's a small step from that notion to the belief that might makes right.

Similarly, the German philosopher Friedrich Nietzsche (1844–1900) disdained conventional morality in general and despised the Christian ethic of humility in particular. Thus, Nietzsche celebrated the will to power and praised the curative effects of war on nations and civilizations.[3]

This theme would be revived with a vengeance half a century later by Adolf Hitler and his ally, Benito Mussolini. Like Hegel and Nietzsche, Mussolini scoffed at pacifism. Said the father of Italian fascism, "War alone brings to their highest tension all human energies and puts the stamp of nobility upon the peoples who have the courage to meet it."[4]

Although war is a constant in human affairs, it has evolved over time. Technology has transformed its ways and means without mitigating its lethal effects or destructive consequences—indeed, quite the opposite. Today, old forms of guerrilla warfare coexist with ultra high-tech robots, drones, and cyberwar.

This ever-present reality of war persists side by side with the dream of a world without war. Throughout the ages, philosophers and theologians have pondered the possibility of perpetual peace. But if war is ever to be eradicated, we must first isolate its causes.

THE CAUSES OF WAR

Why war? There is no simple answer. An observer living in Europe or the Middle East in the twelfth century would probably have attributed the frequency and ferocity of war at that time to religious zealotry. The Crusades, which began at the end of the eleventh century and continued for two hundred years, were marked by the kind of unmerciful slaughter that, paradoxically, has often accompanied the conviction that "God is on our side."

But while religion did help fuel many regional and local wars, it played only a minor role in most of the major wars of the twentieth century. Many observers attribute the outbreak of World War I to **nationalism** run amok. Others stress it was the **arms race** that preceded that war. Still others blame imperialism—the mad scramble for colonial territories in the latter half of the nineteenth century. Ideology was a factor in World War II, but the main "ism" behind the aggressive policies of Germany, Italy, and Japan in World War II was **ultranationalism**, or what scholar Hans J. Morgenthau called **nationalistic universalism**. The Korean Conflict (1950–1953) and the Vietnam War (1963–1975) were fought for both geopolitical reasons, or **reasons of state**, and ideological reasons. Some historians have seen this mix of pragmatism and idealism as a factor in determining the outcome of both of these wars because strategic military decisions were distorted by a crusading anticommunism that defined U.S. foreign policy during the Cold War.

Philosophers and theologians have long sought to discover war's root causes in hope of finding a cure. After World War II, the most destructive war in history, political scientists used statistical and mathematical models to try to learn more. John Vasquez, a leading advocate of this approach, claimed

nationalism
Devotion to one's nation; closely akin to patriotism.

arms race
Reciprocal military buildups between rival states; a process that tends to accelerate research, technology, and development in weapons systems and, according to some experts, is a potential cause of war.

ultranationalism
Extreme nationalism often associated with fascism; a radical right-wing orientation typically characterized by militarism, racial bigotry, and xenophobia.

nationalistic universalism
A messianic foreign policy that seeks to spread the ideas and institutions of one nation to other nations.

reasons of state
The pragmatic basis for foreign policy that places the national interest above moral considerations or idealistic motives; also *raison d'état*.

that philosophy had yielded no breakthroughs: "A substantial advancement in our understanding came only with the development and application of the scientific method."[5] In this view, mathematical rigor has "helped refine thinking about war and raised serious questions about existing explanations of war."[6]

Other political scientists are not so sure.[7] James Dougherty and Robert Pfaltzgraff conclude, "Despite the proliferation of statistical studies of war (both inductive and deductive), . . . [most] are more likely to be relegated to footnotes [in the long run] than regarded as classics."[8] Another scholar, Greg Cashman, argues that "social scientific research has not been completely fruitless." He concedes such studies "have not culminated in the creation of a single, unified theory of war" but thinks they have "certainly added greatly to our understanding."[9]

Clearly, there is no simple explanation for war. To probe deeper, we turn to three broad theories of causation. One emphasizes flaws in human nature. A second stresses defects in society and its institutions. A third sees scarcity as the cause of conflict.[10] After examining each, we look at the findings of several quantitative studies to corroborate or refute them.

Christianity—notably the idea of original sin—has had a profound influence on Western political thought through the ages. According to Saint Augustine (354–430), an early Christian theologian, war is a product of our corrupt nature. Many secular thinkers display a similar pessimism, without citing original sin as the cause. The Greek philosopher Plato attributed wars, at least in part, to the human passion for worldly possessions and creature comforts. The sixteenth-century Italian thinker Niccoló Machiavelli painted an equally depressing picture of the interaction between human nature and politics. In *The Prince*, he asserted that political success and moral rectitude are often inversely related: rulers tend to prosper in direct proportion to the dirty politics they practice for the sake of self-gratifying political ends.

Whereas some have looked to religion and others to philosophy for an explanation of aggressive human tendencies, still others have turned to psychology. Sigmund Freud (1856–1939), the founder of psychoanalysis, believed human beings are born with a "death wish," or innate self-destructive tendencies, that they redirect into other activities most of the time. During times of conflict, Freud theorized, combatants direct these destructive tendencies against each other. Thus, wars serve a psychotherapeutic function: They offer an outlet for otherwise self-destructive impulses. Critics argue this theory is too clever by half—the soldiers who do the fighting and killing are not the ones who decide to go to war, and the decision makers, careful to stay out of harm's way, are not the ones who fight. Most soldiers kill because they have a job to do and because they do not want to be killed, not because they are violent or destructive by nature.

Other psychologists have called aggression an innate human drive constantly seeking an outlet, a normal human response to frustration, or the same "territorial imperative" that supposedly accounts for aggressive behavior in the animal kingdom. According to the territorial imperative theory, latent aggressions are lodged deep in human nature (see "Politics and Pop Culture"), and threats to an individual's or group's territory (property, loved ones, and so on) can trigger aggressive action.

POLITICS AND POP CULTURE

WAR: Coming to a Theater Near You

The term "war theater" denotes a real place where armed conflict takes place. One popular dictionary, for example, defines it as "the entire land, sea, and air area that is or may become involved directly in *war* operations." But war often comes to theaters of a different kind too—theaters that have box offices and movie screens.

War is hell, but films about war can be heavenly for movie studios. *Gone with the Wind*, released in 1939 and set against the backdrop of the Civil War and Reconstruction, was the highest-grossing film ever for a quarter of a century. Adjusted for inflation, it would still be at the very top.

An epic war film about World War II, *Saving Private Ryan*, grossed nearly half a billion dollars worldwide and was the second most profitable movie released in 1998. *Saving Private Ryan* was notable for its grim realism. It gave Steven Spielberg a second Academy Award for Best Director—one of five awards it won. In 2014, the National Film Registry declared it worthy of preservation in the Library of Congress.

Gallipoli (1981) is another equally true-to-life war film—this one set in World War I. The Allies' failed Gallipoli campaign in 1915 was a killing field in which more than 113,000 soldiers died and 123,598 were wounded in just eight months and two weeks of fighting. The film stars Mel Gibson and Mark Lee as two Australian sprinters who join the army despite being underage.

War is also a popular theme in science fiction films. At its peak, *Star Wars* was the second highest-grossing film of all time, and it still makes the Top 20. James Cameron's 2009 science fiction film, *Avatar*, the biggest box office success of all time, is a story about love and war, a kind of antiwar allegory. In fact, Cameron admits that his intent was to raise questions about the U.S. resort to war after 9/11 and the use of "stand-off" weapons (drones, for example) that separate the person pulling the trigger from the target of the attack: "We know what it feels like to launch the missiles. We don't know what it feels like for them to land on our home soil, not in America."

Historically, war is second only to romance in the film industry. Of course, the role of war in popular culture is not confined to movies. If you want learn more about this subject, check out the War and Pop Culture websites at the end of this chapter.

If war is hell, what does it say about human nature that many of the most popular war movies present realistic depictions of the blood and gore of battle? Think about it.

(Hint: Read "The Neuroscience of Aggression: Why Humans Are Drawn to Violence" and "What Attracts People to Violent Movies" in ScienceDaily at www.sciencedaily.com.)

Still other observers find the ultimate cause of war not in the human soul or psyche but rather in the brain. People are neither depraved nor disturbed but obtuse—too stupid to understand the futility of war. In the words of a prominent pacifist writing between World Wars I and II:

The obstacle in our path . . . is not in the moral sphere, but in the intellectual. . . . It is not because men are ill-disposed that they cannot be educated into a world social consciousness. It is because they—let us be honest and say "we"—are beings of conservative temper and limited intelligence.[11]

Human Nature

Thomas Hobbes (1588–1679), living during the Puritan Revolution in England, had a different, but hardly more flattering, explanation for war. He was, above

The frequency of war shows that the law of the jungle still governs human behavior, much as it did before primates evolved beyond the state of nature. In the Nuclear Age, when all-out war is unthinkable, there is still no lasting peace on earth.

Vera Kratochvil/Publicdomainpictures.net

all, a realist who sought to understand human nature as it is, not as it ought to be. The only way to know what people are really like, Hobbes believed, is to look at how they would behave outside civil society as we know it—that is, as brutes of limited intelligence in a **state of nature**. The conclusions he drew from this exercise are fascinating and continue to influence how we think about politics, war, and the possibility of peace even today.

According to Hobbes, life in the state of nature would be "solitary, poor, nasty, brutish, and short." Human beings, like other earth-bound creatures, are governed by a keen instinct for self-preservation. They fear death above all and especially sudden, violent death. This fear does not, however, result in meekness or passivity; on the contrary, aggression and violent behavior are the norm. Hobbes identified "three principal causes" of war:

> First, Competition; Secondly, Diffidence; Thirdly, Glory. The first maketh man invade for Gain; the second, for Safety; and the third, for Reputation. The first cause [men to turn to] Violence to make themselves Masters of other men's persons, wives, children, and cattell; and the second, to defend them; the third, for trifles, at a word, a smile, a different opinion, and other signe of undervalue.[12]

The state of nature, for Hobbes, is a state of war—what he famously called a "war of every man, against every man."

Hobbes applied this same logic to international politics in his own time, which was a perpetual state of war. Just as individuals in the state of nature are governed by base motives and drives, he declared, leaders with similar motives and drives govern nations. And just as the state of nature lacks a government to protect people from each other, so the international system lacks a government to protect nations from each other.

Hobbes theorized that three kinds of disputes correspond to the three defects in human nature: aggressive wars, caused by competitive instincts; defensive wars, caused by fears; and agonistic wars, caused by pride and vanity. Through

state of nature
The human condition before the creation of a social code of behavior and collective techniques to control normal human impulses.

this compact theory, Hobbes sought to explain not only how human beings would act outside the civilizing influence of society and government (human beings constantly at each other's throats if not for government-imposed law and order) but also why nations sometimes go to war over issues that make no sense to outsiders.

The Hobbesian Legacy Hans Morgenthau, like Hobbes, argued forcefully that human beings are deeply flawed. According to Morgenthau, "Human nature, in which the laws of politics have their roots, has not changed since the classical philosophies of China, India, and Greece endeavored to discover these laws," and "politics, like society in general, is governed by objective laws that have their roots in human nature."[13] The key to understanding the operation of these laws is the "concept of interest defined as power." This means human beings are motivated by self-interest, which predisposes human behavior toward an eternal "struggle for power." Morgenthau made this point particularly clear when he stated, "International politics, like all politics, is a struggle for power. Whatever the ultimate aims of international politics, power is always the immediate aim." Like Hobbes before him, Morgenthau rejected the idealist view that "assumes the essential goodness and infinite malleability of human nature." Instead, he embraced the realist view "that the world, imperfect as it is from the rational point of view, is the result of forces inherent in human nature."[14]

According to Morgenthau and the realist school of political theory his writings inspired, human nature and the drive for self-aggrandizement are leading, if not the leading, causes of competition and conflict. Compelling, though not flattering, this view of humankind is not the only plausible explanation of why wars are fought.

Society

Not all political thinkers attribute war to the human psyche or human nature. Some blame modern society in general, organized into a state (an exclusive or "members only" political association), while others contend that particular kinds of political states pose disproportionate dangers to peace. In this section, we examine the different approaches of political theorists and leaders who blame society or the state (the political framework of society) for war's destructiveness.

Rousseau "Man is born free, and everywhere he is in chains." With this attack on the modern nation-state, the French philosopher Jean-Jacques Rousseau (1712–1778) began the first chapter of his classic *Social Contract* (1762), in which he directly challenged Hobbes's assertion that human beings are naturally cunning and violent. Rousseau started from the premise that human beings are naturally "stupid but peaceful" creatures, quite capable of feeling pity for those who are suffering. Hobbes simply erred, in this view, in attributing ambition, fear, and pride to human beings in the state of nature. Rousseau was convinced these are attributes of social man, not natural man (here the term *man* is used in the classic sense to mean all humans, irrespective of gender). Antisocial behaviors, paradoxically, have social causes; they are sure signs of human corruption. Society, not human nature, is to blame. Rousseau is quite explicit on this point:

"It is clear that . . . to society, must be attributed the assassinations, poisonings, highway robberies, and even the punishments of these crimes."[15]

Indeed, Rousseau believed society is the cause of all kinds of problems, including war. Specifically, he blamed the institution of private property—a pre-occupation of all eighteenth-century European societies—for the miseries that have beset the human race since it abandoned its natural innocence for the false pleasures of civilization. Property divides human beings, he argued, by creating unnecessary inequalities in wealth, status, and power among citizens within particular nations and, eventually, among nations:

> The first person who, having fenced off a plot of ground, took it into his head to say this is mine and found people simple enough to believe him, was the true founder of civil society. What crimes, wars, murders, what miseries and horrors would the human race have been spared by some-one who, uprooting the stakes or filling in the ditch, had shouted to his fellow-men: Beware of listening to this imposter, you are lost if you forget that the fruits belong to all and the earth to no one.[16]

Specifically, Rousseau postulated that just as the creation of private property led to the founding of the first political society, that founding mandated the creation of additional nation-states. And because each of these nations faced all the others in a state of nature, great tensions arose that eventually led to the "national wars, battles, murders, and reprisals, which make nature tremble and shock reason."[17] With the "division of the human race into different societies," Rousseau concluded:

> The most decent men learned to consider it one of their duties to murder their fellow men; at length men were seen to massacre each other by the thousands without knowing why; more murders were committed on a single day of fighting and more horrors in the capture of a single city than were committed in the state of nature during whole centuries over the entire race of the earth.[18]

Rousseau's view that private property is the root of all evil has exerted a profound influence on modern intellectual history. Even political thinkers who reject his specific diagnosis of the nation-state have widely accepted his general theory that "man is good but men are bad." Several twentieth-century variations on this theme have appeared. As we shall see, each differs in substantial ways from the others, but all assume the fatal flaw leading to war resides in society rather than in human nature.

Nationalism and War   Many modern thinkers hold that war is inherent in the very existence of separate societies with sovereign governments. The manifestation of these potent separatist tendencies is nationalism, the patriotic sentiments citizens feel toward their homeland (sometimes referred to, in its most extreme forms, as *jingoism* or *chauvinism*). According to one authority:

> Each nation has its own rose-colored mirror. It is the particular quality of such mirrors to reflect images flatteringly: the harsh lines are removed but the character and beauty shine through! To each nation none is so fair as itself. . . . Each nation considers (to itself or proclaims aloud, depending upon its temperament and inclination) that it is "God's chosen people" and dwells in "God's country."[19]

Small wonder that nationalism has been called an idolatrous religion. Although it may foster unity and a spirit of self-sacrifice within a society, between societies it has led, directly or indirectly, to militarism, xenophobia, and mutual distrust.

Nationalism can be manipulated in support of a war policy, and warfare can be used to intensify nationalism. The chemistry between them is sufficiently volatile to have caused many **internationalists**, or theorists favoring peace and cooperation among nations through the active participation of all governments in some sort of world organization, to single out nationalism as the main obstacle to achieving peace and harmony in the world.

To the extent that nationalism is an artificial passion—one socially conditioned rather than inborn—political society is to blame for war. This type of reasoning has led some to suggest a radically simple formula for eliminating war: Do away with the nation-state and you do away with nationalism; do away with nationalism and you do away with war. Others have sought more practical remedies—fix the nation-state rather than abolish it.

Tyranny and War: Wilson Many identify nationalism as the major cause of modern conflict, but others blame despotism for the two calamitous world wars of the last century. President Woodrow Wilson (1856–1924) championed this notion and actually tried to build a new world order on its conceptual foundations.

After World War I, Wilson sought to secure lasting peace through a treaty based on his Fourteen Points—principles he hoped would lead to a world without war. The cornerstone of this proposed new world order was the right of **national self-determination**, or the right of people everywhere to choose the government they wished to live under. Wilson expected self-determination to lead to the creation of democracies, which he viewed as being naturally more prone to peace than dictatorships.

But why should democracies be any more reluctant to go to war than dictatorships? The eighteenth-century German philosopher Immanuel Kant (1724–1804) first provided the explanation, one that appears to have deeply impressed Wilson. So germane are Kant's writings to Wilson's ideas that one authority suggested, "Woodrow Wilson's Fourteen Points were a faithful transcription of both the letter and spirit of Kant's Perpetual Peace."[20]

Kant postulated that to remain strong, nations must promote education, commerce, and civic freedom. Education, he theorized, would lead to popular enlightenment, and commerce would produce worldwide economic interdependence, all of which would advance the cause of peace. Most important, through expanded political freedom, individual citizens would become more competent in public affairs. And because liberty is most pronounced in republican regimes, such governments would be the most peace loving by nature. The reason is simple: in republics—unlike monarchies or aristocracies—the citizens who decide whether to support a war are the same citizens who must then do the fighting. In Kant's own words:

> A republican constitution does offer the prospect of [peace-loving behavior], and the reason is as follows: If . . . the consent of the citizens is required in order to decide whether there should be war or not, nothing is more natural

internationalist
Theorist favoring peace and cooperation among nations through the active participation of all governments in some sort of world organization.

national self-determination
The right of a nation to choose its own government.

Honored in Britain at the end of World War I, American president Woodrow Wilson hoped to make the world "safe for democracy" and end the scourge of war through a world organization—the League of Nations—based on the rule of law, collective security, and national self-determination.

than that those who would have to decide to undergo all the deprivations of war will very much hesitate to start such an evil game. . . . By contrast, under a constitution where the subject is not a citizen and which is therefore not republican, it is the easiest thing in the world to start a war . . . as a kind of amusement on very insignificant grounds.[21]

Kant envisioned an evolution, through steady if imperceptible progress, toward a peaceful world order as governments everywhere became increasingly responsive to popular majorities. Eventually, he felt, war would become little more than a historical curiosity.

Kant's linking of republicanism and peacefulness became Wilson's political credo. Both Kant and Wilson looked to the reconstruction of the nation-state as the key to a world without war. More specifically, both called for the global extension of democracy, education, and free trade to promote peace. Wilson, in particular, placed enormous faith in the morality and common sense of the ordinary person; he became convinced the ideal of national self-determination would be the key to humanity's political salvation. He also believed if the world's peoples were allowed to choose among alternative forms of government, they would universally choose liberal democracy and peace. Finally, if democratic institutions existed in all nations, Wilson felt the moral force of both domestic and world public opinion would serve as a powerful deterrent to armed aggression.

Capitalism, Imperialism, and War: Lenin Among those who did not agree with Wilson was his contemporary, V. I. Lenin, leader of the Russian Revolution and the first ruler of the former Soviet Union. Lenin was as violently opposed to bourgeois democracy as Wilson was enthusiastic about it. Although both supported national self-determination, they held very different interpretations of it. Wilson assumed any nation would choose democracy over any other system. In contrast, Lenin assumed that given a choice between capitalism and Communism, any nation should choose Communism. For Wilson, the pursuit of power was an end in itself and both a necessary and sufficient cause of war; for Lenin, as a follower of Karl Marx, wars were waged solely in the interest of the monopoly capitalists.

In a famous tract titled *Imperialism: The Highest Stage of Capitalism*, Lenin advanced the Marxist thesis that Western imperialism—the late-nineteenth century scramble for colonial territories—was an unmistakable sign that capitalism was teetering on the brink of extinction. Imperialism, according to Lenin, was a logical outgrowth of the cutthroat competition characteristic of monopoly capitalism. Lenin theorized (correctly) that capitalists would always seek foreign markets, where they can make profitable investments and sell (or dump) industrial surpluses. Thus, through their financial power and the political influence that accompanies it, monopoly capitalists push their societies into war for their own selfish purposes. In Lenin's words:

When the colonies of the European powers in Africa, for instance, comprised only one-tenth of that territory (as was the case in 1876), colonial policy was able to develop by methods other than those of monopoly—by the "free grabbing" of territories, so to speak. But when nine-tenths of Africa had been seized (approximately by 1900), when the whole world had been divided up, there was inevitably ushered in a period of colonial monopoly and, consequently, a period of particularly intense struggle for the division and the re-division of the world.[22]

In sum, Lenin held that because war is good business for the capitalists of the world, capitalists make it their business to promote war.

Lenin's analysis of the causes of war seems far removed from the Wilsonian thesis that tyranny leads inevitably to international conflicts, and yet the two views coincide at one crucial point. Lenin and Wilson both believed a particular defect of a certain type of nation-state produces wars—the form of government for Wilson, the economy and resulting social structure (classes divisions) for Lenin. If it could be eradicated, lasting world peace would ensue. Change is the key.

The Environment

Other theorists argue that war is caused by scarcity and the insecurity brought by fear of cold, hunger, disease, snakes, storms, and the like. This view accords with the ideas of philosopher John Locke.

Locke In his *Second Treatise on Civil Government* (1690), Locke argued forcefully that wars reflect conditions inherent in nature that place human beings in do-or-die situations and make conflict inevitable, rather than defects in human nature or society. Like Hobbes before him, Locke saw the imperfections in human beings and believed self-preservation was the most basic human instinct. At this point, however, the two thinkers diverged. In the words of one authority:

> Locke's state of nature is not as violent as Hobbes's. If, as it seems, force will commonly be used without right in Locke's state of nature, it is not because most men are vicious or savage and bloodthirsty; Locke does not, as Hobbes does, speak of every man as the potential murderer of every other man. The main threat to the preservation of life in the state of nature lies not in the murderous tendencies of men but rather . . . in the poverty and hardship of their natural condition.[23]

Locke believed poverty and hardship are inevitable in the state of nature because great exertions are required to provide for our daily needs. Then we still have to protect our property, coveted by neighbors who have less and by others who are hungry and poor. Locke thus saw circumstances rooted in scarce resources as the principal cause of human conflict.

Locke's views on human beings, society, and nature have great bearing on the issues of war and peace. If the origins of war lie within human beings, as Hobbes believed, we can eradicate war only by changing the "inner self." If the problem lies in society, as Rousseau and Lenin contended, the solution is to reconstitute society (or the state) to remove the particular defects giving rise to aggressive behavior. If the problem lies neither in humans nor in society but in nature, the solution must be to transform nature.

The transformation of nature was precisely how Locke proposed to end human conflict in domestic society. Civil government, he asserted, must create the conditions to encourage economic development. Through economic development, a major cause of social tension—that is, the natural "penury" of the human condition—would be greatly eased. At the same time, if the formal rules of organized society replaced the uncertainties of nature, the need for every human being to constantly guard against the depredations of others would be lessened. Human beings would thus finally leave the state of nature, with all its anarchy and danger.

But in leaving one state of nature, humanity ironically found itself inhabiting another—the often-brutal world of international politics. Although Locke did not apply his theory of politics to the realm of international relations, his reasoning lends itself readily to such an application. Before the invention of government, human beings lived in domestic anarchy; likewise, in the absence of an effective world government, nations exist in international anarchy. In this sense, the relationships among nation-states differ little from relationships among individuals before the formation of civil society. The international state of nature, no less than the original, is a perpetual state of potential war. Thus, each nation-state behaves according to the dictates of self-preservation in an environment of hostility and insecurity, just as each individual presumably did in the state of nature.

One of the most common spoils of war is territory. From all appearances, the desire for more land and resources—property, in the Lockean sense—is one of the most common objectives of war. Recall that Lenin attributed the European scramble for colonial territories toward the end of the nineteenth century to the search for new markets, cheap labor, and raw materials—that is, property. Significantly, Lenin held that the propensity to accumulate capital (money and property) that Locke described was directly responsible for imperialism, which Lenin predicted would lead inevitably to war. Even if Lenin overstated the case against capitalism, one thing is certain: Territoriality has always been associated with war, and it always will be.

When Locke wrote, plenty of land in the world remained unclaimed by Europeans and uncultivated. He noted that even in the state of nature, human relations were probably fairly harmonious, so long as no one crowded anyone else. It stands to reason, however, that as growing populations begin to place ever-greater pressures on easily available resources, the drawing of property lines becomes progressively more important. If, as Locke's analysis suggests, prehistoric people felt threatened by the pressures of finite resources, imagine how much greater those pressures have become in modern times.

Nature's Scarcity: Malthusian Nightmares   Many contemporary writers have elaborated on the theme of resource scarcity propounded by Locke and, later, by Thomas Malthus (1766–1834) in his famous *Essay on the Principle of Population* (1798). Richard Falk, for example, identified "four dimensions of planetary danger," including the "war system, population pressures, resource scarcities, and environmental overload."[24] According to Falk, these are interrelated aspects of a single problem that must be treated as a group.

Falk's assumptions about the causes of international conflict are consistent with Locke's political understanding:

> International society is, of course, an extreme example of a war system. Conflicts abound. Vital interests are constantly at stake. Inequalities of resources and power create incentives to acquire what a neighboring state possesses.[25]

Just as humans were constantly vulnerable to the depredations of others in the state of nature, so predatory neighbors continually threaten nation-states. Throughout history, then, violence has played a vital role in the conduct of foreign affairs, because, Falk argued, conditions beyond the control of individual nation-states compel them to regard their own security as directly proportionate to their neighbors' distress.

Hence, even after the unprecedented destruction wrought by World Wars I and II, "many efforts were made, often with success, to moderate the scope and barbarism of war, but no serious assault was mounted to remove the conditions that cause war."[26] What exactly are these conditions? Professor Falk argued that access to food and water supplies had a great bearing on the earliest wars. These considerations remain relevant in the modern world:

> Given the present situation of mass undernourishment (more than two-thirds of the world population), it is worth taking account of the ancient link between war and control of food surplus, as well as the age-old human practice of protecting positions of political and economic privilege by military means.[27]

Plagued by civil war and weakened by famine, an estimated two million people died in Somalia in the early 1990s. A similar tragedy occurred in the Darfur region of Sudan in 2004–2009, but much of the suffering was due to atrocities and violence against unarmed civilians. The Republic of South Sudan gained its independence from Sudan in 2011. Fighting continued in 2015 after a rebel leader replaced South Sudan's ten states with twenty-one new federal states patterned on the former British colonial administration's districts.

The population explosion exacerbates problems of food and water in the least developed countries (LDCs). Population pressures underlie the entire crisis of planetary organization, especially in light of what we now know about the linkages between economic development and urbanization, urbanization and pollution, and pollution and global warming. Nor are the LDCs the only (or primary) source of the problem.

Developed countries, led by the United States, are by far the biggest global polluters. China and India, both emerging economic giants, have a combined population of 2.4 billion, roughly three times that of the United States and the European Union put together, and China and India are exempt from the carbon-emission limits established under the Kyoto Protocol (see Chapter 13). Under such conditions, no nation, no matter how powerful, feels terribly secure in our times. The 2008–2009 world financial crisis served as a dramatic reminder of the vulnerability of even the richest and most powerful countries. Not only oil, but also many other raw materials, such as bauxite, copper, and tin, are unequally distributed and in short supply. At the same time, the poorest countries continue to experience shortages in the most basic of all raw materials—food.

IN SEARCH OF A DEFINITIVE THEORY

The three alternative views on the ultimate causes of war identified in this chapter are based on one of the most fundamental concepts in Western political philosophy: the role of the individual in society, the role of society in shaping individual behavior, and the role of nature in shaping the individual and society. All three theoretical approaches have some validity, and together they point to a multilevel theory on the origins of war. Individually or together, they help explain why war or the threat of war hangs over every nation like a dreaded sword of Damocles. As long as war continues to plague humankind, the search for solutions and for a definitive theory will continue.

Beyond Politics

It seems reasonable to assume that, all else being equal, nations exhibiting intense nationalism are more warlike than are politically apathetic nations. But all else is seldom equal. Indeed, explanations that depend on nationalism "have done a relatively poor job in explaining the incidence of war."[28]

But what about the Wilsonian view that democracies are naturally peaceful, and tyranny is the primary cause of war in the modern world? Through the ages, political thinkers have stressed the relationship between dictatorial rule and belligerent or aggressive behavior. Aristotle called tyrants warmongers who plunge their nations into war "with the object of keeping their subjects constantly occupied and continually in need of a leader."[29] Some modern writers, such as Hannah Arendt, argue that totalitarian governments are inherently aggressive.[30] Two major modern conflicts—World War II and the Korean War—were initiated by totalitarian dictatorships. Stalin in the 1930s, Hitler in the 1940s, Mao in the early 1950s, and Pol Pot between 1975 and 1979 all waged war in the form of bloody purges and mass murder at home. These episodes of lethal state behavior strongly suggest totalitarian rulers are prone to coercive force.

Dictators also exercise absolute control over the armed forces, police, and instruments of propaganda. They have often been war heroes who rode to power on the wings of military victory—successful soldiers who take over governments are rarely squeamish about the use of force. For them, war can provide a popular diversion from the tedium and rigors of everyday life; it can act as an outlet for pent-up domestic hostilities that might otherwise be directed at the dictator; it can help unify society and justify a crackdown on dissidents; and finally, it can rejuvenate a stagnant economy or an uninspired citizenry.

But these observations do not prove despotism often or always causes wars. The Kennedy, Johnson, and Nixon administrations blamed the Vietnam War on communist aggression. Critics of U.S. foreign policy, however, blamed it on misguided or provocative U.S. actions in Southeast Asia. Thus, depending on the evidence we accept, the Vietnam War can "prove" either that dictatorships are more prone to war than democracies or that democracies are no more immune to crusading militarism than are dictatorships.

Democracies have not been notably successful at avoiding war. In the second half of the twentieth century, for example, India, the world's largest democracy,

"The Wall," containing 58,272 names of the deceased as of 2010, is part of the Vietnam War Memorial in Washington, D.C. That war dragged on for well over a decade. Many Americans said "never again." The U.S.-led military forces that invaded Afghanistan after 9/11 have been fighting a fierce Taliban insurgency in rugged mountainous terrain ever since—some claim it is the longest war in U.S. history (others say it isn't so). The conflict spilled over the border into northern Pakistan in recent years, and U.S. drone strikes against targets in Pakistani territory have cast a dark cloud over U.S.-Pakistani relations.

DOD/National Archives

waged several bloody wars against Pakistan, and the United States fought major wars in Korea, Vietnam, and Iraq. More recently, the United States spearheaded large-scale military actions against the Taliban regime in Afghanistan (2001) and Iraq (2003). Nor have democratic nations always been unwilling participants in war. The United States did not go out of its way to avoid fighting the Spanish-American War of 1898. And it is difficult to overlook U.S. intervention in the Mexican Revolution in 1914, when President Wilson ordered U.S. Marines to seize the Mexican port of Veracruz and later sent a punitive expedition into Mexico against the forces of Pancho Villa.

Research shows democratic nations are not less war-like than either authoritarian or totalitarian states.[31] In fact, democratic nations engage in military action about as often as other types of government; some evidence suggests they may start wars less frequently but join them more often.[32] In one respect, however, the Kantian-Wilsonian prodemocracy, antidictatorship theory of war does hold true: In the so-called **paradox of democratic peace**, democratic states rarely, if ever, fight one another.[33] There has not been a real war between democracies in more than a century and a half.[34] One explanation for this paradox goes as follows:

> Expectations of war and threats of war between democracies are almost certainly reduced by the presence of a common political culture, by a mutual identity and sympathy, by stronger people-to-people and elite-to-elite bonds, by the ability of interest groups within these countries to form transnational coalitions, by more frequent communication, and by more positive mutual perceptions.[35]

Public opinion comes into play because government is limited in constitutional democracies, political power is more-or-less widely distributed, popularly elected leaders are inclined to emphasize compromise over confrontation, and constitutional democracies generally respect the individual's rights. All these factors tend to promote the peaceful resolution of political disputes between democracies.

When democracies go to war, they fight nondemocratic states. This suggests that the degree of political difference (or distance) between governments, as well as economic and cultural differences, may be important.[36] Such findings support Wilson's conclusion that dictatorial regimes are the natural enemies of

paradox of democratic peace
Democratic states are often militarily powerful, fight other states, engage in armed intervention, and sometimes commit acts of aggression, but they rarely fight each other.

democracies, as well as Lenin's view that capitalist and communist nations are incompatible. As one study of Latin American politics noted, "The more similar two nations are in economic development, political orientation, Catholic culture, and density, the more aligned their voting in the UN" and the less conflict there will be between them. By the same token, "The more dissimilar two nations are in economic development and size and the greater their joint technological capability to span geographic distance is, the more overt conflict they have with each other."[37]

Beyond Economics

If politics provides only a partial and limited explanation for conflict, Lenin's theory that wars are caused by economic factors, particularly capitalism, explains even less. One problem with this proposition is that wars preceded both capitalism and imperialism, proving that capitalism is certainly not the only cause of war.[38] Furthermore, there is little in the historical evidence to support Lenin's economic theory that capitalist states (as opposed to social-ist or communist states) are particularly warlike. Although some wars can be explained by national economic motives such as imperialism, most cannot.[39]

The relationship between capitalism and imperialism is not clear or consist-ent. Some capitalist states have practiced imperialism and waged war, while oth-ers, like Sweden and Switzerland, have avoided both. Lenin's economic theory has difficulty accounting for such differences or explaining why some social-ist states have engaged in unprovoked armed aggression. Examples include the Soviet invasion of Estonia, Latvia, Lithuania, and Finland in 1939; North Korea's attack on South Korea in 1950; the Soviet invasion of Hungary (1956), Czechoslovakia (1968), and Afghanistan (1979); and China's attack on Tibet (1956), India (1962), and Vietnam (1979).[40]

There is little doubt that economics is a cause of specific wars, if not war in general. For instance, the U.S.-led coalition in the Iraq War was driven in part by economic motives: to protect the vast oil fields of Arabia and to keep the vital lifelines linking the Middle East with Europe, Asia, and North America from Saddam Hussein's control. But other motives are almost always present as well. In the Iraq War these were the belief (false, as it turned out) that Saddam possessed weapons of mass destruction (WMD), that he was aiding and abet-ting international terrorists, that he represented a clear and present danger to Israel, and so on.

There is surprisingly little evidence to support the thesis that one kind of economic system or a country's particular stage of economic development or economics in general is decisive in motivating nations to fight wars. When aca-demic studies point to economics as a contributing cause of war, they often rely solely on a statistical correlation between economics and war, which, as every scientist knows, does not prove causality.

Since World War II, wars have been fought within the territory of develop-ing states. Does this mean countries with less-advanced economies are more warlike? Not necessarily, because it also appears these wars have often been instigated or even fought by industrialized nations. Post–World War II exam-ples of such conflicts include those fought in Suez, Algeria, the Congo, Vietnam, Afghanistan, the Falkland Islands, and Iraq. Although we cannot make a strong correlation between economic development and the frequency of military conflicts, some evidence suggests nations with more-developed economies actually have greater warlike tendencies than countries with less-developed economies.[41]

The Danger of Oversimplification

Simplistic theories of war abound. Some quantitative theorists have described in fine detail recurring patterns that often lead to war-making military alliances, which are then followed by military buildups, the making of threats, a series of crises, and so on.[42] Such studies have also shown that certain actions political leaders take in an effort to reduce the possibility of war (for example, making alliances) may actually increase its likelihood.[43] However, none of these studies proves that making or joining military alliances or any of the other steps associated with the pattern leading to war actually causes war. Fear of war, for example, causes countries to join alliances, but joining alliances does not inevitably lead to war. Thus, virtually all Western democracies joined the NATO alliance and all Communist states of Central and Eastern Europe joined the Warsaw Pact, but NATO and the Warsaw Pact never fought a war. Furthermore, the "typical" pattern is itself somewhat limited, as it represents only those conflicts fought between major states of approximately equal power.[44]

Most war theorists have long believed large states are more inclined to war than are small states,[45] and powerful states more inclined to fight than weak ones. That nations confident of winning are most inclined to fight wars makes intuitive sense.[46] However, defining a state's power is difficult; political leaders may overestimate their own strength and underestimate the adversary's (the Vietnam War is a sterling example).[47] Nations experiencing internal violence are also more likely to be war prone for several reasons. A war may help unify the nation, or internal conflict may make it an easy target.[48] Nations headed by risk-takers are also more likely to go to war.

Another relevant factor is common borders, particularly when there are many or when they are shared by long-standing rivals.[49] Nations with large and growing populations, limited access to necessary resources, and a high level of technology have an obvious environmental incentive to pursue expansionist foreign policy, whereas sparsely populated countries tend to fight fewer wars regardless of technology or access to natural resources. When these latter countries do fight, they tend to be victims rather than aggressors.[50] In sum, a large, powerful nation with a rapidly expanding population and advanced technology, that shares many borders with neighboring states or one border with a traditional enemy (or both), and is governed by a risk-oriented leader is a prime candidate for aggressive war, especially if it faces civil strife or armed rebellion.

Many of the factors we've discussed, from human nature to scarce resources, and many of the characteristics associated with war, including population size, economic development, and border problems, are difficult or impossible to change, especially in the short run. The humorist Will Rogers once suggested that world peace could be advanced if nations—like people—could move, but they can't (although populations can, and do, migrate).

In fact, the false belief that we can eradicate conflict or trace it to a single factor may increase the possibility of war. As European history from 1919 to

limited war
The opposite of all-out war, particularly an all-out nuclear war, a limited war is one in which adversaries choose not to use the most potent weapons available to them.

unconditional surrender
Giving an enemy on the verge of defeat a stark choice between surrendering immediately (placing itself entirely at the mercy of the victor) or being utterly destroyed.

1939 illustrates, concentrating solely on rearranging the international system while ignoring the role of human nature can have the unintended effect of clearing obstacles from the path of megalomaniacs bent on aggression.[51] Had U.S., French, and British leaders in the 1930s heeded Churchill's warnings about the threat posed by Hitler and stood up to him earlier, they might have been able to defeat Nazi Germany quickly or prevent the war altogether. World War II had multiple causes, which does not mean it was inevitable.

An understanding of the complex causes and factors of war can modestly improve the international system of conflict management by dispelling illusions about the prospects for peace. In such important matters, simple solutions can be worse than no solutions at all; some of history's foremost political simplifiers have also been among the foremost contributors to war.

TOTAL WAR: WARS EVERYBODY FIGHTS

Total war is a thoroughly modern phenomenon. It is different from the **limited wars** of the distant past in several crucial respects. First, it is unlimited in that one or more of the belligerents seek total victory and will stop at nothing short of **unconditional surrender**. Second, total war is unlimited as to means. States use advanced technology to enhance the range, accuracy, and killing power of modern weapons. Third, total war is unlimited as to participation: whole societies engage in the war effort.

The Napoleonic Wars are the prototype of total war and the first such war ever fought. Napoléon waged an all-out drive for hegemony that recognized no limits on ends or means. He sought total domination of Europe, and he possessed all the resources available to a modern, centralized state at that time. Of course, there were then no weapons of mass destruction, except conventional armies that could be used to this end once the enemy was defeated. Thus, Napoléon's forces burned much of Moscow, including the Kremlin, to the ground after Russia's defeat. Most important, Napoléon introduced the idea of mass conscription, drafting thousands of young men into the modern world's first people's army. (Prior armies had consisted of professional soldiers and paid mercenaries.) Napoléon also used nationalism, propaganda, and patriotic symbols to mobilize the entire society behind the war effort. These innovations were all harbingers of the future: We can consider the total wars fought in the first half of the twentieth century a single event with an interlude between two incredibly violent spasms—the horrific culmination of processes set in motion more than a century earlier.

After World War II, the concept of total war took on an even more ominous meaning due to major advances in the science and technology of war-fighting capabilities. The advent of the nuclear age utterly transformed both the strategy and tactics of war, the logic of military force and the battlefield. Like the new face of war itself, this transformation was total.

ACCIDENTAL WAR: WARS NOBODY WANTS

We like to think our leaders always know what they are doing, especially when it comes to matters of war and peace. But accidents do happen. What if a Pakistani arms smuggler were passing through India with a package containing "weaponized" anthrax? What if the spores were released in the center of

New Delhi, the capital of India, when the Kashmiri taxi driver ran a red light and collided with a truck at a busy intersection? And what if that happened during a crisis with Pakistan? Might India think Pakistan was launching an all-out war? Pakistan had nothing to do with the incident, but India might decide to retaliate immediately and ask questions later (waiting would be extremely risky in such a situation). In this scenario, an all-out nuclear war could result from accident and misperception, rather than from any rational choice on either side.

War by misperception, or war resulting from the misreading of a situation, is perhaps the most common kind of war nobody wants. **Accidental war** is another possibility. An incorrect translation, a message not delivered, a diplomatic signal missed or misinterpreted—accidents of this kind precipitated unintended wars well before the advent of space-age weapons systems. In a technological era dominated by nuclear weapons and ballistic missiles, the danger of war by accidental means has gone up dramatically, as have the stakes. Nuclear war by escalation could begin as a limited (and presumably localized) conflict between two nations in which neither side originally intended to use its most destructive weapons. But as casualties mount and battlefield reverses occur, one side (most likely the one losing) could be tempted to up the ante by introducing more powerful weapons, which the other side would have little choice but to match. If both sides possess nuclear weapons, the dynamics could move them toward nuclear war.

Catalytic war can also generate violence and destruction well beyond any nation's intention. Historically, such wars reflected alliance arrangements. If one member of the alliance was attacked, the other(s) sprang to its defense, enlarging the war. Nowadays, a catalytic war might originate as a localized conflict between, say, two developing countries that have powerful allies. Local wars have always had the potential to turn into regional or even global wars (as happened in both world wars). Or a saboteur or madman might somehow manage to "pull the nuclear trigger." All such scenarios—sabotage, misperception, accident, escalation, or a catalytic event—show how war can occur without any premeditation or intent.

NUCLEAR WAR: WARS NOBODY WINS

Weapons of mass destruction have been used only once. The United States dropped two atomic bombs on the Japanese cities of Hiroshima and Nagasaki to end World War II. President Truman waited for Japan's High Command to surrender after the first bomb leveled Hiroshima. When three days later they had not, he gave the order to drop the second bomb. This time Japan surrendered. But it would be a mistake to try to repeat that winning strategy. The reason is very simple. When the U.S. president decided to "go nuclear" in 1945, there were only two atomic bombs in the world, and they were both in the U.S. arsenal.

war by misperception
Armed conflict that results when two nations fail to read one another's intentions accurately.

accidental war
In the modern age, the unintentional launching of a nuclear attack because of a mistake or miscalculation.

Nuclear War Survival Skills.

catalytic war
A conflict that begins as a localized and limited encounter but grows into a general war after other parties are drawn into the conflict through the activation of military alliances.

massive retaliation
Strategic military doctrine based on a plausible standing threat of nuclear reprisal, employed by the United States in the 1950s during the short-lived era of the U.S. nuclear monopoly; according to this doctrine, if the Soviet Union attacked U.S. allies with conventional military forces, the United States would retaliate with nuclear weapons.

nuclear monopoly
When only one side in an adversarial relationship possesses a credible nuclear capability; the United States enjoyed a nuclear monopoly for roughly a decade after World War II.

intercontinental ballistic missile (ICBM)
A long-range missile armed with multiple nuclear warheads capable of striking targets anywhere in the world; both the United States and Russia possess large arsenals of these ultimate strategic weapons.

Truman did not have to risk **massive retaliation** (a response in kind) from Japan or any other country. The United States had a (short-lived) **nuclear monopoly**.

The former Soviet Union quickly developed its nuclear weapons program. By the end of the 1950s, it had an arsenal of mass-destruction armaments and was even building long-range rockets called **intercontinental ballistic missiles (ICBMs)**. Moscow actually beat the United States into outer space by launching Sputnik, the first earth-orbiting satellite, in 1957. During the 1960s, the United States lost not only its nuclear monopoly (if it had not already been lost a decade earlier), but also its aura of invulnerability. The era of massive retaliation and **brinkmanship**—reliance on nuclear weapons to intimidate adversaries—was superseded by the era of **mutual assured destruction (MAD)**, or **mutual deterrence**, in which both superpowers had the ability to withstand a nuclear first strike and still be capable of delivering a **second strike** that would result in unacceptable damage to the aggressor.

Neither superpower spared any effort to get (or stay) ahead in the nuclear arms race. By the early 1970s, both sides had a tremendous **overkill** capability; that is, each had enough weapons of mass destruction to destroy the other many times over. Even more alarming, both sides had built nuclear submarines to act as mobile platforms for launching ICBMs and were putting multiple warheads—called **multiple independently targeted reentry vehicles (MIRVs)**—on both land- and sea-based ICBMs (technically known as **submarine-launched ballistic missiles (SLBMs)**. But whereas both sides wanted to win the arms race, neither wanted to lose a war with the other, and both knew there would be no winners if deterrence ever failed. This almost happened during the Cuban Missile Crisis (1963); it was a close call. As a result, the two sworn enemies quickly established the now-famous hotline—a direct communications link between the White House and the Kremlin—to avert a future calamity, one that might just happen by accident.

PROXY WARS: WARS OTHERS FIGHT

Civil wars and guerrilla wars typically pit established governments on one side against rebels or insurgents on the other. During the Cold War, the two superpowers frequently intervened directly or indirectly in civil wars or insurgencies in Third World countries. Vietnam in the 1960s and early 1970s and Afghanistan in the 1970s are two notable examples. In Vietnam, the United States intervened directly with military forces, and the Soviet Union intervened indirectly by sending massive amounts of military and economic aid. In Afghanistan, it was the other way around—the Soviet Union launched a military invasion, and the United States backed the freedom fighters (the mujahideen). Similarly, the Soviet Union intervened in Angola's civil war in the 1970s, and the United States intervened in Nicaragua and El Salvador in the 1980s. These conflicts were sometimes called **proxy wars** because the superpowers would each back one side while relying on indigenous forces to do the fighting with the help of U.S. or Soviet "advisors."

With the collapse of the Soviet Union, only one superpower remained, and the ideological rivalry that fueled the Cold War became a thing of the past. Whether a proxy war will occur again is an open question; if so, it will be in a very different context and, in all likelihood, for different principles.

JUST WARS: WARS OTHERS START

So far, we have been looking at war primarily from the standpoint of the perpetrators of aggression. But what about the victims? Few observers would dispute that nations have the right to resist armed aggression. When national survival is at stake, self-defense is morally justified. So, despite Benjamin Franklin's assertion that "there was never a good war or a bad peace," some wars may be both necessary and proper, but which ones? Who is to say? And how can we know for sure?

The Just War Doctrine

The venerable doctrine of the **just war** holds that, under certain circumstances, a war can be "good"—not pleasant or intrinsically desirable, but serving the welfare of a nation and the cause of justice. This concept was advanced by early Christian theologians such as Saint Augustine and refined by medieval philosophers. Hugo Grotius (1583–1645) and other natural law theorists later reformulated it.

Those who favor the concept of just war unanimously agree defensive wars are justified. A nation that suffers an unprovoked attack is justified in waging war against its assailant. Some theorists further give third-party nations the right to interfere on behalf of hapless victims of military aggression. The 1991 Persian Gulf War, preceded by Iraq's invasion and occupation of Kuwait, is a case in point.

Earlier writers did not always limit the just war doctrine to defensive wars. Saint Augustine abhorred war in all its guises, but he justified even aggressive wars under some circumstances, as when a state "has failed either to make reparation for an injurious action committed by its citizens or to return what has been appropriated."[52] Another early Christian theologian, Saint Ambrose (339–397 CE), argued that nations have a moral obligation, not simply a right, to wage aggressive war for the sake of higher principle. "Man has a moral duty," he wrote, "to employ force to resist active wickedness, for to refrain from hindering evil when possible is tantamount to promoting it."[53] Ambrose

brinkmanship
In diplomacy, the deliberate use of military threats to create a crisis atmosphere; the calculated effort to take a tense bilateral relationship to the brink of war in order to achieve a political objective (for example, deterring a common enemy from carrying out an act of aggression against an ally).

William E Thompson

The U.S.-led military forces that invaded Iraq in the spring of 2003 quickly defeated Saddam Hussein's army, but the subsequent occupation gave rise to a protracted urban guerrilla war of attrition in which the enemy used terrorist tactics that turned key Iraqi cities, including the capital of Baghdad, into bloody battlegrounds. The U.S. withdrew the last combat troops from Iraq in December 2011, but the violence and fighting among factions competing for power continued. As part of a new war-fighting doctrine, the U.S. Army endeavored to establish rapport with the civilian population in an effort to win hearts and minds. The soldier in this photo is deceased.

mutual assured destruction (MAD)
A nuclear stalemate in which both sides in an adversarial relationship know that if either one initiates a war, the other will retain enough retaliatory ("second strike") capability to administer unacceptable damage even after absorbing the full impact of a nuclear surprise attack; during the Cold War, a stable strategic relationship between the two superpowers.

mutual deterrence
The theory that aggressive wars can be prevented if potential victims maintain a military force sufficient to inflict unacceptable damage on any possible aggressor.

second strike
Retaliation in kind against a nuclear attack(er); this capability paradoxically minimizes the likelihood that a nuclear confrontation will lead to an actual nuclear exchange.

overkill
Amassing a much larger nuclear arsenal than is (or would be) needed to annihilate any adversary.

was aware of the need for limitations on this kind of war. Aggressive wars, he declared, should be fought only for a clearly just cause.

The just war doctrine has five postulates. First, war must be the last resort of a legitimate government; there must be no other effective political alternatives available. Second, the conflict must be just, fought only for deterring or repelling aggression or righting a wrong. Third, the war cannot be futile; there must be some probability the nation undertaking it can succeed. Fourth, the war's purpose must justify the cost in money and lives; the means employed must be appropriate to the reason the war is fought. Finally, a just war must minimize injury and death to civilians.

In contrast to the simplistic nationalism represented by such slogans as "My country right or wrong," the just war concept suggests a standard of moral responsibility that transcends narrow national interest. Early Christian theologians based their notions of justice on theological doctrines and scriptural teachings. Modern versions of the doctrine are grounded in a natural-law philosophy holding there are self-evident truths about human welfare that, taken together, point toward the true meaning of the ideal of "justice for all."

Evaluating the Just War Doctrine

Of the criticisms leveled against the just war doctrine, we focus on three of the most substantial: that the doctrine represents moral relativism, that it embodies an ethnocentric bias, and that it is politically unrealistic.

Moral Relativism   Some critics contend the concept of the just war is based on highly subjective, and hence unverifiable, value judgments. Because governments rarely admit to starting wars and almost always blame the other side, any attempt to assign moral responsibility is bound to reflect the opinions of the observer more than the often uncertain facts of the situation. The only way to avoid this **moral relativism** is to confine ourselves to describing what happened before and during wars, sticking to accurate and verifiable facts.

Ethnocentric or Nationalistic Bias   Critics also say Western just war theorists reflect only their own culture, ignoring justifications for war advanced by other cultures or ideologies—an accusation of **ethnocentric bias**. For instance, the traditional Islamic concept of a jihad ("struggle" or "holy war") against temptation, evil, apostasy, or "infidels" offers a moral rationale for aggressive war rarely acknowledged by Western proponents of the just war doctrine. Just war theorists were similarly criticized for rejecting an interpretation advanced until recently by the former Soviet Union—that just wars are waged by the working class against their oppressors, wars of "national liberation" fought by colonized peoples of the Third World against Western "imperialists," and wars waged to prevent the overthrow of socialist governments in Eastern Europe and elsewhere.

Political Naiveté   Several opponents of the just war doctrine raise the practical objection that even a universally accepted standard governing them would be extremely difficult to apply fairly. Just as individuals are not good judges in their own cases, it is argued, so nations are not competent to pass judgment on controversies involving their own interests and well-being. Without an

FIGURE 15.1   Nazi Death Camps. This map shows the location of the Nazi concentration and extermination camps. Notice that concentration camps existed in France, the Netherlands, Austria, Latvia, and Czechoslovakia, as well as in Germany; but the infamous death camps were all located deep inside Poland. Strikingly, not one was located on or near German territory. Hitler obviously did not want the horrors of the Final Solution taking place in his own backyard.

SOURCE: From "Concentration and Death Camps," http://history1900s.about.com/library/holocaust/blmap.htm. Copyright © 2009 by Jennifer Rosenberg. Used with permission of About, Inc., which can be found online at www.about.com. All rights reserved.

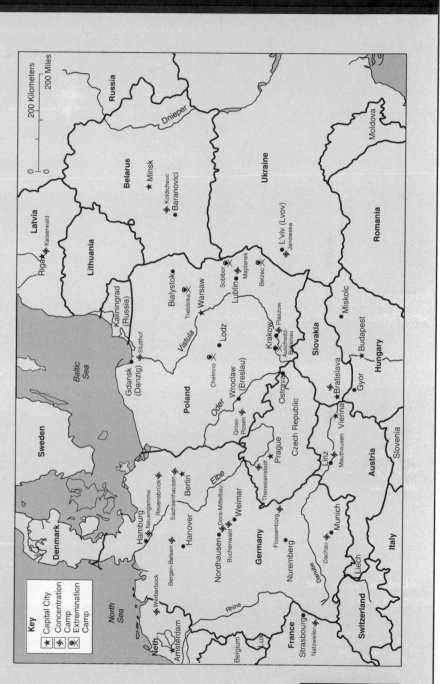

(Continued)

LANDMARKS IN HISTORY

Following World War II, in history's most famous attempt to apply moral standards to wartime conduct, Nazi leaders were charged in Nuremberg, Germany, for several types of crimes. First, they were accused of **crimes against peace**, because they had waged aggressive war in violation of international treaties and obligations. Second, they were charged with **war crimes**, which encompassed violations of the accepted rules of war, such as brutality toward prisoners of war, wanton destruction of towns, and mistreatment of civilians in conquered lands. Third, they were accused of **crimes against humanity**, including the persecution and mass murder of huge numbers of noncombatants. Crimes against peace and war crimes were categories widely accepted under the just war doctrine; the category of crimes against humanity was designed to deal with a specific instance of genocide, the Holocaust.

The decision to punish Nazi leaders for genocide was prompted by an understandable desire for retribution. German actions could not be justified by the exigencies of war (which, of course, Hitler had started). The crimes against humanity concept provided firm support for the just war doctrine (and vice versa).

The Nuremberg trials were justifiable, but it is no simple task to apply the crimes against peace, war crimes, and crimes against humanity labels to concrete and often unique situations. The death camps of the Holocaust violated all standards of law, justice, and decency, (see Figure 15.1). But what about the Allied firebombing of Dresden and many other German cities? Or the brutalities against German civilians tolerated (if not encouraged) by the Soviet army? Or the American firebombing of Japanese cities and the dropping of the atomic bombs on Hiroshima and Nagasaki? These acts, which resulted in hundreds of thousands of civilian

UPI/USAF/HO/Landov

The United States uses drones like this one against the Taliban in Afghanistan and Pakistan. When civilians are killed, Washington calls it "collateral damage," but critics call it a war crime.

(Continued)

(CONTINUED)

deaths, were not covered under the war crimes labels. Critics argue this fact illustrates an important point: the victors write the history of a war. By the same token, the victors alone decide what is and what is not a war crime.

The United States is quick to label auto-genocide in Cambodia or "ethnic cleansing" (a euphemism for genocide) in Bosnia or genocide in Rwanda and Sudan as war crimes. On the other hand, when U.S. drone attacks targeting Taliban fighters in villages along the Afghan-Pakistan border kill civilians, it is labeled "collateral damage"—which makes it legal. Critics of the Bush administration have argued that the methods used in the war on terror—"extraordinary rendition" (seizing

suspected terrorists on foreign soil), leaving detainees in legal limbo by creating a new classification of "illegal combatants," and "enhanced interrogation techniques" such as waterboarding—were war crimes.

As a candidate for the presidency, Barack Obama criticized the harsh methods President Bush approved in carrying out his war on terror. But as Bush's successor, President Obama disappointed many of his most ardent supporters by failing to close the infamous "Gitmo" detention center at Guantanamo Bay, Cuba. And in the spring of 2011, Obama backed off another key campaign pledge when he decided to resume military *trials* for *terrorist* detainees at Guantanamo Bay.

impartial referee, critics contend, the just war doctrine remains a sham advanced by aggressor nations to justify self-serving policies and military interventionism.

Defenders of the just war doctrine point out that moral judgments concerning the conduct of wars have long been thought both natural and necessary: natural in the sense that "for as long as men and women have talked about war, they have talked about it in terms of right and wrong,"[54] and necessary because without them, all wars would have to be considered equally objectionable (or praiseworthy). Admittedly, we cannot prove scientifically that aggressive wars are any worse than preemptive or preventive wars; nor do we need to prove cold-blooded murder is more reprehensible than killing in self-defense—a distinction both criminal law and common sense support.

In the real world, heads of state often engage in moral talk and immoral behavior. The idea of the just war is worth keeping, therefore, if not as a means of controlling that behavior, then as a method of evaluating it (see "Landmarks in History").

A WAR ON *WHAT?* THE POLITICS OF HYPERBOLE

The Bush administration's response to 9/11 was to declare a "war on terror" (see Chapter 16). But terror is not a state—not a place on the map. Waging "war" on terror is thus not like waging traditional war. In fact, calling it war raises major conceptual and strategic problems. President Bush was not the first U.S. commander-in-chief to use the term *war* loosely. U.S. Attorney General Robert F. Kennedy declared a "war on organized crime" in 1961, and every president since John F. Kennedy (Robert's brother) has embraced the "war on

multiple independently targeted reentry vehicle (MIRV) Intercontinental missiles containing many nuclear warheads that can be individually programmed to split off from the nose cone of the rocket upon reentry into the earth's atmosphere and hit different specific targets with a high degree of accuracy.

crime" as his own. President Lyndon Baines Johnson waged a "war on poverty." LBJ's successor in the White House, Richard Nixon, declared a "war on drugs," calling drug abuse "public enemy number one in the United States." These and other domestic "wars" arguably made war appear a kind of permanent condition in a perilous world rather than an extreme step taken only in the most extreme circumstances.

The war on terror identified a subversive organization—al Qaeda—as the source of all evil and a single individual—Osama bin Laden—as the mastermind behind it. Al Qaeda thus became the functional equivalent of world communism, and bin Laden was the new Stalin.

The Bush administration further linked several existing governments—Iraq, Iran, and North Korea—to this conspiratorial organization and branded these states the "axis of evil." (In the 1980s, President Reagan famously called the Soviet Union the "evil empire.") In addition, the war on terror, like the Cold War before it, would be open-ended. Unlike wars of the past, it would go on for generations, possibly forever. Finally, this new "war" was cast as a contest between good and evil, thus turning it into a religious-ideological crusade in much the same way as the Cold War was cast as a struggle between freedom and capitalism, and totalitarian tyranny and Communism.

The means for fighting the war on terror are also reminiscent of the Cold War, including a major military buildup, a soaring defense budget, and a wholesale reorganization of the nation's intelligence, police, and defense establishment. The "national security state" was transformed by creating a new Department of Homeland Security. The central idea of this new department was to integrate the operational procedures of agencies, especially the FBI and CIA, which had operated independently or even competitively during the Cold War.

In the aftermath of the 9/11 attacks, what began as a surgical military operation to wipe out terrorist training camps in Afghanistan became a new global crusade pitting the United States and its allies against the so-called Axis of Evil—Iraq, Iran, and North Korea. Arguably, the prudent course of action was a limited response aimed at a finite evil and a specific target.

Not surprisingly, different observers interpreted the war on terror in very different ways. Conservatives were much more likely than liberals to accept the reasons given for launching an all-out "war" after 9/11, especially for the controversial decision to invade Iraq. But, in fairness, the war was not opposed by leading Democrats in Congress, and even liberal politicians, such as then-Senator Hillary Clinton, supported it. It was only after the occupation turned into a civil war that politicians of all stripes began to jump ship.

What are the lessons of this war? What does it tell us about war in general?

First, the Iraq war combined aspects of various war scenarios discussed earlier in this chapter—**inadvertent war** (war resulting from misperception, misinformation, or miscalculation), accidental war (war touched off unintentionally), catalytic war (war that starts small and gets bigger as other powers are drawn in), and **ABC war** (a war involving atomic, biological, or chemical weapons, otherwise known as weapons of mass destruction). The concept of a just war also came into play because the attack on Iraq was (wrongly) linked to 9/11. Thus, the war was rationalized as a righteous way to punish an aggressor or to avenge a heinous act.

submarine-launched ballistic missile (SLBM) Strategic missiles with multiple nuclear warheads launched from submarines that prowl the ocean depths and that cannot be easily detected or destroyed by a preemptive attack.

proxy war A war in which two adversaries back opposing parties to a conflict by supplying money, weapons, and military advisors, while avoiding direct combat operations against each other.

just war A war fought in self-defense or because it is the only way a nation can do what is right.

moral relativism The idea that all moral judgments are conditional and only "true" in a certain religious, cultural, or social context; the belief that there is no such thing as universal truth in the realm of ethics or morality.

ethnocentric bias The common tendency of human beings to see the world through a cultural lens that distorts reality and exaggerates the good in one's own society and the evil in others.

U.S. Department of Defense

Soldiers in Afghanistan. In late 2009, President Obama ordered a "surge" in troop strength in Afghanistan. Washington pressured NATO allies to commit combat forces to an International Security Assistance Force (ISAF) under U.S. command. U.S. forces never serve under foreign command. PDD-25* decrees, "The chain of command from the President to the lowest U.S. commander in the field [is] inviolate." In this U.S. Army photo, a sniper team scans the area outside a leaders' shura from the rooftop in the village Baki Tana, January 30, 2013.

*PDD stands for Presidential Decision Directive.

Second, the invasion of Iraq was conceived of as part of a larger war; a war not against a specific enemy but against a disembodied "ism." Terrorism, like poverty or crime, is a condition, a fact of life. It does not have a beginning or an end and therefore cannot be eradicated by military means. At best, it can be managed or brought under control. Whether the military as presently constituted is the best instrument for dealing with this type of threat is debatable. In Iraq, traditional military instruments—fighter-bombers, tanks, artillery, and the like—proved highly effective in defeating the Iraqi army but virtually useless in dealing with the guerrilla-style insurrection that followed.

Third, during the course of this war, the Bush administration switched enemies and changed the rationale for fighting. The real enemy was a secretive organization known as al Qaeda rather than another state. To the extent that this enemy had a face, it was the face of Osama bin Laden. For all its military might, the United States was unable to defeat al Qaeda by invading Afghanistan or even to bring the renegade bin Laden, who masterminded the 9/11 attacks, to justice for a decade until a U.S. Navy Seal team finally killed him in 2011. Instead, the Bush administration shifted the focus of attention from Afghanistan and bin Laden to Iraq and Saddam—in other words, from an elusive enemy who could not be defeated militarily to one who could, or so the architects of the Iraq war believed.

That belief proved to be false, as was the evidence that Saddam harbored WMDs, which had been the reason given for launching the war in the first place. As the fighting dragged on and the death toll mounted, the Bush administration changed the rationale for the war once again. Clearly, the original objective—to locate and destroy Saddam's WMD labs and stockpiles—disappeared when no such weapons were discovered. The reason for ousting Saddam then became nation-building, to promote freedom and democracy in the world. Later, as the civil war raged, the reason was simply to stabilize the region because a hasty

crimes against peace
A Nuremberg war crimes trials category, covering the violation of international peace by waging an unjustified, aggressive war.

war crimes
Violation of generally accepted rules of war as established in the Geneva Conventions on the conduct of war. The Geneva Conventions call for the humanitarian treatment of civilians and prisoners of war, and respect for human life and dignity; crimes against humanity, such as genocide and ethnic cleansing, are also war crimes.

withdrawal would, it was argued, leave a dangerous power vacuum. What no one in Washington was saying, however, was what nearly everyone outside Washington was thinking all along: the real reason for invading and occupying Iraq was oil, still the world's most important strategic resource.

On the oil-rich Arabian Peninsula, Iraq's petroleum reserves are second in size only to Saudi Arabia's. The possibility—indeed, the likelihood—that energy security (represented by Iraqi oil) played a major role in shaping the Bush administration's antiterrorism strategy points to one final "lesson learned." The pursuit of security in the modern world is too complex to be reduced to a simple formula or submitted to quick fixes. Any attempt to do so risks producing the opposite effect—that is, greater insecurity.

WEAPONS OF MASS DISRUPTION: CYBERWAR

In 2002, the U.S. Department of the Navy created the Naval Network Warfare Command, known as NETWARCOM. A key element of its mission is information operations (IO), "a warfare area that influences, disrupts, corrupts, or usurps an adversary's decision-making ability while protecting our own." NETWARCOM's "five core integrated abilities" include electronic warfare, computer network operations, psychological operations, military deception, and operational security.[55]

In November 2006, Chinese hackers attacked the U.S. Naval War College computer network, effectively forcing it to shut down for several weeks. Apparently, the attack was aimed at gleaning information about naval war games being developed at the Newport, Rhode Island, facility. The U.S. Navy estimates that hackers try to penetrate its computer systems, which are protected by the Navy Cyber Defense Operations Command, an average of 600,000 times per hour.

In May 2007, Estonia (see Figure 15.2) was the target of an all-out cyberwar attack—the first ever against a sovereign state, but almost certainly not the last. The source of the attack was unknown, but Estonian authorities believed it was ordered by the Kremlin or launched by Russian nationalists in retaliation for Estonia's decision to move a World War II bronze statue of a Soviet soldier from a park in the Estonian capital of Tallinn, the previous month. Angry ethnic Russians living in Estonia staged street demonstrations that led to violent clashes with Estonian riot police. The Kremlin denied any involvement in the subsequent cyberattacks, directed against the executive and legislative branches of Estonia's government, as well as its mobile phone networks, banks, and news organizations.[56]

Although Estonia is a small country, electronic warfare is a big deal no matter what state happens to be the target. When the intended victim is a NATO member and the source of the hostile action implicates Russians (and perhaps Russia), the possibility of a good outcome is not high. Not surprisingly, the cyberwar against Estonia was a matter of intense interest to defense planning agencies, intelligence services, and computer security specialists the world over.

FIGURE 15.2   Estonia is the smallest of the three Baltic states, which became independent when the USSR self-destructed in 1991. Ethnic Russians comprise more than one-fourth of Estonia's 1.3 million people. Tensions between native Estonians and Russians who settled in Estonia during the Soviet period have run high. As a member of both NATO and the EU, Estonia is now politically, economically, and militarily part of the West, but geographically it remains within easy striking distance of Russia's technologically sophisticated armed forces. In 2007 Estonia suffered a major cyberwar attack. In late 2014, North Korea was thought to be the source of a similar attack on Sony Pictures.

Finally, in the summer of 2009, the Obama administration unveiled a plan to create a new Pentagon "cyber command" as the centerpiece of its strategy for defending against a future attack on the nation's computer networks. The plan, still in its infancy, raised major privacy issues, as well as diplomatic questions. President Obama sought to allay fears of "Big Brother" watching what citizens were doing at home, saying the plan "will not—I repeat, will not—include monitoring private sector networks or Internet traffic." But a major architect of the new cyberstrategy was not so reassuring on this point: "How do you understand sovereignty in the cyber domain?" General James E. ("Hoss") Cartwright asked. "It doesn't tend to pay a lot of attention to geographic boundaries."[57]

Another complication raises a delicate diplomatic question: How does the U.S. military respond to a cyberattack initiated in another country without violating international law by invading that country's space? Otherwise put: Does the concept of sovereignty apply in cyberspace?

Clearly, the danger of cyberwar exists in today's world. But key questions have to be answered before adequate defenses can be designed and deployed.

WAR AND DEMOCRACY

Democracies are by nature peace-loving; authoritarian states are warlike. At least that's what most Americans believe. Facing an isolationist Congress, President Woodrow Wilson justified America's (late) entry into World War I by saying that it was necessary to make the world safe for democracy. There is a widely held belief, not without some foundation, that democracies don't go to war against each other. In 1999, scholar Rudolf Rummel published an essay in *Peace* magazine arguing that "democracy is a general cure for political or collective violence of any kind."[58] Pairs of nations had waged war against each other 353 times between 1816 and 1991, said Rummel, and not one of these conflicts was between two democracies. Is this true? Are democracies antiwar? Are they inherently resistant to organized violence? It all depends: (1) on how democracy is defined, (2) on who's counting, and (3) on what counts as war. One thing is certain—democracies can and do fight.

Why Democracies Fight

Often the most vocal patriots are also the most avid defenders of democracy. Typically, when leaders tell citizens and citizens tell each other that war or military intervention is necessary, they say it is to defend freedom or to defeat tyranny. That is sometimes true, but not always. It was clearly true in World War II, for example, but it is now generally conceded that it was not true in Vietnam.

Fear is most definitely a factor when democracies go to war. Fear and prejudice often combine to make a citizenry susceptible to war propaganda. Since World War II, Americans have repeatedly been told that the United States faces grave threats that can only be met with military force. Such an assertion requires careful scrutiny because the consequences of war are always costly and sometimes catastrophic.

Several factors in the modern world work against this kind of "careful scrutiny." One is propaganda, a tool developed into a major instrument of mass manipulation in the last century. Another is television, a "hot" medium that lends itself to hyperbole—or "hype"—and emotional appeals rather than reason. A third is money.

Democracies by definition have market economies that embrace capitalism and the profit motive as necessary and proper. Many scholars who have studied war agree that greed and profit often play a role in boosting military budgets and fostering public attitudes that favor military attitudes over diplomacy.

Superpower or "Chickenhawk Nation"?

Author James Fallows argues that the United States has become the world's leading "chickenhawk economy." popularized the term "chickenhawk nation" and reopened long-festering wounds in American politics: namely, why the military fights unnecessary wars it can't win, and why society doesn't care.[59] The question the article raised was emblazoned on the cover: "Why do the best soldiers in the world keep losing?"

Political satirist Stephen Colbert captures the essence of what it means to be a "chickenhawk" in politics with this statement: "I will do anything in my power to support our military, short of enlisting."

A chickenhawk, as Fallows uses the term, is a person in a position of public prominence or power who displays two traits:

- Aggressive support for military force as a primary instrument of foreign policy.
- A documentable lack of combat experience (usually despite having the opportunity to fight, or even actively dodging it).

Fallows argues that millennials—the generation of Americans born after 1980—are characterized by a near-total separation from the reality of war and the sacrifices that attend it. Compared with preceding generations, far fewer people born in the years after Vietnam—and after the draft was abolished in January 1973—have a soldier in the family or a close friend in the military. He argues there is now a dangerous disconnect between a society that respects and supports the military but does not serve, and the actual institution itself.

The United States spends as much on defense as the next ten nations combined—three to five times as much as China—and 50% more than during the Cold War and Vietnam. Boasting an annual budget of nearly $600 billion and another $200 billion for pensions and veterans benefits in 2014, the Pentagon is wide open to waste, inefficiency, and mismanagement. But unlike other parts of the government, Fallows observes, the military establishment is not held accountable for its expenditures or its failures either by Congress or the American people.

The upshot is a country mired in endless wars, (Afghanistan being the longest in American history), with soldiers in the field (the "grunts") given abundant lip service but little public attention. Fallows contends the situation won't change unless Congress brings back the draft and the people start paying attention again—and the latter won't happen without the former.

Voices raised in recent years in favor of mandatory military or national service include comedian John Stewart and Congressman Charlie Rangel. They are joined by a growing number of savvy social media political activists who believe that without some kind of draft the United States will continue to find itself embroiled in wars the military can neither win nor end.

WAR AND DIPLOMACY

In a world of sovereign states, war is not only the absence of peace but also the failure of diplomacy. Finding a way to keep the peace without compromising one's vital interests or basic principles is the acid test of diplomacy.

Conflict is endemic in international relations, as in everyday life. The mark of a great power is not how many wars it fights and wins but how many conflicts it wins without a fight. The importance of an enlightened foreign policy is the focus of the next chapter.

SUMMARY

Avoiding war is not always an objective of state policy. Some leaders—for example, Italy's fascist dictator Mussolini—have actually glorified it.

We can divide theories of the causes of war into three categories, those that blame human nature, society, or an unforgiving environment. Thomas Hobbes thought war was a product of human perversity; Jean-Jacques Rousseau maintained that human beings are basically good but society corrupts them; John Locke attributed human aggression to scarcities in nature, including hunger and famine, disease, storms, and droughts (that is, circumstances beyond human control).

All simplistic theories fall short of explaining the variety of factors that cause war—social, political, economic, and psychological. A large, powerful nation that shares boundaries with several neighboring states, is ruled by a risk-oriented leader, has access to modern technology, is experiencing (or expecting) internal conflict, and has a rapidly expanding population is likely to be predisposed toward war.

Under conditions of high tension, war may occur even if none of the principals wants it. Such unintended wars may erupt because of misperception, misunderstanding, accident, escalation, or a catalytic reaction and make it difficult to assign moral responsibility. Often when war occurs, it is not clear who or what actually caused it.

Using war as an instrument of state policy violates international law and morality, but not all wars are equally objectionable. The just war doctrine holds that self-defense and the defense of universal principles are legitimate reasons for going to war. This doctrine is frequently criticized on the grounds of moral relativism, cultural ethnocentrism, and political realism.

International lawyers at Nuremberg developed a new category of war crimes—crimes against humanity. Although the trials were justified, such proceedings contain inherent pitfalls and must be approached with extreme caution.

KEY TERMS

war   460
interstate war   460
civil war   460
guerrilla warfare   460
low-intensity
   conflict   460
nationalism   461
arms race   461
ultranationalism   461

nationalistic
   universalism   461
reasons of state   461
state of nature   464
internationalist   467
national self-
   determination   467
paradox of democratic
   peace   473

limited war   476
unconditional
   surrender   476
war by
   misperception   477
accidental war   477
catalytic war   477
massive
   retaliation   478

nuclear monopoly 478

intercontinental ballistic missile (ICBM) 478

brinkmanship 478

mutual assured destruction (MAD) 478

mutual deterrence 478

second strike 478

overkill 478

multiple independently targeted reentry vehicle (MIRV) 478

submarine-launched ballistic missile (SLBM) 478

proxy war 478

just war 479

moral relativism 480

ethnocentric bias 480

crimes against peace 482

war crimes 482

crimes against humanity 482

inadvertent war 484

ABC war 484

REVIEW QUESTIONS

1. Into what general categories do most explanations of the ultimate causes of war fall?
2. According to Thomas Hobbes, what is the root cause of all wars? What arguments did Hobbes offer in defense of his thesis?
3. What did Jean-Jacques Rousseau believe to be the root cause of war? How did his views differ from Hobbes's? What arguments did Rousseau advance to support his thesis?
4. Those who believe society is the ultimate cause of war differ about precisely what aspect of society is most responsible. What are the four alternative theories presented in the text?
5. How did John Locke explain the phenomenon of war? How did his view differ from those of Hobbes and Rousseau? What arguments did Locke offer in support of his thesis?
6. Which explanation of the causes of war seems most plausible? Explain your answer.
7. Why is it difficult simply to condemn the guilty party or parties whenever war breaks out?
8. With the technology of warfare advancing by leaps and bounds, it becomes increasingly probable that a war will start even though nobody intends it to. In what ways might this happen?
9. Are all wars equally objectionable from a moral standpoint? Why or why not?
10. Are the arguments, pro and con, concerning the validity of the just war doctrine equally balanced? Explain.
11. What prompted the Nuremberg War Crimes Trials? What are crimes against humanity? How does the just war doctrine fit into the picture? Should, or could, Nuremberg-type trials be conducted after every war?
12. Critique the concept of a "war on terror" and the strategy the Bush administration used in the conduct of that "war." Compare the Bush administration approach with that of the Obama administration. How do they differ? How are they similar?

WEBSITES AND READINGS

Websites

To find out more about a particular armed conflict, use the title of the conflict as the search term.

War and Pop Culture: http://www.amazon.com/War-American-Popular-Culture-Encyclopedia/dp/0313299080

World War II and Pop Culture: http://www.livinghistoryfarm.org/farminginthe40s/life_07.html

Vietnam War and Pop Culture: http://www.digitalhistory.uh.edu/disp_textbook.cfm?smtID=2&psid=3467

Iraq War and Pop Culture: http://abcnews.go.com/GMA/IraqCoverage/story?id=759253

Cold War and Pop Culture: http://www.telegraph.co.uk/culture/10441108/How-pop-culture-helped-win-the-Cold-War.html

Civil War and Pop Culture: http://www.h-net.org/reviews/showrev.php?id=161

The Crimes of War Project: http://www.crimesofwar.org/

Vietnam War Photos: http://www.vietnampix.com/intro2.htm

Civil War Facts and Photographs: http://www.civilwar.org/battlefields/; http://www.civilwarphotography.org/index.php/exhibits/online-exhibits

Against War and Interventionism: antiwar.com/who.php

PBS Series on World War II: http://www.pbs.org/thewar/

Cost of National Defense (see "Federal Budget 101" and "Our Work"): http://demilitarize.org/income-tax-money-federal-budget-2014-fiscal-year/; https://www.nationalpriorities.org/

World War I: http://www.firstworldwar.com/

Korean War: www.korean-war.com

America's Wars, 1812 to Bush Presidency: http://www.historycentral.com/wars.html

Philosophy of War: http://www.iep.utm.edu/war/

Readings

Aron, Raymond. *The Century of Total War.* Lanham, MD: University Press of America, 1985. One of this century's most influential thinkers examines the causes and conditions of war in our age.

_____. *The Great Debate: Theories of Nuclear Strategy*, trans, by Ernst Pawel. Lanham, MD: University Press of America, 1985. A lucid analysis of strategic alternatives available to the Western alliance. First published in the early 1960s, it is still worth reading.

Bolger, Daniel P. *Why We Lost: A General's Inside Account of the Iraq and Afghanistan Wars.* New York: Houghton Mifflin Harcourt, 2014.

Carr, Edward Hallett. *The Twenty Years' Crisis, 1919–1939*, 2nd ed. New York: St. Martin's Press, 1969. How the stage was set for World War II.

Codevilla, Angelo, and Paul Seabury. *War: Ends and Means.* Dulles, VA: Potomac Books, 2006. A sober discussion of war as a permanent part of the human condition.

Coll, Steve. *Ghost Wars: The Secret History of the CIA, Afghanistan, and bin Laden from the Soviet Invasion to September 10, 2001.* New York: Penguin, 2004. This book won the 2005 Pulitzer Prize.

Fallows, James. "The Tragedy of the American Military," *The Atlantic,* January/February 2015, pp. 73–90. The author calls the United States "a chickenhawk nation in which careless spending and strategic folly combine to lure America into endless wars it cannot win."

Haase, Richard. *War of Necessity, War of Choice: A Memoir of Two Iraq Wars.* New York: Simon and Schuster, 2009. A critical first-person account of the two Iraqi wars by a long-time Washington foreign policy insider who applies the theory and literature on just and unjust wars to the real world of power politics.

Jones, Seth. *In the Graveyard of Empires: America's War in Afghanistan.* New York: Norton, 2009. A detailed account of failed policies and a losing war in Afghanistan.

Junger, Sebastian. *War.* New York: Twelve (The Hachette Group), 2010. A vivid account of the reality of combat by the author of *The Perfect Storm.*

Richardson, Lewis. *Statistics of Deadly Quarrels.* Chicago: Boxwood, 1960. A frequently cited quantitative study of war.

Ricks, Thomas E. *Fiasco: The American Military Adventure in Iraq.* New York: Penguin, 2006.

Russett, Bruce. *Grasping the Democratic Peace.* Princeton, NJ: Princeton University Press, 1995. Why democratic governments do not wage war on one another.

Smith, Rubert. *The Utility of Force: The Art of War in the Modern World.* New York: Knopf, 2007. Reflections on the nature of war in the age of "smart" weapons, urban battlegrounds, and terrorist tactics.

Stoessinger, John. *Why Nations Go to War,* 10th ed. Belmont, CA: Wadsworth, 2007. A standard and highly readable study of war widely used in college courses.

Van Creveld, Martin. *The Changing Face of War: Lessons of Combat, from the Marne to Iraq.* New York: Presidio Press, 2007. On the changing nature of warfare over the past century by a recognized expert on military history and strategy.

Waltz, Kenneth N. *Man, the State, and War: A Theoretical Analysis.* New York: Columbia University Press, 1965. A lucid account of the origins of war emphasizing human nature, the state, and a disorderly world order.

Walzer, Michael. *Just and Unjust Wars: A Moral Argument with Historical Illustrations,* 4th ed. New York: Basic Books, 2006. "[T]he argument about war and justice is still a political and moral necessity."

Wright, Quincy. *A Study of War,* abridged ed. Chicago: University of Chicago Press, 1983. Widely acclaimed. One scholar calls it "the most comprehensive work ever published in any language on the history, the nature, the causes, and the cure of war."

CHAPTER 16

Terrorism
War, Crimes, or War Crimes?

Learning Objectives

1 Trace the origins of terrorism.

2 Discuss the various ways terrorism can be perceived (e.g., heroic, cowardly, an act of war), and explain how one could see it as anything other than a crime.

3 Evaluate the war on terror as a general policy, and critique the strategy adopted in pursuit of this policy.

4 Describe (or prescribe) a sound policy for fighting terrorism effectively.

In February 1993, long before Osama bin Laden became a household name, a yellow Ryder rental van containing a 1,200-pound bomb exploded in the parking garage of the World Trade Center in New York City, blasting a 200-foot crater in the basement. More than a thousand people were injured, and six died. Shocked citizens struggled to grasp the idea that a devastating terrorist attack had taken place against a symbol of U.S. economic might and one of the largest and most famous buildings in the world.

Eight and a half years later, on September 11, 2001, the United States watched in horror as the World Trade Center towers were hit again, this time by hijacked commercial airliners loaded with highly volatile jet fuel. The towers burned for a short time and then imploded with an incredible force that rocked downtown Manhattan, killing thousands of people still trapped inside the towers, creating a firestorm of debris, and sending a huge cloud of smoke, dust, and ash skyward that lingered over the city like an eerie, foul-smelling pall for many days.

No one knew in 1993 whether the first World Trade Center bombing was an isolated act or a sign of things to come. Now we know the answer: Terrorist attacks would become a grim reality of life nearly all across the globe in the coming decades (see Table 16.1).

TABLE 16.1 Twenty-Five Year Terrorism Timeline—1983–2008.

April 18, 1983	Suicide bombing of U.S. embassy in Beirut kills 63.
October 23, 1983	Suicide truck bombing of Marine barracks in Beirut kills 241.
December 21, 1988	Pan Am flight 103 explodes over Lockerbie, Scotland, killing 270 people, including 11 on the ground.
February 26, 1993	Bomb in a van explodes beneath the World Trade Center in New York City, killing 6 and injuring more than 1,000.
March 12, 1993	13 coordinated bomb explosions in Mumbai (Bombay), India, kill 257 people and injure some 700.
June 23, 1993	Federal investigators break up a plot by Islamic radicals to bomb the United Nations and two Hudson River tunnels.
March 20, 1995	Members of Aum Shinrikyo release deadly sarin gas in the Tokyo subway in five coordinated attacks, killing 12, severely injuring 50, and causing temporary vision problems for many others.
April 19, 1995	A truck bomb destroys the federal building in Oklahoma City, Oklahoma, killing 168 and wounding more than 600. Two Americans were charged and convicted.
November 13, 1995	A car bomb explodes outside a U.S. Army training office in Riyadh, Saudi Arabia, killing 7, including 5 Americans, and wounding 60 others.
April 3, 1996	The FBI arrests Theodore J. Kaczynski, a Montana hermit, and accuses him of an eighteen-year series of bomb attacks carried out by the "Unabomber."

(continued)

TABLE 16.1   (continued)

June 25, 1996	A truck bomb explodes outside an apartment complex in Dhahran, Saudi Arabia, killing 19 Americans and wounding hundreds more.
July 1, 1996	Federal agents arrest 12 members of the Viper Militia, a Phoenix, Arizona, group accused of plotting to blow up government buildings.
July 17, 1996	A pipe bomb explodes at a concert during the Summer Olympics in Atlanta, Georgia, killing 1 and wounding more than 100.
August 7, 1998	The U.S. embassies in Kenya and Tanzania are bombed, killing 224 people, mostly Kenyan passers-by, in the capital of Nairobi.
August 15, 1998	A large car bomb explodes in the central shopping district of Omagh, Northern Ireland, killing 29 people and injuring 330.
September 8, 1999	Bombs explode in an apartment block in Moscow, Russia, killing 94 and injuring 152, part of a series of bombings over a two-week period that altogether killed nearly 300 people.
October 12, 2000	A speedboat bomb attack on the USS *Cole* in Aden, Yemen, kills 17.
September 11, 2001	Four commercial jet airliners are hijacked from East Coast airports: two are crashed into the World Trade Center towers; one is crashed into the Pentagon; and the fourth one crashes into a field in Pennsylvania. Thousands are killed or injured.
October 12, 2002	Bomb blast in a Bali resort, blamed on militant Islamic group linked to Osama bin Laden and al Qaeda, kills an estimated 202 people.
August 8, 2003	Car bomb at Jordanian embassy in Baghdad kills at least 11 people.
August 19, 2003	Terrorist bomb attack destroys UN headquarters in Iraqi capital of Baghdad, killing 22, including Sergio Vieira de Mello, the top UN envoy in Iraq.
November 15 & 20, 2003	Suicide bombers in Istanbul attack two synagogues, a British-based bank, and the British consulate, killing as many as 50 people and injuring more than 600.
March 11, 2004	Ten bombs explode at train stations in and around Madrid during morning rush hour, killing 198 and wounding many more in Spain's worst-ever terrorist incident.
July 7, 2005	A series of bombs is detonated in three crowded subway trains and aboard a London bus during peak rush hour, killing at least 191 people and injuring some 1,755.
July 11, 2006	Seven bomb blasts kill 209 people on the Suburban Railway in Mumbai (Bombay), India; another 700 are injured.
September 17, 2008	Al Qaeda in Yemen carries out attack on U.S. embassy in Sanaa, killing 18 people.
November 26–29, 2008	A wave of ten coordinated bombing attacks in Mumbai (Bombay), India, kills at least 173 and injures more than 300; allegedly carried out by Pakistani militants.

SOURCES: *Wall Street Journal*, July 29, 1996, p. A14; *The Economist*, September 15, 2001, p. 18; Country Reports on Terrorism, U.S. Department of State 2006, 2007, 2008; author's updates.

Between 2010 and 2015, terrorist attacks continued worldwide. Many of the worst ones resulted in multiple deaths and injuries and occurred in Iraq, Afghanistan, and Pakistan. In recent years, Baghdad and other major Iraqi cities (including Fallujah, Karbala, Kut, Kirkuk, Najaf, and Tikrit) have suffered frequent car bombings, suicide bombings, and armed attacks. In Afghanistan, three cities—Kabul, Kandahar, Lashkar Gah (the capital of Helmand province)—have been favorite targets of terrorists. In December 2014, a Taliban attack on a school in Peshawar, Pakistan, claimed the lives of 132 children and 13 adults.

Of course, terrorism is not confined to any single country or continent. January 2015 was a harsh reminder that Europe, too, is vulnerable. Barely a month after the tragedy in Peshawar, twelve people were killed in a commando-style terrorist attack on the Paris headquarters of a satirical newspaper, *Charlie Hebdo*. The attack was in retaliation for the paper's unsparing criticism of Islam and a vulgar caricature of the Prophet Muhammad. France is home to Europe's largest Muslim minority population and also to the extreme right-wing, anti-immigrant National Front, France's fastest growing political party. Predictably, this religiously motivated act of mass murder directed against the editor and staff of a secularist French newspaper—and carried out by "foreigners"—triggered a new wave of angst and anger directed at Arabs in France and fed rising anti-Islamic sentiments elsewhere in Europe as well. (Relatively unnoticed on the same day, a suicide bomber killed thirty-seven people and injured sixty-six more in Sanaa, the capital of Yemen.)

In Pakistan, dozens of innocents have died in attacks in remote border regions of North Waziristan and Khyber Pakhtunkhwa, as well as in Islamabad, Bannu, Hangu, Karachi, Lahore, Peshawar, and other cities. On December 25, 2010, a female suicide bomber blew herself up in the middle of a crowd at a United Nations food aid center in northwest Pakistan, killing 46 people and injuring more than 100 others.[1] By mid-November 2014, Pakistan alone recorded 332 major terrorist incidents that claimed the lives 3,283 victims and left another 1,898 injured.

Terrorism is a global problem in today's world; it can happen anywhere and does happen nearly everywhere. In July 2011, for example, a lone gunman killed 77 people and injured 242 in Norway. In a "manifesto" published electronically the day of the attacks, a right-wing blogger named Anders Behring Breivik expressed extreme antipathy toward Islam as a religion, immigrants in general, Muslims in particular, and "multiculturalism." In August 2012, a court in Oslo found Breivik sane and guilty of mass murder.

The terrorism contagion in the post-WWII era had its origins not in Islam or the Middle East but in Europe, where Christianity, with its roots in Roman Catholicism, has long been the predominant religion. In the United Kingdom, Irish Republican Army (IRA) ultranationalists conducted a terrorist campaign against British control of Northern Ireland (also known as Ulster) starting in the late 1960s. In Spain, Basque separatists known as the ETA (Basque Homeland and Freedom) have conducted a long-running terrorist campaign against the Madrid government. In Russia, two female suicide bombers wearing explosive belts detonated the devices on the Moscow Metro system on May 29, 2010, at the peak of the morning rush hour, killing 40 and injuring more than 100.

terrorism
Politically or ideologically motivated violence aimed at public officials, business elites, and civilian populations designed to sow fear and dissension, destabilize societies, undermine established authority, induce policy changes, or even overthrow the existing government.

In May 2009, New York City police arrested four ex-convicts allegedly engaged in a plot to blow up two synagogues in the Bronx and shoot down a military aircraft. Among the weapons they had locked away in a storage container was a surface-to-air missile. In 2011, a decade after the war on terror was launched, the United States still faces terrorist threats at home while continuing to fight two post 9/11 wars abroad.

WHAT IS TERRORISM?

Despite its prevalence, **terrorism** remains an elusive concept. Some definitions emphasize terrorism's use of violence in the service of politics. According to *Webster's New World Dictionary*, terrorism is "the use of force or threats to demoralize, intimidate, and subjugate, especially such use as the political weapon or policy." Another source defines terrorism as "the deliberate attack on innocent civilians for political purposes."[2] *Terrorism* has been defined in many ways, but most definitions take into account several factors, including violence, desire for publicity, political motive, and intimidation aimed at civilian populations.[3] As we will see later in the chapter, our definition of *terrorism* implies both a strategy and tactics (see "Ideas and Politics").

IDEAS AND POLITICS

TERRORISM: Five Definitions

Terrorism, by nature, is difficult to define. Acts of terrorism conjure emotional responses in the victims (those hurt by the violence and those affected by the fear), as well as in the practitioners. Even the U.S. government cannot agree on one single definition. The adage "One man's terrorist is another man's freedom fighter" is still alive and well. Listed here are several definitions of terrorism.

- "Terrorism is the use or threatened use of force designed to bring about political change." —Brian Jenkins
- "Terrorism constitutes the illegitimate use of force to achieve a political objective when innocent people are targeted." —Walter Laqueur
- "Terrorism is the premeditated, deliberate, systematic murder, mayhem, and threatening of the innocent to create fear and intimidation in order to gain a political or tactical advantage, usually to influence an audience." —James M. Poland
- "Terrorism is the unlawful use or threat of violence against persons or property to further

political or social objectives. It is usually intended to intimidate or coerce a government, individuals, or groups, or to modify their behavior or politics." —Vice President's Task Force, 1986
- "Terrorism is the unlawful use of force or violence against persons or property to intimidate or coerce a government, the civilian population, or any segment thereof, in furtherance of political or social objectives." —FBI Definition

In the aftermath of 9/11, the United States declared a "war on terror," yet none of the five definitions listed here describes terrorism as an act of war. Why not? What is terrorism? Who decides? Why does it matter? Think about it.

(Hint: Ponder whether torture is ever justified as an instrument of the state, or why "Gitmo" detainees are not treated as POWs in the "war on terror." Research the Third Geneva Convention of 1949.)

SOURCE: http://www.terror.com

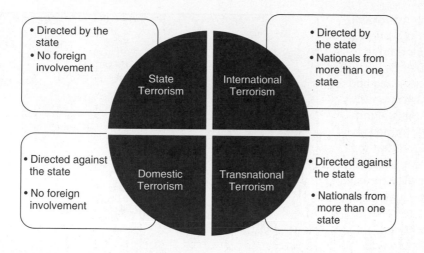

FIGURE 16.1
Classifying Terrorism.

state terrorism
Usually violent methods used by a government's security forces to intimidate and coerce its own people.

international terrorism
Terrorism that involves the governments, citizens, and interests of more than one country; terrorism that spills over into the international arena for whatever reason, whether state-sponsored or not.

state-sponsored terrorism
International terrorism that is aided and abetted by an established state; for example, Libya was linked to many terrorist acts against Western countries until Muammar el-Qaddafi made peace overtures in December 2003 and before he became an international pariah all over again in 2011 in the face of a popular rebellion.

domestic terrorism
A form of terrorism practiced within a country by people with no ties to any government.

Terrorism comes in many forms. Some experts attempt to designate terrorist activities according to whether they (1) are state controlled or directed or (2) involve nationals from more than one country (see Figure 16.1).

State terrorism occurs when a government perpetrates terrorist tactics on its own citizens, such as occurred in Hitler's Germany. In contrast, **international terrorism**, sometimes called **state-sponsored terrorism**, happens when a government harbors international terrorists (as the Taliban government in Afghanistan did in the case of Osama bin Laden and the al Qaeda organization), finances international terrorist operations, or otherwise supports international terrorism *outside* its own borders.

During the Cold War, the United States frequently accused the Soviet Union of underwriting anti-U.S. terrorist groups around the world with money and arms. The Soviet Union responded that the U.S. government did the same when it was in its interests to do so. Iran, Libya, Sudan, Syria, North Korea, and Cuba have all been on the United States' list of suspected state sponsors of terrorism for many years (see Figure 16.2). Afghanistan and Iraq were also on this list prior to the fall of the Taliban regime in Afghanistan in late 2001 and the invasion of Iraq in 2003.

Libya was taken off the list when leader Muammar el-Qaddafi promised to scrap Libya's weapons research programs and open the country to international arms inspections in December 2003. In 2011, he again became a pariah in the eyes of the West when he turned his security forces against his own people in an attempt to resist the tide of democratizing reform—the so-called Arab Spring—sweeping across the region. With UN and NATO backing, President Obama ordered air strikes against the Qaddafi regime on humanitarian grounds (to protect the civilian population, especially in parts of the country, mainly in eastern Libya, known to be rebel strongholds). In the end, rebels caught and killed the deposed tyrant in October 2011.

Domestic terrorism is practiced within a single country by terrorists with no ties to any government. The Tokyo subway sarin gas attacks in 1995, the

FIGURE 16.2   Map of the "Axis of Evil." By far, the largest number of worldwide terrorist incidents in 2006 occurred in two countries President George W. Bush blamed for the 9/11 attacks—Iraq and Afghanistan. President Bush famously declared that these two states, along with Iran and North Korea, formed an "axis of evil." Critics charged that the U.S.-led invasion and occupation of these two countries was disastrously counterproductive—a prelude to anarchy and stepped-up terrorist activity rather than stability or democracy.

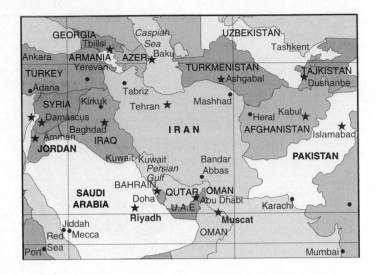

Madrid commuter train bombings in 2004, and the Mumbai Suburban Railway bombings in 2006 (refer to Table 16.1) are examples of this type of terrorism. The aim of domestic terrorism is typically to strike fear and sow seeds of discord in society and to discredit or overthrow existing political institutions. Unlike the United Kingdom, Spain, and several other Western countries, the United States has been largely exempt from such acts but with notable exceptions, including numerous bombings of abortion clinics, the Oklahoma City federal office building bombing in 1995, the summer 1996 bombing at the Olympics in Atlanta, and the April 15, 2013, Boston Marathon bombings that killed 3 people and injured 264 others.

Transnational terrorism arises when terrorists or terrorist groups not backed by any established state and operating in different countries cooperate with each other, or when a single terrorist operates in more than one country. Examples include the bombing of the U.S. embassies in Kenya and Tanzania in 1998, the World Trade Center attacks in 1993 and 2001, and the London subway bombings in 2005 (refer to Table 16.1). The global nature of terrorism today has blurred the distinction between domestic and international forms of terrorism.

Domestic terrorism is often directed against the state. Groups seeking to regain control over their homelands, such as Basques in Spain, Irish Catholics in Northern Ireland, Tamils in Sri Lanka, Sikhs in India, and Chechens in Russia, are motivated by *nationalist* or *separatist* aims. This type of terrorism is usually confined to a specific nation, although its practitioners may receive arms, money, and support from other radical groups, private donors abroad, or even foreign governments. But the distinction between domestic terrorism and violent crime is blurred when multiple killings of innocent civilians occur, as it did in a movie theater in Aurora, Colorado, on July 20, 2012, and at Sandy Hook Elementary School in Newtown, Connecticut, on December 14, 2012.

Groups seeking to destabilize society in the name of some abstract belief are often inspired by *ideological* or *utopian* motives. The specific ideology is less

transnational terrorism
Exists when terrorist groups in different countries cooperate or when a group's terrorist actions cross national boundaries.

School shooting memorial following December 14, 2012, massacre at Sandy Hook Elementary School in Sandy Hook, Connecticut—26 people died. The attack was carried out by a 20-year-old gunman brandishing three firearms, including a Bushmaster semi-automatic AR-15 assault rifle. All 20 children killed were in kindergarten or first grade. For the victims and families, the distinction between terrorism and what happened in Newtown that day is meaningless.

important than the fanatical behavior it encourages. Terrorism is a hallmark of fascism and anarchism, as well as distorted versions of Marxism and Islam.[4] Examples include the Red Army Faction in Germany, the Red Brigades in Italy, the Shining Path in Peru, the Islamic Jihad in Egypt, Osama bin Laden's al Qaeda (the Base), and certain far-right militia groups in the United States. Often such groups also have international links.

Some terrorist organizations defy simple description. Hamas (Islamic Resistance Movement), for example, which has violently opposed peace negotiations between Israel and the Palestine Liberation Organization (PLO) over the future of the Israeli-occupied West Bank and Gaza Strip, won a surprise victory in the Palestinian parliamentary elections of January 2006. Hamas is a nationalist-separatist movement that seeks the destruction of Israel and the establishment of a radical Islamic state. But it is also motivated by ideology, namely, a brand of Islamic fundamentalism that stresses militancy and jihad (holy war). Classifying terrorist groups may be useful as a tool of analysis, but it is not always easy.

THE ORIGINS OF TERRORISM

There is clearly a link between terrorism and religious fundamentalism; Islamic extremism is an obvious case in point. However, many terrorists are not religious, and few religious fundamentalists engage in acts of terrorism. Still, terrorism appears to have its roots in religion—specifically, in obscure religious sects, the names of which have entered into our vernacular.[5]

The Thugs, a Hindu sect that was finally destroyed in the nineteenth century after having operated for many centuries in India, were highway ambushers who secretly killed thousands of other Hindus, apparently out of a perverse sense of religious duty. An extremist Jewish group known as the Zealots killed outsiders and helped provoke rebellion against pagan Rome in 66–73 CE. Beginning in the eleventh century, a Shi'ite Muslim sect, the Assassins, murdered outsiders in a campaign to "purify" Islam. Toward the end of the Middle Ages and later during the Reformation, violent sects arose within Christianity as well.[6]

Modern-day revolutionary terror is usually traced to more secular roots, often to the French Revolution or the writings and deeds of nineteenth-century Russian anarchists.[7] Some experts contend that the type of contemporary terrorism we see on the nightly news sprouted from seeds planted in the late 1960s; a few even cite 1968 as the year of its inception. The confluence of turbulent and unsettling events in the late 1960s included racial strife in the United States, an escalating conflict in Vietnam, and the Arab-Israeli Six Day War of 1967. The year 1968 brought these portents:

- Three Palestinian terrorists seized an Israeli El Al airliner and forced its crew to fly the plane to Algeria, one of the first of many acts of air piracy.
- The Baader-Meinhof gang announced its presence in West Germany by torching a Frankfurt department store.
- Yasir Arafat, an advocate of armed struggle against Israel, became the leader of the PLO.
- The assassination of Martin Luther King Jr. precipitated an outbreak of domestic violence in the United States by such groups as the Black Panthers and the Weathermen.[8]

At least three longer-term historical forces helped create a climate conducive to terrorism. First, direct military confrontations and conflicts became infinitely more dangerous in the nuclear age; what starts as a conventional war between two countries (India and Pakistan, for example) might escalate out of control. Therefore, nations whose interests coincided with certain terrorist objectives sometimes provided moral, financial, or military support to these groups. In this manner, terrorism became a kind of proxy for violence between nations. Second, European colonialism had drawn to a close, leaving many newly formed nations to work out a host of unresolved territorial, national, and religious disputes. The result was a variety of low-intensity wars, many punctuated by terrorist activity, within and between these nations. Third, reverence for life and concern for the individual, common to democratic societies, combined with dramatic "up close and personal" worldwide television news coverage to make terrorist incidents major media events. Consequently, the impact of such incidents—the publicity "payoff" from the terrorist's point of view—has been greatly magnified since the 1960s.

But it was in the 1970s that terrorism and **counterterrorism**, or opposing terrorism, became major growth industries. According to one estimate, the number of terrorist incidents multiplied ten-fold between 1971 and 1985.[9] The level of terrorism remained high throughout the 1980s. Precise figures vary widely and reflect, among other things, differences in how terrorism is defined. Risks International, for example, put the total number of terrorist incidents in 1985 at slightly more than 3,000, but the U.S. government conservatively counted fewer than one-fourth that number.[10]

counterterrorism
Methods used to combat terrorism.

The international terrorist threat to the U.S. homeland culminated in the 9/11 attacks. Both before and after 2001, terrorism plagued Europe, the Middle East, and Latin America far more than it did the United States. Surprisingly, at the end of the 1990s, terrorism was less common in the Middle East than in any other region of the world *except* North America. However, that changed dramatically after the U.S.-led invasion of Iraq in 2003. The National Counter-Terrorism Center (NCTC) reported no fewer than 62,805 worldwide terrorist attacks during the years 2005 to 2009, of which roughly one-third occurred in a single country—Iraq. Given these numbers, it is clear that the war on terror, far from solving the problem, has coincided with a steep rise in terrorism across the globe.

The Logic of Terrorism

Why do terrorists act as they do? Terrorist acts are often designed to undermine support and confidence in the existing government by creating a climate of fear and uncertainty. Terrorists use violence as a form of psychological warfare on behalf of an "overvalued idea" or cause. Terrorists are fiercely anti–status quo and despair of peaceful methods; they seek to bring about change or chaos, the latter either as an end in itself or as a prelude to change. They often aim not so much to spark an immediate revolution as to provoke the government into acts of repression, to make it look weak or inept, and to prepare the way for revolution.

Terrorism strikes at vulnerable societies, not necessarily unjust ones. Indeed, one expert on terrorism noted, "Societies with the least political participation and the most injustice have been the most free from terrorism in our time."[11] By logical extension, democratic societies like the United States and the United Kingdom, with long traditions of respect for civil rights and the rule of law, have both been potential and actual targets of terrorist attacks.

Terrorist Tactics

Terrorism has often been described as the weapon of the weak against the strong. Typically, individuals or tiny groups lacking resources act against defenseless targets. Terrorism requires little money and can be funded by actions normally associated with common crime, such as armed robbery and drug trafficking.

Terrorists' weapons of choice are often crude and cheap (small arms and dynamite). However, as we now know, they can also be highly sophisticated (passenger airplanes used as guided missiles or a particularly lethal form of anthrax). Even before 9/11, terrorism had become a worldwide phenomenon, as news stories of attacks in airports and crowded train terminals, kidnappings of wealthy business executives, and hijacked airliners grew all too familiar.

Although terrorism is usually directed at innocents, it has been blamed for many assassinations of world leaders, including Italy's former prime minister Aldo Moro (1978), Queen Elizabeth's cousin, Lord Louis Mountbatten (1979), Egyptian president Anwar al-Sadat (1981), Indian prime minister Indira Gandhi (1984), her son the former prime minister Rajiv Gandhi (1991), and more recently, Pakistan's former prime minister Benazir Bhutto (December 27, 2007). Terrorists have also attempted to assassinate Pope John Paul II (1981), former British Prime Minister Margaret Thatcher (1984), and her successor John Major (1991). It is possible the White House was one of the intended targets of the September 11 attacks. If so, the conspirators probably hoped to kill the U.S. president.

The relationship between terrorist tactics and objectives is revealed in the Brazilian terrorist Carlos Marighella's chilling but incisive *Mini-Manual of the Urban Guerrilla*, a forty-eight-page do-it-yourself handbook for aspiring terrorists and revolutionaries. It spells out how to blow up bridges, raise money through kidnappings and bank robberies, and plan the "physical liquidation" of enemies. The book offers a range of practical advice: learn to drive a car, pilot a plane, sail a boat; be a mechanic or radio technician; keep physically fit; learn photography and chemistry; acquire "a perfect knowledge of calligraphy"; study pharmacology, nursing, or medicine. It also stresses the need to "shoot first" and aim straight. In general, terrorists champion violence above all other forms of political activity. Furthermore, revolutionaries such as Marighella glorify violence, not as a necessary evil but as a positive form of liberation and creativity.[12] According to Marighella, terrorism succeeds when strategies and tactics come together:

> The government has little or no alternative except to intensify repression. The police roundups, house searches, arrests of innocent people, make life in the city unbearable. [The government appears] unjust, incapable of solving problems. . . . The political situation is transformed into a military situation, in which the militarists appear more and more responsible for errors and violence. . . . Pacifists and right-wing opportunists . . . join hands and beg the hangmen for elections.[13]

Rejecting the so-called political solution, the urban guerrilla must become more aggressive and violent, resorting without mercy to sabotage, terrorism, expropriations, assaults, kidnappings, and executions, heightening the disastrous situation in which the government must act.[14] An urban guerrilla group called the Tupamaros terrorized Uruguay from 1963 to 1972, seeking to overthrow the government. The Tupamaros became the very embodiment of Marighella's revolutionary principles and have since served as an inspiration for terrorists and extremists throughout the world. Significantly, the insurgency in Uruguay ended only after most of the guerrillas were murdered in a brutal government crackdown. Today, Uruguay is a peaceful, democratic country.

Acts of Terrorism versus Acts of War

The al Qaeda operatives who hijacked four commercial airliners on September 11, 2001, were carrying out a terrorist act *by definition* and an act of war *only by inference or interpretation*. When Japanese kamikaze pilots flew fighter planes into U.S. warships anchored in Pearl Harbor on December 7, 1941, and sank most of the Pacific fleet, it was an act of war first and an act of terror only incidentally, if at all. In war-fighting jargon, this attack was a classic example of the preemptive strike. However heinous and treacherous it appeared to U.S.

citizens at the time (and still does), it was extremely successful as a single strategic event.*

The 9/11 attacks and Pearl Harbor are often compared, but the comparison is inapt. Pearl Harbor was the result of a decision made by the government and military high command of an established state with which the United States had diplomatic relations at the time. It was without question an act of war. Moreover, it was directed exclusively against *military* targets—the kamikaze pilots could have hit civilian targets in Hawaii but did not. Finally, the attacks were designed not to overthrow or destabilize the U.S. government or any other government, but rather to cripple U.S. naval power in the Pacific and thus forestall U.S. interference with Japan's imperialist designs in Asia.

The 9/11 attacks contrast sharply on all three points. They were not undertaken by an established state (although Afghanistan harbored al Qaeda network's top leaders and many of its fighters); they were directed mainly at civilians who had nothing to do with making U.S. foreign policy or with the armed forces; and they were clearly aimed at exposing the vulnerability of the United States, embarrassing the government, and undermining U.S. economic might, while tarnishing the Pentagon's image both at home and abroad. Even more to the point, these attacks were designed to rally support for bin Laden's extreme brand of Islamism and lead to the eventual toppling of "apostate" governments in the Arab world (including bin Laden's native Saudi Arabia).

Illegal Enemy Combatants

The very ambiguity of the status of terrorists in domestic and international law raises questions about how captured suspected terrorists ought to be treated. Are they prisoners of war, criminals, or neither? If they are neither, it means they exist in a legal limbo and can be denied even the most basic rights. In theory, they can be tortured or killed in captivity and the world would never know. They can be imprisoned for months or even years without being charged or having legal counsel or contact with family members—this is, in fact, the status of an unknown number of suspected terrorists taken captive by U.S. military forces in Afghanistan, Iraq, and elsewhere after 9/11.[15]

The Bush administration declared these captives were neither common criminals nor prisoners of war (POWs), but rather "illegal combatants"—a category tailor-made for the war on terror but widely rejected by other governments, as well as by experts on international law. Many suspected al Qaeda terrorists rounded up in Afghanistan (about 650 according to published reports) were taken to the U.S. naval base at Guantánamo Bay (also known as "Gitmo") in Cuba, where they were to be kept indefinitely in a maximum-security facility off limits to the press and public.

The constitutionality of indefinite detention without trial was finally challenged in June 2007 in the case of Ali al-Marri, a student at Bradley University who was initially arrested and jailed on charges having nothing to do with

---

*Of course, in the perspective of the entire war, it takes on a very different aspect in that it galvanized the American people, who were up until then resolutely opposed to entering the war, and gave President Roosevelt the green light to ask Congress for a declaration of war on Japan and Germany.

terrorism. Al Marri was eventually classified as an illegal combatant and transferred to the Naval Consolidated Brig in Charleston, South Carolina. In June 2007, a federal appeals court ruled that U.S. residents cannot be incarcerated indefinitely as enemy combatants without being charged. "Put simply, the Constitution does not allow the President to order the military to seize civilians residing within the United States and then detain them indefinitely without criminal process, and this is so even if he calls them 'enemy combatants,'" the court said. The same federal appeals court held a rehearing of the ruling and reversed itself 5 to 4. But in March 2009, the Supreme Court erased that ruling after al-Marri was indicted on federal criminal charges in Illinois, thus belatedly granting his constitutional right to a trial by jury in a civilian court. Al-Marri entered a guilty plea to one count of conspiracy involving a foreign terrorist organization.[16]

The concept of "illegal combatants" does not exist in international law and did not exist in U.S. public policy or jurisprudence before 9/11. Presidents George W. Bush and Barack Obama have both viewed it as a necessary tool in the war on terror. Critics, including the American Bar Association, have questioned the constitutionality of capturing prisoners outside the jurisdiction of the United States, holding them incommunicado, and denying them access to counsel.

Characteristics of Terrorist Groups

Most terrorist groups are short-lived, operate locally, and get very little publicity. Although our national news media covers only a few, hundreds of identifiable terrorist groups exist worldwide.[17] They tend to be small and tight-knit, seldom numbering more than one hundred members and usually fewer than several dozen. Many of the most notorious are found in the Middle East and associated with Islamic fundamentalism—the Abu Nidal Organization, al Qaeda, Islamic Jihad, Hamas, and Hezbollah (Party of God) are five contemporary examples. Because they are often ethnically and politically homogeneous, with members who are close friends or even relatives, terrorist cells are extremely difficult to penetrate or monitor, frequently confounding the best efforts of intelligence agencies.

As the world learned after the release of the fourth post-9/11 bin Laden videotape in mid-December 2001, al Qaeda operates on a need-to-know basis, closely guarding and compartmentalizing information within its own ranks, much like official intelligence services do. This emphasis on secrecy is essential for the success and survival of terrorist groups and networks, especially under greatly heightened security in the United States, Europe, the Arab world, and elsewhere.

Even so, the life span of most terrorist groups is only about five to ten years. By the same token, the leaders of terrorist groups tend to come and go. However, there are exceptions—two of the most notorious being Abu Nidal, who masterminded countless terrorist acts (including airport massacres in Rome and Vienna) for three decades until he was murdered in Baghdad in 2002, reportedly on direct orders from Saddam Hussein; and Osama bin Laden, founder of al Qaeda and the prime mover behind the 9/11 attacks. Finally, terrorist groups seldom operate from a fixed location. Although the perpetrators of the 9/11 attacks were exceptions, terrorists often have relatively little training,

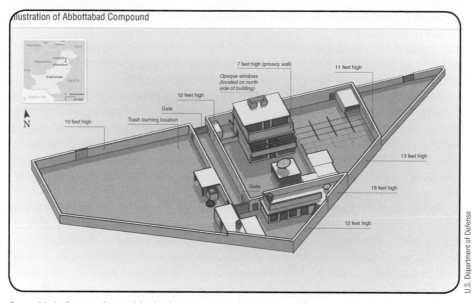

Osama bin Laden was the wealthy Saudi mastermind behind a series of terrorist attacks on U.S. targets that culminated in the destruction of the World Trade Center. On May 2, 2011, U.S. Navy Seals killed bin Laden in a night raid on his walled compound near Abbottabad, Pakistan. Bringing down the architect of the 9/11 attacks on the United States and the supreme leader of the al Qaeda terrorist organization was a major victory for the Obama administration, but the hunt for bin Laden and the decade-old war in Afghanistan it occasioned ultimately came at a high cost in blood and treasure. The unilateral U.S. military action that ended bin Laden's life deepened the distrust between the United States and Pakistan, both because it violated Pakistan's sovereignty and because of U.S. suspicions that Pakistan's Inter-Service Intelligence (ISI), as well as elements in the military, were protecting bin Laden. But when the smoke cleared, the war itself was still far from over.

use unsophisticated equipment, and acquire the "tools of the trade"—some of which could be purchased at any hardware store—by theft.

Algeria in the 1990s: Nightmare and Prelude

In Algeria, the line between Islamic fundamentalism and terrorism—or between revolution and civil war—was difficult to discern in the 1990s. Algeria can be seen as a preview of the political crises that have swept across the Arab world in recent years and destabilized Libya, Egypt, and Syria, among others, where popular anger has become dry tinder for extremists bent on the overthrow of established secular governments in the region. Few stories about Algeria's horrific internecine war appeared in the U.S. press, and even today, few in the United States are aware of what happened there.

Algeria gained its independence from France in 1962 after a long, violent revolutionary struggle. For most of the next thirty years, pro-Marxist military strongmen ruled. Eventually, however, a core of Muslim fundamentalists became dangerously discontented. From this disquiet emerged the political organization Islamic Salvation Front (FIS). Later, when Algeria's first multiparty elections were held in 1991, the FIS gained a dazzling first-round victory. However, in 1992, the military simply canceled the second round of elections and installed a new president. This cynical act radicalized the FIS and prompted it to go underground. Even worse, it split the armed Islamist movement in Algeria and gave the most extreme jihadist elements—advocates of all-out terrorism—the upper hand. At the end of 1992, the Armed Islamic Group (GIA) emerged as a murderous alternative to the somewhat less violent and uncompromising FIS.

Algeria's terrorist nightmare began with GIA attacks primarily on the police, security forces, and government officials. Soon the terrorists began targeting other groups as well. In 1993 and 1994, there were dozens of attacks on opposition groups, foreigners, intellectuals, journalists, and other civilians. Between 1995 and 1998, only about 25% of the attacks were directed against security forces and government officials; the rest struck at civilians. Schools and school employees were among the favorite targets.

As the strategy changed to targeting mainly civilians, the insurgents' tactics changed as well. In 1996, there were more bombings than assassinations, violent clashes with security forces, and organized armed attacks. After the mid-1990s, the bombings increasingly targeted markets, cinemas, and restaurants, as well as schools. According to one Middle East authority on the Algerian Islamist movement:

> Violence reached its ultimate level of cruelty in a series of massacres that began at the end of 1996. At least 67 massacres took place between November 1996 and July 1999, but most . . . took place in 1997 (42 massacres). . . . These massacres involved militants armed with guns, crude bombs, knives, and axes descending on villages at night to kill their inhabitants, often by hacking them to death and slitting their throats. Other atrocities involved fake security checkpoints set up by militants to identify specific targets—e.g., state employees and men with conscription papers.[18]

The government countered with lethal force. In November 1996, constitutional amendments that appeared to move Algeria toward a limited democracy were popularly ratified. The main aim, however, was to curtail radical Islamic groups and ban all political parties based on language or religion, while retaining preponderate power in the executive branch. Thus, during the June 1997 elections, the FIS and similar groups could not run candidates and could only urge citizens not to vote.

The FIS condemned the new constitution and continued to struggle against the regime until September 1997, when its armed wing, the Islamic Salvation Army (AIS), declared a cease-fire. But it was the vicious bands of zealots and thugs that comprised the GIA, not the AIS, that had carried out most of the bloody massacres. Not surprisingly, the hard-line "eradicators" in the government favored finding and killing the terrorists rather than trying to negotiate with them. This stance was not unreasonable given the fact that the GIA had shown no proclivity toward compromise.

The election of a new president in 1999 broke the ice. The government released some political prisoners and pushed through the Law of Civil Reconciliation, extending amnesty to rebels who had not committed atrocities. The AIS, which benefited from a general amnesty due to its 1997 cease-fire, began disbanding its militia under state supervision at the end of 1999. Thousands of AIS rebels took advantage of the general amnesty granted by the regime; at the beginning of 2000, even some GIA militias began declaring they would abide by the cease-fire.

Amnesty International called Algeria the most violent country in the Middle East at the end of the 1990s. The proximate cause of the violence was the military's illegal cancellation of a national election in 1992, but the roots of Algeria's nightmare run deep in social and economic failure. Despite its extensive oil and natural gas reserves, its people are overwhelmingly poor. Unemployment hovers around 25%. Nearly one-third of the population is under 15 years of age. High unemployment hits youth the hardest, which may, in part, explain why terrorists and revolutionaries are disproportionately young. Meanwhile, tensions based on ethnic and linguistic divisions persist. Most notably, Berbers are a sizable minority who feel alienated and powerless, a feeling intensified when Algeria moved to make Arabic its sole official language.

Nevertheless, terrorism still plagues Algeria. One of various terrorist groups operating in Algeria today calls itself al Qaeda in the Islamic Maghreb (AQIM). In 2008, dozens of suicide bombings and other attacks against police, foreigners, government employees, and civilians threatened to plunge the country into anarchy, but Algerian security forces reportedly killed, wounded, or arrested hundreds of terrorists.

The number of terrorist incidents dropped sharply for several years after a bloody 2008, but in August 2011, a suicide attack on a military academy left 18 people dead, including 16 soldiers, and 20 wounded. In December 2013, a terrorist attack on a BP gas facility in eastern Algeria left 37 hostages and at least 32 militants dead. The attack, carried out by anti-Western Islamist elements, "fanned fears of a new terror front,"[19] not least because in 2012 Islamist insurgents seized control of a large swath of territory in neighboring Mali. France sent troops into Mali in early 2013; in February, French and Malian forces succeeded in regaining control of the strategic northern city of Gao, as well as the legendary town of Timbuktu.

Thus, terrorists in Algeria, Mali, and the Maghreb (northwest Africa) continue to find fertile ground for fresh recruits. In retrospect, Algeria in the 1990s was a prelude to the upheavals tearing the Arab societies of North Africa and the Middle East—from Libya to Syria—apart today.

TERRORIST OR FREEDOM FIGHTER?

The terrorism that ravaged Algerian society in the 1990s is hard for people living normal lives to comprehend. Who are the perpetrators of these despicable acts? How do they differ from common criminals, guerrilla fighters, and revolutionaries? Why is terrorism any different from other forms of violence?

Official U.S. policy treats terrorism as an illegal *political* phenomenon. This approach stresses the illegitimacy of terrorism and advocates combating it with swift punishment and due vigilance. Critics (including some European countries and NATO allies) focus on the *socioeconomic* causes of the problem. These divergent views point to quite different policy responses, including targeted programs of trade, aid, and investment designed to alleviate misery, hunger, and disease in poverty-stricken, violence-prone countries and regions, as well as diplomacy that does not exclude talking to regimes and dictators we despise.

Policy differences aside, terrorists are criminals, though by no means ordinary ones. Killing and kidnapping, robbing banks, and hijacking airplanes are heinous crimes, no matter who perpetrates them or why; they become terrorist acts when the *motive* is political. When a serial killer is on the loose in a community, the victims are typically innocent people, but psychopaths are not motivated by religion or ideology. Sometimes the line is blurred, as in the case of narcoterrorists—armed rebels in Colombia associated with powerful drug lords or drug traffickers in Mexico—who use terrorist tactics to intimidate the public, press, and police. In 2008 alone, some 5,700 Mexicans were killed in drug-related violence. In January 2009, drug traffickers staged a grenade attack on Mexico's top TV network, Televisa, during the nightly news broadcast.[20] By May 2011, the death toll from Mexico's drug war had claimed a staggering 34,000 victims and the cost to Mexico's sluggish economy in human resources and lost tourism revenues was inestimable.

If terrorists are not ordinary criminals, neither are they ordinary guerrillas or freedom fighters. Guerrillas often constitute the armed wing of a revolutionary movement or party—Mao's Red Army is one well-known historical example. Guerrilla forces sometimes commit atrocities against civilians (as do soldiers in uniform), but most insurgent violence is directed at the security forces and government. By contrast, terrorists target civilians and noncombatants, as well as police and security forces—a strategy designed to sow the seeds of fear and doubt so people will not cooperate with the police and military, and to show people the government cannot protect them.

Certainly, many revolutionaries in the twentieth century have resorted to terror—both before and after taking power. But, unlike terrorists, revolutionaries seek to overthrow the government *in existing circumstances*, rather than trying to precipitate a political and social crisis by *changing* the circumstances. To that end, revolutionaries attempt to build a subversive party; infiltrate the government, the police, and the military; spread propaganda; agitate among trade unions; recruit and indoctrinate the young; and incite strikes, riots, and street demonstrations. Terrorism in the hands of revolutionaries is a tactic, not a strategy; in the hands of terrorists, terror is both a tactic *and* a strategy. Terrorists often appear to share the view of Émile Henry, a French anarchist who, when charged with throwing a bomb in a Paris café in 1894, replied, "No one is innocent."

TERRORISM AND SOCIETY

Europeans abhor terrorism as much as Americans do, but they tend to sympathize with the social classes or ethnic communities from which terrorists often arise. In sharp contrast to the U.S. pro-Israeli stance, most European governments are openly critical of Israeli policy toward the Palestinians. The best way to defeat terrorism, in their view, is to ameliorate its underlying causes—injustice, despair, and hopelessness. To European critics, Israeli policy exacerbates these conditions and plays into the hands of extremists.

Even where Middle Eastern governments suppress extreme Islamist groups, many people secretly sympathize with them. In Palestine, sympathy with groups like Hamas and Hezbollah is widespread and hardly a secret. Many Arabs admit that throughout the Arab world people expressed admiration for Osama bin Laden. Indeed, in some Arab countries, Osama has reportedly become one of the most popular names for baby boys.

To be sure, any comprehensive theory of terrorism in today's world must take account of its social context, including the dehumanizing effects of life in refugee camps or ghettos, youth unemployment, and the Western intrusion—first colonization and now globalization. People unable to cope with these stresses react in different ways. Some turn to crime, others to alcohol or drugs, and some drop out. A few become terrorists. Of course, not all terrorists are products of poverty. Many are well educated and come from relatively privileged backgrounds; Osama bin Laden was born into a fabulously wealthy family in Saudi Arabia.

Why youths decide to become martyrs is unclear. Perhaps it is from a sense of hopelessness (nothing to lose) or religious zeal, perhaps from idealism, or because they want to be a hero in the eyes of friends and family.

Youthful Recruits

Occasionally young females become suicide bombers, especially in the Middle East. The Shi'ite suicide bomber who drove her explosives-packed Peugeot into an Israeli Army convoy in southern Lebanon in 1985 was 16 years old. But most terrorists are male, single, and young.[21] The Jordanian who tried to assassinate a United Arab Emirates diplomat in Rome in 1984 was 22. The oldest of the four Palestinian terrorists who hijacked a Mediterranean cruise ship (the *Achille Lauro*) carrying 400 passengers in October 1985 was 23; the youngest, 19.

Research puts the median age of terrorists between 22 and 23 years. Twelve- and 14-year-old terrorists have been arrested in Northern Ireland; 14- and 15-year-old children are recruited by Arab and Iranian groups, sometimes for particularly dangerous missions.[22] A German psychologist who interviewed captured members of the Red Army Faction noted elements of an "adolescent crisis" among terrorists, while an expert on the Provisional Irish Republican Army (IRA) observed a "terrorist tradition" at work in some countries where "whole families pass on to their children that [terrorism] is the way you struggle for your rights."[23]

Eric Hoffer touched on the susceptibility of certain youths to fanatical causes in *The True Believer*. He placed them in a group he called "misfits," a category he further broke down into temporary and permanent. Hoffer wrote:

> Adolescent youth, unemployed college graduates, veterans, new immigrants, and the like are of this category. They are dissatisfied and haunted by the fear that their best years will be wasted before they reach their goal.[24]

At the same time, although they tend to be "receptive to the preaching of a proselytizing movement," Hoffer argued that they "do not always make staunch converts."

If the grievances that give rise to terrorism were removed, would there be no terrorists? Possibly, and yet there are many societies where abject poverty and injustice have not given rise to terrorism. The logical conclusion: oppression is a necessary condition of terrorism but not a sufficient one.

The Psychology of Terrorism

According to one expert on the psychology of terrorism, "terrorists with a cause" are the most dangerous to democratic society.[25] Who are these rebels? What motivates them? Not surprisingly, many of the most common traits exhibited by members of terrorist groups are associated with adolescence, including the following:[26]

- *Oversimplification of issues.* Terrorists see complex issues in black-and-white terms; they have no interest in debate; they often live out a "fantasy war," imagining the people overwhelmingly support their cause.
- *Frustration.* Terrorists feel society has cheated them, life is unfair, and they deserve far more; they are unwilling to wait or work for something better and believe the only way to get is to take.
- *Orientation toward risk-taking.* Many terrorists seek situations offering adventure and are easily bored.
- *Self-righteousness.* Terrorists display belligerent assertiveness, dogmatism, and intolerance of opposing views.
- *Utopianism.* They harbor an unexamined belief that heaven on earth is just over the horizon; the only thing standing in the way is the corrupt and oppressive existing order.
- *Social isolation.* Terrorists, one expert noted, are often "people who are really lonely." For some, a terrorist cell may be the only "family" they have.
- *A need to be noticed.* Terrorists share a need to feel important, a desire to make a personal imprint by getting media attention.
- *A taste for blood.* Interviews with captured terrorists, testimony of relatives and acquaintances, and eyewitness accounts by former hostages point to a final, startling characteristic: Some terrorists kill without an ounce of remorse.

Terrorists often oversimplify reality; thus, they may see victims as mere objects—a habit of mind observed among Nazi guards at extermination camps during the Holocaust.[27] In a similar vein, Paul R. McHugh, a distinguished Johns Hopkins School of Medicine psychiatrist, argued that terrorists, like other actors with a "ferocious passion," have an "overvalued idea," defined as "a thought shared with others in a society or culture but in the patient held with an intense emotional commitment capable of provoking dominant behaviors in its service."[28] Adolf Hitler (anti-Semitism), Carrie Nation (temperance), and John Brown (abolitionism) are three examples of historical figures with an obsessive belief in overvalued ideas, though acting on these beliefs had drastically different consequences in each case.

Those who suffer personality or emotional disorders associated with overvalued ideas are commonly called fanatics. Once again, Hoffer's discussion of fanatics in *The True Believer* proves appropriate. Fanaticism—excessive, blind devotion—whether political or religious, is almost always based on hatred, according to Hoffer; the fanatic places hatred in the service of a cause or a vision. Hatred is, in turn, a unifying force for like-minded fanatics, whereas love is divisive. Thus, hatred provides a reason for living, often appealing to individuals who are insecure, have little sense of self-worth, or lack meaning in their lives. Finally, Hoffer noted:

The fanatic is perpetually incomplete and insecure. He cannot generate self-assurance out of his individual resources—out of his rejected self—but finds it only by clinging passionately to [some cause]. This passionate attachment is the essence of his blind devotion and religiosity. . . . And he is ready to sacrifice his life to demonstrate to himself and others that such indeed is his role. He sacrifices his life—for example, in a suicide bombing—to prove his worth.[29]

Nor are fanatics necessarily motivated by a good cause. They embrace a cause not primarily because it is just or holy but because they have a desperate need to hold onto something. It is this need for passionate attachment that turns a cause into *the* cause. From there it can be a short step to jihad or a terrorist campaign.[30] But for normal people fortunate enough to be living normal lives in normal times, it remains a mystery how anyone can commit barbarous acts out of idealism or religious fervor.

Terrorism and the Media

Terrorists seek publicity. As they see it, the more attention they can get, the better. Why? Because media coverage—above all, the dramatic images that flash across our television and computer screens—draws worldwide attention to the act itself and the overvalued idea embraced by those who perpetrated it. This coverage is both politically prized and personally gratifying—it makes otherwise obscure individuals feel important. The prime-time exposure terrorists frequently get on CNN and other network news all over the world is also free. And, of course, the most daring, deadly, or otherwise sensational terrorist acts receive the most extensive media attention. Without question, the two fatal blows struck against the World Trade Center are the most widely and repeatedly televised terrorist acts in history.

In light of terrorists' need for publicity, many political analysts outside the profession of journalism blame the rapid rise of terrorism in part on the media—on television, in particular. After all, bad news makes for better headlines and better copy, and bad news that is also sensational and shocking garners the most attention and the highest Nielsen ratings, which in turn translates into higher advertising revenues for the networks. In this sense, at least, terrorism is tailor-made for television.

In a market economy, simply reporting the news is not enough; the news industry must also sell the news. The audience share that chooses to watch television news determines how much companies will pay to advertise their products on a particular network. Thus, producers of news shows are loath to pass up a good story, even if it means playing into the hands of terrorists. Of course, an airplane hijacking involving hundreds of innocent people is newsworthy by any standard. The media do, after all, have a responsibility to keep people informed. And even if one network decided not to cover a particular terrorist incident or to pay only slight attention to it, the others would not ignore it.

Media self-restraint is the only practical solution. Realistically, the news industry is not likely to cut back significantly on its reporting of terrorism until public opinion turns against such reports. As consumers of news, we often get what we demand and, in that sense, deserve what we get.

COUNTERING TERRORISM

The question facing democratic societies is how terrorism can be curtailed without jeopardizing democratic rights and liberties. The rise of international and state-sponsored terrorism, the danger of nuclear weapons falling into the hands of terrorists, and use of the Internet to plot and coordinate terrorist attacks all underscore the need for governments to coordinate global counterterrorist efforts.

Domestic Legislation

Authoritarian and totalitarian states are free to deal quickly and harshly with terrorists and accused terrorists. Democratic states, however, are committed to following the rule of law whenever and wherever possible. Over the past two decades, many democracies have enacted new laws or adapted old laws to deal more effectively with terrorists and terrorism.

Skyjacking and committing an act of violence against an airline passenger were made crimes in the United States way back in 1961, four decades before 9/11. In the wake of the first World Trade Center bombing in 1993 and the Oklahoma City bombing two years later, Congress passed an antiterrorism act in April 1996 that provided more resources for federal law enforcement to fight terrorism, tightened immigration, and loosened deportation procedures for aliens suspected of being terrorists.

But in 2001, on that fateful day in September, the second assault on the World Trade Center revealed the inadequacy of existing counterterrorist policies. President Bush quickly set up a new cabinet-level Office of Homeland Security, designed to coordinate the work of all federal departments and agencies engaged in any aspect of counterterrorism, and also issued a controversial directive creating military tribunals for suspected terrorists.[31]

The major changes in the government's power over legal aliens in the United States are contained in a law passed by Congress after the 9/11 attacks. The cumbersome name of this law is the Uniting and Strengthening America by Providing Appropriate Tools Required to Intercept and Obstruct Terrorism Act of 2001, more commonly known as the USA Patriot Act. In addition to greatly expanding the FBI's wiretapping authority, this act broadens the notion of who is considered a terrorist suspect and gives the U.S. attorney general sweeping authority to detain Arabs and Muslims, as well as other foreigners; it permits the government to deny entry into the United States to any foreigner who publicly endorses terrorism or belongs to a terrorist group; it expands the definition of *terrorist activity* to include any foreigner who uses "dangerous devices" or raises money for a terrorist group, *wittingly or unwittingly;* finally, it allows the government to detain any foreigner the attorney general considers a menace.

Taken together, the antiterrorist measures growing out of executive orders and the Patriot Act give the U.S. federal government powers of surveillance and infiltration unprecedented in modern times. At first supportive, public opinion is now deeply divided on the wisdom and necessity of warrantless wiretaps and other forms of government spying on civilians. In 2005, a CBS poll found respondents split (49% approved; 45% disapproved); in 2008, the candidate who opposed intrusive government measures—Barack Obama—won the election. As commander in chief, however, President Obama backed extension of the Patriot Act.

In June 2015, the United States Senate passed an act that restricts National Security Agency (NSA) authority to collect phone metadata. (The House passed the measure by a vote of 338 to 88 in mid-May.) Under the proposed new rules, the intelligence services can obtain such data in counterterrorism operations only on a case-by-case basis. The new measure—called the USA Freedom Act—replaces parts of the Patriot Act. Senator Rand Paul, a Republican and outspoken libertarian running for president, advocates nullifying the Patriot Act in its entirety.

The Bush administration's counterterrorist methods and policies were controversial and, according to critics, illegal. One of the most divisive was the use of waterboarding to extract information from prisoners suspected of belonging to Iraqi terrorist groups. These methods also appeared to be counterproductive. Only in 2007 after President Bush ordered a troop surge in Iraq did the insurgency and violence there finally subside, although the level of violence rose again in 2009. Today, after more than a decade of turmoil, Iraq's prospects for social peace and governmental stability are dim.

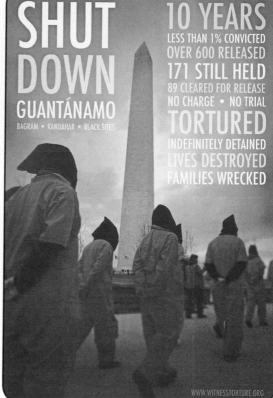

Justin Norman/Shrieking Tree

In the war on terror, the United States used waterboarding as an interrogation technique. Human rights advocates argue that waterboarding is a form of torture and violates the 1949 Geneva Conventions on the treatment of prisoners of war.

President Obama kept his promise to withdraw U.S. combat forces from Iraq by the fall of 2010, but to the dismay of many of his backers, he ordered a troop surge in Afghanistan. At the same time, he fired the commander of U.S.-led NATO forces in Afghanistan, General David McKiernan, and replaced him with a general known for his tough counterterrorism credentials, General Stanley McChrystal.[32] But Obama's problems with his generals did not end there; in June 2010, he ordered General McChrystal back to Washington because he made disparaging remarks to a reporter about Vice President Joe Biden and other top White House officials close to the president. McChrystal resigned rather than be fired, and Obama replaced him with General David Petraeus.

Many democracies, including Italy, France, the Netherlands, and Greece, ban membership in terrorist organizations. In Great Britain, specific terrorist groups are outlawed, including the IRA and the Irish National Liberation Army, as is soliciting funds for them. In 2005, the European Union acted to improve information sharing to combat terrorism through the Schengen Information System (SIS). The EU has also created a European Arrest Warrant to facilitate coordinated action in capturing suspected criminals and terrorists, who can move across national boundaries in Europe easily now that all border controls

Four-star General David Petraeus served as Commander of U.S. Central Command before replacing General Stanley McChrystal as Commander of the International Security Forces (ISAF) in Afghanistan in 2010. Petraeus returned to civilian life as Director of the Central Intelligence Agency in September 2011 but resigned in 2012 amid a sex scandal involving an extramarital relationship with his biographer, Paul Broadwell, whose biography of Petraeus, *All In*, became a favorite joke of late-night comedians.

have been abolished among the twenty-five countries that belong to the Schengen Area. Italy and Sweden have also made it easier for police to tap telephones and open mail to detect letter bombs. In general, most democracies do not protect privacy rights to the extent the United States did before 9/11 and place fewer restrictions on police and investigative agencies. As a result, they did not need a Patriot Act to adopt tough counterterrorism measures. What they did need was better cooperation across borders—which they now have.

Cooperation among Nations

Prior to 9/11, international efforts to combat terrorism undertaken by the United Nations, the Organization of American States, and the Council of Europe were largely ineffective.[33] Bilateral agreements often proved more successful—even between countries otherwise adversarial. For instance, the 1973 agreement between the United States and Cuba brought an end to a wave of skyjackings of U.S. planes to Havana.

After the 9/11 attacks, the Bush administration initially enjoyed the full cooperation of NATO allies, as well as such key countries as Pakistan and Russia, in its war on terror. NATO endorsed, and many NATO members participated in, the U.S.-led invasion of Afghanistan. However, most of this support, with the notable exception of the United Kingdom and former Prime Minister Tony Blair, faded away when the White House made the decision to invade Iraq.

Intelligence sharing across borders has improved since 9/11. Organizations such as Interpol (an international police agency headquartered in France) have reportedly facilitated the capture of terrorists in some instances and possibly prevented some terrorist acts from occurring. Despite many obstacles and continuing challenges, the United States and the European Union have taken steps to achieve closer cooperation on matters related to police, judicial, and border control policy.[34]

In one striking example of bilateral cooperation, high-ranking FBI and CIA officials cooperated with Russian internal security agencies to fight organized crime in Russia and ferret out its suspected links to both international terrorist groups and would-be smugglers of nuclear weapons materials. In another, a retaliatory surgical bombing strike against a dictator with a history of sponsoring international terrorism was facilitated by a close U.S. ally. Specifically, President Ronald Reagan decided to teach Colonel Muammar Qaddafi a lesson.

Qaddafi, Libya's autocratic ruler, was long suspected of sponsoring terrorist attacks in Europe and elsewhere. In April 1986, Reagan ordered the bombing of Tripoli, Libya's capital. Initially, only the British supported the U.S. strike; the French, fearing terrorist reprisals, refused to allow U.S. warplanes based in the United Kingdom to fly over French territory. The punitive U.S. air strike hit Qaddafi's official residence and killed his baby daughter. Thereafter, signs of an emerging multinational consensus began to appear. On April 21, 1986, the

European Community voted to impose economic sanctions against Libya; and in the summer of 1986, Libyans were expelled from Great Britain, West Germany, France, Italy, Spain, Denmark, Belgium, the Netherlands, and Luxembourg.

Libyans accused of blowing up Pan Am Flight 103 over Lockerbie, Scotland, in December 1988, were eventually caught and placed on trial before the International Court of Justice at The Hague in the Netherlands in 2000. In 2003, Qaddafi surprised the world by renouncing terrorism. In September 2008, Secretary of State Condoleezza Rice paid an official visit to Tripoli where she met with Qaddafi, and the United States moved to reestablish normal relations with Libya. But in mid-March, 2011, when Qaddafi used deadly force (including planes, tanks, and cannon) to quell a rising popular rebellion against his rule, President Obama ordered creation of a "no fly zone" and air strikes against loyalist ground forces, ostensibly to protect civilians and prevent a massacre. Few doubted, however, that Qaddafi's pre-2003 reputation as a sponsor of international terrorism also played into the decision to back the Libyan rebels. Unlike the war on Iraq, this intervention was sanctioned by the United Nations and the Arab League. France and the United Kingdom participated actively in the military operations, and NATO assumed full command of the Libya campaign at the end of March.

Unilateral Counterterrorist Measures

Virtually every nation strengthened airport security after the bloody terrorist massacres in Vienna and Rome airports in 1985. But the United States did too little too late; on September 11, 2001, four commercial airplanes were hijacked almost simultaneously from three different East Coast airports in one morning. All the hijack teams apparently managed to get on the planes with weapons (knives and box cutters).

COUNTERTERRORISM IN ITALY: A Success Story

In the 1970s, Italy was the most terror-ridden country in the West. The extreme left-wing Red Brigades kidnapped and killed hundreds of judges, industrialists, and politicians—symbols of capitalism and the establishment. From 1969 to 1983, more than 14,000 acts of terrorist violence were recorded, 409 people were killed, and 1,366 were injured.

In 1978, the Red Brigades kidnapped Aldo Moro, a former prime minister and one of Italy's leading politicians. When the government refused to negotiate with Moro's abductors, he was murdered. In the end, however, it was the terrorists who lost. Shocked and outraged, the public demanded a tough counterterrorist program. Thereafter, the Red Brigades went into sharp decline.

How did Italy do it? First, the police infiltrated Red Brigade terror cells and subsequently arrested hundreds of members. Second, reduced prison sentences were offered to repentant terrorists who supplied information about the activities and whereabouts of other terrorists. Third, the police concentrated on a limited and manageable number of terrorist targets, such as airports, harbors, and border crossings. Finally, new laws gave the police greater ability to tap phones and use other resources more effectively.

Deprived of sympathy for whatever cause they embraced, Italy's terrorists were isolated. Today they pose little or no threat to the country's stability.

Many authorities believe retribution and deterrence are the only effective approach to dealing with terrorism. In this view, deterrence requires, at a minimum, a refusal to make concessions to terrorists. To do otherwise is self-defeating and tantamount to rewarding evil, inviting future attacks of a similar nature. According to one expert, "Where counterterrorism has worked, a unifying thread has been the demonstrated will and ability of the government to take harsh and *preemptive* ("proactive") military or paramilitary countermeasures against terrorists."[35]

The availability of special counterterrorist units such as the British SAS is not enough; governments must also demonstrate a willingness to use them in order "to establish an unmistakable pattern of failure and retribution."[36] There is always the risk of failure (for example, the 1980 U.S. attempt to free hostages in Iran), and the immediate consequences can be tragic. But the long-term consequences of acting indecisively can be even more tragic.

Other steps governments can take include controlling arms and explosives and, perhaps most important (though most difficult), developing better domestic and foreign intelligence-gathering capabilities. Modern technology using satellites, electronic surveillance, advanced search technologies, explosives detection, scanners, robotic vehicles, and drones have greatly enhanced existing counterterrorist capabilities, for only by obtaining information about terrorists' hideouts, movements, and plans can governments prevent attacks. There is also ongoing research in the promising new field of network analysis, using social science techniques to better understand the workings of terrorist networks.

Time is a crucial factor in fighting both insurgencies and terrorism (which often go hand in hand in today's world). The conventional wisdom long held that time was on the side of the insurgents—they are more highly motivated, closer to the people, and so on. There is reason to doubt the truth of this axiom. Consider the case of the Tamil minority in Sri Lanka.

The defeat of the Tamil Tigers, modern Asia's longest-lasting insurgency, in the spring of 2009 demonstrates that a patient strategy, allowing time for terrorists' acts to work against them, can succeed. At one point, the Tamil insurgents controlled a third of Sri Lanka; they used terrorist tactics—child soldiers and suicide bombers—and fought a conventional war, with outside aid from China, Pakistan, and high-earning Tamils abroad. But in the end, the Tamil Tigers' brutality and the Sinhalese-majority government's refusal to negotiate in the face of terrorist blackmail drained the lifeblood from the insurgency.[37]

Obviously, the nature of democratic societies and the constitutional framework in which governments operate present obstacles to police and investigative agencies charged with thwarting terrorism. Citizens are unaccustomed to acting as informants, and intelligence gathering is divided among several agencies, in part to prevent any one of them from gaining too much power. In the United States, for example, intelligence and counterintelligence have traditionally been separated; the CIA is responsible for foreign intelligence and is forbidden to engage in domestic spy operations against U.S. citizens or groups, and counterintelligence is the function of the FBI. Coordinating the work of these two agencies after 9/11 was the prime reason behind President Bush's decision to create the new Office of Homeland Security.

Private Measures

Finally, private citizens and firms have developed strategies to protect them-selves.[38] Just as many governments were "hardening" their embassies and other overseas facilities in the 1980s and 1990s, private companies were spending billions of dollars annually on security services.[39]

With the advent of the Digital Age, a new security threat—so-called cyberterrorism—has arisen. As a consequence, governments, banks, and busi-nesses, as well as private individuals, also spend vast sums on sophisticated software to protect computers, data, financial assets, communications, and state secrets from Internet hackers.

Most citizens cannot afford to hire private security guards, but an alert public can make the terrorist's job more difficult. In Israel, for example, where everyone is acutely aware of the terrorist threat, officials claim 80% of bombs in public places are disarmed because suspicious objects are usually noticed and reported in time.[40] Most security experts agree that success in countering terror-ism depends on vigilant citizens, as well as police and security forces.

THE TERRORISTS AMONG US

Multiple killings such as the massacres in Aurora, Colorado, and Newtown, Connecticut, in 2012 raise serious moral and political issues. Who cares how such heinous acts are labeled? And yet it matters. To understand why, consider the problem of "dirty hands" in politics. We all face moral dilemmas in life; but politicians have to make choices that have far-reaching effects on the whole society—plus, they want to get reelected. So it's no surprise when they clamber to show how tough they are on terrorism.

But the problem of dirty hands becomes a problem of bloody hands when politicians in the U.S. Congress climb into bed with the gun lobby and the National Rifle Association (NRA) because they care more about not getting targeted for defeat in the next election than about the safety of schoolchildren. Arguably, the most dangerous "terrorists" are not the ones we tend to fear the most—imagined "foreigners" who infiltrate our society with malicious intent. Perhaps we have the most to fear from individuals who are "natural-born citizens" and who may even live next door. And, in stark contrast to virtually all other Western societies (with the exception of Switzerland), adult citizens in the United States can legally possess a veritable arsenal of deadly weapons.

CAN TERRORISM BE DEFEATED?

Terrorism poses a continuing threat that shows few signs of abating, despite the ongoing post-9/11 war on terror. Is a "war on terror" winnable? If not, why not? If so, how?

There is no single or totally effective solution to terrorism. Even one terrorist can be too many. One terrorist with a small support system—a few friends, safe houses, and supplies—can inflict enormous damage. Still, as we have seen, there are ways of limiting the opportunities available to terrorists and of deterring, punishing, or simply eradicating terrorism before it becomes an epidemic as it did in Italy in the 1970s and early 1980s, Peru in the 1980s, Algeria in the 1990s, and Pakistan in the late 2000s.

Meanwhile, doomsday scenarios involving terrorist plots to use weapons of mass destruction (WMD)—from anthrax to a "dirty" radiation bomb—cannot be dismissed lightly. No single state can meet this threat alone. Unfortunately, declaring "war on terror" is better theater than public policy, and fear of terrorist attacks can be exploited by governments to silence opposition or erode constitutional rights.

Words matter in politics. *War* is one of the words that matters most. The word, like the phenomenon itself, has a definite meaning and a long history. It is a word we often use loosely—too loosely. Terrorism cannot be defeated the way Germany and Japan were defeated in World War II. Terrorism does not have a territory or a seat of government. It can be contained but not occupied the way Germany and Japan were occupied (and Iraq and Afghanistan are today).

Terrorism is war by other means. War is politics by other means—and the focus of the next chapter.

SUMMARY

Terrorism, a political effort to oppose the status quo by inducing fear in the civilian population through the widespread and publicized use of violence, has become an everyday occurrence in the contemporary world. Although it has ancient roots in religious conflict, contemporary terrorism can be traced to the 1960s.

Terrorists seek to create a climate of chaos and confusion in the belief that political instability will hasten the downfall of a government. They form groups that are close-knit, homogeneous, small, and (often) short-lived. Terrorists can pose great challenges to countries facing political and economic problems; Muslim fundamentalism in Algeria provides such an example.

Although terrorists violate the law, they are not *criminals* in the everyday sense of the term. Nor are they guerrillas or ordinary revolutionaries. All terrorists are revolutionaries, but not all revolutionaries are terrorists. A terrorist is a kind of revolutionary who does not seek to obtain political power, but whose primary objective is to protest and combat the perceived injustice of the existing political order through random acts of violence. Terrorists tend to be young, single males who share a variety of key psychological characteristics, including fanaticism and hatred.

Democracy and terrorism are implacable enemies. Democracy depends for its existence on compromise, tolerance, and mutual trust; whereas terrorists are zealots who seek to radicalize society and destabilize the political system. Furthermore, democratic societies are, by nature, open and vulnerable to terrorist attacks. This vulnerability is both physical and psychological.

The problems democracies face in countering terrorism are complicated by the need to preserve individual freedoms while also protecting national security. Still, various singular and cooperative measures that democracies have undertaken show promise of containing—though not eliminating—terrorism.

KEY TERMS

terrorism 498

state terrorism 499

international
terrorism 499

state-sponsored
terrorism 499

domestic
terrorism 499

transnational
terrorism 500

counterterrorism 502

REVIEW QUESTIONS

1. How is terrorism different from common crime? From guerrilla warfare?
2. What tactics do terrorists typically employ, and how are their ends and means related?
3. What are the psychological roots of terrorism and the characteristics of the typical terrorist?
4. Why are democracies vulnerable to terrorism? Assess the terrorist threat to constitutional democracies.
5. What obstacles stand in the way of an effective counterterrorist policy?
6. What steps did the United States take to protect itself against terrorism after 9/11? Comment on U.S. successes and failures in the fight against terrorism.
7. Cite several examples of successful counterterrorist efforts in other countries, then identify several failures. What have we learned about how to fight terrorism?
8. Is technology on the side of governments or terrorists? Explain.

WEBSITES AND READINGS

Websites

National Counterterrorism Center: http://www.nctc.gov/

Foreign Policy Research Institute: http://www.fpri.org/research/terrorism

Terrorism Research Center, Inc.: http://www.terrorism.com

Center for Nonproliferation Studies: http://cns.miis.edu/pubs/

U.S. Department of Homeland Security: http://www.dhs.gov/ dhs-daily-open-source-infrastructure-report

Readings

Ascencio, Diego, and Nancy Ascencio. *Our Man Is Inside*. New York: Little, Brown, 1983. A gripping account of a hostage situation in Bogotá, Colombia, in which fifteen ambassadors, including the U.S. ambassador to Colombia, were held captive by Marxist terrorists for sixty-one days.

Baer, Robert. *See No Evil: The True Story of a Ground Soldier in the CIA's War on Terrorism*. New York: Crown Publishing Group, 2003. A high-ranking operative's account of how Washington politics perverted the intelligence process and prevented the CIA from playing its proper role both before and after 9/11.

Carr, Caleb. *The Lessons of Terror—A History of Warfare Against Civilians: Why It Has Always Failed and Why It Will Fail Again.* New York: Random House, 2002. The subtitle says it all.

Clark, Richard C. *Technological Terrorism.* Old Greenwich, CT: Devin-Adair, 1980. Deals with the danger of highly enriched uranium being diverted into the hands of terrorists; examines chemical and biological weapons, Andromeda strains, and so on; and makes policy suggestions.

Clutterbuck, Richard. *Protest and the Urban Guerrilla.* New York: Abelard-Shuman, 1974. Examines the roots of protest and violence in Britain and Northern Ireland; surveys the rise of urban guerrilla movements worldwide; and ponders the implications of terrorism for the future of democratic societies.

Combs, Cindy C. *Terrorism in the Twenty-First Century.* Upper Saddle River, NJ: Prentice-Hall, 1997. A balanced, comprehensive text that covers virtually every aspect of terrorists, terrorism, and terrorist acts.

Esposito, John L. *The Islamic Threat: Myth or Reality?* 3rd ed. New York: Oxford University Press, 1999. A balanced book about Arab politics and Islamic fundamentalism by a recognized and sympathetic expert.

Hacker, Frederick J. *Crusaders, Criminals, Crazies: Terror and Terrorism in Our Time.* New York: Norton, 1977. A probing, essential study of the psychology of the terrorist.

Hoffman, Bruce. *Inside Terrorism.* New York: Columbia University Press, 2006. A good choice for anyone who plans to read only one book on this subject; concise, analytical, and thought-provoking.

Jenkins, Brian, ed. *Terrorism and Personal Protection.* Newton, MA: Butterworth, 1985. Essays by an impressive array of experts.

Juergensmeyer, Mark. *Terror in the Mind of God.* Berkeley: University of California Press, 2000. A thoughtful study of the relationship between religious extremism and political violence in the contemporary world by an established scholar in the field.

Kegley, Charles W., Jr., ed. *International Terrorism: Characteristics, Causes, Controls.* New York: St. Martin's Press, 1990. A good collection of essays with well-crafted introductions by the editor to the book's three parts (characteristics, causes, controls).

Kidder, Rushworth M. "Unmasking Terrorism," *Christian Science Monitor,* May 13–21, 1986 (five-part series). Examines the origins and development of terrorism since the late 1960s, the problem of state-sponsored terrorism, the terrorist mentality, the manipulation of the media, and recent efforts to curb terrorism.

Laqueur, Walter. *Terrorism.* New York: Little, Brown, 1979. A penetrating study of the origins, ideology, and sociology of terrorism by a leading scholar and writer; also examines various theories and surveys the modern history of terrorism.

Levy, Michael. *On Nuclear Terrorism*. Cambridge, MA: Harvard University Press, 2007. An insightful examination of everybody's worst nightmare—nuclear weapons in the hands of terrorists. The author describes the danger and prescribes ways of dealing with it.

Napoleoni, Loretta. *The Islamist Phoenix: The Islamic State and the Redrawing of the Middle East*. New York: Seven Stories Press, 2014. From the publisher: "Napoleoni illuminates . . . how [the Islamic State] differs from other jihadist organizations . . . [and] traces the beginnings of IS, its dynamic with al-Qaeda, and its current status as the first official Caliphate in over a century."

Pape, Robert. *Dying to Win: The Strategic Logic of Suicide Terrorism*. New York: Random House Trade Paperbacks, 2005. Delves into the "strategic logic" of suicide bombings. It also draws some conclusions of relevance to policy makers and anyone interested in devising a strategy to defeat the jihadists of the world.

Post, Jerrold M. *The Mind of the Terrorist: The Psychology of Terrorism from the IRA to al-Qaeda*. New York: Palgrave Macmillan, 2007. A top expert on the psychology of violent individuals draws on a rich professional background to explain what motivates terrorists. The result is a both fascinating and frightening.

Rivers, Gayle. *The Specialist: Revelations of a Counterterrorist*. Lanham, MD: Madison Books, 1985. Ostensibly a true story about the underworld of terrorism and counterterrorism, written under a pseudonym by a mercenary who specializes in carrying out antiterrorist operations under contract to Western (and other) governments; reads like a James Bond thriller.

White, Jonathan. *Terrorism and Homeland Security: An Introduction*, 6th ed. Belmont, CA: Wadsworth, 2009. The first chapter is devoted to the vexing problem posed by the many and varied definitions of terrorism. A readable and comprehensive global treatment of all aspects of this timely topic.

Wright, Lawrence. *The Looming Tower: Al Qaeda and the Road to 9/11*. New York: Alfred A. Knopf, 2006. From the publisher: "A sweeping narrative history of the events leading to 9/11, a groundbreaking look at the people and ideas, the terrorist plans, and the Western intelligence failures that culminated in the assault on America."

Politics without Government

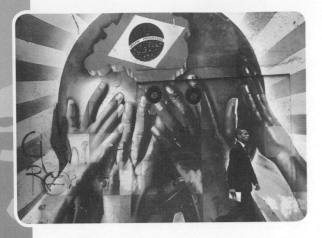

CHAPTER 17

International Relations
The Struggle for World Order

Learning Objectives

1 Define "power politics."

2 Explain the ways world politics differs from other politics.

3 Compare the classical balance of power systems in Europe with the world order that emerged after World War II.

4 Identify and elucidate the three biggest changes in world politics since the end of the Cold War.

5 Elaborate on the role of the United States in the New World Order.

6 Explain the role of international law in world politics and why it is often least enforceable when and where it is most needed.

7 Describe the historical context that made creation of the United Nations appear to be a good idea, and identify its major structures and functions.

In 416 BCE, Athens sent ships and troops against the island of Melos, a colony of Sparta that had remained neutral and wanted no part of the war between Sparta and Athens.[1] Negotiating from a position of overwhelming strength, the Athenians insisted on unconditional surrender, telling the Melians, "You know as well as we do that right, as the world goes, is only in question between equals in power—the strong do what they can, and the weak suffer what they must." The Melians responded, "And how, pray, could it turn out as good for us to serve as for you to rule?" "Because," the Athenians answered, "you would have the advantage of submitting before suffering the worst, and we should gain by not destroying you."

Undaunted, the Melians insisted the interest of all would be enhanced by peaceful relations between the two states. The Athenians would have no part of this logic. With ruthless disregard for justice, they reasoned that if the Melians were permitted to remain independent, they and others would take it as a sign of Athenian weakness. "[By] extending our empire," the Athenians pointed out, "we should gain in security by your subjection; the fact that you are islanders and weaker than others rendering all the more important that you should not succeed in baffling the masters of the sea." Thus, the cold calculus of power politics doomed the Melian state:

> Reinforcements afterwards arriving from Athens in consequence, under the command of Philocrates, son of Demeas, the siege was now pressed vigorously; and some treachery taking place inside, the Melians surrendered at discretion to the Athenians, who put to death all the grown men whom they took, and sold the women and children for slaves, and subsequently sent out five hundred colonists and inhabited the place themselves.

Melos was a real place, and the tragedy depicted in the story really happened. The context was the Peloponnesian War (431–404 BCE), and we know the Melians' cruel fate because the Greek historian Thucydides wrote about it.

GET REAL! MACHIAVELLI AND MORGENTHAU

The greatest political thinker of the Italian Renaissance, Niccolò Machiavelli, taught that the wise ruler must always play to win, for "how we live is so far removed from how we ought to live, that he who abandons what is done for what ought to be done, will rather learn to bring about his own ruin than his preservation."[2] Prudent rulers, he argued, recognize what must be done to preserve and enlarge their dominions and do not allow moral qualms to cloud their judgment. Rulers should keep their promises only when it suits their purposes to do so:

> A prudent ruler ought not to keep faith when by doing so it would be against his interest, and when the reasons which made him bind himself no longer exist. . . . If men were all good, this precept would not be a good one; but as they are bad, and would not observe their faith with you, so you are not bound to keep faith with them.[3]

The teachings of Machiavelli, and the fate of the Melians, suggest morality plays a less significant role in politics *among* nations than *within* nations. As long as international politics resembles the state of nature, tensions between nations will persist, talking will fail, reason will take a holiday, and the only question left will be who lives and who dies. When survival is at stake, necessity is often a tyrant.

Machiavelli's intellectual honesty and relentless realism were the basis for perhaps the most successful and influential political philosophy in the modern world—and evidence for its validity has continually mounted. The theory that nations act on the basis of interests, rather than ideals, is known as political realism. Today, this theory is most closely identified with the writings of Hans Morgenthau (1904–1980).

Following Machiavelli's rationale, political realists pay little heed to the way nations *ought* to act. Rather, they focus on how nations actually *do* act and why they act as they do. Survival is the basic goal of national policy, and the best way to ensure survival is to enhance the nation's power. In international politics, Morgenthau argued, whatever the ultimate aim, the immediate aim is *always* power. Thus, interest is defined as power; indeed, for Morgenthau, these two concepts merge into one—it is in the best interest of every nation to seek power first and other objectives second, and then only as they enhance national power, prestige, and the like.

Political realists stress that success in international politics, even without confrontation, ultimately depends on power. According to Morgenthau, power is "man's control over the minds and actions of other men."[4] Military force is an important but not the only aspect of political power. Geopolitical, economic, and social concerns also contribute. Even the personal charisma or competence of a nation's leader or the effectiveness of its political institutions gives it an edge.[5]

According to Morgenthau, "Realism considers prudence—the weighing of the consequences of political action—to be the supreme virtue in politics."[6] A foreign policy based on realism will avoid "the blindness of crusading frenzy [that] destroys nations and civilizations—in the name of moral principle, ideal, or God himself."[7]

To the political realist, the successful statesman is one who balances national interests and objectives against national capabilities (or power). Prudence demands that a statesman distinguish between what is necessary and what is merely desirable. The essence of statecraft lies in bringing the expectations and desires of a nation into line with its capabilities and correctly differentiating between vital and expendable interests. Political realism places a premium on flexibility, objectivity, and lack of sentimentality in the conduct of foreign policy. Thus, the political realist would say there are no permanent allies, only permanent interests.

In the perilous world of international politics, morality is different than it is in our *domestic* lives. Because other nations act on the basis of their perceived interests, rather than lofty ideals, one's own nation must do likewise; all try to gain an advantage at the expense of others. Therefore, Morgenthau asserted, political realism not only explains *why* nations act the way they do, but in the true spirit of science, it can also predict *how* they will act.

NATION-STATES AND THE BALANCE OF POWER

Machiavelli and Morgenthau were both products of tumultuous but very different times. Machiavelli was influenced by the fierce rivalries, intrigue, and conflict among Italian city-states of the fifteenth and sixteenth centuries. The modern nation-state system, designed to maintain **equilibrium** (or balance) among the participating states, was still in its infancy.

The Classical System: 1648 to 1945

The classical system started with the signing of the Treaty of Westphalia in 1648 more than a century after Machiavelli's death. Morgenthau was born in Germany shortly before World War I. The **balance-of-power system** was one of the casualties of that war.

Although this collective balancing act was based on nations' individual interests, it depended on a common definition of *interest* that emphasized self-preservation of each through a system that depended on the survival of all.

Europe's classical balance-of-power system operated for almost three centuries (see Figure 17.1), beginning with the Treaty of Westphalia and ending with the outbreak of World War I. Although Napoleonic France came perilously close at the start of the nineteenth century, no state was able to establish hegemony on the Continent during this 266-year period—a remarkable achievement for any era.

The **Westphalian system,** or model, depended on the existence of an "honest broker," a so-called **keeper of the balance**—a Power that would consistently oppose the aggressor and back the threatened state or weaker alliance. Great Britain was ideally suited to this role because of its geographic detachment and military (especially naval) prowess.

Britain was an impregnable fortress so long as no single Power succeeded in conquering the Continent. A major British aim was to prevent a Great Power on the Continent from controlling the Lowlands (modern-day Belgium and Holland) just across the English Channel, a mere twenty-two miles wide at its narrowest point. Finally, its unchallenged naval supremacy and economic vitality made it a powerful ally or a formidable foe, while its lack of a large standing army removed any threat of British domination on the Continent.

FIGURE 17.1   Adjusting the Balance of Power. Equilibrium (A) is upset by adding a new participant (B); it is restored (C) by the transfer of one state from one alliance to another.

SOURCE: Edward V. Gulick, *Europe's Classical Balance of Power* (New York: Norton, 1967).

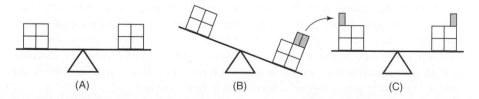

(A)   (B)   (C)

---

equilibrium
A synonym for the word *balance*; also often used interchangeably with *stability* in the literature on international relations.

balance-of-power system
A classic theory of international relations that holds that nations of approximately equal strength will seek to maintain the status quo by preventing any one nation from gaining superiority over the others. In a balance-of-power system, participating nations form alliances and frequently resort to war as a means of resolving disputes, seizing territory, gaining prestige, or seeking glory.

Westphalian system
An old world order based on the emergence of nation-states in 17th Century Europe that depended on the existence of an "honest broker," a power that would oppose the aggressor and back the threatened state or weaker alliance. *See* keeper of the balance.

The Strait of Dover, a narrow channel (less than the distance between Washington, D.C. and Annapolis, Maryland), separates the British Isles from the Europe's mainland. Today, Britain and France are connected by a rail tunnel that runs underneath the Channel. The geographic distance is slight; but the political distance of the Channel has been monumental in the modern history of Europe.

A common outlook—sometimes called "Christendom" or "Western Civilization"—held by nations with certain shared traditions was one key to creating and sustaining this system. Many scholars have stressed the role of cultural and religious traditions that pervaded European society and transcended national boundaries during the heyday of the balance-of-power system.[8]

Under these extraordinary conditions, "international politics became indeed an aristocratic pastime, a sport for princes, all recognizing the same rules of the game and playing for the same limited stakes."[9] Even when war broke out, the belligerents did not seek to annihilate each other. Fanaticism was generally spurned in favor of reason. Ideology was notably absent. Economic and military capabilities were limited: wars were costly, mobilization was a slow process, and military action was constrained by the absence of modern technology. Realignments occurred as circumstances changed and new threats arose.

The Sunset of the Old World Order

What happened to upset the balance-of-power system? First, Napoléon's nearly successful attempt in the early nineteenth century to conquer Europe—creating the first mass-conscription, popular army in modern history—heralded the rise of modern nationalism (see Chapter 15), what Morgenthau famously named **nationalistic universalism**. Although France's bid ultimately failed, it was a harbinger of things to come, and it demonstrated the power of a nation united by a common cause. The cause itself was rooted in the explosive idea of human equality, enshrined in both the American and French revolutions (see Chapter 14). Between the Napoleonic Wars and World War I, ideas such as national self-determination and universal rights changed fundamental assumptions about politics and undermined the old aristocratic order.

In the nineteenth century, the Industrial Revolution's economic and technological changes transformed the art of warfare. Prussia used railroads to move troops in victorious military campaigns against Austria (1866) and France (1870). New instruments of war were not far off—military applications of the internal combustion engine included self-propelled field artillery and, by World War I, combat aircraft.

A final factor that undermined the European system was the rigidity of military alliances. Toward the end of the nineteenth century, coalitions were becoming fixed, while nation-states were steadily accumulating military power. Unprecedented peacetime outlays for military research and development, the creation of relatively large standing armies, and a spiraling arms race reinforced the increasing division of Europe into two opposing alliances. This development set the stage for World War I, which signaled the beginning of the end of the classical balance-of-power system. It would take another world war to finish the job.

The Cold War: 1945 to 1991

World War II produced a new configuration, one that continues to shape world politics today. Replacing the European order was a worldwide system organized into two opposing alliances locked in a "cold war" in which the United States and the Soviet Union competed for the allegiance of the newly independent, nonaligned states in Africa, Asia, and Latin America.

The Dawn of Bipolarity World War II greatly accelerated the transformation that had already begun. Instead of the seven former **Great Powers** at the

keeper of the balance
In a balance-of-power system, the nation-state that functions as an arbiter in disputes, taking sides to preserve the political equilibrium.

nationalistic universalism
A messianic foreign policy that seeks to spread the ideas and institutions of one nation to other nations.

Great Power
During the era of the classical balance of power in Europe from the mid-seventeenth century to the outbreak of World War II in 1939, the states big enough to challenge or pose a threat to the status quo or to lead a coalition in defense of the status quo against acts of armed aggression or territorial expansion were called Great Powers, at one time or another to include Great Britain, France, Russia, Prussia (later Germany), Austria-Hungary, Spain, and Sweden, as well as the United States from the 1890s on.

superpower
A term that evolved in the context of the Cold War to denote the unprecedented destructive capabilities and global reach of the United States and the Soviet Union and to differentiate these two nuclear behemoths from the Great Powers that existed prior to the advent of the Nuclear Age.

Cold War
A worldwide system organized into two opposing alliances in which the United States and the Soviet Union competed for the allegiance of the newly independent, non-aligned states in Africa, Asia, and Latin America after World War II.

bipolar system
Following World War II, the traditional European balance-of-power system gave way to two rival power blocs, one headed by the United States and the other by the former Soviet Union, each with overwhelming economic and military superiority and each unalterably opposed to the politics and ideology of the other.

outbreak of the war, there were now two **superpowers**: the United States and the Soviet Union. To qualify as a superpower, a state has to have a full range of power capabilities, including not only military muscle, but also economic, political, diplomatic, and even moral clout. Second, it must have global reach, the capacity to project power to all parts of the world. Third, it must be willing to assert its leadership role in the international arena.

During the **Cold War**, the United States formed a kind of protectorate over the western half of war-torn Europe. By the same token, the Soviet Union created a "satellite" empire in the eastern half, and a **bipolar system** was born. According to the three-part test for superpowers, the United States became the sole superpower when the Soviet Union self-destructed in 1991.

After World War II, the United States—the first to develop an atomic bomb and the only country ever to use one—enjoyed a short-lived nuclear monopoly. The Soviet Union conducted a successful nuclear test in 1949. In military might, global reach, and economic resources, the United States and the Soviet Union—the two "superpowers"—dwarfed all other nations in the 1950s. And the ideological chasm dividing them was deep and wide.

The Primacy of Ideology Because one superpower was capitalist and democratic and the other was communist and dictatorial, the rivalry between them turned especially acrimonious and dangerous. After World War II, Allied mistrust of Joseph Stalin, the Soviet dictator, was greatly heightened by his nation's permanent occupation of Eastern Europe, which the Red Army had liberated from the Germans, and his attempt to force Western powers to abandon West Berlin. No less alarming was the prospect of a totalitarian Soviet state with nuclear weapons.

The Soviets viewed U.S. foreign policy (the cutoff of lend-lease aid, the refusal to grant large loans, and the massive U.S. foreign aid for Europe under the Marshall Plan) as proof positive that "American imperialism" was aimed at the destruction of the "world socialist system." The United States inveighed against a "world Communist conspiracy," a secret Soviet blueprint to subvert all democratic societies. However exaggerated in retrospect, the constant barrage of Cold War propaganda on both sides lent a certain credibility to this extreme rhetoric.

U.S.-led efforts at **containment** were epitomized in Western Europe by the creation of a powerful military alliance, the North Atlantic Treaty Organization (NATO). The Soviet Union countered with a military pact of its own, the Warsaw Treaty Organization, known as the **Warsaw Pact**, linking Moscow and Eastern Europe. The aura of confrontation that permeated the two alliance systems left little room for compromise or conciliation.

From its inception, the Cold War was waged by two nuclear superpowers whose aims, interests, and values were incompatible. In stark contrast to the Westphalian model, each sought to block the other's ambitions and actively endeavored to hasten the other's collapse (see Figure 17.2). Both now played a **zero-sum game**, in which a win for one side was a loss for the other.

The Danger of Nuclear War Two technological breakthroughs in the twentieth century greatly expanded the destructive potential of military weaponry: (1) the development of airborne bombers and missile delivery systems and

FIGURE 17.2   NATO and the Warsaw Pact. During the Cold War (1947–1991), Europe was divided between East (the Soviet Union and the Warsaw Pact "satellite states") and West (the United States and its NATO allies). Only a handful of European states (Ireland, Sweden, Finland, Austria, Switzerland, and Yugoslavia) managed to remain outside of these two alliance systems.

SOURCE: http://astro.temple.edu/~barbday/Europe66/resources/coldwardivisionmap1.htm.

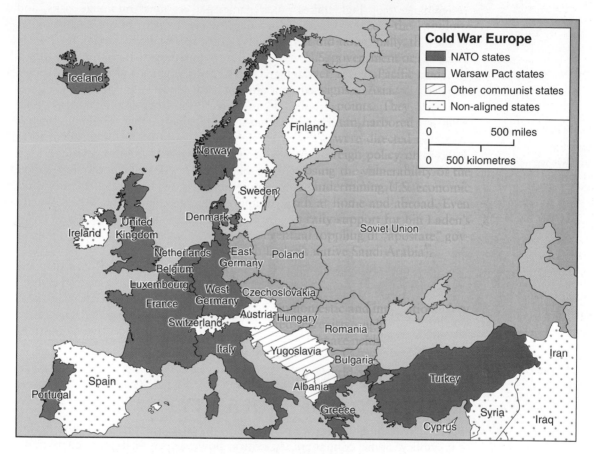

(2) the invention of fission (atomic) and fusion (hydrogen) bombs capable of leveling entire cities. From these advances grew formidable arsenals of increasingly accurate land- and sea-based missiles armed with multiple nuclear warheads.

The two superpowers commanded a vast **overkill** capacity—each held enough nuclear weapons to destroy the other many times over. All-out war had become tantamount to mutual suicide. But how was it possible to safeguard a world threatened with pushbutton destruction?

Mutual Deterrence   The unprecedented power of nuclear weapons made the concept of deterrence paramount during the heyday of Soviet–American rivalry. In 1957, the Soviet Union put the first artificial satellite (Sputnik) into orbit, demonstrating to the world that it had the technology to build long-range rockets capable of striking targets in the United States. By the late 1960s, the era of

containment
The global status quo strategic policy followed by the United States after World War II; the term stems from the U.S. policy of containing attempts by the Soviet Union to extend its sphere of control to other states as it had done in Eastern Europe. NATO, the Marshall Plan, and the Korean and Vietnam wars grew out of this policy.

Warsaw Pact
A military alliance between the former Soviet Union and its satellite states, created in 1955, which established a unified military command and allowed the Soviet army to maintain large garrisons within the satellite states, ostensibly to defend them from outside attack.

zero-sum game
A confrontation in which a win for one side is a loss for the other.

overkill
Amassing a much larger nuclear arsenal than is (or would be) needed to annihilate any adversary.

deterrence
In international relations, the theory that aggressive wars can be prevented if potential victims maintain a military force sufficient to inflict unacceptable punishment on any possible aggressor.

U.S. invulnerability was over, and **deterrence** became the new watchword in a great debate over military strategy and an integral part of the post–World War II balance of power.

According to **deterrence theory**, nations acquire nuclear weapons not to use them but to deter other nations from using them. Deterrence bears a close resemblance to a high-stakes poker game; players must minimize risks, and bluffing is part of the process. Much depends on the perceptions each side has of the other's will, intentions, and resolve in the face of grave danger. If Country A uses military power to keep Country B from pursuing its foreign policy objective, Country B's prestige is damaged and Country A gains a psychological edge.

Deterrence theory is based on a **rational actor** model—that neither side dares to launch a nuclear strike unless it can protect itself from a counterattack. Both sides have to possess a credible second-strike capability—that is, enough nuclear weapons left after an attack to deliver a retaliatory blow (second strike) adequate to inflict unacceptable damage on the attacker. It follows that if both sides are rational and both possesses a second-strike capability, neither side will launch a first strike.

To ensure the survivability of its nuclear forces, the United States built three separate but interrelated nuclear weapon delivery systems after World War II: manned bombers (known as the Strategic Air Command, or SAC), land-based intercontinental ballistic missiles (ICBMs), and submarine-launched ballistic missiles (SLBMs). The Soviet Union developed a similar "triad."

Deterrence and the arms race went hand in hand for decades. Rapid advances in the science and technology relevant to war conduct exerted a powerful influence. On one hand, because technological knowledge cannot be unlearned, both nations were wary of disarmament; on the other, the possibility that one nation might achieve a technological breakthrough provided an incentive to continue investing vast sums in weapons research and development.

AFTER THE COLD WAR: RETURN TO MULTIPOLARITY?

Political realism emphasizes national self-interest as the principal guiding foreign policy. Some contemporary critics, however, say self-centered national interest is outmoded. They argue for "a new diplomacy and for new institutions and regulatory regimes to cope with the world's growing environmental interdependence" because "our accepted definition of the limits of national sovereignty as coinciding with national borders is obsolete."[10] Perhaps, but there is little concrete evidence that state behavior has fundamentally changed.

New World, Old Ideas

The dissolution of the Soviet Union marked the end of the post–World War II bipolar balance of power. The new world order lacks a clearly defined shape and form. The rules of the game remain unclear and contradictions abound. In Europe, for example, the movement toward integration, which transcends traditional nation-state boundaries, competes with the simultaneous rise of religious and ethnic particularism *within* nations, as evidenced in the breakup of the Soviet Union, Yugoslavia, Czechoslovakia, and, most recently, Ukraine.

Problems such as global warming, air pollution, disappearing rain forests, over-population, pandemics, and world poverty are global in scope and require global solutions.[11] The pursuit of narrow self-interests is still possible, of course, but is it still desirable? Is it compatible with a *sustainable* world economy or world order?

These are the kinds of questions serious thinkers are asking. Many climate scientists, for example, are saying the fate of the planet depends on the answers. The need for a new, broader definition of self-interest is implicit in this view.

To old-school realists, talk of a "global community" sounds like soft-boiled idealism. But the new realists advocate policies rooted in enlightened self-interest and argue that global security and self-preservation require a radical rethinking of world politics. In today's world, they contend, yesterday's realism is obsolete—not only short-sighted but also self-defeating.

Globalization

Two contradictory economic trends characterize the new global economy—one toward increased interdependence, the other toward intensified competition. Interdependence and **globalization** are two sides of the same coin. As more economic interactions and transactions occur, national borders remain in place but recede in importance.[12] The forces of globalization are many and varied—multinational corporations (MNCs) seeking to maximize profits and gain competitive advantage from advances in transport, communications, and information technology; sovereign governments seeking allies, influence, and trade advantages; and nongovernmental organizations (NGOs) trying to do good in the world, to name but three.

By the same token, many problems in today's world—trade liberalization, global warming, and arms control, to name a few—are not susceptible of national solutions. Major crises in the global economy occurred in 1997 and 2008. Both times, the **International Monetary Fund (IMF)**—a specialized agency of the UN—was called upon to play an important role in restabilizing the global economy. In 2009, at the G-20* economic summit in London, President Obama declared that U.S. interests were "tied up with the larger world," and leaders agreed to provide $1.1 trillion in new funds to recapitalize the IMF.

Despite "free trade agreements" and other impediments to protectionism, governments still find ways to subsidize domestic industries and agriculture, levy tariffs on imports, and erect nontrade barriers. Relations between the United States and Japan have been strained over Japanese protectionism, for example, and wrangling over agricultural subsidies causes friction in US-EU trade ties. The United States and other countries accuse Beijing of keeping the value of the renminbi (RMB) or yuan (China's currency) artificially low in order to boost its exports. Not surprisingly, China rejects such accusations. The United States treads lightly because China is America's major source of foreign capital. Even so, China has reduced its U.S. bond holdings (the amount it is willing to lend us).

Competition and rivalry remain prominent features of the new world order. At the same time, globalization has greatly reduced America's footprint in the world economy.

---

*The world's twenty major economies constitute the Group of 20 or G-20.

deterrence theory
Holds that states acquire nuclear weapons mainly to deter the use of such weapons by other states; this idea spawned a whole new literature on war in the Nuclear Age in the second half of the twentieth century.

rational actor
A key element in a prominent contemporary theory of international relations predicated on the supposition that decision-makers are rational, that they understand the facts and risks in a crisis, and that nuclear powers regardless of regime type, religion, or ideology will not dare to launch a nuclear strike against each other so long as all are vulnerable to a retaliation in kind.

globalization
The process by which values, attitudes, preferences, and products associated with the most technologically advanced democracies are being spread around the world via mass media and trade.

The IT Revolution

It's no secret that the revolution in information technology (IT) has changed the way the world works and plays. It has also changed the way nations spy on each other and fight wars, including cyberwars.

The carrying capacity of the global communications network of computers, telephone, and television continues to grow exponentially. According to Moore's Law (named for Gordon Moore, cofounder of Intel), computing power per dollar doubles every eighteen months. A $1,500 laptop computer today is far more powerful than a $10 million mainframe was in the mid-1970s. In the 1970s, there were only about 50,000 computers in the world; by the turn of the twenty-first century, there were more than 140 million. A transatlantic telephone cable could carry only 138 conversations simultaneously in 1960; a fiber-optic cable now carries 1.5 million. The number of Internet users stood at about 361 million at the end of 2000; a decade later, estimates put the number at nearly 2 billion.[13]

One consequence of the IT revolution is that governments' hold over societies and individuals has been weakened. People now have greater access to independent sources of information than ever before in history. For this reason, the Internet poses a challenge to dictatorships. China and Iran routinely block certain websites and jam radio broadcasts of the BBC, the Voice of America, and Radio Free Europe/Radio Liberty. But these efforts do not prevent all international contacts via Twitter, Facebook, and other social media, nor can they monitor or prevent all international text messaging.

Paradoxically, computers and the Internet also greatly magnify the potential for government intrusion into the private lives of citizens, as the controversy sparked by Edward Snowden's leak of classified NSA documents in 2013 illustrates. In George Orwell's classic novel, *Nineteen Eighty-Four*, new eavesdropping technology—including a poster of Big Brother with moving eyes and two-way "telescreens" that watched the watcher—enhanced the ruthless grip of tyrannical rulers. In today's world, the kind of technology Orwell imagined is no longer confined to the realm of science fiction. High-tech sensors, meters, cameras, and the like give the modern state the means to monitor most anything and everything it chooses.

The political and social implications of the IT revolution are far-reaching. Computers and the Internet make it more difficult for the state to control what people know and how they know it—and vice versa.

The Rebirth of Europe

When the European Coal and Steel Community (ECSC) was launched in the 1950s, it was a modest effort to integrate two industrial sectors among six countries (France, Germany, Italy, and the Benelux countries). From its seeds grew the world's largest single economy, the twenty-eight-nation European Union (EU). The impressive gains achieved by Europe's integrated economy have inspired efforts to form geography-based trading blocs in other regions of the globe.[14]

The end of the Cold War witnessed a second geopolitical transformation of Europe—three new countries were admitted to the EU in 1995 (Austria, Finland, and Sweden), ten in 2004 (Cyprus, the Czech Republic, Estonia, Hungary, Latvia, Lithuania, Malta, Poland, Slovakia, and Slovenia), and Bulgaria and Romania joined in 2007. Serbia and Croatia are knocking on the door, as is Turkey. Ukraine also wants to join the West (NATO and the EU), but Russia remains adamantly opposed.

European integration has evolved through decades of economic and military cooperation in the West. Its results, however, are revolutionary. Despite the recent euro crisis, the EU symbolizes the success of Europe's post-WWII resolve to end centuries of rivalry, especially between France and Germany.

Some say the nation-state as we know it is being eclipsed by regionalism and globalization. Others emphasize the wisdom of a greater reliance on local production and consumption in a crowded and carbon-polluted world. What that would mean for the future of regional trading blocs, which fall between global and local, is anybody's guess. What do you think?

Weapons of Mass Destruction

As symbols and instruments of national power, weapons of mass destruction (WMDs)—nuclear, biological, and chemical—are in a class by themselves. Typically, states that possess them want to prevent so-called threshold states— including Argentina, Brazil, Egypt, Saudi Arabia, Syria, Iran, Turkey, Japan, both Koreas, and Taiwan—from acquiring them.

Although various arms limitation treaties covering WMDs do exist, many states refuse to sign or be constrained by them. The number of nuclear "haves" is still quite small, yet it has grown from only five in the 1960s to nine at present. Oil-rich Libya, Iran, and Iraq once sought to acquire WMDs. Dictators in both Iraq and Libya have been ousted, but Iran is believed to be close to having "the bomb." Unauthorized nuclear transfers are strictly forbidden under the Nuclear Nonproliferation Treaty (NPT), but Pakistan has never signed the NPT and is therefore not bound by it. The same, of course, is true of Iran and North Korea. Both Iran and North Korea are on the U.S. list of rogue or pariah states.[15] (See "Ideas and Politics").

Following the midterm elections in November 2010, Republican leaders in the U.S. Senate moved to block a vote on a new nuclear arms reduction treaty with Russia, saying the matter was too important to be decided by a lame duck Congress.* But supporters contended that failure to approve the treaty would send the wrong message and jeopardize Russian support for U.S. efforts to stop Iran from acquiring nuclear weapons. In the end, the supporters won and the treaty was approved, a victory for Obama and perhaps a modest step toward deeper nuclear arms cuts in the future.

*Under the treaty, each side within seven years is barred from deploying more than 1,550 strategic warheads or 700 launchers. Because of counting rules and past reductions, however, neither side has to scrap large numbers of weapons to comply with the new limits. Even so, the treaty reestablished an inspection regime that lapsed in December 2010.

PARIAH STATES: An Axis of Evil?

FIGURE 17.3   In addition to the five declared nuclear powers (the United States, Russia, China, France, and the United Kingdom), three other countries (India, Pakistan, and Israel) possess nuclear weapons, and North Korea has successfully tested such weapons. Iran probably does not possess nuclear weapons yet, but the country is widely believed to have the technological capability to do so. Both so-called pariah states reject the rules of international conduct they see as biased toward the United States and Europe. However, India, Pakistan, and Israel have also not seen fit to sign the Nuclear Nonproliferation Treaty (NPT).

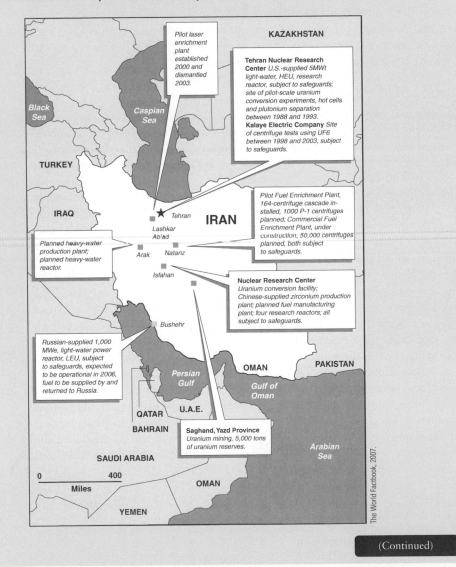

(Continued)

(CONTINUED)

In 2003, the Bush administration justified the invasion of Iraq on the grounds that Saddam Hussein possessed a secret WMD arsenal. As we now know, these allegations were false. Nonetheless, the Iraq war was the first in the Nuclear Age fought for the ostensible purpose of preventing nuclear proliferation.

Having ousted Saddam and set up an interim government in Iraq, the United States confronted two other pariah states, North Korea and Iran, calling them the "axis of evil" while demanding they discontinue all WMD research and development and submit to international inspections.

A defiant North Korea conducted its first-ever atomic test in October 2006, prompting alarm in Japan and the United States as well as in the wider international community. Veiled U.S. military threats, combined with diplomatic pressure from China, compelled President Kim Jong Il to accept a six-nation accord in February 2007, which committed North Korea to shutting down its nuclear weapons program in return for certain trade and aid concessions. But the Pyongyang regime broke the agreement in 2008-2009 when it conducted nuclear tests, ran six short-range missile tests, and twice attempted to test-launch long-range missiles.

In 2007, the United States turned the spotlight on Iran's nuclear weapons program (see Figure 17.3). When President Bush assumed a confrontational stance, the Iranian government responded in kind. For a time, the long-standing diplomatic stalemate appeared to be escalating toward war. Although relations between the United States and Iran have remained icy and adversarial, the United States participated in multilateral negotiations over Iran's nuclear program in 2014, the so-called P5+1 talks involving the five permanent UN Security Council members and Iran. At the beginning of April 2015, the five world powers and Iran agreed to a framework for a nuclear pact to be finalized if certain key sticking points involving an end to economic sanctions and international inspections could be worked out over the next three months. In late May, the world powers led by the United States held "intense" negotiations with Iran in advance of the July 1 deadline.

The United States was the first country in the world to develop nuclear weapons and remains the only country that has ever used them in war. The United States dropped atomic bombs on two cities in Japan to end World War II, and these "weapons of mass destruction" were directed at civilians, not enemy combatants. Today the United States has a massive arsenal of such weapons and the most sophisticated delivery systems on the planet. What right does the world's first and foremost superpower have to tell other countries to do as we say, not as we do? Think about it.

(Hint: Weigh the argument that totalitarian dictatorships like North Korea are more likely to use nuclear weapons in a crisis than are prosperous "open societies" like the United States, UK, or France. Contemplate the dangers inherent in nuclear proliferation.)

The End of the World as We Know It?

Environmental dangers remained largely unrecognized in the United States until the early 1960s, when Rachel Carson's best-selling book, *Silent Spring*, first appeared.[16] Since then, protecting the environment has become more and more political, fueled by declining biodiversity, evidence of global warming, and other signs of climate change. Acid rain, global warming, receding water tables, declining forests and fisheries, and the rapid depletion of the earth's fossil fuels all have contributed to a new sense of urgency.

EVER SINCE WE PRIVATISED THE CLIMATE, IT'S NEVER RUN SO SMOOTHLY!

SANGREA.NET

Sangrea.net

Today, Green Parties exist in virtually every major democracy except the United States, where organizations such as the Sierra Club, the Audubon Society, Save the Whales, and the National Wildlife Federation nonetheless exert considerable political clout. In addition, many research institutes and public policy "think tanks" monitor the state of the environment and advocate ecology-conscious public policies.

The signing of the Kyoto Protocol in 1997 represented a major step toward a global action plan to combat climate change. Kyoto called for the 37 industrialized countries and the European Union to reduce GHG emissions—carbon dioxide, nitrous oxide, methane, and fluorocarbons—by 2012. The Protocol had been endorsed by 192 countries. The United States, Canada, and Afghanistan are the only holdouts now.* (See Chapter 13 for a fuller discussion of environmental policy.)

In 2001, then President George W. Bush announced the United States was withdrawing from the Kyoto accord on the grounds that complying with its provisions would hurt the U.S. economy. Russia announced it would ratify the treaty in 2004, further isolating the United States on this issue. The Bush administration reversed itself and pledged U.S. support for global efforts to combat climate change at a G8 summit meeting in Europe in June, 2007. President Obama created the White House Office of Energy and Climate Change Policy, tasked with developing and directing federal efforts to reduce greenhouse gas (GHG) emissions. In 2015, environmental scientists and activists continued to lament what they saw as a woeful lack of leadership from Washington on this issue.

A More Level Playing Field

unipolar system
In international relations theory, the existence of a single invincible superpower; the international system said to have existed after the collapse of the Soviet Union left the United States as the sole remaining (and thus unrivalled) military and economic superpower on the world stage.

The world changed dramatically after the Cold War ended and again a decade later after 9/11. The changes were economic as well as geostrategic. The U.S. share of global GDP fell from 20% in 2004 to 16% in 2014. In the eyes of critics, the waste of U.S. lives and resources in two unwinnable wars, the unbridled greed of Wall Street in the run-up to the 2008-2009 stock market crash, and gridlock in Washington have resulted in the loss of U.S. standing in the world, eroded the foundations of the post–Cold War world order, and leveled the playing field in the second decade of the twenty-first century.

The emergence of China as a major global economic force also signals a major change in the global balance of power—namely, the end of the U.S.-dominated post–Cold War **unipolar system**. According to a World Bank estimate, the PRC will replace the United States as the world's largest economic power

*Canada ratified it but withdrew in 2011.

in 2015. Other estimates, using a different metric, say that won't happen until 2021. Nobody doubts that it will happen—the only question is how soon.

Long the world's fastest-growing major economy, China achieved average growth rates of 10% for three decades. China's growth rate slowed to a "mere" 7.4% in 2014, but it is still growing much faster than any of the other major world economies. The PRC is now the world's largest exporter and the second largest trading nation. China exports far more to the United States than it imports every year, a chronic imbalance sustained only by heavy U.S. borrowing—from China. As a result, China is mounting a big challenge to U.S. global leadership—arguably, bigger even than that of the Soviet Union during the Cold War.

India and Brazil are potential economic behemoths. If current trends hold, India will soon become the third largest economy, moving ahead of Japan and Germany, and Brazil has overtaken both France and the United Kingdom in GDP (PPP*).

Comparing the United States with the thirty-two other developed countries belonging to the Organization for Economic Co-operation and Development (OECD) reveals some startling facts. In 2008, Turkey and Mexico were the only OECD nations with higher poverty levels than the United States. For those living below the poverty line, only Chile had a lower level of income than the United States. Yet, in per capita gross national income, the United States was 7.4% above the OECD average and 18.8% above the average for the European Union (EU). In 2010, approximately 46.5 million (15%) U.S. residents fell below the poverty line, and 45 to 50 million (16% to17%) were without health insurance coverage. Meanwhile, the top 1% of taxpayers—with incomes of more than $1 million per year—received $95,000 in state subsidies (mainly tax breaks) while families earning $50,000 got less than $500 in benefits.[17]

These numbers reflect the growing concentration of wealth and economic inequality in the United States in recent decades. Of the fourteen high-income OECD countries, the United States had by far the highest cost of health care, the largest portion of the population without health coverage, second from the lowest life expectancy, and the highest rate of infant mortality. In sum, the rapid rise of new global actors, the relative decline in the U.S. share of global GDP, and the precarious state of the once mighty American middle class have combined to level the playing field and undermine the U.S. position as the world's sole superpower.

U.S. FOREIGN POLICY: CONTINUITY AMID CHANGE

Foreign policy is all about ends and means. Think of ends as long-range goals and means as measures—laws, programs, and policies—adopted in pursuit of goals and objectives. Goals are rooted in the traditions, history, and culture of a country and, as such, are resistant to change. By contrast, policies must be constantly adapted to fit changing circumstances.

---

*PPP stands for purchasing power parity, considered by most economists to be the best metric for comparing economies where prices vary greatly. A dollar buys far more in Vietnam, Mexico, Peru, or Indonesia than in France, Finland, or Japan, for example.

Power and the National Interest

A primary purpose of the state is to protect and defend its citizens from acts of aggression by other states. It's a small step from this proposition to the concept of the **national interest** defined in terms of power. Fear of attack or invasion often drives arms races. Paradoxically, the desire for security creates conditions that make war more likely, thus making everyone less secure.

Without power, states cannot deter or resist aggression by other states. But what is power? Does power "grow out of the barrel of a gun," as Mao Zedong famously said? Is it synonymous with brute force—the capability to conquer and coerce? There is no denying the role of military power and prowess in international politics. But powerful military states are not always long-lived or successful. Nazi Germany, for example, lasted little more than a decade and was defeated, occupied, and partitioned. The Soviet Union lasted longer, but it eventually collapsed and broke up into many separate states.

The examples of Nazi Germany and Stalinist Russia suggest that military power alone is not enough for a nation to thrive and prosper in a competitive and perilous world—or to even survive. Clearly, **hard power** in the form of military might is not the whole story. Nations need other forms of power to be viable and sustainable. A robust economy, for example, is vital, as is the power that derives from scientific research, technological advances, industrial innovation, and entrepreneurship—in other words, the kinds of **derivative power** that accompany modernization and are often associated with vibrant market economies. Then, too, a whole host of intangibles—sometimes called **soft power**—are also extremely important. Such things include political stability, social harmony, national character, and the congruence between a nation's self-image and its reputation in the outside world. In the "global village" that is now the arena of international politics, the ability of one country to get other countries to see the world the way it does—and to want what it wants—is a major, often woefully underrated, dimension of power.

Nations seeking to change existing power relationships are typically opposed by nations wishing to freeze them. Dissatisfaction with the status quo is often the motivation for behavior designed to provoke wars, initiate arms races, promote revolutions abroad, and generally destabilize the international system.

Although the distinction between aggressive and defensive states is clear in theory, it blurs in practice (see "Ideas and Politics: Power and Morality"). American foreign policy after World War II provides a vivid illustration of this ambiguity. The United States refused to recognize the existence of the People's Republic of China for more than two decades after the Communist takeover in 1949 on the grounds that China was not a democracy and therefore lacked legitimacy. At the same time, the United States often intervened militarily on the side of friendly dictatorships faced with popular insurrection.

In the 1980s the Reagan administration aided a variety of anti-Communist rebels ("freedom fighters") and insurgencies around the world, including groups in Central America (the Contras in Nicaragua), in Asia (mujahedeen rebels in Afghanistan), and in Africa (UNITA guerrillas in Angola). But in the more recent cases of Iraq and Afghanistan, the United States led invasions that overthrew existing governments.

POWER AND MORALITY: The Struggle for Palestine

In July 2014, war between Israel and Hamas broke out in the miniscule, densely populated Gaza Strip. A withering Israeli offensive, including more than 5,000 air-strikes, started on July 8; for its part, Hamas fired about 4,600 rockets and mortars at Israel. The war claimed 2,104 victims in Gaza (of which 69% were civilians, according to the UN). Sixty-seven Israeli soldiers died, and six civilians were killed in Israel.

The origins of the tragic struggle for Palestine go back at least to World War I and the Balfour Declaration proclaiming Britain's support for a Jewish homeland. After World War II, Jewish nationalists, or Zionists, waged a successful war for a homeland in Palestine. As justification, Zionists cited historical, biblical, and legal authority and argued that, in the aftermath of the Holocaust, Jews could live in security only in a Jewish homeland. But many Palestinian Arab refugees, who had fled rather than live in a Jewish state, regarded the Israelis as imperialists. Palestinian Arabs behaved like people in war zones (or not) everywhere in the world. Some Arabs in Palestine fought and some didn't. Some fled the violence and some stayed put. Indeed, there is still a significant Palestinian minority in Israel to this day. Neighboring Arab states declared a holy war against **Zionism** and vowed to destroy Israel.

Subsequently, radical Palestinian groups directed acts of terrorism against the Israeli population with the complicity of several Arab governments, notably Egypt. In 1956, Egypt seized the Suez Canal from Great Britain and France, which then actively backed Israel in a war with Egypt over which nation would control access to the canal. This episode only strengthened the Arab belief that Zionism and Western imperialism were conspiring to dominate the Muslim nations of the Middle East.

After more than a decade of smoldering hostilities, another war erupted. In 1967, reacting to Egyptian threats and intelligence reports suggesting it was about to attack, Israel launched a preemptive military operation that resulted in the so-called Six Days' War. After less than a week of fighting, the Israelis had routed their enemies and occupied large tracts of Arab territory, including the Sinai Peninsula and Gaza Strip in Egypt, the Golan Heights in Syria, and the West Bank of the Jordan River in Jordan. Jerusalem, until then partitioned, fell under complete Israeli control.

Humiliated by defeat, Egypt and Syria prepared for yet another round of fighting. In 1973, they attempted to revise the post-1967 status quo by attacking Israeli-held territories. The Israelis were again equal to the challenge, but this time they suffered a setback early on. With the United States acting as a mediator, the Egyptians eventually regained the Sinai desert by agreeing to a peace treaty with Israel in 1979 (the Camp David Accords). The other Arab nations charged Egypt with selling out to Zionism and "imperialism."

In the decades that followed, peace has remained elusive. In December 2008, Israel launched air strikes against targets in the Gaza Strip, killing civilians and destroying homes, and then invaded Gaza in an effort to hunt down Hamas militants. Israel claims Hamas is responsible for launching rocket attacks against southern Israel. Meanwhile, about 1.4 million impoverished Palestinians who live in Gaza were cut off from the world by an Israeli embargo.

The Arab states, along with the Palestine Liberation Organization, refused to recognize Israel's right to exist. But Israel has also, at times, been part of the problem, such as when it permitted the establishment of Jewish settlements on land seized from the Arabs. Both sides believe they are blameless victims of religious zealots out to destroy them. Who is right and who is wrong? Think about it.

(Hint: Similar ambiguities crop up frequently in international politics. Real grievances are seldom confined to one side in a dispute. Competing claims do not preclude judgments about right and wrong, but they definitely make them more difficult to reach.)

MANIFEST DESTINY

The United States has always pretended to pursue a status quo policy, even when it was, in fact, expanding. The story of how the United States grew from thirteen states huddled along the Atlantic seaboard (the original colonies) into a vast empire stretching across an entire continent is known to every U.S. schoolchild, but teachers rarely present it as a story about imperialism or expansionism—unless, perhaps, the children and the teacher are Native Americans. Spaniards and Mexicans would have reason to differ over this point as well, as people living in Texas, Arizona, California, or Florida (among other states) ought to know. Having ventured into Alaska before the United States existed, even Russians might object. Expansionists in the U.S. Congress called it Manifest Destiny, but, as Shakespeare said, a rose by any other name is still a rose.

Defense of the status quo is not proof of moral superiority any more than the proponents of change are always in the right. The United States pursued a policy of expansionism in the nineteenth century (see "Landmarks in History: Manifest Destiny") but fought two world wars to preserve the status quo in the twentieth century. The U.S. post–World War II policy of containment was also aimed at defending friendly governments against Soviet-backed "national liberation movements."

The Monroe Doctrine President James Monroe promulgated the **Monroe Doctrine** in his annual message to Congress on December 2, 1823, pledging that the United States would strictly respect the existing political configurations in the Western Hemisphere. "With the existing colonies or dependencies of any European power we have not interfered and shall not interfere," Monroe observed. But, he continued, as for:

> the governments who have declared their Independence, and maintain it . . . we could not view any interposition for the purpose of oppressing them, or controlling in any other manner their destiny, by an European power, in any other light than as the manifestation of an unfriendly disposition towards the United States.[18]

The Monroe Doctrine asserted the right of the United States to maintain a pre-eminent position in half of the world. If there was any question of the extent of the U.S. sway, it was answered in 1898 when the United States fought a war with Spain (the Spanish-American War) and seized Cuba, Hawaii, and the Philippines (across the Pacific some 7,300 miles from the California coast!).

Containment The containment idea was unveiled in a celebrated article in the journal *Foreign Affairs* in July 1947. The anonymous author, "X," turned out to be George F. Kennan (1904–2005), then the director of the State Department's Policy Planning Staff and later an ambassador to the USSR. "It is clear," Kennan wrote:

> that the main element of any United States policy toward the Soviet Union must be that of a long-term, patient but firm and vigilant containment of

Monroe Doctrine
A status quo international policy laid down by U.S. President James Monroe, who pledged the United States would resist any attempts by outside powers to alter the balance of power in the American hemisphere.

Russian expansive tendencies. . . . Soviet pressure against the free institutions of the Western world is something that can be contained by the adroit and vigilant application of counter-force at a series of constantly shifting geographical and political points.[19]

Kennan went on to predict that if a policy of containment were applied consistently for a decade or so, the Soviet challenge would diminish significantly. He also suggested (prophetically) that if containment proved successful, the totalitarian Soviet state would ultimately fall victim to severe internal pressures.

Why containment? World War II had drastically altered the European and thus the global balance of power. In its aftermath, the United States was thrust for the first time into the role of paramount world leader—a role challenged by a formidable adversary under Stalin's leadership. It seemed as if Tocqueville's century-old prophecy that the United States and Russia had each been "marked out by the will of Heaven to sway the destinies of half the globe" was about to be fulfilled.[20]

At bottom, containment was a remodeled status quo policy adapted to a new set of circumstances. Its first major test came in 1947, when Greece appeared about to fall to a communist insurgency. In response, President Harry Truman enunciated what came to be known as the **Truman Doctrine**: "I believe that it must be the policy of the United States to support free peoples who are resisting attempted subjugation by armed minorities or by outside pressures."[21]

After a Communist government gained power in Czechoslovakia in February 1948, the United States countered with the **Marshall Plan**, a $16.5 billion program aimed at reconstructing the war-torn economies of Western Europe—and preventing what happened in Czechoslovakia from happening in France or Italy. In 1949, the United States established NATO, thus "militarizing" containment.

The "loss" of China to the Communists in 1949 provoked another great wave of anxiety throughout the United States. When the Korean War broke out in 1950, the United States stretched containment to cover Asia as well as Europe. During the 1960s, the policy was stretched again—this time to cover the entire Third World. The Cold War strategy of intervention against Communism reached its high-water mark in the 1960s, when hundreds of thousands of U.S. troops were sent to Vietnam in what ultimately proved to be an ill-fated attempt to prevent Communist-ruled North Vietnam from vanquishing the U.S.-backed regime in South Vietnam. Critics called it strategic or imperial **overstretch**.

The collapse of the Soviet Union and the end of the Cold War undercut the rationale for containment and called the need for the NATO alliance into question. In the aftermath of 9/11, the war on terror replaced the Red Menace as the big threat to peace and democracy. Critics charged that fear-mongers and right-wing politicians were exaggerating the threat to justify a bloated defense budget.

Blowback: The Curse of Unintended Consequences

The concept of **blowback** has been at the center of a debate over U.S. foreign policy since the end of the Cold War. Chalmers Johnson, an expert on Asia, who

Truman Doctrine
President Harry Truman's pledge of U.S. support for any free people threatened with revolution by an internal armed minority or an outside aggressor.

Marshall Plan
A post–World War II program of massive economic assistance to Western Europe, inspired by the fear that those war-devastated countries were ripe for communist-backed revolutions.

overstretch
Term used by critics of the Vietnam War and subsequent U.S. military interventions when referring to the ill-fated U.S. attempts to prevent oust and replace repressive governments considered hostile to the West and the postwar world order.

blowback
The unintended consequences of foreign policy often officially downplayed or even kept secret from the general population.

wrote a best-selling book of the same name, popularized the term.[22] According to Johnson:

> [Blowback] refers to the unintended consequences of policies that were kept secret from the American people. What the daily press reports as the malign acts of "terrorists" or "drug lords" or "rogue states" or "illegal arms merchants" often turn out to be blowback from earlier operations.[23]

As examples, Johnson cited the 1988 bombing of Pan Am Flight 103 over Lockerbie, Scotland, which, he asserted, "was retaliation for a 1986 Reagan administration aerial raid on Libya that killed President Muammar Qaddafi's stepdaughter."[24]

Johnson also suggested that terrorist attacks against U.S. targets are blowback, citing a 1997 Pentagon report: "Historical data shows a strong correlation between U.S. involvement in international situations and an increase in terrorist attacks against the United States."[25] Johnson argued that "the most direct and obvious form of blowback often occurs when the victims fight back after a secret American bombing, or a U.S.-sponsored campaign of state terrorism, or a CIA-engineered overthrow of a foreign political leader. All around the world today, it is possible to see the groundwork being laid for future forms of blowback."[26]

The war on terror led to U.S. airstrikes and drone attacks on civilian populations in Muslim countries, including Iraq, Syria, Yemen, Afghanistan, and Pakistan. Washington justified these attacks as deterring terrorism "even if the targets proved to be irrelevant to any damage done to facilities of the United States. In this way, future blowback possibilities are seeded into the world."[27]

Unsurprisingly, Johnson's dissenting views are not universally shared by other academic or policy experts. Indeed, in the wake of 9/11, many in the United States viewed *any* criticism of U.S. foreign policy as unpatriotic.

The Bush Doctrine

After the 9/11 attacks, President Bush declared war on terror. The United States, he warned, would retaliate against terrorists and those who harbor them. When the Taliban ignored Bush's ultimatum to hand over Osama bin Laden and shut down al Qaeda operations, the United States orchestrated a large-scale military invasion of Afghanistan.

But for Bush, overthrowing the Taliban and destroying the al Qaeda training camps in Afghanistan were only the first steps. There still existed an "axis of evil" that included Iraq, Iran, and North Korea. The universal right of self-defense, Bush asserted, justifies the use of preemptive action when an "imminent danger of attack" exists:

> The United States has long maintained the option of preemptive actions to counter a sufficient threat to our national security. The greater the threat, the greater is the risk of inaction—and the more compelling the case for taking anticipatory action to defend ourselves, even if uncertainty remains as to the time and place of the enemy's attack. To forestall or prevent such hostile acts by our adversaries, the United States will, if necessary, act preemptively.[28]

The logic of this foreign-policy stance—the so-called Bush Doctrine—was invoked to justify the invasion of Iraq.

On May 1, 2003, after the U.S. military invaded Iraq, ousted Saddam Hussein, and replaced his brutal regime with a Coalition Provisional Authority (occupation government), President Bush declared "mission accomplished"— the end of the major fighting in Iraq. But it was a premature victory lap. The death toll mounted steadily in the ensuing years as Iraqi insurgents planted bombs, launched missile attacks, and staged ambushes. By mid-June 2009, more than 4,160 U.S. soldiers had died in Iraq *after* the "mission accomplished" pronouncement. Other casualties included 1,306 contract workers, 138 journalists, and 308 coalition troops—and an estimated 1.3 million Iraqis.[29]

President Bush ordered a troop surge in 2008 in a desperate attempt to defeat the urban guerrilla war of attrition in Iraq. He saw his approval ratings fall as a rising chorus of criticism continued to take its toll and cast a shadow over his administration.

Barack Obama campaigned on a promise to withdraw U.S. forces from Iraq, but as president stayed the course. Upon taking office, President Obama ordered a troop surge in Afghanistan. In 2011, amidst tumult in Tunisia, Egypt, Libya, and much of the Arab World, he approved airstrikes against the armed forces of the repressive Qaddafi regime, thus intervening in Libya's civil war. In 2014, he gave the order to bomb the Islamic State of Iraq and Syria (ISIS) and recommit troops in Iraq after withdrawing the last U.S. combat forces from Iraq a few years earlier. This fealty to the Bush Doctrine, however, did nothing to mitigate the vitriolic criticism of Obama's leadership from Republicans in Congress.

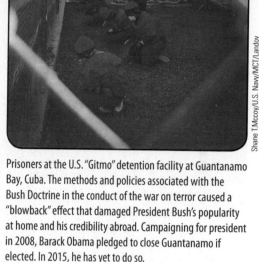

Prisoners at the U.S. "Gitmo" detention facility at Guantanamo Bay, Cuba. The methods and policies associated with the Bush Doctrine in the conduct of the war on terror caused a "blowback" effect that damaged President Bush's popularity at home and his credibility abroad. Campaigning for president in 2008, Barack Obama pledged to close Guantanamo if elected. In 2015, he has yet to do so.

STATECRAFT: BEYOND REALISM

Some international theorists contend that not much has changed in the post–Cold War era. In this view, the United States "must anchor its security and prosperity in a less-than-utopian set of objectives [and] think in terms not of the whole world's well-being but . . . of purely national interest."[30]

Other foreign policy experts argue that the United States has strayed from primary reliance on diplomacy to an overemphasis on military solutions. These critics argue for multilateralism over unilateralism and the use of **statecraft** over force and the threat of force whenever and wherever possible.

What is statecraft? According to Dennis Ross, chief Middle East peace negotiator under Presidents George H. W. Bush and Bill Clinton, "It is the use of the assets or the resources and tools (economic, military, intelligence, media) that a state has to pursue its interest and to affect the behavior of others, whether friendly or hostile." Ross notes, "Plato wrote about statecraft. Machiavelli theorized about it. And Bismarck practiced it, never losing sight of his objectives and recognizing that a nation's ambitions should never exceed its capabilities."[31]

statecraft
Statecraft is the art of achieving political or strategic aims and objectives by force of example, persuasion, and the use of incentives, rather than through coercion and threats; synonymous with *statesmanship* and *far-sighted diplomacy*.

idealism
A political philosophy
that considers values,
ideals, and moral
principles as the keys
to comprehending,
and possibly changing,
the behavior of
nation-states.

Ideals and Self-Interest: The Power of Morality

In sharp contrast to political realism, **idealism** places great emphasis on the role of values, ideals, and moral principles. It not only helps explain why nations act, but it also furnishes guidelines for how nations ought to act. Idealists tend to view war as irrational—a manifestation of misguided ideology or fervent nationalism. They see trade, aid, diplomacy, and international law and organizations as antidotes—and alternatives—to war.

Idealists often regard realists as cynics; realists say idealists are naive. Who is right? Nations *do* sometimes act altruistically—for example, by offering asylum to refugees who flee political persecution, economic disaster, or civil war. Between the two world wars, British leaders sought to alleviate harsh conditions imposed on Germany by the Treaty of Versailles, a stand hailed as "a noble idea, rooted in Christianity, courage, and common sense."[32]

Even the arch-realist Hans Morgenthau did not deny morality's role in international relations. Some actors on the world stage clearly give moral principles more weight than others. President Woodrow Wilson emphasized national self-determination and collective security, Hitler obsessed over territorial expansion *(Lebensraum)*, British Prime Minister Neville Chamberlain sought peace through appeasement, and President Jimmy Carter actively promoted global human rights. President Bill Clinton ordered the U.S. military action in Somalia from 1992 to 1994 to alleviate mass starvation.[33]

Still, it is easier by far to cite instances when leaders and states do *not* act altruistically. President Bill Clinton did not intervene against the genocide in Rwanda, and President George W. Bush did not send troops to stop the savagery in Darfur. The major European nations, too, stayed on the sidelines in both instances.

Most foreign policy contains elements of both ideals and self-interest. Winston Churchill, who measured his words carefully, called the Marshall Plan "the most unsordid act in history."[34] But the Marshall Plan was also consistent with the United States' post–World War II status quo strategic policy of reestablishing a stable Western European community, able to resist armed aggression from without and organized subversion from within. Germany sent massive amounts of aid to Russia in the winter of 1991–1992, partly for humanitarian reasons and partly out of fear a failed Russia would destabilize Western Europe and unleash a horde of refugees in Germany's direction.

Nations have occasionally sacrificed concrete national interests for the sake of moral principle. Although an occupied country during World War II, Denmark was granted much political autonomy by the Nazi government. Many Danes dared to defy German edicts in order to protect Jewish citizens and other refugees, thus creating "an extraordinary obstacle which arose in the path of the German destruction machine: an uncooperative Danish administration and a local population unanimous in its resolve to save its Jews."[35] Denmark, "too weak to seek self-preservation through power," limited its foreign policy "largely to humanitarian causes, and . . . in the end survived Hitler's conquest."[36]

A true understanding of the national interest takes into account both power and morality. Power without morality is mere expedience and, as history shows, can be self-defeating, whereas morality without power rarely goes beyond good intentions.[37]

Aggression: Says Who?

Aggression is strictly condemned in international law and diplomacy. But who starts a fight—who hurls the first insult in a bar or fires the first shot in a war—is often impossible to determine. Third parties seldom agree. The disagreement can and often does lead to a wider conflict.

However, not every state with a territorial claim against another or a desire to change the global distribution of power and wealth is guilty of aggression. A border dispute, for example, does not in itself mean either contending country has an appetite for empire. Neither does the demand by many developing countries for a "new international economic order" (a redistribution of global wealth). Challenging the status quo in this way is hardly proof of aggression, both because the objectives are limited and reasonable and because the methods are political and diplomatic rather than military or economic.

Historically, when one nation's army invaded and occupied the territory of another nation, it was an act of aggression—a violation of international law. Invaders are seldom welcomed by the native inhabitants, and aggressors are seldom embraced by the international community. But, as mentioned previously, since World War II the United States has intervened militarily in some countries and invaded others without *intending* to plunder or seize territory, without intending to take over the country's government, and without intending to stay. Unfortunately, "good" intentions are often misunderstood, misinterpreted, or, in the eyes of others, not good at all. When that happens—and it almost always does—the unintended consequences can be disastrous.

Aggression is often in the eyes of the beholder. It is something others do.

Following the 9/11 terrorist attacks, President George W. Bush called for punitive measures against any state(s) that harbored international terrorists.[38]

Here boys are playing at "ethnic cleansing" in Kosovo in the former Yugoslavia where genocide happened in the 1990s. Is aggression inherent in human nature, a necessity in a dangerous world, or a form of learned behavior?

William E. Thompson

The methods the United States used were violent—bombing and inserting special operations combat teams in order to (1) overthrow the Taliban regime in Afghanistan and (2) kill or capture Osama bin Laden and his al Qaeda terrorist network. Later, the United States led the invasion of Iraq, the ouster of dictator Saddam Hussein followed, and then his capture and execution. These acts were aggressive, but did they constitute aggression? Were they offensive or defensive in nature? What do you think?

Hard Facts about Soft Power

Scholar Joseph Nye argues power in contemporary world politics is "distributed among countries in a pattern that resembles a complex three-dimensional chess game." Imagine three chess games on as many chessboards taking place on three levels simultaneously. On the top board, military power is concentrated in the United States; the world looks unipolar. On the middle chessboard, however, economic power is distributed more evenly among the United States, Europe, Japan, and China; and the world appears multipolar. Finally, there "is the realm of transnational relations that cross borders outside government control" on the bottom of the chessboard:

> This realm includes actors as diverse as bankers electronically transferring sums larger than most national budgets at one extreme, and terrorists transferring weapons or hackers disrupting Internet operations at the other. On this bottom board, power is widely dispersed, and it makes no sense to speak of unipolarity, multipolarity or hegemony.[39]

In a three-dimensional game, Nye argues, you will lose if you focus only on the top board and fail to notice the other boards and the vertical connections among them. Nye draws an even more fundamental distinction between "hard coercive power" and "soft or attractive power," which he defines as "the important ability to get others to want what you want." He concludes: "The paradox of American power in the 21st century is that the largest power since Rome cannot achieve its objectives unilaterally in a global information age."[40]

THE MORE THINGS CHANGE . . .

What does the future hold? During the Cold War, many feared that the world as we know it would be incinerated in a nuclear holocaust. When the Cold War ended, one famous scholar, the late Samuel Huntington, warned that the old clash of ideologies was being replaced by a "clash of civilizations."[41] In his words, "The breaking apart and remaking of the atlas is only now beginning."[42] Then came 9/11, which was widely viewed as a vindication of Huntington's thesis, supposedly pitting the Judeo-Christian West against the Islamic world (an oversimplification that nonetheless has some basis in reality).

About the same time, another scholar, Robert Kaplan, saw a different danger on the horizon—what he called "the coming anarchy." The nation-state as we know it, he argued, is obsolete and destined to be replaced not by larger regional groupings or a world-state (as idealists predicted after World War II) but by a formless force field of political whirlpools energized by the teeming, chaotic, crime-infested cities or "city-states" of the future. The picture Kaplan painted was bleak in the extreme.[43] West Africa in the 1990s presented a glimpse of this grim future, as did the Balkans war after the breakup of Yugoslavia.

There is a famous French adage that goes, *plus ça change, plus c'est la même chose* (the more things change, the more it's the same thing). Apocalyptic visions of the future are titillating and thought-provoking, but they often exaggerate the chaos and minimize the order at work in the world. Containing conflict and avoiding war depends on respect for law, moral norms, and established institutions—our focus in the next and concluding section.

INTERNATIONAL LAW

For roughly 350 years, an evolving body of **international law** defining the rights and obligations of states in relation to one another has helped maintain a modicum of order and peace in the world. The "rules of the game" freely adopted by sovereign states have often assumed the form of treaties. Other widely recognized sources of international law include custom and convention; general legal principles based on such ideas as justice, equity, and morality; and the judicial decisions and teachings of eminent legal authorities.

The most famous codification of international law remains Hugo Grotius's *On the Law of War and Peace*, published in 1625, only twenty-three years before the formal establishment of the nation-state system in the Treaty of Westphalia. International law has since become a vital part of what we might call diplomatic business as usual in the arena of world politics.

Usefulness

If a river ran between two states, who would decide whether the boundary should be drawn along the riverbed, along the river banks, or down the exact center of the river? What would guarantee the safety of diplomatic representatives accredited to a foreign government? How would territorial boundaries on land and sea be determined? How would traffic on the high seas be regulated? Should neutral states have the right to carry on normal commercial relations with belligerents in times of war? The need to answer such practical questions makes international law a vital necessity.

Compliance and Enforcement

During the four hundred years of its existence, international law has in most instances been scrupulously observed. When one of its rules is violated, however, it is not always enforced and, when enforcement action is taken, it's not always effective. Yet to deny that international law plays a vital role in maintaining world order flies in the face of all evidence.[44]

international law
The body of customs, treaties, and generally accepted rules that define the rights and obligations of nations when dealing with one another.

"Put in more references to international law."

ED Fisher/Condé Nast Collection

Enforcing international law is difficult. Governments cannot be arrested, placed on trial, or incarcerated, but they can be made to pay a price for rogue behavior. States perceived as lawbreakers can be subjected to diplomatic censure and economic sanctions. In extreme cases, they can be threatened or attacked, conquered, subjugated, made to pay reparations, or annexed.

Tyrants and mass murderers can be put on trial. One result of political and diplomatic pressure, for example, was the reluctant decision of the Serbian government in 2003 to turn over ex-President Milosevic to the UN War Crimes Tribunal in The Hague.

Fear of political repercussions is not the only reason governments play by the rules. Trade, travel, and tourism would be greatly impeded without rules, as would banking, foreign investment, and cross-border cultural, scientific, and technological exchanges. Few governments would send ambassadors and envoys to foreign capitals without diplomatic immunity.

Still, power is the coin of all politics, and law without adequate means to enforce it is a farce. In the global arena, either the participants (states) police the system or there is no system worthy of the name. Hence, the balance of power is "an indispensable condition of the very existence of International Law."[45]

International Law in the Modern Era

Prior to World War II, the Geneva and Hague Conventions constituted the most important body of international law and set forth the rules of war. Since 1945, international law has advanced in several important areas, most notably in arms control. In the future, international law will likely be increasingly concerned with environmental issues. We look next at each of these important examples of contemporary international law.

Geneva Convention
A body of international law dealing with the treatment of the wounded, prisoners of war, and civilians in a war zone.

Hague Convention
A widely accepted set of rules governing conduct in land wars, the use of new weapons, and the rights and duties of both neutral and warring parties.

Strategic Arms Reduction Treaty II (START II)
A post–Cold War confidence-building treaty aimed at curbing strategic nuclear weapons negotiated between the United States and the former Soviet Union in 1993.

The Geneva and Hague Conventions   In 1856, several Great Powers endorsed the Declaration of Paris, first of a series of multilateral international conventions. It limited war at sea by outlawing privateering and specifying that a naval blockade had to be effective to be legally binding. More important was the **Geneva Convention** of 1864 (revised in 1906), which laid down rules for the humane treatment of the wounded on the battlefield. Of still greater importance was the **Hague Convention** of 1899, which codified for the first time many accepted practices of land warfare. A second Hague Convention, in 1907, revised the 1899 codes and prescribed rules for the use of new weapons such as dumdum bullets, poison gas, and gas-filled balloons for bombing.

Arms Control Treaties   During the Cold War, no global issue was more pressing than the arms control agreements between the two nuclear superpowers. Although they were both numerous and controversial, these agreements altered neither country's dependence on nuclear deterrence to maintain peace.

The demise of the Soviet Union, a perceived improvement in relations between the United States and Russia, and the existence of nuclear weapons in the newly created nations of Belarus, Ukraine, and Kazakhstan spurred the United States and Russia to negotiate new arms control treaties. Most notably, the 1993 **Strategic Arms Reduction Treaty II (START II)** cut nuclear warheads by 60% over levels already reduced two years earlier. START II banned multiple warheads on land-based missiles and reduced submarine-launched multiple warheads. Underlying the treaty was each nation's hope that it "could reduce the chances of a war of annihilation by banning the nuclear weapons that both powers would be most likely to use in a preemptive strike."[46]

Over the past forty years, a number of important arms control measures have been multinational. Some noteworthy agreements include:

- The 1959 **Antarctic Treaty** prohibited all military activity on the Antarctic continent and accorded each signatory the right of aerial surveillance. It also prohibited dumping of nuclear wastes and encouraged cooperation in scientific investigations.
- The 1967 **Outer Space Treaty** banned nuclear weapons from outer space, prohibited military bases and maneuvers on the moon and other planets, and barred claims of national sovereignty in outer space.
- The 1968 **Nonproliferation Treaty** restricted signatories from transferring or receiving nuclear weapons or materials. Although most of the world's nations have signed this agreement, several have not consistently obeyed its provisions; and a number of other nations, including Iran, Iraq, Libya, Pakistan, and India, have not signed it.
- The 1971 **Seabed Treaty** banned nuclear weapons from the bottom of the world's oceans outside each state's twelve-mile territorial limit.
- The 1972 **Biological Weapons Convention** pledged the destruction of biological stockpiles while outlawing the production and storage of such weapons.
- The 1993 **Chemical Weapons Convention** intended to eliminate chemical weapons within ten years. The U.S. Senate ratified this treaty in April 1997.

There are limits to what we can expect such pacts to accomplish. Governments usually do not sign agreements that require them to act contrary to the way they would act in the absence of such agreements. When the United States ratified the Chemical Weapons Convention, it claimed to have no intention of developing such weapons (nor did it rely on those weapons for its national security). When a proposed agreement on international rules of conduct has required the negotiating parties to relinquish something important to them, however, international law has not fared so well.

What Global Warming Treaty? Future international law is likely to include important environmental agreements. Some experts believe past arms limitations treaties will provide a precedent for these.

With a few exceptions, such as the Montreal Protocol (curbing chlorofluorocarbons and other gases that deplete the ozone layer),[47] the number and scope of most international environmental agreements have been limited. Regulations aimed at environmental protection have traditionally come under national sovereignty. Unfortunately, air and water pollution, conservation, wildlife protection, and many other human-induced changes in the biosphere cannot be contained within national boundaries.

The Global Warming Treaty negotiated at Kyoto, Japan, in December 1997 is a good example of the difficulties in fashioning international environmental law. Many scientists, including geophysicists and meteorologists, predict a

Antarctic Treaty An international agreement that prohibits all military activity on the Antarctic continent and allows for inspection of all nations' facilities there. It also nullifies all territorial claims to Antarctic land and pledges the signatories to peaceful cooperation in exploration and research.

Outer Space Treaty An international agreement, signed by the United States and the former Soviet Union, that banned the introduction of military weapons into outer space, prohibited the extension of national sovereignty in space, and encouraged cooperation and sharing of information about space research.

Nonproliferation Treaty An international agreement, drafted in 1968, not to aid nonnuclear nations in acquiring nuclear weapons; it was not signed by France, China, and other nations actively seeking to build these weapons.

significant rise in the earth's temperature over the next century. If these predictions are true, global warming will likely disrupt the world's climate, imperil agriculture, and cause a rising sea level that could threaten many major cities.

A major cause of global warming is carbon dioxide, created when coal, oil, and other fossil fuels are burned in internal combustion engines. However, there is political opposition in the United States to any treaty that would limit energy use. Labor unions, such as the AFL-CIO, worry about lost jobs. Executives from manufacturing industries complain about additional government regulations. Skeptics question the computer models and doubt whether global warming will actually occur or argue that it can be easily or effectively controlled.

Europe has been in the forefront of efforts to combat global warming. A small number of Caribbean and South Pacific nations, seeing themselves most at risk from global warming (even a two-foot rise in sea level would endanger their coastal businesses and poison their drinking water), champion even more stringent standards. Many developing nations, including China, India, and Brazil, have sought to exempt themselves from any agreement. And oil-producing nations, such as Saudi Arabia, see any future treaty as economically harmful and thus have continued to oppose the Kyoto Protocol outright.

The Limitations of International Law

Treaties intended to outlaw war (such as the unsuccessful Kellogg-Briand Pact of 1928, eventually ratified by sixty-four nations) and pacts intended to promote peace and international understanding (such as the UN Charter) seldom withstand the test of time. The world lacks three practical prerequisites necessary to maintain the rule of law. First, there is no world organization with the legitimate authority to pass binding laws. Second, there is no global chief executive with the power to initiate or enforce international law. Third, sovereign states cannot be forced to submit disputes to the World Court for adjudication or to accept the verdict even when they do.

Enforcement must be left to individual nation-states, which too often enforce decisions unreliably or not at all. As long as international law lacks the predictability and coherence that give the rule of law its unique value, it will remain more of a convenience for governments than a constraint on them.

The World Court The lack of international law-enforcement capabilities is reflected most clearly in the workings of the **World Court**, headquartered in The Hague (Holland's old capital). Officially known as the International Court of Justice (ICJ), one of six principal organs established by the UN Charter, the Court is a full-fledged judicial body, complete with judges, procedural rules, and the solemn trappings of a dignified tribunal, but it lacks a clearly defined jurisdiction.

For the Court to gain jurisdiction over an international dispute, the nations involved must confer jurisdiction on it in accordance with Article 36 of the Statute of the International Court of Justice, which stipulates:

> Parties to the present Statute *may* at any time declare that they recognize as compulsory . . . *in relation to any other State accepting the same obligation,* the jurisdiction of the Court in all legal disputes concerning: (1) the interpretation

---

Seabed Treaty
An international agreement that forbids the establishment of nuclear weapons on the ocean floor beyond the twelve-mile territorial limit.

Biological Weapons Convention
A 1972 international arms control treaty that pledged the destruction of biological weapons stockpiles and outlawed the production and storage of such weapons.

Chemical Weapons Convention
A 1993 international arms control treaty to eliminate chemical weapons within ten years. It calls for the destruction of chemical weapons stockpiles and monitoring companies making compounds that can be used to produce nerve agents in order to end production of chemical weapons.

World Court
Also known as the International Court of Justice, the principal judicial organ of the United Nations; the Court hears any case brought before it by parties who voluntarily accept its jurisdiction.

of a treaty; (2) any question of international law; (3) the existence of any fact which, if established, would constitute a breach of an international obligation. [Emphasis added]

In other words, governments are legally obligated to abide by a decision of the Court only when they have given prior consent to the Court's adjudication of a case. They may make a declaration of intent to accept the Court's jurisdiction in advance, as Article 36 invites them to do, or they may simply choose to submit certain cases on an ad hoc basis.

In the first twenty years of the World Court's existence, forty-two governments declared their intent to accept its compulsory jurisdiction. But declarations are not deeds, especially when they involve sovereign states, and appearances can be deceiving. The U.S. "acceptance" of Article 36 in 1946 is a case in point. It was, in fact, a diplomatic sleight of hand. It states, in part:

This declaration shall not apply to: a. disputes the solution of which the parties shall entrust to other tribunals by virtue of agreements already in existence or which may be concluded in the future; or b. disputes with regard to matters which are essentially within the domestic jurisdiction of the United States of America as determined by the United States of America; or c. disputes arising under a multinational treaty, unless (1) all parties to the treaty affected by the decision are also parties to the case before the Court, or (2) the United States of America especially agrees to jurisdiction.

Together, these qualifications meant the U.S. government agreed to compulsory jurisdiction only on the condition that the agreement did not compel it to accept the Court's jurisdiction.

The United States and the World Court In 1985, the Marxist Sandinista government of Nicaragua filed suit against the United States in the World Court, charging Washington with aggression for mining the harbor at Corinto and supporting the Contra rebels. The United States boycotted the proceedings and suspended bilateral talks on the grounds that Nicaragua was using the Court for political and propaganda purposes.

In June 1986, the World Court ruled decisively against the United States. At Nicaragua's initiative, the Security Council voted 11 to 1 to support the World Court's decision (with the United Kingdom, France, and Thailand abstaining). Yet the ruling had no practical effect because the U.S. government rejected the ICJ's jurisdiction.

In 1992, the United States and Great Britain led a successful fight for UN sanctions against Libya when its government refused to extradite two Libyan nationals suspected of masterminding the 1988 terrorist bombing of Pan Am Flight 103 over Lockerbie, Scotland, in which 270 people died. When Libya successfully sought relief in the World Court, the U.S. again argued the Court lacked jurisdiction.

Power and Principle Are principles of justice irrelevant in international politics? There's no simple answer to this question. Strong states can punish weaker states (for example, through economic sanctions or military action). Rogue rulers can also be punished—the International Criminal Court (ICC) trials of former presidents of Yugoslavia (Slobodan Milosevic) and Liberia (Charles Taylor) for crimes against humanity are two examples in recent history.

International law is most effective when it serves the interests of powerful nations. Great Powers typically seek political and military solutions (where they have greater control over the outcomes) rather than judicial remedies (where judges decide the outcomes).

THE UNITED NATIONS: OUR MIRROR IN A MIRROR

The quest for peace in response to two catastrophic world wars in the first half of the twentieth century led to the birth of the United Nations (UN). The UN is the first and only true "world organization" in the sense of having a near-universal membership (North Korea and Taiwan are two rare exceptions). As such, it is a mirror reflecting the realities of a troubled world.

Historical Background

Beginning in the nineteenth century, several international peacekeeping federations were founded, usually in the aftermath of increasingly destructive wars. The Holy Alliance, formed in 1815 in the wake of the Napoleonic Wars, represented an attempt by Europe's major powers to control international events by means of meetings and conferences. A more elaborate organization was the League of Nations, set up in 1919 after World War I.

When the Covenant of the League of Nations was sealed in 1919, Wilsonians (followers of President Woodrow Wilson) hailed it as the advent of a new age. The League's Assembly was a deliberative body of representatives from each member-state, and all votes carried equal weight. Motions required unanimous approval for passage, so no matter how tiny, every member enjoyed veto power over nearly every decision. The much-smaller Council was made up of four permanent and four nonpermanent members who investigated and reported on threats to the peace and proposed or recommended appropriate action to the Assembly. The two bodies were supervised by the Permanent Secretariat, the League's administrative arm.

The League's ambitious aims included, above all, the maintenance of international peace through the promise of swift and certain retribution against aggressor nations—peace and punishment were two sides of the same coin. War was crime, and crime would not pay. In this respect, the League became the institutional embodiment of President Wilson's desire to replace the traditional balance of power with "a single overwhelming, powerful group of nations who shall be trustees of the peace of the world."[48] The key was to create a system of collective security with the combined military forces of all law-abiding nations so formidable that no single challenger would stand a chance against it. The prospect of facing such a potential force would be a sufficient deterrent.

Despite Wilson's inspired advocacy of the League of Nations, the United States was sidelined because Republicans in the Senate opposed the Treaty of Versailles. The U.S. failure to join the League foreshadowed the organization's future

Edward N. Jackson/Foter.com

After defeating Germany in World War I, leaders from the United States, Britain, France, and Italy met at the Paris Peace Conference in 1919 and drafted the Treaty of Versailles. Council of Four at the WWI Paris peace conference, May 27, 1919 (L - R): Prime Minister David Lloyd George, Great Britain; Premier Vittorio Orlando, Italy; French Premier Georges Clemenceau; and President Woodrow Wilson. The treaty imposed harsh terms on Germany and established a League of Nations to prevent future wars.

misfortunes. By the early 1930s, conflicting interests and bitter rivalries had resurfaced with a vengeance.

The League was doomed to failure by several fatal flaws. First, the United States was conspicuously absent. Second, the requirement for unanimity invited inaction in a crisis. Third, although collective security measures were to be triggered by acts of aggression, the Charter failed to define what constituted aggression. Germany remilitarized the Rhineland, Italy invaded Ethiopia, Germany invaded Poland and Czechoslovakia, and Japan embarked on a career of conquest in Asia—none of these actions prompted a collective *reaction* on the part of the League.

World War I transformed the Eurocentric balance-of-power system to one that was truly global and moved the United States front and center on the world stage. The Republican majority in the U.S. Senate rejected the Treaty of Versailles, which ended WWI and established the League of Nations. As a consequence, the Wilsonian idea of collective security as the key to a world without war was stillborn.

The Founding of the United Nations

The shocking death toll and terrifying new weapons of World War II sparked renewed efforts to ensure world peace through a powerful international organization. The United Nations was, in effect, an attempt to build a new and improved League of Nations.

In contrast to the League, the UN Charter created a Security Council entrusted with "primary responsibility for the maintenance of international peace and security" and made up of five permanent members—the United States, the Soviet Union (recently replaced by the Russian Republic), the United Kingdom, France, and China—and ten nonpermanent members. In sharp contrast to the League, the so-called Big Five alone can veto proposed peacekeeping and collective security measures.

The idea was to give major powers responsibilities commensurate with their economic and military capabilities. In Chapter 7, Article 39 specifies "the Security Council shall determine the existence of any threat to the peace, breach of the peace, or act of aggression and shall make recommendations, or decide what measure shall be taken in accordance with Articles 40 and 42, to maintain or restore international peace and security."

Article 41 deals with economic sanctions, including "complete or partial interruption of economic relations and of rail, sea, air, postal, telegraphic, radio, and other means of communication, and the severance of diplomatic relations." Article 42 contemplates situations in which economic sanctions may be inadequate; in such cases, the Security Council "may take action by air, sea, or land forces as may be necessary to maintain or restore international peace and security. Such action may include demonstrations, blockades, and other operations by air, sea, or land forces of Members of the United Nations." Other articles in Chapter 7 deal with organizing the military components of a full-fledged collective security system, including the establishment of the Military Staff Committee (Article 47). The military provisions in the UN Charter far surpass the League's in scope and detail.

The UN Charter was not designed as a blueprint for world government. Article 2, paragraph 7, states that matters "essentially within the domestic jurisdiction of any state" are beyond the purview of UN authority. Article 2 explicitly recognizes the "sovereign equality" of all UN member-states.

Still, many of the UN's creators viewed it as the foundation of a new world order. The wide array of specialized agencies leave no doubt that the UN was committed from the outset to the positive goal of promoting prosperity , as well as preventing war. The Charter mirrors the mix of realism and idealism present at the creation—and shows how patterns from the past often intrude on the best attempts to build a better future.

The United Nations in the Cold War: 1945 to 1991

The United Nations faced problems not unlike those that destroyed the League of Nations. A world government capable of keeping the peace implied nothing less than a wholesale forfeiture of state sovereignty. Anything short of a world government would leave the UN unable to punish an aggressor or preserve the peace unless all the Great Powers—at a minimum, the five permanent Security Council members—were in complete accord.

On one hand, the Charter obligates member-states to act in accordance with the rule of law and empowers the Security Council to punish states when they do not; on the other hand, it provides a number of loopholes and escape clauses for states that wish to evade or ignore their obligations. Article 51, for example, states, "Nothing in the present Charter shall impair the inherent right of individual or collective self-defense." Such a provision invites aggression as long as "self-defense" is a lawful justification to resort to force and individual states are free to define as self-defense any action they deem in their national interest. The dilemma is obvious: without escape clauses such as Article 51, the UN Charter would not have been acceptable; with them, it may not be enforceable.

Another problem plaguing the world body until recently was the persistent state of tension between the United States and the Soviet Union, which seriously hampered the workings of the United Nations during the Cold War. Because each superpower maintained a coalition of allies, followers, and admirers that at one time or another held the majority in the General Assembly, deadlock became the hallmark of most UN deliberations. The consensus necessary to promote peace through collective security was also absent at many critical junctures; when the Soviet Union did not veto a controversial measure, the United States often did. Despite these difficulties, the United Nations has contributed valuable, if limited, efforts toward peace by sending mediators, truce supervision teams, and quasi-military forces to various parts of the world, including the Congo, Cyprus, the Middle East, and the Balkans.

The United Nations after the Cold War: 1991 to the Present

The mid- to late 1980s saw an unprecedented period of cooperation among the five permanent members of the Security Council, particularly between the United States and the Soviet Union. The catalyst was the Soviet Union's new conciliatory foreign policy, initiated by Mikhail Gorbachev. This era of increased cooperation produced two significant results. First, the United Nations embraced a particularly vigorous approach to international peacekeeping, sometimes bordering on peacemaking.[49] Second, it sanctioned collective military action against Iraq after it invaded Kuwait.

After the Cold War, with the superpower rivalry a thing of the past, the United Nations momentarily blossomed. Although balance-of-power politics and nuclear deterrence forged a relatively stable system of order after 1945, the end of the Cold War gave rise not only to new opportunities for order building but also to new dangers and sources of instability. Wherever there was conflict or a humanitarian crisis, the UN was called upon. President Bill Clinton renounced unilateralism and made it a rule to seek UN approval before resorting to military force. The prestige of the UN was at an all-time high.

In 2001, the UN and Secretary-General Kofi Annan were awarded the Nobel Peace Prize for working toward a more peaceful world. It was a fitting tribute to the individual and the organization he served.

Peacekeeping Operations A mere fifty observers helped facilitate the Soviet Union's withdrawal from Afghanistan in 1988, while peacekeeping forces from 109 nations helped secure peace and independence for Namibia in 1989 by creating the conditions for elections and securing the repeal of discriminatory and restrictive legislation, the release of prisoners, and the return of exiles.

During the 1990s, the United Nations launched peacekeeping operations in Kosovo (Yugoslavia), Sierra Leone (West Africa), East Timor (formerly part of Indonesia), the Congo (Central Africa), and Ethiopia, Somalia, and Eritrea (the horn of Africa). In 1991, the UN fielded major peacekeeping operations in El Salvador and Cambodia. Such missions are never risk free, and they come with no guarantee of success. UN troops sent to Somalia in 1992 to facilitate the safe distribution of food to starving people were attacked by rebels who viewed the UN as a cat's paw for the West.

In 1993, the UN dispatched nearly 40,000 peacekeepers to the former Yugoslavia. The presence of this force, combined with NATO military support and UN-sponsored sanctions, induced Serbian President Slobodan Milosevic to negotiate in good faith and helped bring about the U.S.-brokered peace settlement known as the Dayton Accords in 1995. Later, after Milosevic was defeated in national elections and created a popular groundswell when he tried to cancel the results, the United Nations was instrumental in bringing the brutal former president and other accused war criminals in Yugoslavia to justice.

UN peacekeepers generally try to avoid combat but have suffered many casualties over the years, including some 2,591 fatalities (as of mid-2009) since 1948. In the half-century between 1948 and 1999, just over 1,600 UN military personnel were killed in action, compared to nearly 1,400 between 1999 and 2012. Among the 222,000 who died in the 2010 earthquake in Haiti were 102 UN peacekeepers.

Some UN peacekeeping operations have become permanent fixtures without leading to a final settlement—Kashmir, Cyprus, and Lebanon are prime examples. These missions stretch the UN budget to the breaking point, (see "Ideas and Politics: Peace on the Cheap"). Even so, the cost of UN peacekeeping is tiny measured against national defense budgets or the cost of a major war. The war in Iraq, for example, has cost the United States over $3 trillion, according to one authoritative estimate.[50] By comparison, the cost of a peacekeeping operation is a real bargain.

Collective Military Action In August 1990, when Iraq invaded Kuwait, the United Nations responded by authorizing collective military action. This use of

IDEAS AND POLITICS

PEACE ON THE CHEAP: Too Good to Be True?

According to the United Nations:

- UN peace operations are less expensive than other forms of international interventions, and costs are shared more equitably among UN member-states.

- A survey by Oxford University economists found that international military intervention under Chapter 7 of the UN Charter is the most cost-effective means of reducing the risk of conflict in post-conflict societies.

- The approved peacekeeping budget for the period from July 1, 2012, to June 30, 2013, was approximately US$7.23 billion. This represents about 0.5% of global military spending (estimated at US$1.6 trillion for 2010).

- A study by the U.S. Government Accounting Office estimated that it would cost the United States about twice as much as the UN to conduct a peacekeeping operation similar to the UN Stabilization Mission in Haiti (MINUSTAH)—$876 million

compared to the UN budgeted $428 million for the first fourteen months of the mission.

- In 2014, the number of refugees worldwide reached a record 59.5 million, some 8.3 million more than the previous year. Note: The United Nations High Commissioner for Refugees (UNHCR) heads the only international agency that keeps collects and publicizes this information; UNHCR provides relief aid to refugees wherever and whenever possible.

If the United Nations didn't exist, it is often said, it would have to be invented. Is this true? Think about it.

(Hint: Check on the year the UN was launched and consider the context; also, review the causes of war discussed earlier in this book and the types of conflicts that erupted repeatedly in the second half of the twentieth century.)

SOURCE: United Nations, "Peacekeeping Fact Sheet"; http://www.un.org/en/peacekeeping/resources/statistics/factsheet.shtml.

force recalled Woodrow Wilson's failed dream of collective security under the League of Nations flag and an early attempt at collective military action under the auspices of the UN.

In June 1950, when North Korea invaded South Korea, the United Nations, at the urging of the United States, responded with military force. As a permanent member of the Security Council, the Soviet Union was in a position to block this action. But the United States avoided a Soviet veto by taking the matter to the General Assembly (in the form of the "Uniting for Peace" resolution) where it enjoyed an automatic majority. Although the UN flag was raised, the Korean conflict was in truth a war fought by the United States against North Korea and, later, the People's Republic of China. The supreme commander, General Douglas MacArthur, was responsible to the president of the United States, not to the secretary-general of the United Nations.

Four decades later, in 1990-1991 when the United States (backed by the British) launched Operation Desert Storm against Iraq, the Security Council became a forum for the major powers to consult on how to respond to Iraqi aggression. The Council backed resolutions condemning Iraq, establishing tough economic sanctions, and ultimately approving the use of force to expel the Iraqi army from Kuwait. After the Gulf War's end, UN inspectors were allowed access to sites in Iraq suspected of hiding biological, chemical, or nuclear weapons.

The United Nations did not provide any forces of its own. The war was financed in large part by contributions from the richest U.S. allies, including Japan, Germany, Kuwait, and Saudi Arabia. The UN legitimized Desert Storm—nothing more, nothing less. In 2003, the United States invaded Iraq without the authorization of the Security Council and in the face of overwhelming opposition in the General Assembly.

The United Nations and the Iraq War In the fall of 2002, the UN Security Council passed Resolution 1441 requiring Iraq to disarm and allow weapons inspections or face "serious consequences." UN weapons inspectors subsequently found no weapons of mass destruction or weapons laboratories, but the Bush administration claimed to have evidence to the contrary.

The UN Security Council was strongly against an immediate invasion. In opposing a rush to war, France and Germany, longtime U.S. NATO allies, took the lead. Russia and China, both permanent members of the Security Council (like France), also demurred. U.S. polls showed that the public was ambivalent and self-contradictory: a majority favored U.S. action to oust Saddam from power, but an even larger majority agreed the UN Security Council "should make the final decision regarding the disarmament of Iraq"—if the United Nations did not approve the action, the United States should stay out.[51]

When Secretary of State Colin Powell's attempt to persuade the Security Council that Iraq possessed WMDs failed, President Bush decided to act without UN approval. Hawks suggested the United Nations was irrelevant or worse, and the United States was wise to ignore it.

The outcome of the invasion was never in doubt: the United States had overwhelming military superiority and was banking on a quick war with a happy

Ban Ki-moon of South Korea succeeded Kofi Annan as UN Secretary-General in 2007. He thus became the eighth man to be chosen as the UN's top official since 1946. No woman has ever served in this high-profile international role, but past secretaries-general have come from many different countries—Norway, Sweden, Burma, Austria, Peru, Egypt, and Ghana—reflecting the universalistic character and aspirations of the United Nations Charter.

ending—one that would rid the Iraqi people of a sadistic ruler and lead directly to a flourishing democracy. As we now know, the outcome of the occupation was quite a different matter.

Through the Looking-Glass As the history of the postwar world demonstrates, the UN has literally functioned as a life-saver in many conflict-ridden parts of the world. But despite its successes, the world organization has not lived up to all the soaring expectations of its founders, and some problems resemble those of the League, which could not be overcome.

To understand why, we have to peer through the looking-glass, to see what's behind the UN's frequent failure to act effectively to prevent a war or to broker a peace pact. Too often the Security Council is deadlocked; action can be thwarted by the veto of one member, or the General Assembly may fiddle while a village in Nigeria burns.

Procedural difficulties, however, are often rooted in deep-seated political differences. Critics call the UN irrelevant, ineffectual, or even a joke; in truth, the UN is a mirror of the human condition and a testament to the all-too-frequent triumph of emotion over reason in international politics.

THE QUEST FOR WORLD PEACE

No magic formula will resolve the problem of human conflict once and for all. The rule of law will not become the norm in international relations anytime soon, nor will reverence for human life or the sanctity of treaties render national armed forces obsolete.

Exhibit at Disneyland in Hong Kong.

International law and organizations can and do play a vital role in conflict management, but there is still no substitute for goodwill and enlightened leaders. Ending the Cold War rivalry was a significant step toward a safer and saner world, but perpetual peace is as elusive today as it was a century ago.

SUMMARY

The character of international politics differs significantly from that of domestic politics due to the absence of a world government capable of maintaining law and order. The struggle for power, inherent in the international system, is designed to advance national interests. Sovereign states choose a variety of ends, almost always overshadowed by one ultimate aim, to maximize power.

Modern European history saw the rise of the nation-state and the emergence of a multipolar world order sustained by a balance of power characterized by a relatively equal distribution of resources and capabilities among several major states. The traditional balance-of-power system that came into being in Europe in 1648 was limited in size and scope. All members shared certain common values and beliefs; Great Britain acted as keeper of the balance. The system worked because means and ends were limited, alliances were flexible, and crusading zeal was absent.

The demise of the old Eurocentric order following the two world wars fought in the first half of the twentieth century ushered in a bipolar system in the second half of the twentieth century in which two rival "superpowers" were preeminent. In the Cold War, the United States adopted a status quo policy of containment, aimed at preventing the Soviet Union from expanding or upsetting the global balance of power. A bipolar system replaced the old multipolar European system, with ideological differences and the specter of nuclear holocaust characterizing the bitter rivalry between the two superpowers. By the late 1960s, a strategic stalemate based on mutual deterrence made war between these two titans equally irrational for both.

With the disintegration of the Soviet Union and the end of the Cold War, a new international order emerged. Following a brief "unipolar moment" during which the United States was unrivalled as the sole remaining superpower, a new era of multipolarity rapidly emerged characterized by ever-greater interdependence in a dynamic global economy driven by the revolution in information technology; growing concentration of economic power in three regions, namely Europe (the twenty-eight-member EU), northwest Asia (China, Japan, and South Korea), and North America; a deteriorating global economy; the unmitigated danger of nuclear proliferation; climate change and a threatened global environment; and a leveling of the playing field as the share of U.S. GNP in the world economy shrinks.

The world has changed dramatically since the Cold War ended, but U.S. foreign policy has remained basically unchanged. In the Western Hemisphere, the Monroe Doctrine was designed to perpetuate the status quo; after World War II, containment in effect applied the same logic to the entire globe. On many occasions the United States intervened militarily to prevent leftist takeovers in Africa, Asia, and Latin America. Sometimes, these interventions caused "blowback"—self-induced policy problems arising from imprudent past actions—as happened in Vietnam. The Bush Doctrine, asserting a U.S. right to take preemptive measures whenever and wherever it deems necessary, provided the rationale for the U.S.-led invasions of Afghanistan and Iraq.

Political realists run the risk of underestimating the power of moral principles. Aggression is universally denounced in international politics but difficult to define. Neorealists stress the value "soft power"—power derived from goodwill and good works rather than from threats and the use of force. Critics of recent U.S. foreign policy urge a greater reliance on statecraft, or the skillful and prudent practice of diplomacy, as an alternative to overreliance on military force (or "hard power").

To what extent have international organizations and international law contributed to a more peaceful world? In the twentieth century, the League of Nations was torn apart by conflicting national interests. During the Cold War, from the early post–World War II period until the collapse of the Soviet Union in 1991, the United Nations encountered many obstacles, although it had modest success as a peacekeeping institution. Peacekeeping activity expanded in the post–Cold War era when the United Nations authorized collective military action in the Persian Gulf (Iraq), the Horn of Africa (Somalia), the Balkans (Bosnia and Kosovo), West Africa (Sierra Leone and Liberia), and Central Asia (Afghanistan), among others. However, the United Nations refused to back the U.S.-led invasion of Iraq in 2003.

International law facilitates and regulates relations among sovereign and independent states whose interactions might otherwise be chaotic. Examples of international law include the Geneva and Hague Conventions, which set rules for warfare, and the multilateral arms limitations treaties. International environmental agreements, such as the 1997 Kyoto Protocol, are becoming an increasingly important part of international law.

The limitations of international law are starkly apparent in the difficulties encountered by the World Court. The United Nations is similarly constrained by its inability to act against the wishes of the major powers, especially the five permanent members of the Security Council.

Conflict is endemic in the world, always has been and always will be. Apocalyptic visions of the future tend toward alarmism, exaggerating dangers, and focusing on disorder in the world while ignoring evidence of peace and progress.

"If the UN did not exist, it would have to be invented." What do you think?

KEY TERMS

equilibrium   529
balance-of-power
    system   529
Westphalian
    system   529
keeper of the
    balance   529

nationalistic
    universalism   531
Great Power   531
superpower   532
Cold War   532
bipolar system   532
containment   532

Warsaw Pact   532
zero-sum game   532
overkill   533
deterrence   534
deterrence theory   534
rational actor   534
globalization   535

REVIEW QUESTIONS

1. What does Thucydides' account of the confrontation between the Melians and the Athenians reveal about the nature of international politics?
2. What does a Machiavellian approach to politics entail? What sort of world-view does it embrace?
3. What is the meaning of the term *national interest?* How do political realists use this term?
4. What two basic foreign policy goals are available to nation-states?
5. What foreign policy strategies are open to nation-states? Do nation-states usually pursue one strategy at a time? Explain.
6. Explain the difference between "hard power" and "soft power."
7. What is the Bush Doctrine? When and how was it applied? Critique the doctrine and its application.
8. World War II changed the shape and form of the international system. When and how did the present international system come into being? Contrast the new world order with the old one.

WEBSITES AND READINGS

Websites

Author's Website: C:\Users\Tom Magstadt\Desktop\www.isn.ethz.ch http://www.isn.ethz.ch/

International Relations and Security Network: http://www.css.ethz.ch/index_EN

Stock International Peace Research Institute: http://www.sipri.org/

Facts on International Relations and Security Trends: http://www.sipri.org/databases/first

United Nations: http://www.un.org/en/

International Court of Justice: http://www.un.org/en/law/index.shtml

Readings

Bacevich, Andrew. *The Limits of Power: The End of American Exceptionalism.* New York: Holt, 2009. Tightly reasoned critique of the insular world of Washington politics and shop-till-you-drop American consumerism.

Carr, Edward Hallett. *The Twenty Years' Crisis, 1919–1939*. New York: Harper & Row, 1981. Classic study of the relationship between power and morality in international politics.

Cassese, Antonia. *International Law*. Oxford: Oxford University Press, 2005. A good introduction by the president of the International Criminal Tribunal for the Former Yugoslavia.

Claude, Inis L., Jr. *Swords into Plowshares: The Problems and Progress of International Organizations*, 6th ed. New York: McGraw-Hill, 1994. A classic introduction focusing on the theoretical and practical problems of the League of Nations and the United Nations.

Diehl, Paul F., and Brian Frederking. *The Politics of Global Governance: International Organizations in an Interdependent World*, 2nd ed., Boulder: Lynne Rienner, 2009. A useful and informative study of international organizations in the new world order of the early 21st Century.

Doyle, Michael, and Nicholas Sambanis. *Making War and Building Peace: United Nations Peace Keeping Operations*. Princeton, NJ: Princeton University Press, 2006. Compares the results of peace processes the UN was involved in following civil wars with ones it was not.

Hinsley, F. H. *Power and the Pursuit of Peace: Theory and Practice in the History of Relations Between States*. Cambridge: Cambridge University Press, 1967. A scholarly history of proposals and schemes for the international management of conflict from the Middle Ages to the modern age.

Kane, Thomas. *Theoretical Roots of U.S. Foreign Policy: Machiavelli and American Unilateralism*. Oxford and New York: Routledge, 2006. Argues that Machiavelli's political theory goes far toward explaining the historical development of U.S. foreign policy.

Kennan, George F. *American Diplomacy, 1900–1950*. Chicago: University of Chicago Press, 1985. An elegantly written interpretative history of U.S. foreign policy during the first half of the twentieth century.

Kennedy, Paul. *The Parliament of Man: The Past, Present, and Future of the United Nations*. New York: Random House, 2006. "[A] thorough and timely history of the United Nations that explains the institution's roots and functions."

Keohane, Robert O., and Joseph S. Nye. *Power and Interdependence: World Politics in Transition*, 4th ed. New York: Longman, 2011. A groundbreaking work that challenges the realist theory of international relations and attempts to construct an alternative theory based on the concept of interdependence.

Machiavelli, Niccolò. *The Prince*. New Haven, CT: Yale University Press, 1997. Required reading for students and practitioners of diplomacy for several centuries.

Magstadt, Thomas. *An Empire If You Can Keep It: Power and Purpose in American Foreign Policy*. Washington, DC: Congressional Quarterly Press, 2004. Examines present problems in the context of past experience, changing conditions, and enduring principles.

Mearsheimer, John. *The Tragedy of Great Power Politics*. New York: Norton, 2001. A thought-provoking theory of international politics; argues that nations act aggressively for perfectly logical reasons and will continue to do so as long as there is no hegemonic power to impose a draconian peace.

Morgenthau, Hans J. *Politics Among Nations: The Struggle for Power and Peace,* 5th ed. New York: McGraw-Hill, 1992. Sets forth the case for political realism in clear, compelling terms; one of the most famous academic works on world politics ever written; a classic.

Ross, Dennis. *Statecraft: And How to Restore America's Standing in the World.* New York: Farrar, Strauss, and Giroux. 2007. Insights from a seasoned observer and one-time chief U.S. peace negotiator in the Middle East.

Runciman, David. *Political Hypocrisy: The Mask of Power From Hobbes to Orwell and Beyond*. Princeton, NJ: Princeton University Press, 2009. Argues that hypocrisy ("hiding behind a mask") is a necessary and integral part of real politics.

Singer, Max, and Aaron Wildavsky. *The Real World Order: Zones of Peace / Zones of Turmoil*. Chatham, NJ: Chatham House, 1996. An original study of international relations in the post–Cold War era.

Thompson, Kenneth. *Morality and Foreign Policy*. Baton Rouge: Louisiana State University Press, 1980. An illuminating, humanistic look at the relationship between power and morality.

Traub, James. *Best Intentions: Kofi Annan and the UN in the Era of American World Power*. New York: Farrar, Straus, and Giroux, 2006. Kirkus Reviews: "A heartbreaking book about a hardworking idealist's frustrated attempts to restore the stature of the cumbersome United Nations in a world dominated by 'the preemptively belligerent America.'"

Waltz, Kenneth N. *Theory of International Politics*. New York: McGraw-Hill, 1979. Sets forth an interpretation of international relations known as neorealism.

Wolfers, Arnold. *Discord and Collaboration: Essays on International Politics*. Baltimore, MD: Johns Hopkins University Press, 1965. A superb compilation of scholarly essays dealing with key concepts and issues in international relations.

Zakaria, Fareed. *The Post-American World*. New York: W.W. Norton, 2009. Not about the decline of America but about "the rise of the rest . . . [and how it's] changing the way the world works."

Afterword:
The Power of Knowledge

Politics has been called the art of the possible. Experience tells us that banishing conflict in the world is a pipedream. Reducing the ignorance and injustice that are often among the chief causes of violence and venality, however, is an aim no less noble now than it was in Aristotle's day or during the Age of Enlightenment or in Philadelphia in 1787–88. The best hope for humanity in a troubled world is that today's students will never stop learning, will always remember that knowledge is power, and will use the power of knowledge to build a better world.

ENDNOTES

PREFACE

1. Alan Dunn, "Average America vs. the One Percent," *Forbes*, March 21, 2012.

CHAPTER 1

1. See Joseph Nye, *The Paradox of American Power: Why the World's Only Superpower Can't Go It Alone* (London: Oxford University Press, 2002). This quote is from Nye's article, "The New Rome Meets the New Barbarians," *The Economist*, March 23, 2002, p. 24.
2. Baron de Montesquieu's classification of political governments in Book II of *The Spirit of the Laws,* trans. Thomas Nugent (New York: Hafner Press, 1949), has proved most influential. Montesquieu distinguished among republics, monarchies, and despotic governments, further subdividing democratic republics, ruled by the whole people, from aristocratic republics, ruled by part of the people (specifically, by the wealthy class). Republics also have been historically distinguished from direct democracies. Thus, James Madison (perhaps the leading U.S. Founder) called governments in which the people directly participated in their own governing and did not rely on representation *direct democracies*. Because the U.S. government provides for representation, it is called a *republic*.
3. See, for example, Arthur Schlesinger Jr., *The Disuniting of America* (New York: Norton, 1993).
4. Aristotle, *The Politics,* trans. and ed. Ernest Barker (New York: Oxford University Press, 1962), p. 4.
5. Irving Kristol, "The Nature of Nazism," in *The Commentary Reader,* ed. Norman Podhoretz (New York: Atheneum, 1965), p. 16.
6. Hannah Arendt, *Eichmann in Jerusalem: A Report on the Banality of Evil* (New York: Penguin Books, 1964). Compare Gideon Hausner, *Justice in Jerusalem* (New York: Schocken Books, 1968), p. 465.
7. As opposed to Plato, who is sometimes classified as the first political philosopher.
8. Jack H. Nagel and John E. McNulty, "Partisan Effects of Voter Turnout in Senatorial and Gubernatorial Elections," *American Political Science Review* 90 (December 1996): 780–793.
9. See Leo Strauss, *What Is Political Philosophy? and Other Studies* (New York: Free Press, 1959), pp. 10–12.
10. There are variations to this approach; for instance, traditional realist theory has been updated (but not without controversy) by political scientists referred to as *neorealists* or *structural realists*. A leading work here is Kenneth Waltz, *Theory of International Politics* (Reading, MA: Addison-Wesley, 1979). Also see his "Realist Thought and Neo-Realist Theory," *Journal of International Affairs* 44 (Spring/Summer 1990): 21–37.
11. For a scholarly attempt to reconcile the two approaches, see Robert O. Keohane, *International Institutions and State Power* (Boulder, CO: Westview Press, 1989). Keohane's theory is sometimes referred to as *neoliberal institutionalism*.
12. See, Robert Guest, "The few" [A special report on global leaders], *The Economist*, January 22, 2011, pp. 3–20.

CHAPTER 2

1. Aristotle, *The Politics,* trans. and ed. Ernest Barker (New York: Oxford University Press, 1962), 1279a, p. 112.
2. This discussion builds on Andrew Heywood, *Political Ideologies: An Introduction* (New York: St. Martin's Press, 1992), pp. 6–8. Heywood's (and our) discussion, in turn, builds on a definition offered in May Selinger, *Politics and Ideology* (London: Allen & Unwin, 1976).
3. The Anti-Defamation League of B'nai B'rith, *Hate Groups in America: A Record of Bigotry and Violence* (New York, n.d.), p. 11.
4. See, for example, Dianae B. Henriques, "As Exemptions Grow, Religion Outweighs Regulation," *New York Times,* October 6, 2006 (electronic edition).
5. Jack C. Plano and Roy Olton, *The International Relations Dictionary* (Santa Barbara, CA: ABC, 1982), p. 81.
6. Bertrand Russell, *A History of Western Philosophy* (New York: Simon & Schuster, 1965), p. 364.
7. Martin Diamond, Winston Fisk, and Herbert Garfinkel, *The Democratic Republic: An Introduction to American Government* (Skokie, IL: Rand McNally, 1971), pp. 4–5.
8. Baron de Montesquieu, *The Spirit of the Laws,* trans. Thomas Nugent (New York: Hafner Press, 1949), bk. 5, chap. 6, p. 46.
9. Adam Smith, *An Inquiry into the Nature and Causes of the Wealth of Nations* (New York: Modern Library, 1965), p. 14.
10. As is pointed out in Robert Heilbroner, *The Worldly Philosophers: The Lives, Times, and Ideas of the Great Economic Thinkers* (New York: Modern Library, 1965), p. 14.
11. See "A Heavyweight Champ, at Five Foot Two," *The Economist*, November 25, 2006, p. 29.
12. John Stuart Mill, *On Liberty* (Lake Bluff, IL: Regnery/Gateway, 1955), p. 85.
13. Fareed Zakaria, posted June 16, 2011, http://fareedzakaria.com/2011/06/16/how-todays-conservatism-lost-touch-with-reality/.

14. James Davison Hunter, *Culture Wars: The Struggle to Define America* (New York: Basic Books, 1991). The discussion here generally follows, but does not duplicate, Hunter's. See also John Kenneth White, *The Values Divide: American Politics and Culture in Transition* (New York: Chatham House, 2003).
15. Hunter, *Culture Wars*. As Hunter makes clear, members of the same faith often strongly disagree on these issues.
16. See, for example, Marc Ambinder, "A Nation of Free Agents," *Washington Post,* September 3, 2006 (electronic edition): "Independent voters comprise about 10 percent of the electorate, but the percentage of persuadable independents has shot up to about 30 percent. In the 27 states that register voters by party, self-declared independents grew from 8 percent of the registered electorate in 1987 to 24 percent in 2004, according to political analyst Rhodes Cook. Consistently, about 30 percent of U.S. voters tell pollsters they don't belong to a party."

CHAPTER 3

1. See Leo Strauss, *What Is Political Philosophy? and Other Studies* (New York: Free Press, 1959), p. 10.
2. Allan Bloom, "Interpretive Essay," in *The Republic of Plato,* trans. Allan Bloom (New York: Basic Books, 1968), pp. 308–310.
3. Plato's ideal political order is most accurately translated as "city." The Greek word *polis* implies a small, self-sufficient community that provides for all human relationships. Modern distinctions between, for example, society and government or church and state are quite foreign to this concept.
4. Bloom, *The Republic of Plato* p. 410.
5. Ibid.
6. Howard White, *Peace Among the Willows: The Political Philosophy of Francis Bacon* (The Hague: Martinus Nijhoff, 1968), pp. 97, 102.
7. Karl Marx, "Capital: Selections," in *The Marx-Engels Reader,* ed. Robert C. Tucker (New York: Norton, 1972), p. 259.
8. Karl Marx and Friedrich Engels, "Manifesto of the Communist Party," in *The Marx-Engels Reader,* p. 352.
9. Friedrich Engels, "Socialism: Utopian and Scientific," in *The Marx-Engels Reader,* p. 635.
10. Karl Marx, "Outlines of a Future Society, from 'The Germany Ideology,'" in *Capital, Communist Manifesto, and Other Writings,* ed. Max Eastman (New York: Modern Library, 1932), p. 1.
11. Ibid.
12. Joseph Cropsey, "Karl Marx," in *History of Political Philosophy,* eds. Leo Strauss and Joseph Cropsey (Skokie, IL: Rand McNally, 1969), p. 717.
13. Jerome Gilison, *The Soviet Image of Utopia* (Baltimore, MD: Johns Hopkins University Press, 1975), p. 110.
14. Roy Macrides, *Contemporary Political Ideologies* (Cambridge, MA: Winthrop, 1980), p. 180.
15. B. F. Skinner, *Walden Two* (New York: Macmillan, 1962), p. 159.
16. Ibid., p. 161.
17. Ibid., pp. 104–105.
18. Ibid., p. 262.
19. Ibid., p. 193.
20. Ibid., p. 272.
21. Ibid., p. 295.
22. Josiah Warren, The Quarterly Letter: Devoted to Showing the Practical Applications and Progress of Equity, Vol. 1, No. 1 (October 1867) at http://www.crispinsartwell.com/warrennarrative.htm.
23. See also Christopher Hayes, *The Twilight of the Elites: America After Meritocracy* (New York: Crown Publishers, 2012). Hayes dates the "corruption and incompetence" of the meritocracy in politics, government, business, banking, and education, among other professions, to the 1960s and 1970s.
24. Andrew Marantz, "The Virologist," *The New Yorker*, January 5, 2015, p. 26.
25. Anthony Burgess, "The Clockwork Condition," *The New Yorker,* June 4 & 11, 2012, p. 70. The quote at the beginning of this section can be found on p. 74.
26. Ibid., pp. 69–76. The quotes in this paragraph and the next are on p. 71.
27. Ibid., p. 73.
28. Paul Berman, "Terror and Liberalism," *The American Prospect,* October 22, 2001.
29. See, for example, the writings of Daniel Pipes, especially *The Hidden Hand: Middle East Theories of Conspiracy* (New York: Free Press, 1997) and *Conspiracy: How the Paranoid Style Flourishes and Where It Comes From* (New York: Free Press, 1998); see also Fouad Ajami, *The Dream Palace of the Arabs: A Generation's Odyssey* (New York: Pantheon, 1998).

CHAPTER 4

1. See David Held, *Models of Democracy* (Stanford, CA: Polity and Stanford University Press, 1996) and David Held, *Democracy and the Global Order: From the Modern State to Cosmopolitan Governance* (Stanford, CA: Polity and Stanford University Press, 1995).

2. Richard S. Katz, "Models of Democracy: Elite Attitudes and the Democratic Deficit in the European Union." Unpublished paper presented at a meeting of the European Consortium of Political Research, Copenhagen, April 2000.

3. Alexander Hamilton, John Jay, and James Madison, *The Federalist* no. 31 (New York: Modern Library, 1964), p. 190.

4. Ibid., pp. 226–227.

5. Ibid., no. 49, p. 329.

6. Martin Diamond, Winston Fisk, and Herbert Garfinkel, *The Democratic Republic: An Introduction to American National Government* (Skokie, IL: Rand McNally, 1970), p. 136.

7. Stephen Cahn, *Education and the Democratic Ideal* (Chicago: Nelson-Hall, 1979), p. 3.

8. Alexis de Tocqueville, *Democracy in America,* Vol. 1 (New York: Schocken Books, 1961), pp. 299–300.

9. Ibid., p. 301.

10. Jay Hamilton and James Madison, *The Federalist,* no. 9, pp. 48–49.

11. Ibid., no. 10, p. 57.

12. Ibid., no. 51, p. 337.

13. Ibid.

14. Ibid.

15. Ibid., no. 6, p. 27.

16. Ibid., no. 51, p. 37.

17. G. Ross Stephens, "Federal Malignancies." Unpublished paper, March 15, 2009; see also Malcom M. Freeley and Edward Rubin, *Federalism: Political Identity and Tragic Compromise* (Ann Arbor, MI: University of Michigan Press, 2008); and David Cay Johnston, *Free Lunch* (New York: Portfolio, Penguin Books, Ltd., 2007).

18. However, federalism does not protect individuals from abuse by state or local government, which the African American experience in the Deep South well illustrates.

19. Diamond, Fisk, and Garfinkel, *The Democratic Republic,* p. 136.

20. Tocqueville, *Democracy in America,* pp. 304–398.

21. Aristotle, *The Politics,* trans. and ed. Ernest Barker (New York: Oxford University Press, 1962), 1287a, p. 146.

22. John Locke, *Second Treatise on Civil Government* (New York: New American Library, 1965), sec. 202, p. 448.

23. 8 Co. Rep. 114a (1610).

24. See *Youngstown Sheet and Tube Company v. Sawyer,* 343 U.S. 579 (1952), especially the concurring opinion of Justice Jackson.

25. William E. Hudson, *American Democracy in Peril: Eight Challenges to America's Future,* 4th ed. (Chatham, NJ: Chatham House, 2003).

26. Ibid., pp. 10–12.

27. David Held, *Democracy and the Global Order* (Stanford, CA: Stanford University Press, 1996).

CHAPTER 5

1. Bernard Crick, *Basic Forms of Government: A Sketch and a Model* (London: Macmillan, 1980), p. 53.

2. See Robert Kaplan, *The Coming Anarchy: Shattering the Dreams of the Post Cold War* (New York: Vintage Books, 2000), pp. 3–7. The article was later bundled with several other articles by the same author and reprinted in this highly readable little volume.

3. See the Transparency International website at http://www.transparency.org/country; click on Iraq and Afghanistan on the map.

4. Aristotle, *The Politics,* trans. and ed. Ernest Barker (New York: Oxford University Press, 1962), 1279a, p. 112.

5. China's success prompted India to try setting up its own version of SEZs. See, Bruce Einhorn, "India Struggles to Copy China's SEZs," Eye on Asia blog, *BusinessWeek,* posted October 9, 2006; http://www.businessweek.com/globalbiz/blog/eyeonasia/archives/2006/10/india_struggles.html. India announced its intent to create SEZs in 2000. For more information on SEZs in India go to http://www.sezindia.nic.in/index.asp.

6. A. Doak Barnett, "Ten Years After Mao," *Foreign Affairs* (Summer 1986), p. 38.

7. China's military spending grew from $30 billion in 2000 to $120 billion in 2010 according to SIPRI (a Stockholm-based research institute). Beijing announced a double-digit increase for 2012. See, for example, Edward Carr, "Brushwood and gall" (A special report on China's place in the world), *The Economist,* December 4, 2010; see also, "The dragon's teeth: A rare look inside the world's biggest military expansion," *The Economist,* April 7, 2012, pp. 27–32.

8. "Deng's China," *The Economist,* February 22, 1997, p. 21.

9. "Privatization in China," *The Economist,* September 23, 2011 (online edition), http://www.economist.com/node/21528262.

10. "Suddenly Vulnerable," *The Economist,* December 13, 2008, p. 15.

11. "China Learns the World's Rule," *The World in 2001* (London: The Economist Newspaper Limited, 2000), pp. 85–86.

12. P. Ferdinand, "Social Change and the Chinese Communist Party: Domestic Problems of Rule," *Journal of International Affairs* 49, no. 2 (Winter 1996): 478–483.

13. See, for example, "The dragon's teeth," pp. 27–32.

14. Speech by Secretary of Defense Robert Gates at the Air Force Association Convention, September 16, 2009; http://www.defense.gov/speeches/speech.aspx?speechid=1379. Gates repeated this warning in mid-January 2011 during an official visit to Japan. The speech was widely reported in the press.

15. Jane Perlez, "As Dispute Over Islands Escalats, Japan and China Send Fighter Jets to the Scene, *The New York Times*, January 19, 2013, p. A6..

16. "The Revolution is Over," *The Economist*, November 1, 2014. http://www.economist.com/news/leaders/21629338-changes-iran-make-nuclear-deal-more-likelynot-month-perhaps-eventually

17. "That's right Iceman, I am dangerous," *The Economist*, November 14, 2011, p. 53.

18. Aristotle, *The Politics*, 1313b, p. 245; see also, John Dunn, *Democracy: A History* (New York: Atlantic Monthly Press, 2006).

19. Maurice Latey, *Patterns of Tyranny* (New York: Atheneum, 1969), p. 115.

20. Fyodor Dostoyevsky, *The Brothers Karamazov*, ed. Ernest Rhys (London: Dent, 1927), p. 259.

21. Crick, *Basic Forms of Government*, p. 35.

22. See Karl Wittfogel, *Oriental Despotism: A Comparative Study of Total Power* (New York: Random House, 1981).

23. Crick, *Basic Forms of Government*, p. 36.

24. Samuel P. Huntington, "How Countries Democratize," *Political Science Quarterly* 106, no. 4 (1991-1992): 579.

25. Robert M. Press, "Africa's Struggle for Democracy," *Christian Science Monitor*, March 21, 1991, p. 4.

26. "Russia Deserves Pity as Well as Fear," *The Economist*, December 2, 2006, p. 15.

27. Huntington, "How Countries Democratize," p. 579.

28. Juan Forero, "Latin America Is Growing Impatient with Democracy," *New York Times*, June 24, 2004.

29. See, for example, Steven W. Hook and John Spanier, *American Foreign Policy Since World War II* (Washington, DC: CQ Press, 2004), especially chapter 4, "Developing Countries in the Crossfire," pp. 81–111; Chalmers Johnson, *Blowback* (New York: Henry Holt, 2000), especially chapters 3 and 4, pp. 65–118; Thomas M. Magstadt, *An Empire If You Can Keep It: Power and Principle in American Foreign Policy* (Washington: CQ Press, 2004), especially chapter 6.

30. Kaplan, *The Coming Anarchy*, p. 65.

31. Ibid., pp. 65–66.

CHAPTER 6

1. William Kornhauser, *The Politics of Mass Society* (New York: Free Press, 1959), p. 123.

2. C. W. Cassinelli, *Total Revolution: A Comparative Study of Germany Under Hitler, the Soviet Union Under Stalin, and China Under Mao* (Santa Barbara, CA: Clio Books, 1976), p. 225.

3. Leonard Shapiro, *Totalitarianism* (New York: Praeger, 1972), p. 104. Shapiro quotes scholar Hans Buchheim on this point.

4. Carl Friedrich and Zbigniew Brzezinski, *Totalitarian Dictatorship and Autocracy*, 2nd ed. (New York: Praeger, 1966).

5. Eric Hoffer, *The True Believer: Thoughts on the Nature of Mass Movements* (New York: Harper & Row, 1951), pp. 104–105

6. Friedrich and Brzezinski, *Totalitarian Dictatorship*, pp. 279–339.

7. Hoffer, *The True Believer*, p. 86.

8. Raul Hilberg, *The Destruction of the European Jews* (New York: Harper and Row, 1961), p. 12.

9. Cited in Cassinelli, *Total Revolution*, p. 16.

10. Adolph Hitler, speech in Munich, Germany, March 15, 1936.

11. Karl Dietrich Bracher, *The German Dictatorship* (New York: Holt, 1972), p. 181.

12. Adolf Hitler, *Mein Kampf*, trans. R. Manheim (Boston: Houghton Mifflin, 1971), pp. 179–180.

13. Ibid., p. 182.

14. Ibid.

15. Eugene Hadamovsky, *Propaganda und nationale Macht, 1933*, p. 22. Quoted in Hannah Arendt, *The Origins of Totalitarianism* (Cleveland: Meridian Books, 1961 edition), p. 341, n.1. (see footnote #1).

16. See Leo Strauss, *Thoughts on Machiavelli* (Seattle: University of Washington Press, 1968), p. 9.

17. Maurice Latey, *Patterns of Tyranny* (New York: Atheneum, 1969), p. 100.

18. Cassinelli, *Total Revolution*, p. 103.

19. Ibid., p. 186. Cassinelli's observation that Mao "never hesitated to destroy his enemies [including] rival communists, Kuomintang activists, and 'landlords'" can be applied to all successful totalitarian rulers.

20. Quoted in Bracher, *The German Dictatorship*, p. 257.

21. Ibid., p. 272.

22. W. S. Allen, *The Nazi Seizure of Power: The Experience of a Single German Town, 1930–1935* (Chicago: Quadrangle Books, 1965).

23. Peter Drucker, "The Monster and the Lamb," *Atlantic*, December 1978, p. 84.

24. Ibid.

25. Friedrich and Brzezinski, *Totalitarian Dictatorship*, p. 374.

26. Ibid., pp. 9–10.

27. Hannah Arendt, *The Origins of Totalitarianism* (Houghton Mifflin, 1973), Preface to Part III: Totalitarianism (online); http://www.barnesandnoble.com/w/origins-of-totalitarianism-hannah-arendt/1100278208?ean=9780547543154.

28. See Stalin, *Mastering Bolshevism*, p. 10; cited in Merle Fainsod, *How Russia Is Ruled*, rev. ed. (Cambridge, MA: Harvard University Press, 1964), p. 435.

29. Aleksandr Solzhenitsyn, *The Gulag Archipelago, 1918–1956* (New York: Harper & Row, 1974), p. 595.

30. Bracher, *The German Dictatorship*, p. 258.

31. Ibid., pp. 259–260.

32. Ibid., p. 262.

33. Ibid.

34. Hilberg, *The Destruction of the European Jews*, p. 31.

35. Mao Zedong, *Selected Works* (Beijing: Foreign Languages Press, 1960–1965), p. 224.

36. Franz Michaels and George Taylor, *The Far East in the Modern World* (New York: Holt, 1964), p. 479.

37. John King Fairbank, *The United States and China*, 4th ed. (Cambridge, MA: Harvard University Press, 1979), p. 409.

38. Ibid., p. 413.

39. Ibid.

40. Cassinelli, *Total Revolution*, p. 195.

41. Ibid., p. 243. Of course, figures vary widely. For example, using somewhat different criteria, Rummel postulated significantly different individual figures for Hitler, Lenin–Stalin, and Mao. Yet his total of almost 105.5 million people killed is remarkably close to Cassinelli's estimate. See R. J. Rummel, *Death by Government* (New Brunswick, NJ: Transaction, 1996), p. 8.

42. For instance, almost 1.5 million pages of formerly classified documents (German messages intercepted by Britain during World War II as well as newly released Russian documents) revealed that Hitler probably murdered closer to seven million Jews (as opposed to the five or six million, as Cassinelli and others had estimated).

43. Cassinelli, *Total Revolution*, p. 46. See also, Courtois, Stéphane, ed., *The Black Book of Communism: Crimes, Terror, Repression*, trans. Jonathan Murphy and Mark Kramer; consulting ed. Mark Kramer (Cambridge, MA: Harvard University Press, 1999); and Rummel, *Death by Government*.

44. Cassinelli, *Total Revolution*, p. 186. Since Cassinelli published his book, new evidence indicates that these figures vastly understated the actual number of deaths during this period. According to one authority, a three-year famine between 1959 and 1962 *alone* caused at least thirty million Chinese deaths. The immediate cause of the famine was Mao's policy of taking property from Chinese peasants and relocating those peasants in communes. See Jasper Becker, *Hungry Ghosts: Mao's Secret Famine* (New York: Free Press, 1997).

45. Cassinelli, *Total Revolution*, p. 187.

46. Ibid.

47. See Thomas M. Magstadt, "Bleeding Cambodia: The Great Leap Downward," *Reason*, July 1982, pp. 45–50; and "Marxism, Moral Responsibility, and the Cambodian Revolution," *National Review*, July 24, 1981, pp. 831–836.

48. See Thomas M. Magstadt, "Ethiopia's Great Terror," *Worldview*, April 1982, pp. 5–6.

49. "Iran to offer West nuke package soon," *China Daily* (online), April 16, 2009; http://www.chinadaily.net/cndy/2009-04/16/content_7681807.htm.

50. Laqueur applied this concept to the Soviet Union, particularly in his chapter on totalitarianism. See Walter Laqueur, *The Dream That Failed, Reflections on the Soviet Union* (New York: Oxford University Press, 1994), pp. 77–95, 84.

CHAPTER 7

1. Aristotle, *The Politics*, Book 4, trans. and ed. Ernest Barker (New York: Oxford University Press, 1962, 1276b, pp. 101–102; see also, Benjamin Jowett's translation, especially the first three paragraphs in Book 4 (online); http://www.constitution.org/ari/polit_00.htm.

2. The Life Peerage Act of 1958 enables the monarch, upon the advice of the prime minister, to confer nontransferable titles for life on commoners. The rationale for the legislation was to ensure party balance and to increase the number of working members in the House of Lords. Approximately one-quarter of all Lords (and a higher percentage of working members of the House of Lords) are appointed in this way.

3. "Lording it: Britain's Parliament is deadlocked over House of Lords reform. Let the people decide," *The Economist*," July 14, 2012, pp. 10–11.

4. Sydney Bailey, *British Parliamentary Democracy*, 3rd ed. (Westport, CT: Greenwood, 1978), pp. 130–131.

5. Suzanne Berger, *The French Political System*, 3rd ed. (New York: Random House, 1974), p. 368. Berger quotes then Prime Minister (later President) Georges Pompidou in 1964 commenting on the Fifth Republic's institutional balancing act: "France has now chosen a system midway between the American presidential regime and the British parliamentary regime, where the chief of state, who formulates general policy, has the basis of authority in universal suffrage but can

only exercise his functions with a government that he may have chosen and named, but which in order to survive, must maintain the confidence of the Assembly."

6. "Left Bankers: A Socialist landslide, but trouble looms ahead," *The Economist,* June 23, 2012, pp. 56–57.
7. Roy Macridis, ed., *Modern Political Systems: Europe,* 6th ed. (Englewood Cliffs, NJ: Prentice-Hall, 1986), p. 120.
8. Karl Dietrich Bracher, *The German Dictatorship* (New York: Holt, 1970), p. 120.
9. See Thomas M. Magstadt, "Ethics and Emigration: The East German Exodus, 1989," *Carnegie Council on Ethics and International Affairs—Case Studies in Ethics and International Affairs,* No. 6, 1990.
10. Guido Goldman, *The German Political System* (New York: Random House, 1974), p. 56.
11. See John W. Dower, *Embracing Defeat: Japan in the Wake of World War II* (New York: Norton, 2000).
12. See Herbert P. Bix, *Hirohito and the Making of Modern Japan* (New York: HarperCollins, 2000).
13. Franz Michael and George Taylor, *The Far East in the Modern World* (New York: Holt, 1964), p. 263.
14. Ibid, p. 607.
15. Nobutaki Ike, *Japanese Politics: Patron-Client Democracy,* 2nd ed. (New York: Knopf, 1972), p. 17.
16. Michael and Taylor, *The Far East in the Modern World,* p. 603.
17. "India Overheats," *The Economist,* February 3, 2007, p. 11.
18. "Good News: Don't Waste," *The Economist,* May 23, 2009, p. 13.
19. Jodi Roduren, "Tepid Vote for Netanyahu in Israel Is Seen as Rebuke," *The New York Times,* January 22, 2013.
20. Bailey, *British Parliamentary Democracy,* p. 130.
21. *Marbury v. Madison,* 5 U.S. (1 Cranch) 137 (1803).
22. Edward Courtier, *Principles of Politics and Government* (Boston: Allyn & Bacon, 1981), p. 84.
23. See, for example, Norman J. Ornstein and Thomas E. Mann, "When Congress Checks Out," *Foreign Affairs,* November/December 2006, pp. 67–82; see also Norman Ornstein and Thomas Mann, *The Broken Branch: How Congress Is Failing America and How to Get It Back on Track* (New York: Oxford University Press, 2006). The authors take Congress to task for failing to exercise oversight from 2000 to 2006—that is, during most of George W. Bush's tenure in the White House. In the 2006 midterm elections, the Democrats regained control of both the House of Representatives and the Senate but failed to win a large enough majority in the Senate to break a filibuster. (It takes sixty votes to pass a cloture motion to end debate.)

CHAPTER 8

1. Thomas M. Magstadt, *Nations and Governments: Comparative Politics in Regional Perspective,* 5th ed. (Belmont, CA: Wadsworth/Cengage Learning, 2005), pp. 226–238.
2. Susan Dentzer, Jeff Trimble, and Bruce Auster, "The Soviet Economy in Shambles," *US News & World Report,* November 20, 1989, pp. 25–26.
3. Hedrick Smith, *The Russians* (New York: Times Books, 1983), p. 83.
4. Dentzer, et al., "The Soviet Economy in Shambles," pp. 25–29, 32, 35–37, 39.
5. Walter Laqueur, *The Dream That Failed* (New York: Oxford University Press, 1994), pp. 71–73.
6. See Milovan Djilas, *The New Class* (New York: Praeger, 1957); and Smith, *The Russians,* pp. 30–67.
7. "Russia," *World Factbook* (Washington, DC: Central Intelligence Agency, 1996), p. 6 (electronic edition).
8. "Emerging Market Indicators," *The Economist,* March 15, 1997, p. 108.
9. "Emerging Market Indicators," *The Economist,* February 10, 2007, p. 105.
10. See Marshall Goldman, *Petrostate: Putin, Power, and the New Russia* (New York: Oxford University Press, 2008). See also Jason Bush, "Is Russia Blowing Its Oil Bonanza?" *Business Week Online,* October 5, 2005, http://www.businessweek.com/bwdaily/dnflash/oct2005/nf2005105_1326_db089.htm.
11. Vera Tolz, "Thorny Road Toward Federalism in Russia," *Radio Free Europe/Radio Liberty Research Report* 48 (December 1993), p. 1.
12. Claire Sterling, "Redfellas: The Growing Power of Russia's Mob," *The New Republic,* April 11, 1994, p. 19.
13. Xan Smiley, "Russia Wobbles Ahead," *The World in 1997* (an annual publication of *The Economist),* December 31, 1996, p. 39.
14. See, for example, Masha Lipman, "The Third Wave of Russian De-Stalinization," *Foreign Policy* (electronic edition), December 16, 2010. The author asks: "Is the Kremlin finally coming to terms with its dark history?"
15. Ibid. In 1940 on the eve of World War II, Stalin ordered the massacre of 22,000 Poles, including 4,500 Polish officers, by the soviet secret police in the Katyn Forest near the Russian city of Smolensk. The official Soviet history blamed the atrocity on Germany under Nazi rule. Finally, in 2010, almost two decades after the collapse of the Soviet Union, the Russian government admitted the shattering truth about a horrific crime that happened eighty years ago. The admission came in the form of a formal statement issued by the Russian parliament: "The Katyn crime was committed on direct order by Stalin and other Soviet leaders."
16. Neil MacFarquhar and Andrew E. Kramer, "With Russia on Brink of Recession, Russia Faces 'New Reality'," *New York Times,* December 2, 2014.

17. Peter Savodnik, "Skolkovo, Russia's Would-Be Silicon Valley," *Businessweek*, September 1, 2011 (online edition); see also, "Can Russia create a new Silicon Valley?" *The Economist*, July 14, 2012, p. 58.
18. See Luke Harding, *Mafia State: How One Reporter Became the Enemy of the Brutal New Russia* (United Kingdom: Guardian Press, 2012). The book received mixed reviews, but the author's account of the systematic harassment and obstructionism he encountered in his job as Moscow correspondent for a British newspaper (*The Guardian*) is a tale that in its broad outlines rings true.
19. See Matthew Valencia, "Limping Towards Normality: A Survey of Poland," *The Economist*, October 27, 2001, pp. 3–16.
20. Dilma Rousseff, "The Brazilian Model," *The World in 2012* (an annual publication of *The Economist*), December 31, 2011, p. 60.
21. "After Brazil's Election: Diehard Dilma," *The Economist*, November 1, 2014. http://www.economist.com/news/leaders/21629384-after-her-narrow-victory-divided-country-president-must-heed-opponents-well.
22. The term is taken from the title of Alan Riding's much-acclaimed book, *Distant Neighbors: A Portrait of the Mexicans* (New York: Alfred A. Knopf, 1984).
23. "Putting the Brakes on Change," *The Economist*, July 12, 2003, p. 32.

CHAPTER 9

1. Michael Perry, "Malaria and dengue: The sting in climate change," Reuters, November 20, 2008; http://www.reuters.com/article/environmentNews/idUSTRE4AJ2RQ20081120.
2. John Allen, *Student Atlas of World Politics* (Guilford, CT: Dushkin, 1994), p. 16. Thailand was then called Siam, and Iran was named Persia.
3. Ibid, p. 17. However, given the fluidity of contemporary politics, especially in former Yugoslavia, this number is highly unstable.
4. As pointed out by Robert Clark, *Power and Policy in the Third World*, 4th ed. (New York: Macmillan, 1991), p. 26.
5. See Jared Diamond, *Guns, Germs, and Steel: The Fate of Human Societies* (New York: Norton, 1997).
6. Robert D. Kaplan, *The Coming Anarchy* (New York: Vintage Books, 2001), pp. 3–59.
7. These points are generally emphasized in the literature. See James A. Bill and Robert L. Hardgrave Jr., *Comparative Politics: The Quest for Theory* (Websterville, OH: Merrill, 1973), pp. 70–71.
8. For instance, see Seymour Lipset, *Political Man: The Social Bases of Democracy* (Garden City, NY: Doubleday, 1983); Tatu Vanhanen, *The Process of Democratization: A Comparative Study of 147 States, 1980–1988* (Bristol, UK: Taylor & Francis, 1990); and Samuel P. Huntington, "Will More Countries Become Democratic?" *Political Science Quarterly* 99 (1984): 193–218. See also Thomas Scanton, "Democracy's Fragile Flower Spreads Its Roots," *Time*, July 13, 1987, pp. 10–11. An optimistic outlook for democracy, based on such correlates, is offered by Carl Gershman, "Democracy as the Wave of the Future: A World Revolution," *Current* (May 1989), pp. 18–23.
9. Gershman, "Democracy as the Wave of the Future," p. 23.
10. Vanhanen, *The Process of Democratization*, pp. 51–65.
11. See, for example, Justin Yifu Lin, Fang Cai, and Zhou Li, *The China Miracle: Development Strategy and Economic Reform* (Hong Kong: The Chinese University Press, 2003); see also Gregory Chow, *China's Economic Transformation*, 2nd ed. (Malden, MA Blackwell, 2007).
12. Kaplan, *The Coming Anarchy*, pp. 59–98.
13. Samuel Huntington, "How Countries Democratize," *Political Science Quarterly* 106 (1991-1992): 579.
14. See, for example, Robert M. Press, "Africa's Struggle for Democracy," *Christian Science Monitor*, March 21, 1991, p. 4; and Kenneth B. Noble, "Despots Dwindle as Reform Alters Face of Africa," *New York Times*, April 13, 1991, p. 1.
15. Thomas R. Lansner, "Out of Africa," *Wall Street Journal*, December 10, 1996, p. A18.
16. Huntington, "How Countries Democratize," p. 12.
17. Jean Herskovits, "Nigeria: Power and Democracy in Africa," *Headline Series* 527 (January–February 1982): 8.
18. "Transparency International, Berlin." Reprinted from the *Wall Street Journal*, January 2, 1997, sec. 1, p. 5.
19. Lydia Polgreen, "As Nigeria Tries to Fight Graft, A New Sordid Tale," *New York Times*, November 29, 2005 (electronic edition).
20. See, for example, "Big Men, Big Fraud, and Big Trouble," *The Economist*, April 28, 2007, pp. 55–58.
21. "A Nation Divided," *The Economist*, October 25, 2014.
22. Simon Long, "India's Shining Hopes (A Survey of India)," *The Economist*, February 21, 2004, p. 3.
23. "Suddenly Vulnerable," *The Economist*, December 13, 2008, p. 15.
24. World Bank, "India Overview—2014" (online), http://www.worldbank.org/en/country/india/overview.
25. Ibid.
26. Vyvyan Tenorio, "Sri Lanka Peace Process at Delicate Point," *Christian Science Monitor*, September 2, 1986, p. 11.
27. Robert E. Gamer, *Developing Nations: A Comparative Perspective*, 2nd ed. (Dubuque, IA: William C. Brown, 1982), pp. 312–314.
28. See "2013 World Hunger and Poverty Facts and Statistics," World Hunger Education Service, Washington, DC (online), http://www.worldhunger.org/index.html.

29. See, for example, Daniel Pepper, "The Toxic Consequences of the Green Revolution," *US News and World Report*, July 7, 2008 (online edition), http://www.usnews.com/articles/news/world/2008/07/07/the-toxic-consequences-of-the-green-revolution.html.

30. Samuel Huntington, *Political Order in Changing Societies* (New Haven, CT: Yale University Press, 1968), p. 35.

31. See P. W. Singer, *Children at War* (Berkeley: University of California Press, 2006); see also Michael Wessells, *Child Soldiers: From Violence to Protection* (Cambridge, MA: Harvard University Press, 2006). On the use of girls as sex slaves, see, for example, Hannah Strange, "Wounds of sex slaves in Sierra Leone's civil war are a long time healing," *Times Online*, April 30, 2008, http://www.timesonline.co.uk/tol/news/world/africa/article3848621.ece.

32. Jean-Jacques Rousseau, "The First Discourse," in *The First and Second Discourses,* ed. Roger D. Masters (New York: St. Martin's Press, 1964), p. 39.

CHAPTER 10

1. Aristotle, *The Politics,* trans. and ed. Ernest Barker (New York: Oxford University Press, 1962), 1276b, pp. 101–102.

2. Scott Shane, "Waterboarding Used 266 Times on Two Suspects," *New York Times*, April 19, 2009 (electronic edition).

3. Aristotle, *The Politics,* 1274b, p. 93.

4. Immanuel Kant, *The Science of Right,* Vol. 42 (Chicago: Encyclopaedia Britannica, 1952), p. 436.

5. Daniel J. Elazar, *American Federalism: A View from the States,* 3rd ed. (New York: Crowell, 1984). Elazar, a noted expert on U.S. federalism and intergovernmental relations, argued that there are three distinct political cultures in the United States—individualistic, moralistic, and traditionalistic. It is debatable, however, whether these are separate political cultures or merely different aspects of one political culture.

6. John Stuart Mill, *A System of Logic, Ratiocinative and Deductive,* Vol. 2 (London: Longmans, Green, 1879), p. 518.

7. The modern study of political socialization is closely tied to the Greek concern for character formation. One key difference between the two is that whereas behavioral political science focuses primarily on the process by which political opinions are formed, the Greek emphasis is on the traits of character that all good citizens should display.

8. Barbara Defoe Whitehead provided persuasive evidence in "Dan Quayle Was Right," *Atlantic* (April 1993), p. 41. However, single-parent families are only one source of why some families fail. Note James Q. Wilson's comment that one way "the family has become weaker is that more and more children are being raised in one-parent families, and often that one parent is a teenage girl. Another way is that parents, whether in one- or two-parent families, are spending less time with their children and are providing poorer discipline." For a thoughtful review of two-parent families, in light of the academic debate on the subject, see James Q. Wilson, "The Family-Values Debate," *Commentary* 95 (April 1993): 24–31. The quotation is from page 24.

9. See James Q. Wilson, *The Moral Sense* (New York: Free Press, 1995), pp. 141–163.

10. Herbert Winter and Thomas Bellows, *People and Politics* (New York: Wiley, 1977), p. 120.

11. Harry Holloway and John George, *Public Opinion,* 2nd ed. (New York: St. Martin's Press, 1985), pp. 73–77.

12. Dean Jaros, *Socialization to Politics* (New York: Praeger, 1973), pp. 87–88.

13. See M. Margaret Conway and Frank Fergert, *Political Analysis: An Introduction* (Boston: Allyn & Bacon, 1972), p. 106.

14. Holloway and George, *Public Opinion,* p. 79.

15. See M. Kent Jennings, "Preface"; Henry Kenst, "The Gender Factor in a Changing Electorate"; and Arthur Miller, "Gender and the Vote," in *The Politics of the Gender Gap: The Social Construction of Political Influence,* ed. Carol Mueller (Newbury Park, CA: Sage, 1987). Much of the political literature advocating natural differences between the sexes presumes the existence of scholarship in the field of developmental psychology; see Carol Gilligan, *In a Different Voice* (Cambridge, MA: Harvard University Press, 1982); and M. Belenky, B. Clinchy, W. Goldberger, and J. Tarule, *Women's Ways of Knowing: The Development of Self, Voice, and Mind* (New York: Basic Books, 1986).

16. Michael Barone and Grant Ujifusa, *The Almanac of American Politics* (Washington, DC: National Journal, 1994), p. xxvii.

17. Ralph Buultjens, "India: Religion, Political Legitimacy, and the Secular State," *Annals of Political and Social Sciences* 483 (January 1986): 107.

18. James Billington, "The Case for Orthodoxy," *New Republic*, May 30, 1994, p. 26.

19. A. James Reichley, *Religion in American Public Life* (Washington, DC: Brookings Institution, 1985), p. 2.

20. See, for example, Laurie Goodstein, "More Atheists Shout It From the Rooftops," *New York Times*, April 26, 2009 (electronic edition).

21. This is not to deny, of course, that unscrupulous leaders can exploit religion for ignoble purposes.

22. This discussion builds on William Flanigan and Nancy Zingale, *Political Behavior of the American Electorate* (Boston: Allyn & Bacon, 1979), pp.184–187.

23. Kenneth Langton and M. Kent Jennings, "Political Socialization and the High School Civics Curriculum," *American Political Science Review* (September 1968): 851.

24. Conway and Fergert, *Political Analysis,* p. 110. Also see Judith Torney-Purta, "From Attitudes and Knowledge to Schemata: Expanding the Outcomes at Political Socialization Research," in *Political Socialization, Citizenship Education, and Democracy,* ed. Orit Ichilov (New York: Teachers College Press, 1990), p. 99.

25. Or so it would seem. But it is important to determine not only what is studied but also how it is studied. See Albert Speer's comments on German education in Albert Speer, *Inside the Third Reich*, trans. R. Winston and C. Winston (New York: Avon, 1971), p. 35.

26. Robert Erikson, Norman Luttbeg, and Kent Tedin, *American Public Opinion* (New York: Macmillan, 1991), p. 113.

27. Ibid., p. 7.

28. This is commonly recognized. See James MacGregor Burns, J. W. Peltason, Thomas E. Cronin, and David B. Magleby, *Government by the People*, 17th ed. (Upper Saddle River, NJ: Prentice Hall, 1998), p. 293.

29. Ibid., pp. 49–50.

30. James Q. Wilson and Richard Hernstein, *Crime and Human Nature* (New York: Simon & Schuster, 1985), p. 293.

31. See "Radio's Future II: The 2010 American Youth Study," Edison Research (online),http://www.edisonresearch.com/Edison_Research_American_Youth_Study_Radios_Future.pdf.

32. Donna Abu-Nasr, "The Beauty Isn't Skin Deep," *Kansas City Star,* May 7, 2009, p. A18.

33. This section builds on the analysis offered in Montague Kern, *Thirty-Second Politics: Political Advertising in the Eighties* (New York: Praeger, 1989).

34. Thomas E. Patterson, *Out of Order* (New York: Vintage, 1994), p. 25.

35. Daniel Hallin's study is cited as part of a wider discussion of the issue in Samuel Popkin, *The Reasoning Voter: Communication and Persuasion in Presidential Campaigns* (Chicago: University of Chicago Press, 1991), pp. 228–229.

36. University Wisconsin news release, November 21, 2006 (online), http://www.news.wisc.edu/releases/13213.

37. See, for example, Al Franken, *Lies and the Lying Liars Who Tell Them: A Fair and Balanced Look at the Right* (New York: Dutton, 2003). Franken is an unabashed liberal who gained fame as a comic writer on *Saturday Night Live* but has since turned to political satire and is endeavoring to create a new liberal radio network to combat what he believes to be a strong right-wing slant in the corporate-controlled mass media. In 2008, he ran for the United States Senate in Minnesota, won by a few hundred votes, but found himself in a legal battle with the incumbent, Norm Colman, who contested the results in the courts.

38. M. Margaret Conway, *Political Participation in the United States* (Washington, DC: C.Q. Press, 1987), pp. 52–53.

39. Hence, the author of one classic behavioral study long ago concluded, "The principles of freedom and democracy are less widely and enthusiastically favored when they are confronted in their specific or applied forms." See Herbert McCloskey, "Consensus and Ideology in American Democracy," *American Political Science Review* 58 (June 1964): 361–384.

40. Donald Devine, *The Political Culture of the United States* (Boston: Little, Brown, 1972), pp. 187–230. Also see Seymour Martin Lipset, *American Exceptionalism: A Double-Edged Sword* (New York: Norton, 1996) for an extensive discussion of the values that make up the American creed.

CHAPTER 11

1. Howard Schuman and Stanley Presser, *Questions and Answers in Attitude Surveys* (Orlando, FL: Academic Press, 1981), pp. 70–71. This study is illustrated in James Q. Wilson, *American Government*, 4th ed. (Lexington, MA: Heath, 1989), p. 99.

2. See, for example, John L. Fund, "The Perils of Polling," *Wall Street Journal*, August 13, 1996, p. A12; for a commentary on the polls in the 1996 presidential election (Clinton versus Dole), see Everett Carll Ladd, "The Pollsters' Waterloo," *Wall Street Journal*, November 19, 1997, p. A22.

3. Costas Panagopoulos, "Poll Accuracy in the 2008 Presidential Election," November 5, 2008 (online).

4. One study found that almost two-thirds of the promises made in major-party platforms were kept; see Gerald M. Pomper with Susan Lederman, *Elections in America: Control and Influence in Democratic Politics,* 2nd ed. (New York: Dodd, Mead, 1980), p. 161.

5. See Thomas Cronin, *Direct Democracy: The Politics of Initiative, Referendum, and Recall* (Cambridge, MA: Harvard University Press, 1990).

6. Ibid., p. 87.

7. The fact that voters in many democracies do not need to register is often cited as a reason their participation rate is higher. In several democracies (including Australia and Belgium), citizens who do not vote are subject to a fine.

8. Harry Holloway and John George, *Public Opinion: Coalitions, Elites, and Masses,* 2nd ed. (New York: St. Martin's Press, 1986), p. 161.

9. Ibid., pp. 162–163.

10. See Julian L. Woodward and Elmo Roper, "Political Activity of American Citizens," *American Political Science Review* 44 (1950): 822–885.

11. Sidney Verba and Norman Nie, *Participation in America* (New York: Harper & Row, 1972), pp. 79–80.

12. Mark Hugo Lopez, "*Dissecting the 2008 Electorate: Most Diverse in U.S. History*," Pew Research Center, April 30, 2009 (online), http://pewresearch.org/pubs/1209/racial-ethnic-voters-presidential-election on May 2, 2009.

13. Scott Keeter, Juliana Horowitz, and Alex Tyson, *Young Voters in the 2008 Election*, Pew Research Center, November 12, 2008 (online), http://pewresearch.org/pubs/1031/young-voters-in-the-2008-election on May 2, 2009.

14. Students interested in learning more about the changing patterns of wealth and income distribution in America are encouraged to read Daniel Cay Johnston, *Perfectly Legal: The Secret Campaign to Rig Our Tax System to Benefit the Super Rich—And Cheat Everybody Else* (New York: Portfolio, 2003); Joseph E. Stiglitz, *The Roaring Nineties: A New History of the World's Most Prosperous Decade* (New York: Norton, 2003); and Paul Krugman, *The Great Unraveling: Losing Our Way in the New Century* (New York: Norton, 2003), among other recent books on this topic.

15. Alexis de Tocqueville, *Democracy in America,* Vol. 2 (New York: Schocken Books, 1961), p. 18.

16. Ibid., pp. 153, 159.

17. Robert D. Putnam, "Bowling Alone: America's Declining Social Capital," *Journal of Democracy* (January 1995): 65–78.

18. Richard Morin, "Who's in Control? Many Don't Know or Care," *Washington Post,* January 29, 1996, p. A6. The article cited a Harvard University-Washington, D.C. poll.

19. Ibid.

20. Wilson, *American Government,* p. 100.

21. Richard Niemi and Herbert Weisberg, *Controversies in Voting Behavior,* 3rd ed. (Washington, DC: C.Q. Press, 1992), p. 103.

22. Samuel Popkin, *The Reasoning Voter and Persuasion in Presidential Campaigns* (Chicago: University of Chicago Press, 1991), pp. 212–216.

23. C. Wright Mills, *The Power Elite* (New York: Oxford University Press, 1956).

24. Thomas Dye and L. Harmon Ziegler, *The Irony of Democracy: An Uncommon Introduction to American Government,* 4th ed. (North Scituate, MA: Duxbury Press, 1978), p. 374.

25. Andrew Greeley, "Power Is Diffused Throughout Society," in *Taking Sides: Clashing Views on Controversial Political Issues,* eds. George McKenna and Stanley Feingad (Guilford, CT: Dushkin, 1983), p. 23. Also see Arnold Rose, *The Power Structure: Political Process in American Society* (London: Oxford University Press, 1967), pp. 483–493.

26. Thomas Jefferson to Francis Hopkinson, March 13, 1789, in *The Political Writings of Thomas Jefferson,* ed. Edward Dumbauld (Indianapolis: Bobbs-Merrill, 1955), p. 46.

27. Ibid.

28. See, for example, Thomas Magstadt, "This Corrupt(ed) Republic," *Reader Supported News,* September 13, 2012 (online), http://readersupportednews.org/pm-section/78-78/13459-this-corrupted-republic. This article also appeared in *Nation of Change,* August 31, 2012 (online), http://www.nationofchange.org/world-s-most-corrupted-republic-1346419376.

29. G. Ross Stephens, "Our Corrupt, Constitutionally Constipated Government," *Reader Supported News,* January 13, 2013 (online), http://readersupportednews.org/pm-section/26-26/15528-our-corrupt-constitutionally-constitated-government.

30. ""Paul Best, Kul Rai, and David Walsh, *Politics in Three Worlds: An Introduction to Political Science* (New York: Wiley, 1986), pp. 271–272.

31. Gabriel Almond and G. Bingham Powell, *Comparative Politics: A Developmental Approach* (Boston: Little, Brown, 1966), chapter. 4.

32. This discussion is indebted to William Keefe and Morris Ogul, *The American Legislative Process: Congress and the States,* 8th ed. (Englewood Cliffs, NJ: Prentice-Hall, 1992), p. 334.

33. Thomas DiLorenzo, "Who Really Speaks for the Elderly?" *Consumers' Research* 79 (September 1996), p. 15; and Charles Morris, *The AARP: America's Most Powerful Lobby and the Clash of Generations* (New York: Times Books, 1996), pp. 4, 10–11.

34. Jeffrey H. Birnbaum, "Overhaul of Lobbying Laws Unlikely to Succeed Thanks to Opposition of Lobbyists Themselves," *Wall Street Journal,* May 30, 1991, p. A20.

35. Jeffrey H. Birnbaum, "The Road to Riches," *Washington Post,* June 22, 2005 (online edition); see also Jonathan Rauch, "The Hyperpluralism Trap," *New Republic,* June 6, 1994, p. 22.

36. Birnbaum, "Overhaul of Lobbying Laws."

37. John Harwood, "Political Treadmill: For California Senator, Fundraising Becomes Overwhelming Burden," *Wall Street Journal,* March 2, 1994, p. A1. Feinstein's concerted effort to raise money was spurred by the fact that her 1992 election victory was for only a two-year term. Harwood estimated that her 1992 race and her failed 1990 gubernatorial race together cost about $30 million. Another example of spiraling election costs was the 1996 Virginia senatorial election, in which the loser, Mark Warner, spent $11 million (an expenditure of $3.30 per voter, compared with Huffington's $2.03 per voter).

38. Figures obtained from the CQ MoneyLine (formerly PoliticalMoneyLine), http://www.fecinfo.com.

39. See http://www.opensecrets.org/bigpicture/stats.asp.

40. See "Campaign Finance Reform," Pew Charitable Trusts (online), http://www.pewtrusts.com/ideas.

41. Claire Cain Miller, "How Obama's Campaign Changed Politics," *New York Times,* November 7, 2008 (electronic edition), http://bits.blogs.nytimes.com/2008/11/07/how-obamas-internet-campaign-changed-politics/.

42. Ibid.

43. See, for example, Johnston, *Perfectly Legal,* or Krugman, *Great Unraveling.*

CHAPTER 12

1. Robert C. Tucker, *Politics as Leadership* (Columbia: University of Missouri Press, 1995), p. iii.
2. Walter Lippmann, *A Preface to Morals* (Boston: Beacon Press, 1960), p. 280. The quotations that follow are from pp. 279–283.
3. See Harry Jaffa, "The Emancipation Proclamation," in *100 Years of Emancipation*, ed. Robert Goldwin (Skokie, IL: Rand McNally, 1964), pp. 1–24.
4. Douglass Adair, "Fame and the Founding Fathers," in *Fame and the Founding Fathers: Essays by Douglass Adair* (New York: Norton, 1974), p. 10.
5. Ibid., p. 8.
6. Alexander Hamilton, John Jay, and James Madison, *The Federalist* (New York: Modern Library, n.d.), p. 470.
7. Robert J. Alexander, *Rómulo Betancourt and the Transformation of Venezuela* (New Brunswick, NJ: Transaction Books, 1982), p. 435.
8. Ibid., p. 436.
9. Ibid.
10. John Edwin Fagg, *Latin America: A General History*, 2nd ed. (New York: Macmillan, 1969), p. 627.
11. Aaron Wildavsky, *The Nursing Father: Moses as a Political Leader* (Tuscaloosa: University of Alabama Press, 1984). The author makes the point that the mark of a model leader, like a model parent, is to make himself or herself dispensable. Children growing up need to learn how to get along without their parents; likewise, viable nation-states need to be able to survive a change of leadership.
12. Martin Gilbert, *Churchill* (Garden City, NY: Doubleday, 1980), pp. 100–126.
13. Ibid., p. 172.
14. U.S. Department of State, *Selected Documents*, April 1979.
15. Alexis de Tocqueville, *Democracy in America*, Vol. 2 (New York: Schocken Books, 1961), pp. 102–106.
16. Morton Frisch and Richard Stevens, "Introduction," in *American Political Thought: The Philosophic Dimension of American Statesmanship*, ed. Morton Frisch and Richard Stevens (Dubuque, IA: Kendall/Hunt, 1976), p. 5.
17. Quoted in Roman J. Zorn, "Theodore G. Bilbo: Shibboleths for Statesmanship," reprinted in *A Treasury of Southern Folklore: Stories, Ballads, Traditions, and Folkways of the People of the South*, ed. B. A. Brotkin (New York: Crown, 1949), p. 304.
18. James W. Silver, *Mississippi: The Closed Society* (Orlando, FL: Harcourt, 1964), p. 19.
19. Ibid.
20. Hodding Carter, "Huey Long: American Dictator," in *The Aspirin Age: 1919–1941*, ed. Isabel Leighton (New York: Simon & Schuster, 1949), p. 347.
21. Ibid., p. 361.
22. See, for example, Silla Brush, "A Vote of No-Confidence," *U.S. News and World Report*, October 22, 2006 (online edition).
23. Joseph Tussman, as quoted in Marie Collins Swaley, "A Quantitative View," in *Representation*, ed. Hannah Pitkin (New York: Atherton Press, 1969), p. 83.
24. Hannah Pitkin, "The Concept of Representation," in Pitkin, *Representation*, p. 21.
25. Quoted in Harvey Mansfield Jr., *Statesmanship and Party Government: A Study of Burke and Bolingbroke* (Chicago: University of Chicago Press, 1965), p. 23.
26. Edmund Burke, "The English Constitutional System," in Pitkin, *Representation*, p. 175.
27. Ibid.
28. Martin Luther King Jr., "Letter from Birmingham City Jail," in *Civil Disobedience: Theory and Practice* (New York: Pegasus, 1969), pp. 78–79.
29. Ibid., p. 75.
30. David J. Garrow, *Bearing the Cross: Martin Luther King, Jr., and the Southern Christian Leadership Conference, 1955–1968* (New York: Random House, 1988), p. 11.
31. Ibid., p. 12.
32. This famous Mandela quote is found many places in books, articles, and, of course, on the Internet. See, for example, http://prisonphotography.org/2013/12/05/mandelas-1985-refusal-of-release-from-prison/ and here http://news.bbc.co.uk/2/hi/special_report/1998/10/98/truth_and_reconciliation/202394.stm.
33. Margaret Coker, Nour Malas, and Marc Champion, "Google Executive Emerges as Key Figure in Revolt," *Wall Street Journal*, February 7, 2011 (online edition).

CHAPTER 13

1. Aristotle, *The Politics*, trans. and ed. Ernest Barker (New York: Oxford University Press, 1962), 1252b, p. 5.
2. The complete text of this speech can be found at http://www.yale.edu/ lawweb/avalon/presiden/speeches/eisenhower001.htm.

3. James Madison, "Political Observations," 1795. From *The Letters and Other Writings of James Madison* (online), http://www.informationclearinghouse.info/article18562.htm.

4. For a well-documented account of this little-noticed policy change, see P. W. Singer, *Corporate Warriors: The Rise of the Privatized Military Industry* (Ithaca, NY: Cornell University Press, 2003).

5. See, for example, Dean Baquet and Bill Keller, "When Do We Publish a Secret?" *New York Times*, July 1, 2006 (electronic edition) on the Bush administration's secret program to monitor international bank transactions; Peter Dale Scott, "Homeland Security Contracts for Vast New Detention Camps," *New America Media*, February 8, 2006 (online), http://news.newaniericamedia.org/news/; and Laurie Kellman, "Powell Endorses Efforts to Block Bush Terrorist Plan," Associated Press, September 14, 2006 (online), http://www.signonsandiego.com/news/politics/20060914-0755-bush-congress.html.

6. Daniel Patrick Moynihan, "Defining Deviance Down," *American Scholar* 62 (Winter 1993): 1.

7. Thomas Magstadt, "Who Shot the Sheriff: Guns, Governments, and the Rule of Law," Nation of Change, December 20, 2013 (online), http://www.nationofchange.org/who-shot-sheriff-guns-governments-and-rule-law-1387550505.

8. Center on Budget and Policy Priorities (online), http://www.cbpp.org/cms/?fa=view&id=1258; see also, Robert Pear, "Recession Drains Social Security and Medicare," *New York Times*, May 12, 2009 (electronic edition).

9. David M. Walker, "The Debt No One Wants to Talk About," *New York Times*, February 4, 2004 (online edition).

10. Dennis Cauchon, "What Is the Real Federal Deficit?" *USA Today*, August 2, 2006 (online), http://www.usatoday.com/news/ washington/2006-08-02-deficit-usat_x.htm; for a different view, see Center on Budget and Policy Priorities, "Understanding Social Security Trust Funds" (online), http://www.cbpp.org/cms/?fa=view&id=3299.

11. David Cay Johnston, *Perfectly Legal: The Covert Campaign to Rig Our Tax System to Benefit the Super Rich—And Cheat Everybody Else* (New York: Portfolio, 2003), p. 18.

12. Kerry Capell, "Is Europe's Health Care Better?" *Business Week*, June 13, 2007; see also Robert Pear, "Health Spending Rises to Record 15% of Economy, a Record Level," *New York Times*, January 9, 2004 (online edition). Pear writes, "In 2001, . . .—the last year for which comparative figures are available—health accounted for 10.9 percent of the gross domestic product in Switzerland, 10.7 percent in Germany, 9.7 percent in Canada, and 9.5 percent in France."

13. Government Accounting Office, "Climate Change: Trends in Greenhouse Gas Emissions," submitted to the Senate Committee on Commerce, Science, and Transportation by John B. Stephenson, director, Natural Resources and Environment, October 28, 2003, http://www.gao.gov/new.items/d04146r.pdf.

14. Felicity Barringer, "Nations Ranked as Protectors of the Environment," *New York Times*, January 24, 2005 (electronic edition).

15. The author is indebted to the late Martin Diamond for this observation.

16. Johnston, *Perfectly Legal*, p. 16.

17. Ibid., pp. 169–170.

18. Ibid., p. 11.

19. Dawn Kawamoto, "Members of Congress Getting Richer Despite Market Meltdown," *Daily Finance*, November 17, 2010 (online), http://www.dailyfinance.com.

20. Associated Press, "Don't Feel Alone If Tax Is Confusing: 50 Experts Differ Over Family Returns," *Lincoln Star*, February 18, 1989, p. 2.

21. National Center for Education Statistics, "Fast Facts" (online), http://nces.ed.gov/FastFacts/display.asp?id=1.

22. "Viva la différence!" *The Economist*, May 9, 2009, p. 28.

23. Associated Press, "Wal-Mart, Unions Back Universal Health Care," *Star Tribune*, February 7, 2007 (online), http://www.startribune.com/535/story/986879.html.

24. See Ruy Teixeira, Center for American Progress, March 23, 2007 (online), http://www.americanprogress.org/issues/2007/03/opinion_health_care.html.

25. I am indebted to my colleague G. Ross Stephens for the statistical analysis used here. The raw data are from the 1962, 1979, and 2006 Statistical Abstract online at http://www.census.gov/compendia/statab/; see also, Thomas Piketty, *Capitalism in the 21st Century* (Cambridge, MA: Harvard University Press, 2013); and Paul Krugman, *The Great Unraveling: Losing Our Way in the New Century* (New York: Norton, 2003), p. 221.

26. Steven Rattner, "The Rich Get Even Richer, *New York Times*, March 16, 2012; see also, Ezra Klein, "In 2010, 93 percent of income gains went to the top 1 percent," *Washington Post*, March 5, 2012 (online), http://www.washingtonpost.com/blogs/wonkblog/post/in-2010-93-percent-of-income-gains-went-to-the-top-1-percent/2011/08/25/gIQA0qxhsR_blog.html.

27. Thomas Magstadt, "The Myth of the Free Market," *Open Salon* (Editor's Pick), October 25, 2011 (online); http://www.nationofchange.org/myth-free-market-1340630005 (reposted).

28. Johnston, *Perfectly Legal*, pp. 15–16 (among other passages throughout the book).

29. On who benefited most from the Bush tax cuts, see Tax Policy Center analysis at http://www.taxpolicycenter.org/briefing-book/background/bush-tax-cuts/ignore.cfm.

30. Krugman, *The Great Unraveling*, p. 221; Johnston, *Perfectly Legal*, pp. 31–37.

31. *Civil Rights Cases*, 109 U.S. 3 (1883).

32. *Plessy v. Ferguson,* 163 U.S. 537 (1896).
33. *Shelley v. Kraemer,* 334 U.S. 1 (1948).
34. *Sweatt v. Painter,* 339 U.S. 629 (1950).
35. *Brown et al. v. Board of Education of Topeka et al.,* 347 U.S. 483 (1954).
36. And it was upheld as a legitimate exercise of the government's commerce power; see *Heart of Atlanta Motel v. United States,* 379 U.S. 241 (1964), and *Katzenbach v. McClung,* 379 U.S. 294 (1964).
37. *Swann v. Charlotte-Mecklenburg Board of Education,* 402 U.S. 1 (1971).
38. *Milliken v. Bradley,* 418 U.S. 717 (1974).
39. *United States v. Windsor,* 570 U.S. ____ (2013).
40. *Regents of the University of California v. Bakke,* 438 U.S. 265 (1978).
41. In fact, the Supreme Court may have gone beyond *Bakke* by letting stand a federal court's decision that race cannot be a factor for purposes of law school admission. See *Texas v. Hopwood,* 116 S. Ct. 2581, cert denied (1996), 84 Fed. 3d 720 (1996).
42. *Wygant v. Jackson Board of Education,* 476 U.S. 267 (1986).
43. *Johnson v. Transportation Agency, Santa Clara County,* 480 U.S. 616 (1979).
44. *Adarand Construction, Inc. v. Pena,* 515 U.S. 200 (1995).
45. See, for instance, *United States v. Paradise,* 480 U.S. 149 (1987); *City of Richmond v. J. A. Croson Co.,* 488 U.S. 469 (1989); and *Metro Broadcasting, Inc. v. Federal Communications Commission,* 497 U.S. 547 (1990).
46. Elaine Cassels, "Why Citizens Should Be Concerned When Their Government Mistreats Aliens," Findlaw's Book Reviews (online), http://writ.news.fmdlaw. com/books/reviews/2003103l_cassel.html. This article is a review of David Cole's *Enemy Aliens: Double Standards and Constitutional Freedoms in the War on Terrorism* (New York: New Press, 2003).
47. *Romer v. Evans,* 116 S. Ct. 1620 (1996).
48. Adam Gopnik, "Two Views on *Speech,*" *The New Yorker,* January 30, 2015.
49. The FBI memo mentioned here was reported in the *New York Times,* November 13, 2003; cited in Noah Leavitt, "Ashcroft's Subpoena Blitz: Targeting Lawyers, Universities, Peaceful Demonstrators, Hospitals, and Patients, All with No Connection to Terrorism," FindLaw's Writ, February 18, 2004 (online), http://writ.news.findlaw.com/commentary/20040–218.1eavitt.htm.
50. Ibid.
51. Ibid.
52. *Snyder v. Phelps,* 562 U.S. (2011).
53. *Texas v. Johnson,* 491 U.S. 397 (1989).
54. *Brandenberg v. Ohio,* 395 U.S. 444 (1969).
55. This issue was resolved in *R. A. V. v. St. Paul,* 505 U.S. 112 (1992). A white 18-year-old male burned a cross on the lawn of the only black family living in a St. Paul, Minnesota, neighborhood. Although he might have been arrested for trespassing or disturbing the peace, he was charged under a local hate crime ordinance that made it illegal to place "on private or public property, a symbol, object, or graffiti, including but not limited to a burning cross or Nazi swastika, which one knows or has reasonable grounds to know arouses anger, alarm, or resentment in others on the basis of race, color, creed, religion, or gender." The Supreme Court decreed in 1992 that the ordinance, on its face, violated the First Amendment.
56. The Hays Press Enterprise Lecture, Riverside, California, May 7, 2004 (online), http://www.ap.org/pages/about/whatsnew/hayspress.html. Tom Curley, CEO of the Associated Press, gave a chilling speech on this occasion describing a culture of official secrecy and a growing hostility to the press at all levels of government and in the courts.
57. See *New York Times Co. v. United States,* 403 U.S. 713 (1971); and *Nebraska Press Association v. Stuart,* 427 U.S. 539 (1976).
58. *Reynolds v. United States,* 98 U.S. 145 (1879).
59. Most notably in *Abington School District v. Schempp,* 374 U.S. 203 (1963); and *Engle v. Vitale,* 370 U.S. 421 (1963).
60. *Lee v. Wiesman,* 505 U.S. 577 (1992).
61. *Wallace v. Jaffree,* 472 U.S. 38 (1985).
62. Andrew J. Coulson, "Obama's Compromise on D.C.'s School Vouchers Program," *Washington Post.* May 10, 2009 (electronic edition).
63. The original case upholding a woman's right to an abortion is *Roe v. Wade,* 410 U.S. 113 (1973). Other important cases include *Harris v. McRae,* 448 U.S. 297 (1980); *Webster v. Reproductive Health Services,* 492 U.S. 490 (1989); and *Rust v. Sullivan,* 500 U.S. 173 (1991). Also see *Planned Parenthood of Southeast Pennsylvania v. Casey,* 505 U.S. 833 (1992).
64. *N.O. W. v. Scheidler,* 510 U.S. 249 (1994).
65. *Schenck v. Pro Choice Network of Western New York,* 117 S. Ct. 855 (1997).
66. Leavitt, "Ashcroft's Subpoena Blitz." These actions flew in the face of a 1996 federal law requiring doctors, hospitals, and drugstores to issue "notices of privacy practices" and protect personal information of patients and customers.
67. Robert Pear and Eric Lichtblau, "Administration Sets Forth a Limited View on Privacy," *New York Times,* March 6, 2004 (online edition).

68. *Stenberg v. Carhart* (99–830), 530 U.S. 914 (2000). The law in question is the Partial Birth Abortion Ban Act (PBABA) twice vetoed by President Bill Clinton. A similar law was passed again in 2003; the Supreme Court upheld it in a 5–4 decision in 2007.

69. Pear and Lichtblau, "Administration Sets Forth a Limited View on Privacy."

70. *Planned Parenthood of Southeast Pennsylvania v. Casey.*

71. *Washington v. Glucksberg*, 117 S. Ct. 82258 (1997).

72. Burton Leiser, *Liberty, Justice, and Morals: Contemporary Value Conflicts* (New York: Macmillan, 1973), p. 192.

73. The answer provided by the Supreme Court is that the state must provide effective assistance of counsel through the first appeal. See *Douglas v. California*, 372 U.S. 353 (1963), and *Ross v. Moffitt*, 471 U.S. 600 (1974).

74. Pew Research Social & Demographic Trends, August 22, 2013 (online), http://www.pewsocialtrends.org/2013/08/22/chapter-3-demographic-economic-data-by-race/#incarceration; see also, "The Top 10 Most Startling Facts...About...Color and Criminal Justice...," Center for American Progress (online), https://www.americanprogress.org/issues/race/news/2012/03/13/11351/the-top-10-most-startling-facts-about-people-of-color-and-criminal-justice-in-the-united-states/; and Saki Knafo, "1 in 3 Black Males Will Go to Prison," Huffington Post, October 4, 2013 (online), http://www.huffingtonpost.com/2013/10/04/racial-disparities-criminal-justice_n_4045144.html.

75. *Mapp v. Ohio*, 367 U.S. 643 (1961).

76. See, for instance, Chief Justice Burger's dissent in *Bivens v. Six Unknown Agents of the Federal Bureau of Narcotics*, 403 U.S. 897 (1970).

77. *United States v. Leon*, 468 U.S. 897 (1984).

78. National Association of Criminal Defense Lawyers, http://www.nacdl.org/public.nsf/legislation/ci_01_005?opendocument; Laurie Aucoin; "Righting Wrongful Convictions," Northwestern (Spring 1999), http://www.northwestern.edu/magazine/northwestern/spring99/convictions.htm.

79. See, for example, "The Battle in Congress," *The Economist*, October 20, 2001, pp. 31, 34.

CHAPTER 14

1. Jack A. Goldstone, "An Analytical Framework," in *Revolutions of the Late Twentieth Century*, eds. Jack A. Goldstone, Ted Robert Gurr, and Farroyh Moshiri (Boulder, CO: Westview Press, 1991), p. 325.

2. Jack A. Goldstone, "Revolutions in World History," in *Revolutions: Theoretical, Comparative, and Historical Studies*, 2nd ed., ed. Jack A. Goldstone (San Diego: Harcourt, 1993), p. 320.

3. Quoted in Thomas Greene, *Comparative Revolutionary Movements* (Englewood Cliffs, NJ: Prentice-Hall, 1989), p. 5.

4. Ibid., p. 5.

5. Ibid., p. 6.

6. Ted Robert Gurr and Jack Goldstone, "Comparisons and Policy Implications," in *Revolutions of the Late Twentieth Century*, p. 324. The linguistic distinction between *revolution* (a modern term) and *rebellion* is also noteworthy. The distinction is not uniformly made in the literature, however.

7. Barrington Moore Jr., *Reflections on the Causes of Human Misery and upon Certain Proposals to Eliminate Them* (Boston: Beacon Press, 1972), p. 170.

8. James Dougherty and Robert Pfaltzgraff Jr., *Contending Theories of International Relations*, 3rd ed. (New York: Harper & Row, 1990), p. 321. The authors cite the scholarly works of Hannah Arendt, among others.

9. Irving Kristol, "The American Revolution as a Successful Revolution," in *Readings in American Democracy*, ed. Paul Peterson (Dubuque, IA: Kendall Hunt, 1979), pp. 52–53.

10. Cecilia Kenyon, "Republicanism and Radicalism in the American Revolution: An Old-Fashioned Interpretation," in *The Reinterpretation of the American Revolution, 1763–1789*, ed. J. Greene (New York: Harper & Row, 1968), p. 291.

11. See, for instance, Bernard Bailyn, "Political Experience and Enlightenment in Eighteenth-Century America," in *The Reinterpretation of the American Revolution*, pp. 282–283.

12. Martin Diamond, "The Revolution of Sober Expectations," in *Readings in American Democracy*, p. 66.

13. Thomas Jefferson to Roger C. Weightman, June 24, 1826, in *The Political Writings of Thomas Jefferson: Representative Samples*, ed. Edward Dumbauld (Indianapolis: Bobbs-Merrill, 1965), p. 9.

14. Benjamin Wright, *Consensus and Continuity, 1776–1787* (New York: Norton, 1967), p. 3. Here Wright relies on the work of J. Franklin Jameson.

15. Ibid., p. 1.

16. Ibid.

17. Kristol, "The American Revolution," p. 53.

18. Diamond, "The Revolution of Sober Expectations," p. 3.

19. Ibid., p. 65.

20. Crane Brinton, *The Anatomy of Revolution* (Magnolia, MA: Peter Smith, 1990), pp. 122–123.

21. Hannah Arendt, *On Revolution* (New York: Penguin, 1976), p. 60.

22. Kristol, "The American Revolution," p. 6.

23. Ibid., p. 61.
24. Edmund Burke, *Reflections on the Revolution in France* (Indianapolis: Library of Liberal Arts, 1955), p. 197.
25. Thomas Paine, "The Rights of Man," in *Thomas Paine: Representative Selections*, ed. H. Clark (New York: Hill and Wang, 1967), p. 159.
26. Ibid., pp. 184–185.
27. Ibid., p. 162.
28. Ibid., p. 61.
29. Ibid., p. 70.
30. Nonetheless, Burke became something of a supporter of the American cause in the Revolutionary War, urging his nation to recognize the legitimacy of the Americans' grievances.
31. John Locke, "An Essay Concerning the True Original Extent and End of Civil Government," in *Two Treatises on Government* (New York: New American Library, 1963), p. 466.
32. Ibid., p. 463.
33. Ibid., pp. 452–453.
34. See Joseph Cropsey, *Political Philosophy and the Issues of Politics* (Chicago: University of Chicago Press, 1977), pp. 157–162.
35. Goldstone, "An Analytical Framework," p. 50.
36. Alexis de Tocqueville, *The Old Regime and the French Revolution* (Garden City, NY: Doubleday, 1955), p. 176.
37. James C. Davies, "Toward a Theory of Revolution," *American Sociological Review,* February 1962, p. 6.
38. Raymond Tanter and Manus Midlarsky, "A Theory of Revolution," *Journal of Conflict Resolution* 11 (1967): 272, table 6.
39. Ted Gurr, *Why Men Rebel* (Princeton, NJ: Princeton University Press, 1970), pp. 3–21.
40. As pointed out by Jack A. Goldstone in "Theories of Revolution: The Third Revolution," *World Politics* (April 1980), pp. 425–453.
41. This discussion builds heavily on Gurr and Goldstone, "Comparisons and Policy Implications," pp. 324–352.
42. Barry Schutz and Robert Slater, "A Framework for Analysis," in *Revolution and Political Change in the Third World,* eds. Barry Schutz and Robert Slater (Boulder, CO: Lynne Rienner, 1990), pp. 7–9. Also see Gurr and Goldstone, "Comparisons and Policy Implications," p. 331.
43. Since the publication of his *Thinking About Crime* in 1975, James Q. Wilson's writings on crime in America have emphasized that socializing young males is the greatest challenge for a law-abiding society; there are now suggestions in the literature that this demographic fact also has implications for revolution. Compare Gurr and Goldstone, "Comparisons and Policy Implications," p. 335 (who emphasize age, not gender), and Wilson, *Thinking About Crime* (New York: Basic Books, 1975).
44. Walter Lacqueur, "Revolution," in *International Encyclopedia of the Social Sciences* (New York: Macmillan/Free Press, 1968), p. 501. See also Robert Hunter, *Revolution: Why? How? When?* (New York: Harper & Row, 1940), p. 126.
45. Theda Skocpol, *States and Social Revolutions: A Comparative Analysis of France, Russia, and China* (Cambridge: Cambridge University Press, 1979), p. 249.
46. Tocqueville, *The Old Regime,* p. 176.
47. Ibid.
48. Ibid., p. 187.
49. D. E. H. Russell, *Rebellion, Revolution, and Armed Forces: A Comparative Study of Fifteen Countries with Special Emphasis on Cuba and South Africa* (Orlando, FL: Academic Press, 1974).
50. Charismatic leadership is a particularly important element in totalitarian revolution. See Chapter 6.
51. Gurr and Goldstone, "Comparisons and Policy Implications," pp. 353–354.
52. Ibid., p. 334.
53. José Ortega y Gasset, *The Revolt of the Masses* (New York: Norton, 1993). First published in 1930.
54. This quote is taken from an excerpt published at http://www.historyguide.org/europe/gasset.html.
55. Ibid.

CHAPTER 15

1. Paul Seabury and Angelo M. Codevilla, *War: Ends and Means* (New York: Basic Books, 1990), p. 6.
2. G. W. F. Hegel, *Philosophy of Right,* trans. T. M. Knox, in *Great Books of the Western World,* Vol. 46, ed. R. Hutchins (Chicago: Encyclopaedia Britannica, 1952), p. 149.
3. Friedrich Nietzsche, *Human, All Too Human,* trans. Marion Farber (Lincoln: University of Nebraska Press, 1984), pp. 230–231, aphorism #477.
4. Benito Mussolini, "The Doctrine of Fascism," trans. M. Oakeshott, in *Great Political Thinkers,* ed. William Ebenstein (New York: Holt, 1965), p. 621.
5. John Vasquez, "Introduction: Studying War Scientifically," in *The Scientific Study of Peace and War: A Text Reader,* eds. John Vasquez and Marie Henehan (New York: Lexington, 1992), p. xix.

6. Ibid., p. xxii.
7. For an excellent introduction to the statistical methodology associated with quantitative war studies, see Stuart Bremer et al. (adapted by Marie Henehan), "The Scientific Study of War: A Learning Package," in *The Scientific Study of Peace and War*, pp. 373–437.
8. James Dougherty and Robert Pfaltzgraff Jr., *Contending Theories of International Relations: A Comprehensive Study*, 3rd ed. (New York: HarperCollins, 1990), p. 356.
9. Greg Cashman, *What Causes War? An Introduction to Theories of International Conflict* (New York: Lexington, 1993), p. 279.
10. This discussion comprises a variation of the classification scheme presented by Kenneth N. Waltz, *Man, the State, and War: A Theoretical Analysis* (New York: Columbia University Press, 1965). We acknowledge our debt to his scholarship.
11. The quotation is from Sir Norman Angell's "Neutrality and Collective Security," cited in Edward Hallett Carr, *The Twenty Years' Crisis, 1919–1939* (New York: Harper & Row, 1964), p. 39.
12. Thomas Hobbes, *The Leviathan* (London: Everyman's Library, 1965), p. 64.
13. Hans J. Morgenthau, *Politics Among Nations: The Struggle for Power and Peace*, 5th ed. (New York: McGraw-Hill, 1992), pp. 3–4.
14. Ibid., p. 29.
15. Jean-Jacques Rousseau, *First and Second Discourses*, trans. Roger Masters and Judith Masters, ed. Roger Masters (New York: St. Martin's Press, 1964), p. 197. The quotation is from Rousseau's Notes, *Second Discourse*.
16. Ibid., pp. 195–196.
17. Ibid., *Second Discourse*, pp. 141–142.
18. Ibid., p. 161.
19. Frederick Hartmann, *The Relations of Nations* (New York: Macmillan, 1978), p. 32.
20. William Galston, *Kant and the Problem of History* (Chicago: University of Chicago Press, 1975), pp. 26–27.
21. Immanuel Kant, "Eternal Peace," in *Immanuel Kant's Moral and Political Writings*, ed. Carl Friedrich (New York: Modern Library, 1949), p. 438.
22. V. I. Lenin, *Imperialism: The Highest Stage of Capitalism* (New York: International Publishers, 1939), p. 124.
23. Robert Goldwin, "John Locke," in *History of Political Philosophy*, eds. L. Strauss and J. Cropsey (Skokie, IL: Rand McNally, 1963), p. 442.
24. Richard Falk, *This Endangered Planet: Prospects and Proposals for Human Survival* (New York: Vintage Books, 1972), pp. 106–107.
25. Ibid., p. 107.
26. Ibid., p. 113.
27. Ibid., p. 155.
28. Cashman, *What Causes War?* p. 157.
29. Aristotle, *The Politics*, trans. and ed. Ernest Barker (New York: Oxford University Press, 1962), 1313b, p. 245.
30. Hannah Arendt, *Totalitarianism* (New York: Harcourt, 1951), pp. 113–114.
31. William Dixon, "Democracy and the Peaceful Settlement of International Conflict," *American Political Science Review* 88 (March 1994): 14.
32. On democracies' proclivity to join wars more often than other forms of government, see Stuart Bremer, "Are Democracies Less Likely to Join Wars?" Paper presented at the annual meeting of the American Political Science Association, Chicago, September 3–6, 1992.
33. For an extended discussion, see Bruce Russett, *Grasping the Democratic Peace* (Princeton, NJ: Princeton University Press, 1993).
34. As pointed out by Cashman, *What Causes War?* p. 129.
35. Ibid.
36. Ibid., pp. 137–139.
37. Rudolph Rummel, "Some Empirical Findings," *World Politics* 21 (1969): 238–239.
38. This discussion selectively follows Cashman, *What Causes War?* pp. 132–134.
39. Morgenthau, *Politics Among Nations*, pp. 51–57.
40. Ibid., p. 133.
41. Michael Haas, "Societal Approaches to the Study of War," in *The War System*, eds. Richard Falk and Samuel Kim (Boulder, CO: Westview, 1980), pp. 355–356, 365.
42. See John Vasquez, "The Steps to War," in *The Scientific Study of Peace and War*, pp. 343–370.
43. Jack Levy, "Alliance Formation and War Behavior: An Analysis of the Great Powers, 1495–1975," in *The Scientific Study of Peace and War*, pp. 3–36.
44. Vasquez, "The Steps to War," p. 370.
45. Cashman, *What Causes War?* p. 137.
46. Ibid.
47. Dougherty and Pfaltzgraff, *Contending Theories*, pp. 354–355.

48. Ibid., pp. 145–152; however, as Cashman notes, the evidence is not unanimous.

49. The studies are summarized in ibid., pp. 142–145. See also Paul Diehl, "Arms Races to War: Testing Some Empirical Linkages," *Sociological Quarterly* 26 (Fall 1985): 331–349; and his "Continuity and Military Escalation in Major Power Rivalries, 1816–1980," *Journal of Politics* 47 (November 1985):,1203–1211.

50. Nazli Chourci and Robert North, "Lateral Pressure in International Relations: Concept and Theory," in *Handbook of War Studies,* ed. Manus Midlarsky (Boston: Unwin Hyman, 1989), pp. 310–311.

51. Waltz, *Man, the State, and War,* p. 233.

52. Quoted in Lee McDonald, *Western Political Theory: From Its Origins to the Present* (Orlando, FL: Harcourt, 1968), p. 127.

53. Cited in Dougherty and Pfaltzgraff, *Contending Theories.* For an in-depth discussion of St. Ambrose's teachings on ethics and the use of force, see Louis J. Swift, "St. Ambrose on Violence and War," *Transactions and Proceedings of the American Philological Association,* Vol. 101 (1970): 533–543.

54. Michael Walzer, *Just and Unjust Wars* (New York: Basic Books, 1968), p. 1.

55. http://www.netwarcom.navy.mil/;http://www.wvec.com/news/military/stories/wvec_military_080106_cyper_ops_change.4fc6405.html.

56. Tony Halpin, "Putin accused of launching cyber war," *The Times Online* (London), May 18, 2007, http://www.timesonline.co.uk/tol/news/world/europe/article1805636.ece.

57. Thom Shanker and David E. Sanger, "Privacy May Be a Victim in Cyberdefense Plan," *New York Times,* June 13, 2009 (online), http://www.nytimes.com/2009/06/13/us/politics/13cyber.html.

58. Rudolph Rummel, "Democracies Don't Fight Democracies, *Peace,* May-June,1999, online at http://www.peacemagazine.org/archive/v15n3p10.htm.

59. James Fallows, "The Tragedy of the American Military," *The Atlantic,* January/February 2015, pp. 73–90; see also, "Chickenhawk," *Rational Wiki,* http://rationalwiki.org/wiki/Chickenhawk.

CHAPTER 16

1. This story was widely reported in the world press. The UN promptly shut down all of its World Population food aid centers in Pakistan.

2. "Nihilism and Terror," *New Republic,* September 29, 1986, p. 11.

3. See also Martha Crenshaw, "The Causes of Terrorism," in *International Terrorism: Characteristics, Causes, Controls,* ed. Charles W. Kegley Jr. (New York: St. Martin's Press, 1990), p. 113.

4. The distinction between religion and ideology breaks down completely when adherents pursue patently political ends and use religion to justify the means. Islamic extremists, for example, frequently call for jihad (holy war) against Israel and the "Crusaders" (to use Osama bin Laden's epithet). But every Muslim knows that the Koran (Islam's holy scripture) strictly forbids the taking of innocent life and makes no exceptions. Terrorism certainly has no more of a place in Islam than it has in Christianity.

5. For a more complete discussion, see David Rapoport, "Religion and Terror: Thugs, Assassins, and Zealots," in *International Terrorism,* pp. 146–157. Also see Leonard Weinberg and Paul Davis, *Introduction to Political Terrorism* (New York: McGraw-Hill, 1989), pp. 19–23.

6. Weinberg and Davis, *Introduction to Political Terrorism,* p. 22.

7. Compare Rapoport, "Religion and Terror," p. 146, and Weinberg and Davis, *Introduction to Political Terrorism,* pp. 24–26.

8. Rushworth M. Kidder, "Unmasking Terrorism," *Christian Science Monitor,* May 13, 1986, p. 19.

9. Ibid., p. 20.

10. Ibid.

11. Walter Laqueur, *Terrorism* (Boston: Little, Brown, 1979), p. 220.

12. Paul Johnson, "The Seven Deadly Sins of Terrorism," in *International Terrorism,* p. 65.

13. Carlos Marighella, *Mini-Manual for Urban Guerrillas,* trans. by Gene Hanrahan (Chapel Hill, NC: Documentary Publication, 1984.) Originally published in Spanish in 1970.

14. Claire Sterling, *The Terror Network: The Secret War of International Terrorism* (New York: Holt, 1981), pp. 21–22.

15. Neil A. Lewis and Eric Schmitt, "Cuba Detentions May Last for Years," *New York Times,* February 13, 2004 (online edition).

16. See, Adam Liptak, "Justices Erase Ruling That Allowed Detention," *New York Times,* March 6, 2009; see also http://www.cnn.com/2007/LAW/06/11/terror.ruling.ap/index.html.

17. In the 1990s, estimates ranged as high as 600. See, for example, David E. Long, *The Anatomy of Terrorism* (New York: Free Press, 1990), p. 165.

18. Mohammad M. Hafez, "Armed Islamist Movements and Political Violence in Algeria," *Middle East Journal* 4 (Fall 2000):, 584–585.

19. Laura Smith-Spark and Joe Sterling, CNN, January 23, 2013, online at http://www.cnn.com/2013/01/19/world/africa/algeria-hostage-crisis/index.html

20. Sara Miller Llana, "Narcotraffickers Attack Televisa, Mexico's Top TV Network," *Christian Science Monitor*, January 8 2009 (online edition).
21. Long, *The Anatomy of Terrorism*, p. 17.
22. Combs, *Terrorism in the Twenty-first Century*, (Upper Saddle River, NJ: Pearson, 2012), p. 68.
23. Kidder, "Unmasking Terrorism," p. 18.
24. Eric Hoffer, *The True Believer* (New York: Harper & Row, 1951), p. 49.
25. See Frederick J. Hacker, *Crusaders, Criminals, Crazies: Terror and Terrorism in Our Time* (New York: Norton, 1977).
26. Kidder, "Unmasking Terrorism," p. 19.
27. Regarding the lack of remorse, see Long, *The Anatomy of Terrorism*, p. 19.
28. See Paul McHugh, *The Weekly Standard,* December 10, 2001.
29. Hoffer, *The True Believer,* p. 80.
30. Ibid., p. 81.
31. Matthew Purdy, "Bush's New Rules to Fight Terror Transform the Legal Landscape," *New York Times*, December 16, 2001 (electronic edition). According to Purdy, President Bush was also "considering the possibility of trials on ships at sea or on United States installations, like the naval base at Guantánamo Bay, Cuba. The proceedings promise to be swift and largely secret . . . [and] the release of information might be limited to the barest facts, like the defendant's name and sentence. Transcripts of the proceedings . . . could be kept from public view for years, perhaps decades."
32. Tim Heffernan, "Who the Hell is Stanley McChrsystal," *Esquire*, May 19, 2009 (online), http://www.esquire.com/the-side/feature/who-is-stanley-mcchrystal-051909.
33. Weinberg and Davis, *Introduction to Political Terrorism*, pp. 168–170.
34. See Kristin Archick, "U.S.-EU Cooperation Against Terrorism," CRS Report for Congress, October 16, 2006 (online), http://www.fas.org/sgp/crs/terror/RS22030.pdf.
35. Gayle Rivers, *The Specialist: Revelations of a Counterterrorist* (New York: Charter Books, 1985), p. 40. Examples Rivers cites: "The daring July 1976 raid by Israeli commandos at Uganda's Entebbe Airport proved that terrorists are not invincible even after they have taken hostages and dug in, as did the successful comando assault on Túpac Amaru (MRTA) guerrillas holding hostages in the Japanese Embassy in Lima, Peru, in December 1996. Success in hostage rescue operations necessitates highly skilled, quick-hitting commando units, such as Germany's GSG-9, which freed hostages from a Lufthansa airliner hijacked to Mogadishu, Somalia, in 1977; Britain's Special Air Services (SAS); and the U.S. Delta Force. Local police agencies are typically not equipped or trained to deal with terrorism." According to Rivers, "When you are operating with the SAS on the ground in an area like Armagh [in Northern Ireland], you very quickly realize that you are fighting a war, not taking part in a police operation. Night after night, . . . IRA active-service units [infiltrate] from the safety of the South [move] about freely in areas they made safe for themselves by murder, torture, kneecappings and other intimidation. They are using sophisticated weapons, [including] heavy machine-guns, rocket launchers, landmines and massive quantities of explosives. Through audio surveillance, you listen to the planning sessions at which the orders are given for acts of sabotage that will involve indiscriminate civilian casualties. Civilian police procedures cannot deal with this kind of threat. If you locate a team . . . in the process of organizing an attack on a shopping center with milk churns packed with high explosives and nails, you send a fighting patrol to attack it; you don't call the local bobby."
36. Richard Clutterbuck, *Protest and the Urban Guerrilla* (New York: Abelard-Shuman, 1974), p. 287.
37. See, Christopher Hitchens, "The End of the Tamil Tigers: Insurgencies don't always have history on their side," *Slate* (the online daily news magazine), May 25, 2009.
38. See generally Brian Jenkins, ed., *Terrorism and Personal Protection* (Boston: Butterworth, 1985).
39. Kidder, "Unmasking Terrorism," p. 16.
40. Ibid., p. 17.

CHAPTER 17

1. The quotations in this discussion are from Thucydides, "The Melian Conference," from *Readings in World Politics*, 2nd ed., ed. Robert Goldwin and Tony Pearce (New York: Oxford University Press, 1970), pp. 472–478.
2. Niccolò Machiavelli, *The Prince*, in *The Prince and the Discourses* (New York: Modern Library, 1952), p. 56.
3. Ibid., p. 64.
4. Hans J. Morgenthau, *Politics Among Nations: The Struggle for Power and Peace*, 5th ed. (New York: McGraw-Hill, 1992), p. 11.
5. Ibid., pp. 22–23.
6. Ibid., p. 11.
7. Ibid.
8. Ibid., pp. 221–223. Notably, historians Edward Gibbon and Arnold Toynbee, as well as philosophers Emmerich de Vattel and Jean-Jacques Rousseau, have underscored the importance of a common core of religious beliefs and moral norms recognized in—and continually reinforced by—what we call "Western Civilization" or the "Western Heritage" or simply "the West."

9. Ibid., p. 27.

10. Jessica Tuchman Mathews, "The Environment and International Security," in *World Security: Challenges for a New Century,* 2nd ed., ed. Michael Klare and Daniel Thomas (New York: St. Martin's Press, 1994), p. 286.

11. See, for example, Lester R. Brown, *Plan B 3.0: Mobilizing to Save Civilization,* 3rd ed. (New York: Norton and the Earth Policy Institute, 2008).

12. See the "globalization" entry in *The Stanford Encyclopedia of Philosophy* (SEP), http://plato.stanford.edu/entries/globalization/.

13. Internet World Stats, http://www.internetworldstats.com/stats3.htm#asia; see also, Erick Schonfeld, "ComScore: Internet Population Passes One Billion; Top 15 Countries," TechCrunch.com, January 23, 2009, http://www.techcrunch.com/2009/01/23/.

14. "ASEAN Vision 2020," http://www.aseansec.org/1814.htm. In an agreement called ASEAN Vision 2020, the member states pledged "to create a stable, prosperous and highly competitive ASEAN economic region in which there is a free flow of goods, services, investment and a freer flow of capital, equitable economic development and reduced poverty and socioeconomic disparities."

15. See, especially, Kurt M. Campbell, Robert Einhorn, and Mitchell Reiss, *The Nuclear Tipping Point: Why States Reconsider Their Nuclear Options* (Washington, DC: Brookings Institution, 2005).

16. Rachel Carson, *Silent Spring* (Boston: Houghton-Mifflin, 2002). This is the fortieth anniversary edition of the book, originally published in 1962.

17. Eric Eckholm, "Recession raises poverty rate to a 15-year high," *New York Times*, September 16, 2010.

18. Quoted in Alexander de Conde, *A History of American Foreign Policy: Growth to World Power,* Vol. 1, 3rd ed. (New York: Scribner's, 1978), p. 130.

19. George F. Kennan, "Sources of Soviet Conduct," in *Caging the Bear: Containment and the Cold War,* ed. Charles Gati (Indianapolis: Bobbs-Merrill, 1974), p. 18.

20. Alexis de Tocqueville, *Democracy in America,* Vol. 1 (New York: Schocken Books, 1961), p. 522.

21. *Congressional Record,* 80 Cong., 1st sess. (March 1947), 1981.

22. See Chalmers Johnson, *Blowback: The Costs and Consequences of American Empire* (New York: Holt, 2000).

23. Ibid., p. 8.

24. Ibid.

25. Ibid., p. 9.

26. Ibid.

27. Ibid., p. 11.

28. Speech by George W. Bush at West Point, New York, June 1, 2002, published as part of a larger document under the title "National Security Strategy of the United States," released by the White House on September 17, 2002. (The quote here is found on p. 15.)

29. Statistics cited at http://www.antiwar.com/casualties/. This website has a link to a list of U.S. service members killed since May 1, 2008.

30. Alan Tonelson, "What Is the National Interest?" in *America's National Interest in a Post-Cold War World,* ed. Alvin Z. Rubinstein (New York: McGraw-Hill, 1994), p. 56; also see Thomas M. Magstadt, *An Empire If You Can Keep It: Power and Principle in American Foreign Policy* (Washington: CQ Press, 2004), especially pp. 220–242.

31. Dennis Ross, *Statecraft: And How to Restore America's Standing in the World* (New York: Farrar, Straus and Giroux, 2007), p. x.

32. Martin Gilbert, *The Roots of Appeasement* (New York: New American Library, 1966), p. xi.

33. Sadly, the mission failed. Intervention cost U.S. lives and offered no clear political or economic advantages; as such, it cannot be explained by self-interest. A different example of altruism took place in 1920-1921, when a terrible famine occurred in the Soviet Union. Despite the Soviet government's avowed support of anticapitalist revolutions in the West, the U.S. government created a relief organization (known as the Hoover Commission). Millions of dollars in food supplies were sent, and many lives were saved in the severely stricken Volga region. At the time, an official Soviet journal observed, "Of all the capitalist countries, only America showed us major and real help." Quoted in Adam Ulam, *Expansionism and Coexistence: Soviet Foreign Policy, 1917–1973,* 2nd ed. (New York: Praeger, 1974), p. 148. Also see John Lewis Gaddis, *Russia, the Soviet Union, and the United States: An Interpretive History* (New York: Wiley, 1978), pp. 99–101.

34. Quoted in Joseph Marion Jones, *The Fifteen Weeks* (New York: Harbinger, 1955), p. 256.

35. Raul Hilberg, *The Destruction of the European Jews* (New York: Harper & Row, 1961), pp. 358–359.

36. Arnold Wolfers, *Discord and Collaboration: Essays on International Politics* (Baltimore, MD: Johns Hopkins University Press, 1965), p. 93.

37. See, for example, Nathan Tarcov, "Principle and Prudence in Foreign Policy: The Founders' Perspective," *The Public Interest* 76 (Summer 1984):,45–60.

38. See Magstadt, *An Empire If You Can Keep It,* pp. 202–219.

39. Joseph Nye, "The New Rome Meets the New Barbarians," *The Economist,* March 23, 2002, pp. 23–24.

40. Ibid., p. 25.

41. Samuel Huntington, "The Clash of Civilizations?" *Foreign Affairs* 72 (Summer 1993): 22–43; and Samuel Huntington, "If Not Civilizations, What? Paradigms of the Post-Cold War Era," *Foreign Affairs* 72 (December 1993): 24–39; Huntington has since published his view on this subject in *The Clash of Civilizations and the Remaking of World Order* (New York: Simon & Schuster, 1996).

42. Huntington, *The Clash of Civilizations*, p. 40.

43. Robert D. Kaplan, *The Coming Anarchy* (New York: Vintage Books, 2001). This best-selling book is a collection of previously published articles Kaplan wrote. "Imagine *cartography in three dimensions,* as if in hologram. In this hologram would be *the overlapping* sediments of group and other identities atop the merely two-dimensional color markings of city-states and the remaining nations, themselves confused in places by shadowy tentacles, hovering overhead, indicating the power of drug cartels, mafias, and private security agencies. Instead of borders, there would be moving "centers" of power, as in the Middle Ages. Many of these layers would be in motion. Replacing fixed and abrupt lines on a flat space would be a shifting pattern of buffer entities. . . . To this protean cartographic hologram one must add other factors, such as migrations of populations, explosions of birth rates, vectors of disease. Henceforward the map of the world will never be static. This future map—in a sense, the Last Map—will be an ever-mutating representation of chaos." (pp. 50–51)

44. Hans J. Morgenthau, *Politics Among Nations: The Struggle for Power and Peace,* 5th ed. (New York, Knopf, 1978), p. 281.

45. Lassa Francis Oppenheim, *International Law: A Treatise,* Vol. 1, 2nd ed. (London: Longman, 1912), p. 93.

46. See Charles W. Kegley Jr. and Eugene Wittkopf, *World Politics: Trend and Transformation,* 6th ed. (New York: St. Martin's Press, 1997), p. 472.

47. The Montreal Protocol, formally known as the Montreal Protocol on Substances that Deplete the Ozone Layer, was prompted by mounting scientific evidence of the rapid erosion of the ozone layer, which shields the planet from cancer-causing ultraviolet radiation. In 1986, 23 nations endorsed a plan to reduce chlorofluorocarbons (known as CFCs and widely used in automobile air conditioners) by 50 percent by 1999. At a 1990 meeting in London, the agreement was modified, banning all CFCs by the year 2000. Two years later, representatives from more than 80 nations agreed in Copenhagen to move up the ban of CFCs to 1996 and outlaw other harmful substances as well. In 1992, the United States unilaterally announced its compliance with the provisions of the modified Montreal Protocol. The unprecedented scope of the amended plan pleased many who feared for the environment and stressed the need for international cooperation. Still, international funding to help developing nations purchase ozone-friendly technologies was very slow in coming. Criticism of the treaty came from opposite directions—some saw it as unnecessary; others believed it did too little or that loopholes would allow exemptions from the bans. A Dutch study published in 1997 compared three scenarios—one with no restrictions on ozone-destroying chemicals, another with the 1987 Montreal Protocol, and a third with the more stringent Copenhagen Agreement. The results were impressive. " "

48. Inis L. Claude Jr., *Power and International Relations* (New York: Random House, 1962), p. 97.

49. See Margaret Karns, "Maintaining International Peace and Security: UN Peacekeeping and Peacemaking," in *World Security: Challenges for a New Century,* 2nd ed., ed. Michael Klare and Daniel Thomas (New York: St. Martin's Press, 1994), p. 199.

50. Joseph E. Stiglitz and Linda J. Bilmes, "The true cost of the Iraq war: $3 trillion and beyond," *Washington Post*, September 5, 2010 (electronic edition).

51. Karen Tumulty, "The Doubts of War," *Time,* March 3, 2003, pp. 40–43.

ABC war A general term for war involving weapons of mass destruction (WMD), especially atomic (nuclear), biological, and chemical weapons.

accidental war In the modern age, the unintentional launching of a nuclear attack because of a mistake or miscalculation.

affirmative action Giving preferential treatment to a socially or economically disadvantaged group in compensation for opportunities denied by past discrimination.

American Revolution Also called the War of Independence and the Revolutionary War (1775–1783), this epoch-making event led to the end of British rule over the thirteen American colonies and to the formation of the United States of America in 1787–1789; usually dated from the Declaration of Independence in 1776.

anarchism A system that opposes in principle the existence of any form of government, often through violence and lawlessness.

Antarctic Treaty An international agreement that prohibits all military activity on the Antarctic continent and allows for inspection of all nations' facilities there. It also nullifies all territorial claims to Antarctic land and pledges the signatories to peaceful cooperation in exploration and research.

apartheid system The South African system designed to perpetuate racial domination by whites prior to the advent of black majority rule there in the early 1990s.

arms race Reciprocal military buildups between rival states; a process that tends to accelerate research, technology, and development in weapons systems and, according to some experts, is a potential cause of war.

ascriptive status An individual's status and position in society are ascribed on the basis of religion, gender, age, or some other attribute.

Asian flu A term used to describe the widespread financial turmoil in Asian stock markets, financial institutions, and economies in 1997.

authoritarian state Wherever supreme political power is concentrated in one person (dictatorship) or a small group of persons (oligarchy), individual rights are subordinate to the wishes of the state, and all means necessary are used to repress dissent and crush opposition.

authority Command of the obedience of society's members by a government.

autocracy Unchecked political power exercised by a single ruler.

Balanced Budget Act of 1997 Passed by Congress in 1997, this historic measure mandated a balanced federal budget by 2001 but was ironically undone in that very year by the events of 9/11.

balance of power system A classic theory of international relations that holds that nations of approximately equal strength will seek to maintain the status quo by preventing any one nation from gaining superiority over the others. Participating nations form alliances and frequently resort to war as a means of resolving disputes, seizing territory, gaining prestige, or seeking glory.

Balfour Declaration Named for the British foreign secretary who, in 1947, declared that the United Kingdom favored "the establishment in Palestine of a national home for the Jewish people" and pledged to "facilitate the achievement of this object, it being clearly understood that nothing shall be done which may prejudice the civil and religious rights of the existing non-Jewish communities in Palestine or the rights and political status enjoyed by Jews in any other country."

Bastille At the time of the French Revolution (1789), the Bastille was the infamous royal prison in Paris; the mass storming of the Bastille on July 14, 1789, and the freeing of the prisoners constituted a direct attack against the monarchy and symbolized the end of an era in French history; the revolutionaries then used the guillotine against none other than the reigning Bourbon monarch, King Louis XVI, and his extravagant wife, Queen Marie Antoinette.

behavioral engineering The carefully programmed use of rewards and punishments to instill desired patterns of behavior in an individual or an animal.

behavioral psychology A school of psychological thought that holds that the way people (and animals) act is determined by the stimuli they receive from the environment and from other persons and that human or animal behavior can be manipulated by carefully structuring the environment to provide positive stimuli for desired behavior and negative stimuli for unwanted behavior.

behaviorism An approach to the study of politics that emphasizes fact-based evaluations of action.

bicameralism Division of the legislature into two houses.

Biological Weapons Convention A 1972 international arms control treaty that pledged the destruction of biological weapons stockpiles and outlawed the production and storage of such weapons.

bipolar system Following World War II, the traditional European balance of power system gave way to two rival power blocs, one headed by the United States and the other by the former Soviet Union, each with overwhelming economic and military superiority and each unalterably opposed to the politics and ideology of the other.

blowback The unintended consequences of government policies that are kept secret from the general population.

bourgeoisie In Marxist ideology, the capitalist class.

brinkmanship In diplomacy, the deliberate use of military threats to create a crisis atmosphere; the calculated effort to take a tense bilateral relationship to the brink of war to achieve a political objective (for example, deterring a common enemy from carrying out an act of aggression against an ally).

British Raj British colonial rule on the Asian subcontinent from the eighteenth century to 1947, when India and Pakistan became independent.

brokered democracy This theory holds that the interests of major groups cannot be steamrolled by the majority without jeopardizing democracy and that legislators and decision makers should act as brokers in writing laws and devising policies that are acceptable to all major groups in society.

Bundesrat The upper house in the German federal system; its members, who are appointed directly by the *Länder* (states), exercise mostly informal influence in the legislative process (see also *Bundestag*).

Bundestag The lower house in the German federal system; most legislative activity occurs in this house (see also *Bundesrat*).

Camp David Accords A 1979 agreement by which Israel gave the Sinai back to Egypt in return for Egypt's recognition of Israel's right to exist; the two former enemies established full diplomatic relations and pledged to remain at peace with each other.

capitalism An economic system in which individuals own the means of production and can legally amass unlimited personal wealth. Capitalist theory holds that governments should not impose any unnecessary restrictions on economic activity and that the laws of supply and demand can best regulate the economy. In a capitalist system, the private sector (mainly business and consumers), rather than government, makes most of the key decisions about production, employment, savings, investment, and the like; the opposite of a centrally planned economy such as existed in the Soviet Union under Stalin and Stalin's successors.

catalytic war A conflict that begins as a localized and limited encounter but grows into a general war after other parties are drawn into the conflict through the activation of military alliances.

cells Small, tightly knit organizational units at the grassroots level of V. I. Lenin's Bolshevik Party.

charismatic leader A political leader who gains legitimacy largely through the adoration of the populace deriving from past heroic feats (real or imagined), personality traits, oratorical skills, and the like.

checks and balances Constitutional tools that enable branches of government to resist any illegitimate expansion of power by other branches.

Chemical Weapons Convention A 1993 international arms control treaty to eliminate chemical weapons within ten years. It calls for the destruction of chemical weapons stockpiles and monitoring companies making compounds that can be used to produce nerve agents in order to end production of chemical weapons.

citizen-leader An individual who influences government decisively even though he or she holds no official government position.

citizenship The right and the obligation to participate constructively in the ongoing enterprise of self-government.

Citizens United Landmark 2010 Supreme Court decision against campaign finance reform equating money donated to support or oppose political candidates or causes with free speech protected under the First Amendment: the upshot of this ruling is to allow unlimited amounts of money to be poured into political action committees called Super PACs.

civic education The process of inculcating in potential citizens the fundamental values and beliefs of the established order.

civil liberties Basic constitutional rights guaranteed to all citizens, including the right to life and freedom of speech, religion, and association, as well as freedom from arbitrary arrest and incarceration, torture, and slavery. But there is no universally accepted definition or list.

civil war A war between geographical sections or rival groups within a nation.

classless society In Marxist political theory, the ideal society in which wealth is equally distributed according to the principle "from each according to his ability, to each according to his needs."

coalition government In a multiparty parliamentary system, the political situation in which no single party has a majority and the largest party allies itself loosely with other, smaller parties to control a majority of the legislative seats.

co-decision In the European Union, a method of legislation and rule-making that involves both the European Council (heads of government) and the European Parliament.

Cold War A worldwide system organized into two opposing alliances in which the United States and the Soviet Union competed for the allegiance of the newly independent, non-aligned states in Africa, Asia, and Latin America after World War II.

collective memory The history of our country and the world we learn at home and in school and accept as true; what we come to know about our leaders, about crises we have survived as a nation, and about wars we have fought.

collective security In international relations, a system designed to prevent war by combining the armed forces of law-abiding and peace-loving nations in a powerful league capable of deterring or defeating any would-be aggressor.

collectivization The belief that the public good is best served by common (as opposed to individual) ownership of a political community's means of production and distribution; derived from "collective," denoting a form of community or commune in Marxist ideology.

colonialism The policy of seeking to dominate the economic or political affairs of underdeveloped areas or weaker countries (see also *imperialism*).

commercial republic This concept, found in the Federalist Papers, is most closely identified with Alexander Hamilton, who championed the idea of a democracy based on economic vitality, capitalistic principles, and private enterprise free of undue state regulation.

Common Agricultural Policy (CAP) An EU fixture since the inception of the original Common Market in 1958. Sets and collects tariffs on agricultural products coming into the EU and provides subsidies to EU farmers.

common law In Great Britain, laws derived from consistent precedents found in judges' rulings and decisions, as opposed to those enacted by Parliament. In the United States, the part of the common law that was in force at the time of the Revolution and not nullified by the Constitution or any subsequent statute.

Commonwealth of Independent States (CIS) A loose federation of newly sovereign nations created after the collapse of the Soviet Union; it consisted of almost all the republics that previously had made up the USSR.

communism An ideology based on radical equality; the antithesis of capitalism.

concurrent majority John Calhoun's theory of democracy, which holds that the main function of government is to mediate between and among the different economic, social, and sectional interests in U.S. society.

conservative A political philosophy that emphasizes prosperity, security, and tradition above other values (see also *liberal*).

constitutional democracy A system of limited government, based on majority rule, in which political power is scattered among many factions and interest groups and governmental actions and institutions must conform to rules defined by a constitution.

constitutionalism The concept that the power and discretion of government and its officials ought to be restrained by a supreme set of neutral rules that prevent arbitrary and unfair action by government; also called the *rule of law*.

containment The global status quo strategic policy followed by the United States after World War II; the term stems from the U.S. policy of containing attempts by the Soviet Union to extend its sphere of control to other states as it had done in Eastern Europe. NATO, the Marshall Plan, and the Korean and Vietnam wars grew out of this policy.

cosmopolitan democracy A model of democracy that sees the individual as part of a world order, not merely (or even primarily) as a citizen of a particular nation-state; often summarized in the slogan, "Think globally, act locally."

counterterrorism Methods used to combat terrorism.

country As a political term, it refers loosely to a sovereign state and is roughly equivalent to "nation" or "nation-state"; *country* is often used as a term of endearment—for example, in the phrase "my country 'tis of thee, sweet land of liberty" in the patriotic song every U.S. child learns in elementary school; *country* has an emotional dimension not present in the word *state*.

coup d'état The attempted seizure of government power by an alternate power group (often the military) that seeks to gain control of vital government institutions without any fundamental alteration in the form of government or society.

crimes against humanity A category of war crimes, first introduced at the Nuremberg trials of Nazi war criminals, covering the wanton, brutal extermination of millions of innocent civilians.

crimes against peace A Nuremberg war crimes trials category, covering the violation of international peace by waging an unjustified, aggressive war.

Declaration of the Rights of Man Enacted by the French National Assembly in August 1789, this brief manifesto was intended as the preamble to a liberal-democratic constitution to be written later; it affirmed the sovereign authority of the nation but limited that authority by recognizing individual rights to life, property, and security.

delegate theory of representation The theory that elected officials should reflect the views of the voters back home, rather than following their own conscience or substituting their own judgment for that of their constituents; in other words, elected representatives should be followers rather than leaders.

demagogue Someone who uses his or her leadership skills to gain public office through appeals to popular fears and prejudices and then abuses that power for personal gain.

Democracy Wall A wall located near the Forbidden City in the heart of Beijing; on this wall thousands of people wrote criticisms and complaints against the regime in the winter of 1978-1979, a rare opportunity for public dissent that ended in a government crackdown.

democratic correlate A condition or correlate thought to relate positively to the creation and maintenance of democracy within a nation.

Democratic Socialism A form of government based on popular elections, public ownership and control of the main sectors of the economy, and broad welfare programs in health and education to benefit citizens.

democratization Mikhail Gorbachev's policy of encouraging democratic reforms within the former Soviet Union, including increased electoral competition within the Communist Party.

derivative power Political power that arises indirectly as a result of achievements in other areas (art, science, technological prowess, and the like); derivative power is often a product of the heightened prestige or respect that results from such achievements.

deterrence In criminal justice theory, punishing a criminal for the purpose of discouraging others from committing a similar crime. In international relations, the theory that aggressive wars can be prevented if potential victims maintain a military force sufficient to inflict unacceptable punishment on any possible aggressor.

deterrence theory Holds that states acquire nuclear weapons mainly to deter the use of such weapons by other states; this idea spawned a whole new literature on war in the Nuclear Age in the second half of the twentieth century.

developing country Term long used in the West to denote any country that had not achieved levels of economic prosperity and political stability found in North America, Western Europe, Australia, New Zealand, and parts of Asia (particularly Japan, South Korea, Taiwan, and Singapore) during roughly the Cold War era (1945–1989); in general, a country where the ratio of population to land, jobs, and other factors (private capital, infrastructure, education, etc.) is unfavorable and where political stability, public services, and individual safety are lacking. High levels of unemployment, widespread poverty and malnutrition, highly restricted access to education and medical care, official corruption, and social inequality are among the problems often associated with the early stages of economic development.

developmental democracy A model of democracy that emphasizes the development of virtuous citizens: postulates that one essential role of representative government is to serve as a school for civic education to create a politically literate electorate.

dialectical materialism Karl Marx's theory of historical progression, according to which economic classes struggle with one another, producing an evolving series of economic systems that will lead, ultimately, to a classless society.

dictatorship of the proletariat Marx's first stage in the revolution that would overthrow capitalism; the guiding principle would be, "From each according to his abilities, to each according to his needs."

direct democracy A form of government in which political decisions are made directly by citizens, rather than by their representatives.

divided executive Situation in French government in which the president and the prime minister differ in political party or outlook.

domestic terrorism A form of terrorism practiced within a country by people with no ties to any government.

dual executive In a parliamentary system, the division of the functions of head of state and chief executive officer between two persons; the prime minister serves as chief executive, and some other elected (or royal) figure serves as ceremonial head of state.

dual federalism Under this system, which prevailed in the United States between 1835 and 1860, the power of the national government was limited to enumerated powers; during this period, the southern states claimed sovereign powers.

due process A guarantee of fair legal procedure; it is found in the Fifth and Fourteenth Amendments of the U.S. Constitution.

due process of law The established legal and court procedures aimed at ensuring that arrests, interrogations, jury selection, the rules of evidences, verdicts, and sentencing are fair, uniform, and bent toward a common result: justice.

Duma Officially called the State Duma, it is the lower house of the Federal Assembly, Russia's national legislature, re-established in the 1993 constitution, after having been abolished in 1917. It comprises 450 members, half of whom are elected from nation-wide party lists, with the other half elected from single-member constituencies.

dystopia A society whose creators set out to build the perfect political order only to discover that they cannot remain in power except through coercion and by maintaining a ruthless monopoly over the means of communication.

economic stimulus A fiscal tool of government designed to bol-ster a weak economy and create jobs via public works projects and deficit spending.

elitist theory of democracy In political thought, the theory that a small clique of individuals (a "power elite") at the highest levels of government, industry, and other institutions exercise politi-cal power for their own interests; according to elitist theories, ordinary citizens have almost no real influence on governmental policy.

Emissions Trading Scheme (ETS) Europe's major climate change project; a cap-and-trade system that sets limits on the vol-ume of pollutants the five dirtiest industries in any given country can spew into the atmosphere each year.

entitlements Federal- and state-provided benefits in the United States such as Social Security and Medicare funded by mandatory tax contributions; such benefits become a right, rather than a privi-lege, in the public mind because recipients typically pay into the system for many years before they are eligible to take anything out.

equal protection The doctrine enshrined in the Fourteenth Amendment that holds that the prohibitions placed on the federal government and the protections afforded American citizens under the Bill of Rights also apply to the states.

equilibrium A synonym for the word *balance*; also often used interchangeably with *stability* in the literature on international relations.

Estates-General Prior to the French Revolution, a quasi-legis-lative body in France in which each of the three estates (clergy, nobility, and commoners) was represented; it convened in 1789 for the first time since 1614.

ethnic cleansing The practice of clearing all Muslims out of towns and villages in Bosnia by violent means; the term has also been used to characterize genocidal assaults on minority popula-tions in other parts of the world, including the Darfur region of Sudan.

ethnocentric bias The common tendency of human beings to see the world through a cultural lens that distorts reality and exagger-ates the good in one's own society and the evil in others.

eugenics The science of controlling the hereditary traits in a species, usually by selective mating, in an attempt to improve the species.

euro area In the European Union, the euro zone refers to the nineteen member states that have adopted the euro, including Germany, France, and Italy, but not the United Kingdom.

European Union (EU) The successor to the Common Market or European Economic Community; the governing body that pre-sides over a single economy that rivals the United States in size.

exclusionary rule In judicial proceedings, the rule that evidence obtained in violation of constitutional guidelines cannot be used in court against the accused.

exit polling Voters leaving the polling place are asked how they voted; designed to provide a snapshot of the likely outcome of an election before the actual votes can be tallied.

fascism A totalitarian political system that is headed by a popular charismatic leader and in which a single political party and care-fully controlled violence form the bases of complete social and political control. Fascism differs from Communism in that the economic structure, although controlled by the state, is privately owned.

Federal Assembly Russia's national legislature, a bicameral par-liament, established under the 1993 constitution, comprising a lower chamber (State Duma) and an upper chamber (Federation Council).

federal budget deficit In the United States, the difference between federal revenues and federal expenditures in a given year; the national debt is the cumulative sum of budget deficits over many years.

federalism A system of limited government based on the division of authority between the central government and smaller regional governments.

first past the post An electoral method used in the United States and United Kingdom whereby candidates run in single-member districts and the winner is decided by plurality vote; favors broad-based, entrenched political parties and tends toward a two-party configuration.

French Revolution This 1789 war brought down the Bourbon monarchy in France in the name of "*liberté, egalité, et fraternité*" (liberty, equality, and fraternity); introduced the contagion of liberalism in a Europe still ruled by conservative, aristocratic, and royalist institutions; and ushered in the rule of Napoléon Bonaparte. Prelude to the First Republic in France and to the Napoleonic Wars.

functionalism According to functionalist theory, the gradual transfer of economic and social functions to international coop-erative agencies (for example, specialized UN agencies, such as UNESCO) that will eventually lead to a transfer of actual author-ity and integration of political activities on the international level.

gender gap Differences in voting between men and women in the United States; this disparity is most obvious in political issues and elections that raise the issue of appropriateness of governmental force.

Geneva Convention A body of international law dealing with the treatment of the wounded, prisoners of war, and civilians in a war zone.

Gestapo In Nazi Germany, the secret state police, Hitler's instrument for spreading mass terror among Jews and political opponents.

glasnost Literally "openness"; this term refers to Mikhail Gorbachev's curtailment of censorship and encouragement of political discussion and dissent within the former Soviet Union.

Gleichschaltung Hitler's technique of using Nazi-controlled associations, clubs, and organizations to coordinate his revolutionary activities.

globalization The process by which values, attitudes, preferences, and products associated with the most technologically advanced democracies are spread around the world via mass media and trade.

government The persons and institutions that make and enforce rules or laws for the larger community.

gradualism The belief that major changes in society should take place slowly, through reform, rather than suddenly, through revolution.

Great Leap Forward Mao Zedong's attempt, in the late 1950s and early 1960s, to transform and modernize China's economic structure through mass mobilization of the entire population into self-sufficient communes in which everything was done in groups.

Great Power During the era of the classical balance of power in Europe from the mid-seventeenth century to the outbreak of World War II in 1939, the states big enough to challenge or pose a threat to the status quo or to lead a coalition in defense of the status quo against acts of armed aggression or territorial expansion were called Great Powers, at one time or another to include Great Britain, France, Russia, Prussia (later Germany), Austria-Hungary, Spain, and Sweden, as well as the United States from the 1890s on.

Great Proletarian Cultural Revolution A chaotic period beginning in 1966, when the youth of China (the Red Guards), at Mao Zedong's direction, attacked all bureaucratic and military officials on the pretext that a reemergence of capitalist and materialist tendencies was taking place. The offending officials were sent to forced-labor camps to be "reeducated."

Green Revolution A dramatic rise in agricultural output, resulting from modern irrigation systems and synthetic fertilizers, characteristic of modern India, Mexico, Taiwan, and the Philippines.

guerrilla warfare The tactics used by loosely organized military forces grouped into small, mobile squads that carry out acts of terrorism and sabotage, then melt back into the civilian population.

gulag archipelago Metaphorical name for the network of slave labor camps established in the former Soviet Union by Joseph Stalin and maintained by his secret police to which nonconformists and politically undesirable persons were sent.

Hague Convention A widely accepted set of rules governing conduct in land wars, the use of new weapons, and the rights and duties of both neutral and warring parties.

hard power In international politics, the use of military force or the threat to use force or other coercive measures such as freezing foreign assets or imposing strict economic sanctions.

Hare plan In parliamentary democracies, an electoral procedure whereby candidates compete for a set number of seats, and those who receive a certain quota of votes are elected. Voters vote only once and indicate both a first and a second choice.

Hundred Flowers campaign A brief period in China (1956) when Mao Zedong directed that freedom of expression and individualism be allowed; it was quashed when violent criticism of the regime erupted.

idealism A political philosophy that considers values, ideals, and moral principles as the keys to comprehending, and possibly changing, the behavior of nation-states.

ideology Any set of fixed, predictable ideas held by politicians and citizens on how to serve the public good.

imperialism A policy of territorial expansion (empire building), often by means of military conquest; derived from the word *empire*.

inadvertent war A war resulting from misperception, misinformation, or miscalculation; an unnecessary war.

incarceration The isolation of criminals in an effort to protect society and to prevent lawbreakers from committing more crimes.

individualism According to Alexis de Tocqueville, the direction of one's feelings toward oneself and one's immediate situation; a self-centered detachment from the broader concerns of society as a whole. According to John Stuart Mill, the qualities of human character that separate humans from animals and give them uniqueness and dignity.

initiative A mechanism by which voters act as legislators, placing a measure on the ballot by petition and directly deciding whether or not to make it a law on election day.

Institutional Revolutionary Party (PRI) The dominant political party in Mexico from 1929 to the present. The PRI had never lost an election until 2000, when Vicente Fox of the National Action Party won the presidency.

intercontinental ballistic missile (ICBM) A long-range missile armed with multiple nuclear warheads capable of striking targets anywhere in the world; both the United States and Russia possess large arsenals of these ultimate strategic weapons.

interdependence In international politics, a condition in which national economies become inextricably entwined in the global economy, as political and business elites design strategies for continued growth and prosperity around access to foreign markets, labor, and capital.

interest aggregation How the interests, concerns, and demands of various individuals and groups in society are translated into policies and programs; in constitutional democracies, a major function of political parties.

interest group An association of individuals that attempts to influence policy and legislation in a confined area of special interest, often through lobbying, campaign contributions, and bloc voting.

international governmental organization (IGO) A grouping of established states; IGOs are based on treaties, have formal structures, and meet at regular intervals.

internationalist Theorist favoring peace and cooperation among nations through the active participation of all governments in some sort of world organization.

international law The body of customs, treaties, and generally accepted rules that define the rights and obligations of nations when dealing with one another.

International Monetary Fund (IMF) A specialized agency of the United Nations designed to promote worldwide monetary cooperation, international trade, and economic stability. It also helps equalize balance of payments by allowing member countries to borrow from its fund.

international nongovernmental organization (INGO) Comprised of private individuals and groups, an INGO transcends borders in pursuit of common causes.

international terrorism Headline-grabbing, politically motivated acts of violence having consequences and ramifications not confined to a single country; terrorism that spills over into the international arena for whatever reason, whether state-sponsored or not.

interstate war Armed conflict between sovereign states.

intifada An Arabic word meaning "uprising"; the name given to the prolonged Palestinian uprising against Israeli occupation in the West Bank and Gaza in 1987–1993 and again in 2001–2002.

iron law of oligarchy According to this theory, the administrative necessities involved in managing any large organization, access to and control of information and communication, inevitably become concentrated in the hands of a few bureaucrats, who then wield true power in the organization.

judicial review The power of a court to declare acts by the government unconstitutional and hence void.

junta A ruling oligarchy, especially one made up of military officers.

justice Fairness; the distribution of rewards and burdens in society in accordance with what is deserved.

just war A war fought in self-defense or because it is the only way a nation can do what is right.

keeper of the balance In a balance of power system, the nation-state that functions as an arbiter in disputes, taking sides to preserve the political equilibrium.

Knesset The unicameral Israeli parliament.

kulaks A class of well-to-do landowners in Russian society that was purged by Joseph Stalin because it resisted his drive to establish huge collective farms under state control.

Kuomintang The Chinese Nationalist Party, led by Chiang Kai-shek, defeated by Mao Zedong in 1949.

Kyoto Protocol Countries that ratify this treaty, which went into effect in 2005, agree to cut emissions of carbon dioxide and five other greenhouse gases or to engage in emissions trading if they exceed a certain cap; the United States signed it under President Bill Clinton, but President George W. Bush renounced it shortly after taking office in 2001 and President Barack Obama, who was sympathetic to the Kyoto pact as a candidate, in office has shown little inclination to push for a new global climate-change treaty.

law of capitalist accumulation According to Karl Marx, the invariable rule that stronger capitalists, motivated solely by greed, will gradually eliminate weaker competitors and gain increasing control of the market.

law of pauperization In Karl Marx's view, the rule that capitalism has a built-in tendency toward recession and unemployment, and thus workers inevitably become surplus labor.

laissez faire capitalism An ideology that views the marketplace, unfettered by state interference, as the best regulator of the economic life of a society.

least developed countries (LDCs) Countries where the ratio of population to land and jobs is unfavorable, where the economy is not highly diversified, and where literacy rates are low; three criteria used to classify LDCs also indicate the challenges they face: (1) low income; (2) human resource weakness (nutrition, health, education, adult literacy); and (3) economic vulnerability.

legislative referendum A vote through which citizens may directly repeal a law.

legitimacy The exercise of political power in a community in a way that is voluntarily accepted by the members of that community.

legitimate authority The legal and moral right of a government to rule over a specific population and control a specific territory; the term *legitimacy* usually implies a widely recognized claim of governmental authority and voluntary acceptance on the part of the population(s) directly affected.

liberal A political philosophy that emphasizes individualism, equality, and civil rights above other values (see also *conservative*).

liberal education A type of education often associated with private colleges in the United States; stresses the development of critical thinking skills through the study of literature, philosophy, history, and science.

libertarianism The belief that the state is a necessary evil best kept small and weak relative to society; libertarians typically value individual liberty above social services and security.

limited war The opposite of all-out war, particularly an all-out nuclear war, in which adversaries choose not to use the most potent weapons available to them.

list system Method of proportional representation by which candidates are ranked on the ballot by their party and are chosen according to rank.

lobby n. An interest group that operates in Washington, D.C., or in a state capital, and attempts to influence legislators, decision makers, and regulators to bend laws, policies, and rules in ways that benefit its membership or constituency; v. to engage in lobbying activities.

lobbyist One who is paid is lobby lawmakers and high-ranking government officials.

Lok Sabha The lower house of India's Federal Parliament; the directly elected House of the People. In India, as in the United Kingdom and other parliamentary systems, governments are formed by the majority party (or a coalition of parties) in the lower house following national elections (see also *Rajya Sabha*).

low-information rationality The idea that voters can make sensible choices in elections even though they lack knowledge and sophistication about public policy, candidates, and current events.

low-intensity conflict Internal warfare that is sporadic and carried out on a small scale but often prolonged and debilitating to the state and society in which it occurs.

Loyal Opposition The belief, which originated in England, that the out-of-power party has a responsibility to formulate alternative policies and programs; such a party is sometimes called the Loyal Opposition.

Magna Carta A list of political concessions granted in 1215 by King John to his barons that became the basis for the rule of law in England.

majority rule The principle that any candidate or program that receives at least half of all votes plus one prevails.

Marshall Plan A post–World War II program of massive economic assistance to Western Europe, inspired by the fear that those war-devastated countries were ripe for communist-backed revolutions.

Marxism An ideology based on the writings of Karl Marx (1818–1883), who theorized that the future belonged to a rising underclass of urban-industrial workers he called "the proletariat."

Marxism-Leninism In the history of the Russian Revolution, Lenin's anticapitalist rationale for the overthrow of the czar (absolute monarch) and the establishment of a new political order based on communist principles set forth in the writings of Karl Marx.

massive retaliation Strategic military doctrine based on a plausible standing threat of nuclear reprisal employed by the United States in the 1950s during the short-lived era of the U.S. nuclear monopoly. According to this doctrine, if the Soviet Union attacked U.S. allies with conventional military forces, the United States would retaliate with nuclear weapons.

mass media The vehicles of mass communication, such as television, radio, the Internet, film, books, magazines, and newspapers.

Meiji Restoration The end of Japan's feudal era, in 1868, when a small group of powerful individuals crowned a symbolic emperor, embarked on an economic modernization program, and established a modern governmental bureaucracy.

methodology The way scientists and scholars set about exploring, explaining, proving, or disproving propositions in different academic disciplines. The precise methods vary according to the discipline and the object, event, process, or phenomenon under investigation.

mixed regime A nation in which the various branches of government represent social classes.

Moghuls Muslim invaders who created a dynastic empire on the Asian subcontinent; the greatest Moghul rulers were Babur (1526–1530), Akbar (1556–1605), Shah Jahan (1628–1658), and Aurangzeb (1658–1707); Shah Jahan was the architect of the Taj Mahal.

monarchism A system based on the belief that political power should be concentrated in one person (for example, a king) who rules by decree.

monopoly capitalism The last stage before the downfall of the whole capitalist system.

Monroe Doctrine A status quo international policy laid down by U.S. President James Monroe, who pledged the United States would resist any attempts by outside powers to alter the balance of power in the American hemisphere.

moral relativism The idea that all moral judgments are conditional and only "true" in a certain religious, cultural, or social context; the belief that there is no such thing as universal truth in the realm of ethics or morality.

motor voter law A statute that allows residents of a given locality to register to vote at convenient places, such as welfare offices and drivers' license bureaus; the idea behind laws of this kind is to remove technical obstacles to voting and thus promote better turnouts in elections.

multinational corporation (MNC) A company that conducts business in more than one country; major MNCs operate on a global scale.

multiple independently targeted reentry vehicle (MIRV) Intercontinental missiles containing many nuclear warheads that can be individually programmed to split off from the nose cone of the rocket upon reentry into the earth's atmosphere and hit different specific targets with a high degree of accuracy.

mutual assured destruction (MAD) A nuclear stalemate in which both sides in an adversarial relationship know that if either one initiates a war, the other will retain enough retaliatory ("second strike") capability to administer unacceptable damage even after absorbing the full impact of a nuclear surprise attack; during the Cold War, a stable strategic relationship between the two superpowers.

mutual deterrence The theory that aggressive wars can be prevented if potential victims maintain a military force sufficient to inflict unacceptable damage on any possible aggressor.

nation Often interchangeable with *state* or *country*; in common usage, denotes a specific people with a distinct language and culture or a major ethnic group—for example, the French, Dutch, Chinese, and Japanese people each constitute a nation as well as a state, hence the term *nation-state*. Not all nations are fortunate enough to have a state of their own; modern examples include the Kurds (Turkey, Iraq, and Iran), Palestinians (West Bank and Gaza, Lebanon, Jordan), Pashtuns (Afghanistan), and Uighurs and Tibetans (China).

nation-building The process of forming a common identity based on the notion of belonging to a political community separate and distinct from all others.

nation-state A geographically defined community administered by a government.

National Action Party (PAN) The main opposition party in Mexico; the PAN's candidate, Felipe Calderón, was elected president in 2006.

National Assembly Focal point of France's bicameral legislative branch that must approve all laws.

national interest A term often invoked but seldom defined, it is usually associated with power enhancement; shorthand for whatever enhances the power and best serves the supreme purposes of the nation, including prosperity, prestige, security, and, above all, survival.

national security Protection of a country from external and internal enemies.

national self-determination The right of a nation to choose its own government.

nationalism Devotion to one's nation; closely akin to patriotism.

nationalistic universalism A messianic foreign policy that seeks to spread the ideas and institutions of one nation to other nations.

natural harmony of interests According to Adam Smith, what is good for the happiness of the individual is also good for society, and vice versa, because people will unintentionally serve society's needs as they pursue their own self-interests without government intervention.

Nazism Officially called National Socialism, Nazism is a form of fascism based on extreme nationalism, militarism, and racism; the ideology associated with Adolf Hitler and the Holocaust.

neocolonialism A theory holding that unequal and exploitative economic arrangements created by former colonial powers continued to be used to maintain control of former colonies and dependencies long after they gained formal independence in the 1950s and 1960s.

neoconservative In the United States, a term associated with the ideology of top advisers and cabinet members during the presidency of George W. Bush; neoconservatives advocate a strong national defense, decisive military action in the face of threats or provocations, pro-Israeli policy in the Middle East, and a minimum of government interference in the economy. In general, neoconservatives are opposed to federal regulation of business and banking.

nihilism A philosophy that holds that the total destruction of all existing social and political institutions is a desirable end in itself.

no-confidence vote In parliamentary governments, a legislative vote that the sitting government must win to remain in power.

nomenklatura The former Soviet Communist Party's system of controlling all important administrative appointments, thereby ensuring the support and loyalty of those who managed day-to-day affairs.

Nonproliferation Treaty An international agreement, drafted in 1968, not to aid nonnuclear nations in acquiring nuclear weapons; it was not signed by France, China, and other nations actively seeking to build these weapons.

nonstate actor An entity other than a nation-state, including multinational corporations, nongovernmental organizations, and international nongovernmental organizations, that plays a role in international politics.

nonviolent resistance A passive form of confrontation and protest; also called civil disobedience at times.

normativism Applying moral principles—norms—rooted in logic and reason to problems of politics and government; putting moral theory into political practice through good laws, wise legislation, and fair judges.

North American Free Trade Agreement (NAFTA) An agreement signed in 1994 by the United States, Mexico, and Canada that established a compact to allow free trade or trade with reduced tariffs among the three nations.

North Atlantic Treaty Organization (NATO) A permanent peacetime military alliance created by the United States in 1949 to deter Soviet aggression in Europe; today, NATO has twenty-eight members, including twelve Central and East European countries.

nuclear monopoly When only one side in an adversarial relationship possesses a credible nuclear capability; the United States enjoyed a nuclear monopoly for roughly a decade after World War II.

nullification According to this controversial idea, a state can nullify acts of the U.S. Congress within its own borders; John Calhoun and other states' rights advocates put forward this doctrine prior to the Civil War.

oligarchy A form of authoritarian government in which a small group of powerful individuals wields absolute power.

one-party dominant One-party dominant systems are different from authoritarian one-party systems in that they hold regular elections, allow open criticism of the government, and do not outlaw other parties. Until recently, Japan operated as a one-party dominant system, as did Mexico; South Africa is one current example.

order In a political context, an existing or desired arrangement of institutions based on certain principles such as liberty, equality, prosperity, and security. Also often associated with the rule of law (as in the phrase "law and order") and with conservative values such as stability, obedience, and respect for legitimate authority.

Organization of Petroleum Exporting Countries (OPEC) An international cartel established in 1961 that, since 1973, has successfully manipulated the worldwide supply of and price for oil, with far-reaching consequences for the world economy and political structure.

Outer Space Treaty An international agreement, signed by the United States and the former Soviet Union, that banned the introduction of military weapons into outer space, prohibited the extension of national sovereignty in space, and encouraged cooperation and sharing of information about space research.

overkill Amassing a much larger nuclear arsenal than is (or would be) needed to annihilate any adversary.

"overstretch" Term used by critics of the Vietnam War when referring to the ill-fated U.S. attempt to prevent Communist-ruled North Vietnam from vanquishing the U.S.-backed regime in South Vietnam; the term is now frequently applied to other U.S. armed interventions aimed at influencing or interfering in the politics or outcomes of conflicts in other countries directly or indirectly (through proxies, covert action, arms transfers, and the like).

paradox of democratic peace Democratic states are often militarily powerful, fight other states, engage in armed intervention, and sometimes commit acts of aggression, but they rarely fight one another.

parliamentary sovereignty In the United Kingdom, the unwritten constitutional principle that makes the British Parliament the supreme law-making body; laws passed by Parliament are not subject to judicial review and cannot be rejected by the Crown.

parliamentary system In contrast to the U.S. presidential model based on the separation of powers, parliamentary systems feature a fusion of powers in which Parliament chooses the prime minister who then forms a government; Parliament can in turn force the government to resign at any time by a simple majority no-confidence vote.

participatory democracy A model of democracy that seeks to expand citizen participation in government to the maximum possible degree; emphasizes universal suffrage, transparency in government, and opportunities for direct action; includes elements of direct democracy.

partiinost The spirit of sacrifice, enthusiasm, and unquestioning devotion required of Communist Party members.

party discipline In a parliamentary system, the tendency of legislators to vote consistently as a bloc with fellow party members in support of the party's platform.

peer group A group of people similar in age and characteristics—for example, college students.

perestroika Term given to Mikhail Gorbachev's various attempts to restructure the Soviet economy while not completely sacrificing its socialist character.

philosopher-king Wise philosopher who governs Plato's ideal city in *The Republic*.

plebiscite A vote by an entire community on some specific issue of public policy.

pluralist democracy A model of democracy that stresses vigorous competition among various interests in a free society; akin to the idea of market forces and the role of free enterprise in classic economic theory.

plurality Something less than an absolute majority. Where the plurality vote principle applies, the candidate or party receiving the largest number of votes wins; where there are multiple parties or candidates, winners typically receive fewer than half the total votes cast.

plurality vote system A system in which candidates who get the largest number of votes win, whether or not they garner a majority of the votes cast; in a majority vote system, if no candidate gets more than half the votes cast, a runoff election is held to determine the winner.

Politburo A small clique that formed the supreme decision-making body in the former Soviet Union. Some Politburo members also belonged to the Secretariat and were ministers of key government departments.

political action committee (PAC) Group organized to raise campaign funds in support of or in opposition to specific candidates.

political apathy Lack of interest in politics resulting from complacency, ignorance, or the conviction that "my vote doesn't really count" or "nobody cares what I think anyway."

political culture The moral values, beliefs, and myths by which people live and for which they are willing to die.

political development A government's ability to exert power effectively, to provide for public order and services, and to withstand eventual changes in leadership.

political efficacy The ability to participate meaningfully in political activities; relevant factors include education, social background, and sense of self-esteem.

political literacy The ability to think and speak intelligently about politics.

political party An organization whose adherents share a political philosophy and common interests and whose primary reason for existing is to win control of government.

political realism The philosophy that power is the key variable in all political relationships and should be used pragmatically and prudently to advance the national interest; policies are judged good or bad on the basis of their effect on national interests, not on their level of morality.

political socialization The process by which members of a community are taught the basic values of their society and are thus prepared for the duties of citizenship.

politician A public officeholder who is prepared to sacrifice previously held principles or shelve unpopular policies to get reelected.

politics The process by which a community selects rulers and empowers them to make decisions, take action to attain common goals, and reconcile conflicts within the community.

popular referendum A device that allows citizens to approve or repeal a legislative act; the measure is placed on the ballot via a petition signed by voters.

positivism A philosophy of science, originated by Auguste Comte, that stresses observable, scientific facts as the sole basis of proof and truth; a skeptical view of ideas or beliefs based on religion or metaphysics.

power The capacity to influence or control the behavior of persons and institutions, whether by persuasion or coercion.

power of the purse Under the U.S. Constitution, the provision that gives the Congress the exclusive right to impose taxes and the final word on government spending.

prior restraint The legal doctrine that the government does not have the power to censor the press, except in cases of dire national emergency.

proletariat In Marxist theory, a member of the working class.

propaganda The use of mass media to create whatever impression is desired among the general population and to influence thoughts and activities toward desired ends.

proportional representation (PR) Any political structure under which seats in the legislature are allocated to each party based on the percentage of the popular vote each receives.

protective democracy A self-contradictory governing model put in place in the United States after the 9/11 terrorist attacks; a government that places national security above liberty and justifies curtailment of constitutional rights in times of crisis or war; an oxymoron.

proxy war A war in which two adversaries back opposing parties to a conflict by supplying money, weapons, and military advisors, while avoiding direct combat operations against each other.

public good The shared beliefs of a political community as to what goals government ought to attain (for example, to achieve the fullest possible measure of security, prosperity, equality, liberty, or justice for all citizens).

public interest The pursuit of policies aimed at the general good or the betterment of society as a whole; in contrast to special interests that pursue laws or policies more narrowly favoring individuals or groups.

public opinion In general, the ideas and views expressed by taxpayers and voters. When a majority of the people hold strong opinions one way or the other on a given issue or policy question, it tends to sway legislators and decision makers who know they will be held accountable at the next election.

purges The elimination of all rivals to power through mass arrests, imprisonment, exile, and murder, often directed at former associates and their followers who have (or are imagined to have) enough influence to be a threat to the ruling elite.

qualified majority vote (QMV) In the European Union, a form of voting in the European Council and Council of Ministers in which no member state has a veto, but passage of a measure requires a triple majority, including more than 70% of the votes cast.

Question Time In the United Kingdom, the times set aside Monday through Thursday every week for Her Majesty's Loyal Opposition (the party out of power) to criticize and scrutinize the actions and decisions of the government (the party in power); twice each week, the prime minister must answer hostile questions fired at him or her by the opposition or backbenchers.

Rajya Sabha The upper house of India's Federal Parliament; the indirectly elected Council of States (see also *Lok Sabha*).

random sampling A polling method that involves canvassing people at random from the population; the opposite of stratified sampling.

rational actor Nations make rational decisions, and one nation will not dare to launch a nuclear strike unless it can protect itself from a counterattack.

rational choice The role of reason over emotion in human behavior. Political behavior, in this view, follows logical and even predictable patterns so long as we understand the key role of self-interest.

reasons of state The pragmatic basis for foreign policy that places the national interest above moral considerations or idealistic motives; also *raison d'état*.

recall Direct voting to remove an elected official from office.

rectification In Maoist China, the elimination of all purported capitalist traits, such as materialism and individualism.

referendum A vote through which citizens may directly repeal a law.

rehabilitation Education, training, and social conditioning aimed at encouraging imprisoned criminals to become normal, productive members of society when they are released.

Reign of Terror During the French Revolution, Robespierre and his Committee of Public Safety arrested and mass executed thousands of French citizens for the "crime" of opposing the revolution or daring to dissent.

republic A form of government in which sovereignty resides in the people of that country, rather than with the rulers. The vast majority of republics today are democratic or representative republics, meaning that sovereign power is exercised by elected representatives who are responsible to the citizenry.

reserved powers The reserved powers arise from the Tenth Amendment, which provides that powers not delegated to the federal government, "nor prohibited by it to the States, are reserved to the States respectively, or to the people."

retribution The punishment of criminals on the ground that they have done wrong and deserve to suffer as a consequence.

reverse discrimination In effect, going overboard in giving preferences to racial minorities and victims of gender discrimination in hiring, housing, and education; the U.S. Supreme Court has ruled that in some cases, affirmative action quotas are unconstitutional.

revolution A fundamental change in the rules and institutions that govern a society, often involving violent conflict in the form of mass action, insurrection, secession, or civil war.

Revolutionary War The American War of Independence (1775–1783).

right to revolution John Locke's theory that the end of government is the good of society and that when government deprives people of natural rights to life, liberty, and property, it is asking for trouble. If government fails to mend its ways, it deserves to be overthrown.

rule of law The concept that the power and discretion of government and its officials ought to be restrained by a supreme set of neutral rules that prevent arbitrary and unfair action by government; also called constitutionalism.

salami tactics The methods used by Vladimir Lenin to divide his opponents into small groups that could be turned against one another and easily overwhelmed.

Schengen area The visa-free zone within the EU, encompassing twenty-six countries and more than 500 million people who can now travel freely about Europe without being stopped at border-crossings.

scientific method The objective study of nature and society using empirical methods, data collection, and statistical analysis; results of scientific experiments are generally not considered valid or definitive unless they can be repeated and verified.

Seabed Treaty An international agreement that forbids the establishment of nuclear weapons on the ocean floor beyond the twelve-mile territorial limit.

second strike Retaliation in kind against a nuclear attack(er); this capability paradoxically minimizes the likelihood that a nuclear confrontation will lead to a nuclear exchange.

Selective Service System The means by which the United States keeps a list of all individuals eligible for the draft (males 18 to 25 years old); upon turning 18, male citizens are required by law to register within thirty days.

separation of powers The organization of government into distinct areas of legislative, executive, and judicial functions, each responsible to different constituencies and possessing its own powers and responsibilities; the system of dividing the governmental powers among three branches and giving each branch a unique role to play while making all three interdependent.

social contract A concept in political theory most often associated with Thomas Hobbes, Jean-Jacques Rousseau, and John Locke; the social contract is an implicit agreement among individuals to form a civil society and to accept certain moral and political obligations essential to its preservation.

socialism A public philosophy favoring social welfare and general prosperity over individual self-reliance and private wealth.

society An aggregation of individuals who share a common identity. Usually that identity is at least partially defined by geography because people who live in close proximity often know one another, enjoy shared experiences, speak the same language, and have similar values and interests.

soft money Campaign contributions to U.S. national party committees that do not have to be reported to the Federal Election Commission as long as the funds are not used to benefit a particular candidate; the national committees funnel the funds to state parties, which generally operate under less stringent reporting requirements. Critics argue that soft money is a massive loophole in the existing system of campaign finance regulation and that it amounts to a form of legalized corruption.

soft power The ability to get others to want what you want by example and moral suasion, as well as respect and admiration earned through the success of your ideas, institutions, and actions in the world.

sovereignty A government's capacity to assert supreme power successfully in a political state.

sovereign wealth funds A state-owned investment fund made up of financial assets such as stocks, bonds, precious metals, and property; such funds invest globally. China, for example, has invested huge sums in the United States via its sovereign wealth fund.

Special Economic Zones (SEZs) In the People's Republic of China, SEZs are designed to attract foreign investment and facilitate trade with other countries by relaxing state controls; enclaves where market forces are allowed to operate relatively free of state interference; taking a page out of China's playbook, India has also created SEZs in recent years, as have several other countries, including Egypt and Ethiopia.

special interests An organization or association that exists to further private interests in the political arena; examples in the United States are the U.S. Chamber of Commerce or the National Association of Manufacturers (business), the AFL-CIO (labor), and the National Farmers Organization (NFO).

state In its sovereign form, an independent political-administrative unit that successfully claims the allegiance of a given population, exercises a monopoly on the legitimate use of coercive force, and controls the territory inhabited by its citizens or subjects; in its other common form, a state is the major political-administrative subdivision of a federal system and, as such, is not sovereign but rather depends on the central authority (sometimes called the "national government") for resource allocations (tax transfers and grants), defense (military protection and emergency relief), and regulation of economic relations with other federal subdivisions (nonsovereign states) and external entities (sovereign states).

state-building The creation of political institutions capable of exercising authority and allocating resources effectively within a nation.

state capitalism An economy falling somewhere between a Soviet-style command economy and a Western-style market economy. The economy in Communist China after Mao is one contemporary example.

statecraft The art of leading in difficult times, promoting the common good, and protecting vital national interests while avoiding unnecessary conflict. The art of achieving political or strategic aims and objectives by force of example, persuasion, and the use of incentives rather than by coercion and threats; synonymous with *statesmanship* and *far-sighted diplomacy*.

stateless nation People (or nations) scattered over the territory of several states or dispersed widely and who have no autonomous, independent, or sovereign governing body of their own; examples of stateless nations include the Kurds, Palestinians, and Tibetans (see also *nation*).

state of nature The human condition before the creation of a social code of behavior and collective techniques to control normal human impulses.

statesman A political architect who creates new states, a peacemaker who resolves conflicts, or an orator who inspires the popular masses in times of national crisis. He or she is yesterday's founder, today's pathfinder, and tomorrow's legend.

state-sponsored terrorism International terrorism that is aided and abetted by an established state; for example, Libya was linked to many terrorist acts against Western countries until Muammar el-Qaddafi made peace overtures in December 2003 and before he became an international pariah all over again in 2011 in the face of a popular rebellion against his autocratic rule during the so-called Arab Revolution.

state terrorism Usually violent methods used by a government's security forces to intimidate and coerce its own people.

status quo A foreign policy aimed at maintaining the existing balance of power through collective security agreements, diplomacy, and negotiation, as well as through "legitimizing instruments," such as international law and international organizations.

Strategic Arms Reduction Treaty II (START II) A post–Cold War confidence-building treaty aimed at curbing strategic nuclear weapons negotiated between the United States and the former Soviet Union in 1993.

stratified sampling A manner of polling in which participants are chosen on the basis of age, income, socioeconomic background, and the like, so that the sample mirrors the larger population; the opposite of random sampling.

straw poll Unscientific survey; simple, inexpensive poll open to all sorts of manipulation and misuse.

submarine-launched ballistic missile (SLBM) Strategic missiles with multiple nuclear warheads launched from submarines that prowl the ocean depths and that cannot be easily detected or destroyed by a preemptive attack.

superpower A term that evolved in the context of the Cold War to denote the unprecedented destructive capabilities and global reach of the United States and the Soviet Union and to differentiate these two nuclear behemoths from the Great Powers that existed prior to the advent of the Nuclear Age.

Supremacy Clause Article VI, Section 2, of the Constitution, which declares that acts of Congress are "the Supreme law of the Land . . . binding on the Judges in every State."

surplus value Excessive profits created through workers' labor and pocketed by the capitalist or owning class.

sustainable growth A concept popular among environmentalists and liberal economists that emphasizes the need for economic strategies that take account of the high-cost and long-term impact on the environment (including global warming) of economic policies aimed at profit-maximization, current consumption, and the like.

swing vote An independent voter who votes for the Republican Party in one election and votes for the Democratic Party in another.

symbolic speech Forms of expression other than words: for example, flag-burning, provocative gestures, black armbands, and the like.

terms of trade In international economics, the valuation (or price) of the products (commodities, manufactures, services) that countries buy on the world market relative to the valuation of the products they sell; for example, if manufactured goods are generally priced high relative to minerals and agricultural products, then the terms of trade are unfavorable for countries that produce only farm commodities or raw materials.

terrorism Politically or ideologically motivated violence aimed at public officials, business elites, and civilian populations designed to sow fear and dissension, destabilize societies, undermine established authority, induce policy changes, or even overthrow the existing government.

theocracy A state like present-day Iran in which religious leaders monopolize political power, legitimate authority derives from a common belief in one god, and there is no separation of church and state.

Tiananmen Square massacre In 1989, unarmed civilian workers and students marched in Tiananmen Square in Beijing to demand democratic freedom and government reforms. Army troops responded with force, killing 1,500 demonstrators and wounding another 10,000.

ticket splitting A voter who votes for candidates from more than one party; this is the opposite of straight-ticket voting.

totalitarianism A political system in which every facet of the society, the economy, and the government is tightly controlled by the ruling elite. Secret police terrorism and a radical ideology implemented through mass mobilization and propaganda are hallmarks of the totalitarian state's methods and goals.

tracking poll Repeated sampling of voters to assess shifts in attitudes or behavior over time.

traditional societies A common term for often resource-poor societies that continue to observe premodern ways of life, work, and worship; often associated with high infant mortality rates, low life expectancy, poverty, illiteracy, hunger, and lack of the most basic medical services.

transnational terrorism Terrorist groups in different countries who cooperate with one another, or a group that crosses national boundaries to commit acts of terror.

Truman Doctrine President Harry Truman's pledge of U.S. support for any free people threatened with revolution by an internal armed minority or an outside aggressor.

trustee theory of representation The theory that elected officials should be leaders, making informed choices in the interest of their constituencies.

tyranny of the majority The condition arising when a dominant group uses its control of the government to abuse the rights of minority groups.

ultranationalism Extreme nationalism often associated with fascism; a radical right-wing orientation typically characterized by militarism, racial bigotry, and xenophobia.

unconditional surrender Giving an enemy on the verge of defeat a stark choice between surrendering immediately (placing itself entirely at the mercy of the victor) or being utterly destroyed.

unipolar system In international relations theory, the existence of a single invincible superpower; the international system said to have existed after the collapse of the Soviet Union left the United States as the sole remaining (and thus unrivaled) military and economic superpower on the world stage.

unitary system A form of government in which most or all power to make and enforce laws resides in the central government; opposite of a federal system.

USA Patriot Act A post-9/11 expansion of federal law-enforcement powers that greatly enlarged the powers of the executive branch to conduct domestic surveillance including warrantless wiretaps against U.S. citizens.

utopia Any visionary system embodying perfect political and social order.

war Organized violence, often on a large scale, involving sovereign states or geographic parts of the same state or distinct ethnic or social groups within a given state (civil war).

war by misperception Armed conflict that results when two nations fail to read each other's intentions accurately.

war crimes Violation of generally accepted rules of war as established in the Geneva Conventions on the conduct of war. The Geneva Conventions call for the humanitarian treatment of civilians and prisoners of war, and respect for human life and dignity; crimes against humanity, such as genocide and ethnic cleansing, are also war crimes.

war on terror After 9/11, President George W. Bush declared a worldwide "war on terrorism" aimed at defeating international terrorist organizations, destroying terrorist training camps, and bringing terrorists themselves to justice.

war powers The U.S. Constitution gives the Congress the power to raise and support armies, to provide and maintain a navy, to make rules regulating the armed forces, and to declare war; it makes the president the commander in chief of the armed forces.

Warsaw Pact A military alliance between the former Soviet Union and its satellite states, created in 1955, which established a unified military command and allowed the Soviet army to maintain large garrisons within the satellite states, ostensibly to defend them from outside attack.

Weimar Republic The constitutional democracy founded in Germany at the end of World War I by a constitutional convention convened in 1919 at the city of Weimar; associated with a period of political and economic turmoil, it ended when Hitler came to power in 1933.

welfare state A state whose government is concerned with providing for the social welfare of its citizens and does so usually with specific public policies, such as health insurance, minimum wages, and housing subsidies.

Westphalian system An international peace-keeping model that depended on the existence of an "honest broker," a power that would oppose the aggressor and back the threatened state or weaker alliance. *See* keeper of the balance.

winner-takes-all system Electoral system in which the candidate receiving the most votes wins.

withering away of the state A Marxist category of analysis describing what happens after capitalism is overthrown, private property and social classes are abolished, and the need for coercive state power supposedly disappears.

World Court Also known as the International Court of Justice, the principal judicial organ of the United Nations; the Court hears any case brought before it by parties who voluntarily accept its jurisdiction.

zero-sum game A confrontation in which a win for one side is a loss for the other.

Zionism The movement whose genesis was in the reestablishment, and now the support, of the Jewish national state of Israel. The national movement for the return of the Jewish people to the land of Abraham and the resumption of Jewish sovereignty in what is now known as Israel.

INDEX

NOTE: Locators in bold refer to definitions; page numbers followed by *f* and *t* indicate figures and tables, respectively.

A

ABC war, **486**
Abenomics, 195
Abe, Shinzo, 193
Abortion, 29–30, 42
Accidental war, 476–477, **477**
Achille Lauro hijacking (1985), 511
Acquis communataire, 185
Adams, John, 73, 338
Affirmative action, **419**
Affluence, apathy (relationship), 332–334
Affordable Care Act of 2010 (ObamaCare),
    337, 411–412
Afghanistan, failure, 279–280
Africa, 247*t*
    Sub-Saharan Africa, democracy/
        development, 260
Aggression, condemnation, 549–550
Ahmadinejad, Mahmoud, 102, 152
al-Assad, Bashar, 28, 104
al-Bashir, Omar, 28
Algeria, terrorism (1990s), 507–509
Alien and Sedition Acts (1798), 84
Allende, Salvador, 235
al Qaeda, 484–486, 499, 504, 550
    prisoners, interrogation, 290
    terrorist network, 303–304
al-Sadat, Anwar, 368–370, 503
Alternative Vote (AV) system, 167
Amakudari, 192
America. *See* United States of America
American International Group (AIG),
    stock decline, 32
American Nazi Party, 29
American Revolution, 435, **437**, 438–441
    French Revolution, comparison, 444–445
    significance, 438
    social/political changes, 440
Anarchism, **27**
Ancient Greece, 53–54, 53*f*
*An Essay Concerning Human
    Understanding* (Locke), 448
Anomic interest groups, 342
Antarctic Treaty (1959), **553**
Anti-federalism (Thomas Jefferson), 77–78
Antigovernment ideologies, 27
Apartheid, resistance, 360, 382–383
Apathy, affluence (relationship), 332–334
Aquinas, Thomas, 38
Arab-Israeli Six-Day War (1967), 200,
    201, 502
Arab Spring, 236, 248
Arab world, per capita gross national
    income, 270*t*

Arendt, Hannah, 12–13
Argentina, 235, 238–240
Aristide, Jean-Bertrand, 128
Aristotle, 161, 460, 472
Arms control treaties, 552–553
Arms race, **461**
Aryan society/race, 133, 145
Ascriptive societies, **267**
Asian flu, **231**
Asia, tigers/dragon, 230–234, 247*f*, 266
    South Korea, 231–233
    Taiwan, 233–234
Associational interest groups, 342
Atwood, Margaret, 65
Australia, 333, 409*t*
Authoritarian governments, types, 107*f*
Authoritarianism, 109–121
    future, 125–126
    government quality, absence, 125
    qualities, absence, 123–125
    sign of the times, 121
    theory, 121–125
    U.S. foreign policy, relationship,
        126–128
Authoritarian regimes, misconceptions,
    128
Authoritarian rulers
    legitimacy, 122–123
    popularity, absence, 123
    tyranny, 122
    vices, 103–107
Authoritarian state, **101**
    characteristics, 107–109
    modernization, slowness, 108
    virtues, 102–103
Authority, **5**, 5–6
Autocracy, **103**
Axis of Evil, 151–152, 500*f*, 538–539

B

Baburova, Anastasia, 222
Bachelet, Michelle, 235
Bacon, Francis, 51, 55–56, 62, 67
Bakke decision, 419
Bakunin, Mikhail, 27
Balanced Budget Act (1997), 404, **405**
Balanced government (Madison), 78–80
Balance, keeper, **531**
Balance of power, adjustment, 529*f*
Balance-of-power system, **529**, 529–531
Balfour Declaration, **200**
Baltic states, map, 487*f*
Bastille, 442, **443**

Battle of Lexington, 439
Beer Hall Putsch (Hitler), 5
Behavioral engineering, **60**
Behavioral psychology, **59**
Behavioral scientist, god role, 61–62
Behaviorism, **14**
Bellamy, Edward, 51
Betancourt, Rómulo, 364–366
Beyond Freedom and Dignity (Skinner), 65
Bhutto, Benazir, 370–371, 504
Bicameralism, **88**
Bicameral legislative branch, design, 88
Bilbo, Theodore, 374–375
Bill of Rights, 90
bin Laden, Osama, 153, 279, 290, 485,
    507, 550
Biological Weapons Convention (1972),
    553, **554**
Bipartisan Campaign Reform Act of 2002
    (BCRA) (McCain-Feingold Act),
    347
Bipolarity, dawn, 531–532
Bipolar system, **532**
Blackstone, William, 204
Blair, Tony, 167, 516
Block grants, 83
Blowback, **545**, 545–546
Blue Dog Democrats, 44
Boko Haram, 263
Bolsa Familia (Family Allowance), 237
Bolshevik Party, 136, 141, 143
Bonaparte, Napoleon, 1, 123, 444
Bourgeois capitalists, 140–141
Bourgeoisie, 33, **34**
Bourgeois legality, 34
Brave New World (Huxley), 65
Brazil, 235–238, 238*f*
Brinkmanship, **479**
British Raj, **197**
Brokered democracy, **81**
Brokered government (Calhoun), 80–82
Brown, Gordon, 164, 167
Brown v. Board of Education, 417–418
Brzezinski, Zbigniew, 142
Budget deficits
    federal budget deficit, **404**
    national debt, relationship, 404–408
Bundesrat, **178**, 180
Bundestag, **178**, 179–181
Burgess, Anthony, 64, 65
Burke, Edmund, 41, 142, 161, 379,
    445–446
Burr, Aaron, 373–374
Bush Doctrine, 546–547

1001

Things Everyone Should Know About

AFRICAN
AMERICAN
HISTORY

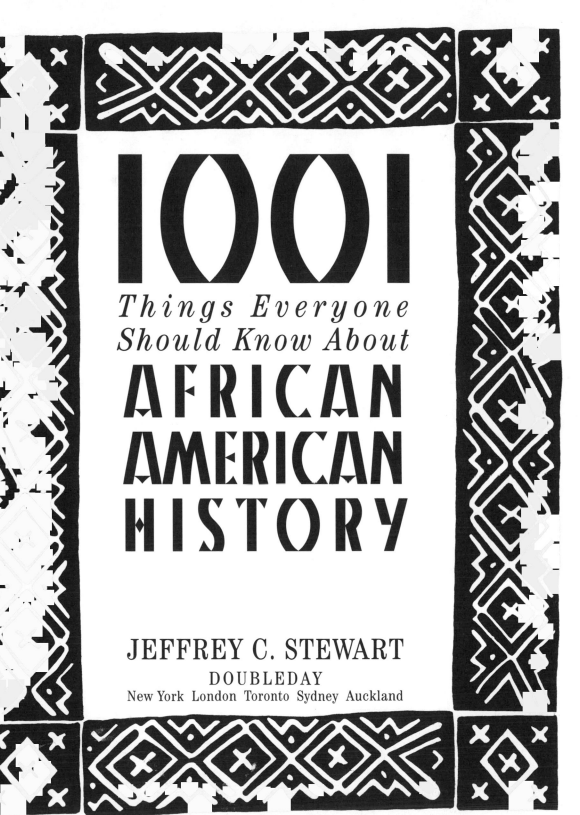

1001

*Things Everyone
Should Know About*

AFRICAN
AMERICAN
HISTORY

JEFFREY C. STEWART

DOUBLEDAY
New York London Toronto Sydney Auckland

PUBLISHED BY DOUBLEDAY

a division of Bantam Doubleday Dell Publishing Group, Inc.

1540 Broadway, New York, New York 10036

DOUBLEDAY and the portrayal of an anchor with a dolphin are trademarks of Doubleday, a division of Bantam Doubleday Dell Publishing Group, Inc.

Book design by Bonni Leon-Berman

Every effort has been made to trace copyright for all the photos in this book. If omissions have been made, please notify the publisher.

Library of Congress Cataloging-in-Publication Data

Stewart, Jeffrey C., 1950–
    1001 things everyone should know about African American history—
1st ed.
        p.   cm.
    Includes bibliographical references (p.   ) and index.
    1. Afro-Americans—History—Miscellanea.   I. Title.
E185.S798   1996
973′.0496073—dc20   95-22199
                                                                       CIP

ISBN 0-385-47309-5

10 9 8 7 6 5 4 3 2 1

First Edition

To James A. Jones, my grandfather, an inventor and an entrepreneur, who inspired me and my family by his accomplishment.

Also honored in fondest memory is Jacqueline Reid Davis, my sister-in-law and supporter of my work in Black history, and Loki, my faithful companion during work for this book.

CONTENTS

INTRODUCTION

I can do no better than my colleague, John A. Garraty, in introducing this work than to repeat what he said about his book, *1001 Things Everyone Needs to Know About American History*: Garraty asserted that his book, like Charles A. Beard's *An Economic Interpretation of the Constitution of the United States*, was an *interpretation* of American history. So is mine, although I am taking aim at a particular part of American history in looking more closely and intensely at African American life and experience in America. But the main point is that I have presented here what I believe is most important and compelling about the African American experience in America—and not what others might select either before or after reading this book. Quite frankly, there is so much to know about African Americans that it would be quite impossible to provide anything truly exhaustive in one volume such as this—especially with such a numerical limit. At the same time, I have tried to be comprehensive rather than idiosyncratic in those topics that I have chosen to explore here. My book is designed to inform as well as to entertain, and to provide those completely unfamiliar with the topic something they can rely upon. While I do not think that these books are substitutes for textbooks in the field, I do believe that this book is an excellent supplement to textbooks and other materials used in high school and college courses. One of the things that I discovered in working on this book is how many contemporary academic books omit the kind of details that students—and I—am interested in finding out, such as when something occurred. I hope, therefore, that the book will be a useful reference work as well as a diverting one.

Actually, this book vibrates with a long tradition in African American history of providing popular histories to a select audience, a tradition that is perhaps most associated with the work of Joel Rogers, whose *World's Great Men of Color* is a classic. Here, however, I have extended considerable effort to overcome an obvious bias of such a work by including the innumerable women who have been not only great, but enormously influential in African American political, social, and cultural affairs. Another popular form of African American historicizing is the books and articles that document the "first" Black person to achieve a distinction. Although denigrated in some academic circles, such books have had an important function in Black popular culture of proving, often to an imaginary and skeptical audience, that Blacks *have* achieved, accomplished, or entered some activity historically associated with whites. Given the history of racism, being the first *inside* some restrictive arena has been important. But in this book, with the exception of sports, where racial barriers have been the stuff of American sports, I have tried to avoid overloading readers of this volume with the first Black persons, and to focus a bit more on the social processes involved. Similarly, in the section on inventions, I am just as interested in the process of invention as the inventor him- or herself. This is especially true in the first section, Great Migrations, which perhaps suggests that migration is a governing metaphor, a trope, as my colleague, Arnold Rampersad, would put it, for the African American experience as a whole.

One word on nomenclature is appropriate. In this work, as in other works of mine, I have used African American to designate Americans of African descent wherever possible, and have capitalized Black, because it refers to an ethnic group, such as Jewish, Chicano, Puerto Rican, etc. White is not capitalized because it does not refer to such an ethnic group. Finally, I also believe, again like Garraty, but perhaps for different reasons, that readers may find this book inspiring. It documents more than three hundred years of change and struggle in African American life that comprises one of the great stories in American history.

Acknowledgments

Finally, I would like to thank Marie Brown, Rob Robertson, Kelly Ryan, Maureen Mineham, Nancy Craig, Melynda Williams, Stefanie Tildon, Deborra Richardson, Betsy Rowe, Larry Hunter, Denise Hawkins, Richard Long, Karin Wisansky, Richard Korn, Kathy Ward, Fath Davis Ruffins, Suzanne Smith, Barbara and Nicholas Natanson, Elizabeth Turner, Martha Jackson Jarvis, Jarvis Grant, Beverly Brannon, Rita Waldron, Mary Lou Hultgren, Ann Stetser, Kelli Bronson, Dorothy Dow, Annie Brose, Richard Powell, Anthony Ruiz, Lawrence Jones, Tom Richards, Jamesetta Verela, Fay Acker, Shirley Tildon, Reginald Clark, David Potter, Tjark and Renate Reiss, Marion Deshmukh, Portia James and, most of all, my wife, Marta Reid Stewart, for help and support on this project.

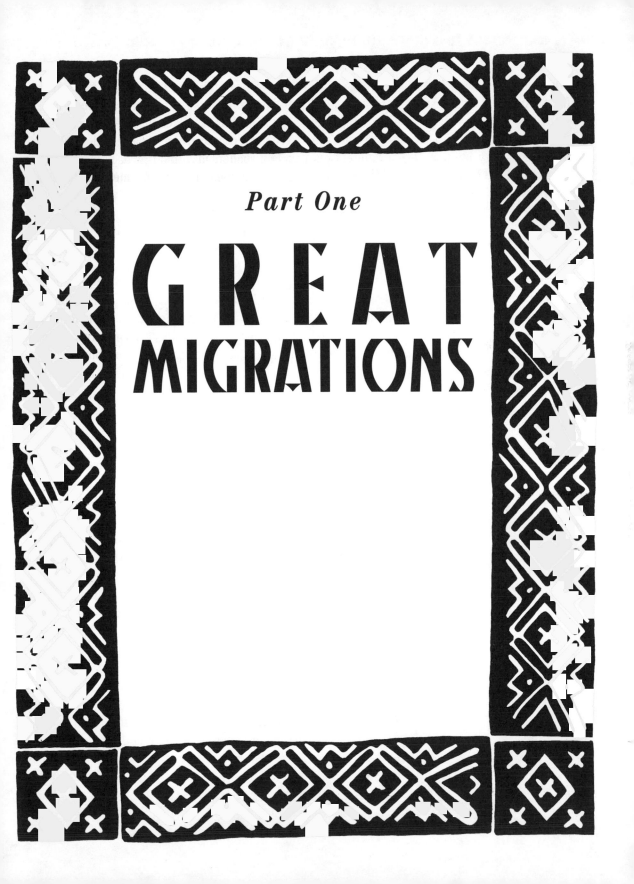

Part One

GREAT MIGRATIONS

FROM AFRICA TO AMERICA

African and African American Explorers

1 • Africans Discovered America

Strong evidence suggests that Africans discovered America before Columbus. When the Spanish explorer Vasco Núñez de Balboa landed in South America in 1513, he found a community of Black people already living there. Later, archaeological excavations uncovered pre-Columbian pottery that bore faces with distinctly African features. Most likely, West Africans who sailed into the Atlantic during the fifteenth century were carried to South America by powerful ocean currents.

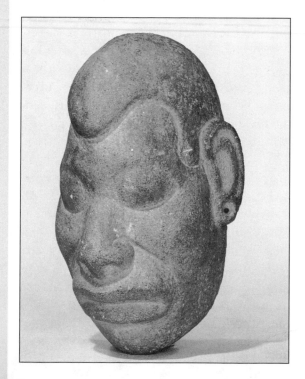

Negro stone head from Veracruz, Mexico. Classic period, c. A.D. 900. Courtesy of American Museum of Natural History, New York

2 • Columbus in the Wake of Africans

Christopher Columbus stopped in the Cape Verde Islands off the coast of Africa on his voyage west to find a shorter route to the Indies. He was emboldened in his daring journey by news from the islanders that Africans had been known to set off into the ocean going west in canoes from the coast of West Africa. When Columbus arrived in the Caribbean islands, he found dark-skinned people who traded with the Indians. He also found Native Americans who told him they had traded gold with Black men who came across the ocean from the southeast. In his diaries, Columbus suggested these dark-skinned peoples hailed from the coast of Guinea, in what is now West Africa.

3 • African Companions of Spanish Explorers

Africans were important members of each of the Spanish expeditions that came to the Western Hemisphere following Columbus. In 1513 Balboa brought with him thirty Africans who helped him cut the first path through Panama to the Pacific Ocean. These Africans also built the first ship ever constructed on the Pacific coast by foreigners. In 1519 Hernando Cortés relied on three hundred Africans to help him defeat the Aztecs. Africans also helped Juan Ponce de León explore Florida; they also filled the army that enabled Francisco Pizarro to conquer Peru.

4 • First Settlers of Jamestown

Africans, along with the Spaniard Lucas Vásquez de Ayllón, were the first to settle what is today Jamestown, Virginia. Ayllón explored the eastern coast of Virginia in the early 1500s and was the first to bring Africans into what is now the United States. Ayllón founded San Miguel de Guadalupe, a colony that flourished until 1527, when Ayllón died and was replaced by a more repressive ruler. Eventually the Africans rebelled, burning the settlement and forcing the Spanish to retreat to Haiti. Many of the Africans who fled the Spanish settlement established their own colony in the area. One could say, then, that this community of Africans was, after those of the Native Americans, the first permanent colony in Virginia.

5 • Estevanico

The most important African explorer of America was Estevanico (also known as Little Stephen), the first foreigner to discover New Mexico. Born in Morocco around 1500, Estevanico left Spain on June 17, 1527, as the slave of Andrés Dorantes, a Spanish explorer. Dorantes and Estevanico had joined a disastrous Spanish expedition led by Pánfilo de Narváez, the Spanish governor of Florida, to explore his new territory. Soon after their arrival in Tampa Bay in 1528, the party fell victim to disease, animal attacks, and Indians vigorously defending their land. When the army of two hundred Spaniards tried to sail from Florida to Mexico, they shipwrecked in Texas. Eventually the party of two hundred was reduced to only four: Dorantes, Stephen, and two other Spaniards. Of these, Stephen was the most important to the success of their eight-year search for the Spanish settlement in Mexico City. Because of his facility for learning new languages quickly, Estevanico became the spokesperson and negotiated for food, shelter, and directions from the Indians. Once the group reached Mexico City, Estevanico was rewarded by appointment to another expedition, led by Father Marcos Niza, to travel northward and locate the legendary "Seven Cities,"

later called the Seven Cities of Cíbola (or Gold). Although Marcos later claimed to be the first to discover New Mexico, he had in fact sent Estevanico ahead of him as a scout. Disobeying Marcos's orders, Estevanico did not wait for his slower compatriot, but pushed on to become the first non–Native American to cross what today is the international border and explore Arizona and New Mexico. In May 1539 Estevanico reached the ridge of the Huachuca Mountains and surveyed much of southern Arizona. But upon reaching his destination, the city of Cíbola, Estevanico was murdered by the Zuni Indians in 1539, seeking to protect their land from further incursions. Although his death allowed others to claim they had discovered Cíbola, Estevanico remains the first foreign explorer of the southwestern United States.

6 • Black Explorer with Lewis and Clark

Lewis and Clark's 1804 expedition through the West from Missouri to Oregon was made easier by York, a Black slave owned by Clark. Over six feet tall and weighing more than two hundred pounds, York was the first Black man that many of the Native Americans had seen. York patiently allowed the Indians to examine his skin to see if the color would rub off. As one Flathead Indian explained, his dark skin inspired respect: "Those who had been brave and fearless, the victorious ones in battle, painted themselves in charcoal. So the Black man, they thought, had been the bravest of his party." York also entertained the Indians with athletic stunts. His antics helped ease the hostility and communication difficulties between the Indians and the exploration party. Clark recorded in his diary that York "amused the crowd very much, and Somewhat astonished them, that So large a man should be active." Some historians believe that York was freed by Clark after they returned to St. Louis and became an Indian chief in the West. Others believe he was never freed and his future after the expedition remained unknown.

7 • James Beckwourth (1798–1866)

Born a slave in Virginia, James Beckwourth ran away from his master in St. Louis, and headed West, where he worked for several years for the Mountain Fur Company and learned the ways of the fur trapper. Always an aggressive, resourceful individual, Beckwourth had his first big break when he stumbled into a Crow village and was claimed by one of the women as her son. Quickly accepting the Crow identity, he also accepted a Crow wife, and thereafter led the Crows in numerous wars against the Blackfeet Indians. Slated to succeed the chief upon his death, Beckwourth bolted to fight in the Seminole wars in Florida. But his greatest contribution came in 1850 when he located a pass through the Sierra Nevada and led the first

James Beckwourth, one of the most famous of the mountain men. Photograph and Print Division, Schomburg Center for Research in Black Culture, New York Public Library, Astor, Lenox and Tilden Foundation

wagon train through it. Located north of Reno, Nevada, Beckwourth's pass still exists as an example of the resourcefulness of this African American warrior-explorer.

8 • Matthew A. Henson (1866–1958)

Matt Henson, as he was known to friends, was the man Robert Peary chose to accompany him on his "final dash" to the north pole in the spring of 1909. The orphaned son of Charles County, Maryland, parents who was already an accomplished seaman and well-read adventurer when Peary met him, Henson had accompanied Peary on his 1887 trip to chart a canal route through Nicaragua and on numerous previous arctic trips before Peary's last attempt to locate the north pole. Donald B. MacMillan, one of Peary's white companions left behind on the final leg of the 1909 attempt, recalled that Henson was

indispensable to Peary and of more real value than the combined services of all four white men. With years of experience equal to that of Peary himself, an expert dog driver, a master mechanic, most popular with the Eskimo, talking the[ir] language like a native, he went to the pole with Peary because he was easily the most efficient of all Peary's assistants.

Henson actually reached what Peary had first projected as the north pole (later called Camp Jesup) forty-five minutes ahead of Peary, but Peary claimed he later crossed over the actual north pole a day later with two Eskimos. After their return to the United States, Peary distanced himself from Henson, who worked at menial jobs in the navy and the New York Customs House. Congress granted Henson a medal, along with Peary's other four assistants, for his efforts. Years after his death, Henson's body was moved to Arlington Cemetery from an unmarked grave in New York, and now rests next to that of Peary.

Matthew A. Henson. The Winold Reiss Collection of Portraits and Studies, Fisk University, Nashville, Tennessee. Photo courtesy of National Portrait Gallery, Smithsonian Institute

The Slave Trade

9 • Africans in the Slave Trade

During its four centuries of operation, the Atlantic slave trade removed approximately 11.7 million people, mostly from West and Central Africa, with the intention of settling them as slaves in Europe, the Americas, or on islands off the coast of Africa. Only about 9.8 to 10 million made it to their destination. The rest perished in port, at sea, or upon arrival in a new land.

10 • Slave Trade Numbers Debate

Controversy over the total number of Africans transplanted by the Atlantic slave trade has raged since Philip Curtin's *The Atlantic Slave Trade: A Census,* the first modern quantitative study of the slave trade, was published in 1969. Some felt Curtin's estimate of 9.8 to 10 million Africans arriving in the New World was too low. But recent revisions tend to uphold Curtin's overall figure, though his numbers for individual nations as destinations are still disputed. Some of the controversy comes from those who feel that calculating the number of Africans who were brought to the New World at only 10 million devalues the scope and horror of the slave trade. Some historians have suggested as many as 100 million men and women were removed from Africa! But such numbers are

Africans of the slave ship *Wildfire*. Prints and Photographs Division, Library of Congress

grossly exaggerated. Neverthe-less, whether it was 10 million or 100 million, the slave trade was still one of the most devastating events in world history. Such a massive population transfer profoundly influenced the development of the American cultures we know today.

11 • Variation over the Centuries

The number of Africans removed by the Atlantic slave trade varied greatly over the centuries. From 1450 to 1600, about 367,000 Africans were taken out of Africa; another 1.868 million were removed in the seventeenth century. The number ballooned to 6.133 million human beings taken from their homeland in the eighteenth century. Then, after 1800, another 3.33 million were removed from Africa, even though the slave trade was outlawed in the United States after 1808.

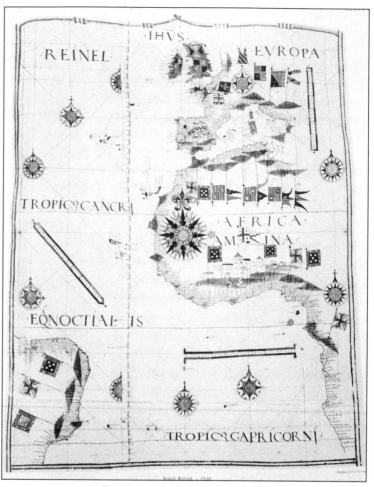

Portuguese chart of Africa c. 1540 by Jorge Reinel. Map and Geography Division, Library of Congress

12 • Portuguese Start Slave Trade

It was the Portuguese who first learned to sail down the Atlantic Ocean to West Africa. As a result, the Catholic Church awarded Portugal the exclusive right to exploration and trade with the continent of Africa in two papal bulls or decrees issued in 1493. The Portuguese had not waited for the papal bulls, however. In 1481 they had built a fort at Elmina over the objections of the West African Asante king, Kwame Ansa. Neither this fort nor its early entry into the trade could ensure Portuguese monopoly, however. By

the middle of the sixteenth century, the Dutch, the French, the English, the Swedes, the Danes, and the Prussians would challenge Portuguese dominance of the slave trade and build forts of their own on the West African coast.

13 • Asiento

Under the asiento system, Spain, and later Spain and Portugal, granted licenses that permitted the direct shipment of Africans to specified destinations, but only after paying a substantial sum to the crown. Such licenses were highly prized, as they guaranteed their owners a huge profit, and the acquisition process was full of theft, intrigue, and murder. Frequently the asiento required international diplomatic skills, as wealthy merchants of Portugal, for example, obtained a license and sub-contracted Dutch or English captains to obtain and transport the Africans to the New World.

14 • Africans React to Portuguese Offer to Build a Fort on African Land

I am not insensible to the high honor which your great master, the Chief of Portugal, has this day conferred upon me . . . but never until this day did I observe such a difference in the appearance of his subjects. They have hitherto been only meanly attired . . . and were never happy until they could complete their lading and return. Now I remark a strange difference. A great number of richly dressed men are eager to build houses and continue among us. Men of such eminence, conducted by a commander who from his own account seems to have descended from God . . . can never bring themselves to endure the hardships of this climate. . . . It is far preferable that both our nations should continue on the same footing they have hitherto done, allowing your ships to come and zgo as usual.

> —West African Asante king Kwame Ansa, upon the occasion of the Portuguese request to build a fort at Elmina

15 • Las Casas Myth

One of the most enduring myths is that the African slave trade to the Americas began in 1517 when Bartolomé de Las Casas, an ordained Spanish priest, suggested that Africans be brought to Haiti to replace the Native Americans who were dying in Spanish mines and plantations. Actually Las Casas was not the first to recommend use of African slaves. Africans were

already at work in the New World when Las Casas approached Charles I, the king of Spain, with his recommendation. As early as 1501, King Ferdinand of Spain decreed, "Negroes born in the power of Christians were . . . allowed to pass to the Indies." In 1505 Ferdinand promised the governor of Hispaniola to "send more Negro slaves as you request" and increased the number of Africans sent to Hispaniola on a yearly basis. In 1516, as Charles I took the throne in 1516 (as Charles I), the use of African slaves in Spanish colonies in the New World was an established practice. By 1528 there were nearly ten thousand Africans in the New World, and although some had come as free people and some as indentured servants, most were enslaved.

16 • Slavery Increased with the Discovery of the Americas

The discovery of the Americas and the building of the transatlantic system of mining and plantation agriculture in the Spanish colonies stimulated a demand for labor, and Portugal was well positioned to supply that labor with African slaves. Portugal remained the dominant slave trader until the end of the sixteenth century.

17 • Portuguese Sugar Plantations in Brazil

Brazil was the primary destination of Portuguese-traded slaves by the end of the sixteenth century. Conquered by Portugal in 1500, Brazil was first valued for its forests full of "brazilwood," not for its agricultural potential. But Portuguese entrepreneurs experimented with the possibility of growing sugar in Brazil, and by 1600 Brazil had thousands of plantations. The word "plantation" meant to "plant" Europeans on overseas land, but by the end of the fifteenth century, it meant a tropical estate that produced a single crop for external consumption and used involuntary labor. The Portuguese had first tried to use Indian labor, but when that failed because of Indian resistance, flight, and insurrections, the Portuguese sugar growers decided to replace Indian laborers with Africans. The rise of Black labor in Brazil began around 1570; although Blacks had been employed as skilled workers and servants before that date, the large number of Indian deaths necessitated the importation of Africans for agricultural work. By the end of the sixteenth century Brazil was the "largest slave importing region in the Atlantic world."

The high mortality rate of slaves in the West Indies derived from harsh work conditions. Here slaves are used to provide power to run the mills. Prints and Photographs Division, Library of Congress

18 • The Caribbean, the Seventeenth- and Eighteenth-Century Destination of Slaves

During the seventeenth century, the Dutch, the British, and the French set up plantation colonies in the Caribbean that were copied from the "Brazilian model." Of these, the British were the most important and the most aggressive. In the seventeenth century the British seized Spanish islands in the Caribbean, most notably Jamaica in 1655, and set up sugar plantations on Barbados and Jamaica that by the end of the seventeenth century were producing more sugar for export than Brazil. The Dutch, who established the Dutch West Indies in the early seventeenth century, yielded to the naval superiority of England and became the banker of the slave trade, supplying capital to trading companies in England and France that brought increasing numbers of Africans into the slave trade in the seventeenth and eighteenth cen-

turies. France also established its plantation system during the middle of the seventeenth century on Martinique and Haiti. By the middle of the eighteenth century, the sugar produced by slaves on Haiti exceeded that of any other Caribbean island. Not surprisingly, the rise in the numbers of Africans forced into the slave trade in the eighteenth century reflected the rise of sugar plantations in the Caribbean and their increased demand for labor. No doubt exists that African labor made this agricultural system profitable. As King Louis XIV of France, on August 26, 1670, noted, "There is nothing which contributes more to the development of the colonies and the cultivation of their soil than the laborious toil of the Negroes." Similarly, George Downing said of Barbados in 1645 that Africans were the "life" of the Caribbean. Europe has seldom been as unanimous on any issue as it has been on the value of African slave labor.

19 • English Trading

Although relative latecomers to the Atlantic slave trade, the English emerged as the nation that transported the largest number of West Africans in the Atlantic slave trade. English slave exports were about 9,000 per year by 1700, and they surged to more than 45,000 per year by the end of the century. English preeminence in the trade was caused in part by her possession of Barbados, the most important sugar-producing island in the Caribbean. The Atlantic slave trade was key to the emergence of Bristol, and later, Liverpool, as the major trading ports in England in the eighteenth century. Indeed, Liverpool became the queen of English slave-trading cities, supplying almost half the ships used in the Atlantic slave trade by the end of the eighteenth century.

Slaves from the British ship *Undine*. Prints and Photographs Division, Library of Congress

20 • Most Slaves from Coast of West Africa

Most of the Africans transplanted to the Western Hemisphere by the Atlantic slave trade came from the coast of West Africa, from such areas as Senegambia, Sierra Leone, the Gold Coast, the Windward Coast, the Bight of Biafra, and the Bight of Benin. Approximately 80 percent of the slaves exported by the British from 1760 to 1807 came from coastal West Africa. But there were other origins as well. Approximately 40 percent of the Africans imported to South Carolina from 1733 to 1807, for example, were Angolans from Central and southern Africa.

21 • Slave Trade in West Africa Prior to European Contact

Slavery and slave trading were well-developed systems in West Africa before Europeans established contact in the fifteenth century. A trans-Saharan trade in gold and slaves had existed with the Muslims for centuries. The Sudanese empires had used slaves to work large plantations, to staff huge armies, and to serve as administrators in state bureaucracies. Slavery was also popular as one of the few ways that economically aggressive individuals could move up in West African societies where ownership of land was not a means of upward mobility. But the very variety of occupations held by slaves in West African societies shows how different a system it was from the one that emerged in the Atlantic system. West African slaves enjoyed a status similar to European peasants, in that they often worked their own plots of land, lived in their own towns and villages, paid tribute to their masters, and held positions of importance in West African societies. Nevertheless, because slavery was an extensive institutional, legal, and commercial system in West Africa, it was easy

for outsiders like the Europeans to acquire African slaves in local markets.

22 • African's View of African Slavery

Those prisoners [of war] not sold or redeemed we kept as slaves but how different was their condition from that of the slaves in the West Indies. With us they do no more work than other members of the community, even their masters' food, clothing and lodging were nearly the same as theirs (except that they were not permitted to eat with those who were free born) and there was scarcely any other difference between them than a superior degree of importance which the head of a family professes in our state.

—Gustavus Vassa

23 • Africans Sell Africans

It is a myth that most Africans who became slaves in America were captured by Europeans in slave raids. Most of the Africans who became slaves were sold into slavery by other Africans. The Portuguese did raid unarmed West African fishermen and their villages in the fifteenth century, but African leaders had organized sophisticated military defenses and delivered costly, bloody defeats to the Portuguese. The Portuguese realized then that the only way to ensure a steady, predictable supply of slaves was to build extensive political connections with African leaders and make the trade work in their interest. By the end of the sixteenth century this had been accomplished. A lucrative trade for European goods, especially weapons, facilitated the selling of slaves to the Europeans. Afterward, most Africans crossing the Atlantic had been captured and traded by other Africans into the hands of Europeans. Most of these captured Africans had become captives as a result of war between rival ethnic groups.

Africans selling Africans on the coast of Africa. Prints and Photographs Division, Library of Congress

24 • Captain's View of Slaves

Those sold by the Blacks are for the most part prisoners of war . . . others stolen away by their own countrymen, and with some there are who will sell their own children, kindred and neighbors. . . . I was told of one who designed to sell his own son after that manner, but he understanding French dissembled for a while and then contrived so cunningly as to persuade the French that the old man was his slave and not his father by which means he delivered him up to captivity. . . . However, it happened that the fellow was met by some of the principal Blacks of the country as he was returning home from the factory with the goods he had received for the sale of his father all of which they took away and ordered him sold for a slave. . . .

—James Barbot

25 • Royals vs. Commoners

Slaves were taken from all classes of African society. Many nobles became slaves as a result of loss or capture in intertribal wars.

My father . . . was a king, and treacherously murdered by the sons of a neighboring prince. To revenge his death, I daily went a hunting with some men, in hopes of retaliating upon his assassins; but I had the misfortune to be surprized, taken and bound; hence these ignoble scars [around his wrists and ankles]. I was afterward sold to your European countrymen on the coast of Guiana—a punishment which was deemed greater than instant death.

26 • Africans Traded Slaves for Firearms

Some African leaders sold slaves to Europeans out of military or political necessity. Once African trading with Europeans for guns and gunpowder expanded in the eighteenth century, West African nations sometimes rose or fell because of their access to European firepower. Some African nations had to engage in the slave trade to acquire weapons to defend themselves against other nations who might attack and make them slaves. The slavers, therefore, exploited the divisions between Africans, who were divided not only by geography but also by language. The 264 Sudanic languages, 182 Bantu languages, and 46 Hamitic languages found in the region made Africa more complex linguistically, culturally, and socially than Europe. Rather than one people, Africans were many peoples each with their own history and rivalries. Europeans seeking more slaves for an expanding Atlantic market capitalized on these preexisting national rivalries. But many of the Africans engaged in the trade believed they were exploiting the Europeans by selling them

unwanted captives from rival groups in return for weapons and other valuable goods.

27 • Bacaroons

Bacaroons were rows of wooden shacks on the coast of Africa where captured Africans were kept while awaiting transport to the Americas.

28 • Coffle

Coffle was the term used for a string of slaves connected by a forked branch or rope. Later, chains were used. Often, slavers used coffles to lead slaves from the interior to the coast, adding newly captured or purchased slaves along the way.

29 • Comments from a Slave on a Slave Ship

. . . the first object which saluted my eyes when I arrived on the coast, was the sea, and a slave

Coffle. Prints and Photographs Division, Library of Congress

ship, which was then riding at anchor, and waiting for its cargo. These filled me with astonishment, which was soon converted into terror, when I was carried on board. I was immediately handled, and tossed up to see if I were sound, by some of the crew; and I was now persuaded that I had gotten into a world of bad spirits, and that they were going to kill me. Their complexions, too, differing so much from ours, their long hair, and the language they spoke, (which was very different from any I had ever heard) united to confirm me in this belief. Indeed, such were the horrors of my views and fears at the moment, that, if ten thousand worlds had been my own, I would have freely parted with them all to have exchanged my condition with that of the meanest slave in my own country.

The Middle Passage

30 • Africans Die in Transit

On the average, two out of every ten Africans who left the coast of Africa on slave ships died during the Middle Passage—the trip from Africa to the Americas. Yet death rates varied greatly from ship to ship and over the four centuries of legal and illegal slave trading. Average death rates declined somewhat during the eighteenth and early nineteenth centuries as methods of travel, ship speed, and medical science improved, but increased after the slave trade was outlawed in the United States in 1808. Average yearly percentages did not reflect the tremendous loss that frequently occurred on particular voyages, and while not typical, some boats lost over half their slave population before reaching America. On the late-eighteenth-century voyage of the *Elizabeth,* for example, 155 out of 602 slaves on board perished before the ship arrived at its destination. Another example

was the *St. Jan,* which left the island of Annobón on August 17, 1659. By the time it reached the West Indies on September 24, 1659, 110 slaves had died and the rest were in such disastrous condition "from want" of food "and sickness . . . that we saved only ninety slaves, out of the whole cargo."

31 • Housing for Slaves on Ships

Once a group of African slaves were boarded onto a slave ship, "the men were shackled two by two, the right wrist and ankle of one to the left wrist and ankle of another. Then they were sent to the hold or, at the end of the eighteenth century, to the 'house' that the sailors had built on deck. The women—usually regarded as fair prey for the sailors—and the children were allowed to wander" around by day, though they slept in separate decks from the men. "All slaves were forced to sleep without covering on bare wooden floors, which were often constructed of rough boards. In a stormy passage the skin over the elbows might be worn away to the bare bones."

32 • Loose/Tight Packers

In the slave trade, one of two techniques was usually advocated by slave ship captains: "loose packing" and "tight packing." The "loose packers" believed that by allowing slaves greater room, air, and sanitary conditions, more would survive the journey and thus bring greater profit. But "tight packers," who tended to dominate the trade after the middle of the eighteenth century, believed that by squeezing more people into the hole, the greater number would offset the increased death rate. An example of the disparity between the two techniques was the *Brookes,* a vessel of 320 tons that was ordered by the Law of 1788 to carry 454 slaves, even though the chart that determined their lo-

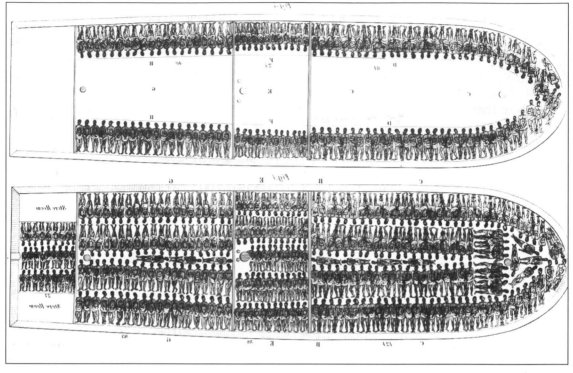

Diagram of the *Brookes*, a slave ship. Photograph and Print Division, Schomburg Center for Research in Black Culture, New York Public Library, Astor, Lenox and Tilden Foundation

cation could only find places for 451. But according to reliable witnesses, the *Brookes* had carried 609 on one voyage.

33 • Small Ships Transported Slaves

Although the famous diagram of the *Brookes* with 454 slaves aboard has created an indelible image of what the typical slave ship looked like, the reality is that most slave ships were much smaller than the 320-ton *Brookes*. In addition, most slave ships were not as completely filled or "tight-packed" before leaving Africa because it was difficult to acquire as many Africans as the 454 specified in the *Brookes* diagram. While the slave trade was a large, complex, and international enterprise, the actual ships were often owned and manned by small companies.

34 • No Link Between Packing and Mortality

Though "tight packing" was usually blamed for the high mortality rate among slaves in the Middle Passage, no proof exists that the practice resulted in dramatically higher deaths. A recent study of Dutch, French, British, and Portuguese slave ships arriving in Rio de Janeiro in the years between 1795 and 1811 did not show any correlation between the number of slaves per ton on each ship and the number who perished in the Middle Passage. In fact, some ships with smaller slave-to-ship tonnage ratios actually showed higher death rates than those with a higher ratio. While overcrowding certainly increased the misery of the slaves, it is debatable whether it actually increased deaths.

35 • Packing

The cargo of a vessel of a hundred tons or a little more is calculated to purchase from 220 to 250 slaves. Their lodging rooms below the deck which are three (for the men, the boys, and the women) besides a place for the sick, are sometimes more than five feet high and sometimes less; and this height is divided toward the middle for the slaves lie in two rows, one above the other, on each side of the ship, close to each other like books upon a shelf. I have known them so close that the shelf would not easily contain one more.

The poor creatures, thus cramped, are likewise in irons for the most part which makes it difficult for them to turn or move or attempt to rise or to lie down without hurting themselves or each other. Every morning, perhaps, more instances than one are found of the living and the dead fastened together.

—Rev. John Newton

36 • Voyage Length Linked to Mortality

The length of the voyage from Africa to the Western Hemisphere was the most important factor in slave mortality. A study of the French slave trade in the eighteenth century showed that ships that took 40 days to reach the New World port of delivery experienced roughly an 8.3 percent loss of slaves, but ships that traveled over 141 days had an average loss of 21.3 percent of their slaves. Even slight increases in distances could have an effect. Dutch slave ships that left Africa from the Guinea coast for the Caribbean instead of the nearer Angola averaged a 6.75 percent increase in the mortality of its slaves.

37 • Slaves Die Before Leaving Africa

Many captured Africans died before they were even loaded onto ships. The Portuguese crammed hundreds of slaves into the dungeon in Elmina, the first and best known Portuguese fort on the western coast of Africa. Often, the captured Africans were forced to wait in the dungeon for the arrival of more Africans so a larger cargo could be carried by the ships to the New World. A study of the Dutch slave trade calculated that an average of 3 to 5 percent of the slaves died before they left Africa, and during some waits, the percentage lost was much higher.

38 • Wait in Port Linked to Slave Deaths

Another factor that contributed to slave mortality was the long wait aboard ships anchored in port. The longer a slave ship remained in an African port, the larger the number of deaths that occurred among the slaves. The wait varied from place to place. At Bonny or Luanda, it might take a month or two to complete the loading process. But on the Gold Coast, where slaves were less numerous, loading of Africans could take from six months to a year. Such long waits had disastrous results, especially for the first people purchased. In 1677–78 the Royal African Company reported that on the *Arthur* fifty-five African men, women, and children died before the ship could leave for the New World.

39 • Psychological Trauma Linked to Slave Deaths

Psychological trauma caused the deaths of many Africans on the Middle Passage. Uprooted from their homelands, separated from their families, sold to Europeans who shackled and transported them to an ocean that many had never seen before, and then forced to inhabit squalid conditions during a long and tumultuous voyage, many Africans were overcome with despondency. On the *Elizabeth*'s tragic crossing, Isaac Wilson, the ship's physician, noted in his journal that many of the Africans were despondent and that he could not treat them. He also ventured that such despair made the Africans more susceptible to the effects of dysentery. Depression also contributed to the high rate of suicide among Africans when they were left unattended for any length of time up on deck.

40 • Greatest Cause of Slave Deaths— Disease

The greatest killer of Africans during the Middle Passage was disease. Scurvy, dysentery, smallpox, and a host of other contagious illnesses called "fevers" often spread like wildfire through the cramped, congested quarters of the slave ship. One French slave ship, *Le Rodeur*, was infected by ophthalmia in 1819. Not only all of the slaves but the entire crew were blinded by the disease. Most eventually recovered their sight. The thirty-nine who did not were thrown overboard, reputedly to avoid reinfecting the rest.

41 • Paying Head Money

Doctors on slave ships were paid a certain amount of money, called head money,

Broadside announcing arrival of Africans from the "Rice Coast" who have been kept "free from the least danger of being infected with the SMALL-POX." Prints and Photographs Division, Library of Congress

for each slave that made it to America in reasonably good health. It was an incentive for the doctor to take good care of the slaves. Many of these men, however, were not doctors in the modern sense. Often, the title merely meant someone skilled in the use of leeches and other pharmacopoeia who could only practice aboard ship. Most of the captured Africans who survived the passage did so because of their own health and fortitude, not because of the ministrations of the shipboard "doctor."

42 • White Man's Grave

Africans were not the only ones to die as a result of the Atlantic slave trade. Indeed, Africa was called the white man's grave because of the high mortality of white crew members both on

African soil and at sea. Disease, poor conditions, inadequate food and water, and exhausting work contributed to the high death rate. Three out of five white men working for the Royal African Company in Africa died between 1684 and 1732. A popular saying among white seamen was "Beware and take care, Of the Bight of Benin; For one that comes out, There are forty go in."

43 • Pinching Doctors

Africans found novel ways to protest the "tight packing" of slave ships. A Dr. Falconridge testified before Parliament that when he had to go down in the holds of tightly packed ships, he took off his shoes because he could not walk without stepping on human beings. But Dr. Falconridge also said the Africans bit and pinched him so much that he had bruises on his feet.

Prints and Photographs Division, Library of Congress

44 • Ship Captain Murders Slaves in Cargo

Slaves were sometimes murdered by the captains of the slave ships. The worst recorded case on a British vessel occurred in late 1781 on the ship *Zong,* commanded by Luke Collingwood. Leaving the African coast for Jamaica with four hundred Africans on September 6, the *Zong* lost several whites and sixty slaves to disease by November 29. Others became sick, and water stores soon became depleted. Thinking that many more would die before he reached port, constituting a big loss to the shipowners, and believing drowned slaves would be covered by insurers, Collingwood decided to throw overboard all those who were sick. First, fifty-four of the sickest slaves were cast into the ocean; soon, forty-two more were similarly drowned. Although a heavy rainfall allowed the crew to collect additional drinking water, twenty-six more Africans were pushed off the deck, and another ten, seeing their fate, jumped overboard with their hands bound. When the *Zong* reached port, the insurers refused to pay and the shipowners sued the captain. The case became a cause célèbre for abolitionists, who seized upon the murders as symbolic of the evils of the slave trade. The *Zong* episode eventually moved the British Parliament to pass laws regulating the terms under which insurance could be paid for losses of slaves during transport.

45 • Slaves Jump Overboard

Many slaves mutinied or committed suicide just before landing in the New World. When the *Prince of Orange* arrived in St. Kitts' Bay, Jamaica, in 1737, for example, at least one hundred Africans leaped overboard to their deaths. In this case, the captain claimed that rumors by Africans that they were about to be eaten by white men caused the suicide. Such suicides may have succeeded in part because the crew, happy to have the Middle Passage over, relaxed their guard as the ship approached port.

46 • Attempted Escapes During Passage

The negroes are so wilful and loth to leave their own country, that they often leap'd out of the canoes, boat and ship, into the sea, and kept under water till they were drowned, to avoid being taken up and saved by our boats, which pursued them; they having a more dreadful apprehension of Barbadoes than we can have of hell, tho' in reality they live much better there than in their own country; but home is home, etc. We have likewise seen divers of them eaten by the sharks, of which a prodigious number kept about the ships in this place, and I have been told will follow her hence to Barbadoes, for the dead negroes that are thrown overboard in the passage.

—Captain Thomas Phillips

47 • The *Little George*

Sometimes slave rebellions at sea were successful despite the overwhelming odds. In early 1730, for example, the ninety-six Africans aboard the *Little George* wrested control of the ship away from the crew. Some crew members were tossed overboard, and the remainder sequestered themselves in a cabin armed with firearms and ammunition, hoping the Africans would be unable to navigate the unfamiliar ship.

Although the journey took longer than usual due to the new crew's inexperience, the Africans successfully piloted the ship back to Africa, where they escaped.

48 • Suicide to Escape Punishment

On the English ship *Don Carlos*, the Africans attempted to overtake the crew with pieces of iron they had torn off the ship and with the shackles they had broken off their feet. One crew member recalled

. . . they fell in crouds and parcels on our men, upon the deck unawares, and stabb'd one of the stoutest of us all, who received fourteen or fifteen wounds of their knives, and so expir'd. Next they assaulted our boatswain, and cut one of his legs so round the bone, that he could not move . . . others cut our cook's throat to the pipe, and others wounded three of the sailors and threw one of them overboard in that condition.

Eventually, however, the crew's firepower overwhelmed the slaves and as the slaves scattered, the ship's captain reported: "many of the most mutinous, leapt over board, and drowned themselves in the ocean *with much resolution, showing no manner of concern for life.*"

49 • Mutinies on the Coast

Mutinies were also typical on the coast of Africa. The following incident took place at Old Calabar.

This Mutiny began at Midnight. . . . Two Men that stood Centry at the Forehatch way . . . permitted four [slaves] to go to that Place, but neglected to lay the Gratings again, as they should have done; whereupon four more Negroes came on Deck . . . and all eight fell on the two Centries who immediately called out for help. The Negroes endeavoured to get their Cutlaces from them, but the Lineyards (that is the Lines by which the

Handles of the Cutlaces were fastened to the Men's Wrists) were so twisted in the Scuffle, that they could not get them off before we came to their Assistance. The Negroes perceiving several white Men coming towards them, with Arms in their Hands, quitted the Centries and jumped over the Ship's Side into the Sea. . . . After we had secured these People, I called the Linguists, and ordered them to bid the Men-Negroes between Decks be quiet; (for there was a great noise amongst them). On their being silent, I asked, "What had induced them to mutiny?" They answered, "I was a great Rogue to buy them, in order to carry them away from their own Country, and that they were resolved to regain their Liberty if possible." I replied, "That they had forfeited their Freedom before I bought them, either by Crimes or by being taken in War." . . . Then I observed to them, "That if they should gain their Point and escape to the Shore, it would be of no Advantage to them, because their Countrymen would catch them, and sell them to other Ships." This served my purpose, and they seemed to be convinced of their Fault.

50 • Fattening Up Slaves

If a surplus of food existed at the end of the passage, captains and crew often overfed the Africans in order to "fatten them up" for market.

51 • Fear of Cannibalism

Many of the captive Africans feared they would be eaten by the Europeans. Cannibalism provided a logical explanation for the failure of the captured to ever return. Traders exploited this fear by threatening to eat the slaves, or turn them over to another group who would, if the slaves did not obey. These cultivated fears led to such expressions of dread that the white slavers eventually relented. Olaudah Equiano recalled that during his experience aboard ship

there was much dread and trembling among us, and nothing but bitter cries to be heard all night from these apprehensions, insomuch that at last the white people got some old slaves from the land to pacify us. They told us we were not to be eaten but to work, and were soon to go on land where we should see many of our country people. This report much eased us.

Landing in the New World

52 • Marching Skeletons

When a captain sold Africans upon arrival in the New World, he often brought them ashore in small boats, forced them to line up onshore, and marched them, like a ragtag army, into town, where they would be taken to market. On some occasions, such marches would be accompanied by the playing of bagpipes. A witness to one of these processions commented, "The whole party was . . . a resurrection of skin and bones . . . risen from the grave or escaped from Surgeon's Hall."

53 • Examination of the Enslaved

Most often, captains sold Africans in consultation with a factor, or broker, who, along with the captain, looked over the assembled Africans and selected out those who were ill, crippled, or near death. These would often be sold separately as "refuse" slaves, sometimes for as low as a dollar. The rest of the Africans were sold at set prices for men, women, boys, and girls. Once the prices were set for all of the purchases, the buyers "scrambled" to select the best-looking prospects. Such a rush of purchasers often frightened the Africans, especially those who

Inspection and sale of a slave. Prints and Photographs Division, Library of Congress

believed they were to be eaten once they landed.

North America

54 • First Twenty Africans as Indentured Servants

In 1619, a year before the landing of the *Mayflower*, the first Africans arrived in British North America aboard a Dutch ship that landed at Jamestown, Virginia. The "twenty Negers," as they were called by the Dutch, were sold not as slaves, but as indentured servants who worked for a term of service, usually seven years. By 1651 several of these original twenty Africans had completed their term of service and received land as part of the usual "freedom duties" that masters gave freed servants, white or Black. One of these twenty, Mr. Anthony John-

son, rose to become a prosperous farmer and master of several white indentured servants. But by the end of the seventeenth century, all Africans brought into or born in Virginia were declared slaves, and any upward mobility like Johnson enjoyed became a near impossibility. In a span of eighty years, Virginia society had evolved into one of the harshest and most severe legal systems of slavery in the Americas.

55 • Africans in Massachusetts

Africans arrived in New England prior to the settling of the Massachusetts Bay Colony in 1629. Records show that Samuel Maverick, the region's first slaveholder, arrived in 1624 and owned two Africans. By the time John Winthrop, later the colony's governor, arrived in 1630, Africans had been living and working in Massachusetts for some time.

Landing at Jamestown, 1619. Prints and Photographs Division, Library of Congress

56 • Slave Trade Latecomers

North Americans were relative latecomers to the slave trade, which had been under way for two hundred years before it became a factor in the development of North America. For the most part, Americans were not involved in the slave trade until the middle of the eighteenth century. This was largely because of the relatively late development of a plantation agricultural system in North America.

57 • The Royal African Company

The formation of the Royal African Company dramatically altered the slave trade to North America. Before its incorporation, British North Americans had to get their slaves from other carriers—Portuguese, Dutch, or French—who had direct contact and bases in Africa. But with the incorporation first of the Royal Adventurers in 1663, and its later incarnation as the RAC in

1672, the British colonies could obtain slaves directly from British traders. Even then, the percentage of slaves coming to British North America was very small. Before the beginning of the eighteenth century, British North America received only a tiny percentage of all slaves being transported by the British to the New World. Most went to the British West Indies, especially Jamaica, which took fully one-third.

58 • Tobacco Cultivation Demanded Slave Labor

It was the successful cultivation of tobacco in Virginia and Maryland that created a demand for labor and ultimately a lucrative trade in slaves to North America in the late seventeenth century. As tobacco shipments to England increased in volume to 105 million pounds in 1771, the demand for slaves increased as well. Tobacco cultivation is extremely labor-intensive, and the tobacco farmers could not persuade enough Englishmen to migrate to North America, so they turned to African labor.

59 • Rice Cultivation

The cultivation of rice in eighteenth-century South Carolina, North Carolina, and Georgia was, like tobacco, a stimulus for the Atlantic slave trade. Rice required not only intensive labor but also agricultural skills that few Englishmen had. People with growing skills from West and Central Africa were especially sought by tobacco planters, and there is considerable evidence that enslaved Africans taught the slave owners how to cultivate rice, since rice did not grow in the colder climate of Great Britain.

60 • Variations in North American Slavery

The daily life of enslaved Africans in North America varied according to what region they lived in and what type of crop they cultivated. The most common system, the "gang-labor method," was found in regions growing tobacco and cotton. Under this system, slaves worked the entire day in groups controlled by a driver or overseer. In South Carolina and Georgia, however, where rice was the predominant crop, a "task system" operated that allocated a certain amount of work to each slave per day. After a slave's task was completed, he could do what he wished with the rest of the day. Many slaves used this time to tend their own crops, which they used to supplement their diets, and if there was a surplus, to sell to other slaves or local traders. Corn, potatoes, tobacco, peanuts, sugar, watermelons, and pumpkins were commonly grown.

61 • Puritans Ardent Slave Traders

Once North Americans entered the international commerce in Africans, the Puritans of New England became some of the most ardent slave traders. After Captain William Pierce of Boston successfully traded captured Pequot Indians for Africans in the West Indies in 1638, other Boston merchants began a lucrative trade between New England and the West Indies. Then, in 1644, Boston traders launched direct trade with Africa to import slaves—a commerce that mushroomed during the eighteenth century, after the British Parliament revoked the Royal African Company's exclusive monopoly on the slave trade. By the middle of the eighteenth century New England had become the biggest slave-trading region in British North America.

62 • Triangle Trade

The slave trade was vital to the emergence of New England as a trading, shipbuilding, and manufacturing center in the eighteenth century. On the famous triangular trade route, New England ships transported food, lumber, horses,

and manufactured goods to the West Indies, exchanged them for rum, and then sailed for Africa, where the rum bought Africans, who were transported back to the West Indies. Often, the routes would be altered to meet current demand; but the important fact was that such trade undergirded the rise of the incredibly profitable rum industry which "became New England's largest manufacturing business before the Revolution." By 1774 there were over one hundred distilleries in Rhode Island and Massachusetts, with those in the latter producing over 2.7 million gallons of rum. On the West African coast, New England rum was bartered and traded more than English, French, and Dutch alcohol, weapons, trinkets, or dry goods.

63 • Slave Trade Fuels War of Independence

Many of the conflicts that led to the War of Independence had their origin in the Atlantic slave trade. Parliament's passage of the Navigation Acts was designed to force colonial planters to do business exclusively with British merchants. In 1723 the British Parliament overturned a Virginia act that reduced the number of Africans being imported into the colony on the grounds that such action would hurt other aspects of British trade with the colonies. In 1764 the Parliament passed the Sugar Act, which attempted to control the growing North American trade with the French West Indies, whose sugar was part of the infamous triangle trade of rum, sugar, and slaves. Not surprisingly, the colony that protested the Sugar Act most vociferously was none other than Rhode Island— the colony most involved in slave trading.

64 • Trade Boycott as Resistance to British

Opposition to the British slave trade was one

way for the North American colonists to resist British colonialism. When the 1774 British Parliament imposed the Coercive Acts on the colonials to punish them for resistance to the earlier Townshend and Tea Acts, the colonists boycotted the British slave trade to America. The First Continental Congress made the slave trade a cornerstone of its resistance against the British when it suspended trade with Britain in 1774, declaring that after December 1, the British could no longer import slaves into the colonies. The resistance continued even after the War of Independence. One of the first acts of the Continental Congress in 1776 was to vote that "no slaves be imported into any of the thirteen United Colonies." Rather than humanity, the cause of this act was a desire to hurt Britain where the colonies knew it would hurt the mother country the most—in the slave trade.

65 • English Profit from the Slave Trade

That resistance by North Americans hurt the British economic interest is certain:

The slave trade is "indeed the best Traffick the Kingdom hath," John Cary affirmed, "as it doth occasionally give so vast an Imployment to our People both by Sea and Land." It was "a Trade of the most Advantage to this kingdom of any we drive, and as it were all Profit." It was linked, of course, with the West Indian trade "and [I] do joyn them together because of their dependence on each other."

66 • Slave Trade Drove a Moral Wedge Between Britain and the Colonies

In 1772 the Virginia House of Burgess declared to King George III: "The importation of slaves into the colonies from the coast of Africa hath long been considered a trade of great inhumanity, and under its present encouragement,

George Mason. Prints and Photographs Division, Library of Congress

we have too much reason to fear will endanger the very existence of your Majesty's American dominions."

After the war, the anti-slavery advocate George Mason concluded that the slave trade "was one of the great causes of our separation from Great Britain."

67 • Original Draft of the Declaration of Independence

The anti-slave trade sentiment influenced Thomas Jefferson's first draft of the Declaration of Independence, in which he indicted the King of England, George III, for foisting the slave trade on the colonists. As originally written, the Declaration of Independence claimed that King George *has waged cruel war against human nature itself, violating its most sacred rights of life liberty in the persons of a distant people who never offended him, captivating and carrying them into slavery in another hemisphere, or to incur miserable death in their transportation thither. The piratical warfare, the opprobrium of infidel powers, is the warfare of the Christian king of Great Britain. Determined to keep open a market where MEN should be bought and sold, he has prostituted his negative for suppressing every legislative attempt to prohibit or to restrain this execrable commerce.*

But the Continental Congress struck this passage from the Declaration. Most likely, Congress did not wish to list slavery in the Declaration for fear that after the war, the new nation might be called on to abolish slavery. Moreover, Jefferson's characterization of slavery and the slave trade as being forced upon the colonists was a half-truth at best: the colonists avidly pursued the slave trade and slavery on their own and had not been blocked by the king from ending the slave trade. The passage remains significant, however, for showing that Jefferson, contrary to some later interpretations, did regard Africans as "MEN . . . bought and sold" who were subject to the Declaration's principles that all men "are created equal, that they are endowed by their Creator with certain unalienable Rights, that among these are Life, Liberty, and the pursuit of Happiness."

68 • Slavery Purchased America's Freedom

While the colonists resisted the British slave trade, they actually benefited from the slave system that depended on the trade. As one historian puts it, Americans actually purchased their freedom with products grown by slaves and then traded to the French during the War of Independence. Before the war, agricultural products such as rice, indigo, and tobacco—all produced by enslaved Africans—were British America's most valuable exports. Without the slave trade and slavery, British North America would never have been able to generate the wealth to gain its freedom from England, at least in the eighteenth century. As a member of the British Parliament acknowledged after the war: "I know not why we should blush to confess that molasses [produced by sugar cultivated by slaves] was an essential ingredient of American independence."

69 • States Dispute Slave Trade Limitations After Independence

Although the colonies made much of the inhumanity of the British slave trade during the conflict with England, the United States could not immediately agree to end the slave trade after the war was over. Virginia, along with several other states, voted to prohibit the future importation of slaves. But South Carolina and Georgia frustrated the effort by threatening to not join the Union if the slave trade was prohibited. The rest of the states capitulated in the interest of unity. But the agreement that the United States would not limit the slave trade before 1808 became the outer limit of tolerance for continuation of the slave trade.

70 • Fear of Rebellion Caused Slave Trade Limitations

South Carolina stopped importing slaves during the War of Independence, partly because it feared the huge concentrations of slaves already in the state and the possibility of a slave rebellion like that which was shaking St. Domingue, now known as Haiti. But in 1803 South Carolina reopened the slave trade to grab as many slaves as it could before the national prohibition of slave trading went into effect in 1808. The new ability to resell slaves in the recently acquired Louisiana Territory also influenced the decision to reopen the slave trade.

71 • British North American Slave Trade Grows

In the period 1701–1810 the United States (and beforehand, British North America) imported only 5.8 percent of the slaves arriving in the Western Hemisphere and slightly more than 20 percent of the slaves that entered British American territories, including the West Indies. As the eighteenth century progressed, however, the American share of the British trade increased, and by the 1740s its trade in slaves exceeded that of Barbados. By 1760 Jamaica's preeminent role in the trade was challenged. In the last years of the slave trade, from 1761 to 1808, the United States received more than 166,900 slaves. Though a late starter in the trade and always a lesser destination for British imported slaves, British North America was quite a significant recipient of enslaved people in the second half of the eighteenth century.

72 • Diseases of Tropics and Sugar Cultivation Increase Slave Mortality

American reliance on the slave trade was relatively low compared to other New World slave societies for one particular reason: the high rate of natural increase of the African American population in British North America, in contrast to the low rate found in the British West Indies. "From 1700 to 1780 the Black population increased twice as rapidly as the rate of importation. In the year 1790 the Negro population stood at 757,000, and by that time perhaps no more than one-half that number of Negroes had been imported." By contrast, Jamaica, Barba-

dos, and the Leeward Islands "held a population of about 387,000, although perhaps 1,230,000 had been imported. Diseases of the tropics and rigors of sugar cultivation exacted a heavy toll in the Caribbean." It was not climate, but the conditions of sugar cultivation and diseases in the tropics, that accounted for the demographic "holocaust" of the British West Indies.

73 • Britain and the United States Abolish Slave Trade

In 1807 Lord Grenville's bill to abolish the slave trade passed the House of Lords and the House of Commons, and was approved by the British crown. That same year, the United States Congress responded to President Jefferson's December 1806 annual message against the "violation" of the slave trade by passing a law prohibiting Americans from involvement in the international slave trade. But it was Britain that aggressively suppressed the slave trade with its powerful navy. Although abolitionist sentiment in Britain played a prominent role in the movement to end the trade, it succeeded in part because of the decline of mercantilism, the reduced profitability of plantation slavery, and the rise of industrialism in England.

74 • Slave Trade Continues

Despite British and American action against the slave trade, the forced migration of Africans continued. From 1780 to 1867, in the period when slave trading was reputedly in decline, more than 5 million Africans—roughly half of the total who arrived in the Americas—were removed forcibly from Africa to the Western Hemisphere. Because the United States possessed a largely self-reproducing slave population after 1800, the U.S. was not the major market for slave trading in the 1800s. But the expansion of sugar plantations in Cuba and coffee plantations in Brazil during the 1800s kept demand for imported slaves high, and illegal slavers continued to meet that demand.

FROM SLAVERY TO FREEDOM

Rebellions

75 • Haitian Revolution Extends Slave Trade End

Britain might have outlawed the slave trade before 1808 if it had not been for the Haitian Revolution. That revolution effectively ended sugar production on St. Domingue (Haiti), a French colony, thereby increasing the value of sugar from the British West Indies. Profits to be made from sugar cultivation soared, and so did the demand for more slaves to work British West Indian plantations. Thus, in 1792, the House of Commons agreed only to the principle that the slave trade ought to be ended, and did not abolish the trade until 1808, four years after the Haitian Revolution was over.

76 • Internal Slave Trade—Rebellion

On October 25, 1841, 135 Blacks were put aboard the *Creole* in Hampton Roads, Virginia, for transfer to New Orleans. On November 7, as the boat neared the Bahamas, the slaves attacked the crew, appropriated all the weapons on board, and retrieved the documents that committed them to slavery. Forcing the crew to take them to an English colony, the ship arrived in Nassau on November 9. Boats piloted by Bahamian Blacks surrounded the ship in the Nassau harbor, permitting the slaves to escape.

77 • Amistad Rebellion

The most famous on-board slave rebellion in U.S. history was the Amistad Incident of 1839. On July 1 of that year, a group of Africans who had been illegally imported to Cuba murdered the captain and took control of the Spanish ship

Death of Captain Ferrer aboard the *Amistad*. Prints and Photographs Division, Library of Congress

Death of Capt. Ferrer, the Captain of the Amistad, July, 1839.

Don Jose Ruiz and Don Pedro Montez, of the Island of Cuba, having purchased fifty-three slaves at Havana, recently imported from Africa, put them on board the Amistad, Capt. Ferrer, in order to transport them to Principe, another port on the Island of Cuba. After being out from Havana about four days, the African captives on board, in order to obtain their freedom, and return to Africa, armed themselves with cane knives, and rose upon the Captain and crew of the vessel. Capt. Ferrer and the cook of the vessel were killed; two of the crew escaped; Ruiz and Montez were made prisoners.

Amistad while it was transporting them from Havana to plantations in Puerto Príncipe, Cuba. Their leader, twenty-five-year-old Joseph Cinque, tried to direct the boat back to Africa, but their purchaser, Montes, steered a course for the United States, where the USS *Washington* captured the vessel and took it and the Africans to New London, Connecticut. The case became a cause célèbre and gained enormous public attention, not only for the captured Africans but also for the abolitionist movement, which assembled an excellent team of lawyers to keep the Africans from being returned to Spain. Eventually Cinque and his fellow Africans were allowed to return to Africa after former President John Quincy Adams successfully argued the Africans' case before the United States Supreme Court.

78 • Fears of Slave Rebellions

Rebellions frequently occurred in the slave trade, especially while ships waited at anchor on the coast. The captain of the *Albion-Frigate* discovered this when he mistakenly allowed his slaves the use of knives to eat meat. After breaking down the forecastle door and breaking off their shackles, the slaves killed several whites before the crew could counterattack and regain control of the ship. Twenty-eight slaves were either killed or jumped overboard to freedom.

79 • Description by an English Captain

An English captain wrote in 1693:

When our slaves are aboard we shackle the men two and two, while we lie in port, and in sight of their own country, for 'tis then they attempt to make their escape and mutiny; to prevent which we always keep centinels upon the hatchways, and have a chest full of small arms, ready loaden and primed, constantly lying at hand upon the quarter-deck, together with some granada shells; and two of our quarter deck guns, pointing on the deck thence, and two more out of steerage.

80 • National Loyalty in Rebellions

The danger of rebellion on a slave ship increased dramatically if all or almost all of the slaves on board were from the same African nation or could speak the same language. The belief existed among slave ship captains that some peoples were more volatile and more revolutionary than others. People along the Gold Coast were considered to be particularly warlike and hateful of other Africans. Ship captains often put this knowledge to good use. "We have some 30 or 40 gold coast negroes, which we buy ... to make guardians and overseers of the Whidaw negroes, and sleep among them to keep them from quarreling; and in order, as well as to give us notice, if they can discover any caballing or plotting among them, which trust they will discharge with great diligence."

81 • Rebellions in North America

Unlike rebellions in South America and the Caribbean, those that occurred in British North America had almost no chance of success. Slaves faced a numerically superior white population in all of the southern states, with the exception of South Carolina. Even when not outnumbered, slaves were poorly armed, usually with only sticks and knives, since slaves were prohibited from bearing arms as early as the late seventeenth century. Nevertheless, slaves still plotted and rebelled against southern slavery, even when it meant certain death.

82 • Revolt Causing 1712 Slave Act

In 1712 a slave revolt threatened to destroy New York City. In April twenty to thirty African

American slaves, along with two Indians, set fire to a building and ambushed several whites who came to put out the flames. When nine whites were killed and at least five more wounded, a general alarm was sounded and soldiers were brought to the scene. Within a day, the slaves' rebellion had been overcome and most of the rebels captured, except those who committed suicide. Following a trial, twenty-one slaves were executed for their participation. As a result of the revolt, New York passed the 1712 Slave Act to suppress insurrections, Massachusetts enacted a law against further importation of slaves into that colony, and Pennsylvania instituted high taxes to restrain African importations.

83 • Garcia and Fort Negro

After the War of 1812, over three hundred Blacks occupied an abandoned British fort on the banks of the Apalachicola River in what is now Florida. Known as Fort Negro, it was headed by an African American man named Garcia. The heavily armed fort became a symbol of Black independence and a threat to the southern slave system. The United States Government made destruction of the fort one of its highest priorities after the War of 1812. In the summer of 1816 the U.S. Navy and Army under Colonel Clinch surrounded Fort Negro and called on the community to surrender. Garcia refused. On July 27, 1816, an attack was launched, but the heavily fortified garrison repelled it. But a second attack succeeded in hitting the ammunition supply, and the fort exploded. Only sixty-four of the three hundred Blacks survived the blast, and only three of the sixty-four were uninjured. Garcia, unhurt, was executed by firing squad. The remaining survivors were returned to slavery.

84 • Slaves Blamed for Fires

Many suspicious or unexplained fires in southern and northern towns were attributed to rebellious slaves. On February 28, 1741, fearful whites in New York City regarded a series of fires as a sign that a slave rebellion was about to begin. Fueled by rumors of a plot, whites rampaged in New York and attacked the Black population. Thirteen Blacks were burned alive, eighteen hanged, seventy shipped to the West Indies, and thirty-three released for a conspiracy that was never proved to have existed. Setting fires was, however, a tactic favored by resistant slaves because it allowed the violent destruction of property valued by whites while avoiding a direct confrontation with slave owners. In the 1790s fires in Charleston, Albany, New York City, Savannah, and Baltimore were blamed on Blacks, and in 1803 Blacks in York, Pennsylvania, attempted to burn major sections of the city after a court convicted a Black woman of attempting to poison two whites. Eleven buildings were destroyed before the militia arrived and enforced a curfew.

85 • Slave Vandalism

The slaves destroyed tirelessly. Like the peasants in the Jacquerie or the Luddite wreckers, they were seeking their salvation in the most obvious way, the destruction of what they knew was the cause of their sufferings; and if they destroyed much it was because they suffered much.

86 • The Stono Rebellion

On September 9, 1739, approximately twelve slaves revolted at Stono, South Carolina, some twenty miles southwest of Charleston. Led by a recently arrived Angolan slave, the group killed two white men guarding a warehouse, took weapons they found inside, and marched southward to escape to freedom in St. Augustine, Spanish Florida. As they marched, other Blacks joined the group, which swelled to more than seventy-five people. Unfortunately for the marchers, they were discovered by a Colonel Bull, lieutenant governor of the colony, who, after narrowly escaping capture by the rebels, rode off to sound the alarm. Bull returned with an armed militia which engaged the slaves, who had stopped ten miles from Stono, in a battle that decimated the rebel force. Some rebels escaped, but most were eventually caught. Twenty-five whites and fifty Africans were killed in the battle. The Stono Rebellion led to a temporary decline in the importation of Africans into a colony that was already described as a "Negro country."

87 • How Toussaint l'Ouverture Led Haitian Revolution

The Haitian Revolution, which began on August 22, 1791, and ended on January 1, 1804, was the only rebellion to liberate an entire slave population. Inspired by the ideals of the French Revolution, slaves on St. Domingue succeeded in overthrowing the white planter class, repulsing the French Army, and defeating Spanish and British forces (the latter invading the island in 1793). The Haitian Revolution's success was largely attributable to its outstanding leader, General Toussaint l'Ouverture, who outwitted all three European forces with tactics that foreshadowed modern guerrilla warfare. The island's mountainous terrain, the spread of yellow fever and malaria among the French, British, and Spanish, and the conflicts among whites and mulattoes on the island enabled this revolution to succeed where others did not. In addition, the huge numerical superiority of slaves ensured success. Though l'Ouverture did not live to see the end of the revolution, its success

Toussaint l'Ouverture. Prints and Photographs Division, Library of Congress

proved that Africans could achieve self-determination in the New World and gave a hope of freedom to millions of slaves in the Western Hemisphere.

88 • Gabriel's Attack on Richmond, Virginia

When a twenty-four-year-old slave named Gabriel Prosser organized a large-scale attack on the city of Richmond in 1800, the entire state of Virginia was shocked. Owned by the barbaric Thomas H. Prosser of Henrico County, Virginia, Gabriel was a six-foot-two-inch man, who in the spring of 1800 began studying the layout of Richmond, recording the location of arms and ammunition, and stockpiling swords, pikes, and bayonets. Gabriel planned to organize slaves into three columns, one to take and hold the city, another to grab arms and ammunition at the city's powder magazine, and another to kill all those who tried to stop them. When Gabriel communicated his plan to numerous slaves, two informed their master, who in turn alerted Governor James Monroe. Even though Monroe amassed six hundred troops in the capital, the one thousand slaves that Gabriel assembled outside of Richmond still had a chance to disrupt the city. But a violent thunderstorm that evening washed out a crucial bridge and the slave army broke up. In the following days, hundreds of Blacks were murdered or arrested. Gabriel was captured in Norfolk on September 25. Neither Gabriel nor his lieutenants would divulge their plans, even in the face of death, and all were executed.

89 • Trial a Mockery?

Gabriel Prosser at his trial for organizing a slave rebellion in 1800:

I have nothing more to offer than what George Washington would have had to offer, had he been taken by the British and put to trial by them. I have adventured my life in endeavoring to obtain the liberty of my countrymen, and am a willing sacrifice to their cause: and I beg, as a favour, that I may be immediately led to execution. I know that you have pre-determined to shed my blood, why then all this mockery of a trial?

90 • Henry Highland Garnet Encouraged Resistance

Some Black militants, like Henry Highland Garnet, exalted:

Brethren, arise, arise! Strike for your lives and liberties. Now is the day and the hour. Let every slave throughout the land do this and the days of slavery are numbered. Rather die freemen than live to be slaves. . . . Awake, Awake, no oppressed people have secured their liberty without resistance.

Henry Highland Garnet. Prints and Photographs Division, Library of Congress

91 • Revolt Led by Dislondes

On January 8, 1811, some thirty-five miles from New Orleans, a group of four hundred to five hundred slaves led by Charles Dislondes, a free mulatto from St. Domingue, revolted on the plantation of Major Andry, wounding the major and killing his son. Arming themselves initially with axes, knives, and clubs, the slaves eventually obtained firearms and marched from plantation to plantation in St. Charles and St. John the Baptist Parishes, wreaking havoc and sending whites fleeing to New Orleans. The next day Major Andry recovered enough to lead eight to ten heavily armed planters against the slaves, whom he claimed he slaughtered in great numbers. Actually it was the arrival of four hundred militiamen and sixty U.S. Army regulars from New Orleans, under the command of Brigadier General Wade Hampton, that routed the slave army. Sixty-six slaves were killed, sixteen more were captured, but seventeen escaped into the woods to die or find freedom. All those captured were executed in the most brutal manner, with the heads of some displayed on the road from Andry's plantation to New Orleans as a message to other would-be rebel slaves.

92 • Denmark Vesey's 1822 Conspiracy

Denmark Vesey's 1822 conspiracy sent fear throughout the South. Vesey was an African-born seaman and former slave who had purchased his freedom and who carried himself as a prideful freeman. Vesey was intelligent, spoke many languages, and chastised other Blacks for obsequious behavior toward whites. Inspired by the Bible description of how the children of Israel were delivered out of Egypt from bondage, Vesey constructed a complex plan to overthrow the city of Charleston on July 14. He enlisted several lieutenants from the artisan class of slaves to spread the word carefully among only trusted slaves, not house servants. Vesey divided his army into divisions according to their presumed African tribal heritage and planned a six-pronged attack on Charleston. When a slave revealed the plan to white planters, two of Vesey's lieutenants were arrested on May 31 and Vesey advanced the day of the attack to June 16 to thwart his enemies. But on June 14 a Charleston slave spied on fellow slaves and revealed to his master that a revolt was planned. Vesey and other conspirators were arrested, and they were hanged on July 2, ironically for acts of rebellion that never occurred.

93 • Slaves Betraying Slaves

Many rebellions were thwarted because slaves told their masters about plots. Some betrayed their fellow slaves because it was one of the surest ways to obtain one's own freedom. One such informer betrayed an 1816 slave rebellion in Camden County and the South Car-

olina legislature purchased his freedom from his master for the sum of $1,100. Devany Prioleau, who revealed plans of the Denmark Vesey conspiracy, obtained his freedom and an annual pension of $50, which was raised to $250 in 1857.

94 • Rise and Take Your Freedom!

Some African Americans, mostly free people in the North, openly advocated violence as the best way for slaves to obtain their freedom. In 1829 *David Walker's Appeal,* a seventy-six-page inflammatory pamphlet, called on slaves to rise and kill their masters. "Remember Americans," Walker, the self-taught, dark-skinned tradesman wrote, "that we must and shall be free and enlightened as you are, will you wait until we shall, under God, obtain our liberty by the crushing arm of power? Will it not be dreadful for you? I speak Americans for your own good." Some attributed Walker's suspicious death in 1830 to the retribution of slavery supporters, but it did not end the influence of the pamphlet, which became a kind of bible to revolutionary-minded Black abolitionists of the period.

95 • Nat Turner's Rebellion

Not long after David Walker issued his radical appeal, the bloodiest slave revolt in U.S. history occurred: Nat Turner's rebellion in Southampton, Virginia, in 1831. Nat was a mystical slave who could read and write, and who interpreted the eclipse of the sun on February 12 as a sign from God that he should "arise and prepare myself...to slay my enemies...with their own weapons." Nat confided his plans only to four trusted slave allies until it was too late for them to be betrayed; then, on the evening of August 21, Turner and his band began their reign of terror by killing all white people they encountered, be-

Discovery of Nat Turner. Prints and Photographs Division, Library of Congress

ginning with Nat's master's family. The group gathered weapons, provisions, horses, and additional slaves. By August 23 the band consisted of seventy slaves, and they had slain more than fifty-seven white men, women, and children. When some in Turner's group went to recruit more slaves, Turner's party was attacked by whites. Though Turner's force initially repulsed this attack, reinforcements for the white forces eventually overwhelmed the group. As Turner's forces scattered, hundreds of white volunteers and militia rushed to the area and began massacring Blacks indiscriminately. Turner eluded capture for months by living in a little cave in the ground near his former home, until he was discovered by Benjamin Phipps on October 30. Unlike Gabriel Prosser and Denmark Vesey, Turner spoke openly during his trial about his role in the uprising. He pleaded not guilty, however, because "he did not feel so," having been directed by God. He was hanged on November 11.

96 • White Newspaper Comments on Nat Turner

Even a white newspaper could treat the subject of Nat Turner with cold sympathy:

Nat seems very humble; willing to answer any questions, indeed quite communicative, and I am disposed to think tells the truth. I heard him speak more than an hour. He readily avowed his motive; confessed that he was the prime instigator of the plot, that he alone opened his master's doors and struck his master the first blow with a hatchet. He clearly verified the accounts which have been given of him. He is a shrewd, intelligent fellow. [Richmond Whig]

97 • Nat Turner's Remains

The bodies of those executed, with one exception, were buried in a decent and becoming manner. That of Nat Turner was delivered to the doctors, who skinned it and made grease of the flesh. Mr. R. S. Barham's father owned a money purse made of his hide. His skeleton was for many years in the possession of Dr. Massenberg, but has since been misplaced.

—William Sidney Drewry

98 • Fear of Rebellions

To those who lived in the midst of slavery, "It is like a smothered volcano—we know not when, or where, the flame will burst forth but we know that death in the most horrid forms threatens us. Some have died, others have become deranged from apprehension since the South Hampton affair" (Mrs. Lawrence Lewis, niece of George Washington, to Mayor Harrison Gray Otis of Boston, October 17, 1831).

99 • Religious Slaves Fomented Rebellions

Sometimes the most religious slaves fomented rebellions. A local paper, writing about the 1816 Conspiracy in Camden County, South Carolina, reported that "those who were most active in the conspiracy occupied a respectable stand in one of the churches, several were professors, and one a class leader."

100 • Hidden Slave Rebellions

If individual acts of revolt are included, it is unknown exactly how many slave revolts occurred in the United States. Hundreds of acts of physical resistance, poisonings, stabbings, shootings, house and plantation burnings, and acts of vengeance must have gone unreported or unrecognized as revolts.

Robert Smalls. Brady Collection, Library of Congress

101 • Frederick Douglass Resists Covey's Brutality

A typical example of individual rebellion was Frederick Douglass's act of resistance against Covey, the "Negro breaker." Douglass's master had hired him out for a year to Covey because Douglass was becoming a difficult slave. Covey succeeded in brutalizing Douglass to such an extent that Douglass ran away and hid in the woods. When he returned to Covey's farm on Sunday, Covey was friendly and forgiving. But on Monday morning, Covey grabbed Douglass in the barn and tried to tie him up, presumably for a whipping. In a split second, Douglass determined to resist, to strike no blow, but to parry all of Covey's and refuse to be beaten. After an hour of wrestling, during which Covey became exhausted trying to beat the younger and stronger Douglass, Covey withdrew and told him, "now, don't you let me get hold of you again." Douglass knew Covey spoke the truth—for Covey had been bested by his young slave. Even more remarkably, Covey never turned Douglass over to the authorities for resisting a white man, an act punishable by death. Admitting that Douglass had successfully resisted him, however, would have destroyed Covey's reputation and business as a Negro breaker. In numerous other instances, it must have been difficult for whites to admit to having been bested by their slaves.

102 • Slave Appointed Navy Captain of Stolen Ship

Rebellious slaves were found even within the Confederate Army. During the Civil War, the Confederacy often used slaves as crew members of its ships, and in at least one instance, the practice backfired. In 1862 the slave pilot Robert Smalls of the steamship *Planter*, along with other slave members of the crew, stole the ship out of the Charleston harbor. Smalls was able to navigate the ship northward into Union hands. As a reward for his accomplishment and in recognition of his skill, Smalls was made captain of the *Planter* when it again set sail under the Union flag.

103 • Punishment of Slaves Pleases God?

I am now to acquaint you that very lately we have had a very wicked and barbarous plott of the designe of the negroes rising with a designe to destroy all the white people in the country and then to take the town [Charles Town] in full body but it pleased God it was discovered and many of them taken prisoners and some burnt some hang'd and some banish'd.

—Anonymous letter to Mr. Boone in London, June 24, 1720

Runaways

104 • The First Runaways

Since the first arrival of Africans to British North America, enslaved men and women have attempted to escape bondage by running away. In the seventeenth century Black and white indentured servants often tried to escape together. In 1640 a Black slave who, with six white indentured servants, tried to steal a small ship stocked with food and weapons was charged with conspiracy to escape. That same year a Black servant ran away with two white servants and was sentenced to lifetime servitude for his action.

105 • Successful Runaways Living in Maroon Colonies

Until recently, Maroon colonies, or settlements of runaway slaves, were thought only to have existed in the Caribbean or South America. Certainly, the quilombos, as they were called in Brazil, and the Maroon colonies of the Dutch and British West Indies lasted longer, were larger, and were able to be more self-sustaining in terms of agriculture, and later, trade, than any such settlements in the United States. The Palmares Maroon colony in Brazil, which numbered thousands of runaway slaves, successfully fought off Portuguese troops that attempted to capture it, and forced the Portuguese to negotiate treaties with them. Similarly, Maroon colonies in Surinam maintained their independence for three hundred years and their descendants live today as the Djulea and Saramaccan peoples.

106 • Recapture of Maroon Colonies

Maroon colonies on the scale of those found in the Caribbean and Latin America did not exist in the United States. Nevertheless, in eighteenth-century Spanish Florida, smaller Maroon colonies, made up of runaway slaves and Indians, survived and maintained their independence until the Creek war of 1813. Other Maroon colonies made up of a dozen or more slaves existed in various southern communities into the nineteenth century and posed an annoying threat to the southern slave regime. In 1729, for example, a group of Virginia slaves escaped into the Blue Ridge Mountains, carrying guns, ammunition, and agricultural supplies. Their presence posed such a temptation to other slaves that eventually a small army of white men was raised and sent into the mountains where, after a fierce battle, the slaves were recaptured.

107 • Maroon Slaves Rather Die Than Be Captured

In Cabarrus County, North Carolina, a ferocious battle erupted in March 1811 when a band of slave catchers discovered a group of fugitive slaves. The fugitive slaves had established a Maroon colony in the area and had already declared their willingness to die rather than be captured and returned to slavery. In the battle that resulted, two African Americans were killed, one injured, and two African American women were captured.

108 • Black Seminoles

Many slaves of South Carolina and Georgia escaped bondage in the eighteenth century by running away to Florida, where, in the marshes and swamps of this Spanish colony, they eluded capture. These runaways eventually bonded with Indian survivors of local wars from the Creek and Cherokee Nations. Known as the Seminole Indians, they created a new ethnic group, the Black Seminoles, and numbered over 100,000 before 1750. Fiercely independent and excellent scouts and traders, the Black Seminoles assumed a prominent role as scouts in the Mexican War of the late 1840s. But their valor and loyalty to the nation were not rewarded with the land promised them, and they were eventually forced onto reservations in Florida and, later, Oklahoma.

109 • Fugitive Slave Act of 1793

In 1793 the United States Congress passed the Fugitive Slave Act that placed the authority of the federal government behind the recovery of slaves by masters. In a clear victory for the South, the law made it more difficult for slaves to escape bondage by allowing masters to follow slaves to the North, capture suspected fugitives, bring them before a judge, and claim them as

Slaves escaping from eastern shore of Maryland. Prints and Photographs Division, Library of Congress

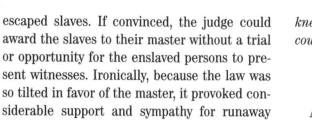

escaped slaves. If convinced, the judge could award the slaves to their master without a trial or opportunity for the enslaved persons to present witnesses. Ironically, because the law was so tilted in favor of the master, it provoked considerable support and sympathy for runaway slaves in the North and led some whites to assist runaways in the underground railroad.

110 • Drapetomania

"Drapetomania, or the Disease Causing Negroes to Run Away" was how one southern doctor, Samuel Cartwright of the University of Louisiana, explained the fact that hundreds of African Americans were fleeing southern plantations in the 1840s. They must be sick! Apparently it did not occur to Dr. Cartwright that it might be slavery that made Black people flee to the North.

111 • Escape to Freedom Seemed Formidable

To look at the map and observe the proximity of Eastern Shore, Maryland, to Delaware and Pennsylvania, it may seem to the reader quite absurd to regard the proposed escape as a formidable undertaking. But to understand, *some one has said, a man must* stand under. *The real distance was great enough, but the imagined distance was, to our ignorance, much greater. Slaveholders sought to impress their slaves with a belief in the boundlessness of slave territory, and of their own limitless power. Our notions of the geography of the country were very vague and indistinct. The distance, however, was not the chief trouble, for the nearer were the lines of a slave state to the borders of a free state the greater was the trouble. Hired kidnappers infested the borders. Then, too, we knew that merely reaching a free state did not free us, that wherever caught we could be returned to slavery. We*

knew of no spot this side the ocean where we could be safe.

—Frederick Douglass

112 • Ellen and William Craft

A talent for cross-dressing and masquerade helped Ellen and William Craft escape from slavery. Around 1847 the two Georgia slaves hit upon the idea of traveling as master and slave, with Ellen Craft, who was light-skinned enough to be mistaken for white, posing as a sickly gentleman. Putting on a man's black suit, cloak, and high-heeled boots, Ellen hid her beardless face by muffling it because of a feigned toothache. Unable to read or write, she placed her arm in a sling as if broken so she would not be asked to sign the register at hotels. She also pretended to be deaf in order to limit having to speak in her natural voice. All of these stratagems worked to perfection, as they were treated as gentleman and slave in first-class hotels in Charleston and in Richmond. But in Baltimore they were almost discovered when officials demanded that Ellen post a bond for William, since a bond was required "for all negroes applying for tickets to go North." But the quick-thinking William objected that he had to travel with his young master to care for him because of his very delicate health, which already threatened to cause the young man's demise before he could reach expert medical treatment in Philadelphia. This overcame the objections and the Crafts made it safely first to Philadelphia and then, after resting awhile, to Boston, where they openly told their story. The story of the escape was celebrated throughout the North and the South, but it also elicited the wrath of their owners, who sent slave catchers to Boston to retrieve them after the Fugitive Slave Act of 1850 was passed. William and Ellen Craft again fled for their lives, this time to London, where they remained until after the Civil War, when they returned, and purchased a plantation outside of Savannah, Georgia, near their old home.

113 • The Obstacles to a Slave's Escape

It is impossible for me now to recollect all the perplexing thoughts that passed through my mind during that forenoon; it was a day of heartaching to me. But I distinctly remember the two great difficulties that stood in the way of my flight: I had a father and mother whom I dearly loved,—I had also six sisters and four brothers on the plantation. The question was, shall I hide my purpose from them? Moreover, how will my flight affect them when I am gone? Will they not be suspected? Will not the whole family be sold off as a disaffected family? But a still more trying question was, how can I expect to succeed, I have no knowledge of distance or direction. I know that Philadelphia is a free state, but I know not where its soil begins, or where that of Maryland ends? Indeed, at this time there was no safety in Pennsylvania, New Jersey, or New York, for a fugitive, except in lurking-places. . . .

Within my recollection no one had attempted to escape from my master; but I had many cases in my mind's eye, of slaves of other planters who had failed, and who had been made examples of the most cruel treatment, by flogging and selling to the far South, where they were never to see their friends more. I was not without serious apprehension that such would be my fate. But the hour was now come, and the man must act and be free, or remain a slave for ever. How the impression came to be upon my mind I cannot tell; but there was a strange and horrifying belief, that if I did not meet the crisis that day, I should be self-doomed—that my ear would be nailed to the door-post for ever.

—James W. C. Pennington, *The Fugitive Blacksmith* (London, 1849)

114 • Fugitive Slave Act of 1850

As part of the Compromise of 1850, Congress passed a more aggressive Fugitive Slave Act that made it relatively easy for masters of slaves to reclaim them. The Fugitive Slave Act stated that a slave owner had to simply produce an affidavit that he or she had ownership of a slave, bring the affidavit to a judge, along with the slave, and the reputed slave would be remanded by the judge to the slaveholder's custody. The law also demanded that all sheriffs and marshals assist those who came North looking for fugitives and provided for the imprisonment, as an enemy of the government, of any person who assisted a runaway. Although the law was included in the Compromise of 1850 to satisfy the South that the North would cooperate in the return of fugitive slaves, the law so angered northerners, who resented the invasion of the North to serve the interests of slave owners, that opposition to slavery became even more fierce and widespread.

115 • First Arrested

The first person arrested under the Fugitive Slave Act of 1850 was James Hamlet, who was seized in New York and returned to the South by slave catchers. Although no firm number exists as to the number of slaves captured under this law, it certainly spread fear among the escaped slave population in the North that despite the best efforts of their abolitionist friends, they could easily be taken back into slavery.

116 • Henry "Box" Brown

Perhaps the most imaginative method of escape from slavery was that devised by Henry "Box" Brown, who mailed himself to freedom. In 1856 Brown, a slave in Richmond, Virginia, ordered a box three feet by two by two feet eight inches deep and put in it a jug of water, a few

The resurrection of Henry "Box" Brown at Philadelphia. Prints and Photographs Division, Library of Congress

biscuits, and a bar to open the box from the inside. His friend James A. Smith addressed the box to William H. Johnson's Philadelphia home on Arch Street, and marked the exterior "Handle with Care" and "This Side Up." Twenty-six hours later, after traveling several miles upside down, Brown arrived in Philadelphia. Abolitionists alerted to the unique cargo had the box picked up from the delivery station and brought secretly to the office of the Anti-Slavery Society. After the assembled Anti-Slavery men pried off the top, up jumped Mr. Brown, who exclaimed, "How do you do, my gentlemen?"

117 • William Peel Jones

In 1859 William Peel Jones succeeded in transporting himself to freedom by steamship from Baltimore to Philadelphia. Jones was moved to action because his master had been selling off his slaves and had threatened the slave with putting him on the market soon. Like Henry "Box" Brown, Jones obtained a box; unfortunately, it was smaller than Brown's and forced Jones to keep his legs folded throughout the trip. Jones almost cried out in pain during his ocean journey, and he suffered such cold from the sea air as to give him constant chills. But such suffering was matched by the devotion of Jones's white ally in his endeavor, who not only mailed Jones in Baltimore but also traveled by land to Philadelphia, where his ally discovered the box on the boat. When the box was transported to safety and opened an hour later, the men rejoiced at their successful teamwork for many hours.

118 • The Theft of Solomon Northrop's Freedom

Often, freemen and freewomen of color were arrested and taken South into bondage. The most celebrated case of a freeman of color being captured and taken South into slavery occurred even before the 1850 Fugitive Slave Act was passed. In this instance, the slave catchers made no pretense of a legal right of ownership. Rather, Solomon Northrop had the unfortunate luck to be spotted by two slave catchers at an evening social playing the fiddle. Realizing that such a good fiddler would bring a handsome price in the South, the two men approached Northrop with a proposition: come to Baltimore and work as a free musician of color. Frustrated by the lack of work in the North, despite his excellent carpentry skills, Northrop agreed, only to awake one morning and find himself in chains. Sold to the highest bidder, Northrop spent twelve years in the Deep South, working on plantations, first as a field hand and then as an artisan slave. A white fellow carpenter who befriended Northrop took pity on him and delivered a letter to his white benefactor back home, who issued legal proceedings that eventually freed Northrop. After returning North, Solomon wrote his famous autobiography, *Twelve Years a Slave*, which became an abolitionist classic, since it was written by an educated free northern Black who had experienced slavery and exposed the conditions of life under which most southern slaves lived.

119 • The Christiana Tragedy

Although most escaped slaves simply fled when slave catchers came North trying to find them, some, as William Still, the Philadelphia conductor of the underground railroad put it, "loved liberty and hated Slavery, and when the slave-catchers arrived, they were prepared for them." Such was the case in Lancaster County, Pennsylvania, on September 11, 1851, when slave catchers tried to capture seven presumedly fugitive African Americans. An Edward Gorsuch, his son, and a small party of armed white men had camped outside a house near Christiana where Gorsuch believed slaves belonging to him were staying. After chasing a Black man back into the house, the party threatened to storm the house by force, even though Gorsuch admitted that the two men he had seen were not his slaves. Gorsuch, however, would not relent in his belief that his slaves were inside the house, even after a body of thirty armed Black men had gathered outside. When one of the Black men inside the house attempted to leave, Gorsuch fired on him, at which point the assembled Black group returned fire, and a fight ensued. When it was all over, Gorsuch was dead and his son seriously wounded, but the Black group sustained only flesh wounds. Despite clear evidence that the group had acted in self-defense, newspapers condemned the "resisting of a law of Congress by a band of armed negroes." Although several Blacks were rounded up and arrested, the two believed to be fugitive slaves escaped, with, according to some, the assistance of the United States marshal supervising the case.

120 • Runaway Reward

Not even passage of the Fugitive Slave Act of 1850 and its compulsion of northern law enforcement officials to help with recapture could replace what had always been the most effective way for slave owners to learn the whereabouts of fugitive slaves: offering a financial reward for information leading to the capture of a slave.

$200 Reward.

RANAWAY from the subscriber, on the night of Thursday, the 30th of Sepember,

FIVE NEGRO SLAVES,

To-wit : one Negro man, his wife, and three children.

The man is a black negro, full height, very erect, his face a little thin. He is about forty years of age, and calls himself *Washington Reed*, and is known by the name of Washington. He is probably well dressed, possibly takes with him an ivory headed cane, and is of good address. Several of his teeth are gone.

Mary, his wife, is about thirty years of age, a bright mulatto woman, and quite stout and strong.

The oldest of the children is a boy, of the name of FIELDING, twelve years of age, a dark mulatto, with heavy eyelids. He probably wore a new cloth cap.

MATILDA, the second child, is a girl, six years of age, rather a dark mulatto, but a bright and smart looking child.

MALCOLM, the youngest, is a boy, four years old, a lighter mulatto than the last, and about equally as bright. He probably also wore a cloth cap. If examined, he will be found to have a swelling at the navel.

Washington and Mary have lived at or near St. Louis, with the subscriber, for about 15 years.

It is supposed that they are making their way to Chicago, and that a white man accompanies them, that they will travel chiefly at night, and most probably in a covered wagon.

A reward of $150 will be paid for their apprehension, so that I can get them, if taken within one hundred miles of St. Louis, and $200 if taken beyond that, and secured so that I can get them, and other reasonable additional charges, if delivered to the subscriber, or to THOMAS ALLEN, Esq., at St. Louis, Mo. The above negroes, for the last few years, have been in possession of Thomas Allen, Esq., of St. Louis.

WM. RUSSELL.

ST. LOUIS, Oct. 1, 1847.

Prints and Photographs Division, Library of Congress

121 • Whites Assist Underground Railroad

Some of the most famous conductors on the underground railroad were white. Levi Coffin, a Quaker, assisted close to two thousand runaway slaves. He often hid runaways in a special compartment built in his house. Thomas Garrett turned his home in Wilmington, Delaware, into one of the most famous stations on the underground railroad. And the Canadian-born physician Alexander Ross made trips throughout the South and rescued slaves from

Fugitives arriving at Levi Coffin's Indiana farm. Prints and Photographs Division, Library of Congress

New Orleans, Richmond, Nashville, and Selma. Not only did whites risk their lives and rescue many slaves, but white participation in the movement gave the underground railroad respectability in the eyes of many whites that it would not have had otherwise.

122 • Harriet Tubman (1820?–1913)

Black conductors on the underground railroad were quite effective at one of the more dangerous activities: going South and making contact with slaves who wanted to flee slavery. The most famous of these conductors was Harriet Tubman, who made dozens of trips into the South, going onto plantations in a variety of disguises and bringing hundreds out of the South. Reportedly Tubman carried a gun with her and

Harriet Tubman. Brady Collection, Prints and Photographs Division, Library of Congress

more than once threatened a slave who suddenly became frightened and wanted to turn back. Such methods kept Tubman from ever being discovered or captured. Leonard A. Grimes, another Negro conductor, was not so fortunate. Working as a cab operator in Washington, D.C., he used his carriage to deliver runaway slaves to freedom as well as to transport wealthy white passengers. But during one of his trips into Virginia, he was arrested for helping a runaway family escape and spent two years in a Richmond prison.

123 • Runaway Assistance

Thousands of largely anonymous African Americans assisted runaways by providing them with overnight housing and food. In addition, the independent Black churches played a vital role as stops along the underground railroad. This was especially important because many escaped slaves had a tremendous fear of white people and were apprehensive about being betrayed by whites offering to hide them from authorities. Ellen Craft, for example, was terrified when she and William Craft were housed with a white man, Barkley Ivers, after reaching Philadelphia. "I have no confidence whatever in white people," she reportedly told William, because "they are only trying to get us back into slavery."

124 • Runaway Meets Adult Brother He Never Knew Existed

A remarkable meeting that occurred in 1850 illustrates the effect of slavery on African American families. William Still, a conductor—and later, historian—of the underground railroad, was working as a clerk in the office of the Philadelphia Anti-Slavery Society when a recently freed slave named Peter walked in. Through a helpful white man, Peter had pur-

William Still. Prints and Photographs Division, Library of Congress

timore by sea in September 1838 by posing as a free Black sailor. But after Douglass became an infamous speaker with William Lloyd Garrison on the abolitionist lecture circuit and authored an autobiography, *Narrative of the Life of Frederick Douglass* (1845), in which he identified his former owners, Douglass again had to flee, this time to England, to escape recapture. His trip to England in August 1845 was a huge success, as he lectured to crowds on the evils of slavery, and his conversations with English intellectuals and activists led to his liberation from the Garrisonian idea that moral suasion was the only way to end slavery. When Douglass returned to the United States in August 1847, a freeman after English friends had purchased his freedom, he moved his family to New York from the Garrisonian stronghold in Boston, started his own newspaper, the *North Star,* and eventually broke with Garrison to advocate political action as a means of bringing slavery to an end.

chased his freedom from his master and then traveled from Alabama to Pennsylvania in search of his parents, Levin and Cidney, who had earlier escaped from slavery but had been forced to leave Peter behind. As Peter relayed this story of his search to William Still, the latter became excited: William Still's own parents were named Levin and Cidney, and as Peter talked further, William realized that he was talking to his long-lost brother, whom he had never met.

125 • Douglass's Intellectual Migration

Often escape to the North was not enough to ensure a runaway's freedom. That was the case for Frederick Douglass, who, with the assistance of a free African American woman, Anna Murray, who became his wife, escaped from Bal-

Colonization Movements

126 • Thomas Jefferson, the Nation's First Colonizationist

Thomas Jefferson was one of the earliest advocates of African American colonization. Jefferson doubted whether whites and Blacks could live together in a multiracial society after slavery. He believed that even the friends of Negro freedom would hesitate if emancipation meant amalgamation of the races. The only way to secure white support for emancipation, in his mind, was to link it to colonization of African Americans outside of the United States. In his *Notes on the State of Virginia,* originally published in 1782, Jefferson described a plan

to emancipate all slaves born after passing the

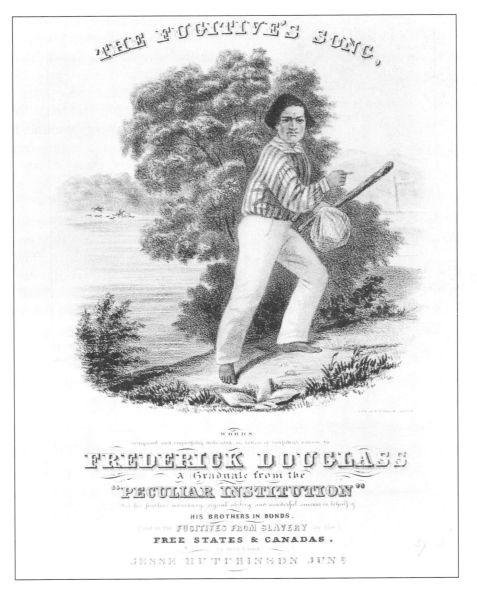

"The Fugitive's Song." Prints and Photographs Division, Library of Congress

act . . . that they should be taken up, and further directing, that they should continue with their parents to a certain age, then be brought up at public expense, to tillage, arts or sciences, according to their geniuses, till the females should be eighteen, and the males twenty-one years of age, when they should be colonized to such place as the circumstances of the time should render most proper; sending them out with arms, implements of household and of handicraft arts, seeds, pairs of the useful domestic animals, &c. to declare them a free and independent people, and extend to them our allegiance and protection, till they shall have acquired strength.

Paul Cuffee and his brig, *Traveller*. Prints and Photographs Division, Library of Congress

127 • Paul Cuffee, the First African-American Colonizer of Africa

The first man to successfully transport Black Americans to Africa was Paul Cuffee (1759–1817), a Black shipowner. Cuffee was a devout Quaker, and he wanted Blacks to return to Africa in order to help Christianize the continent. He was also a successful entrepreneur and saw colonization as a way to open trade with Africa. In addition, he wanted free Blacks to have the choice to return to Africa if they wished. Cuffee appealed to the federal government and free Blacks to support his plan, and he successfully transported thirty-eight African-Americans to Freetown, Sierra Leone.

128 • The American Colonization Society

A year before Paul Cuffee's death in 1817, the American Colonization Society was founded by white philanthropists, slave owners, and Henry Clay. Its goal was to find an outlet for free Blacks who were being manumitted by slave owners in the upper South after the turn of the century. The society transported 86 Blacks to Africa in 1820 and established the settlement of Liberia in 1822. By the end of the decade, the society had relocated 1,162 people to Africa at a cost of $100,000. Because revenue from subscriptions sold to the public was not enough to foot such expenses, Clay and the society lobbied Congress for financial support, but failed to get it. They did, however, receive $30,000 from the state of Virginia in 1850. By then, the society had spent $1.8 million to ship 10,000 African-Americans to Liberia, most of whom were former slaves who had been freed by their masters in order to be shipped out of the United States.

129 • Black Opposition to Colonization

Many free Blacks, including even Paul Cuffee, opposed the efforts of the American Colonization Society. Cuffee wanted emigration to open trade and help Africa and the settlers; but he did not like the implication that the society had to remove free Blacks from American society because they could not succeed and live amicably with whites in America, which was Thomas Jefferson's view. Some free Blacks thought the society was supported by those who believed that Blacks were biologically and socially inferior to whites and unassimilable into a free American society. Others believed that if the society gained federal support, free Blacks might be forced to repatriate to Africa. At the very least, many believed that the society tended to undermine the antislavery effort by removing successful (and to white southerners, dangerous) free Blacks from the population. Ultimately colonization under the auspices of the ACS would threaten the efforts of abolitionists to bring a rapid end to slavery. Thus, many Black leaders organized national conventions against colonization.

130 • Douglass—We Are Here to Stay

We are of the opinion that the free colored people generally mean to live in America, and not in Africa; and to appropriate a large sum for our removal would merely be a waste of the public money. We do not mean to go to Liberia. Our minds our made up to live here if we can, or die here if we must; so every attempt to remove us, will be, as it ought to be, labor lost. Here we are and here we shall remain. While our brethren are in bondage on these shores, it is idle to think of inducing any considerable number of the free colored people to quit this for a foreign land.

For two hundred and twenty-eight years has the colored man toiled over the soil of America, under a burning sun and a driver's lash—plowing, planting, reaping, that white men might roll in ease, their hands unhardened by labor, and their brows unmoistened by the waters of genial toil, and now that the moral sense of mankind is beginning to revolt at this system of foul treachery and cruel wrong, and is demanding its overthrow, the mean and cowardly oppressor is mediating plans to expel the colored man entirely from the country. Shame upon the guilty wretches that dare propose and all that countenance such a proposition. We live here—have lived here—have a right to live here, and mean to live here.

—Frederick Douglass speech published in the *North Star,* January 26, 1849

131 • Peter Williams, a Black Minister, on Colonization

We are natives of this country; we only ask that we be treated as well as foreigners. Not a few of our fathers suffered and bled to purchase its independence; we ask only to be treated as well as those who fought against it.

132 • Black Leaders and William Lloyd Garrison

Black leaders in the antebellum North lobbied the famous white abolitionist William Lloyd Garrison to oppose colonization. "It was their united and strenuous opposition to the expatriation scheme that first induced Garrison and others to oppose it," commented Lewis Tappan, another famous white abolitionist.

133 • Blacks Drop "African" from the Names of Their Organizations

The American Colonization Society also had a more subtle, though no less profound effect on Black leaders and organizations in the antebellum North. Many of them dropped the word "African" from the names of their organizations and the letterheads of stationery, for fear that the use of "Africa" could be manipulated by colonizationists to imply that such Blacks or their organizations desired a return to Africa. Black churches and newspapers, for example, began to use terms such as "Colored American" in their titles.

134 • Abolitionist as Colonizationist

Some late-eighteenth- and early-nineteenth-century abolitionists supported the idea of colonizing African Americans outside of the United States. Benjamin Lundy, a respected abolitionist, even traveled to Upper Canada in January 1832 to scout a place to settle runaway slaves and free people of color from the United States.

He discovered that the Quakers had beat him to it. A settlement, Wilberforce Colony, already existed there, having been established some years earlier by the Society of Friends. Support of colonization was a moderate position of abolitionists before the 1840s that was consistent with their belief that emancipation and integration of the slaves into American society was not possible in the foreseeable future.

135 • Re-created America

Those African Americans who migrated to Liberia in the antebellum period did not leave their American culture behind. Indeed, they re-created an American lifestyle in Liberia. Most spoke the English language and built houses

that resembled regal homes of the South. Indeed, the social life and customs of the migrants more closely resembled those of Victorian America than of West Africa. Many conceived of their role as that of a missionary bringing civilization to otherwise "backward" peoples.

136 • Colonization as Suppression of the Slave Trade

Efforts to expand Liberia before the Civil War were linked to efforts to suppress the continuing if illegal international trade in slaves. In 1849 Joseph Jenkins Roberts, the first Black president of Liberia, requested the United States to buy territories adjacent to Liberia so that his country could police the entire West Coast of Africa from Sierra Leone to Cape Calmas, thereby helping to end the international

House of Joseph Jenkins Roberts, first president of Liberia. Prints and Photographs Division, Library of Congress

slave trade. His proposal was rejected. But Congress did pass a law instructing the U.S. president to send a naval fleet to the coast of West Africa to capture slave ships and resettle Africans in bondage in Liberia. The president put this policy into motion, and by 1867 some 5,700 Africans had been resettled in Liberia.

137 • Emigration Sentiment in the 1850s

African American interest in emigration revived in the 1850s because of the passage of the Fugitive Slave Act, the South's zeal in pursuing runaway slaves, and the North's apparent acquiescence to slave power. Even those like Frederick Douglass who had opposed colonization in the past began to give colonization a second look. Others became convinced that the only salvation for African Americans lay outside of the territorial United States. Martin Delany, a Black doctor, seriously began to plan to transport African Americans to Africa, even though he opposed the work of the American Colonization Society. Rather than going to Liberia, Delany decided to try and establish a colony for emigrating African Americans in what is now Nigeria. Delany even traveled to Nigeria and signed a treaty with its Yoruba king, Abeokuta. But Delany's dream of an African American Nigeria foundered when the Civil War erupted and interest in emigration among American Blacks plummeted. Delany himself became a major in the U.S. Army.

138 • Abraham Lincoln Favored Colonization

At several points in his career, but especially in his annual address to Congress as president on December 1, 1862, Lincoln articulated his support for colonization by proposing an amendment to the Constitution to instruct Con-

gress to appropriate money to colonize free Black people, "with their own consent, at any place or places without the United States." This amendment would accompany the amendment he also proposed to emancipate the slaves, and reflected his long-standing belief in the efficacy of colonization to solve the race problem. But in the same address, Lincoln sought to separate colonization from the arguments against free Blacks remaining in the United States. He discounted arguments that free Blacks would steal labor away from white laborers or demographically overwhelm the nation. He did believe that "deportation" of free Black labor would increase the demand for white labor, a positive in his view. But by February 1864 Lincoln seemed to realize that colonization was not a feasible way to deal with the problem of the freed slaves. That month he directed Edwin M. Stanton to outfit a ship to be sent "to the colored colony established by the United States at the island of Vache, on the coast of San Domingo, to bring back to this country such of the colonists there as desire to return." The experiment to settle free Blacks on Caribbean islands had failed, as most of the African Americans wanted to return. Though not a believer in the social equality of African Americans, Lincoln seemed in 1864 to be moving toward accepting the inevitability of a multiracial postwar American society.

139 • The Afro-American Steamship and Mercantile Company

Whether to Africa or to the American West, the cost of emigration was often prohibitive to potential migrants. When the Reverend Daniel E. Johnson of San Antonio created an all-Black stock company to buy and operate steamships, he hoped to raise the necessary capital by selling shares to Blacks nationwide. Calling the organization the Afro-American Steamship and Mercantile Company, Johnson hoped to encourage emigration, commerce, race organization, and responsibility. Local clubs designed to locate and unite interested people could be formed when one hundred shares were subscribed. People would subscribe to the ten-dollar shares, but then fall behind in the dollar-per-month payments. Ultimately, only Atlanta, Charleston, and Baltimore were able to maintain clubs.

140 • Postwar Revival

Having declined in the 1860s, African American emigration interest rose again after 1877 with the collapse of Radical Reconstruction and the withdrawal of federal troops from the South. Martin Delany and several South Carolinians formed the Liberian Exodus Joint Stock Steamship Company to transport African Americans to Africa. The company's first ship, the *Azor*, set sail for Africa in the spring of 1878. But it soon found its way into debtor's court, reputedly because of the disreputable activities of its white captain, and the ship was eventually sold for debts. Unfortunately the Liberian Exodus Joint Stock Steamship died quickly thereafter.

141 • The Congo Company

The Congo Company, as it was commonly known, was founded in 1886 in Washington, D.C., by three white men from Baltimore who believed it might be profitable to transport Blacks back to Africa. The Congo Free State had been recently established, and these enterprising men hit upon the idea of colonizing the state with African Americans. Its founder, Martin H. K. Paulsen, developed enough interest that the company was incorporated with a Black man from the District of Columbia as president and white men as secretary and trea-

surer. In a manner that foreshadowed Marcus Garvey's Black Star Line, Paulsen sold stock in the company to raise revenue; but when an attempt to exploit a neglected 1862 federal law granting proceeds from the sale of abandoned southern lands failed to net the company an immediate $500,000, the white shareholders abandoned the company to the Blacks. Once a Baptist preacher from Georgia got behind the project, interest among Georgia Blacks ran high. When the company sold tickets for one dollar plus postage to become "preferred passengers," thousands rushed forward to buy what they believed was passage to Africa when, in fact, it only allowed them to buy passage once a ship was secured. Although the company never transported anyone to Africa, the interest generated by the company proved how serious emigration fever was in the South of the 1880s.

142 • Fraud and Redemption

Many would-be emigrants were frustrated by seemingly fraudulent operators. The Congo Company, for example, convinced potential migrants that a ship had been chartered and would leave for Liberia from Savannah in November 1890. The departure date was repeatedly postponed, but in January 1891, fifteen hundred people converged on Savannah in expectation of transport to Africa. Eventually it became clear that no ship was coming. Some Blacks remained in Atlanta hoping it would soon arrive. Others yielded to the stiff pressure from labor agents urging them to move West. But for those who remained in Savannah redemption came in the form of the Danish steamer *Horsa*, which on March 19, 1895, departed Savannah for Liberia.

143 • Bishop Turner's Dream

The most outspoken advocate of emigration

before World War I was Henry McNeal Turner, who used his position as a bishop in the African Methodist Episcopal Church to lobby African Americans to emigrate to Africa. Turner believed that bringing Africans to the United States had been part of God's providential mission to allow American Blacks and whites to join together to redeem and civilize Africa. Whites, however, had reneged on their obligation by blocking Black efforts at improvement, such as education and economic development, in the American South. Ex-slaves, Turner believed, must now shoulder the burden by themselves and redeem Africa from the white missionaries overrunning the mother country. When Turner articulated his views in the AME journal, the *Christian Recorder,* in the 1880s, other Black leaders, including fellow ministers, vigorously opposed his idea. Benjamin Tanner argued that it was foolish for African Americans to abandon the United States when millions of immigrants, even visiting African students, were coming to and staying in the United States.

Marcus Garvey, 1926. Library of Congress, Prints and Photographs Division, NYWT and S Collection

144 • Marcus Garvey's Nightmare

The most famous Black emigrationist was Marcus Garvey (1887–1940), a Jamaican who came to the United States in 1916 and founded the American branch of his Universal Negro Improvement Association. Motivated by the perception gained on his travels around the Caribbean and in England that Black people were oppressed wherever he found them around the globe, Garvey believed that Black people would never be respected until they had their own independent nation in Africa. After he gained widespread support in the United States for his militant critique of imperialism and white racism, Garvey, on June 27, 1919, incorporated the Black Star Steamship Corporation,

the practical basis for realizing his dream of a Black nation. Selling stock for five dollars a share, Garvey raised thousands of dollars, purchased three ships, the *Yarmouth,* the *Kanawha,* and the *Booker T. Washington,* and tried to establish the company as both a profitable shipping company and a propagandist symbol of Black Pride. Unfortunately these goals undermined the effort to repatriate African Americans back to Africa. Garvey's inexperience in running a shipping company, his incompetent assistants, and the real problems with the ships he purchased doomed his Black Star Line to financial catastrophe. Hundreds of thousands of African Americans had bought stock in a company that was bankrupt by the end of 1920, completely unable to send anyone back to Africa. Garvey's financial mismanagement, coupled with organized opposition from the United States attorney general and such other Black leaders as W. E. B. Du Bois and William Pickens, doomed Garvey, and he was arrested in January 1921 for mail fraud. He was found guilty in June 1923 and incarcerated in a federal penitentiary in Atlanta in 1925. Though his sentence was commuted by President Calvin Coolidge in 1927, he was deported back to Jamaica, where he was never again able to generate the kind of enthusiasm for his scheme that he had enjoyed in the United States. Actually the Back to Africa scheme was only one of many of Garvey's programs, but it was the one that brought down his entire operation.

"Go West, Young [Black] Man!"

145 • Horace Greeley's Favorite Saying

Horace Greeley, the nineteenth-century journalist, was fond of urging Americans to "Go West, Young Man." But he meant only young white men. He was adamant that the new lands "shall be reserved for the benefit of the white Caucasian race."

146 • African Americans First Settlers in Ohio Valley

Despite Horace Greeley's wishes, free Black people, like free whites, yearned to move West. African Americans were among the first non–Native American settlers of the Ohio Valley. When Knox County, Ohio, was incorporated in 1808, it already contained a famous Black man—Enoch Harris, known as "Knuck," who was an expert stable hand and handler of horses. Most Black migrants were servants in

white households but generally were not slaves. Most eventually obtained and farmed small parcels of land.

147 • Jean Baptiste Point du Sable

A Black man, Jean Baptiste Point du Sable, was the first to settle what became Chicago, Illinois. Born in Haiti around 1745 to a wealthy Frenchman and an enslaved African woman, du Sable had been educated in Paris before becoming a seaman and sailing to New Orleans. In 1779 he left New Orleans for the Chicago River, where he engaged in fur trapping until he was arrested as war broke out between England and France. But because he spoke English well and had conducted his business and other affairs in an honorable way, he was released and allowed to return to Chicago, where he lived for sixteen more years. During that time he married an Indian woman, built a log cabin that was decorated with European paintings, and became well known to the Indians in the area with whom he traded. Most travelers habitually stopped at du Sable's post to trade their furs and get provisions. Du Sable resided there until he ran for election and lost. Unable to accept his loss, he sold his holdings and left Chicago in 1800. Never as successful afterward as he had been in Chicago, du Sable died in poverty in 1818. Nevertheless, he had established the first outpost in the area that became known as Chicago.

148 • Internal Slave Trade

The opening of passages over the Appalachians to slave owners in the late eighteenth and early nineteenth centuries brought about the first major internal migration of African Americans in American history. Approximately 100,000 African Americans were uprooted from settled communities in the upper South and forced West between 1790 and 1810. This western movement of slaveholders, combined with the closing of the international slave trade, created a strong internal market for slaves in the United States. The internal slave trade further developed as slaveholders in Virginia, South Carolina, and Georgia traded slaves to the burgeoning cotton kingdom of Mississippi, Alabama, Louisiana, and Kentucky in the early nineteenth century.

149 • Texas

As slavery became hotly contested in the South, many farmers took their slaves West in search of greater freedom and better economic opportunities. In 1845, when Texas entered the Union, it contained 100,000 white settlers and 35,000 slaves. By 1861, when it seceded from the Union, it had over 430,000 whites and 182,000 slaves. The movement of slaves and slave owners to the West spread Anglo-American and African American cultures across the continent.

150 • Mexican vs. U.S. Rule

Under Mexican rule, Blacks in Texas were free. The Black population before the mass influx of southerners was relatively small—450 in 1792 and 2,000 in 1834. Many Blacks had Spanish surnames. As southerners moved in, they brought their slaves with them and refused to manumit them as the law required. This led to growing friction between the Mexican and American governments. Many free Blacks supported the United States in the war against Mexico and found themselves in worse positions afterward. As Greenbury Logan recorded it:

My discharge will show the man[n]er in which I discharged my duty as a free man and sol[d]ier, but now look at my situation. Every previleg dear to a freeman is taken away and Logan is liable to be imposed upon by eny that chose to do it. No change to collect a debt without [white] wit-nesses, no vote or say in eny way. Yet Logan is liable for Taxes as eny other person.

151 • Deadwood Dick

Nat Love, or Deadwood Dick, as he called himself, was the most famous and outrageous of the thousands of Black cowboys who migrated West in the post–Civil War era and became cowpunchers. He remains famous today because he was the only Black cowboy to write his own autobiography, which allowed him to infuse his life story with Western myth. His idea for the autobiography as well as the name Deadwood Dick may have come from reading Edward Wheeler's dime novel, *Deadwood Dick,* published in 1877, which told the exploits of *the Black Rider of the Black Hills.* In his own autobiography, *The Life and Adventures of Nat Love, Better Known in the Cattle Country as "Deadwood Dick"* (1907), Nat relates how he was born a slave in Davidson County, Tennessee, in 1854, but left the South for Kansas, arriving in Dodge City in 1869. There his riding, roping, and shooting skills earned him a job on the cattle drives out of Texas to Midwest shipping points. He was also the roughest cowboy on the trail, claiming to have been shot at least fourteen times without being seriously injured and to have excelled at outlandish pranks. He once roped a United States Army cannon in an attempt to steal it. His most famous boast was that he once rode a horse into a Mexican saloon and ordered a drink for his horse and himself. He related that his nickname, "Deadwood Dick," was given to him when he won several roping and shooting contests in a rodeo on July 4, 1876, in Deadwood City in the Dakotas. Although exaggerated, Nat Love's autobiography conveys elements of Black cowboy life out West. There was little formal segregation of Blacks in frontier towns and a great deal of personal freedom. That life came quickly to an end in the late 1880s when the railroad took over transportation of beef to market and ended the lifestyle of the cowboy. In 1890, Deadwood Dick became a Pullman porter.

152 • Free States Prohibit Black Immigration

Four northwestern states denied free Blacks the right to migrate into those states. Iowa passed an act in 1851 prohibiting the immigration of free Blacks into the state. Every free Black found in Iowa was to be given three days to leave the state once notified by a public official. Those that refused were taken to court and, if convicted, ordered to pay a fine of two dollars a day for every day they remained in the state. Then they would be put in jail until they paid the fine or agreed to leave. The other three states, Illinois, Indiana, and Oregon, adopted—in 1848, 1851, and 1857, respectively—anti-Black immigration clauses as part of their state constitution. Oregon went so far as to punish not only Blacks who entered, but also those who brought them. Although these laws were not always enforced, they symbolized the second-class citizenship endured by African Americans already living in those states.

153 • Exodusters

One of the few freedoms that the Civil War brought to African Americans was the freedom to move. Once Reconstruction had ended, sharecropping had reinstalled slavery in a new form on Black farmers, and white terrorism made life and limb unsafe for Blacks in the

Broadside to entice African Americans to follow Benjamin "Pap" Singleton to Kansas. Prints and Photographs Division, Library of Congress

South, two men—Louisiana's Henry Adams and Tennessee's Benjamin "Pap" Singleton—fired the enthusiasm of southern African Americans for migration to Kansas as the one place in America where the former slave could be free. Both men exhorted Blacks to migrate as early as 1877, but Adams led a large, en masse transplanting of between 20,000 and 40,000 African Americans from the South toward Kansas in 1879. The movement of African Americans westward did not go unnoticed: southerners reacted with alarm, claimed northern white Republicans were behind the "Exodus," and forced congressional hearings on the issue. During testimony, Pap Singleton claimed that "I am the whole cause of the Kansas migration," but Adams was at least as significant. Ultimately, however, the cause of the "Exodus" was neither man, but the horrific conditions of life in the postwar South and the promise of better conditions in the West. Actually, though migrants to Kansas were not always met with outright hostility, the welcome was far from enthusiastic, especially as Kansas was forced to absorb close to 100,000 poor, landless African Americans in the late 1870s and early 1880s. In Lincoln, Nebraska, over 150 African Americans from Mississippi were banished from the town. But in other instances, the Freedmen's Relief Association and sympathetic whites from the East supplied food, clothing, and money to the destitute and enabled them to settle and not starve. Seldom did any of the migrants reverse their course and go back to the Deep South.

154 • Nicodemus

In July 1877 thirty Black colonists who had left Lexington, Kentucky, arrived in Kansas and built the town of Nicodemus. Located in Graham County, Nicodemus was one of the earliest Black towns established by former slaves during Reconstruction. The original settlers utilized wood they found along the Solomon River as fuel and as material to build small lean-tos and houses. As the town grew, other former slaves who were disenchanted with postwar life in Mississippi, Missouri, Kentucky, and Tennessee migrated to the town, which was inspired by a spirit of self-reliance. Citizens even went so far as to pass a series of resolutions in 1879 thanking the people of Kansas and other states for helping the town, but refusing any further charitable assistance. Because it was an all-Black town of former slaves, the town had received support from the neighboring communities. Some residents were

afraid that charity would make their people unwilling to work and attract destitute, undesirable persons. By 1880 seven hundred residents populated Nicodemus, which had become quite prosperous. It contained its own post office, stores, hotels, and land office. Although the town declined in 1888 because the Kansas Railroad passed it by, Nicodemus was still a thriving farm community in 1910. Reputedly the town was named after a slave who came on the second slave ship who became an outstanding citizen after he purchased his freedom.

155 • Oklahoma

Some African Americans wanted to establish an all-Black state in the Oklahoma Territory, which had been created by the federal government in 1889. Edwin P. McCabe, a native of Kansas, wanted to settle a Black majority in each voting district of the territory. Over seven thousand Blacks entered the territory in its first year. Several all-Black towns were established, including Langston, named after John Langston, a prominent abolitionist, educator, and politician from Virginia. At its peak, Langston had a population over two thousand, and a university (Langston University) was established in 1897.

FROM RURAL TO URBAN AMERICA

156 • Urban Migration

African Americans have been moving toward cities since Blacks have enjoyed the opportunity to choose their residences. Urban slavery offered better conditions of labor, health, and per-

Migrant. Photograph by Jack Delano. Prints and Photographs Division, Library of Congress

sonal freedom for slaves than rural slavery. Often, urban slaves were domestic servants who lived in the master's house, or just behind it, in the better part of town and enjoyed the freedom to travel unsupervised through streets to carry out errands. In some cases, particularly in the 1840s and 1850s, masters allowed urban slaves to "hire out" their time and contract their own employment. Under such circumstances slaves paid their masters only a portion of their earnings. "Living out" also became popular, because masters found they could save on the costs of feeding, clothing, and housing slaves by allowing the slave to live in a separate residence and pay his or her rent out of earnings. Under such circumstances, slaves who were husband and wife could "hire out" and "live out" and thereby approximate the feeling that they were free. Even though Frederick Douglass hated the experience of having to give part of his wages to his master in Baltimore, Douglass agreed that living in the city was far superior to living in the rural countryside of Maryland.

157 • Urban Discrimination

Frederick Douglass documented the racism and hostility he experienced after he finally escaped from slavery. White workers refused to work with Black workers in many of the trades, and Douglass was beaten up on one occasion when he tried to work. Ironically, in southern cities under slavery, "white and Black carpenters worked side by side in the shipyards," but Douglass could not work as a caulker on a ship in a northern city because "I was told that every white man would leave the ship in her unfinished condition if I struck a blow at my trade upon her." In southern cities, there was plenty of work, but little freedom; in northern cities, there was plenty of freedom, but no work.

158 • Cityward During the Civil War

With the Civil War and the prospect of emancipating the slaves, some northern cities feared that thousands of newly freed slaves would suddenly rush northward and begin competing with white workers for jobs. Emancipation at the end of the war did encourage African Americans to go to the city, but not to the North; many more went to southern cities. The southern city held out the prospect not only of greater freedom but also of nonagricultural employment, and thus a sharp and symbolic break from the labor of plantation slavery. The relative lack of urban and industrial development in the South, the postwar devastation, and the concerted efforts of former planters and the Freedmen's Bureau forced many of the new migrants in southern cities to return to their former plantations and their former jobs as agricultural workers.

159 • Post-Reconstruction Urban Migration

Although many southern Blacks tried to escape the oppression of the rural South by migrating in the period after 1877, most could not migrate to the urban North. The late-nineteenth-century American city experienced a tremendous influx of European immigrants who swelled the urban pool of unskilled laborers and reduced the need and demand for southern Black workers. Moreover, many freedmen still retained the dream of independent landownership as a symbol of their freedom, and there was a much greater chance of owning a farm if a southern Black migrated West. Small numbers of skilled and well-educated African Americans did migrate from southern to northern cities, from 1890 to 1910. But as late as 1910, 52.3 percent of migrants from the South were still going West. This changed with World War I.

160 • Blacks as Strikebreakers

African Americans had worked in northern industry prior to 1916. But they were generally only brought in as strikebreakers. In the Chicago stockyards in 1894, Blacks were hired for the first time in the meatpacking industry when thousands of workers in that industry conducted a sympathy strike with the American Railway Union strike against the Pullman company. That sowed the seeds of race hatred that continued well into the twentieth century in the meatpacking unions. Blacks did not always go along with the strikebreaking formula, however. When Latrobe Steel decided to transport 317 Black workers from Birmingham to break a strike, the workers refused to serve the owner's interest and asked to be returned to Alabama.

Whether they were strikebreakers or not, the situation facing Black workers in the industrial North before 1916 was difficult. The major fact was that there was very little work for African American workers outside of the South before World War I.

161 • Great Migration

World War I transformed Black migration to northern cities into a real option. With the outbreak of hostilities in 1914, the European war dramatically reduced European immigration into the United States and jump-started American industry as it became a source of manufactured goods to the combatants. Suddenly a huge demand for unskilled labor in the urban North emerged, without a local source to supply it. Where years before, the color line in northern industry prevented African Americans from obtaining jobs, suddenly industrial leaders were so eager to hire Black workers that in 1916 recruiters went South to bring Black workers to such cities as Pittsburgh, Chicago, Detroit, and Indianapolis. Fueled by this early encouragement, migration North became a fever that spread by word of mouth throughout the South, and entire Black communities picked up and left Mississippi, Georgia, Alabama, and the Carolinas for good. Approximately 500,000 migrated to the industrial North in the period 1916 to 1919.

162 • Reasons for Leaving

Migrants who left the South during World War I felt pushed out of the South because of the deterioration in the quality of life for Blacks. In the 1890s Jim Crow segregation spread throughout the South, such that railroads, meeting houses, schools, and work sites became legally and drastically segregated. At the same time, laws disfranchising the Black voter through "understanding clauses" that required voters to read and write, poll taxes that required voters to pay registration taxes, and outright voter intimidation dramatically reduced the number of African Americans voting in the South. As if that were not enough, a fever of lynching spread across the South in the 1890s, as Black males, especially businessmen or property owners, were targeted for speaking up or not behaving deferentially to whites. Those conditions, coupled with the lack of equal educational opportunities for Black youth, convinced many Blacks, especially those between the ages of eighteen and thirty-three, that the only future for the younger generation existed up North. As one group of migrants told W. E. B. Du Bois, the editor of the *Crisis,* the journal of the National Association for the Advancement of Colored People, migrants were "willing to run any risk to get where they might breathe easier."

163 • Letters in the *Chicago Defender*

Some southern Blacks wrote to the *Chicago Defender* to explain the brutal conditions of the South that made migration appealing but difficult:

. . . We work but cant get scarcely any thing for it & they dont want us to go away & there is not much of anything here to do & nothing for it Please find some one that need this kind of a people & send at once for us. We dont want anything but our wareing and bed clothes & have not got no money to get away from here with & being to get away before we are killed and hope to here from you at once. We cant talk to you over the phone here we are afraid to they dont want to hear one say that he or she wants to leave here if we do we are apt to be killed. They say if we dont go to war they are not going to let us stay here with their folks and it is not any thing that we

have done to them. . . . [Letter from Daphne, Alabama, April 20, 1917]

164 • Boll Weevil

The devastation caused by the boll weevil also contributed to the Great Migration. The boll weevil, a grayish beetle approximately an inch long, infests cotton plants by depositing its larvae in the boll of the cotton plant. The larvae then feed on the boll, effectively destroying the plant. The boll weevil entered the United States via Mexico in 1892, and by 1903 had cut a swath through Louisiana; by 1907 the weevil had hit Mississippi. Black farmers in Louisiana were hit hardest in the period 1906–10, those in Mississippi in the period 1913–16, and Alabama after 1916. Its impact on Black farmers' attitudes toward the South can be best gauged in the refrain of a song:

> *De white man he got ha'f de crap*
> *Boll weevil took de res'*
> *Ain't got no home,*
> *Ain't got no home.*

165 • Migration North Swells with World War I Industry

In 1916 a trickle of African Americans moving from the rural South to the urban North swelled into a flood, as American industrial production jumped during World War I and European immigration fell. Even recent European immigrants to the United States returned home to fight for their countries. Suddenly an American industrial world that had been all but closed to African Americans was desperate for unskilled laborers and interested in hiring Negroes. And African Americans, tired of mistreatment and abuse in the South, were ready to leave and take a chance on life in the urban industrial North. Pennsylvania and Illinois gained more than 90,000 and

73,000 African Americans in the 1910s, while Michigan's Black population skyrocketed from a mere 17,000 to over 60,000 by 1920.

166 • Labor Agents

Labor agents were often blamed for the migration of large numbers of African Americans out of the South during the Great Migration. Though northern industrialists did initially send agents South to spread the word of work in the North, agents had ceased to be a major factor in the migration by 1917. Long before then, Black southerners had themselves taken over the role of informing their neighbors and friends that the opportunity and necessity to move North had come. Indeed, Black southerners had been ready to leave for years. Once it became widely known that jobs were available in the North, they left.

167 • Letters Home to the South

Those who had migrated and obtained well-paying jobs wrote letters to relatives and friends painting flattering pictures of life up North and encouraging people to follow in their footsteps. These letters were probably the single most important factor in making the decision to leave the South.

I should have been here 20 years ago. I just begin to feel like a man. It's a great deal of pleasure in knowing that you have got some privilege. My children are going to the same school with the whites and I dont have to umble to no one. I have registered—Will vote the next election and there isnt any "yes sirs" and "no sir"—its all yes and no and Sam and Bill.

168 • Migration After a Lynching

Very often a lynching, commonplace in the South of the early twentieth century, would be the catalyst that sent a family or an entire town's Black population up North. One group of African Americans from Florida told investigators that "the horrible lynchings in Tennessee" had prompted them to move. The Chicago Urban League noted that after lynchings, "colored people from that community will arrive in Chicago inside of two weeks."

169 • Black Mississippian Explains

Just a few months ago they hung Widow Baggae's husband from Hirshbery bridge because he talked back to a white man. He was a prosperous Farmer owning about 80 acres. They killed another man because he dared to sell his cotton "off the place." These things have got us sore. Before the North opened up with work all we could do was to move from one plantation to another in hope of finding something better.

Jesse Washington, eighteen years old, lynched and burned, May 15, 1916, Waco, Texas. Prints and Photographs Division, Library of Congress

170 • Economic Reasons for Migrating North

Black migrants were able to make as much for a day's work in the North as they made working for a week in the South. Jobs in the industrial North—from the stockyards in Chicago to the steel mills in Pittsburgh—offered dignified work that was nonagricultural. But just as important as good jobs was the sense of being able to live a real life for the first time, and to expect that they could finally begin to live the American Dream. Many Black migrants expressed the view that for the first time they could believe that life would be better for their children than it had been for them.

Ford worker. Photograph by Arthur Siegel. Prints and Photographs Division, Library of Congress

171 • *Defender* Help-Wanted Ads

The *Chicago Defender*, a Black-owned and edited newspaper, played a pivotal role in fostering the Great Migration. Numerous editorials appeared in the *Defender* during the 1910s urging southern Blacks to vote against southern racism with their feet and come North to work and freedom in Chicago. Perhaps most important, the *Defender* also published thousands of help-wanted ads that convinced those still skeptical that well-paying jobs were waiting for them in Chicago.

Wanted—Men and Women—architects, mechanics, cement masons, carpenters, painters and decorators; cement workers, electricians, plumbers, steamfitters, bookkeepers, steno-type-writers. All must be qualified to take charge of their positions. Apply by letter only, with self-addressed stamped envelope to International Ideal Home and Investment Bankers. Charles D. Basse, 183 N. Wabash Avenue.

172 • Looking for Work

Many people wrote the *Chicago Defender* looking for opportunities or to inquire about conditions in the North.

In reading the Defenders want ad I notice that there is lots of work to be had and if I havent miscomprehended I think I also understand that the transportation is advanced to able bodied working men who is out of work and desire work. Am I not right? with the understanding that those who have been advanced transportation same will be deducted from their salary after they have begun work. Now then if this is they proposition I have about 10 or 15 good working men who is out of work and are dying to leave the south and I as-

sure you that they are working men and will be too glad to come north east or west, any where but the south. [Letter from Port Arthur, Texas, May 5, 1917]

173 • Housing

Although industrial capitalists were willing to provide jobs for African Americans during World War I, none provided housing. This forced Blacks who migrated North during the Great Migration into slum areas of cities such as Chicago that were already overfilled with residents. Eventually such neighborhoods began to impinge on nearby poor white neighborhoods, usually those populated by immigrants. Black migrants were often charged higher rents, as this entry in the Philadelphia Urban League report indicates:

Russell Street Apartment—Ten-family apartment. Apartments taken over in 1923 by colored. Place formerly rented for $30.00 and $35.00 per month. Rent raised $10.00. Apartments each of four small rooms. Steam heat and electricity. General conditions of the interior bad. Needs redecorating. Paper on the walls very dirty and loose. Floors bad. Plumbing fair. Some apartments worse than others. Garbage and rubbish receptacles inadequate for the apartment house. Lawns bad.

174 • Restrictive Covenants

Restrictive covenants were agreements signed voluntarily or involuntarily by property owners in the early twentieth century to prevent Blacks from buying property. There were two distinctive types of restrictive covenants. One was an agreement between existing owners. In Harlem, for example, protective associations forced property owners to sign agreements not to rent apartments to African Americans for ten years. Some covenants even limited the number of African Americans hired to work in a home. The signers all paid one another a fee to make it binding, and the covenants were then notarized and put on file at the city hall of records. Blocks covered by such covenants were sometimes known as Covenant Blocks, and African Americans families took particular delight in being the first to bust a Covenant Block. The other major kind of restrictive covenants were clauses in real-estate deeds, passed from owner to owner of houses or apartment buildings, that prevented selling or subleasing the premises to an African American. Most of the first kind of restrictive covenants had no binding legal value, but constituted a powerful psychological device to enforce residential segregation in northern cities. Often, however, once a Covenant Block was broken, white owners sold to whomever they wanted without legal consequences. The second type was legally binding, although seldom enforced if an owner violated it.

175 • The Second Great Migration

African Americans continued to move northward and cityward after World War I in 1918. In fact, the migration increased during the 1920s as another million southern African Americans picked up their bags and left southern living conditions. The migration expanded in the 1930s as the New Deal Agricultural Adjustment Act of 1933 forced many more to migrate once the AAA paid white southern farmers not to produce crops and made it profitable to dispense with Black sharecroppers. Technological advances such as the cotton picker machine made large numbers of unskilled agricultural laborers obsolete in southern agriculture. Then, as World War II began, Black mass migration exploded and nearly 5 million African Americans left the South for the North from 1940 to 1960. While migrants during the Second Migration were spread over a longer period of time and did not have the immediate impact on racial relations as the Great Migration during World War I, the Second Migration created huge ghettos in all of the major American cities. Whereas in 1890 close to 90 percent of African Americans lived in the South, by 1960 only 50 percent of African Americans still resided there. Moreover, the movement North was also a movement toward urban rather than rural living. By 1990 over 84 percent of African Americans lived in urban areas, making "African American" and "urban" almost synonymous in modern America.

176 • Southward Bound

Ironically, after the huge migration to the North prior to the 1960s, a desire to return to the South gripped the imagination of many African Americans in the early 1970s. Close to 1 million African Americans moved into the South during the period 1970–75. Although the tide slowed in the period 1975–80 to roughly 194,000 African Americans moving to the South, the lure of the southern United States continued. The end of public segregation in the South during the Civil Rights Movement of the 1960s contributed to the desire of African Americans to return to warmer climates and to a region with a closer sense of community.

Part Two

CIVIL RIGHTS AND POLITICS

COLONIAL

Protests, Organizations, and Demonstrations

177 • Quaker Protest

Protest against slavery is as old as the institution in the United States. The Quakers issued the earliest recorded resolution against slavery on May 18, 1652.

Whereas their is a common course practiced among Englishmen, to buy negroes to that end that they may have them for service or as slaves forever; for the preventing of such practices among us, let it be ordered, that no black mankind or white being shall be forced, by covenant, bond, or otherwise, to serve any man or his assignees longer than ten years, or until they come to be twenty-four years of age, if they be taken in under fourteen, from the time of their coming within the liberties of this Colony—at the end or term of ten years, to set them free as the manner is with the English servants. And that man that will not let them go free, or shall sell them away elsewhere, to that end they may be enslaved to others for a longer time, he or they shall forfeit to the colony forty pounds.

The resolution is noteworthy for acknowledging that some Africans were already being held "as slaves forever" in 1652 and that it called for a limited term of service for Africans similar to what existed for indentured whites.

178 • Mennonites

An early protest against the slave trade was recorded in 1688 by Germantown Mennonites in the colony of Pennsylvania. The Mennonites believed the slave trade violated Christian principles. The Germantown Protest stated slavery was wrong because the Negroes were brought to the Americas against their will, that it was wrong to buy and sell them like cattle.

Pray, what thing in the world can be done worse toward us, than if men should rob or steal us away and sell us for slaves to strange countries, separating husbands from their wives and children. Now this is not done in the manner we would be done to; therefore, we contradict and are against this traffic of men. And we who profess that it is not lawful to steal, must, likewise, avoid purchasing things that are stolen, but rather help to stop this robbing and stealing, if possible. And such men ought to be delivered out of the hands of the robbers and set free. . . .

179 • Judge Sewall and the First Abolitionist Tract

Judge Samuel Sewall of Massachusetts wrote one of the first extensive abolitionist tracts, *The Selling of Joseph*, in 1700. As the judge who participated in the Salem witch trials, Sewall believed slavery was wrong because of its sinful effects on ruling whites and its inhumane effects on enslaved Blacks. This negative view of slavery would be reiterated throughout the history of opposition to slavery, even by nineteenth-century abolitionists who, like Sewall, opposed slavery but did not consider African Americans the equals of whites. Sewall's tract is also important because it was the first sustained analysis that used biblical passages for antislavery justifications. For example, Sewall noted that in Exodus 21:16, the Bible commands that "he that stealeth a man, and selleth him, or if he be found in his hand, he shall surely be put to death."

180 • Anthony Benezet on the Slave Trade

A forceful attack on the slave trade was delivered by Anthony Benezet, a Quaker from Philadelphia, who, as a schoolteacher and reformer, popularized the view that the slave trade was both anti-Christian and inhuman. His *Observations on the Inslaving, Importing and Purchasing of Negroes: With Some Advice Thereon, Extracted from the Epistel of the Yearly-Meeting of the People Called Quakers, Held at London in the Year 1748* attacked the abuses and cruelties of the slave trade. *"Did not he that made you, make them?"* his essay queried.

181 • John Woolman, Anti-Slavery Quaker

John Woolman, an itinerant Quaker minister, authored one of the most influential critiques of slavery in the colonial period. Woolman wrote *Some Considerations on the Keeping of Negroes: Recommended to the Professors of Christianity of Every Denomination* in 1746, after traveling through Virginia, Maryland, and North Carolina and observing the conditions and treatment of slaves. Although Woolman, like Judge Samuel Sewall, was concerned about the corrupting effect of slavery on the slave owners, it was the plight of the slaves that moved him to write his essay, for "the general disadvantage which these poor Africans lie under in an enlightened Christian country . . . often filled me with real sadness." There were some good slave owners, Woolman believed, but in general, treating another human being as a slave dimmed the master's spiritual vision. Another reason for Woolman's opposition to slavery was that it devalued the Quaker religion in the eyes of slaves. Woolman practiced his beliefs by individually proselytizing Quakers to give up their slaves. And his essay influenced far more Quakers when the Philadelphia Yearly Meeting, in 1754, distributed it to Quaker groups throughout Pennsylvania and New Jersey. The essay even made its way to England, where it led the London Yearly Meeting of June 1758 to condemn the slave trade. Woolman published a second and more forthright version, *Some Considerations on the Keeping of Negroes, the Second*, in 1762. When the Philadelphia Yearly Meeting, in 1776, finally prohibited Quakers from owning slaves, Woolman's essays were largely responsible.

Title page of Anthony Benezet's *Observations*. Prints and Photographs Division, Library of Congress

Legal Decisions and Their Implications

182 • Hugh Davis Is "Whipt"

Africans and Europeans had been sexually involved with one another from the earliest years of the Virginia colony. The first mention of race in the colonies comes in the case of Hugh Davis, who was brought before the Court of Chauncery in Virginia in 1639 for having had sexual relations with a Black person. "Hugh Davis to be soundly whipt before an assembly of negroes & others for abusing himself to the dishonor of God and shame of Christianity by defiling his body in lying with a negro...." As historian Leon Higginbotham points out, the court record does not reveal the race of Davis or whether the African was enslaved or free, female or male. Probably, Hugh Davis was a free European who in sleeping with an African, whether free or not, violated the still informal English prohibition against interracial sex.

183 • Negro Woman Is "Whipt"

White men were not primarily the ones "whipt" for interracial sex in colonial Virginia. In the Robert Sweat case of 1640, a man who had fathered a child with an African American woman servant was brought to trial. But the "negro woman shall be whipt at the whipping post," while "Sweat shall tomorrow in the forenoon do public penance for his offence," surely a lighter penalty for the "offense." Was she punished more harshly because she was Black, a woman, or a servant? We do not know for certain.

184 • Runaway John Punch

Black and white servants often banded together to run away from servitude in colonial Virginia. It may have been to discourage such unions that John Punch received his severe sentence in 1640. Punch was brought to trial for trying to escape in the company of two white servants. The three were equally guilty, but when sentences were issued, the whites were sentenced to serve an additional year for their masters and three additional years for the colony. But John Punch, the Negro, was required to serve his master and his master's heirs for the rest of his life. Is this proof of racial discrimination? Not quite, since we do not know if John Punch was guilty of some previous infraction. But the trial of Punch is our earliest recorded instance of slavery or lifetime servitude existing in Virginia.

185 • Ambiguous Graweere

We know that Blacks in early seventeenth-century Virginia were utterly degraded, but the case of Graweere in 1641, in which an African American servant successfully secured the freedom of his child, shows that some Blacks were able to take advantage of the legal system. Because his master allowed Graweere to keep livestock and profit from it, Graweere was able to appeal to the court for permission to buy the freedom of his child. By the turn of the century, such a purchase would be largely unthinkable for a Black servant, who by then would be considered a slave, and his children also slaves—servants for life.

186 • The Problem Solved

The real problem English colonists had with interracial sex is that it produced children who were no longer servants or slaves according to English law. Traditional English law held that the status of any child followed that of the father. But in colonial Virginia, which had very few white women, it was difficult to stop inter-racial relations between white men and Black women altogether. In a 1662 act, Virginia solved the problem: "Children got by an Englishman upon a Negro woman shall be bond or free according to the condition of the mother, and if any Christian shall commit fornication with a Negro man or woman, he shall pay double the fine of a former act." This Virginia act is one of the earliest examples of how the institution of slavery changed the English legal practice, a trend that would continue into the new country's legal apparatus.

187 • License to Kill Blacks

By the beginning of the eighteenth century, whites could legally kill Black slaves who resisted their "correcting," as it was called then. In a 1705 act, the Virginia council determined that if a master accidentally murdered his slave while "correcting" him or her for some offense, the master's act would "not be accounted [a] felony; but the master, owner, and every such other person so giving correction, shall be free and acquit[ted] of all punishment. . . ." Ironically this law was put into effect as the rights of white servants were being strengthened.

188 • Intermarriage Punished

Intermarriage between Blacks and whites in seventeenth- and early-eighteenth-century Virginia prompted the passage of a law in 1705 that prohibited the practice and imprisoned whites for six months. Although both white men and white women were punished for marrying African Americans, only white women could have their marriages annulled if it was discovered the woman had sexual relations with an African American prior to marriage. Usually the early birth of a "mulatto child" brought on the discovery. It was not until a 1967 Supreme Court

"Ladies Whipping Girls." Woodcut from *Picture of Slavery*, by George Bourne (Middletown, Conn.: E. Hunt, 1834). Prints and Photographs Division, Library of Congress

decision that all state and local prohibitions against intermarriage were outlawed as unconstitutional (*Loving v. Virginia*, 1967).

189 • Want to Be Free

Perhaps the most important difference between slavery in North America and slavery in Latin America was the drastic curtailment of the possibility of freedom or manumission in North America. In 1691, for example, Virginia passed a law that prohibited the freeing of any African American by a master without first making arrangements for removing the freed Black out of the country within six months. In other words, the ideal society in late-seventeenth-century Virginia was one in which all the Blacks

were slaves ...
masters. In ...
forced the ...
Blacks by pa...
made it unla...
white person ...
a slave. In a colony rapidly becoming a slave colony, exclusion from power to own slaves meant pauperism, and, if not migration out of the colony, perhaps slippage back into enslavement.

"Exchanging Citizens for Horses." Woodcut from *Picture of Slavery*, by George Bourne (Middletown, Conn.: E. Hunt, 1834). Prints and Photographs Division, Library of Congress

190 • Hogs or Real Estate?

A real dilemma for the colonial legal system in North America was how to rank slaves. In 1671 the case of an orphaned child who had inherited Black slaves prompted a decision. If treated like real estate, the slaves could not be disposed of until the child was twenty-one. But if the slaves were considered as hogs or other livestock which might die in the interim and hence lose their value, then the child could sell the slaves now. The court ruled that the latter was the more reasonable to protect the interest of the child. Slaves in North America were thus regularly treated as chattel, as movable and perishable livestock.

191 • 1712 Act: Decline of Rights, but Slave's Human Will Acknowledged

With the passage of the 1712 Slave Act, South Carolina instituted a repressive system of control over slaves who had once enjoyed certain liberties. Seventeenth-century slaves worked in a variety of occupations, such as cooperage, fishing, and cattle herding, and enjoyed a degree of personal freedom, but eighteenth-century slaves in South Carolina were more likely to be forced into rice cultivation and to suffer under a variety of controls on their personal

freedoms. The 1712 code required slaves to have a written pass unless they were accompanied by a white person. Slaves who were caught without a pass were to be whipped. Slaves were also prohibited from trading without their master's permission, thus limiting the money that slaves could acquire on their own. Any property that the slave possessed, moreover, could be forfeited. The 1712 law commanded masters to search slave quarters every two weeks for weapons; and after 1722, justices of the peace could seize horses and other livestock owned by slaves without impunity. The ability of the slave to rise in society through the acquisition of property or wealth was thus severely limited, along with his or her personal freedom. But the 1712 Slave Act also recognized, indirectly, that slaves were human. For example, it stated "that if any Negroes or other slaves shall make mutiny or insurrection, or rise in rebellion against any authority and government of this Province," they would be tried and executed for their

crimes if convicted.
ered responsible fo
of rebellion. Ironic:
recognized that at l
human.

194

ntrol of the Lord Proprietors, a specifically
mmercial and British undertaking. Only after
'21, when South Carolina acquired a royal gov-
nment responsive to the demands of the local
hite population, was voting limited to "Chris-
an" whites, and even then some Blacks still
.ted. Free Blacks exercised their right to vote
from the beginning of colonial America and only
reluctantly relinquished it.

192 • Im

Outbreaks of slave rebellions generally led colonial legislatures to pass even more stringent laws that lowered the status of slaves in the legal system. A prominent example is the 1740 Slave Act passed in South Carolina after the Stono Rebellion of 1739. Rather than defining the slave as necessary to the economic livelihood of the colony, as earlier acts had done, the 1740 act declared that slaves were "mere subjects of property in the hands of particular persons" and thus destined to be *"kept in due subjection and obedience."* While the code tried to suggest that owners needed to provide adequate food and housing to slaves, perhaps with the idea that less well kept slaves might be more likely to rebel, the code also stipulated that only another white person could bring a complaint against a master. It also made it a crime to teach a slave to read or write.

193 • Free Blacks Voted in Colonial South Carolina

Free Blacks voted in South Carolina elections held in 1701 and 1703. After the first election, an assembly was called to try and limit those eligible to vote. In discussing the election in 1701, "the dissenters of Colleton County charged that unqualified aliens, *i.e.* French Protestants, strangers, paupers, servants, and even free negroes, were allowed to vote." Protests were again raised after the 1703 election, because "aliens, Jews, servants, common sailors and negroes were admitted to vote...." Such voting was allowed because the colony was under the

194 • Free Blacks Owned Slaves

Free Blacks owned property, one of the reasons they were able to continue to vote in colonial South Carolina, where voting began to be limited to those who were owners of property. Some free Blacks also owned slaves, an essential possession in an agricultural society rapidly becoming dependent on slavery to supply its spiraling labor needs. But as historian Leon Higginbotham suggests, free Black ownership of slaves might have had an additional motive: many free Blacks purchased slaves, sometimes family members, in order to protect them. As South Carolina tightened manumission laws in the early eighteenth century, it became increasingly difficult to free even relatives; transfer of ownership to a free Black was one way to circumvent the system.

195 • Taxation Without Representation

Even after free Blacks began to lose the right to vote, they were still taxed on their property. Indeed, sometimes free Blacks were taxed more than their white counterparts. In 1792 a law was passed imposing a tax of two dollars on free Blacks irrespective of their property.

196 • Decline of Status of Free Blacks

As the eighteenth century progressed, the legal status and rights of free Blacks declined, and increasingly the courts treated free Blacks and slaves similarly. Free Blacks did continue to possess the right to bring civil suits in court in the eighteenth century, but by the early nineteenth century free Blacks were denied the right to have their testimony honored in court. Perhaps most important, the free Black population dwindled in number during the eighteenth century. The 1722 Slave Act in South Carolina demanded that owners who freed slaves had to transport them out of the state; and after the 1735 act, any manumitted person who returned to South Carolina could be reenslaved. By 1800 the South Carolina legislature passed a law that prohibited free Blacks from being brought into the colony. In the nineteenth century South Carolina's free Black population was limited in numbers and in location to tiny communities in such cities as Charleston.

197 • Georgia Outlaws Slavery!

Georgia, the last colony founded by the British, prohibited the transportation of Blacks into the colony after 1735 and denied its colonists the right to own or use slaves. On one hand, the prohibition of slaves reflected the views of James Oglethorpe, a trustee of the colony, who thought that "slavery . . . is against the Gospel, as well as the fundamental law of England." But as Leon Higginbotham shows, the banning of slaves from Georgia was far from a humanitarian act: it was part of a design to profit from slavery by permitting the government to capture all slaves found in the colony and to sell them into slavery in another colony. Thus, Georgia profited early from its close proximity to such slaveholding colonies as South Carolina. Moreover, the penalty for having slaves in Georgia was merely a fine, not the freeing of slaves. Not surprisingly, as Georgia matured as an agricultural colony in the 1750s, pressure from local planters repealed the prohi-

bition and instituted in the slave codes of 1755, 1765, and 1770 some of the harshest laws governing slaves in British North America.

198 • Pennsylvania Slavery

Although life for slaves in Pennsylvania was considerably less harsh than in Virginia, South Carolina, or Georgia, it was still quite repressive. Slaves in Pennsylvania were tried before a special court in which the principal concern was to protect the master's property. In one trial two slaves were convicted of burglary and sentenced to death in 1707, but the charge was reduced to protect the masters from loss. The masters were permitted to "inflict on [their slaves] such corporal punishment as may be requisite for a terror to others of their color." The masters were then instructed to lead the slaves through the town "with their arms extended and tied to a pole across their Necks, a Cart going before them, and that they shall be severely Whipt all the way as they pass . . . [and] that this punishment shall be repeated for 3 market days successively." Afterward, the owners could transport them out of the colony.

REVOLUTIONARY PERIOD

Protests, Organizations, and Demonstrations

199 • Crispus Attucks

Crispus Attucks, a runaway slave, led a group of rowdy Boston citizens to pelt and taunt a regiment of British soldiers. On March 5, 1770, the British responded by shooting Attucks and ten

Crispus Attucks, the first American to die at the Boston Massacre, 1770. Schomburg Center for Research in Black Culture, New York Public Library, Astor, Lenox and Tilden Foundation

other persons. Though it has been commonly believed that Attucks was the first to die, there is no proof. What is known is that Attucks was believed to have been at the head of the crowd of citizens, and to have provoked the incident by striking one of the British soldiers, Hugh Montgomery.

The people seemed to be leaving the soldiers, and to turn from them, when there came down a number from Jackson's corner, huzzaing and crying, damn them, they dare not fire, we are not afraid of them. One of these people, a stout man with a long cord wood stick, threw himself in, and made a blow at the officer . . . the stout man then turned round, and struck the grenadier's gun at the captain's right hand, and immediately fell in with his club, and knocked his gun away, and struck him over the head. . . . This stout man held the bayonet with his left hand, and twitched it and cried, kill the dogs, knock

them over. This was the general cry; the people then crowded in. . . . I turned to go off, when I heard the word fire . . . I thought I heard the report of a gun. . . . Do you know who this stout man was, that fell in and struck the grenadier? I thought, and still think, it was the mulatto who was shot.

Attucks was one of four men, including Samuel Gray, Samuel Maverick, and James Caldwell, killed that evening and celebrated afterward as America's first martyrs.

200 • Natural Rights Applied to AFAM Freedom

African Americans drafted petitions to be free utilizing the philosophy of the natural rights of man that white colonists used to justify separation from England. In Boston, on April 20, 1773, four slaves petitioned for their freedom by writing:

Sir, the efforts made by the legislative of this province in their last sessions to free themselves from slavery, gave us, who are in that deplorable state, a high degree of satisfaction. We expect great things from men who have made such a noble stand against the designs of their fellow-men to enslave them. We cannot but wish and hope Sir, that you will have the same grand object, we mean civil and religious liberty, in view of our next session. The divine spirit of freedom, seems to fire every humane breast on this continent, except such as are bribed to assist in executing the execrable plan.

The signers of the petition, Peter Bestes, Sambo Freeman, Felix Holbrook, and Chester Joie, went on to state that they did not demand their immediate release from their masters, but only a few days off a week to cultivate their own crops, with the prospect that at a future date, "we can, from our joynt labours procure money to transport ourselves to some part of the Coast of Africa, where we propose a settlement." Other similar petitions followed, including one in 1774, which stated explicitly in the language of John Locke that "your Petitioners apprehind we have in common with all other men a natural right to our freedoms without Being depriv'd of them by our fellow men as we are a freeborn Pepel and have never forfeited this Blessing by aney compact or agreement whatever."

201 • Revolutionary Antislavery Movements

From 1775 to 1804, numerous antislavery societies were founded in northern states. In 1775 the first Quaker antislavery society in America, the Society for the Relief of Free Negroes Unlawfully Held in Bondage, was established in Philadelphia. In 1785 the New York City Manumission Society was organized by John Jay and Alexander Hamilton. Benjamin Franklin founded the Pennsylvania Abolition Society in 1789. The first national antislavery society, the American Convention for Promoting the Abolition of Slavery, was founded in 1794. The latter went beyond earlier societies to

A woodcut of the Anti-Slavery Society of London's Kneeling Slave Medallion, originally designed by Josiah Wedgwood in 1787. Prints and Photographs Division, Library of Congress

protest the legal and political disabilities placed on free Negroes as well as slavery and the slave trade.

202 • The Anti-Slavery Society of London

Antislavery societies were not limited to the United States. In the late eighteenth century, in response to the move to abolish the slave trade, concerned English men and women founded the Anti-Slavery Society of London. Josiah Wedgwood (1730–95) of that society first published what became one of the most famous medallions of the antislavery movement, this picture of a praying slave.

203 • Free African Society

African Americans organized their own societies in the revolutionary period as a way of combating racism and providing for their own survival. One such society was the Free African Society of Boston, which was formed in 1796. This society had more than one purpose: it was committed to the moral uplift of African Americans, but it was also committed to ensuring the economic survival of the Black community in Boston. Toward that end, the Free African Society provided burial insurance and legal representation for its members, the latter in case they might be the victim of reenslavement. The society also provided an opportunity for cultural enrichment, by sponsoring a "Charity Lecture quarterly." Such societies often maintained private lending libraries and offered educational instruction. These societies were needed because it was becoming increasingly clear that African Americans were generally excluded from similar societies that served the white community.

204 • Prince Hall Exhorts

Some African American organizers of fraternal organizations had a more militant agenda than the Free African Society of Boston. That was the case with Prince Hall's African Lodge, established in 1787 after Hall was refused a charter for a Black lodge from the American Masons. After his rejection by the Americans, Hall succeeded in obtaining a charter for a lodge from the British Masons and established the African Lodge, No. 459, in Boston, with Hall as its master. Delivering an address in 1797 to lodge members, Hall exhorted Black Masons to help one another and regard one another with the fellow feeling of the Mason.

205 • Plea for Protection

In 1787 four African American freedmen filed a petition in the House of Representatives to be absolved from having to comply with recent laws passed in North Carolina. Even though these men had been freed legally by their masters, they were still subject to capture and return because of the rewards under North Carolina law. Their petition offered a broader critique of the cruelty of the new nation's fugitive slave laws in practice.

In addition to the hardship of our own case . . . , we believe ourselves warranted, on the present occasion, in offering to your consideration the singular case of a fellow-black now confined in the jail of this city, under sanction of the act of General Government, called the Fugitive Law. . . . This man, having been many years past manumitted by his master in North Carolina, was under the authority of the aforementioned law of that State, sold again into slavery, and, after serving his purchaser upward of six years, made his escape to Philadelphia . . . has been lately apprehended and committed to prison.

Despite such evidence of abuse, the House of Representatives decided not to honor the petition.

206 • Antislavery Petitions Submitted to Congress

On January 2, 1800, a group of Pennsylvania Blacks, including James Forten and Absalom Jones, submitted an antislavery petition to the House of Representatives. The petition sought abolition of the slave trade and repeal of the Fugitive Slave Act of 1793. Congressional reaction was immediate and hostile, as the response of Harrison Gray Otis of Massachusetts illustrates: "To encourage a measure of this kind would have an irritating tendency, and must be mischievous to America very soon. It would teach them [Blacks] the art of assembling together, debating, and the like, and would so soon, if encouraged, extend from one end of the Union to the other." Undaunted, African American organizations continued to submit petitions over the next several decades. In 1836 Congress adopted a rule preventing consideration of such petitions. The rule was finally rescinded in 1845.

207 • Elizabeth Freeman

No better example exists of how African American slaves utilized Republican ideology to free themselves than the case of Elizabeth Freeman, who was born of African parents around 1742. While working in the Sheffield home of one of the wealthiest merchants in Massachusetts, Colonel John Ashley, Freeman's face was scarred for life when the "lady" of the house at-

Portrait of Elizabeth "Mumbet" Freeman by Susan Sedgwick, 1811. Massachusetts Historical Society

tempted to strike Elizabeth's sister with a hot kitchen shovel, and Elizabeth jumped in between and took the blow instead. Furious at such treatment, Elizabeth left the house of Colonel Ashley forever, although Ashley had the gall to attempt to recover her through the law. But Freeman went to a Mr. Theodore Sedgwick, a lawyer, and asked if she could not argue for her freedom under the law. When he asked her what law that might be, she answered "that the 'Bill of Rights' said that all were born free and equal, and that, as she was not a dumb beast, she was certainly one of the nation." Sedgwick accepted her case and Freeman won her suit for freedom against Colonel Ashley. The jury that set her free even awarded her thirty shillings in damages; but the important precedent established by her case was that the Bill of Rights had in fact abolished slavery in Massachusetts.

Legal Decisions and Their Implications

208 • Abolition Laws

Revolutionary-era antislavery sentiment culminated in a series of state laws passed from 1777 to 1804 in Vermont, Massachusetts, New Hampshire, Pennsylvania, Rhode Island, Connecticut, New York, and New Jersey that abolished slavery in those states. Pennsylvania became the first state to end slavery by an act of its legislature when it passed "An Act for the Gradual Abolition of Slavery" in 1780. But as was the case with many such acts, the Pennsylvania law left enslaved those who were already slaves, and freed only those born after the law. Even those freed were still obligated to serve an additional twenty-eight years before they were freed.

209 • Right to Slave Property
The Constitution contains a provision for assisting slave owners in the recapture of fugitive slaves. "No Person held to Service or Labour in one State, under the Laws thereof, escaping into another, shall, in Consequence of any Law or Regulation therein, be discharged from such Service or Labour, but shall be delivered up on Claim of the Party to whom such Service or Labour may be due." This paragraph in the Constitution was part of the reason that Judge Roger B. Taney ruled against the freeing of Dred Scott in the *Dred Scott* decision of 1857.

210 • Constitution Says Slaves Count as Three-Fifths of a Person
That the southern states meant to keep their slaves can be seen from how determined they were to have the slaves counted for purposes of determining their representation. During the 1787 Constitutional Convention, the southern states, led by Georgia and South Carolina, proposed Blacks be counted as equals to whites for representation purposes. The northern delegates considered slaves property and thought they should not be counted at all. A compromise was finally reached whereby slaves would be counted as three-fifths of a person. As it appeared in Article I of the Constitution: "Representatives and direct Taxes shall be apportioned among the several States which may be included within this Union, according to their respective Numbers, which shall be determined by adding to the whole Number of free Persons, including those bound to Service for a Term of Years, and excluding Indians not taxed, *three fifths of all other Persons.*"

211 • The Northwest Ordinance
The Northwest Ordinance adopted in 1787 had two implications for African Americans. First, it outlawed slavery in new territories seeking admittance to the Union, thus incorporating Thomas Jefferson's proposal that slavery be confined to the states in which it already existed. Disappointingly the ordinance also allowed the capture of fugitive slaves found within these territories.

212 • Race and the Naturalization Act
When Congress passed the federal Naturalization Act in 1790, it declared that only "free white persons" of good character who had resided for at least two years in the United States and one year in the state from which they applied could be naturalized. But neither the Constitution nor the Naturalization Act defined citizenship or stated that any person currently living as a native of the United States could not be thought of as a citizen. Thus, the Constitution and the Naturalization Act left open whether free Negroes were in fact citizens and entitled to the enjoyment of all of the privileges of citizenship.

213 • Conflict Between Slave and Free States
The Fugitive Slave Act of 1793 did not answer the question of whether a slave remained a slave when both master and slave traveled from a slave to a free state to reside even temporarily in the free state. For example, the Maryland Court of Appeals ruled in 1799 that a slave who was hired out to work in Pennsylvania became free because of Pennsylvania's laws abolishing slavery. In the early national and antebellum periods, the laws of the state where a slave resided were thought to determine status.

ANTEBELLUM PERIOD

Protests, Organizations, and Demonstrations

214 • African American Celebrations

African Americans celebrated the most important event of the early nineteenth century when on January 1, 1808, the law abolishing the international slave trade took effect. Gathering in New York City, African Americans listened to Peter Williams, a well-versed orator, discuss the impact of the slave trade on Africa, the horrors of the Middle Passage, and the triumph of men like John Woolman, Anthony Benezet, and William Wilberforce over the forces of evil and profit in the slave trade. On July 4, 1827, all slaves became free in New York State under its gradual emancipation plan, originally passed in 1799. The African Zion Church was the festive center of the celebration that year, and was decorated with pictures of famous abolitionists, such as John Jay and Thomas Clarkson. Then, on August 1, 1834, African Americans and abolitionists celebrated the end of slavery in the British West Indies. That celebration was bittersweet, however, because of the realization that slavery was still alive and thriving in the United States.

215 • National Negro Conventions

Beginning in September 1830, African Americans held annual national political conventions until 1835, and then periodically afterward until 1855. Through the conventions, African Americans issued addresses to the nation, called attention to the plight of Black Americans, both free and slave, debated the merits of colonization, and issued calls for the immediate emancipation of all slaves. What these national conventions did was link Blacks from different cities into a national political community, and mark the emergence in the 1830s of a new presence in the American political arena—that of the Black abolitionist.

216 • David Walker's Appeal

Born a free Black in Wilmington, North Carolina, David Walker despised slavery. Migrating to Boston in 1785, he grew increasingly radical. His 1829 publication of an eighty-page pamphlet known widely as *David Walker's Appeal* created an uproar in the South. In the appeal, Walker asserted that American Blacks would not be free until Blacks worldwide were freed, so all must fight for universal emancipation:

Your full glory and happiness . . . shall never be fully consummated, but with the entire emancipation of your universal brethren all over the world. . . . For I believe it is the will of the Lord that our greatest happiness shall consist in working for the salvation of the whole body. When this is accomplished a burst of glory will shine upon you, which will indeed astonish you and the world.

217 • The Liberator

The *Liberator* was the preeminent abolitionist newspaper. Started by William Lloyd Garrison on January 1, 1831, the paper enjoyed immense support from African Americans. In the first edition, Garrison declared:

I will be as harsh as truth, and as uncompromising as justice. On this subject, I do not wish to think, to speak, to write, with moderation. No! No! Tell a man whose house is on fire to give a moderate alarm; tell him to moderately rescue his wife from the hands of the ravisher; tell the

William Lloyd Garrison, editor of the *Liberator*.
National Archives

mother to gradually extricate her babe from the fire into which it has fallen; but urge me not to use moderation in a cause like the present! I am in earnest—I will not equivocate—I will not excuse—I will not retreat a single inch—AND I WILL BE HEARD!

218 • American Anti-Slavery Society

The American Anti-Slavery Society was a benevolent and reform organization founded in Philadelphia on December 4, 1833. Dominated by William Lloyd Garrison, Theodore Weld, Lewis and Arthur Tappan, Henry B. Stanton, and James G. Birney, the society published four periodicals, sent more than seventy lecturers throughout the country, encouraged the formation of local chapters, and tried to dispense antislavery literature throughout the North and South. The multiracial society included five Black abolitionists on its board: Peter Williams,

Robert Purvis, George B. Vashon, Abraham Shadd, and James McCrummell. Although the American Anti-Slavery Society did not create the new abolitionist movement, the organization came to symbolize the two major strains of antislavery activism in the 1830s and 1840s—a wide-ranging moral crusade and an intellectual movement.

219 • Interracial Tensions in the Movement

Even the antislavery movement contained instances of discrimination and segregation of African Americans. For example, when the Anti-Slavery Women met at their first convention in New York in 1837, the society debated the propriety of having African American women in the organization and only allowed them to join after considerable debate. Some African Americans criticized that most antislavery people wished to have all-white antislavery societies. Most antislavery societies were more concerned about ending slavery, and thereby removing its sin from the conscience of whites, than in fighting against the racial prejudice that shackled free Negroes in the North.

220 • The American and Foreign Anti-Slavery Society

A split occurred in the American Anti-Slavery Society in 1840 when William Lloyd Garrison, who had never held an office in the organization, seized control of the society by stacking the convention with votes from Boston, his base of support. The split occurred ideologically between those, like Lewis and Arthur Tappan, who believed in advocating political action as the best method for attaining abolition and those, like Garrison, who favored appeals based on moral principles. In addition, some in the American Anti-Slavery Society opposed the policy of allowing women to speak to the men at the meetings. Garrison supported the right of women as speakers, being a firm advocate of women's rights. Those that supported political action and opposed women speakers broke off to form the American and Foreign Anti-Slavery Society, which became the nucleus of the Liberty Party, which campaigned on an antislavery plank in the early 1840s. Blacks who committed to the American and Foreign Anti-Slavery Society included Christopher Rush, Samuel Cornish, Charles B. Ray, and James W. C. Pennington.

221 • Reaction of South to Antislavery

The Georgia legislature offered $4,000 for the arrest of William Lloyd Garrison. Arthur Tappan was worth $12,000 in Macon and $20,000 in New Orleans. Vigilance committees in North Carolina offered $1,500 for the arrest of anyone distributing the *Liberator* or *David Walker's Appeal.* A Georgian subscriber to the *Liberator* was dragged from his home, tarred and feath-

James W. C. Pennington. Prints and Photographs Division, Library of Congress

ered, set afire, dunked in a river, tied to a post, and then whipped.

222 • The Murder of Elijah Lovejoy

Violent opposition to the abolition movement was not restricted to the South. Elijah Lovejoy, the white publisher of abolitionist literature, was forced to flee St. Louis after he criticized a judge's lenient treatment of defendants accused of burning alive an African American. William Lloyd Garrison was dragged through the streets of Boston with a noose around his neck on one occasion. These sorts of incidents, however, did not deter the bravest abolitionists, some of whom paid with their lives. In 1837 Lovejoy was murdered by a mob that attacked and destroyed for the fourth time the printing press he used to publish the *Alton (Ill.) Observer.* Even in death Lovejoy was a martyr for freedom, as many joined in the struggle not only against slavery but against those forces in American society that sought to curtail free speech.

223 • Garrisonians Abandon Political Action for Passive Resistance and Moral Force

Garrisonians began to advocate passive resistance and nonviolence. William Whipper published an "Address on Non-Resistance to Offensive Aggression" in 1828 that suggested that "the practice of nonresistance to physical aggression is not only consistent with reason, but the surest method of obtaining a speedy triumph of the principles of universal peace." Garrisonians also began to condemn "complexional institutions" such as Black churches, lodges, schools, newspapers, and conventions, thereby widening the gulf between Garrisonians and some of the more radical Black abolitionists.

224 • Frederick Douglass Splits with Garrisonians

When Frederick Douglass returned from England to America in August 1847, he found his freedom of expression and advancement limited by William Lloyd Garrison. Douglass returned from England with money to start his own newspaper, but Garrison opposed it. After a year of complying with Garrison's wishes, Douglass moved to Rochester, New York, began to publish one, and encouraged Blacks to take a more active role in the antislavery movement. Publishing a newspaper strengthened Douglass's connection with the Black community and deepened his sense of race pride. Douglass began to criticize the Garrisonians for their subjugation of Blacks within their organization and argued that "no people that has solely depended . . . upon the efforts of those, in any way identified with the oppressor . . . ever stood forth in the attitude of Freedom." Douglass also began to develop his own analysis of the antislavery struggle and finally rejected Garrison's insistence that abolitionists avoid political action. In developing his independent thinking, Douglass was not forced to segregate himself. The formation of the American and Foreign Anti-Slavery Society in 1840 as an alternative to the Garrison-controlled American Anti-Slavery Society brought Douglass new and powerful allies in Lewis and Arthur Tappan and Gerritt Smith.

225 • Divisions Within the Abolition Movement

Although ostensibly working toward the same goal, interracial and intraracial divisions developed within the abolitionist movement. Charles Lenox Remond, for example, was an early and prominent supporter of the Garrisonian philosophy of passive nonviolence and moral suasion, which rejected political action because the

Charles Remond. Prints and Photographs Division, Library of Congress

Constitution was deemed a proslavery document. When Douglass broke with Garrison over this issue and allied himself with the Liberty Party, his defection split the followers of the Garrisonian position. In a well-attended and well-publicized debate held at Shiloh Church in New York City in May 1857, Charles Remond challenged Douglass to prove that the Constitution was not a proslavery document. But even Remond eventually moved away from the Garrisonian position and even advocated slave revolts. Despite being highly regarded, Remond allegedly resented the greater attention accorded Frederick Douglass. On one occasion, Remond publicly thanked God that he was not a slave or the son of a slave. Douglass, upon hearing of Remond's remarks, replied: "I thank God I am neither a barber nor the son of a barber."

226 • Reaction to Fugitive Slave Law

Black abolitionists were even more divided by how best to respond to the aggressive Fugitive Slave Law passed as part of the Compromise of 1850. Suddenly the idea of settling outside of the territorial United States became a more appealing idea. Not only were former slaves at greater risk of easy capture and return to the South, but many Black abolitionists responded to the bill's passage as a sign that the federal government was not ready to end slavery or grant free Negroes basic civil rights. Although opposition to the American Colonization Society continued, men such as Martin R. Delany became convinced that leaving the United States, perhaps for the Caribbean, was necessary because of the lack of political rights. Others, like James Theodore Holly, believed in emigration regardless of the granting of political rights, because African Americans, in his view, would continue to encounter "a social proscription stronger than conventional legislation." Even staunch anticolonizationists like Frederick Douglass began to give support to the idea, and in the spring of 1861 Douglass accepted an invitation to visit Haiti. The firing on Fort Sumter kept him from making the trip, for he knew that both war and a radical transformation of slavery were imminent.

227 • Further Divisions

The tension between Frederick Douglass and Charles Lenox Remond was in part a tension between Black abolitionists who had been slaves and those who were freeborn. Often, those who had been slaves possessed a greater sense of entitlement to speak upon the issue of slavery, and that led to conflicts sometimes with free Negroes of the North. One such conflict emerged at a Massachusetts meeting of Blacks held on August 2, 1858, in reaction to the *Dred Scott* decision. Remond declared that he was ready to "spit" on Judge Roger B. Taney's ruling in the case and urged the assembly to issue a state-

ment of defiance of the *Dred Scott* decision. He even proposed that the convention issue a call to the slaves to rebel, and though he realized it was bold, he did his best to make sure those assembled would not turn pale at the suggestion of rebellion. Josiah Henson, the subject of Harriet Beecher Stowe's *Uncle Tom's Cabin,* rose and stated that he believed that Remond would be the first to desert a fight to the death with the slaveholders if it ever came to that. Before the furious Remond could get to his feet to rebut the attack, Henson added that he had never in his life turned pale. Remond's proposal was voted down.

228 • John Brown's Raid at Harpers Ferry

John Brown, a fervent abolitionist, believed he was chosen by God to end slavery. Funded by New England antislavery organizations, Brown tried to establish a station in western Virginia to help fugitive slaves. On October 16, 1859, Brown, with fewer than fifty men, attacked the U.S. arsenal in Harpers Ferry hoping to acquire enough ammunition to launch an attack on Virginia slaveholders. After two days, the arsenal was recaptured by U.S. Marines commanded by Robert E. Lee, then a colonel in the U.S. Army. Brown was convicted of "treason, conspiracy, and advising slaves and others to rebel, and murder in the first degree." Although advised by his attorney to plead insanity, he refused and was sentenced to death by hanging. Five African Americans participated in the raid; two were killed in the fight with U.S. troops, two were hanged, and one escaped.

People and Politics

229 • Benjamin Lundy (1789–1839)

One of the most influential antislavery leaders of the early nineteenth century was the European American Benjamin Lundy, founder and editor of the *Genius of Universal Emancipation,* an antislavery newspaper published from 1821 to 1839. Early in his life Lundy was saddened by the sight of slaves in chains in Virginia and became a dedicated opponent who sacrificed a lucrative business to write and proselytize against slavery. Lundy recruited William Lloyd Garrison to the abolitionist movement. Garrison went to Baltimore in 1829 to work on the *Genius* and became its associate editor before going on to publish the *Liberator.* Garrison eventually moved away from Lundy's conservative antislavery views, such as his faith in gradual emancipation of slaves over years and colonization of free Negroes in Africa. Lundy also tried to develop a free-labor colony, possibly in Texas, in the 1830s, which would prosper by using free Black laborers and thereby convince southern planters that hiring free Black workers was even more profitable than slavery. Although Lundy failed to realize his scheme, he was one of the earliest and most inspirational of antebellum antislavery thinkers, and one of the first to successfully publish an abolitionist newspaper.

230 • William Lloyd Garrison (1805–79)

William Lloyd Garrison was a former white indentured servant who was at the forefront of the abolition movement of the 1830s. Garrison first joined the cause of antislavery agitation in Boston in 1828, when he met Benjamin Lundy, who was looking for subscribers for his *Genius of Universal Emancipation,* a quarterly journal of antislavery rhetoric. At the time, Garrison was a printer who had published the early writings of John Greenleaf Whittier and had edited the *Boston National Philanthropist,* a temperance newspaper, and later the *Bennington (Vt.) Journal of the Times.* Lundy recruited Garrison to serve as coeditor of the *Genius* in Baltimore, but their association was brief. Although influenced by Lundy's ideas, Garrison eventually broke away from Lundy, returned to Boston, began publishing the *Liberator,* and launched the New England Anti-Slavery Society in 1831. Over the next thirty years, Garrison would be the most influential intellectual leader of the abolitionist movement. Eventually he would define the new abolitionism as opposition to colonization, advocacy of immediate emancipation of the slaves, harsh attacks on American churches and the United States Constitution for complicity in slavery, and the belief that moral persuasion rather than political action would end slavery in America. Garrison was also responsible for linking abolitionism to the temperance, peace, and women's rights movements. Garrison was also the one white abolitionist who socialized easily with free Blacks in the North. Whereas many abolitionists advocated an end to slavery but eschewed any social contact with free Blacks in the North, believing, as Samuel Ringgold Ward put it, that it was best to "love the colored man at a distance," Garrison frequently dined at the homes of such free Blacks as James Forten, James McCrummell, and William Topp, and stayed with others during his frequent travels.

231 • Theodore Weld (1803–95)

The son of a white conservative Presbyterian minister, Theodore Weld was one of the architects of the agency system of the American Anti-Slavery Society that sent men out to lecture and convert audiences to the cause of antislavery in the 1830s. As a young man, he was a well-known lecturer on temperance and moral reform, and was commissioned by the Tappan brothers to establish the Lane Theological Seminary, which he founded in Cincinnati in 1833. Weld organized the famous Lane Seminary Debate, held in January 1834, which systematized the antislavery argument, which Weld then standardized and made integral to the training of agents for the American Anti-Slavery Society. Weld was responsible for training and sending out men who became the backbone of the agency system. These men were paid to travel and convert audiences to the antislavery position. This education and persuasion campaign proved to be the key to the American Anti-Slavery Society's success in building antislavery sentiment in the United States during the 1830s. Though Weld and others like him were often heckled and sometimes stoned and beaten by crowds hostile to the antislavery position, eventually they converted large portions of the states to which they were sent. Still active as a speaker and lecturer in his nineties, Weld rendered invaluable intellectual service to the abolitionist movement.

232 • James Forten, Sr. (1766–1842)

James Forten was an early American success story as well as a prominent Black abolitionist. Having studied as a boy at a school run by Anthony Benezet, Forten served as a powder boy on an American ship in the Revolutionary War, apprenticed to a wealthy sailmaker, and then assumed control of the firm when the owner died. In 1832 Forten was worth over $100,000, employed white and black workers in his firm, managed considerable rental property, and lived in one of the best homes in his native Philadelphia. But Forten was also an active and

James Forten, Sr. The Historical Society of Pennsylvania

influential abolitionist: the American Anti-Slavery Society was conceived at Forten's home by William Lloyd Garrison; Forten was a member of that society's board of managers; and Forten reputedly persuaded Garrison to oppose colonization. He sponsored a petition in 1832, with William Whipper and Robert Purvis, to block state legislature attempts to enhance enforcement of the Fugitive Slave Act in Pennsylvania. Beyond the abolition of slavery, Forten advanced women's rights, universal peace, and improvement for the free Negro. He authored a pamphlet of protest against a bill in the Pennsylvania senate to bar free Negroes from immigrating into the state, and founded and served as president of the American Moral Reform Society, an association of African American men devoted to moral and educational improvement of the race.

Robert Purvis, Sr. Prints and Photographs Division, Library of Congress

233 • Robert Purvis, Sr. (1810–98)

Born of mixed parentage—his father was a wealthy cotton broker, his mother a freeborn descendant of a native-born African—Robert Purvis came to Philadelphia from Charleston, South Carolina, at age nine, and at age sixteen, upon the death of his father, inherited $120,000. But Purvis's wealth and prominence did not deter him from becoming an avid abolitionist. Having met Benjamin Lundy and William Lloyd Garrison in 1830, Purvis developed a long-term friendship with Garrison, who often stayed at Purvis's home when Garrison stopped in Philadelphia. A number of runaway slaves stayed overnight at Purvis's home too, since as president of the Vigilance Committee of Philadelphia, he was engaged in the underground railroad. He espoused the "free produce movement," and only served food at his house

that was not planted by slaves, supported women's rights, temperance, and prison improvement, and preferred integrated to racially segregated reform movements. Accordingly he was, until 1859, the only African American member of Benjamin Franklin's Pennsylvania Society for Promoting the Abolition of Slavery. Purvis also fought, unsuccessfully, against the proposal to eliminate Blacks from voting in Pennsylvania and successfully blocked the attempt of the school board in his township of Bayberry to bar Black children from public schools when he threatened to withhold the considerable sum he paid in taxes.

234 • William Whipper (1804?–76)

Known as the most articulate writer of the Philadelphia Black abolitionists, William Whipper was also a very successful businessman who pioneered the steam-scouring process into a lucrative dry-cleaning business and ran a successful "free labor and temperance" grocery in Philadelphia. Although not a great speaker, Whipper was very active in the national Negro convention movement, helped organize the American Moral Reform Society, which espoused education, economy, and temperance for all, not just free Blacks, and edited that society's journal, the *National Reformer,* becoming the first African American to edit a national magazine. Whipper was in demand when there was a need to write papers or resolutions. Some of his most important writings were "Address before the Colored Reading Society of Philadelphia" (1828), "Eulogy on William Wilberforce" (1833), and "Non-Resistance to Offensive Aggression," which was published in the *Colored American* in 1837. Whipper, who was a mulatto, was also active in the underground railroad, spending almost $1,000 a year to assist runaway slaves. Despondent over the treatment of

Frederick Douglass. National Archives

African Americans in the United States and the Fugitive Slave Act of 1850, Whipper purchased land in Canada in 1853, with an eye to migrating there. But the Civil War raised his hopes about justice in the United States. Along with Frederick Douglass, Whipper tried, unsuccessfully, to persuade President Andrew Johnson to extend civil rights to Black Americans.

235 • Frederick Douglass (1817–95)

The most famous of the Black abolitionists, Frederick Douglass was born a slave in Talbot County, Maryland, had received favored treatment as a gifted young slave, and eventually escaped to freedom in 1831 by impersonating a free Black sailor. Under the care of David Ruggles, the Black head of the New York Vigilance Committee, Douglass moved to New Bedford, Massachusetts, became an avid reader of the

Liberator, and in 1841, at an abolitionist meeting in Nantucket, Massachusetts, rose and told his story of what it had been like to be a slave. Soon after, Douglass became one of the star attractions for the Massachusetts Anti-Slavery Society. Studying the style of exposition used by Garrison and Wendell Phillips, Douglass evolved from a slave storyteller to an outstanding speaker, whose diction and poise, wit, humor, and sarcasm transformed him into an engaging lecturer. Challenged by those who believed that no one who spoke that well could have been a slave, Douglass, who had taught himself to read and write, authored his autobiography, *Narrative of the Life of Frederick Douglass,* which was published in 1845. It immediately became a classic, for it was one of the few slave narratives authored by a slave himself. It also made Douglass a marked man for recapture by his former master, causing Douglass to flee to England, where he further enthralled audiences. After twenty-one months in England, Douglass returned to the United States with funds enough to purchase his freedom and to assume the reputation of the most highly regarded of the Black abolitionists.

236 • Sojourner Truth (1797?–1883)

Born in Hurley, Ulster County, New York, in 1797, Isabella grew up on a Dutch farm and was sold to a variety of masters before she escaped from her last master, John Dumont, when he reneged on his promise to release her from bondage following a year of particularly hard labor. She decided to leave when God, whom she spoke to often, advised her to leave. That special relationship with God gave her the courage to successfully sue Dumont for the return of a son that he had sold into slavery in the Deep South, which was illegal under New York law. It also gave her the power to change her name and

Sojourner Truth, Randall Studios, c. 1870. The National Portrait Gallery, Smithsonian Institute

transform herself into Sojourner Truth, who by the 1840s would become an abolitionist and a popular speaker in the revival movement then sweeping the Northeast. She became one of the abolitionist movement's most famous speakers, whose folk wisdom and wry humor disarmed angry anti-abolition crowds in Massachusetts, Connecticut, and even Indiana, where, on one occasion, when challenged by men who disbelieved that she was a woman, she bared her breast and embarrassed her critics. Perhaps most important, Sojourner Truth became one of the very few Black women to participate in the women's rights movement. According to witnesses, she rescued the Akron, Ohio, Women's Rights Convention in 1851 from collapsing under the withering assault of male ministers, who countered the call for women's equality with arguments based on the Bible. Sojourner, in her

so-called "Ar'n't I a Woman?" speech, turned the arguments of biblical and intellectual superiority against the men, and asserted her equality with any of them.

237 • Wendell Phillips (1811–84)

Wendell Phillips was a wealthy Bostonian who dedicated himself to lecturing not only on Garrisonian abolitionism but also on the evils of industrial capitalism and the exploitation of labor in America. Like Sojourner Truth, he was regarded as one of the greatest orators of the nineteenth century. After the murder of Elijah Lovejoy, a meeting was called at Faneuil Hall, Boston, on March 26, 1837, to discuss Lovejoy's death. James T. Austin, the attorney general of Massachusetts, referred to Lovejoy's murderers as Revolutionary-era patriots and almost swayed the audience. But Phillips answered the outrageous comparison with a withering verbal speech that sealed his reputation as a first-class antislavery speaker. Phillips supported Garrison's demand that women be allowed the same rights in the American Anti-Slavery Society. He became increasingly militant in the 1840s and 1850s, vigorously opposing the Mexican War, the separation of the North from the South, and the slowness of Lincoln in freeing the slaves. After the Civil War, he became an advocate of a variety of reforms, from American Indian rights to women voting, and the increasing opposition of labor to the rise of moneyed corporations.

238 • Charles Lenox Remond (1810–73)

The son of a Salem hairdresser, merchant, and caterer, Remond was the first Black agent of the Massachusetts Anti-Slavery Society in 1838. Remond was a man of indefatigable energy who lectured every day, sometimes twice a day, to boisterous, hostile crowds, and was reputed to be a great speaker, on par with the great Wendell Phillips. Remond was an unwavering follower of Garrison and believed moral suasion was the only way to bring an end to slavery. He was chosen by the American Anti-Slavery Society as one of its four delegates to attend the 1840 World's Anti-Slavery Convention in London, where, to protest the segregation of women at the convention, he sat in the gallery and entertained Lady Byron, duchess of Sutherland. He remained in Great Britain for eighteen months, lectured in Ireland and Scotland, and brought back to the United States an "Address from the People of Ireland," signed by sixty thousand, urging their opposition to slavery. A frequent victim of Jim Crow segregation on trains, Remond was the first Black person to address the legislative committee of the Massachusetts House of Representatives in 1842, when he delivered the "Rights of Colored Persons in Traveling." Remond was opposed to the growing tendency of Blacks to form their own organizations, being critical of any association based on color. During the Civil War, he enlisted men for the famous 54th Massachusetts, which was the first unit to gain national respect for Black troops.

239 • Sarah Parker Remond (1826–94)

Sarah Remond was a physician and an abolitionist who began lecturing with her brother, Charles Remond, in Groton, Massachusetts, in July 1842 and went on to become a famous speaker and fierce fighter for African American civil rights on her own. She protested segregation in public places and more than once sued establishments that either segregated or removed her because of her color. In one case, she had the agent for Madame Henriette Sontag, who was singing in the Boston Atheneum's production of Mozart's *Don Giovanni,* arrested for

assisting in forcibly ejecting Remond and her friends from the theater. She also sued the theater and won $500 in damages. Appointed a lecturing agent for the American Anti-Slavery Society in 1856, she went to England and lectured on the evils of slavery in Ireland, Scotland, and England, helping to encourage a boycott against purchasing slave-grown cotton. Regarded as a "living refutation to the theory of Negro inferiority," Sarah Remond eventually settled first in Florence and then in Rome, preferring to live abroad rather than face race prejudice at home.

240 • Formation of the Liberty Party

A year before members of the American Anti-Slavery Society left to form the American and Foreign Anti-Slavery Society, some abolitionists decided to create a national political party, the Liberty Party, to bring about the end of slavery. Formed in 1839 by James Birney, a former slaveholder and a prominent Alabama lawyer converted to antislavery by Theodore Weld in 1832, and by such African American abolitionists as Henry Highland Garnet and Samuel Ringgold Ward, the new party ran Birney for president in 1840. Although Birney only received 7,059 votes, the running of an antislavery presidential candidate was the beginning of a process of political activity on the part of antislavery forces that would culminate in the election of Abraham Lincoln in 1860. The Liberty Party was also the first political party to permit African Americans in any office, even nominating Frederick Douglass to run for New York secretary of state in 1855.

241 • White Women in the Antislavery Movement

White women made dramatic contributions to the abolitionist movement beyond the controversy that split the American Anti-Slavery

Society. Philadelphia's Lucretia Mott was one of the founding members of the American Anti-Slavery Society. She preached at a Quaker meeting in 1818 and was well received. But when Sarah Grimké did the same, some objected to having a woman "speak in meeting." In response to this opposition, her sister, Angelina Grimké, wrote an appeal to southern women to oppose slavery, and Sarah wrote a similar appeal to southern clergymen. This led to controversy within the American Anti-Slavery Society as to whether it was appropriate for women to speak to mixed audiences of men and women. When Angelina Grimké undertook a lecture tour in 1839, controversy swirled nationally about the role of women in the movement. Some felt that challenging the old prohibition against women speakers was diverting the resources of the antislavery movement. Much of the opposition came from the clergy, some of whom regarded women who spoke in public as being somehow unnatural. Many felt more comfortable with women playing a supportive role in the movement, confined to such activities as raising funds for the schools, making clothes for runaway slaves, and serving as teachers in schools for Blacks. But as Garrison recognized, abolitionism was part of a larger liberationist movement that could not be easily confined or limited simply to the problem of slavery.

242 • Free-Soil Party

In August 1848 in Buffalo, New York, antislavery Democrats and Whigs came together to form the Free-Soil Party, whose slogan was "Free Soil, Free Speech, Free Labor, and Free Men." The party chose as their presidential candidate Martin Van Buren, who had become an antislavery figure mainly because of his opposition to the annexing of Texas. The Free-Soil Party was not, however, an abolitionist party: it sought merely to keep slavery a state institution and restrain it from spreading into the western territories. The party's platform represented the minimum of slavery opposition—the desire to contain it rather than eliminate it—and lacked any expression of concern for African American civil or political rights. The party mainly reflected the prevailing ideologies of the states in which it emerged: Massachusetts Free-Soilers were far more militant in their opposition to slavery than Illinois Free-Soilers, who advocated internal colonization and separation of free Negroes from whites.

243 • Harriet Beecher Stowe (1811–96)

Called by Abraham Lincoln "the little woman who started the Civil War," Harriet Beecher Stowe contributed mightily to the abolitionist movement when she published *Uncle Tom's Cabin* in 1852, a denouncement of slavery that was particularly effective because of its sympa-

Harriet Beecher Stowe. National Archives

thetic portrait of the African American character Uncle Tom. Although the novel suffered from some of the melodrama typical of abolitionist tracts of the period, the portrayal of Tom as a human being with feelings evidently influenced many northerners to see slavery as an inhuman institution. Even more influential than the novel on antebellum audiences was the play, which toured throughout the North and brought the drama of Tom and Little Eva to life for many Americans.

244 • Republican Party and Slavery

In 1854 remnants of the Free-Soil Party, the Liberty Party, and the old Whig Party combined to form a new, centrist political organization, the Republican Party. In the election of 1860 the Republican Party ran as its presidential candidate Abraham Lincoln, who had a reputation for being opposed to slavery. But the Republican Party was not an abolitionist party. It proposed only to limit the expansion of slavery into the territories and preserve them for settlement by white men rather than for African Americans. Indeed, several of those territories already had ordinances prohibiting the in-migration of free Blacks. "Free soil" meant free of all Negroes, whether slave or free. Neither Lincoln nor the platform of the Republican Party promised to end slavery. As Horace Greeley, a Republican Party spokesperson put it, "Never on earth did the Republican Party propose to abolish slavery. . . . Its object with respect to slavery is simply, nakedly, avowedly, its restriction to the existing states."

245 • David Walker Condemns Whites

David Walker's Appeal was one of the first public documents to harshly condemn whites for their treatment of Blacks.

Yet those men tell us that we are the seed of Cain, and that God put a dark stain upon us, that we might be known as their slaves!!! Now, I ask those avaricious and ignorant wretches, who act more like the seed of Cain, by murdering the whites or the blacks? How many vessel loads of human beings have the blacks thrown into the seas? How many thousand souls have the blacks murdered in cold blood, to make them work in wretchedness and ignorance, to support them and their families? How many millions souls of the human family have the blacks beat nearly to death, to keep them from learning to read the Word of God, and from writing?

Southern reaction to the *Appeal* was swift and hostile. Special sessions of Virginia, Georgia, and North Carolina legislatures were called to discuss the tract, and some southern politicians demanded Boston officials arrest Walker immediately. Walker knew the publication threatened his life but declared himself "ready to be offered at any moment." In June 1830, soon after the third edition of the *Appeal* was published, Walker was found dead outside the clothing store he owned.

246 • New England Anti-Slavery Society Defines Immediate Emancipation

In its annual report of 1833, the New England Anti-Slavery Society explained what was meant by "immediate abolition."

What, then, is meant by immediate abolition?

It means, in the first place, that all title of property in the slaves shall instantly cease, because their Creator has never relinquished his claim of ownership, and because none have a right to sell their own bodies or buy those of their own species as cattle. Is there any thing terrific in this arrangement?

It means, secondly, that every husband shall have his own wife, and every wife her own husband, both being united in wedlock according to its proper forms, and placed under the protection of law. Is this unreasonable?

It means, thirdly, that parents shall have the control and government of their own children, and that the children shall belong to their parents. What is there sanguinary in this concession?

It means, fourthly, that all trade in human beings shall be regarded as felony, and entitled to the highest punishment. Can this be productive of evil?

It means, fifthly, that the tremendous power which is now vested in every slaveholder to punish his slaves without trial, and to a savage extent, shall be at once taken away. Is this undesirable?

It means, sixthly, that all the laws which now prohibit the instruction of slaves, shall instantly be repealed, and others enacted, providing schools and instruction for their intellectual illumination. Would this prove a calamity? . . .

247 • Why a Negro Convention Is Necessary

William Hamilton addressed the fourth Convention of the Colored Peoples in New York City in June 1834 and provided a rationale for the organization.

. . . alas for the people of color in this community! Their interest is not identified with that of other men. From them, white men stand aloof. For them the eye of pity hath scarcely a tear. To them the hand of kindness is palsied, to them the dregs of mercy scarcely are given. To them the finger of scorn is pointed: contumely and reproach is continually theirs. They are a taunt, a hissing, and a byword. . . . Ought they not meet to spread out their wrongs before one another? Ought they not to meet to consult on the best means of their relief? Ought they not to make one weak effort—nay, one strong, one mighty moral effort—to roll off the burden that crushes them? Under present circumstances it is highly necessary the free people of color should combine and closely attend to their own particular interest.

248 • First Editorial from the *North Star*

We solemnly dedicate the North Star to the cause of our long oppressed and plundered fellow countrymen. May God bless the undertaking to your good! It shall fearlessly assert your rights, faithfully proclaim your wrongs, and earnestly demand for you instant and even-handed justice. Giving no quarter to slavery at the South, it will hold no truce with oppressors at the North. While it shall boldly advocate emancipation for our enslaved brethren, it will omit no opportunity to gain for the nominally free complete enfranchisement. Every effort to injure or degrade you or your cause—originating wheresoever, or with whomsoever—shall find in it a constant, unswerving and inflexible foe. . . .

249 • Antislavery Attitudes Toward Free Negro Morality

Much of the antislavery sentiment among northern whites derived from a strongly moralistic and religious consciousness, which was reflected sometimes in moralizing advice to the northern African American community:

We have noticed with sorrow, that some of the colored people are purchasers of lottery tickets, and confess ourselves shocked to learn that some persons, who are situated to do much good, and whose example might be most salutary, engage in games of chance for money and for strong drink.

A moment's thought will show the folly, as well as wickedness of their course. Gambling strikes at the very vitals of society, and surely the laboring but rising classes of the community, have no time to waste, nor money foolishly to hazard. All persons of color who are keepers of places for dram drinking, gambling, lewdness and other infamy, should be faithfully remonstrated with; and continuing their practices should be regarded as most injurious of all your enemies.

250 • Proslavery Attack on the Right to Free Speech

During the 1830s the campaign against the abolitionist movement reached a fever pitch as abolitionist literature was seized by the United States Post Office and antislavery printing presses of James G. Birney were destroyed in Cincinnati in 1836 and those of Elijah Lovejoy in Alton, Illinois, in 1837. In the case of Lovejoy, the mobs not only destroyed his press but took his life. Edward Beecher wrote about that affair and the assault on the freedom of expression in antebellum America.

Resolved, 1. That the free communication of thoughts and opinions is one of the invaluable rights of man; and that every citizen may freely speak, write and print on any subject, being responsible for, the abuse of that liberty. . . . The committee then admit that Mr. Lovejoy has the right to print what he pleases; and to be deprived of this right only for abusing it; and that the question of abuse is to be settled by law, and not by a mob. . . . The simple fact is, and no sophistry can hide it, that Mr. Lovejoy's rights, and those of all his subscribers had been assailed by a mob; and nothing was needed to restore quiet but that the mob should let them alone. But the mob would not; and for this reason the friends of law armed themselves to repel illegal violence.

251 • Justification for the Antiliteracy Law

There might be no occasion for such enactments in Virginia or elsewhere, on the subject of negro education, but as a matter of self-defense against the schemes of Northern incendiaries, and the outcry against holding our slaves in bondage. Many now living well remember how, and when and why the anti-slavery fury began, and by what means its manifestations were made public. Our mails were clogged with abolition pamphlets and inflammatory documents, to be distributed among our Southern negroes to induce them to cut our throats. . . . These, however, were not the only means resorted to by the Northern fanatics to stir up insubordination among our slaves. They scattered far and near pocket handkerchiefs, and other similar articles, with frightful engravings, and printed over with anti-slavery nonsense, with the view to work upon the feeling and ignorance of our negroes, who otherwise would have remained comfortable and happy. Under the circumstances, there was but one measure of protection for the South, and that was adopted. . . .

252 • Reaction of Bostonians to the Return of Anthony Burns Under Fugitive Slave Act

No martial music hear, only the dull tramp of feet and the clatter of horses' hoofs. The men gripped their muskets and stared stolidly down, closing their ears to the jeers and taunts of the crowd.

Windows along the line of the march were draped in mourning and lines of crepe were stretched across the streets. From the window opposite the Old State House was suspended a Black coffin on which were the words, "The Funeral of Liberty." Farther on, the American flag, the Union down, was draped in mourning. The solemn procession was witnessed by fifty thousand people who hissed, groaned and cried, "Kidnappers! Kidnappers! Shame! Shame!..."

Burns was the last fugitive ever seized on the soil of Massachusetts.

253 • Sojourner Truth on Women's Rights

I want to say a few words about this matter. I am a woman's rights, I have as much muscle as any man, and can do as much work as any man. I have plowed and reaped and husked and chopped and mowed, and can any man do more than that? I have heard much about the sexes being equal; I can carry as much as any man, and can eat as much too, if I can get it. I am as strong as any man that is now. As for intellect, all I can say is, if woman have a pint and man a quart— why can't she have her little pint full? You need not be afraid to give us our rights for fear we will take too much, for we can't take more than our pint'll hold. . . . I can't read, but I can hear. I have heard the bible and have learned that Eve caused man to sin. Well if woman upset the world, do give her a chance to set it right side up again. . . . And how came Jesus into the world? Through God, who created him and woman who bore him. Man, where is your part? But the women are coming up, blessed be God, and a few of the men are coming with them. But man is in a tight place, the poor slave is on him, woman is coming on him, and he is surely between a hawk and a buzzard.

—Speech at Women's Rights Convention, Akron, Ohio, June 21, 1851

254 • The Meaning of July Fourth for the Negro

Frederick Douglass, among several others, commented on the alienation African Americans felt in regards to the celebration of the Fourth of July, the date of American independence, when he spoke at a Rochester, New York, celebration in 1852.

Fellow citizens, pardon me, allow me to ask, why am I called upon to speak here today? What have I, or those I represent, to do with your national independence? Are the great principles of political freedom and of natural justice, embodied in that Declaration of Independence, extended to us? and am I, therefore, called upon to bring our humble offering to the national altar and to confess the benefits and express devout gratitude for the blessings resulting from your independence to us?

But such is not the state of the case. I say it with a sad sense of the disparity between us. I am not included within the pale of this glorious anniversary! Your high independence only reveals the immeasurable distance between us. The blessings in which you, this day, rejoice, are not enjoyed in common. The rich inheritance of justice, liberty, prosperity and independence, bequeathed by your fathers, is shared by you, not by me. The sunlight that brought light and healing to you, has brought stripes and death to me. This Fourth of July is yours, not mine. You may rejoice, I must mourn.

255 • Douglass on the Philosophy of Reform

Let me give you a word of the philosophy of reform. The whole history of the progress of human liberty shows that all concessions yet made to her august claims have been born of earnest struggle. . . . If there is no struggle there is no progress. Those who profess to favor freedom and yet deprecate agitation are men who want crops without plowing up the ground; they want rain without thunder and lightning. They want the ocean without the awful roar of its many waters.

—"West Indian Emancipation," 1857

256 • John Rock at the Celebration of the Boston Massacre

John Rock (1825–66) was a dentist, physician, and a Black abolitionist who used the occasion of the celebration of the Boston Massacre of 1858 to attack the treatment of the African American in America.

Our fathers fought nobly for freedom, but they were not victorious. They fought for liberty, but they got slavery. The white man has benefitted, but the black man was injured. I do not envy the white American the little liberty which he enjoys. It is his right, and he ought to have it. I wish him success, though I do not think that he deserves it. But I would have all men free. We have had much sad experience in this country, and it would be strange indeed if we do not profit by some of the lessons which we have so dearly paid for. Sooner or later, the clashing of arms will be heard in this country, and the black man's services will be needed: 150,000 freemen capable of bearing arms, and not all cowards and fools, and three quarters of a million slaves, wild with the enthusiasm caused by the dawn of the glorious opportunity of being able to strike a genuine blow for freedom, will be a power which white men will be bound to respect.

257 • John Brown's Last Remarks

This court acknowledges . . . the validity of the law of God. I see a book kissed, which I suppose to be the Bible, or at least the New Testament, which teaches me that all things whatsoever I would that men should do to me, I should do even so to them. It teaches me further to remember them that are in bonds, as bound with them. I endeavored to act up to that instruction . . . I believe that to have interfered as I have done, as I have always freely admitted I have done in behalf of His despised poor, is no wrong, but right. Now, if it is deemed necessary that I should forfeit my life for the furtherance of the ends of justice, and mingle my blood further with the blood of my children and with the blood of millions in this slave country whose rights are disregarded by wicked, cruel and unjust enactments, I say let it be done.

258 • The Missouri Compromise

When the territory of Missouri applied for statehood, Congress had to decide whether slavery would be permitted or outlawed in the new state. Southern slaveholders had already migrated into Missouri lands, so the question was extremely difficult. In 1820 a two-part compromise was adopted. Missouri gained admission as a slave state, and Maine joined the Union as a free state at the same time, so the balance of slave and free states remained equal—twelve of each. But even more important, the compromise established the principle that slavery could expand into the portion of the Louisiana Territory below 36°30′ north latitude, but not into territory above that latitude. The compromise also reaffirmed that it was legal to capture fugitive slaves in the nonslave territory.

259 • Black Citizenship

Missouri's entry into the Union raised another contentious dispute over its constitution, because it barred free Negroes from entering the state. Barring free Negroes from interstate travel was unconstitutional, some in Congress argued, because free Negroes were citizens. Southerners howled at this suggestion, since they did not regard free Negroes as citizens: certainly they did not enjoy all the rights of citizens in those southern states where they resided in 1820. Some northern congressmen maintained that denying that free Negroes were citizens undermined the entire native basis of citizenship. "If being a native, and free born, and of parents belonging to no other nation or tribe, does not constitute a citizen of this country, I am at a loss to know in what manner citizenship is acquired by birth," stated one. The Missouri Compromise did not resolve the question of whether free Blacks were citizens; and in the 1830s and 1840s not only would free Blacks be barred from entering more free territories and states but their civil rights, such as the right to vote, would be curtailed in many northern states. But since loss of any specific civil right did not mean the loss of all of one's rights as an American citizen and because the Constitution did not limit citizenship for native-born Americans, the argument over whether free Blacks were citizens was not resolved until the *Dred Scott* decision of 1857, and even that decision was soon challenged.

260 • Black Pennsylvanians Lose the Right to Vote

African Americans began to lose one of the principal rights of citizenship, the right to vote, in the 1830s, ironically during the Jacksonian Period when universal suffrage was being extended to white men. In the early National Period, just after the ratification of the Constitution in 1788, the right to vote was restricted to property owners in many states. But in making voting a privilege of class, the provision gave the vote to free Blacks as well as whites. In the 1830s, however, protest arose about the right to vote for unpropertied laboring whites; and when these Jacksonian-era provisions were discussed, the issue was often opposed by those who wished to keep laboring Blacks from obtaining the vote. As a result, in 1837, property-owning African Americans lost the right to vote in reform legislation that awarded the vote to all white men. Such disfranchisement of the well-to-do Black population

actually satisfied the increasingly racist white working class in Philadelphia, which in several anti-Black riots of the 1820s and 1830s had targeted the homes and churches of wealthy African Americans.

261 • Prigg v. Pennsylvania

In *Prigg v. Pennsylvania* (1842) the United States Supreme Court ruled Pennsylvania's "personal liberty" law of 1826 unconstitutional because its sole purpose, in the opinion of the Court, was to block the apprehension and return of fugitive slaves. In doing so, the Court established that a master's right to the return of his or her slave from another state was a national right that could not be abrogated by state law, but could only be legislated by Congress. Since the Court argued that the return of a fugitive slave was essentially a federal responsibility, this decision, ironically, spurred abolitionists to pass even more "personal liberty" laws in such states as Pennsylvania, Rhode Island, Connecticut, Vermont, Massachusetts, and New Hampshire that prevented state authorities from assisting in the recovery of fugitive slaves because it was a federal responsibility. These laws set the stage for the passage of a fugitive slave law in the Compromise of 1850 to compel state authorities to assist the recovery of a master's fugitive slave from another state.

262 • School Segregation in Boston

Brown v. Board of Education (1954) is the most famous school desegregation case, but legal challenges demanding desegregation had been filed as early as 1849. In Massachusetts, for example, African Americans filed a suit (*Roberts v. the City of Boston*) asking the court to enforce the provision of the Massachusetts constitution that declared "all men, without distinction of color or race, are equal before the law" and to allow Black attendance at white schools. Charles Sumner argued the case on behalf of the African American plaintiffs and delivered a famous address criticizing racial discrimination:

Who can say that this does not injure the blacks? Theirs, in its best estate, is an unhappy lot. Shut out by a still lingering prejudice from many social advantages, a despised class, they feel this proscription for the Public Schools as a peculiar brand. Beyond this, it deprives them of those healthful animating influences which would come from a participation in the studies of their white brethren. It adds to their discouragements. It widens their separation from the rest of the community, and postpones the great day of reconciliation which is sure to come. Although the court rejected his arguments and found that school segregation was "neither illegal or unreasonable," school segregation was abolished in 1855 in Massachusetts when the state legislature passed a measure outlawing racial segregation.

263 • The Wilmot Proviso

In 1846 David Wilmot, a Pennsylvania congressman, proposed a bill that would prohibit the extension of slavery into any new territories acquired as a result of the Mexican War. Wilmot opposed the extension of slavery not because he was ideologically opposed to the institution, but because he felt its practice in the new territories would be inimical to the interests of free labor. In arguing for his proviso, Wilmot reminded congressmen from slaveholding states that he had supported the inclusion of Texas in the Union as a slave state. "We are told," Wilmot said, "that the joint blood and treasure of the whole country is being expended in this acquisition, therefore it should be divided, and slavery allowed to share. Sir, the South has her share al-

ready. . . . Now, sir, we are told that California is ours; that New Mexico is ours—won by the valor of our arms. They are free. Shall they remain free? Shall these fair provinces be the inheritance and homes of the white labor of freemen or the Black labor of slaves? This, sir, is the issue. . . ." The Senate rejected the Wilmot Proviso in 1847, but its debate added to the contentiousness over slavery in the territories.

264 • Compromise of 1850

The Compromise of 1850 contained two important elements affecting African Americans. First, it included a new, more stringent fugitive slave law. The new law shifted responsibility for enforcement to federal authorities and permitted assistance from federal marshals and private citizens to pursue and return fugitive slaves. Once apprehended, the fugitive slave would not be allowed to testify on his or her own behalf, and a transcript of an owner's claim of loss was sufficient proof of ownership. The law offered considerable financial rewards to federal commissioners who remanded alleged fugitives back into slavery. The federal commissioners who determined the status of fugitive slaves, for example, received five dollars if the slave was declared free and ten dollars if declared a fugitive and returned to the "rightful" owner. In order to appease abolitionist leaders who were incensed by the Fugitive Slave Act, the second feature of the compromise abolished the slave trade in the District of Columbia. But abolitionists regarded this as woefully insufficient.

265 • Kansas-Nebraska Act

The Kansas-Nebraska Act in 1854 permitted the occupants of the territories seeking admission to the Union to decide for themselves whether the territories would be slave or free, abrogating the agreement established in the Missouri Compromise that all territories above 36°30′ north latitude would be free. Instead, the Kansas-Nebraska Act reflected the belief of Stephen Douglas, its author, that once popular sovereignty became the test of whether a state was slave or free, the controversy over slavery in the territories would be put to rest. In practice, however, the Kansas-Nebraska Act set off a violent struggle between proslavery and antislavery forces as each tried to settle the territories.

266 • *Dred Scott* Case

In 1837 Dr. John Emerson left Missouri to spend four years as an army surgeon in Illinois, a free state. He brought his slave, Dred Scott, with him. Under the Missouri Compromise, Scott also should have been free in the part of the Louisiana Territory in which he had previously lived with Emerson. When he returned to Missouri from Illinois, Dred Scott sued for his freedom, but the court ruled that residence in a free state did not automatically make a slave free. In the meantime, Dr. Emerson had died and his widow became Scott's owner. She married Congressman Calvin C. Chaffee of Massachusetts, a well-known abolitionist. Because Chaffee did not want to be known as a slave owner, Scott was sold to Mrs. Emerson-Chaffee's brother. Scott tried to bring suit in federal court, but when the Supreme Court heard the case in 1857 it decided against Scott because (1) as an African American, Scott was not a citizen of Missouri as set out by the Constitution and had no rights in federal courts, (2) temporary residence in a free state did not make one free, and (3) the Missouri Compromise was unconstitutional. This last decree limited the power of Congress to exclude slavery from any Northwest territories that would subsequently apply for admission to the Union.

Engraving of Dred Scott. Prints and Photographs Division, Library of Congress

267 • Black Civil Rights in the North in the 1850s

Black civil and political rights declined in the 1850s. Although less than 2 percent of the population of the free states (fewer than 250,000 persons), African Americans were severely restricted in their movement and their exercise of basic rights. Blacks lived in the poorest, filthiest, and oldest neighborhoods, worked at the most menial of jobs, attended segregated public schools when they attended school at all, and lacked basic legal protection before the law. All states except Massachusetts denied African Americans the right to serve on juries. Indiana, Iowa, Oregon, California, and Lincoln's own state, Illinois, refused to allow African Americans to testify against whites in court. In California this led to the widespread abuse of Blacks by whites who knew they were immune to prosecution. Ironically the antislavery movement may have indirectly caused an intensifying of restrictions, for as some states witnessed the increasing power of the antislavery movement, fear spread that Blacks would leave the South in droves to compete with white labor in the North and the territories. Accordingly Oregon, Iowa, Indiana, and Illinois barred Blacks from immigrating into the state.

268 • Restrictions on Voting

Five New England states permitted African Americans to vote without restrictions in the presidential election of 1860. In New York, only Blacks who owned $250 or more in property could vote. In Ohio, only those African Americans who visibly appeared to have more Caucasian than African blood in their veins were allowed to vote. In the rest of the country, African American voters played no part in choosing Abraham Lincoln to be the thirteenth president of the United States.

CIVIL WAR

Toward the War

269 • Black Abolitionist View of Lincoln's Election

Most northern Blacks, especially Black abolitionists, approved of Lincoln's election, even if it did not mean he would work to end slavery. According to Frederick Douglass, the election was at least a step in the right direction.

What, then, has been gained to the anti-slavery cause by the election of Mr. Lincoln? Not much, in itself considered, but very much when viewed in the light of its relation and bearings. For fifty years the country has taken the law from the lips of an exacting, haughty and imperious slave oligarchy. . . . Lincoln's election has vitiated their

authority, and broken their power . . . [and] . . . demonstrated the possibility of electing, if not an Abolitionist, at least an anti-slavery reputation to the Presidency.

270 • Southerners React to Lincoln's Election

Regardless of what Lincoln or the Republican Party platform stated, southern states believed the election of Lincoln as president meant the end of slavery. Immediately after the election in November 1860, several states began to hold conventions and debate secession from the Union. Before Lincoln took office on March 4, 1861, seven states had seceded from the Union. South Carolina (December 20, 1860) was the first to secede, followed by Mississippi (January 9, 1861), Florida (January 10), Alabama (January 11), Georgia (January 19), Louisiana (January 26), and Texas (February 1). Although Lincoln and other Unionists were angry that "the functions of the Federal Government were found to be generally suspended within" those states, Black abolitionists were glad to see them go. "Stand not upon the order of your going, but go at once," exclaimed H. Ford Douglass. "There is no union of ideas and interests in this country, and there can be no union between freedom and slavery." Likewise, most Garrisonians supported secession because it would remove the moral evil of slavery from the United States and the Constitution and free the United States from having to defend and protect slavery. Black abolitionists like Frederick Douglass also believed removal of the South from the Union would reduce the influence of the South in trying to erode northern Black political and civil rights, and ultimately prompt more slaves to escape the South and slavery for the North.

271 • Crittenden Compromise of Black Rights

Black abolitionists correctly assumed that compromise with the secessionist South to keep it in the Union would prolong slavery and hurt free Negroes in the North. That such fears were well founded became clear when Senator John Crittenden of Kentucky proposed what became known as the Crittenden Compromise in 1860. Among other things, Crittenden wanted a constitutional amendment that would allow slavery in territories below the 36°30′ line and guarantee that no additional interference with southern slavery would be permitted. Virginia, which was seeking ways not to secede, invited representatives from northern states to Virginia to discuss the proposal, but African Americans in Massachusetts protested. A key ingredient in the compromise was a demand that the few northern states that granted political and civil rights to African Americans rescind those rights and support colonization of free Blacks outside of the country. Black Bostonians wrote that "as citizens of the Commonwealth of Massachusetts who have heretofore felt perfectly secure in the enjoyment of the rights pertaining to such citizenship . . . pray your honorable body . . . to oppose and vote against every proposition which may have in view the withdrawal or injury of those rights." African Americans in the North breathed a sigh of relief when Massachusetts did not support the Crittenden Compromise and Lincoln scuttled it by refusing any extension of slavery into the territories.

272 • African American Reaction to Fort Sumter

African Americans in the North rejoiced when South Carolina's armed forces started the Civil War on April 12, 1861, by attacking Fort Sumter, the federal garrison in South Carolina. After the federal government called up troops and Virginia (April 17), Arkansas (May 6), Tennessee (May 7), and North Carolina (May 20) left the Union, most African Americans in the North approved of the war because they believed it would eventually end slavery. Many African Americans also saw the war as a way for Blacks to prove their citizenship and help liberate the slaves by fighting in the war effort. African Americans throughout the North formed militia companies, began drilling, and volunteered their services. But their offers were rejected. The secretary of war declared in 1861 that "this Department has no intention at present to call into the service of the Government any colored soldiers." The militia commander in Ohio declared inaccurately that "the Constitution will not permit me to issue the order" to raise African American troops. Others in Ohio put the matter more bluntly: "We want you d——d niggers to keep out of this; this is a white man's war." The Lincoln administration and most white northerners argued during its first two years that the Civil War was not a war over slavery, but a way to reunite the Union.

Toward Emancipation

273 • The Slaves as a Military Element in the South

Slavery was an asset to the South, as this article in the *Montgomery Advertiser* dated November 6, 1851, boldly asserted.

The total white population of the eleven states now comprising the Confederacy is 6,000,000, and, therefore, to fill up the ranks of the proposed army (600,000) about ten percent of the entire white population will be required. In any other country than our own such a draft could not be met, but the Southern States can furnish that number of men, and still not leave the material interests of the country in a suffering condition. Those who are incapacitated for bearing arms can oversee the plantations, and the negroes can go on undisturbed in their usual labors. In the North the case is different; the men who join the army of subjugation are the laborers, the producers, and the factory operatives. Nearly every man from that section, especially those from the rural districts, leaves some branch of industry to suffer during his absence. The institution of slavery in the South alone enables her to place in the field a force much larger in proportion to her white population than the North.

274 • Douglass on Lincoln's Early War Policy

In his *Douglass' Monthly* dated July 1861, Frederick Douglass questioned Lincoln's reluctance to emancipate the slaves.

Why? Oh! Why, in the name of all that is national, does our Government allow its enemies this powerful advantage? . . . The very stomach of this rebellion is the negro in the condition of a slave. Arrest that hoe in the hands of the negro, and you smite rebellion in the very seat of its life. . . . Teach the rebels and traitors that the price they are to pay for the attempt to abolish this Government must be the abolition of slavery. . . . Henceforth let the war cry be down with treason and down with slavery, the cause of treason.

275 • Harriet Tubman Was More Positive

Harriet Tubman was more positive about Lincoln than Frederick Douglass in 1861.

God won't let Massa Linkum beat de South till he do de right ting. Massa Linkum he great man, and I'se poor nigger; but dis nigger can tell

Massa Linkum how to save de money and de young men. He do it by setting de niggers free. S'pose dar was awfu' big snake down dar, on de floor. He bite you. . . . You send for doctor to cut de bite; but snake he rolled up dar, and while doctor dwine it, he bite you agin. De doctor cut out dat bite; but while he dwine it, de snake he spring up and bite you agin, and so he keep dwine, till you kill him. Dat's what Massa Linkum orter know.

276 • First Confiscation Act

The first emancipation act was issued by Congress, not by President Lincoln. On August 6, 1861, Congress passed the Confiscation Act, which stated that any slaves owned by masters who were aiding the insurrection against the national government could be captured and set free. This was an act that enabled generals to withhold captured slaves from their masters, in contrast to Union Army policy early in the war. Its impact was limited, however, as the Union forces in 1861 were mainly experiencing losses on the battlefield.

277 • Lincoln Edges Toward Emancipation

Lincoln's views on emancipating the slaves evolved during the Civil War, and on March 6, 1862, he recommended that Congress adopt a resolution to offer funding to any state that voluntarily adopted gradual emancipation. "Resolved that the United States ought to co-operate with any state which may adopt gradual abolishment of slavery, giving to such state pecuniary aid, to be used by such state in its discretion, to compensate for the inconveniences public and private, produced by such change of system." Unfortunately for Lincoln, the border states blocked Congress from passing such a bill.

278 • Lincoln Retreats with Hunter

On April 25, 1862, General David Hunter, commander of the Union forces, declared martial law in South Carolina, Georgia, and Florida. On May 9 he declared: "Slavery and martial law in a free country are altogether incompatible; the persons in these three States—Georgia, Florida, and South Carolina—heretofore held as slaves, are therefore declared forever free." But on May 19 Lincoln revoked Hunter's order.

I, Abraham Lincoln, president of the United States, proclaim and declare, that the government of the United States, had no knowledge, information, or belief, of an intention on the part of General Hunter to issue such a proclamation . . . and that the supposed proclamation, now in question, whether genuine or false, is altogether void, so far as respects such declaration.

I further make known that whether it be competent for me, as Commander-in-Chief of the Army and Navy, to declare the Slaves of any state or states, free, and whether at any time, in any case, it shall have become a necessity indispensable to the maintenance of the government, to exercise such supposed power, are questions which, under my responsibility, I reserve to myself, and which I can not feel justified in leaving to the decision of commanders in the field. These are totally different questions from those of police regulations in armies and camps.

279 • Abolitionists React

I come now to the policy of President Lincoln in reference to slavery. . . . I do not hesitate to say, that whatever may have been his intentions, the action of President Lincoln has been calculated in a marked and decided way to shield and protect it from the very blows which its horrible crimes have loudly and persistently invited. . . . He has steadily refused to proclaim, as he had the constitutional and moral right to proclaim,
complete emancipation to all the slaves of rebels who should make their way into the lines of our army. He has repeatedly interfered with and arrested the anti-slavery policy of some of his most earnest and reliable generals. . . . To my mind that policy is simply and solely to reconstruct the union on the old and corrupting basis of compromise, by which slavery shall retain all the power that it ever had, with the full assurance of gaining more, according to its future necessities.

—Frederick Douglass

280 • Lincoln's Early Views

Lincoln seemed to answer Douglass's charges when Lincoln replied by letter (August 22, 1862) to similar criticisms published by his longtime supporter, the Republican Horace Greeley: "If I could save the Union without freeing *any* slave I would do it, and if I could save it by freeing *all* the slaves I would do it, and if I could save it by freeing some and leaving others alone I would also do that. What I do about slavery, and the colored race, I do because I believe it helps to save the Union."

281 • Second Confiscation Act and Other Pressures from Congress

In addition to the lobbying of abolitionists and Union generals, Lincoln was also increasingly pressured by Congress in 1862. Congress had already issued the first emancipation order that freed the slaves of the District of Columbia and compensated their owners up to $300 each. A resident of Baltimore brought the news to a District of Columbia slave.

Chambermaid at Smith's (my former place) . . . is a slave so this morning I went there to inform her of the passage of the Bill when I entered The cook her and another Slave woman who has a slave son were talking relative to the Bill expressing doubts of its passage & when I entered they perceived that something was ahead and emeadiately asked me "Whats the news?" The Districts free says I pulling out the "National Republican" and reading its editorial when I had finished the chambermaid had left the room sobbing for joy. The slave woman clapped her hands and shouted, left the house saying "let me go and tell my husband that Jesus has done all things well."

In addition to the District bill, a second confiscation act was passed by Congress on July 17 that declared "forever free" the slaves of rebel masters when those slaves came into Union lines. This act did not have the impact of Lincoln's final Emancipation Proclamation, however.

282 • Preliminary Emancipation Proclamation

For largely political reasons—assuaging abolitionists in his party, destabilizing the South, enlisting desperately needed Black troops, pre-venting England from entering the war on the side of the Confederacy, and transforming a lackluster Unionist conflict into an idealistic war to end slavery—Lincoln decided to free the slaves by presidential decree. But Lincoln did not want to issue the proclamation before the North had won a major victory for fear such a proclamation would seem an act of desperation. Thus, Lincoln waited until the Union Army finally won a major battle at Antietam on September 17, 1862, issuing his preliminary proclamation on September 22.

That on the first day of January in the year of our Lord, one thousand eight hundred and sixty-three, all persons held as slaves within any state, or designated part of a state, the people whereof shall then be in rebellion against the United States shall be then, thenceforward, and forever free; and the executive government of the United States, including the military and naval authority thereof, will recognize and maintain the freedom of such persons, and will do no act or acts to

Lincoln reading the Emancipation Proclamation to his cabinet. Prints and Photographs Division, Library of Congress

repress such persons, or any of them, in any efforts they may make for their actual freedom.

Lincoln's proclamation was still tentative and something of a bribe: if any of the Confederate states ceased their resistance to the Union, their slaves would not be freed.

283 • Final Emancipation Proclamation

None of the rebellious states had ceased their armed resistance by January 1, 1863, so Lincoln issued the promised Emancipation Proclamation: "Now, therefore, I, Abraham Lincoln, President of the United States, by virtue of the power in me vested as Commander-in-Chief. . . . as a fit and necessary war measure for suppressing said rebellion, do, on this first day of January . . . declare that all persons held as slaves within said designated States, and parts of States, are, and henceforward shall be free," except the slaves in the four loyal slave states—Maryland, Delaware, Missouri, and Kentucky—thirteen parishes of Louisiana, including New Orleans, forty-eight counties in West Virginia, seven counties in Virginia, including Norfolk and Portsmouth, "which excepted parts are, for the present, left precisely as if this proclamation was not issued."

Actually Lincoln's proclamation did not really free any slaves. Left untouched were the numerous slaves in the border states that had remained loyal to the Union. Lincoln feared he would alienate those states if their slaves were freed, so he exempted them. And those slaves living in the Confederate states would be freed only when, or if, the Union Army won. The proclamation did free those slaves, called contrabands of war, already in Union lines, but this was redundant, as they had already been freed by the Confiscation Act of 1862. Despite this, Lincoln's proclamation was still pivotal. It gave

needed meaning to the conflict as a war to end slavery in America. The Emancipation Proclamation also made it difficult for England to enter the war against a nation fighting to do what England had already done by freeing the slaves in the West Indies. But the most important part of the proclamation was basically neglected: it ordered that Blacks "be received into the armed service of the United States."

284 • Karl Marx on Lincoln and His Proclamation

Even revolutionary thinkers like Karl Marx were impressed with Lincoln's proclamation, which Marx argued represented the largest transfer of property in the history of the world. Marx was also impressed with the democratic style of the president, who, according to Marx,

always gives the most significant of his acts the most commonplace form. . . . Indecisively, against his will, he reluctantly performs the bravura aria of his role as though asking pardon for the fact that circumstances are forcing him to "play the hero." The most formidable decrees which he hurls at the enemy and which will never lose their historic significance, resemble—as the author intends them to—ordinary summonses sent by one lawyer to another on the opposing side. . . . And this is the character the recent Proclamation bears—the most important document of American history since the founding of the Union, a document that breaks away from the old American Constitution—Lincoln's manifesto on the abolition of slavery. . . . Never yet has the New World scored a greater victory than in this instance, through its demonstration that, thanks to its political and social organization, ordinary people of good will can carry out tasks which the Old World would have to have a hero to accomplish!

285 • Southern Slaves Learn of the Proclamation

Most slaves in the Confederate South learned of the Emancipation Proclamation through the slave grapevine, a communication network between Blacks in the Union Army and slaves behind Confederate state lines. But some learned of it through the newspaper. In New Orleans free Blacks published their own bilingual newspaper, *L'Union*, which disseminated information about Lincoln's edict.

Brothers! The hour strikes for us; a new sun, similar to that of 1789, should surely appear on our horizon. May the cry which resounded through France at the seizure of the Bastille resonate today in our ears. . . .

Men of my blood! Shake off the contempt of your proud oppressors. Enough of shame and submission; the break is complete! Down with the craven behavior of bondage! Stand up under the noble flag of the Union and declare yourselves hardy champions of the right. Defend your rights against the barbarous and imbecile spirit of slavery; prove to the entire world that you have a heart noble enough to walk with civilization and to understand its benefits, and a spirit high enough to know and admire the imposing work of the Creator. . . .

286 • Slaves Learn from Union Soldiers

On the South Carolina Sea Islands, the former slaves who were already liberated and attending schools run by northern teachers held a celebration on January 1, 1863.

I wish it were possible to describe fitly the scene which met our eyes as we sat upon the stand, and looked down on the crowd before us. There were the black soldiers in their blue coats and scarlet pantaloons, the officers of this and other regiments in their handsome uniforms, and crowds of lookers-on,—men, women, and children, of every complexion, grouped in various attitudes under the moss-hung trees. The faces of all wore a happy, interested look. The exercises commenced with a prayer by the chaplain of the regiment. . . . Colonel Higginson then introduced Dr. Brisbane, who read the President's Proclamation, which was enthusiastically cheered.

Toward Equality

287 • Reaction in the North: Anti-Black Riots

Some whites in the North welcomed the Emancipation Proclamation. But many others, especially those from the lower classes and of foreign birth, reacted angrily to it. Many white workingmen feared that emancipation would bring job competition with freedmen who might migrate North. Others, many of them from the Irish working class, also reacted angrily to Lincoln's imposition of the draft, which to their minds committed them to fight in a war to free the slaves. On July 13, 1863, these feelings boiled over into four days of bloody rioting in New York City. The rioting started at the draft enrollment office, which was burned down, but it quickly shifted to attacks on the Black section of the city. Twelve hundred people, mostly African Americans, were killed, the Colored Orphan Asylum was set on fire, and hundreds of Blacks were forced to flee from their homes. The ferocity of the attacks on defenseless Blacks, in part a frenzy of anti-Republican feeling whipped up by local Democratic politicians, was unbelievable. "A child of 3 years of age was thrown from a 4th story window and instantly killed. A woman one hour after her confinement was set upon and beaten with her tender babe in her arms. . . . Children were torn from their mother's embrace and their brains blown out in the very face of the afflicted mother. Men were burnt by slow fires." In the end, Union troops were required to quell the rioting.

288 • Northern Treatment of Former Slaves

Mistreatment of African Americans was not confined to the Irish working class in New York. Even soldiers in the Union Army stationed in the Sea Islands off the coast of South Carolina regularly abused and degraded African Americans in the community. But at the same time, many northerners, especially schoolteachers, volunteered to go South and educate the freedmen. These missionaries, both African American and European American, set up schools, provided religious instruction, and helped freedmen make the transformation from slave to free labor.

289 • Lincoln's Plan for Reconstruction

On December 8, 1863, Lincoln issued his Proclamation on Amnesty and Reconstruction for the restoration of the Confederate states into the Union. He offered them a full pardon and restoration of their rights if they were willing to take an oath of loyalty to the Union and accept the end of slavery. When 10 percent of a seceded state's population that had voted in the election of 1860 pledged their future loyalty to the Union, then that state could create a new state government and elect representatives to Congress, subject to the approval of each house of Congress. But Lincoln's proclamation did not demand that the Confederacy give civil or political rights to former slaves or free people of color or promise them the right to vote in the postwar South. As Wendell Phillips noted, Lincoln's plan "frees the slave and ignores the negro."

290 • The Miscegenation Controversy

During Lincoln's reelection campaign in 1864, Democrats sought to exploit the fears of white Americans about the social consequences of the Emancipation Proclamation. Two Democratic strategists, in one of the first examples of election "disinformation," published a pamphlet that they advertised as being produced by an abolitionist. Its title page graphically portrayed what the pamphlet argued—that the point of Lincoln's emancipation of the slaves was to promote "social equality" in general, and sexual intercourse in particular, between the races. The pamphlet introduced a new word in the language—miscegenation—for the latter

WHAT MISCEGENATION IS!

—AND—

WHAT WE ARE TO EXPECT

Now that Mr. Lincoln is Re-elected.

Cover of a pamphlet that falsely represents Lincoln as favoring miscegenation as a consequence of the Emancipation Proclamation, 1864. Prints and Photographs Division, Library of Congress

practice. Despite the boldness of its appeal to racist sentiments, the pamphlet was not believed to be authentic, and Lincoln was re-elected despite an effective attempt by Democrats to use the Emancipation Proclamation against him.

291 • Lincoln on Postwar Black Voting Rights

Like most northerners, Lincoln's belief in the moral rightness of the abolition of slavery did not mean he supported the notion that Blacks were or ever would be the equals of whites. Indeed, Lincoln continued to advance plans for the voluntary colonization of African Americans outside of the United States as the best way to address their postwar status. Yet Lincoln, who showed himself flexible on the subject of emancipation, may have been flexible on the issue of suffrage for Blacks in Reconstruction had he lived to direct it. During the process of Reconstruction in Louisiana, representatives of the wealthy, educated, and cultivated freeborn Negro community in New Orleans met with Lincoln on March 12, 1864, to present a petition to obtain the right to vote in a reconstructed Louisiana. After that meeting, Lincoln wrote to Governor Michael Hahn:

Now you are about to have a Convention which, among other things, will probably define the elective franchise. I barely suggest for your private consideration, whether some of the colored people may not be let in—as, for instance, the very intelligent, and especially those who have fought gallantly in our ranks. They would probably help, in some trying time to come, to keep the jewel of liberty within the family of freedom.

Hahn, however, did not support Lincoln's notion.

292 • Civil Rights Change During the Civil War

The Civil War brought some changes in the civil rights of Blacks in the North, but not without a struggle. After the Emancipation Proclamation was issued in 1863 and Blacks were permitted to fight in the war, California began to allow African Americans to testify in criminal court. Ohio also struck down its Black Laws. But the Civil War also brought enforcement of the anti-immigration statute in Illinois which fined any African American who entered the state. Anyone who could not pay the fine could be arrested and sold into slavery at a public auction. Before the war, this statute was rarely enforced, but when Black migration into the state increased during the Civil War, the courts began to enforce the law vigorously. In 1863, for example, the year of Lincoln's Emancipation Proclamation, eight Blacks were convicted of illegal entry into the state and seven of them were sold into slavery. Black Chicagoans were outraged by the convictions and, led by the wealthy African American tailor John Jones, they prodded, lobbied, and petitioned the Illinois state legislature to eliminate the Black Laws. In February 1865 the laws that kept African Americans from entering the state, serving on juries, or giving testimony in Court were repealed. By the winter of 1865–66 even Indiana had struck down its anti-immigration law. But some things had not changed: only five New England states had allowed Blacks to vote with whites at the beginning of the war, and only those five still granted equal voting rights to Blacks at the end of the war.

293 • Black Convention of 1864

On October 4–7, 1864, more than a hundred African American men gathered at Syracuse, New York, for a "National Convention of Colored

Citizens" to plan a postwar political agenda for Blacks. In attendance were Jonathan C. Gibbs, Richard H. Cain, Francis L. Cardozo, Jonathan J. Wright, Henry Highland Garnet, and Frederick Douglass, who wrote the convention address, "Address to the People of the United States." Although Garnet, a strong Black nationalist, still argued that Blacks should pursue a separate identity, most participants read the events of the Civil War—the imminent demise of slavery, the employment of African American troops, and the success of the abolitionist movement—as signs that African Americans were on the verge of complete acceptance into the mainstream of American society. Among the list of convention recommendations were the abolition of slavery, support of women's rights, full civil and political equality in the law, and extension of the franchise to African Americans. To lobby for these ideas, the convention founded a National Equal Rights League, with the lawyer John Mercer Langston as president. In his "Address to the Colored People of the United States," he urged Blacks to found local auxiliaries of the Equal Rights League in their communities to fight for their rights.

294 • Discrimination on Philadelphia Streetcars

A sign of how far African Americans still had to go to receive equal treatment on public accommodations came in January 1865 when Robert Smalls, the Black Civil War hero who had stolen a Confederate ship and delivered it to the Union Navy, was thrown off a streetcar in Philadelphia because he was an African American. That incident sparked a nationwide outcry about segregation in public accommodations in the North. In May 1865 Massachusetts enacted the first public accommodations law in American history. Ohio soon struck down its Black

Laws. But it was not until 1867, two years after the end of the Civil War, that Pennsylvania desegregated its public transportation and allowed African Americans like Robert Smalls to ride the Philadelphia streetcars like other American citizens.

295 • Rock at the Supreme Court

In February 1865 John Rock became the first African American to be accepted as a lawyer before the Supreme Court. Presented by Charles Sumner and accepted by Chief Justice Salmon P. Chase, Rock became a symbolic repudiation to the 1857 *Dred Scott* decision by the Supreme Court.

296 • Truth Desegregates D.C. Trolleys

In March 1865 a law was passed in the District of Columbia outlawing discrimination on streetcars. But it had not been tested in the streets until Sojourner Truth took on the forces of discrimination. Truth had moved to the nation's capital to work as a nurse tending to the injured and wounded from the war, and during her stay in Washington, she faced difficulty transporting articles for her patients because Blacks were only allowed to ride on a few Jim Crow cars on each line. Even on these cars, Blacks often had to stand because the cars were filled with whites, who, by custom, occupied the seats. After writing to the head of the street railroad, Sojourner believed the practice was ended until she tried to signal a car to stop. Several passed her until finally she began to yell, "I want to ride! *I want to ride!!* I WANT TO RIDE!!" When one car was blocked temporarily from leaving, Sojourner leaped on board to the cheers of the crowd. The conductor, angered by her victory, yelled that he would put her off, but she challenged him and remained on board. After several other conflicts with conductors boarding cars, Truth was finally thrown against the door of a car by a streetcar driver in Georgetown. At the hospital she learned that her shoulder had been broken. Immediately she had the conductor arrested for assault and battery, and the driver lost his job. Sojourner recalled in her autobiography:

It created a great sensation, and before the trial was ended, the inside of the cars looked like pepper and salt; and I felt, like Poll Parrot, "Jack, I am riding." A little circumstance will show how great a change a few weeks had produced: A lady saw some colored women looking wistfully toward a car, when the conductor, halting, said, "Walk in, ladies." Now they who had so lately cursed me for wanting to ride, could stop for black as well as white, and could even condescend to say, "Walk in, ladies."

297 • Freedmen's Bureau

In the last months of the war, southern life was completely devastated. Crusading Union forces and fleeing Confederate stragglers decimated the remaining plantations, destroyed roads, bridges, and cities, and left thousands of people homeless without food or clothing. The pleas of former slaves and free people of color for relief were largely ignored by southern governments more concerned with the plight of former planters and with their own survival as state entities than with helping the newly freed Blacks. So African Americans turned to northerners and abolitionists, who responded by pressuring Congress to provide for the needy in the South. In March 1865 Congress established the Bureau of Refugees, Freedmen, and Abandoned Lands, more popularly known as the Freedmen's Bureau, to aid displaced former

A drawing by A. R. Waud to show the Freedmen's Bureau as a mediator between southern white and freedmen's interests.
Prints and Photographs Division, Library of Congress

slaves and white refugees. It provided food, clothing, supplies, job placement, education, and homestead land to people, and negotiated disputes over contracts between former masters and former slaves. From 1865 to 1869, the Bureau distributed over 21 million rations, set up forty-six hospitals, and spent over $2 million to treat illnesses. But despite its benefits to the South, white southerners denounced the Bureau as an agent of Republican control and an interference in local affairs. When Congress passed a bill to extend the operation of the Freedmen's Bureau in February 1866, President Andrew Johnson vetoed it, claiming that it would create an immense federal bureaucracy, injure citizen's rights, and make freedmen lazy. In July Congress overrode Johnson's veto, extending the life of the bureau until 1870.

298 • Assassination of Lincoln

When Lincoln was shot at Ford's Theater on April 14, 1865, and died the next day, the outlook for postwar African American civil rights changed dramatically. However, Lincoln's death may have improved the outlook for full black political rights. If Lincoln had lived, it is unlikely that the Radical Republican element in Congress would have taken over Reconstruction and pushed through legislation such as the Reconstruction Act of 1867 and the Fourteenth and Fifteenth Amendments. But Lincoln was replaced by the politically less flexible and less astute Vice President, Andrew Johnson, who steered the presidency into a showdown with congressional Republicans that he ultimately lost.

299 • The Wade-Davis Bill

Many of the Republicans in Lincoln's own party disagreed with his mild plan for Reconstruction of the nation, and expressed that dis-

satisfaction by passing their own plan in the Wade-Davis Bill on July 2, 1864. The bill called for a provisional military governor of a state to enroll all white citizens of a state, and after a majority of them took an oath of allegiance to the Union, a constitutional convention would be held to raise a state government. Any southerner who had been a member of the Confederate Army or served in the Confederate government was disqualified from voting or serving as a delegate. The states had to accept, of course, the end of slavery. This bill, by basing representation on a majority of loyal citizens, made it more difficult for states to return to the Union. Lincoln did not support the bill and let it die by simply failing to sign it in time. Given the clamor of Republicans about Lincoln's ignoring of Black rights in his plan, it is interesting to note that the Wade-Davis Bill contained no reference to Black voting rights.

Reconstruction Terms, Phrases, and Slogans

300 • Presidential Reconstruction

Presidential Reconstruction was the process begun by Abraham Lincoln and continued by President Andrew Johnson of bringing the Confederate states back to the Union. Termed a mild reconstruction by Republicans in Congress who proposed harsher terms in the Wade-Davis Bill (July 2, 1864), Presidential Reconstruction only required 10 percent of a seceded state's voting population to pledge their future loyalty to the Union and accept the end of slavery in order to rejoin. Although Lincoln did not sign the Wade-Davis Bill, he was willing to allow states to return to the Union under either his or Congress's plan, but southerners, not surprisingly, preferred Lincoln's plan. Tennessee, Louisiana, Arkansas, and Virginia tried to return to the Union under his plan, but failed because of irregularities. When the less flexible Andrew Johnson assumed the presidency after Lincoln died on April 15, 1865, Johnson discounted Congress's view of Reconstruction and quickly brought all of the seceded states back into the Union while Congress recessed for the summer. When Congress met in December 1865, it noted that the South had returned as its new representatives to Congress old Confederates, including the vice president of the Confederacy. Moreover, the former slave South was passing Black Codes that reinstituted the controls of slavery, and northerners were being harassed on visits through the South. When Congress passed a civil rights bill for Blacks and extended the Freedmen's Bureau, Johnson vetoed both measures and declared Blacks were not ready for citizenship responsibilities. That led to a showdown between Johnson and congressional Republicans that he lost. In the election of 1866, an overwhelming majority of Republicans were reelected to Congress who ended Presidential Reconstruction by pushing through the Reconstruction Act of 1867 over Johnson's veto.

301 • Radical or Congressional Reconstruction

Radical Reconstruction, also known as Congressional or Black Reconstruction, reflected a broader definition of Reconstruction than Presidential Reconstruction. Republicans in the postwar Congress believed that a social and political reconstruction of the South was necessary in addition to bringing the seceded states back into the Union. Thus, in the main bill of Radical Reconstruction, the Reconstruction Act of 1867, the seceded states had to accept the right of Blacks to vote and to serve as represen-

tatives in the state and federal legislature. Southerners had to hold constitutional conventions in which Blacks were participants, draw up constitutions that ensured Black political and civil rights, and have those constitutions approved by Congress. Former Confederates were not allowed to vote in this process, or in state or federal elections. The former Confederate states also had to ratify the Fourteenth Amendment. Beginning in June 1868, Arkansas, North Carolina, South Carolina, Louisiana, Alabama, and Florida were reconstructed and readmitted to the Union. It was not until 1870 that Virginia, Mississippi, and Texas returned, largely because they initially refused to deny the franchise and officeholding to former Confederates. Each also had the additional requirement to ratify the Fifteenth Amendment. With the exception of Virginia, all the southern states were ruled by Republican state governments for varying periods of time: in South Carolina Republican Reconstruction lasted until 1877; in Texas it ended as early as 1874.

302 • The Myth of Black Reconstruction

James Pike and other chroniclers of Radical Reconstruction have called it Black Reconstruction and portrayed it as overwhelmingly negative. Their story of Reconstruction in states such as South Carolina describes illiterate, incompetent ex-slaves, greedy northern white carpetbaggers, and treasonous scalawags who dominated helpless southern white "civilization" in a period of fraud, corruption, and plunder. In truth, Blacks never dominated southern state institutions because, with the exception of South Carolina, Blacks never held a majority of state offices. And in South Carolina the Black elected officials with the most powerful state positions were not ex-slaves, but free Negroes,

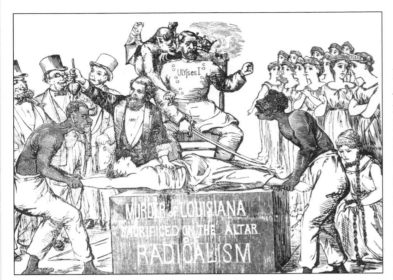

Racist 1871 engraving that characterizes Radical Reconstruction as the murder of southern states under President Ulysses S. Grant's administration. Prints and Photographs Division, Library of Congress

303 • Free Negroes, or Free People of Color

"Free Negroes" and "free people of color" refer to those African Americans who were free before the Civil War and hence were not freed by the Emancipation Proclamation or the Thirteenth Amendment. Often such free Negroes were either mixed-race relatives or descendants of white masters and might possess money, property, or position because of such relationships.

304 • Freedmen

"Freedmen" refers to those African Americans who were formerly slaves and were emancipated by the Civil War.

305 • Freeborn

"Freeborn" refers to African Americans born before the Civil War whose parents were not slaves. The freeborn possessed the highest status in post–Civil War African American social circles, followed by the free Negroes, who were not freeborn, and then the freedmen.

306 • Mulatto

A mulatto is a person of mixed-race parentage, usually with one white and one African American parent. While not enjoying the kind of separate legal and political status of mulattoes in the Caribbean or Latin America, mulattoes in both pre- and postwar southern society often benefited when they were fathered by wealthy or prominent white planters or businessmen. The term is rapidly being replaced by "mixed race" in contemporary usage, since "mulatto" is derived from the Spanish word for mule.

the majority of whom were of mixed-race backgrounds. Many of these mixed-race free people owned property, had some education, and were conservative in their political outlook and public behavior. In general, Blacks in the Congress and in state government served with ability and sometimes with distinction. Corruption *was* rampant in Radical Reconstruction, but it had also been widespread in pre- and postwar southern state government. Although Reconstruction state governments did incur large debts, such was probably unavoidable given the devastation of the postwar South: schools had to be built, roads repaired, railroads established, to bring the South back. And although the later Redeemer governments rewrote Radical Reconstruction state constitutions to delete provisions for Black suffrage, many of the southern states continued to use the constitutions written under Radical Reconstruction with few other changes.

307 • "Who Freed You?"

"Who freed you?" was a question sometimes asked of unknown persons of African descent to determine whether the person had been slave or free prior to the Civil War. If the answerer had been freed by the Civil War, then he or she was viewed by free Negroes as socially inferior. Such ranking of people by their pre–Civil War status was common in the Black Victorian social class that emerged in the post–Civil War era. Charleston, South Carolina, contained one of the wealthiest and most self-consciously free Negro communities. Many of the Charleston free Negroes were descendants of white masters, owners of considerable private property, and members of social clubs, such as the Brown Fellowship Society, which excluded all African Americans except those descended from mixed-race unions. Such social conflicts spilled over into the political realm where free Negro and ex-slave representatives clashed in the South Carolina state legislature over bills to redistribute the property of landowners and protection for Black laborers.

308 • Sharecropper

"Sharecropper" refers to the legal relationship between those who rented parcels of land from landowners in the postwar South. Initially, after the Black Codes were overturned by Congress, ex-slaves refused to work on large plantations in gang labor groups because these were too reminiscent of slavery. Landowners feared ex-slaves would not work without compulsive work routines. Yet landowners needed laborers and laborers lacked land, so sharecropping emerged as a compromise. Tenant farmers rented a parcel of land to work as their own in return for a percentage of their crop at the end of the growing season, usually one-quarter to one-half of the crop, depending on the tools and animals owned by the tenant. Although sharecropping began as a compromise that seemed to satisfy some of the freedmen's demands for autonomy, by the end of the Reconstruction period, a combination of falling prices for cotton, dishonest and unscrupulous planters, the inability of freedmen to read and write, and terroristic activities had transformed sharecropping into a system under which few tenants ever made enough by the year's end to get out of debt, let alone accumulate any capital.

309 • Carpetbagger

A carpetbagger was a northerner who came to the South during Radical Reconstruction (1867–77) to, according to the view of many southern whites at the time, pillage and profit from the economic policies of Republican-dominated state governments. Many white southerners believed the northerners allowed the "rape and pillage" of the South by Blacks in order to reap financial rewards. In reality, however, many northerners who came South devoted themselves unselfishly to helping the freedmen and dispossessed white southerners adjust to change. And some political carpetbaggers, such as South Carolina Governor Daniel H. Chamberlain, were conservative members of the Republican Party who helped undo Black Reconstruction.

310 • Scalawag

A scalawag was a native-born white southerner who joined or supported the Republican Party during Radical Reconstruction. Scalawags were viewed as siding with the freedmen, rather than with the white population, and thus as traitors to the Redeemers, who came after Radical Reconstruction.

311 • Louisiana Murders

The Louisiana Murders, a mass attack that occurred as a result of a disputed election, took place on Easter Sunday in 1873. In Grant Parish, Louisiana, Blacks, afraid white Democrats would take over after the election, "set up armed resistance around the county seat of Colfax." After three weeks, white supremacists overran Colfax, killing over three hundred blacks—many of whom had surrendered. It is called the worst incident of mass racial violence in the Reconstruction period.

312 • "Wave the Bloody Shirt"

Waving a bloody shirt was a practice Republican politicians used in the elections of 1866, 1868, 1872, and 1876 to draw public attention to southern violence against African Americans. The bloody shirt of a lynching victim, for example, would be displayed to whip up enthusiasm for the Republican Party in these elections. At the same time, southern racists who attempted to overthrow Reconstruction were creating such shirts through violent attacks on African Americans. Although Rutherford B. Hayes, the Republican presidential candidate in 1876, used the "bloody shirt" in his election campaign, he willingly complied when southern congressmen demanded he withdraw federal troops from the South to obtain their votes for president. Once the bloody-shirt tactic was no longer useful to Republicans politically, they completely abandoned concern for African American safety.

313 • Redeemers

The Redeemers were white Democrats who led the fight against Radical Reconstruction and replaced Republicans in positions of power in southern state governments after President Rutherford B. Hayes's withdrawal of federal troops from the South in 1877. Redeemers weakened Black political power, rewrote Reconstruction state constitutions, reduced state taxes and budgets, returned land to former planters, and created a legal system that ensured white supremacy and a controlled Black labor force.

314 • The Invisible Empire

The Invisible Empire was a name applied to the Ku Klux Klan, which emerged first in December 1865 as a fraternity of former Confederate officers living in Pulaski, Tennessee. As a *kyklos,* or circle of friends, the Klan practiced strange and mystical rituals, donning robes and masks and riding horseback around the countryside, whooping and yelling. Early Klan members noticed that African Americans were frightened by this cavorting, and the practice spread. But it was not until the passage of the Reconstruction Act of 1867 that the Ku Klux Klan found its real raison d'être and became a regional terrorist organization. Transformed at a meeting in Nashville, Tennessee, into a mystical "empire," with dukes and dominions, the new Klan was ruled by a grand wizard, a Confederate soldier named Nathan Bedford Forrest. While explicitly dedicated to defending the weak and the female, the Invisible Empire was mainly designed to intimidate and torture carpetbaggers, schoolteachers, Republican legislators, Freedmen's Bureau officials, scalawag judges, and all African Americans whose behavior violated southern "traditions." Klan beatings, maimings, and killings became so abhorrent that even Forrest was moved to disband the organization in January 1869. It continued to operate until 1872, however, when Reconstruction was all but over. Most of the upper class and Conservative Democrats sought to distance themselves from the Klan's activities, but many Redeemers praised the Klan as the most important factor in the successful over-throw of Reconstruction.

Laws, Amendments, and Supreme Court Decisions

315 • Compromise of 1877

In the presidential election of 1876, the Republican and Democratic candidates, Rutherford B. Hayes and Samuel Tilden, received equal numbers of electoral votes, which threw the election into the House of Representatives. In the same election, the three states in which Reconstruction governments had not been overthrown—South Carolina, Louisiana, and Florida—reported fraudulent election results and the Democrats and Republicans both claimed victory. In order to gain the votes of southern states in the House to secure his election, Hayes promised to withdraw federal troops from the South and give control of remaining loyal Republican governments to the Conservative Democrats. Hayes also promised to assist the South in getting federal money for internal improvements. Upon his selection by the House as president, Hayes quickly removed the troops and left Black southerners at the mercy of southern white Democratic state governments.

316 • Thirteenth Amendment

Although Lincoln had issued the Emancipation Proclamation in 1863, it was not clear that this liberation of southerners' "property" would have the force of law. Thus, Congress passed the Thirteenth Amendment to abolish slavery throughout the Union on January 31, 1865, and sent it to the states to be approved. President Johnson then made its acceptance a prerequi-

site for readmission of the Confederate states into the Union.

317 • Black Codes

During Presidential Reconstruction, 1865–66, state governments throughout the South passed laws to regulate the status and conduct of the emancipated slaves. These laws, known as the Black Codes, affected almost every aspect of an African American's life. The Black Codes' key objective was to control African American workers by limiting their ability to secure employment outside of plantation work. Although the laws varied from state to state, the Black Codes also regulated mobility and interracial contact. Stiff fines and jail sentences were meted out to those who violated the codes. According to Benjamin F. Flanders, they were the product of state legislatures whose "whole thought and time will be given to plans for getting things back as near as slavery as possible."

318 • Mississippi's Black Codes

Mississippi had some of the toughest Black Codes. It required all blacks to have written proof of employment for the coming year each January. If an employee left a job before the end of a contract, he or she forfeited wages already earned. To discourage an employee's ability to barter for better employment, the state imposed a $500 fine on anyone who offered work to someone under contract. Blacks could not rent urban land. Vagrancy could be punished by fines or involuntary labor on plantations. Blacks were also punished for insulting whites, or, remarkably, preaching the Gospel without a license.

319 • South Carolina's Black Codes

While South Carolina's Black Codes retained a glimmer of the Old Regime's paternalism—

most notably the prohibition against evicting former slaves from plantations—the codes also forbade African Americans from working at nonagricultural jobs. If a Black person worked as anything other than a farmer or a domestic servant, he or she had to pay an annual tax as high as $100 a year. That made it almost impossible for Charleston's Black artisan class to earn a living at its trade. South Carolina's code also forced Blacks to sign annual employment contracts that specified the hours of work, usually from sunup to sundown, and prohibited workers from leaving the plantation during those hours without the owner's permission. Even traveling-circus performers and fortune-tellers could be hauled in for vagrancy and then forced to work on plantations for free.

320 • Northern Reaction to the Black Codes

While initially less concerned with granting Blacks the right to vote or any other civil rights, many white northerners believed the war had been fought to establish a free labor system in the South. The Black Codes convinced northerners that the South had not accepted this lesson of defeat. The suspicion that the South was restoring slavery through the Black Codes galvanized northern opinion against Presidential Reconstruction.

Racist 1866 Pennsylvania governor election poster that highlights northern white opposition to the Fourteenth Amendment and its guarantees of voting rights to African Americans. Prints and Photographs Division, Library of Congress

321 • Civil Rights Act of 1866

With the Civil Rights Act of 1866, passed on April 9, 1866, Congress conferred on African Americans all the civil rights enjoyed by whites, except for the vote, which was regarded as a privilege. The Civil Rights Act of 1866 defined citizenship as coming from the federal government and not the state, and its protection was not limited to the South or the former slaves. It forbade any discriminatory laws by states and it was enacted to render null and void the Black Codes. It also gave African Americans the rights to enter into contracts, to sue, to give evidence in court, and to own property.

322 • Fourteenth Amendment

Proposed in 1866, the Fourteenth Amendment was passed in 1867. "No State shall make or enforce any law which shall abridge the privileges or immunities of citizens of the United States; nor shall any State deprive any person of life, liberty, or property, without due process of law; nor deny to any person within its jurisdiction the equal protection of the laws." The Fourteenth Amendment made civil rights legislation permanent and guaranteed Blacks equal pro-

THE CONSTITUTIONAL AMENDMENT!

GEARY
Is for Negro Suffrage.

STEVENS
Advocates it.

FORNEY
Howls for it.

McCLURE
Speaks for it.

CAMERON
Wants it.

The LEAGUE
Sustains it.

They are rich and want to make

The Negro the Equal
OF THE POOR WHITE MAN,
and then rule them both.

The BLACK Roll
CANDIDATES FOR CONGRESS
WHO VOTED FOR THIS BILL.

THAD. STEVENS
WM. D. KELLEY
CHAS. O'NEILL
LEONARD MYERS
JNO. M. BROOMALL
GEORGE F. MILLER
STEPHEN F. WILSON
ULYSSES MERCUR
GEO. V. LAWRENCE
GLENNI W. SCHOFIELD
J. K. MOORHEAD
THOMAS WILLIAMS

THE RADICAL PLATFORM--"NEGRO SUFFRAGE THE ONLY ISSUE!"
Every man who votes for Geary or for a Radical Candidate for Congress, votes as surely for Negro Suffrage and Negro Equality, as if they were printed on his ballot.

tection under the law. States were required to ratify the Fourteenth Amendment as a condition for readmission to the Union.

323 • The Reconstruction Act of 1867

With the Reconstruction Act of 1867, Congress wrested reconstruction of the South away from the president and imposed new requirements for the reentry of Confederate states to the Union. The act disfranchised former Confederates and divided the eleven Confederate states, except Tennessee, into five military districts under army commanders. It also required each state to elect, through universal male suffrage, a constitutional convention, which would write new constitutions that provided for Black voting in their state constitutions. Once the constitutions were approved by a majority of the voters in each state, and the states had ratified the Fourteenth Amendment, the states could reenter the Union and send representatives to Congress. The Reconstruction Act of 1867 also franchised Blacks in the District of Columbia and extended the term of the Freedmen's Bureau.

324 • Louisiana Liberalism and the Supreme Court

In 1869 Louisiana passed a law forbidding any segregation of Black and white passengers on public transportation. In a clear example of the Supreme Court's tendency to curtail state legislation that was pro–African American, the Court, in its *Hall v. DeCuir* decision, struck down this Louisiana law in 1878. The Supreme Court ruled in this case that the Louisiana law was an abridgment of the right of Congress to regulate interstate commerce, even though the Louisiana law only applied to intrastate carriers.

325 • Slaughterhouse Cases of 1873

In the Slaughterhouse Cases, the Supreme Court gutted the civil rights enforcement of the Fourteenth Amendment. In direct contradiction to the Civil Rights Act of 1866 and the Fourteenth Amendment, the Supreme Court ruled that two classes of citizenship existed—state and federal—and that the Fourteenth Amendment covered only those rights received under federal citizenship. Since most civil rights fell under state citizenship, this decision denied protection under the Fourteenth Amendment for Blacks whose rights were increasingly under attack in the South. When state and local authorities refused to protect Black voters in federal elections from beatings and murder, the Supreme Court denied those victims the right to claim that their voting rights had been violated under the Fourteenth Amendment.

326 • *United States v. Cruikshank*

In the *Cruikshank* decision, handed down on March 27, 1876, the Supreme Court ruled that the Fourteenth Amendment did not protect citizens who were exercising their constitutional right to peaceful assembly from intimidating other citizens. Such intimidation was a local matter, in the Court's opinion, since it believed such rights derived from state rather than national citizenship. What this decision did was to legitimize attacks on Blacks assembling for the purpose of political activity. After this decision, the Ku Klux Klan and other terrorist groups were able to attack Black Republican meetings and conventions in the South with impunity.

327 • Fifteenth Amendment

In 1868 the Republicans argued that the right to suffrage remained a state prerogative, so following Ulysses S. Grant's election, a Republican Congress offered a new constitutional amendment to deal with the question of Black voting. According to the Fifteenth Amendment, "The right of citizens of the United States to vote shall not be denied or abridged by the United States or by any State on account of race, color, or previous condition of servitude." Unfortunately, even after the Fifteenth Amendment took effect on March 30, 1870, it did not insure that African Americans could vote. The Supreme Court had ruled previously that the rules governing suffrage were still the province of the states. States could keep Blacks from voting for nonracial reasons. That loophole was manipulated by southern state constitutions to limit Black suffrage through the understanding, grandfather, and other clauses.

328 • Civil Rights Act of February 28, 1871

Congress passed the Civil Rights Act of 1871 in response to the growing intimidation of Black voters in the South. Known as the "Ku Klux Klan Act" it gave the federal courts a wide variety of powers designed to combat violence if the violence curtailed a person's constitutional rights. Federal courts acquired the power to appoint persons to oversee and supervise elections, and it became a federal crime for anyone to interfere with their work. To specifically counteract the Ku Klux Klan, Congress also outlawed the wearing of disguises upon public highways or in another person's house for the purpose of depriving them of equal protection of the laws.

329 • Civil Rights Act of March 1, 1875

The Civil Rights Act of 1964 was not the first law in American history to guarantee equal access to public accommodations. The Civil Rights Act of March 1, 1875, curtailed the rise of Jim Crow laws in the South, and made as strong a statement of equal rights as the Civil Rights Act

of eighty-nine years later. In unequivocal language the 1875 act declared that

all persons within the jurisdiction of the United States shall be entitled to the full and equal enjoyment of the accommodations, advantages, facilities, and privileges of inns, public conveyances on land or water, theaters, and other places of public amusement; subject only to the conditions and limitations established by law, and applicable alike to citizens of every race and color, regardless of any previous condition of servitude.

The act went on to state that anyone who deprived a person of such "equal enjoyment" because of his or her race could be fined $500, to be paid to the victim. District attorneys were compelled to arrest such violators, and if the district attorneys refused to act, they too could be fined $500, also to be paid to the victim. Federal courts were given jurisdiction in these cases to give federal protection to the civil rights. Unfortunately for American citizens, this landmark legislation was ruled unconstitutional a decade later by the Supreme Court in the 1883 Civil Rights Cases.

330 • *United States v. Reese*

Voter intimidation, in the form of murders and threats of murder against those attempting to vote, increased so drastically in the South during the 1870s that the entire nation became aware of the problem. Faced with an example of such intimidation in *United States v. Reese* (1876), the Supreme Court struck down the federal provisions guaranteeing voting rights. Such action by the Supreme Court sanctioned voter intimidation.

"The Union as it was," cartoon by Thomas Nast for *Harper's Weekly*, October 21, 1876. Prints and Photographs Division, Library of Congress

331 • Supreme Court Nullifies the "Ku Klux Klan Act"

In *United States v. Harris* (1883) the Supreme Court further limited the Fourteenth Amendment as a means of protecting Blacks from civil rights abuses. In this case, a mob had grabbed several African Americans from a Tennessee jail, killed one of them, and beat the others severely. The Supreme Court ruled this was not a violation of the Fourteenth Amendment's equal protection clause because that amendment asserted that no *state* could deprive a person of equal protection under the laws, and did not specifically claim that no *individual* could do so. Regulation of individual behavior was a state matter, the Court argued, and if the state did not deem Black rights important enough to protect, that was not the federal government's business. This decision struck down the Civil Rights Act of 1871, the so-called Ku Klux Klan Act, by holding that congressional action against private actions was not permitted by the Fourteenth Amendment.

332 • Supreme Court Nullifies Public Accommodations Protection of the Civil Rights Act of 1875

In the 1883 Civil Rights Cases the United States Supreme Court ruled that the Civil Rights Act of 1875 was unconstitutional. According to Justice Joseph P. Bradley, who wrote the majority opinion, the Fourteenth Amendment did not give Congress the ability to pass legislation against racial discrimination in public accommodations because "that amendment proscribed only deprivation of rights by *state action*." In a radical reinterpretation of the Fourteenth Amendment, the Court argued that only discrimination by states, not individuals, was prohibited under the Fourteenth Amendment. Discrimination by private businesses amounted to infringement of the "social rights" of African

Americans, not their civil or political rights. The effect of this ruling was to sanction discrimination by individuals.

333 • Possession of Weapons Prohibited

Despite the pervasiveness of guns and other weapons in southern culture, under Section 1 of the Penal Laws of Mississippi, African Americans were unable to possess firearms without authorization from the local government. Rarely was such permission granted. No similar requirements applied to whites.

Quotations

334 • James Pike's View of South Carolina During Black Reconstruction

In a reputedly objective, but actually racist, account of Radical Reconstruction in South Carolina, James S. Pike, a Republican journalist, said:

In the place of this old aristocratic society stands the rude form of the most ignorant democracy that mankind ever saw, invested with the functions of government. It is the dregs of the population habilitated in the robes of their intelligent predecessors, and asserting over them the rule of ignorance and corruption. . . . It is barbarism overwhelming civilization by physical force. . . . We enter the House of Representatives. Here sit one hundred and twenty-four members. Of these, twenty-three are white men, representing the remains of the old civilization. These are good-looking, substantial citizens. They are men of weight and standing in the communities they represent. . . . This negro dense negro crowd . . . do the debating, the squabbling, the lawmaking, and create all the clamor and disorder of the body. . . . The Speaker is black, the Clerk is black, the doorkeepers are black, the little pages are black, the chairman of the Ways and Means is black, and the chaplain is coal black. At some of the desks sit colored men whose types it would be hard to find outside of the Congo; whose costume, visages, attitudes, and expression, only befit the forecastle of a buccaneer. It must be remembered, also, that these men, with not more than a half dozen exceptions, have been themselves slaves, and that their ancestors were slaves for generations. . . .

335 • Another View of Black Political Participation

Although controversial, African American participation in the constitutional conventions held after the Reconstruction Act of 1867 was often praised:

Beyond all question the best men in the convention are the colored members. Considering the influences under which they were called together, and their imperfect acquaintance with parliamentary law, they have displayed, for the most part, remarkable moderation and dignity. . . . They have assembled neither to pull wires like some, nor to make money like others; but to legislate for the welfare of the race to which they belong. [Charleston Daily News]

336 • Henry Turner's Rebuttal

One of the ways southerners undermined Reconstruction was to challenge the seating of African American representatives in the state legislatures. In Georgia in 1868, for example, several representatives were rejected by the state legislature because they were Black. In the following speech, delivered in the Georgia House of Representatives on September 3, 1868, Henry M. Turner attacks those in the legislature who questioned his right to a seat in the body.

Whose Legislature is this? Is it a white man's Legislature, or is it a black man's Legislature?

Who voted for the Constitutional Convention, in obedience to the mandate of the Congress of the United States? Who first rallied around the standard of Reconstruction? Who set the ball of loyalty rolling in the State of Georgia? It was the voice of the brawny-armed Negro, with the few humanitarian-hearted white men who came to our assistance. I claim the honor, sir, of having been the instrument of convincing hundreds— yea, thousands—of white men, that to reconstruct under the measures of the United States Congress was the safest and best course for the interest of the State.

Let us look at some facts in connection with this matter. Did half the white men of Georgia vote for this Legislature? Did not the great bulk of them fight, with all their strength, the Constitution under which we are acting? And did they not fight against the organization of this Legislature? And further, sir, did they not vote against it? Yes, sir! And there are persons in this Legislature to-day, who are ready to spit their poison in my face, while they themselves opposed, with all their power, the ratification of this Constitution.

337 • Violence Rebutted

The following is testimony taken by the Joint Congressional Committee on the Condition of Affairs in the Late Insurrectionary States, July 3, 1871.

Willis Johnson (colored) sworn and examined.

Q.: *Where do you live?*

Johnson: *At Leonidas Sims's, in Newberry County.*

Q.: *How long have you lived there?*

Johnson: *This year. I lived there one year since I have been free before this year. . . .*

Q.: *Have you been at any time visited by men masked and disguised—Ku Klux?*

Johnson: *Yes, sir.*

Q.: *When?*

Johnson: *Last night two weeks ago.*

Q.: *Go on and tell what you saw and what they said and did, telling it in your own way.*

Johnson: *When I awoke, as near as I can tell, it was between 12 and 1 o'clock. I heard some one call "Sims." I held still and listened, and heard them walk from his door to my door. I was upstairs, and I got up and came down-stairs. They walked back to his house again and asked him to put his head out. He did not answer, but his wife asked them who they were. They said they were friends. They walked back to my door again, and just as they got to the door they blew a whistle. Another whistle off a piece answered, and then men seemed to surround the house and all parts of the yard. Then they hallooed, "Open the door." I said nothing. I went to the head of the bed and got my pistol, and leaned forward on the table with the pistol just at the door. They tried with several surges to get the door open, but it did not come open. They went to the wood-pile and got the axe, and struck the front door some licks, bursted it open, and then went to the back door and burst it open. Nobody had yet come into the house; they had not come in. They said, "Strike a light." Then I dropped down on my knees back of the table, and they struck some matches and threw them in the house, and two of them stepped in the front door, and that brought them within arm's length of me as they stood there. As soon as they did that, I raised my pistol quickly, right up to one's back, and shot, and he fell and hallooed, and the other tried to pull him out. As he pulled him I shot again. As they were pulling, others ran up and pulled him out in the yard, and when the whole party was out in the yard I stepped to the door and shot again, and then jumped to the back door and ran. I got off. I staid away until the next morning; then I came back and tracked them half a mile where they had toted this man and laid him down. I was afraid to go further. Mr. Sims and I were together, and I would not go any further, and he told me to go away; that I ought not to stay there; that he saw the men and saw the wounded man, and was satisfied that he was dead or mortally wounded, and I must leave. Mr. John Calmes, the candidate of the democrats for the legislature, advised me to take a paper and go around the settlement to the white people, stating that I would never vote the radical ticket, and he said he did not think they would interfere with me then. He said that all they had against me was that on election day I took the tickets around among the black people; and he said: "You knocked me out of a good many votes, but you are a good fellow and a good laborer, and we want labor in this country." I told him I would not do that. . . .*

People and Politics

338 • Early African American Political Aspirations

Despite the myth that African American Reconstruction leaders were tools of northern Republican leaders, Black political leaders with their own agenda for reconstruction existed in most cities of the Confederate South. Even before the end of the Civil War, African American political groups began to meet and demand political representation in the postwar world. In South Carolina, for example, the Sea Island community sent a group of representatives to the 1864 National Republican Convention, although they failed to be seated and recognized. After Union troops captured Charleston, African Americans met on March 30, 1865, to pass resolutions that publicly declared their support of the Union at a time when violent reprisals by Confederate stragglers were still common.

When South Carolina whites convened to petition readmittance to the Union under Presidential Reconstruction in September 1865, Blacks lobbied unsuccessfully for the same rights accorded to white citizens. Then, in November, Blacks convened their own Colored People's Convention and demanded the state grant equal rights and voting rights to African Americans. Such assertions of and demand for political rights arose from the Black community prior to the Reconstruction Act of 1867 and the introduction of northern Republicans into South Carolina Reconstruction politics.

339 • Economic Insurgency

Along with political activism, African Americans also engaged in an economic struggle for just treatment in the postwar period. Hundreds of Blacks rebelled against exploitative labor contracts, and in some cases took physical possession of plantations and moved into the "big houses," claiming them as rightfully their own. Black urban laborers in Richmond, Virginia, laundry women in Mississippi, longshoremen in New Orleans, and mechanical workers in Georgia all struck for higher wages.

340 • The Constitutional Conventions

When Congress passed the Reconstruction Act of 1867, African American political activity accelerated. Each state of the former Confederacy had to hold constitutional conventions that included African Americans, though in practice the number of African Americans at the conventions varied greatly from state to state in proportion to the percentage of Blacks in the state population. In South Carolina Blacks were the majority at the constitutional convention; in Louisiana the ratio was fifty-fifty; but in Texas only nine of ninety members were African American. The conventions drew up constitu-

"The First Vote," by A. R. Wand in *Harper's Weekly*, November 16, 1867. Prints and Photographs Division, Library of Congress

tions that abolished property qualifications for voting and holding office, extended the ballot to all male residents, banned slavery, and eliminated race distinctions in the possession and inheritance of property. By 1900 most of these constitutions were replaced by constitutions severely limiting the rights of Blacks.

341 • Black Civil Rights Protest After the Reconstruction Act of 1867

Passage of the Reconstruction Act of 1867 led to expectations that discriminatory southern social practices would change. Following the 1867 meeting to approve the Republican Party platform, several African American men climbed aboard a streetcar in Charleston, South Carolina, demanding the right to ride on the cars usually reserved for whites. In Louisiana the demands of Black soldiers of the 39th Infantry to ride on New Orleans streetcars reserved for whites forced General Sheridan to order the urban transit companies to integrate their cars. These accomplishments were not short-lived. When an African American woman was thrown from a streetcar on April 17, 1867, her formal complaint forced the streetcar company to allow Blacks to ride on the streetcars without discrimination until shortly after 1900, when a new wave of Jim Crow segregation was reinstituted.

342 • Thaddeus Stevens (1792–1868)

Thaddeus Stevens, a lawyer and one of the founders of the Republican Party, was perhaps the single most important congressman during the Reconstruction period. As a member of the House of Representatives, he was a vigorous critic of the Crittenden Compromise, of Lincoln for overruling General David Hunter's decision to free the slaves, and of Presidential Reconstruction, with its mild demand that only 10 percent of the southern state voting populations pledge loyalty to the Union. He was one of the principal opponents, along with Charles Sumner, of President Andrew Johnson, and he led the congressional campaign to seize control of Reconstruction, treat the Confederate states as territories, and make them accept African American voting. In the latter, he was motivated not only by a sense of justice for the freedmen but also by practical political considerations: Stevens was shocked by the possibility that former Confederate states might send back Confederate leaders and unrepentant Democrats to Congress. He supported Black suffrage in part to ensure the dominance of the Republican Party in the Congress for years to come. Stevens was a shrill, tough-minded, sharp-tongued legislator who bullied and threatened his opponents to go along with his plan to make the South pay for its treason and to guarantee the political rights of African Americans.

343 • Charles Sumner (1811–74)

Charles Sumner, the United States senator most famous for having been caned by Congressman Preston S. Brooks of South Carolina after Sumner's speech attacking the Kansas-Nebraska Act of 1854 and its author, Stephen A. Douglas, was an outspoken opponent of slavery. For years Sumner spoke out against slavery, the Fugitive Slave Act, and the attacks on abolitionists by proslavery Whig politicians in his native Massachusetts. When he returned to the Senate after his beating in 1857, Sumner resumed his vitriolic, acid-tongued attacks on slavery and its defenders in one of the classics of antislavery speeches, "The Barbarism of Slavery," delivered on the eve of the presidential election. During the war, he was the first congressman to advocate the freeing of slaves and pressed for the granting of civil and political rights to the freedmen after the war. Like Thaddeus Stevens, Sumner demanded that Congress control Re-

construction, blocked Louisiana's readmission to the Union under Lincoln's 10 percent plan, and led the Senate in denunciations of Andrew Johnson. Like Stevens as well, Sumner demanded the extension of all political rights to African Americans while at the same time insisting that those Confederates who had committed treason should not enjoy the franchise in the postwar South.

344 • Blacks in Congress During Reconstruction

During the Reconstruction years, two African Americans served terms in the Senate and twenty African Americans were elected to the House of Representatives. In the House eight of the twenty representatives came from South Carolina, four from North Carolina, three from Alabama, and one each from Georgia, Mississippi, Florida, Louisiana, and Virginia.

345 • Hiram Rhoades Revels (1822–1901)

Hiram Revels was selected by the Mississippi state legislature in 1870 to fill the Senate seat vacated by Jefferson Davis. That made him the first African American chosen to be a member of Congress. Seated on February 25, 1870, he served in the Senate until March 3, 1871, when its short term ended. Born in Fayetteville, North Carolina, Revels was first an ordained minister of the African Methodist Episcopal Church in Baltimore. During the Civil War, he organized colored troops in Maryland and then went to Mississippi in connection with the Freedmen's Bureau effort to create schools for African American youth. After serving as an alderman in Natchez, Mississippi, in 1868, he became a state senator before being selected to represent Mississippi in the United States Senate. Revels was the epitome of politically conservative

Hiram Rhoades Revels, the first African American senator. Photograph by Matthew Brady. Prints and Photographs Division, Library of Congress

Those positions allowed him to acquire wealth and a palatial plantation lost by its owner to Reconstruction taxes, and eventually led to his selection as a U.S. senator. On his climb to power, Bruce made a few political enemies, one of whom was James L. Alcorn, the other Mississippi senator, who broke Senate tradition by refusing to escort Bruce to his Senate seat. New York Senator Roscoe Conkling escorted Bruce instead and became Bruce's lifelong friend. Unlike Senator Hiram Revels, Bruce used his Senate appointment to lobby successfully for colored people's rights: he opposed the Chinese Exclusion Act that was passed in 1878, introduced a bill to desegregate the U.S. Army, recommended federal support of the "Exodusters" migrating to Kansas, and successfully investigated and rescued from bankruptcy the Freedman's Savings Trust Company of Washington, D.C.

African American politicians who gained positions during Reconstruction. After leaving the Senate, Revels sensed the changing political winds of Mississippi and lobbied in 1875 in favor of a white conservative overthrow of the Republican state government.

346 • Blanche K. Bruce (1841–98)

In 1874 Blanche K. Bruce of Mississippi became the second African American selected to serve in the United States Senate. Bruce was the only African American to serve a full term in the Senate until 1972, when Edward Brooke of Massachusetts finished his first term as a U.S. senator. Bruce was a mixed-race slave born in rural Virginia. After running away to freedom in Kansas, attending Oberlin College, and working for a couple of years on a Mississippi riverboat, Bruce migrated to Bolivar County, Mississippi, in 1870, where he was elected sheriff and tax assessor.

347 • Jefferson F. Long (1836–1900)

A vigorous fighter for African American political rights, Jefferson F. Long in January 1871 became the second African American, and the first from Georgia, to be elected to the House of Representatives. Although he served only until the end of the term on March 3, 1871, Long became the first African American to address the House of Representatives when he delivered a speech against a bill removing restrictions on the vote for Confederates. Long argued that Confederates would use the vote to restore white supremacy rule, depicted the rampant hatred expressed toward the American flag and its display, and exposed attacks on Blacks and Republican sympathizers by the Ku Klux Klan. Not until the election of Andrew Young to the House in 1972 would another African American from Georgia be sent to the House of Representatives.

348 • Governor P. B. S. Pinchback (1837–1921)

The first African American to serve as governor of a state was not Douglas Wilder, but P. B. S. Pinchback. His tenure as governor, however, was much shorter than Wilder's. Pinchback had been elected president pro tempore of the Louisiana senate in 1871 and promoted to lieutenant governor upon the death of Oscar J. Dunn. Pinchback was governor of Louisiana for just forty-six days, from December 9, 1872, to January 13, 1873, after the elected governor, Henry Clay Warmouth, was impeached. Pinchback was never able to reach the governor's mansion by election, but he retired to Washington, D.C., where, along with Blanche Bruce, he became a celebrity in Washington social circles.

349 • Robert Carlos De Large (1842–74)

A key myth of Reconstruction is that Black legislators tried to deny white southerners the right to vote. In reality, African American legislators generally lobbied for the removal of political debilities on Confederates. The best example of a conservative Black legislator was Robert De Large, who introduced a bill in the South Carolina legislature in 1868 to remove all political disabilities on former Confederates. Like many of his colleagues, De Large, a mixed-race ex-slave who was distinguished by his muttonchops, believed that the Black Republicans could not afford to appear too radical or vindictive toward the whites. At the same time, De Large, who later served in the House of Representatives and delivered an eloquent speech in favor of the Fourteenth Amendment, was not so conservative as to fail to demand that more of

P. B. S. Pinchback, governor of Louisiana. Photograph by Matthew Brady. Prints and Photographs Division, Library of Congress

Robert Carlos De Large, South Carolina legislator. Photograph by Matthew Brady. Prints and Photographs Division, Library of Congress

the positions of power in the Republican-controlled legislature be given to African Americans. "Why is it that we colored men have become identified with the Republican Party?" De Large asked in 1874.

Is it because there is loadstone which attracts and holds us there, or is it because we are deluded and follow blindly certain men? No! We joined this party because it professed equal rights and privileges to all. . . . We thought, on the ground of expediency we must do nothing to offend them, but some impudent scoundrels in the party now say: "You want too much; you want everything!" We placed them in position; we elected them and by our votes we made them our masters. We now propose to change this thing a little, and let them vote for us. It is no more than reasonable they should do so.

350 • Martin R. Delany (1812–85)

Martin Delany, the Black abolitionist and emigrationist, was one of the most effective nonelected African Americans to work with the South Carolina Freedmen's Bureau. From 1865 to 1868 Delany was effective in protecting African American rights in contracts with employers, in part because he used his reputation as a national Black leader to resist bureau attempts to water down his directives. His efforts included creating an independent cotton press for Black freedmen that circumvented the Charleston cotton factories which controlled cotton processing. This, of course, did not sit well with planters or merchants, and Delany was attacked in the press and in the bureau. Although his cotton press eventually failed because of economic reprisals, Delany continued to work for the freedmen.

JIM CROW

Terms, Phrases, and Slogans

351 • Jim Crow

"Jim Crow" was taken from a white performer named Thomas "Daddy" Rice who caricatured Black styles of walk, talk, and dress in the 1830s. Initially performing in Cincinnati, Rice brought his impressions to the New York Bowery Theater in 1832. His songs became popular American classics, in which he told his working-class white audience that "every time I weel a-bout I jump Jim Crow." "Jim Crow," Rice's portrayal of a handicapped Black man, became an urban stereotype of Black behavior almost as popular as "Uncle Tom." But in the late nineteenth century "Jim Crow" came to symbolize the wide-ranging system of segregation that separated Blacks and whites in almost every aspect of public life in the American South. In recent years the term "Jim Crow" has come to represent the entire system of Black oppression in the South, including not only segregation but also disfranchisement, lynching, rioting, and economic discrimination, which together carved out a place for the Negro in the South as a second-class citizen.

Historians debate the actual beginning of the Jim Crow system in the South. Almost all believe the first attempts at segregation began immediately after the Civil War, codified in the Black Codes. But these efforts were struck down by the Civil Rights Act of 1866, the Reconstruction Act of 1867, and the Fourteenth Amendment. One historian, C. Vann Woodward, has argued that after such suppression, the persuasive segregation of southern life that appeared in the early twentieth century did not begin to develop until the 1890s and the struggle over populism in the South. Other historians, most notably Joel R. Williamson, however, have found evidence of segregation in public life in the South in the 1870s and 1880s, when Blacks began to be refused admittance to first-class cars on trains. That seems plausible, since Congress passed the Civil Rights Act of 1875 in response to the rise of public discrimination against African Americans. Still, that the law was passed and enforcement attempted indicates that segregation in public arenas was not the law of the South in the 1870s. Even after Rutherford B. Hayes, as part of a deal to seal his selection by the House of Representatives to be president, withdrew federal troops from the Confederate South in 1877, African American access to public accommodations varied throughout the South. But in 1887 Florida passed the first segregation statute ordering railroads to segregate their passenger cars. The next year, Mississippi followed suit, and in 1889 Texas passed its own Jim Crow law. The passage of the Florida laws began the Jim Crow period, one of government sanction of segregation, disfranchisement, and terror in the South that lasted until the 1954 *Brown v. Board of Education* (Kansas) decision that declared segregation unconstitutional.

352 • Peonage

Peonage, or the practice of holding people on land against their will, emerged in the late-nineteenth and early-twentieth-century South. Where people worked as sharecroppers, they often found themselves in debt to landowners or merchants at the end of the harvesting season when "settlin'-up time" came. Often they began the next year in debt and were prevented from leaving the plot of land they farmed until they

paid that debt. Although peonage was a class system that affected white sharecroppers and tenants as well as Black ones, it was a particularly devastating form of social control on the former slave. One peon testified:

I am not an educated man. I will give you the peonage system as it is practiced here in the name of the law. . . .

I am brought in a prisoner, go through the farce of being tried. The whole of my fine may amount to fifty dollars. A kindly appearing man will come up and pay my fine and take me to his farm to allow me to work it out. At the end of the month I find that I owe him more than I did when I went there. The debt is increased year in and year out. You would ask, "How is that?" It is simply that he is charging you more for your board, lodging and washing than they allow you for your work, and you can't help yourself either, nor can anyone else help you, because you are still a prisoner and never get your fine worked out. . . . The court and the man you work for are always partners. One makes the fine and the other one works you and holds you, and if you leave you are tracked up with bloodhounds and brought back.

353 • Lynching

Between 1882 and 1901 over a hundred lynchings, almost all of them of African Americans, occurred each year, with several years topping two hundred. Lynching allowed the whites to retain a measure of control by instilling considerable fear among the Black community. By the early 1890s a pattern appeared. More lynchings tended to take place during the hotter months (July was the most popular) and most took place either at or near the scene of the alleged crime. Areas undergoing rapid or extreme economic and political changes were more likely to experience lynchings, and once one

Thomas Shipp and Abram Smith hanging from a tree, Marion, Indiana, 1930. Prints and Photographs Division, Library of Congress

lynching took place, more usually followed. Immediately after a lynching tensions remained high and the Black residential and commercial areas of the city often were burned and looted. Local authorities, if they did not actively assist in it, usually did nothing to stop a lynching. Officials at the highest level of southern governments announced their support of the practice. Cole Blease, for example, a former governor in South Carolina, planted the finger of a lynched man in the gubernatorial garden.

354 • Disfranchisement

Disfranchisement was the process of denying Blacks the right to vote, especially in the late-nineteenth and early-twentieth-century South.

Disfranchisement required considerable ingenuity on the part of southern racists, since the Fifteenth Amendment prohibited denial of the right to vote to a person because of race or color. In order to disfranchise the African American, racists had to devise some other factor that would, in effect, exclude Blacks from the voting rolls. One of the earliest was the poll tax.

355 • Poll Tax

Poll taxes, which made payment of a tax a requirement for voting, first developed in Tennessee in 1890. Usually the voter had to pay the tax before he could vote, but often under confusing conditions that made it difficult for African Americans to pay it. For example, the poll tax might have to be paid on a certain date at a certain time, but the location would only be known by a select few. In addition, the tax was often beyond the restricted salaries of most Blacks. Even though the poll tax was effective in keeping Blacks away from the polls, it was not enough to satisfy the state of Mississippi, with its majority Black population. Mississippi devised an additional device to discourage Black voters, called the understanding clause.

356 • Understanding Clause

The understanding clause demanded that potential voters pass a literacy test to qualify to vote. Developed at Mississippi's 1890 convention, the understanding clause required all citizens to be able to read and interpret a section of the state constitution to the satisfaction of polling officials. First proposed by white conservatives as a demand to elevate the educational qualifications of voters, the clause disfranchised many poor whites, but was mainly aimed at Black voters. In 1894 South Carolina, after years of prodding by Bill Tillman, adopted a similar clause in its constitution. Because of the clause's potential to disfranchise some illiterate southern whites, the grandfather clause was adopted in Louisiana.

357 • Grandfather Clause

Developed at the Louisiana convention of 1898, the grandfather clause exempted all males whose fathers or grandfathers could vote in the election on January 1, 1867, from having to pay poll taxes or pass the understanding test. Because southern Blacks had been denied the right to vote before 1867, they were ineligible for this exemption, which almost all whites enjoyed. Lacking such a qualification, any Black man desiring to vote would then have to pass the poll tax and understanding provisions. It was enormously effective: in 1896, 130,344 Black Americans had been registered voters in Louisiana. But in 1900, after the new clauses had been inserted in the state constitution, only 5,320 African Americans remained as registered voters in Louisiana.

358 • White Primaries

If some Blacks were able to register despite the myriad obstacles to registration, white primaries rendered their votes meaningless. In the solidly Democratic South, the candidate who won the Democratic primary was virtually assured of victory in the actual campaign. Many states adopted laws limiting participation in the primaries to whites only.

Protests, Organizations, and Demonstrations

359 • Ida B. Wells-Barnett Protests Lynching

Ida B. Wells (1862–1931) had been a radical for most of her life. In 1884 she sued the Cleveland and Ohio Railroad for making her leave the first-class accommodations for which she had paid. Wells won the case in state court, and even though it was later overturned by the Tennessee Supreme Court, she believed her protest had been the right thing to do. She became famous as an African American radical when she challenged the South's newest obsession, the lynching of Blacks, in an article published in the *Memphis Free Speech and Headlight,* a Black newspaper, on March 9, 1892. Her article protested the lynching of three young Black businessmen who had tried to defend their store from attack by local whites. "The city of Memphis," she wrote, "has demonstrated that neither character nor standing avails the Negro if he dares to protect himself against the white man or become his rival." These men had been attacked because they had become economic rivals of a local white business. Wells argued lynching was thus a form of economic reprisal. Such an argument was inflammatory enough in the South of 1892, but Wells went further and asserted it was a "thread-bare" lie that most Black men were lynched for raping white women. The white men of the South ought to stop using that excuse because, as she hinted, a closer examination would show that the white women associated with lynching victims had been voluntarily involved with Black men. For those remarks, in a May 1892 issue of *Free Speech* her newspaper office was destroyed, and Wells, traveling in Natchez, Mississippi, was told

Poster portrait of Ida B. Wells and her 1917 words: "I'd rather go down in history as one lone negro who dared to tell the government that it had done a dastardly thing." Prints and Photographs Division, Library of Congress

not to return to Memphis. She didn't, but instead launched a career of writing and agitation about lynching that galvanized an international awareness about the practice. Her books *Southern Horrors: Lynch Law in All Its Phases* and *A Red Record: Tabulated Statistics and Alleged Causes of Lynching in the United States,* published in 1892, were two of the first books to compile statistics on and analyze the causes of lynching. The statistics bore out her contentions: only one-third of those lynched were even accused of rape and most were lynched for acts of economic, educational, or political assertiveness. Ida B. Wells was politically allied with W. E. B. Du Bois and his Niagara Movement, and critical of Booker T. Washington's accommodationist posture toward southern violence.

360 • Booker T. Washington's Counsels Against Politics and Protest

At a Cotton States' International Exposition held in Atlanta, a Black man, Booker T. Washington (1856–1915), head of Tuskegee Institute in Alabama, delivered his famous "Atlanta Compromise" speech. Delivered on September 18, 1895, Washington's speech renounced the attempt of Blacks under Reconstruction to exercise their political rights and assert their social equality with whites. Rather than protest, Washington recommended that Blacks avoid challenging segregation and disfranchisement, work diligently at the agricultural and business occupations open to them, and acquire as much education and economic power as the South would allow them. Washington asked whites to grant Blacks the opportunity to advance independently and economically within their segregated sphere in exchange for Black willingness not to demand political rights. Washington argued that Blacks and whites in the South could be "as separate as the fingers in all things social, but united as a hand in all things fundamental," i.e., economic progress. Washington's speech was a tremendous success, in part because in the year of Frederick Douglass's death, it signaled the rise of a new Black leader and an alternative to Douglass's emphasis on protest as the best means to accomplish Black progress.

361 • Booker T. Behind the Scenes

Despite his public disavowal of Black political resistance and his obsequious manner of presenting himself to white people, Booker T. Washington actually worked behind the scenes to defend African American political and social rights. In 1898, for example, he not only asked the Louisiana legislature to ensure that the understanding clause and other restrictions on voting would be applied fairly, but he also lent

Booker T. Washington. Prints and Photographs Division, Library of Congress

his financial support to legal challenges to the constitutionality of Louisiana's grandfather clause. Secretly he financially supported efforts to end racial discrimination on Pullman cars in southern states. He also provided money to lawyers seeking to overturn statutes in Texas and Alabama that excluded African Americans from participation on juries. Washington did all of this secretly and quietly, usually through organizations like the Afro-American Council, to avoid alerting whites that he was working against segregation and disfranchisement.

362 • Black Opposition to Booker T. Washington

Booker T. Washington's moderate public stance against racism angered many African American intellectuals who formed organizations in the late nineteenth and early twentieth centuries. Richard T. Greener, the first African American to graduate from Harvard College, was one of the founders of the National Association of Colored Men, an organization of Black professionals. With a less avowedly political focus, the American Negro Academy was founded in March 1897 to promote "literature, science and art" among African Americans and also to foster "the defense of the Negro against vicious assault." Ida B. Wells was perhaps one of the earliest to publicly criticize Washington's singleminded public endorsement of Black economic advancement in the South. She argued that following Washington's counsel to forgo demand for civil rights and seek economic parity would increase one's chances of being lynched, as had been the case in Memphis in 1892.

363 • The National Association of Colored Women

Of considerable significance was the formation of the National Association of Colored Women, an outgrowth of the local women's club movement that had begun in earnest in the 1890s. Such clubs as the Phyllis Wheatley Club of New Orleans and the Woman's League of Washington, D.C., were independent associations devoted to self-help, education, and social reform. But in the spring of 1895 these clubs joined together to form the National Association of Colored Women, in part to respond to the increasingly negative portrayals of Black women in the press. Another reason for the formation of the National Association was the rise of segregation in white women's clubs, which before the 1890s had freely admitted African American women. When Mrs. Fannie Barrier Williams, an African American, was recommended for membership in the Chicago Woman's Club in 1894, it led to a national discussion in the media over the appropriateness of Black women in predominantly white women's clubs. While Mrs. Williams was eventually admitted, Mrs. Josephine Ruffin, of the Women's Era Club of Boston, an African American women's club, was refused admittance to the National Federation of Women's Clubs at its meeting in Milwaukee in 1900. Perhaps in response to these incidents, the National Association of Colored Women became increasingly political in the early twentieth century, inviting and hosting lectures from Black leaders from a variety of points of view.

364 • Horrific Lynching Mobilizes W. E. B. Du Bois

When W. E. B. Du Bois, the Harvard Ph.D. graduate and Berlin-trained social scientist, came to Atlanta University in 1897, he launched an impressive series of studies of African American life and culture and settled into a comfortable job as a university professor. But in 1899 Du Bois was shaken out of his academic complacency by the horrific lynching of Sam Hose in April of that year. Sam Hose had killed a white farmer during an argument and was brutally lynched and burned to death by a mob of over two thousand people. After his charred body was dragged to the ground, men, women, and children struggled with one another to take home pieces of his burned flesh as souvenirs. Learning of the lynching stopped Du Bois from working on his monographs to go down to the *Atlanta Constitution* to contribute a letter of mild protest to the editor. Afterward, he learned that Hose had been barbecued and that his burned knuckles were placed on display in a shopkeeper's window in Atlanta. Deeply disturbed by the incident, Du Bois began to pen his landmark book, *The Souls of Black Folk* (1903), in which he criticized Booker T. Washington's accommodationist and educational policies. Three years later, the eruption of the horrific

Atlanta race riot would convince Du Bois that he could not confine himself to scholarly research, but must find some way to protest the worsening conditions of Black life in America.

365 • The Boston Riot

Most white Americans had no inkling of the growing dissatisfaction with Booker T. Washington in the ranks of America's Black intellectual class until a near riot broke out at a Washington address to a National Negro Business League meeting held at an African Methodist Episcopal (AME) Zion church in Boston in the summer of 1903. Boston was the intellectual stronghold of William Monroe Trotter (1872–1934), Washington's most outspoken African American critic. A dapper graduate of Harvard College, Trotter had a fiery disposition and a tremendous animosity toward Washington, devoting columns of his newspaper, the *Guardian,* to anti-Washington news and gossip. Washington had largely ignored Trotter and his group until the July 30 address, when William H. Lewis, another Harvard graduate and a Bookerite, tried to introduce Washington to the crowd of two thousand at the Columbus Avenue church. The audience erupted into commotion, catcalls, and whistles as Washington tried to take the podium. Police advanced into the crowd and were attacked by women with hatpins and pocketbooks, while Trotter stood up and read a series of questions for Washington that could not be heard over the din of the crowd. Trotter was arrested and convicted for conspiracy to disturb the peace. He was sentenced to thirty days in jail. But Washington was also hurt by the event. His wealthy white supporters and Black supporters were stunned by the reaction and looked for explanations. Washington was so embarrassed by the media coverage of the incident that he felt obliged to write to President Theodore Roosevelt to apologize for any concern the incident caused him. Afterward, it would be difficult for Washington to claim he alone spoke for the African American.

366 • The Niagara Movement

On July 10, 1905, thirty young African American professionals gathered at the Erie Beach Hotel in Ontario, Canada (racial discrimination prevented them from obtaining lodgings on the American side of Niagara Falls), to form the Niagara Movement. They were teachers, lawyers, doctors, ministers, and businessmen—whom W. E. B. Du Bois had earlier described as the race's "talented tenth"—who wanted to use their talents to fight for Black rights. Led by William Monroe Trotter and Du Bois, who was chosen the general secretary, the Niagara Movement opposed Booker T. Washington and his control of Black institutions but declined to favor any particular policy. Nevertheless, the group elected an executive committee and drafted a "Declaration of Principles" that celebrated the African American's right to protest. "We refuse to allow the impression to remain that the Negro-American assents to inferiority, is submissive under oppression and apologetic before insults. Through helplessness we may submit, but the voice of protest of ten million Americans must never cease to assail the ears of their fellows, so long as America is unjust." Although it met several more times and reached out to other groups, such as the National Association of Colored Women's Clubs, the Niagara Movement failed to gain much support, because of Washington's opposition and because membership was limited to the tiny "talented tenth." But the Niagara Movement prepared the way for the National Association for the Advancement of Colored People by advocating protest against terrorism and litigation against Jim Crow laws.

367 • The National Association for the Advancement of Colored People (NAACP)

In 1908 a riot broke out in Springfield, Illinois, after an African American shot and killed a white police officer. A mob broke into the jail where the accused was awaiting trial, killed him, hanged him from a telephone pole, and shot the body hundreds of times. After the lynching, the mob destroyed the Black section of the city. William English Walling, a well-known writer, reported from the scene of the Springfield riot in an article entitled "Race War in the North." Walling observed:

Either the spirit of the abolitionists, of Lincoln and Lovejoy, must be revived and we must come to treat the Negro on a plane of absolute political and social equality or [Senators J. K.] Vardaman and [Bill] Tillman will soon have transferred the Race War to the North. . . . Yet who realizes the seriousness of the situation and what large and powerful body of citizens is ready to come to their aid?

Mary White Ovington, one of the founders of the NAACP. Prints and Photographs Division, Library of Congress, Visual Materials from the NAACP Records

Walling answered his own question by issuing a call in 1909 for a select number of socialists, African American protest leaders, and concerned citizens to come together for the purpose of founding a large body to oppose such atrocities. Thus the National Association for the Advancement of Colored People (NAACP), an interracial organization to fight for equal rights for African Americans, was created. In addition to Walling, some of the more prominent founding members were Joel Spingarn, Mary White Ovington, and Dr. W. E. B. Du Bois.

368 • The *Crisis*

The *Crisis* was the official journal of the NAACP. Edited by W. E. B. Du Bois, it was to stand for "the highest ideals of American democracy, and for reasonable but earnest and persistent attempts to gain these rights and realize these ideals." Within several years of its first publication in November 1910, its circulation surpassed 100,000. Its features included a spotlight on African American "Men of the Month," a summary of news on domestic and international race issues, a recap of local and national NAACP activities, and substantial attention to African American literature.

369 • A Silent Antilynching Parade

On July 28, 1917, thousands of African Americans silently marched through New York City to Madison Square to protest lynching and the East St. Louis race riots. Without uttering a sound, the marchers carried antilynching banners and distributed leaflets that proclaimed: "We march because we want to make impossible a repetition of Waco, Memphis and East St. Louis, by rousing the conscience of the country and to bring the murderers of our brothers, sisters and innocent children to justice."

370 • NAACP Legal Defense Activities

From 1910 on, the NAACP devoted much of its activities to seeking legal remedies to the problems of de jure segregation and Black disfranchisement in America. In 1915 the NAACP successfully litigated *Guinn v. United States,* in which the Supreme Court declared the grandfather clauses in Maryland and Oklahoma restrictive to the Fifteenth Amendment and therefore null and void. Two years later the NAACP successfully obtained a Louisville ordinance declaring residential segregation unconstitutional. Then, in 1923, in *Moore v. Dempsey,* the NAACP successfully argued for a new trial of an African American accused of murder. The Supreme Court agreed with the NAACP that the accused had not received a fair trial because Blacks were excluded from the jury.

371 • UNIA Meeting in Madison Square Garden

In 1920 Marcus Garvey's militant organization, the Universal Negro Improvement Association, which he had founded in Jamaica in 1914 and launched in Harlem in 1917, held its first annual mass convention at Madison Square Garden. Thousands of African Americans attended, dozens of street marches and parades were held, and many Blacks joined an organization that advocated "Africa for the Africans," pride in the Black race, independent economic development, and repatriation back to Africa. Garvey's organization grew into the largest mass movement of African Americans prior to the Civil Rights Movement of the 1950s–1960s, but Garvey was handicapped by poor business practices in launching his boldest enterprise, the Black Star Line. The failures of that undertaking, coupled with increasingly hostile attacks by African American leaders and espionage by J. Edgar Hoover, resulted in Garvey's downfall. In

1925 Garvey was convicted of mail fraud and jailed in the Atlanta Penitentiary until 1927, when President Calvin Coolidge commuted his sentence and deported him from the United States as an undesirable alien.

372 • The Right to Self-Defense

In September 1925 hundreds of whites surrounded the Detroit home of Dr. Ossian Sweet, a Black physician. Sweet had, in the eyes of the crowd, overstepped his bounds by moving into the formerly all-white neighborhood. Dr. Sweet, his wife, two brothers, and seven friends decided to stay and defend their home. After the house was attacked with rocks and firebombs, the occupants, armed with guns, opened fire on the crowd. A white man in the crowd was killed, and all the occupants of the home, except Mrs. Sweet, were arrested. A defense team led by Clarence Darrow represented the Sweets and their friends, and the first trial ended in a hung jury. At the second trial, Henry Sweet, Dr. Sweet's brother, was tried first, separately. The all-white jury's verdict of not guilty set a precedent allowing self-defense by African Americans.

373 • Brotherhood of Sleeping Car Porters

In 1925 A. Philip Randolph founded the Brotherhood of Sleeping Car Porters, the first railway union to be open to Black membership. In addition to fighting for the rights of Black Pullman porters, Randolph used the organization to demand better treatment of Blacks within the American Federation of Labor and to agitate for social justice and civil rights for all African Americans. Moreover, Randolph utilized the porters as "civil rights missionaries," because they traveled from city to city and were able to spread and gather information about African American affairs nationwide.

374 • Antilynching Bill

In the early 1920s the NAACP launched a campaign to enact an antilynching law. In 1921 Representative C. C. Dyer of Missouri introduced an antilynching bill that passed the House by a vote of 230–119. Passage in the Senate, however, was much more difficult to attain. The NAACP sent the Senate a letter urging passage that was signed by twenty-four governors, thirty-nine mayors, twenty college presidents, and other important officials. Full-page ads were also placed in leading newspapers such as the *New York Times* and the *Atlanta Constitution.* Southern senators, however, successfully filibustered the bill and it never came to a vote.

The NAACP flew this flag outside its offices in New York every time a lynching took place in the South. Prints and Photographs Division, Library of Congress, Visual Materials from the NAACP Records

375 • Rejection of Judge Parker

Politically blacks exercised increasing influence, especially through the NAACP. President

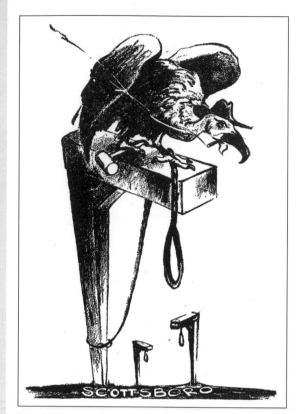

"The Higher Court," cartoon suggesting that the Supreme Court decision overturning the first Scottsboro conviction was part of the same system of injustice as existed in Alabama. Prints and Photographs Division, Library of Congress, Visual Materials from the NAACP Records

Herbert Hoover, for example, nominated Judge John H. Parker to a seat on the Supreme Court. The NAACP requested the withdrawal of Parker's nomination after it became evident that Parker had opposed black suffrage. When Hoover declined, the NAACP conducted mass meetings and write-in campaigns. Pressured, the Senate refused to confirm Parker. A *Christian Science Monitor* article described it as "the first national demonstration of the Negro's power since Reconstruction days."

376 • Scottsboro Case

In 1931 nine young Black men were arrested in Scottsboro, Alabama, on a charge of raping two young white women as they all rode together on a freight train through Alabama. The entire case rested on the testimony of the two women, one of whom was a prostitute, the other a semiliterate cotton mill worker who later recanted her story. Narrowly avoiding being lynched, the nine young men, some of whom were suffering from advanced syphilis, were convicted. But publicity generated by the U.S. Communist Party brought national attention to the case and a new trial. Although the nine were again convicted, several of the men did not serve their full sentence, in part because of the widespread belief in their innocence. The case not only gained favorable opinion for the Communist Party but also embarrassed the NAACP, which, under Walter White, lost the right to represent the "Scottsboro Boys" to the C.P. That embarrassment galvanized White, the executive secretary of the NAACP, to take action and revitalize the NAACP's legal challenge to racism and segregation.

377 • NAACP's Legal Strategy in the 1930s

In 1935 Walter White convinced Howard University Law School Vice-Dean Charles Houston to head up a new legal challenge to educational segregation. Houston's strategy was to test the constitutionality of segregated schooling by showing it was not equal. On tours throughout the South, Houston had previously documented with photographs the inequalities of segregated elementary and high school education. But Houston decided to focus on graduate and professional schools, for tactical reasons. Relatively few states had constructed separate facilities at the graduate level for Blacks, so that it would be easy to show unequal access. Early in the century, few Blacks demanded education beyond the college level; but by the 1920s the number of Blacks entering graduate and law schools had risen. Houston decided to focus on law schools because he believed judges would easily see that makeshift separate law schools for Blacks were not equal in training or reputation to prestigious white law schools. His first victory came in the *Murray* case, where Donald Gaines Murray had been denied admission to the University of Maryland law school. With the assistance of Thurgood Marshall, Houston's former student and a man who himself had been rejected by the University of Maryland law school, Houston argued before the Baltimore city court that Murray ought to be admitted to the law school. Houston and Marshall were successful and the municipal court ordered the University of Maryland to admit Murray. By 1939, the legal work of challenging segregation had grown so much that White created a separate organization, the NAACP Legal Defense and Educational Fund, Inc., with Thurgood Marshall at the helm, to handle the work.

378 • "Buying Power" Movement

During the early 1930s African Americans began using their economic and political power. The "Buying Power" movement, begun in Chicago, used picketing and boycotts to force white employers, especially those with a large Black clientele, to employ Blacks in their businesses. In New York City Adam Clayton Powell, Jr., a future congressman, led a four-year effort that added ten thousand Black workers to the telephone company, the light company, the bus company, dime stores, department stores, and the 1939 World's Fair. Organizations employing similar tactics sprang up in other cities around the country.

379 • The New Negro Alliance

In Washington, D.C., the New Negro Alliance instituted a "don't buy where you can't work" campaign against several local chain stores. In a typical case, the Alliance surveyed a three-block area surrounding an A&P store that refused to hire blacks, and found only five white households. More than ten thousand blacks lived within that area and together they spent an average of $4,700 per month at the A&P, yet company policy prohibited black employees. Alliance leaders tried to negotiate with the A&P management, but after several unproductive meetings, they called on area residents to boycott and picket the store. Over 90 percent of the neighborhood complied, and as economic losses mounted, the A&P management capitulated. Eighteen black clerks were hired by A&P, and several other chains adopted similar policies in an effort to forestall any Alliance action against them.

380 • Southern Tenant Farmers' Union

Organizing against racism and economic subjugation was not limited to Black professionals in northern cities. Following the passage of the Agricultural Adjustment Act of Franklin Delano Roosevelt's New Deal administration, Black and white sharecroppers and farm laborers in Arkansas joined together in 1934 to form the Southern Tenant Farmers' Union (STFU). The organization was designed to fight the eviction of tenants and sharecroppers from land they had worked for years. Under the Agricultural Adjustment Administration (AAA), farmers were paid money not to bring land under cultivation in order to reduce the supply of farm products and drive up prices. But in practice, the AAA policy was disastrous for tenants and sharecroppers, since the AAA simply paid landowners, with the assumption that they would pass on payments to tenants, which did not happen. The STFU also sought to obtain a fairer share of government parity payments for tenants. By 1935 over ten thousand tenants had joined the union; but the union had also come under attack from planters and local southern authorities who raided meetings, arrested members, and beat and shot some who refused to stop attending meetings. In 1936 the STFU organized a strike of cotton pickers in five states that brought national attention to the union. In this effort, African American tenant organizers were most effective in getting tenants to resist inducements to return to the fields. Unfortunately for the union, Roosevelt and those in the AAA administration refused to support the efforts of the STFU, being more concerned with keeping the goodwill of southern politicians to support New Deal legislation. Without that support, the STFU collapsed under the pressure from landowners and state authorities.

381 • Harlem Race Riot of 1935

On March 19, 1935, shoppers in a Kress dime store in Harlem saw a young Black boy grabbed by store workers and taken into a basement, where they believed he was violently beaten. Soon after, an ambulance pulled up in the alley behind the store, and the rumor spread that the boy had been killed. This set off angry protests fueled by six years of the Depression and unemployment in Harlem, neglect of its social services by New York government, and the bitter segregation that denied Blacks, even in Harlem, the ability to work in stores like Kress. When a group of radicals protesting conditions in Harlem assembled outside the store, a riot broke out, even though the boy, Lino Rivera, had been released. Roving bands of people began to break store windows, loot goods, and challenge police and store owners in two days of rioting. It was to be America's first modern race riot.

Harlem radicals claimed that agitation against poor housing, poor city services, high unemployment, high rent eviction rates, and endemic racism even in Harlem had laid the groundwork for the riot.

382 • First March on Washington

The first March on Washington was proposed in 1941 by A. Philip Randolph in response to discrimination in war industries employment and segregation of the armed forces. With the beginning of World War II in Europe in 1939, the U.S. economy pulled out of the Great Depression as the United States began to supply the Allies, principally France, Great Britain, and the Soviet Union, with materials to fight the Axis powers. But as was so often the case in America, Blacks were the last hired in the industrial boom. Randolph, who was head of the Pullman porters' union, gathered together several civil rights leaders and proposed a March on Washington by 100,000 African Americans to focus national attention on the treatment of African Americans in the United States. Randolph had several points he wanted addressed and would not back down, even though President Franklin D. Roosevelt pleaded that a March on Washington would hurt the U.S. war mobilization. Finally, in order to get Randolph to call off the march, FDR issued Executive Order 8802, which banned discrimination in hiring by industries involved in the war effort and established the Federal Employment Practices Commission (FEPC) to hear complaints. Although some critics believed that Randolph sold out for too little and that the FEPC, which could only hear complaints and not impose fines, was a paper institution, establishing the principle of equal employment and the commission was a step forward. Even though industries could not be punished for discrimination, it was nevertheless

A. Philip Randolph. Photograph by Gordon Parks for Office of War Information, Washington, D.C., November 1942. Prints and Photographs Division, Library of Congress

embarrassing for companies to have to appear before the commission, a sign of their lack of patriotism.

383 • Formation of CORE

In April 1942 the Fellowship of Reconciliation (FOR) authorized James Farmer to start an organization to practice Ghandian nonviolent resistance to segregation in the Chicago area. Bob Chino, another of the group's founding activists, argued it should be called the Committee of Racial Equality, or CORE, "because it will be the center of things, the heart of the action." CORE moved away from the pacifist practices of FOR to advocate direct defiance of segregation, and succeeded in desegregating several eating and recreational establishments in Chicago. CORE may have conducted the first successful sit-in when twenty-eight members of the group took seats in booths and at the counter of the Jack Spratt restaurant, which eventually dropped its discriminatory policy of not serving

African Americans. Other such successes followed, but CORE had difficulty raising money in the late 1940s and early 1950s until the Montgomery Bus Boycott jump-started the direct-action movement. CORE would again seize center stage in the civil rights struggle by launching the Freedom Rides in 1961.

Quotations

384 • Letter Warning Those Assisting Voter Registration

In 1920 a prominent white Florida lawyer urged African Americans to register to vote. He subsequently received the following message from the Ku Klux Klan:

We have been informed that you have been telling Negroes to register, explaining to them how to become citizens and how to assert their rights.

If you know the history of reconstruction days following the Civil War, you know how the "scalawags" of the North and the Black republicans of the South did much as you are doing to instill into the Negro the idea of social equality. You will remember that these things forced the loyal citizens of the South to form clans of determined men to maintain white supremacy and to safeguard our women and children.

And now you know that history repeats itself and that he who resorts to your kind of game is handling edged tools. We shall always enjoy white supremacy in this country and he who interferes must face the consequences.

Grand Master Florida Ku Klucks
Copy, Local Ku Klucks, Watch this man.

385 • Jim Crow Railroad Travel

The disparity between accommodations on the railroad for white and Black travelers repudiated the myth that separate did not mean unequal. In *A Black Man's Appeal to His White Brothers* Dr. R. S. Lovingwood, the president of Samuel Houston College in Austin, Texas, described the conditions facing an African American on the railroad during the Jim Crow era:

I went to a station to purchase my ticket. I was there thirty minutes before the ticket office was opened. When the ticket office opened I at once appeared before the window. While the agent served the white people at the other side I remained there beating the window until the train pulled out. I was compelled to jump on the train without my ticket and wire back to have my trunk expressed to me. Considering the temper of the people, the separate-coach law may be the wisest plan for conditions in the South, but the statement of "equal accommodations" is all bosh and twaddle. I pay the same money, but I cannot have a chair car, or lavatory, and rarely a through car. I must crawl out all through the night in all kinds of weather, and catch another "Jim Crow" coach. This is not a request to ride with white people. It is a request for justices, for "equal accommodations" for the same money. . . .

I rode through a small town in Southern Illinois. When the train stopped I went to the car steps to take a view of the country. This is what greeted me: "Look here, darkey, don't get off at this station." I put my head out of the window at a certain small village in Texas, whose reputation was well known to me. This greeted me: "Take your head back, nigger, or we will knock it off."

386 • March on Washington Movement

. . . our nearer goals include the abolition of discrimination, segregation, and jim-crow in the Government, the Army, Navy, Air Corps, U.S. Marines, Coast Guard, Women's Auxiliary Army Corps and the Waves, and defense industries; the elimination of discriminations in hotels, restaurants, on public transportation conveyances, in educational, recreational, cultural, and amusement and entertainment places such as theaters, beaches and so forth.

We want the full works of citizenship with no reservations. We will accept nothing less. . . . As to the composition of our movement. Our policy is that it be all-Negro, and pro-Negro but not anti-white, or anti-Semitic or anti-labor, or anti-Catholic. The reason for this policy is that all oppressed people must assume the responsibility and take the initiative to free themselves. Jews must wage their battle to abolish anti-semitism. Catholics must wage their battle to abolish anti-catholicism. Their workers must wage their battle to advance and protect their interests and rights.

And while the March on Washington Movement may find it advisable to form a citizens committee of friendly white citizens to give moral support to a fight against the poll tax or white primaries, it does not imply that these white citizens or citizens of any racial group should be taken into the March on Washington Movement as members. The essential value of an all-Negro movement such as the March on Washington is that it helps to create faith by Negroes in Negroes. It develops a sense of self-reliance with Negroes depending on Negroes in vital matters. It helps to break down the slave psychology and inferiority-complex in Negroes which comes and is nourished with Negroes relying on white people for direction and support. This inevitably happens in mixed organizations that are supposed to be in the interest of the Negro.

—A. Philip Randolph, keynote address to the Policy Conference on the March on Washington Movement, Detroit, September 26, 1942

387 • Residential Discrimination

The first edition of the *Crisis* in November 1910 applauded the citizens of Baltimore who attempted to break through the residential segregation separating the white and Black communities.

An inevitable step in anti-Negro prejudice is being taken in Baltimore, and threatened elsewhere. The colored folk of that city long ago became dissatisfied with a particularly bad system of alley homes. They saved their money and purchased nearly the whole length of Druid Hill avenue—one of the best colored streets in the world. Then they began to expand into parallel streets, one of which was McCulloh. They had been told that "money talks," and that the surest road to respect in America was financial success. The result was inevitable. The white people of McCulloh street rose in indignation and are importuning the City Council to pass an ordinance prohibiting colored people from "invading" white residential districts, and vice versa.

388 • Violent Attacks on Black Homes in Integrated Neighborhoods

Citizens from across the country appealed to the NAACP to send them legal assistance. The NAACP's second annual report quoted a Kansas City resident's letter that requested aid from the organization's legal department:

We desire to place before the legal department of the NAACP, the case of a group of Negroes of Kansas City, Missouri, who have suffered repeated attempts to destroy their property by an organization of white men who have demanded that they leave the neighborhood. There are nine Negro families in one block and twelve in the next who have purchased or are in process of buying their homes, ranging in price from $1,500 to $4,000. In the block in which I live five explosions of dynamite have occurred in the past year,

causing considerable damage to our homes and much mental uneasiness on the part of our families. The last of these, which happened Saturday, November 11, was by far the most destructive of them all, completely wrecking the home of Mr. Hezekiah Walden. . . .

We have again and again appealed to the mayor and the chief of police to give us protection from these crimes, but the detectives have been of no help either in running the perpetrators to earth or in checking further threats and outrages. We feel that we have a clear case against the city, inasmuch as we have faithfully discharged our duties as citizens, and we are about to retain eminent legal counsel to defend our cause. In addition to this, we beg that we may have the assistance of some member of the legal department of the NAACP who will join us in vigorously prosecuting this case.

People and Politics

389 • John M. Langston (1829–97)

The election of John Mercer Langston to the House of Representatives in 1890 shows that African American political power did not evaporate completely with the end of Reconstruction in 1877. The son of a white planter and a mixed-raced mother, Langston had attended Oberlin College, studied law with a judge, and been admitted to the Ohio bar in 1854. After the Civil War, he organized the Law Department at Howard University before serving as its first dean and then as president from 1873 to 1875. Then, after a brief stint as resident minister and consul general to Haiti and chargé d'affaires to the Dominican Republic, he won the 1888 election to the House of Representatives, but took his seat on September 23, 1890, only after the House had determined that his Democratic rival

John M. Langston. Photograph by Matthew Brady. Prints and Photographs Division, Library of Congress

had cheated. He was a member of the House for less than six months, and his stint showed some of the difficulties of being an African American representative after Reconstruction. When Langston's term ended on March 3, 1891, he failed to get reelected.

390 • Booker T. Washington Dines at the White House

At the turn of the century, African Americans began to believe the federal government might renew its interest in their plight, especially after Teddy Roosevelt broke with segregationist decorum and invited Booker T. Washington to dinner at the White House on October 16, 1901. The meal infuriated much of the white South, but instilled pride and hope in the African American community. Roosevelt's image among

Blacks was further bolstered by his support of William Crum as the collector of port in Charleston, South Carolina. Crum's appointment was vehemently opposed by white South Carolinians, but Roosevelt declared that unless the opponents of the appointment could come up with any reason for opposition other than color, then the appointment would stand. In addition, Roosevelt refused to accept the resignation of Minnie Cox, the postmistress in Indianola, Mississippi. Ms. Cox had been threatened with bodily harm if she did not relinquish her position, but Roosevelt refused to let the post office accept her resignation, and the office was subsequently closed for a period when she continued to decline to return.

391 • The Brownsville Riot

The burgeoning hope African Americans may have felt under Teddy Roosevelt waned with his handling of the Brownsville Riot. On the night of August 13, 1906, a bartender and police officer were wounded in Brownsville, Texas. The 25th Infantry (Colored) was stationed nearby at Fort Brown. Although an immediate roll call at the camp proved everyone accounted for, the Brownsville community suspected a Black military perpetrator. As the Black troops entered the town later that night, fighting broke out. One citizen was killed and another wounded. In response to a preliminary report that blamed the African American soldiers for the disturbances, President Roosevelt dismissed the entire battalion without honor and disqualified every member from civil or military service. In 1970 historian John Weaver published *The Brownsville Raid,* which proved that no Black soldier was responsible for the incident. In 1972, after further review, the dishonorable discharge was finally rescinded.

392 • Woodrow Wilson Preelection Letter to Bishop Walters

Woodrow Wilson wrote to Bishop Alexander Walters, regretting an invitation to address a mass meeting at Carnegie Hall sponsored by the National Colored Democratic League:

It is a matter of genuine disappointment to me that I shall not be able to be present at the meeting on Saturday night. . . . It would afford me pleasure to be present, because there are certain things I want to say, I hope that it seems superfluous to those who know me, but to those who do not know me perhaps it is not unnecessary for me to assure my colored fellow-citizens of my earnest wish to see justice done them in every matter, and not mere grudging justice, but justice executed with liberality and cordial good feeling. Every guarantee of our law, every principle in our constitution, commands this, and our sympathies also make it easy. The colored people of the United States have made extraordinary progress toward self-support and usefulness, and ought to be encouraged in every possible and proper way. My sympathy with them is of long standing, and I want to assure them through you that should I become President of the United States they may count on me for absolute fair dealing and for everything by which I could assist in advancing the interests of their race in the United States.

393 • Wilson Segregates Federal Departments

As with Theodore Roosevelt, African Americans' hopes dimmed with the actions of the newly elected president. Woodrow Wilson's first transgression was the segregation of federal government departments in Washington, D.C. Wilson purported his actions were in the best interests of African Americans because it would allow them to work in peace without fear of racial discrimination. In a letter to Wilson, August 15, 1913, the NAACP disputed this logic:

The National Association for the Advancement of Colored People, through its Board of Directors, respectfully protests the policy of your Administration in segregating the colored employees in the Departments at Washington. It realizes that this new and radical departure has been recommended, and is now being defended, on the ground that by giving certain bureaus or sections wholly to colored employees they are thereby rendered safer in possession of their offices and are less likely to be ousted or discriminated against. We believe this reasoning to be fallacious. It is based on a failure to appreciate the deeper significance of the new policy; to understand how far reaching the effects of such a drawing of caste lines by the Federal Government may be, and how humiliating it is to the men thus stigmatized.

394 • Wilson Meets with Trotter

Woodrow Wilson's second affront to the African American community was his reaction to William Monroe Trotter, editor of the *Boston Guardian*. Trotter and other members of a protest committee from the National Independence Equal Rights League met with Wilson in November 1914. Trotter, as chairman of the committee, served as spokesman. According to the *Chicago Defender*:

In the fervor of his [Trotter's] plea for equal rights for his people he forgot the servile manner and speech once characteristic of the Afro-American and he talked to the president as man to man, addressing the head of the government as any American citizen should, especially when discussing a serious matter. But the president did not like Mr. Trotter's attitude and said that if the committee came to him again it would have to get a new chairman. The president added that he had not been addressed in such a manner since he entered the White House.

Afterward, the President confided to a colleague that he had lost his temper and that Trotter had spoken intelligently and manly.

395 • *The Birth of a Nation*

Perhaps the most striking example of Woodrow Wilson's insensitivity toward racial concerns was the screening of the film *Birth of a Nation* at the White House. Based on the best-selling novel by Thomas Dixon, Jr., *The Clansman,* the film extolled the virtues of the Ku Klux Klan. Using stereotypical portrayals of lusty Black men ravaging defenseless white women, the film exploited the prejudices of the time. After a private screening at the White House, Wilson is alleged to have said: "It is like

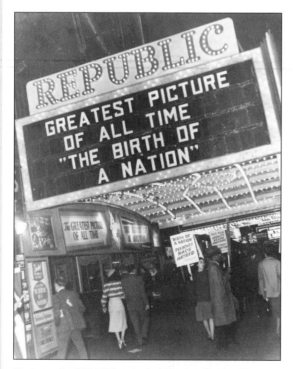

Photograph of NAACP protest at theater showing *The Birth of a Nation*. Prints and Photographs Division, Library of Congress

writing history with lightning and my only regret is that it is all so terribly true."

396 • **Charlotta Spears Bass (1880–1969)**

Charlotta Bass was a bold African American newspaper editor and civil rights activist of the first decade of this century, whose arguments for civil rights were utilized by later spokespersons of the 1950s and 1960s movement. She was a journalist who in 1912 became editor of the *Eagle* (renamed *California Eagle*), the oldest West Coast newspaper for Blacks. Under her guidance (and that of her husband, John Bass), the paper directed its focus to social and political issues important to the Black community. Her motto was "win or lose, we win by raising the issues." She wrote against policies such as harsh sentencing of Black criminals, job discrimination, and the ever-present intimidation and mistreatment of blacks. She even faced down threats from the Ku Klux Klan, which was very strong in California in the 1940s and 1950s. After joining the Progressive Party in the 1940s—"the only party in which there is any hope for civil rights"—she became, in 1952, the first Black woman to run for the second highest political office in the nation when she was nominated as the Progressive Party's vice presidential candidate.

397 • **Oscar DePriest Elected to Congress**

In 1928 Oscar DePriest became the first African American elected to the House of Representatives in the twentieth century. Significantly he was not elected from the South, but from Illinois's 3rd Congressional District, making him the first African American elected to the House from the North. His election symbolized a Black political shift that would continue through the first half of the twentieth century as more African Americans migrated out of the South, which denied them a right to vote, into the urban North, where they could vote. Eventually the growth of Black voting power in the North would force a shift in the racial agenda of the Democratic Party. DePriest was only a forerunner of that shift, because he was a Republican at a time when almost all African Americans voted the Republican Party, "the party of Lincoln."

DePriest used his position to fight for African Americans. His most notable success was passage of the amendment to eliminate racial discrimination in the Civilian Conservation Corps. He defied southern racism by speaking in the South, despite threats on his life, and challenged Senator James Heflin of Alabama by eating in the Senate restaurant. He tried but failed to pass antilynching legislation. DePriest's opposition to Roosevelt's public assistance programs spelled his end, and he was defeated by Arthur W. Mitchell, a Democrat, in 1934.

398 • William Edward Burghardt Du Bois (1868–1963)

William Edward Burghardt Du Bois was the leading African American intellectual and fighter for civil rights in the Jim Crow period. Born in Great Barrington, Massachusetts, educated at Harvard, Fisk, and the University of Berlin, Du Bois made groundbreaking contributions in numerous fields, from sociology to history to fiction to autobiography. While teaching at Atlanta University, he published his most moving work, the *Souls of Black Folk,* in 1903, and then left the university to found, first, the Niagara Movement and then the National Association for the Advancement of Colored People, for which he served as director of research and editor of the *Crisis.* He broke with the NAACP

W. E. B. Du Bois. Prints and Photographs Division, Library of Congress

in 1934 and returned to teaching at Atlanta University, continuing to publish widely in history and political theory. After World War II he committed himself to the cause of world peace, but became a target of government harassment during the cold war for his alleged connections to communists. In 1961, after the State Department was forced to return his passport, which had been seized unconstitutionally, he left the United States and settled in the West African nation of Ghana, where he resided until his death in 1963.

399 • Mary Church Terrell (1863–1954)

In 1884 Mary Church Terrell and two others became the first Black women to receive a B.A. from Oberlin College. Although one of the best educated of the growing African American middle class, she was early acquainted with racism when Matthew Arnold observed her classroom at Oberlin. When Terrell recited several verses in Greek as requested by her teacher, Arnold said he was astounded because he had heard that African Americans could not recite Greek because of the physiological shape of their tongues! Remembering this incident in her autobiography, *A Colored Woman in a White World* (1940), as an example of the ignorance fostered by racism even among the so-called educated, she dedicated herself to uplifting her own race and educating white sensibilities. Moving to Washington, D.C., to teach school, she became a leader in Washington Black society following her marriage to the prominent judge Robert Terrell. But Mary Church was not one to allow her "wifely" duties to deter her from serving the cause of freedom. In 1895 she founded the National Association of Colored Women, which promoted respect and advancement of African American women. A charter member of the NAACP, Mrs. Terrell was also very active in local issues, becoming the first woman to serve on the District of Columbia Board of Education. Mary Church Terrell became a symbol of the cultural and political leadership exercised by African American women in the twentieth century.

400 • Walter Francis White (1893–1955)

Walter Francis White joined the staff of the National Association for the Advancement of Colored People in 1918, and because of the light color of his skin, was able to make a unique contribution to the fight against racism. White posed as a white journalist and traveled through the South to collect information on discrimination, segregation, and most important, lynchings without anyone suspecting that he was African American or a member of the NAACP. His reports helped the association pressure Congress to pass an antilynching law. In 1929

Walter White became acting secretary and then secretary of the NAACP and steered that organization through its difficult years in the 1930s, which included a losing struggle with the Communist Party for control of the Scottsboro Boys case, a failed attempt to win congressional passage of antilynching legislation, and an increasingly successful legal assault on segregation. He was also responsible, according to W. E. B. Du Bois, for forcing Du Bois to resign from the organization in 1934. During the cold war, when other African American leaders were suspected of communist sympathies, White was sufficiently safe to be appointed by President Harry Truman to the U.S. delegation to the United Nations. Forced to accept a ceremonial post of executive secretary of the NAACP in 1950, his death came in the year following the organization's greatest triumph, the Supreme Court decision in *Brown v. Board of Education.*

401 • Asa Philip Randolph (1889–1979)

Asa Philip Randolph was one of the most important but underappreciated African American leaders who made his mark in an area that is often ignored: African American labor. Randolph began to organize workers while a student in college, but became even more energetic in the cause of Black unionization during World War I. He believed that African Americans could not blindly give their loyalty to the United States war effort, but must take advantage of the situation to improve their working status. Toward that end, he founded the *Messenger* to publicize his unionization movement, as well as to provide a critique of organizations like the NAACP, who he believed were too conservative. As founder and head of the Brotherhood of Sleeping Car Porters, he was successful in winning recognition for the union from the Pullman

Company in 1925. He was one of the founders of the National Negro Congress in the 1930s, which sought to galvanize Black thinking on the left, and in 1941 he organized the first March on Washington to protest discrimination. That march was eventually called off when President Franklin Delano Roosevelt capitulated to Randolph's demands and issued Executive Order 8802. In 1963 Randolph was a leader in organizing the second proposed March on Washington, which actually took place.

402 • Henrietta Vinton Davis (1860–1941)

Although men are usually mentioned most prominently in connection with the Garvey movement, one of the most important organizers of the Universal Negro Improvement Association (UNIA) was a woman, Henrietta Davis. A promising actress during the 1880s and a popular public speaker (who was well known in New York City for her speaking recitals), she gave up her performing career to join Garvey in spreading his philosophy of Black nationalism and pride in African heritage. Following Garvey cost Davis her career and many of her friendships. Garvey's dislike of light-skinned African Americans and his calls for Black racial purity and superiority, ideas repugnant to much of the Black elite of the 1920s, made it difficult for her to keep her middle-class, professional friendships. She died in obscurity.

403 • Mary McCleod Bethune (1875–1955)

Mary McCleod Bethune was president of the National Council of Negro Women and a member of President Franklin Delano Roosevelt's "Black Cabinet" of advisers on racial matters after his election to the presidency in 1932. She was also the founder and president of Bethune-

Cookman College, director of the Negro Affairs Division of the National Youth Administration, and one of the American observers who attended the 1945 conference in San Francisco to establish the United Nations.

404 • Paul Robeson (1898–1976)

Paul Robeson graduated from Rutgers University, where he was elected to Phi Beta Kappa and was twice named to Walter Camp's all-white All-American football team. Robeson went on to Columbia University, where he earned a degree in law, but although he worked in a law firm briefly in New York City, his heart was in acting. After appearing in several amateur stage productions, he decided to make the theater his career. After successful appearances in Eugene O'Neill's *The Emperor Jones* and *All God's Chillun Got Wings,* Robeson began to sing on the concert stage, excelling particularly in the singing of African American spirituals. By the mid-1930s his motion picture film credits, his performance of the title role of *Othello* in London, and his acclaimed singing had made Robeson an international star. But because Robeson would not repudiate his ties to the left as others did during the blacklisting of the 1940s and 1950s, his career suffered. He created considerable controversy in 1949 when he stated that African Americans would not fight against the Soviet Union, which as a nation was free of race prejudice. Quickly Robeson was blackballed in the United States, targeted for harassment and investigation, and eventually deprived of his passport (along with W. E. B. Du Bois) by the State Department. His name was removed from the list of All-Americans for the years that he played college football, and the College Football Hall of Fame refused him membership, making him the only All-American not to be included. Still, Robeson never relented in his defense of

Paul Robeson, a world-renowned African American singer, leads Moore Shipyard workers in Oakland, California, in singing "The Star-Spangled Banner." "This is a serious job," he told them, "winning the war against fascists. We have to be together." September 1942. National Archives. Courtesy of A.P./Wide World Photos

his right to speak freely and criticize American racism. He died in Philadelphia in 1976, having seen the success of a new civil rights movement in America.

405 • Adam Clayton Powell, Jr. (1908–72)

The son of the founder of the Abyssinian Baptist Church in Harlem, Adam Clayton Powell, Jr., was a graduate of Cornell University, the pastor of his father's church, and, in 1944, the first representative elected to Congress from Harlem. Powell used his congressional seat, which he held for over twenty-four years, as a bully pulpit for improved civil rights for African Americans. He pressured several presidents and members of Congress to pass substantial civil rights legislation and criticized them for the weak compromise bills that were eventually passed. As a leftward-leaning politician, Powell brought na-

tional attention to the economic conditions of Black and white workers in America. During the 1950s and 1960s he worked closely with civil rights organizations such as the NAACP, the Student Nonviolent Coordinating Committee (SNCC), and CORE, and supported such efforts as the national boycott against five-and-dime stores that refused to serve African Americans at lunch counters in the South. His greatest contribution came after he became, in 1961, chairman of the Committee on Education and Labor in the House of Representatives, where he used his position to promote antipoverty legislation and block the proposals of others who did not support civil rights programs. He also supported legislation for the expansion of educational and artistic opportunities, proposing a National Foundation on the Arts and Humanities in the 89th Congress. But Powell's flair for expensive travel and flamboyant living, often paid for by government funds, led to his expulsion from the Congress. In 1969, after a two-year stint in the Bahamas, he was reelected to Congress by his constituents after the Supreme Court ruled his expulsion unconstitutional. But in 1970 a Harlem newcomer, Charles Rangel, defeated Powell in the Democratic primary by 150 votes and ended the legendary congressman's political career. He died of complications from prostate surgery on April 4, 1972, having been African America's most outspoken congressman.

406 • Ralph J. Bunche (1904–71)

Dr. Ralph J. Bunche was awarded the Nobel Peace Prize in 1950 for his work to establish peace in the Middle East. He received a Ph.D. from Harvard in 1934 and later worked for the U.S. State Department, and still later, the United Nations. After the establishment of a Jewish state in 1948 and the resulting animosity between Jews and Palestinians in the region, Bunche helped design a tentative (and ultimately futile) peace agreement between the two groups in Israel. It was his work in this area that was recognized by the Stockholm committee.

407 • Thurgood Marshall (1908–93)

Thurgood Marshall successfully argued the case that became the Supreme Court's most important twentieth-century decision, *Brown v. Board of Education of Topeka, Kansas,* handed down on May 17, 1954. It was Marshall who decided to switch the Legal Defense Fund's tactics, pioneered under his mentor, Charles Houston, from trying to prove southern schools were unequal to making the case that segregated schooling was inherently unequal, despite the conditions of respective schools. Marshall successfully led the Legal Defense Fund's continued assault on segregation until 1967, when he was chosen by President Lyndon Johnson to be-

Thurgood Marshall, right, leaves Birmingham, Alabama, courthouse with Autherine Lucy, 1956. Courtesy of A.P./Wide World Photos

come the first African American Supreme Court judge. Unlike many others who were appointed to the Supreme Court, Marshall did not abandon his ideological moorings, but continued the campaign for racial justice he had begun before his appointment to the Court. In 1991 he retired from the Supreme Court because of ill health, and he died on January 24, 1993.

Laws, Executive Orders, and Supreme Court Decisions

408 • "Force Bill" Fails

In January 1890 the Republican representative from Massachusetts Henry Cabot Lodge submitted a bill to Congress that would be the last congressional attempt of the Jim Crow period to protect African American voting rights in the South. In what became known as the Force Bill, Lodge sought to obtain federal oversight for federal elections in the South. He brought before Congress extensive evidence of the abuses of Blacks who attempted to vote in such elections in the South. His statistics showed that the percentage of voters in many elections far underrepresented the total population, and in a bill that foreshadowed the Voting Rights Act of 1965, advocated federal intervention. But the bill encountered stiff resistance from southerners who characterized it as another example of the federal government trying to interfere with the state's prerogative to establish its own rules for voting within its boundaries. The bill passed the House, but failed in the Senate on January 26, 1891.

409 • Louisiana's "Act to Promote the Comfort of Passengers"

On July 10, 1890, Louisiana passed a law that "all railway companies carrying passengers in their coaches in this State, shall provide equal but separate accommodations for the white, and colored, races, by providing two or more passenger coaches for each passenger train, or by dividing the passenger coaches by a partition so as to secure separate accommodations." Any passenger who violated this provision could be fined twenty-five dollars and jailed for twenty days. This was the first state law to require segregation of this magnitude, even though other states had barred African Americans from first-class cars on railroads before.

410 • *Plessy v. Ferguson*

Early in the 1890s, Homer Plessy, a man of mixed racial heritage (one-eighth Black, seven-eighths white) refused to ride in the "colored"

section of a Louisiana train and was arrested. Louisiana law stipulated "equal but separate accommodations for the white, and colored, races." Plessy sued to have the law overturned, contending it violated the Thirteenth and Fourteenth Amendments. In 1896 the Supreme Court rejected this argument and upheld Louisiana's contention that separate but equal accommodations did not violate the Fourteenth Amendment's equal protection clause. In doing so, the Court created a distinction between political rights and social discrimination.

The object of the [Fourteenth] amendment was undoubtedly to enforce the absolute equality of the two races before the law, but in the nature of things it could not have been intended to abolish distinctions based upon color, or to enforce social, as distinguished from political equality, or a commingling of the two races upon terms unsatisfactory to either. Laws permitting, and even requiring, racial separation in places where the races are liable to be brought into contact do not necessarily imply the inferiority of either race to the other, and have been generally, if not universally, recognized as within the competency of the state legislatures in the exercise of their police power. . . .

In the aftermath of this decision, state and local governments that had not passed segregation statutes felt free to do so.

411 • *Powell v. Alabama*

In this 1932 decision, the United States Supreme Court ruled that the Scottsboro Boys (nine poor young Black men who had been tried and convicted for rape of two white women migrants) had been denied the counsel of their choice. This was a violation of the Fourteenth Amendment's due process clause. This case was the first time that a conviction for rape of Black men had been overruled by a higher court. It sent the case back to Alabama to be tried again, this time with lawyers representing the Scottsboro Boys supplied by the Communist Party's International Labor Defense. The decision also established that African Americans had a right to adequate legal counsel as part of their constitutional rights as citizens.

412 • *Gaines v. Missouri*

In 1938 the United States Supreme Court ruled that states have to provide equal educational facilities for all citizens *within the state.* Missouri had attempted to send Lloyd Gaines out of state to law school to preserve its "white only" Missouri law school. With this decision, the Supreme Court put the onus of responsibility on states to establish a separate but equal graduate and professional school system, if such a state wished to maintain segregated schooling. The problem for states such as Missouri was that increasing numbers of African Americans were graduating from undergraduate programs at Black colleges and universities.

413 • Executive Order 9808

In the aftermath of World War II, mob violence and lynching of African Americans, in conjunction with the continuing controversy about segregation in American society, led President Harry S. Truman to issue Executive Order 9808 on December 5, 1946, which set up a committee to study the protection of civil rights in the United States. In October 1947 the Committee on Civil Rights published its report, which established the four basic rights a government must protect: the right to safety, the right to citizenship, such as service in the armed service and the exercise of voting, the right to freedom of expression, and the right to equality of opportunity. The report stated that African Ameri-

cans lacked these rights and recommended the President end discrimination and segregation in the armed forces.

414 • Executive Order 9981

In July 1948, four months after his civil rights message to Congress, President Harry Truman issued an executive order to desegregate the armed forces. In doing so, Truman took a bold political risk. Already far behind in the polls to the Republican challenger, Thomas Dewey, Truman needed a dramatic move to revitalize his bid for reelection. Desegregating the armed forces greatly angered the southern segregationists in the Democratic Party, many of whom abandoned the party during the summer convention to vote for Strom Thurmond, a States Rights Party presidential candidate. But Truman's gesture paid off: he edged out Dewey for the victory with majorities in northern urban areas and with support from 69 percent of the African American voters. Truman's victory signaled a shift in the locus of national power in the Democratic Party away from southern Dixiecrats and toward the northern, ethnic, and industrial coalition that Roosevelt's New Deal had built.

415 • *Sweatt v. Painter*

In 1950 the United States Supreme Court ruled that the law school of the University of Texas had to open its doors to a Black applicant despite the fact that the state maintained a separate law school for Blacks. The Supreme Court argued that the benefits of the University of Texas law school—its superior facilities, faculty, and postgraduate contacts—made it a significantly better school for the applicant, and to deny him access to such a school was a denial of his right to due process under the Fourteenth Amendment. This ruling undermined the southern states' strategy creating a dual educational system, since now if inequality could be proved, Black applicants had to be admitted to previously "whites only" schools.

416 • *Brown v. Board of Education of Topeka, Kansas*

Brown v. Board of Education was the landmark decision by the United States Supreme Court that segregated educational facilities were a violation of the Fourteenth Amendment and thus unconstitutional. The Brown case was one of several suits brought by the National Association for the Advancement of Colored People's Legal Defense and Educational Fund on behalf of the parents of Black children in Kansas, South Carolina, Virginia, Delaware, and the District of Columbia, who had watched their children be bused long distances to dilapidated Black schools when quality white schools existed in their neighborhoods. The NAACP had decided to shift from challenging segregation in graduate or professional school education to challenging elementary education. The NAACP had also shifted from showing that segregated educational facilities were unequal to arguing that segregation was degrading to Black children and thus a violation of the Fourteenth Amendment's guarantee of equal protection. The United States Supreme Court agreed and ruled unanimously on May 17, 1954, that segregated schools were "inherently unequal," because to force Black children to attend separate schools purely because of their race "generates a feeling of inferiority as to their status in the community that may affect their hearts and minds in a way very unlikely ever to be undone." After this decision all aspects of segregated life in the South came under pressure, even though the *Brown* decision was limited to elementary school education. This decision overturned the *Plessy v. Ferguson* decision of 1896.

CIVIL RIGHTS MOVEMENT

Protests, Organizations, and Demonstrations

417 • **Racist Reaction to** *Brown v. Board of Education*

Despite the Supreme Court's 1954 ruling in *Brown v. Board of Education,* southern states refused to allow Black children into white schools, and refused to dismantle segregation in public accommodations. Resistance against desegregation, though, was not a view held only by state or local governments. White southerners took it upon themselves to organize opposition to desegregation. One manifestation of that opposition was the White Citizens Councils, made up of citizens who considered themselves more respectable than those engaged in Ku Klux Klan activities. The first meeting of a White Citizens Council occurred in Mississippi on July 11, 1954, at which the group laid plans for resisting the Supreme Court decision in Mississippi. It was this type of active resistance to the Supreme Court decision that made the direct-action Civil Rights Movement necessary. For without the willingness of African Americans and their sympathizers to challenge segregation, the desegregation of the South might not have taken place. Only by creating a crisis in southern segregation could African Americans force the government, especially executive and legislative branches of the federal government, to intervene in the South and force compliance.

418 • **Montgomery Bus Boycott**

The first salvo in the war against segregation in southern society was delivered by a diminutive Black seamstress named Rosa Parks, who, on December 1, 1955, refused to vacate her seat on a Montgomery, Alabama, bus in order for a white passenger to sit. Mrs. Parks was an NAACP activist, who knew that local civil rights leaders were looking for a case to test Montgomery's bus segregation ordinance. But such concerns were secondary in her mind to the indignity of having to get up from her seat just because Montgomery segregation decreed that no African American could occupy a row on a bus with a white person. Contrary to popular misconception, Mrs. Parks was not sitting in the white section: she had taken a seat in the first row of the Black section; but when all the seats in the white section had been filled and a white man was left standing, the bus driver ordered her and two others to get up and let the white man sit. In truth, then, no "Black section" really existed. Upon the bus driver's order, the other two Blacks stood, but Parks refused to get up and was arrested for violating that ordinance. In response, members of the NAACP launched the Montgomery Bus Boycott. After electing the young Rev. Martin Luther King, Jr., as its president, the Montgomery Improvement Association organized a cab service for Black domestic servants and circumvented both the bus company and local officials who sought to break the boycott. The boycott was effective at hurting the bus company financially, but it did not force Montgomery to rescind its bus segregation statute. Again, the Supreme Court came to the rescue: a year after Mrs. Parks refused to give up her seat, the Court ruled that Montgomery's bus segregation ordinance was unconstitutional. Afterward, Black passengers could ride wherever they pleased on Montgomery buses.

419 • SCLC Formed

At a meeting held in Atlanta, Georgia, Janu-

ary 10–11, 1957, the Southern Christian Leadership Conference (SCLC) was founded with Dr. Martin Luther King, Jr., as its president and Ralph Abernathy as its treasurer. First called the Southern Negro Leaders Conference and then the Southern Negro Leadership Conference, the organization was primarily an assembly of ministers who wished to move beyond what the NAACP or the Urban League was doing in the area of civil rights. SCLC focused on building the momentum for direct action in civil rights created by the success of the Montgomery Bus Boycott. Over the next ten years, SCLC would become the most successful of the modern civil rights organizations in carrying out large-scale, well-coordinated, and well-financed demonstrations in a number of southern cities.

420 • Little Rock School Desegregation

In August 1957 nine Black students (later known as the Little Rock Nine) attempted to register at the all-white Central High School in Little Rock, Arkansas. They were denied access to the school by Arkansas Governor Orval Faubus. When the federal government ordered Faubus to allow their registration, he replied he could not guarantee the safety of the students. Local people turned out to taunt and terrorize the students, so much so that eventually their parents would not let them attend the school until the federal government guaranteed their safety. After much delay, President Dwight D. Eisenhower reluctantly ordered federal troops to Little Rock to protect the students and ensure that Faubus would comply with the school integration order.

421 • The Sit-in Movement

The sit-in movement began on February 1, 1960, when four African American students from the North Carolina Central Agricultural

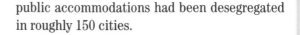
and Technical College sat down at a Woolworth's lunch counter in Greensboro, North Carolina. The aim of the sit-in was to force Woolworth's to serve African Americans at the only lunch counter in the store, where they were not then allowed to sit. Soon after, the idea of the sit-in quickly spread to other cities in five states. Students sat in in Winston-Salem, Durham, Charlotte, and Fayettesville, North Carolina, as well as in Portsmouth, Virginia, and Chattanooga and Nashville, Tennessee. Other students organized nationwide demonstrations and protests outside of segregated Woolworth stores. The Greensboro students were cursed, spit on, and burned with cigarette butts by white youths, but maintained their sit-in until July 25, 1960, at 2:00 P.M., when, without prior notice, the four Black students were served. By 1962 thousands of lunch counters and other public accommodations had been desegregated in roughly 150 cities.

422 • SNCC Founded

The Student Nonviolent Coordinating Committee, or SNCC (pronounced *snick*), was an organization of students who had become active in the sit-in movement. The organization was founded at a conference held April 16–18, 1960, in Raleigh, North Carolina, which Southern Christian Leadership Conference executive director Ella Baker organized. Baker believed that the students needed an organization of their own. Less hierarchical than either SCLC or CORE, SNCC pioneered a "cell" approach to leadership in which group consensus was needed to adopt policy. Critical of the tendency of some SCLC leaders to "invade" a southern city, call demonstrations, and then abandon the Black community afterward, SNCC pioneered a different approach, whereby members lived in and adopted the concerns of the Black community. This experience of close contact with rural Blacks in Mississippi and Alabama led to a radicalization of SNCC, which, along with rising Black anger in the middle 1960s, contributed to the election of Stokely Carmichael as SNCC president in 1966. Carmichael popularized the slogan "Black Power" and steered the organization away from its earlier commitment to interracial democracy toward the goal of separate Black community development. The organization declined in the early 1970s, a victim of governmental repression, white ostracism, and internal conflicts.

A sit-in at a Woolworth's lunch counter in Jackson, Mississippi, on May 28, 1963, turned ugly when whites attacked demonstrators John Salter, Jr., Joan Trumpeter, and Anne Moody, the latter the author of *Coming of Age in Mississippi.* State Historical Society of Wisconsin

Ella Baker. Prints and Photographs Division, Library of Congress, Visual Materials from the NAACP Records

423 • Freedom Rides

The Freedom Rides began on May 4, 1961, when thirteen Blacks and whites who were trained in nonviolence left Washington, D.C., on a bus trip through the South to challenge segregation in interstate bus facilities. Organized by CORE, the Freedom Riders challenged segregated seating requirements, segregated bathrooms, and seating signs in bus terminals. A bus was bombed outside of Anniston, Alabama, and the Freedom Riders were attacked and beaten savagely in Anniston, Birmingham, and Montgomery, Alabama. They were arrested in Mississippi, but

CORE eventually convinced the Supreme Court to order Mississippi to refund the Riders' bond money. At the insistence of Attorney General Robert Kennedy, the Interstate Commerce Commission issued a directive to end bus segregation in the South.

424 • Albany Movement

Begun on November 17, 1961, and lasting until August 1962, the Albany Movement was the first community-based civil rights demonstration. SCLC, SNCC, CORE, and the NAACP all contributed to the Albany Movement. The heart and soul of the movement, however, was a group of local Black professionals and townspeople determined to change the highly segregated southern town of Albany, Georgia. Their task was made difficult, however, by the intransigence and resourcefulness of local white leaders, especially Sheriff Laurie Pritchett, who had learned

Freedom Ride bus destroyed by southern white rioters in Anniston, Alabama, May 15, 1961. Prints and Photographs Division, Library of Congress. Courtesy of Bettmann Archives

from other confrontations with civil rights demonstrators and deliberately sought to minimize national publicity. Albany was also a crisis for the leadership of Martin Luther King, who came to Albany fully expecting a dramatic victory, but not only left without one but received some of the blame from younger activists who felt his unwillingness to defy federal court orders and his adherence to nonviolent methods hurt the Albany Movement. Nevertheless, Albany was an important experience for many young activists and local African Americans. Although it would take six more years to desegregate Albany—a town whose leaders closed parks rather than desegregate them and removed chairs from libraries before admitting Blacks— a grassroots activist movement had been started that eventually transformed even Albany.

425 • James Meredith Integrates Ole Miss

James Meredith's entry into the University of Mississippi was one of the most hard-fought victories of the Civil Rights Movement, mainly because "Ole Miss" symbolized the antebellum traditions of the South. On September 3, 1962, a federal court declared Meredith was eligible for entry into Ole Miss and the school must admit him. This led to a hysterical confrontation between Governor Ross Barnett, a segregationist who believed his reelection chances depended on his ardent defense of Mississippi's state rights, and the federal government. Using television, Barnett whipped up racial feelings among residents and at football games, all the while negotiating with President John F. Kennedy to find a way to comply with the federal order and yet remain an ardent defender of segregation. After Meredith was sneaked into a room in Baxter Hall on campus on September 30, white students attacked federal marshals and full-scale rioting

erupted as Barnett took the radio to call all loyal southerners to Oxford, Mississippi, to defend the southern way of life. Kennedy ordered army troops to Oxford to rescue the federal marshals. When it was over the next morning, 160 federal marshals were injured and two innocent white bystanders were dead. At 7:55 A.M. Meredith was able to walk casually across a now deserted campus and register as a student.

426 • Birmingham April–May 1963

On April 3, 1963, SCLC and the Alabama Christian Movement for Human Rights (ACMHR) launched Project C, a series of demonstrations by Blacks in Birmingham, one of the South's most industrialized yet segregated cities. During the first stage, demonstrators marched to integrate lunch counters, drinking fountains, and downtown businesses, and were peacefully arrested. During the second stage, forty-five people marched to City Hall and kneeled in prayer every day for forty-five days. After Martin Luther King was arrested on April 12 (Good Friday) for violating an injunction against marching, he used his solitary confinement in jail to pen his now famous "Letter from a Birmingham Jail," his answer to eight white clergymen who urged him to stop the demonstration and to work peacefully through the courts. Declaring that to achieve the "positive peace" of the New Testament, social disruption was necessary, King put into practice the third and most controversial phase of the demonstrations as soon as he got out of jail. On May 2, 1963, nearly one thousand children marched every day from Sixteenth Baptist Church to City Hall, where they were arrested. As critics decried the use of children, the commissioner of public safety, Eugene "Bull" Connor, attacked demonstrators with police dogs and powerful fire hoses. Pressured by the Kennedy administration and northern industrialists, Birmingham's business leaders signed an agreement that granted SCLC's and ACMHR's demands to desegregate lunch counters and rest rooms, to hire African Americans in sales and clerical positions, to release jailed demonstrators, who numbered about two thousand, and to form a permanent biracial committee. It was the SCLC's and Martin Luther King's most dramatic and effective victory in the movement since the Montgomery Bus Boycott victory of 1956.

427 • Governor Wallace's University of Alabama Schoolhouse Stand

Days after the successful ending of the 1963 Birmingham demonstrations, Governor George Wallace of Alabama precipitated another confrontation between those seeking to integrate southern institutions and those seeking to keep them segregated. The University of Alabama was ordered by federal court to admit Black students. Wallace believed he could circumvent the order by encouraging whites to stay away from the university. But eventually, on June 11, Wallace personally blocked the doorway to a university building and prevented two Black students, James Hood and Vivian Malone, from enrolling. Wallace then read a statement to Deputy Attorney General Nicholas B. Katzenbach, which argued that the attempt to register Black students at the University of Alabama was an "action in violation of rights reserved for the state by the Constitution of the United States and the Constitution of the state of Alabama." But a few hours after Wallace's "stand in the door" tactic, Wallace left the campus when asked by Alabama National Guard General Henry Graham, along with federal marshals, to remove himself. That same day Black students walked through the door Wallace had previously blocked, and desegregated the University of Alabama.

428 • 1963 March on Washington

Held on August 28, 1963, the March on Washington was organized by A. Philip Randolph, president of the Brotherhood of Sleeping Car Porters and an elder statesman of the Civil Rights Movement. In 1941 Randolph had called a similar march to protest discrimination in wartime hiring; in 1963 he again wanted to draw attention to Black unemployment, which stood at 11 percent, compared to 6 percent for whites. One of his original demands was for job training for Blacks, but after the Birmingham demonstrations and the attacks on Blacks by Bull Connor and his dogs, the March on Washington assumed much broader significance. President John Kennedy's civil rights bill was being argued in the Congress, and the march became a coming together of all of the major civil rights, labor, and religious organizations to urge passage of the Civil Rights Act, rapid integration of the public schools, and passage of a fair employment practices bill. President Kennedy initially tried to dissuade Randolph and Bayard Rustin, the deputy organizer of the march, from holding it, but once Kennedy realized it would take place, he endorsed it. Expecting 100,000 marchers, organizers were surprised when the numbers swelled to 250,000 people, at that time the largest demonstration in the nation's history. Although there was tension between the many different voices and organizations represented, the march went smoothly and was a remarkable show of unity. While some participants, such as SNCC's John Lewis, delivered speeches sharply critical of American practices, Martin Luther King best captured the mood of optimism and hope that day with his now classic "I Have a Dream" speech.

429 • Freedom Schools

As part of SNCC's effort to mobilize the Black

Civil Rights March on Washington, 1963. Prints and Photographs Division, Library of Congress

population in Mississippi, organizer Charles Cobb developed the idea of the "freedom schools" in 1963. Recognizing that Mississippi's educational system was not only inadequate but also counterproductive to the kind of intellectual curiosity and political thinking that SNCC wanted to foster in the Black population, Cobb decided to utilize the hundreds of young college-age students coming South to work in the movement as an educated "fifth column." The radical white professor Staughton Lynd directed a program of study in the spring and summer of 1964 that included academic subjects and also "movement" courses such as Black culture and leadership development. Although tensions developed that year between inexperienced white volunteers and seasoned Black organizers, the Freedom School was a success and a forerunner of later Black Studies curricula.

430 • Mississippi Freedom Democratic Party

Founded at a rally in Jackson, Mississippi, on April 26, 1964, the Mississippi Freedom Democratic Party was SNCC's attempt to create an alternative Democratic Party in Mississippi. The idea began when SNCC workers attempted to create separate voter registration requirements for Blacks who were otherwise prevented from registering to vote under the rules of the Democratic Party in Mississippi. But the idea quickly blossomed into a much more ambitious attempt to challenge the legality of the Mississippi delegation at the Democratic National Convention held that year in Atlantic City, New Jersey. During the Summer Project, SNCC workers encouraged seventeen thousand African Americans to register to vote, although only sixteen hundred were registered by authorities. Another eighty thousand Blacks registered as members of the MFDP, proof of the attractiveness of the alternative party in Mississippi. At the beginning of the

Fannie Lou Hamer speaking truth to power at the Democratic National Convention in Atlantic City, August 22, 1964. Prints and Photographs Division, Library of Congress, U.S. News & World Report Collection. Photo by Warren K. Leffler

national convention, nine Democratic state delegations and over twenty congressmen initially endorsed the MFDP. Fannie Lou Hamer, the charismatic SNCC organizer, electrified the nation when her impassioned request before the Credentials Committee to seat the Freedom Democratic Party was carried on network news. But in the end, President Lyndon Johnson refused to allow any challenge that might threaten his nomination, and when the MFDP refused to accept a White House compromise— "We didn't come all this way for no two seats," Hamer reputedly said—the MFDP effort to unseat the Dixiecrats was defeated.

431 • March from Selma to Montgomery

Beginning on January 2, 1965, SCLC launched a voting registration drive in Selma, Alabama, to dramatize the disparity in voter registration—only 1 percent of the fifteen thousand nonwhite population of Selma was registered to vote in that city. Selma was also important because its sheriff, Jim Clark, and his posse were ardent segregationists. The first month of registration was relatively calm, although Martin Luther King was attacked when he registered on January 18. The drive for voter registration became more violent during the next month. King was arrested on February 1, and after his release, he called on the federal government to enact a voting rights act. But the Selma campaign was going badly and in danger of collapsing when, on March 7, SCLC's Hosea Williams and SNCC's John Lewis led about five hundred people on a march from Brown Chapel African Methodist Episcopal Church in Selma to the state capital of Montgomery to present a petition to Governor George Wallace. King was in Atlanta preaching at his church when the group crossed over Pettus Bridge and was attacked from the front by Major John Cloud's Alabama state troopers and from behind by Jim Clark's tear-gas-throwing posse on horseback. In the chaos that ensued, John Lewis's skull was cracked, dozens of people were beaten and injured, and the marchers were forced back to the church, where Black residents, tired of weeks of harassment, armed themselves and threatened to engage Clark's posse in a shooting war. Through the efforts of Wilson Baker, Selma's director of public safety, who succeeded in getting Clark to retreat, and Andrew Young, who got armed Blacks to return to their homes, a bloodbath was avoided. But the attack was recorded by photographers from major national magazines, and the pictures showed the world southern justice in Alabama. A week later, hundreds of people, including many prominent whites in the religious community, traveled to Selma to participate in a second march along the same route, led this time by Martin Luther King. Bloodshed was avoided when King, by prearranged agreement, limited the march to crossing the Pettus Bridge and returning to Selma. That action was severely criticized by militants in the movement, who argued, in the words of Eldridge Cleaver, that King "denied history a great moment." For if King had attempted to march to Montgomery and the marchers had been attacked, many people— both white and Black—would have been injured. But King didn't want to risk further violence against the marchers either from police or from Ku Klux Klan snipers. The Selma marches did, however, force the federal government to intervene. And on March 1, in his address to Congress, President Lyndon Johnson said he was sending a voting rights bill to Congress and concluded with the movement's own salutation, "And we . . . shall . . . overcome."

432 • Organization of Afro-American Unity

Following his removal as a minister of the Nation of Islam and his trip to Mecca, Malcolm X (1925–65) formed the Organization of Afro-American Unity, a Black nationalist group designed with progressive, militant, and political goals. Beyond simply permitting Malcolm X greater political involvement than he had with the Black Muslims, the OAAU was part of Malcolm X's plan to bring the case of American racism before the United Nations as a human rights violation rather than simply a case of American civil rights. But shortly after forming this organization, Malcolm X was assassinated by two former Black Muslims.

433 • The Black Panther Party

Founded in Oakland, California, in October 1966 by Bobby Seale and Huey P. Newton, the Black Panther Party promoted the idea of militant self-defense for the Black community against police brutality. Originally named the Black Panther Party for Self-Defense, the Panthers advocated a "Ten Point Program" that demanded full employment of Black people in America, decent housing, release of Black prisoners (all of whom were political prisoners in the eyes of the Panthers), payment of the forty acres and a mule (in contemporary currency) promised to former slaves during Reconstruction, and the holding of a United Nations plebiscite for the Black community to determine its future relationship to the United States. Blending the ideas of Malcolm X, Franz Fanon, Karl Marx, and Mao Tse-tung, Seale and Newton rejected cultural nationalism and called for a revolution to address the colonial relationship of the Black community to the larger American society. In the Black community of Oakland, California, the Panthers were

Huey P. Newton poster, artist unknown. "The racist dog policemen must withdraw immediately from our communities, stop their wanton murder and brutality." Permission granted by Gary Yanker

mainly known for wearing black berets and black leather jackets, and for creating a system of armed patrols that followed police whenever they stopped Black citizens. The Panthers gained the attention of the press in 1967 when Bobby Seale and twenty-five armed members marched to the capitol building in Sacramento, California, and read a statement of protest against a gun-control bill introduced by California Assemblyman Don Mulford to limit the Panthers' right to carry weapons in public. That incident also garnered the attention of FBI Director J. Edgar Hoover, who announced that the Black Panthers were "the greatest threat to the internal security of the country" and orchestrated a counterintelligence program to destabilize the party. In 1968 Eldridge Cleaver, a former Black Muslim and in 1968 the Black Panther Party's Minister of Information, ran for U.S. president as a candidate of the Peace and Freedom Party. The Black Panther Party was the victim of police and FBI harassment, and numerous members were killed either in shootouts with police or in raids on the homes of Panther Party members. Although the party contained roughly three thousand members in 1972, it collapsed shortly afterward because of internal divisions and legal problems. Elaine Brown assumed the chairmanship of the party in 1974 when Newton left the United States for Cuba to avoid prosecution on murder charges; he eventually was killed in 1989 in a drug-related shooting. Bobby Seale was tried and convicted for traveling across state lines to incite a riot at the 1968 Democratic National Convention in Chicago. Eldridge Cleaver fled imprisonment by leaving the country, living for a while in Algeria and Cuba, and breaking with the party in 1971. Cleaver returned to the United States in 1976, become a political conservative, and apologized for some of his former statements. *Panther*, a film on the early years of the party, by Melvin and Mario Van Peebles, was released in 1995. The spirit of those years survives in the Dr. Huey P. Newton Foundation, run by Brown and David Hilliard, another former party officer.

434 • Poor People's Campaign

Shortly after the death of Dr. Martin Luther King, Jr., in 1968, Rev. Ralph Abernathy, the southern minister who succeeded King in SCLC, organized a protest demonstration in Washington, D.C., called the Poor People's Campaign. Thousands of African Americans trekked to the nation's capital to draw attention to the continuing problem of poverty and racism in America. Taking up temporary residence in the shadow of the Lincoln Memorial, protesters constructed a shantytown, called Resurrection City, while Martin Luther King's widow, Coretta Scott King, led a demonstration of welfare mothers from around the country. The Poor People's Campaign and Resurrection City symbolized a shift in the Civil Rights Movement politics away from mere racial discrimination toward what was later dubbed the Welfare Rights Movement.

Some Important People Not Yet Mentioned

435 • Daisy Bates (b. 1920)

Daisy Bates was the prime mover behind the Little Rock desegregation movement in 1957 that eventually resulted in the integration of Little Rock Central High School. As the president of the Arkansas chapter of the NAACP, Bates organized the Little Rock Nine, the first Black students to enroll at Central High in September 1957. She became the custodian, confidante, and adviser to the Little Rock Nine. In 1958 she and the nine students won the NAACP Spingarn Medal. Bates continued to struggle against bigotry and institutional prejudice, and in 1972 she organized a movement to expose and critique President Richard Nixon's cutting of funds for economic opportunity programs in Mitchellville, Arkansas.

436 • Fred Shuttlesworth (b. 1922)

Rev. Fred Shuttlesworth was the African American president of the Alabama Christian Movement for Human Rights (ACMHR) in Birmingham, Alabama, an organization founded in 1956. Shuttlesworth was also an active member of SCLC and one of the principal architects of the Birmingham campaign. On May 7, 1963, one of the most violent days of the Birmingham demonstration, Shuttlesworth was seriously injured when water from a fireman's hose slammed him into a building. According to his own account, he returned to the front lines from his hospital bed just in time to veto a deal between Martin Luther King and President John Kennedy to cancel the demonstrations before the demands had been met. More militant than King and some other southern ministers, Fred Shuttlesworth once walked, as James Farmer later recalled, right through a crowd of violent white youths who had surrounded a Baptist church during a riot in 1961. Farmer recalled that "I was scared as hell, but Shuttlesworth . . . shoved his way through the incredulous whites. These goons were standing there, thousands of them with clubs. 'Out of the way, Go on. Out of the way,' he said. He didn't have any trouble. They stopped and looked at him and said: *'That nigger's crazy.'* And I was standing right behind him trying to be little. And we got to the church and got in. . . ."

437 • Diane Nash (b. 1938)

Diane Nash was an undergraduate at Fisk University in 1960 when she became a leader of the student sit-in movement at downtown lunch counters in Nashville, Tennessee. Her most important contribution to the subsequent boycott of downtown stores came on the steps of City Hall when she asked Nashville Mayor Ben West, "Do you feel that it is wrong to discriminate against a person solely on the basis of his race or color." The mayor responded "as a man and not as a politician" that he could "not agree that it [is] morally right for someone to sell them merchandise and refuse them service." Once the mayor had sanctioned the rightfulness of the protest, white resistance wilted, and less than a month later, African Americans were

served at lunch counters in Nashville. Nash also revived the Freedom Rides in 1961, after the first riders were beaten and their buses burned in Anniston, Alabama. Fearing that to end the Freedom Rides would signify that violence could thwart the movement, Nash led a large contingent of Nashville students who boarded new buses in Birmingham and rode to Montgomery, Alabama, and then to Jackson, Mississippi. Eventually the renewed Freedom Rides forced Attorney General Robert Kennedy to make the Interstate Commerce Commission issue tough new guidelines to thwart segregation in interstate travel facilities.

438 • John Lewis (b. 1940)

As a Fisk University student, John Lewis became, along with Diane Nash, one of the organizers of the Nashville Sit-in, and later one of the founders of SNCC. Lewis was savagely beaten by southern whites during the first Freedom Rides in Montgomery, Alabama, in 1961. As chairman of SNCC, Lewis delivered the most militant speech at the 1963 March on Washington, even after it had been edited down to comply with other civil rights organizations. Then, on March 7, 1965, Lewis led the most important

John Lewis, SNCC chairman, at the meeting of the American Society of Newspaper Editors, April 16, 1964. Photo by Marion S. Trikosko. Prints and Photographs Division, Library of Congress, U.S. News & World Report Collection

event of the Civil Rights Movement, the fateful Selma to Montgomery march that elicited attacks from Alabama state troopers. In 1966 Lewis lost the leadership of SNCC to Stokely Carmichael and his more militant Black Power rhetoric. After resigning from SNCC, Lewis worked with the Southern Regional Council and directed the Voter Education Project. In 1986 he ran successfully for Congress from Georgia.

439 • James Farmer (b. 1920)

James Farmer founded CORE in 1941. A student of nonviolent resistance, a technique first developed by Mahatma Gandhi, Farmer served as national director of CORE from 1961 to 1966. Farmer was one of the original organizers of the Freedom Rides that successfully challenged segregated bus facilities along interstate routes in the South. He was succeeded at CORE by Floyd McKissick, who moved the organization in the direction of the Black Power movement. After touring the lecture circuit and teaching, Farmer worked for a short time as an assistant secretary of administration in the Department of Health, Education and Welfare under Richard Nixon from March 1969 to December 1970. In 1985 he published his autobiography, *Lay Bare the Heart.* He now teaches at Mary Washington College in Fredricksburg, Virginia.

440 • Stokely Carmichael (b. 1941)

In 1966 Stokely Carmichael, one of SNCC's most energetic field-workers in Mississippi, became chairman of the organization. Carmichael was most famous for coining the slogan "Black Power," which caught on among young Black militant activists who felt that neither integration nor nonviolence was viable in the Civil Rights Movement of the 1960s. In his transformation of the previously interracial organization into a Black Power organization,

Carmichael kicked whites out of SNCC, a move that alienated many veteran SNCC activists. Leaving SNCC in 1967 (H. Rap Brown became the new chairman), Carmichael joined the Black Panthers and then left the United States for residence in Africa. Changing his name to Kwame Toure, in honor of Dwame Nkrumah and Sekou Toure, the former head of SNCC became a Pan-Africanist, but ironically was arrested in Guinea in West Africa for expressing his desire for revolutionary change. During the 1980s and 1990s Toure has traveled and lectured around the world, organizing chapters of the All African Peoples Revolutionary Party, which he founded in 1969.

441 • Julian Bond (b. 1940)

Julian Bond was one of the organizers of SNCC, the Student Nonviolent Coordinating Committee, for which he also served as communications director from 1960 to 1966. In 1965 Bond was elected to the Georgia state legislature by a predominantly Black district, but he was denied his seat for a year because the legislature refused to seat him: its members objected to his public opposition to the Vietnam War. Many in the Black community argued that Bond's antiwar views were simply an excuse to deny an African American a seat in the Georgia House. Eventually the United States Supreme Court ordered the Georgia House of Representatives to seat Bond. Later, he ran unsuccessfully for a seat representing Georgia in the U.S. House of Representatives, losing to another SNCC leader, John Lewis, in part because Bond refused to accept Lewis's challenge to take a drug test. Bond narrated the voice for the PBS documentary *Eyes on the Prize* and has taught civil rights history at American University in Washington, D.C., and now at the University of Virginia at Charlottesville, Virginia.

442 • Marion Barry (b. 1936)

A superb community organizer, Marion Barry was one of the original founders of SNCC, and one of the people most active in teaching Black teenagers in Mississippi. That expertise came in handy when Barry became the second Black mayor of Washington, D.C., in 1979. In his three terms as mayor, Barry developed summer youth programs, tax relief programs for the elderly, and revitalized the downtown area; he also increased the debt of the nation's capital to pay for such programs during a period of declining revenues. The debate over Barry's performance as mayor was interrupted in 1990 when he was arrested on drug charges after he was videotaped smoking crack cocaine in a hotel room in a FBI sting operation. Convicted for misdemeanor possession of cocaine, Barry served a six-month prison sentence. After his release, he returned to Washington and successfully ran for a seat on the City Council representing the

Marion Barry as mayor, 1995. Courtesy of the Mayor's Office, District of Columbia

city's most desolate sector, Ward 8. In 1994 he stunned his critics and opponents by winning the Democratic primary mayoral election with 47 percent of the vote, employing the same kind of grassroots organizational strategy he had developed in SNCC, and going on to win reelection to a fourth term as mayor.

Quotations

443 • Rosa Parks Remembers

I had had problems with bus drivers over the years, because I didn't see fit to pay my money into the front and then go around to the back. Sometimes bus drivers wouldn't permit me to get on the bus, and I had been evicted from the bus. But as I say, there had been incidents over the years. One of the things that made this get so much publicity was the fact the police were called in and I was placed under arrest. See, if I had just been evicted from the bus and he hadn't placed me under arrest or had any charges brought against me, it probably could have been just another incident. . . . I had almost a life history of being rebellious against being mistreated because of my color.

444 • The Significance of Courageous Lower-Court Judges

Elbert Tuttle was chief judge of the U.S. Fifth Circuit Court of Appeals and an Eisenhower appointee when the 1954 *Brown v. Board of Education* decision was handed down.

You see, the school case dealt with education, and the court said, "Education is somewhat unique, and education is per se unequal if it's segregated." Well, there was the feeling expressed, the clear import, that segregation in any public area must be looked at with great suspicion. But it wasn't said . . . didn't become a precedent that bound anybody, except in school litigation. So when the suits were brought with respect to golf courses and courthouses, voting, jury duty, we faced these problems before the Supreme Court ever reached them.

And the great breakthrough came when Judge Rives and Judge Johnson and Judge Lynne, all from Alabama ... sat as a three-judge district court where there was an attack on the constitutionality of the Montgomery ordinance requiring segregated seating in the bus. Judge Rives and Judge Johnson, in the majority opinion written by Judge Rives, applied the same principles that Brown-against-Topeka had applied in the schools to an ordinance requiring segregated seating on the buses. ... From that time on our [Fifth Circuit] court almost without any serious hesitation applied it to courthouses and these other areas of activity.

445 • "Letter from a Birmingham Jail"

When Martin Luther King was arrested in Birmingham in 1963, he used newspaper corners and scraps of paper to answer eight white clergymen who called on him to avoid direct-action confrontation and allow the courts to resolve southern racial problems. His "Letter from a Birmingham Jail" became the movement's best theological defense of nonviolent direct action.

You deplore the demonstrations taking place in Birmingham. But your statement, I am sorry to say, fails to express a similar concern for the conditions that brought about the demonstrations. I am sure that none of you would want to rest content with the superficial kind of social analysis that deals merely with effects and does not grapple with underlying causes. ...

There can be no gainsaying the fact that racial injustice engulfs this community. Birmingham is probably the most thoroughly segregated city in the United States. Its ugly record of brutality is widely known. Negroes have experienced grossly unjust treatment in the courts. There have been more unsolved bombings of Negro homes and churches in Birmingham than in any other city in the nation. ... We know through painful experience that freedom is never voluntarily given by the oppressor; it must be demanded by the oppressed. Frankly, I have yet to engage in a direct-action campaign that was "well-timed" in the view of those who have not suffered duly from the disease of segregation. For years now I have heard the word "Wait!" It rings in the ear of every Negro with piercing familiarity. This "Wait" has almost always meant "Never." We must come to see, with one of our distinguished jurists, that "justice too long delayed is justice denied."

446 • "The Ballot or the Bullet"

From a speech by Malcolm X delivered April 3, 1964, at Cory Methodist Church in Cleveland, Ohio:

If we don't do something real soon, I think you'll have to agree that we're going to be forced either to use the ballot or the bullet. It's one or the other in 1964. It isn't that time is running out—time has run out! Nineteen sixty-four threatens to be the most explosive year America has ever witnessed. The most explosive year. Why? It's also a political year. It's the year when all of the white political crooks will be right back in your and my community with their false promises, building up our hopes for a letdown, with their trickery and their treachery, with their false promises which they don't intend to keep. As they nourish these dissatisfactions, it can only lead to one thing, an explosion; and now we have the type of Black man on the scene in America today ... who just doesn't intend to turn the other cheek any longer.

447 • Wilson Baker on How SCLC Used Selma's Sheriff, Jim Clark

In 1965 Wilson Baker was Selma's director of public safety.

Dr. King either lost his briefcase or some way it was misplaced in Anniston—a copy of what he called Project Alabama. . . . They mentioned that it was a ready-made situation here for 'em with the posse that Jim Clark had. He had such a large posse. . . . He took his posse to Montgomery during the bus-riding days. . . . We were determined not to give 'em what they wanted and succeeded for two days that first week that they marched in here. We would try to set him down and talk with him.

We found out about two-thirty that morning they had decided that there had been too much homework going on in Selma, that they were going to march one mo' day, and they were going to make every effort to provoke someone in the posse or Jim Clark into committing some kind of violent arrest. And if they couldn't do it, then Dr. King would make a face-saving out and find another community in Alabama to do it in. . . . They were supposed to march at ten o'clock the next morning, and the city attorney, McLean Pitts, . . . came in and said that they could not control Jim, that he was in one of his wild rages . . . they [the marchers] came to the courthouse and when they got'chere Jim Clark started jerkin' 'em around and kicking 'em around. Jim he would want 'em to go in that door of the courthouse, and they'd want to come in this door, and that's really the kind of situation it was. . . . He arrested some several of 'em here that day. . . . If he had made no arrests whatsoever that day, they would have moved out.

448 • Wilson Baker After "Bloody Sunday"

I remember asking Mr. [Nicholas] Katzenbach after he got to be attorney general . . . what did the Justice Department expect if we had realistically registered Blacks as they came in under the existing laws. . . . he said, "About two thousand [Black voters], twenty-five hundred."

I said, "What do you expect if the Voter Rights Bill passes."

He said, "What do you mean if it passes. You people passed that on that bridge. You people in Selma passed that on that bridge that Sunday." . . . And he pulled his finger over there a little further, and he said, "About ten thousand." And we wound up with about fifteen thousand.

Murders and Other Violent Acts

449 • Emmett Till (1941–55)

Emmett Till left Chicago by train in the summer of 1955 for Mississippi, where he would be murdered for speaking to a white woman. Standing outside of a store in Money, Mississippi, on August 24, Till showed a group of Black boys a photograph of a white woman he said was his girlfriend. One of them dared him to prove his familiarity with white people by going into the store and speaking to the white woman working behind the counter. Reputedly Till entered the store, purchased some candy, and said "Bye baby" to Mrs. Carolyn Bryant, the wife of the store owner, who was out of town on a truck run to Texas. Till and the other boys ran off, thinking that the incident would blow over. It didn't. Different versions of the incident—that he whistled at her or asked her for a date—spread throughout the town. When Ray Bryant returned to town, he and his brother-in-law J. W. Milam drove to Mose Wright's home after midnight and demanded to see the boy "who done the talkin'." Although Wright tried to explain that the boy was from "up Nawth" and unfamiliar with southern ways, that did not stop Bryant and Milam from taking Till away in the night, and threatening Wright with death if he spoke a word of what happened that evening. Afterward, Bryant and Milam claimed to a reporter that they did not intend to kill Emmett, but when he would not repent his action or beg for forgiveness, they killed him. "What else could we do?" the brother-in-law recalled. "He was hopeless. I'm no bully; I never hurt a nigger in my life. . . . But I just decided it was time a few people got put on notice."

Emmett Till was discovered three days later at the bottom of a nearby river, with a seventy-five-pound cotton gin fan tied around his neck. The side of his skull had been crushed, an eye had been pushed in, and he had been shot in the head. Bryant and Milam were first charged with kidnaping and then murder, and many Mississippians tried to distance themselves from the murder. The sheriff wanted to bury the body immediately, but Mamie Till, his mother, demanded that the body be sent to Chicago, where she demanded an open-casket funeral so everyone could see what had been done to her son. The picture of the battered, horribly disfigured face was published by *Jet* magazine, and thousands of Black Americans became embittered. As national outrage built, white Mississippians rallied around Bryant and Milam. At the trial, a courageous Mose Wright stood up and did what no other Black Mississippian had ever done before: in open court, when asked to identify the men who had come and carried away Emmett, he rose and pointed to each man, and said, "Thar he." After an hour's deliberation, the jury re-

Emmitt Till. Prints and Photographs Division, Library of Congress, NYWT and S Collection

turned a verdict of not guilty. The Till murder mobilized the Black community, especially the young generation of Till's age, to activism more profoundly than the *Brown v. Board of Education* decision in 1954. The murder also convinced the nation that southern racism was a cancer that must be exorcised from American life.

450 • Martin Luther King, Jr.'s House Bombed

On January 30, 1956, at the height of the boycott against segregated buses in Montgomery, Alabama, Martin Luther King's home was bombed. His wife, Coretta King, jumped into the back room with her newly born child to avoid being injured. As Martin Luther King rushed home to find out if his family was hurt, dozens of Black Montgomery residents flocked to his home with guns in their hands. After months of harassment by whites in cars and by the segregationist legal establishment, many had had enough and were ready to retaliate. But in this first real test of the resolve of the Montgomery Improvement Association that had begun the bus boycott, Martin Luther King articulated forcefully the philosophy of nonviolence as the ruling ideology of the movement. Coming outside of his house to face the growing crowd, he reassured them that all were safe and asked that those assembled go home peacefully. He told them it was for the higher goal of the dignity of their people that they had bound themselves together in this cause, and they must not let this incident take their eyes from that higher goal. The crowd dispersed and went home. And though the segregationists would still try to provoke—E. D. Nixon's home would be bombed on February 1—a corner had been turned in the direct-action movement.

451 • Martin Luther King, Jr., Stabbed in Harlem

On September 20, 1958, Martin Luther King was stabbed by a Black woman, Mrs. Izola Curry, with a letter opener in Blumstein's department store in New York City while he was autographing copies of his book *Stride Toward Freedom*. The woman's motives were never determined, but the stabbing, and the enforced convalescence, may have encouraged King to make a long-postponed pilgrimage to India, where he deepened his study of nonviolence in Gandhi's home country.

452 • Paul Guihard Murdered During the Ole Miss Riot

In the fall of 1962 James Meredith, a native of Mississippi and a veteran of the United States Air Force, tried to enroll in the University of Mississippi. He was blocked from attending by Mississippi Governor Ross Barnett, who continued to assert that no Negro would be a student at the University of Mississippi, even after a federal court ruled Barnett was wrong. After weeks of fruitless negotiations, President John F. Kennedy sent troops to enforce the enrollment of Meredith. But on Sunday evening, September 30, the three hundred federal marshals Kennedy sent were overwhelmed. Hundreds of whites massed around the main buildings of the campus in Oxford, Mississippi, and attacked federal marshals with bricks, rocks, bottles, and guns. On the morning of October 1, reinforcements of regular army troops poured into Oxford, and by the end of the week, close to two thousand federal troops occupied the city. More than two hundred people were arrested and more than forty guns were confiscated. Twenty-eight marshals had been shot and 130 injured. Two white men, one a French reporter named Paul Guihard (1932–62), were shot in the back. In one of his last dispatches from Mississippi, he wrote that "it is in these moments you feel there is a distance of a century between Washington and the segregationists of the South.... The Civil War has never ended."

453 • Herbert Lee (1912–61)

When Bob Moses came to Mississippi in 1961 to launch a voter registration drive, he found that there was only one registered Black voter in Amite County, but there was no shortage of Black people willing to help him start a registration drive. One of the most important was Herbert Lee, a longtime resident of the county who was also one of the few to own a car. Lee took Moses all over the county as the two of them encouraged often reluctant African Americans to try to register. Lee was invaluable in these efforts because he knew the people and he was not afraid. That also made him a threat to the racial establishment in Mississippi. One day, when Lee brought his cotton to the local cotton gin outside of Liberty, Mississippi, he was accosted by Mississippi State Representative E. H. Hurst, who argued with Lee and shot him in the head in front of witnesses. Whites at the scene claimed Lee attacked Hurst with a tire iron. Another witness, a Black man named Louis Allen, was shotgunned later for fear that he might contradict that story. Following Lee's death, over one hundred African American high school students marched through McComb, Mississippi, to protest his senseless murder.

454 • William Moore's One-Man March

William Moore (1927–1963), a World War II Marine veteran, whose recovery from a nervous breakdown made him an idealistic and highly individualistic civil rights worker, was shot and killed outside of Reece City, Alabama, on April 23, 1963. A former social worker and postman, Moore combined elements of both jobs as he took long walks wearing signs that advocated integration. During a 1963 walk from Chattanooga, Tennessee, to Jackson, Mississippi, Moore was yelled at and stoned by motorists, and then shot and killed by a .22-caliber rifle as he sat resting by the side of the road. Although Floyd Simpson, the owner of the rifle, was identified, no one was ever indicted for Moore's murder. Even Governor George Wallace was forced to condemn the killing. But when twenty-nine marchers attempted to finish Moore's walk a month later, Alabama authorities arrested them, showing that the state was still not will-

ing to allow public support for integration to be voiced by American citizens.

455 • Medgar Evers Killed

If relatively obscure citizens could be murdered with impunity in the South for supporting voting rights and integration, it is not surprising that the NAACP's field secretary in Mississippi since 1946 would be murdered as well. Medgar Evers (1925–63) had investigated the cases of George Lee, Emmett Till, and other victims of racist killings, and had even spirited Mose Wright out of Mississippi after he identified the killers of Emmett Till. Evers became more visible when he helped negotiate the successful conclusion of an integrated sit-in at downtown lunch counters in Jackson, Mississippi. Soon after, a Molotov cocktail was thrown into Evers's house, but no one was injured. Then, in the early morning hours of June 13, 1963, as he returned home after watching President John Kennedy's evening speech about the "moral crisis" of civil rights, Evers was shot in his drive-

Funeral procession for Medgar Evers proceeds to Arlington National Cemetery from downtown Washington, June 19, 1963. Courtesy of National Archives

way by White Citizens Council member Byron De La Beckwith. Although he was tried twice for murder soon after the shooting, neither jury convicted Beckwith. In 1994, more than thirty years later, Beckwith was finally convicted for the Evers murder.

456 • Murder of Four Children in a Birmingham Church

Three months after the victory of the 1963 Birmingham demonstrations, a Black church in that city was dynamited. The September 15th blast injured twenty-one and killed four little girls. National outrage and expressions of grief were immediate. President John Kennedy, in a television address the following day, expressed the hope that "if these cruel and tragic events can only awaken that city and state—if they can only awaken this entire nation . . . then it is not too late for all concerned to unite in steps toward peaceful progress before more lives are lost." Unfortunately the blast did not change the attitudes of Birmingham's white community: none of them attended the funeral.

457 • JFK Killed

Many theories have been advanced as to why President John F. Kennedy was murdered in Dallas on November 22, 1963. But many African Americans believed Kennedy's public advocacy of civil rights was a factor in his death. In 1963 Kennedy issued his strongest statement against segregation in his annual address to Congress and proposed sweeping civil rights legislation that was vehemently opposed by the South. Then, rather than oppose the March on Washington, Kennedy met its organizers and made the march part of his overall strategy to improve civil rights in America. Many African Americans interpreted such actions as proof of Kennedy's support for the Civil Rights Movement.

458 • Goodman, Schwerner, and Chaney Killed

On Sunday, June 21, 1964, three civil rights workers drove to Philadelphia, Mississippi, after the Mount Zion Methodist Church in Meridian was bombed. James Chaney, a native of Meridian and longtime CORE activist, was Black. The other two men, Michael Schwerner and Andrew Goodman, both from New York City, were white. All three were targeted by the Ku Klux Klan as troublemakers who deserved to be killed— Chaney because he was a local Black man who dared to challenge racism, and Schwerner and Goodman because they were outsiders. The three were arrested in Philadelphia, Mississippi, by Deputy Sheriff Cecil Price, then released at 10:00 that same evening. As the three continued on their way, they were stopped again—this time by Price and Klan members—placed in Price's police car, and transported to an isolated spot on Highway 19. Each was shot and placed in a ditch that was being converted into a dam. As soon as they were reported missing, a nationwide alarm went off, and President Lyndon Johnson committed the Justice Department and the FBI to finding the three men. After substantial rewards were offered for information on their whereabouts, the three bodies were finally located. Some Blacks and civil rights workers have noted that the FBI undertook the largest investigation in Mississippi only when two white men were killed and that hundreds of murdered Blacks were ignored by the agency. But the murder of the three civil rights workers was highly significant, because it exposed the system of terror operating in Mississippi at that time. Although reluctant to pursue a conviction at first, the Department of Justice indicted Price and several others on federal charges of violating the three workers' civil rights, since no indictment for murder was forthcoming. Seven Klan members, including Price, were found guilty on October 20, 1967, of federal civil rights violations and sentenced to three to ten years in prison. This was the first time that Klansmen had been convicted in Mississippi on charges related to the murder of a black man.

459 • Lieutenant Colonel Lemuel Penn Killed

Lieutenant Colonel Lemuel Penn (1915–64) was driving north with two other Black officers after two weeks of Reserve training at Fort Benning, Georgia, when he was killed by two shotgun blasts fired point-blank by members of the Ku Klux Klan. These Klansmen were part of an Athens, Georgia, "security force" that had been formed to combat civil rights efforts with terror. Having previously beaten an older Black mechanic in March and blinded a teenage boy by shooting into a housing project, the "security force" was on the lookout for civil rights workers trying to change race relations in Georgia. Believing that the soldiers represented some possibly new effort at integration by President Lyndon Johnson, who had recently signed the Civil Rights Act of 1964, Joseph Howard Sims and Cecil William Myers shot Penn simultaneously with shotguns as he was driving the car. The murder, coming a week after the murders of James Chaney, Michael Schwerner, and Andrew Goodman, tested the federal government's resolve to prosecute such acts of violence. After years of legal wrangling, during which the Supreme Court overturned a lower court curtailment of the federal suit, Myers and Sims were convicted of civil rights violations and given the maximum sentences of ten years in jail.

460 • Jimmy Lee Jackson Killed

Jimmy Lee Jackson (1938–65) was beaten and shot on February 18, 1965, when he tried to protect his mother from being beaten by a state trooper who, with others, was attacking scores of civil rights demonstrators in Marion, Alabama. The march, led by SCLC veteran C. T. Vivan, was part of the Selma campaign for Black voter registration led by Martin Luther King. Shot in the stomach, Jackson continued to be beaten by state troopers until he collapsed on the street. He died days later. His killer was never indicted and the state trooper attack was vindicated. Jimmy Lee Jackson's death, however, inspired the March 21 march from Selma to Montgomery led by Coger Lee, Jimmy Lee's grandfather, and Martin Luther King.

461 • Malcolm X Killed

Following his removal as a minister of the Nation of Islam and his trip to Mecca, Malcolm X formed the Organization of Afro-American Unity, a Black nationalist group designed to

Police carry body of Malcolm X out of a New York ballroom on February 21, 1965, after he was shot attempting to address a meeting of his Organization of Afro-American Unity. Library of Congress, NYWT and S Collection

bring the injustices of American racism to the United Nations. Shortly after forming this organization, which allowed for more political involvement than he had enjoyed with the Nation of Islam, Malcolm X was assassinated by two former Black Muslims on February 21, 1965.

462 • Viola Gregg Liuzzo Killed

On March 7, 1965, Viola Liuzzo was so moved watching television reports of the beating of civil rights marchers on Pettus Bridge that she left her home in Michigan and drove to Selma, Alabama, to assist in the struggle. Viola was a remarkable person. After she was married and the mother of five, she went back to school and educated herself to be a lab technician. Then she quit her job as a lab technician to protest the abusive treatment of women secretaries on the job. She was also one of the few white members of the NAACP. Unfortunately, on March 25, 1965, she was on the road returning to Montgomery to pick up more marchers after the successful three-day march when she and LeRoy Moton, a Black civil rights worker, were spotted by Klansmen. Klansmen chased Mrs. Liuzzo and finally forced her off the road, where she was shot twice in the head. The Klan disseminated false information that Mrs. Liuzzo was having an affair with a Black civil rights worker, and the FBI reported these rumors without correction or qualification. In a survey, many readers of *Ladies' Home Journal* said they believed Mrs. Liuzzo had gotten "out of her place" when she went to Selma. Eventually Mrs. Liuzzo's family dispelled the rumors, and three Klansmen—Eugene Thomas, William Eaton, and Collie Wilkins, Jr.—were finally indicted and convicted for conspiring to violate Mrs. Liuzzo's civil rights, after two Alabama juries failed to convict them of murder. Viola Liuzzo became a martyr of the civil rights movement.

463 • Watts Riot

For six days in August 1965, rioting consumed the predominantly Black section of Los Angeles known as Watts. Fed up with years of neglect, impoverishment, and segregation from the rest of Southern California, African Americans in Watts threw rocks at windows and police, burned buildings, looted stores, and brought national attention to the problems of poverty, racism, and police brutality in Southern California. After the rioting was over, more than thirty African Americans had been killed, more than a thousand had been injured, and over $45 million in property had been destroyed.

464 • 1967 "Long Hot Summer"

In the summer of 1967 race riots broke out in Newark, New York, Buffalo, New Haven, Milwaukee, Atlanta, and Boston, with the worst occurring in Detroit. Hundreds of African Americans were killed, thousands injured, and property worth hundreds of thousands of dollars was destroyed.

465 • Martin Luther King, Jr., Killed

Traveling to Memphis in 1968 to champion the cause of striking sanitation workers, Martin Luther King, Jr. (1929–68), was assassinated on April 4 on the second-story balcony of the Lorraine Motel by a bullet fired by James Earl Ray. King had been the most important leader of the Civil Rights Movement, because he combined coolness under pressure, a gift for uplifting oratory, and a vision of an integrated America that enabled him to remain an eloquent spokesperson for the movement, even after nonviolence as a philosophy and a strategy had fallen out of favor. Some of King's critics argued that the movement had passed him by, especially after more radical elements took control of SNCC and CORE in 1966 and articulated a notion of Black

Martin Luther King, Jr., at press conference, Birmingham, Alabama, May 16, 1963. Library of Congress, U.S. News & World Report Collection. Photo by Marion Trikosko

Power and armed self-defense. Refusing to abandon nonviolence or embrace Black Power, King spoke out against the Vietnam War, addressed issues of world peace, and took on the thorny problem of the war against urban poverty in places like Chicago. Indeed, some speculate that it was precisely when King began to address the more fundamental issues of the inequitable distribution of wealth and power in America that he marched down the road toward his death.

Aftermath of District of Columbia rioting, 1968. Prints and Photographs Division, Library of Congress, U.S. News & World Report Magazine Collection, Warren K. Leffler

466 • 1968 Rioting

As news of Martin Luther King's assassination spread, Black residents of urban ghettos in Washington, D.C., Baltimore, Chicago, and other major cities took to the streets and rioted—burning and destroying their own neighborhoods in a fury of frustration. In cities like Washington, blocks of urban development were destroyed overnight in a pillage of rage that set back the economic centers of largely African American inner cities for decades. King's death and the rioting that followed symbolically ended the great period of civil rights advancement.

Legal Decisions and Their Implications

467 • Civil Rights Act of 1957

The Civil Rights Act of 1957 was the first civil rights bill enacted by Congress since 1875. With this act, the U.S. Congress created a Civil Rights Commission of presidential appointees to investigate allegations that citizens were being deprived of their right to vote because of their race, color, religion, or national origin.

468 • Civil Rights Act of 1960

The Civil Rights Act of 1960 was intended to strengthen compliance with the *Brown v. Board of Education* Supreme Court decision of 1954 to desegregate the South. The law addressed the growing recognition that southern Blacks were denied the right to vote. The act provided for the preservation of federal election records, extended the powers of civil rights commissions to take and administer oaths, and gave the courts the right to issue orders declaring persons qualified to vote who had been denied that right by state or local officials. The courts could even appoint voting referees to observe elections and discover whether potential voters were being deprived of their right to vote.

469 • Supreme Court Reinstates Dropped Names

In a major victory for voting rights, the United States Supreme Court ruled in 1960 in *United States v. Raines* that Louisiana must restore to the list of registered voters in Washington Parish thirteen hundred names of Black voters that were dropped for dubious reasons. This decision prefigures the oversight of voting that became the backbone of the Voting Rights Act of 1965.

470 • Interstate Commerce Commission Ruling

Under pressure from Attorney General Robert Kennedy after the Freedom Riders were brutally attacked for trying to integrate waiting rooms on interstate bus lines, the Interstate Commerce Commission barred all segregation in transportation terminals as of November 1, 1961. Afterward, signs that designated "white" and "colored" waiting and rest rooms were illegal, although they persisted in many southern towns.

471 • Civil Rights Act of 1964

In 1964 Congress passed the most important civil rights law of the century. The Civil Rights Act of 1964, signed by President Lyndon Johnson on July 2, created a mechanism to ensure compliance with the Fourteenth and Fifteenth Amendments, as well as the Supreme Court decision of 1954 in *Brown v. Board of Education.* This civil rights law outlawed literacy tests as a qualification for voting in any federal election and guaranteed equal access to "the full and equal enjoyment of the goods, services, facilities, privileges, advantages, and accommodations of any place of public accommodation without discrimination or segregation on the ground of race, color, religion, or national origin." This prohibition of discrimination applied to all hotels, restaurants, lunch counters, theaters, etc., though not to private clubs closed to the public, and empowered the U.S. attorney general to prosecute all those who sought to interfere with an individual's right to utilize such facilities freely with restriction based on his or her race, color, creed, or religion. If the attorney general received information that racially segregated schools did exist, he or she could sue the school district and demand they construct a plan to bring themselves into compliance. The law also appointed a commissioner to report on and approve plans by school boards to desegregate their school districts. The act specified that desegregation meant enrolling students in schools without regard to their race, color, religion, or national origin: it did not sanction assigning students to public schools in order to overcome racial imbalance.

Perhaps the most important part of the bill was Title VII, which outlawed discrimination in employment:

It shall be unlawful employment practice for an employer (1) to fail or refuse to hire or to discharge any individual, or otherwise discriminate against any individual with respect to his compensation, terms, conditions, or privileges of employment, because of such individual's race, color, religion, sex, or national origin; or (2) to limit, segregate, or classify his employees in any way which would deprive or tend to deprive any individual of employment opportunities . . . because of such individual's race, color, religion, sex, or national origin.

Again, the bill contained an important caveat that "nothing contained in this title shall be interpreted to require any employer, employment agency, labor organization, or joint labor-management committee . . . to grant preferential treatment to any individual or to any group because of the race, color, religion, sex, or national origin of such individual or group." The bill also created the Equal Employment Opportunity Commission to investigate charges of discrimination.

Federal registrar registers Black woman to vote in Canton, Mississippi, August 11, 1965. Photograph by Marion S. Trikosko. Prints and Photographs Division, Library of Congress, U.S. News & World Report Collection. Copyright © 1965 by Matt Herron/TAKE STOCK

472 • Voting Rights Act of 1965

Before the passage of the Voting Rights Act in 1965, most Blacks could not vote in the United States. Most Blacks still lived in the South and were denied the right to vote by a variety of covert restrictions and overt intimidation and violence. That fact was made clear by the famous Selma to Montgomery March in 1965, when Alabama state troopers mercilessly beat marchers on their way to the state capital to demand their right to vote. In response, Congress passed the Voting Rights Act of 1965, signed by President Lyndon Johnson on August 6, that declared unconstitutional any state law that imposed qualifications preventing citizens from voting in federal elections because of their "race or color."

The act outlawed all "tests" and taxes required to vote. Moreover, the act created a mechanism for dealing with patterns of race discrimination in voting: if complaints reached the U.S. attorney general that residents of a certain state were denied the right to vote because of their race or color, or if the ratio of nonwhite persons to white persons registered to vote suggested that some voters were unregistered because of their race or color, then the attorney general was to instruct the Civil Service Commission to appoint examiners to maintain lists of persons eligible to vote. The act prevented states from changing their voting qualifications or their voting districts for a period of five years without review by the attorney general.

473 • Ban Against Intermarriage Unconstitutional

In *Loving v. Virginia* the United States Supreme Court ruled in 1967 that a Virginia state law against marriages between African Americans and European Americans was unconstitutional. In this case, a white man and a Black woman, both residents of Virginia, had been married in the District of Columbia. After returning to Virginia, the couple was arrested and convicted of violating the state's antimiscegenation law. Each faced a one-year jail term. The Supreme Court ruled that Virginia's statute violated both the equal protection and the due process clauses of the Fourteenth Amendment and was thus unconstitutional. All similar statutes were also declared unconstitutional. For the first time in three hundred years, marriages between the races were legal in Virginia and the rest of the United States.

474 • Civil Rights Act of 1968

The Civil Rights Act of 1968 contained provisions that banned discrimination in housing and provided penalties for crossing state lines to incite a riot. This bill became the basis for prosecuting civil rights leaders, such as H. Rap Brown, who advocated violence.

REACTION AND BACKLASH

People and Politics

475 • Nixon's Agenda

When Richard M. Nixon was elected president in 1968, he made it clear he represented the growing reactionary feeling in the white electorate against rapid civil rights change. One of his favorite targets was busing students to achieve desegregation, and he urged federal officials not to use "forced busing" to bring about desegregation of southern schools or to integrate across suburban and urban school districts. Nixon suggested such officials might lose their jobs if the practice continued. Nixon even went so far as to threaten to pass a constitutional amendment against the use of busing.

476 • Charleston Confrontation

In 1969, seeking to continue the work begun by Martin Luther King to broaden the Civil Rights Movement to include the working-class struggle, Ralph Abernathy and Coretta Scott King staged a march and demonstration by hospital workers protesting racism and discrimination in Charleston, South Carolina. Hundreds of people were arrested and the governor called in the South Carolina National Guard to restore order.

477 • Affirmative Action

Affirmative action actually began under a Republican administration. In 1969, Arthur A. Fletcher, a Black assistant secretary of labor in the administration of President Richard Nixon, developed the "Philadelphia plan": firms with federal government contracts in the lily-white construction industry would have to set and meet hiring goals for African Americans or be penalized. The plan became a model for other programs such as the "set aside" program, which reserved some contracts for minority-owned businesses; and hiring plans for white women, who gained the most job mobility from affirmative action plans. Because the setting of goals and timetables rationalized the process of compliance, large corporations embraced affirmative action plans in the 1970s; but affirmative action became a political target of the Ronald

Reagan Administration in the 1980s as white Americans faced rising unemployment for professional, middle management, and skilled labor positions. Proportional representation of minorities on jobs became known as "quotas" that took jobs from more qualified white males. The notion that Blacks and women in professional jobs were less qualified than whites became so pervasive that some educated African Americans criticized affirmative action as demeaning Black success. Affirmative action became a campaign theme in 1990 and remains a powerful, divisive national issue.

478 • Cornell Takeover

In 1969 armed Black students took control of campus buildings at Cornell University to protest racial attacks on campus. Students also protested the lack of Black Studies courses and professors. After days of negotiation and tension, the university administration granted student demands. In this period, numerous other elite college campuses experienced similar takeovers and demonstrations by students who had grown up during the Civil Rights Movement, and who were now demanding that their college education reflect the African American experience. These protests led to establishment of Black Studies programs on most major college and university campuses in the North and the West.

479 • Black Manifesto

In April 1969 civil rights activist James Forman led a conference in Detroit to discuss the state of Black America. The conference produced a Black Manifesto that demanded that "White Christian Churches and Jewish Synagogues" and other historically white institutions pay $500 million in reparations to Black people for the sacrifices of African Americans under slavery. The funding was to be used for economic rehabilitation of the urban ghettos. Although the sum was never paid, some churches and synagogues increased their outreach and funding to help the urban poor.

480 • Kenneth Gibson, Mayor of Newark

In 1970 Kenneth Gibson became the first African American mayor of Newark and the first African American mayor of a major industrial center in the North. Not long afterward, James McGhee was elected mayor of Dayton, Ohio, the first Black mayor of that city. Such elections began a trend toward the election of Blacks as mayors of northern cities experiencing "white flight" to the suburbs and an expanding African American population within the city.

481 • Angela Davis (b. 1944)

A brilliant graduate student in philosophy at the University of California at San Diego, where she studied under Herbert Marcuse, Angela Davis developed a powerful interest in the issues of race and class inequality. This led her first to embrace socialism and then to a career as an activist. Involved in the 1960s with both the nonviolent Civil Rights Movement (SNCC) and the more militant Black Panthers, she became disillusioned by the intense sexism she found in both groups. This shy but brilliant and popular professor at the University of California at Los Angeles became a household name when she was accused in 1970 of providing the weapon used in a failed prison escape by Jonathan Jackson. Once accused, she became a fugitive and topped the FBI's Ten Most Wanted list by the end of the year. She was eventually captured, and the furor around the trial led to the "Free Angela movement." She was acquitted of all charges. In 1980 and again in 1984 she ran

FREE ANGELA DAVIS NOW!

FREE ANGELA DAVIS NOW! Poster by New York
Committee to Free Angela Davis, c. 1971. Artist unknown.
Prints and Photographs Division, Library of Congress. Used by
permission of Gary Yanker

for vice president on the Communist Party
ticket. More recently, Angela Davis has lectured
extensively on the issues of gender exploitation
in America.

482 • Wilmington 10

Benjamin Chavis and nine other civil rights
activists were arrested in Wilmington, North
Carolina, in 1971 and charged with burning
down a store. These activists received harsh
sentences, but their cases were publicized by
Amnesty International. In 1980 the convictions
were overturned. One of the Wilmington 10, Ben
Chavis, went on to become the head of the
NAACP in 1993. He was removed from office
over allegations of mismanagement and sexual
harassment in 1995.

483 • Black Caucus

In 1971 the Congressional Black Caucus was
created by the twelve African Americans
elected to the House of Representatives in 1970.
With such new representatives as Ron Dellums
from Northern California, Parren Mitchell from
Maryland, Ralph Metcalfe and George Collins
from Illinois, and Charles Rangel (who defeated
Adam Clayton Powell, Jr.) from New York, Black
Americans had a critical mass of representation
in the House of Representatives. The formation
of the Congressional Black Caucus was an attempt to pressure President Richard Nixon and
the Congress to secure better enforcement of
civil rights legislation.

484 • PUSH

In 1971 the Reverend Jesse Jackson created
PUSH, People United to Save Humanity, in
Chicago. Jackson had founded Operation Bread-
basket, the economic arm of the Southern
Christian Leadership Conference, in 1966, and
had resurrected the use of boycotts against
businesses that discriminated against minorities. After his influence in SCLC waned, Jackson created PUSH as a personal political
organization, although the group also continued
the use of boycotts, usually highly publicized, to
win concessions in the form of money and jobs
from programs that discriminated against
African Americans. PUSH also pioneered educational programs, such as a Los Angeles program
to limit television viewing time of inner-city
schoolchildren.

485 • Barbara Jordan (1936–96)

Barbara Jordan, considered one of the greatest speakers of modern times, is also known for
being the first Black woman to win election to
state office in Texas when she became a Texas
state senator in 1966. She was also the first

African American to sit in the Texas senate in the twentieth century. In 1972 she won election to the House of Representatives in Washington, D.C., where she served until 1978. She gained national attention in 1973 as a member of the House Judiciary Committee when her speech on the House floor recommending impeachment of President Richard Nixon was carried on national television. Her keynote address at the 1976 Democratic National Convention was an outstanding example of inspired political oration, and led to speculation that she would be a candidate for vice president or president someday. But illness forced her to retire from political office in 1978, although she did give a keynote address in a wheelchair at the 1992 Democratic National Convention. In 1994 President Bill Clinton chose Jordan to head the Commission on Immigration Reform in America.

486 • Shirley Chisholm (b. 1924)

Shirley Chisholm was elected to the United States House of Representatives in 1968 as a Democrat after four years as a New York State assemblywoman. She served on the House Education and Labor Committee and instituted programs such as day care and minimum-wage increases to help her predominantly black constituency. Frustrated when President Richard Nixon vetoed much of the legislation, she decided to run for president herself. In 1972 Chisholm became the first African American and first woman to seek a major party's nomination for president. Although she lost the Democratic nomination, she remained in the Congress until her 1982 retirement from politics.

487 • Election of Ronald Reagan

The election of Ronald Reagan, a retired actor and former governor of California, to the presidency in 1980 brought to the White House a man who was hostile to many of the achievements of the Civil Rights Movement, including the use of the federal government to desegregate schools. In 1981 Reagan attempted to obtain federal funding for the Bob Jones College, a school that refused to allow African Americans as students. That effort failed after a storm of controversy confronted the Reagan administration's argument that the federal government should not legislate the practices of private institutions of higher education. In 1982 Reagan did not support renewal of the Voting Rights Act, although after controversy arose, he reluctantly signed the legislation. When Reagan appointed William Bradford Reynolds, a man who opposed most affirmative-action programs, to head the Civil Rights Division of the Department of Justice, he sent a message to African Americans that they should not look to the federal government for relief from discrimination in American society.

488 • Hostage Release

In 1983, in a dramatic demonstration of his international reputation among peoples of color around the world, Jesse Jackson negotiated the release of Lieutenant Robert O. Goodman, Jr., an African American pilot who had been shot down over Syria. Jackson, as a private citizen, had succeeded where the Reagan administration had failed, and his success was a testament to his close connections in the Arab world.

489 • Harold Washington, Mayor of Chicago

In 1983 Harold Washington became the first African American mayor of Chicago after an intense, racially polarized contest. Washington's election was more than the usual African American "first," for Washington represented both a successful mobilization of the Black citizens into a powerful voting bloc and the arrival of a man with a leftist political agenda. With a clear racial mandate, Washington led a campaign to transform the patronage political system of Chicago ward politics. Unfortunately, after weathering another difficult campaign and winning reelection in 1987, Washington died of a heart attack on November 25.

490 • Martin Luther King Day

In 1983 musician Stevie Wonder successfully led a campaign to have Martin Luther King's birthday declared a national holiday. On November 2, in a dramatic White House Rose Garden ceremony, President Ronald Reagan signed the King holiday bill. The first celebration of the holiday took place on January 15, 1986, but some states, such as Arizona and New Hampshire, refused to make King's birthday a state-observed holiday. After these states lost millions of dollars in tourism and convention money because of a well-coordinated boycott, New Hampshire became in 1993 the last state to adopt the King holiday. In January 1995 President Bill Clinton declared Martin Luther King's birthday to be a federal holiday. But even some states that adopted the holiday did so only by combining celebration of King's birthday with those of others. For example, in Virginia, the holiday is officially known as Lee-Jackson-King Day, an amalgam that ironically linked the celebration of America's most successful desegregationist with those who fought to defend slavery.

491 • Jesse's Presidential Runs

In 1984 Jesse Jackson declared his candidacy for the Democratic Party's presidential nomination. While many were skeptical at first, Jackson drew impressive numbers of votes from African Americans and others, and came to the Democratic National Convention with three

Jesse Jackson, July 1, 1983. Photograph by Warren K. Leffler. Prints and Photographs Division, Library of Congress, U.S. News & World Report Collection

hundred delegates. He lost out to Walter Mondale. In 1988 Jackson ran again and in televised debates with other Democratic candidates, acquitted himself well. He received over 6 million votes in the 1988 contest and won seven primaries, but again, lacked enough support to challenge the front-runner, Michael Dukakis. Jackson was the third major African American candidate for the office of president, after James W. Ford, who ran on the Communist Party ticket in the 1930s, and Representative Shirley Chisholm.

492 • Million Man March

On October 16, 1995, roughly 870,000 Black men responded to the call of Nation of Islam Minister Louis Farrakhan and traveled from several states to the mall outside the United States Congress to stage the largest civil rights demonstration to date. Billed as a day of atonement and redemption for Black men to become better fathers, husbands, and citizens of their communities, the Million Man March drew many African Americans who wished to protest the conservative trend in American politics epitomized in attacks on affirmative action, welfare programs, and aid to education. Many people argued that attendance at the march was an endorsement of Farrakhan's anti-Semitic and separatist racial views; but only 5 percent of those who attended the march, according to a *Washington Post* poll, said they came out of allegiance to Farrakhan. Most came to affirm the strength of the Black family, to show Black unity, and to challenge the negative images of Black men in the media by assembling peacefully on the mall. While Jesse Jackson, Congressional Representative Kweisi Mfume, Reverend Al Sharpton, Mayor Kurt L. Schmoke, and other political figures spoke, the poetry of Maya Angelou, the singing of Stevie Wonder, and the testimony of Rosa Parks resonated best with those assembled (which included small numbers of Black women, Hispanics, and whites). Indeed, Farrakhan's two-and-a-half-hour speech, with its mystical, numerological, and historical references, dazed rather than uplifted the crowd. It was his idea of a secular pilgrimage to the mall that had really energized Black men, who had come, seen their strength in numbers, and embraced one another.

493 • Marian Wright Edelman (b. 1939)

Marian Edelman began her involvement in the civil rights struggle during the SNCC voter registration drive in Mississippi in 1963, the same year she graduated from Yale Law School. After becoming the first Black woman to pass the Mississippi state bar in 1964, she decided to practice civil rights law ("mostly getting students out of jail") and to head the NAACP Legal Defense and Education Fund. She founded the Children's Defense Fund in 1973 to develop and provide long-term assistance to children at risk. It became one of the best known and most highly regarded organizations of the Civil Rights Movement. She achieved even greater prominence in 1992 when Bill Clinton, a close friend, was elected president of the United States. Edelman, a trusted adviser of the president, was consulted on numerous decisions made by the president and Mrs. Hillary Clinton.

494 • Myrlie Evers-Williams (b. 1932)

In February 1995, Myrlie Evers-Williams won an upset, one-vote victory over long-time NAACP chairman, William F. Gibson, and was elected the first chairwoman of the NAACP, the nation's oldest living civil rights organization. The former wife of slain NAACP field officer Medgar Evers, Evers-Williams represented a reform movement within the NAACP that sought to put the organization back on the road to financial solvency, after allegations that Gibson had misappropriated funds for his own benefit. Large financial gifts to the NAACP had already begun to dry up in the aftermath of the resignation of former NAACP president Benjamin Chavis amid charges of sexual harassment and financial improprieties. But perhaps most important, Evers-Williams's election in 1995 meant a moral victory for those advocating that the organization return to its original function as an activist, integrationist pressure group at a time when a Republican-led Congress was pushing through a rollback of social programs benefiting the poor and minorities. Beyond restoring financial credibility to the NAACP, Evers-Williams hopes to make the NAACP relevant to younger African American men and women who have been largely alienated from the organization since the 1960s.

Murders and Other Violent Acts

495 • Chicago Panthers Killed

In a raid on the Chicago headquarters of the Black Panther Party on December 4, 1969, police shot and killed Fred Hampton, chairman of the Illinois Black Panther Party, as he lay in bed. Another Panther, Mark Clark, was killed and four other Panthers were seriously injured in the attack. The Chicago police used the wounding of one police officer to substantiate its claim that police fired on Hampton and the others in self-defense. But a later federal grand jury investigation proved that police had massed such a concentration of machine-gun fire that it was impossible any of the police could have been hit by return fire. No police were indicted in the shooting.

496 • Jonathan Jackson's Shoot-out

In 1970 Jonathan Jackson, the brother of inmate George Jackson, kidnaped a judge during a botched attempt to free several Blacks on trial in a San Rafael, California, courtroom. Cornered by police, Jonathan Jackson, along with two defendants, was killed, but he managed to kill the judge before dying. One of the guns used by Jackson was registered to University of California at Los Angeles philosophy professor Angela Davis, who went underground rather than face charges of conspiracy in the murder. Davis was eventually arrested in disguise in New York.

497 • Attica

At the Attica correctional facility in upstate New York in 1971, Black and Puerto Rican inmates rioted, took over the prison, and issued a list of demands, including an end to racial discrimination and improvement in the prison facility. Eventually negotiations with New York Governor Nelson Rockefeller broke down and Rockefeller ordered state troopers to attack the prison. Forty people, including guards held as hostages, were killed in the worst prison riot in history.

498 • Howard Beach

On December 20, 1986, three Black men made the mistake of going to a pizza joint in Howard Beach, an overwhelmingly white section of New York City, to get help with their car. After verbal insults were exchanged, a gang of young whites attacked and chased the three. One of the Black men, Michael Griffith, was struck and killed by a speeding automobile while trying to flee the whites. Three of the white gang members were indicted on second-degree murder and other charges in the case. In 1988 they were convicted of misdemeanor riot charges.

499 • Ku Klux Klan Attack in Georgia

In 1987 four hundred members of the Ku Klux Klan attacked approximately ninety civil rights demonstrators in Forsyth County, Georgia, who were trying to conduct a "brotherhood walk" to honor Martin Luther King, Jr. When the walk was repeated a week later, the now twenty thousand people were guarded by three thousand members of the National Guard.

500 • Rodney King (b. 1966?)

On March 3, 1991, Rodney King, a young African American, was stopped while driving his car by Los Angeles police officers. Once out of the automobile, King was attacked by officers with nightsticks and electric prods, being struck over fifty times in one eighty-one-second period. What made this beating exceptional was that it was captured by a bystander on video-tape, which was repeatedly played over television stations throughout the nation and the world. Many who saw the videotape, including President George Bush, were horrified by it. But a predominantly white jury in Sylmar, California, found the officers not guilty, except for one minor charge. That verdict set off the worst race riot in American history, from April 29 to May 1, 1992, in Los Angeles, during which $2 billion of property was destroyed, fifty people were killed, and dozens of innocent people, such as Reginald Denny, were injured. The verdict and the riot forced the federal government to indict the officers on charges of violating Rodney King's civil rights. After another lengthy trial, three of the four officers were convicted and sentenced to jail. In May 1994 King was awarded $3.8 million in damages from the city of Los Angeles for the beating he received.

Legal Decisions and Their Implications

501 • Bobby Seale on Trial

Under the antirioting provisions of the 1964 Civil Rights Act, Black Panther leader and Chicago Eight member Bobby Seale was tried for conspiracy to incite a riot at the Democratic National Convention in 1968. The Chicago Eight were charged with coming to Chicago in August to incite a riot, for which the penalty was five years in jail. When Seale argued with Judge Julius Hoffman repeatedly in court, Hoffman had Seale chained, bound, and gagged, the only one of the eight defendants to be so treated. A storm of protest ensued as pictures of the gagged and chained Seale were beamed around the world. Seale claimed he had been denied the

counsel of his choice because Hoffman refused to postpone the trial so that lawyer Charles R. Garry could attend the trial. Hoffman eventually separated Seale's case from the other defendants, and convicted Seale of contempt of court, for which Seale was sentenced to four years. The contempt charges, however, were overturned, and Seale served only two years.

502 • Busing

Since residential segregation was one of the most intractable causes of segregated schooling in urban areas, it was logical for federal courts in the late 1960s to require busing of Black children to historically white schools and white children to historically Black schools. But white opposition to busing was swift and virulent, especially after the Supreme Court's 1971 *Swann v. Charlotte-Mecklenburg Board of Education* decision expanded the use of busing to achieve desegregated education in America. Public criticism of busing galvanized Congress to place anti-busing amendments on many bills, and some even proposed a constitutional amendment against busing. Perhaps in response to the public outcry, the Supreme Court reversed itself in *Milliken v. Bradley* (1974) and concluded that busing was not allowable as a solution to the segregated schooling in Detroit and its surrounding suburbs. In the wake of that decision, busing was recommended less by lower federal courts, and desegregation slowed to a halt.

503 • *Bakke* Decision

In 1978 the Supreme Court ruled in the *Bakke* case that race alone could not be used by public schools in their affirmative-action programs to ensure a set number, or "quota," of places for Black students in their incoming classes. Allan Bakke, a Jewish applicant to the University of California at San Diego medical school, who had been turned down by numerous medical schools, was able to argue in this instance that he was denied admission because of his race. Bakke complained that Black students with lower grade point averages and test scores were admitted under a program in the medical school that set aside a "quota" of slots in each admitting class for African Americans. The Court ruled that such affirmative-action programs amounted to reverse discrimination against whites on the basis of race and were unconstitutional. This decision gave rise to the use of "quota" in connection with other civil rights legislation whenever it could be construed as potentially displacing whites. It also spawned new challenges to affirmative-action programs in schools and the workplace. Many in the Civil Rights Movement viewed this decision as the end of affirmative action in America. But affirmative-action programs did not end, because the Court did not say that race could not be one among many factors used by schools to construct a racially diverse student body or class.

504 • *City of Richmond v. J. A. Croson Co.*

In a continuation of the logic of the *Bakke* decision, the Supreme Court ruled in *Richmond v. Croson* (1989) that it was unconstitutional for a city to create a "set-aside program" to award a certain number of public contracts to minority contractors. Because white contractors could not compete for these slots, the set-aside program was deemed a violation of the civil rights of white contractors. This was another blow to affirmative action and to those city governments that had responded to civil rights agitation by awarding contracts to minority businesses.

505 • **Civil Rights Act of 1991**

The Civil Rights Act of 1991, signed by President George Bush on November 21, was the response of Congress to recent decisions handed down by the United States Supreme Court which limited the ability of victims of discrimination to easily sue for compensation. The act provided additional remedies for sexual harassment in the workplace in a response to sexual harassment claims by Anita Hill against Supreme Court Justice Clarence Thomas, and it made claims against employers for discrimination possible retroactively.

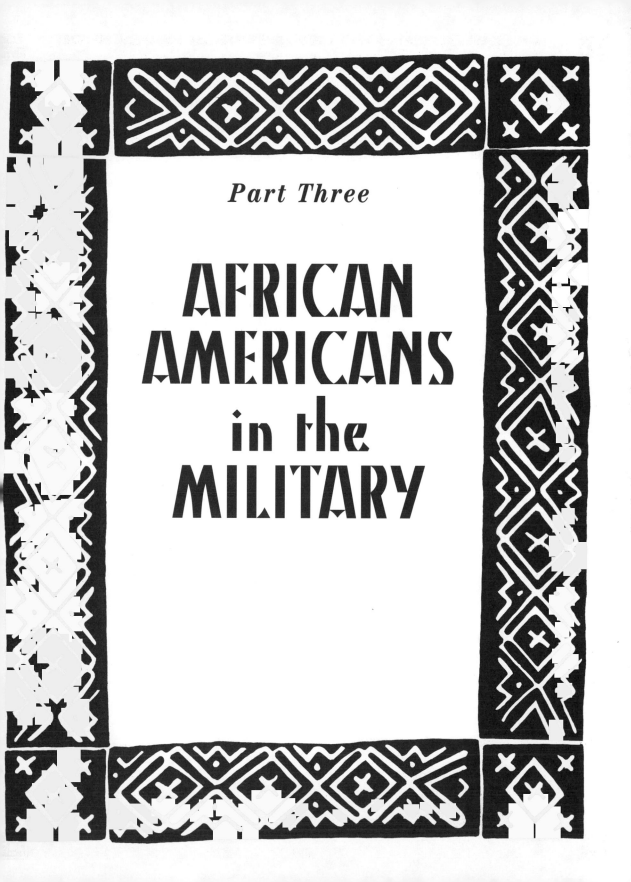

Part Three

AFRICAN AMERICANS in the MILITARY

Because the War of Independence was required to create the American nation, military service has had a special significance in conferring the highest claim to American citizenship on those who served. The great exception, of course, was the case of African Americans, who as slaves and free persons of color defended the nation with their lives and still lacked the privileges of American citizenship. Because it involved questions of race and citizenship, Black military service became a second front of civil rights agitation in American society. Not surprisingly, many American leaders, no less than the ruling elite of the former British colony, were ambivalent about the use of African Americans in the military. Such leaders feared that African Americans would demand equal rights after serving in the military or—worse—turn their weapons on a colony and a nation that denied their civil rights. In addition to their profound patriotism, African Americans threw themselves into the defense of the nation as another way to stake their claim to citizenship and equality in American society. One consequence of the contested nature of military service for African Americans is that the American military not only reflected the racial policies of the larger society but pioneered desegregation among many American institutions.

Black women nurses as part of Field Medical Supply Depot, Washington, D.C., March 22, 1919. National Archives

COLONIAL AND REVOLUTIONARY WARS

Engagements and Policy

506 • Seventeenth-Century Military Role of African Americans

The use of African Americans in military defense varied greatly from colony to colony. Virginia, the father of American slavery, was the first colony to reject the arming of African Americans for defense in the Act of 1639. Massachusetts pursued an ambivalent policy: in 1652 Massachusetts law required African Americans to train and serve in the colonial militia and in some cases, even freed slaves for meritorious service. Four years later, however, Massachusetts reversed itself and banned "Negroes and Indians" from the militia. But a 1660 Massachusetts law required "every person above the age of sixteen" to train, and in 1695 a law exempted African Americans and Indians from military training but provided them with arms and ammunition in case of an emergency! Surprisingly, given its vehement opposition to arming slaves in the Revolutionary War, South Carolina, in 1703, required slaves to serve in emergencies, for it was prudent "to have the assistance of our trusty slaves to assist us against our enemies." The Act of 1703 also promised to free all those who "kill or take one or More of our enemies in case of actual invasions."

507 • Bacon's Rebellion

African Americans fought in the first armed rebellion against British authority in the colonies, Bacon's Rebellion, in 1676. Nathaniel Bacon was a member of the rising generation of colonial planters who resented British rule and, particularly, the British protection of Indian lands that lay just outside of the Virginia settlement. As life expectancy increased in the second half of the seventeenth century, as more and more indentured servants lived beyond the end of their indentures, and as the king gave away huge tracts of arable land to his friends in England, increasing numbers of poor whites found they could not afford land to farm once their indentures were up. Bacon became the leader of a motley crew of poor whites who rebelled against the British governor, seized Williamsburg, and forced the governor to flee the capital. Bacon also offered freedom to any slaves who joined his rebellion. Bacon's substitute government lasted only a few weeks, but it showed the potential to gain the loyalty of the slaves by offering freedom.

508 • Slave Soldiers in the Yamasee War

When the Yamasees, the Creeks, and several other Indian tribes formed a confederation and attacked South Carolina in 1715, South Carolina recruited and armed a free and slave defensive force. Although the turning point in the war came when the Cherokees decided to fight on the side of the whites rather than the Creeks and Yamasees, armed slaves fought and died to defend the colony. Those who could prove that they had killed the enemy on the battlefield were rewarded with freedom and their owners were compensated by the colony. Although the actual number of slaves freed is unknown, there must have been enough to cause South Carolina authorities concern about linking armed service to manumission. In 1719 South Carolina changed the 1703 law and rewarded slaves who killed or captured the enemy with a cash payment, but not freedom.

509 • Black Servicemen in the French and Indian War

Even before the Revolutionary War, a pattern had been established in the British colonies whereby African Americans were enlisted to defend the colonies when they were attacked, but were excluded from military service in times of peace. When Major General Edward Braddock's forces were defeated in the French and Indian War in 1755, Virginia was forced to utilize free African Americans in its colonial military. Yet the colonial legislature refused to use African Americans in combat positions, preferring to relegate them to labor positions and service as scouts. Once armed, African Americans might, it was feared, turn their weapons on the colony in an attempt to free the slaves.

510 • George Gire

George Gire of Grafton, Massachusetts, fought in the French and Indian War (1754–63). Because of the injuries he received in that war, he was awarded an annual pension of forty shillings. Gire, along with Benjamin Negro and Caesar of Rhode Island, was part of an emerging class of free African Americans in the Northeast, where slavery was declining as an agriculturally profitable system of labor. Thus, unlike slaves who were often forced into service by their masters, Gire, along with his Black compatriots, represents the first example in American history of free African Americans fighting for the British colonies.

511 • Colonial Militia Integrated in the War of Independence

The first integrated army in American history was the colonial militia that fought the early battles of the War of Independence. Black minutemen fought on the front lines in the first battles against British authority: Blacks assembled at Lexington and Concord on April 19, 1775, to defend Boston against a threatened attack by His Majesty's regiments. One of the first to see combat was Prince Easterbrooks, a Lexington slave, who was a member of Captain John Parker's company and who was wounded at the battle of Concord. He survived, however, to fight in many other companies throughout the Revolutionary War. Another was Barzillai Lew, who joined the 27th Massachusetts Regiment, fought at Bunker Hill, and served in the army for seven years. Although the Continental Army tried to exclude African Americans at one time during the conflict, and some states raised all-Black units, free Black and slave militiamen served alongside of white militiamen in many battles from Bunker Hill to Yorktown.

512 • Peter Salem

A free Black man, Peter Salem, a private in Captain Simon Edgel's company at the battle of Bunker Hill, was the first military hero of the War of Independence. On June 17, 1775, at a crucial moment in the battle when British Major John Pitcairn had rallied the disorganized British troops and prepared a counterattack, Salem shot the major through the head just after the latter yelled, "The day is ours." Peter Salem, a former slave who had gained his freedom upon enlisting in the militia, had battled Pitcairn and his forces earlier at Lexington and was glad to have dispatched the hated major as he did. Now leaderless, the British lost their nerve and the battle. Afterward, Salem's fellow soldiers took up a collection for him. He was also honored by a visit to meet George Washington and by a monument placed over his grave in Framingham, Massachusetts, in 1882.

513 • Salem Poor

Salem Poor was an African American hero of

The Battle of Bunker Hill, 17 June 1775, detail, by John Trumbull, 1786. "Lt. Grosvenor and Peter Salem after Salem shot the British Major Pitcairne." Yale University Art Gallery

the Revolutionary War. He distinguished himself so in battle that fourteen American officers praised him before Congress. On December 5, 1775, a memorial was dedicated to him at Cambridge, Massachusetts, which carried the citation that "under our own observation, we declare that a negro man called Salem Poor, of Colonel Frye's regiment, Captain Ame's com-

pany, in the late battle at Charlestown, behaved like an experienced officer, as well as an excellent soldier."

514 • African Americans Excluded from the Continental Army

Shortly after George Washington took command of the American forces in July 1775, the council of war decided informally not to enlist "any deserter from the Ministerial army, nor any stroller, negro, or vagabond" in the Continental Army. During the debate on the question in the Continental Congress, Edward Rutledge from South Carolina offered a resolution to "discharge all the Negroes, as well as slaves and freemen, in his army." That failed, but the general recommendation to prohibit African Americans from enlisting in the Continental Army was approved by the council of war on October 8, 1775, and by the delegates to the Continental Congress on October 23. General George Washington made it official on November 12, 1775, when he issued orders that "neither Negroes, boys, unable to bear arms, nor old men unfit to endure the fatigues of the campaign are to be enlisted." But this exclusionary policy would change after 1778.

515 • Black Man Captures British General Prescott

African Americans continued to serve in the colonial militias despite the ban on further enlistment in the Continental Army, and some, like Prince, a Black man in Lieutenant Colonel Barton's Rhode Island army, showed great daring and bravery. Early in August 1777, Colonel Barton conceived a plan to capture British Major General Prescott, commander of the Royal Army at Newport, Rhode Island, to effect a trade for a captured American general. Leading an army of forty men in two boats, Barton landed five miles from Newport and advanced on foot to the headquarters of General Prescott, where the colonel, with "a stout negro close behind him, and another at a small distance," confronted and then overwhelmed a sentry. While the other men surrounded the house, "a negro man, named Prince, instantly thrust his beetle head through

the panel door, and seized his victim [Prescott] while in bed." While Colonel Barton received "an elegant sword" for his exploits, Prince, the actual captor of the general, received nothing. In that sense, Prince was not exceptional: throughout the war, African Americans played a pivotal, decisive role in battles only to have that role forgotten afterward.

516 • Africans Still Serve in Labor Battalions

Despite the ban on using African Americans as fighting soldiers, many of the colonies and the Continental Army used slaves and free African Americans as laborers to build fortifications to defend colonial cities. Even South Carolina, which later refused to raise an all-Black regiment, utilized African Americans to build batteries around Charleston. South Carolina leased such slaves from their masters at a cost of ten shillings a day, which the owners received if their "property" was killed or injured on such duty. The use of African Americans in labor battalions, a sign of their lack of the privileges of full citizenship, would continue until the Korean War.

517 • Lord Dunmore's Declaration

The royal governor of Virginia, John Murray, earl of Dunmore, decided to exploit a weakness of the colonial rebels when he issued a proclamation on November 7, 1775, that freed "all indented servants, negroes or others (appertaining to Rebels)" who joined the British forces. Approximately five hundred slaves rushed to join Dunmore, who organized an Ethiopian Regiment. According to Edmund Pendleton: "The Governor . . . marched out with three hundred and fifty soldiers, Tories and slaves. . . . Letters mention that slaves flock to him in abundance; but I hope it is magnified." It wasn't: as Dunmore wrote the British secretary of state on March 30, 1776: "I have been endeavoring to raise two regiments here—one of white people, the other of black. The former goes on very slowly, but the latter very well. . . ." Defeated more by a smallpox epidemic than battle, Dunmore's Ethiopian Regiment was reduced to 150 by the disease six months after his call to action. In June 1776 rebel forces drove Dunmore and his troops from Gwynn's Island and ended the threat of a British-led slave rebellion in Virginia.

518 • African Americans Replace Reluctant Whites

By 1777 losses on the field of battle and rising white desertions had reduced the Continental Army's ranks of men. Northern colonies began to accept African Americans, free and slave, because these colonies could not fill their quotas with white men. In October 1777 Connecticut adopted a policy whereby masters could avoid service in the army by providing one of his slaves, who would receive his freedom for such service. The policy to allow slaves to substitute for masters spread throughout the northern colonies.

519 • Rhode Island's Black Army

As the war took a turn for the worse for the American forces at the end of 1777 at Valley Forge, the general assembly of Rhode Island passed an act in February 1778 to create a battalion of nonwhite troops. The act declared: "That every able-bodied negro, mulatto, or Indian slave in this State, may enlist into either the said two battalions to serve during the continuance of the present war with Great Britain; that every slave so enlisted shall be entitled to receive all the bounties, wages, encouragements allowed by the Continental Congress to

any soldier enlisted in their service." The act also provided that all slaves offered by their masters would be free after the war and that the masters would receive up to 120 pounds per slave. Although many opposed the plan, in part because of its cost, Rhode Island formed a regiment of emancipated slaves that was one of the three that prevented the British from turning the flank of the American army at the battle of Rhode Island on August 29, 1778.

520 • Rev. Dr. Samuel Hopkins on Why Rhode Island Raised a Regiment of Black Troops

God is so ordering it in his providence that it seems absolutely necessary something should speedily be done with respect to the slaves among us, in order to [insure] our safety and to prevent their turning against us in our present struggle, in order to get their liberty. Our oppressors have planned to get the blacks and induce them to take up arms against us, by promising them liberty on this condition. . . . And should we attempt to restrain them by force and severity, keeping a strict guard over them, and punishing those severely who shall be detected in attempting to join our oppressors, this will only be making bad worse, and serve to render our inconsistence, oppression and cruelty more criminal, perspicuous and shocking, and bring down the righteous vengeance of Heaven on our heads. The only way pointed out to prevent this threatening evil is to set the blacks at liberty ourselves by some public act and laws, and then give them proper encouragement to labor, or take arms in the defense of the American cause, as they shall choose. This would at once be doing them some degree of justice, and defeating our enemies in the scheme that they are prosecuting.

Washington crossing the Delaware with his personal servant, James Armistead.
Prints and Photographs Division, Library of Congress

521 • Washington Accepts African Americans in the Continental Army

Facing mounting desertions and the possibility of losing the war, George Washington reversed himself in 1778 and approved the enlistment of free Negroes in the Continental Army. By the end of the war, over five thousand African Americans had served in the Continental Army. Though many had been assigned to labor units, nearly every battle of the Revolutionary War contained some African American soldiers. Washington's confidence in Black soldiers was such that several, including Oliver Cromwell and Prince Whipple, were among the troops Washington used in his daring nighttime crossing of the Delaware, December 25, 1776.

522 • Black Regiments for South Carolina and Georgia?

Because much of the War of Independence was fought in the South, where American forces were weakest, Henry Laurens and his son John proposed that South Carolina and Georgia arm African Americans for defensive purposes. Henry Laurens first proposed the idea to George Washington when Laurens wrote that "the country is greatly distressed, and will be so unless further reinforcements are sent to its relief. Had we arms for three thousand such black men as I could select in Carolina, I should have no doubt of success in driving the British out of Georgia, and subduing East Florida before the end of July." Colonel John Laurens lobbied both the

South Carolina and Georgia legislatures to raise companies of Black troops for defense of the colonies. But opposition to the plan was high in both states, perhaps because such slaves might have to be freed after the war. Even after Sir Henry Clinton, commander in chief of the British forces, announced on June 30, 1779, that all slaves of rebels who joined the British would be freed, and some slaves did enter the British lines, Colonel Laurens could not overcome South Carolina's opposition to arming Black troops. Evidently most South Carolinians preferred to risk enslavement by the British than end the enslavement of their fellow Americans. But despite the opposition of such southern colonies to arming Black soldiers, African Americans did serve in the army of the South in a variety of ways, as builders of breastworks, dams, and fortifications, as guides in forests, swamps, and waterways, as spies and drummers, and in some rare cases, as men who bore arms.

523 • George Washington on the Failure of South Carolina to Raise African American Troops for Defense

The following is an excerpt from a letter written by George Washington in 1782 to Colonel John Laurens about the latter's inability to persuade his fellow South Carolinians to raise a regiment of Black troops in an hour of desperate need.

I must confess that I am not at all astonished at the failure of your plan. That spirit of freedom, which, at the commencement of this contest, would have gladly sacrificed everything to the attainment of its object, has long since subsided, and every selfish passion has taken its place. It is not the public but private interest which influences the generality of mankind; nor can the Americans any longer boast an exception. Under the circumstances, it would rather have been

surprising if you had succeeded; nor will you, I fear, have better success in Georgia.

524 • Black Reenslavement After Service in the Continental Army and Washington's Response

Many African American slaves were led to believe that if they joined the colonial militia or Continental Army and fought for American independence, they would be freed from slavery at the end of the war. But many slaves were reenslaved after the war by "stay at home" masters. One particularly poignant case was that of Simon Lee, the grandfather of William Wells Brown, the first African American novelist, and a Virginia slave when he joined the war effort. When discharged honorably from the army, Lee was returned to his master to work as a slave on his master's tobacco plantation.

Although himself a slave owner, George Washington was outraged at the practice of reenslaving those who had fought in the war. In one case where a slave owner, Mr. Hobby, demanded return of an African American who had fought in the Massachusetts army, Washington interceded in 1783 and appointed a commission of officers to investigate the claim and the African American's record of service. Eventually the Virginia legislature passed a law that those slaves who had enlisted in a regiment and who had been a substitute for a free person who was obligated to serve would be determined to be free, as if he had been specifically promised such freedom after service.

525 • Fate of African Americans Who Fought for British

As with slaves who fought with the colonies, the slaves who fought on the British side were not guaranteed their freedom or dignity after the war either. According to Thomas Jefferson:

Black sailor in crew of ship at the battle of Lake Erie, 1814. Prints and Photographs Division, Library of Congress

From an estimate I made at that time, on the best information I could collect, I supposed the State of Virginia lost, under Lord Cornwallis' hand, that year, about thirty thousand slaves; and that, of these, twenty-seven thousand died of the small-pox and camp fever; the rest were partly sent to the West Indies, and exchange of rum, sugar, coffee and fruit; and partly sent to New York, from whence they went, at the peace, either to Nova Scotia or England. From this last place, I believe they have lately been sent to Africa.

526 • African Americans Excluded After Revolutionary War

Even though African Americans had helped the Continental Army secure American independence, the new nation, in the Enlistment Act of 1792, limited the right to serve in the national militia only to "each and every free able-bodied white male citizen of the respective States, resident therein, who is or shall be of the age of eighteen years, and under the age of forty-five years."

WAR OF 1812

Engagements, Policy, and People

527 •
Chesapeake-Leopard Affair

Although the U.S. Army did not enlist African Americans after the Revolutionary War, the U.S. Navy continued to use African Americans as seamen because of the perennial shortage of white sailors. The Black presence in the navy placed them at the center of the naval incident that led to the War of 1812. In 1807 the British frigate *Leopard* shelled the USS *Chesapeake* to locate four escaped British sailors. When the *Chesapeake* yielded and the British boarded the American ship, they took into custody four sailors, three of whom—William Ware, Daniel Martin, and John Strachan—were African Americans previously impressed by the British. Although it was obvious that these men were Americans, the British refused to return them for four years, inciting American public opinion and leading President Thomas Jefferson to close American harbors to British ships. The U.S. could not go to war then because it lacked a serious navy; but the seeds of resentment were sown, and in June 1812 the United States declared war on Britain, citing the impressment of American citizens as a principal reason for going to war.

528 • Integrated Navy During War of 1812

An exact accounting of the number of African

Americans in the U.S. Navy during the War of 1812 is unknown. But a surgeon, Usher Parsons, who served on board several ships during the war, recalled:

In 1814, our fleet sailed to the Upper Lakes to co-operate with Colonel Croghan at Mackinac. About one in twelve of the crew was black. In 1816, I was surgeon of the "Java," under Commodore Perry. The white and colored seamen messed together. About one in six or eight were colored. In 1819, I was surgeon of the "Guerriere," under Commodore Macdonough; and the proportion of blacks was about the same in her crew. There seemed to be an entire absence of prejudice against the blacks as messmates among the crew.

529 • American Navy Officers Debate Quality of Black Sailors

Throughout the War of 1812, Captain Oliver Hazard Perry of the American naval forces on Lake Erie complained about the lack of qualified officers and seamen available for his navy. In one instance, after receiving a new allotment of men from Commodore Isaac Chauncey, Perry complained about their quality. "The men that came by Mr. Champlin are a motley set,—blacks, soldiers, and boys. I cannot think you saw them after they were selected. I am, however, pleased to see any thing in the shape of a man." Upset by Perry's comments, Chauncey defended the quality of the men in his reply:

I regret that you are not pleased with the men sent you by Messrs Champlin and Forest; for, to my knowledge, a part of them are not surpassed by any seamen we have in the fleet: and I have yet to learn that the color of the skin, or the cut and trimmings of the coat, can effect a man's qualifications or usefulness. I have nearly fifty blacks on board of this ship, and many more of them are among my best men; and those people you call soldiers have been to sea from two to sev-

enteen years; and I presume that you will find them as good and useful as any men on board of your vessel.

530 • Cyrus Tiffany

Black heroism was not daunted by Captain Oliver H. Perry's opinion of Black sailors; indeed, a Black sailor, Cyrus Tiffany, was instrumental in protecting the life of Perry. When the USS *Lawrence*, the flagship of the American navy on Lake Erie, was sunk during the battle at Put-in-Bay in July 1814, Tiffany and others were rowing Perry to the USS *Niagara*, the new flagship, when the British began to shoot at the rowboat. Tiffany shielded his captain with his body and allowed Perry to escape safely to the new ship.

531 • General Andrew Jackson Reverses U.S. Army Policy

Americans suffered several devastating losses in the first year of the War of 1812 with England. The failed American invasion of Canada, the cessation of the war in Europe, which allowed England to focus its military on the U.S., and the falling morale of American troops and volunteers set the stage for the employment of the African American in the army. When the British prepared to attack New Orleans, General Andrew Jackson issued the following proclamation on September 21, 1814:

To the Free Colored Inhabitants of Louisiana:

Through a mistaken policy, you have heretofore been deprived of a participation in the glorious struggle for national rights in which our country is engaged. This no longer shall exist. As sons of freedom, you are now called upon to defend our most inestimable blessing. As Americans, your country looks with confidence to her adopted children for a valorious support, as a faithful return for the advantages enjoyed under her mild and equitable government. . . . To every noble-hearted, generous freeman of color volunteering to serve during the present contest with Great Britain, and no longer, there will be paid the same bounty, in money and lands, now received by the white soldiers of the United States, vis: one hundred and twenty-four dollars in money, and one hundred and sixty acres of land. . . .

The free African Americans were to be enrolled in a separate regiment, commanded by white officers, and free from negative comments or "sarcasm" from fellow white officers.

532 • Black Battalions of Freemen Respond

African Americans in Louisiana had already organized their own battalion, which, in Sep-

tember 1812, had been recognized by the state legislature of Louisiana and organized as a corps of free African Americans as part of the state militia. After General Andrew Jackson's call to arms, the Battalion of Free Men of Color, as they were called, were joined by a second battalion of Black soldiers organized by a free Black Santo Domingan emigrant, Joseph Savary, and together they were pressed into service in December 1814 to defend New Orleans. While one battalion attended British forces at Chalmette Plains, the other built fortifications against the British attack in January 1815. Both were engaged on January 8 during the main attack by the British, and together they kept the center of the fortifications, the artillery batter-

Black riflemen at battle of New Orleans. Prints and Photographs Division, Library of Congress

ies, from being taken. Although the African Americans had repulsed the British assault, British sharpshooters took up positions after the battle and picked off Americans trying to rescue their wounded on the field. Savary, now a captain, led a group of Black men who routed the British sharpshooters in the last major battle of the contest. Afterward, Jackson praised the Black soldiers as having "not disappointed the hopes that were formed of their courage and perseverance in the performance of their duty."

533 • General Jackson Reneges on His Promise

A negative view of Andrew Jackson's regard for Black troops emerges from *The Narrative of James Roberts,* written by a man who served in Jackson's army at New Orleans. Roberts was a slave who had been returned to slavery after serving in the Revolutionary War.

General Jackson, in order to prepare to meet Packenham, the British General, in the contest at New Orleans, came into our section of the country . . . to enlist five hundred negroes. Jackson came into the field and then addressed us thus: "Had you not as soon go into the battle and fight, as to stay here in the cotton field, dying and never die? If you will go, and the battle is fought and the victory gained on Israel's side, you shall be free."

But after the battle was won and "sixty or seventy or more of the colored men were killed . . . [who] were, without doubt, as Jackson himself acknowledged, the instrumental cause of the victory," Jackson told the men to "go home to your masters." Roberts challenged Jackson about his promise to free them, and Jackson answered: " 'If I were to hire you my horse, could you sell it without my leave? You are another man's property, and I have not money sufficient

to buy all of you, and set you free." Infuriated at the betrayal, Roberts cocked his gun but discovered Jackson had had the guns of the African Americans unloaded. "Had my gun been loaded," Roberts recalled, "doubtless Jackson would have been a dead man in a moment. . . . Jackson asked me if I contended for freedom. I said I did. He said, 'I think you are very presumptuous.' I told him, the time had come for us to claim our rights. He said, 'You are a day too late.' Some of the whites standing round said, 'He ought to be shot.' Now, just think of that! Two days before, I had, with my fellow soldiers, saved their city from fire and massacre . . . now, 'he ought to be shot!' simply for contending for my freedom, which, both my master and Jackson had solemnly before high heaven promised, before I left home."

534 • African American Designs the "Cotton-Bag Fort"

When Andrew Jackson assembled his force at New Orleans, his soldiers, many of whom were African American slaves, were outnumbered by the British forces ten to one. Faced with this disadvantage, Jackson consulted with his men as to what was the best defense. According to *The Narrative of James Roberts,* "There was in Jackson's army a colored soldier named Pompey, who gave Jackson the first idea about the *cotton-bag fort,* and superintended the construction of it. We engaged in making it, and it was completed in the latter part of the second day. The cotton-bags were so placed as to leave port holes for three muskets to point through each." It would be from behind that makeshift cotton-bag fort that Jackson's outnumbered forces would mow down the onrushing British soldiers "like grass before the scythe," and achieve the initial destruction of the center of the British army.

535 • "Major" Jeffrey and American Racism

Among the brave blacks who fought in the battles for American liberty was Major Jeffrey, a Tennessean, who, during the campaign of Major General Andrew Jackson in Mobile, filled the place of "regular" among the soldiers. In the charge made by General Stump against the enemy, the Americans were repulsed and thrown into disorder,—Major Stump being forced to retire, in a manner by no means desirable, under the circumstances. Major Jeffrey, who was but a common soldier, seeing the condition of his comrades, and comprehending the disastrous results about to befall them, rushed forward, mounted a horse, took command of the troops, and, by an heroic effort, rallied them to the charge,—completely routing the enemy, who left the Americans masters of the field. He at once received from the General the title of "Major," though he could not, according to the American policy, so commission him.

A few years ago receiving an indignity from a common ruffian, he was forced to strike him in self-defense; for which act, in accordance with the laws of slavery in that, as well as many other slave States, he was compelled to receive on his naked person, nine and thirty lashes with a raw hide! This, at the age of seventy odd, after the distinguished services rendered his country,—probably when the white ruffian for whom he was tortured was unable to raise an arm in its defense,—war more than he could bear; it broke his heart, and he sank to rise no more, till summoned by the blast of the last trumpet. . . .

—Anonymous, from Joseph T. Wilson's *Black Phalanx*

536 • African Americans in the Navy

Although the U.S. Army returned to its "no African Americans" policy after the War of 1812,

African Americans continued to be present in the navy, not only as cooks but also as seamen. The general lack of white enlistment in the navy disposed this branch of America's antebellum armed forces to not draw the color line. African Americans were so prevalent on American ships that in one case, four Europeans who had seen the USS *Constitution* in port in Trieste were convinced that all Americans were Black because all of the crew members they had seen on the American ship were African Americans!

CIVIL WAR

Engagements and Policy

537 • Black Soldiers Rejected at Beginning of Civil War

When the Civil War erupted in 1861, Blacks rushed forward to volunteer for the Union Army. But they were turned away. "This is a white man's war" was the popular cry. Many northerners believed that servitude rendered slaves unusable as soldiers. Newspaper writers and cartoonists reinforced these feelings by making outrageous examples of how African Americans could be used to aid the Union Army effort.

538 • Lincoln's Early Position

President Abraham Lincoln seemed to reinforce the view that African Americans were inappropriate as Union soldiers by refusing to enlist Black troops. Lincoln's decision was based less on any prejudice against Black soldiers than on his desire to entice the Confederate South back into the Union and to keep the border states from seceding. He believed the use of Black troops would infuriate the southern

Cartoon, "Dark Artillery; or, How to Make the Contrabands Useful." Prints and Photographs Division, Library of Congress

and border states. Moreover, by keeping African Americans out of the fighting, Lincoln hoped to keep the question of slavery out of the war as well.

539 • Slaves as Contraband

Slaves flocked to Union forces whenever they approached plantations, but early in the Civil War Lincoln ordered Union states to return such runaway slaves to their Confederate masters. That policy brought strong public criticism from abolitionist newspapers in the North. The first

challenge to that policy came on May 27, 1861, when General Benjamin F. Butler issued an order that captured slaves coming into his lines would be retained as "contraband of war" and used to aid the Union Army. Butler argued that such confiscation was necessary to deprive the Confederates of their use to construct fortifications. Butler's rationale took hold, and afterward, slaves who had been used on Confederate military projects were not returned. Soon the entire policy of returning any contrabands was reviewed, and early in 1862 the War Department reversed it and prohibited the use of federal troops to return runaway slaves.

540 • Confederates First to Accept Black Volunteers

Ironically the secessionists were the first to use African Americans as soldiers, although they were free Negroes, not slaves. Some of those who served were wealthy landowners in Louisiana and South Carolina who either supported the institution of slavery or believed they must show support of the Confederate cause in order to retain their property in the South. A November 23, 1861, review of Confederate troops at New Orleans showed that these forces contained a company of fourteen hundred free African Americans who were later praised for having supplied themselves "with arms without regard to cost and trouble."

541 • First Law to Enlist African Americans as Soldiers

On June 28, 1861, Tennessee became the first state to pass a law for the enlistment of "all male free persons of color between the ages of fifteen and fifty years." The wording of the law suggested that its primary intention was not to employ these men as soldiers, but to require them "to do all such menial service for the relief of volunteers."

542 • Pressure from Congress

After the Union Army suffered a series of military defeats in 1861 and 1862, pressure mounted on Lincoln to use African Americans as soldiers. As Charles Sumner put it: "I do not say carry the war into Africa; but carry Africa into the war." As desertions from the Union Army increased, and white enlistment plummeted, Congress passed the Confiscation Act of August 6, 1861, which authorized the president

to enlist African Americans in the army. Lincoln still refused. Then, in October 1861, Secretary of War Edwin Stanton authorized General Thomas W. Sherman to use "all loyal persons offering their services for the defense of the Union" at Port Royal, South Carolina. On July 17, 1862, Congress amended the Enlistment Act of 1795 giving the president authority to enlist African Americans, but Lincoln still refused to act on Congress's recommendation. He even went so far as to state he would resign rather than use Negro regiments.

543 • The First African American Regiment

Events on the field of battle advanced ahead of Washington policymaking. In May 1862 General David Hunter, commander of the Department of the South, ordered the formation of the first armed and uniformed Black regiment in the Civil War, what became known as the 1st South Carolina Volunteer Regiment. "Volunteer" was something of a misnomer, since Hunter forcibly pressed into his army African Americans who appeared able-bodied. When news of the regiment reached the press, C. A. Wickliffe, congressman from Kentucky, demanded an explanation from Secretary of War Edwin M. Stanton, as to whether Hunter had raised a regiment of "fugitive slaves." Hunter wrote back that a regiment of "fugitive slaves" did not exist, but rather a "fine regiment of persons whose late masters are 'fugitive rebels.'" Given that these "loyal persons composing this regiment" wished to avoid their masters, the "loyal persons" were working now for the government and helping to "go in full and effective pursuit of their fugacious and traitorous proprietors." Hunter's letter constructed a brilliant argument for raising African American troops out of the language of Secretary Stanton's earlier directive to Sher-

Black soldiers on review, South Carolina. Prints and Photographs Division, Library of Congress

545 • Lincoln Approves

By August 1862, even President Lincoln knew that he could not win the war without the Negro soldier; he just did not want generals making the decision. Accordingly, when Lincoln issued his Emancipation Proclamation on January 1, 1863, he included a provision for enlisting Black troops. The War Department began to aggressively recruit African Americans. By the war's end, approximately 186,000 African Americans had served in the Union Army, with 30,000 casualties. Although all those in the army served in segregated units and mostly in labor battalions, Black soldiers fought in several important battles of the war.

man, but it angered Wickliffe and Lincoln, who disbanded "Hunter's Regiment." Re-formed and reconstituted under Colonel Thomas Wentworth Higginson, the 1st South Carolina was mustered on November 7, 1862, and served throughout the Civil War.

544 • First Appeal for Black Troops in the North

The first northern appeal for African American troops was made on August 4, 1862 by General Sprague of Rhode Island, who asked Black men to enlist as soldiers in the state militia. Rhode Island then organized the first African American artillery regiment. Other appeals for Black soldiers followed, such as General Butler's appeal on August 22 to the free Negroes of New Orleans, which had recently fallen under Union control, to join the Union Army.

546 • First Civil War Battles of African Americans

The first actual fighting done by Black troops occurred on October 28, 1862, by the 79th Colored Infantry from Kansas in a battle at Island Mound, Missouri. A week later, November 3–10, 1862, the 1st South Carolina engaged the enemy in the first extended action and pursuit of the war on St. Helena Island. Under the command of Captain Trowbridge and Lieutenant Colonel Oliver T. Beard, the 1st South Carolina also pursued the enemy along the coast of Georgia and east Florida. Even after these engagements, however, resistance to the use of Black troops in combat remained high. When Frederick Douglass asked Pennsylvania's governor, Andrew Curtin, whether he would accept African American troops, the answer was no—until General Robert E. Lee invaded southern Pennsylvania in

"Make Way for Liberty!" Prints and Photographs Division, Library of Congress

the summer of 1863. Suddenly the prohibition against the use of Black troops evaporated, and by June 23 the first eighty African Americans were recruited into the Pennsylvania forces.

547 • First Publicized Battle

The first publicly documented fighting of Black troops occurred on the night of January 26, 1863. It was part of a deliberate plan to get African Americans into battle so as to end speculation as to whether African Americans could be good fighting men. At the battle of the Hundred Pines in South Carolina, war correspondents accompanied the expedition and reported back that the African American soldiers had acquitted themselves well in combat with the enemy.

548 • Louisiana's *Corps d'Afrique* Enter the Fray

On May 27, 1863, at Port Hudson, Louisiana, free African Americans and former slaves (The *Corps d'Afrique*) in the 1st and 3rd Louisiana Native Guards launched a valiant attack against the Confederate Army. Even though the Confederate stronghold at Port Hudson did not fall until two months later, the courage and heroism of these soldiers was widely reported.

549 • African Americans Repulse Confederate Army

On June 7, 1863, approximately one thousand African American soldiers repulsed an assault by the Confederate Army at Milliken's Bend, Louisiana. General Ulysses S. Grant had withdrawn troops from the garrison at Milliken's Bend to support his attack on Vicksburg. Brigadier General Dennis, who was in command of the troops in Milliken's Bend, was surprised when a Confederate force of three thousand attacked the garrison. When the Confederates mounted the works, Black soldiers fought vicious hand-to-hand combat with Confederate regulars after white Union soldiers had abandoned the field of battle. By the end of the day, the Black troops re-

pulsed the Confederate forces and won the respect of Grant for holding Milliken's Bend.

550 • The 54th Massachusetts at Fort Wagner

Despite the gallantry of African American soldiers at Port Hudson and Milliken's Bend, the belief lingered in the North that African Americans were not fit for the most dangerous and courageous missions of the Civil War. It was with that prejudice in mind that Lieutenant Colonel Robert volunteered the all-Black 54th Massachusetts Volunteer Infantry to lead the largely suicidal assault on South Carolina's Fort Wagner on July 18, 1863. Highly publicized, this attack on a heavily fortressed symbol of Confederate resistance might have succeeded if white troops had reinforced the 54th's heroic assault. After advancing across the open beach side of the fort, during which they suffered many casualties, including the colonel, the 54th Massachusetts briefly took the fort before being

"Storming Fort Wagner." Chromolithograph by Kurz & Allison. Prints and Photographs Division, Library of Congress

repulsed by the Confederates. Still, the 54th's indisputable courage convinced many northerners that Black soldiers were capable of fighting gallantly in the Union Army.

551 • General Grant's Men

Even before the 54th Massachusetts charge against Fort Wagner, Black troops had won the respect of the Union Army's most important general, Ulysses S. Grant. Early in June 1863 Grant had had to withdraw troops from the garrison at Milliken's Bend and thereby left its defense to three infantry regiments of African American troops. The garrison, which then contained fourteen hundred men from the 9th and 11th Louisiana Regiments and the 1st Mississippi, plus a smattering of whites, was attacked on June 7 by three thousand Confederate soldiers. The African American troops repulsed the larger Confederate force, which had mounted the works, with musket fire, bayonets, and hand-to-hand fighting. African American troops gained Grant's respect for holding Milliken's Bend. When Grant left the western front to assume command of the entire Union forces in Virginia, he brought twenty thousand African American soldiers with him. During the last year of the war, thirteen African American regiments were a crucial part of the Union Army that brought victories at Chaffin's Farm, New Market Heights, and Fort Harrison in Virginia.

552 • Fort Pillow Massacre

Black soldiers, along with southern whites who had joined the Union Army, were especially hated by Confederate troops, who made that graphically clear in the spring of 1864 at Fort Pillow, Tennessee. Defended by 295 white men of the 13th Tennessee Union Cavalry and 262 African Americans of the 6th United States Heavy Artillery, Fort Pillow was surrounded on April 12 by a vastly superior force of Confederates. When Major General N. B. Forrest demanded surrender of the fort, Union commanders refused; when the Confederates overwhelmed the fort several hours later, the Confederates slaughtered the Union soldiers, along with women and children in the fort, even though they surrendered. The killing lasted until midnight, as Confederates vented their anger on helpless Black soldiers in the fort: several were shot down as they ran, and others, wounded, were burned alive. Afterward Major Forrest tried to stem the public outcry by claiming that the atrocities were exaggerated, but the massacre lived on in the memory of African American soldiers. In several later engagements, African American soldiers led their charges into battle with the cry "Remember Fort Pillow."

553 • Fatigue Duty

Despite the valor of African American soldiers under fire, most Black soldiers in the Civil War were consigned to labor or fatigue duty. Relegating African Americans to labor battalions reflected the belief that African Americans were second-class citizens and unfit for military service. However, in emergencies, as was true throughout the history of the African American soldier, the army would not hesitate to use African Americans in combat situations. For example, the 14th United States Colored Troops were consigned to fatigue duty until August 15, 1864, when General Joseph Wheeler attacked the Union forces garrisoned at Dalton, Georgia. General James B. Steedman sent the 14th Infantry of ex-slaves to rescue the white Union troops. After the battle had been turned in the Union forces' favor by the quickly dispatched African Americans, they were cheered by the white 51st as the 14th Infantry marched into

Dalton. In recognition of their valor, the 14th Infantry was joined with General Lovell H. Rousseau's command at Pulaski, Tennessee, on September 27, 1864.

554 • Colored Troops' Pay

Throughout the Civil War, Black troops were paid less than white troops. The July 1862 act that gave the president permission to enlist African Americans in the Union Army specified that they were to be paid ten dollars a week, rather than the thirteen a week paid to white soldiers. That act rationalized the lower payment for African Americans with the idea that African Americans were contraband of war and to be used exclusively in labor battalions. But when the 54th Massachusetts was formed, expressly for combat service, it was promised pay as other troops; but the men did not receive it. On June 15, 1864, Congress passed the Army Appropriation Bill that declared Black troops should receive the same uniform, arms, equipment, pay, and bounty as other soldiers. On July 14, 1864, Attorney General Edward Bates declared himself in favor of equal pay and bounty for Black soldiers. But Black soldiers were still paid ten dollars a week until the end of the war.

555 • Gabriel Young Receives Freedom for His Military Service

One of the incentives for military service was freedom. Gabriel Young became free after he joined Captain James Johnson's Regiment of Colored Infantry Volunteers. Subsequently his

Black and white sailors and marines mingle on deck of the U.S. gunboat *Mendota*, 1864. National Archives

wife was also freed, and his son, Charles, was born into freedom in 1865 in Mayslick, Kentucky. Charles Gabriel eventually became the third African American to graduate from West Point.

556 • African Americans in the Navy

Although African Americans in the army were rigidly segregated in the Civil War, they served in the navy on several ships, often in integrated mess and living quarters. This liberalization of racial restrictions resulted from the prevalance of Blacks in the Civil War navy: one out of every four seamen (about 30,000 sailors in the Union Navy) were African American by the war's end; Blacks also served on the infamous Union ship, the *Monitor.*

557 • Robert E. Lee Requests African Americans

When Robert E. Lee became commander in

chief of the Confederate Army on January 31, 1865, one of the first things he did was to ask for the military use of African Americans by the Confederate government. The lower house of the Confederate Congress approved the resolution on January 28, but the senate rejected it. Again, the idea of using Black troops was reintroduced by Lee and again rejected by the Senate, but finally, on March 13, the Congress passed an act to recruit Black troops. On March 23 the 1st Company of Negro state troops joined Confederate active service.

People

558 • African American Leaders Served in the Civil War

Harriet Tubman, the former slave who led hundreds of African Americans North to freedom before the war, became a scout and a spy for the Union Army. Although Frederick Douglass did not accept a commission in the army, two of his sons, Charles and Lewis Douglass, served in the famous 54th Massachusetts, his oldest son, Lewis, becoming a sergeant major. Martin R. Delany, the prewar advocate of African American emigration, accepted commission as a major in the 104th Regiment at Charleston, South Carolina. The war also made some new political leaders. Captain P. B. S. Pinchback of the 2nd Louisiana Volunteers became lieutenant governor of Louisiana during Reconstruction.

559 • Robert Blake at Sea

On December 25, 1863, the USS *Marblehead* was shelled by Confederate batteries on John's Island, South Carolina, killing the powder boy

and throwing the ship into confusion. Robert Blake, the commander's steward, rushed out of his quarters, substituted for the dead powder boy, and brought gunpowder boxes to the ship's artillery throughout the battle. Credited not only with bringing vitally needed gunpowder but also with a sense of humor during the tense battle, Blake was awarded the Navy Medal of Honor on April 16, 1864, for his heroism.

560 • Black Congressional Medals of Honor

During the Civil War, at least sixteen African Americans received the Congressional Medal of

Christian Fleetwood, Medal of Honor man. Prints and Photographs Division, Library of Congress

Honor, a commendation established by Congress on July 12, 1862, to recognize enlisted men of the armed forces who "distinguish themselves by their gallantry in action." Typical of the acts that were honored were those of two men who fought at New Market Heights and Chaffin's Farm in September 1864. Private James Gardner of the 36th United States Colored Troops rushed ahead of his brigade as they stormed the fort at New Market Heights: Gardner shot and bayoneted a rebel officer who was rallying his forces. At Chaffin's Farm, Christian A. Fleetwood, a sergeant major of the 4th United States Colored Troops, grabbed the Union flag after two color-bearers had been shot. With no officers present, Fleetwood then rallied a group of reserves to attack the fort during the final successful battle of the engagement.

POST–CIVIL WAR

Engagements and Policy

561 • Retained but Segregated

Because the army wished to demobilize white troops as quickly as possible and yet retain an effective fighting force after the Civil War, Black troops were retained in the army after the war. The 122,000 Black troops in the U.S. Army as of June 1865 comprised 13 percent of the total—the largest percentage of Blacks in the army in U.S. history. Congress gave official recognition to its continuing need for the African American soldier by passing, in March 1866, a law to create six exclusively African American regiments: four infantries (the 38th, 39th, 40th, and 41st) and two cavalries (the 9th

and 10th). Although the infantry regiments were reduced to two—the 24th and 25th—in 1869, these all-Black regiments proved that the African American soldier had a right to serve in the United States Army. But congressional action also gave a legal basis to a segregated army and made more difficult the effort to desegregate the army in the future.

562 • African Americans in the Army of Reconstruction

After the Civil War, African American troops helped occupy the former Confederacy and enforce the policies of the Reconstruction Act of 1867. Although never a majority of the troops stationed in the South, the eighty thousand African American soldiers serving there became the target of southern white hostility to Reconstruction. Southerners complained bitterly during Reconstruction about Black soldiers who were "uppity" and "disrespectful" of southern whites during the occupation. Black troops had the unenviable task of protecting unpopular Reconstruction governments from the Ku Klux Klan, the White League, and other terrorist organizations. Black soldiers also supported efforts of Black southerners to vote, to hold office, and to organize farm and labor cooperatives. The withdrawal of Black troops in 1877 by President Rutherford B. Hayes ended such protections, but did not end white southerner hostility to Blacks in uniform. Even after World War II, the South greeted Black servicemen with violence, in part because Black soldiers symbolized the occupation of the South during Reconstruction.

563 • Buffalo Soldiers in the Indian Wars

With the decline of Reconstruction, the National Army dwindled in numbers, but African

Americans continued to serve in the U.S. Army and took an active part in the Indian wars in the West. Stationed at such outposts as Fort Snelling, Minnesota, in the 1880s, the 25th Infantry escorted western migrants, protected mail and stage routes, and fought in attacks on the Apaches, Kiowas, Cheyennes, Comanches, and Arapahos. The 10th Cavalry played an even more dramatic role: it was credited with capturing the feared Indian leader Geronimo in 1885. With fewer desertions than white counterparts and greater devotion to the army, the "Buffalo Soldiers," as the Indians named them, distinguished themselves and received fourteen Congressional Medals of Honor for their efforts.

564 • Lieutenant Powhatan Clarke

Congress awarded a Buffalo Soldier the Medal of Honor for a daring rescue during the 1886 campaign to recapture Geronimo. The Apache leader had escaped from the San Carlos reservation in Arizona in May 1885, and after a year-long pursuit that led into Mexico, the K Company of the 10th Cavalry had cornered Geronimo—or so they thought—in the Pinto Mountains, some thirty

HARPER'S WEEKLY.
JOURNAL OF CIVILIZATION.

Vol. XXX.—No. 1548.
Copyright, 1886, by Harper & Brothers.

NEW YORK, SATURDAY, AUGUST 21, 1886.

TEN CENTS A COPY.
WITH A SUPPLEMENT.

Soldiering in the Southwest—the rescue of Corporal Scott. Prints and Photographs Division, Library of Congress

miles south of the Mexican border. But as the K Company marched forward to attack on foot, they found themselves pinned down by Apache rifle fire. Corporal Scott was wounded and lay exposed to enemy fire in an open field. Without regard to his own safety, Lieutenant Powhatan Clarke ran from behind a ridge and dragged Scott to safety. During the commotion created by the rescue, Geronimo escaped from the grasp of the Buffalo Soldiers. Four months later, after a renewed campaign, Geronimo surrendered to the 10th Cavalry.

565 • Why Blacks Out West?

The army stationed a disproportionate number of African Americans in the West for a variety of racially based reasons. First, African American troops were unpopular in the South and in the North, particularly in urban areas. Stationing African American troops in rural areas thus removed them from white opposition. Moreover, in an era of rising scientific racism, the army believed that African Americans were more adapted to the harsh conditions of life in the West. Not only were African Americans believed to survive better in the harsh climate, but also some people, like William Tecumseh Sherman, believed that Blacks survived attacks of typhoid fever better than whites. That such theories were mainly justification for sending African American troops to the worst possible duty, which most white troops would reject, was made plain when the 25th Infantry of presumably "tropical" African Americans was forced to

spend ten years in the frigid conditions in Montana and the Dakotas.

566 • African American Heroes of the Spanish-American War

Teddy Roosevelt and his Rough Riders are credited with winning the Spanish-American War, but Black soldiers turned the most important battles in the Americans' favor. At Las Guásimas, Cuba, on June 23, 1898, the all-Black 10th Cavalry, with more experience from the Indian wars and better arms (machine guns), led the rest of the American forces and overwhelmed the Spanish. Afterward, Roosevelt remarked: "No troops could behave better than the colored soldiers." During the battle of El Caney, Teddy was even more grateful: the 9th and 10th Cavalries rescued his Rough Riders when they were pinned down by a heavily fortified garrison. Advancing quickly through the surrounding woods, the Black troops endured heavy losses from artillery and infantry fire, but freed the Rough Riders from their position. The 10th Cavalry joined with the rest in an assault that crushed the Spanish at El Caney and later

Battle of Las Guásimas. Prints and Photographs Division, Library of Congress

at Santiago. According to one white corporal: "If it had not been for the Negro cavalry, the Rough Riders would have been exterminated." Another put the racial implications of the victory more succinctly: "They can drink out of our canteens."

567 • What a Difference Five Months Makes

Lieutenant John J. Pershing, commander of the 10th Cavalry, heaped praise on his Black soldiers in July 1898 after their valorous assault on San Juan Hill, Cuba, another major engagement of the Spanish-American War. "They had fought their way into our affections, as they have fought their way into the hearts of the American people." But just five months later, in Huntsville, Alabama, two Black members of the same regiment were killed by a Black man. He killed them because local white citizens had announced that a reward would be paid for every Black cavalryman that was killed. As one member of the regiment put it, "Cuba was a paradise. There we expected and looked for trouble. Our enemies were there, but here it is among our supposed friends . . . that we face a more deadly enemy."

568 • Roosevelt's Brownsville Affair

On August 13, 1906, a gun battle broke out in Brownsville, Texas, a town near the Mexican border, that left a white bartender dead and a police lieutenant wounded. White townspeople blamed three companies of the 25th Colored Infantry stationed at nearby Fort Brown for the attack, believing it was retaliation for the town's harassment of the African American troops. The soldiers denied involvement in the affair, and an inspection of their weapons proved none had been fired. Still, when an army investigation concluded that the battalion's "conspiracy of silence" shielded the guilty parties, President Theodore Roosevelt ordered the dishonorable discharge, without a trial, of 167 of the 170 soldiers in the 1st Battalion of the 25th Infantry. His decision forfeited the pension of seasoned soldiers, including six Medal of Honor winners, who not only had fought bravely throughout the American West but also, ironically, had backed up Roosevelt's Rough Riders in their assault on San Juan Hill. Issued a day after African Americans had cast crucial votes for the Republican ticket in several state elections, Roosevelt's decision destroyed his reputation among African Americans, damaged the leadership of Booker T. Washington, a firm Roosevelt supporter, and helped deny Roosevelt and Taft the presidency in 1912.

569 • Colonel Benjamin Grierson

United States Army policy discouraged African Americans from serving as officers, even in all–African American regiments. In the eyes of the army, the stigma of slavery rendered African Americans unfit to lead. Since most whites viewed officer duty as a blight on their careers, African American troops were generally led by white officers who could not avoid such duty—the least qualified. An exception to that rule was Colonel Benjamin Grierson, a fine officer, who organized the 10th Cavalry, molded it into a highly trained fighting force, and led its campaigns against the Comanches, the Mescaleros, and the Chiricahuas in the Southwest.

570 • First Black West Point Cadets

The first African American cadet at West Point was not Henry Flipper or Benjamin O. Davis, as is often believed. Two others—Michael Howard from Mississippi and James Webster Smith from South Carolina—share that distinction. Both entered in 1870, the result of the election of Blacks to Congress under Reconstruction, since entrance to West Point required the recommendation of a member of Congress. Unfortunately neither Howard nor Smith graduated. Smith went on to supervise the training of cadets at South Carolina State College.

571 • Henry Flipper and the Code of Silence

Henry Flipper is rightfully remembered as the first African American to graduate from West Point, on June 15, 1877. That was a considerable achievement, as Flipper's book on his life at West Point disclosed. During his entire four years at West Point, Flipper had to survive a psychological campaign of total isolation during which none of the other cadets would speak with him. Upon graduation, Flipper received a

Lieutenant Henry Flipper. Arizona Historical Society, Tucson

command of a Black unit, the 10th Cavalry "Indian fighters." Unfortunately Flipper was accused of embezzlement of funds and conduct unbecoming of an officer. Although the charge of embezzlement was dropped, he was convicted of the second charge and discharged from the army. He did not let his unfair treatment, however, defeat him. He worked as a special agent in the Justice Department and published several translations of Spanish and Mexican laws that are still used today. Although Flipper failed to vindicate his name by the time of his death in 1940, later investigations concluded he had been wrongfully accused, largely because of his race. He was granted, posthumously, an honorable discharge and burial in Arlington National Cemetery.

572 • The Court-Martial of Johnson Chestnut Whittaker

The perils of being a Black cadet at West Point in the post–Civil War years are illustrated by the experience of Johnson Chestnut Whittaker. On April 6, 1880, this Black cadet was discovered delirious and bound to his bed in his room at West Point, with his ears cut as if he were a hog, his face covered with blood. Incredibly authorities' first reaction was that Whittaker had staged an attack to get "sympathy." A West Point court of inquiry concluded that there was no evidence to support Whittaker's contention that three masked cadets had attacked him. Even when evidence surfaced later in a court-martial that three masked cadets had been seen that evening, the court dismissed that evidence in favor of handwriting experts who claimed that Whittaker had written a threatening note to himself. Although Whittaker was found guilty, the attorney general threw out the decision on the inadmissibility of handwriting evidence. Nevertheless, Whittaker was dismissed from the academy in 1882 for deficiencies on an exam he took shortly after the first verdict. Afterward Whittaker joined the faculty of the Colored Normal, Industrial, Agricultural and Mechanical College in South Carolina and refrained from publicly discussing the issue. His son served in World War I and a grandson in World War II.

573 • Colonel Charles Young

Charles D. Young was the third African American to graduate from West Point. During the Spanish-American War, he commanded the all–African American 9th Ohio Regiment. Then, during the Mexican campaign, he led the 10th Cavalry against Pancho Villa's army at Aguascalientes and Santa Cruz de Villegas. Young's brilliance in the field led to his promotion by John Pershing to lieutenant colonel. But when the United States entered World War I, the U.S. Army forced Colonel Young to retire because of unfounded high blood pressure, in order, many African Americans believed, to avoid giving him a commission as commander of an all-Black regiment. Colonel Young rode by horse from Ohio to Washington, D.C., to disprove such claims, but the army refused to change its decision.

WORLD WAR I

574 • African American Soldiers in World War I

On the eve of America's entry into World War I, approximately 20,000 African Americans were members of the regular army and National Guard, comprising merely 2 percent of the total number of men in the armed forces. Such a low percentage reflected a bias against use of African Americans as soldiers that continued into World War I. Although the United States Army was understaffed when President Woodrow Wilson declared war on Germany in April 1917, the army rejected most of the African Americans who volunteered once war was declared. The situation improved when Congress passed the Selective Service Act on May 18 that called for the enlistment of all able-bodied American citizens. Over 700,000 African Americans signed up on the first day of registration, and ultimately, over 2 million would be registered during World War I. Out of that number, over 360,000 African Americans would be accepted for service and nearly 40,000 of them would serve in two all-Black divisions, the 92nd and 93rd, formed in November and December, 1917, respectively.

575 • The Significance of the Houston Riot

African Americans were not accepted in the marines, or as combat personnel in the navy, which continued to confine African Americans to mess duty on ships. Even in the army, Black soldiers often received inadequate training, served in labor battalions, and languished under white officers who verbally and physically abused them. Perhaps the most negative aspect of joining the army was the experience of being stationed in the South, where white communities often resented and tormented Black troops from the North. In one instance, the constant abuse, goading, and beatings routinely endured by Black regiments flared into a riot. After weeks of harassment, the 24th Infantry retaliated when one of its members, Corporal Charles W. Baltimore, was beaten, shot at, and then arrested by policemen in Houston for having the temerity to ask the policemen about another ar-

Officers of the "Buffaloes," 367th Infantry, 77th Division, in France, c. 1918. National Archives

rested member of the battalion. On the night of August 23, 1917, approximately one hundred soldiers of the 24th marched on the town, opened fire on the police station, and killed sixteen whites, including five policemen, and wounded several others. The army quickly court-martialed sixty-three of the soldiers, convicted and hanged nineteen of them, without appeal, and jailed another sixty-seven. Like the Brownsville Affair, the punishment in the Houston Riot divided African Americans and raised, once again, the question of the kind of justice that African American soldiers could expect from a military that refused to protect them from southern attacks. Moreover, the Houston Riot may have led Secretary of War Newton Baker to abandon plans to recruit sixteen regiments of African Americans; he organized only four.

576 • African American Officers

African Americans were anxious to serve as officers in World War I but were blocked from receiving the training necessary for such service because of the army's refusal to integrate officer training facilities. Joel Spingarn, a board member of the NAACP, began lecturing on Black college campuses, drumming up support for his proposal that the army establish a separate officer training facility in Des Moines, Iowa. Although some African American newspapers criticized the idea as a capitulation to segregation, others, like W. E. B. Du Bois in the *Crisis,* argued that the alternative to a segregated facility was no African American officers at all. When General Leonard of the army promised to establish such a camp if two hundred college-trained African Americans could be found, a Central Committee of Negro College Men was established at Howard University in May 1917 and produced over fifteen hundred names within days. Eventually a camp was established at Fort Des Moines, Iowa, which commissioned 639 Black officers on October 17, 1917. By the end of the war, over fourteen hundred African Americans had received commissions as officers. Although many found themselves in command of labor battalions, others saw combat and distinguished themselves in Europe.

577 • Racial Violence Propels the 369th Abroad

Southern racism actually propelled one regiment, the 15th New York (later the 369th Infantry in France), overseas into combat. In

October 1917 Noble Sissle, the company's drum major and later infamous composer, was beaten viciously by a proprietor of a hotel in Spartanburg, South Carolina, near where the regiment was stationed. The African American militiamen resolved to attack the hotel, but were restrained by Lieutenant James R. Europe, the bandleader, who dispersed them. Later restrained again by their commanding officer, Colonel William Hayward, the regiment's resolve to obtain justice from the town forced the War Department to send the regiment abroad to avoid further trouble. As such, early in 1918 the 369th became the first African American regiment to enter the European war, where it served in the trenches longer than any other American outfit.

578 • The 369th in France and Welcomed Home

The 369th was welcomed when it arrived in France early in 1918, since French forces were exhausted from years of battling the Germans. As part of the American Expeditionary Force, the 369th was attached to a French unit, armed with French weapons, and thrown immediately into combat. Holding off the Germans at Bois d'Hauza and fighting their way to the Rhine, the 369th recorded one of the most impressive records of any American regiment, never retreating and never surrendering any of its men to capture by the enemy. The Germans called them *blutlustige Schwarze* (bloodthirsty Blacks) because of their zealous fighting; the French saw them as saviors, and broke with the American army's tradition of not rewarding black heroism by awarding 171 of them the French Legion of Honor for their bravery. When they returned home to New York, they were given a hero's welcome as they marched down Fifth Avenue to confetti and applause.

579 • U.S. Army Tries to Export Racism

W. E. B. DuBois located an official memorandum about how the U.S. Army advised the French to "deal" with African American troops.

French Military Mission
Stationed with the American Army
August 7, 1918

SECRET INFORMATION CONCERNING
BLACK AMERICAN TROOPS
Conclusion

1. We must prevent the rise of any pronounced degree of intimacy between French officers and black officers. We may be courteous and amiable with these last, but we cannot deal with them on the same plane as with white American officers without deeply wounding the latter. We must not eat with them, must not shake hands or seek to talk or meet with them outside of the requirement of military service.

2. We must not commend too highly the black American troops, particularly in the presence of Americans. It is all right to recognize their good qualities and their services, but only in moderate terms, strictly in keeping with the truth.

3. Make a point of keeping the native cantonment population from "spoiling" the Negroes. Americans become greatly incensed at any public expression of intimacy between white women and black men. . . . Familiarity on the part of white women with black men is furthermore a source of profound regret to our experienced colonials who see in it an overweening menace to the prestige of the white race.

Military authority cannot intervene directly in this question but it can through the civil authorities exercise some influence on the population.

580 • "Close Ranks"

Because African Americans were subjected to racial discrimination when they attempted to join Woodrow Wilson's "War to Make the World Safe for Democracy," many African Americans remained ambivalent about the war effort. W. E. B. Du Bois, editor of the *Crisis,* the journal of the NAACP, addressed the issue in his editorial "Close Ranks," published July 1918, and called on African Americans to put the war effort before their own needs.

This is the crisis of the world. . . . For all the long years to come men will point to the year 1918 as the great Day of Decision. . . . We of the colored race have no ordinary interest in the outcome. That which the German power represents today spells death to the aspirations of Negroes and all the darker races for equality, freedom and democracy. Let us not hesitate. Let us, while this war lasts, forget our special grievances and close our ranks shoulder to shoulder with our white fellow citizens. . . . We make no ordinary sacrifice, but we make it glad and willingly with our eyes lifted to the hills.

Afterward, Du Bois's idealism was marred by the revelation that he wrote the editorial in part to secure an army commission in military intelligence, which, fortunately, he eventually declined.

581 • African American Women

African American women played an important role in World War I. Many Black women organized camps for men about to leave for Europe. Others served as nurses in the Field Medical Supply Depot in Washington, D.C. Although African American nurses were still segregated, in operations such as the Field Medical Supply Depot they were interspersed throughout the group.

WORLD WAR II

582 • Blacks in the Military Prior to World War II

In 1939, on the eve of World War II, African Americans were underutilized and segregated in the armed forces of the United States. In the army, African Americans were restricted to four Black units that had been allowed to decline to 3,640 men. In the navy, African Americans were still segregated and served only in the galley of ships. The Marine and Army Air Corps excluded African Americans altogether. But Black protest against discriminatory treatment, Allied war propaganda against fascism, and the demands of total American mobilization to win the war forced changes in American military policy and set the stage for desegregation of the armed forces after the war.

583 • Discrimination in Mobilization Effort

Having learned from World War I that simply demonstrating their loyalty and patriotism would not automatically improve African Americans' civil rights after the war, African Americans organized protest against discrimination in the armed forces even before the United States entered World War II. In May 1939 the Committee for the Participation of Negroes in National Defense was formed, headed by Howard University history professor Rayford W. Logan and supported by the *Pittsburgh Courier* and the NAACP. The committee secured its first victory when it inserted nondiscriminatory clauses in the Selective Service Bill that passed on September 14, 1940. The bill demanded that men be drafted without regard to race (since many draft boards underrecorded African Americans), and it declared that all servicemen should receive the same training without regard to color (in response to the claim that African Americans often received substandard combat training).

584 • African Americans Challenge the President

On September 17, 1940, the Brotherhood of Sleeping Car Porters' president, A. Philip Randolph, the NAACP's executive secretary, Walter White, and the acting secretary of the National Urban League met with President Franklin Roosevelt to present a seven-point program for African Americans in the American military mobilization. Among other things, the program demanded that African Americans be trained as Army Air Corps pilots, that Black women be admitted to the Red Cross and to army and navy nurse units, and that the fighting units be desegregated. But Roosevelt refused to end segregation in the armed forces, claiming in an October 9, 1940, statement that any change would hurt the national defense. Beyond his promise to enroll Black Americans in the armed forces at a rate equal to their percentage of the population, Roosevelt merely continued World War I policy. African Americans reacted angrily and publicly to the president's statement, especially when it became known that his press secretary, Stephen Early, had lied when he claimed that Randolph and the others had approved the president's statement.

585 • Roosevelt Yields—Somewhat

In response to pressure from African Americans and Republican politicians, the Roosevelt administration made a number of concessions on Black military policy during World War II. Colonel Benjamin O. Davis was promoted to a general, plans were launched to create the first Black flying units, more African Americans

were drafted into the armed forces, and William H. Hastie, the law school dean of Howard University, was made an aide to the secretary of war. An African American, Colonel Campbell C. Johnson, became an adviser to the Selective Service. Perhaps most important, Roosevelt in 1942 ordered the navy and the Marine Corps to accept African Americans into their regular military service units. Blacks would still be segregated in the navy and the marines, and confined in the navy to work in the galleys of most ships.

586 • Protest Against Induction

Some African Americans felt strongly enough about the discriminatory nature of the United States war mobilization to refuse induction. The first man to do so was Ernest Calloway, who in January 1941 wrote his Chicago draft board that he could not "accept the responsibility of taking the oath upon induction into military service under the present anti-democratic structure of the United States Army." Calloway was a member of Conscientious Objectors Against Jim Crow, organized by J. G. St. Clair Drake, which sought to establish the right of African Americans to exempt themselves from service because of segregation. Calloway, however, was jailed, and the group disintegrated. Although organized resistance to induction based on racial grounds collapsed with the entry of the United States into World War II, individuals continued to protest U.S. Army racism by refusing to be inducted. The longest and most significant battle was presented by William Lynn of New York, who refused to be inducted by arguing that the army's induction of African Americans under its "quota" system violated the Selective Service Act's prohibition against racial discrimination. In June 1942 a federal judge demanded that Lynn allow himself to be drafted before the government would hear the case. After submitting for induction and presenting a writ of habeas corpus for his release, Lynn was denied his request to be released because the U.S. Circuit Court of Appeals ruled in February 1944 that Section 4(a) of the Selective Service Act forbade racial discrimination but not segregation! Eventually Lynn's case was argued before the Supreme Court, which declined to rule in the case because Lynn was already serving in the Pacific War. Thus, the Court avoided ruling on a case that would very likely have forced it to overturn United States military policy as a violation of the Selective Service Act.

587 • Double V for Victory Program

Most African Americans responded enthusiastically and patriotically once America entered the war. But Black leaders and newspapers abandoned the World War I strategy advocated in W. E. B. Du Bois's editorial "Close Ranks," to put aside racial activism during wartime. Instead, even the NAACP as well as more militant groups adopted a two-front approach to the war, known as the Double V campaign: African Americans would fight for victory against racism abroad and at home. Black leaders continued to fight publicly against segregation of and discrimination against African Americans even as Blacks rushed forward to serve their country.

588 • Pearl Harbor's Hero

An African American was the first American hero of World War II. When the Japanese bombed Pearl Harbor on December 7, 1941, it was Dorie Miller, a messman on the USS *Arizona*, who rose to the occasion. Coming up from the ship's galley during the attack, Miller, who had had no previous shooting practice due to the segregated nature of navy training, commandeered an antiaircraft gun on his own and shot down four Japanese airplanes before the *Ari-*

Poster of Doris (Dorie) Miller by David Stone Martin, 1943. National Archives

zona sank. Miller was awarded the Navy Cross for his heroism, pinned on his chest by Admiral C. W. Nimitz, on May 27, 1942. But that was not enough to make him a navy gunner. Miller died later in World War II during the Japanese attack on the *Liscome Bay*, an aircraft carrier on which he was still working as a messman.

589 • The Tuskegee Airmen

The first Black pilots in the U.S. armed forces were trained at Tuskegee Institute in Alabama. Beginning on July 19, 1941, African Americans received flying instruction on Booker T. Washington's campus and, on March 7, 1942, the first cadets received their wings. Led by their commander, Colonel Benjamin O. Davis, Jr., the Tuskegee Airmen, as they were known, flew their first combat mission in North Africa on June 2, 1942, and broke a barrier against Blacks

First Lieutenant Lee Rayford of the 99th Fighter Squadron. National Archives

in aerial combat that the army had maintained since World War I. Interestingly, the Tuskegee Flight Training Program was not restricted to males: several women, most notably Willa Brown, who trained pilots later, and Janet Waterford Brogs, a registered nurse, graduated from the program.

590 • "Never Lost a Bomber"

African American pilots amassed an excellent record in World War II. They flew over fifteen thousand sorties, over fifteen hundred missions, and shot down or damaged over four hundred enemy aircraft. Perhaps the most important contribution made by Black fighter pilots was in escort missions with heavy bombers over Germany. They flew two hundred such missions without losing one American heavy bomber to enemy fighter aircraft. The 450 Black pilots of the 99th, 100th, 301st, and 302nd Fighter Squadrons, known collectively as the

332nd Fighter Group, were honored on March 24, 1945, by receiving a Presidential Unit Citation for their " 'outstanding courage, aggressiveness, and combat technique.' "

591 • Capacities of Service

Although Blacks still served in segregated and support units during World War II, many did so in a variety of jobs that drew upon a wide range of capacities in combat and behind the lines. Not only did such African Americans as Benjamin O. Davis, Jr., fly the Mustang P-51 fighter plane in Europe, but African Americans also worked in maintenance crews in Italy.

592 • Black Women Integrated

Some integration crept into the American military despite official policy to the contrary. Interestingly, African American women were more integrated than African American men in the armed forces. In army hospitals and in the Waves, African Americans participated unsegregated in some activities. These islands of integration occurred especially when the number of trainees was so small as to make it grossly inefficient to segregate and when African Americans entered services for the first time.

Right, Lieutenant Harriet Pickens and Ensign Frances Willis, 1944, the first African American Waves to be commissioned. National Archives

593 • Racial Conflicts

Rather than ensuring peace between racial groups, segregation, particularly on and around military camps in the South, was often a source of racial violence. Segregation was strictly enforced on buses that ran between army camps and neighboring towns in the South, such that Black soldiers were often forced to wait until all the whites had boarded and then ride standing up for the duration of trips from town to bases. Resistance to such southern protocols led to Black servicemen being jailed, beaten, and sometimes killed in altercations. Some studies proved that segregation had a negative effect on Black morale. While the overwhelming majority of African Americans entered the military with a strong sense of patriotism, many chafed under segregated life in the military until by the end they were, in the words of Private Bert B. Barbero "indifferent to the whole affair." Many who wrote letters commented that

the "very instrument which our government has organized and built, the United States Armed Forces, to fight for world democracy, is within itself 'undemocratic.'"

594 • Some Prefer Segregation

Not surprisingly, some African American servicemen preferred not to be trained or to serve in integrated units with whites. According to a War Department survey, 38 percent of African American servicemen voiced approval of separate military units, as opposed to 36 percent who demanded integration. While some African Americans certainly preferred to be separated from whites, the polling used to register these feelings was inherently unreliable, since many probably felt compelled not to criticize existing policy or risk harassment. For example, when asked whether they believed army policy was unfair, three-fifths of African American respondents had "mixed opinions."

595 • Morale Booster

The need to raise Black morale led William Hastie to recommend that the War Department launch an educational program about Black contributions in the history of American war efforts that led to the production of the film *The Negro Soldier* (1944), by Frank Capra. The movie detailed the role of African Americans in the American Revolution, the Civil War, and World War I, among others. When the film was shown to Black and white troops in 1944, most of both groups liked the film. An index of the success of the film was that only 4 percent of the whites and 3 percent of the Black servicemen thought the film lacked veracity. While Black critics thought the film romanticized Black life in the military and white critics thought it gave too much importance to the Black role, over 80 percent thought the film

"United We Win," poster by Howard Liberman of integrated aircraft factory workers, 1943. National Archives

504,000 in 1943, over 425,000 of these troops remained in the United States. This allocation of man- and womanpower was especially perplexing given the widespread shortage of American personnel in war zones abroad. The administration claimed that keeping African Americans at home reflected the opposition of foreign governments to Black troops, but in reality, the prejudice came more from United States overseas commanders, who discouraged attempts to send Black troops early in the war. By 1944 the need for American troops was such that some of the barriers to Black combat units began to come down.

597 • The Port Chicago Mutiny

Segregation placed African Americans at the center of the worst home-front disaster in World War II and led to the Port Chicago Mutiny. On July 17, 1944, at the U.S. Navy loading depot at Port Chicago, ammunition being loaded by African Americans exploded, blowing up the dock and two ships, the *E. A. Bryan* and the *Quinalt Victory.* Of the 320 men killed, 202 were Black enlisted men; another 390 were injured. The explosion accounted for 15 percent of all of the casualties suffered by African Americans in World War II. After the explosion, when the Black sailors, who had not been trained in ammunition loading, were ordered to resume the same work, without any change in procedures, 258 refused, citing their fear of another explo-

ought to be shown publicly. White approval ratings suggest the film was most effective at challenging the belief held by many white soldiers that African Americans historically had not been patriotic and had not contributed to the nation's defense.

596 • Labor Battalions

Despite attempts to rehabilitate the image of Blacks as patriots, army officials continued to try to confine Black troops to labor units. Although the number of Black troops rose from 97,725 in the U.S. Army in November 1941 to

sion. Fifty Black sailors were court-martialed for mutiny and sentenced to fifteen years, while the other 208 were tried and sentenced for lesser charges. After the war, the men were granted amnesty, but their convictions for mutiny were not overturned, even though their case was argued by Thurgood Marshall of the NAACP Legal Defense Fund. Some good did come out of their protest: historian Robert L. Allen found that the navy changed its policy of assigning only Black sailors to this dangerous assignment, and afterward assigning white sailors as well.

598 • Blacks in Combat

Despite the policy of segregating Blacks in labor units, many African Americans did serve in combat roles during World War II. Blacks served in the artillery and mortar units. The mortar company of the 92nd Infantry Division was given credit for wiping out numerous Italian and German machine guns in the Italian campaign of the U.S. Army in November 1944.

599 • Silver Star for Bravery

African Americans won distinction for their courage under fire from the elite of the American military. On October 13, 1944, Lieutenant General George S. Patton, commander of the United States Third Army, pinned a Silver Star on Private Ernest A. Jenkins for his bravery during the fierce fighting that liberated Châteaudun, France.

600 • Battle of the Bulge

The greatest challenge to segregation came from the demands of total war against the enemy. For example, in December 1944 in what became known as the Battle of the Bulge, the Germans overran Allied positions in a desperate last attempt to win the war. Faced with a shortage of white soldiers, General Dwight D. Eisenhower, commander of the Allied forces, accepted a recommendation from General John Lee of the Communications Zone to take volunteers from Black service units. More than five thousand African Americans volunteered, many of whom were noncommissioned officers who took reductions in grade to get an opportunity to fight the Germans. Twenty-five hundred men were accepted and trained for six weeks, after which they became thirty-seven platoons that were attached to white units. Such troops fought with valor until the end of the war in 1945; but even in this emergency, the

Black mortar company of the 92nd Infantry Division liquidates several German machine-gun nests near Massa, Italy, c. November 1944. National Archives

Lieutenant General George Patton pins Silver Star on Private Ernest Jenkins. National Archives

when the demands of total war dictated a wider use of Black seamen than simply in the ship's galley. A Special Programs Unit in the Bureau of Naval Personnel suggested that the navy staff entire ships with African Americans. In 1944 two ships, the USS *Mason* and PC 1264, the attack submarine, sailed with all-Black crews. On June 3 of that year, the SS *Harriet Tubman* was launched.

602 • Change at Navy

Much of the navy's zeal for segregation derived from Secretary of Navy Frank Knox, who was a staunch segregationist. His death in 1944 brought the considerably more humane James Forrestal to the helm at the navy. Forrestal established a program to integrate twenty-five ships. He then integrated the auxiliary fleet. In 1945 the Special Programs Unit concluded that integration made for a more effective fighting navy. Restrictions on African Americans in the navy would end in 1947, but the service would not be integrated until 1949.

army rather awkwardly maintained its segregation policy by segregating African Americans into platoons of forty men that were "attached" to companies of two hundred white men.

601 • Black Ships!

The navy found an interesting way to maintain segregation toward the end of the war

People

603 • Benjamin Oliver Davis, Sr. (1877–1970)

Benjamin Oliver Davis was a dedicated soldier whose military career extended from the

Spanish-American War to World War II. Davis left Howard University in 1898 to join the army and fight in the Spanish-American War. He also fought in the Philippines and served in World War I. Partly in response to mounting criticism of its segregated army policy, the Roosevelt administration appointed Davis a brigadier general in 1940, the first Black man to become a general in the U.S. Army. He served in France during World War II.

604 • Benjamin Oliver Davis, Jr. (b. 1912)

Perhaps the most important of the Tuskegee Airmen was Benjamin O. Davis, Jr., who attended West Point, where he survived four years of "silencing" and from which he graduated in 1936, to become captain of the 99th Pursuit Squadron, the "Tuskegee Experiment." After

personally supervising the training of the airmen at Tuskegee, Davis and his fliers were stationed on Sicily in June 1943, when they began to fly defense for American bombers. In September 1943 Davis left the 99th to begin organizing a new, larger flying unit, the 332nd Fighter Group in the United States. To do that, Davis had to make several presentations to military brass to disprove vicious, inaccurate rumors that the 99th had not performed well. Once the record of the 99th was vindicated, the 332nd Fighter Group and the 99th joined forces in escorting bombers over Germany from Italy. His success in those missions earned Davis the Distinguished Flying Cross.

605 • Estine Cowner

The demand for qualified labor in World War II opened up new opportunities for African American women to serve their country in industrial jobs previously closed to them. One of the women who experienced a radical change in her job description was Estine Cowner, a former waitress, who became a scaler on a construction crew at the Kaiser shipyards in Richmond, California, to construct the Liberty ship *George Washington Carver*. The Carver was launched on May 7, 1943.

606 • Warren Capers

African Americans were present when American forces landed on the coast of France on D-Day, August 18, 1944. One of the most important was Private Warren Capers. As a member of a medical detachment, Capers established a dressing station and treated more than 330 soldiers that day. This heroic devotion to wounded soldiers led his superiors to recommend him for a Silver Star.

General Benjamin O. Davis Sr. National Archives

Estine Cowner. National Archives

Josephine Baker sings the national anthem in the
Municipal Theater, Oran, Algeria, May 17, 1943. National
Archives

Warren Capers. National Archives

607 • African American Celebrities

Numerous African American celebrities, sports heroes, and entertainers lent their support to the war effort. In addition to the boxer Joe Louis, who joined the army, and Paul Robeson, who made numerous singing and public appearances, the internationally renowned singer and actress Josephine Baker helped build African support for the Allies by singing the national anthem on May 17, 1943, as the finale to her show in the Municipal Theater, Oran, Algeria.

KOREAN WAR

Engagements and Policy

608 • The Changing Military

Although Franklin Delano Roosevelt has been hailed as a liberal American president, it was Harry Truman, who became president when Roosevelt died in April 1945, who instituted substantial racial change in the American military following World War II. In 1946 Truman established the Committee on Equality of Treatment and Opportunity in the Armed Services, which recommended in its 1947 report, "To Secure These Rights," the elimination of segregation and discrimination within the military. Faced with unlikely reelection in 1948, Truman took the dramatic step of issuing Executive Order 9981, which called for equal treatment and opportunities for all armed services personnel. Despite these orders and recommendations, full integration of African Americans in the United States Army occurred slowly. Two years after Executive Order 9981, for example,

the first African American troops sent to Korea still went in segregated units. But when North Korean attacks substantially reduced the forces of several all-white regiments, African American soldiers were sent in as replacements. By mid-1951, over 20 percent of the African American soldiers in Korea were assigned to integrated units.

609 • Black Troops in the Korean War

The oldest African American infantry, the 24th Regiment, spearheaded the first victory of American forces in Korea. Arriving in Korea on July 13, 1950, the unit, which was part of the 25th Army Division, saw its first action within a week. On July 20 the 24th led a successful drive to recapture Yechon, a vital transportation center overtaken by the North Korean Army. The regiment's victory improved morale for both Black and white troops, and was acknowledged in the *Congressional Record* "for shaming us out of our fears. They demonstrated, the hard way, their faith in a certain cause that has no room for the ignorance and selfishness of racism and bigotry." In later battles, soldiers reportedly yelled "Remember Yechon" as they attacked the enemy.

610 • Removal of Douglas MacArthur Speeds Integration

One of the greatest impediments to army integration was eliminated when President Truman removed for insubordination General Douglas MacArthur, an opponent of integrated forces, from his command of American forces in April 1951. MacArthur was replaced by Lieutenant General Matthew Ridgeway, who immediately sought to integrate every unit. Although Ridgeway's actions were publicly decried by several white southern congressmen, by July 1953, 90 percent of the African Americans serving in

Private Edward Wilson, 24th Infantry, wounded in action near front lines in Korean War. National Archives

Korea were assigned to integrated units. The air force and Marine Corps also integrated their forces during this period, but the navy did not take similar steps until the 1960s.

VIETNAM

Engagements and Policy

611 • Project 100,000

At the beginning of the Vietnam War, African Americans comprised 10 percent of the armed forces, but few served as officers. In 1967, for example, Blacks accounted for 10 percent of the U.S. Marine Corps, but less than 1 percent of the Marine Corps's officers. Throughout the war, the U.S. government tried to control the burgeoning Black Power movement by drafting or recruiting those African Americans to whom the Black nationalist message would most appeal. In mid-1966, for example, the Defense Department launched Project 100,000, aimed at reducing the high rejection rate of African Americans. Billed as a way to "rehabilitate" impoverished or wayward applicants, the project allowed recruitment offices to accept applicants with criminal records or other liabilities for which they would have traditionally been disqualified. The program is credited with supplying over 340,000 new recruits for Vietnam, 40 percent of whom were African Americans. The promised rehabilitation and training failed to materialize, however, as financial difficulties beset the program, and many of the Project 100,000 recruits ultimately saw more extensive combat duty than regular recruits.

612 • Black Opposition to the Vietnam War

Martin Luther King, Jr., strongly opposed the Vietnam War, and after 1965 he worked vigorously to persuade other civil rights leaders and the American public that the conflict was morally wrong. On April 4, 1967, King made a famous antiwar speech at Riverside Church in New York City and led a huge antiwar rally a few days later. King's firm stance caused discomfort among some in the Civil Rights Movement who feared his opposition would create an unwanted backlash or divert attention away from their cause. Other prominent African Americans opposed to the war included Julian Bond, who was denied his seat in the Georgia legislature because of his antiwar views until the courts ordered him seated, and Muhammad Ali, who argued he "had no quarrel" with the Viet Cong. As a Muslim, Ali claimed exemption from military service based on his religious beliefs, but he was convicted of draft evasion, stripped of his boxing title, and sentenced to five years in prison.

People

613 • Medal of Honor Man

Even though the Vietnam War was controversial, African Americans still served bravely and with distinction. This was certainly the case with Clifford C. Sims, a staff sergeant in Vietnam. On patrol with his men during the battle for Hue in 1968, Sergeant Sims heard an ominous click—the sound made by a tripped booby-trap bomb. Without hesitation, Sims leaped onto the bomb to shield his men from the blast. The explosion killed him, and he was awarded the Congressional Medal of Honor posthumously for having given his life to save his men.

Staff Sergeant Clifford Sims, who died saving the lives of his men near Hue, Vietnam. U.S. Army

614 • Colin L. Powell (b. 1937)

It was in Vietnam that Colin Powell won distinction as a hero. Born in Harlem to Jamaican parents, Colin attended the City College of New York, where he enrolled in the Reserve Officers' Training Corps (ROTC). After graduating in 1958, Powell entered the army and Ranger training and later served as a platoon commander in Germany. After becoming a captain, Powell was transferred to Vietnam. On patrol with

General Colin Powell. U.S. Army

his men one day, Colin stepped on a punji stake, a sharpened stick hidden in holes in rice paddies, and was severely injured. In spite of tremendous pain, Powell continued to lead his men to their destination, where they were needed to reinforce other troops. For his persistence and devotion to duty, he was awarded the Bronze Star. After a brief return to the United States, during which he enrolled in the Command and General Staff College at Fort Leavenworth, Kansas, Powell returned to Vietnam. While serving as an operations chief for the Americal Division, Powell again showed his bravery when a helicopter he and his men were flying in crashed in the Vietnam jungle. Being the only member of the craft not to be knocked unconscious by the crash, Powell, with "complete disregard for his own safety, and while injured himself," dragged his injured fellow soldiers from the smoldering craft. For this act of courage, he received the Soldier's Medal. In 1989 Powell became the first African American to be selected Chairman of the Joint Chiefs of Staff, and he orchestrated the successful Operation Desert Storm in 1990. He retired from the army in 1993, published his autobiography, *My American Journey,* in September 1995, and declined to be a candidate for any political office in 1996 at a graceful November 1995 news conference.

Quotation

615 • Return from Vietnam

Those brave soldiers that did make it back from Vietnam did not receive a hero's welcome. African American soldiers, in particular, returned to find that surviving combat on behalf of their country had done little to improve their status. Specialist 4 Richard J. Ford III, who served with the 25th Infantry Division of the army in 1967–68, described his experiences after he was wounded:

You know, they decorated me in Vietnam. Two Bronze Stars. The whiteys did. I was wounded three times. The officers, the generals, and whoever else came out to the hospital to see you. They respected you and pat you on the back. They said, "You brave. And you courageous. You America's finest. America's best." Back in the States the same officers that pat me on the back wouldn't even speak to me. They wanted that salute, that attention, 'til they holler at ease. I didn't get the respect that I thought I was gonna get.... They just wanted another black in the field. Uncle Sam, he didn't give me no justice. You had a job to do, you, you did it, you home. Back where you started. They didn't even ask me to reenlist.

PERSIAN GULF WAR

Engagements and Policy

616 • African American Participation in the Gulf War

The Persian Gulf War helped publicize the disproportionate representation of African Americans serving in the armed forces, especially in combat positions. Led by General Colin Powell, the first African American to chair the Joint Chiefs of Staff, African Americans comprised 25 percent of the troops deployed in the Persian Gulf, yet accounted for only 13 percent of the U.S. population. During the war, many African Americans pointed to these statistics as evidence that career and educational opportunities for young African Americans in American society are still too limited. According to this argument, rather than serving out of a sense of patriotism, many African Americans are forced to consider military service because it is one of the few ways to acquire adequate training or financial support. In times of conflict, then, such as the Persian Gulf War, African Americans disproportionately risk their lives because of economic necessity.

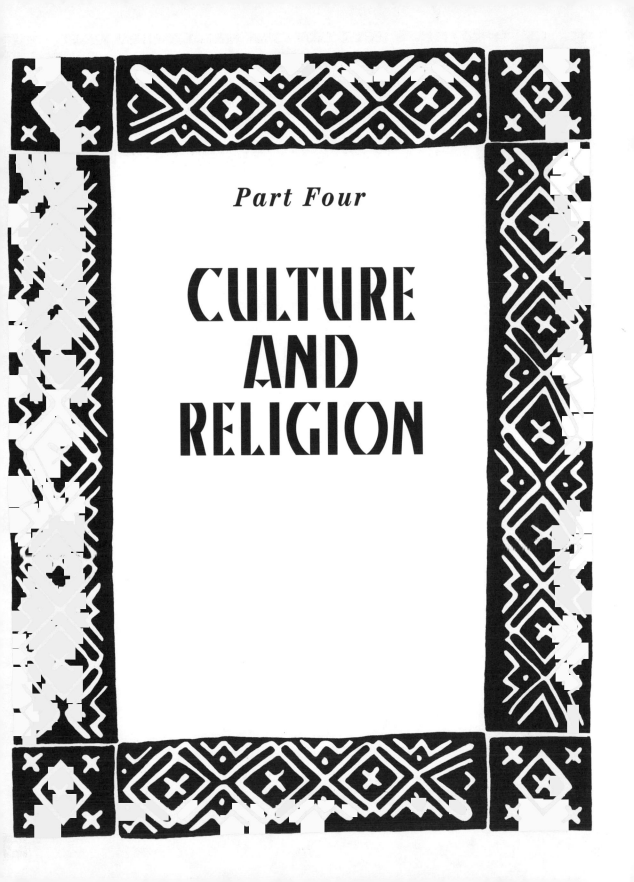

Part Four

CULTURE AND RELIGION

Over the centuries, Africans developed rich traditions in music, dance, sculpture, weaving, mask making, and verbal expression, both literate and oral, which they brought with them to North America. Although sociologists once argued that Africans lost this ancestral heritage during the "shock of enslavement," more recent studies have proven that Africans retained much of that heritage, used it to adapt to their new environment, and melded it with European and Native American forms to create a unique African American culture. The encounter with America, of course, exposed Africans to racism, slavery, and centuries of cultural degradation and thus introduced new themes into African American thought and expression. Generations of African Americans have utilized their culture to contest, satirize, and transcend negative aspects of American life, and some have attempted to win greater respect for African Americans because of their cultural vitality. But while European Americans have often mimicked, borrowed from, and otherwise appropriated African American expressive styles, beginning before the American Revolution, such "adoptions" have seldom resulted in seeing African Americans as the pivotal formative force in American culture that they have been.

Domino Players, 1943. Horrace Pippin (1888–1946). Courtesy of the Phillips Collection, Washington, D.C.

FROM AFRICA TO COLONIAL AMERICA, 1619–1770

Music and Dance

617 • Band and Concert Tradition of African Societies

Music was an integral part of rites, festivals, and ceremonies in West African societies, especially for dignitaries. After Thomas Edward Bowditch led a group of explorers to Africa to meet the king of the Ashanti, he reported:

... more than a hundred bands burst at once on our arrival, [all playing] the peculiar airs of their several chiefs; the horns flourished their defiances [i.e., fanfare melodies], with the beating of innumerable drums and metal instruments, and then yielded for a while to the soft breathings of their long flutes, which were truly harmonious; and a pleasing instrument, like a bagpipe without the drone, was happily blended. . . .

He also noted that "the drummers threw their 'white-washed drums' into the air and caught them again, 'with much agility and grimace,' as they walked along." Bowditch's recollections show the origins not only of the long tradition of African American marching bands and folk music but also the music of African American concert tradition, which is often commissioned for special occasions.

618 • Dance in Africa

The English explorer John Barbot recalled African dances he observed on the coast of Nigeria:

Their dances are commonly in a round, singing the next thing that occurs, whether sense

John Barbot, visiting a West African king, from Awnsham Churchill's *A Collection of Voyages and Travels, Some Now First Printed from Original Manuscripts* (1704; London, 1732). Courtesy of Henry E. Huntington Library, San Marino, California

or nonsense. Some of them stand in the middle of the ring, holding one hand on their head, and the other behind their waist, advancing and strutting out their belly forwards, and beating very hard with their feet on the ground. Others clap their hands to the noise of a kettle, or a calabash fitted for a musical instrument.

619 • Dancing on Ships

Sometimes the Africans' love of dance was used against them. In some cases, they were tricked into bondage by being asked to dance on European ships docked off the coast of Africa. This request, often with the promise of pay, was usually made just before the ship was to depart. Once the ship set sail, Africans would be forced to dance, in a practice called "dancing the slaves," reputedly for health reasons. Dr. Thomas

Trotter, the surgeon assigned to the *Brookes* on its 1783 voyage, recalled that after the morning meal every day, "those who were in irons were ordered to stand up and make what motions they could, leaving a passage for such as were out of irons to dance around the deck." Often, it was difficult to make those in chains dance, so the crew would frequently whip the slaves.

620 • The Atlantic Tradition of Dance

Traditional African dances crossed the Atlantic with the slave trade, landed in the Caribbean, and flourished. Generally, African culture met with less overt opposition from the white planter class in the Caribbean than on the mainland of North America and was able to maintain itself more freely and for a longer time in the West Indies. Conditions of life in West Indian slavery—absentee white ownership of plantations, consequently a low level of concern by whites about the recreational activities of the slaves, frequent arrivals of new Africans due to the higher mortality rate of slaves in the West Indies, and the numerical superiority of Blacks over whites—aided the retention of African culture. Although different African peoples preferred particular dance traditions, four major dances were widespread in the Caribbean. The *calenda,* performed by several couples who circled one another, was a shuffling advance and retreat between partners, who moved mainly with their hips. The *chica* involved mainly the rotation of the hips while the rest of the body was immobilized. The *bamboula,* likely an offshoot of the *chica,* was named after the bamboula drum and performed by a couple inside of a ring. The *juba* was a dance of competition and skill, in which a woman, moving slowly with shuffling feet and contorted limbs, challenged several men to enter the ring and best her dancing, often with the result that they retired ex-

hausted. Although such dances flourished in the West Indies—and drew African American choreographers such as Katherine Dunham to the islands to study them in the 1930s—some variations of them made it to North America. The *chica* spread with the West Indian migration to New Orleans, while the *juba* was danced in selected areas of the southern United States.

621 • Music and Dances for the Masters

Although African American musicians were rarely known nationwide in the seventeenth century, they did perform regularly within the slave quarters and at the plantation owners' homes, also known as the Big Houses. When guests visited plantations, masters often summoned slaves to play music and dance. On these occasions, certain dances were considered appropriate entertainment for the "white folks." The *buck-and-wing* was often performed on such occasions, the "wing" sometimes referred to as the *pigeon wing.* In this dance, slaves flapped their arms and legs, and held the head and neck stiff, like a bird. Some slaves performed the *Irish jig* so well as to be entered in contests with the slaves of other masters. The *cakewalk,* in which couples walked on a straight path with sharp, precise turns, was often danced by slaves at harvesttime. Its name derived from the tradition on some plantations where the mistress would award a cake as a prize to the couple who danced the best. Some learned to play music and dance so well that they were allowed to teach others and to participate in parades for events such as 'Lection Day, a carryover from the days before captivity, in which slaves chose their own officials.

622 • Dirty Dancing

Some dances were considered too risqué to be performed in front of the masters and thus were generally confined to private occasions in the slave quarters. One dance considered particularly primitive was the *ring dance*, which resembled the Congo dances of West Indians. Following a circular path, slaves danced individually in an animated shuffle that vibrated the entire body. Another popular dance was the *buzzard lope*, an animal dance that retained African tradition and sought to represent the behavior of a turkey buzzard "carrying on" about a hen. The *water dance* was performed by slaves who danced while carrying a bucket or glass of water on their heads. This dance looked back to the Africans' tradition of carrying goods on their heads. The West Indian juba became known as the *djouba* in the United States and was a secular dance in which participants "patted" out the juba by clapping, slapping one's chest, thighs, or legs when drums were prohibited. The djouba became the renowned *hambone* dance in modern times.

623 • House Servants' Dances

Caste divisions existed among slaves in the South and were reflected in the kinds of dances that the house servants would perform. Given that the house servants on large plantations in the South often thought of themselves as superior to the field servants, these domestic servants performed dances that integrated West African dance elements with steps from the English square dances and the French quadrille. In New Orleans and Charleston, house servants (and the free persons of color who occupied the "brown societies" of those cities) held balls and cotillions where such "dignified" dancing as the *figure dance* and the *sixteen-figure dance* were popular.

The Old Plantation, watercolor by unknown artist, c. 1800. Courtesy of Abby Aldrich Rockefeller Folk Art Center, Williamsburg, Virginia

624 • Masters' Ambivalence Toward Dancing

While some masters believed that encouraging dance among their slaves was an effective way to keep them happy and contented, other masters refused to allow slaves to hold such dances on their plantations. Some of these masters allowed their slaves to travel to other plantations for dances, but others would not—a restriction that posed difficulties for slaves who enjoyed dancing. Some slaves, however, found ingenious ways to surmount these obstacles. In 1937 a former plantation slave interviewed by the Alabama Writers' Project recalled that

young Massa told Tom . . . one time not to go to de frolic. . . . Tom said "Yassuh" but Marse Nep watch Tom th'oo de do' and atter while Tom slip out and awy he went, wid young Massa right 'hin' him. He got dere and foun' Tom cuttin' groun' shuffle big as anybody. Young Massa called him, "Tom," he say, "Tom, didn't I tell you you couldn't come to dis frolic?" "Yassuh," says Tom, "you sho' did, and I jes' come to tell 'em I couldn't come!"

625 • Alternatives to Drums

Like their West Indian neighbors, southern whites generally prohibited slaves from playing drums, because drums were believed to be used to send signals during a revolt. This prohibition became widespread in the South after the Stono Rebellion in 1739 when Angolan slaves beat drums as they moved through the South Carolina countryside murdering whites. Because of the prohibition, African Americans developed other percussive instruments on which to play. Patting knees, arms, backs, and heads, hand clapping, clinking of spoons, and "playing the bones" became alternative ways for slaves to beat out the time at dances or while generally passing the time on the plantation.

The Bone Player, 1856. Museum of Fine Arts, Boston. Bequest of Martha C. Karolik for the M. and M. Karolik Collection of American Paintings, 1815–65

626 • Coastal Drums

Despite its general prohibition, use of drums did persist in the coastal areas of Georgia, where slaves lived at great distances from one another and from disapproving whites, and in a social environment in which other African-influenced traditions, such as the Gullah language, also survived. Drum use could also be found in parts of Louisiana, because of the nineteenth-century migration of large numbers of West Indian slaves who had been able to practice drum playing in the Caribbean. Both West Indians and native-born African Americans generally made drums by stretching rawhide over one end of hollow logs.

627 • Line Singing

The practice of "line singing" came from the Dutch Reformed Church in colonial New York, where in 1645 church law decreed that the precentor "tune the psalm" for congregational singing. The precentor chanted one or two lines at a time, ended it on a definite pitch, and the congregation followed the precentor's lead with the singing of the same line. This practice became the distinctive feature of African American hymn singing.

628 • Banjar

The "banjar," or banjo, was an African contribution to American music in the eighteenth century. Thomas Jefferson commented on the banjo in his *Notes on Virginia* and acknowledged that it had been "brought hither from Africa, and . . . is the original of the guitar, its chords being precisely the four lower chords of the guitar."

629 • Fiddle

Because masters encouraged its use, the fiddle was probably the most popular instrument played by the slaves in the eighteenth and nineteenth centuries. Some owners purchased fiddles for their slaves to play, hired out talented fiddle players for profit to other slave owners or public functions, and paid more money for slaves who could play the instrument. Such demand was a factor in the enslavement of Solomon Northrop, a free Black man from the North, who was captured and sold into slavery. That African Americans were proficient at fiddle (or violin) playing is attested by the slave orchestras formed in the South, comprised largely of fiddlers and supplemented with tambourine or bones players. Some women fiddlers existed as well. One fiddler, an enslaved woman named Clarinda, was cited by missionaries in the middle of the eighteenth century for having learned the violin, eschewed Christian piety, and played for men and women dancers on the first day of each week.

630 • Whites Act Black

Although Thomas Rice is often credited as the first American white man to perform in Black character on the American stage in 1828, the truth is that white Americans in blackface had been performing on the stage from before the American Revolution. In 1767 the *New York Journal* ran an announcement of a performance by a Mr. Bayly and a Mr. Tea on April 14: at the end of the third part of the performance, Mr. Tea (perhaps the original Mr. T?) offered to the audience a *"Negro Dance, In Character."* A white woman appeared on stage in Boston on November 25, 1796, and performed *"A Comic Dance, In Character of a Female Negro."* A year earlier, the first portrayal of the African American in a serious American drama, *The Triumph of Love,* graced the American stage, containing a "shuffling, cacklin, allegedly comic Negro servant." Ironically the birth of an American political identity coincided with the emergence of a need among American whites to denigrate African American characters through a caricature of Black dance.

Art

631 • African Craft Tradition in the United States

Enslavement destroyed many African artistic traditions, because it rendered obsolete the production of ceremonial masks, throne stools, and musical instruments for kings and rulers by village artists. But the shortage of craftsmen in the colonies created a demand for talented Africans to express their aesthetic sensibilities in pottery, cloth, wood, metal, and architectural production. Some slave owners recruited Africans specifically as artisans rather than agricultural laborers, and profited from their skill under a hiring-out system that rented artisan slaves to white craftsmen. Some enslaved artisans even profited under such a system, moved up from apprentices to journeymen to master craftsmen, and even purchased their freedom in some cases. By the mid-eighteenth century Africans dominated crafts production in such colonies as Maryland, Georgia, South Carolina, and Louisiana.

632 • Personal-Use Artifacts

When slave artisans from West Africa were not working for their masters, they often adorned everyday objects with designs and forms of aesthetic and spiritual significance. The so-called grotesque jugs in slave pottery and the dramatic, carved-wood grave markers are forms that resemble similar objects in West Africa and serve spiritual purposes in North America. Faces on jugs or markers on graves were often designed to frighten away evil spirits.

Folklore, Language, and Literature

633 • African American Folklore

Africans brought to America a body of folklore in the form of humor, poetry, proverbs, and stories that were handed down from generation to generation, but also changed over time to incorporate numerous aspects of the American experience. Satire about the ways and foibles of masters, commentary about the love and marriage relations on the plantation, and slave wisdom of the type that would later be collected in the nineteenth century abounded in African American communities of the seventeenth and eighteenth centuries.

634 • Gullah and Other Pidgin Languages

In all of the southern colonies, the constant importation of Africans via the slave trade brought diverse peoples who spoke different languages into close proximity on plantations. Several generations of Africans continued to see the world through an African worldview and to call objects by their African names and could speak in unadulterated African languages. But most first- and certainly second-generation Africans developed a pidgin language made up of elements from several African languages and English. That process of pidginization began in Africa when speakers from different language groups were thrown together while they awaited deportation to America. It continued and increased once Africans reached colonial North America. In some colonies, such as South Carolina, where Africans were a majority for most of the eighteenth century, such pidginization resulted in Africans developing a distinctive New World language, Gullah, which has survived into the twentieth century.

635 • Koran-Reading Slaves

From 1711 and lasting into the nineteenth century, Muslims, sometimes referred to as Mandingoes, became more numerous in the Atlantic slave trade. These Africans brought with them a literate culture, as reading the Koran was essential to worship. In the 1730s, for example, Job Ben Solomon, the prince of Boudou in the land of Futa, lived as a slave for two years in Maryland. Then, after he wrote a letter in Arabic to his father and it came to the attention of Sir Hans Sloane, an Oxford don, a process began that resulted in Solomon's freedom and return to Africa. Yarrow Mamount was another Muslim who had been kidnaped in Africa and brought to the United States. He purchased his freedom,

Portrait of Yarrow Mamount by Charles Willson Peale. The Historical Society of Pennsylvania

lived to be over a hundred years, and had his portrait painted by the artist Charles Wilson Peale.

Religion

636 • West African Religion

West Africans brought to America a variety of religious beliefs and practices, some of which were shared despite the diversity of African peoples who came to America. One belief was that spirits could take possession of individuals and could be embodied in charms. In the early colonial period, African Americans buried charms with the dead to ensure that the ancestors, some of the most powerful spirits, would not be angered as they passed into the next world. African Americans who also believed in a supreme God continued their West African burial practices well into the nineteenth century. Funeral rites involved a long period of mourning and great feasting as Africans believed that upon dying one

went "home." Such a view of death may have accounted for the frequency of attempted suicides on the journey to America.

637 • First Baptized

The first African child baptized in English America was christened William in the Church of England at Jamestown in 1624. By the English law of the colony in effect at that time, that child became free with the baptism.

638 • Cotton Mather and the First Black Church Service

In 1693 the first recorded church service for Black slaves occurred in Massachusetts. Cotton Mather, a Puritan clergyman, responded to a request from slaves for guidance and produced *Rules for the Society of Negroes* for their benefit. Later Mather published *The Negro Christianized* (1701). In this, he chastised masters who were reluctant to offer religious training to

Cotton Mather. Prints and Photographs Division, Library of Congress

their slaves: "You deny your *Master in Heaven* if you do nothing to bring your Servants into the Knowledge and Service of that glorious Master." However, as he was a slaveholder, he believed that Christianity helped them accept their lot in life and become more obedient slaves: "that is God who has caused them to be *Servants,* and that they serve Jesus Christ, while they are at work for their *Masters."*

639 • Society for the Propagation of the Gospel in Foreign Parts

Established by the Church of England in 1701 to aid the growth of the church in the colonies, the Society for the Propagation of the Gospel in Foreign Parts focused religious instruction on Blacks and Indians. Many planters resisted, as they already allotted their slaves the Sabbath day to tend to their personal chores, such as planting and harvesting food for their own families; the planters had no intention of allowing slaves additional time off. In an effort to persuade the slaveholders to provide religious education for their slaves, the SPG distributed pamphlets indicating that Christian training would convince slaves to be obedient and accept their lot in life: "Scripture, far from making an alteration in Civil Rights, expressly directs that every man abide in the condition wherein he is called, with great indifference of mind concerning outward circumstances." The SPG cited Ephesians 6:5, "Servants, be obedient to them that are your masters," ad nauseam. Slaves were also required to recite the following oath:

You declare in the presence of God and before his congregation that you do not ask for the Holy Baptism out of any design to free yourself from the duty and obedience you owe to your masters while you live; but merely for the good of your soul and to partake of the

grace and blessings promised to the members of the Church of Christ.

640 • The First Great Awakening

It was not until the Great Awakening, which began in the 1730s and climaxed in the 1740s, that large numbers of African Americans were baptized in the English colonies. John and Charles Wesley, who were responsible for founding the Methodist faith in England, traveled to southern colonies in the 1730s to revive religious consciousness and especially to convert African Americans. The Great Awakening rejected the established church, resurrected the notion that anyone could experience God's grace, and stressed the egalitarian nature of Christianity. As such, it rejected the tendency of American Protestantism to avoid conversion of Blacks and Indians. Methodism held that being a Christian was a disposition of the heart, rather than of the head, and thus undermined not only the learned clergy in America but also the intellectual racism that decreed Blacks and Indians were not smart enough to be Christians. The Great Awakening drew many Blacks into white churches for the first time, allowed "called ministry," including Blacks, to preach, and fostered some of the first integrated churches in America.

641 • Black Harry (?–1810)

One of the men most responsible for the spread of Methodism in the United States was Black Harry (Harry Hosier), a close personal assistant of Francis Asbury, the man who increased by 150 percent the number of Methodists in the United States. Sent by Charles Wesley from England in 1771, Asbury took such long and arduous journeys across the United States that the white preacher often broke down under the strain. Asbury turned many of the preaching duties over to Black Harry, including the giving of sermons. Black Harry became one of the most popular draws on the camp meeting circuit of the Great Awakening because of his excellent preaching and rapport with the audiences.

642 • Religious Separatism

An African American desire for religious autonomy and cultural self-determination led to the founding of the first Black churches in the South. These separatists, or Baptists, planted the idea of separate and independent congregations of southern Blacks who saw religion as a way to establish their own social independence. Based on plantation congregations, the first southern Black churches emerged in Virginia and South Carolina.

643 • Black Catholicism

Black Catholicism was established in 1724 by Governor M. Bienville of Louisiana, who encouraged masters to educate and baptize their slaves in the Catholic tradition. Catholicism among slaves had its greatest success in Louisiana and Maryland, states that had sizable Catholic populations before large numbers of slaves had arrived. But even in these states, Catholicism did not flourish among African Americans as it did among slaves elsewhere in the hemisphere. Most notably, the nature of Catholicism—its rituals (difficult for the uninitiated to comprehend), the exclusive nature of its priesthood, and its lessened reliance on the Bible as primary authority—weakened its appeal. Only in the twentieth century did large numbers of African Americans move toward Catholicism.

REVOLUTIONARY AWAKENING, 1760–1820

Movements and Organizations

644 • African American Enlightenment

A generation of African American writers, artists, petitioners, and inventors born around the middle of the eighteenth century produced the first recorded African American intellectual movement. To varying degrees, these thinkers fashioned Protestant Christianity, Enlightenment rationalism, and the revolutionary ideology of equality of opportunity into an argument that Africans were fully human, possessed of all of the human faculties, including reason and the higher emotions, and lacked civilization only because of being forced to live as slaves. This generation believed that displays of ability in literature, the arts, and the sciences would prove that Africans deserved the rights accorded to other American citizens in the new republic. However, Enlightenment African Americans were not glued to one path to freedom. While some, like the slave-born poets Jupiter Hammon and Phillis Wheatley, accommodated to slavery and assimilated Anglo-American traditions and practices, others, like the Black petitioners, used republican ideology to demand their rights as citizens in the new nation. Some, like Richard Allen and Absalom Jones, eschewed remaining in increasingly segregated white churches after the Revolution and established independent churches and fraternal associations that were called African by name. Others, like Prince Hall, first allied with British institutions and then contemplated expatriation from America. Perhaps what was most striking about this generation was its giving voice, unequivocally, to the humanity of African people and their right to be treated with human dignity and respect like other American citizens.

645 • Black Masons Movement

On March 6, 1776, Prince Hall, a well-respected African American, and fourteen other African Americans joined the Masons fraternal organization that was part of a Boston British regiment. After fighting broke out at Lexington and the British soldiers evacuated Boston, Hall and his men retained their permit to have a lodge. Prince Hall may have seen in the Masons the possibility of unity and of support for Black self-determination from the British. In January 1777 Hall would be among eight African Americans who petitioned for the abolition of slavery by citing the need to restore "the Natural Right of all men." After the war, "African Lodge No. 1, Dedicated to St. John," applied for and received a charter in 1787, with Prince Hall as the master. That same year, Hall sent a petition to the general court of Boston to provide "Africans . . . one day in a week to work for themselves" to purchase themselves and transport themselves "to some part of the Coast of Africa, where we propose a settlement." This petition of emigration to Africa was written almost a quarter of a century before Paul Cuffee's voyage to Sierra Leone.

646 • African Union Society

In the fall of 1789 African Americans in Newport, Rhode Island, joined together to ensure their security in the new nation by forming the African Union Society. In one sense, this institution was designed to preserve the identity of the Black community by keeping records of births, deaths, marriages, lawsuits, and diaries and to

provide references and opportunities for employment for the Black citizenry. It was also an organization committed to improvement of the character of African Americans by encouraging them to adopt "good conduct" as the best way for Blacks to raise the esteem of the group in the eyes of the nation.

647 • Literary Society Movement

Free African Americans in the North during the early nineteenth century founded literary and improvement societies in order to elevate the moral and intellectual condition of free Blacks. Separate intellectual institutions, often supported by and based in separate Black churches, were required because African Americans were excluded from participation in benevolent societies and public libraries in the North. Hence, such groups as the Reading Room Society, founded in 1828, collected books, sponsored debates, hosted musical programs and poetry readings, and presented lectures in which a popular history of Africa was invoked to inspire African American achievement.

648 • African Grove Theater Company

Established in 1820 in New York City by James Hewlett, America's first Black tragic actor, the African Grove Theater Company, at Grove and Bleecker Streets in New York, performed Shakespearean plays before African American and white audiences. Hewlett, a West Indian, built an audience for the Grove Theater by acting and singing for parties in homes of the upper classes of New York. Reacting against the segregated audience policy at New York's Park Theater, Hewlett founded the African Grove Theater as a space in which African Americans could present and see such plays as *Richard III* without segregation, and receive training in the dramatic arts. Unfortunately the African Company performed at a time of increasing white working-class hostility toward educated African Americans as "uppity" and English plays as "aristocratic." African Grove Theater performances were negatively reviewed by the press, disrupted by white hoodlums, and shut down by police, who arrested actors for allegedly causing disturbances. Eventually this abuse destroyed the African Company and convinced Ira Aldridge, who studied at the African Grove Theater, that his future as a serious actor lay in Europe and not America.

Some Important Books and Poems

649 • *An Evening Thought* (1760)

The first African American to publish a poem was not Phillis Wheatley but Jupiter Hammon (1711–1800), whose broadside *An Evening Thought. Salvation by Christ, with Penitential Cries: Composed by Jupiter Hammon, a Negro belonging to Mr. Lloyd, of Queen's-Village, on Long Island* was printed more than a dozen years before Wheatley's book of poems appeared. Hammon was a preacher whose poetry reflected the intense religious fervor of African Americans who had converted to Christianity during the Great Awakening. Born a slave on Long Island on October 17, 1711, Jupiter was allowed to attend school and learn to read his master's books, especially the Bible, before moving with his master to Connecticut during the Revolution. Hammon witnessed the tragic 1741 New York slave plot that resulted in the burning of thirteen slaves and hanging of eighteen others, an event that may have conditioned his recommendation in his eighty-eight-line poem (to other slaves?) that humanity seek freedom in heavenly salvation, and not on earth. Hammon's other published poems included *An Address to Miss Phillis Wheatley, Ethiopian Poetess* (1778).

650 • *Poems on Various Subjects, Religious and Moral* (1773)

Before being able to publish her book *Poems on Various Subjects, Religious and Moral,* Phillis Wheatley (1753?–1784), a recent African immigrant and Boston house slave, had to pass an oral examination administered by eighteen of the most important white citizens of Boston at the courthouse. She submitted herself to this examination, as her book had been rejected by Boston publishers the year before. Though no transcript of the examination has survived, it appears likely that Wheatley was questioned on her knowledge of the neoclassical as well as biblical references that appear in her poems. More important, this group of examiners, which included Thomas Hutchinson, the governor of the colony, and John Hancock, a future signer of the Declaration of Independence, sought to determine whether she was capable of writing the poems she claimed to have written. No one, they assured her, would believe that a Negro could write poetry. She passed this examination, for in 1773 her book of poems was published in London (Boston publishers still refused the book!) with a preface that included a written "Attestation" from these citizens that she "is thought qualified to write them." It was the first book to be published that was authored by an African American. "On Being Brought from Africa to America" (1773), perhaps its most famous poem, attested to her faith that although "Some view our sable race with scornful eye . . . Remember, *Christian* Negros, black as *Cain,* May be refin'd, and join th' angelic train."

651 • *The Interesting Narrative of the Life of Olaudah Equiano, or Gustavus Vassa, the African* (1789)

The Narrative by Olaudah Equiano (1745–97) provides a dramatically different perspective from Phillis Wheatley's on the slave trade. Written by an Ibo nobleman, *The Narrative* provides a graphic and detailed account of how African slavery differed from the Atlantic

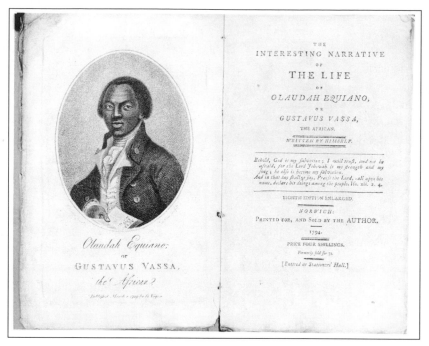

variety, how deeply hurt he was by his separation from his homeland and his sister, and how terrified he was by the huge ships that greeted him when he was brought to the coast of Africa. Vassa, who became an abolitionist, also writes movingly of how he learned to read and write and ultimately acquired enough money to purchase his freedom in Philadelphia in 1766.

Frontispiece engraving of Olaudah Equiano and title page of *The Interesting Narrative of the Life of Olaudah Equiano, or Gustavus Vassa, the African.* Prints and Photographs Division, Library of Congress

Art

652 • Scipio Moorhead

Scipio Moorhead was the painter to whom Phillis Wheatley dedicated her poem "To S.M. a young *African* Painter, on seeing his Works" in her *Poems on Various Subjects, Religious and Moral*. Moorhead was an African slave whose Massachusetts master, like Miss Wheatley's, indulged the talent of his slave. Wheatley's poem describes the effect of seeing two of Moorhead's

paintings—one of Aurora and another on the myth of Damon and Pythias. Perhaps because Moorhead shared Wheatley's interest in classical figures, she lauded his work and hinted it showed the emotional depth of the "bosom" of the African.

To show the lab'ring bosom's deep intent,
And thought in living characters to paint,
When first thy pencil did those beauties give,
And breathing figures learnt from thee to live,
How those prospects give my soul delight,
A new creation rushing on my sight?

Some art historians believe that Scipio Moorhead may have rendered the copperplate engraving of Phillis Wheatley.

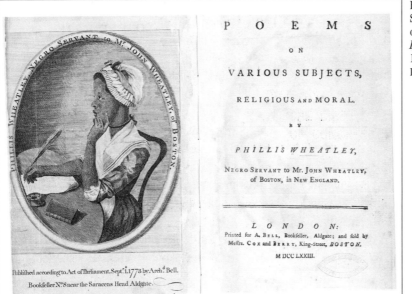

Frontispiece engraving after Scipio Moorhead and title page of *Poems on Various Subjects, Religious and Moral* (London, 1773). Prints and Photographs Division, Library of Congress

depicts a neatly dressed African American whose smile, reminiscent of Leonardo da Vinci's *Mona Lisa,* is slight yet warm and inviting.

654 • Gilbert Stuart's Tutor

The famous American portrait painter Gilbert Stuart reputedly received his first lesson in painting from an African American slave named Neptune Thurston. According to Edward Peterson's *History of Rhode Island* (1853), Stuart "derived his first impression of painting from witnessing Neptune Thurston, a slave, who was employed in his master's cooper-shop, who sketched likenesses on the heads of casks." Thurston may have been the same African whose advertisement appeared in the *Boston Newsletter* on January 7, 1775: "At Mr. M'Lean's, Watchmaker near the Town-House, is a Negro man whose extraordinary genius has been assisted by one of the best Masters in London; he takes fares at the lowest rates. Specimens of his Performances may be seen at said Place."

653 • Joshua Johnston (active 1795–1825)

Although absolute proof of his racial identity has not been found, most art historians regard Joshua Johnston (or Johnson) as the first well-known African American portrait painter. Johnston, who lived and worked in Baltimore, painted primarily affluent European Americans. He may have been influenced by Charles Wilson Peale or Peale's son Rembrandt, also Maryland-based artists. Although his portraits were not signed or dated—a common practice of the day—Johnston nonetheless depicted his subjects in a distinctive, signature style: his figures, both adults and children, appeared stiff, motionless, and posed, with oversize heads that lent a primitive quality to his work. Johnston also produced several portraits of prominent African Americans, whose more relaxed and sympathetic treatment perhaps suggests his identification with these subjects as an African American. In his *Portrait of a Cleric,* Johnston

655 • Slave Artisans

Although enslaved artisans were generally treated better than agricultural laborers, some masters exploited, bartered, and sold them just as vigorously as plantation owners treated their slaves. John Allerwood, an artist, admitted the profitability of enslaving artisans when he advertised his desire to "dispose of his Negro Fellows, Painters. On Wednesday, the Seventh of April Next. . . . As to their abilities . . . they have transacted the Whole of His Business, without any hired Assistance." Perhaps Joe, another enslaved artisan, suspected a similar fate awaiting him when he decided to flee captivity. His master's advertisement in the *South Carolina and American General Gazette* in 1772 sought the return of a runaway silversmith who "is near sixteen years old, . . . is very arch and sensible, and wrought at the silversmith's trade many years, being at work with Mr. Oliphant, jeweller, when he absented himself. . . ."

Music and Drama

656 • Musicians in the Militia

Africans in America were permitted to enter the militia during the colonial period, where many of them learned to play musical instruments. The instruments most commonly played were the fiddle or violin, the French horn, and the drums. Drum-playing soldiers were common throughout the colonial militias and the Continental Army. But, as the late historian Sidney Kaplan observed, seldom was their participation recorded in drawings or portraits from the era.

657 • The First Hymnal

The first hymnal intended for an all-Black religious congregation was *A Collection of Spiritual Songs and Hymns Selected from Various Authors by Richard Allen, African Minister* and was printed in 1801. Such a hymnal was a natural complement to the emergence of an independent church and a sign that by the first

year of the nineteenth century, a distinctive African American religious singing tradition may have already existed.

658 • The Camp Meeting Shout

African Americans improvised upon hymns at camp meetings during the latter part of the Second Great Awakening (1770–1815), and these improvisations were the forerunners to the camp meeting spiritual form. Although most people have assumed that Blacks assimilated these songs from whites, it is not known for sure. Most likely, the camp meeting experience was the first time many slaves were introduced to Christianity, and in this atmosphere, it was much easier for worship and song to take place. Generally the shout was performed at the end of the meeting as the camp was disassembling. Shouting was the climax of this style of music, which included a type of dance step, thigh slapping, and various religious texts mixed with hymn texts, but set to tunes that were more secular in nature.

659 • Ira Aldridge (1807–67)

Recognized as one of the greatest Shakespearean actors, Ira Aldridge was the first African American to perform *Othello* on the English stage. Although the early details of his life are in dispute, Ira Aldridge was apparently born in New York City, where he attended the African Free School and studied at Hewlett's African Theater before he left for England in 1824. On October 10, 1825, Aldridge opened at the Royal Coburg in London and gave his first performance in the play *The Revolt of Surinam or A Slave's Revenge*. But he became internationally famous in 1833 when he debuted at the Theatre Royal, Covent Garden, London, in the title role of *Othello* and won the acclaim of the English press. Nicknamed the African Roscius,

Portrait of Ira Aldridge (as Othello) by Henry Perronet Briggs, c. 1830. National Portrait Gallery, Smithsonian Institution

Aldridge was even more acclaimed when he embarked on his first continental tour in 1852, playing such roles as Mango, Macbeth, Shylock, King Lear, and Richard III, as well as Othello. In 1863 he became a citizen of Great Britain; he was married twice to European women. Though he planned to return to the United States for an acting tour on the eve of his death, Aldridge never set foot in America. A chair dedicated to Ira Aldridge is located in the fourth row of seats of the rebuilt Shakespeare Memorial Theatre at Stratford-upon-Avon.

Religion

660 • First African Baptist Church in Savannah, Georgia

The First African Baptist Church was founded in 1778 by Andrew Bryan (1737–1812), a black pastor and slave. Upon one of the numerous occasions when his gatherings were disrupted by the "pattyrollers" (slave patrols), he "told his persecutors that he rejoiced not only to be whipped, but *would freely suffer death for the cause of Jesus Christ.*" Fortunately his master sought his release and permitted Bryan to continue his ministry in the plantation barn. He soon gained respect as white ministers examined his congregation and found them to be well instructed. Upon his death in 1812, the white Baptist Association of Savannah issued a memorial statement noting his good works.

661 • Lemuel Haynes (1753–1833)

Born in West Hartford, Connecticut, on July 18, 1753, Lemuel Haynes was the first Black minister certified by a predominantly white denomination and licensed to preach in the Congregational Church. His term began on November 29, 1780. Haynes was also the first Black pastor of a white church. In 1785 he was ordained and named pastor of a white church in Torrington, Connecticut. In 1787 he was called to a white church in Rutland, Vermont.

662 • Mother Bethel and St. Thomas Episcopal Church

Racial discrimination caused Blacks to form separate churches in the North. Though Blacks had been a part of St. George's Methodist Church since 1767, the year it was founded, these members found themselves segregated by class from the leadership of the church and by race from common Methodists. As early as the summer of 1791, the society approached several white philanthropists for aid in purchasing two lots on which to erect a church. These plans became more urgent after an incident at St. George's during the summer of 1792. The gallery had just been erected and Richard Allen, Absa-

Bethel African Methodist Episcopal Church. Schomburg
Center for Research in Black Culture, New York Public Library,
Astor, Lenox and Tilden Foundation

churches, in part because many were allowed to attend large camp meetings in which a passionate faith was instilled in those attending. Moreover, the millennialism of the Second Great Awakening, which emphasized universal sin and the coming of God, motivated many to prepare for that event. Such millennialism was a factor in the emergence of spiritual leaders among slaves like Sojourner Truth.

lom Jones, and other Blacks were directed to sit there. As prayers began, the Blacks were ordered to the rear of the gallery. Instead of doing so, Allen states, "all went out of the church in a body and they were no more plagued with us in the church." The Blacks who walked out formed two new congregations: most who left formed St. Thomas Episcopal Church, of which Absalom Jones became pastor; others, followers of Allen, formed Mother Bethel, perhaps the most famous Black church in the early nineteenth century.

663 • Second Great Awakening

Although the First Great Awakening led white masters to encourage conversion of their slaves, it was during the Second Great Awakening (1770–1815) that large numbers of African Americans began joining mainstream Christian

ANTEBELLUM EXPRESSION, 1820–60

Movements, Organizations, and Celebrations

664 • Antislavery Testimony

During the middle of the nineteenth century, several former slaves published autobiographies, called slave narratives, which transformed not only American politics but also American literature. Drawing on eighteenth-century forms of the picaresque novel and nineteenth-century folk and oral traditions, Frederick Douglass, William Wells Brown, Harriet Jacobs, Nat Turner, Harriet E. Wilson, and Sojourner Truth created a new American genre of the heroic slave who discovers an identity through romantic rebellion against American society. David Walker, Martin Delany, and Henry Highland Garnet wrote confessional novels and nonfictional exhortations of rebellion which shaped the work of Henry David Thoreau and other romantic rebels. In folk literature and music, especially the spirituals, African Americans gave voice to the spiritual transcendence of those whose freedom is deferred and the coded escape of those driven to seize freedom now. Such narratives shaped even the expressions of free persons of color who came to believe that none could be free, especially after the Fugitive Slave Act of 1850, as long as the masses remained enslaved.

665 • Slave Festivals

Throughout the nineteenth century, slaves held festivals and carnivals in the United States and throughout the Caribbean. The noisy public performances sometimes lasted for days and included dancing, singing, and music, often with banjos and other slave-made instruments. One of the most famous festivals was Jonkonnu, believed to have originated in Jamaica and been re-created, perhaps by migrating slaves, in North Carolina in 1828. Festivals were occasions on which slaves often reclaimed some of their African heritage: they simulated sounds made by drums, instruments forbidden by slave masters, created and wore outlandish masks and costumes, and danced with "pagan" ringlets, cowbells, and spectacular headdresses. The revelry of Jonkonnu was allowed by masters in part because it took place during Christmas holidays, after the planting of the crop was concluded. While masters looked upon such festivities as merely opportunities for slaves to "let off some steam," the slaves' adornment of masters' and mistresses' clothing, holding of mock courts, and the exchange of gifts symbolized

that slaves also saw the festivals as opportunities to act as if they were free.

666 • Literacy Efforts

Frederick Douglass argued that the only way to permanently keep someone a slave was to keep him or her ignorant. Most antebellum southern states agreed and considered it a crime to teach African Americans, slave or free, to read or write. In Norfolk, Virginia, Margaret Douglass conducted reading lessons in her home for a group of free Black children. Soon a warrant was issued for her arrest and she was indicted by a grand jury and tried for breaking the Virginia law that prohibited assembly of African Americans for religious worship unless the services were led by a white, the gathering of African Americans for instruction in reading and/or writing, and any congregation of Blacks at nighttime for any purpose. Any white person assisting in these assemblies was to be fined and imprisoned. Mrs. Douglass received a one-dollar fine and a one-month jail sentence.

Some Important Books

667 • *Narrative of the Life of Frederick Douglass: An American Slave* (1845)

Frederick Douglass (1818–95), an escaped slave and abolitionist speaker, wrote the *Narrative* to prove to skeptical audiences that he had actually been a slave. When published in June 1845, the *Narrative*, accompanied by William Lloyd Garrison's preface and Wendell Phillips's letter of recommendation, became a best-seller, selling 4,500 copies by the fall and 30,000 by 1850. The book's popularity derived from its having been written by a former slave rather than transcribed by a white abolitionist, and from its compelling story of one man's struggle to emancipate himself mentally and physically from American enslavement. Because it was written by a slave who had taught himself how to read and write, the book not only launched the runaway slave as a powerful figure in American literature but established the self-made African American as a central character in American autobiography. Although Douglass revised his life story in *My Bondage and My Freedom* (1855) and *The Life and Times of Frederick Douglass* (1881), he retained the powerful form of the earlier narrative.

668 • *Clotel; or, The President's Daughter: A Narrative of Slave Life in the United States* (1853)

Clotel, William Wells Brown's allegorical novel of Thomas Jefferson, democratic hypocrisy, and slave life in America, is the first novel published by an African American, appearing in 1853 in London, where Brown (1815–84), a fugi-

Frances Ellen Watkins Harper. Prints and Photographs Division, Library of Congress

tive slave and intellectual expatriate, had been staying for four years. Brown's melodramatic story of the life of three generations of African American descendants of Thomas Jefferson mixes fact, fiction, and political assertion to establish what would become a predominant form for African American fiction—the protest novel. Because of the controversial nature of Brown's assertion that Thomas Jefferson had kept an African American mistress and that he allowed the children from that liaison to remain enslaved, the American edition of the book, published in 1864, substituted a senator for the president. It was not until 1969 that the original version of this inflammatory novel appeared in print in the United States.

669 • *Poems on Miscellaneous Subjects* (1854)

Poems on Miscellaneous Subjects, the first book of poems by Frances Ellen Watkins Harper (1825–1911), contained her classic depiction of

William Wells Brown. Prints and Photographs Division, Library of Congress

the travail of motherhood under slavery ("The Slave Mother") and her indictment of social disdain for women who had slept with men out of wedlock ("A Double Standard"). Although Harper was much more than a poet—a founder of the National Association of Colored Women and a participant in the Equal Rights Association Convention in 1869—she was foremost a writer who is credited with authoring, in addition to her several volumes of poetry, the first short story by an African American, "The Two Offers" (1859).

670 • *Our Nig* (1859)

Harriet Jacobs's novel *Our Nig; or, Sketches from the Life of a Free Black, in a two-story white house, North: showing that slavery's shadows fall even there* is the first novel written by an African American woman to be published. Jacobs's novel, which was discovered by literary scholar Henry Louis Gates, Jr., is an engaging study of the conditions of life in the antebellum North, where "slavery's shadows fall even there" with discrimination, segregation, and abuse the staple of lives led by African American women and men.

671 • *Blake, or the Huts of America* (1859)

Martin Delany's novel of a slave rebellion remains the only revolutionary novel of the antislavery movement. Breaking with the slave narrative tradition of the long-suffering victims of the system and the solitary Frederick Douglass–like rebel, Delany, who was a freeborn African American and student at Harvard Medical School, crafted a novel that imagined what a mass revolt against slavery would look like. Delany's protagonist is an insurrectionist slave who moves stealthily between plantations, being hidden by friendly slaves and informed of

developments by the slave "underground," to organize a full-scale rebellion. Serialized originally in the *Anglo-African,* Delany's novel was one of the most popular novels of the period with the African American reading public.

672 • *Incidents in the Life of a Slave* (1861)

Incidents in the Life of a Slave, the autobiographical novel written by Harriet Jacobs (1813–97), is the best narrative account of slave life from the perspective of a black woman. Jacobs tells the story of Linda Brent (a pseudonym for Jacobs herself), who is sexually harassed by her master and then victimized by her jealous mistress. Jacobs provides an insider's view of the struggles to avoid ongoing rape and reprisal, a conflict that leads Linda to try to escape by entering into a relationship with another white man. When that relationship also becomes problematical, Brent decides to hide in a crawl space on the property for seven years until she can finally escape by boat to the North. Her story also details the prejudice up North, the Fugitive Slave Law in action, and Black women's relationships.

Art

673 • Patrick Henry Reason (1817?–1850?)

Patrick Henry Reason was an engraver from Philadelphia who is most famous for his engraving *Am I Not a Woman and a Sister*—an emblem that signified his commitment to the abolitionist's movement and Black women's rights. He was educated in the African Free School, apprenticed to a white craftsman, and became a skilled engraver himself. Beyond his famous emblem, he contributed numerous images in many antislavery magazines, created the frontispiece for Charles C. Andrews's *The History of the African Free Schools,* published in 1830, and produced portraits of several of the more important abolitionists, including a lithograph (1840) and an engraving (1848) of Henry Bibb.

674 • Julien Hudson (active 1830–40)

Julien Hudson was a freeman of mixed race from New Orleans. Born into the so-called mulatto group, Hudson partook of the French-influenced, flamboyant, upper-class lifestyle that was available to well-born free African Americans in New Orleans. One of his most important works was his painting *Battle of New Orleans* (1815), which documented the contribution made to the War of 1812 by the famous corps of free Black soldiers and its white commander, Colonel Michel Jean Fortier, Jr. Hudson is also distinguished for painting, in 1839, the only known self-portrait of an African American artist in the antebellum period.

Julien Hudson, *Self-Portrait*, 1839. Courtesy of Louisiana State Museum

Advertisement featuring stereotypes "uncle," "auntie," and "pickaninnies." The Warshaw Collection, National Museum of American History, Smithsonian Museum

675 • Caricatures

Racial caricatures flooded the American press in the antebellum period. While caricatures had existed earlier in the eighteenth-century press, the number and viciousness of Black caricatures increased dramatically in the late 1820s and continued to grow through the rest of the nineteenth century. Caricatures seemed to grow in popularity as Blacks made advances in free society, whether northern or southern. Edward Clay began a series of cartoons in the late 1820s called *Life in Philadelphia* that ridiculed the "airs" and conspicuous consumption of Philadelphia's Black elite. These caricatures were very popular because they captured the attention of working-class whites who felt looked down upon by upwardly mobile Blacks, and

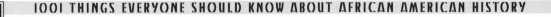

emerged around the time of the horrendous anti-Black riots in cities like Philadelphia and Cincinnati. Caricatures abounded in the 1840s and 1850s in response to the abolitionist movement and continued to spread after the Civil War as a way to critique the ex-slaves and the extension of political rights to Blacks. Racial caricatures were so widely disseminated in the nineteenth century that they came to define the public image of African Americans and limit the publishing opportunities for alternative images created by Black artists.

676 • Robert Scott Duncanson (1821–72)

Robert Scott Duncanson was the first African American landscape painter to gain national and international attention. Born to a Scottish Canadian father and a free woman of color in Seneca County, New York, Duncanson grew up in Canada but moved to a community outside of Cincinnati in the 1840s. In 1842 Duncanson was included in an exhibition sponsored by the Society for the Promotion of Useful Knowledge and secured several important portrait commissions of abolitionists, including that of James G. Birney, the former slave owner and Liberty Party presidential candidate. But Duncanson's true love was landscape painting in the Hudson River School romantic-naturalistic tradition and was distinguished by his use of atmospheric effects in his landscapes. Moving between Detroit and Cincinnati, Duncanson was able to exhibit his work in the annual Western Art and Union exhibitions and was well regarded by his fellow artists. After going abroad in 1853, he returned to the United States and produced a series of murals of Cincinnati for his patron, Nicholas Longworth. Perhaps Duncanson's most impressive work was his series of American landscapes, of which *Landscape with Rainbow*

is a fine example. Because of his need for money and his interest in daguerreotypes, Duncanson began working in 1849 with daguerreotypist J. P. Ball.

677 • J. P. Ball (1825–1904)

Born in Cincinnati, J. P. Ball worked as a waiter on a riverboat and remained something of a showman and entrepreneur for the rest of his life. In 1851 he had one of the most elaborate and fashionable daguerreotype studios in Cincinnati. He did portraits of famous personalities, such as Jenny Lind, and employed Robert Duncanson to transform the daguerreotypes into oil paintings. Ball's most ambitious work, however, was a panoramic history of slavery that consumed a half mile of canvas. Although the work of art has been lost, Ball's lecture notes survived and were published in 1855. The panorama began, according to the notes, with an African village and ended with the recent Cincinnati riots of 1841. Not until Aaron Douglas in the 1930s would another African American artist attempt as sweeping a mural project as that executed by J. P. Ball.

Music and Dance

678 • Work Songs

Sung by both slaves and free people of color in the South, African American work songs were first described by Fanny Kemble in her *Journal of a Residence on a Georgia Plantation in 1838–1839*. Kemble noted that the Black men rowing her boat down a stream

set up a chorus, which they continued to chant in unison with each other, and in time with their stroke, till their voices were heard no more from the distance. . . . [T]hey all sing in unison, having never, it appears, attempted or heard any-

thing like part-singing. Their voices seem oftener tenor than any other quality, and the tune and time they keep something quite wonderful.

Work songs were used extensively in West Africa, in Dahomey and Yoruba, as well as in Haiti, Brazil, and Trinidad, to harmonize the work rhythms mainly of agricultural laborers. In the antebellum South, such songs were sung not only by agricultural laborers but by domestic servants, industrial workers, and steamboat laborers. With one man usually providing the "call" by announcing the verses of the song, the group then echoes those verses in the tempo of his first call. Work songs survived slavery and became characteristic of the "chain gangs" of the convict lease system after the Civil War and can still be heard in certain southern prisons.

679 • Congo Square

Located just outside the northeast limits of New Orleans, Congo Plains (later known as Congo Square) was a vacant plot of land that became a site of Black dancing and music playing in the nineteenth century. After 1805, the year that the United States took over administration of New Orleans from the French, African American slaves began to congregate in Congo Square, along with Indians and Creoles, to play competitive field games, hold dog- and bull-fights, and generally carouse. The proximity of Congo Square to a brickyard where voodoo rites were held also lent a West Indian quality to the square. But Congo Square became famous after the New Orleans City Council ruled in 1817 that "assemblies of slaves" would be confined to Sundays and designated Congo Square as the place for slave entertainments. Although the original impetus was to confine immoral and potentially insurrectionary activities to a particular site where they could be watched carefully, the ordi-

The Love Song, drawn in Congo Square, New Orleans, by E. W. Kemble, in *Century Magazine*, 1886. From *Black Dance: 1619 to Today* by Lynne Fauley Emery

nance turned the square into a tourist attraction where out-of-towners regularly came to see Jamaicans and southern African Americans play drums, dance with long animal tails, and perform complex dances. Congo Square declined after 1880, when the area was divided up into lots.

680 • Frank Johnson (1792–1844)

Frank Johnson was a fiddler, bugler, horn player, and bandleader who acquired a national reputation. Based in Philadelphia, he was sought after for his improvisational, compositional, and orchestration skills. He and his band traveled the country at the request of rich patrons who had heard of his talent to call a tune. The Frank Johnson organization also toured

England and gave a command performance for Queen Victoria at Buckingham Palace.

681 • Elizabeth Taylor Greenfield (182?–76)

Known as the Black Swan, Elizabeth Greenfield was the most celebrated Black concert singer of the antebellum period. Born in the 1820s, and given very little training, she was reputed to be the first African American musician to earn a reputation both in the United States and abroad. After a successful singing tour throughout the free states from 1851 to 1853, Greenfield dazzled audiences on her tour of England in 1854, where she gave a command performance before Queen Victoria. With a singing range of three octaves, she was a vocal curiosity as well as an appreciated singer of classical music songs. Although she toured the U.S. again in 1863 and sang often at charitable events, her singing career was limited by her inability, because of race prejudice, to obtain the kind of training she needed to become a first-rate opera singer. Hence, most of her career was spent as an instructor of music.

682 • Blacks Composed "Dixie"

In 1859 Dan Emmett, a white man in black-face, sang "I Wish I Was in Dixie Land," and the song brought tears to southern eyes and became the Confederate national anthem. But although Emmett claimed to have written the song, historians have now proved that the song was actually composed and sung by a Black musical family from Ohio. The Snowdens, former slaves in Maryland who had migrated to and settled in Knox County, Ohio, were a family of farmers who performed songs for Black and white audiences, usually accompanying themselves on the banjo and the fiddle. Apparently Dan Emmett traveled through Knox County, heard the song,

memorized it, and then made himself famous—for the song. Ironically the song of the South was composed "up North" by African Americans.

683 • Jim Crow Rice

In 1828 Thomas Dartmouth Rice was the first white man to create a successful one-man show based on reputedly dancing like an African American. Rice claimed to have seen a crippled African American sing and dance. Rice's representation of a Black man dancing became known as "to jump Jim Crow." In addition to shuffling in a contorted posture, wheeling his body around to jump high in the air, Rice also dressed in tattered, outlandish clothes, wore a crumpled hat, and rolled his eyes grotesquely. Historians debate whether Rice's performance was an accurate depiction of African American dancing. Some have argued that it was a fusion of a jig and a shuffle. Others have argued that at best it was Rice's imitation of a "lame Negro," and at worst, simply a caricature of Black dance exaggerated and ridiculed in order to entertain a white audience. Whatever its origins, Jim Crow became an instant hit, was hugely successful, and ingrained a stereotype of African American behavior in nineteenth-century American popular culture.

684 • Ethiopian Minstrelsy

Thomas Rice's success spawned numerous imitators and led to the creation of a major American dance and theatrical institution, that of Ethiopian minstrelsy—usually two and sometimes three or more whites performing in blackface several skits, scenes, and songs. Although the performances were supposedly based on African American slave life, the minstrelsy troupes actually provided social commentary upon the events of the day and social issues con-

Juba performing at the Vauxhall Gardens in London, 1848.
From *Black Dance: 1619 to Today* by Lynne Fauley Emery

fronting the masses. Patronized mainly by working-class whites, including many immigrants, the Ethiopian minstrelsy became the most important form of popular entertainment during the pre–Civil War period. It challenged in some instances legitimate theater in America. Eventually Blacks were allowed to form and tour their own minstrel shows, but like the whites, Black performers had to cover their faces with burnt cork and follow closely the pantomimed traditions of the white minstrels, or risk violence. Ironically Blacks by the middle of the century could only perform on the American stage by copying the routines of whites who had mimicked other African Americans.

685 • Juba, the Real Thing

The most famous and most authentic interpreter of African American dance styles in the antebellum period was Master Juba (William Henry Lane), a freeborn African American who emerged in the 1840s on the American popular stage. Juba was an expert in dancing the jig, and his outstanding skill was attested to by many. Marian Winter, who saw Juba dance, stated in 1845 that "it was flatly stated by members of the profession that Juba was beyond question the very greatest of all dancers." In 1846 Juba joined a minstrel show, White's Serenaders, which traveled to London in 1848. Dancing at the Vauxhall Gardens in London, Juba stunned English reviewers, who could not believe they were witnessing such "mobility of muscles, such flexibility of joints, such boundings, such slidings, such gyrations, such toes and heelings, such backwardings and forwardings, such posturings. . . ." A "school of Juba" emerged in the United States, but Master Juba died in London in 1852 before ever returning to his native land. Some critics credited Juba with reviving Black dance on the stage as an authentic rather than a caricature performance.

686 • Blind Tom (1849–1908)

Born near Columbus, Georgia, Thomas Greene was sold with his mother, Charlotte Wiggins, from the Oliver family to the Bethune family while still a baby. When Tom was four, the Bethunes acquired a piano. Tom heard Mrs. Bethune teaching her daughters every day for three years. One day, at age seven, he sat down to the piano and played perfectly the tunes he had heard the previous day. Recognizing his genius, the Bethune family decided to hire out Tom for activities that required music. Armed with a strong memory, Tom developed a huge repertory, on which he could improvise, without formal

Blind Tom. Prints and Photographs Division, Library of Congress

some songs, like "Swing Low, Sweet Chariot" and "Steal Away," possessed a double meaning: the possibility of escape to freedom on earth as well as that promised in heaven. These songs first gained national attention during the Civil War when they were commented on by Thomas Wentworth Higginson in his articles on his service with a Black regiment, and in 1867 when William Allen, Charles Ware, and Lucy McKim Garrison published the first collection of the songs, entitled *Slave Songs of the United States.* Then in 1916 Harry T. Burleigh, an African American singer and arranger, published the first arrangement of a spiritual for solo voice and piano when he arranged "Deep River." With additional arrangements of "Weepin' Mary," "You May Bury Me in the East," and others in 1917, a new period for concert performance of the spirituals began.

musical training. Tom was such a concert draw between 1857 and 1898 that the Bethunes became wealthy. After the war, reformers sued the Bethunes to gain Tom's freedom, but Tom objected that freedom would not help him, given his sightless condition. He remained a ward of the Bethune family until his death.

687 • Spirituals

For generations prior to the Civil War, African Americans had sung songs based on religious hymns, some of which were the English Wesleyan hymns. These "sorrow songs," as they were called by W. E. B. Du Bois, were sung in a distinctive style that was different from the standard phrasing and emphases of the English renditions. European and religious in origin, these songs were distinctively African American in style, and the choice and emphasis of certain songs by the slaves made them into plaintive commentary on the slave system. Moreover,

688 • Slave Songs as Commentary

One former slave recalled how some of the slave songs emerged from the experience of enslavement.

I'll tell you, it's dis way. My master call me up, and order me a short peck of corn and a hundred lash. My friends see it, and is sorry for me. When dey come to de praise-meeting dat night dey sing about it. Some's very good singers and know how; and dey work it in—work it in, you know, till you get it right; and dat's de way.

689 • Underground Railroad Songs

Travelers of the underground railroad used many of the slave songs to pass messages and communicate over long distances. Some songs were used to keep spirits up. Some were meant as a signal to get ready, while others warned of danger. And there were those such as the well-known "Follow the Drinking Gourd" that were intended as maps for the fugitives.

Religion

690 • On White America as Egypt

Maria Stewart, a free Black minister, reform activist, and the first Black woman to give a speech in public, used a speaking occasion in Boston in 1831 to make the biblical connection between Egypt and

America, America, foul and indelible is thy stain! Dark and dismal is the cloud that hangs over thee, for thy cruel wrongs and injuries to the fallen souls of Africa. The blood of her murdered ones cries to heaven for vengeance against Thee. . . . You may kill, tyrannize, and oppress as much as you choose, until our cry shall come up before the throne of God; for I am firmly persuaded, that he will not suffer you to quell the proud, fearless and undaunted spirits of the Africans forever; for in his own time, he is able to plead our cause against you, and to pour out upon you the ten plagues of Egypt.

691 • Those Separate Churches

After the Nat Turner Rebellion in 1831, many independent Black churches in the South, such as the African Baptist Church of Williamsburg, Virginia, responded to white fears by merging with white churches. In the North, hostility toward independent Black churches in Philadelphia led to riots in which the most prominent churches, such as Mother Bethel, were attacked by white mobs. Working-class whites felt that such independent churches were the reason for the success and wealth of Blacks.

692 • The Invisible Institution

The Invisible Institution is the name used by some scholars to describe the secret worship services of African American slaves prior to the Civil War. These secret services took place in "hush harbors," makeshift meeting places in the swamps and bayous away from the plantations. Wet quilts and rags were hung up in the trees around the services in an effort to stifle the sound of the worship. Here they interpreted Christianity according to their personal experience, which inevitably contradicted the messages their masters taught.

693 • Voodoo

Although voodoo, or *vodun* as it was called in Haiti, was never as strong a presence in North America as in the West Indies, it did become quite popular in Louisiana after the eighteenth-century importation of French West Indian slaves. The ruling elite of Louisiana sought to suppress voodoo because they believed it incited rebellion against whites and because prominent voodoo priests or priestesses, such as the renowned Marie Laveau, were free persons of color, who operated outside the social control of planters. Voodoo, called hoodoo by slaves who lived on plantations, involved conjuration, the creation of charms, potions, or other magic, and the prediction of the future. In New Orleans, voodoo was primarily worship of the snake-god, Damballa or Da, from the Dahomey tradition, and involved rituals of spirit possession and animal sacrifice. Voodoo conjurers claimed an ability to predict the future and to fashion charms that protected slaves from masters, but most slaves and free Blacks used voodoo against other African Americans. In the nineteenth century certain voodoo priests, including Marie Laveau, even had a large clientele of whites, especially those who wished to get information, such as on a spouse, loved one, or recently departed relative or friend. Voodoo reached its height in popularity in the 1850s.

Marie Laveau (1794–1881), known as the Voodoo Queen of New Orleans. From the collection of the Louisiana State Museum

POSTBELLUM BLUES, 1865–1915

Movements, Organizations, and Celebrations

694 • Historical Associations

In the post–Civil War environment, a popular theme in African American culture was the celebration of African American heroes, most notably Frederick Douglass. As a former slave who had become a famous and influential abolitionist and citizen, Douglass epitomized the ideology of self-improvement that became dominant in African American intellectual circles. When Douglass died in 1895, his second wife, Helen Pitts Douglass, a white woman, was instrumental in gaining the support of prominent African Americans who joined her in forming the Frederick Douglass Memorial and Historical Association to preserve his Anacostia home at Cedar Hill. Other historical associations and societies, such as the New York Society for Historic Research (1890) and the American Negro Historical Society (1897), were formed during this period, along with such research collections as the Jesse Moorland collection at Howard University, to document the history of exemplary African American individuals and the contributions of Blacks to world history.

695 • African American Folklore Movement

Although African American historical associations represented themselves as preserving the history of all African Americans, the history of the Black masses and the history of slavery were usually understudied in mainstream African American historical associations before the twentieth century. But in the 1890s a group of intellectuals interested in studying the unique qualities of folk culture of the formerly enslaved masses of southern Black people came together and founded the Boston Society for the Collection of Negro Folklore in the 1890s. Similarly, African American historian W. E. B. Du Bois established the significance of African American folk culture in his pathbreaking essay on the "sorrow songs" in *The Souls of Black Folk*. His work and the work of the Boston Folklore Society set the stage for other scholars to collect and preserve the myths, jokes, toasts, and tales of southern Black vernacular culture.

Some Important Books

696 • *A Voice from the South* (1892)

Anna J. Cooper's *A Voice from the South by a Black Woman of the South* is the most forceful indictment of the sexism and racism of late-nineteenth-century reform movements written by an American intellectual. The daughter of a slave and her master, Cooper (1858–1964) graduated from Oberlin College with a B.A. and M.A., became principal of Washington, D.C.'s M Street School (later Dunbar High), and eventually earned a Ph.D. from the Sorbonne in Paris. As a contemporary of W. E. B. Du Bois and Booker T. Washington, Cooper criticized the tendency of Black reform movements to marginalize the plight and potential of Black women in discussions of the "race problem." *A Voice from the South* details the bias against educating women in Black colleges, seminaries, and high schools and critiques the women's movement, especially its leaders, Susan B. Anthony and

Anna B. Shaw, for being unwilling to oppose racism in the women's clubs. *A Voice from the South* also provides an impassioned indictment of the industrial education movement as a conspiracy to deny the humanity of African Americans, both female and male.

697 • *Lyrics of Lowly Life* (1896)

Paul Laurence Dunbar (1872–1906) was an elevator boy in a New York City hotel when he began to compose and publish poetry and short stories, many of which were written in dialect. But it was the publication of 1896 of *Lyrics of Lowly Life*, his third book of poems, with its introduction written by the dean of American letters, William Dean Howells, that made Dunbar famous. While Dunbar's poems were shackled to a degree by dialect he used, they also manifested a directness of expression and sincerity of emotion that eluded dialect poetry produced by Thomas Nelson Page and others. Moreover, in some of his "standard English" poems, Dunbar registered his sense of African American doubleness ("We Wear the Mask") and the bitterness of not being able to live fully in a segregated world.

698 • *The Conjure Woman* (1899)

Charles Chesnutt's first collection of short stories is a subtle and complex retelling of folktales told to a northern carpetbagger and his wife by "Uncle Julius," a trickster ex-slave who worked for the northerner as a coachman. Julius's tales within the northerner's seven tales are written in a North Carolina dialect and conform outwardly to the popular plantation stories written by George W. Cable, Thomas Nelson Page, and others in the late nineteenth century. But unlike those stories, Chesnutt's reveal the tragedy of slavery. In "Sis Becky's Pickaninny," Julius tells of a slave mother sold away from her family and home because of a greedy slave owner, while "Po' Sandy" narrates the tragedy of a slave whose wife turns him into a tree so that he won't be sold away only to have their master cut down the tree for lumber. Perhaps most important, the stories in *The Conjure Woman* narrate an African American folk mysticism in which slaves and ex-slaves identified with supernatural forces and relied on them to gain advantage on white folks. That folk mysticism would become an enduring theme in African American fiction, developed best in the writings of Zora Neale Hurston and Toni Morrison.

699 • *Up from Slavery* (1901)

Up from Slavery, the autobiography of Booker T. Washington (1856–1915), built upon the Black self-made-man genre of Frederick Douglass's *Narrative* but eliminated the earlier book's fiery indictment of American society. Although *Up from Slavery* condemns slavery, it does so mainly for its miseducation of African Americans in a philosophy of labor at odds with the capitalist ethic that one profits from one's labor. Made famous by his 1895 Atlanta Exposition Address that encouraged Blacks to postpone demands for social and political equality for the promise of independent economic development, Washington recounts his rise from slavery to world fame as an allegory of African American success in America if Blacks adopt his philosophy that hard labor is always rewarded. Washington's Horatio Alger–like autobiography not only disseminates his political program for Black advancement in post-Reconstruction America but also, like Benjamin Franklin's *Autobiography*, teaches an ethic of public behavior considerably less sophisticated than the man himself.

700 • *The Souls of Black Folk* (1903)

W. E. B. Du Bois's collection of essays, *The Souls of Black Folk* (1903), is not only one of the most inspiring books in the entire African American canon but also a book that created a genre—the poetic, autobiographical collection of essays—of African American letters. Containing the famous pronouncement "the problem of the twentieth century is the color-line," and the introspective exploration of the "double-consciousness" of the African American, *The Souls of Black Folk* revealed how the educated class of Black Americans felt and thought about life under racism in America. Perhaps even more important than declaring his political independence from the thought of Booker T. Washington, Du Bois (1868–1965) used this book to declare the existence of an African American folk culture that should not be sacrificed to integration. Concluding the book was one of Du Bois's most influential essays, "On the Sorrow Songs," the first published analysis of the spirituals as the building block of African American culture.

701 • *Autobiography of an Ex-Colored Man* (1912)

James Weldon Johnson's only novel is a superb treatment of the problem of the African American identity, which is forced to choose between the material and social success of the white world and the warmth and creativity of the black. On one level, Johnson's novel is the story of an African American light-skinned enough to pass for white. But on another, the *Autobiography of an Ex-Colored Man* is the first cultural pluralist novel of the twentieth century, because it portrays passing into the white world as the choice of personal anonymity and cultural failure for the talented African American. Leaving behind the spirited bo-

hemian New York jazz scene, where his talent as a musician and performer was recognized and celebrated, the narrator laments the rich and vibrant African American culture he is forced to abandon. The *Autobiography of an Ex-Colored Man* is also an excellent guide to the urban folk culture of bohemian New York, which James Weldon and his brother J. Rosamund knew intimately from their days as composers of lyrics and songs for the theater.

Art

702 • Edward Bannister (1828–1901)

Edward Bannister was born and educated in Canada, and when he moved to Boston in 1848, he already possessed a highly developed interest in painting. Working as a barber, he took evening classes at the Lowell Institute and was inspired by the paintings of William Morris Hunt. Exposed to the French Barbizon paintings, Bannister developed into an excellent landscape artist in the heavy-palette style of French naturalism. He gained fame when one of his paintings was accepted in the Philadelphia Centennial Exposition of 1876 and won the first prize bronze medal. The judges wanted to reconsider once they learned that Bannister was African American, but the protest of fellow painters forced the committee to award him the prize. Afterward, he became a leading painter in Providence, Rhode Island. Although the bulk of his work was landscapes, his most sensitive painting remains *Newspaper Boy* (1869), where he captures the expectancy, tentativeness, and mood of a possibly African American newspaper boy.

703 • Edmonia Lewis (1843?–after 1911)

Edmonia Lewis was the first professional African American sculptor. Born of a free

Edmonia Lewis. Photograph by Henry Rocher, c. 1870.
National Portrait Gallery, Smithsonian Institution

704 • Henry Ossawa Tanner (1859–1937)

Henry O. Tanner was the best African American artist of the nineteenth and early twentieth centuries. Born in Philadelphia into the upper-class elite, Tanner enrolled in the Pennsylvania Academy of Fine Arts at age twenty-one and studied with the legendary teacher Thomas Eakins. Eakins steered Tanner away from his first love, landscape painting, toward genre painting. After working for a short while as an art teacher at Clark College, Tanner traveled during the summer of 1889 in North Carolina, where he made numerous sketches of the landscape and its people. Perhaps his most famous work grew out of that trip. *The Banjo Lesson* (1893) depicted a sensitive relationship of an elder teaching a young African American child

African American father and a Chippewa Indian mother, Lewis attended Oberlin College in Ohio in 1859, from which she was dismissed because of unsubstantiated accusations that she had poisoned several of her white female schoolmasters. Moving to Boston, she began to do portrait busts of white abolitionists. In 1865 she took a trip to Europe, settled in Rome, and perfected her neoclassical style. Joining an American community in Rome that consisted of Charlotte Chuman, an actress, and Harriet Hosmer, a sculptor, Lewis remained in Rome in part because of the excellent marble she was able to obtain. Her sculpture of Hagar, an Old Testament Egyptian maidservant of Sarah, the wife of Abraham, who was cast into the wilderness, is one of her most compelling works. It exemplifies her ability to use the neoclassical style to create a dignified rendition of this African and Biblical subject.

The Banjo Lesson, 1893. Courtesy of Hampton University Museum, Virginia

to play a banjo. But Tanner eschewed African American genre studies after the 1890s, went to Paris, and became enthralled with the city, eventually settling there as an expatriate. In the early twentieth century Tanner turned increasingly to religious painting of scenes from the Bible. During World War I he again returned to genre studies of the impact of the war on the people. He received numerous awards in his career, perhaps the most impressive being the French Legion of Honor in 1923.

705 • Collection of African Art

In the late nineteenth century, a museum at Hampton Institute, a Black institution of higher education in Hampton, Virginia, began to collect African art as a way to promote self-knowledge among Black students. Under the direction of curator Cora Mae Folsom, the museum purchased a collection of African artifacts from the Kuba people of the Congo that had been collected by William Sheppard. Sheppard had gone to Africa in 1890 to spread Christianity and European values among the natives but had found himself fascinated by the sophistication and complexity of African civilization. Amassing a large collection of African art and anthropological artifacts, Sheppard came to believe, along with Folsom, that Black Americans needed a positive identification with Africa in order to create a healthy identity. The collaboration of Sheppard and Folsom resulted in Hampton Institute becoming the only American college in the early twentieth century to possess a comprehensive collection of African art.

706 • Meta Warrick Fuller (1877–1968)

Born in Philadelphia and educated in its public schools, Meta Warrick Fuller graduated from the Pennsylvania School of Industrial Art with

honors in 1898. After winning a scholarship to study sculpture for a year, she chose to venture across the Atlantic to Paris, where she was mentored by another Philadelphia-born painter, Henry Ossawa Tanner. Her sculpture *The Wretched* was exhibited at the Paris Salon in 1903 and gained her local acclaim and the attention of French sculptor Auguste Rodin, who took her on as a student. She returned to the United States after three years and opened a studio in her hometown. Her work received little attention until she secured a commission to produce 150 historical Black figures for the Jamestown Tercentennial Exposition of 1907. Although much of her work from this period was destroyed in a fire that consumed a Philadelphia warehouse, she was able to produce a series of historical sculptures when she received another commission from the New York Semi-Centennial of Emancipation. Fuller's commitment to African American portrayal set her apart from the majority of late-nineteenth-century African American artists. Her *Ethiopia Awakening* (1914), a life-size bronze of an Egyptian woman emerging from a mummy's wrapping, testifies to an identification with Africa that looks forward to the Harlem Renaissance.

Music and Theater

707 • Georgia Minstrels

After the Civil War, the first successful all–African American minstrel troupe emerged. The *Georgia Minstrels* was founded by Geo. B. Hicks, a Black Georgian, in 1865. Reorganized by a white manager under the name *Callender's Original Georgia Minstrels* and then in 1878 as *Haverly's European Minstrels,* it was finally known from 1882 on as *Callender's Consolidated Minstrels.* The *Georgia Minstrels* was dis-

Billy Kersands of Callender's Georgia Minstrels. Courtesy of Billy Rose Theater Collection. The New York Public Library for the Performing Arts. Astor, Lenox, and Tilden Foundations

tinguished not only by its all–African American personnel but also by its attempt to elevate minstrelsy to a serious art form. With several outstanding musicians, such as banjoists the Bohee Brothers, the *Georgia Minstrels* excelled at playing serious music and working it into the minstrelsy form. At its peak in 1876, the troupe contained twenty-one performers. It also contained two of the most outstanding minstrels in the history of the form—Billy Kersands and Sam Lucas.

708 • James Bland (1854–1911)

The composer of "Carry Me Back to Old Virginny" and "Oh, Dem Golden Slippers" was a Black minstrel named James Bland, who was born in Flushing, New York, on October 22, 1854. Reared in a mixed-race middle-class family, Bland taught himself to play the banjo as a child. After the family moved to Washington, D.C., and Bland graduated from high school, he entered Howard University to study law, but became infatuated with the songs of the former slaves after hearing them on campus. He dropped out of school to join a minstrel troupe, over the objections of his family, and eventually became famous as a minstrel singer, composer, and performer in the United States and abroad. Quite popular in Europe, where he traveled with the *Haverly Minstrels,* Bland remained abroad by himself in part because he could perform without blackface. This he did for almost ten years until his popularity began to wane with the advent of vaudeville, and he returned to the United States. Of the more than seven hundred songs composed by Bland, the most familiar tunes included "In the Evening by the Moonlight," "There's a Long, Long Trail a-Winding," and "Carry Me Back to Old Virginny," which became the Virginia state song in 1940.

709 • Sissieretta Jones (1868–1933)

Known as the Black Patti, Sissieretta Jones was arguably the most celebrated African American vocalist of the nineteenth and early twentieth centuries. Born into a musical family, she loved to perform from the time she was a toddler. She was a regular entertainer at the White House (she sang for four presidents), performed at several U.S. world expositions, worked with Antonín Dvořák and Harry Burleigh, and toured the West Indies in her early career. Now established, Jones's later career was buoyed by her work with *Black Patti's Troubadoures.* Organized by Jones's managers, the group was created as a vehicle and a platform for her operatic performances. The Troubadoures disbanded and Jones left the stage in 1916.

The first Fisk Jubilee Singers. National Archives

710 • Fisk Jubilee Singers

The Fisk Jubilee Singers emerged in 1871 when George L. White, the European American music teacher at Fisk School in Nashville, Tennessee, decided to present his singing students in a series of fund-raising concerts. Initially White, a fan of Negro music, had the group of five men and four women sing classical music and popular ballads, but these songs received only a lukewarm reception. Gradually White added plantation songs and spirituals to the repertoire, and the white audiences became enthusiastic. By the end of their first tour in 1871, the Singers were able to raise $20,000 after singing in several northern cities and performing before President Ulysses S. Grant. The Fisk Jubilee Singers became world-famous when they sang at the World Peace Jubilee concert in Boston in 1872 and were able to sing "The Bat-tle Hymn of the Republic" flawlessly even though the band had started the song much too high for most of the assembled singers. By the end of their tour in 1878, which had taken them to Europe, the Singers had raised $150,000.

711 • The Blues

Although the exact origin of the blues is a mystery, this type of music appears to have emerged in the Mississippi Delta after the Civil War when African American musicians could travel around the South for the first time and create a repertoire of songs by singing in several towns and cities. Unlike the pre–Civil War spirituals, the blues were sung by solo musicians, and unlike prewar popular Black musicians, the blues singers preferred the guitar to the banjo and fiddle. It was the music of African Americans who had been freed from slavery only to experience perpetual poverty by sharecropping. Actually the blues were more closely related to the work songs of the early nineteenth century, which have been traced back to the work songs heard in West Africa from the seventeenth century forward. Although the blues songs are commonly about such themes as betrayal in love, they are also a poignant commentary on the sadness of African Americans in the post–Civil War period.

712 • Black Musical Comedy

After 1875, minstrelsy declined as a medium for serious African American musical expression, but a new medium emerged in 1891 that revitalized Black theatrical performance. The shift began with *The Creole Show*, which opened in 1891 with Sam Lucas, Fred Piper, Billy Jackson, and Irving Jones, all minstrels, who created something new when they added a chorus of beautiful dancing African American women to the show. With its fancy costumes and new songs, *The Creole Show* was the first modern musical comedy because it emphasized Black music and dancing talent over the buffoonery and caricature of minstrelsy. In 1895 another show, *The Octoroons,* appeared with the same blend of talent and repertoire, and was followed in 1896 by *Oriental America* and later *Black Patti's Troubadoures,* starring the serious concert singer Sissieretta Jones. A new period of the Black musical comedy had emerged, which lured audiences with the promise of comedy but won over their hearts with the music.

713 • Ragtime

The first "rags" appeared in the 1890s in the "coon songs," those humiliating ditties about chicken, watermelon, and razor-wielding Blacks that defined the worst of the minstrel era. But once the "ragging," a speeded-up, jerky, syncopated rhythm, was extracted and fused with

new lyrics, such as in "Clorindy, the Origin of the Cake Walk" (1898), by Will Marion Cook and Paul Laurence Dunbar, ragtime emerged as a distinctive form. Ragtime became popular as a piano style after Ben Harvey transcribed it for piano in his 1897 "Ragtime Instructor" and Scott Joplin created his series of rag compositions like "Maple Leaf Rag" (1898) and "Palm Leaf Rag" (1903). Ragtime attained perhaps its greatest musical expression in the May 1912 Carnegie Hall concert of the Clef Club Orchestra of 125 African American musicians.

Religion

714 • John Jasper's "Visible" Black Church

When the Civil War emancipated millions of slaves, it also freed African Americans from having to worship in white congregations or in secret, and many slave preachers established their own independent congregations. One of the most colorful was John Jasper, an ex-slave, who started a church in a stable but built Sixth Mount Zion Baptist Church into a nationally known congregation. It was famous because of his impassioned, emotional sermons, especially his 1878 sermon "The Sun Do Move," a defense of the Bible against the scientific view that the earth moved around the sun. Although most who heard the sermon were skeptical of Jasper's astronomical views, many, Black and white, liked his preaching style and it made him a popular religious figure until the end of the century.

715 • Benjamin Tucker Tanner (1835–1923)

More respected than John Jasper by fellow African American ministers of the postwar period was Benjamin Tanner, initially a preacher and later a bishop of the African Methodist Episcopal Church. Born in Pittsburgh into a privileged African American family, Tanner had been educated at the historically white Avery College and trained in the ministry in the Western Theological Seminary. Ordained as a minister in the AME Church at the beginning of the Civil War, Tanner went to Washington, D.C., after the war, where he took over the First Colored Presbyterian Church of Washington. He took the lead in bringing religious training and education to freedmen who flocked to Washington from the former slave states of the upper South. During his missionary work, he organized several African American congregations, ministered at Baltimore's Bethel Church, and became the editor of the intellectually oriented AME journal, the *Christian Recorder.*

716 • Militant Black Missionaries

Even Black preachers in northern white congregations went South to minister to the needs of the freedmen, and some of them became involved in the political struggle to advance African American rights. One of the most courageous was the Reverend Jonathan Gibbs (1827–74), a Presbyterian minister from Philadelphia, who traveled to South Carolina in 1865 and assumed leadership of Zion Presbyterian Church and built a

school for the freedmen in Charleston. Moving on to Florida, he expanded his efforts as a missionary and was chosen by his peers to serve as state superintendent of public instruction. But in 1874, while running for the United States Congress, he was found dead. Many suspected that he had been murdered by the Ku Klux Klan, which had threatened him several times.

717 • Women's Day

As the pivotal leader in the National Baptist Convention, Nannie Helen Burroughs sought a way to institutionalize recognition of the contribution of Black women in African American religious circles and found a novel device in Women's Day. At the 1906 meeting of the National Baptist Convention, she proposed a special Sunday be designated as national Women's Day, when women would lead and speak in the

Nannie Helen Burroughs. 1909. Prints and Photographs Division, Library of Congress

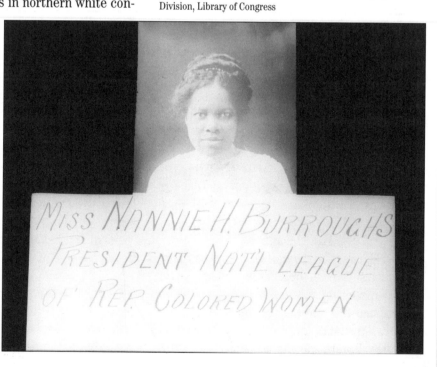

worship service of Baptist churches around the nation. Women's Day was a way for women's voices to be heard at least one day of the year in even the most sexist church. Over the years, Women's Day grew into a series of events, such as a meal served to the women by men of the church, that provided recognition for the essential role played in the Black church by women.

THE NEW NEGRO, 1916–39

Movements

718 • Harlem Renaissance

The Harlem Renaissance emerged after World War I when black writers and artists created poetry, plays, music, painting, sculpture, and cultural criticism that celebrated African American life and captured national attention. Originally called the New Negro Movement, the Harlem Renaissance reflected a sense of racial pride and self-confidence that flourished in Black urban communities of the North as hundreds of thousands of poor Blacks migrated out of the South and into the urban North during World War I. The travail and struggle of such migrants to create lives for themselves in New York City, Chicago, and Washington, D.C., supplied the poems and stories written by Langston Hughes, Claude McKay, and Rudolph Fisher during the period. The Harlem Renaissance benefited from the interest of white American writers in the Black experience, the rise of jazz as America's popular musical form, and the domination of American popular theater by Black musical comedies. Toward the end of the 1920s, another

flowering of creativity occurred in the visual arts when Aaron Douglas, Richmond Barthe, Archibald Motley, William H. Johnson, and Lois Mailou Jones created African American art based on African forms. The Harlem Renaissance plummeted after the stock market crash of 1929, but such African American artists as Zora Neale Hurston, Paul Robeson, and Jacob Lawrence continued to produce powerful works of art that influenced later generations.

Some Important Books

719 • *Bronze* (1922)

Georgia Douglas Johnson's book of racial poetry announced the Black woman's modern voice in poetry. Johnson was the foremother of twentieth-century Black modernism, with close personal relationships with Alain Locke and Jean Toomer. That role comes through clearly in *Bronze,* her collection of racial poetry, in which she constructs, in opposition to the "mammy" stereotype rampant in the early twentieth century, a new, powerful image of the Black mother whose courage and devotion "sandals the feet" of her offspring, balming them against the pain of life in a racist America. At the same time, her poems signal a call for independent womanhood, released from the doldrums of being someone else's caretaker. Carefully crafted and lovingly expressed, Johnson's poems outline paths taken and extended by such later poets as Gwendolyn Brooks.

720 • *Cane* (1923)

Cane, Jean Toomer's modernist homage to African American life and culture, was the Harlem Renaissance's first work of genius and one of the most innovative works of American fiction. Authored by the grandson of P. B. S.

A Poetess (Georgia Douglas Johnson) by Winold Reiss. Copyright Reiss Estate. Collection of J.P. Speed Art Museum, Louisville, Kentucky

Pinchback, the Louisiana Reconstruction lieutenant governor, *Cane* is Toomer's attempt to capture the rhythm and mood of African American life by weaving together short fiction, imagistic poetry, and theatrical dialogue. Divided into three parts, *Cane* begins with a series of impressionistic sketches of southern Black women that Toomer began writing on his return from a summer spent in 1921 as the temporary head of an industrial school in Sparta, Georgia. The second section uses mainly poetry to portray Black life in the North, most powerfully the street life of 7th and T Streets in Washington, D.C., where recent southern migrants congregated, sang songs, and told their life stories. A third section, also cited in the South, narrates the frustrations of an educated African American with religious and educational efforts in the South. Toomer sought to stretch literary form and rebel against the accepted homilies of

African American racial politics in *Cane,* which succeeds best in creating a haunting mood of languid rural life and folk culture in the Black South.

721 • *The New Negro* (1925)

Alain Locke's compendium of poetry, prose, critical and social essays, artwork, and historical commentary is the bible of the New Negro Movement. Announcing a "New Negro," who is culturally self-conscious, racially proud, politically militant, yet socially open to interracial contact, Locke created one of the first mixed-media anthologies in American literary history. With pastel portraits of famous and working-class African Americans, with poems by Countee Cullen, Claude McKay, Langston Hughes, and Jean Toomer, with short fiction by Rudolph Fisher, Zora Neale Hurston, and others, Locke created an open space for the many lights of the

Alain LeRoy Locke, 1925, by Winold Reiss. Courtesy of Reiss Estate

"renaissance" to shine brightly. Moreover, by bringing in such political figures as W. E. B. Du Bois, James Weldon Johnson, and Robert Moton, Locke sought to pose the artistic revival of the twenties as a synthesis of older discourses about how African Americans could win acceptance in American culture.

722 • *The Weary Blues* (1926)

Langston Hughes's (1902–67) first book of poetry may have been his best. It was certainly the best single book of poetry published in the 1920s that captured so powerfully the spirit of the Harlem Renaissance. With poems written on the blues form and in free verse, *The Weary Blues* broke with the traditional English verse forms that dominated the work of Hughes's rivals, Claude McKay and Countee Cullen. By transliterating the speech and music of the urban poor into free-verse poetry, Hughes fulfilled the Harlem Renaissance dictum that the artist should become the voice of his people.

723 • *Home to Harlem* (1928)

Claude McKay (1889–1948), a Jamaican immigrant to the United States, whose book of poetry *Harlem Shadows* (1922) was one of the first books of poems published by one of the new Harlem Renaissance poets, turned to the novel form in the later twenties and produced perhaps the best single novel of the Black twenties. *Home to Harlem* served McKay better than his poetry as a vehicle to portray the color, class, and moral conflicts of the Harlem Renaissance period. Perhaps more than any other novel of the period, *Home to Harlem* captured the urbanism of the Black twenties. It also finds Jake, the urban proletarian, and Ray, the young Black intellectual, to be the perfect pair to carry on a dialogue about the question of Black identity in a modern, urban, American world.

The novel also excelled at weaving discussion of the identity conflicts of African Americans into a complicated yet exciting plot of Black conflict in Harlem during the 1920s.

724 • *The Walls of Jericho* (1928)

Rudolph Fisher's first novel was written on a bet that no one could blend the lives of working- and middle-class Harlemites of the 1920s into one excellent short novel. Fisher did it and thereby portrayed the conflicts of class and skin color better than any other Harlem Renaissance writer. Written from the perspective of working-class men at Padmore's pool hall, Fisher's novel pokes satirically at all of the major characters of the Harlem Renaissance, from race- but not class-conscious striving Black professionals to well-meaning but misguided white philanthropic patrons. Even the working-class pair of Bubber and Jinx do not escape a critique in narrative of the color and class foibles that form their "walls of Jericho." What this novel provides is an excellent portrait of the color and class tensions that divided and sustained Harlem in the twenties.

725 • *Passing* (1929)

Nella Larsen's second novel remains one of the most haunting, suggestive, and contemporary novels written during the Harlem Renaissance. The story is more than just another rehash of the trauma of light-skinned African Americans who can masquerade as white. The story reveals the chance encounter between Irene Redfield and an old neighborhood friend, Clare Kendry. Clare is married to a white man from whom she has hidden her Black ancestry, and in the hands of Larsen, this secret is shaped into a subtle commentary on the "perfect" marriage of an upper-class Black woman of the 1920s. Clare comes to symbolize much that is missing from Irene's bourgeois lifestyle and suggests that the Black bourgeoisie are more fascinated with those who live the double life than this class usually admits. Clare's social and possibly sexual attractiveness for Irene comes from the former's daring energy and boldness of feeling, both of which Irene discovers she needs to survive as a creative woman. More than any other Black writer of the 1920s, Larsen is willing to probe the psychological territory of difference to convey the sense of unexpressed yearning of early-twentieth-century Black middle-class life. As such, *Passing* is a subtle, provocative critique of the Black Victorian propriety in the 1920s.

726 • *Southern Road* (1932)

In his review of *Southern Road,* Alain Locke lauded Sterling Brown for being able to "compose with the freshness and naturalness of folk balladry" and thereby convince skeptics that a Negro poet can achieve an authentic folk-touch. *Southern Road* deserved such praise. For in such poems as "Maumee Ruth," "Sam Smiley," and "Strong Men," Brown captured the poetry and the militancy of the African American blues. Leaving behind the somewhat vague political voice of Hughes's *Weary Blues, Southern Road* possesses the toughness of the 1930s southern folk identity face-to-face with the Great Depression. Perhaps most remarkable, *Southern Road* avoids a note of despair. For in such poems as "Strong Men," Brown constructed a strong male voice that could declare, "The strong men keep a-comin' on, The strong men git stronger."

727 • *Their Eyes Were Watching God* (1937)

Zora Neale Hurston's *Their Eyes Were Watching God* is the first feminist novel of the twentieth century. Situated in Hurston's fictional Eastonville, a kind of idealized world in other Hurston short stories and novels, *Their Eyes Were Watching God* showed that the world of all-Black southern towns was hardly an idyllic one for African American women. Readers follow Hurston's protagonist, Janie, through a series of learning experiences that begin with adopting and then rebelling against the advice given her by her mother. Moving through two marriages, Janie learns to assert her identity in the face of husbands and townspeople who utilize men as "mules." Eventually Janie seizes her right to define her own identity outside of the strictures imposed by such communities. Remarkably Hurston tells her liberation story without portraying these communities as pathological.

Art

728 • Winold Reiss (1886–1953)

In 1924 Paul Kellogg, editor of the *Survey Graphic,* teamed Winold Reiss, the German portraitist and graphic artist, with Alain Locke to illustrate the special Harlem issue of the *Survey Graphic* that appeared March 1, 1925. That issue contained sympathetic pastel studies of Harlem's working class and flattering portraits of Harlem Renaissance Black artists and intellectuals from an artist better known in America for his Indian portraits and commercial design. The latter helped, however, too, for Reiss also produced sharply etched abstract imaginatives of life in Harlem that became the signature design style of the Black twenties. His pastel portraits were exhibited at the 125th Street Harlem Branch of the New York Public Library, and color reproductions enhanced Locke's *The New Negro* (1925). During the late twenties, Reiss

Cover of March 1, 1925, issue of *Survey Graphic*, designed by Winold Reiss, featuring portrait of Roland Hayes.

New York from Kansas in the early twenties, Douglas studied with Winold Reiss, whose cover and illustrations for the *Survey Graphic* had inspired Douglas. Encouraged by Reiss to study African sculpture and motifs, Douglas developed a unique African American interpretive design style that captured the rhythm and energy of African American dances, postures, and consciousness in the twenties. Douglas developed his own signature style that avoided stereotypical images and portrayed a positive and proud African American subject and culture. During the 1920s, Douglas's illustrations graced the covers of many books, journals, and magazines. One of Douglas's best was his cover for *Fire!!*, the aesthetically radical Black journal of the 1920s that produced only one scandalous issue. Douglas's flat, geometric designs were often centered by a monumental, Africanized head and embellished with smaller stylized Africanist motifs. During the 1930s Douglas produced more paintings and murals, especially the marvelous New York Public Library mural of African American history at the 125th Street Harlem Branch (1934).

produced sensitive portraits of African Americans from the Sea Islands in South Carolina and continued to explore the African American subject in the 1930s. Before his death, Reiss donated most of those Harlem Renaissance and South Carolina portraits to Fisk University, while several others are at the Smithsonian's National Portrait Gallery.

729 • Aaron Douglas (1899–1979)

Aaron Douglas rose to prominence in the 1920s because of his willingness and ability to produce Africanist illustrations and designs that satisfied the Harlem Renaissance's need for racially representative images. Migrating to

730 • Richmond Barthe (1901–89)

Richmond Barthe was first a painter who studied at the Chicago Art Institute, but became a sculptor when encouraged to produce some sculptures for the Negro Art Week organized in Chicago in 1927. Like Douglas, Barthe became known for his willingness to produce African American sculpture that utilized African principles of design, particularly the elongation of body forms, to portray African American people. Moreover, in such sculptures as *Blackberry Woman* (1932) and *African Dancer* (1933), which were purchased by the Whitney Museum in 1935, Barthe excelled at capturing motion in clay.

African Dancer, 1933. Photograph by Catharine Kneeland at a one-man show of Richmond Barthe at the Arden Gallery, March 1939. Courtesy of National Archives, the Harmon Foundation Collection

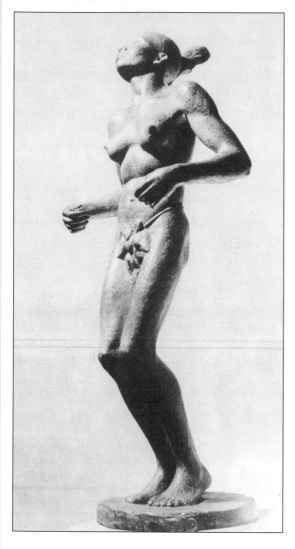

731 • James Van Der Zee (1886–1983)

James Van Der Zee was the most important documentary photographer of the Harlem Renaissance, the man whose photographs have become records of the look, feel, and self-consciousness of Harlem residents between the wars. Migrating to Harlem in 1906, Van Der Zee was at first a pianist, but in 1917 opened a portrait studio on 135th Street in New York City, where he earned a good living by crafting sensitive, often retouched photographs of Black residents, returning servicemen, and white visitors to Harlem. Approaching photography as an art, Van Der Zee used atmospheric effects, soft-focus techniques, and elaborate backdrops to capture the dignity of his subjects, whether they were part of the working class or the educational and financial elite.

732 • Archibald Motley (1891–1980)

Archibald Motley was one of the most versatile artists of the 1920s and 1930s, a man who began with exquisitely detailed portraits of African Americans and then broke into a modernist style of portraying Black urban life that one art historian has called the "blues aesthetic." Born in New Orleans into the Catholic elite of that city, Motley nevertheless acknowledged a Pygmy ancestry and a commitment to documenting African American life. During study at the Art Institute of Chicago, Motley began the type of work that early distinguished his career, portraiture of what might be called the "Old Negro." With his sensitive treatment of an elderly Black woman, *Mending Socks* (1923), Motley evoked an era of the southern servant and grandmother who achieved enduring dignity by helping others. But during the late 1920s Motley's style underwent a dramatic transformation, leaving behind realistic portraiture for modernistic, almost caricaturist, studies of working-class urban African Americans dancing in rent parties; howling in church; and crawling the street in *Chicken Shack* (1936). What these latter pictures conveyed was the energy of African American communities in rich syncopation and color.

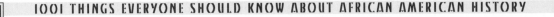

Chicken Shack, 1936. National Archives, the Harmon Foundation Collection. Courtesy of Archie Motley

733 • William H. Johnson (1901–70)

Born in Florence, South Carolina, William H. Johnson was one of the most prolific artists of the twentieth century, and a man whose work went through several styles of expression in his lifetime. Migrating North, he enrolled in the National Academy of Design in New York City, spent summers at the Cape Cod School of Art in Provincetown, Massachusetts, and won several prizes for his work before going to Paris in 1926. There he was influenced by the work of Cézanne and Chaim Soutine, and produced contorted, colorful landscapes that were examples of his expressionist cubism. Returning to the South, he used this technique to produce several studies of southern architecture as well as its people. But it was only after his return to Denmark, his marriage to Holcha Krake, and his subsequent return to the United States in 1938 that Johnson began to paint in his most successful style—that of his silkscreens from the 1930s and 1940s. As in *Going to Church,* Johnson excelled at creating humorous, graphically complex pictures that seemingly reduced his subjects to the bare essentials of design and form.

734 • Horace Pippin (1888–1946)

Horace Pippin was a self-taught African

American artist who stopped painting for years after an injury during service in World War I cost him the use of his right arm. Learning to draw in 1929 by using a hot poker on wood, Pippin developed a technique that communicated his deep emotional response to subject matter. He became well known when one of his paintings was discovered in a shoe repair window in Pennsylvania in 1937 by art critic Christian Brinton. His work was supported by such influential figures as the art dealer Robert Carlen and the flamboyant art collector Albert Barnes. Pippin's painting ranged from arresting winter landscape scenes to such historical narratives as *John Brown Going to His Hanging* (1942) and genre studies as *Domino Players* (1943). Pippin excelled at rendering scenes of life with a combination of warmth and social irony.

735 • Sargent Johnson (1887–1967)

One of the most versatile artists to emerge from the New Negro Movement was Sargent Johnson, who became one of the most provocative sculptors of the 1920s and 1930s. Born in Boston, Johnson was an orphan who moved among several foster homes and cities before taking up residence in San Francisco in 1915, where he studied at the A. W. Best School of Art and the California School of Fine Arts. Through the Harmon Foundation exhibitions, he gained national attention when his bust *Sammy* won a medal in the 1928 exhibition. Self-consciously committed to producing "Negro Art," Johnson adeptly mined the mask traditions of West Africa as inspiration for some of his best sculptures, such as his terra-cotta *Girl's Head* (1929) and *Copper Mask* (1935). His masterpiece *Forever Free* (1933), with its evocation of both African sculpture and African American folk traditions, has become almost iconic in African American art history. But Johnson was not lim-

Sargent Johnson's *Forever Free*, 1933. 36″ × 11½″ × 9″ × ½″. Courtesy of San Francisco Museum of Art. Gift of Mrs. E. D. Lederman. Photo by Marjorie Griffiths. National Archives

ited to small-scale sculpture. During the thirties he worked for the Federal Arts Project and created several monumental and stone relief sculptures. Johnson also created numerous sensitive lithographs, of which *Lenox Avenue* (1938), with its fusion of African American figural and musical elements, is especially beautiful.

736 • Augusta Savage (1900–62)

Despite Augusta Savage's lack of support from her father to become an artist, she persevered to become a well-known portrait sculptor of the 1920s in Harlem, New York. Moreover, Savage was not only a productive sculptor but also an arts administrator who coordinated the Harlem Community Art Center in the 1930s. She was responsible, for example, for promoting the careers of younger artists, most notably Jacob Lawrence, whom she befriended when he was an adolescent. Among her most famous artistic works is *Gamin* (ca. 1930). This piece was modeled in clay, cast in plaster, and then painted. This gamin, or anonymous boy on the street, is a portrait of an individual yet represents the temperament and savvy style of numerous young people during the Harlem Renaissance era. The boy appears to be tough yet compassionate, to have a jaunty sense of self, and to possess the requisite determination to make it.

737 • Lois Mailou Jones (b. 1905)

As an artist who has traversed several historical periods in African American art, Lois Mailou Jones was discovered during the late 1930s by James Herring, James Porter, and Alain Locke as a promising, engaging artist. Born in Boston, Jones attended the Boston Museum School of Fine Arts, New York's Teachers College, and the Académie Julien in Paris. Influenced by the French impressionists, her early work consisted of marvelous studies of French urban life distinguished by their color and design. She took up African American subject matter after Alain Locke's suggestion of "doing something of your own people." Jones responded with the sensitive realism of *Jennie* and the cubistic Africanism of *Les Fétiches* (1938). During several years in Haiti, Jones developed a palette and a technique that combined the aesthetics of Haitian, African, and French cultures, captured in such paintings as *Marche Haiti* (1963). Moreover, as an art teacher at Howard University, she not only taught several generations of African American students but reacted to the emergence of racial self-consciousness in the 1960s and 1970s with such invigorating compositions as *Deux Coiffeurs d'Afrique* (1982).

Music and Dance

738 • *Shuffle Along* (1921)

Shuffle Along was the first musical revue written, produced, and performed by African Americans. It opened in New York to rave reviews. With music by Eubie Blake and lyrics by Noble Sissle, the revue sported a number of hits, including "I'm Just Wild About Harry" and "Love Will Find a Way," and launched the careers of Josephine Baker and Florence Mills. *Shuffle Along* was such a sensation because it showcased African American dance, music, and acting on Broadway that was not imitative of white American musicals. Eubie Blake and Noble Sissle followed up *Shuffle Along* with another Broadway hit in 1923, *Runnin' Wild,* which launched the signature dance of the twenties—the Charleston.

739 • William Christopher Handy (1873–1958)

W. C. Handy, as he was generally known, was a cornet player, a minstrel musician, and a bandleader, but is best known as the composer who first wrote down the blues. Actually, Handy grew up in Alabama hearing spirituals, cakewalks, and minstrel music, and when he began playing the cornet, he performed in what were called novelty music bands, such as the Hampton Cornet Band. He also learned to sing the spirituals and sang with the Mahara's Minstrels. While working as a director of a Black band in Tutwiler, Mississippi, in 1903, Handy first heard the blues, and later came up with the idea of composing and arranging them. In 1912 he published the first blues composition, *The Memphis Blues,* although some interpreters have suggested it was more of a cakewalk than a blues. He quickly followed with *St. Louis Blues* (1914),

Joe Turner's Blues (1915), and *Beale Street Blues* (1917). His autobiography, *Father of the Blues* (1941), made him famous, although it fueled the resentment of some, such as Jelly Roll Morton, who believed that Handy claimed too much in his title.

740 • Jelly Roll Morton (1890–1941)

Jelly Roll Morton became widely known in 1938 when he heard a *Ripley's Believe It or Not!* claim that W. C. Handy was the father of jazz and wrote back that New Orleans was the "cradle of jazz and I, myself, happened to be the creator in 1902." Although many disputed Morton's claim to have originated jazz, he is generally acknowledged as the first complete jazz pianist and the first full-fledged composer of New Orleans–style jazz. Born into the self-consciously superior Creole class that had absorbed French and Spanish musical traditions, Morton got his musical education in the red-light district of New Orleans called Storyville, where he worked as a "house pianist" and won recognition as a "piano professor" by age seventeen. Migrating to Chicago in the early 1920s, he worked briefly for a music company but gained a greater recognition as an intimidating pianist who would elbow lesser players off the piano stool at clubs to teach them and the audience a few piano "lessons." Borrowing from ragtime, the blues, and New Orleans band style, Morton perfected a two-handed piano style that in his own words "imitated a band." With multiple themes, breaks, counterrhythms, and even Latin American accents, Morton's piano playing was incredibly rich. Unfortunately, by the time Morton recorded his music with the Red Hot Peppers in 1926, the New Orleans piano style was falling out of favor. But that did not deter him: Jelly Roll apparently brought a pistol to recording sessions to ensure that his younger sidemen did

not stray too far from the New Orleans jazz line. After his reminiscences, *Mister Jelly Roll*, were published in 1950, Morton's music enjoyed a brief revival, and more recently, has been given fresh reinterpretation by Marcus Roberts. His piano work remains one of the foundations of twentieth-century jazz piano.

741 • King Oliver's Creole Jazz Band

The reputed king of cornet playing in New Orleans in the 1910s, King Oliver (1885–1938) was the first African American to introduce New Orleans jazz to a northern audience. After leaving New Orleans for Chicago in 1918, Oliver formed a band that established itself at the South Side's Lincoln Gardens. The band became a major jazz-performing operation when Louis Armstrong joined the band in 1922. In a series of recordings from April to December 1923, the high-water mark of early Chicago jazz playing was set.

742 • James P. Johnson (1894–1955)

The legendary pianist James P. Johnson was the originator of the Harlem Stride piano playing style that marked the transition from ragtime to jazz. Growing up in the so-called San Juan Hill area of New York City early in the twentieth century, Johnson listened to European music played by middle-class New York African Americans, to ring shouts and gutbucket music favored by Gullah migrants from South Carolina, who danced the original Charleston in the alleyways, and to quadrilles played by New Orleans visitors, and he developed a piano playing style that could appeal to all of these audiences. He became famous while playing piano for the Jungles Casino, a dance hall masquerading as a school. James P., as he was known, created a tradition of piano playing that was continued by Duke Ellington, Fats

Waller, Count Basie, Thelonius Monk, and Herbie Hancock.

743 • Fletcher Henderson (1897–1952)

Fletcher Henderson organized the premier dance band of the 1920s. Initially a studio piano musician, Henderson had numerous publishing and recording connections by the early 1920s, when he put together a pickup band and molded it into a complete orchestra. Dropping the banjos and violins that earlier orchestras such as James Europe's had contained, Henderson streamlined the jazz orchestra and developed the practice of featuring a soloist, such as the legendary Coleman Hawkins, on saxophone. With Don Redman as his arranger, the Fletcher Henderson Orchestra held forth at the Roseland, a whites-only dance establishment, and was the first New York jazz band to play arrangements. But the band really came into its own after September 29, 1924, when Henderson lured Louis Armstrong away from King Oliver and Chicago to come to New York and play with the Henderson Orchestra. Armstrong taught the orchestra to swing, and by the time of Armstrong's departure several months later, the Fletcher Henderson Orchestra had become the most popular dance band in New York.

744 • Louis Armstrong (1898–1971)

Louis Armstrong was the single most important musical innovator of the 1920s. When King Oliver invited Armstrong to join his band in Chicago in 1923, Oliver knew that Armstrong had already eclipsed the "king's" position in New Orleans cornet playing. And although the sidemen in Fletcher Henderson's band laughed at Louis Armstrong's country-bumpkin manners and his simple, ready grin, they listened with awe once he began to play the cornet. Armstrong came out of the same New Orleans tradi-

Louis Armstrong. Prints and Photographs Division, Library of Congress. Used by permission of the Louis Armstrong Educational Foundation

tion of cornet playing that had produced King Oliver, but Armstrong was superior to others of his time in his ability as an improvising soloist. Louis played predictable passages of music with such inventive phrasing, such imagination, such rhythm, and such remarkable accuracy and speed that he pushed bands not only to keep up but also to change their approach to the music. Some of his greatness was lost to later audiences and listeners who were only familiar with him from recordings and broadcasts from the 1940s and 1950s, when his performances were less demanding musically and his contribution clouded by his sometimes obsequious demeanor on stage. But during the 1920s, particularly in the legendary Hot Fives recordings, Armstrong recorded some of the outstanding small combo music in the history of jazz.

745 • Bessie Smith (1894–1937)

The only musical equal of Louis Armstrong in the 1920s was Bessie Smith, the premier blues and jazz singer of the decade, who changed the way that jazz was played with her singing. Although legend has it that Bessie Smith was discovered and taught the blues by Ma Rainey and her husband, the truth is that no one was responsible for the remarkable musical intelligence that Bessie Smith brought to the singing of songs. As a teenager singing in the theater circuit of the 1910s, Bessie Smith first became popular as a stage performer in a vaudeville-like theater world in which Black women performers were required to dance, act, and play the fool before Black and white audiences. But Bessie Smith really came into her own in 1923, when, following Mamie Smith's recording of "Crazy Blues," the first blues record, in August 1920, Bessie began recording songs for the Okeh record company. Her version of "Down-hearted Blues" sold 780,000 copies and propelled her into stardom. When she recorded "St. Louis Blues," W. C. Handy's composition and Ethel Waters's signature piece, with Louis Armstrong in January 1925, Bessie Smith slowed down the tempo, simplified the phrasing, and introduced such depth of feeling that she made hers the definitive version of the song. Bessie Smith's quick rise to popularity was followed by a quick decline in the early 1930s, when her records no longer sold as well. A hard-drinking and verbally abusive woman, Bessie Smith communicated the "hurt" she carried inside in her singing of songs and her acting performance in the film *St. Louis Blues* (1929). Bessie Smith died tragically in 1937 as a result of an automobile accident in Clarksdale, Mississippi, but

Bessie Smith. Photograph by Carl Van Vechten, February 3, 1936. Prints and Photographs Division, Library of Congress. Gift of Carl Van Vechten

contrary to what Edward Albee's play *The Death of Bessie Smith* (1960) reported, it was not a racially motivated tragedy. She did not die because she was refused treatment at a southern hospital. Rather, she was treated for shock by a physician at the scene of the accident and transported to an African American hospital where she died.

746 • Duke Ellington (1899–1974)

Edward Kennedy Ellington was a pianist and composer who emerged in the late 1920s and 1930s to become America's most accomplished jazz bandleader during the so-called swing era. Born into the Black middle class of Washington, D.C., Ellington attended excellent public schools, but left high school in 1917 to devote himself fully to playing music, often solo but increasingly in small combos around town. Early in 1923 he left for New York, where as a pianist he absorbed everything he could from ragtime, Harlem Stride piano, and New Orleans jazz band music, and transmuted it into a remarkably subtle, orchestral piano playing style. Performing initially with a five-piece band known as the Washingtonians, Ellington began writing songs for the group and began recording in 1924. He also expanded the size of the band to ten pieces and moved it to the famous Cotton Club in 1927. By then, it was clear that Ellington was an innovator in his approach to the jazz orchestra. Rather than using the band to feature his piano playing or imposing strict control over the sidemen's playing, Ellington approached the entire orchestra as an instrument, allowed each sideman to develop his own voice, and then used his piano to tie together the overall performance. Ellington was also gaining a reputation for his personal style and sophistication—hence, the title "Duke"—and that was increasingly represented in what could be called his own "sophisticated style" of jazz, which would later be called swing. Having begun recording in 1924, Ellington produced numerous popular songs over the years, including "Mood Indigo," "Down Beat," "Sentimental Lady," and "Harlem Air Shaft." Ellington kept his band alive in the Depression years by touring the South and the North and adding complexity to his compositions. In the 1940s he teamed up with arranger and songwriter Billy Strayhorn to produce a string of hits, including "Take the A Train," "Just a-Settin' and a-Rockin'," and "I Got It Bad and That Ain't Good." After World War II, Ellington was one of the few swing-era musicians and composers who continued to hold the respect of the younger "bebop" generation of jazz musicians and to record with them.

747 • Count Basie (1904–84)

The real master of swing in American jazz during the 1930s was William "Count" Basie, a pianist, but more importantly a jazz bandleader who remained popular with dancers throughout his long career. Born in Red Bank, New Jersey, Basie began playing piano as a teenager, being early influenced by "Fats" Waller. After a stint with the Benny Moten Orchestra in Kansas City in 1926, Basie started his own band and toured the United States from the 1930s on. Known for his distinctive, up-tempo style, Basie not only performed standards but composed such originals as "One O'Clock Jump." Despite the decline of many big bands in the 1940s with the advent of bebop, Basie's brand of swing remained popular. In 1957, he became the first American bandleader to perform before the Queen of England. In the 1970s, he enjoyed a revival of interest in his music by a young generation returning to dancing because of disco music.

748 • William Grant Still (1895–1978)

William Grant Still was the first African American to have a symphony performed by a white American orchestra, the Rochester Philharmonic, conducted by Howard Hanson, in 1931. The son of a bandleader, Grant Still was a medical student at Wilberforce College when he decided to take up music seriously. He studied classical music at Oberlin College; but he played oboe in the orchestra for the musical revue *Shuffle Along.* Further study in composition with such teachers as George Chadwick and Edgard Varèse strengthened his knowledge of musical form. His Symphony no. 1, or the *Afro-American* Symphony, as it is commonly known, was a synthesis of what Still had learned of traditional

Portrait of Lillian Evanti by Lois Mailou Jones, 1940.
Courtesy of National Portrait Gallery, Smithsonian Institution

European symphonic form and what his ear heard in the Black community of the 1920s. Though the dominant tune is not a folk song, Still's melody is nevertheless an improvisation on the blues, especially as they were played by jazz bands in New York. The four movements of the symphony—Longings, Sorrows, Humor, and Aspirations—could be metaphors of the African American outlook on life in the mid-twentieth century. Although known mainly for his *Afro-American* Symphony, Still composed a number of other pieces—*Africa* (1928), *Swanee River* (1939), and a ballet score, *Lenox Avenue* (1936). He received many awards during his career, including the Guggenheim Fellowship in 1934.

749 • Lillian Evanti (1891–1967)

Lillian Evanti was the first African American to sing opera with a major opera company. A coloratura soprano, Evanti (born Lillian Evans) grew up in Washington, D.C., the daughter of the founder of the Armstrong Technical High School. After earning a bachelor of music from Howard University in 1917, she studied voice with Frank La Forge in New York and Madame Ritter-Ciampi in Paris, before singing with the Paris Opéra in 1925. Her debut with the Paris Opéra in Nice in the opera *Lakmé* was acclaimed by those who heard her. She also gained rave reviews for singing in *The Barber of Seville* in Milan in 1930. Perhaps her greatest performance in America came on February 9, 1934, when she sang for President and Mrs. Roosevelt at the White House.

750 • Josephine Baker (1906–75)

Josephine Baker became an internationally famous dancer, singer, and nightclub performer in the 1920s. Fleeing East St. Louis after the pogromlike attack of whites on the Black neighborhoods in 1917, Baker went to Philadelphia, where she obtained her first break as a dancer in the *Dixie Steppers*. Moving to New York, she took a job as a dresser and then filled in for a sick chorus girl in Noble Sissle and Hubie Blake's *Shuffle Along* (1923). After becoming a star in their *Chocolate Dandies,* she gained an international reputation performing the *Danse Sauvage* in *La Revue Nègre* in Paris in 1925. The next year, she created pandemonium among French audiences with her erotic dancing and singing in a banana skirt in the Folies-Bergère. During the 1930s she transformed her image into a more dignified, if no less spectacular, French music hall performer, beginning with her engagement at Casino de Paris in 1931–32. Baker also made several movies. During the 1940s she was awarded the French Legion of Honor for her work during World War II.

Having adopted numerous orphaned children of various nationalities in the 1950s, she came out of retirement to perform in *Paris, Mes Amours* at the Olympia in Paris in 1959.

751 • Marian Anderson (1902–93)

Born in Philadelphia, Marian Anderson was the most accomplished singer of her generation. Having obtained her early music training in church choirs, she studied voice with Giuseppe Boghetti and appeared before the New York Philharmonic Orchestra in 1925. After winning a Rosenwald Fellowship, she traveled to and sang in Berlin in 1930. During the next five years, she studied and performed in Europe before returning to the United States and giving recitals at New York's Town Hall and Carnegie Hall. But her reputation soared in 1939, when the Daughters of the American Revolution (DAR) refused to allow her to sing at Constitution Hall in Washington, D.C., because she was African American. In the uproar that followed, Mrs. Eleanor Roosevelt resigned from the DAR and arranged for Anderson to sing at the Lincoln Memorial on Easter, an outdoor performance witnessed by over 75,000 people. Despite her reputation as a superb contralto, however, not until 1955 did the Metropolitan Opera Company invite Marian Anderson to sing with the company in Verdi's *Un Ballo in Maschera*. She became the first African American invited to perform with the Metropolitan.

752 • Leadbelly (1885–1949)

Born Huddie Ledbetter, Leadbelly, whose nickname referred to his deep-throated singing voice, was the most moving blues singer and guitar player of the 1940s. Early acknowledged as Louisiana's best guitar player, Leadbelly became more widely known when he accompanied Blind Lemon Jefferson to Texas in the 1910s.

Regarded as a "dangerous Negro," who always carried a pistol, charmed and assaulted women, and attempted several murders, Leadbelly spent much of his young adulthood in jail or on the chain gang. Working and singing as the lead man on chain gangs strengthened the worksong elements in his music and added a poignant realism to his crying laments. He literally sang himself to freedom in 1925 when Texas Governor Pat M. Neff freed him in 1925 after hearing him sing. In 1930 Leadbelly was back on a chain gang, this time in Louisiana, but was freed again in 1934 after being discovered and recorded by Alan Lomax for the Library of Congress. Thereafter, Leadbelly became a celebrity entertainer who performed in New York, Hollywood, and at Harvard University, and who influenced such singers as Pete Seeger, Bob Dylan, and Paul McCartney. His songs "Good Night Irene," "Rock Island Line," and "Midnight Special" are classics.

Some Important Plays and Films

753 • *Within These Gates* (1919)

Within These Gates was the second film produced by Oscar Micheaux, the most prolific Black independent filmmaker of the twentieth century, whose Micheaux Film and Book Company was founded in Chicago in 1918. A film of many plots, *Within These Gates* is, on one level, the love story of Jennie, a Black woman with a hidden, compromised past who finds redemption in raising funds for Piney Woods School for African American children. But *Within These Gates* is also Oscar Micheaux's answer to D. W. Griffith's racist Reconstruction film *Birth of a Nation* (1915), because Micheaux shows how a

Oscar Micheaux. Schomburg Center, New York Public Library, Astor, Lenox and Tilden Foundation

white landowner cheats his Black sharecropper, who in turn is lynched after challenging the landowner's figures. *Within These Gates,* whose only surviving print was recently discovered by Thomas Cripps, also details early-twentieth-century Black Victorian color and class consciousness.

754 • *The Emperor Jones* (1920)

The Emperor Jones, written by white playwright Eugene O'Neill, opened by the Provincetown Players in New York in 1920 and starred the African American actor Charles Gilpin. O'Neill's play details how Brutus Jones, an ex–Pullman car porter and former criminal, becomes an evil emperor of a Caribbean island. Ultimately Brutus suffers a nervous breakdown for brutalizing the island people just as the whites. When O'Neill opened *The Emperor Jones* in London in 1924, he replaced the unreliable Gilpin with Paul Robeson in the title role.

The film version of *The Emperor Jones* appeared in 1937, also starring Paul Robeson. *The Emperor Jones* became the signature play of the Harlem Renaissance for its psychological depiction of an African American. It played less well in Harlem, according to Langston Hughes, who recalled that when Jules Bledsoe ran across the Lafayette Theater stage as if in the jungle, Blacks in the audience yelled, "Man, you come on outa that jungle! This is Harlem!"

755 • *The Chip Woman's Fortune* (1923)

The first Broadway play by an African American was *The Chip Woman's Fortune,* which opened in May 1923. Written by playwright Willis Richardson, *The Chip Woman's Fortune* was produced by Chicago's Ethiopian Art Players. The Players were originally brought to Harlem, but after the community reception was lukewarm, the producers moved the serious play to Broadway, where it was well received.

Religion

756 • Storefront Church

During the Great Migration, which began in World War I and continued into the 1940s, southern Blacks abandoned the South for the greater opportunity of the urban North. While many of these migrants were absorbed into established Baptist and Methodist congregations in the North, some found northern styles of worship to be too formal. As some of the southern ministers left behind followed their flock northward, these clergy founded churches in homes or in storefronts—usually rented commercial properties on busy streets in the major northern cities. Visitors to the city on Sundays could regularly hear organ music, tambourine playing, and emotive singing coming from such store-fronts, where parishioners found not only a more emotional style of worship but also temporary housing, food, and fellowship with other southerners.

757 • Longest-Running Radio Program: *Church of God*

Elder "Lightfoot" Solomon Michaux was persuaded by his wife, Mary, in 1917, to build a church to house "Everybody's Mission," a non-denominational, interracial church, in Newport News, Virginia. Although Michaux became an ordained evangelist and Everybody's Mission became affiliated with the Church of Christ, Michaux broke away from the Holiness mother church in 1921 and organized the independent Church of God. Michaux's Church of God became nationally known in 1929, when he decided to begin a radio broadcast to bring religion to those who did not attend church. With a theme song, "Happy I Am," Michaux combined a call for repentance with a message of the power of positive thinking and thereby ensured that his radio message had something for everyone. The popularity of his program declined after 1937 after a scandal over his reputed mismanagement of funds. Undaunted, Michaux continued to broadcast until his death in 1960, making his the longest-running radio program in American history.

758 • Moorish Science Temple of America

The Moorish Science Temple fused Black nationalist ideology and Islamic faith in the United States and laid the groundwork for the Nation of Islam. Derived from the Canaanite Temple that was founded in Newark, New Jersey, in 1913 by Noble Drew Ali (born Timothy Drew), the Moorish Science Temple of America

emerged after Ali and his followers broke with the original temple and set up the Moorish Holy Temple of Science in Chicago in 1925. Ali taught that African Americans needed a nationality before a religion, that they were not Negroes but "Asiatics" who had lost their identity through the domination of Europeans. Ali encouraged followers to replace slave surnames with Islamic ones, identify themselves as Moors on federal, state, and local forms, and practice economic self-sufficiency. Other temples popped up in Milwaukee, Pittsburgh, and Detroit, but the Chicago temple was the most active: followers sometimes challenged "Europeans" on the streets of Chicago with carrying cards that announced the bearers were not Negroes but Moors. In 1930, after a rival was murdered, Ali died mysteriously shortly after being indicted for the other man's murder.

759 • Sweet Daddy Grace (1882?–1960)

Bishop Charles Emmaniel "Sweet Daddy" Grace was the founder of the United House of Prayer for All People who turned his claims of being able to raise the dead into a messianic movement among poor African Americans during the 1930s and 1940s. Born in the Cape Verde Islands in 1881, Sweet Daddy moved to New Bedford, Massachusetts, in 1900 and worked as a short-order cook before he founded the United House of Prayer in 1921. Although the church was located in New Bedford, Grace traveled in North Carolina, South Carolina, Georgia, Michigan, and other states recruiting followers, claiming that he had revived his sister after she had been pronounced dead by doctors. In his famous admonition, Sweet Daddy stated, "Never mind about God. Salvation is by Grace only." He was perhaps most famous for his outstanding appearance—shoulder-length hair, colorful suits, flashy jewelry, and three-inch-long finger-nails—and his superb merchandising. He sold such items as Daddy Grace soap, which supposedly cleansed the body and reduced fat, and the *Grace* magazine, which reputedly could cure a cold or tuberculosis if it was placed on one's chest. Grace was also adept at collecting contributions: in 1956 the Internal Revenue Service estimated his net worth at over $4 million.

Sweet Daddy Grace, 1938, by James Van Der Zee. Courtesy of Donna Van Der Zee

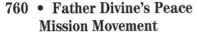

760 • Father Divine's Peace Mission Movement

Born George Baker, on Hutchinson Island, Savannah, Georgia, Father Divine (1880–1965) became a nationally known religious figure in 1932, when residents of Sayville, Long Island, had him arrested. Calling himself God, Divine had established a nondenominational, interracial religious commune on Long Island, and nearby wealthy residents did not like it. But a few days after New York Supreme Court Justice Lewis J. Smith sentenced Divine to one year in Suffolk County Jail on Long Island, the judge died, leading Divine's followers to conclude: "The judge sentenced God to jail, and God sentenced the judge to hell!" Even Divine said from his jail cell, "I hated to do it!" Divine's appeal was based on more than the belief that he was really God: during the Great Depression, Divine's Peace Missions fed hundreds of hungry African Americans and whites, and gave hope when all else seemed to be failing. Divine combined an intensely religious movement with a practical program of action: he ran a lodging house for the homeless, an employment bureau for the unemployed, and several schools for both adults and children. He also registered members to vote in local and national elections, and in 1936 he helped launch the All People's Party by bonding together with Communist Party representatives to run a slate of radical candidates. But when it no longer served his purpose, he repudiated the communists, for Divine was actually an economic conservative. He criticized Franklin Roosevelt's New Deal programs for creating dependency among the people and advocated instead a strict program of self-reliance and Protestant work ethic values. He advised members to pay their debts, to avoid drinking and gambling, and to save, and even held up Andrew Carnegie and Henry Ford as models to be emulated by the masses. Divine also taught that race and color were incidental and developed a strong following among whites. Indeed, he developed at least three movements in one: an eastern United States movement mainly among Blacks; a western movement, sited mainly in California, that appealed largely to the white middle class; and a foreign movement that attracted working-class whites in Canada, Australia, and western Europe. Although the actual scope of his movement is unknown, his membership ranged from 10,000 to 100,000, 75 percent of whom were women.

BLACK SOCIAL REALISM, 1940–63

Some Important Books

761 • *Native Son* (1940)

Born in Mississippi, Richard Wright (1908–60) migrated North to Chicago, where he worked at odd jobs until the Great Depression, when he obtained work on the Federal Writers' Project. His short story "Big Boy Leaves Home," about the racial prejudice and brutality of the South, won the *Story Magazine* prize for the best WPA Writers' Project story, and another, "Fire and Cloud," won a second prize in the O. Henry awards. But it was the publication of *Native Son* that catapulted Wright to national and international prominence. *Native Son* chronicled the tragic trajectory of a working-class Black man in Chicago who finds his manhood in the murder of a white woman, and whose case becomes a cause célèbre for the Communist Party. Part social realist document

Sunday morning breakfast of Richard Wright in his Left Bank apartment, July 1948. National Archives.

and part critique of the communist movement of the 1930s, Wright's *Native Son* ushered in a whole new genre in which racial anger and retaliation against whites was frankly discussed in Black fiction. Moreover, the tremendous popularity of *Native Son* brought Wright recognition as America's leading Black author and showed that social indictment fiction by Blacks could find an audience among white readers.

762 • *The Street* (1946)

Ann Petry's novel of Lutie's struggle to create a life for herself and her son in a disintegrating slum neighborhood did for African American women's fiction what *Native Son* did for Black males. Providing vivid detail about life in Harlem, Petry extracted from the sociological situation of a single Black woman's struggle a measure of universal transcendence. Again, similar to *Native Son,* Lutie's murder of her lover becomes an indictment of the society in which she is forced to live, and not simply a de-

featist caving into environmental forces. Moreover, Petry's use of poetic language to describe life in Harlem and Lutie's psychological motivations gives a narrative elegance to this novel.

763 • *Annie Allen* (1949)

Gwendolyn Brooks's Pulitzer Prize–winning book of poems, *Annie Allen,* is a lyrical masterpiece. Divided into three sections—"Notes from the Childhood and the Girlhood," "The Anniad," and "The Womanhood"—*Annie Allen* narrates the story of a Black woman from the inside. Moreover, in such lines as

> *It is brave to be involved,*
> *To be not fearful to be unresolved.*
> *Her new wish was to smile*
> *When answers took no airships, walked*
> *a while.*

Gwendolyn Brooks. Courtesy of the Contemporary Forum. Photo by Bill Tague

her lyricism touched something universal in the struggle of this young woman for dignity in a Black world. The poems read as well today as they did when they made Brooks the first African American to win the Pulitzer Prize.

764 • *Invisible Man* (1952)

Ralph Ellison's classic novel of the African American as the Underground Man has become the iconic African American novel, particularly so given that its author did not publish another novel in his lifetime. Perhaps one masterpiece was enough, for *Invisible Man* had it all—an existential central character whose alienation from both the white and Black worlds of racial accommodation was nearly complete, an incisive critique of the world of Black education and its compromising hypocrisies, and the probing investigation of the language and culture of the African American folk, still caught in the webs of resistance and accommodation to white power structures. *Invisible Man* still reads today as the indictment of the ways in which the sensitive African American youth habitually have their creativity destroyed by the structures of racial politics in America.

765 • *Go Tell It on the Mountain* (1953)

James Baldwin's first novel about growing up in Harlem as the son of a preacher is his best. It re-creates in excruciating detail the terrors of being reared in a Black slum world that looks on in contempt at the talented young man whose sensibilities unfit him for the stereotypical roles to success available to midcentury Negroes. The central struggle with religion, sexuality, and a sense of community with other African Americans provides a sophisticated, psychological introduction to what life offered the talented exception in modern, pre-integration America.

Moreover, Baldwin's personal style of expression takes this novel to a different level of narrative than that of Ellison's *Invisible Man*, showing the emergence of a fictional versatility in Black letters that had been missing before the advent of this new, social realist generation of the 1940s and 1950s.

Art

766 • Jacob Lawrence (b. 1917)

Recognized as one of America's best artists of the twentieth century, Jacob Lawrence was introduced to art at the Utopia Children's Center in Harlem, New York, and later trained by Augusta Savage at the Harlem Community School. When Savage obtained a position for him on the Works Progress Administration Arts Project, Lawrence began to produce powerful paintings. Lawrence possesses a unique, cubistic style of painting that he uses to comment on the social conditions of Black life. Although he has painted numerous single works in his career, Lawrence is distinguished by his artistic series on Black historical themes, such as his Toussaint l'Ouverture, Frederick Douglass, and Harriet Tubman series. Best known is his sixty-panel Migration Series, with historical captions written by Lawrence, that depict the exodus of African Americans into the North beginning in World War I. His stylized renderings of figures, powerful simplification of forms, and bold use of color make each panel a uniquely artistic interpretation of the social issues. Lawrence's larger theme in the Migration Series and his other works is the necessity of struggle for spiritual realization in this life.

767 • Elizabeth Catlett (b. 1915)

Elizabeth Catlett is one of America's best

sculptors and printmakers. Her large wood and marble sculptures, and stunning linocuts and lithographs, possess remarkable social realism and political significance. Born into a middle-class family in Washington, D.C., Elizabeth Catlett attended Howard University, where she studied under James Herring and Lois Mailou Jones. After graduating in 1937, she continued her art study at the University of Iowa, becoming the first person to receive a master's degree in fine art from that university, in 1940. She then headed the art department at Dillard University in New Orleans before attending the Art Institute of Chicago, where she met and married artist Charles White. She later moved to New York, divorced White, and married Mexican painter Francisco Mora, moving to Mexico City, where she taught art at the National University. Enormously prolific, Catlett has produced numerous strongly modeled portrait sculptures of women. She has also produced fine linocuts, one of the most sensitive being *Sharecropper* (1968). Like all of her studies of African American women, her subject here is tall, strong, and resolute in her eyes and bearing, with her brim straw hat. Her sharecropper has the strength and faith needed to endure the social and economic conditions of tenancy in the rural South.

Music and Dance

768 • Katherine Dunham (b. 1910)

This master dancer, choreographer, anthropologist, teacher, and activist launched the trend among African American modern dancers to ground their choreography in the African dance traditions still alive in the folk culture of the Caribbean. Dunham first gained attention when a dance group she had organized, Ballets Negres, presented one of her compositions, *Ne-*

gro Rhapsody, at the Beaux Arts Ball in Chicago in 1931. Her dancing and choreography reflected not only her race consciousness but her anthropological curiosity about African survivals in the Western Hemisphere, which she researched first at the University of Chicago as a student and then on site in the Caribbean as a Rosenwald Fellow in 1935. Study of African dance in Maroon villages in Jamaica, in urban communities on Martinique and Trinidad, and in voodoo communities on Haiti led to several publications, most notably *Journey to Accompong* (1946), and also to several compositions, such as *Tropics, Tropical Revue,* and *Bal Negre.* While she and her troupe also performed in mainstream productions, such as George Balanchine's *Cabin in the Sky* with Ethel Waters, her heart and creativity went increasingly into her Katherine Dunham School of Arts and Research, founded in 1945. In recent years, she has not only been an authority on the diasporic traditions of African American dance, but also an activist whose hunger strike in 1994 (along with that of Randall Robinson of TransAfrica) forced President Bill Clinton to change American policy toward Haiti, introduce U.S. troops, and restore democracy to her beloved island.

769 • Pearl Primus (1919–94)

Judged by dance critic John Martin to be one of the best dancers in America "regardless of race," Pearl Primus took the American dance scene by storm in 1943 as a dancer in *Folk Dance, Hard Times Blues,* and *African Ceremoniad.* Born in Trinidad, Primus had graduated from Hunter College with a degree in biology before being discovered in a dance unit of the National Youth Administration. After studying briefly with the New Dance Group, she was cast in several productions that she dominated with her remarkable strength and technical abil-

Pearl Primus. The Astor, Lenox and Tilden Foundations. Dance Collection, New York Public Library for the Performing Arts

ity—the "audience audibly gasped," according to Martin, at some of her extremely high leaps. Primus also possessed great dramatic ability and in 1946 was cast in the revival of *Show Boat.* Like Katherine Dunham, however, Primus was interested in the roots of African American dance. She did graduate work in anthropology and psychology before spending nine months in Africa in 1948 on a Rosenwald grant. That experience transformed her into an Africanist, who thereafter molded her dancing, her teaching, and her choreography around the performatory and spiritual benefits of African dance.

770. • Billie Holiday (1915–59)

Billie Holiday (born Eleanor Fagan) was a jazz singer of the blues in the 1930s and 1940s. Born in Baltimore, where she was raped at ten, Billie (a nickname she reputedly got for her tomboyish manner) seemed to carry the scars of a tragic childhood for the rest of her life. As a mature woman, she was also a drug addict who had her cabaret license in New York revoked after an arrest for heroin addiction in 1947. But what made Billie Holiday special was the way she used her personal pain to shape a new lyrical interpretation of the blues song. After listening to the records of Bessie Smith and Louis Armstrong while working in a bordello, Holiday began singing for ten dollars a week in New York in the late 1920s. Her big break came when she met John Hammond, who arranged for her to record with Benny Goodman in 1933 and with small studio bands, most notably Teddy Wilson's. After singing with Count Basie's Orchestra in 1937 and Artie Shaw's in 1938, she recorded her first albums, *Fine and Mellow* and *Strange Fruit,* with its title protest song against lynching, in 1939. During the 1940s she toured as a solo performer and gained a reputation as a unique jazz singer, who changed the rhythm, harmony, and meaning of popular songs as creatively as any jazz instrument player. After her arrest and incarceration in 1947, she emerged to give a triumphant performance at Carnegie Hall; but restricted to playing outside of New York because of her drug problems, she was forced to perform in sleazy nightclubs in California and in Europe for little more than cigarette and drug money. Then, in 1958, two years after the publication of *Lady Sings the Blues,*

Billie Holiday. Photograph by Carl Van Vechten, March 23, 1949. Courtesy of Prints and Photographs Division, Library of Congress. Gift of Carl Van Vechten

her autobiography, and a year before her death, Billie Holiday rallied from deteriorating health to produce—despite her voice's technical limitations—perhaps her best album, *Lady in Satin.* With the dignified treatment of string accompaniments, the autobiographical character of the songs, and the emotional intimacy of her singing, Billie Holiday produced an album not only about love but also her life.

771 • Charlie "Byrd" Parker (1920–55)

Charlie Parker was an improvisational genius on the alto saxophone and one of the main architects of the bebop style that transformed jazz during the 1940s. Born in Kansas City, Missouri, Parker started playing the alto saxophone in 1933, then went to New York in 1939, where he participated in numerous jam sessions and carved out his individual style. Bored with the traditional swing movement changes for the saxophone, Parker hit upon the idea of composing new melodic themes in songs using chord progressions he borrowed from other popular songs. Charlie Parker also broke the pulse and meter of songs, introduced a succession of subdivisions into them, and played the changes at breakneck speed. After playing in Earl Hines's and Billy Eckstine's bands during World War II, Parker emerged as a leader of his own band in New York in 1945 and became nationally recognized after a stint in Los Angeles. But Parker was also suffering from drug and alcohol addiction, and in June 1946 had to be hospitalized at the state hospital in Camarillo, California. Returning to New York in 1947, he entered upon his most productive period. But when the New York narcotics department caused his cabaret license to be revoked in July 1951, he could not work, and entered into a decline of further hospitalization, suicide attempts, and his death in New York on March 12, 1955.

772 • John "Dizzy" Gillespie (1917–93)

Dizzy Gillespie first became well known as the preferred trumpeter sideman for Charlie Parker, whom he had met when the latter joined Earl Hines's band in 1942. Dizzy was the other crucial architect of bebop, whose bent horn, lightning-fast playing, and numerous compositions were the natural complement to Parker's improvisational style. But Dizzy left Charlie Parker's band in Los Angeles in 1946, returned to New York, and became a leader in his own right, recording his own compositions. Even more than Parker, Dizzy worked with

Cuban musicians, wrote compositions utilizing Caribbean themes, and served as a musical bridge between African American and other music of the African diaspora.

773 • Thelonius Monk (1920–82)

Everything about Thelonius Monk—his odd name, curious hats, quirky piano playing, and outlandishly titled compositions—seemed to epitomize bebop, the dominant African American jazz idiom of the 1940s and 1950s. Born in Rocky Mount, North Carolina, Monk learned to play the piano as a child in New York, where he acquired the reputation as the most innovative of the young pianists at Minton's Playhouse in Harlem who, along with Dizzy Gillepsie, Charlie Christian, and Kenny Clarke, created bebop. Monk's piano work was important not only for its strong harmonic structure but also for the creative timing, offbeat syncopation, and uninhibited joy with which he played the piano. Monk was also one of the more memorable bebop composers, whose songs, such as "Round Midnight," "Ruby, My Dear," "Straight, No Chaser," "Well, You Needn't," "Misterioso," "Criss Cross," and "Crespuscule with Nellie," are classics. Relegated to supportive accompaniment of better known beboppers in the forties and fifties, Monk emerged as a star in his own right after his 1959 Town Hall concert in New York. He enjoyed his greatest recording and performance successes in the 1960s when he welded Charlie Rouse (tenor sax), John Ore (bass), and Frankie Dunlop (drums) into the Thelonius Monk Quartet.

774 • Miles Davis (1926–91)

As the man who replaced Dizzy Gillespie in Charlie Parker's Quintet in 1947, Miles Davis became famous as the young boy trumpeter of the bebop generation. But early in the 1950s Miles Davis stepped out from under Dizzy's influence, developed a unique trumpet "voice," and as a bandleader himself, led the way out of the bebop style with his "birth of the cool" movement in the 1950s. During that decade and the next, Davis established himself as the premier bandleader in American jazz, who attracted the best sidemen to work with him, including John Coltrane, Cannonball Adderley, Gerry Morgan, Max Roach, Wayne Shorter, Bill Evans, Herbie Hancock, Chick Corea, Keith Jarrett, Joe Zawinul, Ron Carter, and Tony Williams, and who produced a series of big-band albums using arrangements by Gil Evans. Miles also wrote numerous now classic jazz songs, including "So What," "All Blues," Freddie Freeloader," and "Four," to name only a few. By the early 1960s Miles was more than a musician—he had become a model for young Blacks of how to walk, and talk, and carry oneself in a "cool" manner. In the late 1960s Miles became controversial with fans and critics because he incorporated electric pianos, electric basses, and guitars into his band and began to play a fusion jazz that incorporated the funky rhythms of Jimi Hendrix, James Brown, and Sly and the Family Stone into his music. Yet Miles created some excellent fusion jazz albums, such as "Filles de Kilimanjaro," "Miles in the Sky," "In a Silent Way," and the astonishing 1970 two-record set "Bitches Brew," before a physical and mental decline led him to abandon recording and performing in 1975. Returning in 1980, Miles pursued a mellower electronic synthesis of popular and serious jazz tunes before his death in 1991.

775 • Gospel Music

While African American gospel music has obscure roots in the spirituals, it is a modern form of religious singing that emerged in the 1890s,

Thomas A. Dorsey, the father of gospel music, was known as Georgia Tom in the 1920s blues world. Calyton Hannah Collection, Hogan Jazz Archive, Tulane University Library

predominantly in Holiness or Pentecostal churches of the urban North and South. The formal birth date of gospel music is generally given as 1907, when during a famous revival tent meeting in Los Angeles, Black religious gospel singing came to greater attention. Gospel music got its name from this meeting, designed to recreate the moment when the spirit or gospel came down from heaven to the multitude. Unlike the spirituals, gospel music is an urban rather than rural music, and an instrumental music—with pianos, tambourines, and drums —instead of the often a cappella singing of the spirituals. Initially, Baptist churches, with whom this music is now associated, resisted the new music as a challenge to the authority of ministers. But because of the role of C. Albert

Tindley, who wrote gospel songs in the early 1900s, and Thomas Dorsey, who not only wrote many songs but distributed single sheets of music for sale to singers in churches, the movement spread until at the 1930 National Baptist Convention in Chicago two gospel songs—"How About You" and "Did You See My Savior"—written by Thomas Dorsey were allowed to be performed. The overwhelming enthusiasm for the music broke down the resistance, and gospel music—"feeling" music— spread to Baptist and Methodist church services. Of individual gospel singers, Mahalia Jackson has been the most popular, with the Mighty Clouds of Joy being the most popular gospel singing group.

776 • Leontyne Price (b. 1927)

Leontyne Price was the first African American woman to sing with the Metropolitan Opera when she performed the role of Leonora in *Il Trovatore* on January 27, 1961. Having received a Julliard School of Music scholarship in 1949, Price's first big break came in 1952, when Virgil Thompson chose her to sing in his Broadway revival of *Four Saints in Three Acts.* Soon after followed her singing the role of Bess in the production of Gershwin's opera, her role as Madame Lidoine in the San Francisco production of Poulenc's *Dialogues des Carmélites,* and her debut at the Verona Arena, Vienna, and Covent Garden. After her debut at the Metropolitan Opera, she returned as Cleopatra in Barber's *Anthony and Cleopatra* at the opening of the new Metropolitan Opera in 1966. Known especially for her singing in Verdi's music, she has been renowned for her ability as a musical interpreter.

777 • Chuck Berry (b. ca. 1926)

Chuck Berry was the principal architect of

fifties rock and roll. Despite the accolades and mass popularity given to Elvis Presley, it was Berry, as a songwriter and a performer, who ushered in the transition from rhythm and blues to rock and roll. Growing up in St. Louis, Berry worked as an automobile assembler and then a hairdresser before starting to sing and play the guitar to make extra money. Berry did not forget his cosmetology experience when he went to New York and recorded his first hit song with Chess Records: it was titled "Maybellene" (1955), the name of a popular hair preparation. Berry followed that with a host of other hits, including "Roll Over Beethoven" (1957) and "Johnny B. Goode" (1958). Berry also became an outstanding stage performer, especially noted for his "duck walk"—skating across stage, in a crouched position, while playing the electric guitar. But a conviction under the Mann Act for taking a fourteen-year-old hatcheck girl across state lines almost destroyed his life and career, for after a two-year imprisonment, he emerged in 1964 with a broken family and a different rock music environment. Then, in 1972, his opening in Las Vegas to tremendous ovations signaled a return of attention to this star; and his song "My Ding-a-Ling" shot to number one in October. In 1986 he was still going strong, with a birthday concert in St. Louis with Keith Richards, guitarist of the Rolling Stones, in which Chuck Berry rolled out on stage in a red convertible. A film biography, *Chuck Berry: Hail! Hail! Rock 'n' Roll,* was issued in 1987, the same year that *Chuck Berry: The Autobiography* appeared.

778 • Little Richard (b. 1932)

Little Richard (Richard Wayne Penniman) was born in Macon, Georgia, the grandson of a Baptist minister and the son of a bootleg liquor salesman. That tension between the religious and the nefarious gave his music its special energy. He started singing in a family gospel group, later in church, where he gained a reputation for his tendency to "rock" the gospel—to sing it wildly and extravagantly. When he went on the road at fourteen, he sang rhythm and blues with all the energy of a Holiness church meeting. After touring the South with a variety of rhythm and blues groups, he landed in New Orleans in 1955 with a demo tape and promptly recorded his first hit, "Tutti Frutti." With his pounding keyboard playing and high-energy, punchy singing, "Tutti Frutti" captured the attention of teenage America, who promptly made it number seventeen on the *Billboard* pop chart in January 1956. Reputedly, Elvis Presley was able to record "Hound Dog," his signature song, only after he heard "Tutti Frutti." Richard quickly followed with such hits as "Long Tall Sally," "Slippin and Slidin," "Good Golly, Miss Molly," and an appearance with Jayne Mansfield in a movie, *The Girl Can't Help It* (1956). A sensational performer, with his hair piled high, his makeup packed on, and his eyebrows penciled in, Little Richard did something other Black performers had not yet done—he proved that an African American could enthrall audiences with large numbers of white females, who were attracted by a sexually ambiguous persona that was less threatening than such blatantly heterosexual figures as Chuck Berry. Richard's homosexuality, though hidden in the 1950s, burdened him increasingly as he became more successful, and in 1957 he renounced "sinful" rock and roll and retreated into the church. When Little Richard returned to commercial music in the 1960s, rock music had changed, and his music sounded dated. White artists, such as Pat Boone, had made careers out of "covering"—singing—his songs, but Richard could not collect royalties, because unprincipled recording executives held the ownership rights to his songs. In the 1990s, however, he reemerged as an icon of redemption, who handed out Bibles on talk shows and claimed—as Jelly Roll Morton did before him—that he had invented it all. His 1992 album for children, *Shake It All About,* sold well, and in 1993 the National Academy of Recording Arts and Sciences honored him with a lifetime achievement award.

779 • Motown

Begun in a frame house in Detroit with the sign "Hitsville, U.S.A." outside, Motown Records blossomed into a multimillion-dollar entertainment corporation that produced the best music in America during the 1960s. Motown launched the careers of Mary Wells, Smokey Robinson and the Miracles, Diana Ross and the Supremes, Martha and the Vandellas, the Temptations, the Four Tops, the Jackson 5, Stevie Wonder, Marvin Gaye, Gladys Knight and the Pips, Lionel Richie, and a host of others. Motown's stable of singers produced from 1961 to 1972 over one hundred songs that reached the Top 10 on the pop music charts, with thirty-one of them ranked number one in the country. Such songs as "Please, Mr. Postman," "My Guy," "Baby Love," "Stop! In the Name of Love," "My Girl," "You Keep Me Hanging On," "Reach Out, I'll Be There," "Dancing in the Streets," and "I Heard It Through the Grapevine" became classics still listened and danced to today. Motown was the brainchild of Berry Gordy, Jr., a Ford assembly plant worker, who wrote songs, managed Black rhythm and blues groups, and marketed their music to a national, largely white pop audience. With the songwriting team of Eddie Holland, Lamont Dozier, and Brian Holland, Gordy created the "Motown Sound" of strong bass lines, lush harmonies, and squeaky-clean lyrics that made the music and the groups acceptable to radio and television audiences. A masterful institution builder, Gordy had a knack for attracting new talent just as older groups left the company or broke up. Such strategies netted Motown Records $40 million in sales in 1971 and made it the most profitable Black-owned company in the United States. Motown also contributed to the Civil Rights Movement by creating a spoken-word label that recorded speeches by political leaders, most notably the 1971 Grammy-winning speech, *Why I Oppose the War in Vietnam,* by Martin Luther King, Jr. In 1988 Gordy sold Motown to MCA, Inc., for $61.8 million.

Some Important Plays and Films

780 • *A Raisin in the Sun* (1959)

A Raisin in the Sun, Lorraine Hansberry's first play, made brief appearances in Philadelphia and Chicago before it opened March 11, 1959, on Broadway with Ruby Dee, Sidney Poitier, and Claudia McNeil in the leading roles. *A Raisin in the Sun* won the Drama Critics Circle Award and brought Lorraine Hansberry (1930–65) national acclaim. It was the longest-running play on Broadway by an African American up to that date (847 performances). Opening on Broadway just five years after the Supreme Court's *Brown v. Board of Education, Topeka, Kansas* decision, the play gave theatergoers an insider's look at one Black family's struggle with the costs of residential integration. Transformed in 1973 into a musical, *Raisin* won the Tony Award for the best musical.

781 • *Lilies of the Field* (1963)

Sidney Poitier's portrayal of Homer Smith in this film earned him an Oscar for best actor and made him the first African American to win this award. *Lilies of the Field* epitomized Poitier's emergence as a Hollywood archetype—some might say a new stereotype—of the superlative Negro whose sterling selflessness and devotion to others allowed him to avoid being mistaken for the shiftless, stupid, and incompetent Negro of old Hollywood movies. The film narrates an accidental meeting between Homer Smith (Poitier), a good-natured drifter driving through the western United States, and a group of German immigrant nuns whose leader, played by Lilia Skala, commandeers Smith to build the nuns a chapel. At first, he resists. But after a local boss asks Smith his profession, he replies "a contractor" and builds the church as a way to create a new identity for himself. Criticized by some Black audiences in the 1960s for its saccharine image of a Black man and the implication that he could only find his identity by helping white people, *Lilies of the Field* nevertheless contains memorable scenes. In one, Poitier confronts a man who calls him "boy" by calling *him* "boy"; in another, Poitier teaches the nuns to sing the spirituals and shows that African Americans possess a distinct and vibrant culture. Poitier's portrayal announced to a mass white audience that a new, more prideful Negro had emerged for the 1960s.

Religion

782 • Black Social Gospel Movement

During the 1930s and 1940s a Social Gospel Movement developed in the African American ministry that stressed the need to remember the social dimension of the Christian doctrine and to apply it to transforming the racial situation in America. Black ministers, many of them educated or practicing in Protestant churches in the North, sought to apply the moral reform theology of Reinhold and Richard Niebuhr to transform the Black church into a social reform institution. Religious leaders as diverse as Howard Thurman, Adam Clayton Powell, Jr., and Martin Luther King, Sr., and many others, carved out an engaged ministry that argued Black Christianity was not confined to advocating freedom in the next world, but committed to bringing about social freedom in this one. As a consequence, Black churches became sites of interracial fellowship, community organizing, and protest organizing that brought about the Civil Rights Movement.

BLACK ARTS MOVEMENT, 1959–80

Movements, Organizations, and Celebrations

783 • Black Arts Movement

During the 1960s a new generation of writers, artists, and dramatists emerged in the North to express a Black sensibility in the arts. The movement began in 1959, when Elmer Lewis, Margaret Burroughs, Ossie Davis, Ruby Dee, and LeRoi Jones founded the American Negro Repertory Company, which, like the National Conference of Negro Artists (later the National Conference of Artists), Margaret Burroughs's Ebony Museum of Negro Culture in Chicago, and the San Francisco Negro Historical and Cultural Association, led the way to the 1960s Black Pride movement. Although these institutions grew out of the Civil Rights Movement's belief in integration, they were also committed to the idea that art and history should promote racial self-appreciation. By 1965 this "Black Pride" viewpoint, and a related identification with Africa, led younger artists like LeRoi Jones to change his name to Imamu Amiri Baraka and establish the Black Arts Theater in Newark, New Jersey. Other little theater and writers' groups spurted up around the country in African American ghettos and encouraged young urban Blacks to write about their experiences. By the mid-sixties Black poets, playwrights, and fiction writers linked art to political expression, and articulated a Black aesthetic in the arts that was unavailable to white artists. Influenced by the Pan Africanist Negritude movement of Leopold Senghor and the revolutionary politics of Frantz Fanon, such writers as Larry Neal, Hoyt Fuller, Addison Gayle, Don L. Lee, and Harold Cruse argued for a self-consciously cultural nationalism. The movement was characterized by its multiple media, with groups such as "The Last Poets," which recorded rather than published poetry. In cinema, Gordon Parks, Melvin Van Peebles, and Gordon Parks, Jr., emerged as pro-Black directors in Hollywood. The proliferation of soul music, urban street gangs, and the urban rebellions of the late sixties gave a political urgency to the works of art produced in this period.

Some Important Books

784 • *The Autobiography of Malcolm X* (1965)

Malcolm X's autobiography, ghostwritten by Alex Haley, is a classic Black life story of personal corruption, then redemption through the Nation of Islam, the Honorable Elijah Muhammad's Black nationalist organization. Tracing his life from those early days hustling on the streets of Detroit, Malcolm X chronicles his descent into crime and his personal rejuvenation by the Black Muslim religion, which created a code of behavior as well as a rhetoric of indictment of white racism. As a spokesperson for the Nation in the late 1950s and early 1960s, Malcolm X became more famous and more political than Elijah Muhammad, and when Malcolm disobeyed Muhammad's command and commented on the death of President John F. Kennedy, Malcolm X was censured and eventually left the Black Muslims. He then traveled to the Middle East, and his encounter with Muslims who were white and yet not racist transformed him and led Malcolm to advocate a nonracist but radical critique of American institutions. The story of this transformative life is arrestingly told by Haley, who published the book after Malcolm's assassination in 1965.

785 • *The Man Who Cried I Am* (1967)

John A. Williams's novel *The Man Who Cried I Am* is the most powerful novel of the 1960s. Its power derives from its narrative, which is economic, pungent, fast-paced, and sparkingly provocative. Williams weaves together a forties story of the expatriate Black author who, like Richard Wright and James Baldwin, is vainly searching for African American meaning in Europe, and a sixties plot of the protagonist's encounters with political activism, extremist Black nationalism, and government intelligence programs. As such, Williams turns the problem of the Black intellectual and writer into an engaging narrative. For his central character, Max, pursues the contradictions of the Civil Rights Movement, expatriation, interracial romantic relationships, and rising Black nationalism with an intellectual energy and sophistication that is rare in African American fiction.

786 • *The Crisis of the Negro Intellectual* (1967)

Harold Cruse's autobiographical critique of twentieth-century African American intellectuals became a classic the moment it was published. Cruse defined the problem of the Black intellectual as the failure to develop strong Black cultural nationalism in America. Beginning with the Harlem Renaissance of the 1920s, Cruse traced that failure to the desire in most African American intellectuals to integrate into white cultural institutions, rather than to develop autonomous, self-sustaining Black institutions. According to Cruse, the failure of the Harlem Renaissance was that it allowed Black art and thought to be controlled by white patrons, while the Black intellectuals on the left in the 1930s were guilty of being hoodwinked by Jewish communists into abandoning Black institutions as "chauvinistic," even as such communists maintained their own ethnic identity and institutions. Cruse called on younger Black artists and intellectuals of the 1960s to develop a healthy cultural nationalism that grounded its art and culture in the Black consumer audience. Cruse's book influenced a generation of African American scholarship, much of it dedicated to refuting some of his historical claims.

787 • *The Black Aesthetic* (1971)

This anthology became the bible of the Black Arts Movement because it published in one book the best critical writing of the movement. With essays by LeRoi Jones, Larry Neal, Hoyt Fuller, Don L. Lee, Loften Mitchell, and editor Addison Gayle, the book asserts that a Black aesthetic exists which is distinctive to African American expression. The book was designed to counter arguments by mainly white critics that the new Black arts of the 1960s were an aberration, and merely a capitulation to racial anger. Editor Addison Gayle sought to establish the intellectual canon of ideas in the Black Arts Movement by including in the book's sections "Theory," "Music," "Poetry," "Drama," and "Fiction" essays on Black aesthetics written by Alain Locke, Langston Hughes, J. A. Rogers, and Richard Wright earlier in the century. Moreover, such contemporaries as Larry Neal and Don L. Lee, for example, assert that the Black aesthetic is more than simply a distinctive sense of beauty—it is a characteristic worldview that derives from African culture and differs fundamentally from the Western aesthetic that has dominated American expression.

788 • *Song of Solomon* (1977)

Although Toni Morrison's first two novels, *The Bluest Eye* and *Sula,* were excellent works of fiction, her third novel, *Song of Solomon,* is her masterpiece. In *Song of Solomon,* Morrison creates the world of a Black community that exists, struggles, and nourishes itself completely independent of white control. The novel weaves together the world of myth, ghosts, and African American burial practices, and particularly shows the power of African American naming patterns: characters are named "Macon Dead" and "Milkman" and function in a world where the will of the dead is as important, at times, as that of the living. *Song of Solomon* also shows that such African American naming patterns exist as an act of resistance, as when the Black community first names a street "Doctor" and then "Not Doctor" after the white community attempts to take back the power to name

Toni Morrison. Photo © 1978 by Helen Marcus

streets in the Black part of town. *Song of Solomon* is distinguished by the power of its language, its remarkable detail in description of scenes and surroundings, combined with an imaginative sweep and emotional intensity unseen in American fiction. Perhaps more than any other African American novel of the 1970s, Toni Morrison's *Song of Solomon* drew upon African American folklore not only for the setting but also for the turns of plot.

Art

789 • Romare Bearden (1912–88)

Though born in Charlotte, North Carolina, Bearden grew up in Harlem, where he met such writers, artists, and musicians of the Harlem Re-

naissance as W. E. B. Du Bois, Countee Cullen, Aaron Douglas, and Duke Ellington. After developing an interest in art, Bearden became controversial in the 1930s for his criticism of the Harmon Foundation, a white foundation that held annual exhibitions of Black art, for some of the shoddy art it selected for exhibition. Bearden started as a relatively typical social realist painter who, during the 1930s and early 1940s, documented African American rural and urban life. But in the 1940s and 1950s he broke with current trends: first, he produced small oil paintings on literary themes; but by the late 1950s and early 1960s, he had, belatedly, embraced abstract expressionism. It seemed that Bearden was lurching from one style to another in a vain search for his own distinctive medium when in 1961 he began to construct collages out of cutout photographs of African American figures and other images. In his 1964 series *The Prevalence of Ritual,* Bearden combined disparate elements—photos of African masks, working-class African Americans, rural and urban landscapes, cutouts of teeth, hands, and noses—into a new visual language that evoked Picasso, Braque, Matisse, and the surrealists and embodied African American themes and images. His numerous collages and later his photomontages signaled not only a return to the African American figure but also an ability to use cubistic principles of abstraction to evoke the rhythm and pattern of African American folk culture. Perhaps more than any other artist of his generation, Bearden's work represented the fractured yet triumphant spirit of the Black community in the 1960s, from the optimism of the Civil Rights Movement to the alienation of the urban riots. Something of the richness, complexity, and sophistication of Bearden's artistic vision comes through in his posthumously published art history, *A History of African-American Artists* (1988), which he coauthored with journalist Harry Henderson.

790 • John Biggers (b. 1924)

Born in Gastonia, North Carolina, John Biggers early developed an ability to translate his affective appreciation for African American people and culture into lush, engaging paintings. A trip to Africa under the auspices of Unesco occasioned a process of self-discovery that he chronicled in the book *Ananse, the Web of Life in Africa* and in the painting *Jubilee-Ghana Harvest Festival* (1959), a mixed-media composition that portrayed a public celebration he witnessed in West Africa. More recently, Biggers has combined his sense of the dignity of Black people with his increasing knowledge of African cultural traditions in several stunning compositions, such as *Shotguns* (1987), a tribute to the visual patterns of African American shotgun houses, and *Starry Crown* (1987), his luscious representation of the three Marys of

African antiquity—from Egypt, Benin, and the Dogon of Mali.

791 • Ed Love (b. 1936)

This Los Angeles–born artist recalled that conversations between his father and uncles about Marcus Garvey first inspired in him an interest in things African. Then, in the 1960s, he began to research Egypt, especially Egyptian mythology, and discovered the complexity of Africa. In such powerful steel sculptures as *Osiris* (1972) and *Mask for Mingus* (1974), Love molds scraps of steel, usually from car bumpers he collects, into sculptures that are anthropomorphic and evocative of West African masks and sculptures. Love responds as well in his sculpture to African American music, the violent American traditions of lynching and foreign wars, and the artwork of David Alfaro Siqueiros. Perhaps his masterpiece is the multiple-figure sculpture *Arkestra* (1984–88) that celebrates African American musicians in twenty-seven kinetic steel sculptures. After teaching art for many years at Howard University, Love moved to Miami in 1987 to become dean of the Visual Arts Division of the New World School of the Arts.

The Prevalence of Ritual: Baptism. Photograph by Lee Stalsworth, 1964. Hirshhorn Museum and Sculpture Garden, Smithsonian Institution. Gift of Joseph H. Hirshhorn, 1966. Courtesy of Estate of Romare Bearden

Music and Dance

792 • John Coltrane (1926–67)

John Coltrane eventually occupied the improvisational space vacated by the death of Charlie Parker. Born in Hamlet, North Carolina, Coltrane studied music in Philadelphia in 1945 and then with the Dizzy Gillepsie Orchestra from 1949 to 1951. In 1955 he was recruited by Miles Davis to join his quintet. After a brief stint with Thelonius Monk in 1957, Coltrane rejoined Miles's band in 1958 and made some of his best and most innovative soloing with Davis's band. Leaving Miles Davis again in 1960, he formed his own band, with Elvin Jones, McCoy Tyner, and Paul Chambers. In a series of recordings, Coltrane defined the avant-garde of the early sixties with his rapid-fire delivery of notes and long, complex modal solos on both the tenor and the soprano saxophones.

John Coltrane. Prints and Photographs Division, Library of Congress

793 • Diana Ross and the Supremes

The Supremes set the high-water mark of hit productions for Motown music from July 1964 to April 1965 when they had five consecutive number one singles. That established the Supremes (with Diana Ross as lead singer and Mary Wilson and Florence Ballard as backups) as the most popular American singing group in the 1960s. As if to emphasize the point, the Supremes returned to the number one hit parade in 1966, when the group had another run of four hit songs that lasted until 1967. Singing songs written by the team of Eddie Holand, Lamont Dozier, and Brian Holland, the Supremes epitomized Berry Gordy's ideal of the crossover group: their sweet, sparkling singing of catchy lyrics endeared them to thousands of white Americans. When they appeared successfully on Ed Sullivan's television show on October 10, 1965, they established the mass appeal of the Motown Sound and opened doors for other African American musical groups in the white commercial market. Not surprisingly, their incredible success led to dissension in the Supremes: in July 1967 the group's name was changed to Diana Ross and the Supremes, and Florence Ballard was booted out of the group and replaced by Cindy Birdsong. Then, in January 1970, Diana Ross left the group to pursue what became a very successful solo career: she herself had five number one hit songs over the next ten years and became a popular motion picture actress, starring in *Lady Sings the Blues* (1972), *Mahogany* (1975), and *The Wiz* (1978).

794 • The Temptations and the Four Tops

Most who listened to the Temptations and the Four Tops had a strong preference for one or the other group as the best Black male singing group in America. But together they were clearly the best male singing groups in Motown and the top Black male singing groups in the United States during the 1960s. The Temptations—with a string of Top 10 hits, including "The Way You Do the Things You Do," "The Girl's Alright With Me," and "My Girl," along with such number one hits as "Ain't Too Proud to Beg" and "Just My Imagination"—were considered the top act in Motown, and they were protected as such: in 1970, Gordy gave the Vietnam protest song "War" to Edwin Starr for fear it was too controversial for the Temptations. The Temptations were both polished and versatile, with complex harmonizing, intricate dance routines, flashy clothing, and the ability to sing fast-paced dance tunes and ballads. Interestingly, the Temptations were the only Motown singing group to break out of the conservative Motown Sound formula and embrace (with some criticism) electric, acid rock in the early 1970s. The breakthrough album *Psychedelic Shack* (1970) was the result. Moreover, by singing songs like "Papa Was a Rolling Stone" (1972), the "Temps" (as they were sometimes called) moved beyond simple romantic ballads to social commentary songs. By contrast, the Four Tops (Renaldo Benson, Abdul Fakir, Lawrence Payton, and Levi Stubbs) never abandoned the Motown Sound and remained the undisputed masters of romantic ballad singing. Although their 1965 number one hit "I Can't Help Myself" was an up-tempo tune, the Four Tops are mainly remembered for "Baby I Need Your Loving," "Reach Out, I'll Be There," and "Still Water"—the latter

the title of their best album. In contrast with the numerous personnel changes in the Temptations, the Four Tops have remained the same four singers for over thirty years. Both groups still tour, sometimes together.

795 • Smokey Robinson and the Miracles

The Miracles were formed in 1957 and signed by Motown in 1959, and in 1961 they recorded Motown's first million-unit seller, "Shop Around." The original Miracles contained Warren Moore, Claudette Rogers, Bobby Rogers, Ronnie White, and leader William "Smokey" Robinson, but recorded as a quartet after Claudette Rogers married Smokey in 1965. Not only was Smokey Robinson's smooth, almost falsetto voice the key to the Miracles' beautiful harmonies, but Smokey was an incredibly prolific writer of songs—over one thousand—many of which, like "My Girl," were recorded by other Motown groups. He was also the only artist to become a vice-president of Motown (1963) and to produce other music groups. Smokey left the Miracles in 1972 and the group disbanded in 1978.

796 • James Brown (b. 1928)

James Brown was the most influential bandleader in soul music during the 1960s. He was also a superb performer in concert, with many of his moves, gestures, and antics being copied by hundreds of performers. Born in Pulaski, Tennessee, Brown moved at an early age with his family to Augusta, Georgia. After being arrested as a young man, Brown took up singing, initially with some gospel music groups, during the 1940s, and then expanded his musical knowledge by studying the organ; he also played the drums, and in the 1950s, backed by his

James Brown, 1968. National Archives, photo by Emiloi Grossi

group, the Famous Flames, he got a recording contract and became known to the inner-city ghetto listeners when he recorded "Please, Please, Please" in 1956. After such hits as "Papa Got a Brand New Bag" (1965) and "It's a Man's World" (1966), Brown developed a following among hip young white listeners of rhythm and blues. But his biggest achievements came at the end of the 1960s with "Say It Loud, I'm Black and I'm Proud" (1968), "Mother Popcorn" (1969), and "Give It Up and Turn It Loose" (1969).

797 • Jimi Hendrix (1942–70)

Jimi Hendrix was the greatest guitarist of the 1960s. It was not simply his gifted technical skills that made him great—it was that Hendrix permanently changed the way that electric guitar was played and influenced an entire generation of musicians, guitarists, and others. Born in Seattle, Hendrix listened to records of Muddy Waters and other blues guitarists, learned to reproduce their style of playing, and after a brief stint as a paratrooper in the 101st Airborne Divi-

sion, began to play guitar with numerous rhythm and blues groups during 1961–66, including James Brown. Then, late in 1966, he began singing, went to England, and created the Jimi Hendrix Experience with drummer Mitch Mitchell and guitarist Noel Redding, who played bass. After playing to sellout crowds in England, the Jimi Experience took the United States by storm after its performance during the 1967 Monterey Pop Festival, where the highly amplified music, lurid lyrics, and Jimi's onstage burning of his guitar made the group an "Experience!" During the next two years, the group toured the United States and produced three platinum albums, *Are You Experienced?* (1967), which included such classics as "Purple Haze," "Hey Joe," and "Foxey Lady," *Axis: Bold as Love,* and *Electric Ladyland,* both in 1968, that set a high-water mark for musical creativity. Famous early for his tight, punchy rock songs and his fast, intense, and metallic guitar playing, Hendrix in his later albums expanded his mastery of electric guitar feedback and created special effects that turned the guitar into the most important musical instrument of the decade. He influenced such divergent musicians as the jazz musician Miles Davis and the traditional soul group the Temptations. Unfortunately, at the height of his fame, he became addicted to heroin and died of an overdose in England in 1970.

798 • Stevie Wonder (b. 1950)

At the tender age of eleven, Stevie Wonder joined Motown in 1961 and within two years had a number one hit on the pop charts, "Fingertips, Pt. 2," a live performance recorded at the Regal Theater in Chicago. His *12 Year Old Genius* was Motown's first number one album. After that triumph, Stevie Wonder was a bona fide early-sixties star, who toured the country with the Rolling Stones as his opening act in 1964. In 1972, ironically, it would be Stevie Wonder who would be the Rolling Stones' opening act as he introduced to a new and largely white audience his new album, *Talking Book,* which for the first time in history entered the pop charts at number one. That album was followed by *Innvervisions* in 1973, *Fulfillingness First Finale* in 1974, and the critically acclaimed double album *Songs in the Key of Life* in 1976. These albums established Wonder as one of the most creative musical artists in America, for his ability to weave poetic lyrics and electronic effects into moving songs. In the course of his career, Stevie Wonder has won more than sixteen Grammy Awards and an Oscar for best original song ("I Just Called to Say I Love You," 1985) and has produced eight number one hits, twenty-six in the Top 10. He has also been devoted to social and political causes, participating in the "We Are the World" video and recording to help Africa, and becoming a leader in the campaign to make Martin Luther King's birthday a national holiday.

799 • Alvin Ailey (1931–91)

Alvin Ailey was influenced by, and continued the tradition of, Katherine Dunham in modern dance. In 1953 he gained attention by choreographing two pieces, *Creation of the World* and *Work Songs,* that drew upon the African American folk tradition. Then, in 1954, he appeared as a dancer in *Carmen Jones* with Carmen de Lavallade. Responding to the upsurge in Black consciousness in the late 1950s, Alvin Ailey began giving dance concerts in Harlem at the YMCA and in 1960 formed his own company. During the 1960s he choreographed numerous ballets for his own and other companies, creat-

Alvin Ailey dance troupe in a modern, sensual number, 1972. National Archives. Photo © by Jack Mitchell

ing a distinctive signature style of African American modern dance. Ailey was adept at mining the African American religious tradition for compositions, of which his most famous is *Revelations.* In 1974 he created a series of works based on the music of Duke Ellington. By the mid-1970s Ailey had expanded to become a comprehensive dance theater institution, with not only the Alvin Ailey American Dance Theater but also the Alvin Ailey Repertory Ensemble and Dance Center. Since his death, his company has been guided by his featured dancer, Judith Jamison.

800 • The Dance Theater of Harlem

Founded by Arthur Mitchell in 1969, the Dance Theater of Harlem explored the possibilities of a Black classical ballet rather than modern dance. Mitchell had gained national attention in 1956 in the signature role of George Balanchine's *Agon.* Mitchell then became one of the premier soloists of the New York City Ballet. But Mitchell wanted to be more than simply a featured dancer: after teaching ballet at the Harlem School of the Arts in the 1960s and realizing that considerable interest existed among Black youth for ballet, he, along with Karel Shook, founded the Dance Theater of Harlem. With financial support from many whites who championed his work, Mitchell was able to build the Dance Theater into a major company. With a diverse repertoire that drew upon his Balanchine roots, the Ballet Russe tradition, and the African American heritage of dance, Mitchell developed a distinctive series of compositions that reinterpreted the classical tradition through the lens of African and African American dance expression. His *Firebird* and *Giselle* became signature works; but Mitchell also developed compositions, such as *Streetcar Named Desire,* that blended dramatic and ballet form into truly innovative and provocative performances.

Some Important Plays and Films

801 • *The Dutchman* (1963)

LeRoi Jones's *The Dutchman* was a landmark play that launched a trend in Black drama toward open discussion of racism in American life. The play tells the story of a white woman who makes advances toward a Black man on a subway and then insults him when he begins to respond. Overcome with anger, Clay, the previously soft-spoken African American, ridicules her and all white people for their racism. Lula, the white woman, kills Clay and dumps his body from the subway car. The powerful play suggested that Blacks who told white America the truth about racism and the anger that it produces would be

eliminated. The play ended the period of oblique criticism in Black American literature and ushered in the more direct social criticism associated with the Black Arts Movement.

802 • *Putney Swope* (1969)

This film imagines what happens to a faltering white advertising agency when Putney Swope, the sole Black member of its board of directors, is accidentally elected in a vote of no confidence for its white members. Instead of kowtowing to the white board members, Swope turns the company into a Black-oriented agency whose "Truth and Soul" advertisement really tells the truth about products. In addition to its remarkably funny mock commercial, *Putney Swope* also parodies typical Black characters familiar to participants in the Black Power movement of the 1960s and suggests that even those included in a skin color revolution will sell out to get ahead in capitalist America.

803 • *Sweet Sweetback's Baadasssss Song* (1971)

Melvin Van Peebles produced and financed this classic African American escape saga using credit cards. Peebles recalled that when Hollywood studios turned down his requests for funding, he simply looked in the mirror one morning and stated: "I think I am a studio, therefore I am a studio." Peebles also starred in the movie, which tells the story of an escaped prisoner whose name derives from his expertise as a sexual partner, an expertise that helps him escape capture as he gains the support of numerous women in the Los Angeles ghetto because of his ability as a lover. Eventually Sweetback runs on foot to Mexico. His rebellion against the police, their brutal relationship to the Black community, and the criminal justice system in Los Angeles expressed a militant Black critique of

American race relations. Its angry, unapologetic, and working-class lead character broke sharply with the saccharine assimilationism of Sidney Poitier's roles in major Hollywood movies. The box-office success of the movie alerted Hollywood that movies marketed to a predominantly African American audience would make money. Ironically *Sweet Sweetback's Baadasssss Song* ushered in the wave of less critical blaxploitation films of the 1970s.

804 • *Shaft* (1971)

Directed by Gordon Parks, Sr., and starring Richard Roundtree, *Shaft* epitomizes the blaxploitation films of the early 1970s. It chronicles the adventures of a Black private detective in New York who is hired by a Harlem underworld boss to find his kidnaped daughter. In the course of finding this daughter, Shaft fights the bad guys, woos the women, and "stands up to the Man" in predictable ways; but the movie is embellished by Parks's cinematic ability to portray his hero with a kind of lush adulation. The story is also interesting for its depiction of the dilemma of the "Black spade detective" who must balance his commitment to law enforcement with his loyalty to the Black community. Though Shaft is fundamentally honest and legal in his dealings, he also refuses to "sing a song to the police, baby!" For all its crass commercialism, *Shaft* is a 1970s study of the "double consciousness" that W. E. B. Du Bois decreed in *Souls of Black Folk* as dogging the careers of all thinking African Americans in the twentieth century.

805 • *Superfly* (1972)

This engaging film by Gordon Parks, Jr., takes up where *Shaft* leaves off, but this time from the other side of the legal fence, by glorifying the lifestyle of Superfly (aka Youngblood Priest), who is a cocaine dealer, flashy dresser, and lover man who develops an inappropriate passion—for freedom from working for the Man and the whole system of living in the underworld. What makes this movie more than the usual formulaic blaxploitation film is the way in which it subtly convinces us that Priest is not typical, that he is, in fact, a highly socially competent, intelligent man who has mastered his environment; and the final act of mastery will be to leave it, despite the fact that everyone, from his partner to the white police official who "owns" drug dealers, wants to thwart if not kill him. The film is also interesting for its nonstereotypical portrayal of Black inner-city life and the interesting, atypical angles that the director films the movie. Finally the movie benefits from one of the best movie scores of the period, written and performed by Curtis Mayfield, formerly of the Impressions. Songs such as "Freddie's Dead," "Pusherman," and "Superfly" were outrageously popular during their time, and are enjoying a comeback in the 1990s as they are sampled by rap musicians and television commercial music writers.

806 • *For Colored Girls Who Have Considered Suicide When the Rainbow Is Enuf* (1976)

Ntozake Shange's bold, Black feminist play stunned audiences throughout the United States with its sustained, raplike critique of destructive Black male attitudes and behaviors toward Black women. Shange's play infused the preachy, monologic drama style of Black Arts Movement theater with Black women's anger at the failure of Black men to live up to the rhetoric of Black manhood. By portraying the pain of hurt, tricked, and disillusioned Black women in America, Shange struck a chord with the Black feminist audience searching for its

Poster for play at Booth Theater, 1976. Prints and Photographs Division, Library of Congress. Used by permission of Paul Davis

voice in the mid-1970s. This play's sharp articulation of women's frustrations has kept it alive in the repertory of little theater and college theater groups.

807 • *Roots* (1977)

When Alex Haley translated his fictionalized reconstruction of his family history from West Africa to North America into a television mini-series shown on eight consecutive nights in 1977, he transformed American television as well as America's knowledge and perspective on American slavery. The television series earned the highest ratings of any network program in history as millions of Americans, including Blacks, learned about the evils of slavery for the first time. Dramatic acting by Lou Gossett, Oprah Winfrey, Ruby Dee, Chuck Connors, and many others transformed Haley's powerfully written personal story into an epic narrative of American history, as it brought to a popular audience what historians and other scholars had been writing about the history of slavery for years. Moreover, Haley's story on the little screen became a profoundly American story as it documented the Black family's struggle toward freedom and dignity over generations, while maintaining the tenuous but inspiring folk traditions brought from Africa.

Religion

808 • Nation of Islam

The modern Nation of Islam emerged from the earlier movement of Noble Drew Ali, who founded the Moorish-American Science Temple. When Ali died in 1929, W. D. Fard assumed leadership of the movement, but was replaced, in 1933, by Elijah Muhammad, who was imprisoned in 1942 for refusing to serve in the Army during World War II for his religious beliefs. After his time in jail, during which he recruited many jailed Blacks to the movement, Muhammad organized fifty temples by 1959 and had over one thousand members in his Chicago Temple by 1965. Muhammad restricted membership to nonwhites and rejected the term "Negroes," preferring to call Blacks Muslims (rather than Moslems) in order to emphasize their special religious status as a separate chosen people, whose mission was to redeem the Black nation. Muhammad taught that an apocalypse would occur in the future in which Allah would destroy the United States for its sins against Black people and make nonwhite peoples the sole rulers of the world. While awaiting this apocalypse, Blacks should separate socially and politically from whites, who would never accept Blacks on equal terms, live in autonomous communities, control the institutions in those communities, and live a virtuous Muslim lifestyle. Muhammad sought to create a new positive profile for Blacks by requiring them to be clean cut, businesslike, well dressed, and socially conservative, while confidently articulating a radical critique of white people as permanently racist. From the 1950s onward, Muslims were known for selling a newspaper, *Muhammad Speaks,* and bean pies on the corners of urban ghettos dressed in suits, with white shirts, bow ties, and short haircuts. The Nation became famous in the United States during the 1950s and 1960s, largely because of hostile media coverage and the articulate spokesperson Malcolm X. After Malcolm X's assasination in 1965 and the death of Elijah Muhammad in 1975, Elijah's son, Imam Warith Deen Muhammad, took over the organization, lifted its ban on white membership, and moved it closer to being a traditional Islamic organization. But then Louis Farrakhan revived the older Elijah Muhammad philosophy in a splinter group that has come to be known as the Nation of Islam in the 1990s. Although criticized for his attacks on Jews as "bloodsuckers" and Judaism as a "gutter religion," Farrakhan has gained new respectability with his October 1995 "Million Man March" on Washington, D.C., to protest the demonization of Black men in late twentieth-century America.

809 • Black Theology

Dated usually from the publication of James Cone's seminal books, *Black Theology and Black Power* (1969) and *A Black Theology of Liberation* (1970), a Black theology movement emerged that interpreted Christianity as a theology of liberation for the Black community. Occurring before the formal emergence of the Latin American liberation theology movement, the Black Theology Movement built upon the momentum of the Black Social Gospel Movement, but drew its immediate inspiration from the Black Power Movement of the late 1960s and the tradition of urban Black ministers such as Adam Clayton Powell, Jr., Albert B. Cleage, Nathan Wright, and Ben Chavis who interpreted the urban riots of the 1960s as a stage in the Black revolution. Abandoning the Martin Luther King "turn the other cheek" tradition of Christian social struggle, Cone, C. Eric Lincoln, Leon Watts, and Bill Jones (known for his provocatively titled book, *Is God a White Racist?*) critiqued Christian theology from the perspective of the Black revolutionary movement, interpreted the Bible in terms of the history of the Black community, and argued that a Black theology was necessary because white American Christian theology defended the racial status quo and ignored the Black freedom struggle. After its institutional arm, the National Committee of Black Churchmen, was founded in 1969, the Black Theology Movement spread among young Black ministers and seminarians during the 1970s. But by the beginning of the 1980s, the movement was in decline, in part because of a sustained counterattack against radical Black theology in mainstream American religious organizations and the rise of conservative televangelists, many of whom, like Jerry Falwell and Jim and Tammy Baker, successfully wooed Black worshipers away from Black radicalism with an appeal to family values and interracial reconciliation through Christian fellowship. Nevertheless, the movement spawned several spin-offs in the late 1970s and early 1980s, including a Black womanist theology and an alliance between African Americans and Third World theologians in the World Council of Churches' Commissions on Faith and Order.

810 • Kwanzaa

Kwanzaa is a holiday celebrated from December 26 through January 1 that was initiated in 1966 by Maulama Karenga, now a professor of African American studies, who founded US, a sixties paramilitary cultural nationalist organization. The word "Kwanzaa" means "first fruits" in Swahili and reflected Karenga's belief that African Americans needed a holiday of their own that celebrated what he held as core African values. On each day of Kwanzaa, by eating certain foods, telling stories, and taking part in collective activities, celebrants affirm their commitment to the following values: *umoja* (unity), *kujichangulia* (self-determination), *ujima* (collective work and responsibility), *ujamma* (cooperative economics), *nia* (purpose), *kuumba* (creativity), and *imani* (faith). Although relatively ignored by the masses of African Americans when first proposed, Kwanzaa has become quite popular in the 1990s, and Kwanzaa cards, candles, and other supporting paraphernalia are now commercially available.

AFRICAN AMERICAN RENAISSANCE, 1981–95

Movements, Organizations, and Celebrations

811 • The Second African American Renaissance

The second African American Renaissance began in the early 1980s, largely due to an outpouring of literature, plays, and belles lettres by Black women writers—Toni Morrison, Alice Walker, Toni Cade Bambara, Ntozaka Shange, Terry McMillan, bell hooks, and others—who wrote about racism, sexism, and the Black women's experience with energy, honesty, and imagination not seen before. Their works appear precisely at the time when the production of literature by Black male writers seemed in decline and interest in Black Studies generally seemed to wane. Because these women writers discussed sexism and feminism through Black women's eyes, their works found a white women readership that boosted sales and took some to the top of the best-seller lists. Indeed, in 1993, two African American women garnered recognition never before bestowed on any African American when Toni Morrison became the first African American to win the Nobel Prize for literature and Maya Angelou became the first Black writer to read a poem during a presidential inauguration.

Four other developments have helped usher in the latest renaissance. First, as in the Harlem Renaissance, a sense of the importance of the African past emerged in the 1980s, reflected in the popularity of books such as Martin Bernal's

Black Athena (1987), which documented the influence of Africa on early Western civilization, and in consumer culture items such as videotapes, clothes, educational programs, and paraphernalia that celebrated Africa. Second, an increase in the educated Black middle class during the 1970s and 1980s created a reading and theatergoing audience for books and plays by such authors as Terry McMillan and August Wilson that had been absent, largely, during the first renaissance. Third, and in almost diametrical opposition to the first factor, there emerged in the late 1980s and early 1990s a new freedom among the critical mass of African American writers and artists to create without ideological concerns as their main motivation.

The emergence of figures like Rita Dove, who was the first African American chosen poet laureate of the United States in 1993 on the basis of largely nonracial poetry is a case in point. Fourth, in the early 1990s, a diasporic consciousness that African Americans are part of a worldwide dispersion of African peoples fueled interconnections and "samplings" from the Caribbean and Europe. That development has been evidenced by the increased popularity of reggae music—especially reggae rap artists— in America and the popularity of writings by cultural historian Paul Gilroy that assert African Americans are part of a larger, "Atlantic community." Together, these diverse forces have led to the production of more works of quality than were produced during the first renaissance of the 1920s.

812 • Afrocentricity

Afrocentricity, or Afrocentrism, is a philosophy of culture that revaluates American and world history by looking at it from an African perspective. Afrocentrism emerged in the 1970s in Black Studies programs as a way to challenge Eurocentric values and perspectives in American educational and cultural institutions and to argue that contemporary Black American values, behaviors, and aspirations are only understandable when they are traced back to their African roots. Afrocentrists reject the notion that America can ever be a color-blind society and suggest that successful assimilation into American society by Blacks requires them to abandon their African identity. Afrocentrists see all Black people around the globe as one people and assert that the African past before European contact was a golden age that was preferable to the present. Afrocentrism emerged as a belief system in the early 1970s as professors and students in Black Studies departments searched for a new paradigm to replace outdated notions that Black Studies curricula were needed simply to fill in gaps in Eurocentric college courses or to critique systemic institutional racism in America. Just as feminists in Women's Studies began to demand to look at American history from the perspective of gender, Afrocentrists, such as Molafi Kete Asante, professor at Temple University and author of *Afrocentricity* (1980), argued that retelling the history of America and the world from an African viewpoint would transform our way of understanding history. Such a reinterpretation was already occurring in the work of such scholars as Robert Ferris Thompson, Charles Joyner, Vincent Franklin, Ben Johannon, Janheinz Jahn, Vincent Harding, and many others. Asante's movement met strong resistance in the academic community, but won acceptance in numerous Black Studies programs and among secondary and primary school teachers who saw it as a way to teach African American children and adults a history they could be proud of. With its focus on African kingship and empires, particularly the glorious days of the Egyptian empire, Afrocentric courses gained popularity in the late 1980s. It also spawned a huge commercial industry that produced kente cloth hats, necklaces with African medallions, African beads, dresses, and walking sticks that promoted a positive identification with Africa. Afrocentricity was also helped by its adoption by rap groups in the late 1980s, whose videos and other promotional materials evidenced an African consciousness.

Some Important Books

813 • *The Color Purple* (1982)

Alice Walker borrowed from the nineteenth-century tradition of women's confidential letter writing to construct a powerful novel of two Black women's psychic bonding in the face of male physical and psychological abuse. The novel's innovative form and the power of its focus on gender rather than racial conflict garnered its author a Pulitzer Prize in fiction and instant fame as the woman novelist who temporarily supplanted Toni Morrison's position as the top African American woman novelist writing in contemporary America. The issue of the novel's representation of Black male figures became the focus of a national debate when Steven Spielberg turned Alice Walker's novel in 1985 into a hit movie and made the careers of such new actors as Whoopi Goldberg, Oprah Winfrey, and Danny Glover.

814 • *Ain't I a Woman: Black Women and Feminism* (1981)

In her landmark study of sexism, African American women, and feminism, bell hooks provides a trenchant analysis of the history of sexist treatment of African American women from the beginnings of African enslavement to the contemporary feminist movement. hooks argues that even in West Africa, Black women were oppressed by sexism, and that this oppression was observed and appropriated by white enslavers who conceptualized that African women could be both agricultural laborers and sexual objects in colonial America. Even more, hooks critiques those historians and sociologists who have described Black women's rape by white men as

primarily a feature of slavery, who have perpetuated the myth of Black matriarchal dominance of Black males, and who have failed to delineate the ways in which Black men have participated in and perpetuated oppression of Black women. She provides a theoretical discussion of the relationship between racism and sexism, and the racism of the contemporary feminist movement.

Alice Walker, 1982. National Archives

815 • *Beloved* (1987)

While supervising the publication of *The Black Book* (1974) as an editor at Random House, Toni Morrison came across the story of an enslaved woman who ran away from slavery and then kept slave hunters from recapturing her two children by killing them. That story lodged in Morrison's mind and later emerged as the focal point for her *Beloved,* a novel about slavery and the persistence of its memory in African American women's lives. It is her most extraordinary novel to date. *Beloved* weaves together realistic detail and dreamlike stream-of-consciousness writing that explores the psychological ramifications of enslavement for Black women. In the process, Morrison shows how transfiguring was the struggle of Black women to achieve a sense of dignity in the face of slavery and how even resistance to slavery's oppression often warped those who resisted. The novel engages such universal questions as whether the enslaved life is worth living and the moral question of infanticide, seen through the eyes and heard through the ears of a community aghast at one woman's protest against the system of slavery. By switching point of view, Morrison is able to voice the anger, sympathy, horror, and inhumanity felt by the entire community as a witness to slavery's ultimate inhumanity—its infection of the humanity of the enslaved. *Beloved* brings to light how the memory of slavery, preserved in African American myth and folkore, remains a powerful way of understanding the tortured context of African American experience.

816 • *The Schomburg Library of Nineteenth-Century Black Women Writers* (1988)

Oxford University and Schomburg Library's republication of thirty books in a single edition brought the writings of nineteenth-century Black women writers to an entirely new generation of readers and signaled that African American women writers had come of age. General editor Henry Louis Gates, Jr., blended well-known works by Phillis Wheatley, Harriet Jacobs, and Anna J. Cooper with lesser known writings by Alice Dunbar-Nelson, Elizabeth Keckley, and Pauline Hopkins that balanced efforts in fiction, poetry, autobiography, and social criticism by Black women. Numerous university libraries purchased the entire set and provided a new generation of students and general readers with access to the Black women's literary voice of the nineteenth century. Moreover, the republication of these classics during a period in the 1980s when contemporary Black women writing was flowering signaled that indeed an African American women's renaissance had emerged toward the end of the twentieth century that was as self-conscious and confident of its literary origins as the predominantly male Harlem Renaissance of the early twentieth century.

817 • *Neon Vernacular* (1993)

Yusef Komunyakaa's *Neon Vernacular,* a collection of new and selected poems from other publications, won the Pulitzer Prize for poetry in 1994. The new poems in *Neon Vernacular* continue his autobiographical exploration of years spent in Bogalusa, Louisiana, and thus these poems convey a powerful sense of place and tragedy for a young Black man growing up in the South. But all of Komunyakaa's poems are distinguished for the remarkable physical and emotional detail that they convey. Komunyakaa works as a collagist who layers jazz references, segregationist hypocrises, religious allegories, and a strong, politicized voice into compositions such as "February in Sydney":

Dexter Gordon's tenor sax
plays "April in Paris"
inside my head all the way back
on the bus from Double Bay.

I emerge from the dark theatre,
passing a woman who grabs her red
purse
& hugs it to her like a heart attack.

A loneliness
lingers like a silver needle
under my black skin,
as I try to feel how it is
to scream for help through a horn.

Art

818 • Richard Hunt (b. 1935)

Richard Hunt is one of the nation's prolific and sought-after sculptors. In fact, because Hunt produces mainly large, abstract metal sculptures, most who see his provocative public installations probably do not realize that he is African American. Nevertheless, as a young student at the Art Institute of Chicago, Hunt was introduced to and influenced by the work of fellow sculptor Richmond Barthe. Something of Barthe's elongation of form and rich, vibrant verticality can be seen in Hunt's work, not only his small sculpture but his monumental metal sculptures. There is a rhythm and vitality to Hunt's sculptures that is organic and powerful. Some of his more recent work, such as the projected installation *Middle Passage,* promises an even more strongly narrative response to African American history.

819 • Martha Jackson-Jarvis (b. 1952)

Martha Jackson-Jarvis is a remarkably cre-

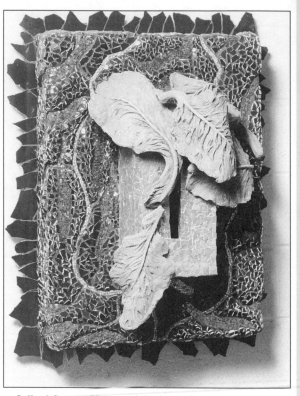

Collard Greens. Photograph by Jarvis Grant. Courtesy of Martha Jackson-Jarvis

ative sculptor who uses clay to create complex, evocative, and rhythmic installations. Beginning as a child with a love for fashioning small clay sculptures, Jackson-Jarvis has continually refined and expanded her control of this medium until she can populate entire galleries with her thematically interesting objects. With pieces on walls as well as floors, she creates a synergy among the objects that makes the installation rooms into vibrant environments. *The Gathering,* installed at the University of Delaware in 1988, was one of her most heralded early works. More recently, Jackson-Jarvis has used her clay sculptures to model one of African American culture's favorite foodstuffs in *Collard Greens,* a provocative set of sculptures that affirm the need of all people to sustain a healthy relationship with our agricultural heritage and ecological future.

820 • Renee Stout (b. 1958)

Renee Stout is one of those contemporary African American artists who seek in their work and the work of West African artists a means to address issues of spirituality in their lives. After obtaining a B.F.A. from Carnegie Mellon University in 1980, Stout's first shift in focus came on a six-month artist-in-residence at Northeastern University in 1984–85, when she shifted from painting to sculpture. She also moved more self-consciously into the study of West African art and culture, especially the *vodun* religion, and began to create box forms and assemblages out of found objects, old photographs, and Kongo spirit-script. An excellent example of this type of sculpture is *Instructions and Provisions: Wake Me Up on Judgment Day* (1987), a mixed-media box containing the instructions and provisions needed for someone to pass through the afterlife. Much of her work seems driven by the desire to bridge the division between life and death, and find in West African ancestral symbols the power to mobilize the self in this world. That project is epitomized in *Fetish #2,* Stout's mixed-media body sculpture. Here the artist cast her own body in plaster, painted the mold with black paint, and added medicine bags, a medicine pouch, a stamp from Niger, a picture of a young girl, dried flowers, cowrie shells for eyes, and monkey hair for the headdress. In effect, Stout has created a full-size West African *nkisi* figure out of her own body that challenges Western conceptions of the female nude and creates instead a powerful symbol of African American womanhood.

821 • David Hammons (b. 1943)

Born in Springfield, Illinois, Hammons began his career as an innovator who utilized the monoprint or body print to create a series of haunting images of African Americans, such as *Injustice Case* (1970). But in the 1980s Hammons expanded into the use of found objects to fashion artwork that challenged prevailing notions of race. His *How Ya Like Me Now?* (1989), a sixteen-foot-high portrait of Jesse Jackson as a white man, was designed to question whether Jesse Jackson would have been an acceptable 1988 presidential candidate if he had been white. But when the portrait was installed over a Metro subway stop in Washington, D.C., as part of an exhibition, "The Blues Aesthetic," created by curator Richard Powell for the Washington Project for the Arts, the portrait was torn down by a group of Black men who believed it was an insult to Jackson and the race. Such provocative, double-meaning art is the specialty of Hammons, who sees the purpose of art to provoke, not to enshrine positive Black images. He has received a MacArthur Foundation Fellowship, twice been awarded National Endowment for the Arts fellowships, and has been a fellow at the American Academy in Rome.

822 • Lorna Simpson (b. 1960)

This multimedia artist has created installations that challenge African Americans as well as European Americans to consider the ways in which control is exercised over African Americans in the American past and the present. In *Self-Possession* (1992), Simpson uses a photograph of a Black woman's body to challenge the structures of domination of Black women's bodies in modern American culture. In *Places with a Past* (1991), Simpson works with an actress, appropriates historical artifacts, and utilizes audiotapes to symbolize the effects of the slave trade as it operated in eighteenth- and nineteenth-century South Carolina. Simpson is con-

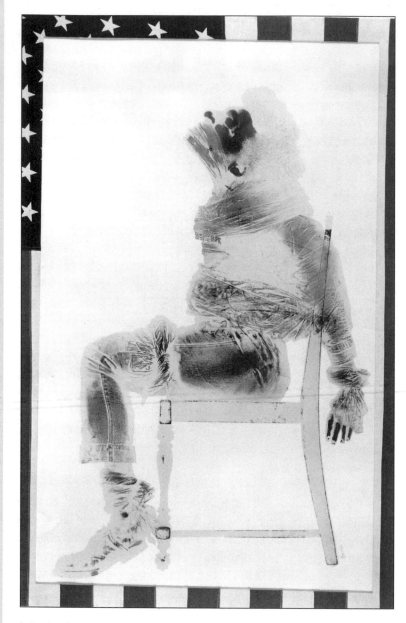

Injustice Case, David Hammons (after Bobby Seale Chicago riot trial in 1968), 1970. Los Angeles County Museum of Art. Museum Purchase Fund

agency in a world of continuing alienation. In her much discussed installation *Wigs*, Simpson challenges us to rethink how notions of what is a proper hairstyle for women are contested by Black women today. She has received numerous honors in her career, perhaps the most important being the first African American woman artist to represent the United States at Venice Biennale.

Music and Dance

823 • Wynton Marsalis (b. 1961)

Wynton Marsalis, whose younger brother, Branford, plays the saxophone, is a trumpeter who has led the neoclassical movement in jazz that has done much to make jazz acceptable again to middle-class audiences in the 1980s and 1990s. Born in New Orleans, Marsalis brought back the sound of the New Orleans trumpeter, made famous earlier by King Oliver and Louis Armstrong, and sought to replace the fusion jazz sound of Miles Davis, his nemesis. Marsalis studied both jazz and classical music, performed both publicly while still a young man in

cerned with the ways in which Western culture has objectified both women and African Americans, and her installations force us to face those forces and thereby restore to us a sense of

New Orleans, and attended the Berkshire Music Center at Tanglewood (Massachusetts) and the Juilliard School of Music in New York. He played with Art Blakey, Herbie Hancock, Ron Carter, and Tony Williams in the 1980s before forming his own quintet in 1982 with Kenny Kirkland, Charles Fambourgh, Jeff Watts, and Branford Marsalis. Then, in 1984, he won Grammys in both jazz and classical music recording categories, becoming the first musician ever to do so. Marsalis's trumpet playing has been distinguished for its speed, brilliance, and sophistication, while his best albums, with the exception of the stunning *Black Codes (from the Underground)* (1985), have been reinterpretations of jazz classics. In 1995 he authored a book about jazz, *Sweet Sing Blues on the Road.*

824 • Michael Jackson (b. 1958)

Michael Jackson was a mere eleven years old when the Jackson 5 (Tito, Jermaine, Marlon, Jackie, and Michael Jackson) signed with Motown Records and had its first single, "I Want You Back." As the Jackson 5 developed into stars in the 1970s, Michael matured from a child dancing attraction into the lead singer and then star of what became by 1975 America's hottest teenage singing group. That year the Jacksons (as they would later be called) left Motown to sign with Epic Records, in part so that they could begin writing and singing their own material. Michael Jackson's solo career blossomed under the new regime: after his first hit, "Got to Be There" (1971), rose to number five on the *Billboard* charts, Michael followed with the number one hit "Ben" (1972), the lead song on the sound track of the movie that chronicled the exploits of a heroic rat. Michael then teamed with talented composer and arranger Quincy Jones to produce two stunning albums, *Off the Wall* (1979) and *Thriller* (1982),

which broke industry records for sales and number of singles (four and six respectively) to become number one from a single album (both of which were also number one). Perhaps as important, *Off the Wall* and *Thriller* were cultural successes: both albums won the approval of white audiences, young and old, garnered praise from pop music critics, and yet retained strong followings among the urban, Black audience. Subsequent albums, *Bad* (1987) and *Dangerous* (1991), were not as popular or critically successful. Among Michael Jackson's other accomplishments are that he was the first to develop the music video format, now a staple with rap and pop artists, and that he is a superb popular dancer whose performances have been praised by such dance experts as Bob Fosse and Fred Astaire. Jackson's decline in music popularity paralleled his increasingly controversial personal life, which included lightening of his skin color and alteration of his face through plastic surgery, a child sex abuse suit lodged against him and settled out of court, and his marriage in 1994 to Lisa Marie Presley, the daughter of Elvis Presley.

825 • Rap Music

Rap was the most influential and controversial Black music form of the 1980s and remains a powerful expression of Black youth culture in the 1990s. Rap music is the rhyming storytelling by one or more speakers over a musical selection often borrowed or "sampled" from another artist. Such rapping has a long pedigree in African American, Caribbean, and African culture, such as the familiar African American "dozens" (rhyming verbal jousts), or the less familiar Jamaican art of "toasting," perhaps introduced to the United States by the DJ Kool Herc, who moved from Jamaica to the West Bronx in New York in 1967. As a musical form, rap began

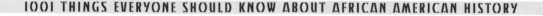

in the 1950s with the "scat" singing of such be-bop jazz groups as Lambert, Hendricks, and Ross and the disc jockey innovation of "Jocko," a fifties "emcee," who used the breaks between songs he played over the radio to deliver rhyming ditties to his listening audience. In the 1960s a kind of rap music could be heard in the Last Poets and Gil Scott-Heron; but it was not until the 1970s that a core group of rapping DJs emerged in New York who also cut between various records to create new songs out of parts of records. At the same time, Black youth street rappers in New York began to narrate stories of love, violence, and betrayal in rhyme over music played on huge cassette players, or "ghetto blasters." Then, in 1979, this art form burst onto radio and the nation when the first rap record hit, "Rapper's Delight," by the Sugar Hill Gang, was released and rose to number forty-one on the disco chart, and coincided with the intro-duction of the term "hip-hop" to characterize the ability to jump between catchy jingles. Af-terward successive waves of rap artists swept American listening audiences, such as Grand-master Flash, Kurtis Blow, Afrika Bambaataa, and the Fatback Band of the "Old School" in the early 1980s, Run D.M.C., LL Cool J, Public En-emy, and Doug E. Fresh of the "New School" of the mid-1980s, and KRS-ONE, Heavy D, Big Daddy Kane, Queen Latifah, and 2 Live Crew of the "Newer New School," and so on. Rap music became controversial because of its connection with the street culture of Black America during a period of rising racial retrenchment and its reflection of Black youth anger in political, crit-ical, and sometimes offensive lyrics. At the same time, rap music has had a tremendous in-fluence on mainstream white American culture, from dress and car styles—the Jeep became an urban vehicle of choice because it was a favorite of rap artists— to television, where such shows

as *The Fresh Prince of Bel-Air* and *Living Single* have been very popular.

826 • Grandmaster Flash

Grandmaster Flash, originally named Joseph Sadler, originated in 1974 the disc jockey tech-nique of "scratching"—moving a record back and forth underneath a needle to produce a rhythmic, jarring sound that has become a sta-ple sound of rap records. His album *The Adven-tures of Grandmaster Flash on the Wheels of Steel* (1981) exhibited this technique for the first time. Flash is also credited for the innova-tion of hooking two turntables up to the same set of speakers and, by putting different records on the turntables, switching quickly from one to the other to mix musical elements from both records into a third, original composition. Such a technique made the disc jockey into a creative musician, whose ability to switch quickly be-tween records required skill and concentration. As Flash became more adept at this technique in the 1970s, he realized that he could not "com-pose" at the turntable as creatively as he wanted and also rap. He then recorded his first rap song using a group of rappers, the Furious Faive, out front to carry the rap, while he man-aged the music. The group received little airplay on radio stations, fueling the view among rap-pers that the "true" rappers are underground artists who are "dissed" by the commercial ra-dio industry.

827 • Queen Latifah (b. 1970)

Queen Latifah (Dana Owens) is an example of how rap music has created its own opposi-tions: she achieved prominence in the late 1980s as both a critic of male dominance and the glorification of conspicuous consumption that was a hallmark of the early 1980s when rappers talked about their material possessions, wore gold chains and gold tooth caps, and drove expensive cars. Reared in East Orange, New Jersey, she broke into the rap scene in 1989 with her first album, *All Hail the Queen,* a powerful statement of both Afrocentrism and female self-respect. Often photographed wearing her Nefertiti headdress, the Queen, as she styles herself, goes further, and has created an identity of female authority to contest the rise of anti-women lyrics in rap music of the late 1980s and early 1990s. Her second album, *Nature of a Sistah* (1991), contains several cuts that state, unequivocally, that the Queen has "had it up to here" with both commercialism in rap and anti-women lyrics and violence. But Queen Latifah is known more today as the star of the television series *Living Single,* on which she plays, in keeping with the Afrocentric economic message, the owner of a Black advertising firm. Reputedly Queen Latifah manages her own economic empire, perhaps realizing better than any other current rap artist the ideology of economic self-sufficiency implicit in both Black feminism and Afrocentrism.

828 • Anthony Davis (b. 1951)

In 1985 Anthony Davis composed an opera, *X: The Life and Times of Malcolm X,* that is a provocative fusion of classical, jazz, and gospel music styles around the theme of the African American hero Malcolm X. Davis, a trained classical pianist, had composed two smaller works—"Hemispheres" (a work in five parts composed for Molissa Fenley's theatrical dance *Hemispheres*) (1983) and "The Ghost Factory" (1984), a violin concerto—before attempting the much larger, three-part opera. The opera form allows Davis to use his romantic music to explore the life of an exemplary African American. By grounding his music in such a narrative, Davis can evoke jazz, gospel, and other African American musical styles within a basically classical operatic format. In chanted songs like "Africa's Time Has Come," Davis choruses champion ideals that were dear to Malcolm X. The entire piece has the feeling of a requiem to a fallen hero. When it was performed by the New York City Opera in 1986, it helped to sustain the growing infatuation with Malcolm X as a source of creative commentary on what it means to be Black in America. Since *X,* Davis has produced *Lost Moonas Sisters for Soprano, Violin, Keyboards, Marimba & Vibraphone* (1990) for the "Urban Diva" and "Emergency Music" series. His *X* was performed by William Henry Curry, Pisteme & Orchestra of St. Luke's and is recorded.

829 • Garth Fagan (b. 1940)

Born in Jamaica, Garth Fagan developed as a dancer in that Caribbean island. He got his start in dance with the Ivy Baxter Company. Upon coming to New York, Fagan studied with Martha Graham, among others. In 1970 he began the Bucket Dance Company in upstate New York, to

Garth Fagan. Photograph by Ron Wu. Courtesy of Garth Fagan Dance

tap urban African American talent. The company has continued to perform compositions choreographed by Garth Fagan and has toured nationally. Working within the tradition of Pearl Primus, Fagan has evolved an abstract but socially relevant choreography. His most important work to date is his critically acclaimed modern ballet *Griot New York*, a sensual full-evening tribute to the energy and frustrations of the modern city that opened at the Brooklyn Academy of Music in 1991 and toured several cities. Wynton Marsalis composed the music, and Martin Puryear sculpted the sets on this collaborative production.

830 • Bill T. Jones (b. 1952)

Bill Jones has emerged as the most inventive modern dance choreographer of the 1990s. Unlike Garth Fagan, Jones has never seen himself as a Black dancer or choreographer. Early in his career, Jones developed an abstract and provocative choreography that was performed by a company started by Jones and Arnie Zane. The most famous of these is *Fever Swamp* (1983), which was also performed by the Alvin Ailey company. After being diagnosed as HIV positive in 1985, and the death of Zane from AIDS in 1988, Jones produced numerous compositions, not only for his own company but also for the Berlin Opera Ballet. Jones has also explored new media in adapting dance to the postmodern aesthetics of the late twentieth century. His multimedia dance composition *Last Supper at Uncle Tom's Cabin/The Promised Land* is a fifty-person extravaganza that begins by interpreting *Uncle Tom's Cabin* and ends with a dialogue between Jones and a clergyman on whether AIDS is a heaven-sent punishment. Rather than seeing himself as working within the Alvin Ailey or Katherine Dunham tradition, Jones seeks to sample all cultural forms to cre-

ate a more universalist choreography. His company, for example, contains more non-Black dancers than African American.

Some Important Plays and Films

831 • *A Soldier's Story* (1981)

This award-winning play narrated the internal conflicts in a Black army unit training in the South during World War II. As such, it documented the pathological and psychological ramifications of racism for African American soldiers, particularly the diversity of social strategies among Black males during segregation for dealing with racism. Written by Charles Fuller, *A Soldier's Story* opened at the Negro Ensemble Company and starred Adoph Caesar, Charles Brown, and Denzel Washington.

832 • *Purple Rain* (1984)

Prince's thinly autobiographical film about an obsessively self-involved rock bandleader and his dysfunctional family life broke new ground in African American rock cinematography. By probing the psychological roots of the lead character's physical abuse of his girlfriend, his psychological abuse of his band members, and his tense relationships with a frustrated Black father and a victimized white mother, Prince's maiden voyage as a film actor engaged many of the issues that still plague the lives of talented media heroes. Confronting such issues as wife abuse, egocentricity, and the sexual politics of success in the commercial world of rock club entertainment, *Purple Rain* suggested that a healing catharsis was possible for those willing to confront the devils in their pasts. The movie was distinguished by its sound track, which was not only one of Prince's best albums but won an Academy Award for best sound track of the year.

833 • *She's Gotta Have It* (1986)

Spike Lee's *She's Gotta Have It* was more than a great film about Black relationships in the 1980s. It also inaugurated the modern era of movies directed by African Americans that were successful at the box office. Produced for $175,000 over twelve days of filming, *She's Gotta Have It* is the story of sexual competition among three Black males—a completely self-involved pretty boy, a frustrated, violent middle-class guy, and a ghetto bicycle homeboy played by Spike Lee—for the love (and sexual fidelity) of one woman, Nola Darling. Because the woman refuses to choose a monogamy that her suitors insist upon, the movie reverses the typical pattern of noncommittal men versus commitment-oriented women; but it also goes further and critiques all of the available options confronting Nola Darling, whose character is far more complex, creative, and likable than any of the males she is pressured to choose. The film introduces several formal cinematic innovations in the way that it is shot in tight close-ups by Ernest Dickerson in gritty black and white. What Lee achieves is a remarkably funny examination of the foibles of sex and love among seemingly overly serious Black people whose characters seem more real than the overly stereotyped and conventionalized representations of Black people coming from mainstream Hollywood in the 1980s.

834 • *Do the Right Thing* (1989)

Spike Lee's mosaic of racial and generational conflict in Brooklyn is a bold challenge to the prevailing genre of race conflict films produced by Hollywood. With outstanding performances by Ossie Davis, Danny Oryeda, and Rosie Perez, the movie shows the depth of interracial attraction in America, the ways in which whites worship Black stars while despising Black people, and the class nature of racial conflict in America. Lee's portrait of the Brooklyn ghetto fused hot sexual scenes, poignant confrontations between the elders and respectless youth of the Black community, and the explosiveness of racial confrontations across class lines. *Do the Right Thing* was also a commercial success as well as extremely popular with Black audiences. The movie grossed over $27 million at the box office, received the accolades of reviewers, and snagged an Oscar nomination for best screenplay.

835 • *The Piano Lesson* (1990)

August Wilson's second Pulitzer Prize–winning play (the first was *Fences,* 1987) is a tight family drama of conflict between a brother and sister over a piano; but it is also conflict over what price African Americans should pay for success, especially if that price is the sacrifice of African American heritage. Set in the Hill neighborhood of Pittsburgh, where Wilson grew up, the drama unfolds in a family's living room after a brother returns home with a not-so-hidden agenda—to sell the family heirloom, a piano with African-inspired carvings that record the family's history, which he co-owns with his sister. He wants to sell the piano, which will bring a good price, in order to buy some land and achieve his economic freedom. But his sister refuses to sell the piano, and the subsequent family argument revolves around whether the piano, which represents the family's past, ought to be sold to create a viable future. What distinguishes August Wilson's plays is not so much their plots, but the powerful poetical language with which his characters argue their case and struggle with their personal demons. After the hot, fast-paced dialogue reaches a peak in which the resolution of the dispute seems to require bloodshed, a spiritual presence, representing the family spirit, makes itself known to the family and resolves the dilemma. Directed by Lloyd Richards, the play opened on Broadway in 1990 with Charles Dutton playing the lead; it was adapted to television (again with Dutton in the lead) and broadcast on CBS on February 5, 1995.

836 • *Boyz N the Hood* (1991)

John Singleton's premier movie about the violence of black urban life in Los Angeles opened to more theater violence than any other movie in American history. It also grossed $55 million and starred Ice Cube, a rapper, in one of its lead roles. The film narrates the struggle of a young urban Black male to be a success, despite growing up in one of the most dangerous neighborhoods in America. With the support of a single-parent father, who instills a dignity and a sense of self-worth in his son, the young man is a success. He is nevertheless constrained by the social dislocation and anomie of his surroundings.

837 • *Twilight: Los Angeles, 1992* (1993–94)

Playwright and performer Anna Deavere Smith's one-woman theater performance *Twilight: Los Angeles, 1992,* which she created, wrote, and performed, is a provocative engagement of the many issues surrounding the Rodney King rebellion. Commissioned by Gordon Davidson of Los Angeles' Mark Taper Forum, Smith conducted interviews with over two hundred people, including African Americans, Koreans, and whites, who were directly or indirectly involved with the beating, the case, or the rioting. She then edited those remarks and skillfully wove them into a stage performance that consists solely of the interviewee's remarks. With numerous costume changes, Smith mimics those interviewed and effectively suggests their personalities without simply duplicating them. The result is a dramatic cross section of America's mind on race. Although the immediate focus is the Los Angeles conflict, Smith's actual goal is to dredge up and expose the terrors, pains, hurts, and angers that fuel contemporary American racial divisiveness. Through her performance, she offers audiences an avenue of catharsis through which they can see themselves and others engaged in the often futile struggle to make America work for them and their ethnic group. *Twilight: Los Angeles, 1992* originally premiered on May 23, 1993, at the Center Theater Group/Mark Taper Forum in Los Angeles, produced by Gordon Davidson, and then opened at the New York Public Theater in March 1994, directed by George C. Wolfe. *Twilight: Los Angeles, 1992* is part of a ten-year-long series of performances on real events called *On the Road: A Search for American Character.* Although the performance could only represent twenty-five of those interviewed, the book script, *Twilight: Los Angeles, 1992: On the Road: A Search for American Character* (1994), by Anna Deavere Smith, contains all of the interviews. Some of those interviewed in the book include Angela King, Rodney's aunt, a Los Angeles Police Department expert on "use of force," a juror in the Simi Valley trial, and Reginald Denny, the white truck driver dragged from his truck and beaten during the rioting.

838 • *Sankofa* (1992)

The movie *Sankofa* is an independently produced and distributed story about a Black fashion model who visits Elmina, the island fortress built by the Portuguese to house Africans before sending them into the Middle Passage. On this visit, this woman, who is considerably lacking in Black consciousness, is suddenly transported back into history to become her ancestor who was shipped from this island into slavery in the sugar islands of the Caribbean. The story is captivating for its frank portrayal of the cruelty and oppression of slavery, the complexity of social relationships between house and field slaves, and the resistance of Africans to the masters.

Filmmaker Haile Gerima, a Howard University professor, states that he produced the film without studio support because Hollywood would not approve the script with such frank criticism of the slave institution. Gerima was also locked out of distribution networks, but rented a Washington, D.C., theater to put on the film. The strategy succeeded: the film garnered critical acclaim and has reaped a profit for the filmmaker, who made the film for $1 million.

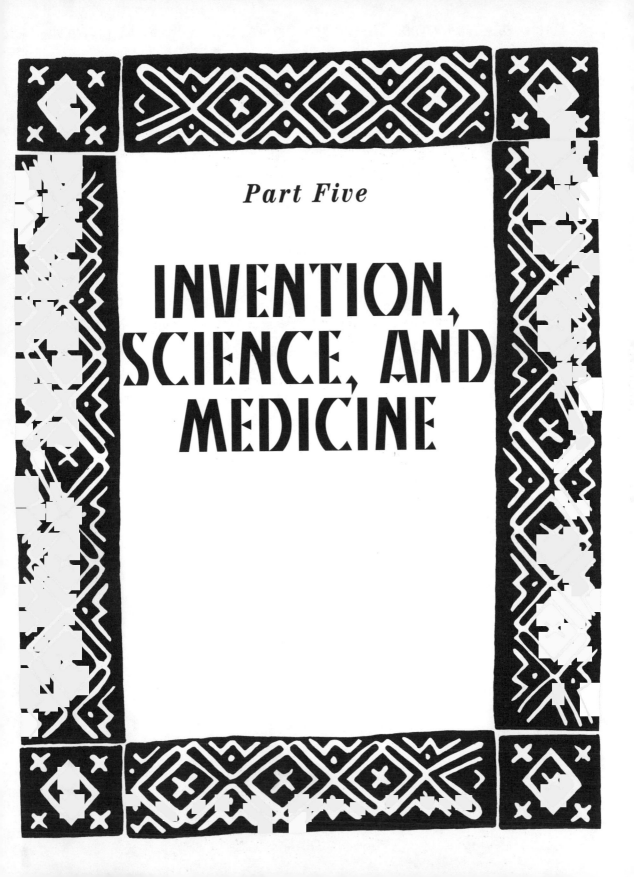

Part Five

INVENTION, SCIENCE, AND MEDICINE

Because of a Eurocentric perspective on the world history of science and technology, the belief has persisted for centuries that Africans lacked scientific and technological sophistication. In addition, many believed that the Middle Passage and subsequent brutal assimilation into a Euro-American culture erased whatever cultural heritage Africans had possessed. But recent research has shown that Africans were creative and inventive problem-solvers in science, medicine, metallurgy, and agriculture prior to European contact. When Africans arrived in the New World, they used their technical knowledge of agriculture, boatbuilding, fishing, iron production, medicine, and textile production to solve many of the problems facing America, both before and after the American Revolution. Slave and free African Americans were often highly skilled and recruited specifically because of those skills. The resultant American culture was less a "white man's culture," and more a multicultural product of African American, Native American, and European American innovation.

INVENTION

Colonial Innovation

839 • Rice and Rice Technology Introduced

West Africans introduced the rice plant and its cultivation to North America. English settlers had no knowledge of rice cultivation until West Africans, who had grown the rice plant since A.D. 100, were transported by English planters on Barbados to South Carolina in the late seventeenth century. Once West Africans showed the English how to plant rice seed in the spring, hoe it in rows during the summer, and harvest it West African style in the fall, the English realized that rice could turn South Carolina into a profitable colony. Indeed, rice became so important to South Carolina's economy that it continued to be that colony's major crop long after the rest of the South had turned to cotton farming in the nineteenth century. Not only did West Africans introduce rice to the colonial American economy, but they also introduced the technology to process the crop. The technique of irrigating the crop by flooding the rice fields was West African in origin. West African mortars and pestles were used to break the husks from around the grains. Then coiled-grass fanner baskets—wide, flat, circular baskets about two feet in diameter—were employed to separate the chaff from the edible grains. Slaves tossed the rice into the air, the wind blew away the lighter husks, and the heavier rice

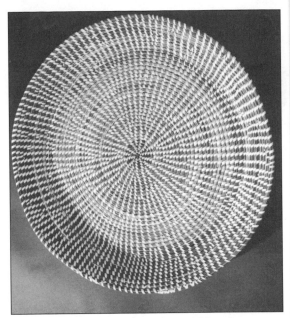

Rice fanner basket. Photograph by Harold Dorwin. Courtesy of Anacostia Museum

grains fell back into the baskets. Baskets made of grasses and palmetto were produced by both Africans and Indians, and some fusion of technologies occurred to create South Carolina's great basket-weaving tradition.

840 • Dugout Canoe

West Africans, along with the Indians, introduced the English in the seventeenth century to dugout canoes, but the English had difficulty learning to row and steer them. Slaves built the narrow canoe by hollowing out a large cypress log, burning the insides so that it could be held open by sticks, and then, after the hull hard-

Dugout canoe. Photograph by Harold Dorwin. Courtesy of Anacostia Museum. Canoe courtesy of Charleston Museum, Charleston, South Carolina

ened, adding log planks to the sides. Two or three such hollowed-out logs would be joined to make the larger and more stable pettiauger, or piragua, a multiple-log dugout canoe. In South Carolina, a colony of numerous narrow waterways and without adequate roads or bridges, African Americans became expert boatmen who used the canoes to fish, hunt, scout, and escape from slavery.

841 • Poisoning Fish

Africans were also some of the colony's best fishermen, in part because of their practice of poisoning fish. Drugging fish was a common West African practice. A particular stream would be dammed up and then quicklime and other plant juices would be added to the water. The intoxicated fish could be captured by hand, and they were still edible. The practice spread

so widely in South Carolina that the assembly passed a law in 1725 to publicly whip any slave convicted of the "pernicious practice," but it continued. Africans also introduced net fishing to the colonies and sometimes combined the two techniques: standing in dugout canoes, Africans hauled in large amounts of drugged fish by flinging nets out into the many waterways of South Carolina. Fishing supplied a lucrative income for slaves and was an important trade source for South Carolina.

842 • Ironsmithing

Ironsmithing was a highly developed technology in West Africa by the sixteenth century when the slave trade began, and Africans brought that technology with them when they crossed the Atlantic. African Americans were highly valued in the South as blacksmiths, not only because they created effective tools but also because of the ironwork they contributed to the decorative architecture in places like New Orleans. Indeed, many of the most famous New Orleans ironworkers employed large numbers of slaves, skilled iron craftsmen, who actually performed the jobs the white supervisors contracted. Often the African American workers in white shops were given the freedom to inscribe motifs in gates and fences that reveal African influences.

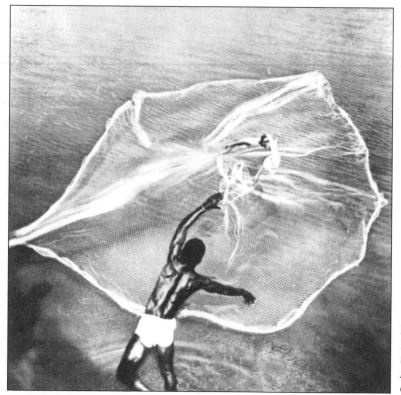

Net fishing. Photograph by Harold Dorwin, Anacostia Museum, Smithsonian Institution. From *Dictionary of Black African Civilization*

843 • Shotgun Houses

The "shotgun" house found extensively in African American neighborhoods throughout the American South was an African American invention. Such rectangular houses are called shotgun houses because if one stood on the porch and fired a shotgun, its pellets would go straight through the house with ease. Usually these houses contain three or more small rooms in succession from the front to the back, the gabled or small end of the house facing the street. This arrangement promotes a great deal of interaction among residents, since one must pass others to get out of the house. These houses led to the southern African American practice of sitting on front porches, one of the few ways to escape the intense interaction within, and also promoted more neighborhood interaction among residents sitting on front porches. Some historians argue that the front porch, an anomaly in English houses, is an African American contribution.

844 • Quilting Language

Although other groups had developed quilts, Africans were some of the most prolific quilt-makers, a testament to their mastery of textile production. But Africans also developed something unique: a language of quilt signs designed to convey messages to those traveling. By the middle of the eighteenth century, a well-developed language of signs had emerged by which quilts could be hung outside a house to impart information surreptitiously to other African Americans, especially runaway slaves. The hanging of the quilt outside of a house meant this was a safe house for a slave to stop at to gain rest and refreshment before going on to the next station on the underground railroad to freedom.

Free Inventors

845 • Benjamin Banneker (1731–1806)

In 1791 inventor and mathematician Benjamin Banneker produced the first scientific book written by an African American. Banneker's almanac consisted of weather data, tidal information for Chesapeake Bay, recipes, medical remedies, poems, abolitionist essays, and information about festivals and holidays. Such almanacs were popular in late-eighteenth-century America when books on natural phenomena were the only secular reading material available. Banneker was already famous in Baltimore for building a wooden clock in 1753, without any instruction, from a pocket watch loaned to him. The clock was still working upon his death. Encouraged by Quaker abolitionists, Banneker sent his almanac, along with a letter offering himself as proof of African American ability, to Thomas Jefferson prior to publishing it. Jefferson's reply was published in the almanac, which was reissued annually until 1797. Jefferson recommended Banneker to Major Andrew Ellicott and Banneker served as an astronomical assistant to Ellicott (not, as some contend, to Major Pierre Charles L'Enfant) during the preliminary survey of the ten-mile square that became the District of Columbia.

846 • Benjamin Banneker and Thomas Jefferson Debate the Doctrine of Racial Inequality

On August 19, 1791, Banneker sent Thomas Jefferson the following letter along with a copy of Banneker's almanac:

I suppose it is a truth too well attested to you, to need a proof here, that we are a race of beings, who have long laboured under the abuse and censure of the world; that we have long been looked upon with an eye of contempt; and that we have long been considered rather as brutish than human, and scarcely capable of mental endowments.... I apprehend you will embrace every opportunity, to eradicate that train of absurd and false ideas and opinions, which so generally prevail with respect to us; and that your sentiments are concurrent with mine, which are, that one universal Father hath given being to us all; ... and endowed us all with the same faculties; and that however variable we may be in society or religion, however diversified in situation or colour, we are all of the same family, and stand in the same relation to Him.... but sir, how pitiable it is to reflect, that although you were so fully convinced of the benevolence of the Father of Mankind, and of His equal and impartial distribution of these rights and privileges, which He hath conferred upon them, that you should at the same time counteract His mercies, in detaining by fraud and violence, so numerous a part of my brethren under groaning captivity, and cruel oppression, that you should at the same time be found guilty of the most criminal act, which you professedly detest in others, with respect to yourselves.

On August 30, 1791, Jefferson wrote back:

I thank you most sincerely, for your letter of the 19th instant, and for the Almanac it contained. Nobody wishes more than I do, to see such proofs as you exhibit, that nature has given to our black brethren talents equal to those of the other color of men; and that the appearance of want of them is owing merely to the degraded condition of their existence, both in Africa and America. I can add with truth, that nobody wishes more ardently to see a good system commenced, for raising the condition, both of their body and mind, to what it ought to be, as far as the imbecility of their present

existence, and other circumstances, which cannot be neglected, will admit.

I have taken the liberty of sending your Almanac to Monsieur de Condorcet, Secretary of the Academy of Sciences, at Paris and Member of the Philanthropic Society, because I considered it as a document to which your whole colour have a right for their justification against the doubts which have been entertained of them.

Curiously, Condorcet never received a copy of Banneker's almanac.

847 • Thomas Jennings (1791–1859)

On March 3, 1821, Thomas Jennings became the first African American to receive a patent. As the owner of a New York dry-cleaning business, Jennings invented and patented a new process for cleaning clothing. Jennings used the money he earned with his invention to buy his family out of slavery. Active as an abolitionist, Jennings published petitions that advocated the end of slavery in New York.

848 • Henry Blair (1804?–60)

On October 14, 1834, Henry Blair of Greenosa, Maryland, became the second African American to obtain a patent. Blair received his first patent for a corn harvester. On August 31, 1836, he obtained his second patent for a cotton seed planter. Blair's entry in the patent registry identifies him as "a colored man," the only entry of this period to do so. It seems likely that other African Americans had received patents, but simply were not identified by race.

849 • Norbert Rillieux (1806–94)

A freeborn African American from New Orleans revolutionized the sugar industry when he invented the multiple-effect evaporator for re-

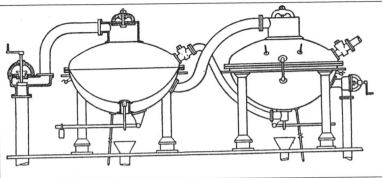

Diagram of the multiple-effect evaporator invented by Norbert Rillieux. Schomburg Center for Research in Black Culture, New York Public Library, Astor, Lenox and Tilden Foundation

Norbert Rillieux. Courtesy of Schomburg Center for Research in Black Culture, New York Public Library, Astor, Lenox and Tilden Foundation

and steam processes that were well received by European scientists. Familiar with the expensive, slow, and dangerous "Jamaica Train" process of refining sugar in use in New Orleans, which at best produced a sugar like molasses in color and texture, Rillieux designed a new process, the multiple-effect evaporation system, in Paris in 1830. Returning to the United States to get funding for his invention, Rillieux operated his new system on a Louisiana plantation in 1845. By 1848 Rillieux's system was successfully producing finer, whiter sugar with a huge reduction in costs and labor. His system was adopted by factories throughout Louisiana, Cuba, and Mexico, and its steam principles found much broader application in manufacturing industries for condensed milk, soap, gelatin, and glue products. Heralded for his work and accepted professionally by the scientific community, Rillieux was nonetheless isolated socially and denied equal access to public accommodations. When Louisiana began to require that every black, free or slave, carry an identification pass, Rillieux returned to Paris in 1861 and studied Egyptology, deciphered hieroglyphics, and continued to perfect his invention until the 1880s. He worked on several other, smaller inventions until his death in 1894.

850 • Sail Positioning Device

James Forten was a sailmaker from Philadelphia who invented and sold an improved version of a sail positioning device, a product that made his company one of the most prosperous sailmaking companies in antebellum Philadelphia. As a young boy, Forten served in the navy during the Revolutionary War and then apprenticed to

fining sugar. The son of Constant Vivant, a free Black woman, and Vincent Rillieux, an engineer and plantation owner who recognized his son's extraordinary mechanical ability, Norbert was sent to Paris to study engineering. Rillieux also taught at the L'Ecole Central in Paris and authored scholarly papers on the steam engine

AN ADDRESS

DELIVERED BEFORE THE

LADIES' ANTI-SLAVERY SOCIETY

OF

PHILADELPHIA.

On the Evening of the 14th of April, 1836,

By JAMES FORTEN, Jr.

—o—••••—o—

PHILADELPHIA:
PRINTED BY MERRIHEW AND GUNN,
No. 7 Carters' Alley.
......
1836.

Title page of address by James Forten, sailmaker. Prints and Photographs Division, Library of Congress

851 • Lewis Temple (1800–54)

Lewis Temple invented the toggle whaling harpoon in the 1840s but never patented his work. A Black ironworker, Temple had established a blacksmith shop in New Bedford, Massachusetts, when in 1848 he designed a harpoon with a movable head that prevented whales from slipping loose from the hook and escaping. The head of the harpoon became "locked" in the whale's flesh, and the only way to remove it was to cut it loose after the whale was killed. Known as the toggle iron, Temple's harpoon became standard whaling equipment; but Temple's failure to patent his work allowed others to reproduce the harpoon themselves, reducing his profits. When he died in 1854, his estate was valued at less than $1,500.

Slave Inventors

852 • Ned and Intellectual Property

The U.S. Patent Office's refusal to award patents to slaves reinforced the predominant view that African Americans were incapable of significant contributions to technology. The policy also kept slave owners from obtaining patent rights for inventions made by their slaves. Such was the result when Oscar J. E. Stuart, a white Mississippi planter, wrote to Secretary of Interior Jacob Thompson, also a southerner, on August 25, 1857, to request a patent for a labor-saving cotton scraper that Ned, a slave blacksmith on Stuart's plantation, had invented. Stuart claimed the invention was his because of his belief that

Robert Bridges, a Philadelphia sailmaker, whose company Forten purchased in 1798. Forten used the fortune he made as a sailmaker to support the abolitionist movement and fund the activities of the emigrationist Paul Cuffee.

Toggle whaling harpoon. Photo by Harold Dorwin, Anacostia Museum. Courtesy of the National Museum of American History

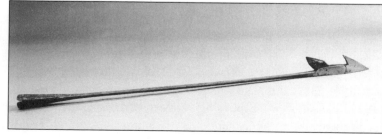

all products of Ned's labor "both intiliectual [*sic*] and manual" belonged to Ned's master. But the commissioner of patents, who ruled on the case, disagreed, contending that the recipient of a patent must be a citizen, and since slaves were not regarded as citizens by the United States government, patents could not be issued in their name. That reading of the matter angered Stuart, who wrote back that he had not applied for the patent in Ned's name but rather his own. The attorney general concurred with the commissioner, however, ruling in 1858 that "a machine invented by a slave, though it be new and useful, cannot, in the present state of the laws, be patented. I may add that if such a patent were issued to the master, it would not protect him in the courts against persons who might infringe it." Nevertheless, Stuart began to sell the cotton scraper in 1860, and even justified the invention as a sign that slavery did not corrupt the intellect of slaves. Neither Ned's intellect nor person was ever heard of again.

HENRY BOYD,

MANUFATURER of Patent Right and Left Wood Screw and Swelled Rail Redsteads, North-west corner of Broadway and Eighth streets, Cincinnati, Ohio, would respectfully invite those wishing to purchase a superior article of furniture in Bedsteads, to call at his ware room and examine for themselves This newly invented Bedstead is warranted superior to any other ever offered in the West; possessing the following decided advantage over all others heretofore us d, they can be put up or taken apart in one fourth the time required to do the same with others, without the possibility of a mistake—are more firm, less apt to become loose and worthless, and without a single harbor for vermin.

CERTIFICATES:

The undersigned, having used the above named Patent Bedsteads, feel no hesitation in recommending them to be the best now in use.

Hon. N. C. Reed,	Milton McLean, Esq,
Hon. Henry Morse,	G. W. H. Evans, Cincinnati Hotel,
Hon. Richard Ayres,	
I. G. Burnett,	Samuel Berresford,
M. Allen,	Wright Smith, Sr,
Rev. L. G. Bingham,	James Eshelby,
D. L. Rusk,	Wm. Holmes,
S. B. Hunt,	Wm. H. Henrie, Henrie House,
Wm. D. Gallagher,	
P. Evens,	T. M. Cockrell, Pearl st House,
Isaiah Wing,	
J. B Russell,	Wm. Marsh, Galt House,
P. Grandin, Esq,	J. W. Mason, 4th st House,
B. Tappin,	Wm. Crossman,) Trus.
Daniel Burritt,	Josiah Foles, } of the
Sam'l L'Hommedieu.	Com. Hospital.

Caution: There are imitations of this Bedstead in market very much resembling it. The genuine, which only he warrants, are all stamped "H. Boyd."

may 18 12-4m

Certificate advertising Henry Boyd's bedstead. Prints and Photographs Division, Library of Congress

853 • Whose Reaper?

Black slave Jo Anderson seldom received credit for his development of the reaper. Instead, Cyrus McCormick is usually given credit for the invention of the automatic reaper. Although McCormick himself gave Anderson some credit for coming up with the idea, it was still McCormick who reaped the financial rewards for the invention.

854 • Brains Buys His Freedom

Henry Boyd invented a bed whose wooden rails screwed into both the headboard and footboard, giving it a much stronger structure than other early-nineteenth-century beds. He used his carpentry skills and his new bedstead idea

to purchase his freedom in 1826. In 1836 he opened his own company using his bed frame design as the foundation. Boyd never patented his device, but he did try to have it protected by having a white man apply for the patent. In addition, Boyd stamped his name on every frame he made to ensure authenticity to his clients. By 1843 he was among Cincinnati's most successful furniture makers with a staff of twenty-five to fifty employees.

855 • Benjamin Montgomery and Jefferson Davis

Benjamin Montgomery (1819–77), while

working as a mechanic on Joseph Davis's plantation in the 1850s, designed an angled blade propeller that enabled steamboats to move efficiently through shallow waters around the plantation. Joseph, along with his brother, Jefferson Davis, who later became president of the Confederacy, tried to obtain a patent for Montgomery's invention. But the attorney general's decision in the Stuart case kept the Davises from profiting from the mental creativity of their slave. Once Jefferson Davis became president of the Confederacy, he had the Confederate Congress pass a law enabling masters to obtain patent rights for slave inventions.

Black Inventions After 1865

856 • Black Patents

Passage of the Thirteenth and Fourteenth Amendments to the Constitution brought a generally unrecognized benefit to African Americans: these amendments gave African Americans the right to patent their inventions. As a result, in the period following the Civil War, the number of patents for inventions filed by Blacks increased dramatically as innovators from all walks of life—farmers, blacksmiths, and scientists—sought recognition for their technological ingenuity. Still, we do not know exactly how many patents were obtained by African Americans, since racial identity was not recorded by the Patent Office.

857 • Agricultural Inventions

Because most African Americans became tenant farmers and continued to work the land after the Civil War, many of the inventions patented by Blacks in the postwar period were agricultural or domestic implements. Former slave Peter R. Campbell, who, like Benjamin Montgomery, had been a slave on Joseph Davis's plantation, patented a screw press in 1879. Charles T. Christmas, another former slave in Mississippi, received a patent in 1880 for a device to simplify the baling of cotton. Lockrum Blue received a patent in 1884 for a corn sheller.

858 • Gong and Signal Chair

Little is known about the Washington, D.C., teacher Miriam E. Benjamin, who received an 1888 patent for a chair with a small flag and a bell that an occupant rang using a rod attached to the seat of the chair. These chairs were used in many hotel dining rooms to summon a waiter. And with the support of a Black congressman, George Washington Murray, Benjamin recommended them to the United States House of Representatives as a way for congressmen to signal for a page.

859 • "The Real McCoy"

The term "the Real McCoy" comes from the automatic engine lubricator that Elijah McCoy (1843–1929) invented to continuously oil train and ship engines, which was immediately adopted by railroad and shipping lines. But soon imitations appeared that did not work as well as McCoy's lubricator and that led many would-be purchasers to inquire, "Is this the real McCoy?" Eventually the phrase was coined as a way to ask whether an item was genuine and of the highest quality. McCoy, born in Canada in 1844 and educated in Scotland, was unable to find work as an engineer after he moved to the United States. Taking a job as a fireman on the Michigan Central Railroad, he noticed that the fireman's duty of oiling the train's engine while stationary added tremendously to the length of

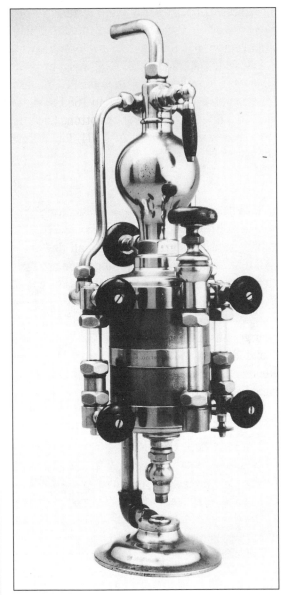

Elijah McCoy's automatic engine lubricator. Photograph by Harold Dorwin. Courtesy of Greenfield Village and the Henry Ford Museum

train trips. McCoy's first invention, a "lubricating cup," patented in 1872, provided a continuous flow of oil over the gears and thus eliminated "the necessity of shutting down the machine periodically." McCoy acquired fifty-

seven other patents for devices designed to streamline the automatic lubrication process of machinery. He is also credited with inventing the ironing board, the lawn sprinkler, and, what McCoy considered his best invention, a graphite lubricator. In April 1915 he received a patent for a graphite lubricator that eliminated the problems of oiling a superheater engine that used large amounts of steam to operate. In 1920 McCoy established the Elijah McCoy Manufacturing Company to manufacture and sell the lubricator.

860 • The "Jenny" Automatic Coupler

Elijah McCoy was not the only African American railroad worker to create innovative solutions to railway problems. In 1897 Andrew J. Beard (1849–1941), an Alabama worker who had seen many men injured while manually coupling train cars, developed the best device for automatically coupling cars. Before Beard's invention, railroad workers had to brace themselves between railway cars while the cars were moved close enough together to drop a metal spike into a slot. The Jenny coupler secured two railroad cars once they were bumped together. Beard was one of the few inventors to actually profit from his invention—receiving $50,000 for his design.

861 • Pullman Car Ventilator

Even those who worked inside the train cars were ingenious in solving some of the mundane problems of riding the railroad. One man, Pullman porter H. H. Reynolds, responded to the constant requests of passengers to open windows by designing a ventilator that allowed air to flow into cars and at the same time kept out dust and soot. When he told his manager about the idea, Reynolds learned what many inventors have learned—that some will try to steal the idea of unsuspecting inventors. After his manager had a working model made, Pullman tried to obtain patent rights for Reynolds's idea. But Reynolds sued the Pullman Company and won the right to profit from his invention.

862 • Shoe Lasting Machine

The shoe manufacturing process in America was revolutionized by a Black immigrant, Jan Ernst Matzeliger (1852–89), who nevertheless died in poverty. Born in Surinam, Matzeliger apprenticed in government machine shops, joined onto an East Indian merchant ship at the age of nineteen, and then left the ship in 1870 to settle in Philadelphia and apprentice as a shoe cobbler. While learning the machinery used in the industry, he noticed that the most difficult part of the production process—"lasting," or con-

Shoe lasting machine. Photograph by Harold Dorwin. Courtesy of the United Shoe Machinery Corporation

necting the upper to the sole of the shoe—had to be done by hand. After he moved to Lynn, Massachusetts, a center of shoe manufacturing, Matzeliger used a discarded forge in the factory where, for five years, he worked to develop a

Jan Ernest Matzeliger. Schomburg Center for Research in Black Culture, New York Public Library, Astor, Lenox and Tilden Foundation

prototype of his shoe lasting machine. In exchange for two-thirds interest in the product, Matzeliger obtained from Melville S. Nichols and Charles H. Delnow the financial assistance he needed to perfect the machine. Finally Matzeliger received a patent on March 20, 1883, for a machine that cut costs in half while greatly increasing production. Not surprisingly, demand for his invention was high, and even though Matzeliger, Nichols, and Delnow formed the Union Lasting Machine Company to produce the machine, the company was too small to handle the huge number of requests. Two more investors were brought in, a larger Consolidated Lasting Machine Company was formed, and Matzeliger had to exchange his patents for a block of stock. Matzeliger lived only six years after his patent was granted, and he bequeathed his stock in the company to the North Congregational Society in Lynn. Apparently Matzeliger had attempted to join several white churches upon his arrival in Massachusetts, and all but the North Congregational Society rebuffed him.

863 • "The Black Edison"

Granville T. Woods (1856–1910) was known as the Black Edison, in part because he competed successfully with the celebrated Thomas Edison to market a telegraph system. Earlier, in 1884, Woods had lost a struggle with Alexander Graham Bell to market an advanced telephone transmitter for which Woods had received a patent. Without the requisite funding to market his device, Woods sold it to the Bell Telephone Company. But later, when Woods's telegraphic device for transmitting messages between moving trains was challenged by a similar device designed by Edison, a court ruled that Woods's design deserved the patent. After that victory, Woods secured the funding in the 1890s to form his own company, the Woods Electrical Com-

pany, to market his inventions, including air brakes and an egg hatching machine. But Woods's career also shows the effects of racism on talented Black inventors: Woods circulated a story in *Cosmopolitan* magazine that he was descended from "full-blooded savage Australian aborigines." Apparently Woods believed that his inventions would not be recognized if it was known that he was an African American.

864 • Carbon Filaments for Lamps

Lewis Latimer received a patent on January 17, 1882, for his unique design of carbon filaments for the electric incandescent lamp sold by Hiram Maxim's U.S. Electric Lighting Company. Primarily a patent illustrator, Latimer had

Drawing by Lewis Latimer to highlight the precariousness of his position as a consulting engineer. Photograph by Harold Dorwin. Courtesy of Dr. Winifred Norman Latimer, the Latimer Collection

begun work on an improved and cheaper carbon filament to make it possible for more people to enjoy electric lighting. His invention also made it possible for U.S. Electric to operate lights safely at a higher temperature.

865 • Edison Pioneers

The changing nature of invention in the late nineteenth century is revealed by the career of Lewis Latimer, who in 1884 was hired away from Maxim's U.S. Electric to join what eventually became known as the Edison Pioneers. As inventions became more scientific and technical in the late nineteenth century, inventors like Thomas Edison and Alexander Graham Bell formed research labs that coordinated a diversity of functions from pioneer research to product development to distribution and patent defense under one roof. Lewis Latimer's multi-faceted genius for invention, patent drawing, and legal writing, made him a natural choice for Edison. Unlike at Maxim's, where Latimer served mainly as an inventor, Latimer became Edison's chief litigator in patent conflicts against those, like Granville Woods, who challenged Edison's patents. Latimer documented

Edison Pioneers. Photograph by Harold Dorwin. Courtesy of Dr. Winifred Norman Latimer, the Latimer Collection

his experience working with Edison by writing the first book on electrical lighting, *Incandescent Electric Lighting: A Practical Description of the Edison System,* in 1890. Then, on January 24, 1918, Latimer was chosen to be the only Black member of the Edison Pioneers, the name Edison gave to the group of distinguished scientists and inventors he had assembled at Menlo Park, New Jersey. Generally speaking, the transition in American invention toward teams of researchers working in labs was not advantageous to Black inventors because it coincided with the rise of segregation in American life, which prevented many talented African Americans from living and working in proximity with other scientists and inventors in research and development labs. Nevertheless, independent Black inventors continued to develop inventions out of their work.

866 • Wrinkle-Preventing Trouser Stretchers

This invention emerged out of Archia Ross's work as a laundress. Wrinkles, obviously, were a problem for laundry and dry-cleaning establishments, and during her work in one, Ross came up with the idea of a wrinkle-preventing trouser stretcher. She received a patent for that invention in 1899. Not only did Ross design this work-saving device, but she also invented a device for keeping handbags closed and a runner to be used on doorsteps.

867 • Bread Crumbing Machine

Master cook Joseph Lee's invention emerged from his work. Lee thought too much bread became stale and was discarded each day. To address this problem, he created the bread crumbing machine to reduce bread to crumbs through a tearing and grinding process. Lee then used the crumbs to make croquettes, escalloped oysters, cutlets, dressing for poultry, cake batter, fried meats, and puddings. He received a patent for his invention on June 4, 1895. Lee sold the patent to the Royal Worcester Bread Crumb Company of Boston, the machine's manufacturer, and the bread crumbing machine became standard equipment in top restaurants around the world. Lee also invented a bread making machine which mixed the ingredients through a more sanitary method than kneading the dough by hand. Variations of this design are still in use today.

868 • Recognition for Black Inventions

Congressman George Washington Murray championed the accomplishments of Black inventors to refute the argument that African Americans should be excluded from the proposed Cotton States Exhibition because African Americans had contributed nothing to American technological progress in the nineteenth century. On August 10, 1894, Murray stood in the House of Representatives and read the names of Black inventors into the *Congressional Record* from a list supplied him by Henry A. Baker, an African American who worked in the Patent Office. Together, Murray and Baker sought to use African American inventiveness as a weapon in the war against Social Darwinist claims of African American racial inferiority. African American invention gained national attention in 1895, when Black inventions were part of the exhibitions in the African American building at the Atlanta Exposition, and received international attention in 1900, when the Paris Exposition featured approximately 350 African American inventors in the African American

Seven African Americans in Hampton Institute exhibit area of the African American Building at the Atlanta Exposition, 1895. Prints and Photographs Division, Library of Congress

section of the United States exhibit. The U.S. Patent Office had collected the information on Black inventors in creating the latter exhibit, which was seen by approximately 39 million visitors, many of which had probably never known that any Black inventors existed.

869 • The Gas Mask

The invention of the protective hood or gas mask in 1912 shows the pathos endured by African American inventors. Garrett Augustus Morgan (1877–1963) was a self-trained sewing machine mechanic who in 1909 had accidentally discovered a chemical solution that straightened hair. Morgan devised a protective hood and smoke protector that enabled firefighters and other personnel to enter smoky or toxic environments without breathing contaminated air. The protective hood covered the head and upper torso and supplied clean air to the

Garrett Augustus Morgan's advertisement for his gas mask. Photograph by Harold Dorwin, courtesy of Anacostia Museum. Used by permission of Western Reserve Historical Society, Cleveland, Ohio

wearer through two tubes from a bag of air that hung on the back of the hood. Garrett patented his invention in 1914 and staged an event in New Orleans where he entered a tent filled with smoke from burning tar sulfur, formaldehyde, and manure and remained for twenty minutes. The *New Orleans Times–Picayune*, reporting the event, described Morgan as "Big Chief Mason," a "full-blooded Indian from the Wolpole Reservation in Canada." Morgan believed that the public and New Orleans officials would be more disposed to believe an Indian had created his safety hood than an African American. His invention gained national attention when the Cleveland Waterworks exploded on July 25, 1916, trapping more than twenty workmen inside with poisonous smoke and gases, and Morgan and his brother donned their masks, entered the tunnel, and retrieved the men. Morgan was celebrated afterward as Cleveland's "most honored and bravest citizen" and his gas mask went into production; but Morgan used white salesmen to promote the mask in the South. Ultimately it was discovered that an African American had invented the mask and it fell into disuse. But Morgan's mask did save the lives of hundreds of American soldiers who wore it in World War I. Its design resembles modern-day suits worn by hazardous chemical fire personnel.

870 • The Stop Sign

Garrett Augustus Morgan was the inventor of a three-way automatic stop sign, a precursor of the present-day traffic light. Before Morgan's invention, traffic signals only had two commands—"Go" and "Stop"—and were generally known as "Go-Stop" signals. Morgan's invention was a tall pole with a bell on top and two flags with "stop" printed on them; the signal controlled traffic by raising and lowering the flags by rotating a hand crank located near the base of the mechanism. Paused in a half-mast position, the flags alerted drivers and pedestrians to prepare to stop. Morgan's traffic light received a U.S. patent on November 20, 1923, and was patented in Great Britain and Canada. So successful was his design that General Electric paid Morgan $40,000 for the rights to his automatic stop sign.

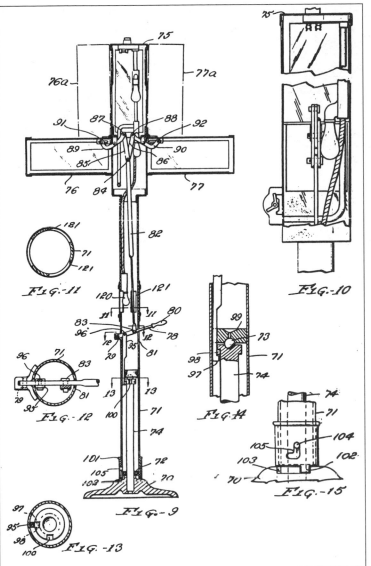

Patent drawing for Morgan's traffic signal. Photograph by Harold Dorwin, courtesy of Anacostia Museum. Used by permission of Western Reserve Historical Society Cleveland, Ohio

also developed a facial cream for lightening African American skin color. Marrying C. J. Walker and moving to Denver in 1906, she sold her products door-to-door and taught African American women how to use these products in beauty salons. She then established a manufacturing plant and headquarters in Indianapolis, Indiana, and began to distribute her products nationwide. Her marketing techniques were just as innovative as her chemical techniques, and she used demonstrations and advertising, especially in African American newspapers, to outsell her competitors, while her "beauty shop" network created independent jobs for thousands of African American women.

871 • Hair Straightening

Sarah Breedlove Walker (1867–1919) discovered a process that would ultimately lift her out of poverty as a washerwoman and make her a millionaire. In 1905, in St. Louis, Missouri, Madam C. J. Walker, as she was later known, perfected a chemical and the use of the hot comb to straighten African American women's hair. She

872 • Adding Machine

Shelby J. Davidson (1869–1931) developed his invention, the adding machine, out of his efforts to make work in the U.S. Postal Service more efficient. Davidson began work in a Washington, D.C., post office in 1893 and found the adding of long columns of figures a tedious task. After an intensive study of applied mechanics, Davidson first sketched, then modeled in cardboard, a working version of his invention.

Photograph of James Andrew Jones. Photograph by Harold Dorwin. Courtesy of Jacqueline Jones Grammer

873 • Convertible Top

On January 21, 1919, James A. Jones of Jackson, Tennessee, received a patent, number 1,292,330, for "The Jones" vehicle spring—a mechanism to raise and lower a top for an automobile. Jones, who had worked as a fireman on the railroad, was a skilled mechanic and designed the device at a time when most automobiles lacked tops.

874 • X-Ray Machine and Refrigerator Equipment

The portable X-ray machine, a refrigerator for military field kitchens, and mechanical refrigeration techniques applied to railroad cars and trucks were invented by Frederick McKinley Jones. Before he started experimenting with refrigeration devices in the late 1930s, truck refrigeration units were too big and wasted space inside the truck. Jones reduced the size of the unit and began, with Joseph Numero, the U.S. Thermo Control Company to manufacture these automatic air coolers for trains, ships, and airplanes in order to keep food fresh. Jones also developed ways to keep the air surrounding food at a constant temperature, devices that produced special atmospheric conditions to prevent fruit from drying out or becoming overripe before reaching supermarkets, and parts for existing refrigeration equipment. Jones received over sixty patents during his lifetime, forty for refrigeration equipment.

875 • Curing Salts

Lloyd Augusta Hall invented curing salts that revolutionized the meatpacking industry while he worked as chief chemist and director of research for Griffith Laboratories in Chicago. Hall received a 1951 patent for the process by which he could cure bacon in several hours rather than the normal time of from six to fifteen days. As a graduate of Northwestern University with a bachelor of science in pharmaceutical chemistry, Hall received more than twenty-five other patents for manufacturing and packing food products.

876 • Medtek 410

It took Michael Croslin nearly twenty years to perfect the Medtek 410, a computerized blood pressure measuring device. Before the Medtek 410, most blood pressure devices relied on the sound of blood pumping to determine blood pressure, but extraneous sounds sometimes disturbed the readings. Croslin's device relied on the motion of the blood, provided almost instantaneous readings, and could be easily calibrated digitally. Unlike many other Black inventors, Croslin successfully created a company—Medtek Corporation—in 1978, and he directly distributed and profited from his invention.

Science

877 • George Washington Carver (1865–1943)

George Washington Carver was an agricultural chemist who won international fame for his research into the uses of peanuts and sweet potatoes. Known as the Peanut Man for his discoveries of 300 products that could be made from the peanut, including a milk substitute, face powder, soap, and printer's ink, Carver also developed 118 uses for the sweet potato, including the production of rubber. Carver was hailed as the pioneer in the new applied science of chemurgy, which involved finding industrial uses for agricultural products. Unfortunately for his later reputation, Carver's career emerged when applied science was increasingly viewed as less respected than theoretical science. Carver was viewed as a mere concocter of products instead of a "real" scientist by the American scientific community, and his relationship with Booker T. Washington and the Tuskegee Institute, which he joined in 1896, diminished his standing among early-twentieth-century militant Black leaders. Nevertheless, Carver's numerous innovations in the applications of peanuts, sweet potatoes, and soybeans revolutionized agriculture in the South particularly, as he used his base at Tuskegee to encourage Black farmers to practice agricultural techniques to increase the yield of and add nutrients to their farmland. In 1923 Carver received the NAACP Spingarn Medal.

878 • Bessie Coleman (1893–1926)

The first licensed African American pilot was Bessie Coleman, a pioneer in women's aviation. Although she was prevented from entering flight school in America, she refused to give up on her passion for flying and traveled to France, where she studied the science of aviation and

George Washington Carver in his laboratory. Photograph by Harold Dorwin. Anacostia Museum, Smithsonian Institution, Tuskegee University Library

Bessie Coleman. Courtesy of Arizona Historical Society, Tucson

received the necessary instruction to get her license. Back in the United States, she flew in many flight exhibitions to raise money for her next dream, a flight school for African Americans. Unfortunately, Coleman died in a plane crash before she could make her flight school into a reality.

879 • Ernest E. Just (1883–1941)

Howard University professor of biology Ernest E. Just was the first to establish, through laboratory experiments, the importance of ectoplasm to the functioning of cells. Born in South Carolina and educated in Charleston's public elementary schools, Just and his family believed he would receive a better education in the North. Just took a job aboard a small ship working its way up the East Coast and eventually arrived in New York City. Once there, he worked long hours to save enough money for tuition and expenses at the Kimball Academy in New Hampshire. After completing the four-year academy curriculum in three years, Just entered Dartmouth, where he became the only person in his class to graduate *magna cum laude* in 1907. That fall, Just accepted a position teaching English at Howard University, but encouraged by President Wilbur Thirkield, Just entered graduate work in biology at the marine biological laboratories in Woods Hole, Massachusetts, where, after 1912, he spent twenty-two of his twenty-four summers. In 1915 Just was awarded the first NAACP Spingarn Medal, less for his accomplishments than for his potential for bringing prestige to Blacks at a time when science was the penultimate arena of intellectual distinction. But Just lived up to his potential after he began receiving an $80,000 Julius Rosenwald grant from 1920 to 1925 that enabled him to spend six months out of every year in research. During the twenties, Just pub-

lished numerous research papers on cell fertilization, coauthored a book, *General Cytology,* published by the University of Chicago Press in 1924, and conducted experiments in parthenogenesis, cell division, and cell mutation. Prior to Just's research, scientists believed a cell's nucleus was the key to the cell's functions and the outer membrane was only of minor importance. But in a series of experiments carried out at Woods Hole Marine Biological Laboratory on Cape Cod, Massachusetts, Just proved that the ectoplasm is just as important as the nucleus to cell function, that ectoplasm regulates the cell's relationship to the external environment, and that without the ectoplasm, cell fertilization is impossible. Perhaps most remarkably, Just established that the nucleus is not the source of hereditary material in a cell. Rather, hereditary factors are located in the cytoplasm and are extracted from the cytoplasm by the genes in the nucleus. Just's research, published in *The Biology of the Cell Surface* (1939), transformed our picture of cells, cell functioning, and human reproduction. Despite numerous discoveries in the field of biology, he was denied appointment to any of the major U.S. laboratories including the Rockefeller Institute for Medical Research, and was never appointed as a full-time faculty member at any historically white American university. Bitter and disheartened, Just, in 1929, accepted an invitation from Max Hartmann to pursue research at the Kaiser Wilhelm Institute for Biology in Germany. After Hitler came to power in 1933, Just continued his research at the Sorbonne in Paris and the Naples Zoological Station in Italy. Despite his tremendous accomplishments, Just felt hampered by the lack of adequate laboratory facilities at Howard University and the institutional racism that constrained his career in the United States. As Frank R. Lillie wrote in an obituary in 1942, "that a man of his ability, scientific devotion, and of such strong personal loyalties as he gave and received, should have been warped in the land of his birth must remain a matter of regret."

880 • Science Doctorates

Although the first doctorate degree in physics was awarded as early as 1876 to an African American, Edward Bouchet (1825–1918), by Yale University, only thirteen African Americans earned doctorate degrees in the biological and physical sciences before 1930, because continuing segregation in higher education meant that African Americans had to attend Black universities that lacked both the faculties and the facilities to sustain Ph.D. programs in science. But during the thirties and forties the breakdown of segregation in postgraduate education and the increased sophistication of faculties at historically Black universities enabled more than one hundred African Americans to receive doctorates in science. By 1972 over eight hundred African Americans had earned doctorates in the natural sciences. Yet even in 1981 most African American science doctorates were confined to teaching positions in historically Black colleges and universities, which still continue to train most Black scientists in America.

881 • Georgia Caldwell Smith

Even those without doctorate degrees have played a significant role in Black scientific education. Born in 1909 in Atchison, Kansas, Georgia Caldwell Smith graduated Phi Beta Kappa from the University of Kansas in 1928 with a bachelor of science in mathematics and earned a master's degree in math at the same university in 1929. That year she began a long and distinguished career as a teacher at Spelman College, the women's college of Atlanta University, where she taught, with brief teaching appointments at other colleges and universities, for over twenty years.

882 • Atomic Negro

Ralph Gardner was a pioneer chemist whose research into plastics led to the development of so-called hard plastics. His innovations in the manipulation of catalytic chemicals led to products for the petrochemical and pharmaceutical industries as well as plastics. Born in Cleveland, Ohio, on December 3, 1922, Gardner was the son of educated parents who provided him with the chemistry set that led to his career. After receiving a B.S. in chemistry from the University of Illinois in 1943, Gardner joined the University of Chicago Argonne National Laboratories and worked on development of the atomic bomb as part of the so-called Manhattan Project. Two other African Americans who worked on the development of the first atomic bomb were William J. Knox and J. Ernest Wilkins. But even though Gardner worked directly under the famed nuclear scientist Dr. Enrico Fermi on the Manhattan Project, Gardner could not find employment when he left the project in 1947.

883 • Earl Shaw, the Laser Man

Born in Mississippi in 1937, Earl Shaw was part of the Second Great Migration North to Chicago, where he enrolled in Crane Technical High School, went on to get a B.A. from the University of Illinois, a master's in physics from Dartmouth, and a doctorate from the University of California at Berkeley in 1969. After teaching for many years at Howard University in Washington, D.C., Shaw joined the Bell Labs in the 1970s where he developed an accelerator that adjusted the wavelength of an electron laser more easily than others did. Shaw, who retired in 1991, was not only an inventor but a pioneer in opening up research labs like Bell to Black participation: after he entered in the 1970s, other Black physicists, such as Shirley Jackson, Roosevelt Peoples, Kenneth Evans, and Walter P. Lowe, were also hired by Bell.

884 • Shirley Jackson (b. 1946)

Shirley Jackson was the first African American woman to be awarded a doctoral degree from the Massachusetts Institute of Technology. An expert on the study of particle physics, Jackson was hired as a theoretical physicist by the Bell Laboratories in 1976. She joined the faculty of Rutgers University in 1991 as a professor of physics. Her particular interest in physics has been the study of how electrons in atoms behave under different experimental conditions, which has yielded her insights into the ways that certain substances conduct electricity. Dr. Jackson has been elected to the American Academy of Arts and Sciences and as a fellow of the American Physical Society.

885 • Black Mathematician (b. 1919)

The first African American mathematician to be elected to the National Academy of Sciences was David H. Blackwell. Blackwell pioneered the study of mathematical game theory, wrote a textbook in the field, and in 1979 received the Von Neumann theory prize. He is best known for his work in the theory of games, especially that of "duels"—military games for deciding when sides in a conflict ought to fire on their enemy. His research has been underwritten by the Rand Corporation.

886 • Carruthers's Ultraviolet Camera/Spectrograph

George E. Carruthers, born in 1939, was one of two naval research laboratory workers responsible for the placement of the ultraviolet camera/spectrograph on the lunar surface. Carruthers designed the instrument that went up on *Apollo 16* in April 1972. Instrumentals designer William Conway adapted the device for the mission. The spectrographs, obtained from eleven targets, include the first photograph of the ultraviolet equatorial bands of atomic oxygen that surround the earth. The spectrograph was the first moon-based observatory and was the first man-made instrument to detect the existence of hydrogen deep in space. Carruthers received a NASA Exceptional Scientific Achievement medal for his work.

887 • Ronald McNair (1950–86)

Dr. Ronald McNair was not the first African American astronaut. That honor goes to U.S. Air Force Colonel Guion "Guy" Bluford, who aboard the shuttle *Challenger* became in August 1983 the first African American to leave the earth's atmosphere. With an M.A. and a Ph.D. in aero-

Ronald McNair. National Archives. Photograph courtesy of NASA

space engineering, Bluford had become an astronaut in 1979 and had flown on the shuttle *Challenger* in 1983 and 1986 before McNair's fatal flight on the *Challenger* on January 28, 1986. McNair was one of America's most accomplished scientists. As a laser physicist who advanced the use of lasers in satellite communications, McNair had flown on earlier *Challenger* missions and was the second African American to orbit the earth on a space mission. On a 1984 *Challenger* flight, McNair had activated the Manned Maneuvering Unit, deployed the Canadian Arm used to move crew members around the *Challenger*'s payload, and assisted the flight crew in the first runway landing of the space shuttle at Kennedy Space Center. On the 1986 mission, McNair was to have deployed the Spartan-Halley satellite which utilized lasers to track Halley's comet. A saxophone player, McNair used his free time aboard the shuttle to become the first person to play the instrument in space.

888 • Dr. Mae C. Jemison (b. 1956)
A pioneering African American astronaut, Mae Jemison, a mission specialist, graduated from Stanford University in 1977. After completing the requirements for a doctor of science in chemical engineering, she entered medical school at Cornell University in September 1977 with the intent on becoming a medical engineering researcher. With a grant from the International Traveling Institute for Health Studies, Jemison went to Africa in January 1983 and became a medical area Peace Corps specialist. After the *Challenger* explosion and the death of Ron McNair, she applied for a position as an astronaut. In 1987 she was accepted into the astronaut program and in 1992 flew on the shuttle *Endeavor*, a joint project of Japan and the United States.

Medicine

889 • Inoculation
Africans introduced the practice of inoculation in America as a cure for smallpox. During the smallpox epidemic of 1721, a Boston slave named Onesimus instructed Cotton Mather, the Puritan cleric, about the technique. Mather injected some infected fluid from a smallpox victim into the blood of another person and found that the second person was immune from catching the disease. In order to overcome white opposition to Mather's use of the technique, he authored the pamphlet "An Account of the Medho and Success of Inoculating the Small-Pox," to show its origin and effectiveness:

A gentleman well known in the City of Boston, had a Garamanee *Servant, who first gave him an Account of a Method frequently used in* Africa, *and which had been practis'd on himself, to procure an easy Small-Pox, and a perpetual security of neither dying by it, nor being again infected with it. . . . in their Country (where they use to die like* Rotten Sheep, *when the* Small-Pox *gets among them) it is now become a* common Thing *to cut a Place or two in their Skin, sometimes one Place, and sometimes another, and put a little of the Matter of the* Small-Pox; *after which, they, in a few Days, grow a little Sick, and a few* Small-Pox *break out, and by and by they dry away; and that no Body ever dy'd of doing this, nor ever had the* Small-Pox *after it: Which last Point is confirm'd by their constant Attendance on the Sick in our Families, without receiving the Infection.*

890 • African Pharmacists
Africans also made important contributions to pharmacological knowledge in colonial America. The use of herbs and other plants to

heal afflictions was widespread and sophisticated in Africa and became very popular in the United States. Sometimes slaves received their freedom for curing the ills of their masters.

891 • Caesarean Midwives

African American women enjoyed a widespread reputation in the eighteenth century for being excellent midwives, practitioners of the art and science of assisted childbirth. From Africa, these midwives brought with them the knowledge of caesarean section, which made them highly valued for their treatment of white as well as Black women. Masters often designated certain African American women as midwives who used their knowledge of various herbs and vegetables to speed healing in women after childbirth. Sometimes midwives' duties were extended into feeding and nursing newborn children whose mothers were forced to return rapidly to plantation labor. At the same time, African American midwives also used their skills to abort unwanted pregnancies, especially those of young slave women raped by their masters or overseers. The tradition of Black women as midwives extends into modern times. A few outstanding midwives are Mattie D. Brewer, born in Tennessee in 1882, who delivered more than one thousand children in her career. She delivered her last child when she was eighty-one years old. Another was Marie Jones Francis from Dublin, Georgia, who was an expert in premature childbirth. And then there was Julia M. Shade, who started midwifing in 1925 in Mississippi and who was known to have delivered over four thousand babies. Her career as a midwife led her to formal study and she earned a degree in nursing from Wayne State University in 1952. In 1939, in recognition of the significance of Black midwives, Tuskegee Institute created a school of nurse-midwifery.

892 • James Derham (b. 1762 or '67?)

The first African American widely recognized as a doctor was James Derham. As a teenage slave owned by John Kearsley, Jr., a Philadelphia doctor, Derham mixed and administered medicines for Dr. Kearsley's patients. Kearsley was impressed with Derham's intelligence and provided him with the beginnings of a medical education. Kearsley was a Tory, however, and he was arrested and imprisoned as a traitor during the Revolutionary War. Kearsley eventually went insane and died in captivity. After Kearsley's death, Derham was sold to a British army surgeon fighting in the war, and with his new owner, he helped care for injured soldiers. After the war, Dr. Robert Dove of New Orleans purchased Derham, and again, Derham acted as a doctor's assistant. Soon, Dove freed Derham as a reward for his outstanding work, and Derham opened his own practice, which served both blacks and whites. Derham was regarded as one of the preeminent doctors in New Orleans and eventually made as much as $3,000 per year. He was recognized as an authority on the relationship between disease and climate. Derham's talents were not limited to the medical field— he was also known as a superb linguist who spoke both French and Spanish fluently.

893 • Black Doctors

In the antebellum South, slaves and free African Americans served as doctors to their masters and other members of the white population. In some cases, Blacks were preferred over white doctors because of the herbal knowledge and the higher success rates of Black doctors. Nevertheless, a prejudice against using Black doctors persisted among whites. Even during the Civil War, the War Department was initially reluctant to use African American medical personnel. That unwillingness to admit

African Americans as doctors and nurses may have contributed to the 35 percent greater total casualties that African American troops suffered in the war as compared to white troops. This greater percentage is particularly striking given that African American troops were not used in the war until 1863. The higher death rate also suggests that white physicians and nursing personnel were not adequately treating African American troops. Only eight African American doctors were commissioned in the Army Medical Corps, and seven of these eight were assigned to hospitals in Washington, D.C.

894 • Medical Schools Discriminate

Medical schools in the South and the North discriminated against prospective African American medical students. Martin Delany, for example, applied to the University of Pennsylvania, Jefferson Medical College, and medical schools in Albany and Geneva, New York, before finally gaining acceptance at Harvard University in 1850. In 1860 eight northern medical schools admitted African Americans: Bowdoin, the medical school of the University of New York, Caselton Medical School in Vermont, Berkshire Medical School in Massachusetts, Rush Medical School in Chicago, the Eclectic Medical School of Philadelphia, the Homeopathic College of Cleveland, and Harvard University Medical School.

895 • James McCune Smith Critiques Craniology

Some African Americans opted to travel abroad for their education. Dr. James McCune Smith (1813–65) received his early education in New York City but, rebuffed by American colleges, went to the University of Glasgow and received his B.A., M.A., and M.D. by 1837. Smith returned to New York and opened a successful practice, but he devoted the majority of his time

to abolitionist activities. He edited both the *Colored American* and the *North Star*. Smith dedicated himself to refuting popular theories of racial inferiority, especially those espoused by Senator John C. Calhoun and Dr. Samuel Cartwright. Cartwright offered a biological justification for slavery in 1843:

... the brain being ten percent less in volume and weight, he [the Negro] is, from necessity, more under the influence of his instincts and animality than other races of men and less under the influence of his reflective facilities. ... His mind thus depressed ... nothing but arbitrary power, prescribing and enforcing temperance in all things, can restrain the excesses of his mental nature and restore reason to her throne.

In addition to Cartwright's theory, Calhoun pointed to the census of 1840 as evidence of African American inferiority. The census allegedly showed that the rate of mental illness among free Blacks was eleven times that of Black slaves—indicating an inability to handle the "burden of freedom." Dr. Smith refuted Calhoun by proving that the results of the 1840 census were fraudulent. Smith showed, for example, that several northern towns said to contain mentally incompetent African Americans had no African American residents at all. In a series of lectures entitled "Comparative Anatomy and Physiology of the Races," Smith successfully repudiated Cartwright's biological arguments.

896 • Freedmen's Hospital

In 1868 General O. O. Howard ordered the Freedmen's Hospital to be established at Fifth and W Streets N.W. in Washington, D.C. The hospital was to serve the thousands of African Americans who had flocked to Washington at the conclusion of the Civil War. Dr. Charles Purvis was chosen to head the three-hundred-bed facility, thereby becoming the first African American to head a civilian hospital. The hospital was vital to improving the health of the African American community. In 1866 some 23,000 of the city's 31,500 African Americans were said to be suffering with some type of illness, and the extraordinary efforts of the hospital and its medical staff helped reduce the number of sick.

897 • Medical Schools Established at Black Universities

In 1868 a medical school was established to serve both white and black students at Howard University. The student body was diverse; in 1871, for example, students came from thirteen states, the District of Columbia, six foreign countries, and the West Indies. The school term lasted almost six months, with classes held from 3:30 to 10:00 P.M. to accommodate those students who worked for the government. Howard was unique because it admitted not only Black and white students but also women. Initially the faculty included several white professors who at the same time held similar positions at the Georgetown University Medical School. Another important medical school was established in Nashville, Tennessee, for the education of African American doctors. Called Meharry Medical College, it differed from Howard in that it educated only African Americans. Between 1877 and 1890, Meharry Medical College awarded medical degrees to 102 students. Many of these students remained in the South following their graduation and provided much-needed services to local African American communities.

898 • William H. Barnes (1887–1945)

In 1887 Dr. William H. Barnes became chief of otolaryngology at Frederick Douglass Hospital in Philadelphia. Born into poverty in Philadelphia,

Barnes was awarded a scholarship to the University of Pennsylvania Medical School based on his outstanding score on a competitive exam. Dr. Barnes is most famous for his bloodless operative techniques, and he created several new or improved surgical instruments to make surgeries easier and cleaner. A firm believer in the relationship between health and environment, as well as racial equality, Barnes fought actively for better housing and living conditions for African Americans in Philadelphia.

899 • Daniel Hale Williams (1856–1931)

Dr. Daniel Hale Williams, who founded the Provident Hospital and Training School on May 4, 1891, was the first person to perform a successful open-heart operation. On July 9, 1893, a man stabbed in the chest during a bar brawl was brought to Provident with a wound considered fatal. Without the benefit of X-rays, breathing apparatus, or blood transfusions, Williams

Daniel Hale Williams. Photograph Courtesy of Schomburg Center for Research in Black Culture, New York Public Library, Astor, Lenox and Tilden Foundation

opened a small trapdoor in the patient's chest, assessed the wound, repaired the damage to the left internal mammary artery, and closed a second wound in the quivering pericardium, which covered the heart. The patient was pronounced healthy and discharged fifty-one days later. Williams wanted to see nurses, both white and Black, trained with high standards and with the newest methods of cleanliness. He also wanted to see training for doctors, especially Black surgeons, improved. At the time, even if Black doctors went to good medical schools, they were not allowed to operate in most hospitals, which prevented them from getting practical experiences or finding consistent work on a hospital staff. Provident insisted on high standards, and only doctors from accredited medical schools were allowed to practice there. Similarly, only the most well-educated women were accepted by the nursing school.

900 • Louis T. Wright (1891–1952)

In 1919 Dr. Louis T. Wright became the first Black physician to be appointed to the staff of a New York hospital when he was hired by Dr. Cosmo O'Neal, the superintendent of Harlem Hospital. At the time, Harlem was a wealthy white community. Dr. O'Neal had heard of Wright's successful work in the army with a smallpox vaccination, using an injection method rather than the previously used scratching method. His reputation enabled him to break the barriers to Black doctors in New York hospitals. In 1948 Dr. Wright entered the field of cancer research. He founded the Harlem Hospital Cancer Research Foundation and dealt with the effectiveness of chemotherapeutic agents to attack and destroy cancer cells. He received a grant from the Damon Runyon Fund to engage in cancer research. He wrote fifteen papers on his work on the effects of various drugs and hor-

mones on cancer cells. Perhaps the crowning achievement of his career came in 1949, when Dr. Wright became the first physician in the world to experiment on humans with the drug Aureomycin. He used it for treatment of patients with lymphogranuloma venereum, a venereal disease caused by a virus that can weaken the body to make the patient an invalid for life. Wright found the drug that helped the patients and cured other diseases such as typhus, pneumonia, and intestinal infections. He published thirty papers on his discoveries with Aureomycin. Dr. Wright is also credited with developing the neck brace used to care for a patient with a broken neck without moving the person and causing further damage to the spinal cord. His successful work on skull trauma led editor Charles Scudder to ask him to contribute a section on skull fractures to the eleventh edition of *The Treatment of Fractures,* published in 1938. Wright also invented a blade plate for surgical treatment of fractures above the knee joint.

901 • Solomon C. Fuller (1872–1953)

Dr. Solomon Carter Fuller was known throughout the medical community for his work on physical or organic changes in the body that cause different forms of mental disorders. Carter was born in Liberia in 1872, the son of a coffee planter and a government official. Educated at Livingstone College in North Carolina, he received his M.D. from Boston University in 1897. Following graduation he was appointed to the faculty at Boston University and remained on staff for over thirty years. His research investigated schizophrenia, old-age mental illness, alcoholism disorders, and inherited brain diseases. It was Fuller who suggested in 1911 that Alzheimer's was caused by something other than the conventional explanation of arteriosclerosis, or hardening of the arteries. Fur-

ther testing confirmed his theory. Fuller was also credited as a pioneer in adapting European psychological research and knowledge in the United States. During his forty-five-year career at the Westborough State Hospital for the Insane in Massachusetts, for example, Fuller was one of the first to practice psychotherapy—the treatment of patients through counseling and discussion to help the patient analyze his own behavior and feelings.

902 • William Hinton (1883–1959)

Dr. William Hinton developed the Davies-Hinton test for syphilis detection that dramatically improved the ability of doctors to accurately test patients for the disease. Born in Chicago, Hinton attended Harvard as an undergraduate and as a medical student, graduating with an M.D. in 1912. Because of his race, he could not obtain an internship at a Boston hospital, but he did secure a position at the Wasserman Laboratory, where he was appointed assistant director in 1915. There he became one of the world's foremost authorities on venereal disease and authored, in 1936, *Syphilis and Its Treatment,* the first medical textbook published by an African American. He also taught at Harvard University, becoming in 1949 the first African American professor at the university. But Hinton's real contribution was to revolutionize the detection of syphilis. Hinton's test was faster, more accurate, and more easily replicated. The U.S. Public Health Service concluded in 1934 that his test was the most efficient for early detection of the disease. In 1931, Hinton started a school at the Boston Dispensary to train women and men to become laboratory technicians. The program grew into one of the country's leading schools for medical technician training. The Hinton program—which continues today as part of the medical training program at North-

eastern University in Boston—was one of the first to help meet the growing demand for technicians well versed in new laboratory techniques, and graduates of the school were hired by laboratories and hospitals nationwide. This brilliant man was also modest: when offered the NAACP's Spingarn Medal in 1938, he refused it because he felt he had not accomplished enough.

903 • Charles R. Drew (1904–50)

Dr. Charles Richard Drew was the first African American to receive the doctor of science degree in medicine. After earning his bachelor's degree at Amherst College in 1925 and graduating from McGill University Medical School in Canada in 1933, Drew came to Columbia University to do research on blood preservation. At the time, blood transfusion was already an established medical procedure, but much remained to be learned about the best ways to

Portrait of Charles R. Drew by Betsy Graves Reyneau, c. 1953. National Portrait Gallery, Smithsonian Institution. Gift of the Harmon Foundation

preserve and handle donated blood. Whole blood, for example, could be stored for no longer than ten days before the blood cells began to break down. Drew's research demonstrated that plasma, or blood fluid, with the cells and platelets separated out, was much easier to preserve than whole blood. His thesis, "Banked Blood," addressed the evolution of the blood bank, the transformations that occur in preserved blood, and the success of the blood bank established at Presbyterian Hospital (New York City) in August 1939 by Drew and Dr. John Scudder.

904 • "Blood for Britain"

In August 1940 the "Blood for Britain" project, designed to generate blood for transfusions for the growing number of men wounded in World War II, was organized. Much of the blood arriving in England from the United States was contaminated and useless. Dr. Charles Drew was offered the position of medical supervisor to address the problem, and upon his acceptance, he immediately standardized blood drawing and storing procedures at all participating hospitals to avoid contamination. He also increased the volunteer pool for blood donation. At the conclusion of this project, the American Red Cross set up a similar program and appointed Drew as the director in January 1941. Ironically, because the U.S. Army prohibited blood donations from African Americans, Drew could not contribute to his own program.

905 • Percy L. Julian (1899–1975)

Dr. Percy Lavon Julian overcame considerable obstacles to make valuable contributions to both organic chemistry and the treatment of arthritis. Born in 1899, the grandson of a former slave, Julian received an inadequate education at the segregated schools of Alabama. Accepted

Percy L. Julian. Courtesy of National Archives

to DePauw University in 1916, Julian was forced to take remedial and supplemental courses during his first two years to make up for the deficiencies of the Alabama system. A tireless worker (the desire for education ran strong in his family—his grandfather was missing two fingers as punishment for learning to read and write as a slave), Julian soon caught up and graduated as a class valedictorian and a Phi Beta Kappa. Discouraged from entering graduate school because of the lack of postgraduate jobs available for African Americans with advanced degrees, Julian accepted a teaching position at Fisk University and remained there until he won the Austin Fellowship in Chemistry position at Harvard University. Again he graduated at the top of his class, and again he was discouraged from further study. After a two-year faculty position at Howard University, Julian traveled to Vienna, where he earned a Ph.D. in organic chemistry. Julian returned to the United States and accepted a position at De-Pauw, where he conducted research until he was offered the position of chief chemist and director of research at the Glidden Company. Dr. Julian developed inexpensive copies of many costly drugs, making them accessible to the general population. In 1935 he developed an exact copy of the rare and expensive drug used to treat glaucoma. His writings about the discovery were the first papers with a Black individual as the senior author to appear in respected American chemistry journals. Julian also produced synthetic cortisone, which cost several hundred dollars less per gram to produce than the cortisone, significantly reducing the cost of treating arthritis and other muscle and bone disorders.

906 • Julian's Struggles

I shall never forget a week of anxious waiting in 1920 to see if I could get to graduate school. I had worked hard for four years. I stood by as day by day my fellow students in Chemistry came by saying, "I am going to Illinois"; "I am going to Ohio State"; "I am going to Michigan"; "I am going to Yale." "Where are you going?" they asked, and they answered for me, "You must be getting the Harvard plum." I could stand the suspense no longer. I went to Professor Blanchard, as staunch a friend as he knew how to be then, and certainly later my most unforgettable friend, and asked timidly, "Professor, did you get me a fellowship?" And then this dear fellow with resignation told me "Now, now, Julian, I knew you would be asking me that. Come in to my office." There he showed me numerous letters from men who had really meant "God" to me—great American chemists of their day. And they had written to him, "I'll take your Mr. ———, but I'd advise you to discourage your bright colored lad. We

couldn't get him a job when he's done, and it'll only mean frustration. In industry, research demands co-work, and white boys would so sabotage his work that an industrial research leader would go crazy! And, of course, we couldn't find him a job as a teacher in a white university. Why don't you find him a teaching job in a Negro college in the South? He doesn't need a Ph.D. for that!" There went my dreams and hopes of four years, and as I pressed my lips to hold back the tears, I remembered my breeding, braced myself, and thanked him for thinking of me.

907 • *Chicago Sun-Times* on Fire Bombing of Julian's Home

As the first black family to move into an all-white community in Oak Park, a suburb of Chicago, Dr. Percy L. Julian and his family were often the targets of racial violence. The following is an editorial that appeared in the *Chicago Sun-Times,* November 23, 1950, after an arson attempt on the Julian home on Thanksgiving Day:

Arsonists tried to burn down the newly purchased home of Dr. Percy Julian to keep him out of Oak Park because he is a Negro. We wonder whether these cowards whose mad prejudice drove them to commit a felony would refuse to use the lifesaving discoveries of Dr. Julian because they came from the hand and brain of a Negro. Would they refuse to take synthetic cortisone if they were wracked with the pain of arthritis? Would they forbid their wives the use of synthetic female hormone now abundantly available because of Dr. Julian's work? Would they refuse to use his synthetic physostigmine if they were afflicted with the dread eye disease, glaucoma? If they themselves were caught in a raging gasoline fire such as they tried to set, would they order the fireman not to use Dr. Julian's great discovery, chemical foam? This stuff saved the lives of thousands of American airmen and sailors after crash landings during the war. No! The bigots welcome the discoveries of Dr. Julian the scientist, but they try to exclude Dr. Julian the human being.

908 • Samuel L. Kountz

Dr. Samuel L. Kountz, noted for his research in immunology, founded the largest kidney transplant research center and participated in the first West Coast kidney transplant in 1959. He worked on methods to combat organ transplant rejection and performed five hundred kidney transplants during his career. In 1964 Dr. Kountz made history by transplanting a kidney from mother to daughter. This was the first transplant between two humans who were not identical twins.

909 • Rebecca Lee

Rebecca Lee was the first African American woman to receive a medical degree. She received her doctorate of medicine degree from the New England Female Medical College in 1864. She conducted a successful practice in Richmond, Virginia, for several years before relocating back to Boston. In 1883 Lee published *A Book of Medical Discourses* that counseled women on how to care for themselves and their children.

910 • Jane Cooke Wright (b. 1919)

Dr. Jane Cooke Wright was appointed associate dean of the New York Medical College in July 1966, attaining the highest post ever granted to an African American woman. She is credited as the first doctor to see remissions in skin cancer mycosis fungoides patients and in solid breast cancer tumor patients. Dr. Wright is an accomplished author, with writings appearing in professional journals and medical text-

Dr. Jane C. Wright, cancer researcher, professor of surgery, and associate dean of the New York Medical College. New York Medical College

books. Wright originally worked with her father, Dr. Louis Wright, at the Cancer Research Foundation testing new alkylating agents for treatment on cancer patients.

911 • Levi Watkins, Jr.

Dr. Levi Watkins, Jr., performed the first surgical implantation of the automatic implantable defibrillator in the human heart in 1980. The device corrects arrhythmia, which prevents the heart from pumping blood.

912 • Ben Carson (b. 1951)

A graduate of Yale University and the University of Michigan Medical School, Ben Carson gained worldwide recognition for his part in the first successful separation of Siamese twins joined at the back of the head, an extremely complex and delicate operation that was planned for five months and took twenty-two hours of actual surgery.

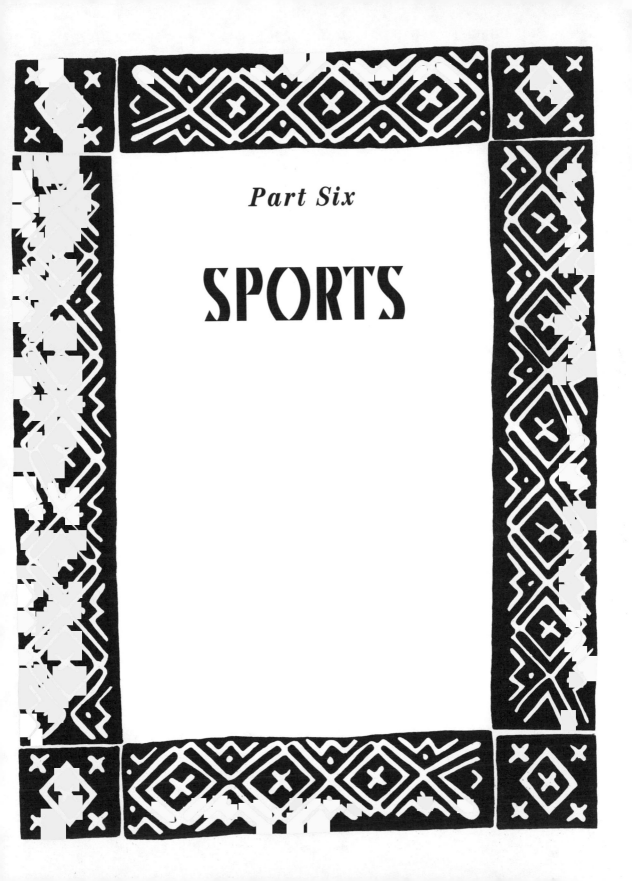

Part Six

SPORTS

Sport in America is not only entertainment and recreation but also an arena of competition that is highly charged with racial stereotypes and feelings. Perhaps the first conflicts over Black participation in sports activities with whites goes back to the days of slavery when African Americans were thought of as bodies without minds. This ideology justified the exploitation of African Americans for the cultivation of tobacco, rice, and cotton; but it also meant that Black Americans would be respected for their physical prowess. For a variety of reasons, not the least of which was that sports offered upward mobility (and in some cases freedom from slavery), African Americans seized on sports as a way to prove first equality and then, in selected sports, the superiority of African American athletes.

913 • Mixed Participation Banned

By the early 1800s the inferiority of slaves in "both body and mind" was accepted as fact. States began to vigorously discourage social interaction between slaves and whites. In 1830, for example, North Carolina enacted legislation making it unlawful "for any white person or free Negro or mulatto, or persons of mixed blood to play at any game of cards, dice, nine-pins, or any game of chance or hazard whether for money, liquor, or property or not, with any slave or slaves."

914 • Slave Participation in Sports

Despite their banishment from organized sports, enslaved African Americans still found opportunities to participate in sports activities. One ex-slave recalled, "Us tho'ed horse shoes, jumped poles, walked on stilts, an' played marbles." Another explained, "Shinny [baseball] was de thing dat I like best." Slave owners considered sports activities disruptive to the daily routine, but they did allow sports and games during holidays. Frederick Douglass believed "those holidays were among the most effective means in the hands of the slaveholders in keeping down the spirit of insurrection." He noted that "everything of rational enjoyment was frowned upon, and only those wild and low sports peculiar to semi-civilized people were encouraged." These wild sports included cockfighting, boxing, and gambling.

915 • Black Colleges and Sports

Black colleges in the post–Civil War period lacked well-developed athletic facilities. Fearing the displeasure of their white patrons, Black college officials were often reluctant to allocate funds to athletic programs. Often, there were no funds to distribute to the athletic department anyway. In 1890, for example, a congressional act appropriated funds to establish land-grant colleges for African Americans (now the Big Ten schools) and earmarked some of the money for recreational facilities. However, the money had to be channeled through the state legislatures, and for more than seventy years, most of these funds were given instead to white land-grant schools.

Boxing

916 • First Black to Contend for a World Title in Any Sport

On October 8, 1805, William Richmond became the first African American to contend for a world title in any sport. Richmond, a free Black born in 1763 on Staten Island, grew up fighting soldiers on the docks of New York Harbor during the British occupation. Richmond's fighting prowess was noticed by the British commander, Hugh Percy, and he brought Richmond with him when he returned to England. Once in England, Richmond accumulated enough semiprofessional wins to challenge then-champion Tom Cribb to a bout. On October 8, 1805, Richmond and Cribb boxed for more than ninety minutes before Cribb was declared the winner. Despite his loss, Richmond continued to box professionally until he was fifty-two. He also gave boxing lessons in London and was responsible for training Tom Molineaux, the next African American to challenge Cribb for the championship.

917 • Tom Molineaux (1784–1818)

Slavery directly influenced the boxing career of Tom Molineaux. Molineaux, born into slavery on March 23, 1784, won thousands of dollars for his owner in matches against other slaves. Slave owners frequently pitted their slaves against

Tom Molineaux, hand-colored etching by Robert D. Dighton, 1812. National Portrait Gallery, Smithsonian Institution

one another, placing huge wagers on the outcome, and Molineaux and his brothers often won double their market worth for their owner. In 1809, in recognition of his service, Molineaux's master agreed to set him free if he won a final bout. After his victory, Molineaux, with $500 in his pocket, sailed first to New York and then to London, where he met William Richmond.

Once in London, Molineaux trained diligently. After winning six bouts against lesser known opponents, William Richmond placed an ad in the *London Times* for Molineaux, challenging Tom Cribb to "unretire" and "meet the Moor." On December 10, 1810, Cribb and Molineaux met in Copthall Hall in Sussex, England.

Although Cribb officially won the fight after forty-four exhausting rounds and collected a $2,000 purse, Molineaux clearly deserved the victory. In the twenty-eighth round, Molineaux had knocked Cribb down and Cribb did not rise within the required thirty seconds. Cribb's trainer leaped into the ring to accuse Molineaux of hiding weights in his gloves, and referee Ap Phys Price, defending the honor of white Britain, waived the rules and gave Cribb two more minutes to revive himself. A disappointed Molineaux finally succumbed fifteen rounds later.

918 • First Black to Hold an American Title

On March 31, 1891, George "Little Chocolate" Dixon became the first Black man to hold an American title in any sport. Dixon, born in Halifax, Nova Scotia, in 1870, became interested in boxing after he moved to Boston with his parents and began an apprenticeship with a photographer specializing in boxing photography. After training in a local gym, the 5'3" 100-pound bantamweight turned professional at age sixteen. In 1888 Dixon fought seventy rounds to a draw against Cal McCarthy for the bantamweight title. In a rematch three years later, on March 31, 1891, he captured the title with a knockout in the twenty-second round. Dixon became the first Black boxer to win an international title on June 27, 1890, when he knocked out British featherweight champion Nunc Wallace for the international bantamweight title. Then, on June 27, 1892, he won the featherweight world title and $4,500 by knocking out Fred Johnson. Buoyed by his victories, Dixon decided to try his luck in the South. On September 6, 1892, Dixon fought the white amateur boxer Jack Skelly at the private New Orleans Olympia Club. At the time, New Orleans was racially very divided and it was assumed that any experienced white boxer in good condition could beat any Black fighter. Through eight rounds on September 6, 1892, Dixon beat Shelly badly. The white community was horrified and discouraged southern white boxers from fighting in future interracial bouts.

919 • White Boxers Refuse to Fight African Americans

It was difficult for African American boxers to challenge for titles against white boxers. John L. Sullivan, one of the country's first national sports heroes and the world heavyweight champion in 1889, for example, refused to fight against Black boxers: "I will not fight a negro. I never have, and I never shall."

John Sullivan's refusal to fight Black boxers was supported by many in the white sports community. Charles Dana, an influential sports editor writing for the *New York Sun,* decried the rise of African Americans in boxing and warned that unless others followed Sullivan's example, Blacks would soon dominate the sport:

We are in the midst of a growing menace. The Black man is rapidly forging to the front ranks in athletics, especially in the field of fisticuffs. We are in the midst of a Black rise against white supremacy. . . . There are two negroes in the ring today who can thrash any white man breathing in their respective classes [George Dixon and Joe Walcott]. . . . What America needs now is another John L. Sullivan. . . . Wake up, you pugilists of the white race! Are you going to permit yourself to be passed by the Black race?"

Jack Johnson. Photograph by Otto Sarony, 1909. Prints and Photographs Division, Library of Congress

920 • First Black Man to Beat a White World Heavyweight Champ

John Arthur "Jack" Johnson, born in Galveston, Texas, in 1878, sought adventure from an early age. Leaving home after finishing fifth grade, Johnson worked on a milk wagon, as a baker's apprentice, and as a cook's helper on a steamship. While working for an ex-boxer in a Dallas carriage shop, Johnson entered his first match and took home twenty-five dollars even though he lost. For the next several years, Johnson traveled the country entering matches, participating in battles royal and serving as a sparring partner for better fighters. On February 3, 1903, Johnson took the Negro heavyweight crown from "Denver" Ed Martin. Not

content to fight within the ranks of African American boxers, Johnson tried to arrange bouts with the 1903 white heavyweight champion, Jim Jeffries, and Canadian Tommy Burns. Burns drew the color line and refused a match, but Johnson followed him to England, France, and Australia, publicly demanding that he fight. Finally Burns agreed, and on December 26, 1908, Johnson and Burns fought for a $40,000 purse—$35,000 for Burns and $5,000 for Johnson. Johnson clearly dominated the fight, staggering Burns with rights to the head and combinations, and in the fourteenth round, with Burns bleeding from the mouth and his eyes swollen almost completely shut, the fight was stopped and Johnson declared the winner.

921 • Johnson vs. Jeffries

Following Jack Johnson's victory over Tommy Burns in 1908, public pressure mounted for Jim Jeffries to come out of retirement and reclaim the crown and white honor. Author Jack London wrote, ". . . one thing now remains. Jim Jeffries must emerge from his alfalfa farm and remove the golden smile from Jack Johnson's face. Jeff, it's up to you!" Jeffries reluctantly agreed, and the fight was set for July 4, 1910, in San Francisco. The fight sparked enormous interest, and six promoters vied for the right to handle the contest. The negotiations with the potential promoters signified the largest legitimate business deal ever conducted by an African American up to that time. Ultimately the $101,000 purse was issued in four installments: $20,000 immediately after signing the contract; $20,000 sixty days after signing; $50,000 forty-eight hours before the bout; and the rest following the fight. The money was split sixty-forty, with the larger percentage allocated to Jeffries.

Jeffries, a 5 to 3 favorite despite his more than five-year absence from the ring, was billed

as the Great White Hope. Throughout the match, Johnson easily outboxed Jeffries and verbally taunted him with remarks about his ability. Early in the fifteenth round, Jeffries was knocked to the ground twice. After a third knockdown several seconds later, he was counted out and Jack Johnson awarded the world heavyweight title. Jeffries was gracious in his loss: "I guess it's my own fault. . . . They started calling for me and mentioning me as 'the white man's hope.' I guess my pride got the better of my judgment." He later acknowledged, "I never could have whipped Johnson at my best. I couldn't have hit him." The Johnson-Jeffries bout was one of the most racially charged fights in history.

922 • Fallout from Johnson vs. Jeffries

The 1910 defeat of Jim Jeffries by an African American infuriated whites. Nationwide, thirteen African Americans were murdered and hundreds injured in postfight racial incidents. The July 5 edition of the *New York Times* contained numerous stories describing the violence, including "Three Killed in Vidalia [Georgia] . . . Omaha Negro Killed . . . Two Negroes Slain . . . Blacks Shoot up Town . . . Houston Man Kills Negro . . . Negro Shoots White Man . . . Negro Hurt in Philadelphia . . . Outbreaks in New Orleans . . . Police Club Rioting Negroes . . . Mob Beats Negroes in Macon . . . 70 Arrested in Baltimore."

923 • The Brown Bomber (1914–81)

It took twenty years after Jack Johnson's victory over Jim Jeffries before another African American was allowed a shot at the heavyweight title. When he was seventeen, Joe Louis, born Joe Louis Barrow, was given fifty cents by his mother to pay for his violin lessons. Instead, Louis used the money to rent a locker at the

Joe Louis. Photograph by Carl Van Vechten. Prints and Photographs Division, Library of Congress. Gift of Carl Van Vechten

Brewster East Side Gymnasium in Detroit, where he began to train as a boxer. After fighting fifty-four matches as an amateur, Louis turned professional on July 4, 1934. Aided by John Roxborough, a local Black businessman, and Jack Blackburn, an ex-boxer, Louis prepared to break into the heavyweight division. Anxious to elude the fate of Jack Johnson, Louis made every effort to avoid activities that would encourage racial discord. He was given lessons in manners and diction, advised to always seek a knockout rather than depend on the judges' decisions, and was repeatedly admonished, "For God's sake, after you beat a white opponent, don't smile." By May 5, 1935, Louis's heavyweight professional record was 22–0. No match had lasted more than ten rounds.

Louis's popularity within the Black community skyrocketed after his defeat of Primo Carnera on June 25, 1935. Making his New York debut, Louis knocked the 6'7" 275-pound Italian out in the sixth round. Louis described his bewilderment at the attention he received:

When I walked in the church, you'd have thought I was the second coming of Christ.... Rev. J. H. Maston ... talked about how God gave certain people gifts ... and through my fighting I was to uplift the spirit of my race. I must make the whole world know that Negro people were strong, fair, and decent.... He said I was one of the chosen. I thought to myself, "Jesus Christ, am I all that?"

924 • Louis vs. Schmeling

The fights that brought Joe Louis his greatest fame came against the German fighter Max

Schmeling. On June 19, 1936, Louis was knocked out in the twelfth round by Schmeling, and Nazi Germany celebrated Louis's defeat. A German magazine, *Der Weltkampf,* printed an article that said "France, England, and white North America—cannot thank Schmeling enough for his victory, for he checked the arrogance of the Negro and clearly demonstrated to them the superiority of white intelligence." This time, however, white Americans were more hesitant to support a boxer solely because of his race. Schmeling was a German, and as news of Nazi atrocities began to cross the Atlantic, the defeat of fascism and a victory for America became more important than racial solidarity. On June 22, 1938, Louis knocked Schmeling out just two minutes and four seconds into the first round. In contrast to the violence that followed Gans's and Johnson's victories over white men, this time the entire country celebrated Louis's feat. Louis would hold the heavyweight title for eleven years, eight months, and seven days.

925 • Sugar Ray Robinson (1920–89)

Born Walker Smith, Jr., Sugar Ray Robinson recorded eighty-nine amateur fights with sixty-nine knockouts, forty-four coming in the first round. Winner of the 1939 featherweight and the 1940 lightweight Golden Gloves titles, Robinson turned professional in 1940 and won his October 4 debut at Madison Square Garden with a second-round knockout of Joe Echeverria. He went on to win thirty-nine consecutive fights, twenty-eight by knockout. Finally, on February 5, 1943, in their second meeting, Jake LaMotta beat Robinson in ten rounds for his first loss. Rebounding, Robinson won ninety-six straight matches over the next eight years.

At age thirty, on February 14, 1951, Sugar Ray Robinson won his first world middleweight crown from Jake LaMotta in a thirteenth-round

technical knockout. He lost the crown to Randy Turpin in England on July 10, 1951, in a fifteen-round bout. In the rematch at the Polo Grounds on September 12, 1951, Robinson regained the title with a tenth-round technical knockout. After retiring to a two-and-a-half-year show business career, Robinson returned to the ring at age thirty-four and won the middleweight crown for the third time from Carl "Bobo" Olson in a second-round knockout. On May 1, 1957, he became the first man to win a world title four times when he scored a fifth-round knockout over Gene Fullmer. Fullmer later beat Robinson in a fifteen-round bout, but Robinson won his fifth middleweight crown on March 25, 1958, against Carmen Basilio. Robinson finally retired in 1965 and was elected to the Boxing Hall of Fame in 1967.

926 • First Heavyweight Champion to Regain Title

Floyd Patterson learned to box at the Wiltwyck School for troubled youngsters in New York City. As an amateur, he developed a peekaboo style of defense and won the 1952 Golden Gloves middleweight title, a gold medal in the 1952 Olympics as a middleweight, and the National AAU middleweight title in 1952. Patterson won the heavyweight title from Archie Moore in a fifth-round knockout in 1955. He lost the title to Swede Ingemar Johansson on June 26, 1959, at Yankee Stadium. Johansson knocked Patterson down seven times during the match on his way to a technical knockout in the third round. Patterson became the first heavyweight to regain the title in June 1960 in a fifth-round knockout over Johansson at the Polo Grounds. He defeated Johansson a second time at Miami Beach on March 13, 1961, on a sixth-round knockout.

927 • Sonny Liston (1932–70)

Charles Liston learned to box in the Missouri State Penitentiary when he was incarcerated for robbing a service station. After his release, Liston won the 1952 Golden Gloves heavyweight title. In 1956 his boxing license was revoked when he was arrested for assaulting a policeman and sentenced to nine months in a workhouse. Liston's prison record and alleged ties to organized crime made it difficult for him to secure matches, but he finally obtained a shot at the heavyweight title in February 1962 after he hired Jack Nilon as a manager. After his second defeat of Floyd Patterson, Liston fought Cassius Clay on February 25, 1964. Liston, a 7 to 1 favorite, alleged Clay "couldn't lick a Popsicle." At the beginning of the seventh round, however, Liston threw in the towel, claiming he was unable to move his left arm. Many speculated Liston threw the fight to pay off a debt to an organized crime figure. A second fight was held on May 25, 1965, with Liston being knocked out two minutes and twelve seconds into round one.

928 • Muhammad Ali Wins Heavyweight Title Four Times (b. 1942)

One day after winning the world heavyweight title by defeating Sonny Liston, Cassius Clay, who had been befriended by Malcolm X, announced his conversion to the Muslim faith and changed his name to Muhammad Ali, which means "worthy of all praise." As part of his new religious faith, Ali refused to submit to the Vietnam War draft because of his opposition to war. He spent twenty-nine months in jail, was stripped of his championship title, and lost his license to fight professionally. He was finally de-

clared free on June 28, 1970, by the United States Supreme Court, and his license was restored. He began training once again and used victories over Jerry Quarry and Oscar Bonavena to prepare for his fight with the new WBA heavyweight title holder, Joe Frazier.

On March 28, 1971, 20,000 fans at Madison Square Garden and 1.3 million fans before closed-circuit televisions watched Muhammad Ali fight Joe Frazier for the WBA heavyweight title. Frazier won the fifteen-round bout but did not fight for ten months following the match. Both boxers were taken to the hospital following the fight. In their second meeting for the NABF title on January 28, 1974, at Madison Square Garden, 20,746 live fans and 1.1 million closed-circuit television viewers witnessed a

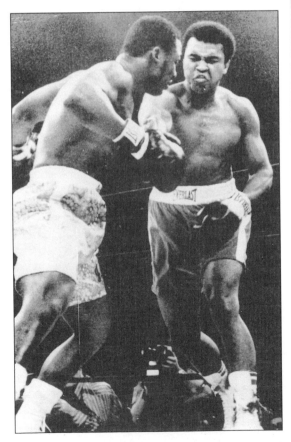

Muhammad Ali battling Joe Frazier in their first championship fight, March 18, 1971. Associated Press. Courtesy of Wide World Photos, Inc. National Archives

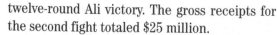

twelve-round Ali victory. The gross receipts for the second fight totaled $25 million.

Muhammad Ali became the second man in history to regain the world heavyweight title on October 30, 1974. An eighth-round knockout over George Foreman was witnessed by 62,000 fans in Kinshasa, Zaire. Ali used what he described as his "rope-a-dope" strategy to defeat Foreman. By leaning back against the ropes, protecting his head, and allowing Foreman to throw numerous punches, Ali correctly guessed Foreman would tire himself out.

Ali's third and final meeting with Joe Frazier came on September 30, 1975, in Manila, the Philippines. Also called Super Fight II, the match was hailed as the greatest fight in the history of the sport. After fourteen difficult rounds, Frazier's trainer, Eddie Futch, refused to let him come out for round fifteen, cutting his gloves off him and telling him, "Sit down, son. It's all over. No one will ever forget what you did here today."

Muhammad Ali lost the world title on February 15, 1978, at age thirty-six to Leon Spinks in a fifteen-round split decision in Las Vegas. Ali became the first man to win the world heavyweight title three times with a fifteen-round unanimous decision over Spinks in the New Orleans Superdome. He retired and then returned at age thirty-nine to lose in eleven rounds to WBC heavyweight champion Larry Holmes on October 2, 1980. Muhammad Ali was elected to the Boxing Hall of Fame in 1987.

929 • One of the Most Financially Successful Boxers

"Sugar" Ray Charles Leonard won the 1973 National Golden Gloves lightweight title, the 1974 National Golden Gloves light-welterweight title, the 1974 and 1975 United States AAU light-welterweight titles, and the light-welter-weight gold medal in the 1975 Pan-American Games and the 1976 Olympics. In his first professional fight, Leonard won $38,000. He won the NABF welterweight title from Pete Banzany on August 12, 1979, in Las Vegas. On November 30, 1979, Leonard won the WBD welterweight title in a fifteenth-round knockout over Wilfredo Benitez. Leonard had earned more than $3 million in his first three years as a professional boxer. He lost his title in a close decision to Roberto Duran on June 20, 1980. In the rematch on November 25, Leonard regained the title. These two bouts grossed Leonard over $16 million, more than the combined career winnings of Joe Louis, Sugar Ray Robinson, Floyd Patterson, and Archie Moore. Leonard elevated to the junior middleweight class and captured the world title from Ayub Kalule in Houston on June 25, 1981, in a ninth-round knockout. After a victory over Thomas Hearns on September 16, 1981, Leonard underwent surgery for a detached retina and retired in 1984.

930 • The "Hit Man" (b. 1958)

Thomas Hearns won the United States National AAU light-welterweight championship and the National Golden Gloves welterweight championship in 1977. His first seventeen professional bouts were won by knockout and he won thirty out of thirty-two fights. Hearns won the WBA title from Pipino Cuevas on August 2, 1980, in a second-round knockout. He lost the bid to unify the WBA and WBC world titles in a fourteenth-round loss to Ray Leonard on September 16, 1981. Hearns did unify the world titles in the junior middleweight class by capturing the WBC title over Wilfredo Benitez on December 3, 1982, and the WBA title over Roberto Duran on June 15, 1984.

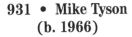
931 • Mike Tyson (b. 1966)

Mike Tyson entered the fighting world of the heavyweights as the enfant terrible, and he has lived up to his billing. Nurtured from the age of thirteen by his father surrogate, Cus D'Amato, Tyson developed early into a very aggressive fighter: in his first sixteen fights, he knocked out twelve of the boxers before the first round was over. With the same ferociousness, he won the heavyweight championship in 1985 and consolidated the heavyweight crown by beating Tony Tucker in 1987. He reached the zenith of his career when he devastated Michael Spinks in less than one round. But things began to go downhill for Tyson shortly thereafter. After he wed actress Robin Givens in 1988, the highly publicized marriage came to an end a year later. Then, uncharacteristically, Tyson seemed listless and unfocused when he was knocked out by the unspectacular Buster Douglas on February 16, 1990. Then, in February 1992, he was convicted of raping an eighteen-year-old contestant in the 1991 Miss Black America pageant in Indianapolis, and was sent to jail in April. Released in April 1995, he plans a return to boxing as a heavyweight.

932 • George Foreman (b. 1948)

George Foreman won the heavyweight Olympic gold medal in the 1968 Olympics. With a second-round knockout of Joe Frazier in January 1973, he became only the second man in his-

George Foreman waves American flag after winning the Olympic heavyweight boxing gold medal, October 26, 1968, in Mexico City. United Press International. Courtesy of Bettmann Archives. National Archives

tory to win both an Olympic gold medal and a world title in the heavyweight division. He defended his title against Jose Roman and Ken Norton in two bouts which together totaled only three rounds. These victories made Foreman eligible for his "Rumble in the Jungle" with Ali, the first-ever heavyweight title match to take place in Africa. After his loss to Ali in that fight, Foreman retired from boxing and became a minister before returning to boxing in 1987. He became the oldest fighter to regain a boxing title when, at age forty-five, he defeated Michael Moorer in November 1994 and took Moorer's International Boxing Federation heavyweight championship belt.

Baseball

933 • The Integrated National Association of Baseball Players

The first national organization of baseball clubs included Blacks. When the National Association of Baseball Players (NABBP) was formed in 1858, it did not exclude Blacks who were members of clubs in the association. However, in 1867, just when African Americans were winning the right to vote, the NABBP banned all Blacks from participation. The guidelines barred both African Americans and any clubs that had African Americans as members, thus creating an incentive for local clubs to refuse to allow Blacks on their teams. The pressure to eliminate Blacks came from Irish and German clubs that did not want to compete with Black players. In 1871 that organization was replaced by the National Association of Professional Baseball Players (NABP), which continued the ban through an unwritten "gentleman's agreement" among club owners. But because professional baseball was relatively unorganized, Black players continued to play for the numerous local all-Black teams that flourished in the post–Civil War period. Often these teams were comprised of members of the Black upper class who had the time and leisure to travel playing baseball. Bud Fowler, a player from one of these Black teams, the Washington Mutuals, became the first African American to play professional baseball full-time. He joined a local white team from New Castle, Pennsylvania, in 1872, before Reconstruction ended and the national organizations consolidated their control over baseball.

934 • First Black Player in Organized Baseball

Rivalry between national organizations helped create an opportunity for Moses Fleetwood Walker to become the first African American to play what is known as organized baseball. When the National League of Professional Baseball Clubs (NLPBBC) arose in 1876 to replace the NABP, the NLPBBC continued the earlier clubs' ban on Blacks. But in 1880 rebels against what became the National League formed their own competing American Association. Moses Walker was the Toledo Mudhens' full-time catcher when the team joined the Northwestern League of the American Association of Baseball Clubs in 1884. Walker had been the first African American to play on a white college varsity team, catching in 1878 for Oberlin College in Ohio and later at the University of Michigan Law School. Racism still blunted his baseball career, however. He had a nasty run-in with Adrian Cap Anson, the star of the Cincinnati Red Stockings and a known racist. Walker was also jeered by fans when the team played in Louisville and threatened with bodily harm when the team planned to play in Richmond, Virginia. Despite such harassment, Walker compiled an excellent record in 1884: he batted .251 over forty-six games, including four doubles and two triples, and was a superb fielding catcher.

935 • Blacks Forced out of Professional Baseball

African American players were becoming popular in the league again in 1887 when Cap Anson, the manager of the Chicago White Stockings, refused to field his team against Newark until Moses Walker and George Stovey left the field. Anson's personal boycott galvanized the opposition of several white players who refused to play against Black players. The same year, players on the St. Louis Browns, a white team, sent a letter of protest to the team president on the eve of a scheduled game before fifteen thousand against the Cuban Giants that read: "We, the undersigned members of the St. Louis baseball club, do not agree to play against negroes tomorrow. We will cheerfully play against white people at anytime, and think by refusing to play we are only doing what is right, taking everything into consideration." The protest worked, the game was called off, and the St. Louis Browns played against and lost to the Detroit Tigers instead. It was then understood throughout the league that no Black players would be signed in the future.

Most Black baseball players were paid much less than white players. This pay disparity was one of the reasons white players increasingly objected to playing with Blacks. White players feared large numbers of Black players on a team might lower the salaries for all.

936 • The Negro National League

At the urging of Rube Foster, a select group of Black baseball club owners met at the Colored YMCA in Kansas City on February 13–14, 1920, to form the Negro National League. The owners present were Rube Foster of the Chicago American Giants; C. I. Taylor of the Indianapolis ABCs; Joe Green of the Chicago Giants; J. L. Wilkerson, a white owner of the Kansas City Monarchs; Lorenzo S. Cobb of the St. Louis Giants; and J. T. Blount of the Detroit Stars. The NNL was the first long-term Black league in any professional sport. In the league's debut game on May 2, 1920, the Indianapolis ABCs defeated the Chicago Giants 4–2 in front of eight thousand fans at home. The NNL disbanded in 1931 due to bickering among owners, weak financial backing, few stars for the Black press to write about, and the death of Rube Foster on December 9, 1930. The NNL finally received serious competition in 1937 when the Negro American League was formed. The NAL consisted of the Kansas City Monarchs, the St. Louis Stars, the Indianapolis Athletics, the Cincinnati Tigers, the Memphis Red Sox, the Detroit Stars, the Birmingham Black Barons, and the Chicago American Giants.

While Black baseball teams often played each other, more often they barnstormed, traveling from town to town in the United States, Cuba, Mexico, and the Dominican Republic to play local Black teams and semiprofessional white teams. While no records of these contests have survived, evidence suggests such Black teams were competitive with white professional baseball teams. In 1911 Ty Cobb and the Detroit Tigers played a Black baseball team in Cuba. Cobb batted .370 for the five-game series, but the Black team's John Lloyd averaged .500. Cobb refused to play any more Black teams after the series was concluded.

937 • Josh Gibson (1911–47)

Known as the Black Babe Ruth, Josh Gibson, born in Buena Vista, Georgia, on December 21, 1911, was probably the most powerful baseball player of his time. Roy Campanella, who played with both Hank Aaron and Josh Gibson, once said: "I think Josh was the greatest home-run hitter I ever saw. Now it's true, nobody ever counted the home runs this man has hit, but I'll say one thing, I'll put him with anybody, not taking anything away from Babe Ruth. I think Josh Gibson was the greatest home run hitter that ever lived." He was easily the best player on his favorite team, the Homestead Grays, where he played catcher. In one game, he hit four home runs out of Griffith Stadium. According to his teammate Buck Leonard, "I saw him almost hit one out of Yankee Stadium. At the Polo Grounds I saw him hit one between the upper deck and the roof. It hit an elevated train track outside the park. Josh hit seventy to seventy-two home

Josh Gibson. Photograph by Charles "Teenie" Harris, c. 1942. Courtesy of Pittsburgh Courier Photographic Archives

runs in one year. In 1939 he hit more home runs in Griffith Stadium than all the right-handed hitters in the American League combined." Unfortunately there are no official records of Gibson's performances and he died before the desegregation of baseball.

938 • Judy Johnson

Another outstanding player was third baseman Judy Johnson of the Pittsburgh Crawfords. Johnson was regarded as one of the best all-around players in baseball. He was an excellent

fielder, able to roam to the right and left to catch balls, he bunted and hit well, and he was a defensive punisher who often threw out men at the plate with his powerful arm. In March 1975 Judy Johnson was inducted into the Baseball Hall of Fame.

939 • Satchel Paige (1906–82)

Leroy Paige earned his nickname while carrying satchel bags at the train station in Mobile, Alabama. He began pitching at age eighteen in 1924 with the Mobile Tigers. In 1926 Paige pitched for the Chattanooga Black Lookouts and the New Orleans Black Pelicans for $50 to $200 a month. Legendary as a pitcher in the Negro Leagues, Paige played in the 1948 World Series in game five between the Cleveland Indians and the Boston Braves at Cleveland. Paige pitched relief for two-thirds of an inning. He went on to play for the St. Louis Browns in 1951–53. To qualify him for a major league pension, the Kansas City Athletics signed Paige in 1965 for one game in which he pitched three innings. He was fifty-nine years old at the time. Satchel Paige was inducted into the Baseball Hall of Fame in 1971.

940 • First African American to Play in the Major League

On October 23, 1945, Branch Rickey, owner of the Brooklyn Dodgers of the National League, announced the signing of Jack Roosevelt Robinson to the organization. Robinson, who lettered in football, baseball, track, and basketball at UCLA, had been playing for the NNL's Kansas City Monarchs since March 1945 for $400 a month. In August 1945 Robinson signed with the Dodgers and was assigned to the Dodgers' minor league affiliate, the Montreal Royals, for a $3,500 signing bonus and $600 a month. On April 9, 1947, Rickey announced Robinson

African American baseball players of the Brooklyn Dodgers (from left to right): Roy Campanella, catcher, Don Newcombe, pitcher, and Jackie Robinson, second base, 1949. Courtesy of Bettmann Archives. National Archives

941 • MVP Three Different Years

Roy Campanella was the only Black baseball player to be named Most Valuable Player for three separate years (1951, 1953, and 1955). In 1948 he became the fourth Black player in the modern major leagues after he signed with the Brooklyn Dodgers. Campanella was originally asked by Branch Rickey to join the Dodgers organization in October 1945 because he did not want Robinson to be the only Black player, but Campanella declined because he thought Rickey was referring to the Brooklyn Brown Dodgers. In the 1955 World Series, he had two home runs, four runs batted in, and seven hits. On January 28, 1959, Campanella's car skidded into a pole on an icy road in New York and left him paralyzed from the chest down. After intensive physical therapy, he returned as an instructor with the Dodgers. In May 1959, 93,000 fans, a league record, crowded into the Los Angeles Coliseum to honor Campanella's courage and accomplishments. He was inducted into the Baseball Hall of Fame in 1969.

would be moved up to the Dodgers. In his first season, he batted .297 with twelve home runs, forty-eight runs batted in, and sixteen errors at first base. He led the National League in stolen bases with twenty-nine. He dominated on the field despite name-calling, racial epithets, a Black cat being thrown at him in Philadelphia, and brushback pitches from opposing pitchers.

Jackie Robinson's best year came in 1949, when he finished first in the National League in batting average (.342) and stolen bases (37). He finished second in RBIs (124) and hits (203). In 1951 Robinson set a new National League record for double plays by a second baseman with 137. He retired in 1956 and during his ten years in the league, he completed six World Series and played every position except pitcher and catcher. In 1962 he became the first African American inducted into the Baseball Hall of Fame in his first year of eligibility.

942 • Willie Mays (b. 1931)

Willie Howard Mays joined the Birmingham Black Barons in the late 1940s. His contract was bought by the Giants for $10,000 from the Barons. He joined the Giants on May 25, 1951, and signed for $5,000 a year. Mays was chosen as the National League's Rookie of the Year in 1951. Mays was known for his basket-style technique of catching fly balls, holding the glove waist-high and palms-up. His over-the-head basket-style nab of Cleveland Indian Vic Wertz's long fly ball in the first game of the 1954 World Series at the Polo Grounds was his most famous catch. The score was tied 2–2 in the top of the eighth with two men on base and Mays saved a run. Mays was named the National League Most Valuable Player in two seasons over ten years apart—1954 and 1965.

In 1954 Willie Mays won the major league batting title and made the cover of *Time* magazine. He hit 30 home runs and stole 30 bases in the 1956 and 1957 seasons. Mays was also the first man to hit 200 home runs and steal 200 bases. He spent his last two seasons, 1972 and 1973, with the New York Mets. Over his career, Mays played in 2,992 games, had 3,283 hits, 660 home runs, led the league three times in triples, four times in home runs, five times in slugging average, and four times in stolen bases. He was inducted into the Baseball Hall of Fame in 1979. Although Mays had an outstanding career, he received some criticism for not using his position as a premier athlete to speak out against racial injustice. Mays explained in 1960: "I don't picket in the streets of Birmingham. I'm not mad at the people who do. Maybe they shouldn't be mad at the people who don't."

943 • Discrimination in the Major Leagues

Although both the American and National Leagues were successfully integrated by the 1960s, Black baseball players still faced discrimination and limited opportunities. A December 1970 report by the Rand Corporation found that no Black baseball player prior to 1959 had received a signing bonus over $20,000, although such bonuses had been paid to twenty-six white players during the same period. Between 1959 and 1961, forty-three whites and only three Blacks received $20,000 or greater

signing bonuses. Black baseball players were often forced to accept less favorable terms because even fewer opportunities existed for them off the field. Hank Aaron remembered, "I'd always been easy to deal with. They'd offer me a contract and I'd nearly always sign without any argument." Black players were also handicapped by lack of education. Few white colleges recruited Black baseball players and few Black colleges had baseball programs, so African American baseball players had more limited access to higher education than their white counterparts, who often played on scholarships at white colleges.

944 • Hank Aaron (b. 1934)

On March 13, 1954, Hank Aaron broke into the Braves lineup when Bobby Thompson injured his leg. In his third year with the Braves, Aaron led the National League with a batting average of .328, 200 hits, 340 total bases, and 34 doubles. He was second in the National League with 14 triples, third in slugging average with .558, and third in runs scored with 106. In 1957 Aaron was named National League Most Valuable Player and he helped the Braves win the World Series.

On Monday, April 8, 1974, Hank Aaron hit his 715th home run, breaking Babe Ruth's record. At the time of his retirement, he had 755 home runs. Aaron was named captain of the Braves in 1969 and retired after the 1976 season. Over his career, Aaron hit 40 or more home runs eight times, had 100 or more RBIs eleven times, and had a batting average of .300 or higher fourteen times. He set a record with twenty consecutive years of hitting at least 20 home runs. He was inducted into the Baseball Hall of Fame in 1982.

945 • First Black Major League Manager

On October 3, 1974, Cleveland Indians General Manager Phil Seghi announced that Frank Robinson would become a player-manager for the Indians with a one-year, $180,000 contract. Robinson had played for the Cincinnati Reds, had led the league with 38 home runs, and 122 runs scored, and won National League Rookie of the Year honors. In 1956 he was the only major league baseball player to be voted Most Valuable Player in both the National and American Leagues. In 1966 he won the triple crown, finishing the season first in batting average, home runs, and runs batted in. Robinson became the first player to hit the ball completely out of Baltimore's Memorial Stadium in 1966 with a 451-foot home run. As the Cleveland Indians manager, he hit a home run in his first at-bat. Ejected three times and suspended once over the season, Robinson felt the officiating was biased against him because he was Black. His first season record was 79–80, a fourth-place finish. Robinson was fired by the Indians and hired by the San Francisco Giants in 1981 and was replaced in 1984 after a 268–277 record.

946 • Baseball's Complete Integration

The Boston Red Sox finally completed the total integration of Black players in every major league franchise when they signed Elijah "Pumpsie" Green in 1959. It had been twelve years since Jackie Robinson's first day in the majors. Nineteen fifty-nine was also the first year that Black players dominated the record books. Black players led the league in nine of twelve batting categories and two of twelve pitching categories. The top five stolen-base leaders—Willie Mays, Jim Gilliam, Orlando Cepeda, Tony Taylor, and Vada Pinson—were Black.

947 • "The Stacking Phenomenon"

From 1960 to 1971, Black players were limited on team rosters by position. African Americans were mostly confined to the outfield, first base, or second base. In 1968, Black players made up the following proportions of major-league positions: 53 percent of outfielders, 40 percent of first basemen, 30 percent of second basemen, 26 percent of shortstops, 14 percent of basemen, 12 percent of catchers, and 9 percent of pitchers. This stacking phenomenon was originally described by Black University of California at Berkeley professor Harry Edwards. Reasons given for the arrangement were that (1) Blacks were thought of as untrustworthy in the crucial positions of pitcher and catcher, (2) pitchers and catchers required more pre–major league experience and interaction with coaches and many Black players found it difficult to relate to their white coaches, and (3) aspiring young Black players wanted to emulate their heroes and had few non-outfield examples to follow.

Distinctions were also made among African Americans when assigning positions. According to the June 1969 issue of *Ebony*, the skin tone of Black players also determined a player's position. It reported that 80 percent of very light-skinned Black players were assigned non-outfield roles; 67.9 percent of light brown players; 56.8 percent of medium brown players; 53.5 percent of dark brown players; and 25 percent of very dark-skinned players.

948 • Reggie Jackson (b. 1946)

Reginald Martinez Jackson began his career in 1967 with the Kansas City Athletics. The Athletics moved to Oakland in 1968. Jackson became a first-string player in his rookie season with the A's after thirty-five games. Through 1984, Jackson led the American League in home runs four times. In the 1977 World Series in the sixth game, Reggie Jackson walked in his first at-bat, hit a two-run homer in his second, hit another two-run homer in his third, and hit a solo home run in his fourth at-bat. No one had ever hit three consecutive home runs in World Series competition on three consecutive pitches. Jackson is known for his outstanding play during play-offs. He tied or set seven World Series records: most homers in a World Series (five); most runs scored (ten); highest slugging average in a six-game Series (1.250); most total bases (twenty-five—tied with Willie Stargell); most extra-base hits in a six-game Series (six); most home runs in consecutive at-bats (four); most total bases in one Series game (twelve—tied with Babe Ruth); and most homers in one game (three).

949 • Youngest All-Star to Win Cy Young Award

In his first year with the New York Mets in 1984, Dwight "Doc" Gooden compiled a 17–9 record, a 2.60 earned-run average, and a league-leading strikeout total of 276. He broke the rookie strikeout record of 245 by Herb Score. In September 1984 Gooden set the National League record by striking out thirty-two total batters in two consecutive games. He also set a record of 11.39 strikeouts-per-nine-innings performed over the 1984 season. Gooden was the youngest player to ever appear in an All-Star game at age twenty and was voted National League Rookie of the Year. In his second season in the major leagues, Doc Gooden became the youngest pitcher to win at least twenty games with his 24–4 record. Gooden's 268 strikeouts and 1.53 ERA led the major leagues and helped him become the youngest player to win the triple crown, leading the major leagues in wins, strikeouts, and ERAs.

950 • Why Blacks Were Kept Out

Judy Johnson recalled asking Connie Mack, the owner of the Philadelphia Athletics, why he did not field a Black player on his team. "He told me, 'There were too many of you to go in. It would have taken too many jobs away from the white boys.' "

951 • The Significance of Jackie Robinson (1919–72)

In 1947, my mother couldn't wait to see Jackie Robinson play, so we wandered up to the Polo Grounds one hot July day to see a Giant-Dodger double-header. It was a really weird feeling to see so many Blacks in a major-league park at one time. My mother laughed and said, "Who's playing today, the Black Yankees and the Homestead Grays?" Man, my people were raising hell in the ballpark that day. I think they would have applauded if Robinson had urinated on home plate. But what the hell, it had been a long time coming. A Black ballplayer in the major leagues!

—Art Rust, *Get That Nigger off the Field!*

I don't know anyone who could have stood all the abuse Jackie had to take in breaking into baseball and stuck it out to become the great player he was. When you know the true nature of Jackie . . . what a fighter he was and how he had to keep it inside of him . . . it's just unbelievable. Thinking back on it, I'm just glad I got to play alongside Jackie and be a part of history.

—Pee Wee Reese

Basketball

952 • First Full-Salaried Pro Team

Robert J. Douglas, the father of Black basketball, organized the Spartan Braves of Brooklyn, which became the New York Renaissance (the Rens) in 1923. Douglas's talent and business sense enabled the team to survive until the late 1940s. The players earned $800 to $1,000 per month and traveled annually in the spring through the South to play Black college teams. On March 30, 1932, the Rens won their first world professional championship against an all-white squad, the Original Celtics, beating them 37–34. In a rematch on April 3, the Rens prevailed again, 30–23. The New York Renaissance was inducted into the Professional Basketball Hall of Fame in 1963.

953 • The Harlem Globetrotters

In 1927 Black basketball was enhanced by the organization of the Harlem Globetrotters

team. By 1940 the Globetrotters were considered better than the Rens, but both teams were handicapped by the lack of a Black league. After the integration of the National Basketball Association in the 1960s, the Globetrotters lost their monopoly on the best Black players, and they switched to playing as an entertainment team using comical routines and fancy ball handling.

954 • First African Americans to Play in NBA

In 1951 the Boston Celtics signed Chuck Cooper out of Duquesne University and made him the first African American to play in the National Basketball Association. Cooper played in sixty-six games, had 562 rebounds and 174 assists, and scored 615 points in his first season. Nathanial "Sweetwater" Clifton of Xavier University was also signed in 1950 by the New York Knickerbockers. He played in sixty-five games and had 491 rebounds, 162 assists, and 562 points.

955 • First Rookie to Win NBA All-State MVP Award

Elgin Gay Baylor attended Spingarn High School in Washington, D.C., and the College of Idaho on a football scholarship. He transferred to Seattle University and was the MVP of the 1958 NCAA Tournament. He was chosen in the first round of the 1958 draft by the Los Angeles Lakers and was the first player to impress crowds with his seeming ability to defy gravity. Over his fourteen-year career, Baylor was a member of a championship team once. The Lakers lost to the Celtics in the play-offs six times during Baylor's career. He was inducted into the Basketball Hall of Fame in 1976 and was chosen to the NBA 35th Anniversary All-Time Team in 1980.

The Harlem Globetrotters against the Boston Whirlwinds, 1958. National Archives. Courtesy of A.P./Wide World Photos, Inc.

956 • Wilt the Stilt (b. 1936)

Wilton Norman Chamberlain played for the University of Kansas for two seasons and played for the Harlem Globetrotters in the 1958–59 season. He later signed with the Philadelphia Warriors. In his first NBA game, October 24, 1959, Chamberlain scored 43 points and had 28 rebounds against the New York Knicks. He was the first and only NBA player to score 100 points in a game. In what was his finest year, 1960, he was chosen NBA Rookie of the Year, the Most Valuable Player in the NBA All-Star Game, and the NBA's Most Valuable Player. He was again the league's Most Valuable Player in 1966, 1967, and 1968. Chamberlain is the all-time leading NBA rebounder with 23,924. He was inducted into the Basketball Hall of Fame in 1978 and was chosen to the NBA 35th Anniversary All-Time Team in 1980.

957 • Women Basketball Players

In 1931 the *Philadelphia Tribune* Black newspaper sponsored a female basketball squad that became the first Black female sports team to experience success in the United States. The team rarely lost behind star center Ora Washington. The typical style of women's basketball until the 1960s was six players per team with separate threesomes for offense and defense. The squad was named national champion by most Black newspapers throughout most of the 1930s.

Cheryl Miller played on the 1984 Olympic gold medal women's basketball team. In one game at Polytechnic High School in Riverside, California, Miller scored 105 points. She was a member of two NCAA championship teams at the University of Southern California and the All-America team in 1983 and 1984.

958 • "The Russell Rule"

Consistently voted the most valuable player in NBA history, William Fenton Russell (born 1934) led his University of San Francisco basketball team to two NCAA titles, while suffering only one loss in his college career. He was chosen Most Outstanding Player of the 1955 NCAA Tournament and was a member of the 1956 United States Olympic basketball team. So dominant was Russell as a rebounder that the NCAA adopted what was known as the Russell Rule: at the end of 1955, the NCAA doubled the width of the field goal lane, from six to twelve feet. Still, Russell dominated NCAA rebounding.

Bill Russell has more championship titles than any other American athlete in major

Bill Russell succeeds Arnold "Red" Auerbach as coach of the Boston Celtics and becomes the first African American head coach of a major-league sport in the United States, 1966. United Press International. National Archives. Courtesy of Bettmann Archives

sports. As a Celtic, Russell led the team to eleven NBA titles, beginning in 1957. Russell was named Most Valuable Player of the National Basketball Association in 1958, but was not named by sportswriters to the all-NBA team. He also won the MVP award in 1961, 1963, and 1965 and the NBA All-Star Game MVP award in 1963. For the 1966–67 season, Russell was named player-coach of the Celtics and later coached the Seattle Supersonics and the Sacramento Kings. He was inducted into the Basketball Hall of Fame in 1974 and chosen to the NBA 25th Anniversary All-Time Team in 1970 and the 35th Anniversary Team in 1980.

959 • Kareem (b. 1947)

In 1967, 1968, and 1969, Ferdinand Lewis Alcindor, Jr., was an NCAA All-America selection and Most Outstanding Player in the NCAA Tournament. He was United Press International's Player of the Year in 1967 and 1969. Alcindor was 1970 NBA Rookie of the Year, NBA All-Star 1970–74 and 1976–88. He was NBA MVP 1971, 1972, 1974, 1976, 1977, and 1980. Alcindor changed his name to Kareem Abdul-Jabbar and holds the NBA all-time lead in points scored with 38,387, field goals made with 15,837, and games played with 1,560. Because of Lew Alcindor, the NCAA changed its rules and outlawed the "dunk." Later the ruling was reversed.

960 • Dr. J (b. 1950)

With his huge Afro, his frenetic, fast-paced drives to the basket, and his monster dunks, Dr. J (Julius Erving) came to symbolize the new style of basketball and personal appearance of the American Basketball Association (known as the ABA, founded in 1967) when he began to play for the New York Nets in 1972. During his ABA career, Erving was clearly the best player on the best ABA team: he was chosen MVP of

Lew Alcindor (Kareem Abdul-Jabbar) as a member of the Milwaukee Bucks, 1972. National Archives. Courtesy Milwaukee Bucks

the ABA three times and led the Nets to two ABA championship titles (1974–76). With the merger of the four ABA teams—the Denver Nuggets, Indiana Pacers, San Antonio Spurs, and the New York (now New Jersey) Nets—into the NBA, Dr. J faced and met a new challenge—to prove that the open, hectic, fast-paced ABA style of basketball that he played could be successful in the more plodding, defense-minded NBA. Growing with the change,

Erving developed into an excellent defensive player and outside shooter, to go along with his slashing, driving style of offense. He was selected five times as a member of the All-NBA first team, was MVP of the league in 1981, and in 1983 he led the Philadelphia 76ers to the NBA championship title. Perhaps just as important, the "Doctor," as he was affectionately called by teammates and fans, became a graceful, debonair, and respectable businessman and spokesperson after he decided to end his professional basketball-playing career in 1987.

961 • Magic (b. 1959)

In Lansing, Michigan, Earvin Johnson guided his Everett High School team to the state title. As a sophomore at Michigan State University in 1979, Johnson led the team to the NCAA title. In 1981 he was signed by the Los Angeles Lakers to a twenty-five-year, $25-million contract, the largest total sum in team sports history at that time. Within five years, Magic had helped the Lakers win two NBA titles. In the fall of 1991 he announced that he had contracted the AIDS virus and was retiring from professional basketball. He went on to play on the 1992 Olympic gold medal basketball "Dream Team." Johnson coached the Los Angeles Lakers for a temporary period in the 1993–94 season.

962 • Michael Jordan (b. 1963)

At the University of North Carolina at Chapel Hill, Michael Jordan earned the College Player of the Year Award two years in a row. His final shot won UNC its first title in twenty-five years. In 1983 Jordan helped the United States team win a gold medal at the Pan-American Games. A member of the 1984 and 1992 gold medal U.S. Olympic teams, Jordan was named the 1985 NBA Rookie of the Year, led the NBA in scoring for 1987–93, won the Most Valuable Player

award in 1988, 1991, and 1992, and set the record for points scored in a play-off game (63). Jordan led the Chicago Bulls to three consecutive NBA titles in 1991, 1992, and 1993 and was voted MVP of the play-offs for those years. Jordan led the NBA in all-time scoring average at 32.2 points per game, before retiring from professional basketball in 1993. He returned to basketball in 1995 after a year and a half of trying to play professional baseball. His comeback as the star of the Chicago Bulls was spoiled when the Orlando Magic defeated the Bulls in the 1995 semi-finals championship.

Rodeo

963 • Bill Pickett (1860?–1932)

Bill Pickett is renowned as the inventor of the modern art of bulldogging, which became the most popular act at rodeos in the late nineteenth century. Historians differ on the origin of Pickett's special technique. Some argue that when a steer escaped its pen one day around 1900 on a farm where Pickett was working, he jumped on his horse and gave chase. Rather than roping the runaway animal from his perch on his horse, Pickett jumped onto the steer's back from his horse while moving, grabbed the steer's horns, and by turning them, forced the steer over onto the ground. Reputedly, he would also bite into the steer's lip while wrestling it over onto its side. Others suggest that Pickett may have imitated a bulldog of the type that was used to extricate steers from underbrush by jumping up and biting the steers on their necks. Whichever version one accepts, Pickett was a brave, innovative wrestler of steers, and he perfected his technique into a popular rodeo act. In 1908, Pickett even bulldogged a bull in Mexico in a stunt that almost took his life. That he lost in 1932 when he was kicked in the head by a horse. Pickett's exploits lived on in the entertainment careers of Will Rogers and Tom Mix, both of whom worked as Pickett's assistants.

Bicycling

964 • Fastest Bicyclist in the World

Marshall W. "Major" Taylor (1878–1934) was literally "the fastest bicyclist in the world" from 1898 to 1910, the year he retired from professional bicycling competition. Beginning in 1898, he was champion of America for several years; in 1899, he established a new one-mile world record and secured the world championship in Montreal. On his first European tour in 1901, he competed in sixteen cities, raced against the best European riders on their own courses, and won all but two single man-to-man races;

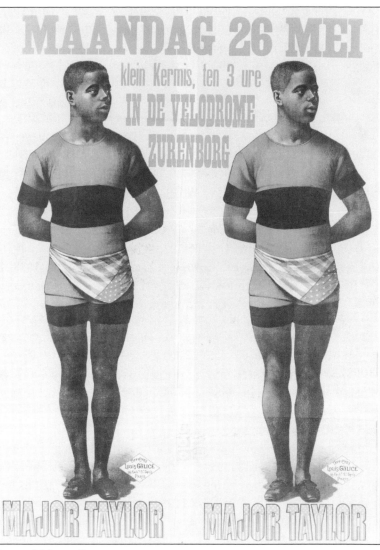

Poster announces the appearance of Marshall W. "Major" Taylor at a fair in Antwerp, Belgium, 1902, the year he beat the Belgium national champion. National Portrait Gallery, Smithsonian Institution

returning to Europe in 1902, he topped his earlier record by winning every single man-to-man match race he entered, and beating the former world champion, Thorwald Ellegaard, in Paris. Taylor raced against and beat all of the outstanding bicyclists of his time in the United States, Canada, Europe, Australia, and New Zealand. He was so good that the League of American Wheelmen (L.A.W.) tried to ban him from its races; and when that failed, his white competitors, especially Americans, used a combination of dirty tricks—from running him off of the track to surrounding him with other riders, creating "pockets"—to keep him from winning. But Taylor, whose strategic ideas and competitive will equaled his physical skills, learned to avoid and escape such traps, and dominated bicycling for sixteen years. Taking three years off from competition in 1905, he staged a thrilling comeback in 1908 when he regained his championship form and established two world records, before retiring for good in 1910.

Bowling

965 • Black Bowling Association Formed

The National Negro Bowling Association was organized on August 20, 1939, in Detroit because of the ban on Black bowler participation in the American Bowling Congress (ABC) and the Women's International Bowling Congress (WIBC). The first NNBA tournament was held in 1939, and in 1944 the organization changed its name to the National Bowling Association (NBA). The best bowlers in the association hailed from Chicago, Cleveland, and Detroit. In 1950 the ABC and WIBC finally lifted the ban on Blacks because of the threat of a lawsuit, and by 1951 any qualified bowler was admitted to ABC and WIBC events. On May 24, 1951, in St. Paul, Minnesota, a Black bowling team from Detroit finished in seventy-second place in the ABC national competition. The Black participants were awarded $600 in prizes and became the first African Americans to participate in any ABC competition. In 1960, Fuller Gordy of Detroit became the nation's first Black professional bowler, and the first to have a career on the Professional Bowlers' Association (PBA) tour.

Golf

966 • Patent for Golf Tee

In 1899 Dr. George F. Grant received United States patent number 638,920 for his invention of a golf tee, a small cone-shaped, solid piece of wood with slightly concave tops. Before Grant's invention in Boston, golfers had to construct small mounds of dirt on which to place their balls. A Harvard University graduate and prominent dentist, Grant never made an attempt to capitalize on his invention. The tees used in modern golf games were adapted from Grant's invention.

967 • First African American Member of PGA

The Professional Golfers' Association had no formal restrictions on membership when it formed in 1916, but it banned Black membership in 1943. Dewey Brown became the first Black member of the PGA in the 1920s, but he was too old to play competitively in tournaments. He served as a golf teacher and caddy in southern New Jersey country clubs.

968 • First Case in Black Sports to Reach Supreme Court

In October 1950 Joseph Rice and his NAACP attorney, Franklin Williams, appealed a decision made by the Florida Supreme Court to the United States Supreme Court. Rice had sued Miami Springs to protest the restriction of Black golfers to one day per week of play on the city's only public golf course. The U.S. Supreme Court ordered the Florida Supreme Court to reconsider its decision to uphold the rights of Miami Springs as opposed to the rights of Black golfers. The case encouraged more Black golfers across the country to press for equal access to public facilities.

969 • First African American to Win a Major PGA Event

By winning the Los Angeles Open in 1969, Charlie Sifford became the first African American to win a major PGA event. He also won the

1964 Puerto Rico Open, the 1967 Hartford Open, the 1975 PGA Seniors Open, and the 1980 Suntree Seniors. His career earnings were $339,000 on the PGA tour and $251,000 on the PGA Senior tour.

970 • First African American to Play in the Masters

Robert Lee Elder won the UGA Professional title four times, turned professional in 1959, and received his PGA card in 1967 and played as a thirty-three-year-old rookie. Elder was financially successful in his first nine PGA events in 1968. In 1971 he won the Nigerian Open and became the first African American to play in the South African Open. Elder became the Masters Tournament's first Black entrant when he teed off at the Augusta, Georgia, course on April 10, 1975, his seventh year on the PGA tour. His admittance to the Masters was heralded as a

Calvin Peete. Copyright *Washington Post*. Reprinted by permission of D.C. Public Library

breakthrough of the color line in golf. Yet, twenty years later, the country club that hosts the Masters has only one Black member.

971 • Most Successful 1980–84 Player on the PGA Tour

In 1983 Calvin Peete won the PGA Georgia-Pacific Atlantic Classic and the Anheuser-Busch Classic. He was placed on the Ryder Cup Team, won the Golf Writer's Association's Ben Hogan Award and *Golf Digest* magazine's 1983 All-America Team. In 1982 Peete won the Greater Milwaukee Open for the second time, the Anheuser-Busch Classic, the BC Open, and the Pensacola Championship, and finished third in the PGA championship. He won the Vardon Trophy in 1984 for lowest scoring average with a 70.56 score. Peete ended 1984 as the winningest player on the PGA tour for the preceding four years. Calvin Peete had never been a caddy, never played in the UGA, and had not played golf until he was in his early twenties. Many had believed he would never succeed as a golfer because a childhood injury had limited his arm swing.

972 • Youngest U.S. Amateur Champion

In 1994, at age eighteen, Tiger Woods became the youngest amateur golfer to win the United States Amateur Championships. Because he was the U.S. Amateur Champion, he was automatically invited to the Masters, becoming the second Black golfer to play in that tournament.

Horse Racing

973 • First Black Jockey

African Americans played an important role in the early years of horse racing in the United States. Aware that a horse's success was often dependent on the skills of its jockey, southern horse owners turned to their Black slaves, who had long been responsible for the physical care of their owners' horses. These slaves proved extremely adept at riding, and by 1800 diminutive Blacks accounted for almost all the jockeys in the southern United States. The first known African American jockey was 4'6" Monkey Simon. Considered the country's best jockey in the early 1800s, Simon was able to earn more than $100 per ride for himself or his master. Despite the slave jockeys' achievements, credit was usually given to the horses' owners instead.

974 • Isaac Murphy (1861–96)

After the Civil War, African American jockeys became active again. Between 1880 and 1905, Black riders won more than 110 major races, including 13 Kentucky Derbys. Isaac Murphy, born in Kentucky, was one of the best jockeys of the

Isaac Murphy, three-time winner of the Kentucky Derby.
Prints and Photographs Division, Library of Congress

time, Black or white. When he was twelve, Murphy obtained his jockey apprentice license and began his career as an exercise rider. After developing excellent skills as a hand rider, a jockey who rarely needed a whip to motivate his horse, Murphy won his first major victory aboard Lady Greenfield at Louisville in 1875. By 1882 he was earning $10,000 per year, $25 per winning ride and $15 for every loss. In 1884, with four different horses, Murphy won six races, including the Kentucky Derby. He was the first jockey to win three Kentucky Derbys, a record that stood until 1948. In 1891 the *Louisville Times* said of Murphy, "His integrity and honor are the pride of the Turf, and many of the best horsemen pronounce him the greatest jockey that ever mounted a horse." Murphy died in 1896 of pneumonia at the age of thirty-five.

As the nineteenth century drew to a close, segregation and discrimination in American society worsened. This development was reflected in events on the horse track. An observer noted:

The white riders retaliated [against the victories of Black jockeys] ganging up against the black riders on the rails. A black boy would be pocketed, thrust back in a race; or his mount would be bumped out of contention on a white boy's stirrup, and toss him out of the saddle . . . those white fellows would slash out and cut the nearest Negro rider. . . . they literally ran the black boys off the track.

975 • The Jockey Club

African Americans were essentially forced out of racing with the establishment of the Jockey Club in 1894 to license riders. The Jockey Club refused to grant Black jockeys their licenses, and Jess Conley, who finished third aboard Colston in 1911, became the last African American to ride in the Kentucky Derby. Although unable to ride, Blacks remained in the sport working as trainers, dockers, hot walkers, exercise boys, stable hands, and groomers.

Some Black riders turned to steeplechase events after being forced out of "flat" racing events. Water jumps, hedgerows, and railings served as obstacles in steeplechase riding, and many African Americans proved adept at the sport. Charlie Smoot, the most successful and visible African American steeplechase rider, won the Beverwyck Steeplechase in 1916, 1926, and 1933.

Gymnastics

976 • First Internationally Ranked Black Woman Gymnast
Diane Durham was the first Black gymnast to achieve prominence at an early age. She was the 1981 and 1982 United States Junior Champion in the floor exercise, vault, parallel bars, and balance beam. In 1983 Durham was named National Senior Champion in the same four events. She was injured just before beginning the 1984 Olympic competition.

977 • 1994 U.S. Champion
In the 1992 Seoul Olympics, Dominique Dawes helped the United States gymnastics team win a bronze medal. Dawes was the 1994 United States champion in the all-around competition. She also placed first in individual competition in the uneven bars, beam, floor, and vault events.

Ice Skating

978 • First Black Winter Olympic Medalist
In 1980 Debra Thomas finished second in the

United States Novice Ladies ice skating competition. She finished thirteenth in the 1983 Senior Ladies competition and won the 1983 Critérium International du Sucre in France. She placed sixth in the 1984 National Seniors event and second in 1985 competition. Thomas won the United States and World Figure Skating titles in 1986 and the United States championship in 1988. The first African American woman figure skater to be widely covered in the media in 1988, she won a bronze medal in the 1988 Winter Olympics.

Weight Lifting

979 • First Man to Win Eight Straight World and Olympic Weight Lifting Championships
John Davis won the 1938 world light-heavyweight championship when he was seventeen years old. He won the 1946–47 and 1949–51 world heavyweight titles, the 1939–40 U.S. light-heavyweight title, and the 1941–43, 1946–48, and 1950–53 U.S. heavyweight titles. In 1951 he became the first amateur weight lifter to clean and jerk more than 400 pounds. The first man to win eight consecutive world and Olympic championships, Davis was elected to the Helms Hall of Fame and the Black Athletes Hall of Fame.

Football

980 • First-Team All-American
In 1915 Paul Leroy Robeson began attending Rutgers University on an academic scholarship. In his second year, Robeson was promoted to first string on the football team at the tackle and guard positions, but was left off the team for Rutgers' game against Washington and Lee

University because that school refused to play against Blacks. In 1918 Walter Camp, the initiator of the All-America team, said that Robeson was the finest end to ever play the game and named him to his first-team All-America roster. Robeson graduated Phi Beta Kappa with honors, and after graduation, played professional football to support himself through Columbia University Law School. Robeson later became a successful concert singer, stage and motion picture actor, and civil rights activist. Because Robeson had the temerity to criticize American racial practices and voice support for the Soviet Union during the McCarthy era, he became the target of a blacklisting campaign that affected the record of his football accomplishments. When lists of football All-Americans were published in the 1950s, there was a blank space where Robeson's name had been.

981 • First African American to Win Bert Bell Trophy

In his first year with the Cleveland Browns in 1957, Jim Brown led the National Football League with 942 rushing yards and was selected as NFL Rookie of the Year. He led the league in rushing for eight seasons. In seven of his nine career seasons, Brown rushed for 1,000 yards or more. He was selected as a football All-Pro in 1957, 1958, and 1959. His 12,312 total career rushing yards was the record in the National Football League for nineteen years. Brown was given the Bert Bell Trophy as the Most Valuable Player in the NFL in 1963, becoming the first African American to win the award. Brown was voted Football Back of the Decade for 1950–60. He was elected to the Professional Football Hall of Fame in 1971.

982 • First African American in Hall of Fame

In 1968 Marion Motley became the first African American player to be inducted into the National Football Hall of Fame. A running back out of the University of Nevada at Reno, Motley began his professional career with the Cleveland Browns of the All-American Football Conference (AAFC) in 1946 and played with the Pittsburgh Steelers in 1954–55.

983 • Rookie of the Year in 1965

University of Kansas running back Gale Sayers was voted Rookie of the Year in his first season in 1965 with the Chicago Bears. In a November 5, 1965, game versus the San Francisco 49ers, Sayers scored six touchdowns. He led the league in rushing in 1969 with 1,032 yards and was the highest-paid player in the league. Sayers retired in 1970 and was inducted into the Professional Football Hall of Fame in 1977.

984 • O.J. Simpson (b. 1947)

While at the University of Southern California, running back Orenthal James "O.J." Simpson won the 1968 Heisman Trophy. He signed a three-year, $250,000 contract with the Buffalo Bills in 1969.

On December 16, 1973, O.J. Simpson set an NFL record of 2,003 rushing yards in one season. On November 25, 1976, in a game against the Detroit Lions, he set a new single-game rushing record of 273 yards. Over his eleven total seasons in the National Football League, he rushed for 1,000 yards or more in five seasons. Simpson received the 1973 Bert Bell Trophy as Most Valuable Player in the National Football League. He was the United Press International's American Football Conference Player of the Year in 1972, 1973, and 1974. Simpson was in-

O.J. Simpson playing for the University of Southern California in the Rose Bowl, January 1, 1969. National Archives. Courtesy of USC Sports Information

ducted into the Professional Football Hall of Fame in 1985.

Arrested and charged with the June 12, 1994, murder of his former wife, Nicole Brown Simpson, and her friend Ronald Goldman, Simpson was found not guilty on all murder charges by a Los Angeles jury on October 3, 1995.

985 • All-Time Leading NFL Rusher

Walter "Sweetness" Payton broke Jim Brown's career rushing record on October 7, 1984, in a game with the New Orleans Saints. Payton, out of Jackson State University, became the only runner to set the all-time rushing record for his college conference and for the National Football League.

Walter Payton broke O.J. Simpson's single-game rushing record on November 20, 1977, by rushing for 275 yards on forty carries against the Minnesota Vikings. Over his ten-year career,

Jim Brown playing lacrosse. 1957 Onondagan, Syracuse University Archives

Althea Gibson, the first African American to win women's singles at Wimbledon, rides up Broadway in New York during ticker-tape parade in her honor, 1957. Courtesy of the *New York Times.* National Archives

Arthur Ashe in action during the United States National Tennis Championship, September 8, 1965. Courtesy of Wide World Photos, Inc. National Archives

Payton rushed for 1,000 yards or more in eight seasons. He finished his career with 13,309 total rushing yards.

Lacrosse

986 • First African American to Play in Lacrosse's North-South Game

Jim Brown, the star football player, was also a Syracuse lacrosse midfielder in 1955–56. He initially tried the sport out of curiosity and came to be known for his speed on the field. In 1957 Brown became the first African American to participate in the North-South game. He played

for half the game, scoring five goals and making two assists to lead the North squad to a 14–10 upset victory.

Tennis

987 • Althea Gibson (b. 1927)

Althea Gibson was given her first tennis racket in 1940. In 1955 she won eighteen of the nineteen tennis events she participated in. In the spring of 1956 Gibson became the first Black to win a Grand Slam event when she won the singles and doubles title at the French Open. In 1956 she also won the doubles title at Wimbledon and the Asian Championships in Ceylon. In 1957 and 1958 Althea Gibson was ranked as the number one female tennis player in the world. She won her first Wimbledon singles title in 1957 over Darlene Hard 6–3, 6–2.

[handwritten: 1017]

e the first Black athlete to
lon courts in 1951. She was
nis player to play at Forest
n won the U.S. Lawn Tennis
ls at Forest Hills in 1957 by
ough 6–3, 6–2. Gibson re-
ies in 1958. She was a mem-
ber of the 1957–58 United States Wightman Cup
Squad and was awarded the Female of the Year
Babe Didrickson Zaharias Trophy.

988 • Arthur Ashe, Jr. (1943–93)

Arthur Ashe, Jr., became the first African
American to receive a USLTA national ranking
when he ranked fifth among all United States
junior players in 1958. Ashe won three ATA
Boys' titles. From 1960–62 Ashe won three consecutive ATA men's singles titles. He became
the first Black member of the United States Junior Davis Cup Team in 1960 and won the 1960
USLTA National Junior Indoors title. After winning the U.S. Open Singles Championship in
1968, Ashe appeared on the cover of *Life* magazine and was the first African American athlete
to appear on the talk show *Face the Nation.* In
1975 Ashe defeated Jimmy Connors at Wimbledon and took over the World Championship Tennis singles title from Bjorn Borg. Ashe retired
on July 31, 1979, after suffering a mild heart attack. He died in 1993 after suffering with the
AIDS virus contracted through blood transfusions during heart surgery.

Track and Field

989 • First Black Medals in Modern Olympics

George Coleman Poage won a bronze medal
in the 400-meter hurdles in the 1904 St. Louis
Olympics, becoming the first African American
to receive a medal in the Olympic Games. The
next day, Poage won a bronze medal in the 200-
meter hurdles. At the University of Wisconsin,
Poage set the collegiate record for the 440-yard
sprint and low hurdles.

At the 1908 London Olympics, John Baxter
Taylor, Jr., ran the third leg of the 1,600-meter
relay, which the American team won by twenty-
five yards. Taylor's gold medal in this event was
the first gold received by any Black member of
the United States Olympic team.

990 • First Black Individual Gold Medal Olympian

At the 1924 Paris Olympics, William Hubbard
won a gold medal in the long jump with a leap of
24 feet 5$\frac{1}{8}$ inches. He tied the 100-yard dash
world record at 9.6 seconds in a meet against
Ohio State and later won the national title in
the 100-yard dash. Hubbard set the world
record in the long jump on June 13, 1925, at 25
feet 107/8 inches at the Stagg Field NCAA
Championships.

991 • Jesse Owens (1913–80)

James Cleveland "Jesse" Owens won a then-
unprecedented four gold medals at the 1936
Berlin Olympics. On Monday, August 3, Owens
tied the Olympic record in the 100-meter dash
with a time of 10.3 seconds. On Tuesday, August
4, he set an Olympic record in the long jump
with a leap of 26 feet 5$\frac{1}{2}$ inches. In the college
conference championships in 1935, Owens had
set the world record in the long jump at 26 feet
8$\frac{1}{2}$ inches. On Wednesday, August 5, Owens set
an Olympic record in the 200-meter dash at 20.7
seconds. In his last competition on Friday, he
helped set a world record in the 400-meter relay
at 39.8 seconds. Jesse Owens won as many track
and field events alone as did any other country.

In 1950 the Associated Press named Jesse

Jesse Owens sprints to an easy victory in the 200-meter race during the 1936 Summer Olympics. United Press International. Courtesy of Bettmann Archives. National Archives

Hall of Fame, and the Bob Douglas Hall of Fame.

993 • Decathlon Olympic Record

In the 1956 Olympics, Rafer Johnson won a silver medal in the decathlon with 7,568 points in ten events: the 100-meter dash, the broad jump, the shot put, the high jump, the 400-meter run, the 100-meter hurdles, the discus throw, the pole vault, the javelin toss, and the 1,500-meter run. In the 1960 Olympics, Johnson set an Olympic record in the decathlon, capturing the gold medal with 8,001 points. He carried the American flag in the 1960 Olympics and lit the Olympic torch above the Coliseum in the 1984 Olympics in Los Angeles.

Owens the Athlete of the Half-Century. He was given an honorary award from his alma mater, Ohio State University, in 1971. The NCAA presented Owens the 1974 Theodore Roosevelt Award for collegiate contribution, and he was made a charter member of the Track and Field Hall of Fame. In 1976 President Gerald Ford awarded Owens the highest award a civilian could receive, the Presidential Medal of Freedom.

992 • First Black Woman to Win Olympic Gold

Alice Coachman (Davis) was the only United States woman to win a gold medal in a track and field event at the 1948 Olympics. She set an Olympic record in the high jump with a leap of 5 feet 6 inches. Between 1939 and 1948, Coachman set a record for the most victories in the National AAU Outdoor High Jump without a loss at 10. She is a member of the National Track and Field Hall of Fame, the Helms Hall of Fame, the Tuskegee Hall of Fame, the Georgia State

994 • First Black Female Sprinter to Win Gold

Wilma Rudolph, out of Tennessee State University, won a bronze medal in the 440-meter relay in the 1956 Olympics. She returned in 1960 to win three gold medals, becoming the first African American female to win a gold medal in a sprint event at the Olympic Games. She had sprained her ankle the day before her first race, but won the 100-meter dash in 11.0 seconds, the 200-meter dash in 24.0 seconds, and the 400-meter relay in 44.5 seconds. Rudolph won the AAU Outdoor 100-meter title from 1959 to 1962.

Tommie Smith crosses finish line in 200-meter dash at 1968 Olympics in Mexico. Associated Press. Courtesy of A.P./Wide World Photos, Inc. National Archives

Wilma Rudolph wins the 200-yard dash at the 1960 Summer Olympics in Rome. Copyright *Washington Post.* Reprinted by permission of the D.C. Public Library

995 • "Arch of Unity and Power"

Tommie Smith and John Carlos finished first and third respectively in the 200-meter dash at the 1968 Olympic Games. In a victory stand demonstration during the playing of the American national anthem, Smith raised his right Black-gloved fist high above his head. Both men bowed their heads and closed their eyes during the entire national anthem. Afterward, Smith explained to Howard Cosell, "My raised right hand stood for the power in Black America. Carlos' raised left hand stood for the unity of Black America. Together they formed an arch of unity and power." Both runners were ejected by the International Olympic Committee from the Olympic Village.

996 • Long Jump Too Long

Before the 1968 Olympic Games, Bob Bea-

mon had won twenty long jump titles in twenty-one meets. He set an indoor world record of 27 feet 1 inch at the NAIA Indoors and extended the record to 27 feet 2¾ inches at a later meet. At the 1968 Olympics, he noticed a rain cloud approaching and wanted to accomplish a good jump before the rain started. After Beamon's jump, the meet marshals discovered that their optical equipment was not designed to measure a jump of that distance. They got a new tape and officially measured his jump twice at 29 feet 2½ inches. Beamon's new Olympic and world record extended the previous world record by almost 2 feet.

997 • Unbeaten in 102 Races

Edwin Moses, out of Morehouse College, set an Olympic and world record in the 400-meter hurdles at 47.64 seconds in the 1976 Olympics. He went on to lower this record on several occasions. Before the 400-meter hurdle final in the 1984 Los Angles Olympic Games, Moses had an unbeaten streak of 102 races, with 89 consecutive wins in the finals. He won the gold medal in 1984.

998 • Six Olympic Medals

Jackie Joyner-Kersee won gold medals in the long jump and high jump in the 1988 Olympics and gold in the heptathlon and high jump in the 1992 Olympics. Her bronze medal in the long jump in 1992 and her silver in the heptathlon in 1984 brought Joyner-Kersee's total medal count through the 1992 Olympics to six. After her silver medal performance in the 1984 Olympics, Jackie Joyner-Kersee was awarded the 1986 James E. Sullivan Award for Most Outstanding Amateur Athlete.

999 • Carl Lewis (b. 1961)

Carl Lewis, out of the University of Houston, became the first Olympian since Jesse Owens in 1936 to win four gold medals in one Olympiad at the 1984 Olympics. Lewis won the 100-meter dash in 10.97 seconds, the long jump in 8.54 meters, and set an Olympic record in the 200-meter dash at 19.80 seconds. He helped set a new Olympic and world record in the 400-meter relay at 37.83 seconds. Lewis won the 100-meter by eight feet, the largest winning margin in history. His winning long jump was achieved on his first attempt. In the 1988 Olympics, Carl Lewis was awarded the gold medal in the 100-meter dash after the disqualification of Canadian Ben Johnson for steroid use. Lewis also won the gold medal in the long jump. Lewis returned to the 1992 Olympics to defend his long title and won the event for the third straight time. He also anchored the record-setting United States 400-meter relay.

1000 • Three Golds, One Silver

In the 1988 Seoul Olympics, Florence Griffith-Joyner won gold medals in the 100-meter dash (10.54 seconds), the 200-meter dash (21.34 seconds—world record), and the four by one hundred-meter relay. Flo-Jo had set the world record for the 100-meter dash at 10.49 at the United States Olympic Trials. She won the James E. Sullivan Trophy in 1988.

1001 • Long-Jump Record

In the 1988 Olympics, Mike Powell won the silver medal in the long jump. In fifteen attempts, Powell had never beaten Carl Lewis. Finally, at the 1991 World Track and Field Championships in Tokyo, Powell beat Lewis for the first time. He also broke Bob Beamon's twenty-three-year-old world record. Powell's jump of 29 feet 4$\frac{1}{4}$ inches came on his fifth attempt in the meet. He won the 1991 James E. Sullivan Trophy.

SELECT BIBLIOGRAPHY

This bibliography is by no means a complete record of all the works and sources I have consulted in making this book. Rather, this bibliography indicates the substance and range of my readings and my suggestions for those who wish to pursue further the study of African American history.

Allen, Robert L. *The Port Chicago Mutiny.* New York: Amistad, 1993.

Applegate, Katherine. *The Story of Two American Generals: Benjamin O. Davis, Jr., Colin Powell.* New York: Dell, 1992.

Aptheker, Herbert. *American Negro Slave Revolts.* New York: Columbia University Press, 1944.

———. *A Documentary History of the Negro People in the United States.* Vol. 2. New York: Citadel Press, 1968.

Ashe, Arthur. *A Hard Road to Glory: A History of the African-American Athlete, 1619–1918.* New York: Warner Books, 1988.

Baer, Hans A., and Merril Sanger. *African American Religion in the Twentieth Century.* Knoxville: University of Tennessee, 1971.

Bedini, Silvio. *The Life of Benjamin Banneker.* New York: Charles Scribner's Sons, 1972.

Bennett, Lerone. *Before the Mayflower: A History of Black America.* Chicago: Johnson Publishing Co., 1969.

Bianco, David. *Heat Wave: The Motown Fact Book.* Ann Arbor: Popular Press, 1988.

Black Art Ancestral Legacy: The African Impulse in African-American Art. New York: Harry N. Abrams and Dallas Museum of Art, 1989.

Blaustein, Albert P., and Robert L. Zangrado, eds. *Civil Rights and the American Negro: A Documentary History.* New York: Washington Square Press, 1969.

Bogle, Donald. *Blacks in American Films and Television.* New York: Garland Publishing, 1988.

Brier, Stephen, et al. *Who Built America?* Vol. 1. New York: Pantheon Books, 1992.

Brodie, James. *Created Equal: The Lives and Ideas of Black American Innovators.* New York: Morrow & Co., 1993.

Bullard, Sara. *Free at Last: A History of the Civil Rights Movement and Those Who Died in the Struggle.* Montgomery: Civil Rights Education Project, Southern Poverty Law Center, 1989.

Bussey, Lt. Col. Charles M. *Firefight at Yechon: Courage and Racism in the Korean War.* Washington, D.C.: Brassey, 1991.

Carson, Clayborne. *In Struggle: SNCC and the Black Awakening of the 1960s.* Cambridge: Harvard University Press, 1981.

Clarke, John Henrik. *Harlem: A Community in Transition.* New York: Citadel Press, 1969.

Cohen, Bernard, ed. *Cotton Mather and American Science and Medicine.* Vol. 2. New York: Arno Press, 1980.

Conniff, Michael. *Africans in the Americas: A History of the Black Diaspora.* New York: St. Martin's Press, 1994.

Curtin, Philip D. *Atlantic Slave Trade: A Census.* Madison: University of Wisconsin Press, 1969.

David, Jay, and Elaine Crane, eds. *The Black Soldier: From the American Revolution to Vietnam.* New York: William Morrow & Co., 1971.

Davis, David Brion. *The Problem of Slavery in the Age of Revolution.* Ithaca: Cornell University Press, 1995.

Davis, Marianna W., ed. *Contributions of Black Women in America.* Vol. 2. Columbia, S.C.: Kenday Press, 1982.

Dawson, Joseph G., III. *Army Generals and Reconstruction: Louisiana, 1862–1872.* Baton Rouge: Louisiana State University Press, 1982.

Dees, Morris. *A Season for Justice: The Life and Times of Civil Rights Lawyer Morris Dees.* New York: Simon & Schuster, 1991.

Donaldson, Gary. *The History of African-Americans in the Military: Double V.* Malabar, Fl.: Krieger, 1991.

Driskell, David. *Two Centuries of Black American Art.* Venice, Calif.: Environmental Communications, 1976.

Dumond, Dwight L. *Anti-Slavery: The Crusade for Freedom in America.* Ann Arbor: University of Michigan Press, 1961.

Emery, Lynne Fauley. *Black Dance: From 1619 to Today.* 2nd rev. ed. Princeton, N.J.: Princeton Book Co., 1988.

Fletcher, Marvin. *The Black Soldier and Officer in the United States Army, 1891–1917.* Columbia: University of Missouri Press, 1974.

Foner, Eric. *Reconstruction: America's Unfinished Revolution, 1863–1877.* New York: Harper & Row, 1988.

Franklin, John Hope, and Alfred A. Moss. *From Slavery to Freedom: A History of African Americans.* New York: McGraw-Hill, 1994.

Frazier, Thomas, ed. *Afro-American History: Primary Sources.* New York: Harcourt, Brace & World, 1970.

Goldman, Martin S. *Nat Turner and the Southampton Revolt of 1831.* New York: Franklin Watts, 1992.

Grant, Joanne. *Black Protest: History, Documents, and Analyses, 1619 to the Present.* Greenwich, Conn.: Fawcett Publications, 1974.

Greene, Robert E. *Black Defenders of the Persian Gulf War.* Fort Washington, Md.: privately printed, 1991.

Grossman, James R. *Land of Hope: Chicago, Black Southerners, and the Great Migration.* Chicago: University of Chicago Press, 1989.

Haber, Louis. *Black Pioneers of Science and Invention.* New York: Harcourt, Brace & World, 1970.

Ham, Debra Newman, ed. *The African-American Mosaic: A Library of Congress Resource Guide for the Study of Black History and Culture.* Washington, D.C.: Library of Congress, 1993.

Hayden, Robert L. *7 African American Scientists.* Frederick, Md.: Twenty-First Books, 1992.

Higgenbotham, Leon, Jr. *In the Matter of Color: Race & the American Legal Process: The Colonial Period.* New York: Oxford University Press, 1978.

Hine, Darlene Clark. *Black Women in America: An Historical Encyclopedia.* New York: Carlson, 1993.

Hughes, Langston, and Milton Meltzer. *A Pictorial History of the Negro in America.* 3rd ed. New York: Crown Publishers, 1968.

James, Portia. *The Real McCoy: African-American Invention and Innovation, 1619–1930.* Washington, D.C.: Smithsonian Institution Press, 1989.

Johnson, Paul E. *African-American Christianity: Essays in History.* Berkeley: University of California Press, 1994.

Jones, Howard. *Mutiny on the Amistad: The Saga of a Slave Revolt and Its Impact on American Abolition, Law and Diplomacy.* New York: Oxford University Press, 1987.

Kaplan, Sidney. *The Black Presence in the Era of the American Revolution, 1770–1800.* Washington, D.C.: Smithsonian Institution, 1973.

Kate, William Loren. *Black People Who Made the Old West.* New York: Crowell, 1977.

King, Donald. *Legal Aspects of the Civil Rights Movement.* Detroit: Wayne State University Press, 1965.

Klein, Aaron. *The Hidden Contributors: Black Scientists and Inventors in America.* Garden City, N.Y.: Doubleday & Co., 1971.

Leckie, William H. *The Buffalo Soldiers: A Narrative of the Negro Cavalry in the West.* Norman: University of Oklahoma Press, 1967.

Lee, Irvin H. *Negro Medal of Honor Men.* New York: Dodd, Mead & Co., 1967.

Lewis, Samella. *African American Art and Artists.* Berkeley: University of California Press, 1990.

Lincoln, C. Eric. *Race, Religion, and the Continuing American Dilemma.* New York: Hill & Wang, 1984.

Locke, Alain. *Race Contacts and Inter-racial Relations.* Washington, D.C.: Howard University Press, 1992.

Logan, Rayford W., and Michael R. Winston, eds. *Dictionary of American Negro Biography.* New York: W. W. Norton & Co., 1982.

Long, Richard A. *The Black Tradition in American Dance.* New York: Rizzoli, 1990.

Lyttelton, Humphrey. *The Best of Jazz: Basin Street to Harlem.* New York: Taplinger, 1979.

McClendon, Robert Jr. James. *The Origin of Rap Music.* Del Rio, Tex.: "We the Negro People" Film and Non-Commercial Venture, Etc., 1994.

McCloud, Aminah Beverly. *African American Islam.* New York: Routledge, 1995.

McPherson, James. *The Negro's Civil War.* New York: Vintage Books, 1965.

Mannix, Daniel P., and Malcolm Cowley. *Black Cargoes: A History of the Atlantic Slave Trade, 1518–1865.* New York: Viking, 1972.

Marszaler, John F. *Assault at West Point: The Court Martial of Johnson Whittaker.* New York: Macmillan, 1972.

Maultsby, Portia. *Afro-American Religious Music.* Springfield, Ohio: Hymn Society of America, 1981.

Mitchell, Loften. *Black Drama.* New York: Hawthorn Books, 1967.

Morgan, Edmund. *American Slavery, American Freedom.* New York: Norton, 1975.

Nalty, Bernard C., and Morris J. MacGregor, eds. *Blacks in the Military: Essential Documents.* Wilmington, Del.: Scholarly Resources, 1986.

———. *Strength for the Fight: A History of Black Americans in the Military.* New York: Free Press, 1986.

Pierson, William Dillon. *Black Legacy: America's Hidden Heritage.* Amherst: University of Massachusetts Press, 1993.

Quarles, Benjamin. *Black Abolitionists.* New York: Oxford University Press, 1969.

———. *The Black American: A Documentary History.* Glenview, Ill.: Scott, Foresman, 1976.

Raboteau, Albert J. *Slave Religion.* New York: Oxford University Press, 1978.

Raines, Howell. *My Soul Is Rested: The Story of the Civil Rights Movement in the Deep South Told by the Men and Women Who Made It Happen.* New York: Bantam Books, 1978.

Rawley, James A. *The Transatlantic Slave Trade: A History.* New York: W. W. Norton & Co., 1981.

Reagon, Bernice Johnson. *We'll Understand It Better By and By: Pioneering African-American Gospel Composers.* Washington, Smithsonian, 1992.

Redkey, Edwin S. *Black Exodus: Black Nationalist and Back-to-Africa Movements, 1890–1910.* New Haven: Yale University Press, 1969.

Rust, Art. *"Get That Nigger off the Field!": A Sparkling, Informal History of the Black Man in Baseball.* New York: Delacorte Press, 1976.

Sacks, Howard L. *Way Up North in Dixie: A Black Family's Claim to the Confederate Anthem.* Washington, D.C.: Smithsonian Institution Press, 1993.

Smith, Edward D. *Climbing Jacob's Ladder: The Rise of Black Churches in Eastern American Cities, 1740–1877.* Washington, D.C.: Smithsonian Institution Press, 1988.

Smith, Jessie Carney. *Notable Black American Women.* Detroit: Gale Research, 1992.

Sollors, Werner, and Maria Diedrich, eds. *The Black Columbiad: Defining Moments in African American Literature and Culture.* Cambridge: Harvard University Press, 1994.

Southern, Eileen. *The Music of Black Americans.* New York: W. W. Norton & Co., 1971.

Still, William. *The Underground Railroad.* New York: Arno Press and the New York Times, 1968.

Story, Rosalyn M. *And So I Sing: African American Divas of Opera and Concert.* New York: Warner Books, 1990.

Tate, Claudia, ed. *The Selected Works of Georgia Douglas Johnson.* New York: G. K. Hall, 1996.

Terry, Wallace. *Bloods: An Oral History of Vietnam by Black Veterans.* New York: Random House, 1984.

Vlach, John. *The Afro-American Tradition in Decorative Arts.* Athens: University of Georgia Press, 1990.

Williams, Eric. *Capitalism and Slavery.* Chapel Hill: University of North Carolina Press, 1944.

Williams, George W. *Negro Troops in Rebellion, 1861–1865.* New York: Kraus Reprint, 1969.

Williams, Juan. *Eyes on the Prize: America's Civil Rights Years, 1954–1965.* New York: Penguin, 1988.

Wilson, Joseph T. *The Black Phalanx.* New York: Da Capo, 1994.

Wolff, Miles. *Lunch at the 5 & 10.* Chicago: Ivan R. Dee, 1990.

Wood, Peter H. *Black Majority: Negroes in Colonial South Carolina from 1670 Through the Stono Rebellion.* New York: W. W. Norton & Co., 1974.

Wuthenau, Alexander von. *Unexpected Faces in Ancient America.* New York: Crown Publishers, 1975.

INDEX

Page numbers in italics refer to illustrations.

coffee, 25–26
rice, 21
sugar, 7–8, 9, 25
tobacco, 21
Planter (ship), 33–34
Plessy, Homer, 146
Plessy v. Ferguson, 146, 148
Poage, George Coleman, 381
Poems on Miscellaneous Subjects (Harper), 244–45
Poitier, Sidney, 290, 301
Poll taxes, 56, 124
Poor, Salem, 184–85
Poor People's Campaign, 157
Porter, James, 271
Powell, Adam Clayton, Jr., 133, 144–45, 291, 303
Powell, Colin L., *223*, 223–24
Powell, Mike, 384
Powell v. Alabama, 146–47
Price, Cecil, 165, 167
Price, Leontyne, 288
Prigg v. Pennsylvania, 91
Primus, Pearl, 284–85, *285*, 314
Prince, 314–15
Prioleau, Devany, 31
Pritchett, Laurie, 151–52
Proclamation on Amnesty and Reconstruction. *See* Reconstruction
Professional Bowlers' Association, 374
Professional Golfers' Association, 374
Progressive Party, 140
Project C, 152
Prosser, Gabriel, 29–30
Protests
    antebellum period, 74–78
    Civil Rights Movement, 148–57
    colonial period, 62–63
    military, 212–13
    Revolutionary period, 68–72
Public Enemy, 312
Pulitzer Prize, 282, 306, 307, 315
Punch, John, 64
Puritans, 22
Purvis, Charles, 343–44
Purvis, Robert, 75, 80, 81, *81*
Puryear, Martin, 314
PUSH. *See* People United to Save Humanity

Quakers, 40, 44, 46, 62, 63, 70, 85, 323
Queen Latifah, 312–13
Quilombos, 34

Quilting, 323
Quotas, 173, 179–80, 212

Rainey, Ma, 274
A Raisin in the Sun (Hansberry), 290
Randolph, A. Philip, 131, 134, *135*, 136, 142–43, 153, 212
Rangel, Charles, 145, 174
Rape, 125, 140, 146–47
Ray, Charles B., 76
Ray, James Earl, 168
Rayford, Lee, 214, *214*
Reading Room Society, 236
Reagan, Ronald, 172–73, 175, 176
Reapers, 327
Reason, Patrick Henry, 245–46
Rebellions, 24, 26–34
    Amistad incident, 26–27
    effect of, 67
    fear of, 27, 32
    Haitian, 26, 29, 30–31
    hidden, 33
    Nat Turner's Rebellion, 31–32
    New York City, 27, 28
    Stono Rebellion, 28–29, 67, 230
Reconstruction, 48, 52, 101, 102, 105–10
    Black, 106–7, 115, 121
    congressional, 106
    presidential, 105–6, 110, 117, 118
    radical, 106, 107, *107*, 108, 109
Reconstruction Act of 1867, 105, 106, 109, 112, 115, 117, 118, 122, 203
Redeemers, 109
Red Hot Peppers, 272
Redman, Don, 273
Reiss, Winold, 266–67
Religion, 252–54, 278–81
    baptism, 233
    camp meetings, 242
    Church of England, 234
    colonial period, 233–35, 241–42
    Great Awakening, 234, 235, 240, 242
    mainstream churches, 242
    post-Civil War, 261–63
    separate churches, 241–42, 252
    spirits, 233
    storefront churches, 278–79
    voodoo, 252
    West African, 233
Remond, Charles Lenox, 77, *77*, 78, 83–84
Remond, Sarah Parker, 84